Authors, Illustrators, and Representa...

1989 Jon Scieszka
The True Story of the Three Little Pigs
ILLUSTRATED BY LANE SMITH

1989 Laurence Yep
Rainbow People
ILLUSTRATED BY DAVID WIESNER

1989 Ed Young
Lon Po Po: A Red Riding Hood Story from China

1988 Paul Fleischman
Joyful Noise: Poems for Two Voices
ILLUSTRATED BY ERIC BEDDOWS

1988 Eloise Greenfield
Nathaniel Talking
ILLUSTRATED BY JAN SPIVEY GILCHRIST

1988 Virginia Hamilton
Anthony Burns: The Defeat and Triumph of a Fugitive Slave

1987 Russell Freedman
Lincoln: A Photobiography

1987 John Steptoe
Murafo's Beautiful Daughters: An African Tale

1987 Jane Yolen
Owl Moon
ILLUSTRATED BY JOHN SCHOENHERR

1986 Nicholasa Mohr
Going Home

1985 Patricia Maclachlan
Sarah, Plain and Tall

1985 Chris Van Allsburg
The Polar Express

1982 Toshi Maruki
Hiroshima No Pika

1981 Yoshiko Uchida
Jar of Dreams

1970s

1978 Paul Goble
The Girl Who Loved Wild Horses

1977 Katherine Paterson
Bridge to Terabithia

1977 David McCord
One at a Time

1976 Jean Fritz
What's the Big Idea, Ben Franklin?
ILLUSTRATED BY MARGOT TOMES

1976 Byrd Baylor
Hawk, I'm Your Brother
ILLUSTRATED BY PETER PARNALL

1976 Mildred Taylor
Roll of Thunder Hear My Cry

1975 Tomie Depaola
Strega Nona

1975 Natalie Babbitt
Tuck Everlasting

1975 Sharon Mathis
The Hundred Penny Box

1975 Laurence Yep
Dragonwings

1974 Virginia Hamilton
M. C. Higgins the Great

1973 Susan Cooper
The Dark Is Rising

1972 Arnold Lobel
Frog and Toad Together

1971 Miska Miles
Annie and the Old One
ILLUSTRATED BY PETER PARNALL

1971 Muriel Feelings
Moja Means One: Swahili Counting Book
ILLUSTRATED BY TOM FEELINGS

1970 Betsy Byars
Summer of the Swans

1960s

1969 John Steptoe
Stevie

1968 Don Freeman
Corduroy

1968 Ursula K. Le Guin
Wizard of Earthsea

1967 Virginia Hamilton
Zeely
ILLUSTRATED BY SYMEON SHININ

1964 Maurice Sendak
Where the Wild Things Are

1964 Lloyd Alexander
The Book of Three

1962 Madeleine L'Engle
A Wrinkle in Time

1962 Ezra Jack Keats
The Snowy Day

LITERATURE AND THE CHILD

· · · EIGHTH EDITION · · ·

Lee Galda
UNIVERSITY OF MINNESOTA

Lawrence R. Sipe
UNIVERSITY OF PENNSYLVANIA

Lauren A. Liang
UNIVERSITY OF UTAH

Bernice E. Cullinan
NEW YORK UNIVERSITY

WADSWORTH
CENGAGE Learning™

Australia • Brazil • Japan • Korea • Mexico • Singapore • Spain • United Kingdom • United States

Literature and the Child, Eighth Edition

Lee Galda, Lawrence R. Sipe, Lauren A. Liang, and Bernice E. Cullinan

Editor-in-Chief: Linda Ganster

Executive Editor: Mark Kerr

Managing Development Editor: Lisa Mafrici

Developmental Editor: Kate Scheinman

Editorial Assistant: Greta Lindquist

Media Editor: Elizabeth Momb

Brand Manager: Melissa Larmon

Senior Market Development Manager: Kara Kindstrom

Content Project Manager: Samen Iqbal

Art Director: Jennifer Wahi

Manufacturing Planner: Doug Bertke

Rights Acquisitions Specialist: Thomas McDonough

Production Service: Joan Keyes, Dovetail Publishing Services

Photo Researcher: Wendy Granger

Text Researcher: Pablo D'Stair

Copy Editor: Susan Gall

Text Designer: Marsha Cohen

Cover Designer: Jeff Bane

Cover Illustration: Judith Caseley

Compositor: MPS Limited

For product information and technology assistance, contact us at **Cengage Learning Customer & Sales Support, 1-800-354-9706**.

For permission to use material from this text or product, submit all requests online at **www.cengage.com/permissions**. Further permissions questions can be e-mailed to **permissionrequest@cengage.com**.

Library of Congress Control Number: 2012942201

Student Edition:

ISBN-13: 978-1-133-60207-1

ISBN-10: 1-133-60207-X

Paper Edition:

ISBN-13: 978-1-133-96396-7

ISBN-10: 1-133-96396-X

Loose-leaf Edition:

ISBN-13: 978-1-133-96388-2

ISBN-10: 1-133-96388-9

Wadsworth
20 Davis Drive
Belmont, CA 94002-3098
USA

Cengage Learning is a leading provider of customized learning solutions with office locations around the globe, including Singapore, the United Kingdom, Australia, Mexico, Brazil, and Japan. Locate your local office at: **www.cengage.com/global**.

Cengage Learning products are represented in Canada by Nelson Education, Ltd.

To learn more about Wadsworth, visit **www.cengage.com/wadsworth**

Purchase any of our products at your local college store or at our preferred online store **www.CengageBrain.com**.

Printed in the United States of America
1 2 3 4 5 6 7 16 15 14 13 12

Brief Contents

Contents

PART II
Formats and Genres in Literature for Young Readers

CHAPTER

3

Picturebooks: A Unique Format in Children's Literature / 59

CHAPTER
4
Poetry and Verse / 127

CHAPTER 7
Contemporary Realistic Fiction / 219

CHAPTER 8
Historical Fiction / 251

CHAPTER
9
Biography and Memoir / 279

CHAPTER
10
Nonfiction / 303

accompanying instructor website offers access to password-protected resources such as an electronic version of the instructor's manual, test bank files, and PowerPoint® slides. Create an account at login.cengage.com.

WebTutor

Jumpstart your course with customizable, rich, text-specific content within your Course Management System. Whether you want to Web-enable your class or put an entire course online, WebTutor™ delivers. WebTutor™ offers a wide array of resources including access to the eBook, quizzes, videos, web links, exercises, and more.

Instructor's Manual with Test Bank

An online instructor's manual accompanies this book. The instructor's manual contains information to assist the instructor in designing the course, including a sample syllabus, learning objectives, teaching and learning activities, and additional print and online resources. For assessment support, the updated test bank includes true/false, multiple-choice, matching, short answer, and essay questions for each chapter.

Online ExamView

Available for download from the instructor website, ExamView® testing software includes all the test items from the printed test bank in electronic format, enabling you to create customized tests in print or online.

PowerPoint Slides

These vibrant, Microsoft PowerPoint lecture slides for each chapter assist you with your lecture, by providing concept coverage using images, figures, and tables directly from the textbook.

• • ACKNOWLEDGEMENTS • •

Since the beginning, this book has been shaped by the legacy of Bee Cullinan, whose foundational first two editions continue to influence new editions. Bee's legacy to the field remains vibrant in the work of the many she taught and influenced. I am fortunate to have studied with her, to have written with her for many years, and to have the opportunity to pass on her knowledge and love of books to my own doctoral students at the University of Minnesota, who also have shaped this edition.

They, however, have influenced me as much as I have influenced them. Aimee Rogers has managed to convert me to a great appreciation of graphic novels, and her suggestions influenced those that I discussed in this text; she also did the children's literature references and vetted many author websites for many chapters, allowing me to focus on my writing. Lori Laster's knowledge of fantastic literature has significantly enhanced my own, and her influence is apparent in Chapter 6, as is the work of Richa Kapoor, a former doctoral student. She contributed one of the Close Looks in Chapter 6 and did the preliminary selection of books to include in that chapter. Lauren Causey did considerable research on culturally diverse literature, and her personal insights into African American literature have honed the way that I look at those books; her work helped shape Chapter 1. Kate Wu's work on the children's literature references was also significant and allowed me more time to write than I would have had. Amy Frederick contributed ideas for working with English language learners, which were incorporated into several Teaching Ideas. My dear friend and colleague, Rebecca Rapport is also present in this text, as she and I "talk books" on a regular basis. T. J. Wilson, doctoral student at the University of Utah, helped with references for Chapter 9. A resounding thank you is due to Naomi Watkins, University of LaVerne, who has graciously taken over the work on the instructor's manual.

I also continue to be inspired by the wonderful teachers with whom I have had the privilege to work. Terry Nestor, Lisa Stanzi, Karen Bliss, Betty Shockley, and Rene Goepfrich demonstrate what can be accomplished by a gifted teacher.

It has been a pleasure to work with Kate Scheinman as developmental editor. Her unfailing good humor and prompt responses kept me happy, and her suggestions were invaluable. A special thank you to Joan Keyes, of Dovetail Publishing Services, for shepherding this, the fourth edition that we have worked on together. Similarly, Susan Gall, Copy Editor, is part of the team for another edition. Without Kate, Joan, and Susan, the quality of this book would be diminished—and it wouldn't have been as much fun to write! And of course, thank you to Mark Kerr, Executive Editor; Ashley Cronin, Senior Media Editor, and Greta Lindquist, Editorial Assistant for their help in shaping and producing this new edition.

We also acknowledge the many good ideas that our reviewers provided to us. It is always gratifying to have a reviewer like the text, and it's really wonderful to have them not only like the text but give us good ideas. Thank you to:

John Beach, St. John's University

Mary Drucker, Utica College

Tonja Fillippino, Arkansas State University

Carolyn Hayes, The Ohio State University/Newark Branch

Gwen Marra, Dordt College

Zelda McMurtry, Arkansas State University

Peg Moneypenny, Trinity International University

Deborah Norland, Luther College

Margaret Petersen, Nova Southeastern University

Kathy Phillips, University of Nebraska Lincoln

Jacquelin Smith, University of Northern Iowa

Denise Tallakson, University of Northern Iowa

Finally, and especially, I am most grateful that Dr. Lauren Liang joined the author team this year. Lauren's experience as a reviewer for *The Horn Book Guide* and her work as a professor at the University of Utah were reason enough to ask her to write Chapters 9 and 10. That she is a terrific writer, utterly reliable, and a wonderful person only made it even better to work with her. Lauren is grateful for the endless love and support of her family, Bernie, Zev, Zoë, and Lexie. My own family is now familiar with the intensity with which I write this book. As always, they are the beginning, the delicious middle, and the end of all that really matters.

Lee Galda

About the Authors
and Illustrator

Lee Galda

After teaching in elementary- and middle-school classrooms for a number of years, Lee Galda received her Ph.D. in English Education from New York University. She is the Marguerite Henry Professor of Children's Literature at the University of Minnesota where she teaches undergraduate and graduate courses in children's and young adult literature. Lee is a member of the International Reading Association and the United States Board on Books for Young People, working on various committees related to literature. She was children's books department editor for *The Reading Teacher* from 1989 to 1993; a member of the 2003 Newbery Committee; a member of the International Reading Association Book Award Selection Committee for the past five years, co-chairing that committee in 2010–2011 and 2011–2012; and a member of the USBBY Bridge to Understanding Award Committee in 2008 through 2011, chairing that committee in 2011. She sits on the review boards of several professional journals and on the editorial boards of *Children's Literature in Education* and *Journal of Children's Literature*. Author of numerous articles, books, and book chapters about children's literature and response, she was lead author of the first chapter on children's literature appearing in the *Handbook of Reading Research (Volume III)*. In 2011, Lee received the International Reading Association Arbuthnot Award for excellence in teaching children's literature. Lee lives in Minneapolis, Minnesota, with her husband.

Lawrence R. Sipe

Lawrence R. Sipe was a professor in the University of Pennsylvania's Graduate School of Education for sixteen years, where he taught courses in children's and adolescent literature and conducted research on young children's responses to picturebooks. He taught in primary and elementary classrooms for six years, including a two-year stint in an isolated one-room school in the province of Newfoundland, Canada. He also was the coordinator of professional development for K–6 teachers for a school board in Newfoundland for thirteen years. His Ph.D. was in Children's Literature and Emergent Literacy from Ohio State University. His awards include Outstanding Dissertation of the Year from the International Reading Association, the Outstanding Dissertation Award from the College Reading Association, the Promising Researcher Award from the National Council of Teachers of English, and the Early Career Achievement Award from the National Reading Conference. He also won several awards for teaching, including the Teaching Excellence Award for the province of Newfoundland; the Graduate School of Education Teaching Award; and the Lindback Award for Distinguished Teaching from the University of Pennsylvania. He was the North American editor of the journal *Children's Literature in Education*. His book *Storytime: Young Children's Literary Understanding in the Classroom* was published in 2008 by Teachers College Press.

Lauren A. Liang

Lauren Aimonette Liang is an associate professor in the College of Education at the University of Utah. She teaches courses in children's and young adult literature, including a course on international children's literature, and was awarded the University of Utah's Early Career Teaching Award in 2010. Lauren's research in children's literature and comprehension has been published in journals such as *Reading Research Quarterly*, *Journal of Children's Literature*, and *The Reading Teacher*, as well as in both professional and practitioner books. Lauren serves on editorial boards and committees for the International Reading Association, the American Library Association, and the Literacy Research Association. She is a long-time reviewer for *The Horn Book Guide* and other review publications and has served on the International Reading Association's Children's and Young Adult Book Awards committee for the past three years. She lives in Salt Lake City, Utah, with her husband and three children, all younger than age six.

Bernice E. Cullinan

Bernice E. Cullinan is known both nationally and internationally for her work in children's literature. She has written more than thirty books on literature for classroom teachers and librarians, including *Literature and the Child*, *Poetry Lessons to Dazzle and Delight*, and *Three Voices: Invitation to Poetry across the Curriculum*. She also has written a book for parents, *Read to Me: Raising Kids Who Love to Read*. Dr. Cullinan was editor in chief of *Wordsong*—the poetry imprint of Boyds Mills Press, a Highlights for Children Company—and has collected poems written by the recipients of the National Council of Teachers of English Award for Poetry in *A Jar of Tiny Stars* and subsequent volumes. She served as president of the International Reading Association, was inducted into the Reading Hall of Fame and The Ohio State University Hall of Fame, and selected as the recipient of the Arbuthnot Award for Outstanding Teacher of Children's Literature. Dr. Cullinan lives in New York City.

Judith Caseley

Judith Caseley has written and illustrated forty books for children and young adults, published by HarperCollins, Farrar, Straus and Giroux, and more recently, Tanglewood Press. All of Caseley's books are gently based on real life experiences that she and her two children, Jenna and Michael, have lived through. *Dear Annie* is about her father writing letters to his granddaughter, Jenna. *Bully* is about Michael's school problems with Jack, a troubled classmate. *On the Town: A Community Adventure* is based on the town where Caseley lives. *The Kissing Diary*, a t'ween novel, was very loosely based on her divorce and how it affected her children. *Do You Hear Me, Mr. Lincoln* is a teen novel that honors Caseley's love for Abraham Lincoln and her love for her niece, Jessica, whose father died when she was a little girl. The books are based on small moments, nuggets of life that to a child are monumental. The frivolous and fun author/illustrator continues painting, doing mosaics, and writing pithy blogs about life. Check out her website at www.judithcaseley.com or read her blogs on www.geopalette.com.

PART 1

Children
and
Books

Children's and Adolescent Literature

Our centuries-long struggle for freedom and equal rights had helped make the American promise of life, liberty, and the pursuit of happiness a reality for all Americans. We have come a mighty long way, honey, and we still have a good ways to go, but that promise and the right to fight for it is worth every ounce of its weight in gold. It is our nation's heart and soul.

—KADIR NELSON

Heart and Soul: The Story of America and African Americans, p. 99

Again this year at Oak Middle School, the library is full of students talking about the newly announced Newbery, Printz, King, and Belpré Award winners, some pleased that their favorites have been selected, others disappointed. Because Lauren, their librarian, has read Kadir Nelson's **Heart and Soul: The Story of America and African Americans** (I–A) out loud, the students are thrilled to hear that Nelson had won the Coretta Scott King Author Award for 2012, that his illustrations for the book had garnered a King Illustrator Honor, but surprised that the book wasn't on the list of Sibert Awards for nonfiction. This is a good opportunity for Lauren to talk about how award committees work and the politics involved in book awards. Having also seen Patricia McKissack's **Never Forgotten** (I–A) and Eloise Greenfield's **The Great Migration: Journey to the North** (I–A), the students are pleased that these books were King Author Honor books. Many students have already read the Newbery medalist, Jack Gantos's **Dead End in Norvelt** (A), attracted to it because they had loved Gantos's **Joey Pigza** series, and they loved it; others wonder why Gary Schmidt's **Okay for Now** (A) wasn't on the Newbery list. Still others wanted to get their hands on the Newbery Honor books, **Inside Out & Back Again**, by Thanhha Lai and **Breaking Stalin's Nose** by Eugene Yelchin. As they talk, the students realize that the books they are discussing are all historical fiction, which surprises many of them and leads to a discussion of favorite genres.

Not too far away, the fourth- and fifth-grade students at Green Elementary School also have been avidly following the awards process especially the Caldecott, Newbery, Belpré, and King Awards. They have read many of the books that were nominated as contenders on a "mock Newbery" website, they have voted for their favorites, and they are ready when their librarian, Ms. Rebecca, announces the official American Library Association winners that afternoon. In both schools, students argue passionately about their personal favorites, often seeking out the opinions of the adults in the room. They ask Lee, a visitor who has come to share the excitement, invited because she has served on a previous Newbery selection committee and can explain the awards processes, her opinion about the winners. These students, too, had heard Kadir Nelson's book read aloud, as well as those of McKissack and Greenfield and Yelchin, and Lee asks the students what they enjoyed about those books. From that opening, the conversation grows to include authors and titles not related to the Newbery Award at all. The pleased smiles of students whose favorite books also have been read and enjoyed by their visitor demonstrate the powerful nature of sharing in the joys of engaged reading.

Just down the hall from the library, the sound of cheering from the second- and third-grade classrooms indicate that they, too, are engaged with books and heartily approve this year's Caldecott Award, **A Ball for Daisy** (N–P), a wordless book illustrated by Chris Raschka. Raschka's illustrations are among the children's favorites, and his first Caldecott Medal winner, **The Hello, Goodbye Window** (P), written by Norton Juster, as well as his Caldecott Honor–winning **Yo! Yes?** (N–P) are familiar to all of them. They are also excited about Shane Evans winning the King Illustrator Award for **Underground: Finding the Light to Freedom** (P), which happens to be on the "award contenders" table in the library, along with Caldecott Honor books **Me . . . Jane** (P), by Patrick McDonnell and Lane Smith's **Grandpa Green** (P), which surprised them because it is so different from the books he has produced with Jon Scieszka such as **The True Story of the Three Little Pigs** (P–I). On this important day in the world of literature for young readers, it is clear that this literature has captured the imagination and inspired engaged reading for most of these students.

*This painting from **Heart and Soul** captures the immense significance of the story of America and African Americans, from colonial times to the election of the first African American president.*

If you walk into the children's room at your local library, you are likely to see children and their parents, reading together, sprawled on the floor in front of bookshelves, several books on the floor and in their laps, or in chairs at tables, with piles of books beside them. Older children are finding their own books, debating which ones to check out, and the adolescents in the young adult room are using computers, selecting books, and talking among themselves. Libraries today are busy places. Children's bookstores, as well, are full of vibrancy as readers from toddlers to adolescents find books that they just *have* to read. Obviously, books, whether picturebook, poetry, novel, or nonfiction are *alive and thriving*.

At your local elementary school, you can pop into a classroom during read-aloud time, and you'll see children whose eyes are riveted to the pictures in a picturebook or staring off into space as they visualize the words in a novel. Dropping by during independent reading time, you might see individual students intensely engaged with books, reading a novel and lost to the world, or looking so closely at a detailed illustration in a nonfiction text that nose almost touches book. You might notice individual readers as well as pairs of students reading together. In middle schools, too, you are likely to see young readers in library and classroom, reading and often sharing books written especially for them.

What happens when good books, time to read them, and a supportive context are available to young readers? Like the students just described, they learn to read and to love reading, on their way to becoming lifelong readers. This text is not about teaching reading, although there are instructional suggestions throughout the text, but rather, about the books that make it worthwhile to do the hard work of learning to read and reading to learn. Why is it important that young readers become engaged readers, readers who turn to books for pleasure, eager to experience the fictive worlds that authors create and to find out about their own actual world through books? The opportunities that lie between the covers of a book are multifaceted, when unleashed by an engaged reader.

The Power of Literature

Avid readers read poetry to stir their souls, narrative fiction to help them discover who they are, and nonfiction to help them understand their worlds. The importance of reading good books is apparent in both theory (Nodelman, 1996, 1997; Galda, Ash, & Cullinan, 2000; Rosenblatt, 1938/1976;

Sipe & McGuire, 2008) and research (Cunningham & Stanovitch, 1998). The opportunity to discover new experiences and ideas is enticing to readers, leading to the engagement and motivation that it takes to become a successful, and lifelong, reader (Guthrie & Wigfield, 2000). Those who engage with books from a young age and become avid readers have an academic advantage that continues to support their success, regardless of intelligence or circumstances. Avid reading really does make you smarter (Cunningham & Stanovitch, 1998, p. 14).

Reading literature contributes to language growth and development. When children and adolescents read or hear stories read to them, they learn new vocabulary; they encounter a greater variety of words in books than they will ever hear in spoken conversation or on television. Each reader builds an individual storehouse of language possibilities and draws on that wealth when speaking, writing, listening, and reading. Literature also develops readers' facility with language because it exposes them to carefully crafted poetry and prose. Young people who read literature have a broad range of experiences and language to put in their storehouse; they have greater resources on which to draw than do people who do not read.

Outstanding literature helps readers become better writers as well. When students read a lot, they notice what writers do. They see that writers choose from a variety of language possibilities in their writing. When readers write, they borrow the structures, patterns, and words from what they read.

Reading literature promotes skill and growth in reading. Engaging stories, poetry, and information appeal to readers and entice them to read: The more they read, the better they get. The better they read, the more they learn. The more they learn, the more curious they become. And the more curious they become, the more they read. Thus, good books provide a way for young people to become motivated and engaged readers.

This love of reading leads to readers seeking out exciting stories, interesting information, and compelling poems; they turn to reading as a source of knowledge, pleasure, and enlightenment. Thus, literature enables young people to explore and understand their world. It enriches their lives and widens their horizons: They learn about people and places on the other side of the world as well as those down the street. They travel back and forth in time to visit familiar places and people, to meet new friends, to see new worlds, to discover new ideas. They can increase their own knowledge, explore their own feelings, shape their own values, and imagine lives beyond the ones they live.

Literature prompts readers to explore their own feelings. Avid readers gain insight into human experience and begin to understand themselves better. When they explore their own feelings, they also understand why others react as they do. Writer Jill Payton Walsh argues that "we cannot understand ourselves at all until we understand ourselves 'longways.' This is the [narrative] mode of understanding that stories promote" (2007, p. 251). Indeed, Nodelman (1996, 1997) and Nodelman & Reimer (2003) argue that it is crucial that children have books that offer them varied depictions of what it is to be human and the tools to understand that there are many ways of being for all people. Nodelman also comments that reading literature gives children a much broader view of the way the world works than the narrow band of normality offered by television and popular culture. Literature enables us to see beyond the messages given to us daily by our own culture. Thus, while some scholars valorize popular culture for the relevance it has to children's lives (Dyson, 2003; Carrington & Luke, 2003), we believe that this is a short-sighted approach. Such scholars argue that children's literature is an elitist, middle-class phenomenon, not realizing or acknowledging how controlled by hegemonic interests the texts of popular culture are. All young readers, everyone's children, need and deserve a rich diet of literature.

Many wonderful books are available to enrich the lives of millions of children and adolescents worldwide, readers who are diverse in their ethnicity, religion, abilities, nationality, and social and economic status, but united by commonalities of youth. Literature provides insights into the realities and dreams of young people and of the authors and illustrators who depict those dreams and realities. It reflects life throughout the course of time and across national boundaries. Literature keeps people's dreams alive, presenting a vision of what is possible, helping to shape readers' views of the world. Frye (1970) underscores the role of literature in "educating" the imagination. He argues that the fundamental job of the imagination in ordinary life is to produce, out of the society we *have* to live in, a vision of the society we *want* to live in. In this sense, we live in two worlds: our ordinary world and our ideal world. One world is around us, the other is a vision inside our minds, born and fostered by the imagination, yet real enough for us to try to make the world we see conform to its shape. Literature fuels this imagination. Glenna Davis Sloan (2009) provides an excellent summary of Frye's work, arguing for the continued relevance

of his ideas as they relate to literature for young readers. Literature can and does enrich the moral, intellectual, social, and spiritual lives of young readers (Coles, 1989).

Many speak to the potential of literature:

> Any child who finds the healthy escapism of books—one that enlarges the mind rather than narrows it—has gained a lifelong ally. Every human spends a portion of his or her life searching for solace: a kindred spirit, a non-judgmental friend, a sympathetic mirror showing dreams and possibilities. At birth, our parents fill this need. Next, a favorite stuffed animal may take on the same burden, or a pet. How wonderful for a child to discover a similar respite in books that do not preach obvious lessons but instead hold up a mirror revealing something we suspected, but had not yet articulated. At their best, children's books shed light on our inner selves and the world around us, leading us down rabbit holes and over rainbows. (Robinson, 2008, p. 34)

Books are a powerful force in the lives of young readers. Even in today's world of standards, accountability, testing, and electronic media, books form the vital core of an education for the twenty-first century. The richness and diversity that typifies literature today means that teachers, librarians, parents, and young people have a wealth of books from which to select. The power of books to open new worlds, to cause readers to think in new ways—in short, to transform their ways of knowing—makes books the greatest single resource for educating our children to become contributing members of our society.

Today, excellent children's books and young adult literature abound. There are thousands of wonderful books just waiting to be put into the hands of young readers. This text will help you learn about those books.

In the remainder of this chapter, we:

- Present a brief historical overview of the development of children's and adolescent literature
- Describe the current state of literature for young readers while discussing
  - Fiction and nonfiction
  - The elements of narrative
  - The major types, or *genres*, of literature
  - Picturebook, graphic novel, and e-book formats
  - Global and multicultural literature for young readers

We then go on to

- Consider the basis for selecting literature for young readers
- Briefly describe some resources for selecting books
- Discuss how literature for young readers supports working toward mastery of the Common Core Standards for the English Language Arts

First, though, we define literature for young readers.

Defining Literature for Children and Adolescents

A basic definition of literature for children and adolescents might state that it encompasses books written for this particular audience; we add that it can also include books that children and adolescents enjoy and have made their own. In short, this literature consists of books that children and adolescents read. In this textbook we focus on those books written for and marketed to an audience of young readers. This audience begins at birth and ends at adulthood, which is, for the purposes of this text age eighteen. Although our primary focus is on literature for young readers from birth through middle school, we do also discuss some of the trends in and major contributions to literature for older adolescents. We indicate in parentheses following the title the general age range of the books we discuss in this text with the following designations:

> N = **Nursery (birth to age five)**
>
> P = **Primary (ages five to eight)**
>
> I = **Intermediate (ages eight to twelve)**
>
> A = **Advanced (ages twelve to eighteen)**

Many books, however, appeal in different ways to a wide range of ages, so there is considerable overlap in these designations. Today, we are fortunate to have a wealth of wonderful books from which to select. This text will help you discover some of those books. In Chapter 2, we turn to a consideration of the readers of this literature and some general theoretical constructs that describe how readers read and respond to texts, and how this looks in today's classrooms. In Chapters 3 through 10, we present detailed information about the major formats and genres in children's and adolescent literature. Finally, in Chapters 11 and 12 we describe teachers and children working with literature, from primary through middle school levels, as they teach to the standards through the use of children's books.

A Brief History of Literature for Children and Adolescents

• • THE EARLY YEARS • •

In 1744, John Newbery (1713–1767) opened a bookstore in St. Paul's Churchyard, London, where he published and sold books for children. Up until that time, children had been given chapbooks (crudely printed little books sold by peddlers or chapmen), battledores (folded sheets of cardboard covered with crude woodcuts of the alphabet or Bible verses), and hornbooks (small wooden paddles with lesson sheets tacked on with strips of brass and covered with a transparent sheet of cow's horn). These materials, like other books of their day, were meant to instruct children. Newbery's books were meant to teach children proper behavior, but did not threaten them with fire and brimstone if they did not behave, as did most early literature.

Originally, most children's books came to North America from England. They clearly were intended for instruction, but it soon became apparent that the books nurtured children's imagination as well. For example, Lewis Carroll's *Alice's Adventures in Wonderland* (1865/1992) was soon reprinted in English-speaking countries all over the world. The revolutionary quality of Lewis Carroll's two books, *Alice's Adventures in Wonderland* and *Through the Looking Glass* (1871/1977), derives from the fact that they were written purely to give pleasure to children. There is not a trace of a lesson or moral in the books. Nathaniel Hawthorne is considered the author of the first American book written specifically for children, *A Wonder Book for Boys and Girls* (1851/1893). England, however, continued as a major source of literature for North American children for generations and led the way to global publishing. American children made no distinction among British and American books or those from other countries. They read Carlo Collodi's *Pinocchio* originally published in1883, from Italy, Johanna Spyri's *Heidi*, published in 1879–1880, in Switzerland, and Selma Lagerlöf's *The Wonderful Adventures of Nils*, originally published in 1906–1907 in Sweden with equal enthusiasm.

The first child labor laws, which were passed in 1907, freed children to go to school. As more children learned how to read and write due to universal first- through eighth-grade public schools, the quantity and the types of books published for them rapidly increased. At the same time, new technologies helped reduce publishing costs, and the generosity of charitable individuals allowed public library systems to develop rapidly, putting books in the hands of vast numbers of children worldwide. Literature written especially for children became profitable, and publishers began to establish departments of children's books.

• • THE TWENTIETH CENTURY • •

In 1919, the US publishing house Macmillan launched a department devoted entirely to children's books. Louise Bechtel Seaman, who had worked as an editor of adult books and taught in a progressive school, was appointed department head. In 1922, the John Newbery Award was established by the American Library Association, followed by the Randolph Caldecott Award in 1938. (See Appendix A for a complete list of the winners and honor books.) In 1922 and 1923, two women, Helen Dean Fish and May Massee, became the first children's books editors, each at a different company. In 1924, *The Horn Book Magazine* was published by the Bookshop for Boys and Girls in Boston under the guidance of Bertha Mahony and Elinor Whitney. In 1933, May Massee moved to open a children's books department at Viking. Other publishers began to open children's books departments, and children's literature blossomed into the twentieth century. Modern picturebooks began to develop during the 1920s and 1930s; from the 1940s through the 1960s, children's and young adults' books became an increasingly important part of libraries, schools, homes, and publishing houses. The spread of public libraries with rooms devoted to children's and adolescents' reading interests opened the floodgates, inviting an eager audience to read books and magazines and to listen to stories told aloud. Leonard Marcus (2008) traces the history of children's literature in the United States in *Minders of Make-Believe: Idealists, Entrepreneurs, and the Shaping of American Children's Literature*. Figure 1.1 contains some milestones in the history of literature for children and young adults.

The field of children's books changed considerably during the last half of the twentieth century as it slowly began to reflect the diversity that marks North America and also to include more literature from around the world. Whereas early publications sought to instill a seemingly unified community's values in the young to socialize them and to teach them, this approach changed to one that reflects a broad spectrum of social values that come from many cultures and cross international boundaries. The percentage of culturally diverse books in relation to the entire corpus of books published each year remained woefully low, however, despite the increasing diversity of our population. In 1975, disturbed by the lack of picturebooks that reflected diversity, Harriet Rohmer established Children's Book Press, devoted to the publication of bilingual picturebooks that reflected a diversity of cultural experiences. Other small presses such as Just Us Books, founded in 1988, were established to address the lack of diversity in the field, and forward-thinking editors such as Phyllis Fogelman, at Dial, encouraged and supported the work of several now-notable African American authors and illustrators (Marcus, 2008).

A study conducted in the final decade of the twentieth century confirmed that the number of children's books that present pluralistic, balanced racial and ethnic images of children seldom paralleled census figures (Bishop, 1994). Although the number of US presidents from parallel cultures (Hamilton, 1993) had increased dramatically, few books representing those groups were published between the 1960s and 1980s. In 1994, Bishop found that only 3 to 4 percent of the children's books published in 1990, 1991, and 1992 related to people of color. Since 1999, less than 3 percent of books published each year were by or about people of color (Hansen-Krening, Aoki, & Mizokawa, 2003). Considering that more than five thousand books for children and early adolescents were published in the United States alone each year, there were not enough books that reflected diversity published in any given year.

The situation was similar in terms of international literature. Although books published in English-speaking countries were often available internationally, less than 1 percent of books published in the United States were books that had been translated (Tomlinson, 2002; see also Stan, 2002, and Tomlinson, 1998). Books that contained characters who are gay, lesbian, bisexual, or transgendered were also few and far between, as were books that contained characters with exceptionalities.

Whereas it was difficult in the 1960s and 1970s to find books that presented girls and women in what at the time were "nontraditional" roles, that was not the case at the end of the twentieth century. Rather, female characters in contemporary realistic fiction reflected a profound change in society's perceptions of roles for women and girls. Social class as presented in contemporary fiction also seemed to have been slightly transformed, with a greater number of books in which the characters are poor or working class, but again, the numbers did not reflect the census figures.

At the same time that literature for children was slowly beginning to reflect diversity, young adult literature was enjoying a robust renaissance. The genre began in earnest in the 1960s and 1970s with the publication of novels such as S. E. Hinton's

FIGURE 1.1

Milestones in Literature for Children and Adolescents

1865	Lewis Carroll, *Alice's Adventures in Wonderland*
1902	Walter de la Mare, *Songs of Childhood*
	Rudyard Kipling, *Just So Stories*
	E. Nesbit, *Five Children and It*
	Beatrix Potter, *The Tale of Peter Rabbit*
1908	Kenneth Grahame, *The Wind in the Willows*
	L. M. Montgomery, *Anne of Green Gables*
1911	James M. Barrie, *Peter Pan*
1922	Margery Williams, *The Velveteen Rabbit*
1924	A. A. Milne, *When We Were Very Young*
1933	Jean de Brunhoff, *The Story of Babar*
	P. L. Travers, *Mary Poppins*
1936	Edward Ardizzone, *Little Tim and the Brave Sea Captain*
1938	Marjorie Kinnan Rawlings, *The Yearling*
1939	Ludwig Bemelmans, *Madeline*
	T. S. Eliot, *Old Possum's Book of Practical Cats*
1940	Maud Hart Lovelace, *Betsy-Tacy*
	Eric Knight, *Lassie Come-Home*

1941	Robert McCloskey, *Make Way for Ducklings*
	H. A. Rey, *Curious George*
1943	Esther Forbes, *Johnny Tremain*
1950	C. S. Lewis, *The Lion, the Witch, and the Wardrobe*
1952	Mary Norton, *The Borrowers*
	E. B. White, *Charlotte's Web*
1954	Lucy M. Boston, *The Children of Green Knowe*
	Rosemary Sutcliff, *The Eagle of the Ninth*
	J.R.R. Tolkien, *The Fellowship of the Ring*
1958	Philippa Pearce, *Tom's Midnight Garden*
1962	Ezra Jack Keats, *The Snowy Day*
	Madeleine L'Engle, *A Wrinkle in Time*
1963	Maurice Sendak, *Where the Wild Things Are*
1964	Lloyd Alexander, *The Book of Three*
	Louise Fitzhugh, *Harriet the Spy*
1967	Virginia Hamilton, *Zeely*
	S. E. Hinton, *The Outsiders*
1968	Ursula Le Guin, *A Wizard of Earthsea*
	Paul Zindel, *The Pigman*

The Outsiders (A), Paul Zindel's *The Pigman* (A), Robert Lipsyte's *The Contender* (A), Robert Cormier's *The Chocolate War* (A), and Judy Blume's *Forever* (A), among others. The subsequent resurgence of adolescent literature was marked by the establishment of the Michael L. Printz Award in 2000; this award is administered by the American Library Association.

Similarly, the increasing attention paid to nonfiction in the final decades of the twentieth century is reflected in the establishment of the OrbisPictus Award, administered by the National Council of Teachers of English, in 1990, and the Robert F. Sibert Award for outstanding informational books, administered by the American Library Association, in 2001.

Understanding Children's Literature in the Twenty-First Century

Literature for young readers continues to evolve along many dimensions in both content and form. The continuing popularity and increasing numbers of series books, the availability of outstanding books for emerging readers, more young adult fiction that casts an unrelenting eye on life, the continuing popularity of post-modern texts, the rise of graphic novels, the popularity of *crossover* books, and an explosion

1971	Virginia Hamilton, **The Planet of Junior Brown**	2005	Lynne Rae Perkins, **Criss Cross**
	Robert C. O'Brien, **Mrs. Frisby and the Rats of NIMH**		Jacqueline Woodson, **Show Way**
		2006	Gene Luen Yang, **American Born Chinese**
1974	Robert Cormier, **The Chocolate War**		Markus Zusak, **The Book Thief**
1976	Mildred Taylor, **Roll of Thunder, Hear My Cry**	2007	Sherman Alexie, **The Absolutely True Diary of a Part-Time Indian**
1977	Katherine Paterson, **Bridge to Terabithia**		Brian Selznick, **The Invention of Hugo Cabret**
1983	Anthony Browne, **Gorilla**		Shaun Tan, **The Arrival**
1988	Paul Fleischman, **Joyful Noise: Poems for Two Voices**	2008	Kathi Appelt, **The Underneath**
			Mark Reibstein, **WabiSabi**
1993	Lois Lowry, **The Giver**		Suzanne Collins, **The Hunger Games**
1997	Karen Hesse, **Out of the Dust**	2009	Rebecca Stead, **When You Reach Me**
1998	J. K. Rowling, **Harry Potter and the Sorcerer's Stone**	2010	Sy Montgomery, **Kakapo Rescue: Saving the World's Strangest Parrot**
	Louis Sachar, **Holes**		Grace Lin, **Ling & Ting: Not Exactly the Same**
1999	Walter Dean Myers, **Monster**		
2000	Philip Pullman, **The Amber Spyglass**		Joyce Sidman, **Dark Emperor & Other Poems of the Night**
2001	Marilyn Nelson, **Carver: A Life in Poems**	2011	Herve Tullet, **Press Here**
	David Wiesner, **The Three Pigs**		Kadir Nelson, **Heart and Soul: The Story of America and African Americans**
2003	Kate DiCamillo, **The Tale of Despereaux: Being the Story of a Mouse, a Princess, Some Soup, and a Spool of Thread**		
2004	Russell Freedman, **The Voice That Challenged a Nation: Marian Anderson and the Struggle for Equal Rights**		

of dystopian novels for young adults have added to the rich mix of books available for young readers. Further, the continued experimentation with innovative techniques and genre mixing, the development of electronic books (e-books) and apps, and the slow but continual rise in global and multicultural literature continue to alter the field of children's literature.

The content of literature for children and adolescents is as broad as the hopes, fears, dreams, experiences, and interests of the audience it reaches. It reflects the increasing diversity and globalization of the lives of young readers. This literature also demonstrates the amazing talent of those who write and illustrate books for young readers, who find unique ways of presenting their imaginative visions. Here, we present some basic literary concepts to help you understand how children's books work.

• • FICTION OR NONFICTION • •

One of the most basic distinctions in literature for children is that between fiction and nonfiction. Fiction, by definition, is "something made up." Some fiction may *seem* real, but it is not; no matter how realistic it seems, it is something invented, an author's vision of a realistic or a fantastic world. The task of the author is to make the fiction seem plausible, or possible, within the story world that the author has created. Nonfiction, on the other hand, is based on facts and theories. It presents information that is real, verifiable by a reader. The task of the author is to be as truthful as possible, based on what is known at the time of the writing. Narrative, poetic, and expository writing can be fiction or nonfiction, depending upon the intent of the writer.

● ● NARRATIVE, POETIC, ● ● AND EXPOSITORY TEXTS

The basic distinction between narratives and other types of writing such as non-narrative poetry and expository writing is that *narratives* tell a story that occurs over time. They often have a *character* or characters who encounter some kind of problem and work to resolve it. The narrative is developed through the *plot*—the temporal events or actions that lead to the solution of the problem—which progresses to a *climax*, or solution to the problem, and sometimes, but not always, ends with a *resolution*, or closure to the story. Texts that are not narratives do not tell a story, but rather may present content through expository writing that seeks to explain, describe, or inform, or through the many poetic forms that are not narrative.

Narratives are abundant in literature for children and adolescents; story is popular with these readers. Poetry is abundant, as well, with children's poets exploring both narrative and many other forms of poetry. Marked by condensed language, poems for young readers span a wide variety of topics and forms. Expository writing, or writing to explain, describe, or inform, is found primarily in biography and other nonfiction, and is the preferred choice of many young readers. There are also books for young readers that combine these basic text types in innovative ways.

Literary Elements in Narrative

Narratives contain certain literary elements that authors and illustrators work with to create memorable stories. They include setting, characterization, plot, and theme.

Setting is the time and place in which story events occur. In most stories, the setting is important and thoroughly described. In others, the setting is less important, with few details. Picturebooks with vague settings in the text offer artists the opportunity to create images that present their own vision of the physical surroundings of the story. In other stories, setting is very important; details about a particular city, a part of the country, a historical period, or an imaginary place affect the development of the characters and the plot.

Characterization refers to the means by which an author establishes credibility of character.

Characters are the personalities that populate literature. Like people, main characters—protagonist(s) and antagonist(s)—are multidimensional, with varied strengths and weaknesses, and dynamic, growing and changing over time. This change or development is most often due to the events that occur as the characters seek to resolve some kind of problem. Authors develop characters by describing how they appear, what they do or say, what others *say* about or to them as well as what others *do* to them, and by what the narrator reveals. In picturebooks, character is also interpreted by illustrators who reveal appearance, thoughts, and actions.

Plot refers to the sequence of story events. In fiction for children, the plot is often a straightforward chronology, but sometimes authors use flashbacks, episodic plots, or alternating plots, especially those writing for an adolescent audience. Flashbacks provide background information about earlier events that led to the creation of the problem the character faces. Episodic plots highlight particular events in characters' lives, and alternating plots enable authors to tell parallel or contrasting stories from different points of view.

The plot usually revolves around a central conflict or conflicts. Common conflicts include: self against self, in which the main character engages in an internal struggle; self against other, in which the struggle is between the main character and one or more others; self against society, in which the main character combats societal pressures or norms; and self against nature, in which the main character struggles with the forces of nature. In most fiction for children, the conflict is positively, or at least hopefully, resolved by the end of the story; fiction for adolescents often ends with an unclear or a less-than-happy resolution.

A *theme* is a central, unifying idea, a thread that stitches the story together. Often a theme is the reason authors write in the first place: a story allows them to say what they want to say about something important. Most stories have several interwoven themes. Interpretation of themes varies among readers; each internalizes it in an individual way.

Style

Style is how an author writes—the vocabulary, syntax, and structure that create a story, poem, or piece of nonfiction. In story, style needs to reflect the time, place, and characters through dialogue that sounds natural and descriptions that are vivid and fresh. *Point of view* is part of style. Many stories are told through the voice of the main character, who reports events in a first-person narrative, solely from his or her point of view. This allows readers to understand thoroughly the thoughts of that character and often provokes a strong identification with that character. Another point of view, third-person limited, limits the information that is conveyed to what a particular character could logically know, but it does so in a more detached tone, using third-person rather than first-person pronouns. Omniscient narrators, ones who are all-knowing, can reveal the thoughts and inner feelings of several characters. They can move about in time and space to report events from an unbiased position. This point of view allows readers to know a great deal about what all the characters are thinking and doing. It also puts more distance between the reader and the main character because the reader is viewing the protagonist through the narrator's eyes rather than viewing the story world through the protagonist's eyes. Authors generally select one point of view and stick with it throughout the story, although some alternate between two or among several narrators. In a well-written story, the point of view provides a perspective that enriches the story.

Poets and authors who work with nonfiction also work with elements of style as they seek to illuminate the concept or idea that unifies their work. In poetry, style is evident in word choice, form, and use of poetic devices; we discuss this in Chapter 4. In nonfiction, style is reflected in word choice, structure, and tone; we discuss this in Chapters 9 and 10. In the chapters that follow, we examine the unique qualities of the literary elements that distinguish each genre.

• • GENRES • •

A genre is a category of composition that has such defining characteristics as type of characters, setting, action, and overall form or structure. The defining characteristics of each genre help us recognize the organization of the discipline of literature, provide a framework for talking about books, and help guide our selection. In this text, we explore the genres of poetry, folklore, fantastic literature (fantasy and science fiction), contemporary realistic fiction, historical fiction, biography and memoir, and nonfiction.

Distinguishing features help readers recognize genres. For example, *poetry* is marked by condensed language that contains various poetic devices to call attention to something in a fresh way. Ancient stories that were told by word of mouth are known as *folklore*. *Fantastic literature* includes *fantasy*, or stories could not happen in the real world and *science fiction*, which might happen in the future. Stories focusing on events that could happen in the real world today are works of *contemporary realistic fiction*; realistic stories set in the past are called *historical fiction*; and stories that tell the tale of a person's life are

biography or *memoir*. Books that explain, describe, or inform are called *nonfiction*.

Within these general distinctions, however, lies amazing variation. Some writers deliberately cross the rather arbitrary boundaries of genre by, for example, setting a story in both contemporary and historical times, or using fantasy devices or folkloric elements in contemporary or historical fiction. Within many of these genres, readers can find subgenres such as mystery stories, romances, quest tales, sports stories, and adventure stories. Humorous stories as well as serious stories populate each genre, as do series books. Some authors even blend fiction and nonfiction. We summarize the basic genres in Figure 1.2; the remainder of this text shows you how to recognize different genres and the variation within them. Following, we discuss each genre, presenting some examples of books that exemplify each genre, and then go on to consider more examples in greater depth in Chapters 4 through 10. As you read these chapters you will come to appreciate the inventiveness of those who create books for young readers.

Poetry and Verse

Poetry is the shorthand of beauty; its distilled language captures the essence of an idea or experience and encompasses the universe in its vision. Emerson suggests that poetry says the most important things in the simplest way. A lot of poetry is rhythmic and rhymed, appealing to the ear as well as to the mind and emotions, but many wonderful poems are in free verse or concrete forms as well. The best poetry and verse—from nonsense rhymes and limericks through lyrical and narrative poetry—shape an experience or idea into thoughts extraordinary.

Poetry not only varies across form, but also across audience and content. Paul Fleischman's Newbery Medal–winning *Joyful Noise: Poems for Two Voices* (I), a collection of poems about insects, has delighted countless teachers and young readers for more than twenty years with its witty word play and brilliant use of sound to evoke meaning. In Marilyn Singer's *Mirror Mirror: a Book of Reversible Verse* (I), illustrated by Jósee Masse, the poet has created a new form, one that allows her to play with familiar characters from folklore, presenting a familiar scene from two opposite points of view. Joyce Sidman's *Ubiquitous: Celebrating Nature's Survivors* (I), with illustrations by Beckie Prange, is a collection of poetry about science, accompanied by explanatory notes. This book is a perfect example of the blurring of genres—in this case, poetry and nonfiction—that is a hallmark of twenty-first century literature. Cynthia Grady's *I Lay My Stitches*

FIGURE 1.2

Genres in Children's and Young Adult Literature

Category	Brief Description
Poetry and Verse	Condensed language, expression of imaginative thoughts and perceptions, often containing rhythm and other devices of sound, imagery, figurative language.
Folklore	Traditional stories, myths, legends, nursery rhymes, and songs from the past. Oral tradition; no known author.
Fantasy	Stories set in places that do not exist, about people and creatures that could not exist or events that could not happen.
Science Fiction	Based on extending physical laws and scientific principles to their logical outcomes, usually futuristic.
Contemporary Realistic Fiction	Stories could happen in the real world; characters seem real; contemporary setting.
Historical Fiction	Stories reconstruct life in the past, using realistic actual or fictional characters, events, and historical setting.
Biography/Memoir	An account of a person's life, or part of a life history by someone else or the person him- or herself.
Nonfiction	Informational books that explain, describe, or inform about a subject or concept using facts about the real world.

Down: Poems of American Slavery (A), illustrated by Michele Wood, and Ntozake Shange's *Freedom's a-Callin Me* (A), with illustrations by Rod Brown, speak eloquently through both words and pictures, of the emotional toll and strength of slaves in America before emancipation.

In the past twenty years, there has been an increasing number of verse novels for young readers. Verse novels tell a story—they are narrative—in a poetic form, often but not always free verse. In *Never Forgotten* (I–A), illustrated by Leo and Diane Dillon, Patricia C. McKissack uses free verse to create a story of how those lost to the African slave trade were remembered. The verse novel continues to be popular with both authors and readers. *Pearl Verses the World* (I) by Sally Murphy with illustrations by Heather Potter, depicts the final days of Pearl's grandmother, who has dementia. This verse novel is also contemporary realistic fiction. Caroline Starr Rose tells a story of survival on the Kansas prairie in *May B*. (A), with free verse poems from the point of view of the young protagonist, sent to work on another homestead by her parents and stranded there for the winter. This verse novel is also historical fiction.

Teachers have discovered that poetry encourages reading, expands oral language development, provides techniques for young writers to experiment with, and enriches experiences across the curriculum. Researchers have found that poetry learned by heart in childhood stays in the mind for a lifetime. Today, publishers who once published only one or two poetry books per year create entire divisions devoted to poetry. We explore poetry in Chapter 4.

Folklore

Folklore is composed of stories passed down through generations by word of mouth. As such, they have no known author. As people told the stories to one another, they changed and molded them to suit their fancy. Eventually, collectors such as Charles Perrault and the Brothers Grimm wrote the stories down. Over time, other retellers have continued to shape the stories. Folklore reflects the values of the culture in which it grew; it encompasses universal experiences as shaped by individual cultures.

Folklore comes in many forms, including *nursery rhymes* such as those from Mother Goose; *folktales* and *fairy tales* such as the Brer Rabbit stories or Cinderella tales; *tall tales* exaggerating the strength and riches of America such as John Henry and Paul Bunyan; *fables*—simply told, highly condensed morality tales—such as "The Boy Who Cried Wolf"; *mythology*, which explains the origins of the Earth and the relation between humans and gods; *pourquoistories*, which explain why things are as they are; *hero tales*, *epics*, and *legends* such as Robin Hood and Beowulf; and *folksongs*.

Folklore comes from around the world, and what is available today reflects an increasingly international view. Similarly, as the composition of North America has become increasingly multicultural, folklore for children has expanded beyond a predominantly Western European tradition to include folklore of many cultures. Virginia Hamilton's posthumously published picturebook retelling of a Gullah tale, ***Bruh Rabbit and the Tar Baby Girl*** (P), illustrated by James Ransome, is a wonderful addition to a growing number of books that are retellings of African American tales. Paul Fleischman has highlighted the multiple cultural origins of the classic Cinderella tale in ***Glass Slipper, Gold Sandal: A Worldwide Cinderella*** (I).

Ancient Greek and Roman myths continue to be popular, and authors often expand beyond a simple retelling. Lise Lunge-Larsen combines etymology and mythology in ***Gifts from the Gods: Ancient Words & Wisdom from Greek & Roman Mythology*** (I–A), illustrated by Gareth Hinds. Donna Jo Napoli taps the same source in ***Treasure of Greek Mythology: Classic Stories of Gods, Goddesses, Heroes & Monsters*** (I–A), illustrated by Christina Balit. We discuss folklore in Chapter 5.

Fantasy

Fantasy, a type of fantastic literature, is imaginative literature distinguished by characters, places, or events that could not happen in the real world. Animals might talk, inanimate objects are endowed with feelings, time follows the author's rules, and humans can accomplish superhuman feats. Fantasy ranges from picturebooks containing talking animal stories for very young children to complex novels for older readers. Although fantasy stories could not possibly happen in reality, their carefully constructed plots, well-developed characters, and vivid settings cause readers to suspend disbelief.

The fantasy genre continues to grow as modern fantasy writers create powerful stories redolent with the legacy of folklore and ancient tales. From E. B. White's well-loved ***Charlotte's Web*** (P–I) to the success of ***Harry Potter and the Sorcerer's Stone*** (I) and the subsequent books in the series, to the great popularity of the genre today, fantasy for young readers is thriving.

Fantasy series books continue to be immensely popular with intermediate and advanced readers. Rick Riordan is a prolific writer of fantasy series, and in the second book in his **Heroes of Olympus** series, ***The Son of Neptune*** (I–A), Percy Jackson, hero of an earlier series, continues to struggle with being a "half-blood," son of a Roman god and a human mother. Janice Hardy's ***Darkfall*** (A) is the final book in her **Healing Wars** trilogy, which is based on the unusual premise of pain as a valuable commodity. Paranormal romance, in series or not, such as Myra McEntire's ***Hourglass*** (A), are quite popular with middle- and high-school girls.

Fantasy is often set in fully realized fantasy worlds such as the world of Avalon as created by T.A. Barron. Sometimes, however, the fantastic occurs within a realistic setting. In ***The Cabinet of Earths*** (I–A), by Anne Nesbet, young Maya, living in Paris with her family for a year, finds herself part of an ongoing fantasy, when she discovers that she is the next keeper of the cabinet of earths. Sometimes writers craft their tales around ancient folklore, giving it a unique twist, as Jane Yolen does in ***Snow in Summer: Fairest of Them All*** (A), a Snow White story set in Depression-era West Virginia.

Magic realism, when the magical is considered realistic by those encountering it, has become increasingly popular in fantasy. Pam Muñoz Ryan combines magic realism, biography, and poetry in ***The Dreamer*** (I), a fictional story of the acclaimed Chilean poet Pablo Neruda. Illustrations by Peter Sís combine beautifully with Ryan's text. Sally Nicholls employs magic realism and draws on stories of Celtic and Greek mythology in ***Season of Secrets*** (I). We explore fantasy in Chapter 6.

Science Fiction

Another type of fantastic literature, science fiction is an imaginative extrapolation of fact and theory: stories project what could happen in the future through a logical extension of established theories and scientific principles. Science fiction describes worlds that are plausible and that could possibly exist someday. Scientific advances cause writers to speculate about the consequences of those advances; science fiction is the result. For example, space travel led to stories of space colonies and intergalactic wars. Cloning led to stories of the human implications of using cloned cells to prolong life.

Science fiction is enjoying a record popularity today, with authors from around the world creating possible future worlds for young readers to ponder. Dystopian novels such as Lois Lowry's classic

The Giver (A) have virtually exploded in numbers. As in fantasy, science fiction series abound. Suzanne Collins's *The Hunger Games, Catching Fire*, and *Mockingjay* (A) enjoyed record sales, and there is a movie based on the first novel. "Steampunk" science fiction novels are also becoming increasingly prevalent and popular. A type of science fiction, steampunk is set in an anachronistic nineteenth or early twentieth century and often includes alternate world history; some describe it as "retro-futurism." In *Goliath* (A), the final volume in Scott Westerfeld's **Leviathan** trilogy (A), the alternate history of World War I and the fantastic steampunk machinery are extended by Keith Thompson's detailed illustrations. Further discussion of science fiction appears in Chapter 6.

Contemporary Realistic Fiction

Contemporary realistic fiction is set in modern times with events, settings, and characters that could occur in the real world. Authors create characters, plots, and settings that stay within the realm of possibility, and many readers respond to these stories as if the characters were actual people.

Realistic fiction grapples with a wide range of human conditions and emotions. Writers address contemporary problems such as hunger, divorce, drugs, and homelessness as well as themes such as growing up, making friends, and falling in love. Both picturebooks and novels address the experiences of today's world, as Patricia Reilly Giff does in *Pictures of Hollis Woods* (I–A).

Contemporary realistic fiction contains books that are about sports, adventure stories and animal stories, mysteries and romances. Many of the series books that primary-grade readers devour are also realistic fiction, including Sara Pennypacker's **Clementine** (P) series and Annie Barrows's **Ivy + Bean** (P) books. *Ivy + Bean: No News Is Good News* (P), illustrated by Sophie Blackall, is warmly funny. Grace Lin's *Ling & Ting: Not Exactly the Same* (P) is a transitional chapter book for newly independent readers.

Contemporary realistic fiction writers are from many cultures and lifestyles and present realistic stories of life as they see it, which means that there are many stories to both affirm and challenge perceptions about how things "really" are. No matter who we are, most of us want to have meaningful relationships with others; poet Naomi Shihab Nye's *There Is No Long Distance Now: Very Short Stories* (A) speak of this longing through the voices of adolescents in thirty-nine stories. We discuss contemporary realistic fiction in Chapter 7.

Historical Fiction

Historical fiction tells stories set in the past; it portrays events that actually occurred or possibly could have occurred. Authors create plot and character within an authentic historical setting. Once a genre in which history was retold from an all-white, and usually all-male, point of view, today we are fortunate to have skilled authors writing from careful research and from various cultural perspectives. Historical fiction ranges from stories set in prehistoric times to those reflecting the issues and events of the twentieth century. The stories are usually told through the perspective of a child or adolescent who is living life in a particular time and place. Collectively, historical fiction for children and young adults now represents a broad range of voices and cultures.

A great deal of historical fiction is written for intermediate and advanced readers and is often popular with adults as well; the 2012 Newbery winner and the two honor books are all historical fiction. The days of history being recounted by only white authors are over, and rich historical narratives from African American writers are now plentiful. Christopher Paul Curtis's books include *The Mighty Miss Malone* (I), who was a supporting character in his Newbery-winning *Bud, Not Buddy* (I). Barbara Wright's *Crow* (A) is based on the true but not widely known story of how the black middle class that flourished in Wilmington, North Carolina, at the end of the nineteenth century was systematically destroyed by a white minority who begrudged them their power . . . and their humanity. In addition to novels, there also are many fine picturebooks—such as Margaree King Mitchell's *When Grandmama Sings* (P), illustrated by James Ransome—that bring the past, in this case life in the segregated South, to life for younger readers. We discuss historical fiction in Chapter 8. Teaching Idea 1.1 offers suggestions to help students distinguish among fantastic literature, historical fiction, and contemporary realistic fiction.

Biography and Memoir

Biography tells about a real person's life. The subjects of biography are usually people who are famous, such as national leaders, artists, sports figures, writers, or explorers, but there are also many biographies and memoirs that are about "ordinary" people who do extraordinary things. Like historical fiction, biography has become increasingly diverse; today, the stories of many people from many cultures and parts of the world are available for young readers. These stories are told both in picturebooks and in lengthy texts. Every biography bears the imprint of its author; although the story of the person's life provides the basic facts, the writer selects, interprets, and shapes elements to create an aesthetic work. Sometimes, although

TEACHING IDEA 1.1

Distinguish among Fantasy, Contemporary Realism, and Historical Fiction

 **COMMON CORE STATE STANDARDS** This Teaching Idea addresses the Common Core English Language Arts, Reading: Literature standard 9, grades 6 through 8. The suggestions in this Teaching Idea may need to be adapted to suit your particular grade level and the needs of your students.

Choose three picturebooks (use the Booklists at the end of Chapters 3, 6, 7, and 8)—one fantasy, one contemporary realistic fiction, and one historical fiction. If you can find three with similar themes, your comparisons will be richer. Read the books aloud and compare them on relevant points, including genre, characters, plot, setting, theme, and any important details. Ask students to answer the following questions, using both the text and the illustrations to explain their answers:

- Which stories could really have happened? How do you know?

- Which stories could not really have happened? How do you know?

- Which story is contemporary, set in today's world? How do you know?

- Which story is historical? How do you know?

- How are these stories alike?

- How are these stories different?

Next, help students generate some descriptors of each of the three genres.

---

based on fact, biographies are so fictionalized as to be considered biographical fiction rather than true biography, straddling the line between fiction and nonfiction. Deborah Hopkinson's story of the childhood of a famous writer, ***A Boy Called Dickens*** (P), illustrated by John Hendrix, is one such biography. It is a terrific biographical story, great for introducing Dickens to young readers, but not necessarily "true." Most contemporary biographies are, however, very well grounded in fact and present accurate information to young readers. Charles R. Smith Jr.'s ***Twelve Rounds to Glory: The Story of Muhammad Ali*** (I–A), illustrated by Bryan Collier, incorporates accurate information in a beautifully written text, with additional detail and emotion supplied by the paintings; the book ends with a time line of Ali's life.

Autobiographies and memoirs are stories of a person's life, but they are written by the subjects themselves. Over the years, a number of memoirs from children's and young adult authors have been produced. Peter Sís's ***The Wall: Growing Up Behind the Iron Curtain*** (I), winner of the Sibert Award, is a brilliant visual depiction, supported by text, of his childhood and young adulthood in Prague. The book explores his quest for freedom, and freedom of expression, as it shaped his artistic life. Allen Say, in ***Drawing from Memory*** (I), a Siebert Honor book, writes compellingly of his childhood growing up in Japan, until his eventual move to the United States. His struggles to become an artist are depicted in words, black-and-white sketches, photographs, and color panels. Another Caldecott medalist, Ed Young, describes his own childhood in ***The House Baba Built: An Artist's Childhood in China*** (I). We discuss biographies and memoirs in Chapter 9.

Nonfiction

Nonfiction books are informational sources that explain or describe a subject. Children are naturally curious about the world they inhabit. They observe and explore, question and hypothesize about how this world works. Nonfiction outnumbers fiction in most children's libraries and is available for children from preschool through the advanced grades. Nonfiction presents information in a variety of formats: as picturebooks and photo essays, as how-to manuals, and as descriptive or expository texts. Books intended to inform have evolved into books designed to inform and delight.

Nonfiction covers diverse topics, ranging from dinosaurs to endangered species, cathedrals to igloos,

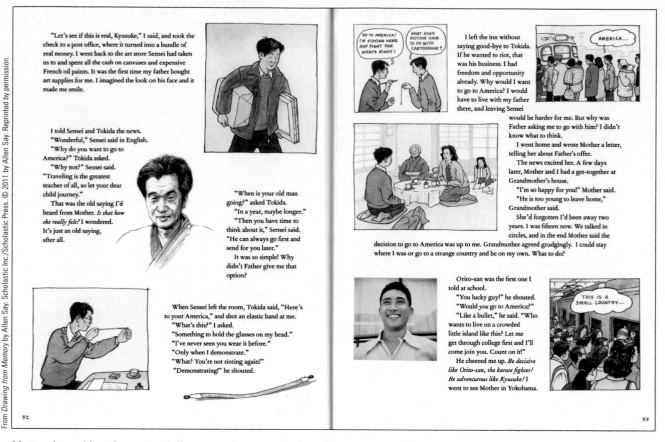

*Notice how Alan Say uses different techniques and media to create illustrations to help tell his story in **Drawing from Memory**.*

triangles to probability, history to philosophy, artistic design to book construction. Most contemporary nonfiction books are works of art as well as works of fact. For example, Kadir Nelson's **We Are the Ship: The Story of the Negro Baseball League** (A) reflects Nelson's passion for the game and the men who played it in both text and illustration. Winner of the Sibert Award for nonfiction, this book also received the King Author Award and was a King Illustrator Award Honor book. He also received the King Author Award for **Heart and Soul: The Story of America and African Americans**, described at the beginning of this chapter.

Nonfiction books about any topic you might imagine appear on library shelves. The interests of contemporary society, current events, and new insights into history, science, art, or other disciplines appear in nonfiction for young readers. Oil (resources, prices, and pollution) is a frequent topic in the news today, and noted nonfiction author Albert Marrin explains how oil has shaped the economy, politics, and social structures in our world in **Black Gold: The Story of Oil in Our Lives** (A); he also makes clear the environmental consequences of our reliance on this fossil fuel. The passion with which the story of oil is told engages readers, and references, an index, and a glossary make this a useful resource as well as an interesting mix of science, history, and politics. The history of the civil rights movement is the subject of Charlayne Hunter-Gault's **To the Mountaintop: My Journey through the Civil Rights Movement** (A). Although there are many excellent treatments of this period in history that have been created for young readers, this one offers the personal viewpoint of the author, one of the first two African American students to enroll at the segregated University of Georgia. Hunter-Gault's viewpoint is augmented by black-and-white photographs and articles from the *New York Times*. Shane Evans's **We March** (P) offers a picture of what participating in the 1963 March on Washington was like in a manner that allows young children to grasp the enormity of what the protesters were doing.

Jonah Winter relied on the memories of his own father to create his touching portrayal of life during the Great Depression in East Texas. **Born and Bred in the Great Depression** (P) opens and closes with black-and-white photographs of Winter's father and family, but the text itself is illuminated by Kimberly

Bulcken Root's detailed pencil, ink, and watercolor illustrations. Even though the text describes extreme poverty, the overall feeling is one of happiness and warmth of family.

There are also outstanding nonfiction books that present scientific information, concepts, and methods to young readers. Nicola Davies focuses on the many ways in which animals communicate in ***Talk, Talk, Squawk!: Animal Communications*** (P–I), illustrated by Neal Layton. Migration is the topic of Nick Dowson's ***North: The Amazing Story of Artic Migration*** (P). Whales, wolves, cranes, and many other animals that move north for the summer are beautifully illustrated by Patrick Benson. The theory of evolution has been presented for young readers for decades, with books such as Lisa Westberg Peters's ***Our Family Tree: An Evolution Story*** (N–P), illustrated by Lauren Stringer, enabling children to understand the interrelatedness of living organisms. Laurence Pringle's ***Billions of Years, Amazing Changes: The Story of Evolution*** (I–A), with illustrations by Steve Jenkins, is aimed at older readers. Pringle traces the scientific history that preceded Darwin's work, explaining important concepts such as natural selection, and then discusses contemporary work in evolutionary biology, genetics, and other scientific fields that supports Darwin's theory.

History and science are but two of the many fields that nonfiction writers explore; there are books on language, the arts, mathematics, engineering, and many other fields, books that need to find their way into the hands of a young reader eager to learn. In addition to concept books for the youngest readers, discussed in Chapter 3, and authentic biographies, discussed in Chapter 9, we explore nonfiction in Chapter 10.

The examples briefly discussed in each genre section are but a few of the thousands of examples of the wonderful books that are available today. Each year we see innovations in what our talented writers and illustrators offer to these readers, including experimentation with genre and technique, blurring of audience boundaries, as well as increasing diversity and globalization.

• • FORMATS • •

Special formats, such as picturebooks, graphic novels, as well as audio, video, and electronic versions of books for young readers have had a major impact on what today's children have the opportunity to read.

Picturebooks

Picturebooks are a special format in children's literature; we call them "picturebooks" rather than "picture books" to stress their unique combination of text and art. Unlike an "illustrated book," or indeed, a book with no illustrations whatsoever, in a picturebook the words, if present, do not convey the content alone. The words tell us things not in the pictures, and the pictures tell us things not in the words, and, together, they create an essential unity that marks excellent picturebooks. Picturebooks span the genres; this format works well for poetry, folklore, fantastic literature, contemporary realistic fiction, historical fiction, biography, and nonfiction.

Chris Raschka's ***A Ball for Daisy*** (N–P), mentioned at the beginning of this chapter, is completely wordless, relying entirely on the illustrations to tell the story of a small dog who loved playing (and sleeping) with her big red ball, was devastated when a doggie friend accidentally punctured it, and is delighted when presented, by the doggie friend's owner with a new, blue ball. Raschka conveys emotions, action, and theme through use of line, color, and the sequence of the illustrations—and for this, he was awarded the 2012 Caldecott Medal. Another wordless picturebook, Stephen Savage's ***Where's Walrus?*** (N) invites very young readers to look closely at the clean-lined illustrations to spot the walrus, no matter what hat he is wearing.

Lita Judge's beautiful ***Red Sled*** (N) uses words only to indicate sounds, such as the "scrunch scrunch" of walking in the snow, as readers watch woodland animals enjoying an after-hours romp with the sled. Laura Vaccaro Seeger uses very few words to draw young readers into her picturebook ***What If?*** (N–P), as she poses three choices and their possible results through her vivid, color-filled illustrations. The minimal text in Monica Carnesi's ***Little Dog Lost: The True Story of a Brave Dog Named Baltic*** (N–P) tells the story of a small dog adrift in the ice-filled Vistula River, headed out to an equally icy sea, but with a happy ending. With illustrations carrying much of the action, this picturebook also appeals to children beginning to be able to read on their own. Jon Klassen's minimal, repetitive text in large font also lends itself to being read both to and by young children, but not until they've had an opportunity to hear and look closely at the illustrations in ***I Want My Hat Back*** (N–P).

The lyrical text in ***And Then It's Spring*** (P) by Julie Fogliano with illustrations by Erin E. Stead depict a small boy, a dog, a rabbit, and a turtle on a search for spring. Stead's quietly beautiful illustrations enhance the anticipatory tone and are also full of subtle humor. Readers who enjoy this book should also like her Caldecott Medal–winning ***A Sick Day for Amos McGee*** (N–P) by Philip C. Stead. Another picturebook that captures young children's curiosity about the natural world, ***Over and Under the Snow*** (N–P) by Kate

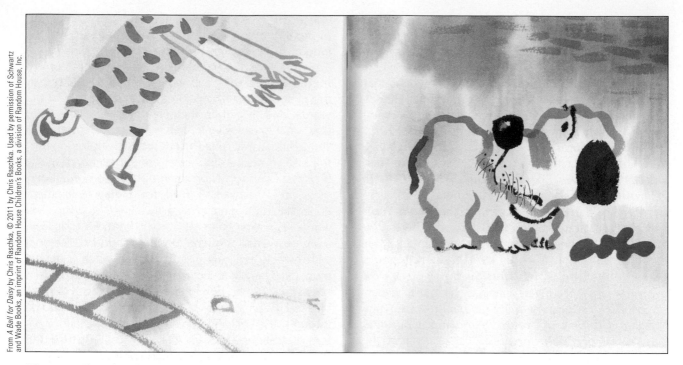

The way Chris Raschka captures emotion in a few lines and colors resulted in **A Ball for Daisy** *winning the 2012 Caldecott Medal.*

Messner, follows an adult and a child cross-country skiing through a snowy forest. Christopher Silas Neal's clever illustrations display the activities of the animals around them, both above and below the snow. Marla Frazee's illustrations and Mary Lyn Ray's meditative text combine to create a top-notch picturebook, **Stars** (P). After spending time with this book, the word *star* takes on new connotations. A book aimed at slightly older readers, **Which Side Are You On?: The Story of a Song** (P–I), by George Ella Lyon with illustrations by Christopher Cardinale, is a fictionalized version of the true story of how this iconic union anthem was created by a mother of seven during the coal miners' struggle to unionize. Though fiction, the end material includes an author's note and bibliography.

The world of picturebooks encompasses books both with and without words, but always with illustrations. Generally, but certainly not always, these books are thirty-two pages in which words, if present, and illustrations are artistically arranged, most often together. In 2008, however, the classic description of a picturebook was shaken with the awarding of the Caldecott Medal, given for the most distinguished picturebook of the preceding year, to Brian Selznick for **The Invention of Hugo Cabret** (I). Selznick's book contains more than five hundred pages of text with hundreds of pictures. **Hugo** has been made into a movie, and Selznick's **Wonderstruck: A Novel in Words and Pictures** (I) is yet another distinguished

contribution to children's literature that expands our ideas about picturebooks.

In a picturebook for young readers, Emily Gravett's **The Rabbit Problem** (P) is designed as a calendar and can actually be hung on the wall; it is extremely engaging as it presents a rather sophisticated topic—the Fibonacci sequence. We discuss the special characteristics of picturebooks and how they work in Chapter 3. They also appear, along with graphic novels and other formats, in Chapters 4 through 10 where appropriate.

Picturebooks have also changed conceptually in the last few years. Children seem more tolerant of ambiguous endings, books that make references to other texts, and books that play with the seemingly solid distinction between fiction and reality. These picturebooks are labeled with the broad term *postmodern*. Why would these types of picturebooks be important? New types of texts teach children different things about reading. Just as historical fiction and poetry are different types of texts that children must learn to read differently, so, too, do postmodern picturebooks force readers to read in new ways. For example, readers learn to be satisfied with ambiguous endings; to accept multiple interpretations, to play with stories instead of taking them at face value, and to understand the humor of combining different texts together. In these ways, postmodern picturebooks give children the opportunity to become more critical and more thoughtful readers.

The very concept of "story" has been radically altered in postmodern picturebooks. This word is difficult to define and is used by theorists in a variety of ways, but the types of picturebooks we might call "postmodern" seem to have some identifiable characteristics.

Sipe and McGuire (2008), combining and synthesizing the work of several scholars, list six characteristics of postmodern picturebooks:

1. Blurring the distinctions between "high culture" and popular culture, the categories of traditional literary genres, and the boundaries among author, narrator, and reader.

2. Subversion of literary traditions and conventions, and undermining the traditional distinctions between the story and the outside "real" world.

3. Intertextuality—texts referring to other texts—is present in all writing, but in postmodern texts, this layering of texts is made explicit and often results in strange and amusing juxtapositions.

4. Multiplicity of meanings, so that there are many possible pathways through the story, a high degree of ambiguity, and endings that are often ambiguous and open-ended.

5. Playfulness, in which readers are invited to manipulate the text, "enter" it and control it, and generally subvert the story.

6. *Self-referentiality*, a term that refers to the types of stories that refuse to allow readers to have what Louise Rosenblatt (1978) calls a "lived-through" experience of the story. Instead, the story pushes readers away, as if to say, "What you are reading is not real—remember that it's just a story."

Post-modern picturebooks appeal to a wide range of readers, from young children through adolescents.

Graphic Novels

In Japan, graphic novels, in the form of manga, have been popular for many decades, and the increasing globalization of children's and adolescent literature brought them to the attention of North American readers (Michaels, 2004). Older children and adolescents responded with great delight. Although Art Spiegelman's **Maus** books were not intended for an adolescent audience, young readers quickly made them their own. Other popular adult authors, such as Neil Gaiman in his **Sandman** series, have produced graphic novels that enthrall young readers.

The graphic novel, with its resemblance to a long and complicated comic book, has come into its own as another form of art that combines words and visual images in synergistic ways. A graphic novel for adolescents, Gene Luen Yang's **American Born Chinese** (A), won the Printz Award in 2007. It was also a National Book Award finalist. This alone signals a new respect for a sophisticated art form that many had dismissed as "light reading." In fact, many graphic novels such as David Almond's graphic novel within a novel, **Savage** (A); Don Wood's **Into the Volcano** (I–A); and Sid Jackson and Ernie Colon's graphic biography, **Anne Frank: The Anne Frank House Authorized Graphic Biography** (A) have extremely serious themes and plots and have given inspiration to those who work in the world of picturebooks. The enormous potential of this new form has yet to be realized. Publishers, such as First Second, are devoting resources to graphic novels, and beginning in 2009, The American Library Association's Young Adult Library Services Association (YALSA) publishes a list of "Great Graphic Novels for Teens" as well as a "Top Ten" list each winter.

Just as the distinctions among various literary genres are becoming less clear, the distinctions among the formats of picturebooks, graphic novels, and comics are blurring. We predict that this trend will continue until the distinctions become less and less useful, and we begin to think of picturebooks, graphic novels, and comics as forms of "sequential art" (Eisner, 2008). An exemplar of this, Australian Shaun Tan was awarded a Boston Globe–Horn Book Special Citation for Excellence in Graphic Storytelling for his stunning **The Arrival** (I–A). This gorgeous book is part wordless picturebook, part graphic novel, wholly imaginative, and eloquently speaks to the immigrant experience.

Audio, Video, and Electronic Books: Beyond the Printed Page

In the twenty-first century, audiobooks for young readers are a lucrative market. Publishing houses such as Random House and HarperCollins are increasing their production of audiobooks, and parents, teachers, and librarians are thinking and talking about their place in the world of children's reading (Varley, 2002). Listening to a book is certainly not the same as reading it, but listening to a wonderful recording of a great book offers its own opportunities for engagement, literary appreciation, and comprehension. Listening to Listening Library's full-cast recording of Philip Pullman's **His Dark Materials** trilogy is as amazing an experience as reading the books. Audiobooks have become so popular that *The Horn Book Magazine* reviews them in a special section that follows their book reviews. The American Library Association (ALA) publishes an annual list of Notable Children's Recordings as well.

The American Library Association also publishes an annual list of Notable Children's Videos. Filmmakers, too, have successfully adapted several popular books, such as J. K. Rowling's **Harry Potter** series and Lemony Snicket's **A Series of Unfortunate Events**, Chris Van Allsburg's **The Polar Express**, and Kate DiCamillo's **Because of Winn-Dixie** and **The Tale of Despereaux**, and the Oscar nominee, **Hugo**, from Brian Selznick's novel.

In addition to books, we have an extensive array of electronic media that relate to books, aimed to engage children and adolescents in a variety of ways such as book-group blogs, and other Internet activities for a visually oriented audience. To help parents and teachers select the best, the ALA provides an annual list of great websites for children.

It is clear that children, even the very youngest, are intrigued by the electronic books that are increasing in availability and popularity. A brief story about one young reader illustrates this development:

> One-year-old Lexie loves to sit on her father's lap and and read Dorothy Kunhardt's **Pat the Bunny** (P). She quickly reaches forward to play "peek-a-boo" with Paul, put her nose on the talcum-powder scented flowers, and stroke the soft fur on Bunny's back. But she also enjoys cuddling up with her sister, brother, and the family's iPad to listen to it read aloud **Pat the Bunny**. With her older siblings, she giggles as she "pops" the bubbles and delights in seeing herself reflected in the mirror. Lexie watches her brother recording and then listening to himself reading Marc Tolon Brown's interactive e-book **Arthur Turns Green** (P) and sees her sister laughing at puppy Rocket's surprised reactions while she clicks away on Tad Hill's interactive e-book **How Rocket Learned to Read** (P). Lexie's older cousin is reading her way through the **Ivy & Bean** (P–I) series on her mom's Kindle as well as the "hardcopy" versions in the school library.

Lexie's experiences with print are still dominated by actual books, but e-books, apps, and other interactive book experiences will likely change the way her generation views reading. Those in the reading and children's literature fields have been discussing this new dimension in reading fervently the last few years. Articles about teaching with e-books have popped up in all the major journals for reading teachers, librarians have explored how many and what sort of e-books they should begin to purchase, and researchers have explored possible effects of reading electronically versus reading in print. Although electronic books seem to be more gradually being embraced in the classroom, it is the apps and the more interactive-style e-books that appear to be causing a stir. E-books are slightly more print-bound; they present the text in digital form with simple additions such as dictionary help, or some, aimed more at children, offer the ability to record and listen or have the text read aloud. The interactive e-books and apps offer opportunities for animation of characters, coloring, and even little games, and thus open up new, and perhaps challenging, possibilities. Roger Sutton, editor of *The Horn Book Magazine*, and award-winning author and illustrator Mo Willems have addressed interactive e-books and apps in the pages of *The Horn Book Magazine* ("Why Books," 2011 and "A is for App," 2010), both drawing the conclusion that, for now, regular print books offer something that the digital books cannot. Sutton focuses on what young readers will turn to after reading and/or playing with a book app; Willems speaks to the opportunities for creativity he believes print books uniquely offer. Currently, the *Horn Book* has not offered "What Makes a Good Interactive Digital Book" in their "What Makes a Good . . . ?" series, but *The School Library Journal* already has established a blog that reviews the best apps and interactive books available for children called *Touch and Go: A Guide to the Best Apps for Children and Teens*.

Oceanhouse Media and Random House Children's Books perhaps dominated the early offerings of the children's interactive book scene, offering many app versions of existing popular children's books, but more publishers with more new interactive book apps appear daily. Beyond the interactive books, several book- and reading-related apps for young readers are available. How will it change students' reading experiences to read along with Booktracks—an app that plays background music and sound effects for well-known stories, or to use Crazy Faces in readers' theater—an app that provides masks for fairy-tale characters, masks that have mouths to move along to your speech?

Beyond the apps and interactive books, we now have regular promotion videos for books appearing online (easily accessible on Amazon.com, for example) and highly visited websites for fans of popular series, often including space for authors of fan-fiction. One of the more exciting developments in this area is J. K. Rowling's inventive **Pottermore.com**, a website community offering a complex series of ways to interact with the **Harry Potter** series (I–A). A community element allows visitors to interact with one another, "casting" spells and winning house points, but the website moves past this to offer what Rowling terms "[a website] that can be enjoyed alongside the Harry Potter books." A labyrinth maze traces the books chapter by chapter, and as visitors move along the site, they can engage with new, additional material related to the characters, setting, and action of that chapter. The popularity of the website in its beta version has exceeded even the most optimistic expectations, and it is likely that other similar websites linked to popular series may appear. As the digital world of books expand, the face of publishing and marketing children's books will likely change. Perhaps, however, the book will remain as the center, the inspiration for the rapidly evolving electronic world.

Global and Multicultural Literature

In the first twelve years of the twenty-first century, innovative authors and illustrators and technological advances have changed literature for children and adolescents. So, too, have increasing globalization and the recognition of a rich multiculturalism within the United States.

• • GLOBAL LITERATURE • •

In the late fall of 2002, the International Children's Digital Library (ICDL) was launched, a joint project of the Human-Computer Interaction Laboratory at the University of Maryland and the Internet Archive in San Francisco. By early 2004 there were almost four hundred books online, with plans for an additional ten thousand more by 2009 (Cummins, 2004). The ICDL now reports almost five thousand books in sixty-one languages. The more than three million users come from 228 different countries; 53 percent are from the United States. Strides toward the ICDL's goal of providing free access to children's books from around the world to the children of the world are impressive; a great deal has been accomplished in the past ten years. Organizations such as the International Board on Books for Young People (IBBY), with members from around the world, help sustain a global perspective. IBBY has national sections in many countries, such as the United States Board on Books for Young People (USBBY). IBBY sponsors the Hans Christian Andersen Awards, an international prestigious award given annually for writing and illustration. USBBY publishes an annual list of Outstanding International Books.

Members of USBBY, the International Reading Association, the National Council of Teachers of English, and the American Library Association produce books about international literature, such as *Bridges to Understanding: Envisioning the World*

through Children's Eyes (Pavonetti, 2011), the fourth volume in an undertaking that began in the late 1990s. *Reading Globally, K–8: Connecting Students to the World Through Literature* (Lehman, Freeman, & Scharer, 2010) explores literature from other countries as well as that written by those who have immigrated to the United States and those books written by persons living outside of the United States but first published here. The authors ground their discussion in the real world of classrooms in the United States. Additionally, annual annotated bibliographies such as "Notable Books for a Global Society" from the International Reading Association and that compiled by the ALA's Association for Library Service to Children's International Relations Committee, as well as the USBBY Outstanding International Books list, begun in 2006, and reviews of translated books in the USBBY newsletter, offer titles for those interested in global literature. Selected titles from the 2012 list appear in the Booklist at the end of this chapter.

Literature reflects the interests and concerns of the culture that produces it. Currently, the United States is focused on the people and places in the Middle and Far East. Although in the past there were excellent books set in these countries, such as Suzanne Fisher Staples's **Shabanu** and **Haveli** (A), there has been an increase in books set in that region or about people who have fled from that region. **Running on Eggs** (A), a story of friendship between a Jewish girl and a Palestinian girl by Anna Levine, is a positive picture of possibilities for friendship and peace. Daniella Carmi's **Samir and Yonatan** (I–A) also explores Palestinian-Israeli friendship but is less hopeful. Randa Abdel-Fattah's **Where the Streets Had a Name** (I–A) is set in Palestine and depicts the restrictions of life under occupation. Deborah Ellis sets **No Ordinary Day** (A) in India, and **The Breadwinner** (I) in contemporary Afghanistan, where Trent Reedy's **Words in the Dust** (A) is also set. In the United States, books such as the titles just mentioned that are set in other countries include those written by American authors, those with family roots in other countries, and those who are knowledgeable about other countries. This practice has long been a part of literature for young readers, and most contemporary writers take great pains to research their material carefully so that they present as accurate a picture of life in another country as they are able. Patricia McCormick's **Sold** (A) is a good example of this type of book, with its powerful portrayal of the experience of a young Nepalese girl sold into a life of prostitution in India. Although the accurately depicted circumstances of Lakshmi's life are unbearable, her indomitable spirit never flags. Linda Sue Park's **A Long Walk to Water: Based** *on a True Story* (A) is partially the story of a friend of hers, one of the Lost Boys of Sudan who escaped the war that was raging in the mid-1980s and returned years later to create a company to drill wells in remote Sudanese villages. His story is entwined with the story of a contemporary Sudanese girl whose village receives one of these wells.

Books from other English-speaking countries are the most plentiful type of international literature. Canada, Great Britain, and Australia produce the majority of books that are imported to the United States (Stan, 2002). In most cases, these books are published in the United States, usually, but not always, a little while after publication in the home country. Irishman Eoin Colfer's best-selling **Artemis Fowl** series was a runaway success in America. His 2008 novel **Airman** (I–A) is a rip-roaring adventure set on islands off the Irish coast. Siobhan Parkinson's novel set in Ireland, **Blue Like Friday** (I–A), explores family dynamics and friendship in a manner that crosses national boundaries. Mimi Grey's **Traction Man Meets Turbo Dog** (P), a companion to her popular **Traction Man Is Here** (P), a Boston Globe–Horn Book Award winner, appeals to young readers in many countries other than her native England, with its spirited graphics and text. Helen Ward's **Varmints** (I), hauntingly illustrated by Marc Craste, is an imaginative science fiction picturebook from England that poses questions important to young readers everywhere. Venezuelan Menena Cottin offers young readers an intriguing experience in **The Black Book of Colors** (P), illustrated by Rosana Faria and translated by Elisa Amado. Raised black line drawings on black paper, accompanied by both Braille and English text, offers sighted readers an opportunity to "see" color in a new way and to experience making meaning through their fingertips.

Laurel Croza's **I Know Here**, illustrated by Matt James, is a beautifully evocative story of a young girl's emotions as she prepares to move with her family from Saskatchewan to Toronto, a place that is only a star on a map of Canada to her. Atinuke's **Anna Hibiscus** (P), illustrated by Lauren Tobia, is set in contemporary Nigeria and introduces young readers to a loveable and spunky young girl; the author spent her childhood in Nigeria and now lives in Wales.

A compilation of three previously published but not easily accessible picturebooks by Shaun Tan, **Lost & Found: Three by Shaun Tan** (A) are welcome additions to the many American fans of Tan's work. Tan received the 2011 Astrid Lindgren Memorial Award, honoring his contributions to international children's literature. Another illustrator and storyteller from Australia, Jeannie Baker's **Mirror** (P–I) contains two parallel wordless stories that depict differences and similarities between a boy from Sydney, Australia, and one from rural Morocco, and includes a bilingual introduction. Innovative design allows the boys' stories to unfold side by side. Patrick Ness built upon a story idea from another well-respected international author, the late Siobhan Dowd, in **A Monster Calls: Inspired by an Idea from Siobhan Dowd** (I–A), with a setting that evokes Great Britain. David Almond's **Raven Summer** (A) is another book that has crossed the Atlantic to find an audience in the United States. You will find many examples of books written and illustrated by children's book creators from other English-speaking countries in the chapters that follow.

Translated books are less plentiful, less than 1 percent annually, but awards such as the American Library Association's Mildred L. Batchelder Book Award encourage a truly international exchange. The 2012 Batchelder winner, **Soldier Bear** (I–A), by Bibi Dumon Tak, was translated from the Dutch by Laura Watkinson. The Honor book was Annika Thor's **The Lily Pond** (A), translated from the Swedish by Linda Schenck. Both books are discussed in Chapter 8. Other translated books include Mirjam Pressler's **Let Sleeping Dogs Lie** (A), a welcome addition to her several other novels for young readers that have been translated from the German, and Anne-Laure Bondoux's **A Time of Miracles** (A), translated from the French by Y. Maudet. Two picturebooks, Philippe Coudray's **Benjamin Bear in Fuzzy Thinking: A Toon Book** (P), translated from the French by Leigh Stein, and Yukiko Kato's **In the Meadow** (N), illustrated by Komako Sakai and translated from the Japanese by Yuki Kaneko, offer the youngest readers lovely experiences reading books that were created in other parts of the world.

• • MULTICULTURAL LITERATURE • •

Although literature by and about people of color, what Virginia Hamilton (1993) called "parallel cultures," remains a small percentage of all publications for children and young adults, stunning talent, stalwart publishers, and the cultural and social changes in the last few decades of the twentieth century came together to create a twenty-first-century demand for quality books from parallel cultures (Bader, 2003b). In a three-part series of articles in *The Horn Book Magazine*, Barbara Bader (2002, 2003a, 2003b) describes the gradual growth of literature from parallel cultures. Rudine Sims Bishop's (2007) brilliant **Free Within Ourselves: The Development of African American Children's Literature** details the struggles and triumphs of those committed to bringing African

American literature to young readers. Special recognition of authors and illustrators of particular parallel cultures, such as the Coretta Scott King Awards (for African American literature) and the Pura Belpré Awards (for Latino literature), were established in 1970 and 1996, respectively, and are administered by the American Library Association. The history of these awards reflects increasingly robust publication. The King Award has expanded from the original single award for an author to awards for both authors and illustrators, including honor awards. The Belpré has always honored both authors and illustrators, but, since 2009, is an annual, rather than biennial, award. Winners of these and other awards are listed in Appendix A.

Who are the authors and illustrators who have helped shape the literature we have today? Many of their names appear in Appendix A as winners of not only the King or the Belpré Awards, but also as winners of the Caldecott and Newbery Awards. We provide suggestions for resources for finding multicultural and global literature in the section on selecting literature for young readers later in this chapter. In the Booklist at the end of this chapter, we present the names of selected authors and illustrators working within various cultural traditions in the United States as a beginning resource for you as you seek out children's literature that reflects the many cultures that contribute to the vibrancy of the United States.

Race and ethnicity are important aspects of diversity within America, and children's and adolescent literature reflect this diversity. Of the many parallel cultures in North America, African Americans are presented in literature for children and adolescents more frequently than other cultural groups. In the "Thoughts on Publishing" issued by the Cooperative Children's Book Center in 2011, they offer the following statistics on multicultural literature:

> Out of the 3,400 books that CCBC received in 2010, 156 books had significant African or African American content, 22 books featured American Indian themes, topics, or characters, 64 books had significant Asian Pacific or Asian/Pacific American content, and 66 books had significant Latino content. Clearly, while the state of literature from parallel cultures has improved due to years of publishing quality books, it is still troubling that so few books by and about parallel cultures are being published, especially when one considers the 2010 census data on race in the United States.

Over the past few decades, books about African Americans have reflected the wide range of African American culture, including the experience and consequences of slavery; the civil rights movement; and life in the late twentieth and early twenty-first centuries, ranging from inner-city poverty to middle-class African American experiences. The Coretta Scott King Awards continue to honor some of the many excellent books produced by African American writers and illustrators. Established authors and illustrators create beautiful books, and new talent continues to appear.

The first African American to win the Newbery Award, in 1975 for **M. C. Higgins, the Great** (I–A) and the international Hans Christian Andersen Award, the late Virginia Hamilton was also the first writer for children and adolescents to receive the prestigious MacArthur "genius" grant. Angela Johnson, another prolific African American author, was also honored with this grant. Mildred Taylor won the Newbery in 1977 for **Roll of Thunder, Hear My Cry** (A), and Christopher Paul Curtis, with a 1996 Newbery Honor for **The Watsons Go to Birmingham— 1963**, was the Newbery winner in 2000 for **Bud, Not Buddy** (I–A). These authors, along with writers such as Patricia and Fredrick McKissack, Sharon Draper, Andrea Davis Pinkney, Tanya Bolden, Lesa Cline Ransome, Julius Lester, and Jacqueline Woodson have won many awards and honors, including the King Awards and Honor Awards and Newbery Honors. Walter Dean Myers was the first recipient of the Printz Award for **Monster** (A), a ground-breaking book for adolescents. Major African American and Caribbean poets include Ashley Bryan, Gwendolyn Brooks, Lucille Clifton, Maya Angelou, Eloise Greenfield, Nikki Grimes, Nikki Giovanni, and Marilyn Nelson, who won both a King and a Newbery Honor for **Carver: A Life in Poems** (A), featured in Chapter 4. Rita Williams-Garcia was showered with recognition for her novel **One Crazy Summer** (I–A), which won the 2011 Coretta Scott King Book Award, was a 2011 Newbery Honor book, won the 2011 Scott Odell Award for historical fiction, and was a 2010 National Book Award finalist.

In 2010, the beloved illustrator Jerry Pinkney won the Caldecott Award, for **The Lion & the Mouse** (N–P); he has many Caldecott Honors and King Awards and Honors as well as several international awards. Other outstanding African American illustrators include James Ransome, E. B. Lewis, Christopher Myers, Javaka Steptoe, Bryan Collier, Floyd Cooper, Donald Crews, Leo Dillon, Synthia Saint James, Kadir Nelson, Brian Pinkney, and the late Tom Feelings, many of whom have garnered Caldecott and Coretta Scott King Awards and Honors. Ashley Bryan was named the winner of the 2012 Coretta Scott King– Virginia Hamilton Award for Lifetime Achievement;

in 1962, Bryan was the first African American to both write and illustrate a children's book. The rich and varied heritage of the African American experience is indeed reflected in its literature for children and adolescents; it is also reflected in the remainder of this text. These and other talented African American writers and illustrators give all readers the gift of wonderful books, books that everyone can read and enjoy.

Latino literature for children and young adults is also growing at a slow pace, but marked by outstanding authors and illustrators. Like books by and about African Americans, the number of books for children portraying Latino characters stands in stark contrast to the number of Latinos in the population. A very small portion of children's books, 2 percent, represent a Latino culture (Nieto, 2002). Compared to the number of Latino children who need to see themselves represented in books, and to the number of other children who need to understand something of Latino culture, we have a long way to go. Fortunately, awards such as the Pura Belpré Awards and the Americas Awards draw attention to the many Latino gifted writers and illustrators.

Happily, these writers, illustrators, and poets produce outstanding literature. Latino literature began to become increasingly popular with the paperback publication of Sandra Cisneros's *The House on Mango Street* (A) in 1991. This was followed by Judith Ortiz Cofer's *An Island Like You: Stories of the Barrio* (A). Both of these books were originally published by Arte Publico, the same house that reissued Nicholasa Mohr's early books about life in the New York City barrio, *Nilda* and *In Nueva York* (both A), originally published in the 1970s (Bader, 2003b). As Latino writers began to produce more books, our literature for young readers began to be enriched by their contributions. Victor Martinez won the 1996 National Book Award for his powerful novel, *Parrot in the Oven: Mi Vida* (A). Francisco Jiménez's *The Circuit: Stories from the Life of a Migrant Child* (A), a collection of stories based on his own experiences as a child in a migrant farmworker family, won the 1998 Boston Globe–Horn book Award for fiction. Julia Alvarez, whose *Before We Were Free* (A), a coming of age story set in the Trujilo dictatorship of the Dominican Republic, was the Pura Belpré winner in 2002; she was the 2010 winner of the Pura Belpré and the Americas Award for her novel *Return to Sender* (A), a powerful indictment of the way we treat the children of undocumented workers in the United States. She is also the author of the *Tia Lola* series as well as highly acclaimed books for adults.

Other Latino/a authors include Ana Veciana-Suarez, George Ancona, Francisco X. Alarcón, Nancy Osa, Carmen Agra Deedy, Patricia Mora, Pam Muñoz Ryan, Alma Flor Ada, Carmen T. Bernier-Grand, Gary Soto, and Margarita Engle, who won a Newbery Honor and the Belpré Award in 2009 for her book, *The Surrender Tree: Poems of Cuba's Struggle for Freedom*; her *Hurricane Dancers: The First Caribbean Pirate Shipwreck* (A), was a Belpré Honor book in 2012 and is discussed in Chapter 6. Meg Medina's *Tia Isa Wants a Car* (P), illustrated by Claudio Munoz, gracefully incorporates Spanish words in this story of a family saving to bring other family members to America. Many of these writers span the genres of fantasy, contemporary fiction, and historical fiction, poetry, and memoir for older and younger readers alike. Illustrators include Lulu Delacre, Enrique O. Sanchez, Carmen Lomas Garza, Susan Guevara, Yuyi Morales, Robert Casilla, Raul Colon, Joe Cepeda, and David Diaz, whose *Smoky Night* (P–I), by Eve Bunting, was a Caldecott Medal winner.

Although still disproportionally small, the number of high-quality books featuring Asian and Pacific-Islander Americans is increasing in number and becoming increasingly diverse, as literature by immigrants from Laos, Vietnam, Thailand, and the Pacific Islands joins with that from Japanese, Chinese, and Korean Americans. Years ago, Yoshiko Uchida wrote powerful novels about her experiences as a first-generation Japanese American living in California after the outbreak of World War II. She and Laurence Yep, who has been telling the stories of the Chinese American experience for thirty years, has been joined by authors such as Linda Sue Park, whose historical fiction novel, *A Single Shard* (A), was the 2002 Newbery Award winner, and Cynthia Kadahota, whose moving story *Kira-Kira* (A), won the 2005 Newbery Award. Thanhha Lai was a Newbery Honor winner in 2012 for *Inside Out & Back Again* (A), a moving story of a family who flees Vietnam for the American south. An Na was the recipient of the Printz Award for *A Step from Heaven* for her powerful novel exploring the experience of one Korean child who emigrates with her parents to the United States only to find that the streets are not paved with gold for them. Grace Lin's *Where the Mountain Meets the Moon* (A), a Newbery Honor book, is a fantasy inspired by Asian folklore. Other authors include Minfong Ho and Ken Mochizuki.

Several Asian American authors write contemporary realistic fiction or poetry about being Asian American today. Grace Lin, Lisa Yee, Lenore Look, Lensey Namioka, and Marie Lee create books that explore being a child or adolescent in America today; Janet Wong's poetry often explores this as well. Ying Chang Compestine's *Crouching Tiger* (P), illustrated by Yan Nascimbene, depicts a family that balances their Chinese and American cultures. Allen Say explores being multicultural and biracial in some of his many picturebooks. His *Grandfather's Journey* (P–I) won the Caldecott Award in 1994. Ed Young, another prolific illustrator, was the recipient of the 1990 Caldecott Award for *Lon Po Po: A Red-Riding Hood Story from China* (P). He won the 2008–2009 Asian Pacific American Award for Picture Book illustrations for his gorgeous art for Mark Reibstein's *Wabi Sabi* (I). The Asian Pacific American Award for Literature honors books by and about Asian Pacific Americans.

Native American experiences have been interpreted in literature for children by members of various tribal groups, anthropologists, folklorists, and others. Unfortunately, much of the literature that portrayed Native Americans did so with erroneous or stereotyped information and images. Literature for young readers by and about Native Americans began to flower in the late 1970s, as Native American voices, so long suppressed, began to be heard. Children's literature now includes Native American poetry, folklore, historical fiction, and biography, as well as historical nonfiction from a Native American perspective. There are some, but not nearly enough, books about contemporary Native American experiences.

One of the earliest authors to express Native American values was Craig Kee Strete in novels such as *When Grandfather Journeys into Winter* and *The World in Grandfather's Hands* (both A). Cynthia Leitich Smith explores contemporary life in books such as *Rain Is Not My Indian Name* (I–A). Joseph Bruchac's many books span a wide range of genres and reach both intermediate and advanced readers. His *Eagle Song* and *The Heart of a Chief* (both I–A), are contemporary realistic fiction; *Sacajawea* and *The Winter People* (both I–A) are historical fiction. Other important historical fiction from a Native American perspective includes books by Michael Dorris, whose *Morning Girl* imagines the perceptions of a young Taino Indian girl upon the landing of Columbus. Louise Erdrich, acclaimed writer for adults, also writes wonderful books for young readers. Her novels for upper-elementary grade students, *The Birchbark House, The Game of Silence*, and *The Porcupine Year* are discussed in Chapter 8. *The Birchbark House* won the 2006 American Indian Youth Literature Award, which honors the best writing and illustrations by and about American Indians. Outstanding Native American illustrators include Shonto Begay and George Littlechild.

The Arab American experience has recently begun to be found in literature for young readers. Ibtisam Barakat's *Tasting the Sky: A Palestinian Childhood* (I–A) is a memoir recounting her experiences as a young girl caught up in war. Naomi Shihab Nye, a Palestinian American writer, has given us *Sitti's Secrets* (P–I), a lovely picturebook describing an Arab American girl's visit to her Palestinian relatives; her novel *Habibi* (I–A) is based on the same premise but graphically explores the political and social realities of living in Palestine. Her book of poetry, *19 Varieties of Gazelle: Poems of the Middle East* (I–A), is again focused on Palestine and offers older readers a glimpse of a culture that is on the brink of being shattered. Reflecting the increasing numbers of books that the Arab American community produces, the Arab American Book Award for literature for young readers was established in 2007. Acknowledging books that "preserve and advance the understanding, knowledge, and resources of the Arab American community by celebrating the thoughts and lives of Arab Americans," the Arab American Book Award honors a children's or young adult book each year. These and other books that explore the experiences of contemporary characters straddling two cultures are discussed in Chapter 7.

Other aspects of diversity have also enriched literature for young readers. Books that explore exceptionalities seem to be increasing, with powerful novels such as Sharon Draper's *Out of My Mind* (I–A) joining Terry Trueman's Printz Honor Book, *Stuck in Neutral* (A) as riveting stories of the bright minds hidden behind conditions such as cerebral palsy. Mark Haddon won the 2003 Whitbread Book of the Year Award for his portrayal of a young man with Asperger's syndrome in *The Curious Incident of the Dog in the Night-Time* (A). In 2010, Kathryn Erskine's *Mockingbird* (I–A) won the National Book Award for Young People's Literature; her novel was informed by her daughter's experiences with Asperger's syndrome. Books that explore life with other physical and mental challenges include stories of children who struggle in school. Some of the first, and most well known, are Jack Gantos's *Joey Pigza* (I) books. These and many other books are discussed in Chapters 7 and 8 of this text. In 2004, the Schneider Family Book Award, administered by the American Library Association, was inaugurated to honor an author or illustrator for his or her expression of the disability experience for young readers.

There have also been an increasing number of books exploring sexual preference, mostly in books for young adult readers. Since the 1982 publication of Nancy Garden's *Annie on My Mind* (A), noted authors such as David Levithan have created stories about being gay or lesbian as a contemporary American adolescent. Many of these books are discussed in Chapter 7. Other aspects of diversity reflected in literature for young readers include religion and socio-economic status, though these stories are less prevalent than those reflecting race, culture, exceptionalities, and sexual orientation.

Selecting and Using Literature for Children and Adolescents

Books can play a significant role in the life of our youth, but the extent to which they will do so depends on the adults surrounding them. Books and children aren't made of Velcro; they don't stick to one another without a little help from significant others, including parents, grandparents, teachers, librarians, community leaders, volunteers, and others who come into contact with them. Adults are responsible for determining a child's literary heritage by selecting and presenting nursery rhymes, traditional tales, beautiful poetry, arresting picturebooks of all kinds, great novels, and riveting nonfiction. This selection process is neither easy nor without pitfalls. Knowing the literature is important. Knowing children and their community is equally important.

● ● CONSIDERING LITERARY ● ● EXCELLENCE

Selecting books to offer to young readers is a multidimensional task. For teachers and librarians, this process is even more difficult because they are selecting a large number of books to use with many children from varied backgrounds. Because of the diversity and richness in children's literature today, readers' experiences with books can be infinitely varied. With so much to choose from, we as teachers and librarians can select high-quality literature: books that use interesting language in creative ways, develop important ideas, are potentially interesting to children, and (through picturebooks) contain artistically excellent illustrations. Characteristics of excellence in the format of picturebooks are discussed in Chapter 3. Those for each genre are summarized in Figure 1.3.

FIGURE 1.3

Characteristics of Good Books by Genre

Genre	Text	Illustration
Poetry	Condensed, evocative language	Interprets beyond literal meaning
Folklore	Patterned language, fast-paced plot Sounds like spoken language	Interpretive of the tale and cultural origins
Fantasy	Consistent, logical fantasy world	Extends fanciful elements
	Clearly defined conflict Strong characterization	Reflects characterization and events
Science Fiction	Speculative extrapolation of scientific possibility, vivid and logical	Visualizes imaginative worlds
	Strong characterization	Enhances characterization and plot
Contemporary Realistic Fiction	Story is plausible	Enhances characterization and plot
	Well-defined conflict	
	Strong characterization	
Historical Fiction	Setting affects plot and character	Enhances setting, characterization, and plot
	Authenticity of details and language	
Biography/ Memoir	Authentic, vivid representation	Authentic images of life segments
Nonfiction	Clarity, accuracy	Clarifies and extends facts and concepts
	Stimulating writing	
	Artful design	

We elaborate on and explore these characteristics in Chapters 4 through 10. In this text, we focus on "literary quality" because we believe that the books we put into the hands of young readers should be the best we have to offer. We also acknowledge, as Deborah Stevenson has pointed out, that "'good' is a tremendously complicated and shifting idea" (2006, p. 511) given that readers' needs and experiences as well as cultural values and practices always influence our definition of "good."

• • EVALUATING CULTURAL • • CONTENT

Diversity is a complex notion. Too often those in the mainstream make the mistake of thinking that cultural diversity refers only to people who are different from them, but everyone belongs to a culture, and in fact, to several cultural communities. Our cultures are woven from many diverse strands; we all live in families and communities that draw on a wealth of knowledge and skills to help them function (Moll, 1994). Cultural diversity is wider than race, ethnicity, gender, sexual preference, or exceptionalities; it also involves values, attitudes, customs, beliefs, and ethics. From this perspective, all children's books could be considered culturally diverse in relation to one another. Because for so long literature for young readers was a literature of the white middle class, however, it is necessary to pay special attention to books coming from people who are not representative of that group. Selecting good books that reflect a diversity of nationalities, races, and ethnicities, contain a wide configuration of family structures, explore diverse sexual orientations, make readers think about issues of class and gender, and contain characters with exceptionalities that shape their worlds is important. Doing so means that young readers will have a wider, more realistic view of how lives are lived in our global society.

Today, all genres contain books from a variety of cultural perspectives, which means that it is now possible to make diversity a central tenet of any literature collection. There are many aspects to consider when selecting books to build a culturally diverse collection. For example, consider the role of culture in a book. Some books have characters that are from a variety of ethnicities or cultures, and often indicate diversity through visual information, such as skin color, eye shape, hair color and style, or the presence of a wheelchair, but present no cultural content. You might think of books of this type as "painted faces" books. If the inclusion of culturally diverse characters is gratuitous or stereotyped, select another book. Sometimes,

however, the diversity subtly reinforces the idea that we live in a culturally diverse world, one populated by people of different colors, people in wheelchairs, people who live in a variety of situations. Norman Juster's ***The Hello-Goodbye Window*** (P), illustrated by Chris Raschka and winner of the Caldecott Medal, features an interracial family, but being interracial is not the focus of the book, or of the companion book, ***Sourpuss and Sweetie Pie*** (P). Culture, as such, is not an important aspect of this book, but the theme of the strength of family is broadened by the diversity depicted.

Other books are about "culture as a concept." Their theme or unifying idea is that culture is important, that people are different yet the same, and, often, that both differences and commonalities need to be acknowledged. Many of these books explicitly state this idea, such as Mem Fox's ***Whoever You Are*** (P) and ***Same, Same But Different*** (P) by Jenny Sue Kostecki-Shaw.

Other books are "culturally rich," depicting experiences that are explicitly embedded in a particular culture, with setting, plot, and characters inextricably tied to culture (Bishop, 1997, 2007), such as ***My Man Blue*** (P) by Nikki Grimes and illustrated by Jerome Lagarrigue. Culturally rich books allow readers to look through a window at characters similar to or different from themselves, to recognize their own culture or learn about another. These books offer young readers the opportunity for a more-than-superficial experience with diverse characters and concepts.

Regardless of the role culture plays in a book, the depiction of culture should be accurate, authentic, and free from stereotypes. Good literature portrays what is unique to an individual culture. It accurately portrays the nuances and variety of day-to-day living in the culture depicted. It does not distort or misrepresent the culture it reflects (Bishop, 1997). At the same time, most stories are about the experience of an individual character, not necessarily representative of a cultural "norm." As Barbara Bader points out, "It is important, too, to have the cultural details be right, although just what *is* right is not always easy to determine. People's experiences and understandings of their experiences vary. Cultures are large, and individuals within cultures are distinct—even in cultures that don't stress individualism. Blatant misinformation and the perpetuation of demeaning stereotypes are one thing, minor mistakes are another" (2007, p. 420).

Determining authenticity, accuracy, and the absence of stereotypes can be difficult. Fortunately, there are a number of resources that can help you make good decisions about which books to include in your collection. The Multicultural Booklist Committee of the National Council of Teachers of English (NCTE) periodically prepares *Kaleidoscope*, an annotated bibliography of multicultural books (defined as books about people of color residing in the United States, Africa, Asia, South and Central America, the Caribbean, Mexico, Canada, and England) as well as books that focus on intercultural or interracial issues. As they read and evaluate books, the committee eliminates those that demonstrate stereotyped images in text or illustration, demeaning or inaccurate use of language, and inaccuracies in text or illustration. The committee does not consider books multicultural when culture is mere tokenism or when it is reflected through the gratuitous inclusion of a sprinkling of words from another language or an occasional character of color in the illustrations (Bishop, 1994).

Problems with perspective are another concern of the committee, and they are a source of debate among the children's literature community. Some argue that anyone outside a particular cultural group cannot hope to write with the understanding and knowledge of an insider and therefore should not try. Some grant that being an outsider makes it more difficult, but contend that good writers such as Paul Goble transcend their outsider status. A good book will "contribute in a positive way to an understanding of the people and cultures portrayed" (Bishop, 1994), whether its author is an insider or an outsider to the culture. It helps, however, to note the perspective of the author when deciding on the quality of any book. In *Stories Matter: The Complexity of Cultural Authenticity in Children's Literature*, editors Dana Fox and Kathy Short (2003) have collected a number of previously published articles that explore this issue.

Books representing a particular culture must represent it accurately and, in most cases, with depth. Look for books that avoid stereotypes, portray the values and the cultural group in an authentic way, use language that reflects cultural group usage, and validate readers' experiences while also broadening vision and inviting reflection. As you begin to evaluate books for their cultural authenticity, think about aspects listed in Figure 1.4.

In Chapters 4 through 10, we discuss the criteria for quality literature in each genre and give examples of books that are among the best of the genre. When appropriate, we also evaluate books on criteria that speak to the quality of the cultural content. If you think of the genre criteria summarized in Figure 1.3 and elaborated in Chapters 4 through 10 as one lens through which to view children's books critically, think of cultural content as another, equally important lens, one that is

FIGURE 1.4

Considering Culturally Diverse Literature

- The book is an excellent piece of literature.
- The book depicts diversity as an important but not gratuitous backdrop in a nonstereotyped manner.
- The book explores cultural differences and similarities in an accurate and sensitive manner.
- The book explores a particular culture accurately, demonstrating diversity within as well as across cultures if appropriate, and avoiding stereotypes.
- The book is a positive contribution to an understanding of the culture portrayed.

additional to, rather than a replacement for, the genre criteria. Each informs the other, and any book can and should be evaluated in terms of both its quality as an example of its genre and its cultural content.

Further, we can evaluate a collection of books—whether in a classroom, a school library, or a public library—in terms of both the depth and breadth of the diversity that it represents. It is up to all of us to select individual books that are of the highest merit, both in literary and in cultural terms, and to make sure that a collection is culturally diverse, no matter who the readers are. All readers need outstanding books that are also richly diverse.

It is important to build a diverse collection because culturally diverse books portray the uniqueness of people while demonstrating a common humanity that connects us all. Human needs, emotions, and desires are similar; books can help us appreciate the similarities as well as celebrate the uniqueness of cultural groups. North America, once considered a melting pot where cultural differences disappeared, is more like a patchwork quilt today—patches of varying colors, textures, shapes, and sizes, all held together by a common thread of humanity (Jackson, 1992).

Children's books offer opportunities for building background knowledge and understanding about the world. Picturebooks, poetry, folklore, realistic and historical fiction, biographies, and nonfiction that

FIGURE 1.5

Resources for Considering Culturally Diverse Literature

The following is a selection of the many books that you might want to consult when selecting culturally diverse literature.

Bishop, Rudine Sims, *Free Within Ourselves: The Development of African American Children's Literature*

Brooks, Wanda & Jonda McNair, *Embracing, evaluating, and examining African American Children's and Young Adult Literature*

Fox, Dana, and Kathy Short, *Stories Matter: The Complexity of Cultural Authenticity in Children's Literature*

Harris, Violet, *Teaching Multicultural Literature in Grades K–8*

_____, *Using Multiethnic Literature in the K–8 Classroom*

Helbig, Althea, and A. R. Perkins, *Many Peoples, One Land: A Guide to New Multicultural Literature for Children and Young Adults*

Kaleidoscope (Various editors over four editions available through the National Council of Teachers of English)

Lehman, Barbara, Freeman, Evelyn, and Scharer, Patricia, *Reading Globally, K–8: Connecting Students to the World Through Literature*

Lehr, Susan, *Beauty, Brains and Brawn: The Construction of Gender in Children's Literature*

Miller-Lachmann, Lynn, *Our Family, Our Friends, Our World*

Pavonetti, Linda, *Bridges to Understanding: Envisioning the World through Children's Eyes*

Pratt, Linda, and Janice Beaty, *Transcultural Children's Literature*

Quintero, Elizabeth, and Mary Kay Rummel, *American Voices: Webs of Diversity*

Seale, Doris, and Beverly Slapin, *A Broken Flute: The Native Experience in Books for Children and Young Adults*

Smith, Henrietta, *The Coretta Scott King Awards: 1970–2004*

Stan, Susan, editor, *The World through Children's Books*

Tomlinson, Carl, editor, *Children's Books from Other Countries*

A committee of the International Reading Association also generates a list, "Notable Books for a Global Society," published annually in the February issue of *The Reading Teacher*. There are also many on line resources available. Go to CengageBrain.com to access the Education CourseMate website where you will find links to relevant websites.

---

demonstrate cultural diversity are available for a wide range of readers. With the help of these books, we can work toward the goal of cross-cultural understanding. In Figure 1.5 we list some resources that will help you make decisions about what books you will need in a culturally diverse collection.

• • STANDARDS, MANDATES, • • TESTS, AND TIME TO READ

Although there are many joys in sharing books with young readers, there are also many challenges. One such challenge is finding time in the school day to read with students. In the past few years, our schools have been under extreme scrutiny, and teachers under extreme time pressure.

We now have Common Core Standards, as well as standards in most states that describe what schoolchildren should be able to do at each grade level. This is a good thing when the standards are sound, given that we all should know the goals we are trying to reach. National organizations, too, have set national standards. The International Reading Association (IRA) has created a set of standards for professionals—for teachers. Happily, it is apparent that to meet the Common Core English Language Arts Standards for grades K through 8, and the IRA Professional Standards, a teacher must use children's books! Indeed, Appendix B of the Common Core Standards lists many titles for children and young adults that are "exemplars" of books that might be used to meet those standards. The exemplars, however, are relatively dated, older titles that, although appropriate for the Standards, might not be appropriate for all of our students today. The books described in this chapter and in Chapters 3 through 10 in this text are also exemplary, and are a wonderful resource as you decide what literature to use.

A look at just one standard demonstrates how necessary children's literature is. In the Common Core English Language Arts Standards/Reading: Literature, standard 7 concerns using both visual and verbal texts to understand aspects of literature. To meet this standard for grades 2 through 5, teachers and students would have to read, study, and discuss picturebooks with their students. For grades 6 and 7, graphic novels, multimedia, audio, video or live presentations of fiction or poetry are necessary. The point is that children's literature can help you teach so that your students meet the standards; in fact, they cannot meet the standards without it. Throughout this text we have included teaching ideas that can help you meet Common Core Standards. Although our primary focus is the literature standards, some of the teaching ideas relate to writing and oral language standards as well. We suggest which standards are relevant in a note at the beginning of each Teaching Idea. As you read the Teaching Ideas, remember that they can be altered to suit varied grade levels by adjusting the questions you ask, the procedures you use, and the literature you choose. Also remember that the standards are constructed so that they build in strength across the grades, from, for example, grade 2, Standard 1, "Ask and answer such questions as who, what, where, when, why, and how to demonstrate understanding of key details in a text" to grade 8, Standard 1, "Cite the textual evidence that most strongly supports an analysis of what the text says explicitly as well as inferences drawn from the text."

Whereas standards can be beneficial and can serve to promote reading, too many national and state-mandated tests can work against the inclusion of children's literature in the curriculum. When a high-stakes test looms, and both a teacher's job and the students' futures are on the line, time to read seems to evaporate. Yet reading a variety of texts for a variety of purposes does serve students well, even when they are taking tests. Generally, students who read the most are also among the best readers and the best test-takers. Creative teachers, knowing that they have an obligation to prepare their students to do their best but not wanting to allow standardized tests to take over their curriculum, often teach their students how to take the tests—how to read and answer questions—much as they teach their students how to read and understand a genre of literature. Tests, like literary genres, have structures and formats that can be taught so that they are familiar to students. When treated in this manner, preparing for these tests becomes simply another unit.

It is vital that we do not let testing take over our teaching, for if time to read and savor books disappears, there will be fewer avid readers and probably fewer accomplished readers as well. Books are the secret ingredient that keeps children doing the hard work of learning to read, learning to read fluently, and learning to read with comprehension. Much of the recent research on motivation indicates that children's literature plays a central role in engaging readers (Pressley et al., 2003). Reading engaging books and thinking, writing, and talking about them with others also provide opportunities for students to develop the higher-order thinking skills that will enable them to be successful citizens of the twenty-first century (Galda & Graves, 2006). For these reasons, and others mentioned at the beginning of this chapter, it is important that we offer wonderful books to our students so that they view books as a vital part of their lives.

• • RESOURCES FOR SELECTING • • LITERATURE

The voluminous body of high-quality children's and adolescent literature shows that the field attracts talented writers and illustrators. Creative people respond to and change their world; innovation is abundantly evident in the children's book world. The number of books published continues to grow, which makes selection even more difficult. Our job as teachers, librarians, and parents is to select the best from the vast array of books. The primary goal of this textbook is to help you recognize good literature and to develop your ability to select quality material. Resources that you will find useful are review journals, awards lists, and other material that calls attention to literature for children. Although all of the resources suggested following are helpful, the best of all is your informed, critical knowledge of the literature that is available for young readers.

Review Journals

Sources of information about new children's and adolescent literature include review resources: *Booklinks, Booklist, Bulletin of the Center for Children's Books (BCCB), The Horn Book Magazine, The Horn Book Guide, Publisher's Weekly*, and *School Library Journal*. Although not primarily review journals, *Language Arts, The Reading Teacher, Journal of Children's Literature,* and *Journal of Adolescent and Adult Literacy* contain useful book reviews as well. Descriptions of these and other resources are found in Appendix B.

Book Awards

Many awards, such as the Newbery, Caldecott, and Coretta Scott King Awards, are based on experts declaring that the winners are the outstanding examples of children's literature for the year. The awards have significant educational, social, cultural, and financial impact. Books that receive these awards are read by millions of children around the world. In the United States alone, every public and school library will purchase the appropriate books that win major awards. Winning one of these awards, therefore, also guarantees considerable financial reward for the author, illustrator, and publisher. The awards receive widespread media attention, and winning authors and illustrators receive numerous speaking invitations. A list of the winners and honor books of the major awards, both national and international, appears in Appendix A. There are also many lists of outstanding books published each year, such as the American Library Association's "Notables" list for both children's books and young adult literature. Other, more specific lists are included in Appendix B as well.

Websites

Teachers and students can access an infinite amount of current information about children's books, authors, illustrators, professional publications, teaching ideas, library collections, conferences, and other activities through the World Wide Web. You need only access to the Internet, a search engine, and a few key terms: "children's literature," "adolescent literature," "young adult literature," "children's books," "children's authors," or "children's illustrators" to get started. You will find numerous websites to help you find out about children's and adolescent literature. Many of them, such as the Children's Literature Network, will have live links to other sites, including authors' sites.

Many authors have a home page; typing an author's name into a search engine will usually get you there. At the home page you can initiate a conversation, ask questions, learn about the authors' new books, and find out about their speaking appearances. Many publishers have programs online that provide access to teaching ideas, books, and author information. Several publishers sponsor online interviews with authors, illustrators, librarians, teachers, book reviewers, and editors. To explore the many online resources available today, go to CengageBrain.com to access the Education CourseMate website, where you will find links to relevant websites.

Summary

The story of children's and adolescent literature intertwines with the social, political, and economic history of the world. Children's and adolescents' books are shaped by prevailing views of what adults believe children should be reading, but also by the amount of time children have to explore books and by competing sources of entertainment available to children. Today, we have a wealth of literature for children and adolescents. We have moved from crude horn books and religious tracts to books of artistic and literary excellence. Young readers are the beneficiaries of this wealth.

Given the history and durability of children's and adolescent literature, the future will certainly be interesting. No doubt we will have more international literature; more culturally diverse writers and artists will present their culture more accurately; global economics will play a stronger role; readers will have ready access to interviews with authors and illustrators on the World Wide Web; and projects such as the IDCL will help bring literature to all children. The many talented writers and illustrators who fill our lives with wonderful books will continue to do so, and new talent and new permutations of genre will never cease to emerge. At the same time, pressures are mounting on schools and libraries in the form of lack of funding, mandated high-stakes testing, and increasing numbers of children who need food, clothes, and stability as well as books. Our world is changing, and literature for children and adolescents will change with it. We, too, have to change as well as to keep up with the literature that is available for young readers.

Exploring the field of literature for children and adolescents can seem overwhelming at first, but knowledge about books is addictive. The more you know, the more you want to know and to share with young readers. With each new day there is more to know. This textbook will help you begin to explore the wonderful world of books. Enjoy!

Booklist

This Booklist contains the names of authors and illustrators to look for as you build a multicultural children's literature collection. These names are followed by a list of the 2012 USBBY Outstanding International Books to introduce you to specific titles and authors from around the world.

Writers and Illustrators to Look For

AFRICAN AMERICAN WRITERS

Maya Angelou
Tanya Bolden
Gwendolyn Brooks
Lucille Clifton
Christopher Paul Curtis
Tanita S. Davis
Sharon Draper
Sundee T. Frazier
Nikki Giovanni
Eloise Greenfield
Nikki Grimes
Virginia Hamilton
Angela Johnson
Julius Lester
Frederick McKissack
Patricia McKissack
Walter Dean Myers
Kadir Nelson
Marilyn Nelson
Vaunda Micheaux Nelson
Angela Davis Pinkney
Lesa Cline Ransome
Jewell Parker Rhodes
Margaree King Smith
Mildred Taylor
Carole Boston Weatherford
Rita Williams-Garcia
Jacqueline Woodson

AFRICAN AMERICAN ILLUSTRATORS

Ashley Bryan
R. Gregory Christie
Bryan Collier
Floyd Cooper
Donald Crews
Leo Dillon
Tom Feelings
E. B. Lewis
Christopher Myers
Kadir Nelson
Brian Pinkney

Jerry Pinkney
Sean Qualls
James Ransome
Synthia Saint James
Charles R. Smith
Javaka Steptoe

ARAB AMERICAN WRITERS

Randa Abdel-Fattah
Ibtisam Barakat
Hena Khan
Naomi Shihab Nye

ASIAN AND PACIFIC ISLAND AMERICAN WRITERS

Debjani Chatterjee
Ying Chang Compestine
Demi
Chen Jiang Hong
Cynthia Kadahota
Marie Lee
Thanhha Lei
Grace Lin
Lenore Look
Adeline Yen Mah
Ken Mochizuki
An Na
Lensey Namioka
Linda Sue Park
Yoshiko Uchida
Janet Wong
Lisa Yee
Wong Herbert Yee
Lawrence Yep
Ed Young

ASIAN AND PACIFIC ISLAND AMERICAN ILLUSTRATORS

Yan Nascimbene
Alan Say
Ed Young

LATINO WRITERS

Alma Flor Ada
Francisco X. Alarcón
Julia Alvarez
George Ancona
Anilú Bernardo
Carmen T. Bernier-Grand
Diane Gonzales Bertrand
Sandra Cisneros
Julia Ortiz Cofer
Ina Cumpiano

Carmen Agra Deedy
Margarita Engle
Francisco Jimenez
Victor Martinez
Guadalupe Garcia McCall
Meg Medina
Nicholasa Mohr
Patricia Mora
Nancy Osa
Pam Muñoz Ryan
Gary Soto
Ana Veciana-Suarez

LATINO ILLUSTRATORS

George Ancona
Robert Casilla
Joe Cepeda
Raul Colon
David Diaz
Lulu Delacre
Enrique Flores-Galbes
Carmen Lomas Garza
Susan Guevara
Rafael Lopez
Yuyi Morales
Sara Palacios
Enrique O. Sanchez
Duncan Tonatiuh
Eric Velasquez

NATIVE AMERICAN WRITERS

Sherman Alexie
Joseph Bruchac
Michael Dorris
Louise Erdrich
Gayle Ross
Cynthia Leitich Smith
Virginia Driving Hawk Sneve

NATIVE AMERICAN ILLUSTRATORS

Shonto Begay
Christopher Canyon
Murv Jacob
George Littlechild
Leo Yerxa

United States Board on Books for Young People 2012 Outstanding International Books

GRADES K–2

Devernay, Laëtitia, **The Conductor** (France)
Gormley, Greg, **Dog in Boots**, illllustrated by Roberta Angaramo (UK)
Könnecke, Ole, **Anton Can Do Magic**, translated by Catherine Chidgey (Germany)
Padmanabhan, Manjula, **I Am Different! Can You Find Me?** (India)
Schubert, Ingrid and Dieter, **The Umbrella** (Netherlands)

Maxiner, Trottier, **Migrant**, illustrated by Isabelle Arsenault (Canada)
Tullet, Herve, **Press Here**, translated by Christopher Franceschelli (France)
Van de Griek, Susan, **Loon**, illustrated by Karen Reczuch (Canada)
Van Mol, Sine, **Meena**, illustrated by Carianne Wijffels (Belgium)
Young, Cybèle, **Ten Birds** (Canada)

GRADES 3–5

Abela, Deborah, **Ghosts of Gribblesea Pier** (Australia)
Andrews, Jan, **When Apples Grew Noses and White Horses Flew: Tales of Ti-Jean**, illustrated by Dušan Petričić (Canada)
Arrigan, Mary, **The Rabbit Girl** (UK)
Ibbotson, Eva, **The Ogre of Oglefort**, illustrated by Lisa K. Weber (UK)
Jordan-Fenton, Christy, and Margaret Poklak-Fenton. **A Stranger at Home: A True Story**, illustrated by Liz Amini-Holmes (Canada)
Kojo, K. P., **The Parade: A Stampede of Stories about Ananse, the Trickster Spider**, illustrated by Karen Lilje (UK)
Naidoo, Beverley, **Aesop's Fables**, illustrated by Piet Grobler (UK)
Smith, David, **This Child, Every Child: A Book about the World's Children**, illustrated by Shelagh Armstrong (Canada)
Wang, Gabrielle, **The Garden of Empress Cassia** (Australia)
Williams, Karen Lynn, **Beatrice's Dream: A Story of Kibera Slum**, illustrated by Wendy Stone (UK)

GRADES 6–8

Ashley, Bernard, **Aftershock** (UK)
Brooks, Martha, **Queen of Hearts** (Canada)
Gerszak, Rafal, and Dawn Hunter. **Beyond Bullets: A Photo Journal of Afghanistan** (Canada)
Hartnett, Sonya, **The Midnight Zoo**, illustrated by Andrea Offermann (Australia)
Lewis, Gill, **Wild Wings**, illustrated by Yuta Onoda (UK)
Morpurgo, Michael, **An Elephant in the Garden** (UK)
Nicholls, Sally, **Season of Secrets** (UK)
Reeve, Philip, **A Web of Air** (UK)
Tak, Bibi Dumon, **Soldier Bear**, illustrated by Philip Hopman, translated by Laura Watkinson (Netherlands)
Tan, Shaun, **Lost & Found** (Australia)

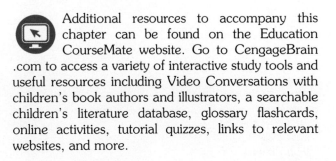 Additional resources to accompany this chapter can be found on the Education CourseMate website. Go to CengageBrain .com to access a variety of interactive study tools and useful resources including Video Conversations with children's book authors and illustrators, a searchable children's literature database, glossary flashcards, online activities, tutorial quizzes, links to relevant websites, and more.

2

Literature in the Lives of Young Readers

- **A Transactional View of Reading Literature**

- **Readers**

- **Texts**
  Diversity
  Ideology

- **Contexts**
  Classroom Contexts
  Censorship and Selection

- **Summary**

- **Booklist**

But the dam still stood, its great bulk defying the puny efforts of the Minnipins.

Glocken could not believe his eyes. His hand went out to the Whisper, and he struck it again, this time from the other side. And then again. And again. And again. And again. And still the dam stood.

Until suddenly—it simply disappeared.

One moment it was there defying them. And the next moment it had gone into a thousand cracks. And the earth, the stone, the washed-limestone simply went to powder and slid away. With a roar, the released river shot out from under them, roaring down the valley, roaring across the waste, roaring to freedom!

In his excitement Glocken struck the Whisper one last time. There was a sudden fearful crack! Over their heads.

Then the whole mountain fell down on top of them.

—CAROL KENDALL
The Whisper of Glocken, p. 218

Anna, her head bent forward so that her dark hair makes a tent around her face and the book she is reading, is totally engrossed in the world of ***The Whisper of Glocken*** (i). When she gets to the part where Silky finds a little gray creature and calls him Wafer, she looks up, sighs, and says, "Mom, Wafer is a perfect name for a gray kitten." She then goes back to her reading, once more lost to the world. Later, when she is finished with the book,

Anna is totally absorbed in the book she is reading. A frequent traveler in the world of books, she knows the pathway well.

she talks about it, wondering aloud how the Minnipins had the courage to leave their valley and venture out into the bigger world, questioning whether she would be that brave. From one book she's found the perfect name for her new gray kitten, has experienced a dangerous journey into an unknown land, and has thought about her personal courage, all without leaving her own living room.

She's been doing this forever. She careened down a hill in a buggy with Max, Rosemary Wells's captivating rabbit, even as she chewed the corners of the sturdy board book. She went with another Max in his private boat to the land of the wild things, played in the rain with Peter Spier's children, and learned to understand the natural world through Joanne Ryder's imaginative nonfiction. She's laughed, cried, absorbed information, experienced danger, engaged in adventures, solved mysteries, and learned a great deal about the world and about herself as she's read book after book. Anna's a lucky child. She's been engaged with wonderful books all of her life.

Memories of special books stay with us all our lives. The experiences we have during our lives shape and are shaped by the books that are important to us. Like Anna, many who love to read get so engrossed in their books that the real world disappears. What happens when a reader engages with a book has been explored by many researchers, has delighted many parents and teachers, and, most importantly, creates the opportunity for literature to transform the lives of its readers.

In Chapter 1, we discuss the power of literature as we introduce the world of books for young readers. In Chapters 3 through 10, we explore varied formats and genres of literature for children and adolescents, and in Chapters 11 and 12, we present some effective ways to engage young readers in the classroom and beyond. In this chapter:

- We describe our overarching theory, that reading is a transaction between reader and text in a particular sociocultural context—a transactional view of reading.

- We then consider the readers themselves, for it is through response that young readers engage with books and powerful things happen.

- We then explore the role of the text in the response process and consider how both texts and readers reflect the beliefs and attitudes of the contexts in which they are produced and read.

- Finally, we discuss the delicate nature of reading and discussing books with students and the very real possibility of book challenges, including resources and procedures for handling these challenges.

A Transactional View of Reading Literature

A *transactional* view of reading postulates that meaning does not reside in the text alone, waiting for a reader to unearth it, but rather is created in the transaction that occurs between a text and a reader. As a reader reads, many factors guide the selection and construction of meaning including personal experiences, abilities, knowledge, feelings, preferences, attitudes, cultural assumptions, and reasons for reading. At the same time, the text itself—the words on the page—guides and constrains the meaning that a reader builds. No matter what kind of book they are reading, readers build meaning that is shaped by the text, even as they shape the meaning. The construction of meaning is a transaction in which text and reader act on each other.

Iser (1978) argues that when we read we engage in anticipation and retrospection: we both anticipate what will happen based on our prior reading and we look back and revise our ideas about what we have read in light of what we have just read. Thus, good readers move back and forth when they read. Good readers also know that no text contains all they need to know; they realize that they themselves must fill in the gaps or indeterminacies in the text from their own knowledge of the world. This kind of reading is very much influenced by personal experience: the closer a text is to a reader's own experience of the world, the easier it is to read; the farther away, the more work a reader must do in order to understand the worldview from which the text is written (Iser, 1978).

P | R | O | F | I | L | E

Louise Rosenblatt

Louise Rosenblatt was a remarkable woman with exceptional talent. Her work, which presents theories about the nature of reading and the literary experience, substantially shaped the teaching of literature in schools and colleges.

Rosenblatt brought a scholarly approach to literary criticism, combined with an active concern for the teaching of literature. At a time when it was assumed that the reader's role was to passively receive a meaning from a text, she stressed the idea of the reader actively making meaning by engaging in a transaction with the text, bringing background, interests, and purposes to bear. She also stressed the difference between reading and responding with attention to what is being lived through (an aesthetic experience) and reading with attention focused on what is to be taken and used for a purpose, an "efferent" reading.

Rosenblatt graduated with honors from Barnard College, Columbia University, and went on to receive her doctorate in comparative literature from the Sorbonne. Postdoctoral work in anthropology with Franz Boas and Ruth Benedict at Columbia University inspired her feeling for the contributions of diverse cultures that encourage the creation of a democratic American society, a feeling that permeates her seminal work, *Literature as Exploration*, published in 1938 and currently in a fifth edition. Rosenblatt's primary professorship was at New York University, where she directed the doctoral program in English education. She received a John Simon Guggenheim Fellowship in 1943, the Great Teacher Award from New York University in 1972, the Distinguished Service Award from the National Council of Teachers of English in 1973, and the National Conference on Research in English Lifetime Award in 1990. She was inducted into the Reading Hall of Fame by the International Reading Association in 1992 and the National Council of Teachers of English honored her with a full day of programs to celebrate the fiftieth anniversary of the publication of *Literature as Exploration*. This and her many other works, including *The Reader, the Text, the Poem* (1994), have profoundly influenced how we read and understand literature and the teaching of literature.

Louise Rosenblatt was married to Sidney Ratner, scholar in philosophy and history, for more than sixty years. She died in 2005 at one hundred years of age.

Rosenblatt (1938/1976; 1978), Britton (1970), and Langer (1995) describe two primary ways to approach a text: aesthetic and efferent (Rosenblatt) stances, spectator and participant stances (Britton), and reading toward a horizon of possibilities versus reading toward a point (Langer). Although there are differences in the theories that each have developed, they all agree that there are different approaches to and outcomes from reading. Readers approaching a text from an aesthetic stance (Rosenblatt, 1978) read for the experience, for the opportunity to enter the story world. Although this experience is often visceral and "real," it is virtual rather than actual, requiring not action on the part of the reader but, rather, thought and emotional connection. This kind of reading offers readers the opportunity to contemplate, to reflect on the ideas presented in the text and their reactions to those ideas, and to develop their own values (Britton, 1970). As a young reader said, "When I was reading I was thinking, what would I do if this happened to me?" (Galda, 1982). In contrast, approaching a text from an efferent stance (Rosenblatt, 1978) means reading for information, for knowledge to use to act in the world. Generally, readers would approach a poem or fictional narrative from a primarily aesthetic stance, a biography or other nonfiction work from a primarily efferent stance. Rarely, however, are these stances purely one or the other. Rather than being polar opposites that are exclusive of each other, they exist along a continuum, with an aesthetic stance often containing elements of the efferent, and an efferent stance often containing elements of the aesthetic.

For example, if we read a beautiful poem, we would enjoy the experience of the reading but also note the way the poet has crafted those experiences. Reading a piece of historical fiction results in being in that historical story world for the duration of the reading, but probably also results in knowing some facts about that particular time in history. Reading a well-crafted piece of nonfiction offers the opportunity to learn about a particular aspect of our world (perhaps birds) and then to use this knowledge (in this case to identify birds), but the reader also experiences an aesthetic response to the subject, language, format, design, and illustrations. The important point here is that differences in the predominant stance that is adopted lead to different ways of reading and to more or less successful realization of the potential that waits between the covers of any book. Stance helps determine the response that readers develop over time as they read.

It is important to note that, according to Rosenblatt, the stance lies in the reader, not the text. In other words, although some texts may lend themselves to reading from an aesthetic stance, stance is not "in" a text. Poetry and literary texts that are fiction are, from Rosenblatt's point of view, most effectively read and understood when the reader first adopts an aesthetic stance. After this, the reader (or a classroom of readers) can talk about the text's structure, its major images, and the way the author's craft has influenced their reading. In other words, Rosenblatt envisions that readers will first adopt an aesthetic stance and follow this by adopting an efferent stance. Rosenblatt believes that the most complete and mature understandings and interpretations of text involve both stances, though she also stresses the importance of beginning with the

© Lee Galda

This first grader used both words and pictures to respond to the many nonfiction books he is reading about the natural world. The efferent and the aesthetic are both evident in his response.

aesthetic stance when reading stories and poems. Reading and understanding nonfiction are primarily efferent tasks, although most successful readers will also read aesthetically, especially given the outstanding quality of nonfiction for young readers today.

Building on the notion of an actively engaged reader described by Rosenblatt, Britton, and Iser, Langer (1995), Benton (1992), and others discuss how reading is *temporal* in nature because the linear processing of language means that readers read over time (rather than instantaneously). Further, as readers move through their reading time, they make predictions and engage in retrospection as they think about the meaning they have created in light of the new ideas they are developing (Benton, 1992). Langer (1995) describes active readers as first being out and stepping into a text, then being in and moving through, perhaps being in and stepping out to think, and, when finished reading, stepping out and thinking about the reading experience, regardless of text or stance. Other cognitive activities that occur across time during aesthetic reading are creating mental images, interacting with the text (as in identifying with characters in narrative fiction), and valuing the text, either through questioning or acquiescing to the ideas presented (Benton, 1992). The journey through the world of story that Rosenblatt, Langer, and Benton describe was summed up nicely by a ten-year-old who declared, "I love books that inhale me!" (Galda, 1982). Many writers and illustrators of books for young readers comment on the role of the reader/viewer; they recognize that their words and images are inert until given life by a reader.

The valuing of ideas encoded in a text relates to the *social and cultural dimensions* of reading and responding. Although it is easy to think of reading literature as a private, personal activity, it is actually thoroughly embedded in the social and cultural milieu of the author, the reader, and the reading itself. The creators of texts—the authors—bring to their writing the sum of who they are, and who they are is the result of the expectations of their social and cultural groups. The texts they create reflect these ideologies, existing "within a complex network of ideas and images and cultural values" (Nodelman, 1997, p. 5), just as readers bring their own cultural assumptions with them as they read.

Fish (1980) proposed that readers read in various "interpretive communities" of readers, with each community helping to shape attitudes and beliefs, as well as preferences and ways of interacting with any given text in a particular situation. Readers in communities generally do what they have to do—share their responses with a book group, write a paper, make a diorama, give a report—and these post-reading tasks help shape the way they read. Reading in order to discuss with peers results in responses that are not only the product of an individual reader's transaction with an individual text, but also of that reader's knowledge that he or she will be sharing with others in a specific, community-sanctioned manner. Reading in order to answer the low-level recall questions that comprise many computerized reading programs pushes readers to read everything in a manner that allows them to retain discrete facts, which is problematic when reading poetry and fiction, as discussed previously. Every interpretive community has both explicit and implicit rules for what "counts" as response.

Teachers and scholars (Carter, 2005; Sumara, 1996) point out that, although reading is often public, especially in schools, private reading—reading done with books of one's choice, in a place of one's choice, with no post-reading task to complete—is not only important for readers, but also appropriate for what Carter calls "interior" books (2005). Even private reading, however, is steeped in cultural assumptions and social routines.

Whether private or public, when readers engage with books, the experience can be *transformational*. Engaged reading increases knowledge and helps build values and attitudes (Britton, 1970; Galda, 1998; Rosenblatt, 1978; Sipe, 2000). Reading beautifully crafted nonfiction increases knowledge exponentially. Seeing things as yet unseen, coming to understandings of experienced phenomena, even figuring out how things work transforms the knowledge that readers call upon to make sense of the world around them. Reading poetry and stories allows readers to bring texts into their lives in a way that helps them define and shape their lives. Reading books in which they recognize themselves or come to know others offers readers the opportunity to reconstruct themselves, to understand themselves and others. These transactional, temporal, social, and cultural aspects of reading and responding to literature intertwine as readers engage with texts in ways that can be transformational. This is where the power of books lies—in the opportunity for transformation that reading affords.

Readers

Who readers are determines how they read. Instead of absorbing "one right meaning" from a text (an elusive concept at best), readers construct meaning as they read based on their own background knowledge, experiences, and skills (Goodman, 1985; Rosenblatt, 1938/1976, 1978). A text that makes one reader cry might bore another; a book read as a ten-year-old brings a different kind of response when read again as a

thirteen-year-old; and the cultural values that permeate a text will trigger varying responses in culturally diverse readers. Even though the text remains the same, readers are constantly changing, and therefore will have differing responses depending on their life experiences. Even on rereading, we never experience the same text in quite the same way. Think, for example, of Shel Silverstein's popular **The Giving Tree** (I). Many readers find this book a charming depiction of selfless love; the tree gives her all to the boy. Others, however, find this an expression of selfishness; the boy takes everything the tree gives and asks for more, giving little in return. Both groups read the same text and view the same illustrations, but construct entirely different meanings.

As Iser (1978) and others have argued, who readers are and what they have experienced influence their responses to the books they read. The places they have been, the people they know, the attitudes they hold, who they are, what they know, and the way they present themselves to the world all influence how readers read and respond. Although there are several category systems that serve to describe frequent responses by a variety of readers, research also has shown that individuals seem to have characteristic ways of responding. For example, three fifth-grade girls with similar backgrounds and schooling were quite different in their approaches to books, but each was individually consistent (Galda, 1982). Four first- and second-grade students showed remarkably different response styles; for example, one reader demonstrated sensitivity toward the feelings of the story characters and another used the story as a springboard for oral performance (Sipe, 1998). Beach, Thein, and Parks (2008) have described how adolescent readers approach texts in ways that reflect who they are and what they have experienced. Hickman's (1981) groundbreaking work on response in elementary schools gave us a glimpse at what it might look like, as presented in Teaching Idea 2.1.

For many years, researchers have sought to postulate general response patterns. For example, Bogdan (1990) describes three basic types of response to literature: stock response, kinetic response, and spectator response, although her use of the term is different from Britton's use of the same term. For Bogdan, *stock response* involves evaluating a text in terms of whether its worldview, ideology, and so on conform to the reader's own worldview. In this type of response, readers say something is good or bad based on their own view of how things are or should be and whether the book does or does not support their view. A response such as "I don't think that books about magic should be in school libraries" would be a stock response. *Kinetic response* consists of evaluation of a book in terms of whether it packs an emotional punch

Recognizing Response when You See It

COMMON CORE STATE STANDARDS

This Teaching Idea is a general description of teaching in ways that address many of the Common Core English Language Arts standards across grade levels. The suggestions in this Teaching Idea may need to be adapted to suit your particular grade level and the needs of your students.

Hickman (1981, p. 346) described seven different types of responses that occurred in the elementary classrooms she observed across the course of a school year. Her observations remind us that a response does not have to be an activity, but ranges from individual thoughtfulness to a simple sharing with another to a formal activity. She saw children engaged in:

- Listening behaviors, such as laughter and applause.
- Contact with books, such as browsing, intent attention.
- Acting on the impulse to share, reading together.

- Oral responses, such as storytelling and discussion.
- Actions and drama, such as dramatic play.
- Making things, such as pictures, games, or displays.
- Writing using literary models, summarizing, and writing about books.

Provide your students ample time, an opportunity to linger for a while in the spell of a good book. Provide them with structured response activities, such as the Teaching Ideas that are in every chapter in this text. And provide them with a supportive environment in which to engage with books and make them their own.

---

for the reader, as in "I loved this book because it made me cry." *Spectator responses*, for Bogdan, evaluate a book on formal structure, use of images, patterns, and language—all traditional literary elements, such as "I thought this book was great because of the striking use of metaphors." Bogdan argues that none of these responses is wrong but that they are all incomplete, that readers need to learn to respond in all three ways.

In his work with young readers, Sipe (2008) has determined that there are five basic ways children respond to picture storybooks. First, some analyze in the traditional manner of talking about the language, characters, plot, setting, theme, and mood of the story. Second, they may make intertextual connections to other texts such as books, movies, videos, and so forth. Third, children also make personal connections, drawing the self to the story or the story to the self. Fourth, they may make "transparent" responses that indicate that, for the moment, the children are "in" the story world (as when they "talk back" to the characters in the text). Finally, children may display "performative" responses that use the story as a platform in imaginative play.

Readers also learn to make connections between their own experiences and knowledge and those portrayed in story or presented in nonfiction. These links between text and world, as Cochran-Smith (1984) describes, not only help readers understand the texts

they read, but also allow them to use what they read to understand their own lives. A six-year-old who is living in a new city and, upon seeing a vine-covered building on a corner, asks, "Mommy, are we in Paris?" is using her experience with Ludwig Bemelmans's *Madeline* (N) to understand where she is now living.

Thus, readers use their prior life experiences to understand literature, but they also use literature to illuminate and make sense of their own lives. For example, a combination first/second-grade class, upon hearing Charlotte Huck's *Princess Furball* (P) read aloud by their teacher, engaged in a long discussion (prompted by the frontispiece, which depicts the funeral of Princess Furball's mother) of death and how it affected them. Some children spoke of relatives (grandmothers, uncles, and aunts) who had died and how it had affected them. The children's mood during this discussion was not sorrowful or depressed; on the contrary, the experience of interpreting the frontispiece of *Princess Furball* had enabled them to work through and interpret their own lives in light of the book they were hearing (and seeing).

These ways of categorizing responses flow from the theoretical descriptions of reader response and reflect the observed behavior of readers. The important thing to note is that readers *do* things as they interact with books, and those things they do help shape the meaning they create.

How young readers respond to books is, of course, learned; past experience with books influences how readers read and respond. As Fish (1980) argues, often this relates primarily to the contexts in which these experiences occurred. The readers described by Bogdan or Sipe or any of the many researchers offering us categories of response have all learned to respond as they do through their interaction with others around books. For example, years of reading stories in classrooms in which the teacher asks questions that prompt recall of specific information from stories and poems will force young readers away from their naturally aesthetic responses into a less-productive efferent stance. One parent, for instance, talking about how her son learned to hate reading in school, described how he first reads the questions that he has to answer at the end of each reading selection, and then scans the story or poem to find the answers to those questions. Of course, he misses the story or poem, and never connecting means that he misses the pleasure that aesthetic reading can bring. Another middle-school boy, an avid reader of long, complex animal fantasies at home, felt that he had become a "poor" reader because of his performance on the tests in a popular computer-based reading program. He had learned to read fiction for the virtual experience; the tests asked him to read efferently, for very specific and often unimportant details. Consequently, he chose less complex novels for his school reading. Readers who take great delight in nonfiction and seek it out, only to have adults dismiss this kind of reading material as not important, eventually come to think of themselves as nonreaders. It is only through positive experiences with an array of books that the tremendous benefits of avid reading described by Cunningham and Stanovich (1998) are realized.

Readers who have had an array of pleasurable experiences with books will spontaneously compare stories, share information, knowledgeably discuss authors, and bring their ideas about how literature works and their experiences with other texts to their reading. Many researchers such as McGinley and Kamberelis (1996); Sipe (1999); Many and Wiseman (1992); Short and Pierce (1990); Galda, Rayburn, and Stanzi (2000); Maloch (2002); Martinez-Roldan (2003); McIntyre, Kyle, and Moore (2006); Wood, Roser, and Martinez (2001); Pantaleo (2008); Sipe (2008); and Roser, Martinez, Fuhrken, et al. (2007), have documented the richness of young readers' responses when they are in an environment that encourages exploration and consideration of books.

Experience with reading also encompasses the actual texts with which young readers have engaged. Once they understand that thinking about one book in comparison to another, or making "intertextual links," is not only interesting but also productive, readers of all ages engage in forging connections among books. When reading the Egielski version of **The Gingerbread Boy** (P), which takes place in New York City, first graders noted the similarities and differences in this version and the more traditional versions (like the one by Galdone) where the setting is rural. They noticed that instead of a "little old man and a little old woman," the makers of the gingerbread boy were a young couple. They also noticed that the construction workers that chase the gingerbread boy in the Egielski version were "like farmers." Here they were making an intertextual connection based on what Vladamir Propp (1958) calls "character function": construction workers are nothing like farmers, *except* that they chase the gingerbread boy in a group, just like the farmers. The children also commented that perhaps the Egielski version was "the original version." When the teacher asked them why they supposed it was the original version, one of them reasoned, "Well, probably they lived in the city and made a gingerbread boy and lost him. And then when they got older, they retired to the country and tried again. And that would make these two gingerbread boys [the one from the Egielski version and the one from the Galdone version] brothers!" Thus, the children were using their knowledge of another version of **The Gingerbread Boy** to interpret the text at hand; moreover, they were stitching the two stories together by postulating that the couple in the Egielski version was the same as the couple in the Galdone version, only younger!

The second-grade readers in Lisa Stanzi's class immediately took up her invitation to make an intertextual link, and with great enthusiasm. They spent the bulk of the school year weaving links between the many texts they were reading. In this way they came to many different realizations about literature. They decided that different stories might have the same themes, that characters in different stories might be both the same and different, and that some dinosaur books were factual while others wove together both fact and fiction, to name just a few of the ideas they developed as they read and compared texts (Galda, Rayburn, & Stanzi, 2000). Most importantly, they learned to use their experiences with previously read texts to understand new texts. Older readers, especially those with a rich reading diet, also rely on intertextual links to develop their understanding of new texts. Author Jane Yolen (2000) has said that "stories lean on stories," and J.R.R. Tolkien (1938/1964) wrote that "there are no new stories, only a cauldron of stories into which we dip as we write." Of course, these links encompass the texts all readers encounter in movie, song, video,

TEACHING IDEA 2.2

Creating Links across Stories

 **COMMON CORE STATE STANDARDS**

This teaching idea addresses Common Core English Language Arts, Reading: Literature standards 5, 9 grade 2; 3, 9 grade 3; 3 grade 4; 2, 3 grades 5 and 6. The suggestions in this Teaching Idea many need to be adapted to suit your particular grade level and the needs of your students.

Talking about characters enables students to make comparisons among characters from various stories. These comparisons can lead to generalizations about character types that readers will meet as they read widely. Discussing plot results in identification of various kinds of plots and in understandings about archetypal plots that underlie literature. Finding similarities and differences in the underlying conflicts of stories also helps readers make connections among books, just as considering themes can bring the recognition that different authors treat the same general theme in infinitely varied ways. Readers who explore how literature works learn to look at books as works of art crafted by a writer.

Some questions that you can consider as you read and respond with your students include:

- Plot: What are the key events? How are they structured? How does this relate to other books we have read?

- Character: How do we learn about the characters? What are they like and how are they developed? Are they similar to other characters in books we have read? Do they have similar problems? Similar reactions to problems?

- Setting: How are characters and events influenced by the time and place in which the story takes place? How does this affect their similarity or differences with other characters we know?

- Theme: What are the big ideas that hold the story together? Are there other stories that you know that have similar themes?

---

and other electronic sources as well. Teaching Idea 2.2 offers suggestions for creating links across texts.

Once they are reading for themselves, readers' reading abilities also influence the act of reading. Fluent readers read with an ease that enables them to concentrate fully on the text they are reading; those who struggle with words often miss the meaning. In a discussion of Madeleine L'Engle's **A Wind in the Door** (A), a complex science fantasy that contains some difficult-to-pronounce proper nouns, one reader remarked that he had been doing well until he tried to figure out all the names, when he became mixed up. Another reader then told the group how he had "replaced" the names with familiar ones because it "did not make any difference" to the story (Galda, 1990, 1992).

Different concepts about literature certainly influence response. What readers know about literature—its creation, its forms, its purposes, and its effects—as well as their experience with particular texts, influences the meaning they create. Understanding how literature works, and having multiple experiences with multiple texts, helps readers understand each new text encountered. Again, the context in which readers read and respond makes a difference in the way they respond; supportive contexts allow children to stretch

their ideas. Lehr (1991), for example, found that young children who are in literature-rich classrooms and have many experiences reading and discussing literature over time in a supportive context can, and do, discuss themes and character motivation and make generalizations about stories—behaviors usually associated with older children. Galda, Rayburn, and Stanzi (2000) demonstrated the depth of understanding evident in the discussions of second-grade readers in a safe, supportive literature-based classroom. After reading Patricia MacLachlan's **Arthur, for the Very First Time** (I) in November, and again in January, the second graders discussed what "looking through the faraway end," a piece of advice given to the main character, might mean. The discussion was brief. Three months later, in April, Amarachi ran up to one of the researchers, who had just entered the room, and said, out of the blue, "I know why you might want to look through the faraway end. Well, I was looking through my binoculars at a bird in a tree. When I looked through the close-up end, I saw the bird, but when I looked through the faraway end, I saw the whole tree" (p. 1). This eight-year-old had tucked the story into her heart and, three months later, brought it together with a bit of life experience to understand how altering perspective changes everything.

Who readers are includes the cultural values and assumptions that they have developed over time. We all are influenced by others, as each person is shaped by the social and cultural worlds that surround them. For example, most American readers respond negatively to the idea of arranged marriage and positively to books that portray this custom in a negative light (Stewart, 2008). Yet, the attitude toward arranged marriage is cultural, as author Suzanne Fisher Staples (2008) points out when she recounts a discussion about arranged marriage with some of her Pakistani acquaintances in which they asked her, "Do you really send your children out to do the most important thing in their life without the wisdom of their elders?" These women would view a negative portrayal of arranged marriage with alarm. The point is not the validity of either opinion about arranged marriage, but the undeniable cultural influence on response to a book that portrays arranged marriage. Even young children bring cultural attitudes and assumptions with them as they read. Urban kindergarteners, on hearing Beatrix Potter's **The Tale of Peter Rabbit** (N), made that Edwardian classic relevant for themselves by bringing their own cultural attitudes and assumptions to the text. For example, they called Peter a "chip off the old block" because Peter disobeys, just as his father went into Mr. McGregor's garden and got killed. They also interpreted Mrs. Rabbit as a "harried single mother" with three children, one of whom (Peter) was always getting into trouble. One of them poignantly said, "My dad's in jail, but my grandma helps take care of us." They were pointing out that Peter's father wasn't on the scene, just as some of their own fathers were absent. Nevertheless, they also pointed out that they had extended family to help take care of them, unlike poor Mrs. Rabbit, who seems to be all alone. They were able to compare and contrast Peter's family situation with their own because they had clear ideas about their own cultural identities.

Reading interests and preferences also influence response, and we can make some generalizations about young readers' interests and preferences, about what they *might like* to read or what they *actually select* to read, but within each generalization lies a lot of individual variation. This variation is humorously captured in Barbara Bottner's **Miss Brooks Loves Books! (and I don't)**, illustrated by Michael Emberley, in which a first-grader rejects every book that her enthusiastic school librarian offers, only to be seduced when her mother offers her William Steig's **Shrek!** (P). Many children, regardless of age, enjoy humor. Primary-grade children often enjoy stories with animal characters and are usually fond of folklore. There is a period of time during the elementary years when many readers are engrossed in mysteries. As children enter the intermediate grades and solidify friendships outside their immediate families, they often like to read realistic stories about children "just like" themselves, especially stories that are exciting and full of action. Older children and adolescents often diverge in their interests along gender lines, with girls preferring romance and contemporary realistic novels and boys preferring nonfiction and fantasy/science fiction. There is some evidence that girls tend to prefer the "discourse of feeling" in books that emphasize the feelings and relationships of the characters, whereas boys tend to prefer the "discourse of action," where an exciting plot is key (Cherland, 1992). Of course, the greater society also impacts young readers' preferences, as the recent surge in delight in fantasy demonstrates.

Young readers who do not yet purchase books for themselves or older readers who do not buy books are at the mercy of the adults who offer books to them. Sometimes, the books that adults offer are not the same as the books that readers prefer. A number of studies point to the discrepancy between awards for literary quality, such as the Caldecott, Newbery, and Printz, selected by adults, and awards for popularity, decided by young readers. Carter (2010) writes compellingly of the role that popular books that don't win awards play as children become avid readers. Two national awards reflect the choices of young readers, although the initial selection of books and the awards are administered by adults. The International Reading Association's Children's Choices and Young Adult Choices appear in the Booklist at the end of this chapter.

As each individual reader matures and reads an increasing number of books with an increasing degree of understanding, the preferences of that individual will change along lines that reflect the individual's interests, development, and experiences (Galda, Ash, & Cullinan, 2000; Sebesta & Monson, 2003). As readers' preferences change, so too do their overall responses to literature. When children read widely, they seem to develop an appreciation for a broad range of characters, styles, and genres, regardless of their own specific preferences.

While readers certainly change, as both people and readers, over the course of their development, at any age a rich diet of books to read and a supportive context in which to read them affords readers the best chance to become avid, thoughtful, responsive readers for life. This kind of reader, however, goes well beyond being "inhaled by books." Lewis (2000) argues that being a thoughtful reader involves going beyond personal response and considering the social and political dimensions of texts, an idea that revolutionizes the way we might teach literature.

Texts

The richness of literature available for children and adolescents means that *every* reader can find books with which they engage deeply. Picturebooks and graphic novels enrich the lives of their readers with their carefully crafted visual and verbal texts. For most children, picturebooks are their primary connection to fine art, and one of the ways they learn to "read" pictures, as well as a source for varied models of language. The impact of a rich diet of picturebooks on children's literate lives is profound. Children who live with poetry in their lives turn to poetry again and again for pleasure, delight, and sometimes solace. Poems offer readers strong images, feelings, and ideas in language that calls attention to itself. Readers respond to poetry in visceral ways and learn to delight in language play. Folklore helps modern children understand the basic principles of cultures around the world, offering absolutes of good and evil, recurring patterns and motifs, and basic structures that are foundational for building an understanding of the family of stories. Fantasy offers readers the opportunity to explore big issues in the world in a way that is manageable and can be a force for moral and spiritual growth. Science fiction allows readers to consider ethical dilemmas that may result from physical and technological advances. Realistic fiction presents stories that allow readers to reflect on their own lives. So, too, does historical fiction help readers reflect on life in the past and on the idea that history was created and lived by people not unlike themselves. Biography offers much the same, allowing readers to come to know biographical subjects as human beings impacted by and having influence on their society. Nonfiction offers readers the opportunity to both learn about and reflect on the world they live in. All of these genres have something unique and universal to offer engaged readers, and they increasingly reflect varied cultural experiences and viewpoints.

How, then, do we determine quality of text? As we discuss in Chapter 1, quality certainly involves a multilayeredness, or openness to multiple interpretations, and an absence of superficiality. Nodelman (1996) puts it this way: What distinguishes the most important literature is its "ability to engender new interpretations from its readers" (p. 187). Who we are as readers and the quality and variety of the texts we have experienced help us build our own personal "canons" of valuable literature, no matter who we are. In Chapters 3 through 10 we consider quality in various formats and genres. Here, we look more broadly at another aspect of quality—the diversity of experiences and ideas presented in a collection of books that are offered to students. Although it is difficult if not impossible for any single book to represent all aspects of diversity, it is possible for a collection of books to be diverse.

• • DIVERSITY • •

We know that it is vital that young readers have the opportunity to see both themselves and others different from themselves in the books they encounter. The opportunities for diverse readers—all readers—to see themselves in literature as well as to learn about others, to find their own values depicted as well as to consider new values, to find books a source of both comfort and challenge are available when young readers have the opportunity to read and respond to a rich diet of literature. Teaching Idea 2.3 suggests how readers can use literature to learn about themselves.

As we discussed previously, readers shape their view of the world and of themselves partly through the books they read, and the texts themselves are an integral part of this shaping. If children never see themselves in books, they receive the subtle message that they are not important enough to appear in books and that books are not for them. Conversely, if children see only themselves in the books they read, the message is that those who are different from them are not worthy of appearing in books. Further, stereotyped images of an ethnic group, gender, nationality, region, religion, or other subculture are harmful not only to the children of that group but also to others who then get a distorted view. By the same token, "essentializing" cultures by depicting certain "universal" qualities as reflecting all members of a culture also presents a skewed viewpoint. Rich depictions of multiple ways of being part of a culture make diverse literature a rich source of experience for all readers.

Author Jane Kurtz has written many books that are set in Ethiopia, where she spent her childhood. Her experience and her books, such as ***Jakarta Missing*** (I) and ***Faraway Home*** (P), have implications regarding the issue of cultural authenticity discussed in Chapter 1. Jane is not Ethiopian, but she spent her childhood there. She is American, but she didn't grow up here. Describing her "culture" is complicated, just as is describing anyone's culture in simplistic terms.

Literature can act as both mirror and window for its readers (Galda, 1982), and Bishop (1997) has applied this metaphor to culturally diverse literature in particular. Although it is true that literature allows readers to envision themselves and those different from themselves, perhaps the best books offer an experience that is more like looking through a window as the light slowly fades. At first one sees clearly through

TEACHING IDEA 2.3

Making Thematic Connections: Learning about Yourself

COMMON CORE STATE STANDARDS This Teaching Idea addresses Common Core English Language Arts Reading: Literature standards 2, 3 grades 4, 5; and Speaking and Listening standard 1 grades K through 8 and is the basis for meaningful discussions about theme for all grade levels. The suggestions in this Teaching Idea may need to be adapted to suit your particular grade level and the needs of your students.

Begin the year by asking students to write down several characteristics that describe themselves, as well as several likes and dislikes. If you plan ahead, you can ask questions that will enable them to think about certain aspects of their lives before they read the books you have selected. As you read books depicting varied cultural groups and experiences, explicitly talk about the similarities among the experiences, emotions, attitudes, relationships, and personalities that students find in the book and those they find in their lives. Periodically ask students to write or talk about what they have learned about various characters and what they have learned about themselves. For example, it might surprise some students to realize how terrible it would be not to be able to go to school or to be separated from a sibling. As an end-of-year activity, ask students to revisit and revise their original descriptions of themselves.

the window into another's world—but gradually, as the light dims, one's own image becomes reflected as well (Galda, 1998). Children's books at their best highlight the unique characteristics of the cultures represented by their characters but also speak to universal

On Your Education CourseMate

CONVERSATION WITH JANE KURTZ

In a conversation with Lee Galda, Jane talks about how after returning to America and beginning her family and career, she put Ethiopia behind her, only to return to it through her writing. Go to CengageBrain.com to access the Education CourseMate website and watch the video conversation with author Jane Kurtz.

Questions to Consider

1. How would you describe Jane's culture? She is American but didn't grow up here; spent her childhood in Ethiopia but wasn't born there.

2. What implications does this have for the idea of cultural authenticity?

emotions. With them, we can understand, recognize, and appreciate differences; call attention to commonly held values and experiences and those that differ; and promote empathy, respect, and a sense of common humanity. Thinking about, talking about, and developing an understanding of others are natural outgrowths of reading diverse literature, especially when readers discuss their reading with others. An example of powerful response to an engaging text is evident in the conversation of a diverse group of fourth- and fifth-grade students discussing Christopher Paul Curtis's Newbery Honor–winning story of the experiences of an African American family, **The Watsons Go to Birmingham—1963** (i). This book captured the interest of every single student, those who liked and did not like to read, those who were African American and those who were not, those who spoke English as a second language and those who did not. The guest reader and students read the final chapter together, aloud. After a few moments of quiet, as everyone digested the ending, the talk began. They talked about how the characters of Kenny and Byron changed across the course of the book, and then about what Byron said to Kenny about fairness: "Kenny, things ain't ever going to be fair. How's it fair that two grown men could hate negroes so much that they'd kill some kids just to stop them from going to school? How's it fair that even though the cops down there might know who did it nothing will probably ever happen to those men? It ain't. But you just gotta understand that that's the way it is and keep on steppin'."

One boy asked, but *why* would the police not arrest the people who killed the little girls if they knew that they did it, and the conversation exploded with cries of "That's not fair." They offered thoughts about prejudice and hatred, about the Klan, about an event in their city ten years earlier in which a cross was burned in the yard of a black family who had moved into a white suburb. The conversation moved on to corrupt law enforcement in the 1960s, police brutality then and now, and racial profiling, a topic that was currently on television and in the papers. They finished by considering the various responses to the influx of immigrants and refugees in their city, with one child asking, "If the United States has a war in the country they [the immigrants] came from, would they get mad at us and make a war here?" (Galda, 2007). These young readers took Curtis's book into their hearts and used it to make sense of the imperfect world around them even as they were using what they knew to makes sense of the book, and they were working together to expand their understandings of their own and others' experiences. They did this by thoughtfully considering the ideas about racial discrimination and power that Curtis offered in his text. These ideas are the ideology embedded in the story.

• • IDEOLOGY • •

Lewis's (2000) call for moving beyond the personal to consider the social and political dimensions of reading and responding is a call to encourage young readers to discover the ideology, the "assumptions" in a text. This is difficult to do if the ideology in a text reflects one's own because then it seems an obvious "truth" rather than an assumption. Sometimes, when the ideology of a text is markedly different from that of a reader, the reader reacts with resistance to the text. This is often the case when varied readers are reading literature from other cultures, as we discuss shortly. Stephens (1992) claims that simply encouraging young readers to engage with a text through identification, or "being inhaled," is actually dangerous, as then they never learn to recognize the ideologies in a text, especially those that are implicit. Literature is an expression of cultural values; but whose values, in addition to those of the author, are being expressed? Cultures, as we discussed previously, are not uniform, and not everyone believes the same thing or sees things the same way. For example, as we discuss in Chapter 8, many picturebooks and novels for young readers extol the bravery and resourcefulness of the pioneers who settled the West; Manifest Destiny as a national ethos permeates these stories. Other books take a different perspective, presenting the inexorable march westward as the destruction of culture after culture. Different ideologies make a significant difference.

Once we understand that texts express, both explicitly and implicitly, an ideology—cultural assumptions and attitudes that the author expresses consciously or unconsciously—we can become aware of how texts manipulate readers and of how our own ideologies shape our responses to texts. Ideology in both texts and readers is socially constructed. For example, the antiwar sentiment of the Vietnam era—the assumption that war is bad—permeates Collier and Collier's ***My Brother Sam Is Dead*** (A), written during that era. Charlotte Zolotow's ***William's Doll*** (P) reflects the heightened consciousness of gender stereotypes that the feminist movement precipitated. The cultural assumption in many of these books, while appealing to those who agree with it, is nevertheless an ideology.

As society changes, so do books for young readers. Sutherland (1985) argues that authors approach social and cultural norms and ideologies in one of three ways: assent, which reflects those norms; advocacy, which promotes particular practices; and attack, which denounces particular practices (Sipe, 1999). We might describe the Collier novel as advocating the antiwar stance of the peace movement while at the same time attacking the prowar stance of the political establishment. Zolotow advocates for young boys being allowed to cross gender barriers and play with dolls, although she does not attack those who engage in more traditional male sports.

Some of our cherished "classics," such as Louisa May Alcott's ***Little Women*** (A) or Carol Ryrie Brink's ***Caddie Woodlawn*** (A), are interesting to consider in terms of ideology. Jo, in Alcott's novel, is different from most girls, and generations of readers have loved her for that. She eventually accepts the role that society insists upon, however, and abandons many of her dreams for the love of a good man. Caddie, in Brink's novel, also gives up her freedom so that she can grow up to be a young woman, just as her mother and society want her to do. Thus, these books and others like them seem to value the adventuresome and the rebellious in girls, while disallowing those qualities as those girls become young women.

Apol claims that texts written for children are:

> Deeply tied to the ideologies of a culture and a time. Children's literature is a form of education and socialization, an indication of a society's deepest hopes and fears, expectations and demands. It presents to children the values approved by adult society and (overtly or covertly) attempts to explain, justify, and even impose on its audience what could be considered "correct" patterns of behavior and belief. Whether deliberate or

not, children's literature functions as a form of social power, for adults control most, if not all, of a child's reading. Adults write, edit, publish, market, and purchase books; they select, read, and even teach them to children. And in each of these capacities, the choices made by adults are motivated: adults want children to read particular books for particular reasons. (1998, p. 34)

She, like Lewis (2000), argues for helping young readers learn to approach texts from a critical perspective.

Because readers rely on their own experiences and the assumptions and attitudes they have developed as a result of those experiences, it is not surprising that, when the reader's assumptions are generally similar to the ideology of the text, most readers do not even notice the presence of these ideas. When they are different from those expressed in the text, however, readers challenge the text in different ways. Research on readers responding to texts has dubbed this behavior "resistance."

Sipe and McGuire (2006) document how kindergarten, first-, and second-grade children resist texts in six distinct ways. Some children push texts away when they differ from texts they already know. Others resist when the type of text is not that which they prefer. Children who expect texts to reflect the reality they themselves have experienced will resist texts that present a different reality; they will also resist a text that inscribes a potentially painful reality. Some children also resist texts if they cannot identify with the characters. Finally, children resist texts they perceive are somehow faulty in their craft, language, or illustration. Other research on response documents similar resistance in older readers (Encico, 1994; Hemphill, 1999; Lewis, 1997).

Studies of resistance often focus on readers engaging with multicultural texts. Although adults might want young readers to embrace cultural pluralism or to "experience" historical attitudes and events, resistance to texts, however ideologically problematic, does indicate that readers are not simply passively accepting the text but are actively engaged in thinking about and even talking back to the text, the very behavior that Lewis (2000) calls for. Readers resist texts for any number of reasons. For example, as Beach, Thein, and Parks (2007) describe, white readers of multicultural texts often resist the ideologies in those texts. Moller and Allen (2000) describe the "engaged resistance" of some African American readers of Mildred Taylor's **The Friendship** (I), who found the depictions of intolerance and prejudice too painful to read. Beach, Thein, and Parks (2008) document how classroom practice modified students' stances toward texts. Likewise, we now turn to the contexts in which readers respond to text, as these contexts have a great deal of influence on those responses. In Figure 2.1, you will find suggestions for understanding how your own ideological stance affects your responses to what you read.

FIGURE 2.1

Questions for Critical Readings by Teachers

When you read, be aware of how much you assume about the way things are, or ought to be, in the stories you read. Assumptions about life profoundly influence an individual's response to text, shaping those responses without our awareness. The following questions are one way to begin recognizing how your own ideology shapes you as a reader and how ideologies are encoded in the books you read.

1. What explicit messages does the text present? What are the implicit, or underlying, assumptions? How do they relate to each other?

2. What parts of the story are "obvious" or "natural" to you? Which assumptions do you find yourself agreeing with? Consider why you feel this way.

3. What parts of the story do you find yourself resisting? What assumptions do you disagree with? Consider why you feel this way.

4. What are some possible ways to interpret this text? How do your own experiences and beliefs influence these interpretations?

These questions are taken from Laura Apol's "But what does this have to do with kids?": Literary theory and children's literature in the teacher education classroom. *Journal of Children's Literature, 24*(2), p. 38. They do not represent all of the questions she poses in the article; read it in its entirety for more comprehensive suggestions.

Contexts

Learning occurs in a social context that depends on interaction, and literature plays an important role in that context. Children gain experience with life and literature in the company of others. How readers read and how they respond to the books they read is influenced by the contexts in which they are reading. Hearing a bedtime story is different from hearing a story at the library's story hour; reading on a rainy Saturday afternoon in the most comfortable chair in the house is different from reading from eight-thirty to nine every morning at a school desk. Reading in a space that has plenty of books, that provides time to read them, and that includes other readers who support developing ideas is much different from reading for homework or contests, and much different from reading privately. All kinds of reading opportunities belong in all readers' lives. Not all books are meant to be shared and talked about, even in a supportive classroom, as sometimes the experience of reading is so moving and important that readers might choose to keep their thoughts to themselves. Given that, a safe and supportive classroom environment allows for those private readings while also supporting a lively exchange of responses and ideas among students.

• • CLASSROOM CONTEXTS • •

One of the goals of a response-centered curriculum is to create lifelong readers. This involves helping students understand their own responses to what they read, make connections between books and their lives, and read widely for different purposes. As students become lifelong readers, they grow to appreciate the use of language by a variety of writers, make intertextual connections, and understand that stories and poems vary in meaning across readers and across time. The development of lifelong readers occurs in many contexts, but here, we consider some important components of the classroom context.

Young people become engaged readers when we surround them with opportunities to read and respond to a variety of genres, styles, and authors; when we appreciate individual differences and offer opportunities to explore and share diverse responses; and when we provide time and encouragement for responding in a variety of ways. Rosenblatt (1938/1976) argues that the *experience* of the book must come first, with teachers then building on readers' connections to a text through various activities, one of which is discussion. Talking about books encourages readers to articulate their own responses to books and to find out how other readers responded. In many cases, talking about books adds new dimensions to individual responses, as the ideas of others provide new perspectives. As one young reader remarked, "I never thought about it that way, but now it makes a lot of sense"—a sentiment that anyone who has discussed books with friends can understand. When young readers share books with peers and adults in collaborative, supportive contexts, they develop positive feelings about books and about themselves as readers. Teaching Idea 2.4 suggests ways to support English language learners as they talk and write about their responses to the books they read.

TEACHING IDEA 2.4

Scaffolding Written Response for English Language Learners

ELL

COMMON CORE STATE STANDARDS This Teaching Idea meets the Common Core English Language Arts, Reading: Literature standards 4, 5, 6 for grades 2 and 3; standards 1, 2, 3 for grades 4 through 6. The suggestions in this Teaching Idea may need to be adapted to suit your particular grade level and the needs of your students.

One way to support English language learners as they attempt to respond in writing to the books they are reading and hearing is to use a small group, shared writing format. Ask students to first discuss their ideas (in their first language if the group shares that language), and then to record the group's views as one document for which each student shares ownership. Individuals can copy, illustrate, reread, or add to their response as their language allows. In this way, even the newest language learners can express their ideas, clarify confusions, practice the language of literary response, and feel a part of the reading community in the classroom.

TEACHING IDEA 2.5

Book Buddies

 **COMMON CORE STATE STANDARDS** This Teaching Idea does not relate directly to the Common Core English Language Arts, Reading: Literature standards, but is one effective way to encourage students to share their reading and responses with others. The suggestions in this Teaching Idea may need to be adapted to suit your particular grade level and the needs of your students.

There are many different ways to shape a community of readers, one of which is Book Buddies. Sharing books with other readers benefits older and younger students. When students talk about books, it increases their understanding and improves their ability to express themselves orally. It also offers the opportunity to hear what another reader thinks, and thus enlarge their own responses. A Book Buddies program is one aspect of a classroom or school-wide community.

Classmate Book Buddies

To implement Book Buddies in your classroom:

- Have students choose partners; one reads aloud, or they both read silently.

- After they have finished reading, partners discuss the book quietly.

- Discussions are generally open-ended, with no teacher prompts.

Cross-Age Book Buddies

To implement cross-age Book Buddies, connect with another teacher in a grade level two or three years higher than yours and proceed as follows:

- The older students come to visit and get acquainted with your students.

- The older students receive training in how to select books, read aloud, engage in discussion, and plan appropriate follow-up activities (if desired).

- Book Buddies meet on a regular schedule to read together and talk about what they read.

The social and cultural context in which young readers grow and learn shapes their view of the world and the role of literature in it. Readers belong to a community, in fact to varied communities of readers, and in these interpretive communities they learn different ways of approaching a text, different ways to think about a text, and different ways to talk about a text (Fish, 1980). One such interpretive community might be Book Buddies, as described in Teaching Idea 2.5.

Sipe (1999) points out that contexts are multiple, ranging from the immediate context—perhaps the classroom library with comfortable pillows and attractive bookshelves—to the wider context of the classroom and its interpretive community, to the even wider context of the reader's social world and cultural background, including popular culture. Langer (1995) describes reader-based literature instruction based on transactional theory and research on response. Lewis (2001) details how power, status, and cultural norms shape what occurs in one particular classroom. Apol (1998), Nodelman (1996), Nodelman and Reimer (2003), and others argue for classroom communities in which teachers and children participate in

critical readings of texts. We present varied classroom contexts in Chapters 11 and 12.

Because of the power of books to shape our lives, it is important that we offer wonderful books to our students so they view books as a vital part of their lives. We must be careful in what we choose, selecting the best books for the best reasons. Even when we are cautious, however, it is not unusual to have a book "challenged" by a parent, community member, or even administrator. Challenges to your students' right to read are called *censorship*.

• • CENSORSHIP AND SELECTION • •

Books about virtually any topic or issue in the world are found in children's and especially adolescent literature. For example, Laurie Halse Anderson's main character in ***Speak*** (A) remains silent for most of the novel but finally reveals that she has been sexually abused and identifies her attacker. Walter Dean Myers's ***Monster*** (A) involves the murder of a Korean storekeeper and the trial of a teenage boy for that murder. The wide range of topics covered in children's and adolescent literature gives young people access to a comprehensive picture of their world; it also invites serious attempts to censor what they read. Many people feel that children should not face difficult issues; others believe that difficult issues should be presented in books that reflect the real world children face. Sometimes an author's realistic portrayal of language or customs disturbs adults, as in Kris Franklin's **The Grape Thief** (I–A), which caused some argument about whether the ethnic slurs present in the book—as used by the characters in the 1920s small-town setting—were too nasty or not nasty enough to be realistic.

Even books that seem quite harmless, such as Beatrix Potter's **The Tale of Peter Rabbit** (N–P), can cause some adults to want to keep them from children. In the case of **Peter**, many felt that it was sexist because the girls were good and the boy got to have all the fun, and they wanted the book removed from nursery schools in London. The outpouring of challenges to the use of the Harry Potter books, and fantasy in general, occurred because many people believe that magic is not fantasy at all, but real, and as such is the work of evil. The point is that although we all have beliefs and preferences, we cannot prevent others from reading, viewing, or listening to the material they choose. That is what the First Amendment is all about. The ALA's Office for Intellectual Freedom publishes a list of frequently challenged books. *Hit List for Children 2* and *Hit List for Young Adults 2* provide resources for withstanding challenges to the targeted books.

Most professional organizations, such as the ALA, the International Reading Association (IRA), and the National Council of Teachers of English (NCTE), believe that parents have the right to decide what their own children read but not the right to tell other people's children what they should read. Sometimes books that teachers and librarians choose for school study provoke criticism from parents or community members. Often parents simply request that their child not read a particular book; it is easy to make provisions for that. Sometimes, however, an individual parent, school board member, or member of the larger community will request that no child be allowed to read a particular book; this is a bigger problem.

Suppressing reading material is *censorship*, a remedy that creates more problems than it solves. Choosing reading material that does not offend our taste, however, is *selection*—not censorship. Censorship is the attempt to deny others the right to read something the censor thinks is offensive. Selection is the process of choosing appropriate material for readers according to literary and educational judgments.

The NCTE (1983, p. 18) differentiates between selection and censorship in five dimensions: (1) Censorship *excludes* specific materials; selection *includes* specific material to give breadth to collections. (2) Censorship is *negative*; selection is *affirmative*. (3) Censorship intends to *control* the reading of others; selection intends to *advise* the reading of others. (4) Censorship seeks to *indoctrinate and limit access* to ideas and information, whereas selection seeks to *educate and increase access* to ideas and information. (5) Censorship looks at specific aspects and *parts of a work in isolation*, whereas selection examines the relationship of *parts to each other and to a work as a whole*.

The controversy surrounding many books is rooted in a blatant attempt to impose censorship, to limit student access to materials, and to impose the religious and political views of a small segment of society on those whose views may differ. The IRA, the NCTE, the ALA, and the National Coalition Against Censorship condemn attempts by self-appointed censors to restrict students' access to quality reading materials. Professional associations and most school districts have established procedures for dealing with attempts at censorship. School media specialists or principals need to have a standard process to follow if a book is challenged.

NCTE's Anti-Censorship Center offers a wealth of information about what to do if a book is challenged. There is a site for reporting a censorship incident as well as a listing of sites that contain news reports of censorship. A listing of helpful online resources includes instructions on how to obtain a series of written rationales for the most commonly challenged books as well as the site for Students' Right to Read, which gives detailed procedures for responding to challenges, including a copy of the "Citizen's Request for Reconsideration of a Work." This form asks those who complain about a book for detailed information through questions that stress the sound educational reasons that the book was selected by the teacher or school. To learn more about this center, go to CengageBrain.com to access the Education CourseMate website, where you will find links to relevant websites.

If a book you have chosen is challenged, don't panic. Get the complaint in writing and take it to your media specialist, principal, or other appropriate school-based person. The most important thing to remember is to select wisely—know your resources for making good selections as well as your reasons for selection. We know now that even very young children are capable of making meaningful connections with text and responding in ways that are both deeply felt and critically astute (Cochran-Smith, 1984; Lehr, 1991; McGee, 1992; Sipe, 2008). And there is ample evidence, much of which is cited

On Your Education CourseMate

HANDLING CENSORSHIP ATTEMPTS

IRA, ALA, NCTE, and the National Coalition have wonderful websites that provide information and guidance about censorship. For example, the NCTE offers *Guidelines for Selection of Materials in English Language Arts Programs*, in which they advocate for a clear written policy that reflects local interests and issues for the selection of materials in any English language arts program. Go to CengageBrain.com to access the Education CourseMate website, where you will find links to relevant websites.

Questions to Consider

Because selection must be tied to community standards, there is no one set of guidelines, but rather general principles: material must have a clear connection to established educational objectives and must address the needs of the students. Select a piece of literature and ask:

1. What educational objectives and needs would this book meet?
2. Why is this book an important book for you to include in your classroom?

previously, that readers continue to do so as they mature, encountering new texts in the context of classroom and world, and adding them to the "family of stories" (Stott, 1987) they know. This is one reason why those who seek to control what others read feel threatened by particular books. Perhaps the most intriguing development in the research literature is a realization of just how important context is as it shapes how readers read the texts they encounter. Chapters 3 through 10 explore the texts of children's and adolescent literature. In Chapters 11 and 12, we turn once again to one important context in which children read them—the classroom.

SUMMARY

Reading is a transaction that occurs between a reader and a text and is embedded within multiple sociocultural contexts. All readers actively construct meaning, under the guidance of a text, bringing experiences with life and literature to any act of reading. The text guides them as they use prior understandings to construct new meaning. Texts are also shaped by sociocultural contexts and reflect either implicitly or explicitly the values that their authors have developed. The ideologies of both texts and readers, and of the contexts in which writing and reading occurs, play an important role in shaping meaning as readers either accept or resist the ideas presented in a text by judging that idea in terms of their own values while also reading in a socially sanctioned manner.

Booklist

International Reading Association Children's Choices, 2011 (Books published in 2010)

BEGINNING READERS (GRADES K–2)

A Balloon for Isabel, by Deborah Underwood, illustrated by Laura Rankin (Greenwillow)

Banana! by Ed Vere (Henry Holt)

Born Yesterday: The Diary of a Young Journalist, by James Solheim, illustrated by Simon James (Dolly Parton's Imagination Library)

City Dog, Country Frog, by Mo Willems, illustrated by Jon J Muth (Hyperion)

Daddy's Little Scout, by Janet Bingham, illustrated by Rosalind Beardshaw (Cartwheel)

Dogs Don't Do Ballet, by Anna Kemp, illustrated by Sara Ogilvie (Simon & Schuster)

Even Monsters Need Haircuts, by Matthew McElligott (Walker)

Frankie Stein Starts School, by Lola M. Schaefer, illustrated by Kevan Atteberry (Marshall Cavendish)

Furious George Goes Bananas: A Primate Parody, by Michael Rex (Putnam)

Hattie the Bad, by Jane Devlin, illustrated by Joe Berger (Dial)

Hot Rod Hamster, by Cynthia Lord, illustrated by Derek Anderson (Scholastic)

How Rocket Learned to Read, by Tad Hills (Random House)

If You're a Monster and You Know It, by Rebecca Emberley and Ed Emberley (Orchard)

Is Your Buffalo Ready for Kindergarten? by Audrey Vernick, illustrated by Daniel Jennewein (Balzer & Bray)

Let's Save the Animals, by Frances Barry (Candlewick)

Little Pink Pup, by Johanna Kerby (Putnam)

Memoirs of a Goldfish, by Devin Scillian, illustrated by Tim Bowers (Sleeping Bear)

Miss Brooks Loves Books! (and I don't), by Barbara Bottner, illustrated by Michael Emberley (Knopf)

Mr. President Goes to School, by Rick Walton, illustrated by Brad Sneed (Peachtree)

Pete the Cat: I Love My White Shoes, by Eric Litwin, illustrated by James Dean (HarperCollins)

Roly Poly Pangolin, by Anna Dewdney (Viking)

Shark vs. Train, by Chris Barton and Tom Lichtenheld (Little, Brown)

Taking Care of Mama, by Mitra Modarressi (Putnam)

YOUNG READERS (GRADES 3–4)

Adrian Peterson, by Michael Sandler (Bearport)

Amazing Greek Myths of Wonder and Blunders, by Mike Townsend (Dial)

Animal Rescue Team: Gator on the Loose! by Sue Stauffacher, illustrated by Priscilla Lamont (Knopf)

Babymouse #12: Burns Rubber, by Jennifer L. Holm and Matthew Holm (Random House)

Bad Kitty vs. Uncle Murray: The Uproar at the Front Door, by Nick Bruel (Roaring Brook)

The Bat's Cave: A Dark City, by Joyce Markovics (Bearport)

Bones: Skeletons and How They Work, by Steve Jenkins (Scholastic)

Chester's Masterpiece, by Mélanie Watt (Kids Can Press)

Combat-Wounded Dogs, by Sonita Apte (Bearport)

Copper, by Kazu Kibuishi (Graphix)

Drizzle, by Kathleen Van Cleve (Dial)

Encyclopedia Mythologica: Gods & Heroes, by Matthew Reinhart and Robert Sabuda (Candlewick)

Finally, by Wendy Mass (Scholastic)

Finn McCool and the Great Fish, by Eve Bunting, illustrated by Zachary Pullen (Sleeping Bear)

Goliath: Hero of the Great Baltimore Fire, by Claudia Friddell, illustrated by Troy Howell (Sleeping Bear)

Heart-Stopping Roller Coasters, by Meish Goldish (Bearport)

I Survived #1: The Sinking of the Titanic, 1912, by Lauren Tarshis (Scholastic)

Lunch Lady and the Summer Camp Shakedown, by Jarrett J. Krosoczka (Knopf)

Miniature Horses, by Natalie Lunis (Bearport)

Missile Mouse #1: The Star Crusher, by Jake Parker (Graphix)

The Odious Ogre, by Norton Juster, illustrated by Jules Feiffer (Scholastic)

Older Than the Stars, by Karen C. Fox, illustrated by Nancy Davis (Charlesbridge)

Potbellied Pigs, by Natalie Lunis (Bearport)

Swim! Swim! by Lerch (Scholastic)

There Was an Old Monkey Who Swallowed a Frog, by Jennifer Ward, illustrated by Steve Gray (Marshall Cavendish)

Young Zeus, by G. Brian Karas (Scholastic)

Zen Ghosts, by Jon J. Muth (Scholastic)

ADVANCED READERS (GRADES 5–6)

31 Ways to Change the World. We Are What We Do (Candlewick)

Big Nate: In a Class by Himself, by Lincoln Peirce (HarperCollins)

The Billionaire's Curse, by Richard Newsome, illustrated by Johnny Duddle (Walden Pond)

Blindsided, by Priscilla Cummings (Dutton)

Calamity Jack, by Shannon and Dean Hale, illustrated by Nathan Hale (Bloomsbury)

Chemistry: Getting a Big Reaction! by Dan Green, created and illustrated by Simon Basher (Kingfisher)

Dark Labyrinths, by Michael Goodman (Bearport)

The Dreamer, by Pam Muñoz Ryan, illustrated by Peter Sís (Scholastic)

Explorers: Dinosaurs, by Dougal Dixon, illustrated by Peter Bull (Kingfisher)

Ghostopolis, by Doug TenNapel (Graphix)

The Grimm Legacy, by Polly Shulman (Putnam)

How I, Nicky Flynn, Finally Get a Life (and a Dog), by Art Corriveau (Amulet)

I Dreamed of Flying Like a Bird: My Adventures Photographing Wild Animals from a Helicopter, by Robert B. Haas (National Geographic)

It's a Book, by Lane Smith (Roaring Brook)

Kid vs. Squid, by Greg van Eekhout (Bloomsbury)

The Line, by Teri Hall (Dial)

Love Puppies and Corner Kicks, by R. W. Krech (Dutton)

Lynn Visible, by Julia DeVillers (Dutton)

Micro Monsters: Extreme Encounters with Invisible Armies (Kingfisher)

NERDS Book Two: M Is for Mama's Boy, by Michael Buckley (Amulet)

Other Goose: Re-Nurseried!! and Re-Rhymed!! Children's Classics, by J. Otto Seibold (Chronicle)

Planet Earth: What Planet Are You On? by Dan Green, created and illustrated by Simon Basher (Kingfisher)

The Popularity Papers: Research for the Social Improvement and General Betterment of Lydia Goldblatt & Julie Graham-Chang, by Amy Ignatow (Amulet)

The Red Pyramid, by Rick Riordan (Disney Hyperion)

Smile, by Raina Telgemeier (Graphix)

The Sons of Liberty, by Alexander and Joseph Lagos, illustrated by Steve Walker and Oren Kramek (Random House)

The Strange Case of Origami Yoda, by Tom Angleberger (Amulet)

Super Human, by Michael Carroll (Puffin)

Tower of Treasure, by Scott Chantler (Kids Can Press)

Turtle in Paradise, by Jennifer L. Holm (Random House)

Versus: Pirates, by Richard Platt, illustrated by Steve Stone (Kingfisher)

The Wimpy Kid Movie Diary: How Greg Heffley Went Hollywood, by Jeff Kinney (Amulet)

X-treme X-ray, by Nick Veasey (Scholastic)

Yours Truly, Lucy B. Parker: Girl vs. Superstar, by Robin Palmer (Puffin)

Zebrafish, by Peter H. Reynolds and FableVision (Atheneum)

International Reading Association Young Adult Choices 2011 (Books Published in 2010)

The Big Ideas that Changed the World (Dorling Kindersley)

Candy Bomber: The Story of the Berlin Airlift's "Chocolate Pilot," by Michael O. Tunnell (Charlesbridge)

City of Glass, by Cassandra Clare (Simon & Schuster)

Halo, by Alexandra Adornetto (Feiwel and Friends)

Happyface, by Stephen Emond (Little, Brown)

Hush, Hush, by Becca Fitzpatrick (Simon & Schuster)

I Am Number Four, by Pittacus Lore (HarperCollins)

If I Stay, by Gayle Forman (Speak)

If You Live Like Me, by Lori Weber (Lobster)

Incarceron, by Catherine Fisher (Firebird)

It Started with a Dare, by Lindsay Faith Rech (Graphia)

Jumping Off Swings, by Jo Knowles (Candlewick)

Leviathan, by Scott Westerfeld (Simon Pulse)

The Lost Hero, by Rick Riordan (Thorndike)

Low Red Moon, by Ivy Devlin (Bloomsbury)

Matched, by Ally Condie (Dutton)

Mockingjay, by Suzanne Collins (Scholastic)

The Necromancer, by Michael Scott (Delacorte)

Out of My Mind, by Sharon M. Draper (Atheneum)

The Pale Assassin, by Patricia Elliott (Holiday House)

Ruined, by Paula Morris (Point)

Rules of Attraction, by Simone Elkeles (Walker)

Sea, by Heidi R. Kling (Putnam)

Shiver, by Maggie Stiefvater (Scholastic)

The Sky Is Everywhere, by Jandy Nelson (Speak)

The Sons of Liberty, by Alexander Lagos and Joseph Lagos (Random House)

The Strange Case of Origami Yoda, by Tom Angleberger (Amulet)

The Summer I Turned Pretty, by Jenny Han (Simon & Schuster)

Sweet Treats & Secret Crushes, by Lisa Greenwald (Amulet)

You Wish, by Mandy Hubbard (Razorbill)

 Additional resources to accompany this chapter can be found on the Education CourseMate website. Go to CengageBrain .com to access a variety of interactive study tools and useful resources including Video Conversations with children's book authors and illustrators, a searchable children's literature database, glossary flashcards, online activities, tutorial quizzes, links to relevant websites, and more.

PART 11

Formats and Genres in Literature for Young Readers

3

Picturebooks: A Unique Format in Children's Literature

The integrity, the dignity, the quiet strength of Rosa Parks turned her no into a YES for change.

—NIKKI GIOVANNI
Rosa, illustrated by Bryan Collier, unpaged

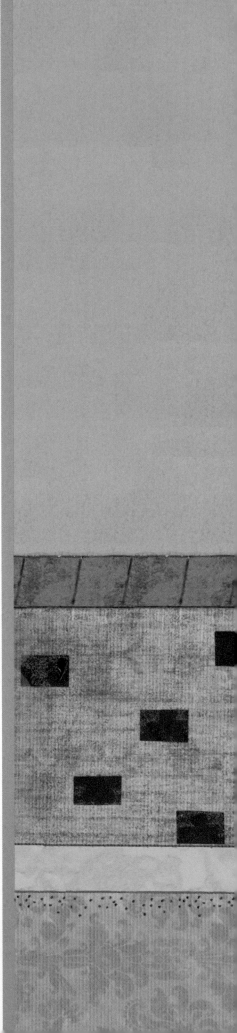

During read-aloud time, Bev has been discussing picturebooks that exemplify various types of heroes with her third graders. These Philadelphia children—all African Americans—have heard stories of courage (**Henry's Freedom Box**, P–I), self-sacrifice (**Martin's Big Words**, P–I), and folk heroes (**John Henry**, P–I). Today, Bev has chosen to read Nikki Giovanni's **Rosa** (P–I). As they examine the front cover, the children notice two things. Jamal says that the "white man with the cap" "looks like he's angry at the woman," and Debra notices that "it looks like there's a halo around the woman's head." The children have already identified the central conflict in the story, and their comments suggest a developing sense of its theme, which is racial inequality. Bev always spends time examining the front and back covers, endpapers, and title page with the children because she feels that these elements of the picturebook provide the best introduction to the story rather than her own "purpose-setting" questions.

Bev reads the dedication page. The children already understand the idea of dedicating a book to someone and comment that Giovanni's dedication of the book to her sister "courageously facing down lung cancer" shows that the sister is a hero, too. As she reads, Bev explains that there was a time when black people and white people could not sit on buses together. The children are incredulous when they hear that black people had to sit in the back of the bus or stand. Alexis suddenly remembers that she knows something about the story: "I remember someone named Rosa and she wouldn't give up her seat on the bus." On the fifth opening of the book, they notice that the illustration is the same as the one on the front cover. When Bev reads the text, which describes the bus driver's angry confrontation with Rosa Parks, Alexis says, "I knew it—she's Rosa Parks, and she's not goin' to give up her seat!" As the story continues through Rosa's arrest and the resulting bus boycott, the children hear of Dr. Martin Luther King's involvement, and many children make personal comments that show their knowledge of Dr. King's resolve to make life better for African Americans. Keith mentions that there is a picture of Dr. King in his own living room. The children also make intertextual connections to **Martin's Big Words** and remember that Dr. King was "shot and killed." When the book closes with the results of the Supreme Court decision that segregation—in schools, on buses, and everywhere else—is wrong, the children want to talk about how white people still treat African Americans intolerantly. Although this is not an easy conversation for Bev, who is white, she understands that the book has touched a resonant chord for the children and encourages them to continue to talk. She has created the space for children to feel comfortable talking about these issues by explicitly mentioning issues of race.

[handwritten margin note: Many thoughts and insights came about before even reading be of cover discussions.]

On the last page of the story, the children again notice the "halo" around Rosa Parks, and several compare her to a "saint." Patricia remembers that at the end of **Martin's Big Words** there is an illustration with candles burning in front of an image of Dr. King and makes a beautiful connection: "This is like **Martin's Big Words** because it's like Martin Luther King was a saint, and so is Rosa."

Bev's plan is to continue the theme of heroes with a read-aloud of **Something Beautiful** (P–I), the story of a little girl who realizes that by changing her attitude about her neighborhood, she can make a positive difference. In this way, Bev will continue the idea of heroes by giving children the opportunity to talk about how they might be heroes, not by actions that would appear in newspaper headlines but by smaller actions that will make the world a better place.

Thus, both the words and illustrations of **Rosa** have added another dimension to the children's understanding of heroes: heroes can exhibit determination and "quiet strength" in the face of injustice and intolerance. The book has also invited exploration of several other aspects of the civil rights movement and has elicited serious discussion of social inequities, which will continue during the rest of the year. All of this from a thirty-two-page picturebook!

Defining Picturebooks

For as long as there have been written texts, there have been illustrations that accompany them. Ancient Egyptian, Middle Eastern, and Asian scrolls contain both words and pictures; and medieval European manuscripts frequently include visual images along with texts. *Illustrated* books such as these have a very long history and many precedents; however, *picturebooks* (we use the compound word to differentiate them from books with pictures, or illustrated books) are something quite different and relatively recent. Unlike an illustrated book, in a picturebook the words cannot present information or tell the story alone. The words tell us things that are not in the pictures, and the pictures tell us things that the words do not reveal. This, in short, is what picturebooks do; the central idea is the essential unity, harmony, or "synergy" (Sipe, 1998) of the words and illustrations. Each is as important as the other; unlike in illustrated books, where the visual images are clearly subordinate to the words. Indeed, there are picturebooks with few or no words at all; in these wordless picturebooks, the visual images carry the narrative by themselves. Awards given for picturebooks can be based on either the text, as is the Charlotte Zolotow Award for outstanding writing in a picturebook, or the illustrations, in the case of the Caldecott Medal. Lists of Caldecott-winning picturebooks are found in Appendix A.

Whether wordless or composed of text and illustration, picturebooks occupy a unique place in the world of children's literature. Because we classify picturebooks according to format rather than content, they actually span other genres. We have picturebooks that are folklore, fantasy and science fiction, contemporary realistic fiction, historical fiction, or nonfiction—including informational books, concept books, and biographies—as well as poetry and song. These genres are defined in Chapter 1, and books that represent particular genres in picturebook format are discussed in Chapters 4 through 10. Teaching Idea 3.1 offers ideas for exploring genres within a picturebook format with children.

Picturebooks not only span a number of genres; they also span a wide range of readers, from babies through adolescents. From board books that present simple concepts or tell simple stories to books that pose significant questions and explore complex issues, picturebooks have an important place in children's lives.

A Brief History of Picturebooks

In the form we know them now, picturebooks were virtually invented by the talented illustrator Randolph Caldecott in the 1870s and 1880s. This is the person for whom the American Library Association's highest

[handwritten margin note: Words + pics combine to tell the story.]

TEACHING IDEA 3.1

Using Picturebooks to Help Students Learn about Literature

 **COMMON CORE STATE STANDARDS** This Teaching Idea addresses Common Core English Language Arts, Reading: Literature standards 4, 5, 6 grades 2 through 8 according to the concepts you choose to address. The suggestions in this Teaching Idea may need to be adapted to suit your particular grade level and the needs of your students.

Because picturebooks span the range of genres and include examples of outstanding writing, they can be used to teach students—from kindergarten through high school—whatever you want them to learn about literature. If we read picturebooks aloud and talk about them without ever talking about their literary quality, we miss a wonderful opportunity to help students learn how literature works. Here are some things to think about in planning literature lessons using picturebooks:

- What do you want students to learn?
- What books do you have in your classroom library that will help you teach this concept?
- What kinds of activities can you do with students that will help them explore this concept?
- How can you build on initial understandings as you go on to read more books with your students?

If, for example, you are working with younger students and want to help them make the basic distinction between fact and fiction, then you will want to collect picturebooks about the same topic that are fiction, fact, or factual information embedded in fiction. For example, you could collect imaginative stories about dinosaurs, expository nonfiction about dinosaurs, and narrative nonfiction (information set within a story frame) about dinosaurs. Read the books with your students and talk about them, noting characteristics of each in a chart that allows you to

list what is fictional and what is factual. If you are working with older students, they can take a more sophisticated look at this same idea by talking about what is "true" and what is "plausible" in the historical fiction they read.

Or you might want to look at how authors and illustrators develop characters and at how characters grow and change over the course of a story. If so, then you would select picturebooks with strong, engaging characters. You can help students learn to think about theme, or big ideas, by selecting picture storybooks and asking them to tell you the "most important word" in the story. After collecting their answers, you can lead them into a discussion of those words, which turns naturally into a discussion of theme. You can study metaphor, allusions, foreshadowing, parallel plots—whatever you care to study—using picturebooks. The possibilities are almost endless.

To help you get started, you might want to consult *Using Picture Storybooks to Teach Literary Devices* by Susan Hall (1990); *Looking through the Faraway End: Creating a Literature-based Reading Curriculum with 2nd Graders* by Lee Galda, Shane Rayburn, and Lisa Stanzi (2000); Mary R. Jalongo's *Young Children and Picture Books*, Second Edition (2004); and *A Picture Book Primer: Understanding and Using Picture Books* by Denise Matulka (2008), as well as the various genre chapters in this textbook.

[handwritten: Resources for using picture books in various ways.]

---

award for picturebook illustration, the Caldecott Medal, is named. What was new about Caldecott's "toy books" for children, as they were called?

Instead of merely illustrating a text that could stand perfectly well by itself, Caldecott invented a form in which both words and pictures were equally important—and necessary—to tell the story. His illustrations were not lovely embellishments, but an integral part of the whole experience of his books. For

example, one of his most famous children's books took the nonsense rhyme "Hey, Diddle, Diddle" and injected it with new life through his illustrations, which are still admired and enjoyed today. The last line of the rhyme, "And the dish ran away with the spoon," is accompanied by an illustration of the dish (a male) dancing with the spoon (his girlfriend) to the tune of the cat playing the fiddle, and a whole assemblage of dishes and plates joining in the celebration. Another

[handwritten: Caldecott's illustrations provided an entirely different perspective on the nursery rhyme.]

illustration shows the dish and spoon romantically snuggling beside each other on a bench. But this is not all: on the following page, disaster has struck. In the center of the illustration the dish lies, broken in pieces, and the other dishes and plates are wailing with mourning. On the right-hand side of the illustration, a knife and fork (the spoon's father and mother, respectively) flank the devastated spoon, haughtily leading her away. We're invited to speculate that the knife and fork didn't think the dish was worthy of their daughter and that they took violent action against him! By themselves, the words tell us nothing of a romantic involvement between the dish and spoon, let alone the tragic result of their love. In other words, this set of illustrations greatly expands and extends our understanding and enjoyment of the words. Today's picturebooks may look different, due to the great advances in printing reproduction techniques, but the essence remains the same.

Randolph Caldecott, along with illustrators Walter Crane and Kate Greenaway, showed that books for children with many colorful illustrations could be quite successful. At the turn of the century, Beatrix Potter published her first picturebook, **The Tale of Peter Rabbit** (1902). As literacy rates improved and more children became readers, and as printing techniques for reproducing illustrations made great progress, the stage was set for a veritable explosion of children's picturebooks in the 1920s, here in the United States.

In the late 1930s and early 1940s, picturebooks like **Goodnight Moon** (N–P) began to focus on the everyday lives of children rather than on fantasy and fairy tales. This trend continues to the present day, though of course fantasy and anthropomorphized animals are still an important feature of many picturebooks. Some milestones of children's picturebook publishing are listed in Figure 3.1. All of these picturebooks are considered classics, are still in print, and continue to sell well.

As in most books for children, until the 1950s and 1960s, the presence of children of color and children from diverse cultures in picturebooks was rare, and what representations there were tended to

[handwritten: classics, in print, sell well]

FIGURE 3.1

Milestones in the History of Picturebooks

1878	**The House that Jack Built** by Randolph Caldecott
1902	**The Tale of Peter Rabbit** by Beatrix Potter
1928	**Millions of Cats** by Wanda Gág
1930	**The Little Engine that Could** by Watty Piper
1933	**The Story of Babar** by Jean de Brunoff
1936	**The Story of Ferdinand** by Munro Leaf, illustrated by Robert Lawson
1937	**And to Think I Saw It on Mulberry Street**, Dr. Seuss's first book
1938	Creation of the Caldecott Medal by the American Library Association—this greatly spurred the interest in (and availability of) picturebooks
1939	**Madeline** by Ludwig Bemelmans
	Mike Mulligan and His Steam Shovel by Virginia Lee Burton
1941	**Make Way for Ducklings** by Robert McCloskey

1942	Simon & Schuster begin publishing the Little Golden Books, which marketed picturebooks at a price low enough (25 cents) for almost every family to afford.
1947	**Goodnight Moon** by Margaret Wise Brown, illustrated by Clement Hurd
1955	**Harold and the Purple Crayon** by Crockett Johnson
1957	**The Cat in the Hat**, Dr. Seuss's most famous book
1962	**The Snowy Day** by Ezra Jack Keats
1963	**Where the Wild Things Are**, Maurice Sendak's most famous book
1967	**Brown Bear, Brown Bear, What Do You See?** by Bill Martin (Eric Carle's first picturebook)
1969	**Stevie** by John Steptoe (one of the first picturebooks to represent African American children from the perspective of an African American author/ illustrator)

be stereotypical and racist. **The Snowy Day** (N–P) by Ezra Jack Keats (1962), himself not an African American, was the first picturebook with an African American protagonist to win the Caldecott Medal. John Steptoe's **Stevie** (P) (1969) is generally recognized as one of the first picturebooks to represent the everyday lives of African American children from an insider's perspective, although an overwhelming percentage of picturebooks published today still do not contain images of children of color (Martin, 2004). Further advances in color reproduction techniques in the 1960s and early 1970s made it possible for printing companies to separate the colors in illustrations, so that illustrators did not have to do this themselves. Prior to this, illustrators had to create a separate illustration for each color they used—an unbelievable amount of labor! This advance alone increased the number of picturebooks illustrators produced. Today, we are living in the golden age of color reproduction techniques, where any illustration, no matter what medium has been used to produce it, can be used in a picturebook.

[handwritten margin note: How tedious!]

Since about 1990, picturebooks that are decidedly unusual have piqued the interest of children and adults alike. These picturebooks may contain multiple narratives of the same incident (such as Anthony Browne's **Voices in the Park**, P–I), or they may contain interlocking narratives that it is the reader's job to connect to one another, as in David Macaulay's **Black and White** (P–I–A). In many of these postmodern picturebooks, characters talk directly to the reader. In **Do Not Open This Book!** (P–I) by Michaela Muntean, the pig who is in the process of writing a book keeps telling us not to turn the page, but of course, we do, and it's the pig's interactions with us that make the story amusing. In Mélanie Watt's **Chester** (P–I), the story consists of the author/illustrator's attempts to tell a story about a mouse; but she is continually interrupted by her cat Chester, who inserts his own ideas for the story (of course starring him, not the mouse) on every page. **Chester's Back!** (P–I) provides a hilarious and equally postmodern sequel. Postmodern picturebooks often refer to many other texts; that is, they are heavily intertextual. For example, in **Ivan the Terrier** (P–I) by Peter Catalanotto, the title character keeps barging in on other stories: the dog invades the stories of "The Three Billy Goats Gruff," "The Three Bears," "The Three Little Pigs," and "The Gingerbread Boy." Part of the pleasure of this book is the idea that stories are permeable to one another. In David Wiesner's version of **The Three Pigs** (P–I–A), for example, the pigs are literally blown out of their own story by the wolf's huffing and puffing, and enter a series of other stories before they return to their own tale. In Lauren Child's delightful **Who's Afraid of the Big Bad Book?** (P–I), Herb, the main character, enters his own badly damaged book of fairy tales and has adventures with many fairy tale characters, including Goldilocks, the Three Bears, Hansel and Gretel, and Cinderella. Allan Ahlberg's **Previously** (P–I), with illustrations by Bruce Ingman, tells a story backward, with intertextual links and visits to a similar list of commonly known tales, ending the book with "Once upon a time."

Rather than enticing the reader to enter the world of the story, many of these postmodern picturebooks push the reader away, as if to say, "Remember this is not true—it's just a story." Emily Gravett's **Wolves** (P–I–A) is an example of such a self-referential book. When a rabbit gets eaten by a wolf, the narrator breaks into the story with the comment, "No rabbits were eaten during the making of this book. It is a work of fiction," then proceeds to provide an "alternative ending" for squeamish readers. Finally, some postmodern picturebooks play with the conventions of picturebooks themselves. In Jon Scieszka's collection of hilarious parodies of traditional fairy tales, **The Stinky Cheese Man and Other Fairly Stupid Tales** (P–I–A), the table of contents falls on the story characters, knocking one of the stories entirely out of the book. Jack, the narrator (we don't know for sure whether he is Jack from "Jack and the Beanstalk" or Jack from the rhyme "Jack and Jill went up the hill") moves the back endpage forward so that the giant, who is chasing him, "will think the book is over." The satisfaction of these types of picturebooks is our delighted shock that both the conventions of stories and the conventions of the picturebook format are playfully subverted.

Both young and older readers must do a lot more active reading and thinking in these books than in picturebooks with more standard plots and structures. Moreover, such picturebooks make us aware of our own thought processes as we encounter elements that contradict or defy our own expectations. In this way, postmodern picturebooks teach readers to be consciously aware of their own knowledge of stories and how they work. These books are decidedly not just for older readers; research proves that young children can understand, interpret, and appreciate their violations of literary conventions (Pantaleo, 2008; Sipe, 2008). See Figure 3.2 for a list of postmodern picturebooks.

[handwritten margin note: Is this why pic books reach older audiences metacognition]

In this chapter,

- We first look closely at the art of picturebooks, beginning with the elements that are common to all visual art, as well as the various styles of art that illustrators employ to create meaning with pictures.

FIGURE 3.2

Blurring the Boundaries: Postmodern Picturebooks

Ahlberg, Janet, and Allan Ahlberg. (1986). *The Jolly Postman or Other People's Letters*. Boston: Little, Brown

Browne, Anthony. (1998). *Voices in the Park*. New York: DK

_____. (2004). *Into the Forest*. Cambridge, MA: Candlewick

Catalanotto, Peter. (2007). *Ivan the Terrier*. New York: Atheneum

Child, Lauren. (2000). *Beware of the Storybook Wolves*. New York: Scholastic

_____. (2002). *Who's Afraid of the Big Bad Book?* New York: Hyperion

Feiffer, Jules. (1997). *Meanwhile*. New York: HarperCollins

Felix, Monique. (1988). *The Story of a Little Mouse Trapped in a Book*. La Jolla, CA: Green Tiger

Grey, Mini. (2005). *Traction Man Is Here*. New York: Knopf

_____. (2006). *The Adventures of the Dish and the Spoon*. New York: Knopf

_____. (2008). *Traction Man Meets Turbo Dog*. New York: Knopf

Hawkins, Colin, and Jacqui Hawkins. (2004). *Fairytale News*. Cambridge, MA: Candlewick

Hopkinson, Deborah. (2008). *Abe Lincoln Crosses a Creek*. Illustrated by John Hendrix. New York: Random House

Lehman, Barbara. (2004). *The Red Book*. Boston: Houghton Mifflin

_____. (2006). *Museum Trip*. Boston: Houghton Mifflin

Macaulay, David. (1990). *Black and White*. Boston: Houghton Mifflin

_____. (1995). *Shortcut*. Boston: Houghton Mifflin

Muntean, Michaela. (2006). *Do Not Open This Book!* New York: Scholastic

Scieszka, Jon. (1994). *The Book That Jack Wrote*. New York: Viking

_____. (1992). *The Stinky Cheese Man and Other Fairly Stupid Tales*. New York: Viking

Vail, Rachel. (1998). *Over the Moon*. Illustrated by Scott Nash. New York: Orchard

Van Allsburg, Chris. (1995). *Bad Day at Riverbend*. Boston: Houghton Mifflin

Watt, Mélanie. (2007). *Chester*. Toronto, Ontario: Kids Can Press

_____. (2008). *Chester's Back!* Toronto, Ontario: Kids Can Press

Wattenberg, Jane. (2000). *Henny Penny*. New York: Scholastic

Whatley, Bruce. (2001). *Wait! No Paint!* New York: HarperCollins

Wiesner, David. (2001). *The Three Pigs*. New York: Clarion

Wilson, April. (1999). *Magpie Magic*. New York: Dial

- We then consider the special aesthetic qualities specific to picturebooks and how picturebooks are put together from cover to cover as carefully designed art objects.

- Next, we explore the various types of picturebooks, ranging from storybooks to nonfiction, and from simple board books and concept books for very young children all the way to picturebooks that have intellectual and aesthetic appeal to much older readers.

- Lastly, we address teaching and learning with picturebooks in the classroom.

Here, we take a close look at the exemplary picturebooks with which we open this chapter, Nikki Giovanni's *Rosa* (P–I) illustrated by Bryan Collier.

* * *

A CLOSE LOOK AT
Rosa

A good picturebook can always be read on several levels. Nikki Giovanni's *Rosa* (P–I), illustrated by Bryan Collier, tells the familiar story of Rosa Parks (1913–2005), whose refusal to give up her seat to a white person on a bus in Montgomery, Alabama, in December 1955 was one of the landmarks of the civil rights movement. In simple but elegantly subtle language, Giovanni tells Rosa's story, with allusions to other important civil rights events. Collier's illustrations also deserve careful examination and portray Rosa Parks as a revered icon in this history. Collier also includes details that invite readers to pursue further study of the whole civil rights movement. Thus, this book can be read and enjoyed by a wide range of ages, from the primary through intermediate grades.

The central event of the whole story is captured dramatically on the front *dust jacket* (defined in Figure 3.6 on page 95), which is identical to the front *board cover*. We see an arresting close-up of the confrontation between Rosa and the bus driver. From the top right of the picture space, the bus driver glares down at Rosa, the brim of his stiff cap pointing directly at her. Only the top half of Rosa's head is depicted, from her carefully parted black hair to the bottom of her wire-rimmed eyeglasses. Her eyes and eyebrows suggest calm but intense determination. Rosa's head is surrounded by a round design of irregular rectangles in thick gold paint, suggesting a glowing halo. Even the front cover, therefore, suggests her saintlike qualities, as well as the eventual triumph of justice and freedom over repression.

The front *endpapers* show a crowded bus, in shades of monochromatic dark (almost black) purple, with Ms. Parks seated beside another African American who holds a newspaper with the headline "The Life of Emmett Till," referring to the horrific story of a fourteen-year-old's brutal murder and mutilation at the hands of white racists who believed he had insulted a white woman. This event, which also galvanized support for the civil rights movement, happened in August of the same year. This is one of the details that Giovanni also refers to later in the story. Rosa Parks's refusal to give up her seat came "only weeks" after the trial in which all of Emmett's "killers were freed" near the end of September. Also present in the front endpapers is the familiar symbol of the Confederacy, with its X-shaped design of thirteen stars, representing the thirteen states that fought against the Union in the Civil War. This illustration is repeated on the fourth *opening* of the story, but in full color.

*Bryan Collier draws attention to Rosa Parks by placing her near the center of the illustration in **Rosa**. A newspaper with the headline "The Life of Emmett Till" suggests the terrible story of an African American teenager who was brutally killed for allegedly whistling at a white girl.*

P R O F I L E

Bryan Collier

Bryan Collier's childhood was spent in a small town on the eastern shore of Maryland. He was the youngest of six children in his family. Like many future artists, he developed an interest in art at an early age, and both his parents and teachers encouraged him. He began painting seriously at the age of fifteen, developing his own style of watercolor and collage, which won several awards. He enrolled in the prestigious Pratt Institute in New York City, winning a scholarship in a national talent competition. He graduated from Pratt in 1989 with honors.

Despite this success, however, it took Bryan a long time—seven years—to break into the world of children's publishing with his book **Uptown** (P–I), which is a celebration of the vibrant life of Harlem; **Uptown** won both the Ezra Jack Keats Book Award and the Coretta Scott King Award for Illustration. Prior to this, he showed his commitment to encouraging young artists by volunteering at the Harlem Horizon Studio and Harlem Hospital Center, then went on to become the program director. At the Hospital Center, he worked with young people who had experienced traumatic events, helping them to express their feelings and achieve healing through making art. He feels a great responsibility to be a positive role model for children and teenagers, and believes that art can play an important role in building kids' self-esteem and steering them "away from negative influences." As a successful full-time illustrator who resides in New York, he now works on his own art as well as visiting schools and libraries. He also directs mural programs throughout the city, retaining his determination to help young people improve their lives through art.

Bryan's intensity extends to his chosen style of collage and watercolor; he comments, "Collage is more than just an art style. Collage is all about bringing different elements together. Once you form a sensibility about connection, how different elements relate to each other, you deepen your understanding of yourself and others." **Rosa**, the story of Rosa Parks's role in the civil rights movement, was done in collaboration with the poet Nikki Giovanni. Bryan's illustrations, coupled with Giovanni's poignant language, garnered the Coretta Scott King Award and a Caldecott Medal. He has won King and Caldecott recognition for his other work, including the Coretta Scott King Award and a Caldecott Honor in 2011 for **Dave the Potter: Artist, Poet, Slave** (P–I). This is an artist who truly has a social conscience, believes wholeheartedly in the power of art, and whose sincerity and dedication are evident in his art as well as his life.

To learn more about Bryan Collier and to read his 2011 Caldecott and King acceptance speeches, go to CengageBrain.com to access the Education CourseMate website, where you will find links to relevant websites.

The *dedication, frontmatter,* and *title page,* with a background of warm yellow, contain a rectangular illustration of Rosa, smiling broadly as she seems to step off a bus. Her left hand holds the bus rail, and her right hand is raised vertically in a gesture that can be interpreted either as a simple wave or a saint's benediction. This illustration also suggests the triumph at the end of this serious story.

The great majority of the openings of this book consist of illustrations that cross the gutter, so that three-quarters of the page is illustration and one-quarter is a column of varying colors overprinted with the words of the text, as the illustration on page 67 demonstrates. This arrangement gives room for both Giovanni and Collier to share in telling the story. Collier's accomplished watercolor and collage images do not merely illustrate the story but add considerably to its power and extend it. The openings alternate between positioning the illustration to the left and the print to the right, and vice versa, adding to the visual interest.

Alabama's state capitol building is a recurring image in Collier's illustrations, appearing four times. This building holds great significance as a background for the story because it was on the steps of this edifice that Jefferson Davis was sworn in as president of the Confederacy. Until fairly recently, the Confederate flag flew just below the American flag on the staff surmounting the capitol dome, and there are still disputes about whether this potent symbol of the Confederacy should be represented anywhere on the building. In this way, Collier reminds readers and viewers of the connection between the Civil War and the civil rights events that happened almost one hundred years afterward.

The illustrations allow the reader to learn about other relevant events in history that are not part of the text.

The pattern of three-quarters illustration and one-quarter text is dramatically broken on the thirteenth opening, which consists of a *double-page spread* of many people, some holding American flags, and the text, which explains that there were people who walked to work rather than taking buses for almost a year to protest Rosa's arrest and the injustice of having to sit at the back of public transportation. The illustration seems to be set in Selma, Alabama, and not in Montgomery because of the presence of the Edmund Pettus Bridge in Selma, which in 1965 was the scene of violence toward African Americans who were marching from Selma to Montgomery and were brutally attacked by state troopers wielding billy clubs and tear gas. This illustration is a *double-gatefold*, which readers can open to reveal a four-page illustration of many people, steadfast in their resolve, and the text that explains the Supreme Court's 1956 ruling that "segregation of the buses, like segregation at schools, was illegal." At the extreme right of this impressive illustration is the image of the state capitol, still with its Confederate flag flying beneath the American flag, suggesting the conflict between the federal and state laws.

The last opening contains another iconic image of Rosa, surrounded by the same golden sunburst as on the front cover; she is looking down at several children, who hold their hands out to her as if venerating her and seeking her blessing. The book ends with the back endpapers, rendered in the same monochromatic dark purple as the front endpapers, with an image of a bus passing a house and leaflets and posters in support of Ms. Parks and the bus boycott.

Collier's illustrator's note states that he made trips to both Montgomery and Selma, during which he felt the intense heat of the summer. He wanted his paintings to "have a yellow, sometimes dark, hue. I wanted the reader to feel in that heat a foreshadowing, an uneasy quiet before the storm." He also states that it was his intent to make Rosa look "as if light is emanating from her."

Naturally, not all the details of this book will be explored by teachers of young children, but the potential is there for the book to provide an entrée into a serious study of the civil rights movement as well as a study of how text and art work together in a brilliant picturebook.

Considering Quality in Picturebooks

There are many things to consider when evaluating the quality of a picturebook: the quality of the text, if there is any; the quality of the art; and the quality of the overall design of the book. There are so many outstanding picturebooks from which to choose that it is never necessary to give an inferior book to a reader. In Figure 3.3, we offer some general guidelines for picturebooks as well as guidelines for picturebooks that are storybooks, nonfiction, and

FIGURE 3.3

Considering Quality in Picturebooks

All Picturebooks

- Language is rich, with interesting words used in interesting ways.
- Illustrations are artistically excellent.
- Size, shape, and overall design of the book are appropriate to the subject or story.

Picture Storybooks

- Text and illustrations establish the mood, setting, characters, and theme of the story.
- Illustrations expand on the story appropriately and do not merely duplicate what is described in the text.
- Layout and design are visually appealing.

Nonfiction

- Text and illustrations are accurate.
- Text and illustrations are organized in an appropriate manner.
- Text and illustrations are attractive, and show verve and style.

Poetry and Song

- Language is lyrical.
- Illustrations enhance the feeling established by the text.

poetry for you to think about as you select books. These guidelines will help you determine what you might want to talk about with your students as you help them learn about the art of the picturebook and how it manifests itself in various genres. Following this, we consider specific aspects of art and overall design as they are present in picturebooks.

In addition to the guidelines presented in Figure 3.3, you will want to consider the artfulness of the book as a whole. What is the relationship between the illustrations and the text? How do the illustrations support or extend the text? Are the medium, technique, and style appropriate to the text? How do the elements of design work to enhance the meaning, in both individual pictures and across the book as a whole? What makes the book special? These and other aspects of picturebooks are discussed following.

A Focus on Illustration: Artistic Quality

Artists have many resources and techniques at their disposal. They can choose a medium, technique, and style that fit the text they are illustrating, or they can choose texts for which their unique style is suitable. When the right art is combined with a memorable text, the result is a superb book.

• • ELEMENTS OF VISUAL ART • •

Art in children's picturebooks involves the entire range of media, techniques, and styles used in all art. The *medium* (the plural is *media*)—the material used in the production of a work—may be watercolors, oils, acrylics, ink, pencil, charcoal, pastels, tissue paper, construction paper, acetate sheets, real objects (such as fabric or leaves), or any other material that artists employ. The *technique* might be painting, etching, woodcut or linoleum block printing, airbrush, collage, photography, or many other means. Currently, an increasing number of illustrators use computer software specifically intended for the production of digital images. Some illustrations are thus produced without any of the more traditional means. William Low's illustrations for **The Day the Stones Walked** (P–I), about the last days of the Easter Island civilization, seem to be rendered in oil pastels, but a note at the back of the book tells us that they were done completely "on the computer using Adobe Photoshop." Other illustrations are the product of a sensitive combination of traditional media and the

tools of the computer. For example, a note in **Wave** (N–P) informs readers that "The illustrations in this book were rendered in charcoal and acrylics and digitally manipulated." The images in Stephen Savage's **Where's Walrus?** (N–P) feature traditional artistic elements such as strong lines, color, and shape, and are created in Adobe Illustrator. The individual artist combines medium and technique in his or her own particular style to evoke setting, establish character, convey theme, display information, explain a concept, or create a mood.

When illustrating a picturebook, artists decide what media and techniques they will use, and they make other aesthetic choices as well. They must decide about color, style, and composition in their illustrations. They must make choices about line, shape, placement on a page, the use of negative space, and texture. Artists work with the basic elements of art (line, shape, color, and texture) and with the principles of design (rhythm, balance, variety, emphasis, spatial order, and unity) to create a unified image that conveys meaning.

• • LINE • •

Line is a mark on paper or a place where different colors meet. Each stroke starts with a dot that grows into a line that may be slow and rolling, sleek and fast, quiet or frenetic, flowing or angular. Line is perhaps the most expressive element in the artist's arsenal. Artists create lines that move in the direction in which they want to focus the viewer and pull the eye in a particular direction. Lines can suggest delicacy (thin lines) or stability (thick lines). Artists use the angle, width, length, and motion of line to express the meaning they want to convey. David Diaz, Rosemary Wells, Peter Sís, David Wiesner, Suzy Lee, Kadir Nelson, and Brian Selznick all use line in different and effective ways.

One use of line is to create a series of thin parallel lines that are then crossed at right angles with another set of lines. This technique, called *crosshatching*, gives the impression of energy or intensity. A classic example of cross-hatching is found in Maurice Sendak's **Where the Wild Things Are** (N–P), where most of the illustrations contain a great deal of cross-hatching in thin lines of black ink that overlay the watercolor images. The effect is particularly noticeable on the endpages of this picturebook, which seem to represent a series of colorful overlapping leaves or flowers. The addition of crosshatching over the entire surface of the illustration gives readers a feeling of excitement: What could be hiding behind this screen of foliage? If you try to imagine what the illustration would look like without any cross-hatching, you will understand that it would seem rather flat and uninteresting, despite the different colors. It's the cross-hatching that gives the illustration its vibrancy. A more recent example of the extensive use of cross-hatching to add energy and excitement to the illustrations is found in Susan Marie Swanson's ***The House in the Night*** (N–P), a Caldecott Medal winner, where Beth Krommes's black-and-white cross-hatched images, colored by touches of yellow, provide a vibrant counterpoint to the repetitive, cumulative text, which is almost hypnotically calm.

Mo Willems uses line to create a memorable character in ***Don't Let the Pigeon Drive the Bus!*** and its several sequels (P). Soft textured black lines (rendered with crayon) convey motion, and emotion, as the pigeon's dream is left unfulfilled but not forgotten. Willems won a Caldecott Medal for this book. Eric Rohmann uses thick black lines to define his characters, depict movement, and propel readers from one page to another in his Caldecott Medal–winning book, ***My Friend Rabbit*** (N–P). He uses the same

technique in ***Bone Dog*** (P). Kevin Henkes uses bold lines to create movement in ***Little White Rabbit*** (N). Arthur Geisert masterfully employs the precision of thin etched lines to create the meticulously detailed and hilarious illustrations in ***Hogwash*** (P–I). Robert Sabuda in Marguerite Davol's ***The Paper Dragon*** (P–I) uses cut paper as line.

Richard Michelson's ***As Good as Anybody*** (I–A) is a moving and uplifting story about the friendship between Dr. Martin Luther King Jr., and Rabbi Abraham Joshua Heschel and their joint commitment to justice and equity for all people. Raul Colón's illustrations for this picturebook use subtle lines that are lighter than the background colors to give a sense of movement and definition to the subdued palette and hazy shapes. In a scene depicting dogs attacking Freedom Marchers on the road from Selma to Montgomery, Alabama, for example, Colón adds a great deal of energy to the illustration through subtle curved and swirling lines that accentuate the clothing of the police and the marchers as well as the movement of the police dogs. This use of line is a common feature of Colón's style and can be seen in the illustration below.

Raul Colón's accomplished illustrations for **As Good as Anybody** *add drama and a sense of movement with curving lines that cover the figures of civil rights marchers, police, and dogs.*

In **Scribble** (N–P), Deborah Freedman's fantasy of a child who magically follows her scribbled cat into another drawing, the lines perfectly mimic the playfulness and uninhibited nature of children's drawings. We can almost see the hurried, pulsating movements of Scribble, the cat, as they are embodied in the lines quickly and chaotically drawn with black Magic Marker.

• • COLOR • •

Artists use color—or the lack of it—to express character, mood, and emotion. Color conveys warmth or coolness, personality traits, indifference or engagement, and other feelings. Color can vary in *hue*—ranging across the rainbow of colors—and *intensity*. Subdued colors can express weariness, boredom, and serenity, whereas intense (or *saturated*) colors evoke feelings of energy, vibrancy, and excitement. Colors can also vary in *value*, or the amount of light and dark. A range of values creates drama or movement; an absence of contrast creates a quiet or solemn mood. A *shade* of a color is created by adding black to the pure hue, whereas a *tint* results when white (or water, in the case of watercolors or acrylics) is added.

Chris Raschka combines both line and color to convey emotion in his wordless storybook, **A Ball for Daisy** (N-P), with watercolor washes and lines ranging from tentative to bold revealing Daisy's moods. Allen Say employs a very limited range of shades in gray and brown to emphasize the desolation and loneliness of inhabitants of the US World War II internment camps for Japanese people in **Home of the Brave** (I–A). A limited palette, however, does not necessarily convey bleakness: the muted shades of color in a limited range of values in Jonathan Bean's **At Night** (N–P) are appropriate for the gentle and quiet story of a little girl who sleeps on the roof of her apartment building during the summer months. Fittingly, Ted Lewin uses shades of blue, gray, brown, and black to illustrate Marion Dane Bauer's **The Longest Night** (P), adding dawn's rose and yellow hues to the final openings. In contrast, in Christopher Myers's hip, urban version of Lewis Carroll's nonsense poem **Jabberwocky** (P–I–A), the colors are almost all saturated hues of neon colors, adding to the energy of the intense basketball game played by the hero (the "beamish boy") and the Jabberwock, who is imagined as an enormously tall and menacing basketball player. Carll Cneut's vibrant illustrations for Marilyn Singer's **City Lullaby** (P) depict busy city life through warm, saturated colors.

Peter Sís's strategic use of color in **The Wall: Growing Up behind the Iron Curtain** (I–A) draws a dramatic contrast between the dull and fearful atmosphere of Prague during communist rule and the exuberance of the introduction of mainstream Western popular culture. In this autobiographical picturebook, Sís uses an intense hue of red to symbolize the repressions of communism in otherwise black-and-white drawings. Whenever creativity and imagination are highlighted, however, Sís's palette becomes much more expansive, reaching a high point as he describes the "Prague Spring," where the communist authorities allowed more freedom of expression in art, music, and literature, culminating in The Beatles' rock music and the daring poetry of Allen Ginsberg. In the double-page spread that illustrates the Prague Spring, Sís uses a combination of truly psychedelic colors and intense hues to convey the excitement of that short-lived time period.

In John Light's **The Flower** (I), Lisa Evans's illustrations reflect the change in mood from the dull and lonely life of a boy who lives in a big city (rendered in a very narrow range of values of shades of gray and brown) to one of quiet joy as he discovers a book full of pictures of flowers, which are depicted in colorful tints of pinks, reds, and greens. As he searches in vain for a flower, the palette again turns gray, until he discovers an old packet of flower seeds in a junk shop. As the planted seeds grow, the palette brightens along with his mood and the mood of the story to reflect the hope that the city might one day be filled with flowers.

• • SHAPE • •

Shape is an area or form with a definite outline. It, along with line, directs the viewer's eye and suggests feelings and ideas. Shapes can be geometric (circles, triangles, squares), abstract (suggestive, less well-defined shapes, such as clouds), or realistic and representational. Shape can contribute to the volume or three-dimensional quality of an illustration. In some illustrations, shapes seem to jut out from the front, or plane, of the picture, coming toward the viewer. Artists make decisions about the placement of shapes (positive space) on the background (negative space).

Manuel Monroy extends Jorge Luján's spare, poetic text—in Spanish, with an English translation by Elisa Amado below the Spanish, set in a smaller, different-colored font—in **Rooster/Gallo** (N–P), a mythic hymn to the dawn. The colors are dramatic, and the shapes of rooster, beak, and star are a rhythmic accompaniment to the lyrical text.

Colors depict an array of moods and emotions.

And I grew up,
tall and straight-boned,
writing every day.
And the words became books
that told the stories of
many people's Show Ways.

*In this double-page spread from **Show Way**, the theme that runs through the story is emphasized by the common geometric shapes used in quilting.*

Hudson Talbott's illustrations for Jacqueline Woodson's **Show Way** (P–I) rely heavily on the geometric shapes that are characteristic of quilts, which feature prominently in Woodson's history of her own family from slave times until the present. In the books of Saxton Freymann and Joost Elfers (such as **Dog Food**, **Fast Food**, and **Baby Food**, all N–P), the shapes of cleverly carved assemblages of fruits and vegetables delight all readers. Who would have thought that a piece of cauliflower could be carved into a fluffy white poodle? The strong and beautifully photographed shapes take center stage in these lively books. The combination of strong geometric shapes of blast furnaces and other machinery used in the steel-making industry with the rounded shapes of workmen give much visual interest to **Steel Town** (I) written by Jonah Winter and illustrated by Terry Widener, resulting in a visual style similar to that of the American artist Thomas Hart Benton. Lois Ehlert highlights geometric shapes in many of her books, including **Color Zoo** (N) and **Oodles of Animals** (N). Her books are marked by bright colors, clear lines, and shapes that seem to jump off the page. Shape is an essential element of Ashley Bryan's **Let It Shine** (P–I), and Steve Jenkins's **Living Color** (I). In these two books, shape combines with color to produce vivid illustrations.

Yuyi Morales's **Little Night** (P), a Golden Kite Award winner, is an excellent example of the use of shape to indicate mood and feeling. In all the illustrations for this dreamy and magical picturebook, there is hardly a shape that is not composed of rounded curves. The round, curved shapes give the mood of comfort, softness, and warmth as Mother Sky gently proceeds through the bedtime rituals. How inappropriate sharp, angular shapes would be in this calm and loving story! In addition, the color palette for this bedtime book is appropriately muted, combining with the shapes to produce a dreamlike atmosphere.

Attention to shape and color are evident in Lauren Stringer's many picturebooks, including **The Princess and Her Panther** (N–P), written by Wendy Orr, in which glowing, saturated colors and rounded, comforting shapes draw readers into the world of the story.

● ● TEXTURE ● ●

Some illustrations seem smooth, others rough. Some, like collage, do have a rough texture in the original art, whereas in others texture is entirely visual. Texture conveys a sense of reality; interesting visual contrasts or patterns suggest movement and action, roughness, or delicacy.

Denise Fleming uses an unusual process to create illustrations for **Barnyard Banter** (N–P), **Lunch** (N–P), **In the Small, Small Pond** (N–P), **Sleepy, Oh so Sleepy** (N), **The Everything Book** (N–P), and **Shout! Shout It Out!**. She pours colored cotton pulp through hand-cut stencils, which results in handmade paper images. The art is satisfyingly textured and more softly edged than most cut-paper illustrations. The softness of the paper tempers the intense colors and active composition to make her art appealing to children and fascinating to adults.

Lois Ehlert's **Red Leaf, Yellow Leaf** (P–I), with its use of real objects, such as strips of burlap, string, and twigs, has a marvelous combination of textures that delight the eye. Another master of the use of real objects, Jeannie Baker creates the illusion of a landscape through the use of real sand, bits of moss, vines, leaves, and tree bark in **Where the Forest Meets the Sea** (P–I). The use of these organic objects creates such an illusion of texture that readers want to touch the pages. Javaka Steptoe's exuberant collage illustrations for Karen English's **Hot Day on Abbott Avenue** (P) are textured with layers of tissue paper and construction paper on painted planks of wood, and his use of various materials gives us a sense of the different texture of each person's hair, from spiky and straight to smooth and flowing. David Diaz's textured collages for Eve Bunting's story **Smoky Night** (I–A) convey the turmoil, fear, and anxiety caused by riots. Diaz uses material that reflects the events in the text: wooden matches texturize the illustration for fire; plastic bags and hangers symbolize the looting of the dry cleaners. Diaz won the Caldecott Medal for this book. Barbara Reid's unique plasticine illustrations in picturebooks such as **The Subway Mouse** (P) demonstrate her ability to convey a great range of textures, from the soft fur of a mouse to the rough concrete walls of a subway to the smooth shiny surface of ripe blackberries.

*Barbara Reid's expert use of plasticene and real objects creates a multitude of textures in her illustrations for **Subway Mouse**.*

It was their favourite time of day.

35

In the Caldecott Medal book **Snowflake Bentley** (P–I)—Jacqueline Briggs Martin's biography of William Bentley, a photographer of natural phenomena—Mary Azarian's hand-colored woodcuts have a folksy, down-home quality that is appropriate for this story, which takes place in the Vermont countryside at the end of the nineteenth century. As we look at the rustic woodcuts, we can almost feel the rough wood furnishings, the scratchy wool knits, and the coarse weave of the lumber jacket. We can see the diversity of textures of fields and flowers, and of course the beauty of the snowflakes that became Bentley's favorite subject matter.

Texture can be achieved by painters as well, as in Francois Roca's illustrations for Jonah Winter's **Muhammad Ali: Champion of the World** (I). Roca manages to convey the warm smoothness of skin, the silkiness of boxing shorts, and the shiny softness of boxing gloves with the medium of oil paint.

*Giles Laroche's beautifully rendered front dust jacket cover for **What Do Wheels Do All Day?** by April Jones Prince exemplifies the best of all the elements of visual design.*

• • DESIGN • •

Artists use the basic elements of art to create meaning and feeling; they manipulate these elements through principles of design to express their unique visions. Artists work to achieve unity, or a meaningful whole, through *composition* of their art. To achieve unity, artists make use of balance, repeated rhythms, variety, emphasis, and spatial order. Balance means giving equal weight to the lines, shapes, textures, and colors in a picture; without it the picture seems awkward (Greenberg & Jordan, 1991, 1993). *Repetition* in art helps achieve visual harmony and balance, whereas *variety* sets up a paradox or a progression that leads the eye from one point to another. Artists draw attention to a particular part of their piece by emphasizing size, placement, color, or line; these elements work together to force the viewer's eyes to focus on a particular place in an illustration.

For example, examine the front cover of April Jones Prince's **What Do Wheels Do All Day?** (P–I) illustrated by Giles Laroche. Repetition is certainly present, in the many circles of wheels and gears; however, variety is also much in evidence—no two wheels are the same, either in size or color. There is a balance between more simple wheels, such as the one in the upper right-hand corner, and more complex ones, such as the circular gear mechanism and the large wheel at the bottom left, with its multiple colors and smaller circles inside larger ones. In addition, the range of vibrant colors is balanced. The cool colors, such as blue and green, are balanced by the spectrum of warm colors, such as yellow, orange, and red. The curved lines of the wheels are balanced by the straight spokes in several of the circles. The use of negative and positive space is pleasing; some wheels seem to overlap with each other, giving a three-dimensional effect. The background (the negative space) is light beige with a texture much like sandpaper, contrasting effectively with the darker and brighter colors of the wheels. Finally, the curved lines of the title and the author's and illustrator's names are pleasingly integrated into the total design. The main word in the title, "Wheels," jumps out at us because it is presented in a larger font than the rest of the title, as well as being red, in contrast to the black used for the rest of the title. The combination of all these elements results in a superbly designed cover that invites us into the book.

In her book *Picture This: How Pictures Work* (2002), Molly Bang describes the formal principles of design; we have summarized them here:

- Smooth, flat, horizontal shapes present a sense of stability and calm. (p. 42)
- Vertical shapes are more exciting and active, implying energy and reaching. (p. 44)
- Diagonal shapes are dynamic, implying motion or tension. (p. 46)
- The upper half of a picture connotes freedom, happiness, triumph, and spirituality. (p. 54)
- The bottom half connotes threat, heaviness, sadness, and constraint. (p. 56)
- An object in the upper half carries "greater pictorial weight" and emphasis. (p. 56)

Interesting

- The center of the page is the point of "greatest attraction." (p. 62)
- The edges and corners of the picture are the ends of the picture world. (p. 66)
- White or light backgrounds feel safer than dark backgrounds. (p. 68)
- Pointed shapes frighten; rounded shapes or curves comfort and feel safe. (p. 70)
- The larger an object is, the stronger it feels, whereas the smaller an object is, the weaker or more insignificant it seems. (p. 72)
- We link the same or similar colors more readily than the same or similar shapes. (p. 76)
- Contrasts enable us to see. (p. 80)

Artists such as Molly Bang work with these principles to compose their illustrations so that a reader's eye is guided by the art as the artist intends. In a similar way, Mark Gonyea's two books for children, **A Book about Design: Complicated Doesn't Make It Good** (I) and **Another Book about Design: Complicated Doesn't Make It Bad** (I) present similar design elements in ways that primary and intermediate students can understand, using many simple and effective examples.

The text becomes part of the illustration in **Hot Day on Abbott Avenue**, mentioned previously. In an illustration of the girls playing double dutch jump rope, the artist has left room for the words of the rhyme to be printed in curved lines that follow the curves of the rope. This integration of text and picture results in a pleasing circular design that gestures toward the rhythmic energy of the girls playing their game.

• • MEDIA AND TECHNIQUE • •

Artists make choices about the media and techniques they use. As mentioned earlier, *media* refers to the material used in the production of a work. *Technique* refers to the method artists use to create art with the chosen medium. Artists can work with virtually any medium—various types of paper, clay, wood, metal, watercolors, oils, gouache (a thick tempera paint), fabric, acrylics, ink, graphite pencil or colored pencil, charcoal, pastels—or with any combination of media. A combination of media in the same book is referred to as *mixed media*. For example, the publishing information for Steve Johnson's and Lou Fancher's exquisite illustrations for Maya Angelou's **Amazing Peace: A Christmas Poem** (P–I) lists "oil, acrylic, and fabric on canvas" as the media used. Artists may use the same medium for several books but produce a very different effect by using different

In **Hot Day on Abbott Avenue**, *Javaka Steptoe's collage illustrations include the words of the story as an integral part of this design by curving them parallel to the girls' jump rope.*

techniques. Other artists employ different media that seem appropriate for different books. As well, no two artists use the same medium in the same way.

Stephen T. Johnson uses pastels to create gentle, delicately colored drawings in Lenore Look's **Love as Strong as Ginger** (P–I), whereas the pastel drawings in Rachel Isadora's **Uh-Oh!** (N) are full of intense, highly saturated color to complement the story of a toddler's day. Chris Van Allsburg's masterful use of pastels changes from book to book. In **The Wreck of the Zephyr** (I), Van Allsburg's illustrations give the impression of great calm and stillness, but in **The Polar Express** (P–I) and **The Stranger** (P–I), there is a luminous quality to the images that highlights the excitement and mystery in the stories.

David Shannon uses acrylics in his humorous signature illustrations for **No, David!**, **David Goes to School**, and **David Gets in Trouble** (all N–P). R. Gregory Christie's use of acrylic with colored pencil illustrations for Tonya Bolden's **The Champ: The Story of Muhammad Ali** (P–I) emphasizes the head and hands of this boxer, famous for his intellectual stance on war as well as for his boxing ability. Watercolor is a favorite medium of many artists. Meilo So's watercolor illustrations for Janet

Schulman's ***Pale Male: Citizen Hawk of New York City*** (I–A) convey both the serenity of New York's Central Park and the hustle and bustle of the city; in a completely different palette, Phil Huling reflects the vibrancy of the Mexican setting in Eric Kimmel's ***Cactus Soup*** (P). Emily Arnold McCully's watercolors in ***Squirrel and John Muir*** (P) depict the beauty of Yosemite as well as the relationship between Muir and a young girl who learns from him how to observe nature. E. B. Lewis, Ted Lewin, and Jerry Pinkney each have a distinctive style of watercolor illustration, as can be seen in ***The Legend of the Cape May Diamond*** (I) and ***Across the Alley*** (I) (Lewis); ***Horse Song: The Naadam of Mongolia*** (I) and ***The Always Prayer Shawl*** (I) (Lewin); and ***The Little Red Hen*** (P) and ***Little Red Riding Hood*** (P) (Pinkney).

Artists also use a variety of techniques in addition to painting, such as etching, linoleum block printing, airbrush, collage, stitching, computer art, and photography. Photographs in Maya Ajmera and John Ivanko's ***Be My Neighbor*** (N–P) are clear and focused on conveying information, as are Michael Doolittle's photographs for Susan Goodman's ***Skyscraper: From the Ground Up*** (P–I). Frank Serafini's series of nature books, ***Looking Closely through the Forest***, ***Looking Closely along the Shore***, ***Looking Closely across the Desert***, and ***Looking Closely inside the Garden*** (all P–I) present close-up shots and invite readers to speculate on what larger object the close-up might be a part of. Turning the page reveals the secret, along with some information. For example, in ***Looking Closely across the Desert***, we see a mysterious maroon circle with bumps and the words "What do you see? A pincushion? Monster skin? What could it be?" The page turn reveals a photograph of a prickly pear cactus.

In Martin Waddell's ***Tiny's Big Adventure*** (N–P), John Lawrence's lush engravings in blues and golds extend the mood of the story, as do Barry Moser's more somber-colored wood engravings for Virginia Hamilton's ***Wee Winnie Witch's Skinny: An Original African American Scare Tale*** (I). Mary Azarian uses woodcuts to good effect in ***A Gardener's Alphabet*** (N–P) and in Jacqueline Briggs Martin's ***Snowflake Bentley*** (P–I). Jim Meyer's stunning woodcuts, which beautifully evoke the beauty of the northern wilderness in Phyllis Root's ***If You Want to See a Caribou*** (P–I), are another example of the effective use of this time-intensive and difficult medium.

Two related media that produce very intriguing illustrations are represented by the work of Brian Pinkney and Chris Gall. Pinkney (who is Jerry Pinkney's son) specializes in scratchboard. Using thick cardboard that has a heavy black coating, Pinkney employs various sharp tools to scratch away the areas he wants to appear white and finishes by handcoloring the images. The result is visually interesting because of the bold contrasts of the black-and-white portions of the illustration, overlaid with color. Fine examples of Brian Pinkney's scratchboard media and technique are found in ***Duke Ellington: The Piano Prince and His Orchestra***, ***The Adventures of***

*Jim Meyer is a master of the exacting art of colored woodcuts, as shown in his illustrations for **If You Want to See a Caribou** by Phyllis Root.*

Sparrowboy, and *Wiley and the Hairy Man* (all P–I). In a similar way, Chris Gall hand-engraves clay-coated board and applies his vibrant colors digitally with Adobe Illustrator. The tools he uses to scrape away the coating of clay are similar to Pinkney's, but they produce thicker, more forceful lines in contrast to Pinkney's fine and more flowing lines. Gall's work is well represented by *America the Beautiful*, *Dear Fish*, and *There's Nothing to Do on Mars* (all P–I).

Many artists use collage materials but create different effects using a variety of techniques and supplies. Rachel Isadora brushes oil paints on thick palette paper, which she allows to dry and then cuts into the shapes of people and objects in *Yo, Jo!* (P–I). In this way, it is reminiscent of Eric Carle's collage style, which employs a similar method of prepainting sheets of tissue paper, letting them dry, and then cutting out the shapes for his illustrations (see *The Art of Eric Carle*, 1996, for an excellent description of the process). Isadora also includes bits of newspaper or magazine texts and pieces of patterned wallpaper to add interest to her work. Holly Meade uses torn-paper collages in *Sleep, Sleep, Sleep: A Lullaby for Little Ones Around the World* (N–P) by Nancy Van Laan. Ed Young uses crisply cut collage shapes in *Seven Blind Mice* (P–I). In *Balancing Act* (N), Ellen Stoll Walsh creates her narrative using cut-and-torn paper collages that almost pop out from the white space surrounding each illustration. Steve Jenkins is perhaps the master of the type of collage style, which relies on many types and colors of handmade paper, as shown in *Sisters and Brothers: Sibling Relationships in the Animal World*, *Animals in Flight*, *Actual Size*, and *Prehistoric Actual Size* (P–I). Jenkins's

studio contains literally thousands of papers in a great variety of colors and textures, so that he can choose exactly the right type and hue for the image he is constructing, whether it be the smooth skin of a snake, the fur of a bear, or the soft down of a newly born chick. Christopher Myers uses ink and gouache with cut and torn pieces of collage in *Harlem* (P–I) by Walter Dean Myers. Simms Taback uses mixed media—watercolor, gouache, pencil, ink, and photography—and collage on craft paper in *Joseph Had a Little Overcoat* (N–P–I). Susan Roth illustrates *Hard Hat Area* (P) with collage overlaid on a photomontage of the skyline of New York City, and Kyrsten Brooker combines oil paints and collage in Patricia McKissack and Onawumi Jean Moss's *Precious and the Boo Hag* (P). Raul Colón's illustrations, a combination of watercolor washes, etching, colored pencils, and litho pencils, are easily recognized in his many picturebooks, for example Pat Mora's tall tale *Doña Flor* (P–I) and Jonah Winter's *Roberto Clemente: Pride of the Pittsburgh Pirates* (I). Bryan Collier's brilliant combinations of paint and paper or fabric collage are discussed in his profile and the close look at *Rosa*.

Computers are making an impact in illustration for picturebooks. Although computer-generated art was initially considered inferior, enormous technological advances have changed that perception. Now, with proper training one can draw with a penlike stylus and approximate any medium, which then appears on a monitor; the images can be corrected, adjusted, and enhanced. After an initial period where artists seemed infatuated with the new technology and treated it as an end in itself rather than subordinating it to their aesthetic

Davey hopped on his scooter. His dog, Polaris, chased after him.

"Okay, you know the rules," Davey reminded Polaris. "Don't bark at the moons and be careful what you sniff—you might overload your circuits."

Polaris couldn't fetch, and sometimes his batteries leaked all over the floor, but he did have a remarkable nose. Once he even smelled some old socks Davey left behind on Earth.

Polaris beeped and clicked, and together they raced across Mars.

The clay engraving technique used by Chris Gall in **There's Nothing to Do on Mars** *is similar to Brian Pinkney's scratchboard, though Gall's lines are thicker and more definite.*

purposes, they are now using it in more sophisticated ways (Salisbury, 2007). Such artists as Janet Stevens and Mo Willems make use of the computer to great effect. In Mo Willems's Caldecott Honor–winning **Knuffle Bunny: A Cautionary Tale** (N–P) and **Knuffle Bunny Too: A Case of Mistaken Identity** (N–P), Willems digitally incorporates his brightly colored cartoon characters into sepia-toned photographs. Janet Stevens used the computer to enhance her original art in Anne Miranda's **To Market, to Market** (P), and the resulting illustrations are full of energy.

Figure 3.4 presents examples of the variety of media and techniques found in picturebooks. This is followed by Teaching Idea 3.2, which suggests ways to explore various media with children.

FIGURE 3.4

Media and Techniques Used in Picturebooks

In the following list, we begin with the name of the illustrator and include the author's name following the title if the author is someone other than the illustrator. We mention only one or two books for each illustrator, but their other books might include similar art. Also review the chapter text for other ideas. Some publishers now state the media, technique, and typography used in their books. Check the copyright page of each book for this information. Following each list, there are some suggestions for activities you can do with children to explore these media further. Please note that some of the entries are preceded by an asterisk, which indicates that that book is either international or from a parallel culture.

Acrylic

* Austin, Michael, **Martina the Beautiful Cockroach: A Cuban Folktale** by Carmen Agra Deedy (2007) (P–I)

Beeke, Tiphanie, **I'm Going to Grandma's** by Mary Ann Hoberman (2007) (N–P)

Egielski, Richard, **The End** by David LaRochelle (2007) (P)

* Gomez, Elena, **Mama's Saris** by Pooja Makhijani (2007) (P–I)

* Gonzalez, Maya Christina, **Nana's Big Surprise: Nana, Qué Sorpresa!** by Amada Irma Pérez (2007) (P)

Hall, August, **When I Met the Wolf Girls** by Deborah Noyes (2007) (P)

Keller, Laurie, **Do Unto Otters: A Book about Manners** (2007) (P)

Klise, M. Sarah, **Imagine Harry** by Kate Klise (2007) (N–P)

Pratt, Pierre, **Roar of a Snore** by Marsha Diane Arnold (2007) (N–P)

Shannon, David, **David Goes to School** (1999) (N–P)

———, **No, David!** (1998) (N–P)

Shannon, George, **Rabbit's Gift** by Laura Dronzek (2007) (N–P)

Stringer, Lauren, **The Princess and Her Panther** by Wendy Orr (2010) (N–P)

Cut Paper and Collage

Baker, Jeannie, **Home** (2004) (P–I)

Barner, Bob, **Penguins, Penguins, Everywhere!** (2007) (N–P)

* Bryan, Ashley, **Beautiful Blackbird** (2003) (N–P)

Carle, Eric, **The Very Hungry Caterpillar** (1981) (N–P), painted tissue paper

Frasier, Debra, **On the Day You Were Born** (1995) (N–P–I)

* Isadora, Rachel, **Yo, Jo!** (2007) (N–P)

Jenkins, Steve, **Biggest, Strongest, Fastest** (1995) (P–I), commercially handmade paper

Keats, Ezra Jack, **The Snowy Day** (1962) (N–P)

Laroche, Giles, **What Do Wheels Do All Day?** by April Jones Prince (2006) (N), bas relief cut-paper collage

McCarthy, Mary, **A Closer Look** (2007) (N–P)

Walsh, Ellen Stoll, **Mouse Shapes** (2007) (N–P)

Young, Ed, **Seven Blind Mice** (1992) (N–P)

(Continued)

Computer-Generated or Computer-Augmented Art

Auch, Mary Jane and Herm Auch, **Beauty and the Beaks: A Turkey's Cautionary Tale** (2007) (P)

Nash, Scott, **Rainy Day** by Patricia Lakin (2007) (N–P)

Savage, Stephen, **Where's Walrus?** (2011) (N–P)

Willems, Mo, **Knuffle Bunny Too: A Case of Mistaken Identity** (2007) (N–P)

Gouache

* Christie, R. Gregory, **Jazz Baby** by Lisa Wheeler (2007) (N–P)

Falconer, Ian, **Olivia Helps with Christmas** (2007) (N–P)

* Paschkis, Julie, **Glass Slipper, Gold Sandal: A Worldwide Cinderella** by Paul Fleischman (2007) (P)

Yaccarino, Dan, **All the Way to America: The Story of a Big Italian Family and a Little Shovel** (2011) (N–P)

———, **Who Will Sing a Lullaby?** by Dee Lillegard (2007) (N–P)

Yee, Wong Herbert, **Abracadabra!: Magic with Mouse and Mole** (2007) (P–I)

Graphite and Pencil

Browne, Anthony, **My Brother** (2007) (N–P)

Dale, Penny, **Jamie and Angus Together** by Anne Fine (2007) (P)

Ramá, Sue, **Fix It, Sam** by Lori Ries (2007) (N–P)

Van Allsburg, Chris, **Jumanji** (1981) (P–I)

———, **Zathura** (2002) (P–I)

Yee, Wong Herbert, **Who Likes Rain?** (2007) (N), colored pencil

Mixed Media

* Blackall, Sophie, **Red Butterfly: How a Princess Smuggled the Secret of Silk out of China** by Deborah Noyes (2007) (P), Chinese ink and watercolor

Breen, Steve, **Stick** (2007) (N–P)

Briggs, Raymond, **The Puddleman** (2006) (N–P), colored pencil and gouache

Church, Caroline Jayne, **Digby Takes Charge** (2007) (N–P), acrylic and collage

Debon, Nicolas, **The Red Sash** by Jean E. Pendziwol (2005) (P–I), gouache and mixed media

Denton, Kady MacDonald, **A Second Is a Hiccup: A Child's Book of Time** by Hazel Hutchins (2007) (P), watercolor and spot art

* Diakité, Baba Wagué, **Mee-Ann and the Magic Serpent** (2007) (P), paintings on glazed tile

Duke, Kate, **The Tale of Pip and Squeak** (2007) (N–P), watercolor and gouache

Dunbar, Polly, **Penguin** (2007) (N–P), outlined drawings in mixed media

Fleming, Denise, **The Cow Who Clucked** (2006) (N), colored cotton fiber, hand-cut stencils, and squeeze bottles

Gorbachev, Valeri, **Red Red Red** (2007) (P), pen-and-ink and watercolor

Gore, Leonid, **Danny's First Snow** (2007) (P), acrylic and pastel

Grey, Mini, **The Adventures of the Dish and the Spoon** (2006) (P)

Hillenbrand, Will, **What a Treasure!** by Jane Hillenbrand (2006) (N)

* Isadora, Rachel, **The Princess and the Pea** (2007) (N–P), oils on patterned paper

Jackson, Shelley, **The Chicken-Chasing Queen of Lamar County** by Janice N. Harrington (2007) (N), paintings plus blend of printed paper, fabric, photos, and other items

James, Ann, **Ready, Set, Skip!** by Jane O'Connor (2007) (N), pencil and watercolor

* Johnson, Steve and Lou Fancher, **Amazing Peace: A Christmas Poem** by Maya Angelou (2008) (P–I), oil, acrylic, and fabric on canvas

* Juan, Ana, **The Jewel Box Ballerinas** by Monique de Varennes (2007) (P–I), acrylic and crayon

Kellogg, Steven, **Clorinda Takes Flight** by Robert Kinerk (2007) (P–I)

* Meade, Holly, **Sky Sweeper** by Phyllis Gershator (2005) (P–I), collage and paint with delicate lines

McFarland, Richard, **Grandfather's Wrinkles** by Kathryn England (2007) (P–I), pencil, watercolor, and pastel

Milgrim, David, **Time to Get Up, Time to Go** (2006) (N), digital pastels

Myers, Christopher, **Blues Journey** by Walter Dean Myers (2003) (P–I)

* ———, **Harlem** by Walter Dean Myers (1997) (P–I)

* Nelson, Kadir, **Henry's Freedom Box** by Ellen Levine (2007) (P–I), pencil, watercolor, and oil paint

Niland, Deborah, **Annie's Chair** (2006) (N–P), gouache and digital art

Perkins, Lynne Rae, **Pictures from Our Vacation** (2007) (P–I), pen-and-ink and watercolor

Reiser, Lynn, **Hardworking Puppies** (2006) (N–P), Sharpie markers, White-Out, watercolor, scissors, tape, and a copy machine

Seeger, Laura Vaccaro, **Dog and Bear: Two Friends, Three Stories** (2007) (N–P), ink pen, and paint

Small, David, **Once Upon a Banana** by Jennifer Armstrong (2006) (P), line and watercolor

Sneed, Brad, **The Boy Who Was Raised by Librarians** by Carla Morris (2007) (P), watercolor and gouache

* Taback, Simms, **Joseph Had a Little Overcoat** (1999) (P), watercolor, gouache, pencil, ink, and collage

* Talbott, Hudson, **Show Way** by Jacqueline Woodson (2005) (I), chalk, watercolor, and muslin

Varon, Sara, **Chicken and Cat** (2006) (N), digital and ink art

* Young, Ed, **My Mei Mei** (2006) (P), gouache, pastel, and collage

Oil Paintings

* Caravela, Elena, **A Night of Tamales & Roses** by Joanna H. Kraus (2007) (P)

de Monfried, Dorothée, **I'd Really Like to Eat a Child** by Sylviane Donnio (2007) (P–I)

Goossens, Philippe, **Sam Tells Stories** by Thierry Robberecht (2007) (N–P)

Hallensleben, Georg, **Fox** by Kate Banks (2007) (N)

* Ransome, James E., **The Old Dog** by Charlotte Zolotow (1995) (P–I)

Zelinsky, Paul, **Rapunzel** (1997) (P–I)

Outline Drawing and Comic Strip

deGroat, Diane, **Last One in Is a Rotten Egg!** (2007) (N–P)

McLeod, Bob, **SuperHero ABC** (2006) (N), comic-book illustration

Phillips, Louise, **I Heard a Little Baa** by Elizabeth MacLeod (2007) (N, board book)

Thomas, Jan, **What Will Fat Cat Sit On?** (2007) (N–P)

Pastels, Crayon, and Charcoal

Owens, Mary Beth, **Panda Whispers** (2007) (N–P)

Phelan, Matt, **Very Hairy Bear** by Alice Schertle (2007) (N–P)

Pigni, Guido, **The Story of Giraffe** by Ronald Hermsen (2007) (P)

Pinel, Hervé, **I'm Bored!** by Christine Schneider (2004) (N–P)

Rayyan, Omar, **To Catch a Burglar** by Mary Casanova (2007) (P–I)

Shapiro, Michelle, **A Piece of Chalk** by Jennifer Ericsson (2007) (N–P)

Williams, Sam, **Tummy Girl** by Roseanne Thong (2007) (N–P)

Yee, Wong Herbert, **Who Likes Rain?** (2007) (N–P)

Pen-and-Ink

Gravett, Emily, **Meerkat Mail** (2007) (N–P)

* Kwon, Yoon-duck, **My Cat Copies Me** (2007) (N–P), brush calligraphy

Rogers, Gregory, **Midsummer Knight** (2007) (P–I)

van Haeringen, Annemarie, **Little Donkey and the Birthday Present** by Rindert Kromhout (2007) (N–P)

(Continued)

Photographs or Photomontage

Crews, Nina, **Below** (2005) (N), photomontage

Fisher, Valorie, **Moxy Maxwell Does Not Love Stuart Little** by Peggy Gifford (2007) (P–I)

✳ Global Fund for Children, **Global Babies** (2007) (N–P) , board book

✳ Jiménez, Moisés and Jiménez, Armondo, **ABeCedarios: Mexican Folk Art ABCs in English and Spanish** by Cynthia Weill and K. B. Basseches (2007) (N–P), photographs of wood sculpture

Rotner, Shelley, **Senses at the Seashore** (2006) (N)

Stanton, Brian, **Dog** by Matthew Van Fleet (2007) (N), board book

Scratchboard and Engraving

Pinkney, Brian, **Duke Ellington: The Piano Prince and His Orchestra** by Andrea Davis Pinkney (1998) (P–I)

✳ ———, **The Faithful Friend** by Robert D. San Souci (1995) (P–I)

———, **Peggony-Po: A Whale of a Tale** by Andrea Davis Pinkney (2006) (P)

Watercolor

Brooks, Karen Stormer, **Piggy Wiglet and the Great Adventure** by David L. Harrison (2007) (N–P)

✳ Daly, Niki, **Happy Birthday, Jamela!** (2006) (P)

Davenier, Christine, **Has Anyone Seen My Emily Greene?** by Norma Fox Mazer (2007) (N–P)

✳ Dodson, Bert, **Kami and the Yaks** by Andrea Stenn Stryer (2007) (P–I)

✳ Domi, **Napi Goes to the Mountain** by Antonio Ramirez (2006) (P)

✳ Glick, Sharon, **Perros! Perros! Dogs! Dogs!: A Story in English and Spanish** by Ginger Foglesong Guy (2007) (N–P)

Henkes, Kevin, **A Good Day** (2007) (N–P)

Jeffers, Oliver, **Lost and Found** (2006) (N–P)

Jorisch, Stéphanie, **Granddad's Fishing Buddy** by Mary Quigley (2007) (P)

Kennedy, Anne, **Callie Cat, Ice Skater** by Eileen Spinelli (2007) (N–P)

King, Stephen Michael, **Piglet and Papa** by Margaret Wild (2007) (N–P)

✳ Lewis, E. B., **Night Boat to Freedom** by Margot Theis Raven (2006) (P)

———, **Pitching in for Eubie** by Jerdine Nolen (2007) (P)

Mammano, Julie, **Rhinos Who Rescue** (2007) (N–P)

Parker, Robert Andrew, **Across the Blue Pacific: A World War II Story** by Louise Borden (2006) (P–I)

Pinkney, Jerry, **The Lion and the Mouse** (2009) (N–P)

Polacco, Patricia, **The Butterfly** (2000) (I)

✳ Reiser, Lynn, **My Way/A mi manera: A Margaret and Margarita Story** (2007) (P–I)

Roberts, David, **The Dumpster Diver** by Janet S. Wong (2007) (P)

Tallec, Olivier, **This Is a Poem that Heals Fish** by Jean-Pierre Siméon (2007) (N–P)

Tafuri, Nancy, **The Busy Little Squirrel** (2007) (N–P)

Tjong Khing, Thé, **Where Is the Cake?** (2007) (N–P)

Tusa, Tricia, **Fred Stays with Me!** by Nancy Coffelt (2007) (P)

✳ Ungar, Richard, **Even Higher** (2007) (P)

Wiesner, David, **Flotsam** (2006) (P–I)

Woodcuts and Other Printing Techniques

Azarian, Mary, **Snowflake Bentley** by Jacqueline Briggs Martin (1998) (P–I)

Meyer, Jim, **If You Want to See a Caribou** by Phyllis Root (2004) (P)

✳ Louis, Catherine, with calligraphy and chop marks by Wang Fei, **Legend of the Chinese Dragon** by Marie Sellier (2007) (P–I)

Matthews, Tina, **Out of the Egg** (2007) (N–P)

TEACHING IDEA 3.2

Experiencing Media and Technique

COMMON CORE STATE STANDARDS

This Teaching Idea is foundational to Common Core English Language Arts, Reading: Literature standard 7 grades K through 4. The suggestions in this Teaching Idea may need to be adapted to suit your particular grade level and the needs of your students.

- Diluted acrylic can be painted onto transparencies, and several monoprints can be made from these in the copier. Children can then experiment by painting on the copies.

- Use tissue paper, construction paper, magazines, newspaper, wallpaper, and gift wrap to make book illustrations, collages, mosaics, and paper sculptures.

- Use a computer program to create art. Illustrate a picturebook or a poetry book with it.

- Using black or white crayons, have children make an under-drawing or outline, and then paint over it in gouache or tempera to fill in the spaces not waxed with crayon.

- Provide children with pencils of varying softness and hardness and experiment with different stroke techniques to show how artists develop tone and shading.

- After exploring a variety of media with children and looking at a variety of mixed media picturebooks, ask students how many different combinations they can come up with and then try some of these to illustrate a story. Have the students bring various materials from the recycling bin at home and see how these might be included in an illustration.

- Consult with an art teacher before exposing children to oil paint. Oils can damage clothing and may even be dangerous for some children if they are allergic to the chemicals involved.

- Write characters' dialogue in speech balloons. Illustrate the action. Examine different framing techniques and how they affect the flow of the narrative.

- Use crayons, pastels, water crayons, charcoal, and markers on a variety of textured papers. Include crayon scratch drawings and any other combination of media.

- Examine different ways artists use pen and ink for outlining and shading, and have children see if they can reproduce some of these techniques in their own illustrations.

- Give children disposable cameras and have them take photographs to illustrate stories or informational pieces about their own life and neighborhood.

- Provide children with cardboard strips of varying widths and have them experiment with the different strokes they can achieve. Dipping Q-tips in watercolor and stamping them on paper can be a fun way to experiment with pointillism. Show students how to graduate washes in different colors mixed with water and how various colors are mixed.

- Use linoleum blocks, wood blocks, potato halves, Styrofoam, cardboard, sandpaper, and yarn. Create shapes to dip into paints and stamp onto paper. Make relief prints, etchings, cardboard cuts, and potato prints.

Styles of Art

In **Art & Max** (P–I), David Wiesner explores the effects of style and technique when Arthur the painter attempts to help Max, an irrepressible amateur, learn to paint. Although an artist's style is what makes his or her work recognizable as unique to that artist, sometimes artists like Arthur break out of their norm to surprising results. *Style* refers to a configuration of artistic elements (line, shape, color, texture, and artistic medium) that together constitute a specific and identifiable manner of expression (Cianciolo, 1997). Although artists display individual styles, they are also situated in a wider context of various established traditions of art that influence their idiosyncratic styles.

Some artists consciously imitate traditional styles of individual artists or schools of art. D. B. Johnson's **Henry** books (**Henry Hikes to Fitchburg**, **Henry**

Would be a good way to get children to explore different methods.

Builds a Cabin, *Henry Climbs a Mountain*, and *Henry Works*) as well as his *Four Legs Bad, Two Legs Good!* (P–I) give a nod to the Cubist style of Georges Braque and Pablo Picasso, and Neil Waldman's *The Starry Night* (I) expertly renders scenes from New York City in Vincent Van Gogh's instantly recognizable style. Rachel Isadora's *ABC Pop!* (N) draws heavily on the 1960s pop art style of Roy Lichtenstein. Leo and Diane Dillon's illustrations for the biblical text *To Everything There Is a Season* (I–A) evoke the universality of the words by imitating fifteen different styles of traditional art, ranging from ancient Egyptian, Greek, and Roman art to medieval European woodcuts to fourteenth-century Pueblo art. Even more ambitiously, Jon Scieszka and Lane Smith's *Seen Art?* (I–A) follows a young boy named Art through the Museum of Modern Art in New York as he passes sixty-four famous paintings and sculptures. Anthony Browne parodies the styles of twenty-four different painters in *Willy's Pictures* (I–A), amusingly inserting images of gorillas and other primates instead of people. Laurent de Brunhoff's *Babar's Museum of Art* (P–I–A) parodies many styles as well, with elephants substituted for people. Elisa Gutierrez's *Picturescape* (P–I–A), a finely crafted wordless picturebook, is a fantasy about a boy who takes a trip to an art museum and magically enters paintings by twelve famous Canadian painters. To learn more about this book, go to CengageBrain .com to access the Education CourseMate website, where you will find a link to the book that contains information about the twelve painters and their work. Indeed, there is a growing number of picturebooks that either parody or imitate the style of particular artists, specific paintings, or specific cultural time periods in which an artistic style was prevalent. These types of picturebooks can be used to teach children some rudiments of the history of art (Sipe, 2001).

Nevertheless, each artist strives for his or her own unique style. In addition to reflecting the individuality and artistic strength of the artist, style is influenced by the content and mood of the text as well as by the intended audience (Cianciolo, 1976). In very general terms, a *painterly* style refers to works of art in which individual brushstrokes are immediately visible, as in the bold use of oil paints by James Ransome in his illustrations for Deborah Hopkinson's *Under the Quilt of Night* (I) and Lesa Cline-Ransome's *Young Pele: Soccer's First Star* (I). This contrasts with styles that are smoother or more "finished" in appearance, where the individual brushstrokes are blended together so that they are not noticeable except on very close inspection. Teaching Idea 3.3 suggests one exercise that might help your students grasp the concept of artistic style.

Some artists' styles remain constant across many books, so that their work is immediately recognizable. The styles of Tomie dePaola and Jerry Pinkney, for example, are remarkably uniform across their many picturebooks, as is the style of Lauren Stringer. Other artists may vary their styles to suit the subject matter or setting of the story. In the illustrations for *Saint Valentine* (I), Robert Sabuda chose small squares of colored paper to give the effect of mosaic, a common artistic technique in ancient Rome, the setting for the book. For the medieval setting of *Arthur and the Sword* (P–I), Sabuda imitated the effect of medieval stained glass by painting on clear acetate, and then photographing the translucent illustrations with strong light shining behind them. In *King Tutankhamen's Gift* (I), he painted on papyrus in the formalized style of ancient Egypt. Diane Stanley is another artist who sometimes employs a particular style to complement stories she illustrates, as in *Joan of Arc* (medieval European miniatures, I); *Shaka, King of the Zulus* (South African beadwork, I); and *Fortune* (ancient Persian miniatures, I).

Artistic styles available in books for children are thus many and varied, ranging across six general styles that are frequently found in picturebooks for children and adolescents, which we now turn to.

• • REPRESENTATIONAL ART • •

Representational art consists of literal, realistic depictions of characters, objects, and events. Paul Zelinsky creates exquisite, realistic oil paintings in the style of the French and Italian Renaissance painters to illustrate the Grimm's fairy tale *Rapunzel* (P–I). Beautifully rendered settings and emotionally evocative portraits of the leading characters add drama and dimension to the old tale. Ted Lewin is an illustrator whose watercolors are often so realistic they resemble color photographs, as in *One Green Apple* (I), Eve Bunting's moving story of a young immigrant Muslim girl who makes her first steps in becoming friends with her US classmates during a field trip. Lewin also captures the excitement of a county fair at night in his brilliantly realistic watercolors for *Fair!* (P–I). Jan Peng Wang's beautiful realistic paintings provide detail and elaborate character in Paul Yee's moving story, *A Song for Ba* (I). Ntozake Shange's poetic remembrance of some of the African American men who changed the world, *Ellington Was Not a Street* (P–I), is brought to life by Kadir Nelson's realistic oil paintings. Nelson's work in this book received a Coretta Scott King Award. In *Windows with Birds* (P), Karen Ritz's beautiful realistic watercolor illustrations capture the

This morning there are birds.

Karen Ritz's carefully rendered realistic style captures the sleeping boy, alert cat, and distant birds in **Windows with Birds**.

The surrealistic and whimsical qualities of David Wiesner's exquisite detailed watercolors for **Flotsam** *are shown to their best effect in this colorful illustration.*

difficulty and delight of adjusting to a new home—from a cat's point of view.

• • SURREALISTIC ART • •

Surrealistic art contains "startling images and incongruities" that often suggest an "attitude or mockery about conventionalities" (Cianciolo, 1976, p. 40).

Surreal pictures are often composed of the kinds of images experienced in dreams or nightmares or in a state of hallucination. Chris Van Allsburg's surrealistic paintings in **Jumanji** (I) extend the clever challenge of the text and are full of garishly funny details. Anthony Browne's surrealist paintings in his many books, such as **Changes** (P) and **Voices in the Park**

TEACHING IDEA 3.3

Teaching Style to Children

Compare & Contrast lit works (handwritten margin note)

COMMON CORE STATE STANDARDS This Teaching Idea is foundational to Common Core English Language Arts, Reading: Literature standard 7 grades K through 4. The suggestions in this Teaching Idea may need to be adapted to suit your particular grade level and the needs of your students.

It may seem as if style is a slippery concept to teach; however, students quickly learn to recognize the individual styles of artists, especially those artists who employ a consistent style in most of their books. After encountering a few books illustrated by Tomie dePaola, for example, students can spot a new dePaola book from across the room! They may not be able to articulate what makes his books so easily recognizable, but we can help students put into words what they have already noticed unconsciously. Here are a few suggestions for teaching the idea of style.

- First, start with two illustrators who have fairly consistent yet very different styles, such as Tomie dePaola and Jerry Pinkney. Then talk with the students about what makes work by these two illustrators so different. Discussion might result in these observations:

  - dePaola uses an outline style, often in dark brown (sepia), in either watercolor or diluted acrylic paint. His people are full of rounded shapes, and the facial features are often suggested by dots for eyes and minimal lines for nose and mouth. His colors are almost always tints—a pleasing pastel palette. Colored shapes are always surrounded by outlines. He commonly includes features such as fluffy white clouds and religious symbols as well as hearts and doves in his illustrations.

  - Pinkney draws in pencil first (this is called the underdrawing), and then paints over the pencil drawing with vibrant watercolors. The pencil, however, still remains visible. His shapes and figures are not done in outline style. His renderings of people are much more realistic

than dePaola's: they look like carefully done portraits, and every face and body is different, like real people's faces and bodies. Indeed, he carefully poses models who wear the clothing he intends to depict in his preliminary drawings. His colors tend to be bright and saturated, and because the shapes are not outlined, colors often "bleed" and blend into one another. He rarely includes "signature" features, in contrast to dePaola.

- Second, after you have compared and contrasted several illustrators whose styles are quite different, try something a little more difficult: have the students examine the illustrations of two artists who are similar, but distinct, for example Jerry Pinkney and Ted Lewin.

Pinkney and Lewin both use watercolors, however Pinkney's underdrawing of pencil always shows through, whereas Lewin's work, without any underdrawing, appears less spontaneous. As well, Pinkney has a "loose" watercolor style, using a fair amount of water, and his backgrounds are usually suggested by dappled shade and light that suggests impressionist painting. In contrast, Lewin's watercolor style is "tighter," with more discernible clear outlines and more controlled use of the brush. The effect is that Lewin's illustrations look more detailed and finished. Both illustrators are master watercolorists, but a close look at their work reveals very different styles. When you have finished closely examining Pinkney and Lewin's work, take a look at E. B. Lewis's watercolors, which seem to lie somewhere between Pinkney's loose style and Lewin's tight style.

(P–I), enhance the ideas he conveys in the texts. In David Wiesner's wordless books, such as **Tuesday** (P–I), and **Flotsam** (P–I), both Caldecott Medal winners, strange phenomena occur, and totally surreal events unfold in the skies or under water. Lane Smith's surrealist illustrations for several of Jon Scieszka's books, including **The Stinky Cheese**

Man and Other Fairly Stupid Tales (P–I–A) match the bizarre, subversive stories.

• • • **IMPRESSIONISTIC ART** • • •

Impressionist artists emphasize light and color; they create a fleeting impression of reality. They may break an image into many small bits of color to mimic the way the eye perceives and merges color to create images. The result is often reminiscent of dappled sunlight. Jerry Pinkney's watercolor illustrations often convey this beautiful dappled effect, for example in the lush jungle backgrounds of Julius Lester's **Sam and the Tigers** (P–I). Ed Young's **Lon Po Po: A Red Riding Hood Story from China** (N–P–I) and Emily Arnold McCully's **Mirette on the High Wire** (P) both won Caldecott Medals for their beautiful, impressionistic paintings. Jerome Lagarrigue's impressionistic paintings in Janice Harrington's **Going North** (P–I) beautifully depict the experiences of a young African American girl and her family in the 1960s as they drive from Alabama to Nebraska, seeking a better life "up north."

• • FOLK ART AND NAÏVE ART • •

Folk art is a broad designation for the style of artistic expression of a particular cultural group. Folk art may simplify, exaggerate, or distort reality, but it does so in a way that is characteristic of the traditional art of a culture, often through the use of traditional motifs, symbols, and techniques.

There are as many folk art styles as there are folk cultures. Many artists illustrate folktales told in the style of a particular culture using the characteristics, motifs, and symbols found in the art of that culture, as Gerald McDermott does in many picturebooks, including **Zomo the Rabbit** (West African, P), **Raven** (Pacific northwest Native American, P), **Coyote** (American southwest Native American, P), and **The Stonecutter** (Japanese, P). Anita Riggio and You Yang's illustrations for Pegi Dietz Shea's **The Whispering Cloth** (P–I) are *pa'ndaus*, Hmong tapestries that contain traditional symbols and images. Holly Berry relies on traditional Romanian folk art designs to illustrate Sabina Rascol's retelling of the classic Romanian tale **The Impudent Rooster** (P–I). John Parra's folk art acrylic illustrations for Pat Mora's **Gracias/Thanks** (P), translated into the Spanish by Adriana Dominguez, are a perfect match in mood to the text and setting.

Naïve art is often difficult to distinguish from folk art; indeed a particular style of art may be described interchangeably as folk or naïve art. Martin Jarrie's illustrations for **ABC USA** (I–A) are a good example of the blurring of folk art and naïve art. Naïve art may look technically unsophisticated, but it is usually marked by an artist's clear, intense emotions and visions. The conventions of folk and naïve art include adherence to frontal posture or profile and a disregard for traditional representation of anatomy and perspective. Backgrounds, including trees, plants, and flowers, are rendered simply, and there is often a lack of three-dimensional perspective. Naïve art presents the essence of experiences and objects in a deceptively simplified fashion, using clearly recognizable forms for people and places. Jude Daly's illustrations for Kelly Cunnane's **Chirchir Is Singing** are excellent examples of naïve/folk art.

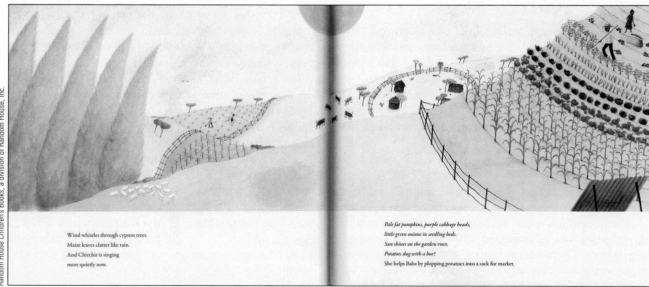

Wind whistles through cypress trees.
Maize leaves clatter like rain.
And Chirchir is singing
more quietly now.

Pale fat pumpkins, purple cabbage heads,
little green onions in seedling beds.
Sun shines on the garden rows.
Potatoes dug with a hoe!
She helps Baba by plopping potatoes into a sack for market.

Jude Daly's naïve style is a perfect accompaniment to Kelly Cunnane's story, **Chirchir Is Singing**, *providing visual details that enhance the simple text.*

TEACHING IDEA 3.4

Study the Art of Your Favorite Illustrator

 COMMON CORE STATE STANDARDS

This Teaching Idea does not directly relate to Common Core English Language Arts, Reading: Literature standards but does suggest activities that will help students better understand picturebook art. This can increase both comprehension and appreciation. The suggestions in this Teaching Idea may need to be adapted to suit your particular grade level and the needs of your students.

Many artists develop a characteristic way of presenting ideas visually; some vary their style according to the text. Read aloud some books by the illustrators discussed in this chapter or in Pat Cummings's *Talking with Artists*, volumes 1 and 2, and ask listening students to respond to the art. Later, see if they can recognize the artist's style when you cover up the names and titles. Play "Name that Illustrator": Hold up an illustration and ask "Who is the illustrator?"

If you collect several books by one illustrator, you can ask students to compare them. Is the art similar across books? Does the art represent a distinct approach? Ask students to describe each illustrator's work and to use examples of the work to illustrate their points.

Gunnella's oil paintings for Bruce McMillan's *How the Ladies Stopped the Wind* (P) use rounded and simplified shapes with little shading to portray the humans and animals in this folk story. Ashley Bryan, in *Let It Shine* (P–I), an exuberant illustrated version of three spirituals (P–I), uses flat, unshaded frontal or profile depictions of people, a flattened perspective, and vivid colors.

• • OUTLINE STYLE • •

Outline style art emphasizes line and often reduces features to simplified shapes. A special type of outline style, cartoon art, often uses exaggeration in two dimensions to create caricature (Cianciolo, 1976). The artist may employ such cartoon techniques as slapstick and may use ludicrous distortions of characteristics to depict absurdities and incongruities of situations so as to evoke laughter or at least a smile. Both adults and children are regularly exposed to outline style art through comic strips, political cartoons, and, of course, animated films and videos. Because of its exaggerated expressive qualities, outline style art communicates directly and can often be understood without words or very sparse text. The cartoon outline art of comic books is perfectly adapted to the picturebook format in George O'Connor's *Kapow!* (P–I), the story of a boy and his friends who pretend to be superheroes. Tedd Arnold's outline art in comic strip panels is a perfect

Humor →

match for the hilarious story line of Steve Metzger's *Detective Blue* (P), a superb takeoff on nursery rhymes and folk stories.

There used to be a tendency to disparage outline style art, perhaps because of its connection to cartoons, comic books, comic strips, and animated films. Outline style art has become more sophisticated, however, and is increasingly popular with artists and readers. Many of our greatest children's illustrators were clearly inspired by cartoon art, and they continue to work in that style. Outline style, though, is an umbrella term for any art in which shapes are clearly delineated by lines. Such brilliant author/illustrators as Maurice Sendak, creator of *Where the Wild Things Are* (N–P), William Steig, creator of *Sylvester and the Magic Pebble* (P–I), Tomi Ungerer, creator of *The Moon Man* (P–I), and James Marshall, creator of a comic version of *Goldilocks and the Three Bears* (P), all use their various outline styles to create award-winning books. Rosemary Wells, author of *Max's Bunny Business* (N–P) and the many other Max books, uses her cartoon humor to tell of the escapades of the mischievous boy bunny, Max. In *My Rhinocerous* (P), Jon Agee's outline art fits perfectly with this humorous story of a boy whose unusual pet seemingly can't do anything fun.

Olivier Dunrea's cartoon ink and watercolor art in *Peedie* and *Boo-Boo* (P) is beautifully drawn and full of energy and the humor of surprise. In his

*Chris Gall's bold outline style uses surrealism with exciting results in his illustrations for **Dear Fish**.*

David books, David Shannon uses full-color outline style to create a portrait of a perfectly believable but impossible little boy. The simple and energetic outline style of Mo Willems's Pigeon books (***Don't Let the Pigeon Drive the Bus!***, ***The Pigeon Finds a Hot Dog!***, ***Don't Let the Pigeon Stay Up Late***, and ***The Pigeon Wants a Puppy***), as well as ***Knuffle Bunny*** and ***Knuffle Bunny, Too*** (P) is a perfect accompaniment for his minimalist texts. Emily Arnold McCully is a master of outline style, as shown in ***Cat Jumped In!*** (N–P) by Tess Weaver, where the loose watercolor style is "anchored" and given shape by the thin black ink outlines. Another master, David Small, won the Caldecott Medal for his illustrations for Judith St. George's ***So You Want to Be President?*** (I–A). Small's many books with his wife, Sarah Stewart, such as ***The Friend*** (P), have helped bring outline style into a new, sophisticated realm. Similarly, Ian Falconer's ***Olivia*** books (N–P) display a very delicate outline style that manages to convey an enormous range of actions, feelings, and thoughts. All of these outline styles, each quite different from one another, show how varied this style can be in picturebook art.

• • COMBINING STYLES • •

Some artists purposefully combine styles to produce intriguing illustrations. For example, Pamela Patrick's pastel illustrations for Richard Ammon's ***An Amish Year*** (I) are an interesting juxtaposition of realistic and impressionistic styles. Human figures, especially faces, are rendered in almost photographic realism, whereas landscape foregrounds and backgrounds are drawn in an impressionistic style that includes many strokes of different colors that combine to suggest a sun-drenched field or meadow. In Chris Gall's ***Dear Fish*** (P–I) outline style combines with surrealism to match the story. While at the beach for the day, a boy writes a letter beginning "Dear Fish," inviting the fish to come for a visit on dry land. The resulting magical chaos—including a school of fish invading a school classroom—is perfectly matched by the combination of styles.

All these many styles of art—representational, surrealistic, impressionistic, folk and naïve, and outline style—are found in picturebooks. Teaching Idea 3.4 offers ideas for studying the style of a favorite illustrator, and Figure 3.5 suggests professional resources for studying illustrators and illustrations in picturebooks.

FIGURE 3.5

teaching ideas for various books.

Illustrations and Illustrators: A Suggested Bookshelf for Teachers

The following books may be useful to you as you learn more about illustrations for picturebooks and the artists who produce them, as well as the uses of picturebooks in the classroom. The list is arranged in order from the latest-published books to the ones published earliest.

No author noted. (2012). *The Best Children's Books of the Year: 2012 Edition. Books Published in 2011.* Distributed by Teachers College Press, New York.

This very carefully considered list, which has been produced for some years, is now available through Teachers College Press and will reach a well-deserved wider audience. It contains annotated lists of books (divided by age and topic) chosen by a committee of Bank Street instructors and covers books from preschool through young adult.

Charles, Z., and L. Robinson, (2008). *Over Rainbows and Down Rabbit Holes: The Art of Children's Books.* Amherst, MA: Eric Carle Museum of PictureBook Art

Featuring thirteen illustrators from classics such as Arthur Rackham and Edmund Dulac to contemporary masters such as Chris Van Allsburg and David Wiesner, this gorgeous book will acquaint readers with the best illustrations for children over a broad span of time.

Evans, Dilys. (2008). *Show & Tell: Exploring the Fine Art of Children's Book Illustration.* San Francisco: Chronicle

In this beautifully crafted book, Evans takes twelve eminent picturebook illustrators/authors and writes insightful comments about both their art and their lives.

Marcus, L. S. (2008). *Pass It Down: Five Picture-Book Families Make Their Mark.* New York: Walker & Company

Marcus traces the work of members of five influential families in the world of picturebooks: Crews/Jonas, Hurd, Myers, Pinkney, and Rockwell.

Thompson, Terry. (2008). *Adventures in Graphica: Using Comics and Graphic Novels to Teach Comprehension, 2–6.* Portland, ME: Stenhouse

This very practical book will be interesting to educators who want to know how to use "graphica" (Thompson's own term) in teaching children critical thinking skills and visual literacy.

Carter, J. B., Ed. (2007). *Building Literacy Connections with Graphic Novels: Page by Page, Panel by Panel.* Urbana, IL: National Council of Teachers of English

A companion piece to the Thompson book listed previously, this book's contributors focus on teaching English using graphic novels to middle-school and high-school students.

Marcus, L. S., J. B. Curley, and C. Ward, (2007). *Children Should Be Seen: The Image of the Child in American Picture Book Art.* Amherst, MA: Eric Carle Museum of Picture Book Art

This volume is a treasure trove of eighty-four contemporary American artists and focuses on the changing images of children and childhood present in their picturebooks.

No author noted. (2007). *Knock, Knock!* New York: Dial

A companion to *Why Did the Chicken Cross the Road?* (following), this picturebook contains fourteen more illustrators' works. Only one artist—Chris Raschka—appears in both books, so together the books present work by twenty-seven different illustrators.

No author noted. (2007). *Artist to Artist: 23 Major Illustrators Talk to Children about Their Art.* Amherst, MA: Eric Carle Museum of Picture Book Art

Each of the 23 artists writes in a way that is accessible to children while also captivating adults with interesting details about their motivations to become illustrators and their artistic styles.

Salisbury, Martin. (2007). *Play Pen: New Children's Book Illustration.* London: Laurence King

If you're interested in international children's picturebooks, this is a book you will consult again and again. Salisbury includes insightful biographies and discussions of the work of thirty-six international illustrators.

Blake, Quentin (2006). *Magic Pencil: Children's Book Illustration Today.* London: The British Council and the British Library

This lavishly illustrated book, with a foreword by Quentin Blake and an informative essay on the history of British children's illustration by Joanna Carey, contains information about thirteen British illustrators for children and includes reproductions of many of their works.

No author noted. (2006). *Why Did the Chicken Cross the Road?* New York: Dial

This age-old question is answered by fourteen illustrators, giving us a large sample of the range of contemporary illustration.

No author noted. (2005). *The Art of Reading: Forty Illustrators Celebrate Reading Is Fundamental's 40th Anniversary.* New York: Dutton

This is another feast for the eyes: forty illustrators from around the world write about their lives as artists and include original art inspired by their favorite books as children. Sales of the book benefit the organization Reading Is Fundamental (RIF), which has put millions of books in children's hands.

Aldana, Patricia, Ed. (2004). *Under the Spell of the Moon: Art for Children from the World's Great Illustrators.* Toronto, Ontario: Groundwood

This is an international collection of thirty-two illustrators whose work represents the best in children's illustration. Each illustrator is showcased by reproductions of double-page spreads from their books. This is an artistic feast, sponsored by the International Board on Books for Young People (IBBY).

Frohardt, Darcie Clark (1999). *Teaching Art with Books Kids Love.* Golden, CO: Fulcrum Resources

This useful book encourages teachers to connect famous fine artists with picturebooks that imitate or parody their styles and to help children make art that is related to these styles.

From Cover to Cover: Artistic and Design Elements Specific to Picture Storybooks

Now, we continue our discussion of artistic features by concentrating on elements that are particular to narrative picturebooks, or picture storybooks. To help you conceptualize these features more clearly, we will frequently refer to three very different picturebooks, **Henry's Freedom Box** (P–I), **Trainstop** (P–I–A), and **Don't Let the Pigeon Drive the Bus!** (N–P), as well as several other examples of excellent picturebook art and design. **Henry's Freedom Box** (hereafter referred to as **Henry**) retells the true story of one slave's ingenious and courageous escape to freedom by mailing himself in a box to a free state. **Trainstop** is an imaginative wordless fantasy about a girl's adventure on a city train as she gets magically transported to the countryside where she helps rescue an inhabitant of a village of tiny people. **Don't Let the Pigeon Drive the Bus!** (hereafter referred to as **Pigeon**) is a hilarious recounting of a pigeon's unsuccessful attempts to convince the reader to let it drive a bus, bringing to mind the various strategies preschoolers will use to achieve a goal: nagging, reasoning, bribing, whining, and throwing tantrums.

• • BREVITY • •

Most picturebooks differ dramatically from novels by being relatively brief. The standard length is thirty-two pages, such as in **Trainstop** or **Pigeon**. Some authors and illustrators need a little more to tell their story completely: **Henry** is forty pages long. Some need a little less (see the Close Look at **Monkey and Me** [N–P]). What you will notice is that the number of pages is almost always a multiple of eight. This is because of the printing process; generally, eight pages are printed on each side of very large sheets of paper. When these pages are folded and cut, the sixteen pages (counting both sides) are called a *signature*, and generally two signatures are bound together for a picturebook. Leaving aside several pages for the title page, dedication page, and publishing information, you can see that there are a limited number of pages left. Pages are rarely numbered in picturebooks, so that two facing pages are referred to as *openings* or *double-page spreads*. The left-hand side of the opening is called the *verso*, and the right-hand side is called the *recto* (think "recto" = "right"). The "first opening" is the double-page spread where the text of the story begins. Writing (and illustrating) a picturebook is similar to writing a sonnet; every word must count, and every illustration must be used to its fullest advantage because there is a limited amount of space.

• • ELEMENTS "SURROUNDING" • • THE STORY

Every part of the picturebook, literally from cover to cover, is used to convey meaning and contributes to our perception of it as one complete artistic whole. The *dust jacket* surrounds the front and back covers, folded inside the covers at the front and back to keep it in place. The front inner *flap* of the dust jacket often gives a general description of the story as an enticement to the reader, and the back inner flap often gives information about the author and illustrator. The front and back covers themselves (called the *case*) are either thick cardboard or cloth-covered board. The covers may be identical to the dust jacket, or they may have a different illustration. In *Trainstop*, the dust jacket and the front and back covers are subtly different. The dust jacket of this book depicts a train with the city in the background, and the title of the book on a horizontal stripe of the train, along with a girl looking out of one of the train windows. The front and back board covers show the train with a strip of green grass beside the tracks and the same girl with a surprised look on her face; as well, the title word is missing from the train. Thus, the differences between the dust jacket and the case prefigure the girl's adventure.

Some front and back covers contain only the title of the book, stamped or printed on the case, as in *Woolvs in the Sitee* (I–A). In addition, some books, like *Trainstop*, have a dust jacket or case that contains one continuous illustration. In other books, the front cover and front dust jacket contain one illustration whereas the back cover and back dust jacket depict another illustration. In *Henry*, the front cover shows Henry, an African American boy, sitting outdoors, silhouetted against a blue sky and tiny birds, whereas the back cover resembles part of a wooden box. In this way, Kadir Nelson, the illustrator, conveys Henry's longing for freedom on the front cover, whereas the back cover shows us the method he uses to escape from slavery.

Contemporary dust jackets and covers are often enriched by sophisticated printing techniques. For example, *Trainstop*'s jacket and board covers feature the use of thin coatings of mylar, a clear plastic, to highlight the windows of the train; this, of course, makes the windows look more realistic because they reflect light like glass. In addition, the title word is not only covered in mylar, but also is embossed, raising the letters slightly for a three-dimensional effect. The letters of the title and names of the author and illustrator are also covered in mylar in *Henry*, drawing our attention to them and causing them to appear closer to us than the matte surface of the underlying illustration of Henry.

When we open a picturebook, the first things we see are the front *endpages* (sometimes called endpapers). The part of the endpage that adheres to the inside of the cover is called the *pastedown*, and the part that is like a normal page is called the *fly-leaf*. Every hardcover book has endpages because they are used to attach the covers to the rest of the pages in the book. In picturebooks, however, special attention is often paid to the endpages because they are like the closed curtains on the stage of a theater before a performance begins. Picturebook endpages may be plain or illustrated, but even if there is a plain color, there is a reason for this choice; the color may correspond to the palette used in the book, or it may give a hint about the mood of the story. Both *Trainstop* and *Henry* have plain-colored endpages, but the colors have a definite relationship with the stories. In *Henry*, the endpages are a warm shade of metallic bronze, which harmonizes well with the palette used throughout the book and also suggests the hope and overcoming of adversity in the story. *Trainstop* has green endpages that are the same color as both the bright grass of the countryside and the little girl's slacks. For the ochre-colored endpages in the Caldecott-winning *The Hello, Goodbye Window* (P–I), illustrator Chris Raschka spent hours matching hand-painted color swatches to printer's samples to find the perfect color to harmonize with his palette for the images in the book. In some books, such as Mary Lyn Ray's *Mud* (N–P), illustrated by Lauren Stringer, the plain endpages change color, in this case beginning with the brown of mud and ending with the green of spring.

Other endpages are illustrated. Moreover, some front endpages are identical to the back endpages, and other back endpages are different from the front. For example, in **Pigeon**, the front endpages present us with a pigeon, eyes closed, and a "thought bubble" containing multiple images of the pigeon driving a bus. The back endpages are similar, except that the pigeon seems to be thinking about driving a large red tractor-trailer truck. Thus, the endpages in this book give us a hint about the pigeon's aspirations at the beginning and the end of the story. Another good example of differently illustrated front and back endpages is found in Matthew Baek's **Be Gentle with the Dog, Dear!** (N–P), the story of a toddler who learns that her expressions of affection are sometimes a bit too physically hurtful for the family dog. The front endpages show Elisa, the toddler, chasing Tag; the erratic dotted line suggests the chaotic route the chase has taken. The other family pet, a kitten, lies curled up observing the chase. At the end of the story, Elisa turns her attention to the kitten, and the back endpages show her energetically chasing the kitten while Tag looks on. Here again, the front and back endpages frame the story by suggesting the beginning and the ending. Therefore, when you read picture storybooks to students, it's a good idea to take a look at both the front and back endpages before you start reading the story and see if they are different in any way. All of these options are the result of careful choices by the author, illustrator, editor, and designer, and we can speculate about these choices with students.

Upon turning the flyleaf, we come to either the *half-title page* or the *title page*. The half-title page has only the title of the book—a famous example of a half-title page is found in **Where the Wild Things Are**, with its stark title against white space. The next page (the full-title page) usually contains the title, the names of the author and illustrator, the name of the publisher, the city in which the publisher has its office, and the date the book was published. Some picturebooks (like **Henry** and **Trainstop**) dispense with the half-title page and go straight to the full title page. In some books, the story actually begins with the title page. In **Pigeon**, this page contains not only the title but a speech bubble from the bus driver, asking readers to "watch things for me" to make sure that the pigeon doesn't drive his bus.

The next page of the typical picturebook contains the *front matter*—all the fine print about the copyright, ISBN number, Library of Congress cataloging data—the print almost nobody ever reads.

There is often a *dedication page* as well. Sometimes, the fine print occurs at the very end of the book; then it's called the *publishing information*. Some of the fine print is worth reading because there is often a note informing the reader about what art medium or media were used to produce the illustrations. The publishing information on the last page of **Henry** notes that "The artwork was created with pencil, watercolor, and oil"; a similar note in the front matter of **Trainstop** tells us that "The illustrations are watercolor, gouache, and ink."

In many books, all of these elements occur before we actually get to the beginning of the story! It's tempting to skip over them, or at most to talk briefly just about the cover illustration and title and predict what the story might be about. But this would be a mistake. William Moebius (1986) perceptively comments that skipping all these surrounding elements and going straight to the story would be like arriving at the opera after the overture is finished. Just as the opera overture contains musical motifs and themes that will occur throughout the opera, thus giving us an idea of what to expect, so the surrounding elements of the picturebook contain much information for prediction and speculation about the characters, plot, setting, mood, and theme of the story.

Elisha Cooper utilizes every part of the picturebook in **Beaver Is Lost** (N–P), a wordless storybook. The story is introduced by the dust jacket which, when opened, shows an empty landscape on the verso leading to a large city on the recto, with a river running from left to right and beaver, sitting upright, holding a twig that points to the right, as his nose does, inviting us to turn the page. Once turned, the jacket flap, depicting three beavers looking left and one heading right, into the river, perfectly matches the lines of the endpages, creating a seamless entrance into the beaver's adventure. (The case and the back endpages depict the river at night.) The first opening comes next, before a title page, dedication page, or publishing information, and depicts beaver riding a log, head poised above a small stick pointing right, on the recto, with the family across the gutter on the verso, looking after him, followed by the second opening, a close-up of beaver floating past machinery and a truck loaded with wood. The third opening features a close-up of beaver, stick in hand, having arrived in the city on the verso, with a white page with the words "Beaver is lost" in black letters on the recto. The fourth opening functions as a title page, with the title, the author's name, the publisher, and the dedication embedded in a double-page spread of the busy city.

[handwritten margin note: Get out of this habit!]

Elisha Cooper depicts beaver's travel homeward with panels, as well as changing light and background details in **Beaver Is Lost**.

The next nine openings depict beaver's adventures in the city in an interestingly varied series of boxes until, on the thirteenth opening, a full bleed double-page spread depicts beaver finding and entering the river that will take him home, where he arrives on the sixteenth opening to the word *Home* centered on the whitespace in the verso, and the family, looking left at him as he approaches in a full-bleed painting on the recto. He has come full circle, always swimming to the right, yet appearing home from the left. The final opening contains the publishing information and dedication on a full-bleed double-page spread. Cooper has created a virtually wordless picture storybook that uses many artistic and design elements particular to picture storybooks in an innovative fashion.

At this point, you may be feeling as if you are learning a new language—all these special terms may be a bit overwhelming. Remember that you might introduce these elements to students over the course of examining many books, perhaps over an entire school year. Also remember that we must never underestimate the ability of even young children to learn this terminology and use it themselves. For example, if you casually say, "Here are the end-pages" when you show them to students, they will pick up this language and use it when they discuss other books. Educators who make a point of talking about all these surrounding elements with students before actually beginning the story are surprised by how much information and food for thought are generated that help the students understand and

interpret the story better. In other words, discussion about the surrounding elements is not a frill or a waste of time: this discussion sets the stage for children's literary and aesthetic understanding and is often a better preparation for the story than "purpose-setting" questions. Trust the picturebook itself to be its own best introduction, and trust the children to use their speculations, predictions, and questions to assist them as they interpret the story. All of the specialized terms we use in this chapter are defined in Figure 3.6.

● ●   THE RELATIONSHIP OF   ● ●
WORDS AND PICTURES

At the beginning of this chapter, we mentioned that the pictures and words in a picturebook are both necessary to tell the story. Another way of thinking about this is that a picturebook actually has three stories—the story told by the sequence of pictures; the story told by the words; and the *complete* story told by both the words and the pictures (Nodelman & Reimer, 2003). Reading a picturebook is as much a matter of "reading" the illustrations as it is reading the words. Words tell us things that the pictures omit, and vice versa. Pictures may extend the meaning of the words. For example, in **Henry**, when the protagonist marries and has children, the text mentions that "Henry knew they were very lucky. They lived together even though they had different masters." The illustration that accompanies this text shows the interior of a house, with a cozy fire in the fireplace, a colorful quilt on the wall,

Use the terminology in everyday language & conversation

FIGURE 3.6

Picturebook Terminology

Bleed When the illustration extends to the very edge of the page, with no white space or border, it is said to "bleed." When the illustration extends to all four edges of the page, this is called a "full bleed." An illustration can bleed to one, two, three, or all four edges.

Borders Illustrators often design a border for their illustrations. Sometimes the border is used to tell more of the story or to tell a parallel story.

Case The front and back fixed covers of a book, usually thick cardboard or cloth-covered board. The covers may be laminated for protection and a glossy appearance. The covers are frequently embossed or stamped with a design or words.

Composition The way in which an artist achieves unity in art through balance, repetition, variety, emphasis, and spatial order.

Continuous narration Joseph Schwarcz's term for the use of several separate illustrations on the same page (a montage), which indicate motion, action, or the sequence of time.

Cross-hatching Fine parallel lines, usually in black, which are crossed with another set of parallel lines to produce the effect of shading.

Cut-out An illustration which has no frame, but simply appears against the background.

Dedication page A page that contains a note by the author and sometimes illustrator, honoring some person or persons.

Double-page spread Picturebooks are planned as a series of facing pages called double-page spreads or openings. An illustrator may choose to spread the illustration over both pages of an opening. This is called a double-page spread illustration.

Dust jacket The thick paper wrapper around the outside of a picturebook, folded inside at the front and back to keep it in place.

Edition The *trade edition* of a book contains the fullest expression of the art of the picturebook, containing a dust jacket, case, endpages, and so on. The *library edition*, which has a stronger binding, frequently omits the dust jacket, reproducing the same illustration on the front case. The *paperback edition* omits the dust jacket and frequently omits the endpages and/or illustrations on the back cover of the book.

Endpages or endpapers The inside of the front and back board cover, consisting of two parts: a pastedown (affixed to the inside back or front cover) and the flyleaf (the part of the endpage that is not pasted down).

Flap The part of the dust jacket that is folded inside the front and back covers (the case) of a book. Often, the front flap has a summary of the story, and the back flap has short biographies of the author and/or illustrator.

Flyleaf The part of the endpage that is not pasted down, opposite the pastedown.

Fold and gathers Before a picturebook is bound, all the printed pages are gathered and folded so that reviewers can see what the finished book will look like. Often abbreviated as "F and Gs."

Frame In a picturebook, the illustrations are sometimes surrounded by an illustrated border, by white space, or by lines, giving the impression of a framed picture. Sometimes, part of the illustration may "break the frame," seemingly breaking out of and overlapping the straight edge of the illustration.

Front matter Page containing the fine print indicating publishing information, copyright, ISBN number, and Library of Congress cataloguing data. Sometimes, there is a note about what artistic medium was used in the illustrations. This information is occasionally located at the back of the book, in which case it is usually simply termed *publishing information*.

Gutter When the book is opened, the middle of the spread where the pages are bound.

Half-title page A page containing only the title of the book.

Hue A pure color, such as red, blue, green, purple, and so on, without any addition of white or black.

Illustrated books Books in which visual images add interest to a text but are clearly subordinated to the words.

Illustrational sequence In a picturebook, the illustrations do not stand alone, but in

(Continued)

an ordered sequence that conveys meaning, chronological order, and narrative.

Intensity The relative use of shade and tint in pure hues.

Line A mark on paper or a place where different colors meet.

Medium The material used to produce an illustration. Plural is *media*.

Montage The inclusion of several separate illustrations on the same page.

Opening The "first opening" is the two facing pages where the story or text begins, usually, but not always, occurring after the title page.

Page break/Page turns Picturebooks are a series of openings, or double-page spreads. In storybooks, gaps between one opening and another are carefully planned; they are called page breaks. Readers/viewers often make inferences about what occurred during the page breaks.

Pastedown The part of the endpage that adheres to the cover, opposite the flyleaf.

Peritext Gerard Genette's term for anything in a book other than the printed text or illustrations. This includes the dust jacket, front and back covers, endpages, title page, and so on. In a picturebook, the peritext conveys meaning.

Point of view An illustration is planned from a certain point of view, so that viewers feel themselves to be in a certain position in relation to the scene in the illustration. We can seem to look down on a scene, or to be placed below a scene, or on a level with it.

Publishing information Front matter that appears at the back of a book.

Recto The right-hand side of a page opening, or double spread.

Saturated Colors that are intense rather than subdued.

Shade A pure color to which black has been added, to darken it.

Shape An area or form with a definite outline.

Signature A single large sheet of paper is printed with eight book pages on one side and eight on the other side. When this sheet is folded and cut, it is called a signature. The standard-size picturebook contains two signatures, or thirty-two pages.

Spine The bound edge of the book, which is frequently reinforced with an extra strip of cloth or cardboard.

Synergy Reference to the fact that the illustrations and the verbal text of a picturebook combine to produce an effect that is greater than the sum of either part.

Technique The method artists use to create art with the chosen medium.

Text box The text of a picturebook may be printed below or above the illustrations, in a plain white space. It may also be printed directly on the illustration. Additionally, it may be printed in a box placed on top of part of the illustration. This is known as a text box.

Texture In an illustration, the appearance of having a smooth or rough surface.

Tint A pure color to which white (or water in the case of watercolors or acrylics) has been added to lighten it.

Title page A page containing the title, the names of the author and illustrator, the name of the publisher, the city, and the date the book was published.

Trim size The overall size and proportion of a book.

Typography The typeface or font used for the text, the title, and other printed portions of the book. This coordinates in some way with the meaning of the text and the overall look of the book.

Value The proportion of darkness or lightness in a color. Lighter colors are higher in value and darker colors are lower in value.

Verso The left-hand side of page opening or double spread.

Vignette A small illustration used to break up sections of text or otherwise decorate a page.

Wash Watercolor or ink that has been much diluted with water, producing a pale effect. Oil paints may be diluted with a great deal of turpentine.

and Henry playing the banjo while his three children cuddle on their mother's lap. The illustration does much to extend our understanding of their domestic tranquility: it shows *how* they are "lucky."

According to Nodelman (1988), words "limit" the illustrations by telling us what to pay attention to and how to interpret them. In **Pigeon**, the pigeon is shown with one wing placed over its chest. The accompanying words are "True story." Thus, we're led to interpret the pigeon's physical gesture as a "cross my heart and hope to die" expression of honesty.

The art in some books not only reflects and extends the text but also presents visual information that creates a story within a story. Marla Frazee does this brilliantly in **Roller Coaster** (P–I), in which she tells multiple side stories through her illustrations. In the text, the book tells the story of a roller coaster ride, focusing on one young girl who has never ridden a roller coaster before: her initial trepidation, joyful ride with her big brother, and desire to do it over again. The illustrations tell several stories, all of them humorous. For example, behind the girl and her brother in line are three big men, bulging with muscles and, in one case, fat. The biggest one, in a muscle shirt with

a tattoo on his arm, doesn't even make it onto the ride; he abandons his friends to sit and watch. The other two nonchalantly get on, arms casually draped on the sides of the car, sunglasses in place—until the first downhill, when they grab the seat in front of them (and one of them loses his cap). They hang on for dear life, close their eyes (and lose their sunglasses), and grimace until they get off, clutching their stomachs. In this case, the illustrations tell much, much more than the single story told by the text.

In some cases, the illustrations in picturebooks provide a much richer, broader context than the words can possibly convey. For example, in **Henry**, the last double-page spread ends the story with Henry emerging from his box, having finally arrived in Philadelphia, a city where he would be a free man. One detail of the illustration rewards close inspection: the ceramic pitcher, resting on a wooden stand, at the extreme left. On the pitcher there is an image of a slave kneeling on one knee, his hands bound in chains, with the words "Am I not a man and a brother?" The image was the emblem of the Society for Effecting the Abolition of the Slave Trade, which was formed in 1787, well over fifty years before

*Kadir Nelson's background for the culminating illustration in Ellen Levine's **Henry's Freedom Box** contains a pitcher whose message turns out to have a fascinating history of its own.*

Henry's courageous escape from slavery in 1849. Kadir Nelson's illustration thus hints at the long history of abolitionist sentiment through this seemingly insignificant detail, as well as placing Henry's story in a fascinating historical context. The words of the story could not possibly convey this amount of detail; however, the illustration invites us to research the meaning behind this image on the pitcher, leading to much greater understanding.

The words in a picturebook can also have visual qualities that underline or extend their literal meaning. In *Pigeon*, the illustration of the pigeon's tantrum is accentuated by the large, bold letters of the words "LET ME DRIVE THE BUS!!!" in all capital letters. The "look" of the font chosen for the book is important to examine because it, too, is the result of a conscious choice by the designer. In *Henry*, for example, the title is rendered in a font that looks as if it were designed in the nineteenth century, the same time period in which the story is set.

The relationships of words and pictures can also be ironic, subversive, or even completely contradictory. Marla Frazee's hilarious text and illustrations for *A Couple of Boys Have the Best Week Ever* (P–I), a Caldecott Honor book, often stand in this type of relationship. For example, when James visits his friend Eamon "with just a couple of his belongings," the illustration depicts James standing in front of an enormous pile of boxes, baskets, and duffel bags stuffed to overflowing. The boys go to day camp together, and when they get back home at the end of the day, the text comments that "the campers would decide to practice quiet meditation downstairs," while the accompanying illustration shows them boisterously and competitively playing a video game. See Teaching Idea 3.5 for more examples of this type of ironic or contradictory text–picture relationship.

The positioning of words and pictures on the openings of a picturebook is also part of the word–picture relationship. Some text is printed in an outlined *text box*, which is simply placed on top of an unimportant part of the illustration. Other text is printed in a column beside the illustration, or under it or over it in a blank space. In other cases, the words are printed directly over the illustration, again taking care not to obscure a crucial part of the illustration. Often, artists will leave a light-colored or white area in the illustration itself so that the words can be printed easily. In this case, the words are printed in black or a dark-colored ink. In other cases, where the background of the illustration is very dark, the words will be printed in white. Examine *Henry*, and you will see that every one of these techniques is used. This adds variation and interest to the story.

Teaching Idea 3.5 presents one example of how to help students understand the relationship between words and pictures in one particular book.

• • SIZE AND SHAPE OF • • THE BOOK AND THE ILLUSTRATIONS

The *trim size* (the final dimensions of the pages of the book) varies according to the subject matter of the book and its purposes. Beatrix Potter is famous for remarking that she made her books rather small so that they could be easily held by little hands. Beyond this, designers work with authors and illustrators to determine whether a book will be in "portrait" or "landscape" form. If a story will contain many broad vistas, landscape form is appropriate. If, on the other hand, the story will contain many close-ups of human beings, portrait form is sensible. In *Trainstop*, the horizontal quality of the train, the rectangular windows that are longer than they are wide, and the countryside vista all make a landscape format appropriate. For Suzy Lee's *Wave* (N–P), a wordless book about a little girl's day at the shore, the pronounced horizontal line of the beach and the ocean are conveyed by the trim size—when the book is opened, the length is far more than three times the width, giving the illustrator plenty of space to depict the large expanse of sand, ocean, and sky. By contrast, *Henry*, with its many dramatic close-up illustrations of characters, uses a portrait orientation to the best advantage.

Illustrations can stretch across both pages of an opening, thus giving the artist a large space in which to work. An even larger space is provided if the illustrations "bleed" to the edges of the page. The illustrator can also decide to have one or many illustrations on an opening. In *Pigeon*, all of these choices contribute to the interest of the design of the book. At one point (the tenth opening), illustrator Mo Willems has chosen to divide the opening into eight boxes, delineated by slightly different background colors, for multiple illustrations of the pigeon's barrage of persuasive techniques. In *Henry*, except for four openings where a text panel reduces the size of the illustration slightly, Kadir Nelson uses double-page-spread full bleeds, which convey the intensity of emotion and the dramatic quality of the story most effectively. In *Wave*, mentioned previously, every one of the illustrations takes up the entire double-page spread with full bleed, effectively conveying the infinity of the horizon line.

When illustrations have borders, either constituted by thin lines, white space, or thicker strips of

Pictures and Words in Picturebooks

 This Teaching Idea addresses Common Core English Language Arts, Reading: Literature standard 7 grades K through 4. The suggestions in this Teaching Idea may need to be adapted to suit your particular grade level and the needs of your students.

To really understand and interpret a picturebook, children must "read" the illustrations as well as the words and integrate the knowledge they gain from both pictures and words. We can't assume that all children (or adults) will do this naturally, so we can explicitly teach it. The following examples of word–picture relationships are from Kevin Hawkes's *The Wicked Big Toddlah* (P–I), a hilarious modern-day tall tale about a baby from Maine (thus the "toddlah," imitating the Maine accent) who is as tall as a big tree. Consider a few of the illustrations in this book in terms of what the pictures and the words tell us.

> **Text**: The narrator says that when she and her brothers visited the new baby in the hospital, he "grabbed hold of my finger."

The technique you might employ is to read the text without showing the picture and ask students to talk about whether they have ever seen a baby grasp someone's finger. Then show the illustration and ask how their interpretation has changed.

> **Illustration**: Shows a group of people at the hospital, including the mother, father, and "Uncle Bert," and an array of balloons with messages: "Ayuh, It's a Buoy" and "It's anuthah Mainah." The top third of the illustration shows an enormous fist and forearm stretching almost the whole way across the double-page spread. The little girl (the narrator) is being hoisted into the air, and the baby's huge fist envelops her entire hand and part of her arm. Of course, the illustrations also tell us that the baby is from Maine, something the text never mentions.

What the text describes is a normal circumstance with a normal-size baby: babies often grab people's fingers. The illustration, however, gives this common action an entirely new meaning!

A Second Example from the Same Book

> **Text**: The narrator says that Toddie (the huge baby) likes taking baths and playing with boats.

> **Illustration**: Shows Toddie, waist deep in the ocean, hoisting a lobster boat and two lobster fishermen out of the water with one hand and a rowboat in the other. Toddie's relatives are approaching him with a rubber dinghy with the label "S. S. Bathtime," and one of the figures in the dinghy is holding a mop with a bucket full of soapy water.

If you read the text, students will have associations with playing with toy boats in their bathtubs, either remembering themselves doing this or seeing another baby engaged in the same activity. When they see the illustration, the meaning naturally changes: the "boats" are full-size, real boats in the illustration, corresponding to Toddie's huge size, and "taking baths" has a new meaning, too—Toddie is going to be scrubbed with a mop. From the looks of it, bathtime is going to take a long, long while!

A Third Example

In this case, you might consider showing the illustration first, asking the students to describe the details they see, and then read the text.

> **Illustration**: Shows Toddie in a huge hammock, sleeping outdoors. A rope is attached to the hammock, and Mother (inside the house, in her bed) is pulling the hammock to and fro. "Uncle Bert" is sitting near Toddie's head, playing bagpipes, and the rest of the relatives (six of them) are sitting on Toddie's enormous stomach, with their mouths wide open.

> **Text**: The narrator says that everyone sings to make Toddie go to sleep and that his uncle "plays a soft lullaby."

The "soft lullaby" that would soothe a normal baby would not even be heard by Toddie—he needs blaring bagpipes instead! Talking with students in this way makes them aware of the ironies of the illustrations versus the text. They can understand that a great deal of the humor of the book depends on the interesting relationship of words and pictures

(Continued)

in **The Wicked Big Toddlah**. If you single out a few pages every so often when you read aloud to students and talk with them about what the illustrations tell them versus what the words tell them, this will alert them to the possible ironies, subversions, and potential humor of other books' text–picture relationships. This book, of course, represents only one of the many relationships that text and pictures can have. Words and illustrations can extend each other or amplify each other. The words never tell us *exactly* what the picture shows, nor vice versa. Other good books to try this with are **Rosie's Walk** (N–P) by Pat Hutchens; **Officer Buckle and Gloria** (P–I) by Peggy Rathman, and **A Couple of Boys Have the Best Week Ever** (P–I) by Marla Frazee.

color that look like picture frames, the effect is to render the illustration a bit less intense because we feel less as if we are "in" the illustration than if it bled to the edge of each side of the page. Notice that in **Trainstop** there are only two full bleeds, which both indicate large expanses of space: first, when the girl is running behind ten tiny people to begin her rescue of a person caught in a tree, and second, at the end of the story when, after the tiny people bring her a small tree as a gift, the scene broadens to include a panorama of the city, with several other trees, suggesting that the little people have made other visits to the city from their magical country. Most of the images in **Trainstop** are framed by thick black lines and the white space surrounding the images. "Breaking" the frame occurs on the fifth opening, in which a tiny person signals the train to stop with a large banner. In this illustration, part of the banner extends beyond the black line border, and the top of the train and its horn also break the frame. Breaking the frame often accentuates action or drama, and in this case, the train's size and speed, as well as the rapidly waving banner, are indicated by this technique. Breaking the frame can also signal a change of some kind. The illustrations in **Where the Wild Things Are** begin breaking the frame just at the point where the story changes from a realistic narration of Max's naughtiness to the magical fantasy of a forest growing in his room. Thus, the change from realistic fiction to fantasy is suggested by the frame break.

Illustrations that have no straight lines for borders but appear to "float" against a white background are called *cut-outs*. In **Henry**, there is an excellent example of cut-outs on the seventeenth

Mo Willems's deftly simple series of vignettes in **Don't Let the Pigeon Drive the Bus!** *suggests a progression of Pigeon's unsuccessful persuasive techniques.*

In **Trainstop,** *Barbara Lehman makes excellent use of the technique of continuous narration as she tells the story of a girl who rescues some tiny people in a magical land.*

opening, where a series of four borderless illustrations show Henry's box (with a view of him inside) being moved to and fro by two men, who want to use it to sit upon. The lack of a border for these cutouts adds to the impression of topsy-turvy freedom of movement.

An artist may choose to include several illustrations on one page that show action or what Schwarcz (1982) calls "continuous narration"; in other words, the sequence of small illustrations is intended to convey motion or to be interpreted as a rapid sequence of actions. The sequence of eight illustrations on the tenth opening of **Pigeon,** mentioned previously, is an example of continuous narration.

Similarly, **Trainstop** has several instances of continuous narration. For example, on the verso of the tenth opening, there is a sequence of six illustrations. First, we see a close-up of the girl's hand trying to reach the tiny person who is stuck in the tree, but not getting quite close enough. Second, the girl is puzzling out what to do. Third, a tiny person pulls on the bottom edge of her slacks to get her attention. Fourth, she bends down to listen to him. Fifth, she holds him in the palm of her hand. Sixth, she stretches up to the tree, and the additional height

provided by the tiny person allows her to reach his friend and rescue him.

• • ILLUSTRATION SEQUENCE • •

In contrast to paintings, which stand by themselves, picturebook illustrations have a critical relationship with the illustrations that come before and after them. The sequence of illustrations (with the accompanying words) is what makes the picturebook a special type of art. The variation as the sequence proceeds can take many forms. The perspective can change from close-up to far away. One of the most dramatic moments in **Henry** occurs when Henry worries about whether his wife and children will be sold to another master. At this point in the story, the illustration pans in for an extreme close-up of Henry's face, which takes up almost all of the opening. In this way, the illustrator conveys Henry's deep anxiety.

The viewpoint of the viewer can also change, from seeing the scene from the same level as the characters, or viewing the scene from above or below. A number of Chris Van Allsburg's picturebooks are notable for their changes in perspective from one illustration to the next, adding to the surrealistic quality of many of his stories. (Look, for example, at the dramatic sequence of perspectives in *Jumanji*.) The sequence can also move from a large double-page-spread illustration to a series of small illustrations in the next opening. More importantly, the sequence of openings should be considered to be like watching a slow-motion film, though with the opportunity of turning back and revisiting a page rather than the relentless succession of images in a film. In successful picture storybooks, the sequence of illustrations and words support the plot and characterization.

Taking a look at part of the sequence of *Train-stop,* we see that the title page illustration shows a little girl and her parents about to walk down steps, and on the dedication page, we see them waiting in the station. The following double-page spread contains two illustrations; on the verso, we see the girl sitting contentedly by herself while her parents read the newspaper, and other passengers sleep, read books, work on their laptop computers, or use their cell phones. The recto shows a close-up view of only the little girl, looking out the train window, with a dull gray, beige, and brown city landscape as a background. In the next spread, the verso shows the train going through a tunnel, while the recto contains four rectangular illustrations of the girl, again looking out the window. The upper left rectangle is quite similar to the previous illustration, with the dull city landscape, and the upper right and lower left rectangles depict the train's swift passage through the dark tunnel. The lower right, however, changes perspective; we as viewers are now outside the train, and we see the girl's face looking excitedly through the window. This is followed by the next spread, which again changes perspective as the large rectangular illustration on the verso gives us our first glimpse of a country landscape, with trees, a windmill, houses, and towers. The recto shows a similar landscape, but we see the girl from the back, her hands pressed against the glass of the window. Thus, the sequence leads us seamlessly from the entrance to the train station to the waiting area. Then we are inside the train, first with a wide-angle view of the whole car of passengers next with a close-up of the girl looking out the window. The perspective thus keeps changing, giving us a variety of views while also advancing the plot.

• • PAGE TURNS • •

Another element of picturebooks that receives very careful attention from authors and illustrators is what Barbara Bader (1976, p. 1) refers to as "the drama of the turning of the page." As the previous section on sequence indicates, no opening or double-page spread stands alone; turning from one opening to the next is part of the pleasure of reading/viewing a picturebook. In illustrator Remy Charlip's words, "A thrilling picture book not only makes beautiful single images or sequential images, but also allows us to become aware of a book's unique physical structure by bringing our attention, once again, to that momentous moment: the turning of the page" (quoted in Selznick, 2008, pp. 403–404). Because picturebooks are so brief, what is omitted is just as important as what is included. Talking about what might have happened between one opening and the next therefore gives students the opportunity to make inferences and to speculate. For example, in *Pigeon*, the reader is continuously engaged in answering the pigeon's pleas: on one opening, the pigeon asks if it can drive the bus and on the next opening, it says "Please?" Readers may infer that we have refused Pigeon's request. On another opening, Pigeon says that his cousin drives a bus "almost every day." In the next opening, Pigeon says, "True story." Children in one classroom, when asked what might have happened between these two openings, suggested that they might say, "We don't believe you—you probably don't even have a cousin!" or "You're lying!" Research (Sipe & Brightman, 2009) has shown that, given the opportunity, even young children make inferences about characters' actions, thoughts, and feelings, and create dialogue when asked what might happen during the page turns between two openings. They also notice changes in perspective ("It looks like we've moved away from the pigeon"), speculate about how much time might have elapsed between openings ("The pigeon probably takes a long while to get over his tantrum"), or how the setting might have changed from one opening to the next ("Maybe the pigeon went to another part of the parking lot"). If students are accustomed to discussing books in an open, interactive manner, they will take on the challenge of speculating about page turns, and this speculation will result in greater understanding of the coherence of the story, as well as deepening their interpretive and inferential capacities.

• • THE CHALLENGE • • OF THE GUTTER

Yet another concern of picturebook illustrators, authors, and designers is that when illustrations cross both sides of the double-page spread, attention must be paid to the *gutter*, the middle of the spread where the pages are bound. If it crosses the gutter, a small bit of the illustration is lost in the binding. Thus, in planning the illustration, the artist needs to make sure that nothing important is located in the gutter. For example, an artist would rarely position a human

FIGURE 3.7

Questions to Ask about the Overall Design and Artistry of Picturebooks

Overall Design

- Is the overall design of the book—including the dust jacket, front and back board covers, endpages, title and dedication pages, and the sequence of openings for the story—coherent and integrated?

- Is the trim size—the overall size and proportions of the book—appropriate for the subject or story?

- How is the challenge of the gutter handled in each opening? Are any important parts of the illustration obscured by the gutter?

- How are page turns handled? Is there a surprise or a shift that invites us to infer what happened between the openings? Is there an opportunity to make inferences about what occurs during the page breaks?

- Does the sequence of openings that tell the story through words and pictures seem to flow smoothly?

- How do the individual openings work in sequence?

- If there are several illustrations in one opening, are they related in a way that is easy to follow?

- Is the choice of font—shape and size—appropriate for the story being told? How is the text visually integrated with the illustrations—in text boxes, overprinting, beside, over or under the illustration?

Text–Picture Relationships

- How do the words and pictures integrate to produce a story that is more than either text or pictures could tell alone?

- Are there a variety of ways text and pictures relate to each other? Do pictures and text extend each other or amplify on each other? Do they stand in an intentionally ironic or contradictory relationship with each other? Do the pictures merely repeat what the words say, or do they add something? Do the words merely repeat what the pictures show, or do they add something?

Individual Illustrations

- According to the principles of art and design, are the individual illustrations well constructed?

- Is there balance, proportion, repetition, and variety in the colors and shapes?

- Does the artist's line correspond to the tone/mood/feeling conveyed in the story?

- Do the shapes correspond to the tone/mood/feeling conveyed in the story?

- Is the overall style of the illustration congruent with or complementary to the tone/mood/feeling conveyed in the story?

---

figure or an animal in the gutter. As you look at picturebook illustrations that do cross the gutter, think about how the artist has designed the illustration so that the gutter is not obscuring an important part of the image. Also, words almost never cross the gutter because some of the letters would be hidden. So designers must ensure that the gutter does not interfere with our reading of the text. Notice how the double-page spread on the third opening of **Henry** depicts Henry and his mother standing at the bedside of their master, who is dying. The illustration is perfectly arranged so that the gutter does not interfere with the images of any of the characters: the master

and Henry are on the verso and the mother stands off by herself on the recto. Even the bedposts are not split by the gutter. In fact, the placement of Henry and his mother on opposite sides of the page suggests their approaching separation, as Henry must go to work for the master's son.

Many adults mistakenly think that picturebooks are simple. As you now know, they are not. Figure 3.7 contains questions that you can ask as you are evaluating the overall design and artistry of any picturebook. Following that, Figure 3.8 contains an annotated bibliography of books about picturebook design and children's responses.

FIGURE 3.8

An Annotated List of Books about Picturebooks: Picturebook Design and Children's Responses

This list is arranged chronologically rather than alphabetically to give a sense of the development of book-length treatments of picturebooks over time. This list is for practitioners who want to learn more about picturebook theory and design, and who also want to know more about children's incredibly sophisticated responses to these books.

Nodelman, Perry. (1988). *Words about Pictures: The Narrative Art of Children's Picture Books*. Athens: University of Georgia Press

This book was one of the first book-length treatments of picturebooks from an academic perspective, and is still one of the best. Nodelman lucidly describes the relationship of text and pictures as one that is frequently characterized by ironic tension. An ambitious comprehensive theoretical approach.

Doonan, Jane. (1993). *Looking at Pictures in Picture Books*. Stroud, Glouchestershire: Thimble

Brief but packed with theoretically sound techniques for analyzing picturebooks; contains extensive examples.

Kiefer, Barbara. (1995). *The Potential of Picturebooks*. Englewood Cliffs, NJ: Prentice Hall

Written from the perspective of an educator with an arts education background, this beautifully composed book has a wealth of information about art techniques/media, the history of picturebooks, and the use of picturebooks in classrooms, as well as careful analysis of the picturebook as an aesthetic object.

Lewis, David. (2001). *Reading Contemporary Picturebooks: Picturing Text*. New York: Routledge Falmer

Lewis packs a great deal into this slim volume. It is notable for his exploration of the "ecology" of the picturebook, in which *every* part (including word–picture relationships) relates to *every* other part, much the same way each part of the physical environment has a relationship to *every* other part. Lewis also very usefully discusses Kress and Van Leeuven's *Grammar of Visual Design* and applies it specifically to picturebooks.

Nikolavja, Maria, and Carole Scott. (2001). *How Picturebooks Work*. New York: Garland

Another very ambitious and comprehensive theoretically based approach. Especially noteworthy for its typology of word–picture relationships. Considers a wide range of international picturebooks.

Arizpe, Evelyn, and Morag Styles. (2003). *Children Reading Pictures: Interpreting Visual Texts*. New York: Routledge Falmer

Includes discussions of visual literacy and text–picture relationships but is primarily a careful report of a large, two-year research study with English children, ages four to eleven, in seven primary schools, representing a large range of sociocultural diversity. The focus is on children's responses to picturebooks by Anthony Browne and Satoshi Kitamura.

Martin, Michelle. (2004). *Brown Gold: Milestones of African-American Children's Picture Books, 1845–2002*. New York: Routledge

The first book to focus exclusively on African American picturebooks, this volume takes a historical approach to contextualize the development of the representation of African Americans over 150 years.

Salisbury, Martin. (2004). *Illustrating Children's Books: Creating Pictures for Publication*. London: Quarto

Similar to Shulevitz's 1985 book *Writing with Pictures: How to Write and Illustrate Children's Books*, this beautifully illustrated guide for illustrators is packed with insights and information for a wider audience, including teachers and other practitioners who want to discover more about the current state of children's book illustration, including picturebooks; illustration for older children; and nonfiction illustration.

Matulka, Dense. (2008). *A Picture Book Primer: Understanding and Using Picture Books*. Westport, CN: Libraries Unlimited

The title says it all: if you want an introductory text on understanding picturebook design and terminology, this book will help you get started.

Sipe, Lawrence R. (2008). *Storytime: Young Children's Literary Understanding in the Classroom*. New York: Teachers College Press

The result of twelve years of research with kindergarteners as well as first and second graders and their teachers, this book offers a comprehensively grounded theory of young children's literary understanding of picture storybooks.

Sipe, Lawrence R., and Sylvia Pantaleo. (2008). *Postmodern Picturebooks: Play, Parody, and Self-Referentiality*. New York: Routledge Falmer

This edited volume, the first to focus specifically on postmodern picturebooks, contains sixteen chapters from contributors who represent the fields of English, library science, and education, and who also hail from the United Kingdom, Scandanavia, Canada, the United States, and Australia—thus, it is both multidisciplinary and international in scope.

Pantaleo, Sylvia. (2008). *Exploring Student Response to Contemporary Picturebooks*. Toronto: University of Toronto Press

In this volume, Pantaleo discusses her extensive research over four years with first and fifth graders reading and interpreting postmodern picturebooks, as well as explaining how the children used what they learned in their own writing.

Evans, J. (2009). *Talking Beyond the Page: Reading and Responding to Picturebooks*. New York: Routledge

This edited volume explores how children respond to visual images and other aspects of picturebooks and use them to make sense out of the books; how their responses can be qualitatively improved by encouraged conversations on picturebooks before, during, and after reading; how different types of picturebooks (e.g., wordless, postmodern, and multimodal, etc.) are structured; and how picturebooks can help children cope with complex issues in their lives.

Nikolajeva, M. (2010). *Power, Voice and Subjectivity in Literature for Young Readers*. New York: Routledge

Considering the use of children's and young adult literature as an instrument of power and attempting to reach a balance between empowering and educating the child, this book examines the canonical works from the eighteenth century to the present. Key topics such as genre, gender, cross-vocalization, species, and the power structure in picturebook images are included, whereas contemporary power theories such as cultural studies, feminism, postcolonialism, and queer studies are considered as well.

Colomer, T., Kummerling-Melibauer, B., & Silva-Diaz, C. (2010). *New Directions in Picturebook Research*. New York: Routledge

Including essays contributed by children's literature scholars from twelve different countries, this book shows the new foci of picturebook research, such as the challenges of first-person narratives, ellipsis, frame breaking, and mindscape, through interdisciplinary approaches from literary studies, art history, linguistics, narratology, cognitive psychology, sociology, memory studies, and picture theory. Other topics such as intervisuality, twist endings, autobiographical narration, and metaliterary awareness in picturebooks are also discussed.

On Your Education CourseMate

CONVERSATIONS WITH JAMES RANSOME AND DEBRA FRASIER

In a conversation with Lee Galda, James Ransome talks about his creative process, how he works with someone else's ideas and words to create illustrations to bring those words to life, and to make the story his own. In a visit to Debra Frasier's studio, Lee Galda saw how Frasier develops her own ideas through words and pictures. Go to CengageBrain.com to access the Education CourseMate website and watch these two video conversations.

Questions to consider

1. What are the similarities in the processes of these two illustrators?

2. What are the differences?

3. If you didn't know, do you think you would be able to tell which books were illustrated by separate authors and illustrators and which were not? How or how not?

Narrative Elements in Picture Storybooks

Picture storybooks, as the name implies, tell a story and contain the traditional elements of narrative that we discuss in Chapter 1: setting, characterization, plot, theme, and style of writing. The narratives that picture storybooks tell may be folklore, fantasy, contemporary realistic fiction, or historical fiction. Whatever the type of narrative, we evaluate the quality of the literary elements for a particular genre as revealed through text and illustration. Illustrations in picture storybooks work with the words to provide visual representations, elaborations, or extensions of the setting, characters, and plot that is presented through the text. The illustrations also reflect the theme and the mood of the text.

• • SETTING • •

Setting—the time and place of a story—is often presented succinctly in the text of picturebooks, given that visual details about time and place can be portrayed clearly and economically through the illustrations. In Michael Bania's **Kumak's Fish: A Tall Tale from the Far North** (P), the Arctic setting is clear in both text and pictures. Her light watercolor washes outlined in ink with plenty of white space highlight the icy setting, as do the details of place and the Inupiat people.

• • CHARACTERIZATION • •

Characterization—establishing characters—varies according to genre in picture storybooks. In folklore, characters are usually stereotypes. In well-written realistic or fantasy narratives, the characters are well-developed personalities that often show some evidence of growth and change over the course of the story. Whether animal or human, characters in picture storybooks are most often children or adolescents, depending on the intended audience. They reflect the actions, thoughts, and emotions of children and adolescents in the narration, the dialogue, and the art.

As the text describes a personality trait, the art interprets that trait and presents a portrait of the character. As the story progresses, the art reflects characters' emotions and the growth and change that occurs. Jacqueline Woodson uses words to develop her characters, young Ada Ruth and her grandma, with whom Ada Ruth stays home when Mama goes north to Chicago to earn money during World War II. E. B. Lewis uses watercolor paintings to visually convey Ada Ruth's emotions as well as the time and place. The combination of words and pictures creates the memorable story **Coming on Home Soon** (P), a Caldecott Honor book.

• • PLOT • •

In picture storybooks, plot—the sequence of events—is usually presented in a straightforward chronological order. Plot usually centers on a problem or conflict, generally a problem that children recognize and relate to. As the character works to solve the problem, the plot unfolds into an event or series of events that lead to a solution. The action of the story is apparent in both the text and the illustrations. As we discussed earlier, sometimes the illustrations offer a subplot that the text does not. Peggy Rathman's text in the Caldecott Medal–winning **Officer Buckle and Gloria** (P) tells only part of the story. The story behind the story, and the humor, is carried entirely by her illustrations.

• • THEME • •

Theme, a major overriding idea that ties the whole together, often reflects a child's or adolescent's world.

Picturebooks for younger children are often organized around the theme of growing up—increasing independence and self-reliance, ability, and understanding. Memorable themes are neither blatantly stated, as in an explicit moral to a story, nor so subtle that they elude young readers. The theme evolves naturally from plot and character, and permeates the illustrations. Helen Recorvits's *My Name Is Yoon* (N–P), illustrated by Gabi Swiatkowska, gently traces the ways in which a young Korean girl becomes accustomed to the tasks of American schooling. Both the rebellion and the resiliency of young immigrants are portrayed in this story.

• • STYLE • •

Style of language is essential to quality in a picturebook; because words are limited, they must be carefully chosen. Most picturebooks for young readers contain rich language—well beyond the reading ability of the intended audience—because they are meant to be read aloud. Picturebooks are most often introduced to babies, toddlers, or preschool children by an adult reading *to* the child. The language in most picturebooks for younger children is language that adults can read and that children can understand. Most picturebooks are not meant for beginning reading material. Those that are should still contain language that is interesting, even if simple, and that is a pleasure to read aloud. For older readers, the text can be more complex. In any case, good picture storybooks have interesting words used in interesting ways, with language that builds excitement, creates images, and has an internal rhythm and melody. If it sounds natural when read aloud, it is probably well written. *makes sense- helps keep listeners attention*

Many adults underestimate the ability of young children to understand the language of picturebooks that are read to them; even difficult vocabulary is often understood through a combination of the context of the story and the illustrations. A wonderful example of this understanding is from Beatrix Potter's classic, *The Tale of Peter Rabbit* (N–P). At the point when Peter is being chased by Mr. MacGregor, he gets caught by his coat buttons in a gooseberry net. Sparrows, according to Potter's text, "flew to him in great excitement and implored him to exert himself." Contemporary urban kindergarteners had no difficulty in understanding this sophisticated language: "It means the sparrows are trying to help him to keep trying—they're saying, don't give up, Peter, you can do it!" (Sipe, 2002). Potter was wise in never "writing down" to children and in trusting them to comprehend and infer meaning from her stories.

The choice of words helps create the *mood* of the text—humorous or serious, lighthearted or thoughtful—and the style of art should be congruent. It might, for example, be inappropriate to illustrate books about a serious theme with bright, happy colors. Most of Loren Long's illustrations for Angela Johnson's *I Dream of Trains* (P–I) are somber and serious, in shades of gray and brown. The colors warm up, however, when the narrator, an African American boy, associates the sounds of trains with leaving his life in the rural South for the greater freedom and hope associated with going north. Thus, the varying moods of the story are captured by the changing palette of the illustrations.

Picture books reach a wide audience.

Picture Storybooks from Nursery through Adolescence

Although most picturebooks are for readers from birth through age eight or so, there are picture storybooks for all ages of readers. Here, we describe a variety of picture storybooks that appeal to readers from preschool through high school.

• • SIMPLE STORYBOOKS FOR • • YOUNG CHILDREN

Stories for the very young have a simple plot line, are about familiar childhood experiences, and contain clear illustrations. All are present in James Ransome's *New Red Bike!* (N–P). Tom is understandably thrilled with his new bike and rides it everywhere, and when his friend Sam "borrows" it, Tom could have been angry. Instead, he shares. Young children completely understand these emotions. They also appreciate reminders of parents' unconditional love, as in Emily Jenkins's *Love You when You Whine* (N–P), as a mother cat patiently reassures her child that she loves her even when she doesn't say "please" or when she screams "Lollipop!" over and over while waiting with her mother in line at the bank. Other favorite topics of young children include common everyday activities, as in *Time to Get Dressed!* (N) by Elivia Savadier, in which a little boy wants to dress himself but still needs help. Mo Willems tells the classic tale of the "blankie" or "lovey" lost and found again in *Knuffle Bunny: A Cautionary Tale* (N–P), a Caldecott Medal book. Young listeners identify with the child who misplaces her bunny and then utters her very first words when it is finally found.

As young children turn pages and point to pictures in books, they develop concepts about books and how they work. Simple storybooks introduce them to stories and help them learn about narrative by capturing and holding their interest even if they have short attention spans; these books often are the ones children turn to again and again. Kevin Henkes's Caldecott Medal–winning book, *Kitten's First Full Moon* (N), is a quiet story of one kitten's adventure as she tries to drink the bowl of milk that she mistakenly thinks is waiting for her in the full moon. Expressive pictures and a brief, lyrical text hold the attention of young listeners. The illustrations are black and cream, with thick black lines and soft shading that both define Kitten's shape and personality and highlight the full moon. Henkes's simple words and simple lines combine to form a story that is satisfying to young readers.

The 2011 Caldecott Medal–winning *A Sick Day for Amos McGee* (N), by Philip C. Stead with illustrations by Erin E. Stead, is another perfect example of an excellent story for young children. Amos, a friendly and thoughtful zookeeper, can't go to work one morning because he has a terrible cold. Elephant, tortoise, penguin, rhinoceros, and owl miss their daily activities with Amos, so they go to visit him at home. The detailed drawings, spare use of soft color, and obvious delight on Amos's face (along with a pink-tipped nose) when his friends arrive combine to make this a quietly reassuring story of friendship and loyalty.

Tao Nyeu's *Bunny Days* (N) is a collection of three brief stories that appeal to young children. When the bunnies get muddy, bear washes them. When they get dusty because Mrs. Goat inadvertently sucks them into her vacuum, bear sets up a fan to blow the dust away. And when Mr. Goat accidently snips off some bunny tails while trimming his hedge, Bear gets out his sewing machine. The last double-page spread reassures that all are happy. There is a lot to look at on each opening, and the limited palette of soft colors enhances the gentle tone. Mo Willems also offers a collection of stories in *Hooray for Amanda & Her Alligator!: $6\frac{1}{2}$ Surprising Stories about 2 Surprising Friends* (N–P). With episodic chapters, lively action, a humorous tone, and surprisingly complete character development for both Amanda and the alligator, the seventy-two pages in this book just fly by. James Rumford's *Tiger and Turtle* (N–P) is another charming story of unlikely friendship.

Emily Gravett uses colors quite effectively, and fittingly, in *Blue Chameleon* (N). The chameleon is, both literally and figuratively, blue; he's lonely. Looking for companionship, he tries to fit in by changing his color and shape to imitate a banana, a cockatoo, a snail, a boot, a sock, a ball, a goldfish, a grasshopper,

a rock, and, finally, a white page on which the chameleon, barely visible, is embossed. Happiness reigns when he meets another colorful chameleon. Young children enjoy the story, the color identification, object identification, and the happy ending.

Emily Gravett is a favorite with young readers and the adults in their lives. Her book *Monkey and Me* (N) amply demonstrates the potential of a picture storybook for young children. We take a close look at it now.

* * *

A CLOSE LOOK AT
Monkey and Me

Many young children love to play with their stuffed animals, and the little girl in this picturebook imaginatively visits several other animals with her stuffed monkey. With her sparse text and lively illustrations, British author/illustrator Emily Gravett does not need any more than twenty-eight pages to tell her story. The dust jacket (identical to the board cover) shows off Gravett's elegantly simple drawing, with the girl holding a smiling monkey whose curved, outstretched arms seem to embrace the hand-lettered title. Together, the title and the monkey's arms form an elliptical shape that frames the author's name. The monkey's elongated tail is accentuated by continuing off the left side of the front cover and onto the back cover. The front endpapers show a sequence of illustrations of the little girl getting dressed and ready for her adventures with Monkey, thus beginning the story. There is clever use of the dedication page with its publishing information and the facing title page: Gravett depicts Monkey holding a poster with the publishing information and the little girl (unnamed throughout the story, which is narrated by her) holding a poster with the title and some scribbled drawings.

The left side of the next opening continues this story with the words "Monkey and me [repeated three times],/We went to see" accompanied by three illustrations of the girl with a firm grasp on Monkey's forearm. The right-hand side of the opening continues with a larger illustration of the girl with Monkey's arms, legs, and tail in a new position and the words "We went to see some . . ." Gravett makes excellent use of the page turns in this book because, in each case, the ellipsis encourages readers to turn to the next opening to discover what the girl and Monkey "went to see"—it's a procession of penguins, some with their baby chicks. The word "PENGUINS!" is in a very large font with an exclamation point. Readers attending to details will notice that the girl's arms and legs on the previous page (arms outstretched and one leg stiffly held up in

P | R | O | F | I | L | E

Emily Gravett

Emily Gravett is a relative newcomer to the world of children's books, but she has already made quite an impact. This author/illustrator grew up in Brighton, England, in a family that valued the arts—her mother was an art teacher and her father a printmaker. Although she enjoyed drawing when she was a youngster, it didn't occur to her until much later that she might become a professional artist. She was a quiet child, enjoying reading. In her late teens and early twenties, she spent eight years living on the road in impoverished circumstances, which certainly changed her outlook on life! When her daughter Oleander was born, the only thing that would quiet the infant was for Emily to read to her. She kept a journal full of drawings and doodles. Finally, despite her lack of good high school credentials, she persuaded the University of Brighton to let her study art. Her first book, **Wolves** (P–I–A), which was written and illustrated when she was studying at the university, won the Kate Greenaway Medal—the British equivalent of the Caldecott Medal—and she's been busy ever since. In interviews, she seems somewhat surprised and puzzled (but absolutely delighted) by her sudden success in children's publishing.

Her books almost always have some personal connection to her own life. For example, **Monkey and Me** was based on the daughter of a friend of hers who was a very "bouncy" child and couldn't sit still for long. Emily wanted to make a book that this child could relate to. **Meerkat Mail** (P–I), which tells the story of a meerkat named Sunny who decides to go on a trip because he is tired of his large family, contains many postcards sent by Sunny to his family. It's no surprise to find that Emily is "obsessed" with making and receiving postcards. **Meerkat Mail** also owes its existence in part to Emily's long time traveling on the road, with no fixed address. Her style is spontaneous and emphasizes flowing lines. She is known for leaving a lot of white space in her work, and most of her illustrations are done with pencil and watercolor wash; she says that she likes the fresh look of pencil rather than the more studied line of pen and ink. Her books often make something out of very little: who would have thought that "orange," "pear," "apple," "bear," and "there" could be the only words in a charming story for young children (**Orange Pear Apple Bear**, N–P)? There is a very attractive economy in both her illustrations and language, making them accessible to beginning readers; there is also, however, a subtlety and cleverness that appeal to older children as well.

Emily now lives in a cottage outside Brighton with her partner, Mik, who is a plumber, their daughter, and several pets. It seems as if this wanderer has finally found her vocation as an author/illustrator whose work has already delighted thousands of children, teachers, and parents.

 For more information about Emily, go to CengageBrain .com to access the Education CourseMate website where you will find a link to relevant websites.

the air) exactly echo the position of the lead penguin's arms and legs on the following opening.

The stage is thus set for the comfortably predictable quality of both illustrations and text. The next opening also contains the words "Monkey and me" [repeated three times], and "We went to see some ..." inviting us to turn the page to see three lively "KANGAROOS!" with the word again in a very large font and three bounding kangaroos. As well, the illustrations of the girl show her holding Monkey partly inside her red-and-white striped shirt, in the same way the kangaroos hold their babies, and leaping in the same bouncy rhythm as the kangaroos. The predictable structure continues with the same words accompanied by an illustration of the girl, holding Monkey and hanging upside down, so readers can predict that the following illustration of the animals they "went to see" are "BATS!" The next animals the pair visit are "ELEPHANTS!" followed by the most energetic illustrations in the book when they visit "MONKEYS!" After all this activity, we are not surprised to see a page opening showing a tired-looking girl and Monkey with all limbs drooping, and the words "Monkey ... and ... me [repeated three times], We went ..." The ellipses slow readers down, imitating the drowsy girl, and the last page of the story shows the sleeping girl at a table, her head resting on her arm, having barely finished a meal, and her other arm still holding Monkey.

Gravett surprises us with an image of a real monkey peeking over the table's edge, prompting us to speculate how much of this story was real and how much was fantasy. Did the girl take a trip to the zoo? Did she merely imagine the whole sequence of animal visits? The back endpapers nicely recapitulate the story sequence, with a line of penguins, a kangaroo, bats, elephants, and monkeys.

Gravett's palette and design are as simple as the words of the story. She limits herself to shades of brown and gray, except for the bright red of the girl's striped shirt, all rendered in pencil and watercolor. As well, the large amounts of white space surrounding all the illustrations suggest freedom of movement and activity, appropriate for the exuberance of the girl's adventure.

• • STORYBOOKS FOR • • PRIMARY-GRADE READERS

Children in first through third grade also enjoy listening to picture storybooks and, in some cases, reading them on their own. Books for this group are more complex than the simple stories for young children, and they reflect the increasingly wider worlds of children in the primary grades.

Monica Brown's **Waiting for the Biblioburro** (P), illustrated by John Parra, is another picture storybook inspired by the life of Luis Soriano, of Colombia. The young protagonist loves stories but lives in the country and, lacking money and library, has only one book. She compensates for this by making up stories to tell her little brother. Imagine her joy when she awakes one morning to the sound of burros' hooves and sees a traveling library. Both text, which artfully includes Spanish words, and the folk-art illustrations bring an important story from another country to young readers in the United States.

Another language and culture also play a role in Christine McDonnell's **Goyangi Means Cat** (P), illustrated by Steve Johnson and Lou Fancher. When a young Korean girl is adopted by American parents, she faces many new experiences. The family cat helps her adjust to her new life, until the cat escapes outside, only to return home. Korean words that relate to each scene appear in the illustrations.

Primary-grade children enjoy humor. In **The Day Ray Got Away** (P), Angela Johnson combines humor and fantasy with a serious theme. Ray, a sunburst balloon with a big smile, wakes on the morning of the parade and decides that this is the day to break his ties and soar, free. This, of course, creates havoc with the rest of the balloons and completely disrupts the parade. Clever word play and humorous illustrations by Luke LaMarca are perfect for primary-grade readers, who will cheer Ray on in his quest for

freedom. Jon Klassen's simple story, **I Want My Hat Back** (P), has few words, but requires close attention as bear goes through the forest looking for his red hat. Attentive listeners/readers will note something odd about rabbit's reply and will also know what happens to rabbit when bear discovers what happened to his hat. The sly humor engages readers of all ages, young and old.

Shane W. Evans tells a more serious story with spare text and mesmerizing illustrations in **Underground: Finding the Light to Freedom** (P–I). This story of the Underground Railroad introduces young readers to the danger and the glory of the flight of so many slaves, highlighting the courage of those who fled and those who helped them. The dark blue and gray palette is broken only by white in the eyes of the people and the stars in the sky or the gold gleam of a torch or lantern until the journey is almost complete when the sun, and freedom, dawns. The simplicity of the text makes the book accessible to many readers.

• • WORDLESS STORYBOOKS • •

Wordless storybooks tell a story through illustration alone, though of course the title of a wordless book often contains important clues regarding what the story will be about; moreover, many wordless books incorporate words in the illustrations, often in the form of street signs or other public text. Young children who do not yet read can retell a story from looking at the pictures; beginning readers, through their developing concept of *story*, are able to narrate the story with character and narrator voices. Older, struggling readers can grasp the story elements in wordless books. All students can use wordless books as a springboard to writing and oral storytelling. Good wordless storybooks contain all the important elements found in all good storybooks—except for the dialogue and narration, which are supplied by the reader. Teaching Idea 3.6 contains suggestions for working with English language learners using wordless books, although the suggestions are effective for English speakers as well.

Lita Judge's almost wordless **Red Sled** (N-P) engages young readers with its bold illustrations that shine (literally) on each page and onomatopoetic words that accompany the actions depicted in the illustrations. Framed, horizontal double-page spreads capture the cumulative action when bear takes the red sled left outside of a cabin and his friends join him for a wild and wonderful ride. In **Breakfast for Jack** (P), Pat Schories tells the charming story of a little boy who gets out of bed and feeds the family

TEACHING IDEA 3.6

Interactive Writing with Wordless Picturebooks and English Language Learners

ELL

 **COMMON CORE STATE STANDARDS** This Teaching Idea addresses Common Core English Language Arts, Reading: Literature standards 1, 2, 7 grade 2; and 1, 2 grade 3. The suggestions in this Teaching Idea may need to be adapted to suit your particular grade level and the needs of your students. For older students, this can be an excellent way to help them become familiar with various story structures.

Interactive writing builds bridges between oral language and writing, especially for English learning students. In interactive writing, students and teachers collaborate to construct a text based on some shared experience or conversation. Interactive writing can be used in a number of ways, such as retelling stories, sequencing events, responding to literature, or summarizing children's thinking. Following is a way of using a wordless picturebook to create a collaboratively authored book with elementary-grade students.

- Read a wordless picture storybook out loud to all students.

- Engage in plenty of conversation around the book. Talk about details students notice in the illustrations, what might happen next in the story, and how they're making sense of the story. Also, think ahead about new vocabulary words English learning students may need in order to write about the pictures. Introduce a few words during the

discussion and write them somewhere students can see them when they're doing their own writing.

- Have pairs of students draw pictures similar to those in the book. Be sure to leave space at the bottom of each page.

- Have students work with a partner and write about their illustrations. With newer English learners, you will want to work with them in a small group to facilitate the writing process. Be sure to welcome the language of the students whenever possible; don't make corrections or add your own words. Students have more difficulty reading the text if it does not reflect their own words.

- Ask students to create a title page and bind the book. Use the story for shared and independent reading.

These ideas were adapted from Patterson, E., Schaller, M., & Clemens, J. (2008). A closer look at interactive writing. *The Reading Teacher, 61*(6), 496–497.

---

cat, but forgets to feed his dog, Jack. Luckily, the boy remembers just as he goes out the door along with the rest of his family. Dennis Nolan's gorgeous wordless book, **Sea of Dreams** (N–P), imagines a sand castle populated by tiny people who embark on a dangerous adventure. Chris Raschka's **A Ball for Daisy** (N–P), evokes many emotions as Daisy and her owner enjoy playing with the ball until it is destroyed by another dog. Jeanne Baker's wordless book for older readers, **Mirror** (P–I), offers parallel stories, as side-by-side stories mirror each other, highlighting differences and similarities between the lives of two boys with her signature detailed collage, a bilingual introduction, and a very clever ending. The book may be wordless, but readers will want to talk about it.

Barbara Lehman's **The Red Book** (P–I), a Caldecott Honor winner, is, appropriately, bright red. The watercolor, gouache, and ink illustrations, with their straightforward, geometric shapes, present the story of a young girl who finds a red book in the snow on the city sidewalk, picks it up, and takes it to school. When she opens the book, she sees a map of islands. The illustrations then zoom into a close-up of the island on which a boy walks along a beach, and he finds a red book in the sand. When he opens the book, he sees a city and, as the pictures zoom in again, the girl. They gaze at each other, entranced, and the story builds from there. With its clever plot, expressive characters, and exploration of the power of books and the imagination, this wordless book is a treasure. Her other books include **Museum Trip** (P–I), **Rainstorm** (P–I), and **The Secret Box** (P–I), as well as **Trainstop** (P–I), described in detail previously. All of these celebrate the power of the imagination and the blurring of realism and fantasy, and are a great stimulus to writing and an inspiration to children's creative capacities.

Chicken and Cat (P) by Sara Varon relates Cat's visit to Chicken in a big city in wordless cartoon format. This amusing story includes Cat's initial fascination with the interesting things to do in the city and Cat's growing discontent with the drab urban landscape. The witty storyline, with its resolution (Cat helps Chicken plant a garden to improve the view) appeals to a range of readers. In **Invisible** (P–I), Katja Kamm amusingly explores how things and people can disappear against backgrounds of the same color or pattern. Charlotte Dematons gives children a lot to look at in **The Yellow Balloon** (N–P), as the illustrations, through a series of aerial views, present the world travels of an escaped balloon. The visually stunning **Yellow Umbrella** (P–I) by Dong Il Sheen and Jae-Soo Lieu, though it contains no words, is accompanied by a CD with music to play while turning the pages.

Wordless books can be very sophisticated, appealing primarily to an older audience, such as Thé Tjong Khing's **Where Is the Cake?** (I–A), which presents an intricate cast of characters and weaves together many stories. Istvan Banyai's **The Other Side** (I–A) takes a look at the same scene from different perspectives; it is quite challenging for even sophisticated readers/viewers.

All students learn about story structure and form when they translate the pictures of a wordless storybook into language. The structure of the story, along with the character development, provides a good model for writers and for students to explore the visual characterization, setting, and theme that wordless books provide.

● ● PICTURE STORYBOOKS ● ● AND GRAPHIC NOVELS FOR OLDER READERS

Today, publishers offer a variety of picture storybooks, graphic picturebooks, and graphic novels that appeal to older readers. These books entice visually sophisticated students; they are also accessible to struggling readers who learn more easily using books with more pictures and sparser text. Students learning English also appreciate picturebooks and graphic novels. Fortunately, the graphic novel is becoming increasingly popular, and more are published each year.

Like picturebooks, graphic novels are not defined by their content, but rather by their form. They almost always contain "the representation of time through sequential panels" and are an "interaction between word and image" (Tucker, 2009, p. 28). In the past decade, there have been increasing numbers of graphic picturebooks or, as some call them, graphic novels in which the story is told through a combination of cartoons with speech bubbles and, sometimes, a brief narrative text below each cartoon. Dav Pilkey's **Captain Underpants** (P–I) series and the **Babymouse** (P–I) series by Jennifer and Matthew Holm are popular with younger readers. Older readers are captivated by graphic novels targeted at both adolescent and adult audiences. Art Spiegelman's **Maus** (A) books are an example of these "crossover" books.

Graphic picturebooks and novels have become popular with upper elementary and adolescent readers. The visual nature of these books is especially appealing to many students. Nicolas Debon uses this format to present his biography of artist Emily Carr in **Four Pictures by Emily Carr** (I–A), in which he tells his entire story through cartoon art and speech bubbles with handwritten text. **Little Vampire Goes to School** (I) by French author Joann Sfar, was a Children's Choices Award Winner in 2004. This book is an interesting mix of cartoon style and creepy content and is appealing to many readers, including reluctant ones. Avi's graphic picturebook, **Silent Movie** (I–A), illustrated by C. B. Mordan, is, appropriately, black and white and told only through images and title cards. The rags-to-riches immigrant story, complete with villain, appealing young child and mother on their own, and happy ending is perfect fare for the silent movie and the audience. The melodrama is a wonderful stimulus for some extended dramatic writing.

Marcia Williams created two graphic picturebooks: **Tales from Shakespeare** and **Bravo, Mr. William Shakespeare!** (I–A). Each book contains seven of Shakespeare's most popular plays. The first contains *Romeo and Juliet, A Winter's Tale, Macbeth, A Midsummer Night's Dream, Julius Caesar, Hamlet,* and *The Tempest.* The second contains *As You Like It, Richard III, Antony and Cleopatra, Much Ado about Nothing, Twelfth Night, King Lear,* and *The Merchant of Venice.* **King** (A) by Ho Che Anderson, subtitled **A Comics Biography of Martin Luther King, Jr.**, combines black-and-white comic book cells with larger illustrations that have speech bubbles and spare but effective use of color in mixed media for a powerful and unforgettable visual and literary experience. Other not-to-be-missed graphic novels for older readers include **Persepolis 1 and 2** (A) by Marjane Satrapi and Gene Luen Yang's **American Born Chinese** (A). The latter won the Michael Printz Award for Young Adult Fiction. **The Magical Life of Long Tack Sam** (A), an illustrated memoir by Ann Marie Fleming, uses a combination of old photographs, historical documents, and drawings to tell the fascinating story of her great-grandfather, who was one of the most famous Chinese magicians. **500 Essential Graphic Novels: The Ultimate Guide** (A) by Gene Kannenberg Jr., is an excellent resource for this proliferating format. In the realm of comic books, an equally impressive array is present in **The Best American Comics** series (A) for 2006, 2007, and 2008.

Other new graphic novels include both fiction and biographical fiction. Greg Neri takes on the serious topics of gangs and death in **Yummy: The Last Days of a Southside Shorty** (A), with illustrations by Randy DuBurke. Sarah Stewart Taylor and illustrator Ben Tawle use a graphic novel form to tell the story of Amelia Earhart's Atlantic Ocean crossing through the eyes of a teenager in Newfoundland in 1928, in **Amelia Earhart: This Broad Ocean** (I). Gloria Jablonski's historical fiction account of the French Resistance in World War II, **Resistance: Book 1** (A), illustrated by Leland Purvis, illuminates that part of history. Sara Varon's **Robot Dreams** (I–A) is one of several graphic novels published by Roaring Brook Press's First Second Books imprint, which also includes Jane Yolen's **Foiled** (I–A), illustrated by Mike Cavallaro. Both of these fantasies are highly entertaining.

Recently, writers and illustrators have begun blurring forms and formats, creating new forms of what artist Will Eisner (2008) calls "sequential art" or what Terry Thompson (2008) calls "graphica," such as comic books, graphic novels, and films. In all of these art forms, there is a sequence of visual images, and there is also a verbal component, with either written or spoken words that accompany the visual images. In addition, all require both words and pictures working in concert and synergy to communicate their meanings. Recent years have seen a hybridization of these forms and formats that is quite exciting for both older and younger readers. A very high-profile example of this hybridization was the awarding of the 2008 Caldecott Medal to Brian Selznick's **The Invention of Hugo Cabret** (I–A). Remember, the Caldecott Medal is given by the American Library Association "to the artist of the most distinguished American picture book for children" (quoting the ALA website, www.ala.org). At first glance, **The Invention of Hugo Cabret** (hereafter referred to as **Hugo**) looks like a novel:

it's more than five hundred pages long. Opening it, we see that it contains sections of text and long sequences of black-and-white illustrations, though the words are never printed on the same page as the illustrations. Is this a picturebook? According to the Caldecott committee, it is! This decision by the committee marks a new way of conceptualizing picturebooks; it means that it is no longer easy (or perhaps even useful) to draw rigid distinctions among graphic novels, comic books, picturebooks, and films. The layout of **Hugo** resembles a graphic novel, cells in a very long comic book or a series of stills from a film presented in slow motion. The recognition given to **Hugo** may spur those who write and illustrate literature for children and adolescents to even greater inventive departures from the traditional format of the picturebook. The many fans of **Hugo Cabret** were thrilled to find Selznik's **Wonderstruck** (I–A) on bookstore shelves.

Another excellent example of the blurring of forms and formats is Shaun Tan's **The Arrival** (I–A), a beautifully illustrated wordless book that tells the story of an immigrant to a country whose culture and language are quite different from his own. We learn along with the immigrant about the new culture and rejoice with him when he is able to afford to send for his wife and young daughter to come to be with him. On the last page, the exquisite illustrations show the youngster giving another recent immigrant directions. **The Arrival** combines the forms of the wordless picturebook and the graphic novel in a wonderful work of art that might have given **The Invention of Hugo Cabret** some stiff competition for best picturebook; however, it was ineligible, due to being published first in Australia. Shaun Tan's **Tales from Outer Suburbia** (I–A) is a series of "illustrated stories" around the common theme of encountering the new and surprising in the humdrum life of the suburbs. His **Lost and Found** (I–A) is a compilation of three stories previously published in Australia, all of which are disturbing, visually arresting, and thought-provoking. Tan was recently awarded the Astrid Lindgren Memorial Award for the body of his work by the International Board on Books for Youth.

Although not as abundant as those for preschool and elementary school readers, an increasing number of picture storybooks are intended specifically for an audience of older readers. These books offer adolescents the opportunity to consider serious themes as presented in both text and art. One of the most exciting examples of picturebooks for adolescents is Margaret Wild's **Woolvs in the Sitee** (A), a book at which we now take a close look.

*The sinister mood and the despair of the teenager in Margaret Wild's **Woolvs in the Sitee** are powerfully conveyed in Ann Spudvilas's illustrations. The invented spelling suggests that Ben has been unable or unwilling to go to school for quite a while, causing readers to wonder why.*

Would the invented spelling be a detriment to some readers?

✳ ✳ ✳
A CLOSE LOOK AT
Woolvs in the Sitee

There are few contemporary picturebooks for older readers that have as powerful an impact as **Woolvs in the Sitee** (I–A) by the Australian team of Margaret Wild and Anne Spudvilas. The title alone unsettles us; the phonetic spelling, which continues throughout the book, accentuates the chaos and deeply disturbing tone of the book, which will provide many opportunities for mature readers' speculations and inferences. Set in an unnamed, perhaps futuristic urban area, **Woolvs** is narrated by Ben, a young teenager who is terribly afraid to even step outside his own derelict building, so afraid is he of the "woolvs" that he thinks prowl the city where he used to live happily with his family. Now an orphan, he lives alone, his only friend a neighbor, "Missus Radinski," an older woman who fails (or pretends to

fail) to perceive the danger of the ominous "woolvs" that roam the streets. Are the "woolvs" figments of Ben's disordered imagination? Or are they metaphors for the distrust, fear, and terror that are everyday features of urban life, even in our contemporary cities, where the fabric of society is so tattered that no one trusts anyone else?

The front and back dust jacket of this book read as one continuous illustration. The top half has a black background, with the names of the author and illustrator in red and the title, crudely hand-lettered, in stark white. Just visible on the top half of the back dust jacket are the words "they spare no won," a phrase that occurs repeatedly in the book. The bottom half of the front and back dust jacket contains similar disquieting phrases on a red background. Clearly, this is not going to be a light-hearted book. The cloth board cover is plain black, and the endpapers (front and back) are an equally somber black with child-like scribbled drawings of wolves. The title

P | R | O | F | I | L | E

Margaret Wild

One of the most prolific and distinguished writers of children's literature in Australia, Margaret Wild was born in South Africa in 1948 but has lived "down under" since 1972. She has written more than forty books for children, from picturebooks to young adult fiction. Wild is a private person and does not share much of her personal life with the public.

Wild has never shrunk from topics and issues that some might consider taboo for children's books. She has dealt with death, dying, and the mourning process; divorce; anxiety; the betrayal of friendship; bullying; and the Holocaust—all in picturebook format. Her book *Jenny Angel* (P–I), about a little girl whose brother is dying, was inspired by Wild's brother's death when he was seven years old. *Fox* (I–A), one of Wild's most thought-provoking picturebooks, concerns Fox's rage and jealousy over the friendship between Magpie (whose wing has been injured in a forest fire) and Dog. Despite these serious themes, however, Wild's books are never ultimately depressing; on the contrary, they are full of hope and the examples of protagonists who overcome adversity and end up making good decisions. In our Close Look at *Woolvs in the Sitee*, for example, the protagonist musters up courage and determination to look for a lost neighbor, despite his fears and anxieties.

Serious topics do not exhaust Wild's creativity: *Loosey Goosey* (about a young goose who is afraid to fly and needs reassurance from her mother, N–P); *Kiss, Kiss* (featuring a young hippo who scampers out to play without remembering to kiss his mother good-bye, N–P); and *Tom Goes to Kindergarten* (the adventures of a young panda on the first day of school, N–P) will delight preschoolers and early primary-age children with anthropomorphized animals.

Wild is not above taking an irreverent and upbeat look at subjects that are frequently presented in an overly sentimental way. Wild has two children and currently lives in Sydney, one of Australia's most vibrant cities.

---

page has a red background, with illegible handwritten words. The reader turns to the first opening, which begins, *There are woolvs in the sitee. Oh yes!*

The palette for the illustrations is appropriately dark and foreboding, in tones of black and sick yellows, with occasional splashes of brighter colors that only add to the eerie quality of the story. Ben says, "I longs for bloo skys. I longs for it to rane. But the seesons are topsee-turvee. Nothing is rite," suggesting that something cataclysmic—a nuclear war? A severe societal upheaval?—has reduced the city where once the streets were his "rivers, these parks my vallees" to a ruin where only an occasional person rides by on a bicycle, looking over his shoulder in apprehension. One day, seduced by a blue-painted wall, he thinks things are back to normal and runs out of the building, only to be paralyzed by fear of the "woolvs." "Missus Radinski" rescues him and drags him back inside. Then the worst happens: Missus Radinski disappears. Ben has to summon up all his courage to look for her, all the while terrified of the "woolvs." He gathers a few things in a knapsack and goes looking for her, his heart "jakhammering." But he is determined that he "will no longer let the woolvs forse me to scrooch." On the last,

almost unbearably poignant opening, he turns to the reader, his face a combination of fear and determination, and says, "Joyn me." So the story ends.

What are we to make of this apocalyptic and desperate narrative? Older readers will find endless opportunities to hypothesize about both what caused this situation and what will become of Ben. Why is Ben so afraid? Is his childish spelling the result of his having been unable, or too afraid, to go to school for many years? Is any of this real, or is he an unfortunate victim of paranoid schizophrenia? How are we to respond to his plea to "joyn" him? The book offers no answers, with its sinister tone and unrelenting sadness. Spudvilas's full-bleed illustrations are the perfect complement to the ominous text, which is printed over the illustrations in black or white depending on the color of the backgrounds. The only hope offered in this haunting book is the luminous white background of the last opening, with its pale blue and orange tints and Ben's courageous face, gazing at us with imploring eyes.

This book will explode older readers' ideas that picturebooks are for little children and will elicit deep and provocative discussion.

Picturebooks of Poetry and Song

Some picturebooks present an artist's visual interpretation of a song, poem, or verse. In these books, the artist arranges the text across the pages, often with only one or two lines per page, and then illuminates each thought expressed by the text. The lyrical language of the text should be both interesting to and understandable by the intended audience. Brief, rhythmic verses, narrative verses, and children's and folk songs make excellent picturebook texts. Some books contain several separate poems; others present single poems or songs. Many picturebooks of poetry are discussed in Chapter 4, and we consider a few examples here as well.

In beautifully designed picturebooks of poetry and song, the arrangement of the text across the pages reflects the natural breaks in the meaning and sound of the original. Illustrations depict both action and feeling, matching the mood established by the author as interpreted by the artist. Lynne Rae Perkins's **Snow Music** (P) is a perfect example of a beautifully designed picturebook containing a single poem. Tracey Campbell Pearson charmingly illustrates Robert Louis Stevenson's poem **The Moon** (P–I) in loose, dreamy watercolors whose setting seems to be the rocky coast of Maine. Each double-page spread illustrates a line or phrase from the poem, while the back endpages reprint the entire text. Marla Frazee brings new life to a Woody Guthrie song with her clever and energetic illustrations for **New Baby Train** (P). Holly Meade's exuberant hand-painted woodcut illustrations for David Elliott's **On the Farm** (P) are a wonderful accompaniment for the individual poems about farm animals on each double-page spread.

Susan Campbell Bartoletti created a lovely and soothing lullaby using an ancient Arabic verse form in **Naamah and the Ark at Night** (N–P), with illustrations by Holly Meade. This is a perfect one-on-one bedtime book. Nina Crews takes on a different task, that of creating a book for sharing with a larger group, **The Neighborhood Sing-Along** (N–P). Like her earlier **The Neighborhood Mother Goose** (N–P), this book invites readers to celebrate multi-ethnic city neighborhoods with her lively text and visually arresting photographs. In **Looking Like Me** (P–I), Walter Dean Myers celebrates the many things that any one child can be. Christopher Myers's exuberant mixed-media illustrations pop from the pages, and text boxes and varied fonts and colors add to the excitement.

A much quieter tone permeates Liz Garton Scanlon's **All the World** (N–P), a book that celebrates the small joys found everywhere in our world as a family goes about its day. Illustrator Marla Frazee uses double-page spreads and small vignettes to reflect the words of this celebration of the beauty of the world, from small shell to sunset. George Ella Lyon celebrates water in **All the Water in the World: The Water Cycle in Poetry** (N–P), with digital illustrations by Katherine Tillotson.

Picturebooks of poetry and song contain voices from exuberant to quiet, celebratory to contemplative. Their illustrations are as varied as their topics; all offer readers the opportunity to experience poetic language in a format that allows visual interpretation by some of our most gifted illustrators.

Nonfiction Picturebooks

Nonfiction picturebooks include concept books that seek to present a particular concept in a way that young readers can understand, informational books designed to provide readers with knowledge about a particular topic, and biographies based on factual information about a subject. The text should be accurate, organized in a manner appropriate to both the information presented and the intended audience, designed in an attractive and appropriate fashion, and written and illustrated with verve and style. We focus on biography in Chapter 9 and other nonfiction in Chapter 10. Although many of these books are highly illustrated, those we discuss here have the unique relationship between text and illustrations that mark a true picturebook. Thus, the illustrations and the text together create a book that imparts information to its readers.

Nonfiction picturebooks reach a broad range of students, enabling students at many different ability levels to access information. Producing picturebooks appropriate to a young reader's age or to a struggling older reader's ability creates a special challenge for nonfiction writers, who have to find ways to explain a subject simply enough to be understood and still be accurate. Nonfiction picturebooks for older, more advanced readers can present more complex, detailed information, but still retain the interdependence of text and illustration.

• • CONCEPT BOOKS • •

Concept books, which are simple nonfiction books, appeal to young children as they learn about the world. For very young children, Kaaren Pixton's series of virtually indestructible books, such as **Farm Charm** (N), present pictures of different sorts of birds, insects, and animals with no words so that caregivers can engage children in labeling and talking about the pictures.

Concept books contribute to a child's expanding knowledge and language by providing numerous examples of an idea. Some books present abstract ideas, such as shape, color, size, or sound, through many illustrations, as Tana Hoban does in **Cubes, Cones, Cylinders, and Spheres** (N–P). Hoban, a master of the art of concept books and a skilled photographer, uses no words in the book about shapes. Instead, she uses crystal-clear photographs of objects that children could find in their own environment. Petr Horacek combines the concepts of color and different types of animals in **Butterfly, Butterfly** (N–P) and adds further interest with die-cut holes. Animals, colors, and the idea of camouflage are all present in Satoru Onishi's **Who's Hiding?** (P). Michael Hall's story of the **Perfect Square** (N–P) features color, shape, and the days of the week in the simple story of a perfectly happy square who, through various transformations, decided that four equal sides and matching corners were much too confining. Beautifully designed with collages set off by white pages facing solid color pages containing white text, the book is, fittingly, a perfect square.

A book such as **Chicken, Chicken, Duck!** (N), written and illustrated by Nadia Krilanovich, uses very few words as it both labels animals and presents the sounds they make for very young readers. The large, realistic, colorful illustrations, rendered in acrylic paint, are set on spacious white space, with words printed in black near each animal. This basic concept book definitely invites labeling and imitating as it presents information to very young readers. Concepts of sight, sound, smell, taste, and feel allow Anne Crausaz to explore the natural world in **Seasons** (N).

The mother-daughter team of Marthe Jocelyn and Nell Jocelyn present the concept of single and pairs in **Ones and Twos** (P) in a narrative of two young friends who go to the park together. Patricia Intriago embeds the concept of opposites in the arc of a child's day in **Dot** (N–P). In **RRRalph** (N), Lois Ehlert questions the general belief that dogs cannot talk. Does Ralph say "Ruff" or "Rough?" It all depends on how you listen. It all depends on how you think about shape in Mary Lyn Ray's **Stars** (N–P). The book begins and ends with stars in the night sky, but in between we see many other stars, like dandelion seeds and sheriff badges. Illustrator Marla Frazee surprises us with a sky full of fireworks stars at the end. Keith Baker, creator of the popular

LMNO Peas (P), explores the concept of the unique nature of many things, from snowflakes to humans, in **No Two Alike** (P).

G. Brian Karas brings a village garage to life with text and illustrations in **The Village Garage** (N–P). Readers can observe how municipal workers take care of many tasks around town, and the illustrations of various trucks and machines are an extra bonus for big vehicle lovers. Peter Mandel capitalizes on young children's interest in machines as well. In his **Jackhammer Sam** (N), illustrated by David Catrow, rhymed couplets present Sam's description of what he does, a description that becomes a tall tale as he drains the Milky Way. In **Everything Goes: On Land** (N), Brian Biggs offers interestingly detailed spreads of cars, trucks, and many other machines that operate on land, as seen by a young boy on his way from his suburban home to the train station in the city.

• • NONFICTION • • FOR PRESCHOOL AND PRIMARY-GRADE READERS

Virtually everything you need to know could be learned from a children's nonfiction picturebook. The topics presented in these books are many, the language is clear, and the illustrations work with the text to convey information that young readers want and need to know.

Preschool and primary-grade children are developing their concept of time, and Geraldine McCaughrean's **My Grandmother's Clock** (N–P), illustrated by Stephen Lambert, will help them do that. This is a simple story, redolent with the affection between grandmother and granddaughter, that looks at time from a much larger perspective than minutes and hours. Time is also the focus in **While You Are Sleeping: A Lift-the-Flap Book of Time Around the World** (N–P), by Durga Bernhard. The design of this book allows young readers to lift flaps to see simultaneous events around the world. Steve Jenkins looks at time in a different way in **Just a Second** (P–I), illustrated with his signature cut-paper collage and including informative back matter on the history of the universe, Earth's population, and the lifespan of species.

Older readers are sure to understand the concept of zero after spending time with Betsy Franco's **Zero Is the Leaves on the Tree** (P), illustrated by Shino Arihara. Zero may be egg-shaped, and it certainly is a number, but the presence of zero is most clearly understood through the metaphors that Franco employs, such as the tree in late fall of the title or the empty ball holder at recess. Nicola Davies's

Surprising Sharks (P), intended for a primary-grade audience, presents many different sizes and shapes of sharks, pointing out some of the surprising results of adaptation as well as the commonalities of anatomy and behavior. The text is humorous and informative, and the bright colors and clever art of James Croft add to both the humor and the information. This book blends accuracy with fun, a perfect combination for the subject and the intended audience. Jim Arnosky tells the true story of a pregnant manatee, injured by a boat propeller, in *Slow Down for Manatees* (P). Not only does this book inform young readers about the plight of the manatees, it demonstrates that a simple act, slowing down boats in a manatee habitat, can make a difference.

Steve Jenkins and Robin Page challenge a broad range of readers to expand their knowledge about the function of body parts in *What Do You Do with a Tail Like This?* (P–I). The authors include information about each animal in the back of the book. *Actual Size* and *Prehistoric Actual Size* (P–I) are books that Steve Jenkins created to help children understand the concept of size. The book contains pictures of the eyeball of a giant squid and the head of an Alaskan brown bear, among other animals. Each page includes the height and weight of each animal; additional information about each animal is included in the back of the book.

Spirals are the focus on Joyce Sidman's *Swirl by Swirl: Spirals in Nature* (N–P). With simple, poetic text and lush, detailed scratchboard illustrations by Beth Krommes, this book makes readers aware of some of the many spirals around them, their function, and their beauty. Jacqueline Briggs Martin's *The Chiru of High Tibet* (P–I), illustrated by Linda Wingerter, presents information about Chiru, an endangered antelope-type animal that lives only in the high plains/mountains of Tibet, through succinct prose and gorgeous realistic landscape paintings that are supplemented by boxed facts. Pamela Turner's *Project Seahorse* (I), part of the **Scientists in the Field** series, is all about teamwork, which is emphasized in Scott Tuason's photographs of American scientists and their Philippine coworkers engaged in their effort to save the tiger tail seahorse.

Farms have always been subject of nonfiction for all ages of readers, and two recent books serve as beautiful examples of the marriage of text and art to relay information. Elisha Cooper's *Farm* (P–I) combines an informative text with Cooper's beautiful watercolor illustrations, from spot art arranged on spacious pages to full-bleed, double-page spreads, as it follows life on a farm through the growing season. Arthur Geisert uses an ABC format to impart information in *Country Road ABC: An Illustrated Journey through America's Farmland* (P–I). Copperplate etchings hand colored with acrylic and watercolor take us on a visual exploration of a real place and people, a small farming community in Iowa. Each letter is accompanied by a word important to twentieth-century farm life, such as fencing for the letter F, with accompanying close-up and panoramic images. On the double-page F spread, we see a farmer stringing fence, while at the bottom we see farms surrounded by fence.

For older readers, David Macaulay, a master of nonfiction, presents *Built to Last* (I–A), a compilation of his earlier *Castle* (I–A), *Cathedral: The Story of Its Construction* (I–A), and *Mosque* (I–A) with new research, information, and additional drawings, as well as adding color to the original black-and-white drawings for *Castle* and *Cathedral*. The painstakingly detailed illustrations are fascinating, as we see these buildings and the structures that surround them being created and changing the worlds of the people who constructed them.

• • PICTUREBOOK BIOGRAPHIES • •

Many nonfiction picturebooks are biographies, stories of real people. Picturebooks offer a way to read about and see the lives of others. Details offered by illustrators present information in a way that allows a wide range of readers to learn a great deal of detail, without extensive text. Many picturebook biographies are discussed in Chapter 9.

Jeanette Winter's *Biblioburro: A True Story from Colombia* (P) is a brief biography of the avid reader and teacher who created the burro-powered mobile library described in Brown's fictional *Waiting for the Biblioburro*, described previously. Winter tells the story of Luis Seriano's decision to bring books to others in the isolated villages of his homeland. Her brightly colored, naïve illustrations work with the text to create the setting and depict the emotional impact of books on people's lives. Author/illustrator Dan Yaccarino tells the autobiographical story of his own family in *All the Way to America: The Story of a Big Italian Family and a Little Shovel* (P). A classic story of immigration and success, this warm-hearted picturebook, like many others, can trigger conversations about family origins and values. Similarly, the illustrations of Bryan Collier for Laban Carrick Hill's *Dave the Potter: Artist, Poet, Slave* (P–I) add depth, resonance, and a deeper understanding of this man's life and work. The gatefold in which we see four views of Dave's dark hands as he works the clay to shape a pot evokes the experience of actually making a pot and extends the impact of the eloquently simple text. Collier's art earned the Coretta Scott King Award for illustration and a Caldecott Honor.

Collier also illustrated Charles R. Smith's ***Twelve Rounds to Glory: The Story of Muhammad Ali*** (I–A), which has much more text than most picturebooks, yet the illustrations convey so much information that the text alone would be diminished. ***A Nation's Hope: The Story of Boxing Legend Joe Louis*** (I–A), written by Matt de la Pena and illustrated by Kadir Nelson, focuses on Louis's 1938 rematch with German Max Schmeling. Although the book is certainly about Louis as a boxer, it is also about Louis as a figure who challenged and, for a brief time, overcame the racism that permeated the United States at the time. Nelson's illustrations are superb, showing the intense joy of African Americans at his win as well as the sheer physical power of this iconic boxer.

• • ALPHABET BOOKS AND • • BOOKS ABOUT NUMBERS

Alphabet books serve many useful purposes, only one of which is related to learning the alphabet. Children ages two to four years old point to pictures and label objects on the page; five-year-olds may say the letter names and the words that start with each letter; six-year-olds may read the letters, words, or text to confirm their knowledge of letter–sound correspondence. However they are read, alphabet books help children develop an awareness of words on the page; they increase language learning and serve as a pleasurable activity for children.

We never need to settle for a mediocre alphabet book because magnificent ones are available, such as Alison Jay's ***ABC: A Child's First Alphabet Book*** (N–P), Lisa Campbell Ernst's ***The Turn-Around, Upside-Down Alphabet Book*** (N–P), Andy Rash's ***Agent A to Agent Z*** (P), ***Max's ABC*** (N) by Rosemary Wells, ***ABC Pop!*** (N–P) by Rachel Isadora, and Brian Floca's ***The Racecar Alphabet*** (N–P). Jon Agee's ***Z Goes Home*** (N–P) combines fun with bold graphics as it follows the journey of Z, heading home across a bridge, eating a donut, and so on until it arrives home, the Z in the City Zoo. Ross MacDonald treats the alphabet humorously in ***Achoo! Bang! Crash! The Noisy Alphabet*** (P). Children who are just becoming interested in superheroes will love Bob McLeod's ***SuperHero ABC*** (P).

Some authors use the ABCs to structure the information they want to present, as Arthur Geisert did in ***Country Road ABC***, discussed previously as a piece of nonfiction about farming. Indeed, many alphabet and counting books are nonfiction about particular subjects other than letters and numbers. Kristin Joy Pratt uses the alphabet for ***A Walk in the Rain Forest*** and ***A Swim through the Sea*** (P). Similarly, Paul Kratter's ***The Living Rain Forest*** (P) is as much about tropical rain forests as it is an alphabet book. David McLimans's Caldecott Honor–winning book, ***Gone Wild*** (I), is a fascinating inquiry into endangered animals from A to Z. Each letter becomes the animal it represents, and information about the animals is presented in an accompanying box and back matter.

These books are organized by the alphabet, but don't really focus on the alphabet as such. Martin Jarrie's ***ABC USA*** (P–I) contains much information about the United States and its culture ("J is for jazz" and "L is for Liberty Bell"). Deborah Lee Rose's ***Into the A, B, Sea: An Ocean Alphabet*** (P–I) with Steve Jenkins's outstanding paper collage illustrations contains many animals and plants, all linked with a continuous rhyme, and also includes a short description of each creature at the end of the book.

Celeste Davidson Mannis's ***The Queen's Progress: An Elizabethan Alphabet*** (I–A) lures readers by providing alphabetical bite-size nuggets of information about the reign of Elizabeth I. Reflecting the Elizabethan Age, the illustrations complement the text. Another example is Arthur Yorinks's ***The Alphabet Atlas*** (I–A). This alphabetical atlas transforms geography into stunning quilted artwork. ***Q Is for Quark: A Science Alphabet Book*** and ***G Is for Googol: A Math Alphabet Book*** (I–A), written by David M. Schwartz, are directed to upper-grade students. Some teachers use these books to complement their math and science curricula by providing a "letter-a-day" read-aloud experience or by reinforcing a topic such as "D" for DNA when it connects to the subject students are studying. The two books make complicated topics friendly and fun. "D" for DNA, for example, employs plain, simple language and silly drawings that make DNA comical and intriguing rather than boring and difficult to understand. Teaching students how to say "rhombicosidodecahedron" (the biggest polyhedron, with 240 faces) adds linguistic sparkle to a geometry lesson because it becomes a fun word to say and "show off" to others.

Some counting books help children learn numbers, numerical concepts, days of the week, months of the year, and the four seasons. Anita Lobel does all that and wraps it in an engaging story in ***One Lighthouse, One Moon*** (P). Many counting books are available for the nursery and primary grades, starting with those that use simple pictures to illustrate the progression from one to ten, such as Rachel Isadora's ***1 2 3 Pop!*** (P). Lynn Reiser's ***Ten Puppies*** (N) illustrates paired integers whose sum is ten with adorable puppies that make young readers want to look closely at the *nine* pink tongues and *one* blue tongue as they count. Reading Maurie Manning's **The Aunts Go Marching** (N), a cheerful, engaging text with plenty of things to count, leads children into singing along, movement, and counting out loud. Leo and Diane Dillon's delightful **Mother Goose: Numbers on the Loose** (P) highlights rhymes with numbers, and readers will enjoy counting the representations of objects and people in the illustrations. For example, in "Baa, baa black sheep," the "three bags full" are carried by a procession of characters across the double-page spread. Sarah Weeks's **Counting Ovejas** (N) begins with parents tucking their child into bed. When the ticking clock and dripping water keep him awake, he begins counting sheep of different colors. The progression from one to ten is lushly illustrated by David Diaz, and the rhythmic, repetitive text is first in Spanish, then English, with a pronunciation guide for the Spanish directly beneath. It will not surprise young readers that many of the sheep end up in bed as the child, finally, sleeps.

Carll Cneut's vibrant, busy illustrations combine with Marilyn Singer's rhymed text in **City Lullaby** (P) to present a humorous story of a baby who slumbers through "10 horns beeping," "9 phones ringing," "8 dogs barking" . . . until, in the surprise ending, "1 bird begins to twitter" and the baby awakens. Counting books help children develop concepts of quantity and numerical order through fine visual portrayal of number concepts. The best illustrations for young children avoid distracting clutter so that the objects to be counted can be identified and counted without confusion. Molly Bang's delightful **Ten, Nine, Eight** (N–P), recently reissued, also counts backward; as a father helps his daughter at bedtime, they count down from ten toes to one sleepy child all ready for bed. Books for older children can be more complex. Other counting books go far beyond ten or count in sets, such as **Anno's Counting Book** (P–I), by Mitsumasa Anno, which moves from zero to twelve and from January to December.

Unique Formats

● ● BOARD BOOKS AND ● ●
PARTICIPATION BOOKS

Board books are a particular format that appeals to adults as well as infants, toddlers, and children in preschool; the books are often six to twelve pages long, made of sturdy cardboard. There are also cloth books, shape books, pudgy books, lift-the-flap books, toy books, and plastic bathtub books. Books of this type, appropriate for children in the picture identification stage, are also good for those in the earliest stages of reading. **Max's First Word** (N) by Rosemary Wells, is a favorite board book. Big sister Ruby tries time and again to get Max to say a word. He responds only with "Bang." Just to surprise Ruby and show that he is no dummy, when she holds up an apple, Max says, "Delicious."

A combination board book and fascinating participation book by Rufus Butler Seder, **Gallop!** (N–P) is a "runaway success" because every time a page is turned, the animals seem to move; Seder's **Swing!: A Scanimation Picture Book** (N–P) is likewise an animated book with a story about playing baseball. A similar interesting participation book is **Magic Moving Images: Animated Optical Illusions** (N–P) by Colin Ord, in which an acetate overlay, provided in the book, brings images such as a moving horse or a waving flag to life.

Fruit (N–P) by Sara Anderson contains memorable illustrations that help young children identify both shapes and colors of common fruits; and **Global Babies** (N) contains wonderful photographs of babies from many countries around the world. Donald Crews created **Inside Freight Train** (N), a sturdy board book with sliding doors that open on each railroad car. Children's fascination with trains starts early and continues for many years. This book is a treasure. Children also enjoy books about children and parents. Barbara Joosse's **¿Me quieres, mama?** (N) is a Spanish version of the very popular **Do You Love Me, Mama?**. David Shannon, Kevin Henkes, Mo Willems, and Ian Falconer have all created board books based on the well-beloved characters in their picture storybooks. Shannon, for example, has published the **Diaper David** series (**David Smells!**, N); Henkes uses characters from his mouse books (**Wemberly's Ice-Cream Star**, N); Willems has produced humorous board books based on his Pigeon character (**The Pigeon Loves Things that Go!**, N; and **The Pigeon Has Feelings, Too!** N); and Falconer has used Olivia, his pig character, in **Olivia Counts** (N) and **Olivia's Opposites** (N). These board books are not simply picture storybooks converted into board books; they are much shorter and especially created for the board book format.

Participation books provide concrete visual and tactile materials for children to explore: textures to touch, flaps to lift, flowers to smell, and pieces to manipulate. A classic by Dorothy Kunhardt, **Pat the Bunny** (N) asks children to look in a mirror, play peek-a-boo, and feel a scratchy beard; babies love touching this book. Eric Carle's **The Very Busy Spider** (N), reissued as a twenty-four-page board book, has brightly colored collages and tactile renderings of the spider's growing web. **Dog** (N) by Matthew Van Fleet enables young children to pull tabs that cause many dogs to wag their tails, shake, and scratch themselves. Young children also love lift-the-flap books that reveal the location of animals, such as **Ruff! Ruff! Where's Scruff?** (N) by Sarah Weeks. Other lift-the-flap books such as Christopher Inns's **Peekaboo Puppy and Other Pets** (both N–P) contain flaps, which when lifted give the answers to riddles. A new kind of participation is called for in Hervé Tullet's **Press Here** (P–I). With a board cover and sturdy pages, this sixty-two-page book demonstrates that, with a little bit of imagination, a book can be just as interactive as an iPad. Denise Fleming's **Shout! Shout It Out!** (N), discussed previously, requires a more vocal participation.

• • PREDICTABLE OR • • PATTERNED BOOKS

Learning to read and being able to unlock the secrets of a printed page mark an important step toward maturity. Many storybooks and nonfiction books are available for developing readers, including some we have already discussed. There are also many picture-books that are written with a high degree of predictability and not much text—predictable books that support children's attempts at independent reading.

Books with sparse text and predictable books are ideal material for the child who is beginning to pay attention to print. Beginning-to-read books are perfect for children who have just become independent readers but still need the support of simple but interesting texts. Picture storybooks, with and without words, books of poetry and song, and nonfiction books continue to play an important role in a child's reading as well.

Predictable books are structured using strong language patterns, such as repeated phrases, rhyme, and rhythm; cumulative story structures that add, or accumulate, information; and familiar concepts, songs, or sequences (like days of the week). Detailed illustrations reinforce the language patterns and provide a visual reproduction of the text. These attributes help children anticipate what is going to happen next and predict the next word to come. Many four- and five-year-old children can make predictions and use their knowledge of phonics to read books on their own after hearing them read aloud once or twice. In **The Seals on the Bus** (N–P) Lenny Hort replicates the pattern of a familiar song, turning the wheels on the bus into the seals on the bus who go "errp, errp, errp" all around the town. Emily Gravett's storybook, **Monkey and Me** (N) is predictable, as is her **Orange Pear Apple Bear** (N–P), which contains only five words, with the illustrations providing heavy support for the streamlined plot, which involves a bear who finds, and eventually eats, each of the fruits in the title of the story.

Dayle Ann Dodds's **Where's Pup?** (N–P) contains simple text consisting of two- and three-word sentences, rhyming words, and a limited vocabulary, yet manages to tell an engaging story that young children can actually read on their own. Pierre Pratt's colorful illustrations provide a context that both engages and supports young readers. In **Red Sled** (N–P), Patricia Thomas signals by the title that the book will be composed of pairs of rhyming words that tell the story of a boy and his father who go sledding and finish their winter's evening by having some hot chocolate and going to bed. Reading involves sampling, predicting, and confirming (Goodman, 1985; Smith, 1978). Fluent readers build hypotheses about text meaning as they read. They predict a probable meaning based on the information sampled, and then confirm it by checking to see if it makes sense, matches the letter–sound correspondence in the print, and sounds like real language. For beginning readers, patterned books are ideal fare because they match expectations every step of the way. Poetry also meets the criteria. Through rhythm, repetition, and rhyme, Jane Yolen creates a story in **How Do Dinosaurs Say Goodnight?** (P) that uses dinosaurs to capture childlike behavior. Beginning readers chime in the second time through the book and soon can read it on their own.

Patterned, predictable books help beginning readers confirm their knowledge of sound–letter correspondence. Often the books have an illustration followed by a single line of text. For example, Mem Fox's **Where Is the Green Sheep?** (N–P), illustrated by Judy Horacek, contains patterned, lilting, rhyming statements with art that precisely reflects the language until, toward the end of the story, readers are cautioned to turn the page quietly because the green sheep is fast asleep.

• • BEGINNING TO READ BOOKS • •

Beginning-to-read books are those that children who have just become independent readers can enjoy on their own; they combine controlled vocabulary with creative storytelling and engaging illustrations. Good beginning-to-read books have strong characterization, worthy themes, and engaging plots. The sentences are generally simple, with few embedded clauses, and the language is often direct dialogue. Lines of text often are printed so that sentence breaks occur according to natural phrases; meaningful chunks of language are grouped together. Illustrations depict the characters and action in ways that reflect and extend the text, which contains a limited number of different words and tells an interesting story. David McPhail's *Boy, Bird, and Dog* (N–P) has just the right combination of simple, repetitive text, intriguing characters, and charming illustrations to intrigue emergent readers.

Sometimes simple stories such as Cynthia Rylant's *Brownie and Pearl See the Sights* (N–P) offer just enough support for young readers to be able to read on their own after hearing it read once. The illustrations by Brian Biggs help these readers guess words they may not know. Jon Scieszka's *Trucktown* series for beginning readers offers a very simple text with the jazzy illustrations that mark the books in this popular series.

Arnold Lobel's classic series, including *Frog and Toad Are Friends* (N–P), is a favorite with newly independent readers. Frog and Toad, humanlike characters in animal form, solve understandable problems with naïveté and wit. Cynthia Rylant, a wizard with words, creates *Henry and Mudge* (P), the first book in a wonderful series of stories about a large dog and the boy who loves him. The **Annie and Snowball** books, such as *Annie and Snowball and the Book Bugs Club* (N–P), utilize the same characters. Illustrations depict the action and provide emotional details about the characters. Rylant chooses words wisely; her stories are so well written that they are a pleasure to read. Denys Cazet's **Minnie and Moo** series has a loyal following of young readers. In *Minnie and Moo: Will You Be My Valentine?* (P) the humor is high and the text easy for young readers to decode. Kevin Henkes's *Old Bear* (P) gently relates the dreams of a bear during its long winter hibernation, culminating in the arrival of spring.

Other beginning to read books and transitional chapter books, often highly illustrated although they are not true picturebooks, are an important part of a young child's development as an independent reader. These books offer young readers the opportunity to read longer, more complex texts that are still supported by illustrations. We discuss them in the appropriate genre chapters.

As children grow in their reading ability, they move beyond listening to picturebooks and working with easy-to-read materials on to chapter books and then toward full-length texts. Even though children grow beyond their early reading experiences, however, they remember their happy, successful encounters with these books. These strong, positive experiences propel them into more positive connections with literature.

Studying Picturebook Art in the Classroom

In all of the previous discussion, and in the ideas for the classroom that follow, *we focused on the trade edition* of the picturebooks—the edition you would find in the children's or young adult section of a bookstore. There is also the *library edition*, the *soft-cover* (or paperback) *edition*, and the versions of picturebooks found in reading anthologies. In the library edition, the dust jacket is frequently omitted, so if the dust jacket contains a different illustration from the board covers, this element is lost. In the case of paperback editions of picturebooks, there is never a dust jacket, and endpages are frequently omitted. In anthologies, if picturebooks are reproduced, a number of elements are always omitted, and the sequence of the illustrations is sometimes shortened or otherwise changed. In anthologies, as well, page turns are changed so that the careful attention to the "drama of the turning of the page" is also lost. In all these cases, losing an element of the picturebook means losing the opportunity of talking about its possible meaning with students and the way it contributes to the picturebook as an integrated art object. Thus, we recommend, when possible, using the trade edition because it is the fullest expression of the artistic design of the whole picturebook.

Children and adolescents learn how to think and talk about the art of picturebooks by reading and responding to outstanding picturebooks. If they are guided by teachers like Bev from the opening vignette, they will learn to notice the careful use of words; the way color, shape, texture, and line are used; and the varied styles, media, and techniques that artists choose. Conversations about picturebooks help students develop their visual literacy skills.

Students who encounter excellent picturebooks learn how to read not only the words but also the pictures. They pay close attention to what they see, often discovering things in the illustrations that most adults would miss. Just as students notice the writer's craft, they notice the artist's craft and discuss it. In fact, a good question to ask students after reading a picturebook is "What do you notice?" Kiefer (1986) listened to students of all ages talk about what they noticed about elements of design in picturebooks. First graders discussed line, shape, texture, and color with ease; older students considered the expressive qualities of illustrations. In every case, teachers provided time for students to explore books, to discover and develop individual responses, and to share those responses with others. Teachers also provided a wide selection of books and gave students varied opportunities for response while sharing their knowledge of the elements of language and visual art, as well as their own critical aesthetic responses. Another powerful question begins "Why do you suppose . . ." For example, "Why do you suppose the designer chose red endpapers for this book?" or "Why do you suppose we never see the wicked stepmother's face in Nancy Elkholm Burkert's version of **Snow White**?" These types of questions invite readers to give their opinion and interpretation and to make high-level inferences, rather than suggesting, however subtly, that there is one and only one right answer.

We often think of selecting books that contain similar themes, structures, or literary devices. We can also select books that demonstrate similarities and differences in visual art. Careful selection of these "text sets" (Harste, Woodward, & Burke, 1984) can lead students to compare the use of line and color, for example, or to note how different artists use texture, light, and space. A thoughtful selection of books that demonstrate particular qualities of visual art can educate students' eyes as well as their minds and hearts. Students can also explore art first-hand, by working with various media and techniques.

Children and adolescents come to school full of images and ideas, with the imagination to expand on them. By providing them with the opportunity to explore the thousands of wonderful picturebooks that are available, we can feed their imaginations and encourage them to think about the symbol systems of language and art that we use to convey our ideas.

SUMMARY

Picturebooks hold a special place in the lives of those who read them. These books are the first exposure to fine art for many children. They enrich readers' worlds by providing opportunities for experiences through pictures and print. Illustrators use a full range of artistic elements and styles as they create picturebooks, seeking to interpret an author's words through his or her art. There are picturebooks in all genres and for all readers, each of which poses particular constraints as well as possibilities. When we experience excellent picturebooks and share them with our students, we are educating their—and our—imaginations.

In the Booklist following, we have grouped picturebooks in a manner that is different from the way we discuss them in the chapter—by the most common themes that are present in this wide-ranging and ever-changing format. We believe that the groupings may be suitable for a broad range of readers as you plan units of study that are organized around certain themes, giving you suggestions for picturebooks that you might use as part of your curricular decisions. In this Booklist are examples of the other genres that we cover in Chapters 4 through 10; use this list as a resource to enhance your knowledge as you read farther. Most, but not all of the titles in the Booklist are in addition to those discussed in the body of this chapter; most have been published since 2005, although some "classics" also appear.

Booklist

* Indicates some aspect of diversity

Family Relationships

* Atinuke, **Anna Hibiscus' Song**, illustrated by Lauren Tobia (2011) (N–P)
Bang, Molly, **In My Heart** (2006) (N)
* Bertrand, Diane Gonzales, **We Are Cousins/Somos Primos**, illustrated by Christina E. Rodriguez (2008) (N–P)

Blackall, Sophie, **Are You Awake?** (2011) (P)
Brown, Lisa, **How to Be** (2006) (N)
Brown, Ruth, **The Tale of Two Mice** (2009) (N–P)
Browne, Anthony, **My Brother** (2008) (N–P)
_____, **My Dad** (2001) (N–P)
_____, **My Mom** (2005) (N–P)
Bunge, Daniela, **The Scarves** (2006) (P)
Bunting, Eve, **Hurry! Hurry!** illustrated by Jeff Mack (2007) (N)

✳ Cisneros, Sandra, *Hairs/Pelitos*, illustrated by Terry Ybanez (1997) (P–I)

Coffelt, Nancy, *Fred Stays with Me!* illustrated by Tricia Tusa (2007) (P)

Cruise, Robin, *Only You*, illustrated by Margaret Chodos-Irvine (2007) (N–P)

Crum, Shutta, *A Family for Old Mill Farm* (2007) (N–P)

_____, *Thunder-Boomer*, illustrated by Carol Thompson (2009) (P)

✳ Cunnane, Kelly, *For You Are a Kenyan Child*, illustrated by Ana Juan (2006) (P)

Daly, Cathleen, *Prudence Wants a Pet*, illustrated by Stephen Michael King (2011) (P)

✳ Daly, Niki, *Happy Birthday, Jamela!* (2006) (P)

Davies, Nicola, *White Owl, Barn Owl*, illustrated by Michael Foreman (2008) (P–I)

✳ Diakité, Penda, *I Lost My Tooth in Africa*, illustrated by Baba Wagué Diakité (2006) (P)

✳ Dorros, Arthur, *Abuela*, illustrated by Elisa Kleven (1997) (P)

_____, *Isla*, illustrated by Elisa Kleven (1999) (P)

Duke, Kate, *The Tale of Pip and Squeak* (2007) (N–P)

England, Kathryn, *Grandfather's Wrinkles*, illustrated by Richard McFarland (2007) (P–I)

Funke, Cornelia, *The Wildest Brother*, illustrated by Kerstin Meyer (2008) (N–P)

✳ Garza, Carmen Lomas, *In My Family/En mi familia* (1997) (P)

✳ Global Fund for Children, *Global Babies* (2007) (N–P)

✳ Gravett, Emily, *Meerkat Mail* (2007) (N–P)

✳ Havill, Juanita, *Jamaica's Find* (1986/2011) (P)

Hoberman, Mary Ann, *I'm Going to Grandma's*, illustrated by Tiphanie Beeke (2007) (N–P)

Holmberg, Bo R., *A Day with Dad*, illustrated by Eva Eriksson (2008) (P)

✳ Isadora, Rachel, *What a Family!* (2006) (N–P)

_____, *Yo, Jo!* (2007) (N–P)

Jenkins, Emily, *Love You when You Whine*, illustrated by Sergio Ruzzier (2006) (N)

Johnson, Angela, *When I Am Old with You*, illustrated by David Soman (1993) (P)

✳ Joosse, Barbara M., *Mama, Do You Love Me?* illustrated by Barbara Lavallee (1991) (N–P)

✳ Kraus, Joanna H., *A Night of Tamales & Roses*, illustrated by Elena Caravela (2007) (P)

Lindbergh, Reeve, *My Little Grandmother Often Forgets*, illustrated by Kathryn Brown (2007) (N–P)

Liwska, Renata, *Little Panda* (2010) (N)

Lloyd-Jones, Sally, *How to Be a Baby . . . By Me, the Big Sister*, illustrated by Sue Heap (2007) (P)

✳ Makhijani, Pooja, *Mama's Saris*, illustrated by Elena Gomez (2007) (P–I)

Markle, Sandra, *A Mother's Journey*, illustrated by Alan Marks (2006) (P)

Matthews, Tina, *Out of the Egg* (2007) (N–P)

McAllister, Angela, *Mama and Little Joe*, illustrated by Terry Milne (2007) (N–P)

McMullan, Kate, *Papa's Song*, illustrated by Jim McMullan (2003) (N)

Nolen, Jerdine, *Pitching in for Eubie*, illustrated by E. B. Lewis (2007) (P)

Pennypacker, Sara, *Clementine*, illustrated by Marla Frazee (2008) (P)

✳ Pérez, Amada Irma, *Nana's Big Surprise: Nana, Qué Sorpresa!* illustrated by Maya Christina Gonzalez (2007) (P)

Perkins, Lynn Rae, *Pictures from Our Vacation* (2007) (P)

Polacco, Patricia, *My Rotten, Red-Headed Older Brother* (1998) (P)

Quigley, Mary, *Granddad's Fishing Buddy*, illustrated by Stéphanie Jorisch (2007) (P)

✳ Ramirez, Antonio, *Napi Goes to the Mountain*, illustrated by Domi (2006) (P)

Ransom, Jeanie Franz, *What Do Parents Do? (When You're Not Home)*, illustrated by Cyd Moore (2007) (N–P)

Ries, Lori, *Fix It, Sam*, illustrated by Sue Ramá (2007) (N–P)

✳ Stryer, Andrea Stenn, *Kami and the Yaks*, illustrated by Bert Dodson (2007) (P–I)

Sturges, Philemon, *How Do You Make a Baby Smile?* illustrated by Bridget Strevens-Marzo (2007) (N–P)

Tinkham, Kelly A., *Hair for Mama*, illustrated by Amy June Bates (2007) (P–I)

Wild, Margaret, *Piglet and Papa*, illustrated by Stephen Michael King (2007) (N–P)

✳ Williams, Vera B., *"More More More" Said the Baby* (1996) (P)

✳ Woodson, Jacqueline, *Coming on Home Soon*, illustrated by E. B. Lewis (2004) (P)

Yaccarino, Dan, *Every Friday* (2007) (N–P)

✳ Young, Ed, *My Mei Mei* (2006) (P)

Fears

Allen, Jonathan, *I'm Not Scared* (2008) (N–P)

Arnold, Tedd, *There Was an Old Lady Who Swallowed Fly Guy* (2007) (P–I)

Fine, Anne, *Jamie and Angus Together*, illustrated by Penny Dale (2007) (P)

Graves, Keith, *The Unexpectedly Bad Hair of Barcelona Smith* (2006) (N–P)

Klise, Kate, *Imagine Harry*, illustrated by M. Sarah Klise (2007) (N–P)

Kwon, Yoon-Duck, *My Cat Copies Me* (2007) (N–P)

McPhail, David, *Boy on the Brink* (2006) (P)

Pitzer, Susanna, *Not Afraid of Dogs*, illustrated by Larry Day (2006) (N–P)

Sendak, Maurice, *Mommy?* paper engineering by Matthew Reinhart; scenario by Arthur Yorinks (2006) (N–P)

Feelings

Aliki, *Feelings* (1986) (N–P)

Atkins, Jeannine, *Anne Hutchinson's Way*, illustrated by Michael Dooling (2007) (P–I)

Bang, Molly, **When Sophie Gets Angry—Really, Really Angry . . .** (2004) (N–P)

Beaumont, Karen, **Where's My T-R-U-C-K?** illustrated by David Catrow (2011) (N–P)

Brown, Ruth, **The Tale of Two Mice** (2009) (N–P)

Castello, Lauren, **Melvin and the Boy** (2011) (P)

de Varennes, Monique, **The Jewel Box Ballerinas**, illustrated by Ana Juan (2007) (P–I)

Fleming, Denise, **Mama Cat Has Three Kittens** (2002) (N–P)

Gravett, Emily, **Blue Chameleon** (2011) (N–P)

Henkes, Kevin, **Chrysanthemum** (1991) (N–P)

_____, **A Good Day** (2007) (N–P)

Hermsen, Ronald, **The Story of Giraffe**, illustrated by Guido Pigni (2007) (P)

Lakin, Patricia, **Rainy Day**, illustrated by Scott Nash (2007) (N–P)

Menchin, Scott, **Taking a Bath with the Dog and Other Things that Make Me Happy** (2007) (N–P)

Raschka, Chris, **A Ball for Daisy** (2011) (N–P)

Rosenthal, Amy Krouse, **One of Those Days**, illustrated by Rebecca Doughty (2006) (P–I)

Shannon, David, **No, David!** (1999) (N–P)

Steig, William, **Pete's a Pizza** (1998) (N–P)

Friendship

Becker, Bonny, **The Sniffles for Bear**, illustrated by Kady MacDonald Denton (2011) (N–P)

Bley, Anette, **And What Comes after a Thousand?** (2007) (P–I)

Bruel, Robert O., **Bob and Otto**, illustrated by Nick Bruel (2007) (P)

Bunge, Daniela, **Cherry Time** (2007) (P)

Bynum, Janie, **Nutmeg and Barley: A Budding Friendship** (2006) (N–P)

Chodos-Irvine, Margaret, **Best Best Friends** (2006) (N–P)

Consentino, Ralph, **The Marvelous Misadventures of … Fun Boy** (2006) (N–P)

Coombs, Kate, **The Secret-Keeper**, illustrated by Heather M. Solomon (2006) (P)

Grey, Mini, **Three by the Sea** (2010) (N–P)

Hillenbrand, Jane, **What a Treasure!** illustrated by Will Hillenbrand (2006) (N)

Hills, Tad, **Duck & Goose** (2006) (N)

Jeffers, Oliver, **Lost and Found** (2005) (N–P)

Juster, Norton, **Neville**, illustrated by G. Brian Karas (2011) (P)

Kromhout, Rindert, **Little Donkey and the Birthday Present**, illustrated by Annemarie van Haeringen, translated by Marianne Martens (2007) (N–P)

Lehman, Barbara, **Rainstorm** (2007) (N–P)

Lin, Grace, **Lissy's Friends** (2007) (P–I)

Lobel, Arnold, **Days with Frog and Toad** (1979) (P–I)

_____, **Frog and Toad Are Friends** (1970) (P–I)

_____, **Frog and Toad Together** (1972) (P–I)

McCarty, Peter, **Fabian Escapes** (2007) (N–P)

Niland, Deborah, **Annie's Chair** (2006) (N)

✳ Reiser, Lynn, **Margaret and Margarita/Margarita y Margaret** (1993) (P)

✳ _____, **My Way/A mi manera** (2007) (P)

Sakai, Komako, **Emily's Balloon** (2006) (N)

Seeger, Laura Vaccaro, **Dog and Bear: Two Friends, Three Stories** (2007) (N–P)

Shannon, George, **Rabbit's Gift**, illustrated by Laura Dronzek (2007) (N–P)

Silverman, Erica, **Cowgirl Kate and Cocoa: School Days**, illustrated by Betsy Lewin (2007) (P–I)

Stead, Philip, **A Sick Day for Amos McGee**, illustrated by Erin Stead (2010) (N)

Stein, Mathilde, **Mine!** illustrated by Mies van Hout (2007) (N–P)

Weeks, Sarah, **Pip Squeak**, illustrated by Jane Manning (2008) (P–I)

Willems, Mo, **I Am Invited to a Party!** (2007) (N–P)

_____, **Knuffle Bunny Too: A Case of Mistaken Identity** (2007) (N–P)

_____, **My Friend Is Sad** (2007) (N–P)

_____, **There Is a Bird on Your Head!** (2007) (N–P)

_____, **Today I Will Fly!** (2007) (N–P)

Humor

Agee, Jon, **My Rhinocerous** (2011) (P)

Armstrong, Jennifer, **Once upon a Banana**, illustrated by David Small (2006) (P)

Ashman, Linda, **Samantha on a Roll**, illustrated by Christine Davenur (2011) (P)

Bliss, Harry, **Bailey** (2011) (P)

Bottner, Barbara, **An Annoying ABC**, illustrated by Michael Emberley (2011) (P)

Breen, Steve, **Stick** (2007) (N–P)

Casanova, Mary, **Some Dog!** illustrated by Ard Hoyt (2007) (P–I)

Catalanotto, Peter, **Ivan the Terrier** (2007) (N–P)

Chaconas, Dori, **Virginnie's Hat**, illustrated by Holly Meade (2007) (N–P)

Church, Caroline Jayne, **Digby Takes Charge** (2007) (N–P)

Cronin, Doreen, **Click, Clack, Moo: Cows that Type**, illustrated by Betsy Lewin (2000) (P–I)

Denise, Anika, **Pigs Love Potatoes**, illustrated by Denise Christopher (2007) (N–P)

Dodds, Dayle Ann, **Teacher's Pets**, illustrated by Marylin Hafner (2006) (P)

Donnio, Sylviane, **I'd Really Like to Eat a Child**, illustrated by Dorothée de Monfried (2007) (P–I)

Flaherty, A. W., **The Luck of the Loch Ness Monster: A Tale of Picky Eating**, illustrated by Scott Magoon (2007) (N–P)

Friend, Catherine, **The Perfect Nest**, illustrated by John Manders (2007) (N–P)

Gran, Julia, **Big Bug Surprise** (2007) (N–P)

Grey, Mini, **The Adventures of the Dish and the Spoon** (2007) (P)

Harrington, Janice N., **The Chicken-Chasing Queen of Lamar County**, illustrated by Shelley Jackson (2007) (P)

Hawkes, Kevin, **The Wicked Big Toddlah Goes to New York** (2011) (N–P)

Johnson, Paul Brett, **On Top of Spaghetti** (2006) (N–P)

Jones, Sylvie, **Who's in the Tub?** illustrated by Pascale Constantin (2007) (N)

Keller, Laurie, **Do Unto Otters: A Book about Manners** (2007) (P)

Kitamura, Satoshi, **Me and My Cat** (2000) (N–P)

Krensky, Stephen, **Big Bad Wolves at School**, illustrated by Brad Sneed (2007) (N–P)

Landström, Lena, **Boo and Baa Have Company**, illustrated by Olof Landström; translated by Joan Sandin (2006) (N–P)

Lodge, Bernard, **Custard Surprise**, illustrated by Tim Bowers (2008) (P–I)

Metzger, Steve, **Detective Blue**, illustrated by Tedd Arnold (2011) (P)

Murray, Laura, **The Gingerbread Man Loose in the School**, illustrated by Mike Lowery (2011) (P)

Offill, Jenny, **17 Things I'm Not Allowed to Do Anymore**, illustrated by Nancy Carpenter (2006) (P–I)

Pennypacker, Sara, **The Talented Clementine**, illustrated by Marla Frazee (2008) (P–I)

Rocco, John, **Wolf! Wolf!** (2007) (P–I)

Root, Phyllis, **Aunt Nancy and the Bothersome Visitors**, illustrated by David Parkins (2007) (P–I)

Sierra, Judy, **Thelonius Monster's Sky-High Fly Pie**, illustrated by Edward Koren (2006) (P–I)

Steig, William, **Pete's a Pizza** (1998) (N–P)

Stevens, April, **Waking Up Wendell**, illustrated by Tad Hills (2007) (P)

Stevens, Susan Crummel, **Ten-Gallon Bart,** illustrated by Dorothy Donohue (2006) (P)

Swallow, Pamela Curtis, **Groundhog Gets a Say**, illustrated by Denise Brunkus (2005) (P)

Tomas, Jan, **What Will Fat Cat Sit on?** (2007) (N–P)

Watt, Mélanie, **Chester** (2007) (P–I)

———, **Chester's Back!** (2008) (P–I)

Weaver, Tess, **Cat Jumped In!** illustrated by Emily Arnold McCully (2007) (N–P)

Weston, Carrie, **If a Chicken Stayed for Supper**, illustrated by Sophie Fatus (2007) (N–P)

Willems, Mo, **Don't Let the Pigeon Drive the Bus!** (2003) (P)

———, **Don't Let the Pigeon Stay Up Late!** (2006) (P)

———, **Edwina, The Dinosaur Who Didn't Know She Was Extinct** (2006) (N)

———, **The Pigeon Finds a Hot Dog** (2004) (P)

Books for Older Children and Adolescents

✳ Bruchac, Joseph, **Crazy Horse's Vision**, illustrated by S. D. Nelson (2007) (A)

✳ Bunting, Eve, **Smoky Night**, illustrated by David Diaz (1994) (A)

———, **The Wall**, illustrated by Ronald Himler (1990) (A)

✳ Feelings, Tom, **The Middle Passage** (1995) (A)

✳ ———, **Soul Looks Back in Wonder** (1993) (A)

✳ Hopkinson, Deborah, **Sweet Clara and the Freedom Quilt**, illustrated by James E. Ransome (2003) (I)

Innocenti, Robert, **Rose Blanche** (1985) (A)

Macaulay, David, **Black and White** (1990) (A)

✳ Maruki, Toshi, **Hiroshima No Pika** (1982) (A)

✳ McKissack, Patricia, **Never Forgotten,** illustrated by Leo and Diane Dillon, (2011) (I–A)

✳ Polacco, Patricia, **Pink and Say** (1994) (I–A)

✳ Say, Allen, **Grandfather's Journey** (1993) (I–A)

Sciezka, Jon, **Math Curse**, illustrated by Lane Smith (1995) (I–A)

———, **Science Verse**, illustrated by Lane Smith (2004) (I–A)

———, **The Stinky Cheese Man and Other Fairly Stupid Tales**, illustrated by Lane Smith (1992) (I–A)

Sís, Peter, **The Tree of Life: Charles Darwin** (2003) (I–A)

———, **The Wall: Growing Up Behind the Iron Curtain** (2007) (I–A)

Steig, William, **Caleb and Kate** (1986) (A)

Tan, Shaun, **Lost & Found** (2011) (I–A)

Van Allsburg, Chris, **Bad Day at Riverbend** (1995) (I–A)

———, **The Wretched Stone** (1991) (I–A)

Additional resources to accompany this chapter can be found on the Education CourseMate website. Go to CengageBrain .com to access a variety of interactive study tools and useful resources including Video Conversations with children's book authors and illustrators, a searchable children's literature database, glossary flashcards, online activities, tutorial quizzes, links to relevant websites, and more.

Poetry and Verse

In his careful welter of dried leaves and seeds,
soil samples, quartz pebbles, notes-to-myself, letters,
on Dr. Carver's bedside table
next to his pocket watch,
folded in Aunt Mariah's Bible:
the Bill of Sale.
Seven hundred dollars
for a thirteen-year-old girl named Mary.

—MARILYN NELSON
"Bedside Reading" in **Carver: A Life in Poems,** *p. 41**

When Lila finishes reading "Bedside Reading" the room is silent as the eighth-grade students understand that the girl, Mary, was George Washington Carver's mother. Lila has been reading a handful of poems aloud each day, and the discussion has been lively. Students have argued about what kind of a book **Carver** (A) is—poetry to be sure, but also historical fiction, perhaps, or possibly even a biography. At this point they seem to have agreed that it is both poetry and biography, and are now wondering if this could be called a novel in verse, like Karen Hesse's **Out of the Dust** (A), which several of the students in class have read. Lila welcomes this discussion but also wants her students to consider the content of the poem they have just heard. Words such as *love, slavery, loneliness,* and *belief* soon push the discussion to a consideration of how alone Carver must have felt, how difficult it was to be an educated black man in the late nineteenth century in America, even with a position at Tuskegee Institute. They go back to the poems "My People" and "Odalisque" and talk about the difficulty of being different, something they have all experienced, or at least worried about. Eventually, Lila guides the discussion to a consideration of what they are coming to understand about George Washington Carver and his life, how he is now much more than the "peanut man"—now that they understand something about his spirit because of Marilyn Nelson's poems.

Poetry is a window to the soul of a poet, whose choice of words and ideas and emotions reveal it. Perhaps it also stirs the soul of the reader engaged by a poem. Perhaps, in this case, it is also the soul of the subject of the poems. George Washington Carver is revealed as a deeply spiritual man living a life of service, struggle, and abiding love. At its best, poetry such as this offers readers the opportunity to explore emotions, ideas, and the extraordinary use of language.

Defining Poetry

Defining poetry is perhaps the most difficult thing about poetry. It is easier to say what poetry does than to describe what it is. We know that poetry can make us chuckle or laugh aloud, startle us with insight, or surprise us with its clarity. Some poems express feelings that we did not even know we had until we read them, presenting the familiar in a way that surprises.

Carver: A Life in Poems is a biographical novel in verse that captures much more than the life of George Washington Carver.

Then we say, "Yes, that's just the way it is!" Poetry deals with the essence of life and experience. "Poems have a unique sense of contained energy, made as they are from words used in the most precise and evocative form," say anthologists Michael and Peter Benton. "Poems have their effects upon us as much by sounds, rhythms, associations, shapes, and forms as by lexical definition" (2008, pp. 136–137). Although good prose and poetry share many of the same stylistic devices, poetry is marked by the "saturation" of its language.

Poets themselves are often the best source for a definition of poetry. Robert Frost (1939) notes that "a poem begins in delight and ends in wisdom." Poetry, says poet Gregory Corso (1983, p. 11), is "the opposite of hypocrisy." Poet Ron Koertge agrees with Emily Dickinson that writers of poetry need to "tell all the Truth, but tell it slant" (2006, p. 539). Poetry combines rich meaning with sounds of language arranged in an interesting form. Poet J. Patrick Lewis calls it "ear candy." Poets select

words and arrange them carefully to call attention to experiences in a fresh, new way. Samuel Taylor Coleridge distinguished between prose, "words in their best order," and poetry, "the best words in the best order." Poetry has an economy of form that prose rarely contains. Eve Merriam once remarked that poetry is like a can of frozen juice, becoming prose only when diluted.

Many poets write poems about poetry. Bobbye Goldstein's ***Inner Chimes: Poems on Poetry*** (P–I–A) contains several poems about poetry. In "Inside a Poem," from ***It Doesn't Always Have to Rhyme*** (P–I), Eve Merriam captures the essence of poetry and reveals some of its characteristics. She says poetry has a beat that repeats, words that chime, an inner chime, and images not imagined before. Eleanor Farjeon gives a more elusive definition in ***Poems for Children*** (P–I) when she says that it is "Not the rose, but the scent of the rose." Poet Kristine O'Connell George writes about herself as a poet in "The Blue Between" in Paul B. Janeczko's ***Seeing the Blue Between: Advice and Inspiration for Young Poets*** (A), pointing out that poets view the world in a special way, not looking at the shapes of the clouds in the sky, but at the sky between those shapes—unlike most people.

Poets and critics also often distinguish between poetry and verse. Noted poet and anthologist Myra Cohn Livingston argued that there was a clear difference; generally, the variation in emotional intensity distinguishes verse and poetry, with verse being much less intense than poetry. Anthologist Liz Rosenberg puts it succinctly: "Shel Silverstein … worked in a tradition of light verse … [but] has moments of poetry in his light verse, just as Shakespeare deliberately plants ditties in the midst of his great poetic plays. But by and large verse and poetry are two separate creatures, like the difference between standup comedy and *A Midsummer Night's Dream*" (2005, p. 375). Verse, such as Jon Agee's ***Orangutan Tongs: Poems to Tangle Your Tongue*** (P), and Alma Flor Ada and F. Isabel Campay's bilingual ***¡Muu, Moo!: Rimas de animales/Animal Nursery Rhymes*** (N), illustrated by Viví Escrivá, is often amusing and generally not intense. It is meant to delight, and does so all over the world as books such as Halfdan Rasmussen's ***A Little Bitty Man and Other Poems for the Very Young*** (N/P), illustrated by Kevin Hawkes and translated from the Danish by Marilyn Nelson and Pamela Espeland demonstrate. Poetry is intense, an intricate combination of the sounds, meanings, and arrangement of words to call attention to something in a fresh, compelling manner. In this chapter we explore both poetry and verse for young readers.

A Brief History of Poetry for Young Readers

Verse written especially for children appears in folklore, with Mother Goose verses some of the earliest poetic forms to delight the ears and tickle the tongues of children. Whereas doggerel, sentimental lines, riddles, and traditional rhymes were plentiful, poetry written especially for children began to flower only in the nineteenth century. Some truly great works, though written for adults, preceded this. For example, the English poet William Blake (1757–1827) captured the spirit of childhood in verse. The poems in **Songs of Innocence and Experience** (1789) portray the human mind with a childlike quality. Blake's poems show the child as refreshingly curious and responding intuitively to unfathomable beauty.

Ann Taylor (1782–1866) and Jane Taylor (1783–1824) published **Original Poems for Infant Minds by Several Young Persons** in 1804. These verses reflected a childlike spirit despite subtle lessons. "Twinkle, Twinkle, Little Star" is a song that children sing today. This and other early poems, such as "Mary Had a Little Lamb" (1830) by Sarah Josepha Hale and "Will You Walk into My Parlor? Said the Spider to the Fly" in **Hymns and Fire-side Verses** by Mary Howitt (1799–1888), were dispersed so widely it is difficult to remember that they are not folklore.

Most nineteenth-century poets had a strong desire to teach lessons, but some went beyond preachy moralistic verses. A few early English poets portrayed life from a child's point of view and sang the pleasures of childhood as children might have seen them. Some of these include Edward Lear, **A Book of Nonsense** (1846); Robert Louis Stevenson, **A Child's Garden of Verses** (1885); and A. A. Milne, **When We Were Very Young** (1924) and **Now We Are Six** (1927). An American, Clement C. Moore, wrote **A Visit from St. Nicholas** (1823), a poem that is a rarity because it is free from the didactic teachings of the time. It is now generally known as "The Night before Christmas."

In the last half of the twentieth century, poetry for children flourished, with poets such as Aileen Fisher, David McCord, Eve Merriam, Myra Cohn Livingston, John Ciardi, and Karla Kuskin providing young readers with opportunities for delight. Some classics, such as Langston Hughes's work, continue to speak to young readers. Hughes's **The Dream Keeper and Other Poems** (A) is currently available in a beautiful seventy-fifth anniversary edition, illustrated by Brian Pinkney.

Late twentieth-century authors, such as Shel Silverstein and Jack Prelutsky, were both prolific and successful, as were others who penned the "urchin verse" that children so delighted in (Thomas, 2007). There were also three Newbery Awards given to poets. The first went to Nancy Willard in 1982 for **A Visit to William Blake's Inn: Poems for Innocent and Experienced Travelers** (I), the second to Paul Fleischman in 1989 for **Joyful Noise: Poems for Two Voices** (I–A), and the third to Karen Hesse in 1998 for her verse novel, **Out of the Dust** (A). In 2002, Marilyn Nelson received a Newbery Honor for **Carver: A Life in Poems** (A), and Joyce Sidman received a Newbery Honor in 2011 for **Dark Emperor & Other Poems of the Night** (I–A). We take a close look at these books later in this chapter. In 2006, Jack Prelutsky became the first children's poet laureate in the United States, followed by Mary Ann Hoberman and. J. Patrick Lewis, the current children's poet laureate.

A late twentieth-century phenomenon, the verse novel for children, began in 1993 with Virginia Euwer Wolff's **Make Lemonade** (A). Verse novels are narrative in structure, contain the condensed language found in poetry, and are usually intensely focused on characters' feelings (Campbell, 2004, p. 614). Most scholars agree that Karen Hesse's Newbery Award brought mainstream attention to the verse novel, increasing with a National Book Award for Virginia Euwer Wolff's **True Believer** (A) and a Printz Award for Angela Johnson's **The First Part Last** (A). Since that time, many writers have experimented with verse novels, with more than a dozen published for adolescents in 2004 alone. We look at verse novels closely later in this chapter.

In 1977, the National Council of Teachers of English (NCTE) established an award to honor poets who write for children. The award, established in memory of Bee Cullinan's son Jonathan (born 1969, died 1975), recognizes the outstanding contribution of a poet who writes expressly for children. The award is given for the entire body of a poet's work for children. This was an annual award from 1977 through 1982. In 1983, a new policy was instituted to present the award every three years. In 2008, things changed again, and the award is now bestowed every other year, with the latest given in 2011. The combined works of the poets who have received the award thus far form the foundation for poetry study in the field of children's literature. Brief profiles of the NCTE award winners—David McCord, Aileen Fisher, Karla Kuskin, Myra Cohn Livingston, Eve Merriam, John Ciardi, Lilian Moore, Arnold Adoff, Valerie Worth, Barbara Juster Esbensen, Eloise Greenfield, X. J. Kennedy, Mary Ann Hoberman, Nikki Grimes, Lee Bennett Hopkins, and J. Patrick

P R O F I L E S

David McCord, 1977

Poetry, like rain, should fall with elemental music, and poetry for children should catch the eye as well as the ear and the mind. It should delight; it really has to delight. Furthermore, poetry for children should keep reminding them, without any feeling on their part that they are being reminded, that the English language is a most marvelous and availing instrument.

David McCord is considered the dean of children's poets. His collected works appear in **One at a Time**. Other popular collections of his work appear in **Every Time I Climb a Tree** and **For Me to Say**. "Nature abounds in McCord's poetry," noted David A. Dillon (1978), "and the reader is treated to a sensual feast of sights, sounds, and touch, captured as a result of the poet's careful observation of common things which many of us fail to notice[:] colors, speeds, sizes, textures, shapes" (p. 379). David McCord was the first recipient of the NCTE Award for Excellence in Poetry for Children.

Aileen Fisher, 1978

Poetry is a rhythmical piece of writing that leaves the reader feeling that life is a little richer than before, a little more full of wonder, beauty, or just plain delight.

"Since the early 1930s," commented Lee Bennett Hopkins (1978), "Aileen Fisher … has reached and touched thousands upon thousands of children with her warm, wise and wonderful writing" (p. 868). A nature poet, Fisher lived as a child on forty acres of land near the Iron Range on the Upper Peninsula of Michigan. She returned to the country as an adult to write full time. Her popular books include **Sing of the Earth and Sky: Poems about Our Planet and the Wonders Beyond; Always Wondering; The House of a Mouse; Like Nothing at All: Out in the Dark and Daylight; Rabbits, Rabbits**; and **Anybody Home?**.

Karla Kuskin, 1979

If there were a recipe for a poem, these would be the ingredients: word sounds, rhythm, description, feeling, memory, rhyme, and imagination. They can be put together a thousand different ways, a thousand, thousand … more.

An artist as well as a poet, Karla Kuskin designed the medallion for the NCTE poetry award; when she won the same award three years later, friends teased her about designing awards she would win. "Her pictures and her verse and poetry," noted Alvina Treut Burrows (1979), "are brimming over with the experiences of children growing up in a big city" (p. 935). Fittingly, Kuskin's poetry appears in New York subways as part of the Poetry in Motion program. Her most popular books include **Near the Window Tree: Poems and Notes; Dogs and Dragons, Trees and Dreams: A Collection of Poems; The Upstairs Cat; The Sky Is Always in the Sky**; and **I Am Me**. Her anthology, **Moon, Have You Met My Mother?**, is a collection of all her poems.

To learn more about the poets honored with this award, go to CengageBrain.com to access the Education CourseMate website where you will find links to relevant websites.

The opening quotations for these profiles are from the poets' acceptance speeches for the NCTE poetry award. (The speech is given in November of the year the award is received.)

Lewis appear throughout this chapter. Visit the Education CourseMate site at CengageBrain.com for links to relevant websites including more information about this award.

Today, we find poetry in many formats, ranging from picturebooks containing a single poem to picturebooks and longer collections containing a number of poems by either one (*individual*) or many (*collective*) poets. If the collection is focused on one topic, it is called a *specialized anthology* and can be either individual or collective. A collection of one poet's work may be either a *specialized* or *general* anthology; *general, collective* anthologies contain works by many poets on several subjects. All of these types of anthologies allow young readers to browse through poetry and discover favorites.

*This picturebook, **Harlem**, contains a single poem by Walter Dean Myers, which celebrates the community of Harlem. The stunning collage art by Christopher Myers illuminates the people and the place.*

Single-poem picturebooks with beautiful illustrations provide excellent opportunities to explore poetry as visually interpreted by fine artists, as we discuss in Chapter 3. This can lead to some surprises. For example, illustrator Christopher Myers takes a single text, Lewis Carroll's **Jabberwocky** (I–A), to a new place by illustrating it in a unique, contemporary fashion as a basketball game. Christopher Myers also collaborates with his father, writer Walter Dean Myers, on stunning books such as the Caldecott Honor– and Coretta Scott King Award–winning **Harlem**. This powerful poem explores the strength and depth of this vibrant community while the collage art illuminates Harlem's spirit. Other book-length single poems include Alice Walker's **Why War Is Never a Good Idea** (I), illustrated by Stefano Vitale, and Giselle Potter's stunning visual interpretation of the Eugene Field classic **Wynken, Blynken, and Nod** (N).

Picturebooks that are also specialized anthologies may be created by one poet, as in Joyce Carol Thomas's **The Blacker the Berry** (I), illustrated by Floyd Cooper, and Jane Yolen's **Birds of a Feather** (I), illustrated by Jason Stemple. Kristine O'Connell George created a series of poems that explore sibling relationships in **Emma Dilemma: Big Sister Poems** (P–I), illustrated by Nancy Carpenter. In **Roots and Blues: A Celebration** (I–A), with illustrations by R. Gregory Christie, Arnold Adoff has created a series of poems and poetic prose pieces that celebrate the blues, exploring its roots in the rhythms of Africa, development during the tribulations of slave times, and its place in our time.

Some of the best of these books are structured so that the poems build on one another to create a book that is tightly woven, as exemplified by Joyce Sidman's individual specialized anthology **The World According to Dog: Poems and Teen Voices** (A). Sidman's poems capture the essence of four-legged friends and their relationships with the teens who love them in images that empower advanced readers to almost reach out and pet the dogs featured in the anthology. Sidman uses her poet's eye to create poems about color in another specialized anthology, **Red Sings from Treetops: A Year in Colors** (P–I–A), beautifully illustrated by Pamela Zagarenski, who won a Caldecott Honor for her work.

Specialized anthologies also may contain the selected works of several poets, as in Lee Bennett Hopkins's **Dizzy Dinosaurs: Silly Dino Poems** (P), a poetry collection especially for newly independent readers. His **I Am the Book** (P–I), illustrated by Yayo, celebrates books and reading. Jane Yolen and Andrew Peters's collection, **Switching on the Night: A Very First Book of Bedtime Poems** (N), is wonderful to read aloud while exploring Brian Karas's paintings, which accompany the poems.

Anthologies might focus on a form of poetry rather than a particular topic, although sometimes these go hand in hand, as in Betsy Franco's collection of concrete poems, **A Dazzling Display of Dogs** (P), with digital illustrations by Michael Wertz. In **Dogku** (P), illustrated by Tim Bowers, Andrew Clements tells the story of a stray dog who finds a home in a series of haiku, which, together, form a narrative.

Palestinian American poet Naomi Shihab Nye's **19 Varieties of Gazelle: Poems of the Middle East** (A) contains sixty of her own poems that bring the sights, sounds, smells, and tastes of Palestine to adolescent readers while also serving as a commentary on the tragedy of 9/11. Her **Honeybee: Poems & Short Prose** (A) is a blend of more than eighty poems and prose paragraphs that explore prejudice, war, peace, kindness, and Arab Americans.

The collective, generalized anthology by X. J. Kennedy and Dorothy Kennedy, **Talking Like the Rain** (P–I), contains poems arranged under informative headings. The book is a pleasure to skim, read, or savor. David McCord's individual general anthology, *One at a Time* (P–I), is an impressive volume containing most of his poetry. Karla Kuskin's collected works, *Moon, Have You Met My Mother?* (P) and Valerie Worth's *All the Small Poems and Fourteen More* (P) are wonderful resources for adults who share poetry with primary-grade students. Collections of works by authors such as Shel Silverstein, such as *A Light in the Attic* (I–A), and Jack Prelutsky, including *The New Kid on the Block* (I), delight upper elementary and even middle-school readers.

In this chapter we will:

- Consider quality in poems and anthologies.
- Explore how poets use language.
- Discuss examples of poetic structure.
- Suggest why poetry is vital in classrooms.

Considering Quality in Poetry and Poetry Anthologies

We value poems that have stood the test of time as well as poetry books that have won significant awards and have received positive reviews from literary critics. Most of all, however, we treasure poems that speak to our sense of delight, wonder, recognition, or emotional state. The final test, after all, is the level of reader engagement. When evaluating individual poems for young readers, consider how well they speak to their intended audience, the quality of their use of language, and the aptness of their form. The intended reader should easily be able to understand the content of a poem, and it should prove meaningful to him or her as well. Outstanding poets know how to use language in ways that enhance meaning. So, too, do poets structure a poem in a manner in which the form conveys meaning.

We judge anthologies of poetry both by the quality of the individual poems they contain and by the overall structure and content of the entire collection. Excellent anthologies have "a generous *inclusiveness* which acknowledges [the range] of poems students may enjoy, feel provoked by, remember, and, maybe, find valuable" (Benton & Benton, 2008, p. 137). The arrangement of poetry in an anthology and the overall impact of that arrangement also determine the quality. Figure 4.1 suggests some criteria to use as you evaluate books of poetry. Keep

FIGURE 4.1

Checklist for Assessing Quality in Poetry

Individual Poems Demonstrate:

- Content that is interesting to and understandable by intended readers.
- Language that is innovative, with careful word choices and use of poetic devices to enhance meaning.
- Form or structure that helps readers understand more about the poetic subject or mood.

Anthologies Demonstrate:

- Purposeful selection of quality poetry.
- Arrangement that is logical.
- Inclusiveness of a range of poetry.

the criteria in mind as you search for excellent poetry books to delight young readers.

• • CONTENT THAT • • SPEAKS TO READERS

Research tells us that young readers like poetry they can understand. Of course, they do! This does not mean, however, that poetry for children or adolescents has to be simple or lighthearted. The emotions expressed in poetry run the gamut from humor to delight to despair. Indeed, many poems originally intended for adults have found their way into young readers' anthologies—and into their hearts. Readers of all ages find content engaging when it relates to their own interests and experiences. Because young readers have so many varied interests and experiences, we cannot really decide which topics are "best" for any reader because readers vary so widely. We can, however, evaluate the presentation of that content. Here are two poems that explore the same general topic—the absence of a father from a child's life—written from two different perspectives, a young child's and a young adult's point of view.

The first, from the book *Fathers, Mothers, Sisters, Brothers* (N–P), by Mary Ann Hoberman, is understandable by young children.

MY FATHER*

My father doesn't live with us.
It doesn't help to make a fuss,
But still I feel unhappy, plus
I miss him.

My father doesn't live with me.
He's got another family;
He moved away when I was three.
I miss him.

I'm always happy on the day
He visits and we talk and play;
But after he has gone away
I miss him.

MARY ANN HOBERMAN

Contrast the feeling of loneliness in this poem with that same feeling in a poem found in Paul Janeczko's anthology **Looking for Your Name: A Collection of Contemporary Poems** (A).

THE ABSENT FATHER**

Perhaps a wish, perhaps a memory of rocking
in your arms.

Reaching up to you expecting to be lifted to
the sky.

Riding piggyback. Playing Trust Me:
standing straight and falling back and you
would catch—
no, that was Uncle Dan.

Hiking down a grassy slope, across a dusty
field
to a huge yellow tent, roped and staked,
and inside: girls in pink
swivel on circling elephants, trapeze families
swing from the roof, wide-mouthed clowns
pratfall, lunge at us in the front row —
me and Uncle Jerry.

Summer days at the ocean, I learn the math
of waves, the pulse of tide with Mother.

With you, what voyage?
What event or conversation, you and I?
What skill, what lore?

Not learning to ride a bike
or skate or read or write
or dance or sing in any language
or play a finger game or pray—

For a moment, you put down your paper,
let me kiss your cheek good night.

But nothing! Nothing
to remember I learned to live
to love us by.

LEE SHARKEY

Both of these poets speak of loneliness, of missing a close relationship with a father, yet they are very different in the *way* they speak about it, with Sharkey presenting a much more implicit, complex notion of what is missed than Hoberman does. Hoberman uses rhyme, meter, and repetition to explicitly state what is missed. The topic of both poems is understandable to all levels of readers. The manner in which the content is presented—the voice that speaks the words and the way they are spoken—varies according to the intended audience.

When selecting poems, however, it is important to not underestimate the verbal and emotional intelligence of young readers. Further, even if we are looking for poetry only to enhance a particular curricular topic, the poetry still needs to be excellent. For example, books such as Jane Yolen's **Fine Feathered Friends: Poems for Young People** (P) combine beauty with information. The photographs by her son, illustrator Jason Stemple, and the poetry are spectacular, and the information that appears in inserts is accurate and engaging. Francisco X. Alarcón's bilingual **Animal Poems of the Iguazu/Animalario del Iguazu** (P) uses humor and beauty to allow the creatures of the Iguazu rain forest to plead for continued existence. Maya Christina Gonzalez's mixed-media illustrations draw the eye with color and texture that bring the rain forest to life.

Joyce Sidman's **Butterfly Eyes and Other Secrets of the Meadow: Poems** (I), combines beautiful language in various poetic forms, all of which are riddles, with stunning illustrations by Beth Krommes, as it explores the hidden world of a meadow. In **Song of the Water Boatman and Other Pond Poems** (I), she combines a variety of poetic forms accompanied by an informational paragraph as she explores life in a wetland from spring through fall. Becky Prange's gorgeous woodcuts add to the information given, but also heighten the aesthetic impact of the book. In **Ubiquitous: Celebrating Nature's Survivors** (I), her poems again vary in form, but all center on nature's evolutionary successes. The additional informational boxes on each double-page spread and Beckie Prange's linocuts and watercolor illustrations make this book of poetry a useful science text as well. Douglas Florian's cycle of seasonal books, **Summersaults** (P), **Autumblings** (P), **Winter Eyes** (P), and **Handsprings** (P) capture the spirit of each season with word play, humor, and striking watercolor illustrations. David Elliott's brief, simple verse in **On the Farm** (P) offers brief, insightful

P|R|O|F|I|L|E|S

Myra Cohn Livingston, 1980

rained as a traditionalist in poetry, I feel strongly about the importance of order imposed by fixed forms, meter, and rhyme when I write about some things; yet free verse seems more suitable for other subjects. It is the force of what I say that shapes the form.

Myra Cohn Livingston was highly respected for her "commitment to the need for higher standards for children's creative writing" (Porter, 1980, p. 901). She published approximately eighty books of poetry and writings about poetry. Her work includes such titles as *Riddle-Me Rhymes, Lots of Limericks, Call Down the Moon,* and *Poem-Making: Ways to Begin Writing Poetry.*

Eve Merriam, 1981

here is a physical element in reading poetry out loud; it's like jumping rope or throwing a ball. If we can get teachers to read poetry, lots of it,

out loud to children, we'll develop a generation of poetry readers; we may even have some poetry writers, but the main thing [is] we'll have language appreciators.

It is the physical thrill of poetry "that Eve Merriam want[ed] children to experience for themselves" (Sloan, 1981, p. 958). She felt that "Children, like poets, are intrigued by the wonderful things that words can do: how their sounds mimic what is being described, how puns are possible, how language can be made . . . to 'natter, patter, chatter, and prate.' " Merriam's poetry is widely anthologized. Some of her books include *It Doesn't Always Have to Rhyme; There Is No Rhyme for Silver; The Singing Green: New and Selected Poems for All Seasons*; and *Higgle Wiggle: Happy Rhymes.*

John Ciardi, 1982

oetry and learning are both fun, and children are full of an enormous relish for both. My poetry is just a bubbling up of a natural

foolishness and the idea that maybe you can make language dance a bit.

"There is magic in the poetry John Ciardi has written for children," said Norine Odland (1982, p. 872). She felt that the "humor in his poems allows a child to reach for new ways to view ordinary things and places in the world." John Ciardi began writing poetry for his own children. His first book was *The Reason for the Pelican.* Other favorites include *You Read to Me, I'll Read to You; You Know Who; The Monster Den: Or Look What Happened at My House—and to It; The Man Who Sang the Sillies*; and *I Met a Man.*

To learn more about the poets honored with this award, go to CengageBrain.com to access the Education CourseMate website where you will find links to relevant websites.

The opening quotations for these profiles are from the poets' acceptance speeches for the NCTE poetry award. (The speech is given in November of the year the award is received.)

---

observations of farm life while Holly Meade's colored woodcuts draw readers in.

• • LANGUAGE THAT ENHANCES • • MEANING

Scholars have noted that with poetry what matters is not so much "what" it means as "how it says what it means" (Nodelman, 1996). Outstanding poems capture readers' attention with innovative ways to use words. Nothing about poetic language is mundane or prosaic. Poets choose words carefully to describe objects, events, feelings, or ideas in new and surprising ways. Although their words, like their subjects, may be familiar ones, poets select and arrange them purposefully to capture

our imagination. The experience conveyed in poetry may be commonplace, but it becomes extraordinary when seen through the poet's eye. Those who enjoy jazz, for example, will find new ways to think about that music when reading Walter Dean Myers's *Jazz* (I), vibrantly illustrated by Christopher Myers; and those who have never listened to jazz will find themselves wanting to do so after experiencing these poems.

The language of poetry startles us into seeing with wide-open eyes just how extraordinary are our thoughts and experiences, even seemingly ordinary subjects as those studied in school. Jon Scieszka and illustrator Lane Smith brought their trademark humor and brilliant collaboration to the making of *Math Curse* (I) and *Science Verse* (I). J. Patrick Lewis, also a master at writing poetry on various school topics, such as **Mathmatickles!** (I), created **Scien-Trickery: Riddles in Science** (I), a text in which the answers to his science riddles are hidden on the pages.

Sometimes the language that poets use contains strong rhythm and rhyme to express meaning; others write in free verse in which there is no regular rhyme or rhythm, but rather a specific structure built to reinforce meaning. Many use alliteration, assonance, or onomatopoeia to express their ideas; others do not. The elements of sound—whichever a poet chooses to use—are so important in poetry that it is often said that a poem cannot be truly understood until it is read aloud. Sometimes what a poet wants to convey is best expressed through figurative language, such as metaphor, simile, and personification, or through vivid imagery; at other times, this would be inappropriate. In all poetry, however, word choice and arrangement is central because the connotation, or what a word suggests, is often as important as the denotation, or the literal meaning of a word. How these carefully selected words are arranged also affects the sound of a poem and helps to shape the connotations of individual words. These and other poetic techniques, listed and defined in Figure 4.2, are the linguistic tools of a poet's trade, and success or failure can be judged by how carefully the poet has selected and used these tools.

We explore how various poets use these devices later in this chapter. Here, we take a close look at Joyce Sidman's Newbery Honor–winning **Dark Emperor & Other Poems of the Night** (I), illustrated by Rick Allen.

***

A CLOSE LOOK AT
Dark Emperor & Other Poems of the Night

A glance at the cover of this book entices readers to open it up. A huge owl takes up most of the page, tail on the lower left, head on the upper right, eyes looking down at the viewer. This, clearly, is the "dark emperor" of the title. The endpages continue the nocturnal feeling with a purple that ought to be called "twilight." They are followed by the title page, which precedes a double-page, full-bleed illustration of the cover owl flying over a woods at sunset. Throughout the book, Rick Allen's block linocut prints with gouache tints are richly textured, inviting touch. The opening double-page spread is followed by the publishing information and a table of contents. The heart of the book follows a consistent pattern of poem and small close-up illustration on the verso with a larger illustration placing the focus within a wider nocturnal context, on the recto, along with an explanatory paragraph of information in a column along the right edge. Thus, readers have four things to consider: the poems, the spot art, the larger illustration, and the prose information. This continues until the final double-page, full-bleed spread, an echo of the opening spread, but at sunrise, with the owl on a tree branch, blending into the background. This is followed by a glossary and then the endpages, now a warm golden hue.

The information in the prose sections is clear and concise. The language in the poems, in contrast, is

FIGURE 4.2

Glossary of Commonly Used Poetic Techniques

Alliteration The repetition of initial consonant sounds at close intervals

Assonance The repetition of vowel sounds at close intervals

Connotation The individual emotional implications or private meaning of a word

Consonance The repetition of internal consonant sounds at close intervals

Denotation The commonly understood or public meaning of a word

Imagery Words that appeal to the senses

Metaphor An implied comparison of unlike things

Meter A beat or measure in a line of poetry

Onomatopoeia Words that sound like their meanings

Personification Human traits given to inanimate objects

Repetition Using a word or sound over and over for effect

Rhyme Words whose ending sounds are alike. May occur at end of lines (**end rhyme**) or from the end of one line to the beginning or middle of the next (**link rhyme**)

Rhythm A recurring pattern of strong and weak beats in language

Simile A stated comparison of unlike things using *like* or *as*

Symbol A word that stands for more than its denotative meaning

Each double-page spread in Sidman's **The Dark Emperor & Other Poems of the Night** *offers detailed, textured illustrations, beautiful language, and solid scientific information.*

richly layered, replete with imagery, metaphors, personification, and other poetic techniques that help Sidman answer the question she sets out to answer: Why and how do some creatures love and thrive in the dark? In "Love Poem of the Primrose Moth," Sidman creates a mask, or persona poem and the moth speaks directly to us, describing evening and the moon as holding primroselike qualities before forthrightly declaring his love, which extends into the following day when, as we discover in the explanatory prose, the moth clings to the stem of a primrose, camouflaged to look like a primrose bud. "Dark Emperor," the title poem, is from the point of view of a small mouse, who sees the owl as a "missile." Notice the shape of the poem, in the illustration above. Sidman has created a shape, or concrete poem that visually reflects the way the mouse thinks of the owl. Do you see an owl, or a missile, or both? With other metaphors such as "sleek satellite dish" to describe the owl's swiveling head, the "cool moons" of the owl's eyes, and "symphonies" of sounds, and, of course, the "Dark Emperor" of the title, Sidman paints a picture of the owl that helps human readers perceive its power and the resulting fear of the small creatures it hunts.

Sidman's deft hand with language was recognized by the 2011 Newbery committee when they awarded her a Newbery Honor.

• • STRUCTURE THAT • • SUPPORTS MEANING

In well-constructed poems, the shape and patterns of words, lines, and stanzas, indeed of whole poems, says something about what the poem means. Poets structure their poems to reveal more about their subjects than words alone can. Skillful poets use form in sophisticated ways to convey their ideas. Word choice, arrangement, and poetic devices all come together to create a poem; poets manipulate language in many ways to best express what they want to show us. Eloise Greenfield employs a free verse form with alternating and combined voices to create the picturebook narrative poem **The Friendly Four** (P), illustrated by Jan Spivey Gilchrist. Written as a script, with each child's voice in a different color typeface, the poems tell of an unexpectedly satisfying yet challenging summer in the lives of four children. In some anthologies, poetic form is the point; all of the poems are the same form or present varied forms along with simple explanations. Marilyn Singer's **Mirror Mirror: A Book of Reversible Verse** (P–I), illustrated by Josée Masse, contains free verse poems that capture twelve folktales in two "mirror" poems each, with lines top to bottom in one, bottom to top in the mirror. This, of course provides two very different perspectives on the same tale. In this case, the structure truly *is* the meaning. In **Lemonade: And Other Poems Squeezed from a Single Word** (I), Bob Raczka also invents a new form—an amalgam of anagram, riddle, and rebus, to invite young readers and writers to play with language themselves. We look at the different ways poets structure poems throughout the remainder of this chapter. In Teaching Idea 4.1 we explore free verse.

Break It Up! Exploring Line Breaks in Free Verse Poetry

This Teaching Idea addresses the Common Core English Language Arts, Reading: Literature standard 4 Grade 2; 4, 5 Grade 3; 5 Grade 4; 4, 5 Grade 5; 5 Grades 6, 7, 8. The suggestions in this Teaching Idea may need to be adapted to suit your particular grade level and the needs of your students.

Line breaks in free verse poems are precise and purposeful; each break helps the reader understand something about the poem (Livingston, 1991; Heard, 1989). Primary and more advanced students can explore how poets use line breaks to communicate meaning in free verse poems by arranging and rearranging the words of a free verse poem in different ways. The following steps are adaptations of excellent teaching ideas presented by Georgia Heard (1989) in *For the Good of the Earth and Sun: Teaching Poetry* and by Myra Cohn Livingston (1991) in *Poem-Making: Ways to Begin Writing Poems*.

Before the Lesson

- Select a free verse poem that describes an experience you can easily help students visualize, then record the poem on chart paper or computer for projection. Create copies of the words of the poem arranged in a continuous manner, with space between each so that students can cut them apart.

During the Lesson

- Have students close their eyes as you lead them in visualizing the experience depicted in the poem, using as many descriptive words as you can (Heard, 1989). Help the students see, hear, and touch the subject of the poem. After they have visualized and talked about the experience you described, tell them that a poet described that same experience using free verse.

- Give students a copy of the words of the poem in a continuous line and ask them to cut them apart. Challenge them to arrange the words in an order that will captures their visualized experience. For example, if the poem is about a person feeling lonely, students may choose to put the word *lonely* by itself in a line to emphasize the meaning of the word and the mood of the poem.

- As students arrange the words with different line breaks, encourage them to be thoughtful about their choices; ask them to explain how their choices capture the meaning of the poem. Encourage students to think innovatively—get excited about their poetic decisions! Participate and revise the model. Talk out loud as you consider and reconsider your own line break choices; rearrange "your" index cards to reflect more clearly what the class considers to be the essence of the poem's subject.

- After students have arranged their words, have them tape them onto a sheet of paper and then read what they have done with the whole class. If you are the one reading, you can help them learn to "read" line breaks by talking about why you paused, why you read as you did. You can discuss how the line breaks convey in form what the poet describes in words.

- Reveal (dramatically, if possible!) the poem as written and discuss how the poet made line break decisions that were both similar to and different from the decisions the class made. Talk about how both the poet and the class made their decisions based on how line breaks convey meaning in free verse poetry.

After the Lesson

- Encourage students to continue to physically manipulate the words of their own free verse poems, and provide them with time to practice using line breaks purposefully to help readers understand their poems.

Resources for Teaching about Line Breaks

- Heard, Georgia, *For the Good of the Earth and Sun: Teaching Poetry*
- Livingston, Myra Cohn, *Poem-Making: Ways to Begin Writing Poems*

Poets Use Language in Interesting Ways

Poets manipulate language to create an impact more powerful than any found in prose. Their economy of language, precision of word choice—not just the best word, but the *only* word—and placement, as well as their manipulation of poetic devices that employ sound and image to create meaning, all coalesce in stunning examples of poetry. Stylistic brilliance saturates the condensed language of poetry.

• • WORDS AS SOUND • •

Of all the elements of poetry, sound may offer the most pleasure to young readers. From an early age, children delight in hearing and chanting nursery rhymes, finger games, and lullabies. Older children also enjoy the rhyme and rhythm of jump rope chants and sidewalk games, and adolescents love their music. The use of poetic elements that relate to sound is friendly through familiarity; it invites young readers into a poem to experience a familiar pleasure in an unfamiliar manner. The choice and arrangement of sounds make poetry musical and reinforce meaning. Rhythm, rhyme, alliteration, assonance, and onomatopoeia are among the language resources of sound.

Rhythm is a common and familiar poetic device that many poets call upon. Rhythm is everywhere in life—in ocean waves, in the tick of a clock, in a horse's hoof beats, in one's own pulse. In poetry, the recurrence of specific beats of stressed and unstressed syllables creates rhythm, the repeated use of syllables and accents, and the rise and fall of words spoken or read.

The rhythm in poetry is often metrical, or ordered rhythm, in which certain syllables are regularly stressed or accented in a more or less fixed pattern. *Meter* is a "measure," and metrical language in poetry can be measured. The meter in poetry can range from that of tightly structured verse patterns to the irregular, but important, rhythms of free verse. When prominent, rhythm helps create and reinforce a poem's meaning. As you read a poem aloud, think about the rhythm of the lines; tap the rhythm you hear. What is the pattern of stressed and unstressed syllables? Whereas basic rhythmic patterns have formal names, the most important question to ask yourself is, How does this pattern enhance meaning? Good examples of the connection between rhythm and meaning appear in **Circus** (N–P) by Jack Prelutsky. Hear how he adjusts his rhythms to the subject by reading aloud the following lines:

Over and over the tumblers tumble
with never a fumble
with never a stumble
top over bottom and back over top
flop-flippy-floppity-flippity-flop.*

JACK PRELUTSKY

Notice the speed in the flow of these lines. The first line's ten beats; the six beats in each of the second and third lines and ten beats in the fourth and fifth lines reflect the speed and rhythm of a parade of acrobats flipping across the ring. The tumblers pass by, followed by the elephants, whose lumbering, plodding walk is captured in the new rhythm:

Here come the elephants, ten feet high
elephants, elephants, heads in the sky.
Eleven great elephants intertwined
one little elephant close behind.*

JACK PRELUTSKY

Rhythm, of course, is achieved by word choice and placement. In the first excerpt, notice how Prelutsky uses the repetition of initial "t" and "f" consonant sounds, as well as rhymes that close the lines with a rather abrupt sound. In the elephant excerpt, he uses the vowel sound of "e" quite deliberately to slow down the rhythm, selecting words such as the three-syllable "eleven" (rather than, for example, "ten"), and ending the lines with a long "i" sound to create the plodding beat. He uses rhyme, assonance, and alliteration in the service of rhythm, all of which underscore the images he is trying to convey.

Alliteration refers to the repetition of the initial consonants of words at close intervals; consonance, often called internal alliteration, is the repetition of internal consonant sounds at close intervals. Tongue twisters such as "rubber baby buggy bumpers" play with alliteration. *Assonance* is the repetition of vowel sounds at close intervals. Rhoda W. Bacmeister uses alliteration and assonance in "Galoshes":

GALOSHES

Susie's galoshes
Make splishes and sploshes
And slooshes and sloshes
As Susie steps slowly
Along in the slush.
They stamp and they tramp
On the ice and concrete
They get stuck in the muck and the mud;
But Susie likes much best to hear

P|R|O|F|I|L|E|S

Lilian Moore, 1985

Poetry should be like fireworks, packed carefully and artfully, ready to explode with unpredictable effects. When people asked Robert Frost—as they did by the hundreds—what he meant by "But I have promises to keep/ And miles to go before I sleep/ And miles to go before I sleep," he always turned the question aside with a joke. Maybe he couldn't answer it, and maybe he was glad that the lines exploded in so many different colors in so many people's minds.

Lilian Moore taught school in New York and worked in publishing for many years. Her work, characterized by "the truth of accurate observations, without sentimentality" (Glazer, 1985, p. 647), may be found in her collections of poetry, including *I Feel the Same Way, Something New Begins: New and Selected Poems, Poems Have Roots*, and *Adam Mouse's Book of Poems*.

Arnold Adoff, 1988

I look for craft and control in making a form that is unique to the individual poem, that shapes it, holds it tight, creates an inner tension that makes a whole shape out of the words. (from Pauses [Hopkins, 1999, p. 219])

Many of Adoff's anthologies reflect the varied experiences of African American people and frequently celebrate racial pride and family strength. "Another unique feature of Adoff's work," commented Mary Lou White (1988, p. 586), "is his technique of creating a series of poems within a book that acts as a prose work yet is different from both a single narrative poem or a prose story. Read together, the individual poems tell a story." Some of Adoff's popular works include *I Am the Darker Brother: An Anthology of Modern Poems by African Americans, Black Is Brown Is Tan, All the Colors of the Race: Poems, My Black Me: A Beginning Book of Black Poetry*, and *Make a Circle, Keep Us In: Poems for a Good Day*.

Valerie Worth, 1991

Never forget that the subject is as important as your feeling: The mud puddle itself is as important as your pleasure in looking at it or splashing through it. Never let the mud puddle get lost in the poetry—because in many ways, the mud puddle is the poetry.

Valerie Worth's small poems are crystal-clear images, luminous word jewels about the simplest things—coat hangers, pebbles, or marbles. Sharing these images with others was important to Worth; she commented that winning the NCTE Award for Excellence in Poetry for Children was "proof that poetry is not just a solitary pursuit, not just a rare flower blooming in isolation, but actually a very effective means of communication" (quoted in Hopkins, 1991, p. 501). A collection of her small poems and others can be found in *All the Small Poems and Fourteen More*.

To learn more about the poets honored with this award, go to CengageBrain.com to access the Education CourseMate website where you will find links to relevant websites.

The opening quotations for these profiles are from the poets' acceptance speeches for the NCTE poetry award. (The speech is given in November of the year the award is received.)

The slippery slush
As it slooshes and sloshes
And splishes and sploshes
All around her galoshes!*

RHODA BACMEISTER

Notice the alliteration in the repetition of the initial consonant "s," as in "sl" or "sp," and the assonance in the short "i" in "splish," as well as the "osh" of "galoshes," "sloshes," "sploshes," and the "oo" of "slooshes" and "Susie." She also employs *consonance*, or the repetition of consonant sounds (other than initial) at close intervals with the many internal "sh" repetitions. These techniques help her employ *onomatopoeia*, or words created from natural sounds associated with the thing or action designated—for example, *slush, slooshes, sloshes, splishes*, and *sploshes.* Onomatopoeia is yet another tool poets use to delight the ears of readers. In **Snow Sounds: An Onomatopoeic Story** (P), David A. Johnson uses visual images—his illustrations—to tell the story of a snowfall, with onomatopoetic words evoking the sounds and feelings of that experience.

Poets' ears are tuned to the *repetition* of consonants, vowels, syllables, words, phrases, and lines, separately and in combination. Anything may be repeated to achieve effect. Repetition is like meeting an old friend again; children find it reassuring. Repetition underscores meaning, as it does in Hoberman's repetition of the words "I miss him." It establishes a sound pattern and is sometimes a source of humor, as in this chant by David McCord from his book **One at a Time** (P):

III.

THE PICKETY FENCE*

The pickety fence
Give it a lick it's
The pickety fence
Give it a lick it's
A clickety fence
Give it a lick it's
A lickety fence
Give it a lick
Give it a lick
Give it a lick
With a rickety stick
Pickety
Pickety
Pickety
Pick

DAVID MCCORD

Perhaps the most identifiable and well-known poetic device, *rhyme* refers to words whose ending sounds are alike (lick/stick/pick). Although much wonderful poetry does not rhyme, young readers often relish the way rhyme clicks phrases together in melodic ways. Generation after generation of children attest to this enjoyment of rhyme when they chant jump rope jingles and rhyming street games.

An example of the familiar *end rhyme,* in which the rhyming words appear at the ends of lines, appears in Jane Yolen's **Sky Scrape/City Scape: Poems of City Life** (P) in her title poem:

SKY SCRAPE / CITY SCAPE**

Sky scrape
City scape

High stone
Steel bone
Cloud crown
Smog gown

Hurry up
Hurry down.

JANE YOLEN

When the final word or syllable of one line rhymes with the first word or syllable of the second line, we have *link rhyme.* In **Easy Poetry Lessons that Dazzle and Delight** (I), David Harrison uses link rhymes to consider the child he was and the person he will become:

THE FUTURE ME[†]

Looking back, I see
Me, unafraid
Eager, teasing
Pleasing, first grade.

Part on the right
Light cowlick hair
Lopsided grin
Thin, blue eyes, fair.

Who am I now?
How am I to be?
Looking behind
To find the future me.

DAVID HARRISON

Harrison uses end rhyme ("unafraid/grade," "hair/fair," and "be/me") as well as link rhyme ("see/me," "teasing/pleasing," "right/light," "grin/thin," "now/how," and "behind/find"). In some cases these link rhymes occur within a *run-on line,* also called "enjambment" (Shapiro and Beum, 1975), in which the grammatical sense of one line carries over into the next, as in "see/me" in the previous example. This is quite different in, for example, the second stanza where each line is *end-stopped,* or a separate grammatical entity.

On first reading a poem, it is *easy* to focus entirely on the sound of the poem. It is very rewarding, however, to go beyond this delight and begin to explore how sound, pattern, and images develop meaning. In Teaching Idea 4.2 we offer an example of using poems written for multiple voices as a way of moving from a discussion of the devices of sound to a consideration of how meaning is shaped.

TEACHING IDEA 4.2

Choral Reading with Poems for Multiple Voices

ELL

COMMON CORE STATE STANDARDS This Teaching Idea addresses the Common Core English Language Arts, Reading: Literature standard 4 grade 2; 4 and 5 grade 3; 5 grade 4; 4 and 5 grade 5; 5 grades 6, 7, and 8. The suggestions in this Teaching Idea may need to be adapted to suit your particular grade level and the needs of your students.

One effective way of introducing choral speaking to your class is to use poems that are written for multiple voices, such as Paul Fleischman's *I Am Phoenix; Joyful Noise: Poems for Two Voices*; and *Big Talk: Poems for Two Voices* (all I). These poems are printed in such a way that it is apparent when solo or combined voices are meant to be used. Even with these cues, it still requires some practice to be able to read well. When students work with these poems, they being to realize the close connection between sound and meaning, and they learn to work together to produce the sound that most effectively captures the meaning they want to convey. This also provides important oral language practice for English language learners.

Many poems, not just those written for multiple voices, work well for choral reading. Put one of your favorite poems on an overhead, then explore how different ways of reading the same poem can create different effects. Even a simple tempo or stress change alters the effect and often the meaning

of the poem. Here are some ways to explore the connections between meaning and sound in poetry.

- Vary the tempo. Read faster or slower and discuss the effects.

- Experiment with stress, discussing which words might be emphasized, and why.

- Play with tone; some poems seem to call for a deep, somber tone, whereas others need a light tone.

- Try different groupings of voices. Poems can be read in many ways—in unison, with choruses, using single voices paired with other single or blended voices, or cumulatively, with voices blending to an increasingly powerful effect.

After you have worked with several poems this way, encourage students to experiment in small groups with choral speaking as a way to explore meaning and sound in poetry.

• • WORDS AS PATTERNS • •

Word order contributes to the sound and meaning of poetry as well. Arranging words is central to creating a poem, and delight in poetry is heightened when we notice how word order, the sound and connotations of the words arranged in a particular way, affects meaning. Just as Jane Yolen arranges the words in "Sky Scrape/City Scape" to reflect the height of the skyscrapers she is depicting, poets manipulate syntax until they find an order and rhythm that is both pleasing to them and communicates more than the literal message. As Nodelman notes, poets express ideas "in words that do more and say more than the prose version, and say it much more specifically . . . by creating patterns . . . that depend on these exact words being said in this exact order" (1996, p. 195).

Gwendolyn Brooks creates pattern through alliteration, assonance, rhyme, and careful word

placement in "We Real Cool," a poem from her anthology *Selected Poems* (A).

> WE REAL COOL. THE POOL PLAYERS.
> SEVEN AT THE GOLDEN SHOVEL.*
>
> *We real cool. We*
> *Left school. We*
> *Lurk late. We*
> *Strike straight. We*
>
> *Sing sin. We*
> *Thin gin. We*
>
> *Jazz June. We*
> *Die soon.*
>
> GWENDOLYN BROOKS

Nodelman (1996) notes that the repetition of "we" both establishes the rhythm and allows for the significance of its absence at the end of the last line.

*From Gwendolyn Brooks, "We Real Cool." Reprinted by permission of Brooks Permissions.

Word order, or patterns, helps create meaning, calling attention to the words themselves as well as the images they create. Whether this order is in part dictated by particular forms, as we discuss later in this chapter, or entirely by meaning, it is perhaps the core of poetry—the only words arranged in the only way possible to convey the poet's idea, and thus to trigger new ideas in the reader.

• • WORDS AS PICTURES • •

Word choice and placement, or how words are juxtaposed or separated, help create meaning. Poets also have at their disposal several poetic devices including *connotation, figurative language,* and *imagery.* Writers use all of these poetic devices to suggest that the words mean more than meets the eye or ear. As in "We Real Cool," something left unsaid is often as important as what is on the page.

Poetry often carries several layers of meaning and, as is true of other literature, is subject to different interpretations. The meaning readers create relates directly to what their experience prepares them to comprehend; who we are determines what we can understand. Although the words that poets choose do have a public, shared meaning, or *denotation,* the *connotations* that surround those words, are both public and private. It is often the resonance of a particular word in the heart of a reader that creates a powerful poetic experience. Think of the word *school* and what it means to you.

Although also found in prose, figurative language—metaphor, simile, and personification—often saturates the language of poetry. Complex comparisons using the devices of metaphor and simile, which compare one thing to another or view something in terms of something else, are frequent in poetry. The comparison in a simile is stated and uses the words *like* or *as* to draw the comparison. A comparison in a metaphor is inferred; something is stated as something else. As poets create vivid experiences and use language metaphorically, they help us see or feel things in new way, as in this poem from Eve Merriam's ***It Doesn't Always Have to Rhyme*** (I):

METAPHOR*

Morning is
a new sheet of paper
for you to write on.

Whatever you want to say,
all day,
until night
folds it up
and files it away.

The bright words and the dark words
are gone
until dawn
and a new day
to write on.

E v e M e r r i a m

This poem functions as both a perfect example of its title and as a wonderful way of looking at the possibilities inherent in a new day, a sentiment uttered to the point of triteness by many other writers and speakers but seen as fresh through Merriam's metaphor.

Personification refers to representing a thing or abstraction as a person. When we say "Fortune smiled on us" or "If the weather permits," we are giving human qualities to an idea—fortune—and to the weather. Poets often give human feelings or thoughts to plants and animals. In her poem "Crickets," Valerie Worth uses personification to make ideas more vivid or unusual when she says that crickets "talk" and dry grass "whispers." Langston Hughes uses personification in "April Rain Song" when he advises to let the rain "kiss" you and "sing you a lullaby." Notice how Sarah Hansen uses both simile and personification to craft a new way to think about morning in "Rising," found in Lee Bennett Hopkins's ***Sky Magic*** (I).

RISING**

Like a fresh loaf
Sun rises,
Tempting dawn
To break
Her golden crust.

Taste morning!

S a r a h H a n s e n

The sun, infused with a distinctly human energy, "tempts" dawn to break. No longer is sunrise merely the consequence of earth's rotation, but it is the sun's motivation to coax morning into existence. Like Hansen's readers, the sun is brimming with agency. She makes things happen, and in many ways, large or small, we can relate to that. Personification, at its best, invites us not only to observe the plants, animals, and inanimate objects populating our world, but to connect with them in ways that reveal or clarify our own thoughts, feelings, and behaviors.

Poets create *imagery* by using words that arrest our senses; we can imagine that we almost see, taste, touch, smell, or hear what they describe. Little escapes the poet's vision; nothing limits the speculations upon what he or she sees. In a poem from ***All***

the Small Poems and Fourteen More (P), Valerie Worth creates a fresh vision of a common flower through metaphor and imagery:

DANDELION*

*Out of
Green space,
A sun:
Bright for
A day, burning,
Away to
A husk, a
Cratered moon:*

*Burst
In a week
To dust:
Seeding
The infinite
Lawn with
Its starry
Smithereens.*

VALERIE WORTH

Comparing the dandelion to a "sun" and a "cratered moon" calls up visions of hot yellow and cool, creamy gray. Words such as *green space, bright, burning,* and *husk* create an image of the flower in the phases of its life cycle, and "starry smithereens"

forever changes the way we view the humble weed that grows everywhere.

Barbara Juster Esbensen creates vivid word pictures in **Words with Wrinkled Knees** (I):

*Touch it with your
pencil
Splat! The word lands wet
and squat
upon the page F R O G*

*Feed it something light
With wings Here's one!
Tongue flicks bright
wing caught!
Small poem
gone***

BARBARA JUSTER ESBENSEN

This and the other poems in this collection go beyond the skillful use of imagery to describe an object, place, or person, and give readers an opportunity to consider not just the thing itself, but the word that represents it. The frog, and the word itself, is "squat," "wet," with "flicking tongue," while the prey, "light" with "bright wings," is a "small poem."

Strong images allow readers to have—through language—experiences and ideas that perhaps they have never before known. Imagery helps readers stretch their sensory selves. In **Toasting**

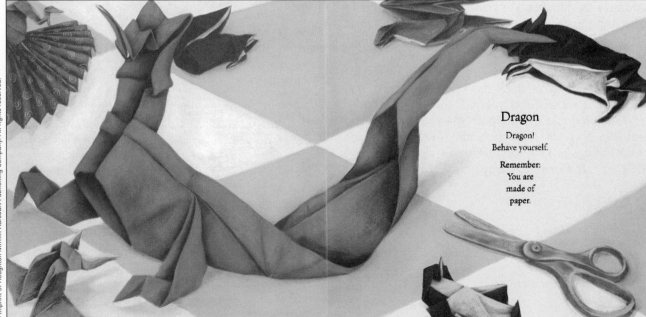

Dragon

Dragon!
Behave yourself.

Remember:
You are
made of
paper.

Lauren Stringer's illustration of the dragon in Kristine O'Connell George's **Fold Me a Poem** *affirms the nature of the beast—even one made out of origami paper!*

Marshmallows: Camping Poems (I), Kristine O'Connell George uses imagery to describe the sights and sounds of camping in the woods—a subject that appeals to many children. A close look at her *Fold Me a Poem* (P–I), beautifully illustrated by Lauren Stringer, shows how a poet's words create pictures that inspire both illustrator and reader to go beyond the literal.

* * *

A CLOSE LOOK AT
Fold Me a Poem

Kristine O'Connell George composed the thirty-two free verse poems in *Fold Me a Poem* (P) because she realized how alike origami and poetry were. Perfect words used well create an image, emotion, or idea in a poem, just as the precise folds of origami create wondrous things out of a simple sheet of paper. George uses perfect words to create images, mostly animals, that appeal to many children. Through these images the imagination in her poet's mind spills onto the pages to be interpreted by Lauren Stringer's vibrant illustrations. For example, "Wind Storm" implores "Hurry, animals!/Get inside the barn./My brother/just turned on/the fan." and the illustration depicts a pair of hands hastily placing origami animals in a cardboard box while the cat pounces on another and a paper lion leaps toward safety. The sly humor in the fifteen syllables of "Dragon" represents the tone of the entire book: "Dragon!/Behave yourself./Remember:/You are/made of/paper." Stringer's illustration adds to the humor by depicting a dragon stretching across a full-bleed, double-page spread, with decimated origami animals strewn around the edges.

George's poems, all "small," reflect the spareness of the Japanese tradition. With Stringer's expressive origami animals, created in order to paint the illustrations almost leaping off the page, *Fold Me a Poem* becomes an enticing poetry book for young readers as well as an example of the marriage of art and text that marks an outstanding picturebook.

Poetic Structures

Poems look different from prose writing; there is a lot more white space. Within that extra white space, however, are an astounding variety of poetic forms. Generally, we speak of two basic types of poetry—narrative and lyric—but there are a plethora of poetic forms that poets play with, either to tell a story, to express emotion, or to amuse.

• • NARRATIVE POETRY • •

Narrative poems tell a story, sometimes in amazingly few lines and sometimes at length. Narrative poems can take many forms, ranging from unstructured free verse to tightly structured ballads. Think about stories from childhood that you first heard through poetry. Perhaps "Casey at the Bat," "Hiawatha," "Paul Revere's Ride," or another poem comes to mind. Many readers enjoy narrative verse, and this is not surprising—they enjoy and are familiar with stories of all kinds. A book-length narrative poem (one that is longer than a picture book) is called an epic, but most contemporary story poems for young readers are relatively short and relate only one or a few episodes.

Ballads

Ballads are a specific form of narrative poetry, with "rules" for poets to follow. Within these rules, they tell a story relating a single incident or thought. Some poets use dialogue to tell a story in repeated refrains. There are folk ballads and literary ballads. Folk ballads have no known author; they have become anonymous and are handed down in song. "John Henry" is a well-known folk ballad. Myra Cohn Livingston's *Abraham Lincoln: A Man for All the People* (I) extols the trials and tribulations of Lincoln's life. Livingston's *Keep on Singing: A Ballad of Marion Anderson* (I) focuses on the triumphs of the great singer. As ballads are essentially story in song, many modern vocalists express themselves through ballads.

Narrative Poems and Verse Novels

Narrative poetry sets a story with characters, plot, and theme—like any other story—into a poetic framework, which can make even a humble story memorable. Poets experiment with the narrative form. Books such as Joyce Carol Thomas's picturebooks, *Gingerbread Days*, *Brown Honey in Broomwheat Tea* (P), and *I Have Heard of a Land* (P) or Nikki Grimes's *Oh, Brother!* (P) contain a series of short poems that, taken together, tell a story. Eloise Greenfield created narrative poetry for *Night on Neighborhood Street* as does Nikki Grimes in *Come Sunday; Danitra Brown, Class Clown* (P); and *What Is Goodbye?* (I).

In *The Great Migration: Journey to the North* (I–A), Eloise Greenfield captures the strength and determination of the African Americans who left the Jim Crow south for work and the promise of a better life in northern industrial regions. Jan Spivey Gilchrist's illustrations provide both historical details and images of the spirit of the people. Patricia C. McKissack's *Never Forgotten* (I–A), stunningly illustrated by Leo and Diane Dillon, contains a series of powerful free verse poems that create a fictional narrative of a young African man stolen into slavery and thematically explores the unbreakable bonds of memory. Each poem tells a part of the larger story. This can be considered a verse novel, although its brevity, trim size, and abundance of illustration make it appear to be a picturebook for older readers.

Verse novels are another way to tell a story through poetry. Like ballads and other narrative poems, verse novels tell stories through poetry but most often consist of a series of one- or two-page poems rather than a single long poem The individual poems within the verse novel may be narrative themselves, but often they are not. Rather, the story is constructed through the arrangement and accumulation of emotions and events presented in individual poems, often through the first-person voice of one or more characters. The immediacy inherent in first-person narration makes the poems intensely emotional.

There is some controversy about whether verse novels are really poetry. They certainly resemble poetry, with condensed language saturated with poetic devices. Campbell (2004) points out that the rhythms found in verse novels are more often that of ordinary speech than of formal metrics, but this is true of much other poetry as well. The best verse novels go well beyond the criticism of being merely prose chopped into short lines.

Verse novels, like so many other literary forms, do not fit neatly under one general category. They do all tell a story, but vary widely within that description. Some verse novels consist of free verse, as in Karen Hesse's *Out of the Dust* (A), Lindsay Lee Johnson's *Soul Moon Soup* (A), Andrea Cheng's *Where the Steps Were* (I), and Janet Wong's *Minn and Jake* (I), but poets also explore various forms of poetry to great effect. Ron Koertge's *Shakespeare Bats Cleanup* (A), Sharon Creech's *Love that Dog* (I) and the sequel *Hate that Cat* (I), Nikki Grimes's *Bronx Masquerade* (A), and Jacqueline Woodson's *Locomotion* (I) contain poems in a variety of forms, with the narrators experimenting with a form as they are learning how poetry can help them come to terms with an emotional crisis in their lives. In *Love that Dog* (I) and *Hate that Cat* (I), the narrator, Jack, uses poems by various writers as models as he struggles to come to terms with the death of his beloved pet. His biggest inspiration is Walter Dean Myers's poem, "Love that Boy," and the writer behind it.

In *The Braid* (A), set in Scotland and Nova Scotia in the nineteenth century, Helen Frost uses narrative poems in two alternating voices—sisters separated by the North Atlantic—interspersed with "praise poems" that sing of something named in the narrative poems.

The praise poems are linked by last and first lines, and the narrative poems are linked by the last words of each line and the first words of each line in the following poem. This complex structure echoes the closeness of the "braid" that the sisters carry with them as a symbol of their love. Elizabeth Alexander and Marilyn Nelson work within a sonnet form while also innovating on that form in *Miss Crandall's School for Young Ladies & Little Misses of Color* (A). Multiple voices of students and Floyd Cooper's illustrations combine to tell the story of the violent history of this school begun in Connecticut in the 1830s.

Margarita Engle's *The Poet Slave of Cuba: A Biography of Juan Francisco Manzano* (A) is another riveting biography in verse. Stephanie Hemphill's Printz Honor–winning *Your Own, Sylvia: A Verse Portrait of Sylvia Plath* (A) is also biographical. Hemphill writes in a range of verse forms and voices, with approximately 150 poems arranged to give insight into the life and work of a great poet.

Marilyn Nelson's *Carver: A Life in Poems* (A), which so captivated the students described at the beginning of this chapter, contains free verse poems arranged to carry the narrative of Carver's life forward. The book is also biographical, so perhaps we might label it as a "biographical verse novel." Here, we look closely at Marilyn Nelson's *Carver: A Life in Poems* (A).

On Your Education CourseMate

CONVERSATION WITH LINDSAY LEE JOHNSON

In a conversation with Lee Galda, Lindsay Lee Johnson discusses her verse novel, **Soul Moon Soup**. In that discussion, she talks about the power of poetic language, and especially of narrative poetry, to help young readers connect to books. Go to CengageBrain.com to access the Education CourseMate website and watch the video conversation with Lindsay Lee Johnson.

Questions to Consider

1. Do you think that poetic language is more or less accessible to young readers?

2. What properties of poetic language might make it more appealing than prose?

* * *

A CLOSE LOOK AT
Carver: A Life in Poems

Marilyn Nelson brings a poet's ear to ***Carver: A Life in Poems*** (A), her biography-in-verse of the life of George Washington Carver. Nelson's ear is as attuned to the nuances of Carver's life as it is to the nuances of her own words, and the complexity of both are clearly evident in the fifty-nine separate poems that make up this slim volume. Her poems offer readers verbal portraits of important people, events, ideas, and beliefs that influenced Carver's life. Far from mere snapshots, her poems are richly textured, a verbal equivalent to a detailed oil portrait of the man and his times.

The content of these poems—Carver's life—is well worth knowing about, and Nelson provides a birth-to-death picture, beginning shortly after Carver's birth when he and his slave mother are stolen by bushwhackers. When his owners, the Carvers, have George rescued they are overjoyed because the childless couple love him and his older brother. The poem that tells us this also makes clear how unusual this is because Mrs. Carver speaks of George's tenuous freedom in a "hate-filled land." This effective combination of the personal and the societal permeates the entire book.

Many voices speak these poems, from the hired man who rescued Carver, to the white folks with whom he lived in Missouri, Kansas, and Iowa, to those who were jealous of him at the Tuskegee Institute, to those who considered him a hero. All of these speakers view Carver in a slightly different manner. Nelson also employs an anonymous poetic voice that speaks of Carver in his private moments—as he shakes when reading that his brother is dead, witnesses a lynching, paints, or absorbs information from the natural world. This combination of exterior and interior perspectives is powerful. We see Carver's deeply devout soul, his dedication to helping his people learn to be more successful farmers (and thus better feed their families), and his doomed relationship with a white teacher who loved him. Other poems reveal his artistic talents—ranging from painting to needlework—and his close friendships with many young men across the country. Nelson calls these young men "lovingly sons," after the closing on one of the many letters that Carver received from "his boys," whom he inspired with his lectures, his letters, and his prayers.

These poems often depict the ugliness of racism, but are also often filled with heartbreakingly beautiful passages, such as Nelson's description of Booker T. Washington and George Washington Carver as "two veil-raisers,/Walking our people/into history." (p. 61), or Nelson's comparison of the flights on the Tuskegee Airfield to a flower: "Behind them the amaryllis on the sill surrenders/to the cold sky its slow-motion skyrocket./Beyond the clasped flame of its bud/a P-40 zooms in at five o' clock,/high as a negro has ever been." (p. 96). Nelson also weaves Carver's actual words into poems, as in "My Dear Spiritual Boy." His own words and period photographs add significantly to the emotional impact of the poems. In these fifty-nine poems, Nelson shows us the strength of the bonds between faith and science, intellect and spirit, which defined Carver's life.

• • LYRIC POETRY • •

Rather than telling a story, lyric poetry is a statement of mood or feeling. It offers a direct and intense outpouring of thoughts and emotions. Any subjective, emotional poem can be lyric, but most lyric poems are melodic and are expressive of a single mood. As its Greek name indicates, a lyric was originally sung to the accompaniment of a lyre. Like ballads, lyric poems are songlike, as is Eleanor Farjeon's "Morning Has Broken," from her book ***The Children's Bells: A Selection of Poems*** (P–I).

Many poems are lyrical because of their singing quality and their expression of intense emotion. Songs are often the first lyric poems children hear. For ***Hush Songs: African American Lullabies*** (N–P–I), Joyce Carol Thomas collected traditional songs sung by cradling mothers and caring fathers to lull a child to sleep. A soothing melody sung with comforting words works its magic on sleepy children:

ALL THE PRETTY LITTLE HORSES

Hush-a-bye
Don't you cry
Go to sleep
My little baby.

When you wake
You shall have
All the pretty little horses.

ANONYMOUS

Walter Dean Myers captures the feelings and emotions of Harlem residents during the 1940s in ***Here in Harlem: Poetry in Many Voices*** (A), an excellent example of lyric poetry for advanced readers. Myers's descriptions of the pride, heartache, aspiration, determination, and elation felt by the people of Harlem resonate in the text; his words depict an emotional world in which the experiences of individuals shout—and sometimes whisper—across borders of time, speaking directly to modern readers' sensitivities. Eloise Greenfield offers primary-grade students lyric poetry in *Honey, I Love and Other Love Poems* (I).

• • A VARIETY OF FORMS • • AND VOICES

There are many poetic forms that are clearly defined, although poets alter conventional and traditional forms often as they manipulate word meanings. Poets experiment with form. In *A Wreath for Emmett Till* (A), Marilyn Nelson worked within the strict form of the sonnet, a fourteen-line poem with a strict rhyme scheme, in this case Petrarchan. Moreover, she wrote the poem as a "heroic crown" of sonnets, which contains fifteen interlinked sonnets, in which the last line of one becomes the first line of the next, with the final sonnet consisting of the first lines of the preceding fourteen. In her introduction to the book, she comments on how this form helped to insulate her, helped her to contain the sorrow and pain of the 1955 lynching of this young black man. Her choice of form was dictated by the content of the poem, as was Helen Frost's choice in *The Braid* (A), discussed earlier.

Form is the focus of recent anthologies that celebrate the rich variety of forms that are available to today's poets. Some poets invent their own new forms, as Marilyn Nelson did in *Mirror Mirror* (P–I), discussed earlier. Bob Raczka has taken word puzzles and turned them into poetry, combining anagrams, rebus, and riddle in *Lemonade and Other Poems Squeezed from a Single Word* (I), illustrated by Nancy Doniger.

Concrete Poetry

We saw how Jane Yolen structured her skyscraper poem so that the shape contributed to meaning. Concrete poetry uses the appearance of words on a page to suggest or illustrate the poem's meaning. Children call these poems *shape* (or *picture*) *poems*. The actual physical form of the words depicts the subject, so the work illustrates itself, as shown following in Joan Bransfield Graham's "Popsicle." Note how Chris Raschka's torn-paper collage adds humor and whimsy but does not interfere with the shape of the poem itself.

"Popsicle," along with many other examples of shape poems, appears in Paul Janeczko's indispensable *A Poke in the I: A Collection of Concrete Poems* (I). *Doodle Dandies: Poems that Take Shape* by J. Patrick Lewis and *Splish Splash* and *Flicker Flash* by Joan Bransfield Graham (P) are also terrific resources for young readers discovering concrete poems. Joyce Sidman's *Meow Ruff* (P) is full of onomatopoeia and

other poetic devices, and the words are hidden in Michelle Berg's innovative illustrations. Douglas Florian often uses form to convey meaning in his poems. When writing about a sawfish in his anthology *In the Swim: Poems and Paintings* (I), he arranges his lines in a zigzag pattern to make his words "saw" down the page. His salmon poem hurtles diagonally upward across the page, reinforcing the fish's dramatic movement.

Limericks

Limerick, a form of light verse, has five lines and a rhyme scheme of a-a-b-b-a. Usually, the first, second, and fifth lines (which rhyme) have eight beats, whereas the third and fourth (which rhyme) have six. Limericks appeal to young readers because they poke fun and have a definite rhythm and rhyme. Edward Lear (1812–1888) is credited with making limericks popular, although he did not create the form. Limericks often make fun of people who take themselves too seriously.

Readers with a good sense of humor devour limericks. Some limericks have been passed down by word of mouth, becoming folklore when their original authorship is forgotten. One such is:

> *A flea and a fly in a flue*
> *Were imprisoned, so what could they do?*
> *Said the fly, "Let us flee."*
> *Said the flea, "Let us fly."*
> *So they flew through a flaw in the flue.*
>
> ANONYMOUS

Many young readers enjoy Myra Cohn Livingston's *Lots of Limericks* (P–I), James Marshall's *Pocketful of Nonsense* (P–I), and Arnold Lobel's *The Book of Pigericks: Pig Limericks* (P–I).

Haiku and Cinquain

The word *haiku* means "beginning." Haiku frequently refer to nature, to a particular event happening at one moment, and to an attendant emotion or feeling, often of the most fragile and evanescent kind. This Japanese verse form consists of three lines and seventeen syllables: the first line contains five syllables; the second line, seven; and the third, five. A haiku usually focuses on an image that suggests a thought or emotion. Experimenting with the form is much more than counting syllables; meaning should be central. Paul Janeczko notes that haiku often feature nature in rural areas, but he sought out haiku that show the natural beauty of everyday city streets in his collection *Stone Bench in an Empty Park* (A).

Poets who master the haiku form sometimes stretch its boundaries by varying the five-seven-five syllable

POPSICLE
Joan Bransfield Graham

```
P o p s i c l e
P o p s i c l e
t i c k l e
tongue fun
l i c k s i c l e
s t i c k s i c l e
p l e a s e
d o n ' t  r u n
d r i p s i c l e
s l i p s i c l e
melt, melt
t r i c k y
s t o p s i c l e
p l o p s i c l e
h a n d   a l l
          s
          t
          i
          c
          k
          y
```

17

*Chris Raschka's torn-paper collages add whimsy to Paul Janeczko's collection of concrete poems in **A Poke in the I: A Collection of Concrete Poems**.*

count while maintaining the essence of its meaning. Kobayashi Issa, a noted Japanese poet, demonstrates in ***Don't Tell the Scarecrow, and Other Japanese Poems*** (I) the beauty of haiku in these two variations:

> *Where can he be going*
> *In the rain,*
> *This snail?*

> *Little knowing*
> *The tree will soon be cut down*
> *Birds are building their nests in it.*

ISSA

G. Brian Karas arranged and illustrated haiku by Kobayashi Issa in ***Today and Today*** (P), a poetic view of one year in the life of a contemporary family. Other poetry books that help young readers explore haiku include Bob Raczka's ***Guyku: a Year of Haiku for Boys*** (P), illustrated by Peter Reynolds; Paul B. Janeczko and J. Patrick Lewis's ***Wing Nuts: Screwy Haiku*** (I); Lee Wardlaw's ***Won Ton: A Cat Tale Told in Haiku*** (P), illustrated by Eugene Yelchin; and Michael Rosen's ***The Hound Dog's Haiku: And***

Other Poems for Dog Lovers (P–I), with woodcut illustrations by Mary Azarian. Nikki Grimes combines lyrical free verse and haiku in ***A Pocketful of Poems*** (P–I), with collage illustrations by Javaka Steptoe.

Linda Sue Park uses the Korean variant of haiku in her book ***Tap Dancing on the Roof: Sijo (Poems)*** (I). The twenty-six poems in this anthology reflect the traditional sijo structure, three lines of fourteen to sixteen syllables each in which the first introduces the idea, the next lines develop it, and the final line gives it an unexpected or ironic twist. As Park says in an introductory note, however, sijo in English are sometimes divided into six shorter lines, and her collection contains both versions.

A cinquain consists of five unrhymed lines usually in the pattern of two, four, six, eight, and two syllables each. A simplified variation has five lines with one, two, three, and four words, with the fifth line just one word that is a synonym for the title.

Other Forms

Young readers enjoy reading and writing poems in a variety of other forms as well. Mask, or persona, poems are written from the point of view of an object or animal—anything that's not human. Myra Cohn Livingston writes from the point of view of her bed in "What My Bed Says" from *O Sliver of Liver and Other Poems* (I).

WHAT MY BED SAYS*

*You squirm and settle down in me
when the day goes.
I feel the ends of your toes
naked and free
from shoes and socks, and I cover
all the laughter and tears of your day.
Here in my snug world you stay,
and the dreams we discover
in the dark patterns of the night
make us feel as one.
Then comes another sun,
and its first light
tears us apart, for you wake and turn
from me, battered, wrinkled, in folds.
Leave then—see what the day holds
and share it with me when you return.*

MYRA COHN LIVINGSTON

Alice Shertle gives voice to pieces of clothing in *Button Up!: Wrinkled Rhymes* (P), illustrated by Petra Mathers. Paul Janeczko's collection *Dirty Laundry Pile: Poems in Different Voices* (P), illustrated by Melissa Sweet, offers many examples of persona, or mask poems.

Janeczko is also the editor of a selection of apostrophe poems, poems addressed to things such as bugs, statues, buildings, or toothbrushes. *Hey, You!: Poems to Skyscrapers, Mosquitoes, and Other Fun Things* (I), illustrated by Robert Rayevsky, presents humorous, whimsical, and serious poems of address.

J. Patrick Lewis and Paul B. Janeczko teamed up to compose a series of renga, or linked verse, in *Birds on a Wire: A Renga 'round Town* (I), a clever introduction to this specialized form that young readers will want to try. Janeczko's *A Kick in the Head: An Everyday Guide to Poetic Forms* (I), with illustrations by Chris Raschka, is a collective specialized anthology that also offers examples and explanations of a variety of poetic forms. Avis Harley's *Fly with Poetry: An ABC of Poetry* (I), *Leap into Poetry: More ABC's of Poetry* (I) present clever examples of a variety of forms with brief explanatory notes that help readers—and writers—learn the conventions of the forms.

Poetry in the Classroom

Having a good collection of poetry available for young readers is the first step in helping them to know and love poetry. Although knowing and loving poetry has its own internal rewards, there are also academic benefits to engaging with poetry.

Poetry draws young readers into listening. Students pay attention to poetry because it plays with the sounds of language; uses interesting, intriguing words; and deals with fascinating topics. Poetry increases readers' language resources. We all learn the language we hear; if we hear ordinary conversational language, we will use ordinary language when we speak and write. Fortunately, we also learn the language we read. If we read or hear poetic language, we will use poetic language in our writing and speaking.

Poetry is excellent material for developing phonemic awareness, the ability to segment and manipulate speech sounds. Children learn to discriminate sounds, hear parts of words, and make connections between sounds they hear and letters they see. Because poetry and verse are often patterned, predictable, and repetitive, children know what a word should be and probably is going to be. When they recognize beginning consonants, they are likely to say the right word. Alliteration and rhyme help beginning readers make sense of print.

Poetry helps students learn how to write by giving them a storehouse of words and patterns to draw from in their own writing. Playing with various poetic forms allows students to explore various options. This often pushes students to work within a structure, something that is both challenging and reassuring. The clearly visible framework of poetry helps students understand.

Poetry helps students learn to think by showing them how to look at their world in a new way. It presents fresh perspectives on life. Poetry builds on paradox, ambiguity, and contradictions; it sets these features in stark relief so they become apparent to naive readers.

Building a poetry collection takes time. Begin with those books that speak to you as a reader, knowing that you will want to add many more based on your students' needs and interests. All readers have personal favorites they like to read from, poets they return to again and again. Just as some books are clearly for younger or older readers—because the way the content is presented helps determine the audience—poetry can also appeal to a wide range of ages. Just as young readers vary widely in their interests, abilities, and experiences, your collection should do the same.

P R O F I L E S

Barbara Juster Esbensen, 1994

As a child growing up in Madison, Wisconsin, I read everything in sight and drew pictures on anything that looked like it needed decoration. I wrote stories with my two best friends, and we all intended to be writers. When I was fourteen and a half, my teacher looked at a poem I had written and told me I was "a writer." When she introduced me to poets like Amy Lowell, Stephen Vincent Benét, and Emily Dickinson, she literally changed my life. Until then, I had not known that it was possible to use words in such exciting ways.

What impressed the NCTE Poetry Award Committee about Barbara Juster Esbensen's work was "the clarity of [her] images, the differentness of [her] images" (Greenlaw, 1994, p. 544). When asked if her work as an artist influenced her poetic images, Esbensen said, "I'm sure that I'm looking all the time. I'm sure of that because I am an artist, and that's what I have really been doing all my life. I'm a looker! And I'm an exaggerator . . . I tell children you are allowed to say things that are absolutely off-the-wall in poetry" (p. 544). Esbensen's poetry anthologies for children include *Cold Stars and Fireflies, Words with Wrinkled Knees: Animal Poems*, and *Who Shrank My Grandmother's House?*.

Eloise Greenfield, 1997

There's a desperate need for more black literature for children, for a large body of literature in which black children can see themselves and their lives and history reflected. I want to do my share in building it.

Eloise Greenfield has played a significant role in contributing to African American literature in several genres; her poetry books are frequently cited by teachers and scholars. She received ALA Notable citations, the Coretta Scott King Award, and the Mary McLeod Bethune Award for her work, particularly for *Honey, I Love and Other Love Poems* and *Nathaniel Talking*. "[Greenfield's] poetry reflects or comments on the specific cultural experience of growing up African American in this society," noted Rudine Sims Bishop (1997, p. 632), "but the topics and themes—love, family, neighbors, dreams, the joy of living, the resilience of the human spirit— reach out to all children."

X. J. Kennedy, 2000

Rhyme and meter have been in the doghouse of adult poetry lately, and some have claimed that children, too, don't like such old-fangled devices. But children do. This makes me glad, for I have never been able to write what is termed "free verse." I love the constant surprise one encounters in rhyming things, and the driving urge of a steady beat.

For years, X. J. Kennedy wrote poetry for children but kept it in the bottom drawer of his desk until Myra Cohn Livingston asked him to send some of it to her editor, Margaret McElderry. McElderry published his first book of poetry for children, *One Winter Night in August, and Other Nonsense Jingles*. Since then, Kennedy has authored more than a dozen collections of verse for children. Daniel L. Darigan (2001) observed, "[Kennedy's] topics are timely and accessible, his use of the language sophisticated, and his humor leads children and adoring adults into a genre that often gets overlooked and ignored. Children who read his collections as well as his anthologies will receive a better understanding of what poetry is and the joys it holds for them" (p. 298).

To learn more about the poets honored with this award, go to CengageBrain.com to access the Education CourseMate website where you will find links to relevant websites.

The opening quotations for these profiles are from the poets' acceptance speeches for the NCTE poetry award. (The speech is given in November of the year the award is received.)

P R O F I L E S

Mary Ann Hoberman, 2003

isual language . . . is for writers. So are word games and word play. Just think of what you can do with words. . . . Each time you discover the perfect word for your purpose, each time you shape a sentence, each time you awaken a reader's imagination, you will feel fulfilled. (Quoted in Ernst & McClure, 2004)

Mary Ann Hoberman is a master of rhyme, rhythm, and wordplay. She began publishing for children in 1957 with **All My Shoes Come in Twos**. Since then, Hoberman has created lasting favorites, including **A House Is a House for Me; Fathers, Mothers, Sisters, Brothers: A Collection of Family Poems**; and **The Llama Who Had No Pajama: 100 Favorite Poems**.

Nikki Grimes, 2006

hen I grow up, I thought, I'll write books about children who look and feel like me. (Quoted in Something About the Author, *2007)*

Poet, novelist, and picturebook author, Nikki Grimes has received many honors as the author of approximately fifty published books. In most of these she did, indeed, write about children like the child she had been. Her poetry speaks to the heart in stark yet beautiful language. She began

publishing for young readers in 1977 and is beloved for her books of poetry, which include **Meet Danitra Brown; Danitra Brown Leaves Town; Danitra Brown, Class Clown; My Man Blue; A Pocketful of Poems; Bronx Masquerade; It's Raining Laughter; What Is Goodbye?**; and **Oh, Brother!**.

Lee Bennett Hopkins, 2009

oetry and I fit together. I can't imagine being without it. Were it in my power I would give poetry to every single child everywhere. (www.booksense.com; Meet the Author/Illustrator Archives)

Lee Bennett Hopkins is a prolific anthologist and writer. His many anthologies offer children the opportunity to experience wonderful poetry written about a variety of topics and ideas. His autobiography in poetry, **Been to Yesterdays: Poems of a Life**, received the Christopher Medal and a Golden Kite Honor. Among his latest anthologies are **America at War: Poems Selected by Lee Bennett Hopkins** and **Sky Magic**. Mr. Hopkins has also endowed two awards for poets, the Lee Bennett Hopkins Poetry Award, presented annually since 1983, and the Lee Bennett Hopkins/International Reading Association Promising Poet Award, presented every three years since 1995.

J. Patrick Lewis, 2011

ou can be a writer! Oh, my, if only someone had told me that when I was young. (www.jpatricklewis.com; interview with Carolyn Brodie School Library Media Activities Monthly, *April 2009)*

J. Patrick Lewis, the Poetry Foundation's current Children's Poet Laureate, is a prolific writer. Author of more than sixty-five books for children, Lewis also writes extensively for adults, often on the subject of economics, in which he holds a Ph.D. from The Ohio State University. Lewis's books of poetry for young readers are often funny, always clever, and have won numerous awards. His popular titles include **Doodle Dandies: Poems that Take Shape, Scien-Trickery: Riddles in Science, Once Upon a Tomb: Gravely Humorous Verses**, and **Wing Nuts: Screwy Haiku**. He writes also in other genres, and has several books for teachers.

To learn more about the poets honored with this award, go to CengageBrain.com to access the Education CourseMate website where you will find links to relevant websites.

The opening quotations for these profiles are from the poets' acceptance speeches for the NCTE poetry award. (The speech is given in November of the year the award is received.)

FIGURE 4.3

Resources for the Poetry Teacher

Appelt, Kathi, *Poems from Homeroom: A Writer's Place to Start* (A)

Booth, David, and Bill Moore, *Poems Please! Sharing Poetry with Children* (P–I)

Brown, Bill, and Malcolm Glass, *Important Words: A Book for Poets and Writers* (I–A)

Chatton, Barbara, *Using Poetry across the Curriculum* (P–I)

Cullinan, Bernice, Marilyn Scala, and Virginia Schroder, with Ann Lovett, *Three Voices: An Invitation to Poetry across the Curriculum* (P–I)

Denman, Gregory, *When You've Made It Your Own: Teaching Poetry to Young People* (I–A)

Esbensen, Barbara Juster, *A Celebration of Bees: Endless Opportunities for Inspiring Children to Write Poetry* (P–I)

Fletcher, Ralph, *Poetry Matters: Writing a Poem from the Inside Out* (P–I)

Fox, Mem, *Radical Reflections: Passionate Opinions on Teaching, Learning, and Living* (P–I)

Graves, Donald, *Explore Poetry: The Reading/Writing Teacher's Companion* (P–I)

Grossman, Florence, *Listening to the Bells: Learning to Read Poetry by Writing Poetry* (I–A)

Harrison, David L., and Bernice Cullinan, *Easy Poetry Lessons that Dazzle and Delight* (P–I)

Heard, Georgia, *Awakening the Heart: Exploring Poetry in Elementary and Middle School* (I–A)

——, *For the Good of the Earth and Sun: Teaching Poetry* (I–A)

——, *Writing toward Home: Tales and Lessons to Find Your Way* (I–A)

Hewitt, Geof, *Today You Are My Favorite Poet: Writing Poems with Teenagers* (A)

Hopkins, Lee Bennett, *Pass the Poetry, Please* (I)

——, *Pauses: Autobiographical Reflections of 101 Creators of Children's Books* (P–I)

Janeczko, Paul, *The Place My Words Are Looking For: What Poets Say About and Through Their Work* (I–A)

——, *Poetry from A to Z: A Guide for Young Writers* (I–A)

——, *Poetspeak: In Their Work, About Their Work: A Selection* (I–A)

——, *Seeing the Blue Between: Advice and Inspiration for Young Poets* (I–A)

Kennedy, X. J., and Dorothy M. Kennedy, *Knock at a Star: A Child's Introduction to Poetry* (P)

Kuskin, Karla, *Dogs and Dragons, Trees and Dreams* (P)

Larrick, Nancy, *Let's Do a Poem: Introducing Poetry to Children Through Listening, Singing, Chanting, Impromptu Choral Reading, Body Movement, Dance, and Dramatization; Including 98 Favorite Songs and Poems* (P–I)

Livingston, Myra Cohn, *Climb into the Bell Tower* (I–A)

——, *Poem-Making: Ways to Begin Writing Poetry* (I–A)

McClure, Amy, with Peggy Harrison and Sheryl Reed, *Sunrises and Songs: Reading and Writing Poetry in an Elementary Classroom* (I–A)

Nye, Naomi Shihab, *Salting the Ocean: 100 Poems by Young Poets* (A).

Reading reviews in professional journals and noting the winners of the NCTE poetry award will help keep you up-to-date on poetry for children. Look at the poetry books that have won awards such as the Caldecott, Newbery, or Printz, and also look at Children's Choices or Young Adult Choices to see what young readers are enjoying. There are also some wonderful resources available that are full of ideas for exploring poetry with young readers. These are listed in Figure 4.3.

Researchers have studied the kinds of poems young readers like, as well as the kinds of poems teachers like to read to them. Not surprisingly, the poems they hear influence what kinds of poems they like. Researchers (Fisher & Natarella, 1982; Terry, 1974) found that children in their studies liked:

- Contemporary poems
- Poems they could understand
- Narrative poems
- Poems with rhyme, rhythm, and sound
- Poems that related to their personal experiences

What young readers prefer and what they can learn to appreciate in the company of others and an enthusiastic teacher, however, are often very different.

McClure (1985) found that classroom experiences change children's responses to poetry. In supportive environments, children respond more positively to a wider variety of poetry, showing that teachers' attitudes and practices make a tremendous difference. In other words, what you do with poetry in the classroom determines how your students respond to poetry.

A case study focusing on the classroom poetry experiences of a combined fourth/fifth-grade class in the Midwest also supports the idea that children may change their poetry preferences when their school experiences support their exploration of the genre (Hansen, 2004). After six months of classroom poetry experiences, during which students explored poetry with enthusiastic teachers, students' appreciation for varied techniques and devices such as free verse and simile increased. They also became more articulate about what they liked and disliked about specific poems after participating in the classroom poetry experiences.

Poetry grows increasingly popular as more poetry is published in appealing formats. The International Reading Association's (IRA) annual Children's Choices lists show that children consistently select poetry books as among their favorites. Delight in poetry prevails amid opportunities to choose from hundreds of other picturebooks, novels, and nonfiction.

We may not know why a particular poem appeals to young readers, but we do know that poems read aloud with enthusiasm are likely to become their favorites. Teachers' selections soon become children's choices. Results of the IRA Teachers' Choices project show that teachers frequently choose poetry as their favorite books for teaching. Teachers choose poems that reflect our multicultural heritage, poems with beautiful language, and poems that help them teach subject-area content. When teachers select poems they like, their enthusiasm is apparent to their students.

Immerse, or as poet Ralph Fletcher (2002) says, "marinate" students in poetry—lots of poetry over lots of time. Students need to feel comfortable using the books you have gathered; talk about the books and display their covers to attract readers. Shelve poetry with other books by the same author or about the same subject. Your students need time and space to browse, to pull out several volumes at once, and to compare poems or look for favorites. Give students time to browse through the poetry collection during a free period; encourage them to read poetry for their independent reading.

Reading poetry in a manner that highlights the meaning and talking about the reading helps students understand the link between sound and meaning. Listening to a poem read aloud well brings insight into how poetry works, what a poem might mean to another reader, techniques for oral interpretation, and strategies for reading that can be employed silently. Learning these techniques gives young readers tools for their own reading; they develop an understanding of the importance of how a poem sounds. Teaching Idea 4.3 offers ideas for helping students explore poetry.

Young readers learn to love poetry when they explore it freely. Unfortunately, some learn to dislike poetry when someone insists they search for elusive meanings or rhyme schemes that make no sense to them. Close attention to students' comments can supply a basis for thought-provoking questions that will lead them to discover the substance of poetry for themselves. The object is to develop a positive response to the music of words and to give students the terminology to talk about their responses. Appropriate discussions of poetry take readers back into the experience of a poem, not away from it, as students discover how poetry works. Let their questions be your guide.

Poets themselves have good suggestions for young readers. When Eve Merriam accepted the NCTE poetry award, she encouraged children with these words:

> Read a lot. Sit down with anthologies and decide which pleases you. Copy out your favorites in your own handwriting. Buy a notebook and jot down images and descriptions. Be specific; use all the senses. Use your whole body as you write. It might even help sometimes to stand up and move with your words. Don't be afraid of copying

Fifteen Minutes, Fifty Poems!

This Teaching Idea addresses the Common Core English Language Arts, Reading: Literature standard 4 grade 2; 4 and 5 grade 3; 5 grade 4; 4 and 5 grade 5; 5 grades 6, 7, and 8. The suggestions in this Teaching Idea may need to be adapted to suit your particular grade level and the needs of your students.

Teachers who write poetry have students who write poetry. Let them see you write! This teaching idea is perfect for those fifteen-minute intervals between specials or as a warm-up activity before a language arts lesson. Teachers find that it works well with both primary and more advanced students.

Before the Lesson

- Be sure each student has a poetry notebook (a blank composition notebook) and a pencil.

- Prepare a poetry notebook for yourself as well.

- Place an overhead projector in a location where all students will be able to see its projection from their desks.

During the Lesson

- Invite students to sit at their desks with their poetry notebooks and pencils.

- Dim the lights to create a "writing" mood.

- Tell students that you have a poem on your mind; invite them to watch as you try to capture it in words.

- Talk out loud as you project your writing on the overhead projector. Scribble out words. Sketch ideas in the margins. Consider line breaks and talk about how you will use them to convey meaning.

- Keep writing, even if you are not sure what words will come next. Remember, you are modeling for students what to do if they become "stuck" while writing. Demonstrate how to play with language until your words match your thoughts.

- Stop at a point when you are visibly excited about what you will next compose. Tell students that your poem simply cannot wait to emerge on paper and that you must spend the next ten minutes writing silently in your poetry notebook.

- Invite students to write poems in their poetry notebooks as you write in yours.

- Continue writing in your poetry notebook as students work independently. It will be tempting to circulate to observe students at work, but students need to observe *you* writing. When they glance up from their notebooks during moments of frustration, they will need to see that their teacher is a writer—and that writers persevere, even when the words do not come easily. They will also need to see you smile to yourself when you write something "really good"; they will do the same when they write words that please them. Your actions teach your students how to *be* poets—keep your pencil moving!

After the Lesson

- When students ask you (and they most likely will) if they can bring their poetry notebooks outside for recess or home for the weekend, say yes! Your fifteen minutes of modeling will lead students to create a multitude of poems that they may share with you, with friends, or with the class. The more you model, the more your students will write. The more poems your students write, the more poetic devices and forms they will notice in the poems they read. It is a cycle that sweeps children into exploring and experimenting with language. Teachers have the power to set the cycle in motion.

a form or convention, especially in the beginning. And, to give yourself scope and flexibility, remember: It doesn't always have to rhyme.

You don't need gimmicks, elaborate plans, or detailed instructions. You do need lots of poetry books, time to savor them, and pleasurable poetry experiences.

Poetry is a valuable tool for fully realizing life's many and varied experiences. It allows us to participate in the imaginative experience of others and thereby better understand our own experiences. The more readers participate, the more they create, and the more personal and enjoyable the experience of poetry becomes. The rewards are more than worth the effort.

SUMMARY

Listening to, reading, and writing poetry helps us learn about the world, about ourselves, and about the power and potential of language. Poets write about everything, using devices of sound and meaning to present their own unique visions. Poetry comes in varied forms and is available in many formats. Young readers are attracted to poetry, and teachers can build on this attraction, providing experiences with poetry that will lead children to enjoy poetry and thus to consider how poetry works. Children who experience a poetry-rich environment will become lifelong readers and writers of poetry.

Booklist

Although books are arranged primarily under age of intended audience, many books of poetry can be enjoyed across ages. This is just a small sample of poetry available for young readers. There are more mentioned in the text of this chapter, and many others unlisted, but created by the poets listed here.

* Indicates some aspect of diversity

Books for Preschool Readers

* Bryan, Ashley, **Sing to the Sun: Poems and Pictures** (1992)

Calmenson, Stephanie, **Kindergarten Kids: Riddles, Rebuses, Wiggles, Giggles, and More!** (2005)

Cullinan, Bernice, Andi MacLeod, and Marc Nadel, **A Jar of Tiny Stars: Poems by NCTE Award-Winning Poets** (1996)

* Delacre, Lulu, **Arrorró, Mi Niño: Latino Lullabies and Gentle Games** (2004)

Elliott, David. **In the Wild** (2010)

Hoberman, Mary Ann, **Fathers, Mothers, Sisters, Brothers: A Collection of Family Poems** (1991)

_____, **A House Is a House for Me** (1978)

Johnson, David A., **Snow Sounds: An Onomatopoeic Story** (2006)

Kennedy, X. J., and Dorothy Kennedy, **Talking Like the Rain** (1991)

Kuskin, Karla, **Moon, Have You Met My Mother?** (2003)

McCord, David, **One at a Time** (1974)

* Mora, Pat, **The Desert Is My Mother/El desierto es mi madre** (1994)

* Thomas, Joyce Carol, **Hush Songs: African American Lullabies** (2000)

Worth, Valerie, **All the Small Poems and Fourteen More** (1994)

Yolen, Jane, and Peters, Andrew Fusek, **Switching on the Moon: a Very First Book of Bedtime Poems** (2010)

Poems for Primary-Grade Readers

* Adoff, Arnold, **Black Is Brown Is Tan** (1973)

Agee, Jon, **Orangutan Tongs: Poems to Tangle Your Tongue** (2009)

Ahlberg, Allan, **Everybody Was a Baby Once: And Other Poems** (2010)

* Alarcón, Francisco X., **Animal Poems of the Iguazu/ Animalario del Iguazu** (2008)

Elliott, David, **On the Farm** (2008)

Florian, Douglas, **Autumblings** (2003)

_____, **Handsprings** (2006)

_____, **Poetrees** (2011)

_____, **Summersaults** (2002)

Franco, Betsy, **A Curious Collection of Cats** (2010)

_____, **A Dazzling Display of Dogs** (2011)

George, Kristine O'Connell, **Emma Dilemma: Big Sister Poems** (2011)

_____, **Fold Me a Poem** (2005)

_____, **Little Dog and Duncan** (2002)

_____, **Little Dog Poems** (1999)

* Greenfield, Eloise, **Honey, I Love and Other Poems** (1998)

* _____, **Night on Neighborhood Street** (1991)

* Greenfield, Eloise, and Jan Spivey Gilchrist, **The Friendly Four** (2006)

* Grimes, Nikki, **Danitra Brown, Class Clown** (2005)
* _____, **A Dime a Dozen** (1998)
* _____, **Hopscotch Love: A Family Treasury of Love Poems** (1999)
* _____, **Meet Danitra Brown** (1994)
* _____, **My Man Blue: Poems** (1999)
* _____, **Stepping Out with Grandma Mac** (2000)
Hopkins, Lee Bennett, **Good Books, Good Times!** (1990)
_____, **Side by Side: Poems to Read Together** (1988)
* Issa, Kobayashi, *et al.*, **Today and Today** (2007)
Lobel, Arnold, **The Book of Pigericks: Pig Limericks** (1983)
Marshall, James, **Pocketful of Nonsense** (2003)
* Newsome, Effie Lee, **Wonders: The Best Children's Poems of Effie Lee Newsome**, compiled by Rudine Sims Bishop (1999)
Sidman, Joyce, **Red Sings from Treetops: A Year in Colors** (2009)
_____, **Meow Ruff** (2006)
* Smith, Hope Anita, **Keeping the Night Watch** (2008)
Stevenson, James, **Candy Corn: Poems** (1999)
_____, **Cornflakes: Poems** (2000)
_____, **Popcorn: Poems** (1998)
_____, **Sweet Corn: Poems** (1995)
* Thomas, Joyce Carol, **The Blacker the Berry** (2008)
* _____, **Brown Honey in Broomwheat Tea** (1993)
* _____, **Gingerbread Days** (1995)
* _____, **Hush Songs: African American Lullabies** (2000)
_____, **I Have Heard of a Land** (1998)
Worth, Valerie, **All the Small Poems and Fourteen More** (1994)
_____, **Animal Poems** (2007)
_____, **Peacock and Other Poems** (2002)
Yolen, Jane, **Alphabestiary: Animal Poems from A to Z** (1995)
_____, **Color Me a Rhyme: Nature Poems for Young People** (2000)
_____, **Fine Feathered Friends** (2004)
* _____, **Street Rhymes around the World** (1992)

Poems for Intermediate Grade Readers

Adoff, Arnold, **Chocolate Dreams: Poems** (1989)
_____, **Eats: Poems** (1979)
_____, **Sports Pages** (1986)
_____, **Street Music: City Poems** (1995)
* Cassedy, Sylvia, **Red Dragonfly on My Shoulder: Haiku** (1992)
* Cheng, Andrea, **Where the Steps Were** (2008)
Creech, Sharon, **Hate that Cat** (2008)
_____, **Love that Dog** (2001)
Esbensen, Barbara Juster, **Dance with Me** (1995)
_____, **Echoes for the Eye: Poems to Celebrate Patterns in Nature** (1996)
_____, **Who Shrank My Grandmother's House?: Poems of Discovery** (1992)

_____, **Words with Wrinkled Knees**: Animal Poems (1986)
Fleischman, Paul, **Big Talk: Poems for Four Voices** (2000)
_____, **I Am Phoenix: Poems for Two Voices** (1985)
_____, **Joyful Noise: Poems for Two Voices** (1988)
Florian, Douglas, **Beast Feast** (1998)
_____, **Bing Bang Boing: Poems and Drawings** (1994)
_____, **In the Swim: Poems and Paintings** (1997)
_____, **Laugh-eteria: Poems and Drawings** (1999)
_____, **Mammalabilia: Poems and Paintings** (2000)
_____, **On the Wing: Bird Poems and Paintings** (1996)
_____, **Summersaults**: Poems and Paintings (2002)
Froman, Robert, **Seeing Things: A Book of Poems** (1974)
George, Kristine O'Connell, **Hummingbird Nest: A Journal of Poems** (2004)
_____, **Swimming Upstream: Middle School Poems** (2002)
_____, **Toasting Marshmallows: Camping Poems** (2001)
* Giovanni, Nikki, **Knoxville, Tennessee** (1994)
* _____, **Spin a Soft Black Song: Poems for Children** (1985)
* Gollub, Matthew, **Cool Melons—Turn to Frogs! The Life and Poems of Issa** (2005)
* Greenfield, Eloise, **The Great Migration: Journey to the North** (2011)
* _____, **Honey, I Love and Other Love Poems** (1972)
* Grimes, Nikki, **A Pocketful of Poems** (2001)
_____, **What Is Goodbye?** (2004)
Harley, Avis, **Fly with Poetry: An ABC of Poetry** (2000)
_____, **Leap into Poetry** (2001)
_____, **The Monarch's Progress: Poems with Wings** (2008)
Harrison, David, **The Boy Who Counted Stars: Poems** (1994)
_____, **Easy Poetry Lessons that Dazzle and Delight** (1999)
_____, **Somebody Catch My Homework: Poems** (1993)
_____, **A Thousand Cousins: Poems of Family Life** (1996)
Heard, Georgia, **Creatures of Earth, Sea, and Sky: Poems** (1992)
Hopkins, Lee Bennett, **Hand in Hand: An American History through Poetry** (1994)
_____, **Home to Me: Poems across America** (2002)
_____, **My America: A Poetry Atlas of the United States** (2000)
_____, **Sky Magic** (2008)
Janeczko, Paul B., **Dirty Laundry Pile: Poems in Different Voices** (2001)
_____, **Hey, You! Poems to Skyscrapers, Mosquitoes, and Other Fun Things** (2007)

———, *A Kick in the Head: An Everyday Guide to Poetic Forms* (2005)

———, *A Poke in the I: A Collection of Concrete Poems* (2001)

———, *That Sweet Diamond: Baseball Poems* (1998)

Janeczko, Paul B., and J. Patrick Lewis, *Hey, You!: Poems to Skyscrapers, Mosquitoes, and Other Fun Things* (2007)

———, *Wing Nuts: Screwy Haiku* (2006)

Kennedy, X. J., *Exploding Gravy: Poems to Make You Laugh* (2002)

———, *The Forgetful Wishing Well: Poems for Young People* (1985)

———, *Fresh Brats* (1990)

Kurtz, Jane, *River Friendly, River Wild* (1999)

❋ Lewis, J. Patrick, *Black Swan White Crow: Haiku* (1994)

———, *Doodle Dandies: Poems that Take Shape* (1998)

———, *A Hippopotamusn't and Other Animal Verses* (1990)

———, *Mathmatickles!* (2007)

———, *Ridicholas Nicholas: Animal Poems* (1995)

———, *Scien-Trickery: Riddles in Science* (2004)

Lewis, J. Patrick, and Paul B. Janeczko, *Birds on a Wire: Or a Jewel Tray of Stars* (2008)

Livingston, Myra Cohn, *Abraham Lincoln: A Man for All the People* (1993)

———, *Keep on Singing: A Ballad of Marion Anderson* (1994)

Myers, Christopher, *Jabberwocky* (2007)

❋ Myers, Walter Dean, *Brown Angels* (1993)

❋ ———, *Harlem* (1997)

❋ ———, *Jazz* (2006)

❋ Park, Linda Sue, *Tap Dancing on the Roof: Sijo (Poems)* (2007)

Prelutsky, Jack, *The Frogs Wore Red Suspenders: Rhymes* (2007)

❋ ———, *If Not for the Cat: Haiku* (2004)

———, *My Dog May Be a Genius* (2008)

———, *The New Kid on the Block* (1984)

———, *A Pizza the Size of the Sun: Poems* (1996)

———, *Scranimals* (2006)

———, *The Swamps of Sleethe: Poems from Beyond the Solar System* (2009)

Scieszka, Jon, *Math Curse* (1995)

———, *Science Verse* (2004)

Sidman, Joyce, *Butterfly Eyes and Other Secrets of the Meadow: Poems* (2006)

———, *Dark Emperor and Other Poems of the Night* (2010)

———, *Song of the Water Boatman & Other Pond Poems* (2005)

———, *Ubiquitous: Celebrating Nature's Survivors* (2010)

Silverstein, Shel, *Falling Up: Poems and Drawings* (1996)

———, *A Light in the Attic* (1981)

———, *Where the Sidewalk Ends* (1974)

Singer, Marilyn, *Mirror Mirror: A Book of Reversible Verse* (2011)

❋ Smith, Charles R. Jr., *Black Jack: the Ballad of Jack Johnson* (2010)

❋ Sneve, Virginia Driving Hawk, *Dancing Teepees: Poems of American Indian Youth* (1989)

Walker, Alice, *Why War Is Never a Good Idea* (2007)

Willard, Nancy, *A Visit to William Blake's Inn: Poems of Innocent and Experienced Travelers* (1981)

Wong, Janet S., *Behind the Wheel: Poems about Driving* (1999)

———, *Knock on Wood: Poems about Superstitions* (2003)

———, *Night Garden: Poems from the World of Dreams* (2000)

———, *The Rainbow Hand: Poems about Mothers and Children* (1999)

Yolen, Jane, *Once Upon Ice: and Other Frozen Poems* (1997)

———, *Snow, Snow: Winter Poems for Children* (2005)

———, *Water Music: Poems for Children* (1998)

Poems for Adolescent Readers

❋ Alexander, Elizabeth, and Marilyn Nelson, *Miss Crandall's School for Young Ladies & Little Misses of Color: Poems* (2007)

❋ Angelou, Maya, *Soul Looks Back in Wonder* (1993)

❋ Bierhorst, John, *In the Trail of the Wind: American Indian Poems and Ritual Orations* (1971)

❋ Brooks, Gwendolyn, *Bronzeville Boys and Girls* (1956/2007)

❋ ———, *Selected Poems* (2006)

Fletcher, Ralph, *I Am Wings: Poems about Love* (1994)

———, *Relatively Speaking: Poems about Family* (1999)

❋ Giovanni, Nikki, *Shimmy, Shimmy, Shimmy Like My Sister Kate: Looking at the Harlem Renaissance Through Poems* (1996)

Grandits, John, *Blue Lipstick: Concrete Poems* (2007)

Hopkins, Lee Bennett, *America at War: Poems Selected by Lee Bennett Hopkins* (2008)

———, *Been to Yesterdays: Poems of a Life* (1995)

❋ Hughes, Langston, *The Block*, selected by Lowery S. Sims and Daisy Murray Voigt (1995)

❋ ———, *The Dream Keeper: And Other Poems* (2007)

Janeczko, Paul B., *Looking for Your Name: A Collection of Contemporary Poems* (1993)

———, *Stone Bench in an Empty Park* (2000)

———, *Wherever Home Begins: 100 Contemporary Poems* (1995)

❋ Johnson, Angela, *The Other Side: Shorter Poems* (1998)

❋ ———, *Running Back to Ludie* (2001)

Lewis, J. Patrick, *The Brother's War: Civil War Voices in Verse* (2007)

＊ Myers, Walter Dean, *Here in Harlem: Poems in Many Voices* (2004)

＊ Nelson, Marilyn, *Carver: A Life in Poems* (2001)

_____, *A Wreath for Emmett Till* (2005)

Nye, Naomi Shihab, *Honeybee* (2008)

_____, *Is This Forever, or What? Poems and Paintings from Texas* (2004)

＊ _____, *19 Varieties of Gazelle: Poems of the Middle East* (2002)

＊ _____, *The Space Between Our Footsteps: Poems and Paintings from the Middle East* (1998)

Rosenberg, Liz, *Light-Gathering Poems* (2000)

_____, *Roots and Flowers: Poets and Poems on Family* (2001)

Rosenberg, Liz, and Deena November, *I Just Hope It's Lethal: Poems of Sadness, Madness, and Joy* (2005)

Sidman, Joyce, *The World According to Dog: Poems and Teen Voices* (2003)

＊ Soto, Gary, *Canto Familiar* (1995)

＊ _____, *Fire in My Hands* (1990)

_____, *Neighborhood Odes* (1992)

Vecchione, Patrice, *The Body Eclectic: An Anthology of Poems* (2002)

_____, *Revenge and Forgiveness: An Anthology of Poems* (2004)

Novels in Verse

Creech, Sharon, *Hate that Cat* (2008)

_____, *Love that Dog* (2001)

Creech, Sharon, and Margarita Engle, *The Poet Slave of Cuba: A Biography of Juan Francisco Manzano* (2006)

Frost, Helen, *The Braid* (2006)

*Greenfield, Eloise. *The Great Migration: Journey to the North.* (2010)

＊ Grimes, Nikki, *Bronx Masquerade* (2002)

＊ _____, *What Is Goodbye?* (2004)

Hemphill, Stephanie, *Things Left Unsaid* (2005)

_____, *Your Own, Sylvia: A Verse Portrait of Sylvia Plath* (2007)

Hesse, Karen, *Out of the Dust* (1997)

＊ _____, *Witness* (2001)

Janeczko, Paul B., *Worlds Afire* (2004)

Johnson, Angela, *The First Part Last* (2003)

Johnson, Lindsay Lee, *Soul Moon Soup* (2002)

Koertge, Ron, *Shakespeare Bats Cleanup* (2003)

_____, *Shakespeare Makes the Playoffs* (2010)

＊ McKissack, Patricia C. *Never Forgotten* (2011)

＊ Nelson, Marilyn, *Carver: A Life in Poems* (2001)

＊ Soto, Gary, *Fearless Fernie: Hanging Out with Fernie and Me* (2002)

Testa, Maria, *Becoming Joe DiMaggio* (2002)

＊ Williams, Vera B., *Amber Was Brave, Essie Was Smart: The Story of Amber and Essie Told Here in Poems and Pictures* (2001)

＊ Wolff, Virginia Euwer, *Make Lemonade* (1993)

_____, *True Believer* (2001)

Wong, Janet, *Minn and Jake* (2003)

＊ Woodson, Jacqueline, *Locomotion* (2003)

＊ _____, *Peace, Locomotion* (2009)

Additional resources to accompany this chapter can be found on the Education CourseMate website. Go to CengageBrain .com to access a variety of interactive study tools and useful resources including Video Conversations with children's book authors and illustrators, a searchable children's literature database, glossary flashcards, online activities, tutorial quizzes, links to relevant websites, and more.

Folklore:
A Literary Heritage

- **Defining Folklore**

- **A Brief History of Folklore for Young Readers**

- **Considering Quality in Folklore**
  A CLOSE LOOK AT *Bruh Rabbit and the Tar Baby Girl*

- **Patterns in Folklore**
  Conventions
  Motifs
  Themes

- **Types of Folklore**
  Nursery Rhymes
  Folktales
  Fables
  A CLOSE LOOK AT *The Lion & the Mouse*
  Myths and Pourquoi Stories
  Hero Tales: Epics and Legends
  A CLOSE LOOK AT *Beowulf*
  Folk Songs
  Fractured Fairy Tales and Literary Folklore

- **Folklore in the Classroom**

- **Summary**

- **Booklist**

Watch out behind you, Bruh Wolf! Better look out for Bruh Rabbit when next the day leans over and night falls down.

—VIRGINIA HAMILTON

Bruh Rabbit and the Tar Baby Girl, *illustrated by James Ransome, unpaged*

Dan's first/second-grade class in Minnesota has just heard Virginia Hamilton's **Bruh Rabbit and the Tar Baby Girl** (P) read aloud. This tale from the South Carolina Sea Islands was just what they needed to warm them up on this cold January day. James Ransome's sun-washed illustrations add to the warmth as well as the humor of the tale, and everyone was giggling by the time Dan finished reading the story. Comments such as "Served him right!" and "He got tricked himself!" indicate the degree of involvement of these young listeners.

Dan chose this particular book to read aloud because it meets three of the goals he has set for the winter months. He is collaborating with the art teacher to help students learn how to recognize the work of different illustrators, one of whom is James Ransome. This book is a bit different from most of Ransome's work because it is painted in watercolors rather than oils and of animal rather than human characters, so it will expand their understanding of Ransome's art. Dan also is trying to encourage his students to pay close attention to the words they read and hear, and then to use them in their own speaking and writing. Virginia Hamilton's use of Gullah words and phrases has delighted the students, and they will probably all go home tonight and tell their parents that dawn is really "dayclean" and evening is "daylean." Finally, Dan and his class are going to study trickster tales from around the world, and this is a great introduction to a classic African American trickster, a perfect way to begin their study of trickster tales—one of the most engaging types of folklore. Dan wants to help his students understand that all stories are part of a larger "family" of stories that share certain characteristics, that writers often borrow the elements and structure of old tales when they write, and that oral tales, the kind that many of the children hear at home, are the beginnings of the more polished written stories that they can produce themselves.

From just one thirty-two-page folktale comes the opportunity to learn about folklore, about art, about language, about an American culture, and about literature itself—as well as the occasion for a great deal of delight. Dan will go on to use a variety of trickster tales to not only delight his students, but to build upon their oral skills through storytelling and drama, to encourage their own writing, and to reflect on the many cultures that have produced these tales—cultures that the students in his class bring with them to school every day. Folklore offers him these unique opportunities for teaching and learning.

Defining Folklore

Creating stories is an essential part of being human. The oldest of stories—folklore, or traditional literature—includes those nursery rhymes, folktales, myths, epics, legends, fables, songs, and ballads that have been passed down by storytellers for hundreds, even thousands, of years to enlighten and entertain generations of listeners, young and old. Today, when we think of stories, we often think of books, of stories that are created by an author and written down, frozen just as they are for all time. Long ago, however, before most people could read or write, stories were told aloud to captivated listeners. Each time a teller told the tale, it was revised and reborn. Many of these tales have survived over the centuries, eventually finding their way into the books we share with children; some are still shared today through the ancient art of storytelling. It is important to remember, though, that they all began as oral stories.

There are many different types of folklore available to young readers: nursery, or Mother Goose, rhymes; folktales such as talking animal stories, noodlehead tales, fairy tales, and tall tales; fables; myths and pourquoi stories; hero tales, such as epics and legends; and folk songs. Today, we can select from all of these types of folklore, from a wide variety of cultural traditions, and from stunning books in which the stories are retold and illustrated by some of our finest authors and artists. This abundance, however, has not always been the case.

A Brief History of Folklore for Young Readers

No one knows who the first teller of any particular story was, only that with countless tellers, over long periods of time, the stories evolved into the written, literary tales that we know today. An accomplished teller of tales, Jane Yolen explains that "the oldest stories were transmitted and transmuted, the kaleidoscope patterns of motif changed by time and by the times, by the tellers and by the listeners, by the country in which they arose and the countries to which they were carried. The old oral tales were changed the way culture itself changes, the way traditions change, by an erosion/eruption as powerful in its way as any geological force" (2000, p. 22).

Stories of the folk of many different world cultures explained why the world is as it is, showed that wishes could come true, gave hope to the young and

the powerless, made even the fiercest fiend vulnerable, proved that good could vanquish evil, and taught all who listened how to live and work in harmony. Lise Lunge-Larsen (2004) suggests that "folktales grow out of the shadowy borderland between what is known and what is unknown. Or as ancient maps warned: Beyond here there be dragons."

Storytelling began with the songs and tales early societies composed to describe their daily work. "The first primitive efforts," notes storyteller Ruth Sawyer (1962, pp. 45–46), "consisted of a simple chant set to the rhythm of some daily tribal occupation such as grinding corn, paddling a canoe or kayak, sharpening weapons for hunting or war, or ceremonial dancing." As they speculated about the power of nature, the forces behind it, and human behavior, the people of primitive societies created stories to explain the unexplainable. These were the stories that grew into hero legends, pourquoi tales, and myths. When the ancient Greeks, for instance, were frightened by thunder, they invented a story about an angry god who shook the heavens. When they did not understand how and why the sun moved, they imagined a god who drove a chariot across the sky. With the passage of time, the folklore that had been passed from one generation to the next became our cultural heritage. Love, hate, heroic acts, values, morality, and other human qualities and concerns play an important part in myths of all cultures.

At one time, common belief held that all folklore emerged from one prehistoric civilization. The Grimm brothers, who collected tales from all over Germany, ascribed to this view, speculating that as people migrated, they took their stories with them. This theory would account for regional differences in folktales, such as the evolution of West Africa's trickster Ananse the spider to Anansi in the Caribbean and then to Aunt Nancy in the United States. As folklorists studied the tales of many diverse cultures, however, it became apparent that some stories must have originated spontaneously in a number of separate places, which would account for the hundreds of variants of the Cinderella tale told all over the world. Today, cultural anthropologists believe that both theories about the origin of folktales are correct. Folklore scholars Iona and Peter Opie (1974) note that no one theory "is likely to account satisfactorily for the origin of even a majority of the tales. Their wellsprings are almost certainly numerous, their ages likely to vary considerably, their meanings—if they ever had meanings—to be diverse" (p. 18). What we do know is that people everywhere tell and listen to stories and have done so for a long, long time.

The transition from oral retelling to printed versions of folktales dates back centuries. Some Eastern stories appeared in print as early as the ninth century.

In Europe, Straparola (1480–1557) gathered one of the earliest and most important collections of traditional tales in mid-sixteenth-century Venice in **Piacevoli Notti**, volumes 1 and 2 (published in 1550 and 1553). The work contains twenty folktales, including "Beauty and the Beast" and "Puss in Boots." Perrault's French publication of **Histoires ou Contes du Temps Passé, avec des Moralités (Stories or Tales of Times Past, with Morals)** in 1697, helped folk literature flourish in Europe. Perrault included "Sleeping Beauty," "Little Red Riding Hood," "Cinderella," and "Puss in Boots" along with other familiar tales in his collection, including many nursery rhymes that are still popular today.

As in all folklore, we do not have conclusive evidence of the origins of nursery rhymes, but we do know that these rhymes were linked with various political and social events (Opie & Opie, 1951). Many of the rhymes probably have a simple origin. They may have been created to teach children to count, to learn the alphabet or the days of the week, to share important customs and beliefs, or to remind them to say their prayers; others were probably intended simply for amusement. The literary name "Mother Goose" was probably first associated with Charles Perrault's 1697 publication. The frontispiece shows an old woman spinning and telling stories and is labeled **Contes de ma Mère l'Oye (Tales of My Mother Goose)**. Today, the name *Mother Goose* is associated primarily with nursery rhymes and no longer with the folktales first recorded in the late 1600s.

Folktales have deep literary roots. During the eighteenth century, La Fontaine's **Fables**, Countess d'Aulnoy's **Fairy Tales**, and de Beaumont's **Beauty and the Beast** were published. Toward the end of the eighteenth century, philologists such as the brothers Grimm studied folklore to find out about customs and languages in different societies. The German brothers traveled through the countryside asking people to tell stories they remembered. The Grimms eventually wrote a German dictionary and a book of grammar, but they are best remembered for their retellings of the stories they heard. The two volumes of the first edition of **Kinder-und Hausmärchen** were published in the early nineteenth century.

German Popular Stories, an English translation of the Grimms' tales illustrated by George Cruikshank, became an instant success when it was published in 1823. It raised the respectability of the old tales among scholars and educators, who had held them to be "an affront to the rational mind" (Opie & Opie, 1974, p. 25). Following the popularity of the Grimm brothers' tales, enthusiasm for collecting folklore spread around the world. Joseph Jacobs and Andrew Lang collected folktales in England; Jacobs's **English Fairy Tales** includes many well-loved stories, and Lang's series, in which the books are identified by color—**The Blue Fairy Book**, for example—continues to serve as a primary source of British tales. During the mid-1800s, Norse scholars Peter Christian Asbjornsen and Jorgen E. Moe collected most of the Scandinavian tales we have today.

Although most adults today recognize the importance of sharing folklore with children, some feel the tales are too sexist or too violent. Historically, though the tales were shared orally by everyone for many centuries, by the 1600s, many adults did not approve of them, finding the stories crude, brutal, dishonest, and of questionable moral value—certainly not appropriate for children. Jack Zipes (1979) points out that "the tales were often censored and outlawed during the early phase of the rise of the middle classes to power because their fantastic components which encouraged imaginative play and free exploration were contrary to the precepts of capitalist rationalization and the Protestant ethos" (p. 196).

It wasn't until the end of the nineteenth century that the tales were no longer generally considered dangerous to young minds and became widely available in print, but even well into the twentieth century arguments about their worth continued, with librarian Anne Carroll Moore a vociferous champion of the old stories (Marcus, 2008).

The beloved American writer Wanda Gág translated and illustrated the Grimms' stories in her **Tales from Grimm** (I) in 1936 and **More Tales from Grimm** (I) in 1947. Maurice Sendak handsomely illustrated Lore Segal's translation **The Juniper Tree and Other Tales from Grimm** (A) in 1973, a collection containing many gritty tales suitable for adolescent readers. In **The Annotated Brothers Grimm**, Maria Tatar translates 37 of the 210 tales, along with 9 adult tales, from the Grimms' final edition of the stories, giving readers valuable background information for each. Nancy Willard converted the Norwegian tale **East of the Sun and West of the Moon** into a dramatic play (A) of the same name, illustrated by Barry Moser. More recently, Lise Lunge-Larsen has collected Norwegian troll stories in **The Troll with No Heart in His Body** (I), with rough-textured woodcuts by Betsy Bowen that echo the age of the tales. Isaac Bashevis Singer's collections of Yiddish tales, in such books as **Naftali the Storyteller and His Horse, Sus** (P–I), and **When Shlemiel Went to Warsaw and Other Stories** (I), are inspired by old Jewish stories he heard as a boy in Warsaw.

In the 1960s and 1970s, interest in folklore from other than western European cultures began to grow, and in the almost fifty years since, the genre has grown to include stories from many countries and from various cultural traditions in North America. Although there are still more retellings of stories from the western European tradition, young readers now have access to tales from Australia to Zaire. Those tales include not only stories from other countries, but also tales that Africans brought with them to America and retold as they struggled with slavery, to those brought by immigrants from all corners of the world, to those from Native American cultures across the continent. With this new richness of cultural traditions came important questions surrounding cultural authenticity and appropriation (Bader, 2006), with many calling for the importance of acknowledging sources and respecting cultural origins. Picturebook versions of traditional tales dominated the market in the 1980s and 1990s, with 555 folklore picturebooks published in the 1990s, many of which came from small presses. Such was America's hunger for ethnic variety in picturebooks for young readers (Bader, 2010). The publication of folklore has slowed since, but there are still wonderful new books being created each year, such as Jerry Pinkney's **The Lion & the Mouse** (N–P), which was awarded the Caldecott Medal in 2011.

Stories such as Virginia Hamilton's stunning collections **The People Could Fly: American Black Folktales** (A) and **In the Beginning: Creation Stories from around the World** (A), Ed Young's illustrations of single stories from China such as **Lon Po Po: A Red-Riding Hood Story from China** (P–I) and Ai-Ling Louie's **Yeh Shen: A Cinderella Story from China** (P–I), Joseph Bruchac's retellings of Native American tales such as **Between Earth and Sky: Legends of Native American Sacred Places** (I–A), and Isabel Schon's **Doña Blanca and Other Hispanic Nursery Rhymes and Games** (P) greatly enrich the choices for young readers. Collections such as Shirley Climo's **Monkey Business: Stories from around the World** (I), illustrated by Erik Brooks, enable young readers to savor tales from varied places, in this case Africa and Madagascar, the Americas, and Asia. The collection contains fourteen tales, a scattering of proverbs, fables, myths, legends, and folktales, and the sources are documented in the concluding commentary. Although he does not include source notes, Sam McBratney's **One Voice, Please: Favorite Read-Aloud Stories** (I), illustrated by Russell Ayto, offers fifty-six tales of wise men, fools, and tricksters from across the world. Rafe Martin has produced an extensive culturally diverse collection of work, which includes folklore from India, such as **The Brave Little Parrot**, illustrated by Susan Gaber, and **Foolish Rabbit's Big Mistake**, illustrated by Ed Young. **Dear as Salt, The Language of Birds, Mysterious Tales of Japan**, and **The Shark God** draw on the oral traditions of Italy, Russia, Japan, and Hawaii. Martin retells a Chinook tale in **The Boy Who Lived with Seals**, and **The Rough-Face Girl** is a Cinderella story in the Algonquin tradition.

Denys Johnson-Davies retells **Goha, the Wise Fool** (I), with illustrations of hand-sewn tapestries by Cairo tent maker Hany El SaedAhmed and illustrations by Hag Hamdy Mohamed Fattouh. Patricia Santos Marcantonio sets her retellings in the American southwest in **Red Ridin' in the Hood: And Other Cuentos** (I–A), illustrated by Renato Alcarcão. This collection contains eleven stories, a glossary for the sprinkling of Spanish words, and detailed, if satirical, full-page drawings.

Whatever the explanation of the origins or purposes of the tales, it is clear that similar archetypes—images, plot patterns, themes, or character types that recur in the oldest stories—appear in the myths, legends, and folktales of all people across time and in all places. Traditional heroes from many cultures share similar traits: they often have unusual births, leave home to go on a quest, have magical help, have to prove themselves through many trials, and are richly rewarded for their heroism. Other familiar character examples that reappear in many tales include the good mother (fairy godmother), the bad mother (wicked stepmother or old witch), and the evil underside of every person (the shadow). The same archetypes of these primal stories appear in realistic and fantasy novels; characters continue to battle the forces of evil to ensure the survival of good. Some retellers reposition the tales by setting them in modern times, as does Jude Daly in **Sivu's Six Wishes: A Taoist Tale** (P), an ancient tale of a stonemason's greed and perhaps the origin of the old adage "Be careful what you wish for."

Folklore gave us the stories that underlie so many modern stories, the stories of the people, all the people, which continue to play a vital role in the lives of children. The bravery, loyalty, and daring embodied in some of these tales continue to thrill young readers, while the humor and exaggerations of other tales make them laugh. Folklore from the world over also helps young readers understand the universal family of stories, providing them with many examples of common human values.

In this chapter we will:

- Consider how to determine the quality of a retelling
- Explore common patterns in folklore
- Discuss examples of different types of folklore
- Suggest why folklore can be an important genre for classroom study

Considering Quality in Folklore

These old tales are at their best when the style of the written story reflects the oral origins of the tale. Vivid phrases and rhythmic language capture the attention of a listener, and these remain in good retellings. Listen for language that sounds natural when read aloud—that contains imagery, melodious rhythms, and the cadences of speech. Oral origins mean that most folklore gets into the action, or plot, immediately. Characters are delineated sparingly, such as the stereotypical beautiful princess, and settings are vague, such as the oft-used "Once upon a time." The themes of these stories represent age-old values and beliefs that formed the basis for how ancient peoples lived in the world; they should be readily apparent to young readers.

Stories that maintain the cultural integrity of early versions best represent those cultures. Excellent retellings note the cultural origins of the tale and often cite their sources, so look for this information in the books you select. Artists present an immense amount of cultural detail in their illustrations—detail that the honed language of folklore may not provide. Further, artists have a unique opportunity to create their own visions because the oft-told tales present only general descriptions of setting and character. Look for artistically excellent illustrations that complement and

extend the narrative and accurately reflect the cultural heritage of the tale. When evaluating folklore, look for qualities of authenticity and excellence in language, theme, and illustration, as presented in Figure 5.1.

FIGURE 5.1

Considering Quality in Folklore

Language

- Echoes spoken language, with rich, natural rhythms
- Reflects the cultural integrity of early retellings
- Preserves the straightforward structure of oral stories
- Explores significant universal themes

Illustrations

- Serve as examples of artistic excellence
- Complement and extend the narrative
- Offer authentic cultural detail

P R O F I L E

Virginia Hamilton

Books can and do help us to live; and some may even change our lives.

The late Virginia Hamilton has been lauded as the most important author for children. Indeed, in her groundbreaking work, she created more than forty books, ranging from folklore and biography to historical fiction, contemporary realistic fiction, and fantasy—all of which reflected her African American roots, her unflinching willingness to tackle difficult subjects, and above all her unsurpassed talent as a writer. This talent as well as her innovative contributions to literature for children was recognized by

numerous awards. *M. C. Higgins the Great* was the first book ever to win both the National Book Award and the Newbery Medal. She won several Newbery Honor and Coretta Scott King Awards, and in 1992 was honored with the Hans Christian Andersen Medal, the "Nobel prize" in children's literature. She was also awarded the Laura Ingalls Wilder Award for lifetime achievement and was the first writer of children's literature to receive a MacArthur "genius" grant.

Her notable works of folklore include *The People Could Fly: American Black Folktales; In the Beginning: Creation Stories*

from around the World; Her Stories: African American Folktales, Fairy Tales, and True Tales; When Birds Could Talk and Bats Could Sing: The Adventures of Bruh Sparrow, Sis Wren, and Their Friends; A Ring of Tricksters: Animal Tales from America, the West Indies, and Africa; The People Could Fly: The Picturebook; and *Bruh Rabbit and the Tar Baby Girl*.

 To learn more about Virginia Hamilton, go to Cengage Brain.com to access the Education CourseMate where you will find links to relevant websites.

*The humor of **Bruh Rabbit and the Tar Baby Girl** is evident in the sight of Bruh Rabbit, with a sheepish look in his eyes, perched on the back of the Tar Baby Girl.*

We now turn to an examination of a familiar trickster tale retold by one of America's most gifted storytellers and illustrated by an outstanding artist.

* * *

A CLOSE LOOK AT
Bruh Rabbit and the Tar Baby Girl

James Ransome's brilliant artistic interpretation and Virginia Hamilton's exciting text make **Bruh Rabbit and the Tar Baby Girl** (P) a special book. In it Hamilton retells the familiar trickster tale as it is told by the Gullah people of the South Carolina Sea Islands.

Hamilton's gift with language is evident from the opening of the story with the words "It was a far time ago." She tells her story with a perfect balance of distinctive Gullah dialect and standard written English. The Gullah constructions that she chooses to use are all understandable to young readers, such as those who appear in the opening vignette for this chapter, who are captivated by the unusual words. Such words as *Bruh, tricky-some, nary, scarey-crow, daylean, croker sack*, and *dayclean* are understandable within the context of the story and in their relation to standard written English or their descriptive properties.

Sentences such as "Guess me, somebody been into my peanuts" or "For true, somebody been here" convey the thoughts of the characters, the events of the story, and the flavor of the Gullah dialect. Indeed, the link between the written text and the oral genesis of the original tale is a close one. You can hear the storyteller's voice in Hamilton's prose as the lazy rabbit "sneakity-sneaks" along until—"WHOOM!"—he sees the scarey-crow. The text simply begs to be read aloud, as a good retelling of an oral story should.

Ransome's watercolor with pen-and-ink illustrations are beautiful. Further, they not only reflect the events of the tale but create a detailed setting, develop the stock characters, and extend the humor. We know this will be a lighthearted story from the front cover because of the way the title and the author's name curve around the huge sun that fills the center of the page, anchored by the brown wooden fence and green grass running horizontally across the bottom, as well as the predominance of yellow and gold. The two title characters—the rabbit and the tar baby girl—are centered on the page, directly in front of the sun. The fence, the briars that are visible behind it, and the size of the sun are the first hints of the setting.

Ransome continues to develop the setting in the endpages. As we open the book, we see, literally, a bird's-eye view of a countryside scene; the particular bird has a bonnet on her head. There's an old frame house, with a typical southern chimney and roof, a pond with ducks being watched by an alligator almost hidden in the bushes, and bluish mountains off in the distance. Everything is green, except where the grass has worn away to the orange-brown dirt. In this scene Ransome also begins to develop the characters. We see Bruh Wolf at work in his garden, while Bruh Rabbit is racing down the path from his burrow door toward the pond, fishing pole and bucket in hand. Upon turning the page, on the verso, opposite the title page, we see Bruh Rabbit throwing horseshoes, and on the dedication page he is fishing while Bruh Wolf pushes a wheelbarrow in the background. Before the story even begins, it is clear from the illustrations that Bruh Rabbit likes to have fun. The character development and the humor continue as we see Bruh Rabbit asleep in the first two pictures, and then Bruh Wolf working hard on his scarey-crow.

The seamless integration of text and illustration makes **Bruh Rabbit and the Tar Baby Girl** an outstanding example of a picturebook retelling of a classic folktale. Ransome's touching dedication of the book to the late Virginia Hamilton and the endnote about the origins of the tale add to the impact of the book. To learn more about James Ransome, go to CengageBrain.com to access the Education Course-Mate where you will find links to relevant websites.

Patterns in Folklore

Students who read widely soon recognize recurring patterns in the folklore of many countries. As characters, events, and resolutions recur in their reading, students begin to recognize the conventions, motifs, and themes that form these tales. They then use this literary knowledge in their subsequent reading and writing. Teachers and librarians can help students recognize these patterns if they provide exposure to a wide array of stories that exemplify characteristic structures.

● ● CONVENTIONS ● ●

Literary devices called conventions are the cornerstones of folktales. One of the easiest conventions for children to recognize and use in their own writing is the story frame, such as the one that begins with "Once upon a time" and ends with "They lived happily ever after." Opening variations such as "Long ago and far away" or "Once there was and once there was not," which are used by storytellers in some cultural groups, contribute to children's ability to generalize the patterns; seeing a different frame serve the same purpose helps children appreciate the flexibility of the device. Early in their literary education, children search for formulaic patterns in language, plots, and characters that they can identify.

The repeated use of the number three is another familiar convention in the western European tradition. In addition to three main characters—three bears, three billy goats, three pigs—there are usually three events. "Goldilocks and the Three Bears" contains three bears, of course, but also three more sets of three: three bowls of porridge, three chairs, and three beds. Goldilocks tries each bowl of porridge and each chair and bed before deciding which is "just right." Many other folktales feature three tasks, three adventures, three magical objects, three trials, or three wishes. The number seven appears frequently, too, as in "Snow White and the Seven Dwarfs," "The Seven Ravens," and "The Seven Swans." In stories from other cultural groups, such as Native American tales, the convention might be four rather than three because the four seasons anchor many Native American tales. These various story structures add richness to our understandings of "story" and become an important resource for children learning to read and write narrative. Teaching Idea 5.1 offers suggestions for helping English learners develop their understanding of story structure; the suggestions are, however, applicable to all students.

● ● MOTIFS ● ●

A motif is a recurring salient element, the smallest unit used to classify tales: the intentional repetition of a word or phrase, an event or unit of action, characters, objects, or ideas that run through a story. Motifs have been used by folklorists to categorize and analyze tales, as in Stith Thompson's five-volume *Motif-Index of Folk-Literature* (1955–1958). Many stories share similar stock characters (for example, the youngest son, the trickster), many contain magical objects (such as flying carpets, cooking pots, or boots and other footwear), and many include episodes in which characters sleep for a very long time or make wishes. Beasts and frogs are really princes, and evil creatures and human beings are easily tricked. These are the folklore elements that make these stories so appealing to children from one generation to the next. Margaret Read MacDonald and Brian W. Sturm have created *The Storyteller's Sourcebook: A Subject, Title, and Motif Index to Folklore Collections for Children, 1983–1999* (2001), a valuable resource for teachers and librarians who want students to compare folktale variants and their motifs.

TEACHING IDEA 5.1

Discovering Story Structures with English Learners

ELL

COMMON CORE STATE STANDARDS

This Teaching Idea addresses Common Core English Language Arts, Reading: Literature standards 2, 5 grade 2; 2 grade 3. The suggestions in this Teaching Idea may need to be adapted to suit your particular grade level and the needs of your students.

In Western European cultures, we think of the structure of narratives as following a particular pattern with predictable elements. There are characters engaged in a problem, with a beginning, a middle (often with three episodes), the climax, and then the ending, or resolution. In some cultures, however, there is more emphasis on plot, while others emphasize character. In many cultures there is also the presence of an explicit moral, or lesson to be learned. For English language learners who come from a culture in which stories are structured differently than they are in the Western European tales that dominate school libraries, comprehension can be difficult. How, for example, can a student sense foreshadowing or make accurate predictions if there is no inherent sense, based on knowledge of narrative structures, of where the story is going.

One way to support English language learners who may be familiar with different story structures is to be deliberate about including stories from many different cultures, exhibiting different story structures. Both familiarity with a variety of tales and time spent comparing and contrasting the way stories work in different cultures, help English language learners comprehend new stories.

Another way to support English language learners is to encourage all students to bring their oral stories to the classroom. A storytelling time offers everyone opportunities to tell and hear a variety of tales. By listening closely, responding with interest, and asking questions that extend students' language, teachers help English language learners extend their ability to speak English as well as strengthen their comprehension toolbox.

Many stories contain a number of different motifs that students can identify when comparing folktales. Cinderella stories often contain a small shoe, a flight from a gathering, a youngest daughter who is ill-treated, a wealthy man or prince, a mean stepmother, and a magical wish-granter. Characters—gods, witches, fairies, tricksters, noodleheads, or stepmothers—behave in stereotypical ways, so readers learn to predict how they will act in certain situations.

A second kind of motif involves magical objects, spells, curses, or wishes as the center of the plot. Magic beans tossed carelessly out a window lead the way to a magical kingdom in "Jack and the Beanstalk." "The Magic Porridge Pot" and its variants hinge on the magical properties of said pot. Sometimes the magical element is a spell or enchantment. Both Snow White and Sleeping Beauty are victims of a witch's evil curse and are put to sleep until a kiss from a handsome prince awakens them. In some stories, the evil spell causes a transformation; only love and kindness can return the frog, donkey, or beast to its former state. "The Frog Prince," "The Donkey Prince," "The Seven Ravens," "The Six Swans," "Jorinda and Joringel," and "Beauty and the Beast" are all transformation tales.

A third type of motif involves trickery, or outwitting someone else. A spider man is the trickster in African and Caribbean tales, a rabbit in West African tales, a coyote in many Native American tales, and a tortoise in the Brazilian tale ***Jabuti the Tortoise*** (P–I), by Gerald McDermott. Trickery and cunning also appear in French and Swedish folktales, such as "Stone Soup" and "Nail Soup." The wiliest trickster of all, Brer Rabbit, is almost always able to outsmart his larger opponents, except when he himself is tricked.

• • THEMES • •

Themes in folktales, obvious although not stated explicitly, express the values of the people who created them and reflect their philosophy of life. The theme in a folktale revolves around a topic of universal human concern. Time and time again, the struggle between good and evil is played out: hate, fear, laziness, and greed contrast with love, security, industriousness, and generosity. The themes are usually developed through stock characters who personify one trait. For example, the bad fairy in "Sleeping Beauty," the witch in "Hansel and Gretel," and the

TEACHING IDEA 5.2

An Exploration of Theme in Folklore

COMMON CORE STATE STANDARDS This Teaching Idea addresses the Common Core English Language Arts, Reading: Literature standards 2, 9 grades 2 through 5; 2 grades 6 through 8. The suggestions in this Teaching Idea may need to be adapted to suit your particular grade level and the needs of your students.

Reading a wide range of folklore helps students develop a sense of its basic elements. Gradually, they become aware of various archetypes and motifs in the folklore they read and are able to identify images, characters, and patterns that occur frequently. To develop an awareness of the dominant themes in folklore, ask students to identify the important lessons conveyed through the tales and to list them along with the titles of the stories. Compare their discoveries with those of other students. Ask students which themes and stories appeal to them most. Why do these big ideas resonate? What do they say about what students value and believe to be true? About who they are? Some books that contain evocative themes include the following:

Hero's Quest

Hodges, Margaret, **St. George and the Dragon: A Golden Legend**

McKinley, Robin, **The Outlaws of Sherwood**

Rumford, James, **Beowulf: A Hero's Tale Retold**

Good versus Bad

San Souci, Robert D., **The Talking Eggs: A Folktale from the American South**

Steptoe, John, **Mufaro's Beautiful Daughters**

Yolen, Jane, **Tam Lin: An Old Ballad**

Young, Ed, **Lon Po Po: A Red-Riding Hood Story from China**

Transformations and the Power of Love

Brett, Jan, **Beauty and the Beast**

Cooper, Susan, **The Selkie Girl**

Ormerod, Jan, and David Lloyd, **The Frog Prince**

Steptoe, John, **The Story of Jumping Mouse**

Yagawa, Sumiko, **The Crane Wife**, translated by Katherine Paterson

---

stepmother in "Snow White" all represent evil. Each is destroyed, and the virtuous characters triumph. Such themes are reassuring; we would all like to believe that good prevails and evil is punished. In enchantment and transformation tales, the struggle between good and evil materializes as a contrast between surface appearances and deeper qualities of goodness. A beautiful princess sees the goodness of the prince hidden beneath the loathsome or laughable guise of a beast, frog, or donkey, or a prince sees beauty beneath the dirt and rags of a young woman. In other stories, such as some versions of "Sleeping Beauty," the entire world lies under an evil spell, veiled and hidden from clear view until goodness triumphs.

Another theme, that of the quest, centers on the hero's search for happiness or lost identity, which he undertakes in order to restore harmony to life. The hero succeeds only after repeated trials, much suffering, and extended separation, and he often exhibits courage, gallantry, and sacrifice. Teaching Idea 5.2 offers suggestions for exploring themes in folklore with students.

Types of Folklore

Folklore has many categories. Those most commonly available to young readers include nursery rhymes; folktales such as animal tales, noodlehead tales, fairy tales, and tall tales; fables; myths; hero tales such as epics and legends; and folk songs. Beginning in infancy and continuing through the primary grades, children delight in nursery rhymes. As they grow, they begin to understand and enjoy folktales, tall tales, myths, legends, and the simple stories and morals of fables. This literary background helps them form their ideas about how stories work.

• • NURSERY RHYMES • •

Mother Goose and other nursery rhymes form the foundation of many children's literary heritage. Surprising as that may sound, the rhythm and rhyme of the language as well as the nursery rhyme's compact structure and engaging characters produce bountiful models for young children learning language. Children learn about characters, themes, and structures that become the foundation for subsequent literary education. As they chant the phrases, mimic the nonsense words, and endlessly recite the alliterative rhymes and repetitions, children also develop phonemic awareness—the ability to segment sounds in spoken words, something that is a prerequisite to learning phonics and linked to proficient reading. Exposure to nursery rhymes improves children's phonological skills and thereby their later reading ability (MacLean, Bryant, & Bradley, 1987). More important, children delight in language play.

Nursery rhymes know no regional, ethnic, cultural, or language boundaries. People around the world have crooned similar verses to their young children. The magic of Mother Goose is still handed down by word of mouth, though there are many collections available. When selecting books to share with children, it is important to choose versions that maintain the original, robust language.

Characteristics

The *rhythmic words* of nursery rhymes strengthen a child's sense of language. The cadence of the language—its beat, stress, sound, and intonation— reflects the oral origins and charms the listener's ear. It is almost impossible to keep from bouncing when hearing:

> Ride a cock horse
> to Banbury Cross
> to see a fine lady
> upon a white horse.

A second characteristic of nursery rhymes is the *imaginative use of words and ideas.* Nothing is too preposterous! Children delight in the images conjured up by:

> Hey diddle, diddle,
> The cat and the fiddle,
> The cow jumped over the moon;
> The little dog laughed
> To see such sport,
> And the dish ran away with the spoon.

These verses feed the fancy, spark creativity, and stretch imagination: three wise men of Gotham go to sea in a bowl; an old woman is tossed up in a basket nineteen times as high as the moon; another old woman lives in a shoe with her entire brood of children. Anything can happen in nursery rhymes.

A third characteristic, *compact structure*, establishes the scene quickly and divulges the plot at once.

In four short lines, we hear an entire story:

> Jack Sprat could eat no fat,
> His wife could eat no lean,
> And so between them both, you see,
> They licked the platter clean.

As in all folklore, the consolidation of action and the economy of words result from the rhymes being said aloud for many generations before being set in print. As the verses were passed from one teller to the next, they were honed to their present simplicity.

The *wit* and *whimsy* of the characters also account for the popularity and longevity of Mother Goose. Children appreciate the humorous nonsense in:

> Peter, Peter, pumpkin eater,
> Had a wife and couldn't keep her;
> He put her in a pumpkin shell,
> And there he kept her very well.

Collections of Nursery Rhymes

Such old favorites as Alice and Martin Provensen's **The Mother Goose Book**, Blanche Fisher Wright's **The Real Mother Goose**, Arnold Lobel's **The Random House Book of Mother Goose**, and Iona and Peter Opie's **Tail Feathers from Mother Goose: The Opie Rhyme Book** (N–P) provide many familiar and some less familiar rhymes to share. More recently, Rosemary Wells and Iona Opie worked together to produce **My Very First Mother Goose**, **Mother Goose's Little Treasures**, and **Here Comes Mother Goose** (N–P). Leo and Diane Dillon's **Mother Goose: Numbers on the Loose** (P) is a verbal and visual treasure. Nina Crews has added a lively urban collection, **The Neighborhood Mother Goose** (P–I). **The Charles Addams Mother Goose** (A), with its darkly droll, comic illustrations, will appeal to older students who will see the familiar rhymes in a totally novel way. Sally Mavor's **Pocketful of Posies: A Treasury of Nursery Rhymes** (N) contains sixty-four familiar rhymes and is illustrated with photographs of needlework tapestry. It won the 2011 Boston Globe–Horn Book Award for picturebooks. Chris Duffy has edited a collection of fifty nursery rhymes as interpreted by fifty cartoonists in **Nursery Rhyme Comics** (N–P–I) in which the outline art transforms the words into a visual delight. The cartoon format appeals to a wide range of readers.

Authors, editors, and publishers, aware of the international makeup of our population and the global village view of our world, search for new books to reflect that vision. Patricia Polacco includes verses and images from her Russian grandmother in **Babushka's Mother Goose**; Nancy Van Laan depicts a mother and a child from seven different continents in **Sleep, Sleep, Sleep: A Lullaby for Little Ones Around the World**; and Jane Yolen selects from an international palette in **Sleep Rhymes around the World** (N–P). For their collection **Chinese Mother Goose Rhymes** (N–P), illustrator Ed Young and editor Robert Wyndham have chosen rhymes from the Chinese oral tradition that may sometimes seem familiar even to modern American children. **¡Pío Peep! Traditional Spanish Nursery Rhymes** (N), by Alma Flor Ada and F. Isabel Campoy, with English adaptations by poet Alice Schertle, is a bilingual collection of rhymes that may be well known to Latino children and will appeal to children from other cultures as well. These, and other books of rhyme discussed in Chapter 4, are wonderful fare for exploring language shaped by cultures around the world.

• • FOLKTALES • •

Folktales have delighted young and old for countless generations. These stories, which include talking animal stories, noodlehead tales, fairy tales, and tall tales, are narratives in which heroes and heroines triumph over adversity by demonstrating virtues like cleverness or bravery, or loveable vices like supreme silliness. Their themes, obvious though not always stated explicitly, express the values of the people who created them. Authors Alice McGill and Virginia Hamilton have both retold the African American slave tale, in which slaves "fly" to freedom, in language that captures the spirit of people longing to be free. Hamilton's retellings appear in her collected stories in **The People Could Fly: American Black Folktales** (A), illustrated by Leo and Diane Dillon, and in a sumptuous picturebook version, also illustrated by the Dillons, **The People Could Fly** (I). Alice McGill's version, **Way up and over Everything** (P), illustrated by Jude Daly, presents the same story to a younger audience. All three versions are powerful statements of the solace of imagined freedom.

Characteristics

Folktales have an artistic yet simple form that derives from the oral tradition. The *plot structure* is clean and direct. A succinct beginning establishes characters, setting, and problem; the body develops the problem and moves toward the climax; and the ending quickly resolves the problem without complications. Folktales are, in fact, minidramas. See Teaching Idea 5.3 for ideas for involving students in folklore theatre.

The plot of a folktale unfolds with little ambiguity: the good characters are supremely good, the evil ones are outrageously evil—and justice prevails

TEACHING IDEA 5.3

Create a Folklore Performance

ELL

This Teaching Idea addresses Common Core English Language Arts, Reading: Literature standards 1 through 5 grade 2; 2 through 5 grade 3; 5 grade 4. The suggestions in this Teaching Idea may need to be adapted to suit your particular grade level or the needs of your students. This oral language activity helps all students develop their oral language skills; it is especially suited to English language learners.

Folklore is ideal material for readers' theatre, puppetry, or choral reading. Folktales contain simple plot lines, a limited cast of well-defined characters, and decisive endings, making them ideal for young scriptwriters and dramatists. To create a folklore performance with your students:

1. Ask book groups to choose several folktales to read.

2. Generate criteria for selecting a good story for dramatizing. What elements make stories easier to tell?

3. Have them choose their favorite folktale that fits the selection criteria to share through creative drama.

4. Prepare a script for readers' theatre, a puppet play, or choral reading.

5. Practice and share the performance with others.

Folklore performances help all children develop oral language skills, no matter what first language they speak. Working with their simple structure also supports important comprehension skills.

without compromise. The problem, or conflict, is identified early, and only incidents that build on the problem or add complexity to it have survived oral transmission. Problems are resolved decisively and succinctly, resulting in classic happily-ever-after endings. Margaret Willey's books set in the far north woods, ***Clever Beatrice: An Upper Peninsula Conte*** and ***Clever Beatrice and the Best Little Pony*** (P–I), which introduce a spunky and very capable young girl who first outsmarts a giant and then a lutin—a cunning little man—are excellent examples of tales that fit this pattern.

Because folktales are more concerned with situation than personality, characters are delineated economically and usually exemplify one salient trait. These one-dimensional stock characters crystallize in the form of the foolish, the wise, the wicked, or the virtuous. All perform in predictable ways and rarely change throughout the course of a story. The language is direct, vivid vernacular that reflects the oral heritage of the tale; they are tempered to the tongue, having been honed and polished through centuries.

Although folktales use precise language, the verbal *setting* remains vague; the stories take place in unidentified times, in places defined by minimal detail, allowing illustrators to let their imaginations soar. Folktales know no geographical or temporal boundaries; they come to life everywhere for each new generation of children. Figure 5.2 summarizes folktale characteristics.

FIGURE 5.2

Folktale Characteristics

- Characters represent such traits as cleverness, bravery, or supreme silliness.
- Characters are delineated economically.
- Plot lines are direct and uncluttered by side issues (this varies by culture).
- Stories contain very little ambiguity.
- Conflict is identified early.
- Resolution is decisive.
- Themes express the values of the people who created them.
- Language is a direct, vivid vernacular.
- Setting and time are vague, other than as depicted in illustrations.

Types of Folktales

TALKING ANIMAL AND TRICKSTER TALES In this type of tale, animals talk with human beings or with one another. Like human characters, the talking animals may be good or evil, wise or silly. Those who are good and wise are rewarded. Young children especially enjoy talking animals. Perennial favorites include "The Three Little Pigs," "The Three Billy Goats Gruff," "Henny Penny," "Brer Rabbit," and the Anansi spider stories. Talking animal tales come from everywhere. Jessica Souhami retells a traditional tale from India in ***No Dinner! The Story of the Old Woman and the Pumpkin*** (N–P). With the help of her granddaughter, the old woman outsmarts a bear, wolf, and tiger that want to eat her for dinner. Lisbeth Zwerger illustrates the classic Grimm tale, ***The Bremen Town Musicians*** (P), translated by Anthea Bell, in which a dog, cat, rooster, and donkey outwit robbers and find a home. Rebecca Emberley and Ed Emberley retell ***Chicken Little*** (N–P) to hilarious effect with side-splitting illustrations and silly sound effects.

Children appreciate the humorous situations and rhythmic language of Eric Kimmel's retelling of the West African trickster tale ***Anansi Goes Fishing*** (P), an exemplary talking animal tale, as is his tale ***Anansi and the Moss-Covered Rock*** (P), with Janet Stevens's humorous illustrations of the scheming spider and all the animals he tricks and is tricked by. Native American tribal tales also have tricksters, such as the coyote and raven. Gerald McDermott's series of trickster tales includes ***Coyote: A Trickster Tale from the American Southwest*** (P–I), telling the story of a prideful, comic mischief-maker with "a nose for trouble." He brings another comic mischief-maker to life in ***Pig-Boy: A Trickster Tale from Hawai'I*** (P–I). His ***Monkey: A Trickster Tale from India*** (P–I) concludes the series. The rabbit in ***Brother Rabbit: A Cambodian Tale*** (P–I), by Minfong Ho and Saphan Ros, is clever enough to repeatedly outsmart the hungry crocodile. Animal tricksters such as these are common in stories from many different cultures. Julius Lester (2004) writes that "a prime characteristic of the trickster tale is the absence of morality. Uncle Remus said, 'Creatures don't know nothing about that's good and that's bad. They don't know right from wrong. They see what they want and they get it if they can, by hook or crook'" (p. 114). Perhaps tricksters and their stories are so appealing to children for just that reason: tricksters will do anything to get what they want.

Brer Rabbit trickster stories were carried by enslaved people from Africa and Jamaica to the

American rural South. Storyteller Joel Chandler Harris retold these slave tales and they were popularized by Disney in the movie *Song of the South*. New retellings that respect the cultural origins of the tales are now available. Van Dyke Parks's outstanding renditions of these traditional tales include ***Jump! The Adventures of Brer Rabbit***; ***Jump Again! More Adventures of Brer Rabbit***, and ***Jump on Over! The Adventures of Brer Rabbit and His Family*** (P–I), all illustrated by Barry Moser. Julius Lester's retellings ***The Tales of Uncle Remus: The Adventures of Brer Rabbit; More Tales of Uncle Remus: Further Adventures of Brer Rabbit, His Friends, Enemies, and Others***; and ***Further Tales of Uncle Remus: The Misadventures of Brer Rabbit, Brer Fox, Brer Wolf, the Doodang, and Other Creatures*** (I–A) are also marked by melodious language that reflects the authentic speech patterns of the culture that gave rise to the stories. ***The Butter Tree: Tales of Bruh Rabbit*** (I), retold by Mary Lyons and illustrated by Mireille Vautier, and Hamilton's ***Bruh Rabbit and the Tar Baby Girl*** (P) show that Brer Rabbit is just as sly as ever.

Margaret Hodges retells ***Dick Whittington and His Cat*** (P), with illustrations by Melisande Potter, a picturebook that is sure to charm a new generation. Shirley Climo retells a story from the Philippines in ***Tuko and the Birds: A Tale from the Philippines*** (P), illustrated by Francesco X. Mora, in which a gecko is a nuisance to the other animals. Other talking animal stories appear in the Booklist at the end of the chapter.

NOODLEHEAD TALES Humorous noodlehead stories focus on characters that are pure-hearted but lacking in good judgment. In ***Noodlehead Stories from around the World*** (I), Moritz A. Jagendorf describes a noodlehead as a simple blunderer who does not use good sense or learn from experience. Storyteller Colleen Salley's ***Epossomandus*** (P) and ***Epossomandus Saves the Day*** (P), both illustrated by Janet Stevens, engage young listeners as they laugh at the antics of the characters and cheer Epossomandus on. Jessica Souhami's ***Sausages*** (N–P) is a funny retelling of the classic three wishes tale, one that pairs foolish characters with magic, just as in ***The Fisherman and His Wife*** (P), retold by Rachel Isadora with illustrations that set the tale of the foolish couple in a generic African country setting. The same essential tale, ***The Boy from the Dragon Palace: A Folktale from Japan*** (P), retold by Margaret Read MacDonald and illustrated by Sachiko Yoshikawa, is brief, patterned, and predictable, with a less than happy ending, as the poor flower-seller learns, much to his dismay, that greed destroys happiness.

Every cultural group has noodlehead stories that provoke hearty laughter: the wise men of Gotham in England, the fools in the Jewish ghetto of Chelm in Poland, Juan Bobo in Puerto Rico, the Connemara Man in Ireland, the Montieri in Italy, and the Ti-Jean stories from the French Canadian tradition. Jan Andrews reinvents three Ti-Jean tales in ***When Apples Grew Noses and White Horses Flew: Tales of Ti-Jean***, with the humor enhanced by illustrations by Dušan Petričič. In ***The Rooster Prince of Breslov*** (N–P), illustrated by Eugene Yelchim, Ann Redisch Stampler retells an old Yiddish tale in which too much of a good thing is a huge problem. Other examples of noodlehead stories are listed in the Booklist at the end of the chapter.

FAIRY TALES Fairy tales contain magic. Though fairy tales are structured like other folktales, their deeply magical character sets them apart. Wee people, fairy godmothers, and other magical beings intervene to make things happen. Enchantment aside, these stories paint an ideal vision of life based on the hope that virtue will be recognized and hard work rewarded, while greed and wickedness are punished. Fairy tales show us that courage, honesty, and resourcefulness are valued.

There are a prodigious number of fairy tales available to young readers, including Rachel Isadora's beautifully illustrated retelling of the Grimm brothers' ***The Twelve Dancing Princesses*** (P). Interestingly, Isadora sets this story from the Germanic tradition in a generic African countryside. She does the same with ***Hansel and Gretel*** (P). Stephen Mitchell's ***Genies, Meanies, and Magic Rings: Three Tales from the Arabian Nights*** (I), illustrated by Tom Pohrt, is a clever retelling of these magical stories. Aaron Shepard's ***One-Eye! Two-Eyes! Three-Eyes!: A Very Grimm Fairy Tale*** (P) is accompanied by droll illustrations by Gary Clement that delight primary-grade readers. ***Little Red Riding Hood*** (P) is beautifully retold and illustrated by Jerry Pinkney, while Laura Amy Schlitz offers a less well-known tale in ***The Bearskinner: A Tale of the Brothers Grimm*** (I), illustrated by Max Grafe, in which the virtues of endurance and heroism are highlighted. Lise Lunge-Larsen's collection, ***The Hidden Folk: Stories of Fairies, Dwarves, Selkies, and Other Secret Beings*** (P–I–A), with lushly patterned scratchboard illustrations by Beth Krommes, is a comprehensive introduction to the folk characters who populate many European fairy tales. Jane Yolen shares a dozen tales of strong women in *Not One Damsel in Distress: World Folktales for Strong Girls* (I), and Judy Sierra has gathered enchanting tales in *Nursery Tales around the World* (N–P). Eight very cheeky cartoon versions of classic Grimm stories appear in Rotraut Susanne Berner's *Definitely Not for Little Ones: Some Very Grimm Fairy-tale Comics* (I), translated from the German by Shelley Tanaka.

There are many variants of fairytales. Indeed, the origins of folktales are clouded in prehistory, and variants come from many cultures. Contemporary writers and artists breathe new life into the many versions of ancient folktales. Many stories from folklore have hundreds of variants from countries all over the world. Comparing the motifs, characters, and themes of the different versions can be a very illuminating activity for readers. Here we briefly discuss three variants of fairy tales: "Cinderella," "Rumpelstiltskin," and "Jack and the Beanstalk." See Figure 5.3 for a list of some of these variants to explore.

Cinderella. Folklorist M. R. Cox, a pioneer in folklore research during the 1890s, described the Cinderella motif in his book for adults, *Cinderella: Three Hundred and Forty-Five Variants* (1893). In the foreword to the Cox collection, Andrew Lang states, "The märchen [fairy tale] is a kaleidoscope: the incidents are the bits of coloured glass. Shaken, they fall into a variety of attractive forms; some forms are fitter than others, survive more powerfully, and are more widely spread" (p. x). Today, we know that there are more than 1,500 variants of this timeless

FIGURE 5.3

Variants of Familiar Fairy Tales

Books in this section are appropriate for primary–intermediate–advanced readers in a study of variants.

Cinderella

* Climo, Shirley, *The Egyptian Cinderella*
* ———, *The Irish Cinderlad*
* ———, *The Korean Cinderella*
* Fleischman, Paul, *Glass Slipper, Gold Sandal: A Worldwide Cinderella*

Greaves, Margaret, *Tattercoats*

* Hayes, Joe, *Little Gold Star/Estrellita de Oro: A Cinderella Cuento*

Hooks, William, *Moss Gown*

Huck, Charlotte, *Princess Furball*

* Louie, Ai-Ling, *Yeh Shen: A Cinderella Story from China*

Manna, Anthony, and SoulaMitakidou, *The Orphan: A Cinderella Story from Greece*

Martin, Rafe, *The Rough-Face Girl*

* San Souci, Robert D., *Cendrillon: A Caribbean*
* ———, *Sootface: An Ojibwa Cinderella Story*
* ———, *Cinderella*
* Silverman, Erica, *Raisel's Riddle*

Jack Tales

Briggs, Raymond, *Jim and the Beanstalk*

Compton, Kenn, and Joanne Compton, *Jack the Giant Chaser: An Appalachian Tale*

Fleischman, Sid, *McBroom and the Beanstalk*

Haley, Gail E., *Jack and the Fire Dragon*

———, *Mountain Jack Tales*

Kellogg, Steven, *Jack and the Beanstalk*

Osborne, Mary Pope, *Kate and the Beanstalk*

Rumpelstiltskin

* Hamilton, Virginia, *The Girl Who Spun Gold*

Jacobs, Joseph, *Tom Tit Tot*

Stanley, Diane, *Rumpelstiltskin's Daughter*

Zelinsky, Paul (reteller), *Rumpelstiltskin*

Zemach, Harve, *Duffy and the Devil: A Cornish Tale*

Multiple Stories

Alley, Zoe B. *There's a Princess in the Palace*

Brooks, William, *A Telling of the Tales*

tale. Paul Fleischman has gathered thirty-six variants of this story from seventeen cultures across the world in his clever **Glass Slipper, Gold Sandal: A Worldwide Cinderella** (I), stunningly illustrated by Julie Paschkis. Pieces of the tale are strung together as one continuous story, reflecting many variants. Accompanying art incorporates appropriate cultural details (and a small label) that reflect the origin of the specific text, placed on a background color that differs for each culture. The result is a kaleidoscope of stories, reflecting both the variety and the constancy of this well-loved tale.

The romantic rags-to-riches story of "Cinderella" based on Charles Perrault's version has been illustrated by many noted artists, including Marcia Brown, Susan Jeffers, and Errol Le Cain. Perrault's fairy godmother, coach, and lush costumes are familiar to most children. Barbara McClintock's retelling of Perrault's **Cinderella** (P) includes richly detailed illustrations both of the French court and a loyal little gray cat, who is rewarded at the end of the tale. In the less-familiar German version by the Brothers Grimm, **Cinderella** (I–A), illustrated by Nonny Hogrogian, the story takes on a macabre tone. In order to make their feet fit into the tiny glass slipper, the sisters take drastic measures: one cuts off her toe and the other cuts off her heel. In the end they are blinded by vengeful doves. Other versions include Appalachian, Chinese, Creole, Yiddish, Egyptian, English, Indonesian, Irish, Korean, Persian, Spanish American, and Vietnamese, as well as Native American versions such as **The Turkey Girl: A Zuni Cinderella Story** (I), retold by Penny Pollock and illustrated by Ed Young, and the Algonquin variant, **The Rough-Face Girl** (I). The storyteller's voice is clear in **The Orphan: A Cinderella Story from Greece** (I), retold by Anthony Manna and Soula Mitakidou, with illustrations by Giselle Potter.

Rumpelstiltskin. The story of the little man who, for a cruel fee, helps a poor girl spin straw or flax into skeins of gold is another well-loved tale. The best-known version, Grimms' **Rumpelstiltskin** (I), has been retold and illustrated by Paul Zelinsky, among others. The Grimm variant tells the story of a dwarf who demands the queen's firstborn child as payment for his help. Joseph Jacobs's **Tom Tit Tot** (P), retold and illustrated by Evaline Ness, is a version from Suffolk, England, in which an impet (dwarf) spins five skeins of gold from flax. In Devonshire and Cornwall, England, the devil knits stockings, jackets, and other clothing for the Squire, as recounted in **Duffy and the Devil: A Cornish Tale** (P), retold by Harve Zemach. The character that corresponds to

Rumpelstiltskin is Trit-a-Trot in Ireland and Whuppity Stoorie in Scotland. Each version's cultural origins are reflected in the clothing, dialect, and settings. Virginia Hamilton uses a colloquial style to present a West Indian variant in **The Girl Who Spun Gold** (P–I). Leo and Diane Dillon illustrate the book in magnificent paintings made with acrylic paint on acetate overpainted with gold. The embossed paintings appear on pages edged with gold leaf. The gold of the art conveys the importance of gold in the story.

Jack and The Beanstalk. "Jack and the Beanstalk" first appeared in Joseph Jacobs's collection of English folktales. It has since been illustrated by many contemporary artists. In Lorinda Bryan Cauley's **Jack and the Beanstalk** (N–P), the beanstalk is a lush green forest peopled with dour folks who sense danger and are heavy with foreboding. In contrast, Paul Galdone's characters in **Jack and the Beanstalk** (N–P) are oafish, laughing bunglers who create a lighthearted story.

Many Americanized versions of Old World tales revolve around a boy named Jack and are therefore known as "Jack Tales." One of the most familiar is a variant of "Jack and the Beanstalk" known as "Jack's Bean Tree." It is found in Richard Chase's **The Jack Tales** and in **Jack and the Wonder Beans** (I), by James Still. Appalachian dialect permeates these versions of the familiar tale. For example, the giant's refrain in **Jack and the Wonder Beans** is "Fee, fie, chew tobacco [pronounced "tobacco"], I smell the toes of a tadwhacker." Gail E. Haley's Appalachian retelling, **Jack and the Bean Tree** (P), is set in the context of a storyteller's tale. Family and neighbors gather around Grandmother Poppyseed, who gives a local flavor to her tales: A banty hen lays the golden eggs; the giant chants "Bein' he live or bein'/ he dead,/I'll have his bones/To eat with my pones." Haley paints her bold, energetic illustrations on wood, and the brilliant colors reflect the intensities of light and shadow.

Mary Pope Osborne chose a girl to climb the beanstalk in **Kate and the Beanstalk** (P), illustrated by Giselle Potter. Kate outsmarts the giant and makes a fortune for herself and her mother. Raymond Briggs wrote a parody of the Jack Tales in **Jim and the Beanstalk** (P–I). The giant has grown old and has lost his appetite, his teeth, and his eyesight. Jim helps him get false teeth and glasses. Nina Crews's **Jack and the Beanstalk** (N) is modern. We see the giant getting a pedicure as Jack arrives. The illustrations are photographs manipulated with Adobe Photoshop. Variants of this tale and others appear in the Booklist at the end of the chapter.

TALL TALES Tall tales are primarily indigenous to the United States and are a peculiarly American form of folktale. They are a combination of history, myth, and fact. Tall tales gave the early American settlers symbols of strength, and offset with a little humor the harsh realities of an untamed land. The exaggerated strength and blatant lies in tall tales added zest and lightened a life of hard labor. As the settlers built a new country, they created heroes who were the mightiest, strongest, and most daring lumberjacks, railroad men, coal miners, riverboat drivers, and steel workers possible.

Many heroes of tall tales were real people, but their improbable stories have made them larger than life. Davy Crockett, Daniel Boone, and Johnny Appleseed accomplished feats no mortal would dare. John Henry, Pecos Bill, and Mike Fink exemplify the brawn and muscle that developed America. Children love the exaggerations that mark the tall tales. They laugh when Paul Bunyan's loggers tie bacon to their feet and skate across the huge griddle to grease it. And when the infant Pecos Bill falls out of the covered wagon, children can picture the abandoned baby scrambling toward the coyote mother, who eventually raises him with the rest of the coyote pack. The heroes in tall tales are powerful, so readers know they will meet their challenges. The suspense is in *how* the challenge will be met.

Julius Lester describes the mighty battle between a steam drill and the legendary hero in **John Henry** (P–I), illustrated by Jerry Pinkney. Steven Kellogg's tall tale biography, **Johnny Appleseed** (P–I), and Reeve Lindbergh's poetic version, **Johnny Appleseed: A Poem** (P–I), illustrated by Kathy Jakobsen, both tell the story of John Chapman, who traveled across the Allegheny mountains planting apple orchards. Alvin Schwartz gathered his entertaining and informative research into the language, superstition, and folk history of America's legendary past in many books, including **Whoppers: Tall Tales and Other Lies** (I–A). Not all the heroes are male: Robert D. San Souci collected twenty tales about strong women in **Cut from the Same Cloth: American Women of Myth, Legend, and Tall Tale** (I).

Years ago author Zora Neale Hurston collected a slightly different kind of tall tale—outrageous lies—and Christopher Myers has adapted and illustrated them in **Lies and Other Tall Tales** (P–I); Hurston's stories are a beautiful example of the power of language in these old tales. The style reflects the original language, whereas the illustrations create a visual community of the black tellers of the tales. These and other tall tales are listed in the Booklist at the end of the chapter.

• • FABLES • •

A fable is a brief tale that presents a clear and unambiguous moral. Fables make didactic comments on human nature using dramatic action to heighten the effect. They differ from other traditional literature in that the moral of the story is explicitly stated.

Many common sayings come from fables. "Better beans and bacon in peace than cakes and ale in fear" comes from "Town Mouse, Country Mouse." "Slow and steady wins the race" is from "The Tortoise and the Hare," one of the tales retold and illustrated by Jerry Pinkney in **Aesop's Fables** (P–I). "Knowing in part may make a fine tale, but wisdom comes from seeing the whole" is illustrated in **Seven Blind Mice** (P–I), by Ed Young. "Do not put off until tomorrow what you should do today" is one of the morals from **Unwitting Wisdom: An Anthology of Aesop's Fables** (P–I), by Helen Ward. Such injunctions, explicitly stated as morals, are taught by allegory, or symbolic narrative. Animals or inanimate objects take on human traits in stories that clearly show the wisdom of the simple lessons. In the single-incident story typical of the fable, we are told not to be vain, not to be greedy, and not to lie. John Kilaka's **True Friends: A Tale from Tanzania** (P) tells the story of the friendship between Elephant and Rat, which erodes when hunger results in Elephant stealing Rat's grain. This retelling reflects traditional Tanzanian storytelling in that it is meandering rather than taut, a characteristic of most Western tales.

The origins of fables are ascribed to both Greece and India. Reputedly, a Greek slave named Aesop used fables for political purposes, and though some scholars doubt that he ever lived, his name has been associated with fables since ancient times. Jean de La Fontaine, a seventeenth-century French poet, adapted many of Aesop's fables into verse form. Brian Wildsmith illustrated several of these, including **Hare and the Tortoise** (P). Jerry Pinkney chose the story of the lion and the mouse, one of his childhood favorites, to retell in pictures in his Caldecott Medal–winning **The Lion & the Mouse** (N–P), which we look at closely here.

✳ ✳ ✳

A CLOSE LOOK AT
The Lion & the Mouse

The front cover of **The Lion & the Mouse** is intriguing at first glance: a full-bleed portrait of the lion's face is perfectly centered, nose and muzzle seeming to extend out from the page, but the eyes

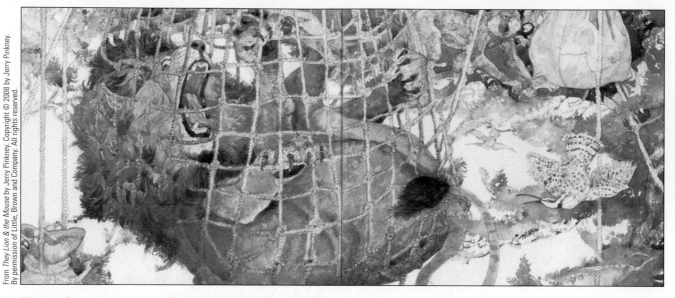

Notice the emotion in the lion's eye, the texture of his fur and the rope, and the many details that Jerry Pinkney includes in this illustration from **The Lion & the Mouse**.

looking toward the spine of the book. Why? On the back cover, we find the answer: the mouse stands in the center, surrounded by grass, looking toward the spine as well, a friendly look on its face. The illustrations on the front of the case are vertical panels, one of the lion, looking right, one of the mouse on a chewed rope, looking left, and an ampersand in the center space. With the story having begun on the cover, the endpages depict the setting with a panoramic view of several of the iconic animals and vegetation of the Serengeti, followed by the dedication and title pages, a double-page-spread close-up of huge paw prints, with a small mouse filling a portion of one on the bottom right corner. The next opening, another double-page, full-bleed illustration, depicts the mouse in the foreground, small against the immensity of the Serengeti plain, as day begins to break, with the "who, who, whoooo" of an owl appearing in the upper left corner. In the next opening, we see the owl swooping down to catch the mouse on the full-bleed recto, with a panel illustration of the mouse running through a hollow log, on the recto. In the next opening, we see the mouse in the grass, with something suspiciously like a lion's tail almost hidden in the grass. On the verso we see the mouse climbing up—oh, no!—the body of the lion!

The suspense doesn't end here, as the next opening contains another full-bleed, double-page spread with the lion resplendent across the gutter, a puzzled snarl on his face, eyes looking down to the right at the mouse, who dangles from the lion's paw. In the next opening, we see the lion's head, front paws holding the mouse, with the creatures looking at each other, mouths slightly open as if talking. The following opening, another double-page spread, shows the lion, a quizzical look on his face, with paw open and the mouse climbing down. Told in a pleasing arrangement of detailed illustrations with animal sounds the only words, this timeless fable ends with the back endpages depicting the lion, his mate, and their cubs strolling across the plain with the mouse and her family riding upon his back, a fitting finale. The lion and his mate seem to be talking. Although they do not actually talk, the viewer is sure of what they are talking about: she is wondering why they are taking the mouse family for a ride, and he is explaining what has just happened. The vivid personalities that Pinkney has shaped for both lion and mouse are the result of careful attention to the expressions on their faces and their body language.

The theme of the fable has been interpreted in several different ways. The illustration on the back cover is Pinkney's beautiful version of a "peaceable kingdom," making it clear that he views the fable as presenting the possibility for peace and harmony among diverse creatures. Indeed, in his Caldecott acceptance speech he says: "To me the story represents a world of neighbors helping neighbors, unity and harmony, interdependence" (Pinkney, 2010, p. 23).

Rand Burkert retells the same tale in words, and his lion dreams happily of "small things" at the end of the tale of **Mouse and Lion** (N–P), with illustrations by Nancy Ekholm Burkert. Burkert's illustrations, with softer colors and more white space, create

P | R | O | F | I | L | E

Jerry Pinkney

Jerry Pinkney has been making picturebooks for young readers since the early 1960s. In those almost fifty years, he has created more than one hundred books, won five Caldecott Honors, five Coretta Scott King Awards and five Coretta Scott King Honors, as well as receiving many other honors and awards. He is the father of four, and some of his family are also in the children's book business, including his wife, Gloria Jean, and sons, Myles and Brian. He has mentored other illustrators, such as James Ransome, and has worked tirelessly for groups and causes, such as the NEA's National Council of the Arts.

He is a generous man: generous with his time, his talent, his imagination, and his enthusiasm.

Many of Pinkney's books depict some aspect of African American history or African American life; many are folklore, such as *Little Red Riding Hood, The Little Red Hen, The Talking Eggs,* and *Aesop's Fables* (all N–P). He does meticulous research for the books he illustrates, knowing that getting the details "right" is as important as making beautiful art. His signature style, described by his editor, Andrea Spooner, is "intricate yet organic line . . . defltly meshed with layers and layers of transparent [water]

color," (2010, p. 28), yet, although his art is quickly recognized as his, each book varies significantly according to the needs of the story. He and others have said that he relishes an artistic challenge, and evidence that he rises to those challenges is present in every book he has created. His books have been referred to as a "national treasure," but those who know him would argue that it is the man himself who is that treasure.

To learn more about Jerry Pinkney, visit CengageBrain.com to access the Education CourseMate website where you will find links to relevant websites.

---

a different mood from that of the Pinkney version, although her illustrations also reflect an African setting. Two collections of the fables of Aesop offer "the lion and the mouse" as well as other fables. *Aesop's Fables: A Pop-Up Book of Classic Tales* (N–P), engineered by Kees Moerbeek and illustrated by Chris Beatrice and Bruce Wheeley is a spectacular visual experience. Beverley Naidoo retells sixteen fables in *Aesop's Fables* (N–P), illustrated by Piet Grobler. While the small do help the strong, as in the lion and the mouse, this collection also contains some of the tales that end with unfortunate consequences.

The source of early collections from the East is the Indian "Panchatantra" (literally, five *tantras*, or books), known to English readers as the "Fables of Bidpai" or "Jataka Tales." The Jatakas are stories of the Buddha's prior lives, in which he took the form of various animals. Each story is intended to illustrate a moral principle. *Foolish Rabbit's Big Mistake* (P–I), by Rafe Martin, is an early version of a "sky is falling" tale, with frenetic action vividly illustrated by Ed Young. B. G. Hennessy retells *The Boy Who Cried Wolf* (P) and adds dialogue to the story. Boris Kulikov's watercolor and gouache illustrations span time by, for example, mixing articles of clothing from wildly varied time periods, adding humor even though the wolf is always frightening.

Because fables are short and are told in simple language, some adults mistakenly give fables to children who are too young to comprehend or fully appreciate them. Researchers have found that seven-year-olds often miss the point of widely used fables (Pillar, 1983). Because fables are constructed within the oblique perspective of satire, allegory, and symbolism, their intent may elude young children's literal understanding. However, richly illustrated fables such as *The Lion & the Mouse* provide enough scaffolding through the illustrations that young children can, in their own way, understand the point of these brief stories. Examples of individual and collected fables appear in the Booklist at the end of the chapter.

• • MYTHS AND POURQUOI • • STORIES

The special group of stories we call myths developed as humans sought to interpret both natural phenomena and human behavior. They were used to answer fundamental questions concerning how human beings and their world were created. Myths express the beliefs and religious customs of ancient cultures and portray their visions of destiny. Myths relate to one another; taken together, they build a complex picture of an imaginative world (Frye, 1970). Many

TEACHING IDEA 5.4

Search for Mythical Allusions

 **COMMON CORE STATE STANDARDS**

This Teaching Idea addresses Common Core English Language Arts, Reading: Literature standard 4 grades 4 through 7; 4, 9 grade 8. The suggestions in this Teaching Idea may need to be adapted to suit your particular grade level and the needs of your students.

Students who read widely recognize frequently used *allusions* (references to a literary figure, event, or object) drawn from mythology. Classical allusions—such as Pandora's box, an Achilles heel, the Midas touch, the Trojan horse, and the face that launched a thousand ships—appear in our language, literature, and culture; they are part of our common vocabulary. A winged horse (Pegasus) appeared on old gas station signs, Mercury delivers flowers, Vulcan repairs tires, and many of us wear our Nike shoes to work or play every day.

The English language reflects origins in Greek, Roman, and Norse myths: *erotic* comes from Eros, *titanic* comes from the Titans, and *cereal* comes from Ceres. The days of the week also derive from myths: Sunday = Sun-day; Monday = Moon-day; Tuesday = Tiu's-day; Wednesday = Odin's-day; Thursday = Thor's-day; Friday = Freya's-day; Saturday = Saturn's-day. In **Words from the Myths**,

Isaac Asimov presents many words that have their origins in myths. To encourage students to learn more about allusions:

1. Ask students to note words, symbols, and allusions to myths as they read newspapers, magazines, and books, and as they watch television and movies. Having a collection of these instances yourself is a good way to begin, and any students who read fantasy such as Rick Riordan's **Percy and the Olympians** series will have much to share.

2. Have them find out who Odysseus, Medea, Achilles, Circe, Oedipus, Hector, and other mythical characters and creatures are and why their names are important to us today.

3. Post the allusions on a bulletin board as they find them. Who can find the most unusual?

---

myths are so integral to Western culture that they appear as literary allusions, as discussed in Teaching Idea 5.4.

Northrop Frye (1970) traces the origins of all literature back to one central story: how man once lived in a golden age (also referred to as the garden of Eden, the Hesperides, and a happy island kingdom in the Atlantic), how that world was lost, and how we someday may be able to get it back again (pp. 53, 57). Penelope Farmer (1979), translator of many myths, describes their purpose this way: "Myths have seemed to me to point quite distinctly—yet without ever directly expressing it—to some kind of unity behind creation, not a static unity, but a forever shifting breathing one. . . . The acquisition by man of life or food or fire has to be paid for by the acceptance of death—the message is everywhere, quite unmistakable. To live is to die; to die is to live" (p. 4).

The great archetypal theme of life and death appears again and again throughout the stories told by all cultures. In images and symbols, mythic themes

reappear under many guises that students can recognize through their study of myth. Literature throughout the ages echoes the themes of the ancient myths.

The literary value of myths lies in their exciting plots, memorable characters, heroic actions, challenging situations, and deep emotions. They are compelling stories of love, carnage, revenge, and mystery. At the same time, they transmit ancient values, symbols, customs, art, law, and language. Isaac Asimov explores the roots of hundreds of mythic images in **Words from the Myths** (I), a handy reference for students interested in etymology. Penelope Proddow compiled **Art Tells a Story: Greek and Roman Myths** (I–A), a collection of myths accompanied by photographs of the artwork they inspired. **Gods, Goddesses and Monsters: A Book of World Mythology** (A), by Sheila Keenan, provides information about mythic characters from countries all around the globe. **Encyclopedia Mythologica: Dragons and Monsters** (I), a pop-up book created by Matthew Reinhart and Robert Sabuda, depicts six major monsters of myth and legend, each illustration accompanied by depictions of smaller related creatures.

In myths, as in all folklore, a great deal depends on the telling. Much also depends on the illustrating, and myths offer artists an excellent opportunity for presenting their own interpretation of some elemental stories. Katrin Hyman Tchana's **Changing Woman and Her Sisters: Stories of Goddesses from around the World** (I), illustrated with collage portraits by Trina Schart Hyman, is an anthology of tales from ten different cultures ranging from Navajo to Buddhist, ancient Sumer to Ireland. The extensive source material illuminates the origins of the tales. Brian Karas takes a much less reverent tone in his funny farce, **Young Zeus** (P).

All cultures have creation myths, and these stories are popular and are suitable for students in elementary and middle school. They describe the origin of the earth and the phenomena that affect it. Some books are collections of creation myths from around the world; others focus on myths from one culture. Jacqueline Morley collected eleven creation myths in **Egyptian Myths** (I), illustrated by Giovanni Caselli. Her graceful retellings focus on the struggle between good and evil, the creation of the world, and the relationships between gods and humans. Virginia Hamilton's definitive collection, **In the Beginning: Creation Stories from around the World** (I–A), gives students many different cultures' explanations of how the world began and how people were created.

The simplest myths are *pourquoi* stories, from the French word for "why." They tell how the Earth began and why the seasons change, how animals got their colors and why they behave as they do. We humans lose our fear of things we can name and explain. "Given a universe full of uncertainties and mysteries, the myth intervenes to introduce the human element: clouds in the sky, sunlight, storms at sea, all extra-human factors such as these lose much of their power to terrify as soon as they are given the sensibility, intentions, and motivations that every individual experiences daily" (Grimal, 1965, p. 9). **Why the Sky Is Far Away: A Nigerian Folktale** (N–P), by Mary-Joan Gerson, illustrated by Carla Golembe, and **Why Mosquitoes Buzz in People's Ears: A West African Tale** (P), by Verna Aardema, illustrated by Leo and Diane Dillon, are two excellent examples of African pourquoi tales. Native Americans also have many stories to explain animals' traits, human conduct, and natural phenomena. Joseph Bruchac's stories, such as **The First Strawberries** (P) and **How Chipmunk Got His Stripes: A Tale of Bragging and Teasing** (P), as well as Paul Goble's **The Gift of the Sacred Dog** (I), will give students an idea of the significance of this type of story to North American tribes. More pourquoi tales are listed in the Booklist at the end of the chapter.

Greek and Roman Mythology

Myths are only tenuously related to historical fact and geographical location, but they played an important role in the lives of the ancients, especially in the art, music, architecture, and culture of ancient Greece. The Greeks believed that gods and goddesses controlled the universe. Zeus, the most powerful god, controlled the weather—the lightning and thunder—and ruled over all the other gods who lived on Mount Olympus and the mortals who lived around it. Greek myths are replete with wondrous monsters. Young readers are fascinated by these half-human, half-beast creatures that frightened early people and wreaked havoc on their lands. Just as young children delight in tales of witches and giants, older students, too, love to read about Medusa, who grew hissing snakes on her head instead of hair; Cerberus, the huge three-headed dog; and the horrible one-eyed Cyclops. Lynn Curlee's **Mythological Creatures: A Classical Bestiary: Tales of Strange Beings, Fabulous Creatures, Fearsome Beasts, & Hideous Monsters from Ancient Greek Mythology** (I) brings to vivid life sixteen mythical creatures of ancient Greece.

Stories of individual heroes tell of great adventures, tests, victories, and losses. They feature relationships between gods and mortals and show how life must be lived with morality and conscience. Countless myths focus on the love between a god or goddess and a mortal, like that between Psyche and Cupid. Students familiar with this myth recognize its presence in many modern romances.

Lise Lunge-Larsen's **Gifts from the Gods: Words and Wisdom from Ancient Greek and Roman Mythology** (I) explores the power of these old stories and their influence on modern language. Excellent retellings of Greek myths include Shirley Climo's **Atalanta's Race: A Greek Myth** (I–A), illustrated by Alexander Koshkin. In **Olympians: Great Gods and Goddesses of Ancient Greece** (I–A), Leonard Everett Fisher presents handsome portraits and describes the origins and characteristics of the deities. In **King Midas** (I–A), illustrated by Isabelle Brent, Philip Neil brings the king's sorrowful curse to life. Jane Yolen's **Wings** (I–A) tells the story of Daedalus, a mortal who is exiled to the island of Crete. Jeanne Steig's collection, **A Gift from Zeus: Sixteen Favorite Myths** (A), is retold in vivid language and enhanced by the wittily gruesome illustrations of William Steig. George O'Connor's **Zeus: King of the Gods** (A) graphic novel format brings the Olympians to life as superheroes.

Mythology from Other Cultures

Equally rich stories exist in other cultures. The tales that grew from the cold, rugged climate of northern Europe burn with man's passionate struggle against the cruelty of nature and the powerful gods and monsters that ruled the harsh land.

In **Favorite Norse Myths** (I–A), Mary Pope Osborne explains how the universe began, according to the creation story of Norway. She quotes from the *Poetic Edda*, the oldest written source of Norse mythology. In it, Odin, the Norse war god, trades an eye for all the world's wisdom. Thor, god of thunder, defeats a vicious giant with a hammer, and mischief-maker Loki creates trouble wherever he goes. Padraic Colum, an Irish poet and master storyteller, first published **The Children of Odin: The Book of Northern Myths** (I) in 1920; his classic collection remains available today. Ingri and Edgar Parin d'Aulaire have told these bold stories in **Norse Gods and Giants** (I–A), an entertaining account based on Norse mythology.

Although Greek, Roman, and Norse mythologies have traditionally been the most studied and the most readily available, today we have access to books of mythology from many cultures. Mythology from Africa has taken its place alongside European stories, and hauntingly beautiful versions of Native American and Inuit myths are being published with increasing frequency. Ngangur Mbitu and Ranchor Prime have collected the myths of Africa in **Essential African Mythology: Stories that Change the World** (I). Isaac Olaleye describes a contest on a rainfield in Africa in **In the Rainfield: Who Is the Greatest?** (P–I), illustrated by Ann Grifalconi. Wind, fire, and rain are portrayed as regal Africans competing to determine who is the greatest. Richard Lewis retells the Aztec myth that explains how music came to Earth in **All of You Was Singing** (I–A), a poetic version that is infused with his own imagination. Ed Young's illustrations combine Lewis's images, Aztec cultural motifs, and his own vision. The result is a stunningly beautiful book that echoes the splendor of creation. John Bierhorst has gathered many other Aztec tales in **The Hungry Woman: Myths and Legends of the Aztecs** (A). Myths from many cultures are listed in the Booklist at the end of the chapter.

• • HERO TALES: EPICS • • AND LEGENDS

Hero tales focus on the courageous deeds of superhuman mortals in their struggles against one another as well as against gods and monsters. The heroes embody universal human emotions and represent the eternal contest between good and evil. Hero tales contribute to an appreciation of world history and literature, to an understanding of national ideals of behavior, and to our understanding of valor and nobility.

Epics are usually written in verse and consist of a cycle of tales that center on a legendary hero. Some well-known epics of the Western world include that of Beowulf, King Arthur and Camelot, and Robin Hood, as well as the account of the Trojan War retold in Homer's *Iliad* and *Odyssey*. **The Odyssey** (I–A), as adapted by Gareth Hinds, offers pencil and watercolor art that interprets this classic story, a visual translation of Homer's Greek epic.

Language is often key in setting the drama of the tales, as is evident from the first line of Robert Sabuda's **Arthur and the Sword** (I): "Long ago in a time of great darkness, a time without a king, there lived a fair boy called Arthur." The elegant language foretells the majesty in the story. **Merlin and the Making of the King** (I–A), retold by Margaret Hodges and illustrated by Trina Schart Hyman, introduces three of the famous Arthurian legends that chronicle Arthur's life from his birth until his death. The dramatic tales are accompanied by equally dramatic illustrations surrounded by tiny flowered borders inspired by illuminated manuscripts. Kevin Crossley-Holland has written an authoritative resource on Camelot, Arthur, his knights, and the history of chivalry in **The World of King Arthur and His Court: People, Places, Legend and Lore** (A), a book that gives historical knowledge of England at the time Arthur may have lived as well as information about the Arthurian ideal created by storytellers through the ages. The illustrations by Peter Malone, inspired by medieval art, clarify the information provided by the text.

The epic of the hero Gilgamesh, who travels the world with his friend Enkidu fighting monsters, is the oldest known recorded story in the world. In the foreword to her retelling, **Gilgamesh the Hero** (I–A), Geraldine McCaughrean relates that the story was carved onto twelve tablets that were smashed into thousands of shards over thousands of years. The story of this ancient Sumerian king of Mesopotamia (now Iraq), which may not be complete, was painstakingly restored by scholars. Gilgamesh, though a powerful hero, suffers terribly: "Gilgamesh knelt on the bank of the pool vomiting his misery in great retching sobs. He beat his torn fists on the ground and howled like a wild animal" (p. 88). Like the theme of so many others to follow, his story ends, "He walked through darkness and so glimpsed light" (p. 95).

Gilgamesh's father, Lugalbanda, is the hero in Kathy Henderson's retelling, **Lugalbanda: The Boy**

Who Got Caught Up in a War (A), illustrated by Jane Ray. This Sumerian epic, recorded on tablets about forty-five hundred years ago, is another of the oldest stories in the world. This retelling comes from the many fragments of stories from ancient Iraq and includes notes and an introduction. Now we take a close look at the retelling of the story of another warrior hero, Beowulf.

* * *
A CLOSE LOOK AT
Beowulf

Beowulf: A Hero's Tale Retold (A) by James Rumford is a succinct, yet magnificent retelling of the epic first recorded in about 800 A.D. The endnote gives readers a brief history of the tale itself and the language that it was first written down in—Old English, or Anglo Saxon. Rumford notes that the poem was "lost" when English became heavily dominated by French, and not rediscovered until the eighteenth century. The language history is important because Rumford chose to retell this epic in words that can be traced back to their Anglo-Saxon origins, or at least usage (in the case of "dragon," "ogre," and "giant"), with the exception of "they," "their," and "them," all from Old Norse.

Rumford begins and ends his tale by speaking directly to the audience, much as the old bards would have done: "Listen! For I will sing of Beowulf. . . ." The subsequent tale is straightforward, spare, and passionate. Rumford includes the original names of characters and places, and inserts two important statements in Old English, always with the pronunciation in brackets following the first usage. This judicious use of Old English as well as Rumford's use of words descended from that language extend the power of the retelling. The two statements that he reproduces in Old English are in red, and they mark the beginning and end of Beowulf's story. "Beowulf is min nama" is how the hero announces himself, and the language and structure of this sentence alerts readers and listeners that Beowulf is the important character here. Similarly, Beowulf's final words, "Ic him aeftersceal," mark the end of his story.

Rumford's pen-and-ink and watercolor illustrations are beautiful, even as they supply details of time and place. The three sections of the story—the slaying of the ogre, Grendel, the subsequent battle with the ogre's mother, and the final battle with the dragon—are visually separated by different colors (green, blue, gold) in the background full-bleed, double-page-spread paintings. Superimposed on the background paintings are both text and illustration panels, framed in narrow

black line. The first letter of the first word of each section is reminiscent of ancient illuminated manuscripts and is the same blood red as the two Anglo-Saxon statements. In the first two sections, the dragon who eventually slays the hero lurks behind text and illustration panels, a stunning visual foreshadowing.

This ancient epic speaks to young readers today with its revelation of loyalty, courage, friendship, and honor. A hero, a slayer of evil, Beowulf is even more a man whose sense of honor took him from his hearthside, even though he was old and white-haired, into his final battle with a dragon that threatened the land he protected and loved as its king.

Legends also grow around places and phenomena. Barbara Juster Esbensen's poem about the aurora borealis, *The Night Rainbow* (P), presents images from many cultures, including white geese, dancers, whales, and battles. Esbensen also provides scientific explanations as well as information about the legends in this celebration of the northern lights. *The Sons of the Dragon King: A Chinese Legend* (I–A), retold and illustrated by Ed Young, shows how the many tribes of China were combined into one

James Rumford incorporates gorgeous design, detail in image, and a bit of foreshadowing in the background as he retells the epic, **Beowulf.**

by the Dragon King and his nine sons, and thus an entire culture is influenced by an ancient story.

Hero tales that are not technically epics are often referred to as legends. Legendary heroes may be real or imaginary people. Even if legends have some factual basis, they are often so fanciful that it becomes difficult to tell where fact stops and imagination takes over. Many storytellers elaborated on reports of their hero's exploits until the stories became full-blown legends that interwove fact and fiction yet contained a grain of truth at their core.

In *La Llorona/The Weeping Woman: An Hispanic Legend Told in Spanish and English* (I–A), Joe Hayes retells the Hispanic legend of La Llorona (the Weeping Woman), the jilted wife who turned her rage against her beloved children and is still believed to wander the banks of the river where she died of grief after she drowned them. Hayes asserts that no one knows whether the story is true, but in notes to the reader at the end of the book he writes, "When children ask me if I believe in La Llorona, I answer as I do whenever I'm asked about a story: I don't think the things I told you really did happen, but if you think about the story you can find a lot of truth in it." In Demi's tale *The Hungry Coat:*

A Tale from Turkey (I), Nasrettin Hoca, a legendary wise Turkish hero, teaches an old friend and his guests, "If you want to look deeply, look at the man and not at his coat. You can change the coat, but you cannot change the man." Students will appreciate the humor in Demi's tale enhanced by her illustrations, inspired by Turkish art. Demi's *The Legend of Lao Tzu and the Tao TeChing* (I) is another outstanding tale of an international hero. Mary Quattlebaum chose a legendary character from historical Virginia for *Sparks Fly High: The Legend of Dancing Point* (P), in which Colonel Lightfoot outsmarts the devil, complete with source notes. Julius Lester's *The Old African* (A), illustrated by Jerry Pinkney, is a powerful verbal and visual portrait of the horrors and the courage of the Middle Passage, a legend based on stories from Ybo Landing, Georgia.

● ● FOLK SONGS ● ●

Songs serve as powerful vehicles for both shaping and preserving our cultural heritage. Ballads and folk songs inform and unify people. Work songs, often developed as a diversion from boredom, capture the rhythm and spirit of the labor in which their creators were engaged. They sing of the values and lifestyles of the people who laid the railroads, dug the tunnels and canals, sailed the ships, and toted the bales.

Folklorist Benjamin A. Botkin (1944) observed in *A Treasury of American Folklore* that we sing folk songs for self-gratification, power, or freedom (pp. 818–819). We also sing songs to lighten our labor, fill our leisure time, record events, and voice praise or protest. Civil rights marchers led by Martin Luther King Jr. were united by the experience of singing "We Shall Overcome" together.

We use songs to teach young children to count or to say the ABCs and, most often, to soothe them and sing them to sleep. Joyce Carol Thomas collected African American songs for **Hush Songs: African American Lullabies** (N–P–I), illustrated by Brenda Joysmith. These songs have worked their sleepy-time magic for generations. Jane Hart compiled 125 songs in her splendid **Singing Bee!: A Collection of Favorite Children's Songs** (N–P–I), which is beautifully illustrated by Anita Lobel. She

augments the nursery rhymes, lullabies, finger plays, cumulative songs, holiday songs, and activity songs with piano accompaniments and guitar chords. Lobel uses historical settings, eighteenth-century garb, and stage production scenes to illustrate the traditional songs.

Children celebrate their own culture or learn about others through song; they can even learn a second language through song. The best published versions include guitar or piano scores, historical notes, and appropriate illustrations that coordinate with the text. Lulu Delacre selected and illustrated **Arroz con Leche: Popular Songs and Rhymes from Latin America** (P), with English lyrics by Elena Paz and musical arrangements by Ana-Maria Rosada. Jose-Luis Orozco selected, arranged, and translated Latin American songs for **De Colores and Other Latin American Folk Songs for Children** (P), illustrated by Elisa Kleven. David Diaz highlights the single song "De Colores/Bright with Colors" (P) in his beautifully illustrated celebration

TEACHING IDEA 5.5

Identify Folkloric Style

COMMON CORE STATE STANDARDS
This Teaching Idea addresses Common Core English Language Arts, Reading: Literature standard 9 grade 8. The suggestions in this Teaching Idea may need to be adapted to suit your particular grade level and the needs of your students.

Contemporary stories are often written in a folkloric style: they contain elements, themes, or recurring patterns found in folklore. Read aloud and discuss fiction containing folklore elements, motifs, or allusions to illustrate the idea. Encourage book discussion groups to continue the search for transformations, magic objects, wishes, trickery, and other folklore conventions. Do the following to help students learn about folkloric style:

- Collect stories written in folkloric style.
- Discuss folklore elements. What characteristics suggest that a work is folklore?
- Have students work in groups to discover folklore elements.
- Discuss the devices, allusions, and patterns found. Make a list of commonly used folklore elements.
- Encourage students to use the elements in stories they write.

Many of the literary variants discussed in Chapter 5 are good materials to use, as are the books listed below:

Arnold, Caroline, **The Terrible Hodag and the Animal Catchers**

Bang, Molly, **Dawn**

———, **The Paper Crane**

Cowley, Joy, **The Wishing of Biddy Malone**

Della Chiesa, Carol, **Adventures of Pinocchio**

French, Fiona, **Anancy and Mr. Dry-Bone**

Gregory, Valiska, **Through the Mickle Woods**

Isaacs, Anne, **Swamp Angel**

Melmed, Laura Krauss, **Rainbabies**

Nolen, Jerdine, **Big Jabe**

Paterson, Katherine, **The King's Equal**

Wisniewski, David, **The Warrior and the Wise Man**

of love and peace. Gary Chalk chose humorous illustrations depicting events of the American Revolution to accompany the original verses of "Yankee Doodle" in **Yankee Doodle** (P). Gerald Milnes shares traditional songs, rhymes, and riddles from the mountains of West Virginia in **Granny, Will Your Dog Bite and Other Mountain Rhymes** (I–A). Other authors of folk songs include Robert Quackenbush, Aliki, Glen Rounds, John Langstaff, and Peter Spier.

● ● FRACTURED FAIRY TALES ● ●
AND LITERARY FOLKLORE

When is folklore not "real" folklore? Many writers, especially those who write fantasies, have been influenced by the structure, motifs, problems, and characters of tales from the oral tradition. Hans Christian Andersen, Rudyard Kipling, Oscar Wilde, and contemporary author Jane Yolen among others have created their own literary fairy tales and pourquoi stories, sometimes referred to as "fakelore," stories that are patterned after traditional tales but go well beyond them. Other writers create parodies and fractured versions of favorite tales. David Wiesner's **The Three Pigs** (P–I) relies on the fact that readers know something about the original tale so that they can fully enjoy the pigs' plight and ingenious means of escape in his story. Jon Scieszka's **The True Story of the Three Little Pigs** (P–I), illustrated by Lane Smith, is told from the point of view of a harmless-looking and misunderstood wolf. Zoe B. Alley, with help from illustrator R. W. Alley, weaves several tales together in **There's a Princess in the Palace** (P–I). The outrageous humor of the pun-filled text is perfectly extended by the comic book panel art. Their earlier collaboration, **There's a Wolf at the Door** (P–I), is equally entertaining.

Older readers enjoy novel-length, embellished retellings of familiar folktales such as Cinderella in **Ella Enchanted**, by Gail Carson Levine and **Beauty** by Robin McKinley. Writers also are inspired by mythology. Gerald McDermott's **Creation** (P–I–A) and Phyllis Root's **Big Momma Makes the World** (N–P–I) echo Genesis and other cultures' creation myths while inventing their own joyous celebrations of the beginning of life. In **Wings** (P–I–A), Christopher Myers tells the modern story of Ikarus Jackson, who proudly flies using his powerful wings just as did his namesake in Greek mythology. We discuss these literary narratives based on folklore traditions in Chapter 6, Fantastic Literature: Fantasy and Science Fiction. Teaching Idea 5.5 offers suggestions for helping children identify folkloric style in more contemporary stories that are not from the oral tradition.

Folklore in the Classroom

Because folklore is a foundation for future literary understanding, it is beneficial for children and young adults to spend time reading from the vast body of folklore. We shortchange our students if we deny them the background information necessary for understanding the countless references to folklore in contemporary books and society. Students who do not comprehend the significance of the wolf in folklore will not understand the meaning of the wolf-shaped bush in Anthony Browne's **Piggybook** (P–I), nor will they appreciate the humor of folktale parodies, such as Jon Scieszka's **The True Story of the Three Little Pigs**. Children enjoy knowing that common phrases like "sour grapes" and "slow and steady wins the race" come from Aesop's fables and that "Pandora's box" and "the Midas touch" originated in Greek mythology.

Good teachers give their students opportunities to *discover* recurring patterns. Teachers who facilitate students' discovery of archetypes find that the primal patterns, themes, and characters become the structural framework for viewing all literature as one overarching story. The most effective approach is to immerse students in traditional stories until they begin to recognize similarities, distinguish patterns, and make predictions. Young children who have heard many folktales will tell you that they often begin "Once upon a time" and end "They lived happily ever after," that the good people win, and that the youngest son gets the princess. These responses show that children recognize the motifs, themes, and story conventions of folklore. Older readers who have been introduced to basic folktales and pourquoi stories will understand the roots of hero tales and mythology as well.

Folklore provides an opportunity for increasing multicultural understanding; it reflects the values, hopes, fears, and beliefs of many cultures. By recognizing recurring themes in folklore from around the world, we can begin to build a bridge of understanding among all people. The oral origins of folklore make it a wonderful resource for storytelling and language development. Dramatic readings or performances offer one venue for creativity. Teaching Idea 5.6 presents suggestions on how to select stories for telling and becoming a storyteller. Children who are familiar with folklore also learn to use similar patterns and conventions in their own writing, borrowing and exploring folkloric frameworks and characters for their own personal stories.

The Ancient Art of Storytelling

ELL

COMMON CORE STATE STANDARDS This Teaching Idea addresses Common Core English Language Arts, Reading: Literature standard 2, grades 2, 3. The suggestions in this Teaching Idea may need to be adapted to suit your particular grade level and the needs of your students.

Telling stories is an art that allows for students from all cultures and abilities to express themselves. It is particularly suited to helping English language learners develop oral proficiency, and it allows all students to bring stories from their own culture into the classroom. Both teachers and students can become storytellers of the tales they bring from home, as well as of those they have read or heard.

The Student Storyteller

1. With younger students, beginning with stories that they bring from home is a wonderful way to integrate their home and school experiences and to honor their cultural heritage. Beginning a day with a sharing circle, a place for sharing stories, allows students to express themselves. If telling a particular folkloric story is the goal, students can pour over folklore looking for the perfect tale to tell. It may be one that has cultural significance to them or one that is particularly funny or exciting or that mirrors their values.

2. After discovering the ideal tale, students should read it aloud a few times to really hear the language and become familiar with the characters and plot. They should also learn to recognize the climax and the slower parts of the tale.

3. Students should then memorize any recurring refrains and learn the order of important events to recognize the pattern of the story.

4. After putting the book aside, students should practice telling the story a few times, making the story theirs.

5. Then students should decide how to introduce the story to the audience to help them get ready to listen.

A good way to begin with younger students is to focus on a tale that has a cumulative structure in which each incident grows from the preceding one, as in "This Is the House that Jack Built" and "The Old Woman and Her Pig." Jeanette Winter's ***The House that Jack Built*** (N–P) uses rebuses in the text so that even younger children can predict what is coming next. These stories are often called "chain tales" because each part of the story is linked to the next. The initial incident reveals both central character and problem; each subsequent scene builds on the previous one, continuing to a climax and then unraveling in reverse order or stopping with an abrupt surprise ending. Cat is so very hungry in Meilo So's Indian folktale, ***Gobble, Gobble, Slip, Slop: A Tale of a Very Greedy Cat*** (P–I) that he eats everything and everyone he encounters, with ridiculous results. Chain tales often have repetitive phrases such as "Run, run as fast as you can. You can't catch me. I'm the Gingerbread man," from "The Gingerbread Boy" and its variants, "Johnny Cake," "The Pancake," and "The Bun." It is easy for young children to grasp the structure of these tales, and the telling is almost always humorous.

To hear how professional storytellers tell tales that engage their audiences, students can listen to tapes such as those by Robert Munsch, Michael Parent, or the many actors, such as Robin Williams and Denzel Washington, who tell tales for the Rabbit Ears series **We All Have Tales**. Rafe Martin tells the story of ***The Rough-Face Girl*** on *Rafe Martin Tells His Children's Books* (Yellow Moon Press), and James Earl Jones has recorded the stories in Virginia Hamilton's ***The People Could Fly***. There are also many other storytelling resources available, including *The Way of the Storyteller* by Ruth Sawyer (1962); *The Story Vine: A Source Book of Unusual and Easy-to-Tell Stories from around the World* by Anne Pellowski (1984); *Tell Me a Tale: A Book about Storytelling* by Joseph Bruchac (1997); and *Pete Seeger's Storytelling Book* by Pete Seeger and Paul DuBois Jacobs (2000).

SUMMARY

Folklore began as stories and poems told across the generations, as people sought to entertain, to explain the world, and to pass down their cultural values and beliefs. Folklore helps us understand not only ourselves but people from other cultures and other times. Folktales, fables, myths, hero tales, and songs add depth to our literary knowledge.

Each type of folklore has its own characteristics. Rhythmic nursery rhymes enchant young children. Folktales—which include fairy tales, talking animal stories, noodlehead tales, and tall tales—have universal themes and motifs, and appear in different guises around the world. Fables incorporate explicit moral statements that are intended to guide behavior. Myths explain the origins of the world, natural phenomena, and human behavior. Hero tales reveal cultural beliefs and values. Folk songs celebrate the values and circumstances of those who first sang them.

Teachers in all grades recognize that folklore, in addition to being a source of pleasure for students of all ages, is a valuable resource for developing language, learning about literature, and learning about other cultures. As it did in the past, folklore today continues to educate and entertain. Above all else, these are stirring stories that have entertained listeners for centuries because they are filled with harrowing adventures and horrific monsters as well as mythic and everyday heroes who triumph in the end. When teachers share these memorable stories with their students, they link them to people in the distant past from all corners of the world. In the following Booklist we first group some representative folklore titles by geographic region as a way to highlight the worldwide scope of this vibrant genre. We then offer more titles for different types of folklore.

Booklist

✳ Indicates some aspect of diversity

Folklore around the World

WORLDWIDE COLLECTIONS

✳ Climo, Shirley, *Monkey Business: Stories from around the World* (2005) (I)

✳ Fleischman, Paul, *Glass Slipper, Gold Sandal: A Worldwide Cinderella* (2007) (I)

✳ Hamilton, Virginia, *The Dark Way: Stories from the Spirit World* (1990) (A)

✳ _____, *In the Beginning: Creation Stories from around the World* (1988) (A)

✳ Keenan, Sheila, *Gods, Goddesses and Monsters: A Book of World Mythology* (2000) (A)

✳ Kherdian, David, *Feathers and Tails: Animal Fables from around the World* (1992) (P–I)

✳ McBratney, Sam, *One Voice, Please: Favorite Read-Aloud Stories* (2008) (I)

✳ Norman, Howard, *Between Heaven and Earth: Bird Tales from around the World* (2004) (I)

✳ Shannon, George, *More True Lies: 18 Tales for You to Judge* (2001) (I–A)

✳ Tchana, Katrin Hyman, *Changing Woman and Her Sisters: Stories of Goddesses from Around the World* (2006) (I–A)

✳ Yolen, Jane, *Mightier Than the Sword: World Folktales for Strong Boys* (2003) (I)

✳ _____, *Not One Damsel in Distress: World Folktales for Strong Girls* (2000) (I)

✳ _____, *Sleep Rhymes around the World* (1994) (N–P)

✳ _____, *Street Rhymes around the World* (1992) (I)

NORTH, SOUTH, AND CENTRAL AMERICA

✳ Aardema, Verna, *Borreguita and the Coyote: A Tale from Ayutla, Mexico* (1991) (P–I)

✳ Ada, Alma Flor, *Mediopollito/Half-Chicken* (1995) (P–I)

✳ _____, *Three Golden Oranges* (1999) (P–I)

✳ Anaya, Rudolfo, *My Land Sings: Stories from the Rio Grande* (1999) (I)

Aylesworth, Jim, *The Mitten* (2009) (N–P)

✳ Bernier-Grand, Carmen T., *Juan Bobo: Four Tales from Puerto Rico* (1994) (P–I)

✳ Bierhorst, John, *Is My Friend at Home? Pueblo Fireside Tales* (2000) (P–I)

✳ _____, *The People with Five Fingers: A Native Californian Creation Tale* (2000) (P–I)

✳ Bruchac, James and Joseph Bruchac, *The Girl Who Helped Thunder and Other Naïve American Folktales* (2009) (I)

✳ Bruchac, Joseph, *Between Earth and Sky: Legends of Native American Sacred Places* (1996) (I)

✳ _____, *The Boy Who Lived with the Bears and Other Iroquois Stories* (1995) (I)

✳ _____, *Gluskabe and the Four Wishes* (1995) (P–I)

✳ _____, *The Story of the Milky Way: A Cherokee Tale* (1995) (P–I)

✳ Brusca, María Cristina, and Tona Wilson, *When Jaguars Ate the Moon and Other Stories about Animals and Plants of the Americas* (1995) (P–I)

✳ Gerson, Mary-Joan, *People of Corn: A Mayan Story* (1995) (P–I)

✳ Goble, Paul, *Adopted by the Eagles: A Plains Indian Story of Friendship and Treachery* (1994) (P–I)

✳ _____, *Crow Chief: A Plains Indian Story* (1992) (P–I)

✳ _____, *Iktomi and the Coyote* (1998) (I)

✳ Gonzalez, Lucia, *The Bossy Gallito: A Traditional Cuban Folktale* (1994) (P)

✳ Hamilton, Virginia, *Her Stories: African American Folktales, Fairy Tales, and True Tales* (1995) (I–A)

✳ _____, *The People Could Fly: American Black Folktales* (1985) (A)

✳ _____, *The People Could Fly: The Picture Book* (2004) (I–A)

✳ _____, *When Birds Could Talk and Bats Could Sing: The Adventures of Bruh Sparrow, Sis Wren, and Their Friends* (1996) (I–A)

✳ Hayes, Joe, *La Llorona/The Weeping Woman: An Hispanic Legend Told in Spanish and English* (2004) (I–A)

Irving, Washington, *The Legend of Sleepy Hollow* (2007) (I–A)

✳ Joseph, Lynn, *The Mermaid's Twin Sister: More Stories from Trinidad* (1994) (I–A)

✳ Kilaka, John, *True Friends: A Tale from Tanzania* (2006) (P)

✳ Kimmel, Eric A., *The Two Mountains: An Aztec Legend* (2000) (P–I)

✳ Lester, Julius, *John Henry* (1994) (P–I)

✳ Lyons, Mary E., *The Butter Tree: Tales of Bruh Rabbit* (1995) (I)

✳ Marcantonio, Patricia Santos, *Red Ridin' in the Hood: And Other Cuentos* (2005) (I–A)

✳ McDermott, Gerald, *Raven: A Trickster Tale from the Pacific Northwest* (1993) (P–I)

✳ McGill, Alice, *Way up and over Everything* (2008) (P)

✳ McKissack, Patricia C., *The Dark-Thirty: Southern Tales of the Supernatural* (1992) (A)

✳ Morales, Yuyi, *Just a Minute: A Trickster Tale and Counting Book* (2003) (N–P)

Moses, Will, *Johnny Appleseed: The Story of a Legend* (2001) (I)

✳ Philip, Neil, *Horse Hooves and Chicken Feet: Mexican Folktales* (2003) (I)

✳ Pinkney, Jerry, *Little Red Riding Hood* (2007) (P–I)

✳ Rockwell, Anne, *The Boy Who Wouldn't Obey: A Mayan Legend* (2001) (P–I)

✳ Rodanas, Kristina, *Dance of the Sacred Circle: A Native American Tale* (1994) (I)

✳ _____, *Dragonfly's Tale* (1991) (P)

✳ Root, Phyllis, *Aunt Nancy and the Bothersome Visitors* (2007) (P)

✳ Ross, Gayle, *How Turtle's Back Was Cracked: A Traditional Cherokee Tale* (1995) (P–I)

Salley, Coleen, *Epossumondas Saves the Day* (2006) (P)

San Souci, Robert D., *The Faithful Friend* (1995) (P–I)

_____, *Six Foolish Fishermen* (2000) (P–I)

✳ _____, *Sukey and the Mermaid* (1992) (P–I)

✳ _____, *The Talking Eggs* (1989) (P–I)

✳ Sierra, Judy, *Wiley and the Hairy Man* (1996) (P–I)

✳ Stevens, Jane, *Old Bag of Bones: A Coyote Tale* (1996) (P)

✳ Van Laan, Nancy, *In a Circle Long Ago: A Treasury of Native Lore from North America* (1995) (I–A)

✳ _____, *With a Whoop and a Holler: A Bushel of Lore from Way Down South* (2001) (I)

EUROPE, AFRICA, AND THE MIDDLE EAST

✳ Aardema, Verna, *Bringing the Rain to Kapiti Plain: A Nandi Tale* (1981) (P)

✳ _____, *The Lonely Lioness and the Ostrich Chicks* (1996) (P)

✳ _____, *Misoso: Once upon a Time: Tales from Africa* (1994) (I–A)

✳ _____, *Why Mosquitoes Buzz in People's Ears: A West African Tale* (1975) (P)

✳ Bryan, Ashley, *Ashley Bryan's African Tales, Uh-Huh* (1998) (I)

✳ _____, *Beautiful Blackbird* (2003) (P)

✳ _____, *Lion and the Ostrich Chicks* (1986) (I)

✳ Doyle, Malachy, *Tales from Old Ireland* (2000) (I–A)

✳ Gerson, Mary-Joan, *Why the Sky Is Far Away: A Nigerian Folktale* (1994) (N–P)

✳ Gregor, C. Shana, *Cry of the Benu Bird: An Egyptian Creation Story* (1996) (P–I)

✳ Haley, Gail E., *A Story, a Story* (1970) (P–I)

✳ Huck, Charlotte, *The Black Bull of Norroway: A Scottish Tale* (2001) (P–I)

✳ Huth, Holly Young, *The Son of the Sun and the Daughter of the Moon: A Saami Folktale* (2000) (P–I)

Isadora, Rachel, *The Fisherman and His Wife* (2008) (P)

✳ _____, *Hansel and Gretel* (2009) (P)

✳ _____, *Twelve Dancing Princesses* (2007) (P)

Johnson-Davies, Denys, *Goha the Wise Fool* (2005) (I)

Karas, G. Brian, *Young Zeus* (2010) (P)

✳ Kimmel, Eric A., *The Adventures of Hershel of Ostropol* (1995) (I)

✳ _____, *Count Silvernose: A Story from Italy* (1996) (P–I)

✳ Lupton, Hugh, *Pirican Pic and Pirican Mor* (2003) (P)

✳ Mitchell, Stephen, *Genies, Meanies, and Magic Rings: Three Tales from the Arabian Nights* (2007) (I)

✳ Mollel, Tololwa M., *The Orphan Boy: A Maasai Story* (1990) (P–I)

✳ _____, *Shadow Dance* (1998) (P–I)

✳ _____, *Subira Subira* (2000) (P–I)

✳ Morley, Jacqueline, *Egyptian Myths* (1999) (I–A)

✳ Onyefulu, Obi, *Chinye: A West African Folk Tale* (1994) (P–I)

✳ Paye, Won-Ldy, and Margaret Lippert, *Head, Body, Legs: A Tale from Liberia* (2002) (P–I)

✳ _____, *Mrs. Chicken and the Hungry Crocodile* (2003) (P–I)

✳ Philip, Neil, *Celtic Fairy Tales* (1999) (I–A)

Schlitz, Laura Amy, *The Bearskinner: A Tale of the Brothers Grimm* (2007) (I)

Shepard, Aaron, *One-Eye! Two-Eyes! Three-Eyes!: A Very Grimm Fairy Tale* (2006) (P)

✳ Sierra, Judy, *The Beautiful Butterfly: A Folktale from Spain* (2000) (P–I)

✳ Singer, Isaac, *When Shlemiel Went to Warsaw and Other Stories* (1968) (I)

✳ _____, *Zlateh the Goat and Other Stories* (1966) (I)

✳ Souhami, Jessica, *The Leopard's Drum: An Ashanti Tale from West Africa* (1995) (P)

_____, *Sausages* (2006) (P)

✳ Taback, Simms, *Joseph Had a Little Overcoat* (1999) (P)

✳ Tchana, Katrin, *Sense Pass King: A Story from Cameroon* (2002) (I)

✳ Washington, Donna, *A Pride of African Tales* (2004) (I)

✳ Wisniewski, David, *Elfwyn's Saga* (1990) (I)

✳ _____, *Golem* (1996) (I)

✳ Yolen, Jane, *Tam Lin: An Old Ballad* (1990) (I)

CENTRAL ASIA

✳ Brett, Jan, *The Mitten: A Ukrainian Folktale* (1989) (P)

✳ Demi, *Firebird* (1994) (P–I)

✳ _____, *The Hungry Coat: A Tale from Turkey* (2004) (I)

✳ Hastings, Selina, *The Firebird* (1992) (P–I)

✳ Hogrogian, Nonny, *One Fine Day* (1971) (P)

✳ Ransome, Arthur, *The Fool of the World and the Flying Ship: A Russian Tale* (1968) (P–I)

✳ Shah, Idries, *The Boy without a Name* (2000) (P–I)

✳ _____, *The Clever Boy and the Terrible, Dangerous Animal* (2000) (P–I)

✳ _____, *Neem the Half-Boy* (1998) (P–I)

✳ _____, *The Old Woman and the Eagle* (2003) (P–I)

THE FAR EAST

✳ Climo, Shirley, *Tuko and the Birds: A Tale from the Philippines* (2008) (P)

✳ Daly, Jude, *Sivu's Six Wishes: A Taoist Tale* (2010) (P)

✳ Demi, *The Empty Pot* (1990) (P)

✳ _____, *The Magic Boat* (1990) (P–I)

✳ Greene, Ellin, *Ling-Li and the Phoenix Fairy: A Chinese Folktale* (1996) (P–I)

✳ Ho, Minfong, and Saphan Ros, *Brother Rabbit: A Cambodian Tale* (1997) (P–I)

✳ _____, *The Two Brothers* (1995) (P–I)

✳ Kajikawa, Kimiko, *Yoshi's Feast* (2000) (P–I)

✳ Kimmel, Eric, *Three Samurai Cats: A Story from Japan* (2003) (I)

✳ Nishizuka, Koko, *The Beckoning Cat: Based on a Japanese Folktale* (2009) (P)

✳ Xiong, Blia, *Nine-in-One Grr! Grr!: A Folktale from the Hmong People of Laos* (1989) (P–I)

✳ Young, Ed, *The Lost Horse: A Chinese Folktale* (1998) (I)

✳ _____, *Seven Blind Mice* (1992) (P)

✳ _____, *The Sons of the Dragon King: A Chinese Legend* (2004) (I–A)

Types of Folklore

NURSERY RHYMES

Books in this section are appropriate for nursery–primary readers unless otherwise noted.

Addams, Charles, *The Charles Addams Mother Goose* (1967) (A)

Crews, Nina, *The Neighborhood Mother Goose* (2004) (P–I)

dePaola, Tomie, *Tomie de Paola's Mother Goose* (1985)

✳ Griego, Margot C., Betsy Bucks, Sharon Gilbert, and Laurel Kimball, *Tortillas para Mama and Other Nursery Rhymes: Spanish and English* (1981) (P–I)

Lobel, Arnold, *Random House Book of Mother Goose* (1986)

Mavor, Salley, *Pocketful of Posies: A Treasury of Nursery Rhymes*, (2010) (N–P)

Opie, Iona, *Here Comes Mother Goose* (1999)

_____, *My Very First Mother Goose* (1996)

_____, *Tail Feathers from Mother Goose: The Opie Rhyme Book* (1988)

Opie, Iona, and Peter Opie, *I Saw Esau: The Schoolchild's Pocket Book* (1992)

✳ _____, *The Oxford Dictionary of Nursery Rhymes* (1951)

✳ Polacco, Patricia, *Babushka's Mother Goose* (1995)

Slier, Debby, *The Real Mother Goose: Book of American Rhymes* (1995)

Sutherland, Zena, *The Orchard Book of Nursery Rhymes* (1990)

Watson, Clyde, *Wendy Watson's Mother Goose* (1989)

Yolen, Jane, *Jane Yolen's Mother Goose Songbook* (1992)

TALKING ANIMAL TALES

Books in this section are appropriate for primary–intermediate readers unless otherwise noted.

Emberley, Rebecca, and Ed Emberley, *Chicken Little* (2009) (N–P)

Grimm, Jacob, and Wilhelm Grimm, *The Bremen Town Musicians* (2007) (P)

✳ Hamilton, Virginia, *Bruh Rabbit and the Tar Baby Girl* (2003) (P)

✳ Knutson, Barbara, *Sungura and Leopard: A Swahili Trickster Tale* (1993)

✳ Lester, Julius, *Further Tales of Uncle Remus: The Misadventures of Brer Rabbit, Brer Fox, Brer Wolf, the Doodang, and Other Creatures* (1990) (I–A)

✳ _____, *More Tales of Uncle Remus: Further Adventures of Brer Rabbit, His Friends, Enemies, and Others* (1988) (I–A)

✳ _____, *The Tales of Uncle Remus: The Adventures of Brer Rabbit* (1987) (I–A)

✳ McDermott, Gerald, *Coyote: A Trickster Tale from the American Southwest* (1994)

✳ _____, *The Pig-Boy: A Trickster Tale from Hawai'I* (2009)

✳ _____, *Zomo the Rabbit: A Trickster Tale from West Africa* (1992)

✳ McGill, Alice, *Sure as Sunrise: Stories of Bruh Rabbit & His Walkin' Talkin' Friends* (2004)

✳ Parks, Van Dyke, *Jump Again! More Adventures of Brer Rabbit* (1987)

✳ _____, *Jump on Over! The Adventures of Brer Rabbit and His Family* (1989)

✳ Parks, Van Dyke, and Malcolm Jones, *Jump! The Adventures of Brer Rabbit* (1986)

✳ Rascol, Sabina, *The Impudent Rooster* (2004)

✳ So, Meilo, *Gobble, Gobble, Slip, Slop: A Tale of a Very Greedy Cat* (2004)

FAIRY TALES

Grimm, Jacob, and Wilhelm Grimm, *The Annotated Brothers Grimm*, translated and edited by Maria Tatar (2004) (A)

✳ _____, *The Twelve Dancing Princesses* (2007) (P)

Lunge-Larsen, Lise, *The Hidden Folk: Stories of Fairies, Dwarves, Selkies, and Other Secret Beings* (2004) (I–A)

Manna, Anthony, and Christodoula Mitakidou, *Mr. Semolina-Semolinus: A Greek Folktale* (1997) (I)

Perrault, Charles, *Beauty and the Beast*, adapted by Nancy Willard (1992) (I)

_____, *Cinderella*, adapted by Barbara McClintock (2005) (P)

Smith, James, *Book of a Thousand Days* (2007) (I)

Steig, Jeanne, *A Handful of Beans: Six Fairy Tales* (1998) (I–A)

Willey, Margaret, *Clever Beatrice* (2001) (P–I)

_____, *Clever Beatrice and the Best Little Pony* (2004) (P–I)

TALL TALES

Arnold, Caroline, *The Terrible Hodag and the Animal Catchers* (2006) (P–I)

✳ Hurston, Zora Neale, *Lies and Other Tall Tales* (2005) (I)

Johnson, Paul Brett, *Old Dry Frye: A Deliciously Funny Tall Tale* (1999) (P–I)

Kellogg, Steven, *Paul Bunyan* (1984) (P)

_____, *Pecos Bill* (1986) (P)

✳ Lester, Julius, *John Henry* (1994) (P)

Osborne, Mary Pope, *American Tall Tales* (1991) (P–I)

San Souci, Robert D., and Jane Yolen, *Cut from the Same Cloth: American Women of Myth, Legend, and Tall Tale* (1993) (I)

Walker, Paul Robert, *Big Men, Big Country: A Collection of American Tall Tales* (1993) (A)

FABLES

Books in this section are appropriate for primary–intermediate readers.

Anno, Mitsumasa, *Anno's Aesop: A Book of Fables by Aesop and Mr. Fox* (1989)

✳ Bierhorst, John, *Doctor Coyote: A Native American Aesop's Fables* (1987)

Brett, Jan, *Town Mouse, Country Mouse* (1994)

✳ Climo, Shirley, *The Little Red Ant and the Great Big Crumb: A Mexican Fable* (1995)

✳ Demi, *A Chinese Zoo: Fables and Proverbs* (1987)

✳ Galdone, Paul, *The Monkey and the Crocodile: A Jataka Tale from India* (1969)

✳ Heins, Ethel, *The Cat and the Cook: And Other Fables of Krylov* (1995)

Hennessy, B. G., *The Boy Who Cried Wolf* (2006)

MacDonald, Suse, and Bill Oakes, *Once upon Another* (1990)

✳ Martin, Rafe, *Foolish Rabbit's Big Mistake* (1985)

McDermott, Gerald, *The Fox and the Stork* (1999)

Pinkney, Jerry, *Aesop's Fables* (2000)

_____, *The Lion & the Mouse* (2009)

Stevens, Janet, *The Tortoise and the Hare: An Aesop Fable* (1984)

_____, *The Town Mouse and the Country Mouse: An Aesop Fable* (1987)

Ward, Helen, *The Hare and the Tortoise: A Fable from Aesop* (1999)

_____, *Unwitting Wisdom: An Anthology of Aesop's Fables* (2004)

Young, Ed, *Seven Blind Mice* (1992)

MYTHS AND POURQUOI TALES

AFRICAN

Aardema, Verna, *Princess Gorilla and a New Kind of Water* (1988) (P–I)

_____, *Why Mosquitoes Buzz in People's Ears: A West African Tale* (1975) (P–I)

Gerson, Mary-Joan, *Why the Sky Is Far Away: A Nigerian Folktale* (1994) (P–I)

Knutson, Barbara, *How the Guinea Fowl Got Her Spots* (1990) (P–I)

_____, *Why the Crab Has No Head* (1987) (P–I)

Lester, Julius, *How Many Spots Does a Leopard Have? And Other Tales* (1989) (P–I)

GREEK AND ROMAN

Curlee, Lynn, *Mythological Creatures: A Classical Bestiary* (2008) (I)

Hutton, Warwick, *Odysseus and the Cyclops* (1995) (I)

———, *Persephone* (1994) (I)

Rylant, Cynthia, *The Beautiful Stories of Life: Six Greek Myths, Retold* (2009) (I)

Steig, Jeanne, *A Gift from Zeus: Sixteen Favorite Myths* (2001) (I–A)

NATIVE AMERICAN

Esbensen, Barbara Juster, *Ladder to the Sky: How the Gift of Healing Came to the Ojibway Nation* (1989) (P–I)

Goble, Paul, *Her Seven Brothers* (1988) (P–I)

———, *Mystic Horse* (2003) (P–I)

———, *Star Boy* (1983) (P–I)

Martin, Rafe, *The Boy Who Lived with the Seals* (1993)

Oughton, Jerrie, *How the Stars Fell into the Sky: A Navajo Legend* (1992)

Troughton, Joanna, *How the Birds Changed Their Feathers: A South American Indian Folktale* (1976)

———, *How Rabbit Stole the Fire: A North American Indian Folktale* (1986)

HERO TALES

Crossley-Holland, Kevin, *Beowulf* (1968) (I–A)

———, *The World of King Arthur and His Court: People, Places, Legend and Lore* (1998) (I-A)

✳ Demi, *The Legend of Lao Tzu and the Tao Te Ching* (2007) (I)

Gretchen, Sylvia, *Hero of the Land of Snow* (1990) (I–A)

✳ Henderson, Kathy, *Lugalbanda: The Boy Who Got Caught Up in a War* (2006) (A)

Hodges, Margaret, *The Kitchen Knight: A Tale of King Arthur* (1990) (I–A)

Hodges, Margaret, and Margery Evernden, *Of Swords and Sorcerers: The Adventures of King Arthur and His Knights* (1993) (I–A)

———, *Merlin and the Making of the King* (2004) (I–A)

———, *St. George and the Dragon* (1984) (I–A)

✳ Lester, Julius, *The Old African* (2005) (A)

✳ McCaughrean, Geraldine, *Gilgamesh the Hero* (2002) (I-A)

Perham, Molly, *King Arthur: The Legends of Camelot* (1993) (I–A)

Philip, Neil, *Tale of Sir Gawain* (1987) (I–A)

✳ Quattlebaum, Mary, *Sparks Fly High: The Legend of Dancing Point* (2006) (P)

✳ Running Wolf, Michael B., and Patricia Clark Smith, *On the Trail of Elder Brother: Glous'gap Stories of the Micmac Indians* (2000) (I–A)

Sabuda, Robert, *Arthur and the Sword* (1995) (I–A)

San Souci, Robert D., *Young Guinevere* (1993) (I–A)

———, *Larger Than Life: The Adventures of American Legendary Heroes* (1991) (I–A)

Williams, Marcia, *King Arthur and the Knights of the Round Table* (1996) (I–A)

Yolen, Jane, *Camelot* (1995) (I–A)

✳ Young, Ed, *Monkey King* (2001) (I–A)

Additional resources to accompany this chapter can be found on the Education CourseMate website. Go to CengageBrain .com to access a variety of interactive study tools and useful resources including Video Conversations with children's book authors and illustrators, a searchable children's literature database, glossary flashcards, online activities, tutorial quizzes, links to relevant websites, and more.

Fantastic Literature: Fantasy and Science Fiction

Every theory of the course of events in nature is necessarily based on some process of simplification of the phenomena and is to some extent therefore a fairy tale.

—SIR NAPIER SHAW

*Manual of Meterology, in **The Storm in the Barn** by Matt Phelan*

Rose decided to engage her sixth-grade students with a book that challenges many traditional genre boundaries, so she began the year by sharing Matt Phelan's **The Storm in the Barn** (I–A), a graphic novel that is historical fiction with a significant aspect of magic realism incorporated into a powerful story of an eleven-year-old boy struggling with both personal and environmental challenges. Many of her students were thrilled that they were "reading" a graphic novel for a school assignment; they usually read them as independent reading. Those who weren't familiar with the format quickly rose to the challenge of creating story out of illustrations, probably calling up their picturebook reading skills.

As they read, students responded in writing to the story, sometimes in an open-ended manner and sometimes in response to specific prompts that Rose gave them. They have just finished talking in small groups, sharing their ideas and questions. Now, they are gathered in a circle so that they can see one another, discussing the story as a whole class. After students share some of the comments they made during the small-group discussions, Rose poses a question: "Were any of you puzzled or surprised when Jack saw the figure of a man 'with a face like rain' in the barn?" After most students answer in the affirmative, she poses another: "What do you think that figure was?" This time, answers range from "like a mirage," to "an illusion," to "a hallucination because he was sick," to "magic." After the discussion winds down, Rose reads the introductory quote from Sir Napier Shaw, and then talks a bit about "magic realism" and human perception. After she reveals that this book has won a prize for outstanding historical fiction, the discussion becomes an argument about whether this book is fantasy or historical fiction, or both. The conversation ends with Rose's promise that they will share more books that are "unusual." She's planning to begin an exploration of postmodern picturebooks soon.

Defining Fantastic Literature

Fantastic literature, which includes folklore, fantasy, and science fiction, seeks to explain and explore the mysteries of the world, the universe, and the behavior of we humans who inhabit it. As Rabkin (1976) explains, the readers of fantastic literature are "astonished" when their preconceptions of what is possible, grounded in natural laws, are challenged in the narrative world of fantastic literature. Wolfe (1986) describes fantastic literature as the "polar opposite" of reality, a reversal of the "ground rules" of reality (Laster, 2011). This break with reality, many argue, allows authors to explore ideas that would be difficult to confront through realistic fiction.

Jane Yolen reminds us that "stories lean on stories" (2000, p. 15), and fantasy and science fiction derive strength from themes, traditions, and structures established in ancient myths and legends. There is a significant difference, however, between stories that came to us through oral tradition and ones we call fantasy or science fiction. Ancient tales were shaped and honed through cultural belief and the voice of the storyteller. Modern tales are shaped through the author's artistic vision and stylistic choices. Egoff (1981) considers this the difference between a public dream (folklore) and a private, metaphorical vision (modern fantasy and science fiction). For example, the appearance of the Holy Grail in Thomas Malory's *Le Morte d'Arthur* was not taken as fantasy in the fifteenth century; it was a public dream, meant to be believed. Weaving this and other legends from Arthurian days into the fabric of modern life, Susan Cooper creates a private vision—fantasies that dramatize the risks of failing to stand up for what is right and just. Cooper bases her award-winning series on English and Celtic myth, beginning with **Over Sea, Under Stone** and continuing with **The Dark Is Rising, Greenwitch, The Grey King**, and **Silver on the Tree** (all A). As our ancestors created myths to explain the sun's apparent movement, so modern writers spin imaginative tales to explain things we do not fully understand and to probe the dimensions of areas we do not fully know.

Heroes of ancient legend confront great danger and rise to impossible challenges, and modern heroes also take on a larger-than-life nature in fantasy and science fiction. For example, in Philip Pullman's magnificent trilogy **The Golden Compass, The Subtle Knife**, and **The Amber Spyglass** (A), Lyra and Will, the youthful heroes, battle powerful forces as they seek to fulfill their own destinies. These stories and many others also rely on structural patterns found in the oral tradition. In many cases, characters go on a quest that turns out differently than what they expected, they rise to the occasion, and they are transformed in some way. In the Pullman trilogy, Lyra and Will travel to several worlds, including the world of the dead, and they end up discovering the magnificence of love.

Writers of fantastic literature often grapple with issues and ideas so serious that they would be difficult to explore in realistic fiction for children. The consequences of war, cruelty, enslavement, and greed are some of the many aspects of life explored in these genres. The "imaginative exploration of human nature and metaphysical truths" (Baker, 2006, p. 624) that marks fantastic literature offers readers an opportunity to develop their personal codes for how they will operate in the world. Susan Cooper speaks of fantasy as "the metaphor through which we

discover ourselves" (1981/1996, p. 16). She argues that rather than helping us escape out of ourselves and into a fantasy world, fantasy draws readers into themselves, pushing them to consider who they are and what the world is. Serious fantastic literature "is probably the most complex form of fiction [readers] will ever find" and demands a great deal from its readers (1996, p. 16). Hunt (2007) argues that fantasy speaks to young readers in a special way. "Above everything else—the terrific plotting, the nifty world-building, the sense of awe and wonder and magic— the potent appeal of fantasy for me was that while so many of the mundane, ordinary things of life were controlled by adults, the *really* important things— the fate of the universe, the battle between good and evil—were left in the capable hands of children" (p. 645).

Scholars and writers have argued for decades about the labels of "fantasy" and "science fiction" (Card, 1990; Wolfe, 1986). For the sake of simplicity, we define fantastic literature as imaginative narratives that explore alternate realities, although what exactly constitutes an alternate reality is a slippery concept. Fantasy suspends scientific explanations and natural laws; it is not "possible," but the logic that governs a fantasy world makes it "plausible." Within the fantasy world, authors ask age-old questions about life, goodness, and harmony. Science fiction is "possible," as it explores scientific possibilities, asking and answering the question "If this, then what?" Although both fantasy and science fiction are often set in worlds that do not correspond to present realities, science fiction differs from fantasy in that the future realities it depicts are based on extrapolation from scientific principles.

Of course, it is sometimes difficult to draw the line between what is scientifically possible and what is not, and some critics talk about "science fantasy" books in which the line between the fantastic and a scientific possibility is a fine one. Madeleine L'Engle's **A Wrinkle in Time, A Wind in the Door**, and **A Swiftly Tilting Planet** (A) all involve travel through time and space. Is this fantasy? Or, because this travel is theoretically possible, is it science fiction? What is truly important is that L'Engle's powerful novels, however one chooses to classify them, offer readers opportunities to think about the power of love in a deeper, more profound way than our daily lives permit.

Rebecca Stead's Newbery Medal–winning **When You Reach Me** (I–A), set in the upper west side of Manhattan in 1979, is seemingly a realistic coming-of-age story for young adolescents, until it is apparent that the letters that twelve-year-old Miranda is getting are coming from someone in the future. As she and the reader figure out who is sending the letters, she is also figuring out how to leave childhood for the more complicated adolescent world and how to stay friends with her childhood buddy, Sal, while making new ones. An interesting twist is that Mira's favorite book is L'Engle's *A Wrinkle in Time*. Susan Fletcher's **Dragon Chronicles** series, which includes ***Dragon's Milk, Flight of the Dragon Kyn, Sign of the Dove***, and ***Ancient, Strange, and Lovely*** (all A), combine adolescent life, raising a dragon, and environmental concerns. The dragon is commonly found in fantasy; the microbes that eat environmental toxins are science fiction. The stories, however one might label them, are gripping.

Similarly, stories that contain magic realism, also called magical realism, blur the boundaries between fantastic and realistic literature because magic realism involves something that is not part of the common Western conception of reality being accepted as "real" in an otherwise realistic fiction text. Stories such as David Almond's **Skellig** (A) and Patrick Ness's **A Monster Calls: A Novel** (A) challenge readers to consider what is real and what is fantastic. We discuss this and other stories that contain magic realism later in this chapter. Books with magic realism, such as ***The Storm in the Barn*** (I–A), discussed in the opening vignette for this chapter, challenge the boundaries between fantasy and other traditional genres.

A Brief History of Fantastic Literature

Children had little time to be children in the mid-nineteenth century. Social and economic conditions dictated that many young people work, often in horrendous circumstances. The society that tolerated grim conditions for children developed a literature that provided a fantasy escape from the harsh workaday world while still giving a justification for the work ethic. Much of that fanciful literature came from England, and hardworking American children welcomed it with open arms.

Alice's Adventures in Wonderland (1865) and ***Through the Looking Glass*** (1871) by Charles Dodgson are the first significant works of fantasy for children. Dodgson, a clergyman and scholarly math professor at Oxford, chose the pen name Lewis Carroll to avoid being identified with books for children, ironically the very reason that he is remembered today. Legend says that Dodgson often told stories to the three Liddell girls, daughters of a friend. One afternoon, Alice, one of the sisters, asked for a

story with nonsense. The story she heard that day became world famous: Dodgson wrote it out for her the following Christmas, and it was then published with John Tenniel's brilliant illustrations. Contemporary artists offer their own interpretations of this still-popular fantasy, as demonstrated by Lisbeth Zwerger's **Alice in Wonderland** (I), first published in 1999 and reissued in 2008.

Fantasy flourished in the twentieth century, with publication of books such as the classic story-play ***Peter Pan*** (P–I) by J. M. Barrie (1904), Beatrix Potter's ***The Tale of Peter Rabbit*** (N) (1902), and E. B. White's ***Charlotte's Web*** (I) (1952). The "series" book in the fantasy genre was increasingly frequent, with books such as Frank Baum's ***The Wizard of Oz*** (I) (1900), J.R.R. Tolkien's ***The Hobbit*** (I–A) (1938), C. S. Lewis's **The Chronicles of Narnia** (I) (1950), Lloyd Alexander's ***The Book of Three*** (I) (1964), and Susan Cooper's ***The Dark Is Rising*** (I–A) (1973) being parts of an expansive story told across multiple books. Books such as Philip Pullman's **His Dark Materials** (I–A) trilogy, J. K. Rowling's **Harry Potter** (I–A) series, and J.R.R. Tolkien's **Lord of the Rings** (I–A) are so popular today that they have been made into movies, fueling and reflecting the current "fantasy renaissance." Interestingly, fantastic literature from Great Britain is now easily available and immensely popular in the United States, with books from authors such as Philip Pullman, Patrick Ness, Catherine Fisher, Saci Lloyd, Philip Reeve, Rachel Ward, and, of course, J. K. Rowling added to the venerable J.R.R. Tolkien, very popular with intermediate and young adult readers.

Science fiction as a term was introduced by Hugo Gernsback in the late 1920s to describe a "pulp magazine," what we might think of as "escapist literature," or "trash." Although writers and critics argued about the term, and in fact still do, the genre grew in popularity and prestige as gifted writers produced what is now commonly called science fiction for a range of audiences. Writers Andre Norton and Robert Heinlein are generally credited with popularizing science fiction for young readers, with Heinlein's ***Rocket Ship Galileo*** (I), published in 1947, considered the first piece of science fiction especially for the juvenile market. Today, most science fiction for young readers is targeted primarily to the twelve and older group. The World Science Fiction Society created the Hugo Award, given to the best science fiction of the previous year, to honor Gernsback, and the Andre Norton Award for science fiction and fantasy, to honor Norton (Laster, 2011).

As fantastic literature for young readers has continued to blossom over the past decade, subgenres, or types, have become popular. For example, "steampunk" is used to describe a type of fantastic literature that is set in an anachronistic, nineteenth-century society and often includes alternate world history or a strong fantasy component. It can take the form of a "retrofuturism" featuring scientific innovations as imagined by Victorians, or fully imagined secondary fantasy worlds that reflect science and culture from the Victorian era (Laster, personal communication).

Alongside the growth of the genre, many writers and critics have insisted on a distinction between "high" fantasy, stories placed in a fully realized fantastic setting, and "low" fantasy, stories in which something fantastic intrudes on the real world. A similar distinction is made in science fiction between "hard" and "soft" science fiction. The former is based on possibilities suggested by the "hard" sciences of biology, chemistry, physics, and so forth; the latter is based on possibilities suggested by "soft" sciences such as sociology (Laster, 2011). Lois Lowry's Newbery Medal–winning ***The Giver*** (I–A) would be in the latter category, what some call "social-science fiction," although genetic engineering certainly plays an important role in that novel. Once again, authors defy boundaries, causing us to rethink our accepted category systems.

Today, there is still debate about whether fantasy and science fiction are one genre, fantastic literature, rather than two; about the relative literary quality of "high" versus "low" fantasy or "hard" versus "soft" science fiction; and about the place of fantasy in young readers' lives. What is apparent, however, is that young readers do not much care about these debates. What they do care about is the books themselves, books that they devour, share with friends, and love passionately.

In this chapter, we first:

- Consider how to determine quality in fantasy and science fiction
- Explore various types of fantasy
- Examine themes in science fiction
- Discuss the role of fantasy and science fiction in the classroom

Considering Quality in Fantastic Literature

The passion with which children love fantastic literature is in part because of the talent of the writers of that literature. As with all quality narrative literature, good fantasy and science fiction stories—whether

FIGURE 6.1

Considering Quality in Fantastic Literature

- The story meets the criteria for excellence in narrative fiction.
- The fantastic or future world, characters, and events are detailed and believable within the context of the story.
- The story events are imaginative, yet logically consistent within the story world.
- The characters are multidimensional, with consistent and logical behavior.
- The writing is rich, and the structures are clear.
- The themes are meaningful, causing readers to think about life.

they are serious or playful—tell an interesting story and have well-developed characters, an engaging plot, and an important theme—all presented through a well-crafted style. Authors manipulate these literary elements to create the fantastic. If the writer is successful, readers willingly suspend disbelief. Although not "real," fantastic literature is, in a very important way, "true." We judge the quality of a writer's private vision by how thoroughly it convinces us of its truth, by how long it haunts our memory, and by how deeply it moves us to new insights. As Baker points out, "Every great fantasy is great in its own way,… because real insight and artistic originality must be unique to its author" (2006, p. 624). Within that originality, however, it is possible to recognize certain qualities that usually are present in excellent fantasy and science fiction. Criteria for evaluating fantastic literature appear in Figure 6.1.

• • SETTING • •

No matter how fantastic they are, settings become believable when an author provides rich details that enable a reader to envision them. Some authors set their stories entirely in an alternate reality, providing detailed verbal "maps" of fantastic worlds, often with accompanying visual depictions. Others gradually lead readers from a fictional real world into a richly detailed fantasy world through some device,

TEACHING IDEA 6.1

Teaching Genre: Setting in Fantasy and Science Fiction

COMMON CORE STATE STANDARDS   This Teaching Idea adresses Common Core English Language Arts, Reading: Literature standard 9, grades 3 through 6. The suggestions in this Teaching Idea may need to be adapted to suit your particular grade level or the needs of your students.

Good fantasy writers establish believable settings by carefully presenting them in intricate detail. Because the reader must envision the fantasy world, a writer's words ought to stimulate pictures in the mind's eye. Some writers add a map or make a scale drawing of an area; some paint scenes that are so vivid you can smell them.

Read outstanding fantasies aloud to savor the descriptive language used to establish setting. Read aloud scenes and ask students to create dioramas, paintings, or three-dimensional scenes of the ones described. Ask students to describe in writing the scene they envision. Discuss these and other examples of vivid writing in a writing workshop to show effective techniques, and then ask young writers to create their own vivid settings.

Following are a few suggestions of books for intermediate and advanced readers and pages where

you will read vivid scenes. As you continue to read in this genre, you will find many more. Younger readers can look closely at illustrations in fantasy picture storybooks and then try to describe those scenes in words.

- Farmer, Nancy, *The House of the Scorpion*, see chapter 33, p. 324, "The Boneyard."

- Jacques, Brian, *Redwall*, see the frontispiece: "Redwall stood foursquare along the marches of the old south border, flanked on two sides by Mossflower Wood's shaded depths . . ."

- Jansson, Tove, *Tales from Moominvalley*, see p. 11: "The brook was a good one . . ."

- White, E. B., *Charlotte's Web*, see p. 13: "The barn was very large . . ."

---

such as a magic door, a magic object, or the belief of realistic characters in the fantasy setting. In science fiction the setting is usually a time in the future, a future shaped by a present-day scientific possibility that has been realized. It may be, for example, a dystopian world overcrowded due to medical advances, or one in which genetic engineering has run amuck, or a world that has been devastated by global warming. Many, but not all science fiction novels are set in dystopias. In fantastic literature, effective settings are detailed and believable within the context of the story. Teaching Idea 6.1 suggests ideas for examining some believable settings with your students.

● ● PLOT ● ●

Even though events might not be realistic, what happens in a story should be logically consistent within the story world. If characters move through time, they do so for a reason; they may walk through a door, press a magic button, or visit a particular place. If the fantastic operates in the real world, then

there is consistency in how real people are affected by the fantastic events. In science fiction, the plot is usually logically driven by the problems that scientific advances have created for the characters in the story world.

● ● CHARACTERS ● ●

Main characters in excellent fantasy and science fiction are multidimensional personalities who behave consistently, respond to events in a believable fashion, and grow and change across the course of the story. There is strong unity of character and action: characters both influence and are influenced by the events in the story. If a character that lives in a realistic story world enters a fantastic situation, the character does not magically change, but remains consistent across both worlds. Characters in science fiction struggle as they try to live in a future world as imagined by a writer. Even if characters are superheroes in a story, they are so carefully delineated that readers easily accept their otherworldly powers.

How a writer chooses to tell a story—through structure, syntax, and word choice—makes the difference between a mediocre book and an excellent one. Some of the best writing in books for young readers appears in fantasy and science fiction. Style works to establish the setting; rich images and vivid figurative language help readers envision the created world. Style makes the characters and the plot believable; authentic dialogue and clear structure help readers build characterizations and follow the action. Well-written stories have clear structures supported by vivid, interesting images and rich language.

• • THEME • •

Although some fantasy and science fiction is lighthearted, many other books have serious themes of great import. The monumental struggle between good and evil, what it means to be human, and the consequences of pride are all examples of recurring themes in fantastic literature. In science fiction, writers additionally challenge readers to consider the emotional, psychological, and physical effects of particular scientific advances. These profound themes weave throughout the story, logically radiating from character and plot. At their best, these stories ask questions that arise naturally from the unity of character and action and are meaningful for readers, causing them to ask questions about life. Excellent fantastic literature can carry "us from the concrete to the abstract, from a satisfying narrative experience to a moment of articulate wisdom" (Baker, 2006, p. 264). A close look at Kathi Appelt's Newbery Honor–winning **The Underneath** (I) demonstrates these characteristics of quality.

* * *

A CLOSE LOOK AT
The Underneath

The very first words of this story draw the reader in, for who can resist a lonely cat, especially if they notice that there are two very small kittens on the cover. Within the first few pages, several "characters" are introduced and questions are raised that propel readers immediately into the story. There are the cat and her unborn kittens; an old, lonely hound; an ancient serpent; a man, emotionally wounded in childhood, who is filled with hate; and the piney woods, themselves a character.

The setting, seemingly an antagonist in the story, is lushly depicted—with trees detailed by name, and careful descriptions of the forest floor and the waters that surround it. The tall, ancient loblolly pine rises above the rest even though it is hollowed and has been cracked by lightning strikes and age. "This pine," Appelt tells us, "did not fall to the earth or slide into the creek. Not then. And not now. It still stands." And thus we are alerted to both the strength and the vulnerability of this particular tree. Other kinds of trees, and the waters, too, are named and described in such detail that Bayou Tartine, Petite Tartine, and Sorrowful Creek become familiar places in which many wild creatures, but especially snakes, alligators, and the man called Gar Face, make their home.

The characters are both varied and memorable, with each demonstrating particular qualities. Gar Face, for example, is unutterably mean, chaining and beating his hound, killing not only for money but for pleasure, yet many readers also feel slightly sympathetic as we read about his miserable childhood, his disfigurement, and his isolation. The calico cat radiates love even as she radiates purrs, meeting the need of the lonely old hound for a loving companion, and the hound rewards her, and her kittens, with loyalty. Together, they are a family. The cat and the hound watch over the kittens from underneath the porch of Gar Face's house, warning them to stay out of his view. The kittens themselves are completely vulnerable, with individual personality traits that make them recognizably "human." The ancient serpent, woven from native lore, seems at first to be pure evil, but even she loved her long-lost daughter. The immense alligator king, who lies in the marshes between the Tartines, a menace to everything that comes his way, also has a saving grace: he is wise. Thus, reflecting folkloric tradition, each character represents a unique quality, but all have at least one other dimension.

The plot is complex, with each character's stories weaving together to form a complete and satisfying whole. We follow the angry fixation of Gar Face in his battle with the alligator king; the courage of the calico cat as she saves her kitten's life; the determination with which that kitten, Puck, seeks to reunite with his sister, Sabine, and Ranger, the hound. Woven around these strands are the stories of Grandmother Moccasin and her daughter, Night Song, who left her mother to love Hawk Man, and of their daughter, Grandmother Moccasin's granddaughter. The trees, too, have their own story, one even more ancient than those of the grandmother and the alligator. These narrative strands intertwine in a way that is inevitable, so carefully foreshadowed that a second reading reveals just how tightly woven this novel is.

An omniscient narrator enables the structure of the book to be based on multiple narrative strands

P | R | O | F | I | L | E

Kathi Appelt

I feel particularly committed to children and the difficult odds facing them in this country. One of my own personal missions is to change what we call children—that is, I would like to see them called a "priority" rather than a "resource." I don't feel we've done a very good job with our resources and I don't like the connotation that children are something that can be mined or exploited. Rather, they should be something that gets our top attention, something that receives our most intensive care and love.

The author of more than thirty books for children and young adults, Kathi Appelt published her first book for children in 1986 and the next eighteen between 1993 and 2000. A gifted writer, she creates books as diverse as her lyrical, picturebook texts in verse, nonfiction, poetry for adolescent readers and writers, short stories, and *The Underneath*, her first novel. She has won Pick of the Lists and Teachers' Choice Awards and has had her books selected by the American Library Association for their Best Books for Young Adults and Quick Picks for Reluctant Readers lists.

The Underneath is a 2008 National Book Award finalist and a Newbery Honor winner.

Kathi serves on the faculty at Vermont College of Fine Arts in their Master of Fine Arts in Writing for Children and Young Adults Program, and occasionally teaches a course in creative writing at Texas A&M, her alma mater.

To learn more about Kathi Appelt, go to CengageBrain.com to access the Education CourseMate website where you will find links to relevant websites.

---

and also allows the development of characters as we see into the minds and hearts of them all. The story, woven as it is from rage and abuse, hate and violence, but also love and loyalty, is surprisingly beautiful. The language is lyrical, begging to be read aloud, and the story is life-affirming in the depiction of the triumph of love. Over all of the events stand the trees—ancient, wise, and telling their own stories—stories that resonate with ancient themes of love and hate, life and death, stories that have been and will be told as long as those ancient trees stand, and beyond.

Fantasy

Fantasy that explores the human condition is often deeply serious. This type of fantasy, often called "high" fantasy, lies closely beside ancient folklore and contains archetypal themes. It is often set in a fully realized fantasy world, explores the struggle between good and evil, and depicts a quest for personal identity. Sometimes these stories are so steeped in ancient tales that it's difficult to remember that they are, indeed, not folklore, but created by the imagination of an author. Other fantasies are more lighthearted, sometimes simply creating a veil of unreality to disguise the real world in some way. Many fantasy picturebooks for younger readers are simply animal characters "standing in" for humans.

The fantastic element may be as simple as animals that act like humans or as complex as fully developed worlds that reflect real life with a significant twist. Fantasy writers, playfully and seriously, use such devices as fully developed fantastic settings, nonhuman characters, and magic or magic realism to create fantasy. By so doing, writers are able to explore complex issues with a depth that might be too disturbing when considered in realistic settings. The metaphorical nature of fantasy allows young readers to consider ideas about things such as prejudice, death, war, the consequences of beauty, and other serious matters in a manageable way.

In Shaun Tan's *The Arrival* (I–A), a lengthy graphic picturebook for older readers discussed earlier, Tan uses fantasy to heighten the emotional impact of an immigrant entering a new culture. Just as the character is bemused by new customs, fashions, places, and people, readers also are forced to notice the surroundings because everything is new to them as well—the new world is a fantasy world. In his Caldecott Award–winning *Flotsam* (P–I), David Wiesner asks readers to consider, and reconsider, the possibilities of the world under the sea and the structure of time. When the main character, who seems to have the habit of looking closely at things, finds an old camera washed up on the beach, new worlds and possibilities open to him as he looks at the photographs that were on the film in the camera. Fantasy, whether in novel or picturebook format, serious or lighthearted, asks readers to open their eyes and imagine.

• • QUESTS AND FANTASY WORLDS • •

As in ancient folklore, many fantasy stories are quest tales set in well-developed fantasy worlds, stories in which a protagonist leaves home to accomplish a goal, finds him- or herself, and returns a wiser, better person. T. A. Barron's **The Lost Years of Merlin** epic (A) is a magnificent quest based on legend. **The Great Tree of Avalon** series, including *Child of the Dark Prophecy, Shadows on the Stars*, and *The Eternal Flame* (all A), is set in a wholly imagined world that was created when Merlin planted a seed and the tree of Avalon sprang into being. The **Merlin's Dragon** trilogy, *Merlin's Dragon, Doomraga's Revenge*, and *Ultimate Magic* (all I–A) chronicle the adventures of Basil, an unlikely hero who becomes a magnificent dragon as he fights to save Avalon from destruction. Barron is a riveting storyteller, and his readers are never disappointed with the time they spend in his world of Avalon.

Archetypal quest themes from folklore become vividly evident in high fantasy. Quest stories that are most memorable describe characters' outer and inner struggles and may involve Herculean journeys during which they overcome obstacles and vanquish foes. Quests often become a search for an inner, rather than an outer, enemy. Inner strength is required as characters are put to a variety of challenges that often seem endless and unbeatable. It is the indomitable goodness of character that prevails. Books such as *The Book of Three* from Lloyd Alexander's beloved series **The Prydain Chronicles** (I), which has been reissued in beautiful matched editions, continue to enchant young readers eager to test their metaphorical mettle against all odds. Cornelia Funke, author of *The Thief Lord* (I) and *Dragon Rider* (I), tells the story of young Igraine, daughter of two magicians, who wants desperately to be a knight. *Igraine the Brave* (I) is full of high spirits and good cheer, and she's a very spunky hero. Christopher Paolini's series **Inheritance Cycle**, which includes *Eragon, Eldest, Brisinger*, and *Inheritance: Or the Vault of Souls* (all A), creates an alternate reality, new languages, and memorable characters who engage in an epic battle between good and evil.

Many fantasies portray the anxieties of adolescence. Margaret Mahy creates an epic quest for identity in *The Magician of Hoad* (A), replete with suspense and romance, as Heriot learns to balance his identities as farm boy and magician. As Heriot and his friends discover the extent of their powers and how they can use them for good, it is evident that their struggles are also the struggles of adolescence, realized here in a fantasy world. Terry Pratchett's *I Shall Wear Midnight* (I–A), a Tiffany Aching adventure in Pratchett's extensive **Discworld** series, is marked by his consistently brilliant writing. Pratchett masterfully combines humor with deep seriousness as he explores the human character, in this case the potential for viciousness, with great insight. This series is both critically acclaimed and wildly popular, with Pratchett receiving many awards, including the Nebula.

This is also apparent in Philip Pullman's **His Dark Materials** trilogy (A). Readers are introduced to Lyra, the young and engaging protagonist, in *The Golden Compass*. Lyra is an interesting blend: she is both a street urchin and the highly intelligent daughter of eminent and powerful people. She thinks herself an orphan but soon discovers, to her horror, who her mother and father really are. Lyra sets out on a quest to save herself and the children who are being kidnapped and sent north to be the victims of a horrible experiment. By the end of the story, she has come to realize that her quest is bigger than this, and she unhesitatingly steps into a new world, determined to carry on. Continue she does, in *The Subtle Knife*, where she meets her partner, Will, a hero not unlike herself but from a different world. They pursue their quest, moving between worlds, aided by witches and angels, running from the evildoers of the church, until the triumphant ending of *The Amber Spyglass*. This series has it all: young heroes, alternate worlds, time slips, magic objects, fantastic creatures, imagination at its height. It is all anchored in an overarching theme, the struggle between good and evil and the overwhelming power of love.

Nancy Farmer taps the ancient stories of the northlands to construct the world in which she explores adolescence in her three-volume series *The Sea of Trolls, The Land of the Silver Apples*, and *The Islands of the Blessed* (all I). Jack, an apprentice Bard, is actually an unwilling hero, a young boy who is thrust into his quest by a series of events that shatter his assumptions about life. Set in Britain in 790 A.D., these stories also depict the clash between Christianity, the "new" religion, and the ancient lore of the Druids, as well as the hostility between the British and the Norsemen.

Tamora Pierce has been entertaining readers for many years with her fantasies set within the imaginary land of Tortall. One of her memorable heroines is Beka Cooper, a brave young woman who rises to the challenges posed by life in her world. In *Mastiff* (A), book three in a trilogy, Beka grapples with betrayal and corruption in the Tortallan government. Pierce's *Tortall and Other Lands: A Collection of Tales* (I–A) is both an introduction to her fantasy worlds and a pleasant visit for those already familiar with them. In Susannah Appelbaum's **Poisons of Caux** trilogy, *The Hollow Bettle, The Tasters Guild*, and *The Shepherd of Weeds* (I), eleven-year-old Ivy is the heroine as she continues her quest to defeat greedy evildoers, save Caux, and fulfill an ancient prophesy. Yet another brave girl is the protagonist of Catherynne Valente's Andre Norton Award–winning **The Girl Who Circumnavigated Fairyland in a Ship of Her Own Making** (I), illustrated by Ana Juan. This book combines classic fairy-tale elements, unusual characters, humorous banter, and an engaging heroine in a beautifully crafted story. Elaborate fantasy worlds and significant quests draw young readers into books that help them think about the age-old struggle inherent in growing up and finding out what special gifts we bring to our world.

● ● MAGIC AND MAGIC REALISM ● ●

Along with detailed fantasy worlds and sweeping quest tales, there is often some kind of magic in fantasy narratives. This magic may consist of objects or places that enable characters to slip across time and space into a fantasy world, an object or action that changes characters into fantastical beings, enchanting objects that do not exist in the real world, or characters who possess magical powers. Readers recognize the possibilities that magic entails; they willingly enter a world that does not operate by natural law, and they stay immersed in that world as long as the magic operates logically.

Magic can be lighthearted or deeply serious. A personal fairy—with a bad attitude—creates the magic in Liz Kessler's **Philippa Fisher's Fairy Godsister** (I), illustrated by Katie May. Another kind of magic is that constructed by writers such as Neil Gaiman—ghost stories. In the Newbery Medal–winning **The Graveyard Book** (A), illustrated by David McKean, Gaiman combines a ghost story with a coming-of-age novel that is spellbinding, even to the point of tears at the artful ending. Tonya Hegamin and Marilyn Nelson's **Pemba's Song: A Ghost Story** (A) uses verse and prose to tell the tale of how Phyllys, the ghost of an eighteenth-century slave girl visits Pemba in the old house in Connecticut, where she is unhappily missing

her friends back home in Brooklyn. The characters are engaging, the evolving mystery enticing, and the themes of freedom, redemption, and honest friendships speak to today's readers.

One of the more unusual objects to possess magical powers is at the center of Laurel Snyder's **Bigger than a Bread Box** (I). Twelve-year-old Rebecca is very upset that her mother has taken her and her little brother from Baltimore to Atlanta, to her grandmother's house, leaving Rebecca's father behind. As she struggles to understand how her family could be falling apart, she discovers that the old bread box she finds in her grandmother's attic will give her what she asks for, if it fits inside of the box. She learns that objects and money don't make her happy and that her wishes don't help get her parents back together.

Diane Stanley sets her novel **The Silver Bowl** (I–A) in a fictional world of castles, royalty, and dark magic. This fantasy adventure story has a wonderful heroine, a bumbling kitchen maid, Molly, who is finally sent to polish the royal family's silver. When she is polishing one particularly beautiful silver bowl, the carvings in it alter themselves so that she can see both past and future. Discovering the source of the dark curse that has blighted the royal family, Molly is determined to help. Full of suspense, the story closes with a perfect ending; sometimes the good are, indeed, rewarded.

J. K. Rowling's **Harry Potter** series (I–A) contains a vast array of magic devices, such as Harry's famous Quidditch broom, owls that deliver mail, invisibility cloaks, and a map that shows people and their locations. The books are also firmly anchored in the well-developed fantasy world of the Hogwarts School of Witchcraft and Wizardry, which is peopled by teachers and students who practice an assortment of bizarre and intriguing magic. All of this magic is carefully placed, and the actions within the fantasy world are ultimately logical. Rowling never violates the rules she creates.

The premise in Polly Shulman's **The Grimm Legacy** (I–A) is that the powerful magical objects from the Grimm tales exist and are safely locked away in the New York Circulating Material Repository, where Elizabeth, unhappy at school, takes a job hoping to make new friends and a little money. When the objects, not as safely locked up as they should have been, begin to disappear, Elizabeth and friends search for the thief before bad things can happen. Mystery and romance combine in this innovative fantasy.

Natalie Babbitt's classic fantasy, **Tuck Everlasting** (I), postulates a magic spring that, like the water so long sought by explorer Ponce de Leon, bestows eternal life. The magical water has given eternal life to the Tuck family, and young Winnie Foster discovers their secret. What she learns about the impact of eternal life on the Tucks influences the decision she makes—not to drink from the spring. The magic in this tale allows Babbitt to explore some important life questions. In Cornelia Funke's trilogy *Inkheart, Inkspell*, and *Inkdeath* (all A), the magic, fittingly, is in a book that draws young Meggie and her father into its story world. As the story world becomes more chaotic and dangerous, it is clear that the characters in that world are out of the control of the author.

The twelve-year-old protagonist in Nnedi Okorafor's *Akata Witch* (A) is, like the author, born in America of Nigerian parents. She is also albino, and she contains her own magic. She is a witch, possessing magical powers that her new friends, also magical, help her uncover as they work together to stop a serial killer. The African perspective that is clearly present in this book, set in Nigeria, the explicit discussion of "fitting in" across cultures, and the boxed informational asides as well as the Nsibidi symbols that appear in the text, add an extra depth to this outstanding coming-of-age fantasy.

In Janice Hardy's *The Shifter* (A), book one in **The Healing Wars** series, Nya has the ability to draw pain out of a sufferer and into her own body. This is a prized power in the world of occupied Geveg, recently defeated in a brutal war, where the government regulates the "pain trade" to support its fragile economy. Nya's power, however, is complicated by the ability to then transfer pain to another person rather than simply ridding herself of it by transferring it to pynvium, a metal that absorbs pain. This coming-of-age novel confronts ethical dilemmas that, although fantastic in Nya's country, are too possible in our world. *Blue Fire* and *Darkfall* (both A) complete the trilogy as Nya struggles to save her sister and protect her own love as she tries to sort out the moral implications of how pain is used.

Many fantasy writers use the device of characters moving across time and space to create and sustain the fantasy in their stories. In these stories, time and space are carried beyond the realm of everyday experience as characters move between their current reality and other times and places. For many writers, the past and future are part of the present; by challenging our understanding of time as sequential, these authors are making a statement about the meaning of time itself. One such writer, Eleanor Cameron (1969), describes a globe of time in which the past, present, and future are perceived as a whole.

Joseph Bruchac plays on the interconnectedness of time in *Dragon Castle* (I–A), with parallel plots, dragons, and mystery, and echoes of Slovakian origins in the setting and the Gypsy proverbs. Humor also abounds, and the multiple plotlines come together to form a terrific whole. Authors of fantasy invent a dazzling variety of devices to permit their characters to move in and out of conventional time and from one world to another. The children in C. S. Lewis's *The Lion, the Witch, and the Wardrobe* (I) enter the land of Narnia through a wardrobe door; while they are in Narnia, time does not pass in their real world. Many, if not most of the fantasies discussed in this chapter, focus on a central character going through a difficult adjustment period, often adolescence, and loneliness, alienation, and extraordinary sensitivity seem to be associated with moving from world to world and across time. Lyra and Will, Harry, and Jack, hero of *The Storm in the Barn*, are all such characters. In *The Emerald Atlas* (I), the first in a planned trilogy, **The Books of Beginning**, John Stephens's protagonists, fourteen-, twelve-, and eleven-year-old siblings, have bounced from orphanage to orphanage after their parents' mysterious disappearance ten years earlier. When they find a blank book in their latest residence in upstate New York, they are transported back through time to fifteen years earlier to the middle of a battle between an evil witch and a kindly wizard. As the children realize that they can intervene to change the course of events and discover what happened to their parents, they move through an inventive magical world.

Magical, or magic realism in art, including literature, presents what may seem to be, to some, magical occurrences, but in a manner that suggests the "reality" of those occurrences; magical occurrences are not logically explained. Many artists and writers consider what we might call "magic" as more real than what we refer to as "reality." There are an increasing number of books that make use of magic realism, blurring the line between historical or contemporary realistic fiction and fantasy. The magic realism of David Almond's *Skellig* (A), a beautifully haunting, moving tale, involves a being that seems to be an angel, at least to the two young protagonists who see and talk with him. How you categorize this book and most of the others he has written depends on your perception of who Skellig was and where you place magical realism. For some, this makes it a fantasy novel; for others, it is grippingly realistic.

In Sid Fleischman's *The Dream Stealer* (I), illustrated by Peter Sís, an eight-year-old girl encounters a creature who steals nightmares. This book explores the boundary between realism and magic, a boundary that we might call the unconscious. Martin Mordecai sets *Blue Mountain Trouble* (I–A) in the Blue mountains of Jamaica. The dialogue and description are vivid and engaging, and it's quite easy to believe, along with the characters, that the mystical goat they discover really does have magical powers.

In *Keeper* (I), Kathi Appelt blends folkloric elements with magic realism in a story of a ten-year-old girl who is longing for the mother who left her behind so many years ago. The alternating flashbacks to her past and the forward action of her quest (into the ocean in the middle of the night in a stolen rowboat) to free a batch of crabs and find her mermaid mother, allow us to see beneath Keeper's often rough surface. Themes of identity and the meaning of family speak to readers.

Franny Billingsley's **Chime** (A), a National Book Award finalist, is a hauntingly beautiful tale of adolescent angst. Briony, the narrator, hates herself for having caused her twin sister's brain damage, her stepmother's death, and a host of other problems. In fact, she hates herself so much that she punishes herself by staying away from the swamp, her favorite place, where she can talk to the Old Ones who haunt it. The daughter of a clergyman but sure that she is a witch, Briony also worries about being discovered and hanged,

punishment for all witches. And then Eldric appears, beautiful Eldric, who thinks that Briony is wonderful, and with whom she is falling in love. This is a romance, a mystery, and a family story wrapped in fantasy and period details of early-twentieth-century rural England.

We now take a close look at a graphic novel that incorporates magic realism, Matt Phelan's **The Storm in the Barn** (I–A).

* * *

A CLOSE LOOK AT
The Storm in the Barn

The Storm in the Barn is a story of coming of age in hard times. Set in 1937 Kansas, it is an artful introduction to the world of the Dust Bowl, as seen

In **The Storm in the Barn**, *Matt Phelan's combination of historical fiction and magic realism results in a story beautifully told in images.*

through the struggles of one family—the Clarks— and in the making of an unlikely hero in the figure of eleven-year-old Jack Clark. It mines the genres of both historical fiction and tall tale, and combines them effectively with elements of fantasy and magic realism. The story employs minimal text, relying primarily on Phelan's panel art to tell a rich story.

The setting for this graphic novel is richly depicted in the illustrations, with panels frequently showing billowing clouds of dust shrouding the town and featuring grim, thin-lipped townspeople, creating a realistic vignette of those desperate times. Phelan then injects elements of both fantasy and tall tale into this realistic setting.

Jack Clark, a reticent, sensitive, eleven-year-old, is facing life's ordinary and extraordinary challenges. At school, he has to contend with bullies, and at home he has to live down the acute sense of having disappointed his father. The reader also sees the troubling effects of a Dust Bowl existence through the eyes of Jack. Often shown slouched over or hiding behind the brim of his hat, Jack Clark, like other heroes of tales that are named Jack, gathers his courage when it matters the most.

The two vignettes that open **The Storm in the Barn** are key pieces that help unfold the plot and take it to its logical conclusion. In the first, Jack's father gets a glimpse of a tall, shadowy figure as he is trying to escape town. In the second, Jack briefly stands up to the bullying ways of his schoolmates. These two pieces are brought together at the end, when Jack battles the shadowy figure and defeats him. Phelan's pacing of the plot of **The Storm in the Barn** is measured and masterful.

Phelan chooses to tell the story of **The Storm in the Barn** primarily through his art panels, which are mostly wordless. Their almost cinematic composition, with both perspective and scale being adroitly manipulated to give the reader a vivid sense of those times, results in a story that unfolds like a silent film, its many powerful images staying in the reader's mind long after the page is turned. Phelan's use of color— or rather the lack of it—is also a strategic, stylistic device, a visual reminder to the reader of what living in a perpetual haze of grit must have been like.

A recurring theme in **The Storm in the Barn** is the power of stories and storytelling. Jack's mother's stories about the time when their land was fertile and yielded bountiful harvests serve to remind of happier times gone by. For Jack's sister, Dorothy, bedridden and battling what the family physician calls "dust dementia," stories are a refuge. She escapes the present by losing herself in the adventures of another Dorothy, the one in **The Wizard of Oz**. Jack's triumph over the mysterious figure at the end of the story affirms the power of storytelling in an emphatic way, with Jack deriving inspiration from tall tales of other brave heroes also called Jack. Story, for Jack, helps him manage both the difficult time and place in which he lives and the difficult landscape of adolescence.

The intriguing quote that prefaces the story— "Every theory of the course of events in nature is necessarily based on some process of simplification of the phenomena and is to some extent therefore a fairy tale"—hints at the author's artful use of elements of realism, folklore, and fantasy. Phelan injects the fantastical element of a shadowy Rain figure, lurking in an abandoned barn, into a realistic setting of a small town in Kansas, re-created in all its Dust Bowl details. Rather than burden the tale with scientific explanations of overplanting and soil erosion, Phelan's stylistic use of such a fantastical element seems fitting given that the Dust Bowl years were a time of historical convulsions and personal upheavals. His imaginative depiction of rain as the tall, dark, sinister figure whom Jack Clark must triumph over results in a deeply satisfying story of an ordinary boy successfully facing up to some extraordinary challenges. Note that **The Storm in the Barn** also won the Scott O'Dell Award for historical fiction.

P|R|O|F|I|L|E

Matt Phelan

After studying film and theater in college, Matt Phelan planned to write and direct movies. Instead, he worked at several different jobs until he realized that drawing was what he really enjoyed. He began creating illustrations in 2004. In the past eight years, he has illustrated many picturebooks and created the covers for several novels, including Susan Patron's Newbery Award–winning, **The Higher Power of Lucky** (i). We discuss his graphic novel, **Around the World** (i), in Chapter 8. He did a great deal of research before creating **The Storm in the Barn**, including looking at photographs of the Dust Bowl era by Dorothea Lange and Walker Evans.

 For more information about Matt Phelan, visit CengageBrain.com to access the Education CourseMate website, where you will find links to relevant websites.

• • LITERARY LORE • • •

The literary tale, a story crafted by a writer who intentionally imitates the traditional qualities of ancient folklore, has become increasingly popular over the past several years. As discussed in Chapter 5, these stories are not cultural variants of well-known folktales, but rather the deliberate construction of a writer intending to imitate, embellish, or alter traditional folktales. Today, there are many picturebooks and full-length novels with characters and action based on traditional lore, using traditional stories and characters, but elaborated to create a wholly original tale. Teaching Idea 6.2 offers suggestions for exploring these tales with students.

Jon Scieszka's *The True Story of the Three Little Pigs* and *The Stinky Cheese Man and Other Fairly Stupid Tales* (I) are well-loved examples of this type of story for younger readers. Increasingly, writers for both young and older readers have created stories that weave around traditional tales. Zoe Alley retells five wolf stories in *There's a Wolf at the Door* (P), to the delight of young readers. A text that is full of funny one-liners, a comicstrip format, and varied, humorous illustrations by R. W. Alley make this a terrific book to share. Janet Stevens and her sister, Susan Stevens Crummel, draw on the classic tale of "the little red hen" in their hilarious picturebook, *The*

Little Red Pen (P–I). Who knew that teachers got so much help correcting student papers!

Anthony Browne's *Me and You* (P) is a wholly original rendition of the classic "three bears" story. In this version, the bears are privileged and rather smug, whereas Goldilocks is living in poverty, which completely changes the way we view these characters. Browne's illustrations heighten the differences between the two sets of characters and propel both character development and action. This is considered appropriate for primary-grade readers but would generate interesting discussions with intermediate and advanced readers as well.

William Joyce has been creating **The Guardians of Childhood** series for a very long time, and the first of those books, *The Man in the Moon* (P) is a visual and verbal feast for the imagination. Joyce's guardians are familiar ones: Santa, the Tooth Fairy, the Sandman, the Easter Bunny, the Man in the Moon, all of those companions of childhood who existed just beneath the surface of our lives. In this first book, Joyce gives us the backstory for MiM, as he is familiarly called, answering the question of how he came to be and why he created Nighlight to watch over children as they sleep.

In *Breadcrumbs* (I), Anne Ursu explores the pain of growing up and growing apart. She weaves this tale around the motif of Andersen's snow queen,

TEACHING IDEA 6.2

Literary Tales and Folkloric Themes

 **COMMON CORE STATE STANDARDS**   This Teaching Idea addresses the Common Core English Language Arts, Reading: Literature standard 9, grades K through 8. The suggestions in this Teaching Idea may need to be adapted to suit your particular grade level and the needs of your students.

It is easy to confuse literary tales with folklore because the two genres are quite similar. Modern writers intentionally use folkloric elements in their stories, and sometimes they do this so well that their work is mistaken for folktales. For example, Hans Christian Andersen captures the essence of folktales so artfully that it's hard to distinguish his work from the massive body of anonymous traditional literature. Other authors, such as Donna Jo Napoli, Jane Yolen, Gail Carson Levine, and Kevin Crossley-Holland, build on essential elements of well-known folklore and craft novel-length stories around their central core. As you read literary tales with your students, build on their

knowledge of folklore elements and discuss those that they notice in the literary tales they are reading. After you have read several literary tales with your students, ask them to consider the following:

● What folklore elements do the tales contain?

● How subtly does the author weave in the folklore elements? Give an example.

● Compare a literary tale to the original piece of folklore on which it was modeled.

● Discuss the differences between the original and the elaborated tale.

as eleven-year-old Hazel braves the wintery woods, which are full of threatening and magical beings, to find her best friend, Jack, and bring him home. There are also many lovely literary allusions that help create this multilayered tale. Gail Carson Levine's *A Tale of Two Castles* (I–A) plays on the story of "puss in boots." A clever and determined heroine, mystery and adventure, and themes of friendship and developing independence mark this book, similar to her *Ella Enchanted* (I–A).

A Tale Dark & Grimm (I–A), by Adam Gidwitz is indeed both dark and Grimm, as in the Grimm brothers. The book begins with a rather cheeky narrator challenging readers to continue to read, promising them a journey through "darkest zones" to find "brightest beauty" and "luminous wisdom" and "the most blood." Those who do continue to read meet Hansel and Gretl, not in the familiar tale, but in a rather obscure tale in which they are introduced, the problem parents are described, and the siblings begin a quest for better parents. As they wander through a series of tales, linked by Gidwitz in a logical narrative arc, the narrator is there to guide readers along with them. This is truly literary lore, masterful retellings that are faithful to the original stories but cast in a new light by a very inventive author.

For older readers, Robin McKinley's *Beauty* (A), an early example of an elaborated tale based on folklore, has been followed by *Rose Daughter* and *Spindle's End* (A). Older readers can also appreciate Donna Jo Napoli's mastery of style in such books as *Crazy Jack, Beast, Spinners, Zel*, and *The Magic Circle* (A). Elizabeth Bunce's *A Curse Dark as Gold* (A) is an elaboration of the Rumpelstiltskin tale, complete with gritty details of small-town life and unflinching observations about loyalty, pride, and determination.

Shannon and Dean Hale's *Rapunzel's Revenge* (I–A) is a graphic novel that depicts a spunky sixteen-year-old heroine with some guy named Jack . . . guess who! We first meet Jack in their *Calamity Jack* (I–A), where Jack's escapades are set against a turn-of-the-twentieth-century steampunk setting. Then Jack gets involved with the events in *Rapunzel's Revenge* and eventually takes Rapunzel back to New York, only to find his mother being held hostage by a giant and the city under attack by ant people. Nathan Hale's illustrations further both action and character development in both of these entertaining graphic novels.

Jane Yolen is one of the masters of literary lore. Her novels in **The Young Merlin Trilogy** re-create the legend of King Arthur with her own deft touches. In *Sword of the Rightful King: A Novel of King Arthur* (I), she re-creates the story of Excalibur with

a new twist, creating ultimately human characters out of the stuff of legend. Kevin Crossley-Holland's **The Seeing Stone** and *King of the Middle March* (I–A) move between the often uncomfortable, filthy reality of the Middle Ages and the magical world described in the legend of King Arthur. These novels, like Elizabeth Wein's **Arthurian/Aksumite** cycle, are a unique blend of historical fiction and fantasy. Philip Reeve re-imagines part of King Arthur's story in *Here Lies Arthur* (A). Another gifted writer who retells ancient tales, Gerald Morris brings to life both the Middle Ages and the famous story of the doomed love of Tristram and Iseult in *The Ballad of Sir Dinadan* (A), one of his **Squire's Tales** series of ten books. His **Knight's Tales** series, written for younger readers, includes *The Adventures of Sir Gawain the True* (I). This series allows readers ready for chapter books an opportunity to read well-told tales of a manageable length, thus providing an entry into the extended world of fantasy.

Even more ancient legends are at the core of other examples of literary lore. Mary Pope Osborne's **Tales from the Odyssey** series retells and embellishes well-known stories from Homer's epic poem. *The One-Eyed Giant, The Land of the Dead, Sirens and Sea Monsters, The Gray-Eyed Goddess*, and *Return to Ithaca* (all I) are written with verve and style in a manner that appeals to middle-grade readers. These same readers enjoy Rick Riordan's **Percy Jackson and the Olympians** series, in which children of the ancient Greek gods go on quests and struggle with their powers. *The Lightning Thief* (I) is the first book in the series; it introduces readers to an array of characters. A unique combination of humor, mythological allusions, and adventure, this series is great fun.

• • ANIMAL FANTASY • •

Animal fantasy attributes human thought, feeling, and language to animals. Children like to see animals dressed like people and believe in them readily; young children are often willing to invest any kind of creature or object with human characteristics. Because books that extend and enrich this developmental tendency strike a responsive chord in children, animal fantasy in picturebook form is well loved. Like the folktale, it becomes part of children's literary experiences before they make clear distinctions between fact and fancy. This early pleasure in animal fantasy often continues as children mature into readers who devour animal fantasy novels.

Some of the most memorable characters from children's literature populate animal fantasy. Naïve

Wilbur of *Charlotte's Web* (I) by E. B. White, incorrigible Toad of Toad Hall, Peter Rabbit, and Babar are some classic characters of this genre. Today's readers enjoy these classic tales as well as new stories, such as Kate DiCamillo's **Mercy Watson** (P) series of transitional chapter books, illustrated by Chris Van Dusen, in which Mercy, a pig, behaves as a human, and her human owners treat her as such! Jill Barklem's **Brambly Hedge** series presents realistic, everyday events as experienced by a community of mice. The detailed, beautiful illustrations create a setting that heightens the pleasure.

The protagonist in Cynthia Voigt's *Young Fredle* (I), with illustrations by Louise Yates, is also a mouse, one who leaves the safety of the nest behind the pantry and ventures outside, into the unknown. The outside has many dangers in addition to the cat and mousetraps of the kitchen, such as owls, snakes, and raccoons, and Fredle feels increasingly vulnerable, frightened, and, for the first time in his life, lonely. Even so, he also thrills to the things he sees and experiences and, when he returns home, he is profoundly changed by his journey.

Richard Peck's rollicking adventure, **Secrets at Sea: A Novel** (I), illustrated by Kelly Murphy, also features mice as protagonists. These mice, however, are traveling with their human family to England. Set in turn-of-the-twentieth-century England, this is a great adventure story, a social commentary on the ways of some humans at that time, and a wonderful book to read aloud. Lois Lowry's mouse tale, **Bless This Mouse** (P–I), illustrated by Eric Rohmann, has an unusual setting: the church of Saint Bartholemew. Lowry turns upside down the assumption that life in a church would be peaceful and safe.

There are many other stories featuring animals that face serious challenges that mirror the challenges children face. Kate DiCamillo's *The Tale of Despereaux: Being the Story of a Mouse, a Princess, Some Soup, and a Spool of Thread* (P–I) is a wonderful combination of animal fantasy, literary lore, and quest tale. Winner of the 2004 Newbery Medal, **Despereaux** is an engaging, multilayered story that asks fundamental questions about life. On the surface this is a story about a very small mouse with very large ears, his love for a princess, his quest through the dungeon to rescue her, and a mostly happily-ever-after ending. Beneath the surface tale, important questions about love, honor, perfidy, self-worth, and determination combine to elevate the story to one that explores the human heart with great seriousness.

Despereaux is the hero on a quest, and, as in all good quests, his mettle is tested, allowing him to grow and develop from a small mouse who faints into a brave hero. The sweetness of Despereaux's love for the princess, his pleasure in music and books, and his wavering but ultimately resolute determination to rescue the princess raise the mouse above a stock hero and elevate his quest beyond the confines of a fairy tale. The narrator's voice is funny, haughty, and often sarcastic, yet serves to remind readers that this fantasy may seem to be about a mouse and a princess, but relates directly to our lives. DiCamillo's use of imagery and symbolism, such as in the constant interplay between dark and light, heightens the impact of her tale.

Avi also uses a small mouse to raise large questions. His **Tales from Dimwood Forest** series, which includes *Poppy*, *Poppy and Rye*, *Ragweed*, and *Ereth's Birthday* (all I), follows the adventures of one special mouse, Poppy, and her friends. As they seek to make a safe home in Dimwood Forest, they encounter many dangers from humans and other predators, as well as prejudice, fear, and resistance from their fellow mice. The combination of adventure, humorous dialogue, notable characters, and a vividly detailed setting makes these books perfect for readers who enjoy animal fantasy and are ready for short novels. *Poppy* is also a wonderful introduction to the classic quest tale.

Brian Jacques's **Redwall** (I–A) books, a multivolume series that provides quests filled with high

---

On Your Education CourseMate

CONVERSATION WITH KATE DICAMILLO

In a conversation with Lee Galda, Kate DiCamillo talks about the writing of **Despereaux** and the power of fantasy. Go to CengageBrain.com to access the Education CourseMate website and watch the video conversation with DiCamillo. There you will also find links to relevant websites.

Questions to Consider

1. Why do young readers need the opportunity that fantasy provides to think about powerful ideas?

2. Consider your own responses to fantasy and realistic fiction. How do these reading experiences differ?

adventure, memorable characters, and intriguing descriptions of battles and weapons, are enticing to those who are ready to move to more extensive texts. The many volumes in this series provide years of good books to read. Kenneth Oppel's novels in his Silverwing saga—***Silverwing, Darkwing, Firewing***, and ***Sunwing*** (I–A)—consider courage, loyalty, prejudice, and honor; contain echoes of traditional tales; and portray gripping adventures in a fantasy world in which bat communities serve as metaphors for humanity.

Lynne Jonnell's ***Emmy and the Incredible Shrinking Rat*** (I) and ***Emmy and the Home for Troubled Girls*** (I), both with art by Jonathan Bean, are fast-paced, funny, and immensely readable. In this case the protagonist is human, ten-year-old Emmy, who saves herself and her parents from the wicked magic of her evil nanny, Miss Barmy, in the first book, with the help of her soccer star best friend, Joe. In the second book, she and Joe are attempting to rescue the missing girls who were shrunk and trapped by Miss Barmy before she attempted to do the same to Emmy. All of this is possible because Emmy can talk to and understand rats, and one magic rat can shrink her, with a bite, so that she can visit the underground world of the rodents as well as defeat the evil nanny. The problem is, she just wants to be a normal ten-year-old girl, which she most definitely is not. In ***Masterpiece*** (I), illustrated by Kelly Murphy, Elise Broach creates a memorable character out of another interesting creature, a kitchen beetle. Marvin the beetle's kindness toward eleven-year-old Jack takes them both into the world of art forgery and theft, a big adventure, and a remarkable friendship.

Animal fantasies for older readers often create an allegorical world in which the nature of the human condition is explored. Such books as ***The Underneath*** (I–A) and ***Watership Down*** (A), by Richard Adams, use animal fantasy to comment on human frailties and foibles. In ***Watership Down*** we confront, among other issues, the consequences of war.

• • MINIATURE WORLDS • •

Every cultural group has its folkloric sprites, elves, trolls, hobbits, or leprechauns, which go unseen about houses and villages. Tales about these and other small beings such as toys that come to life, engage audiences, young and old alike. Just as older readers continue to enjoy animal fantasy as they move on to longer books, they also continue to respond to the call of miniature worlds. There is something compelling about smallness that pulls readers into a story world. What and how do small beings eat, dress, and move about? How does smallness transform daily life as we know it? What extra challenges does it pose? What advantages might it offer? Miniature worlds, like animal fantasy, fascinate readers interested in details.

As with other types of fantasy, stories set in miniature worlds might take a lighthearted look at what life in miniature would be like or seriously explore human needs and desires. Fantasies about toys and miniature beings highlight human emotions by displaying them in action on a miniscule scale. From Arriety in ***The Borrowers*** (I) by Mary Norton to the Minnipins in ***The Gammage Cup*** and ***The Whisper of Glocken*** (I) by Carol Kendall, the best and worst in human nature are magnified by the small size of the characters.

Emily Jenkins infuses toys with life in ***Toys Come Home: Being the Early Experiences of an Intelligent Stingray, a Brave Buffalo, and a Brand-New Someone Called Plastic*** (P), with illustrations by Paul Zelinsky. A companion to her earlier ***Toys Go Out*** and ***Toy Dance Party*** (both P), this engaging story explores friendship and the meaning of life—at least for the toys who live in the Little Girl's room. In two engaging transitional chapter books, Marion Dane Bauer tells the story of ***The Very Little Princess*** (P). Both ***Zoey's Story*** and ***Rose's Story*** depict a three-and-a-quarter-inch china doll, a perfect princess to look at, but not so much fun to take care of when she comes to life. When ***Rose's Story*** begins, it is apparent that Rose and her mother do not get along well. It is also obvious that the mother has had her own less than wonderful experience with the doll. In spite of her mother's warnings, Rose takes the doll and soon learns that it is difficult to care for something that is alive, and demanding, and not very nice. By the story's end, she has learned a lot about herself and about relationships with others. Rose finally puts the doll into the dollhouse where she stays, until ***Zoey's Story***, when she is again brought to life by an unhappy little girl, Rose's daughter, who is also at odds with her mother. Although the fantasy is charming, the underlying seriousness of the theme is compelling, balanced by the intimacy of direct address by the narrator.

In Ellen Booraem's ***Small Persons with Wings*** (I–A), thirteen-year-old Mellie, a social outcast with high intelligence and a snarky voice, narrates the story of how her family got involved with helping the small persons with wings, also known as fairies, or "Parvi Pennati," regain their waning powers. In this engaging story, the realistic setting, populated by the small persons with wings, allows readers to understand Mellie's struggles as similar to their own. She wants to be something she is not—skinny and popular—but finds that who she is is more than good enough.

Timothee de Fombelle constructs a fantasy world and a complicated plot in **Toby Alone** (A), illustrated by Francois Place and translated from the French by Sarah Ardizzone. Small people populate the world of the Tree, an agrarian society that is threatened by developers who think only of profit. When his father is arrested and sentenced to death, it is up to Toby to negotiate the dangers in Tree, his own self-doubts, and betrayal at the hands of friends in order to save his family and his world. Although it's impossible to miss the strong environmental and political messages, they are so integral to the story that de Fombelle escapes didacticism. This very exciting adventure ends with a cliffhanger, harbinger of the sequel, **Toby and the Secrets of the Tree** (A).

Science Fiction

Although it is possible to find lighthearted science fiction for younger readers, this genre is generally serious and geared to an adolescent audience. An early example of serious science fiction for younger readers, **The Green Book** (I), a classic story by Jill Paton Walsh, is the story of young Pattie, who takes her green-covered blank book with her when she and her family escape from the dying planet Earth. When they arrive at their new settlement, Pattie and her friends explore their new world, Shine. Their courage and perseverance lead the community to find a way to exist, and Pattie's book becomes the place where the community can write the story of their survival. The occasional soft illustrations by Lloyd Bloom help describe what life is like on Shine.

Most science fiction, however, is written for older readers, and these stories offer the same kind of deep questioning that fantasy offers, although in this case, the questions asked relate to future realities based on scientific possibilities. Just as fantasy has become an increasingly popular genre, science fiction has as well, with many new series that are immensely popular with readers. Dystopian science fiction, such as Suzanne Collins's **Hunger Games** (A) trilogy, with more than 2.3 million copies of the first two books printed before the third was released, has found a huge audience in young adult readers. Whether the aftermath of nuclear war, the results of genetic engineering, technology overwhelming humanity, mind control, or environmental degradation, stories of potential futures abound. Like fantasy, these tales are also depictions of the struggles of adolescents for identity, independence, and, in many cases, a sense of purpose. Unlike science fiction for adults, in most

young adult novels there is hope for a future, and often the reason for hope is the adolescent protagonist.

Science fiction often examines anthropological and sociological aspects of life in the future and considers questions of individual commitment and ethical behavior. These include the results of aggression and competition as opposed to peace and cooperation, a consideration of what it means to be human, the quality of life in an increasingly crowded world, and the ethical and social consequences of technological and medical advances. Dystopian worlds abound, created by technology run amuck, war, environmental degradation, or space exploration, among other causes. Authors are quite inventive in their premises for the existence of these worlds as well as their nature.

Over the past eighteen years, Lois Lowry's Newbery Medal–winning **The Giver** (A) has become a book frequently read in middle-school classrooms. This dystopian novel explores the consequences of genetic engineering, a world without memories, and the veneration of safety and harmony as absolute goals. Companion novels **Messenger** and **Gathering Blue** (both A) continue her exploration of the possibilities of controlled communities. In the final book in the trilogy, Lowry brings together characters from the first two books and creates a new hero, a young boy named Matty, who is on the brink of discovering his true power. Lowry's dystopian novels probe issues of mind control, individuality, honor, and courage in a future world, the seeds of which are visible today.

Suzanne Collins, author of the popular **Underland Chronicles** (A), captivated readers with the first novel in her trilogy, **The Hunger Games** (all A). **The Hunger Games** takes place in a dystopian society in which teenagers are sacrificed through mortal combat with others. Survival, fierce family love, loyalty, and romance combine to create a riveting story with a remarkable female hero. **Catching Fire** and **Mockingjay** continue the adventure of Katniss and her family and friends, to its logical and reassuring conclusion.

Technology can be both a blessing and a curse, and dystopian science fiction often examines the implications of technological advances outstripping our ability to keep them from encroaching on our humanity. Mary Pearson considers the ethical and social implications of advanced medical technology in **The Adoration of Jenna Fox** (A), raising questions that are similar to those that permeate Peter Dickinson's classic, **Eva** (A). Jenna sets out to discover exactly what happened to her in the days following an automobile accident that should have killed her.

Victoria Forester explores one possible result of intolerance for those who are "different," even if these differences are the result of unusual talents, in **The**

Girl Who Could Fly (I) in which Piper fights family, church, and society for her right to be different. In his **Cyberia** (I) series for younger readers, Chris Lynch has created a dastardly protagonist, Dr. Gristle, who is trying to control every living thing on Earth, and an engaging protagonist, Zane, an animal rights crusader living in a world overwhelmed by technological possibilities. *Cyberia; Monkey See, Monkey Don't*; and *Prime Evil* are packed with action and humor.

A school that seems wonderful to Benson, a smart teenager who has been bounced from one foster home to another, hides a dangerous secret in Robison Wells's *Variant* (A). As Benson discovers, the school is a dangerous place, with students developing allegiances and fighting other groups, students disappearing, razor wire, video monitors, and rigid rules that, if broken, are punishable by death. Part mystery, part thriller, this suspenseful story leaves readers wanting the promised next book. The real-world setting and the idea of human beings conducting a brutal psychological experiment on adolescents who are "expendable" makes this a chilling novel.

In Patrick Ness's **Chaos Walking** series, which includes *The Knife of Never Letting Go, The Ask and the Answer*, and *Monsters of Men* (all A), the dystopian world of Prentisstown, a world in which everyone can hear everyone else's thoughts, is suddenly a dangerous place to be when Todd discovers a disturbing secret. With Viola, Todd flees before a relentless army only to find himself in even more danger as different factions fight for control, and none of them are interested in peace.

James Dashner's *The Maze Runner* (A) begins his exciting trilogy of dystopian novels. Thomas, the protagonist in all three, wakes up to no memory other than his first name and begins his life as a maze runner, living in the Glade with other adolescent boys, which is surrounded by stone walls that open into a maze, a maze through which they repeatedly try to escape. When they finally do, they end up in a world much more difficult and dangerous. In *The Scorch Trials* (A), the Earth is a wasteland, government is nonexistent, and people who suffer from the Flare, the result of governmental release of a virus, roam the disintegrating cities, hunting for their next meal. Thomas and his friends struggle to survive. In *The Death Cure* (A), the final volume of the trilogy, Thomas and the Gladers, memories restored, are targeted to help Wicked finally cure the Flare, but Thomas knows he can't trust Wicked. The suspense is high as Thomas fights to stay alive until the very end. The series ends with a glimmer of hope for his future and the future of the world, but also a grim reminder of what government can, and has, done.

Philip Reeve's **Mortal Engines** quartet (A), *Mortal Engines, Predator's Gold, Infernal Devices*, and *The Darkling Plain* are set over the span of twenty years in the "traction era," in which cities move across the land, hunting smaller towns and harvesting their "raw materials." In this inventively detailed futuristic world, there are also pieces of nonbiodegradable technology, leftovers from a past war, which will be useful in the approaching conflict between the cities and those who seek to destroy them. *Fever Crumb, A Web of Air*, and *Scrivener's Moon* (all A) are prequels to the series, introducing Fever, a girl living in London just before it begins to turn into a mobile city.

The dystopic future in Catherine Fisher's *Incarceron* (A) is a complex combination of political intrigue, technological advances leading to a world controlled by a few, and a sentient technology that has more power than the humans who created it. We take a close look at *Incarceron* here.

In **Incarceron**, *Catherine Fisher creates a fantastic world in which a sprawling prison is sentient, and no one knows exactly how to control it.*

* * *

A CLOSE LOOK AT
Incarceron

World-building is an important facet of many works of fantastic literature, and it is vital to the novel **Incarceron**. The story begins with a heart-grabbing first sentence: "Finn had been flung on his face and chained to the stone slabs of the transitway," and immediately the action begins in a place that is dark, strange, and dangerous, more so than subway lines as we know them. Who is the "Civicry," and how can the "Prison" be watching him? Where is Finn? That question, and the answer to it, constitutes the main plot of the story.

In the first few pages then, it is clear that Finn is in a place unlike any we have experienced. He calls the Prison "Incarceron" and speaks of it as a being that can "sense his peril" with "harsh amusement," . . . "watch[ing]" him and not "interfer[ring]." Page by page the world of Incarceron is carefully constructed. There are the Civicry, a group who seems to have some humanity, the Scum, of which the Comitatus seems to be the most dangerous. The characters are somewhere underground, and it's clear that it's a dangerous place, populated by many who deceive and murder, even Finn. And then the scene reverses to a much lovelier place, but with odd characteristics, revealed in the first line of the second chapter: "The oak tree looked genuine, but it had been genetically aged." In this second setting, we are outside, in a world that seems medieval but is clearly futuristic because of the technology that has constructed it. In this world, Claudia, daughter of the warden of Incarceron, is the protagonist. Both worlds are complex, with sociological and technological themes underpinning their construction.

It is clear from the first two chapters that the stories of Finn and of Claudia will intersect, and they do, via a crystal key that Finn hopes will help him discover his past, before Incarceron, because he has an image of the key etched on his wrist. Claudia, desperate to find the door to Incarceron, a secret carefully held by her father, steals a key from his study. Through the keys, the two meet, and soon Claudia is sure that Finn is, indeed, the prince whom she was supposed to marry but who "died" many years before. For the remainder of the book, we observe Finn as he and three others try to escape Incarceron and discover just how vast it truly is. We see Claudia struggling to become the woman she wants to be rather than the one her father and their social circle feel she needs to be, which includes marriage to Finn's loathsome stepbrother. As they continue in their separate struggles, those struggles increasingly intertwine. As Finn braves dangers to find a way out of Incarceron, and Claudia does the same to find a way into Incarceron, they work together toward unmasking the secrets of the Prison. As they do, we realize that Incarceron is alive, sentient, and out of control, even that of the Warden.

Both Finn and Claudia are multidimensional characters, with strengths and weaknesses that propel the action, even as they are influenced by the events occurring around them. The secondary characters are a mix of stock—the wicked stepmother queen—and more complex—the imperious Warden who comes to love his daughter—which allows for unpredicted plot twists. Yet these twists are always logical within the world of Incarceron and of that outside. Heart-pounding suspense, characters to care about, and two fully realized fantasy worlds are bound together by themes of identity, coming of age, and developing

P R O F I L E

Catherine Fisher

I*ncarceron and its sequel are certainly the most complex books I've written.*

Catherine Fisher is a poet and a novelist, and writes in many genres. She lives in Wales, where she grew up and attended college, majoring in English. She has worked in education and archaeology and was a lecturer in creative writing. She is a Fellow of the Welsh Academy. When she began **Incarceron**, she wanted to write a book about a prison, a "vast, talking, dreaming living edifice, which contains villages and forests as well as cells and corridors," and so she created the world of Incarceron, the prison. Her books **The Oracle Betrayed, The Sphere of Secrets**, and **Day of the Scarab** (all I) comprise a very popular fantasy trilogy.

To learn more about Catherine Fisher, visit CengageBrain.com to access the Education CourseMate website, where you will find links to relevant websites.

inner strength, all things that adolescent readers are seeking for themselves. Many of these readers turn eagerly to the sequel, *Sapphique* (A).

A technological wonder created by humans that has gained power over those humans is also part of Catherine Jink's *Living Hell* (A). The seventeen-year-old protagonist has lived his life onboard a spaceship that has been seeking a habitable planet for the past forty-six years. When it flies through a radiation wave, the ship becomes sentient and identifies the human passengers as hostile parasites, its systems become "immune" and seek to destroy the very humans who created them.

An invasion by aliens is the premise of Stephen Wallenfels's *POD* (I–A). When sixteen-year-old Josh, one of the narrators, and his father awake to a horrible screeching sound outside of their home in Washington state, they find that all of their machines—computer, telephone, clock, and so on—other than the furnace have stopped working and that a series of massive black spheres are descending, using beams of light to destroy things at will. Meanwhile, in Los Angeles, where Josh's mom is attending a conference, twelve-year-old Megs, the second narrator, is experiencing the same invasion. How humanity responds to the invasion, in both Washington and in Los Angeles, creates the action. Many characters act horribly, focusing on their own comfort and power, while others act nobly, seeking to help others. As the tension mounts, it becomes clear that the stranger in Los Angeles who takes care of Megs is, in fact, Josh's mother. The end makes it clear that there will be a sequel, as mother and son search for each other.

Sometimes, it is the technology of an all-too-possible nuclear war that precipitates the need for survival. Although most nuclear scenarios are extremely depressing, an entire body of books exists that shows children surviving a nuclear war. Post-nuclear holocaust books such as Louise Lawrence's classic *Children of the Dust* (A) offer young readers the opportunity to consider deep, abiding questions. L. J. Adlington's *Cherry Heaven* (A) creates a futuristic society that parallels the holocaust, and S. A. Bodeen's *The Compound* (A) explores what it means to live in a compound for years. Is it truly living? Are those in the compound truly human?

Stories about survival are also often linked to environmental degradation. The problems of life as it is today—the overcrowding, the pollution, the extinction of animal and plant species, the question of an adequate food supply, and climate change—provide science fiction writers with unlimited opportunities to project how humans will survive on Earth.

Environmental degradation has been a theme in science fiction for many years. The Newbery Honor–winning *The Ear, the Eye, and the Arm: A Novel* (A), by Nancy Farmer, deals with life in Zimbabwe in the year 2194 when people live in armed fortresses and in tunnels under toxic waste dumps. Thirteen-year-old Tendai and his younger sister and brother are kidnapped and forced to work in miserable surroundings. Their parents engage the Ear, Eye, and Arm Detective Agency to find them, but the detectives get near to the children only moments after they have moved on. The mystery and close calls keep readers turning the pages to find out what happens.

In *The Boy at the End of the World* (I–A), by Greg van Eekhout, Fisher awakes in his Ark, alone, the other pods having been destroyed. The world is in ruins, and his robot, Click, tells him that he is the last human being. Fisher and his Ark-mates were genetically engineered to contribute to the common good, and thus halt the rush toward environmental degradation that was overtaking the world. With the others dead, however, he must set out, with Click, to traverse this strange new world, hoping to find others who have also survived.

Paolo Bacigalupi's *Ship Breaker* (A), posits a dystopian future America in which the effects of human greed and climate change have fundamentally changed our society and the world in which we live. A very disturbing vision of the effects of how we are living now, this novel is full of action, with an engaging teenage protagonist who must make a momentous decision, one that will have consequences for many others.

Nancy Farmer's *The House of the Scorpion* (A), winner of both the Printz and Newbery Honor Awards, presents the potential ramifications of the scientific possibility of cloning to prolong life and the social possibility of drug cartels making political deals in order to create their own laws and countries. Matteo, the protagonist, is a clone, the property of El Patron. He is considered a "beast" by most of the people around him because he was born from cow, a being existing only to be killed in order for El Patron to continue to live.

Surrounded by people with twisted morals, he sometimes stumbles into anger and revenge, but he carefully tries to create a soul for himself, building on the love of Celia, who took care of him as a baby; the example of Tam Lin, the bodyguard who cares for Matt; and his love for Maria, daughter of one of El Patron's supporters. By the time he escapes, it is not surprising that he has the inner resources to confront new dangers and challenges or that he is determined, once he returns to Opium, to change it for the better. Science fiction, adventure, and quest, this novel explores the age-old struggles between good and evil, powerful and powerless.

TEACHING IDEA 6.3

Science Changes the World

 This Teaching Idea addresses the Common Core English Language Arts, Writing standard 3, grades 6 through 8. The suggestions in this Teaching Idea may need to be adapted to suit your particular grade level and the needs of your students.

Many people believe that each small change in our world results in a chain reaction of alterations. We cannot foresee subsequent modifications, nor can we control them. Some may bring good results; others, undesirable ones. Science fiction writers take the possibility of change to its ultimate extreme.

After reading several science fiction novels that use new scientific and technological advances as the premise for their futuristic depictions, discuss how these writers extrapolate from a possibility to a fully realized depiction of what might happen. Then ask students to consider both the pros and cons of the new technology they use and to describe an application of that technology in a possible future world. How might such technology affect life?

After these reading experiences and discussions, ask students to select one piece of technology, imagine the furthest limits of its application, and create a future scenario that describes what might happen.

Science fiction at its best invites readers to think about the effects of scientific advances in their own lives and how these advances might influence their own futures. Teaching Idea 6.3 describes a way to get students to do so.

Both fantasy and science fiction offer many opportunities to explore powerful questions about life. One of the themes that students who have read these books often discuss is self-knowledge. This is not at all surprising given that this audience is frequently concerned with discovering who they are, who they want to be, and who they might become. Teaching Idea 6.4 offers some suggestions for writing prompts or discussion questions that can lead to a consideration of how characters such as Puck, Despereaux, and Matteo discovered who they were, decided what they wanted to be, and acted on this self-knowledge.

TEACHING IDEA 6.4

Thematic Exploration: Self-Knowledge

COMMON CORE STATE STANDARDS This Teaching Idea addresses the Common Core English Language Arts, Reading: Literature standard 3, grades 6 through 8. The suggestions in this Teaching Idea may need to be adapted to suit your particular grade level and the needs of your students.

In most of the books discussed in this chapter, the protagonists are seeking self-knowledge as they pursue their various quests. These heroes realize their differences and weaknesses and discover their strengths. As you read, discuss passages from these books in which the heroes discover something about themselves and act on it. Ask students to write or talk about the following general questions:

- What did [the protagonist] discover about him- or herself in this passage?

- How did [the protagonist's] actions reflect his or her increasing self-knowledge?

- What are some of the special things that define you as a person?

- Have you ever felt as different from others as [the protagonist] felt?

Fantastic Literature in the Classroom

For many children, fantastic literature is the first literature they love. Children in preschool and primary grades love books with animal characters that act like human beings. Children have no trouble understanding what the stories are about and what questions they raise about real life. As they mature, children experience many kinds of literature. Sometime during the elementary-school years, some children become enraptured with realistic fiction, giving themselves completely over to this genre. Others become avid consumers of nonfiction and biography. Some continue to enjoy fantastic literature, moving from picturebooks to more fully developed narratives.

As children mature they either move toward science fiction and fantasy or learn to avoid them entirely in their personal selection of books (Sebesta & Monson, 2003). Those who like these genres love them passionately, and those who do not are just as passionate. For some young readers, these genre preferences may last the rest of their lives; others will become more eclectic with development and will once again enjoy fantasy. The record-breaking popularity of J. K. Rowling's **Harry Potter** (I–A) series has enticed many readers to fantasy and perhaps converted some of them into avid readers of fantasy. It has certainly spawned increased interest in writing and publishing fantasy, and there is an abundance of outstanding books from which to choose.

Once children have enjoyed and made their own the many picturebooks that are also fantasy, it is an easy step into longer, more complex stories. Many children will find these stories on their own, moving naturally from books like Mem Fox's **Possum Magic** (N–P) to such books as E. B. White's **Charlotte's Web** (I), Natalie Babbitt's **Tuck Everlasting** (I), or Kate DiCamillo's **The Tale of Despereaux: Being the Story of a Mouse, a Princess, Some Soup, and a Spool of Thread** (P–I). As children move into adolescence and develop as readers and thinkers, they discover the intellectual enchantment of Ursula Le Guin's **Earthsea** novels, ponder the questions of Nancy Farmer's **The House of the Scorpion** (A), or relive ancient stories with such books as Adele Geras's **Troy** (A). They are intrigued by the powerful questions that fantasy and science fiction writers ask and answer.

To encourage students to explore fantastic literature, many teachers turn to reading aloud as the very best way to encourage readers to expand their interests. A read-aloud program offers the opportunity to experience books that are thoughtful considerations of some of life's most important questions: Who am I? What am I capable of? How do I live in this new world of adolescence? An added plus, many fantasy and science fiction novels explore the idea of discrimination, something that students are aware of and interested in. Some teachers who work with immigrant and English language learners feel that fantastic literature offers a more equitable opportunity for their students to enter the world of story given that *no one* is familiar with the physical setting, the social rules, or the special challenges of a fantastic world. Books that are well written and thought-provoking are excellent choices to read aloud, both to pique and to fuel developing interest in these genres.

Fantasy and science fiction books can also be read and discussed by literature groups, an idea that is discussed in Chapter 12. These books fit well into genre studies as well as within many thematic units. The kinds of questions about values, self, good and evil, and courage that fantasy and science fiction writers consider are also themes in contemporary realism and historical fiction. Looking at books from various genres that contain similar themes, such as self-knowledge, can be a powerful reading experience.

Benefits of fantasy and science fiction include the flexibility and expansion of the imagination they encourage and the important questions they push readers to consider. As our students read stories about people and events that are real and familiar to them, they also need to read stories that make them wonder, cause them to reassess values and ideals, and stretch their souls. Fantasy and science fiction can do just that.

SUMMARY

There has been an impressive increase in fantastic literature available for young readers today, with many fantasy and science fiction series dominating the market. Fantasy is concerned with beings, places, or events that could not occur in the real world. Science fiction is concerned with the impact of present-day scientific possibilities on the world of the future. Both explore the human heart, society, and morality. In both genres we find many excellent stories that are well written, present multidimensional characters engaging in exciting plots, and contain profound themes. Fantasy often presents heroes on a quest to achieve a goal as well as discover personal identity. It may contain fully developed fantasy worlds and magic. It may be set in our world and include magic realism. Often, animal characters act as humans or miniature beings reflect human activity. Science fiction is set in the future with characters who must learn to live in difficult circumstances, situations brought about by the results of scientific advancements. Fantastic literature offers young readers the opportunity to think about choices, actions, and consequences at a profound level.

The following Booklist contains both fantasy and science fiction titles that represent both the older, "classic" stories and those newer works that are popular with today's young readers. With few exceptions, we have listed only one book per author; many have multiple books and extensive series. Most of the books mentioned within the body of this chapter are not listed in the Booklist, which is meant as a supplement to those titles. The Booklist is not marked for diversity, as most books go beyond the boundaries of the way we think about diversity and, for the most part, consider themes that relate to diverse cultures and people.

Booklist

Fantasy

Abbott, Ellen Jensen, *The Centaur's Daughter* (2011) (I–A)

_____, *Watersmeet* (2009) (I–A)

Adams, Richard, *Watership Down* (1974) (A)

Ahlberg, Allan, *The Improbable Cat* (2004) (I)

Alexander, Lloyd, *The Black Cauldron* (1965) (I)

_____, *Book of Three* (1964) (I)

_____, *Taran Wanderer* (1967) (I)

Alley, Zoe, *There's a Wolf at the Door* (2008) (P)

Almond, David, *Heaven Eyes* (2001) (I)

Anderson, M.T., *Zombie Mommy* (2011) (I)

Avi, *The End of the Beginning: Being the Adventures of a Small Snail (and an Even Smaller Ant)* (2004) (P–I)

_____, *Perloo the Bold* (1998) (I)

Babbitt, Natalie, *Tuck Everlasting* (1975) (I)

Barron, T. A., *Fires of Merlin* (2007) (A)

Bass, L. G., *Sign of the Qin: Outlaws of the Moonshadow Marsh, Book One* (2004) (I–A)

Bell, Hilari, *The Goblin War* (2011) (I)

_____, *Last Knight: A Knight and Rogue Novel* (2007) (I)

Billingsley, Franny, *The Folk Keeper* (1999) (A)

Bond, Michael, *Paddington Here and Now* (2008) (P–I)

Boyne, John, *Noah Barleywater Runs Away* (2011) (I)

Broach, Elise, *Masterpiece* (2008) (I)

Brosgol, Vera, *Anya's Ghost* (2011) (I)

Bruchac, Joseph, *The Dark Pond* (2004) (I)

Bunel, Elizabeth, *A Curse Dark as Gold* (2008) (A)

Burtenshaw, Jenna, *Shadowcry* (2011) (I)

Cadnum, Michael, *Starfall: Phaeton and the Chariot of the Sun* (2004) (A)

Cameron, Ann, *Spunky Tells All*, illustrated by Lauren Castillo (2011) (P)

Carroll, Lewis, *Alice in Wonderland*, illustrated by Lisbeth Zwerger (2008) (I)

Cassedy, Sylvia, *Behind the Attic Wall* (1983) (A)

Chima, Cinda Williams, *The Demon King* (2010) (A)

Collins, Suzanne, *Gregor and the Code of Claw* (2007) (I)

Compestine, Ying Chang, *A Banquet for Hungry Ghosts*, illustrated by Coleman Polhemus (2009) (I)

Conrad, Pam, *The Tub People* (1996) (P)

Cooper, Susan, *The Dark Is Rising* (1973) (A)

Coville, Bruce, *Jennifer Murdley's Toad* (1992) (I)

Cowley, Joy, *Chicken Feathers* (2008) (I)

Creech, Sharon, *Castle Corona* (2007) (I)

Cross, Gillian, *Nightmare Game: Book Three* (2007) (A)

Dahl, Roald, *Charlie and the Chocolate Factory* (1964) (I)

Dakin, Glenn, *The Society of Unrelenting Vigilance* (2010) (I–A)

Delaney, Joseph, *Night of the Soul Stealer* (2007) (I)

Deutsch, Barry, *Hereville: How Mirka Got Her Sward*, illustrated by author & Jake Richmond (2010) (I)

Dickinson, Peter, *Angel Isle* (2007) (A)

Divakaruni, Chitra Banerjee, *The Conch Bearer* (2003) (I)

Dunmore, Helen, *The Tide Knot* (2008) (I)

DuPrau, Jeanne, *The Diamond of Darkhold* (2008) (I)

Farmer, Nancy, *The Sea of Trolls* (2004) (I–A)

Ferris, Jean, *Once upon a Marigold* (2002) (A)

Fisher, Catherine, *The Oracle Betrayed* (2003) (A)

French, Vivian, *The Robe of Skulls* (2008) (I)

Funke, Cornelia, *Dragon Rider* (2004) (A)

_____, *The Thief Lord* (2002) (A)

Furlong, Monica, *Wise Child* (2004) (A)

Gaiman, Neil, *The Graveyard Book* (2008) (I–A)

Gardner, Lyn, *Into the Woods* (2007) (I)

Geras, Adele, *Troy* (2001) (A)

Going, K. L., *Garden of Eve* (2007) (I)

Grahame, Kenneth, *The Wind in the Willows* (1961) (I)

Hamilton, Virginia, *The Magical Adventures of Pretty Pearl* (1983) (A)

Harding, Frances, *Well Witched* (2008) (I)

Higgins, F. E., *Black Book of Secrets* (2007) (I)

Hodges, Margaret, *Merlin and the Making of a King* (2004) (P–I)

Hoffman, Alice, *Green Angel* (2003) (I)

Howe, James, *Bunnicula* (1979) (I)

Ibbotson, Eva, *The Dragonfly Pool* (2008) (I–A)

_____, *The Ogre of Oglefort* (2011) (P–I)

Jacques, Brian, *Lord Brocktree* (2001) (A)

James, Mary, *Shoebag* (1990) (I)

Jansson, Tove, *Finn Family Moomintroll* (1989) (I)

Jones, Diana Wynne, *House of Many Ways* (2008) (I)

Joyce, William, *George Shrinks* (1985) (P)

Juster, Norton, *The Phantom Tollbooth* (1961) (I)

Kendall, Carol, *The Gammage Cup* (1959) (I)

Kessler, Liz, *Philippa Fisher's Fairy Godsister* (2008) (I)

Kindl, Patrice, *Goose Chase* (2001) (I)

King-Smith, Dick, *Martin's Mice* (1988) (I)

Lanagan, Margo, *Red Spikes* (2007) (A)

Le Guin, Ursula, *Tehanu: The Last Book of Earthsea* (1990) (A)

Levine, Gail Carson, *Ella Enchanted* (1997) (I)

Lewis, C. S., *The Lion, the Witch and the Wardrobe* (1950) (I)

Lisle, Janet Taylor, *The Ruby Key* (2008) (I–A)

Llewellyn, Sam, *Lyonesse: the Well Between the Worlds* (2009) (I–A)

Lofting, Hugh, *The Story of Doctor Doolittle* (1997) (P–I)

Mages, Jane Kelley, *The Girl Behind the Glass* (2011) (I)

Maguire, Gregory, *What-the-Dickens: The Story of a Rogue Fairy* (2007) (I)

Mahy, Margaret, *Alchemy* (2003) (A)

McCaffrey, Anne, *Dragonsong* (1976) (A)

McKinley, Robin, *The Blue Sword* (1982) (A)

_____, *Dragonhaven* (2007) (A)

_____, *Pegasus* (2010) (A)

Milne, A. A., *Winnie-the-Pooh* (1954) (I)

Morris, Gerald, *The Princess, the Crone, and the Dung-Cart Knight* (2004) (I–A)

Mould, Chris, *Something Wickedly Weird: The Wooden Mile* (2008) (I)

Murdock, Catherine Gilbert, *Wisdom's Kiss* (2011) (A)

Napoli, Donna Jo, *Crazy Jack* (1999) (A)

Newbery, Linda, *At the Firefly Gate* (2007) (I)

Norton, Mary, *The Borrowers* (1953) (I)

Oppel, Kenneth, *Starclimber* (2009) (A)

Osborne, Mary Pope, *Return to Ithaca* (2004) (I)

Paolini, Christopher, *Eragon* (2003) (A)

Paterson, Katherine, and John Paterson, *The Flint Heart*, illustrated by John Rocco (2011) (I)

Pearce, Philippa, *Tom's Midnight Garden* (1958) (I)

Peterson, John, *The Littles* (1967) (I)

Pierce, Meredith Ann, *The Darkangel* (1982) (A)

_____, *Treasure at the Heart of Tanglewood* (2001) (I)

Pierce, Tamora, *Mastiff* (2011) (A)

Pinkwater, Daniel, *Neddiad* (2007) (I)

Potter, Beatrix, *The Tale of Peter Rabbit* (1902) (P)

Pratchett, Terry, *Nation* (2008) (A)

_____, *The Wee Free Men* (2003) (I)

Prevost, Guillaume, *Book of Time* (2007) (I)

Prineas, Sarah, *The Magic Thief* (2008) (I)

Prue, Sally, *Cold Tom* (2001) (I)

Pullman, Philip, *I Was a Rat* (2000) (I)

Riordan, Rick, *The Last Olympian* (2011) (I)

_____, *The Lost Hero* (2010) (I–A)

Rowling, J. K, *Harry Potter and the Sorcerer's Stone* (1998) (I)

Rubenstein, Gillian, *Under the Cat's Eye: A Tale of Morph and Mystery* (2001) (A)

Rutkovski, Marie, *The Cabinet of Wonders: The Kronos Chronicles* (2010) (I–A)

Sage, Angie, *Dark (Septimus Heap)* (2011) (I–A)

Said, S. F., *Varjak Paw* (2005) (I)

Sanderson, Brandon, *Alcatraz versus the Shattered Lens* (2010) (A)

Schlitz, Laura Amy, *The Night Fairy*, illustrated by Angela Barrett (2011) (P–I)

Scieszka, Jon, *Marco? Polo!* (2006) (I)

Seidler, Tor, *Gully's Travels* (2008) (I)

Selden, George, *Cricket in Times Square* (1997) (I)

Shusterman, Neal, *Everfound* (2011) (A)

Slade, Arthur, *Dust* (2003) (I)

Smith, Cynthia Leitich, *Tantalize* (2007) (A)

Snyder, Lauren, *Any Which Wall* (2010) (I)

Speck, Katie, *Maybelle in the Soup* (2007) (P–I)

Springer, Nancy, *I Am Mordred: A Tale from Camelot* (1998) (A)

Steig, William, *Sylvester and the Magic Pebble* (1969) (P)

Stewart, Paul, and Chris Riddell, *Hugo Pepper* (2007) (I)

Stewart, Trenton Lee, *The Mysterious Benedict Society Collection* (2010) (I–A)

Stiefvater, Maggie, *The Scorpio Races* (2011) (A)

Swope, Sam, *Jack and the Seven Deadly Giants* (2004) (I)

Thompson, Kate, *The Last of the High Kings* (2008) (I–A)

Tolkien, J.R.R., *The Hobbit* (1937) (A)

_____, *The Lord of the Rings* (1954–1955) (A)

Townley, *The Door in the Forest* (2011) (I)

Ursu, Anne, *Siren Song: The Cronus Chronicles, Book Two* (2007) (I)

Van Allsburg, Chris, *Jumanji* (1981) (I)

Vande Velde, Vivian, *Stolen* (2008) (A)

Wein, Elizabeth, *The Empty Kingdom* (2008) (A)

Weston, Robert Paul, *Zorgamazoo* (2008) (I)

White, E. B., *Charlotte's Web* (1952) (I)

White, Ruth, *Way Down Deep* (2007) (I)

Wiesner, David, *Tuesday* (1999) (P–I)

Wilce, Ysabeau, *Flora Segunda: Being the Magical Mishaps of a Girl* (2007) (A)

Wilson, N. D., **100 Cupboards** (2007) (I)

Wrede, Patricia, **Thirteenth Child: Frontier Magic** (2010) (A)

Yolen, Jane, **Dragon's Heart** (2011) (A)

————, **Foiled**, illustrated by Mike Cavallaro (2010) (I–A)

Science Fiction

Adlington, L. J., **Cherry Heaven** (2008) (A)

Anderson, M. T., **Feed** (2002) (A)

Bodeen, S. A., **The Compound** (2008) (A)

Booraem, Ellen, **The Unnameables** (2011) (A)

Brooks, Kevin, **Being** (2007) (A)

Card, Orson Scott, **Pathfinder** (2010) (A)

Christopher, John, **The White Mountains** (1967) (A)

Clements, Andrew, **Things Not Seen** (2002) (A)

Collins, Suzanne, **The Hunger Games** (2008) (A)

Cross, Gillian, **New World** (1994) (A)

Dickinson, Peter, **Eva** (1988) (A)

DuPrau, Jeanne, **The People of Sparks** (2005) (I–A)

Gaiman, Neil, and Michael Reaves, **InterWorld** (2007) (A)

Gee, Maurice, **Salt** (2011) (A)

Haddix, Margaret Peterson, **Among the Hidden** (1998) (I–A)

Hatke, Ben, **Zita the Spacegirl** (2010) (I)

Hautman, Pete, **Hole in the Sky** (2001) (A)

Hughes, Monica, **Keeper of the Isis Light** (1981) (A)

Klass, David, **Stuck on Earth** (2010) (I–A)

L'Engle, Madeleine, **A Wrinkle in Time** (1962) (A)

Lawrence, Louise, **Children of the Dust** (2002) (A)

Lee, Marie, **Legend** (2011) (A)

Link, Kelly and Grant, Gavin, **Steampunk!: An Anthology of Fantastically Rich and Strange Stories** (2011) (A)

Lloyd, Saci, **The Carbon Diaries 2017** (2009) (A)

Logue, Mary, **Dancing with an Alien** (2008) (A)

Lowry, Lois, **The Giver** (1993) (A)

Mulligan, Andy, **Trash** (2010) (A)

O'Brien, Robert C., **Mrs. Frisby and the Rats of NIMH** (1971) (I)

Paton Walsh, Jill, **The Green Book** (1982) (I)

Reeve, Philip, **Mothstorm: The Horror from Beyond Uranus Georgium Sidus!** illustrated by David Wyatt (2008) (A)

Rubenstein, Gillian, **Galax-Arena: A Novel** (1993) (I)

Sanderson, Branden, **Alcatraz versus the Shattered Lens** (2010) (I)

Service, Pamela, **Tomorrow's Magic** (2007) (I)

Seuss, Dr., **The Lorax** (1971) (P)

Sleator, William, **Singularity** (1985) (A)

Stead, Rebecca, **First Light** (2007) (I)

Strahan, **Life on Mars: Tales from the New Frontier** (2011) (A)

Thompson, Kate, **The White Horse Trick** (2010) (A)

Varon, Sara, **Robot Dreams** (2007) (I)

Ward, Rachel, **ThƐ Cha0s** (2011) (A)

Westerfield, Scott, **Extras** (2007) (A)

————, **Goliath: Leviathan Trilogy** (2011) (A)

Additional resources to accompany this chapter can be found on the Education CourseMate website. Go to CengageBrain .com to access a variety of interactive study tools and useful resources including Video Conversations with children's book authors and illustrators, a searchable children's literature database, glossary flashcards, online activities, tutorial quizzes, links to relevant websites, and more.

Contemporary Realistic Fiction

"I want to show you something," I told Steven. I reached into my pocket for the crumpled-up W picture I had taken out of my backpack before I'd left. "I've had it since I was six."

We sat on a ledge, our feet dangling, and he smoothed the picture on his knee, stared at it, then looked over at me.

"We had to find pictures with W words," I said.

"It's a wishing picture," he said slowly, "for a family."

I could feel my lips trembling. Oh, Mrs. Evans, I thought, why didn't you see that?

"It's too bad you didn't come when you were six." He smiled. "I knew you had to stay with us when you let me win that checkers game."

His hair was falling over his forehead and his glasses were crooked, almost hiding his eyes. I thought of the X-picture day and walking out of school. I thought of sitting in the park on a swing, my foot digging into the dirt underneath.

"I run away sometimes," I said. "I don't go to school."

He kicked his foot gently against the ledge, his socks down over his sneakers.

"Someone called me incorrigible."

Now that I'd begun, I didn't know how to stop. "Kids never wanted to play with me. I was mean. . . ."

Steven pulled his glasses off and set them down on the ledge next to him. He rubbed the deep red mark in the bridge of his nose.

I stopped, looking out as far as I could, miles of looking out. For a moment I was sorry I'd told him. But he turned and I could see his eyes clearly, and I wondered if he might be blinking back tears. I wasn't sure, though. He reached out and took my hand. "You ran in the right direction this time, didn't you?"

And that was it. He knew all about me, and he didn't mind.

—PATRICIA REILLY GIFF
Pictures of Hollis Woods, pp. 123–125

Sarah had to stop a few times to wipe the tears from her eyes as she read this climactic scene aloud to her fourth-grade class. Several students wipe away tears too, but they don't seem at all ashamed. The moving story of the foster child, Hollis, and her missed opportunity to be part of a loving family has captured them all. They have been talking about family, and loving relationships, and what it is like for Hollis never to have experienced them. They have been talking about how Josie, an elderly artist with whom Hollis eventually goes to live, helps her understand that she is a good person with a special talent. And now they are about to discover why Hollis ran away from her one chance at being part of a family, fled the love and understanding that were offered to her.

When they hear the end of the scene, in which Steven and Hollis are about to have an accident, they erupt with comments and questions: "Oh, no! Steven is going to die!" "Giff's been hinting at this all along, this about the truck." "It's not Hollis's fault! It's not!" "How can this happen to her?" Ms. Hansen lets the comments flow freely for a minute, then brings the class back together. She begins, "I can tell that you were all engrossed in the scene as I was reading. I was even crying, wasn't I? I heard someone say that Giff has been hinting at this event. Was that you, Joelle? You're right; she has been hinting at this. This kind of hinting is called foreshadowing. How did she foreshadow this accident with the pickup?" Various students tell her about parts of the story in which either Steven or his father talks about his lack of skill as a driver and the danger of the road up the mountain. Ms. Hansen then changes the focus a bit, commenting, "I also heard someone say, 'How could this happen to her?' and I felt that way, too. What had just happened to Hollis before they got into the truck?" The class continues to talk, noting how Hollis had finally realized that Steven cared for her even though she wasn't perfect and how that seemed like a big breakthrough for her. They have been discussing how little she liked or valued herself, and this scene seemed to resolve some of that. And then the accident occurs. "We could say that this is ironic," comments Ms. Hansen, "that just when Hollis realizes that the Regan family really does like her for who she is, she and Steven crash in the truck. What do you think will happen next? Remember, we already know that she runs away from them. Take a few minutes to write in your response log and speculate on what happens. There are only forty-one pages left before we see how Giff ends it herself."

Characterization is the soul of great literature. When readers connect with the emotions of the characters in a book, they experience the events of the story virtually, almost as though they were happening to them. Thus, through the magic of fiction, children accumulate the experience of many lives and grow in their understanding of themselves and others. These fourth graders empathized with the loneliness and despair of Hollis as the story unfolded, and at this point they are so involved that this climactic event evoked their cries of protest. Fortunately for them, a happy ending is only pages away.

Defining Contemporary Realistic Fiction

Realistic fiction has a strong sense of actuality. Its plausible stories are about people and events that could actually happen. Good *contemporary* realistic fiction illuminates life, presenting social and personal concerns in a fully human context as it is experienced today or in the very recent past. The line between contemporary and historical is ever shifting and understood differently by readers of different ages. Here, we consider books written about life in the late twentieth and early twenty-first centuries to be contemporary realistic fiction.

Realistic fiction portrays the real world in all its dimensions: it shows the humorous, the sensitive, the thoughtful, the joyful, and the painful sides of life. By its very nature, it deals with the vast range of sensitive topics prevalent in today's world. Author Lloyd Alexander (1970) reminds us that stories explore polarities, such as love and hate, birth and death, joy and sorrow, loss and recovery. Life's raw materials, questions, and polarities appear most starkly in realistic fiction.

Good stories do not resolve complex problems with easy answers; they consider these problems with the seriousness they require. Because literature reflects the society that creates it, children's contemporary realistic fiction reflects many of the problems that our society is concerned with today. It also reflects the things that we value in our lives: love, personal integrity, family, and friends. Thus, although many realistic novels grapple with realistic problems, many are also stories of courage in which people transform their lives into something worthwhile by drawing on their inner strength. Others are accounts of ordinary people living ordinary lives; their stories are illuminated through the careful consideration of a talented author.

No definition of *realism* is simple, and to say that realism is fiction that could happen in the real world—as opposed to fantasy, which could not—is simplistic. Every work of fiction, like the stories we tell ourselves, is part fanciful and part realistic. We selectively remember and reshape events of our past and present; the same thing happens in books. A realistic story is an author's vision of what might really happen (the plot) in a particular time and place (the setting) to particular people (the characters). Fantasy offers young readers the opportunity to consider elemental questions. Contemporary realistic fiction offers the opportunity for young readers to think about and measure their own lives; we might say that contemporary realistic fiction can put us in touch with our lives. Teaching Idea 7.1 shows how students can use a writer's notebook to keep track of their own observations of life as they live it, compiling ideas that they might one day turn into a realistic story.

TEACHING IDEA 7.1

Keep a Writer's Notebook

ELL

This Teaching Idea addresses Common Core English Language Arts, Writing: Literature standard 3, grades K through 8. The suggestions in this Teaching Idea may need to be adapted to suit your particular grade level and the needs of your students.

Authors of realistic fiction develop plot lines in which they portray real people with real feelings. To do this, they observe themselves and others living their lives and record their observations in journals—not only when they are working on a story, but every day.

Ask your students to collect material for future stories by recording their observations in small notebooks that they can carry around with them.

1. Have students start notebooks of their own by recording events that happen to them. Have them describe events they observe as well as their feelings about what they see happening.

2. After they have kept the notebook for a period of time, have them go back through their notes and highlight items that might lead to a story. At the same time, read what established authors have to say about where they get their ideas for writing. The July/August issue of *The Horn Book Magazine* always contains the acceptance speech of that year's Newbery winner; in these speeches, authors frequently talk about why they wrote their books.

3. Have students discuss in groups what ideas might lead to interesting stories. If they do this with direction from you, followed by regular discussions with a writing group, they will develop their abilities to recognize good ideas.

4. Find resources that will help you and your students develop a writer's notebook. Ralph Fletcher's *Writer's Notebook* is an excellent place to begin, as is Janet Wong's book for younger readers, *You Have to Write*.

A Brief History of Contemporary Realistic Fiction

One of the interesting aspects of this genre is that it becomes dated over time. Thus, some popular contemporary realistic fiction that was written years ago seems "quaint," with characters acting in ways that are not quite the way they might act today. Reading what was contemporary realistic fiction in the past reveals that books for children at that time were very didactic. As children's book publishing developed in the late eighteenth century, the earlier focus on religious education gave way to fanciful stories for entertainment. Despite the desire for pure pleasure in stories, authors generally tucked lessons in as well. At the end of the eighteenth century, children in books were polite, diligent, dutiful, and prudent, just the opposite of Hollis Woods. Well-behaved boys and girls searched relentlessly for information and guidance, when parents, teachers, ministers, and librarians were revered as sources of information and translators of God's prescription for behavior.

In an attempt to expand the bookselling market started by John Newbery, some publishers commissioned people to write expressly for children. Most of the writers were women such as Maria Edgeworth (1767–1849), who wrote stories to entertain her seventeen siblings. One of Edgeworth's stories, **The Purple Jar**, illustrates how books often encouraged children to obey elders. After the American Revolution, writers composed stories that attempted to develop a sense of national pride. Books for children featured adventure stories of travel on the American frontier and courageous battles with the Indians. The books were still didactic, with the American ethic of "work hard and make good" embedded in the stories they told. And they were all from a white American point of view.

In the first half of the nineteenth century, Samuel Goodrich, who believed books could guide children along the right path, collaborated with other writers such as Nathaniel Hawthorne to produce the **Peter Parley** series, a forerunner of the series book that is so popular today. Once begun, series books flourished. Jacob Abbott's series, **Rollo's Tour in Europe**, reads like a travelogue, with wise Uncle George serving as mentor to young Rollo. Rollo eventually returns to America, knowing that it is the "best" place to be. The desire to indoctrinate children in the American work ethic was evident in a series begun by Horatio Alger in 1868. In more than one hundred stories, male characters acquired power and wealth through great effort, courage, and impeccable morality. At this time, books for boys and girls differed. Boys' books were filled with adventure, travel, and the desire to succeed; girls' books centered around homemaking, caring for others, and piety.

Gradually, a new type of literature appeared in which characters were portrayed more realistically. Boy characters, but not girls, began to act more realistically, even devilishly. Those girls who did break the mold almost always reverted to standard gender roles. For example, although most of the female characters in Louisa May Alcott's **Little Women** (1868) are portrayed in conventional roles, Jo was a breath of fresh air compared to most female characters of the time. By the end of the book, though, even Jo has moved toward becoming a wife and mother, understanding that her writing will suffer for it, as it does in the sequel. With the publication of Margaret Sidney's **The Five Little Peppers and How They Grew** in 1880, girls had a series of family stories to enjoy, albeit a sentimental one in which generosity, humility, and proper manners are rewarded in a family with little money but lots of love. Around the same time, many inexpensive, aesthetically weak, mass-produced series written to formula were devoured by children in spite of adult objections. Edward Stratemeyer was perhaps the foremost producer of series with his plot outlines and hired writers. His **Hardy Boys** and **Bobbsey Twins** were immensely popular, and updated versions of these and his **Nancy Drew** books still sell well today. Although most contemporary realistic fiction for young readers published in the United States was also set in America, as provincialism waned, children were able to read about characters from other lands in books such as Mary Mapes Dodge's **Hans Brinker; or The Silver Skates** (1865) and Johanna Spyri's **Heidi** (1884).

In the early twentieth century, adventure stories for boys and home stories for girls continued, giving way in the middle of the century to a new realism in books for young readers. This new realism appeared in books for readers of all ages, with books such as Louise Fitzhugh's **Harriet the Spy** (I) and Judy Blume's **Are You There God? It's Me, Margaret** (I) captivating children and sometimes shocking adults. Adolescent literature began to explode in 1967 through 1968 with the publication of S. E. Hinton's **The Outsiders** (A), closely followed by Paul Zindel's **The Pigman** (A), Robert Lipsyte's **The Contender** (A), the anonymously written **Go Ask Alice** (A), Judy Blume's **Forever** (A), Robert Cormier's **The Chocolate War** (A), and other novels for adolescent readers. Thus, social concerns such as violence, sex, drugs, and difficult life decisions became literary issues. Publication of "social issues" books was dramatically curtailed in the 1980s when censorship intensified (Marcus, 2008), whereas the 1990s saw a boom in publishing children's books and a stunningly varied approach to form, style, and issues.

Beginning in the 1960s and 1970s, waning in the 1980s, and increasing from the 1990s to the present, we have benefited from an accumulating number of books that embrace all types of diversity, and variations within cultures, portraying unique characters who live in the world of today. There were few books that presented girls and women in what, at the time, were "nontraditional" roles during the years prior to the late 1960s; that is not the case today. Female characters in contemporary realistic fiction reflect the profound change in society's perceptions of gender roles. Consideration of social class continues to be a part of realistic fiction, although now class issues are questioned rather than softened with platitudes. Over the past several years, the number of engaging books by and about contemporary people of color has grown, albeit slowly. Similarly, books about characters with exceptionalities also are increasing in number, as are books that explore cultural differences, sexual orientation, mental illness, and many contemporary concerns such as war and violence.

As the world changes, literature reflects those changes. The stories that today's young readers have access to encompass both familiar types of stories—such as animal stories, adventure stories, or sports stories, available for many years—and new themes that are increasingly important to contemporary readers. Romance has taken on a gritty realism, school stories now sometimes encompass violence, and coming-of-age stories might reflect drug use and the dissolution of families. War stories, always with us as war has always been with us, are set in new locations, such as Afghanistan and Iraq, and terrorism plays a role. Contemporary realistic fiction challenges readers to think about race, class, and gender, about sexual orientation, exceptionalities, and lifestyles. Today, contemporary realistic fiction reflects the contemporary world with its joys, triumphs, and dangers—it is a passport to experiences in all parts of the world.

In this chapter we first:

- Consider how to determine quality in contemporary realistic fiction

- Discuss some popular formats for and various types of contemporary realistic fiction

- Explore broad themes that appear in contemporary realistic fiction

- Examine ways that contemporary realistic fiction functions in today's classrooms

Considering Quality in Contemporary Realistic Fiction

We can think of contemporary realistic fiction, like many other genres, in terms of the setting, characters, plot, theme, and style. If the book is illustrated, the quality of the art is important as well. Specific considerations for realistic fiction include the plausibility of setting, characters, and plot.

• • SETTING • •

When creating story settings, realistic story authors choose times and places that do or could possibly exist. The setting may be general or specific, depending on the needs of the story. Sometimes the setting may be a backdrop to the story, with little influence on characters or action. Often, however, the setting is important. A small town might be the very reason why a young character desires to be free; an ocean, a forest, or a desert might be an antagonist that challenges a character to survive. Schools or cities that are large and anonymous might provoke feelings of invisibility and isolation in characters; and cultural values and standards might challenge a character. Settings in contemporary realism work in many ways. When evaluating a setting, look for a vivid, realistic setting and note how it functions in the story.

• • CHARACTERIZATION • •

Characters in realistic fiction reflect human beings we know; they exhibit the powers and failings of a real person in a real world. Like real people, they change over time as they affect and are affected by the world surrounding them. When evaluating characterization in realistic fiction, look for main characters that are believable, authentic, and not stereotypical; are fully developed as multidimensional human beings; and show change or development during the course of the story.

• • PLOT • •

The central conflict in a realistic fiction story is one that is probable in today's world and that matters to today's children. When selecting realistic fiction, look for plot structures that are appropriate for the target audience and events that are probable given the setting and characters of the story. Note how the action is influenced by the characters and how plot events impact the characters as well.

• • THEME • •

Themes in realistic fiction generally reflect important issues of contemporary society. Although no one

FIGURE 7.1

Considering Quality in Contemporary Realistic Fiction

- The story exemplifies characteristics of excellence in narrative fiction.
- A vivid, realistic setting supports the events of the story.
- The characters are credible and not stereotypes.
- The main characters are multidimensional, and they change and develop over time.
- The problems are believable and are solved in realistic, culturally grounded ways.

- The intended age group can understand the plot structure.
- There is a theme that is intrinsic to the story and applicable to readers' lives.
- The dialogue and thoughts of the characters sound natural, with dialect and diction that reflect the setting and characters but do not overwhelm the reader.

book will—or should—reflect every current issue, there are often multiple themes in contemporary realistic fiction. A story about coming of age, for example, might also explore family relationships, peer pressure, and/or cultural tensions. Books in which the protagonist struggles with some physical challenge might also raise issues of loneliness or self-discovery. Many books today explore social and political issues while also focusing on individual yet universal concerns. Well-developed themes are intrinsic to the narrative.

• • STYLE • •

As in any book, the writing should be superb. Structure should support character development and plot. The dialogue in realistic fiction should reflect today's language forms, including current slang and appropriate dialect variations, yet not be overwhelming. Style that engages the reader and includes realistic dialogue that reflects the characters and their cultural milieu is vital to the development of setting, characterization, plot, and theme. Figure 7.1 summarizes the criteria for evaluating a work of contemporary realistic fiction.

A close look at Patricia Reilly Giff's *Pictures of Hollis Woods* (I–A) demonstrates how the qualities of excellence in contemporary realistic fiction come together to create a memorable story.

✱ ✱ ✱
A CLOSE LOOK AT
Pictures of Hollis Woods

Patricia Reilly Giff's *Pictures of Hollis Woods* (I–A) is an outstanding example of contemporary realistic

fiction. Winner of a 2003 Newbery Honor, this book exemplifies the criteria for excellence in realistic fiction. It engages young readers in a search for love and acceptance that is sure to affect the way they regard their own lives.

The story is set in two different places: the primary setting is the Regans' summer home by the East Fork of the Delaware River; Josie's house is the secondary setting. Both settings are described vividly, with a great deal of visual imagery that makes both come alive for the reader. Josie's house is full of color and odd bits and pieces of her long life. The Delaware house is old, somewhat decrepit, and full of warmth and color. The river and the mountain that the house rests beside are also clearly depicted, and much of the action takes place there. The warmth and comfort of the houses and the beauty of their surroundings are important to the development of character and plot.

The story is told as a series of flashbacks that are interspersed with Hollis's ongoing life with Josie, until the final climax. These flashbacks are triggered by Hollis's perusal of the pictures that she drew during her summer with the Regans. As she looks and remembers, we learn of her past life, how she came to spend the summer with the Regans, how she gradually became a part of their family, and why she left them. This plot line is juxtaposed with her growing love for Josie and her decision to stay with her. Tragically, Josie's deteriorating mental health precipitates yet another move for Hollis, and she flees with Josie to the only other place she has ever felt loved—the Delaware River house. It is there, in the middle of winter, the day after Christmas, that the two parts of her life come together and the conflict is resolved.

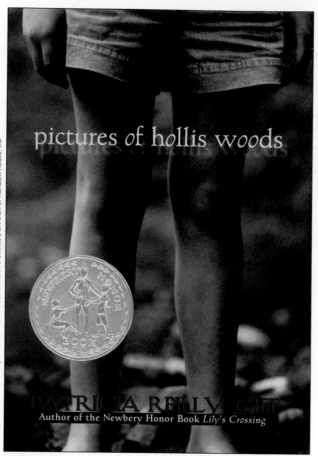

Patricia Reilly Giff creates a heartbreakingly real story in **Pictures of Hollis Woods**.

The conflict in the story is primarily an internal one, as Hollis struggles with herself, caught between her intense longing for family yet afraid of the potential for pain that loving others opens us up to. Minor conflicts between Hollis and her former foster mothers and caseworkers help set up her character as a difficult child, but her internal dialogue allows us to understand that her actions spring from her desire to be loved. Finally, the climax of her story with the Regans, when she and her foster brother, Steven, crash while trying to drive down the mountain, pits the two children against this formidable force of nature, a conflict that has been foreshadowed throughout her time with them.

Because we experience the story through Hollis's point of view, and in part through her direct memories, we feel immediate sympathy for her. From the outset, we see her as a loving child in untenable circumstances. Like the heroes in the ancient Greek dramas, she carries within herself the seeds of her own downfall. Her habit of running away from foster homes is repeated with the Regans when Hollis feels responsible for the crash and again when she flees with Josie. Her intense lifelong desire for a family has led her to idealize family life, and that idealization causes her to feel guilty about her role in the arguments that Steven and his father have, even though they have nothing to do with Hollis. The seeds of her redemption are also within her. Hollis is an artist, and it is through her drawings that she comes to understand her life. Her own vision, realized in her art, allows her to see those whom she loves with a clarity that is perhaps beyond that of a typical twelve-year-old. These tight causal connections between character and plot create a unity of character and action that helps make this a very compelling novel.

Hollis is the primary character, but Giff also pays close attention to Josie and the Regans as well, creating characters that we recognize as human beings, complete with foibles as well as strengths, characters we would like to know. Just as Hollis does, we come to love these people in her life.

Giff's lyrical, intensely visual style is filled with imagery so strong that colors and shapes are almost palpable. Hollis sees the world in precise colors: French blue, iridescent silver, the yellow kitchen, the mix of greens and grays and blues of the river and the mountain. This imagery allows Giff to develop the setting, the character of Hollis, the unity of character and action that is evident in the novel, and the themes that permeate the novel.

Themes in this novel are multilayered. The sustaining metaphor of art as a clearer vision of life becomes the vehicle through which Hollis grows and changes. Through this sustaining metaphor, Giff also explores what it means to be a family; the importance of loving and being loved and how to love oneself; belonging; how actions lead to consequences; and how the misinterpretations of actions and events can lead to destruction rather than redemption. This ultimately triumphant story of the power of art and love to transform life stays in the hearts of readers long after they read the final words, through which they look with Hollis at the last picture, the one that doesn't exactly match the W picture she's been holding on to for so long:

> But the picture, and why it doesn't match the first one, the W picture: It's because I'm holding my sister, Christina, six weeks old, in my arms.
> . . . So there are five of us now: a mother, a father, a brother, and two sisters. A family.
> (p. 166)

P | R | O | F | I | L | E |

Patricia Reilly Giff

I want to write books that children will laugh over even if their own lives are not happy, books that say ordinary people are special.

Patricia Reilly Giff's characters, full of authentic spunk, adroitly demonstrate how ordinary people are special in everyday ways. The genuineness of Giff's characters reflects her tendency to build books around the people in her life. Giff hopes her books inspire young readers to write the stories of their own lives: "I want [children] to make the connection that books are people's stories, that writing is talking on paper, and I want them to write their own stories. I'd like my books to provide that connection for them" (Bantam Doubleday Dell, n.d.).

Giff has written prolifically since 1979, producing more than seventy books for children. Her popular series include the **Polk Street** books. She has won Newbery Honor Awards for *Lily's Crossing* and *Pictures of Hollis Woods*.

To learn more about Patricia Reilly Giff, go to CengageBrain.com to access the Education CourseMate website, where you will find links to relevant websites.

Ways to Think about Contemporary Realistic Fiction

Like other genres, realistic fiction encompasses a variety of literature. One variation is in format. There are contemporary realistic fiction stories that are what primary and intermediate grades readers call "chapter books," books that are created especially for those readers who are moving toward being able to read and comprehend increasingly complex texts. These chapter books often come in series. We also find contemporary realistic fiction stories that are novels in verse, discussed in Chapter 4, in which realistic stories are the content, with verse the style through which the content is presented. Contemporary realistic fiction comes in graphic novel form as well, in which pictures and text work together to tell a story. Presently, most contemporary realistic fiction for young readers is in the form of picture storybooks and prose novels.

Contemporary realistic fiction also contains various distinctive types, or subgenres, of stories, which include adventure and survival stories, mysteries and thrillers, animal stories, sports stories, and others that contemporary readers enjoy and ask for. These categories are not discrete; many books fall into more than one. Because children often ask for books by saying that they want "an adventure story," or "a real story about animals," it is useful to think about contemporary realistic fiction in this manner.

Another useful way to consider contemporary realistic fiction is by theme. Not surprisingly, most contemporary realistic fiction reflects what its readers are doing: growing up, or coming of age. Some of these books explore peer relationships both in and out of school, including a range of romantic relationships, as well as family relationships. Sometimes these themes are accompanied by a consideration of how particular attributes, such as various exceptionalities and learning challenges, or circumstances, such as cultural dislocation, political strife, or violence affect the lives of young people. Still others consider the effects of contemporary social practices, issues, and events. The best of this fiction explores these themes in fresh ways. Teaching Idea 7.2 uses **Pictures of Hollis Woods** as an example of how readers can make connections between themselves and characters in fiction, although any other book could lend itself to this exercise as well.

We begin our discussion of contemporary realistic fiction by first considering some currently popular formats, then explore types of stories, and finally address this genre in terms of themes.

• • POPULAR FORMATS • •

Transitional Chapter Books in Series

Series books of narrative fiction of any genre contain the same characters in varying situations across many different books. The best of these narrative fiction books contain memorable, vivid characters that readers remember from book to book. Series books are very popular with readers young and old. Many children like to read series books; their familiarity makes

TEACHING IDEA 7.2

Thematic Connections: Discovering the Self

This Teaching Idea addresses the Common Core English, Language Arts, Reading: Literature standard 2, grades 4 through 8. Discussing theme with students younger than grade 4 is also effective practice. The suggestions in this Teaching Idea may need to be adapted to suit your particular grade level and the needs of your students.

In Patricia Reilly Giff's *Pictures of Hollis Woods*, Hollis is engaged in a journey of self-discovery. Ask your students to list the things that Hollis discovers about herself and how she did so. Then ask them to compare their own journeys of self-discovery with Hollis's. Is their own easier? More difficult? Have they completed it? Do they think they will? Other books that lend themselves to this same question are Lindsay Lee Johnson's *Soul Moon Soup*, Ron Koertge's *Shakespeare Bats Cleanup*, Sharon Creech's *Heartbeat*, and Jacqueline Woodson's *Locomotion*.

Compare the ways that art helps the protagonists of *Soul Moon Soup, Heartbeat,* and *Pictures of Hollis Woods* heal themselves, and the way that writing helps the protagonists of *Shakespeare Bats Cleanup* and *Locomotion*. Ask students to think about some of the things each of them can do that might help them come to know themselves and heal their own emotional wounds.

Find other books with themes that might resonate with your students.

---

readers comfortable. Feitelsen, Kita, and Goldstein (1986) studied the effects of reading series books on first-grade readers. They found that series books facilitate reading comprehension because the reader knows the character and setting, the framework, and the background of the story. Knowing what to expect from a particular book makes reading easier; it's like meeting a good friend again. Series books also motivate reluctant readers. Knowing that there are other books in the series increases the anticipation; if the first book was good, then the next one is sure to be enjoyable as well. In addition to the many contemporary realistic fiction series, many popular series books are from other genres as well—fantasy, science fiction, and historical fiction, not to mention biography and nonfiction—and we discuss those books in the appropriate chapters.

Here, we consider a special type of series book, contemporary realistic fiction stories that are written for readers who are transitioning from brief, simple texts into longer, more complex texts. Although many chapter books for transitioning readers from second through fourth or fifth grade are series books, many of which we discuss following, not all "transitional chapter books" appear in a series. For example, Atinuke's chapter book, *The No. 1 Car Spotter* (P–I) contains four stories set in contemporary Africa, supported by Warwick Johnson Cadwell's black-and-white illustrations. Bonnie Graves's *Taking Care of Trouble* and *No Copycats Allowed* (both P), are brief, humorous

stories in manageable chapters and appeal to newly independent readers in second or third grade.

On Your Education CourseMate

CONVERSATION WITH BONNIE GRAVES

Bonnie Graves is the author of several transitional chapter books for young readers. In our conversation, she talks about how she develops and maintains a character's voice in her books, a voice that is often humorous. Go to CengageBrain.com to access the Education CourseMate website and watch the video conversation with author Bonnie Graves.

Questions to Consider

1. What did you notice about how Bonnie Graves thinks about language as she writes?

2. What do you think about the role of humor in helping to entice children to read extended text?

As we mention in Chapter 3, the easy-readers series books such as Cynthia Rylant's **Henry and Mudge** series (P) are designed to support newly independent readers with their large type, careful word placement, and supportive illustrations. Longer books, such as Megan McDonald's **Judy Moody** series (P), Paula Danziger's **Amber Brown** books (P), and Patricia Reilly Giff's **Polk Street School** series (P) are popular with young readers who are outgrowing easier books and are eager to move on to longer "chapter books." The supportive illustrations, simple texts, usually episodic chapters, and familiar cast of characters (once the first book is read) allow newly independent readers to rise to the challenge of longer texts.

Stephanie Greene's ***Princess Posey and the First Grade Parade*** and ***Princess Posey and the Perfect Present*** (both P), illustrated by Stephanie Roth Sisson, like many other series books, are full of humor, and engage young readers who enjoy sharing Posey's "great days" in first grade. Jessica Harper's **Uh-oh, Cleo** books, such as *I Barfed on Mrs. Kenly* (P), prompt young readers to laugh at situations that, in real life, can be really embarrassing. Lois Lowry's **Gooney Bird Greene** series, including *Gooney Bird Is So Absurd* and *Gooney Bird on the Map* (both P–I), with illustrations by Middy Thomas, are humorous looks at life in the second grade for a one-of-a-kind youngster.

Michelle Edwards's **Jackson Friends** series (P–I) is narrated by a young African American girl who attends a contemporary American magnet school, and young readers relate to the multicultural school environment that Edwards creates. These same readers enjoy the **Gym Shorts** series, including *Basketball Bats* and *Goof-Off Goalie* (both P), written by Betty Hicks with illustrations by Adam McCauley. This series consists of short chapter books that follow a fourth-grade boy, Henry, and his friends who love sports. Pencil sketches decorate each spread and support the text. Peter Catalanotto and Pamela Schembri's **Second Grade Friends** series offers yet another choice for newly independent readers. In *The Veteran's Day Visitor* (P), the third book in the series, readers consider some of the less comfortable aspects of aging and the bittersweet joys of having a close relationship with an older person.

Young readers enjoy being able to recognize the characters in Annie Barrows's *Ivy + Bean Take Care of the Babysitter* (P) and *Ivy + Bean Doomed to Dance* (P) in the **Ivy and Bean** series, with illustrations by Sophie Blackall. Kimberly Willis Holt's *Piper Reed, Navy Brat* (P) introduces readers to nine-year-old Piper, irrepressible and full of spunk, and most will be eager to go on to *Piper Reed, the*

Great Gypsy (P). Peggy Gifford's ***Moxie Maxwell Does Not Love Stuart Little*** and ***Moxie Maxwell Does Not Love Writing Thank-You Notes*** (P–I), blend humor and family stories in a satisfying chapter book format. In Gail Gauthier's ***A Girl, a Boy, and a Monster Cat*** and ***A Girl, a Boy, and Three Robbers*** (P–I), Brandon and Hannah develop a true friendship as they learn to play together after school while Brandon's mother is at work. Joe Cepeda's cartoon illustrations capture the humor and liveliness of the pair.

Relying more on text and less on illustration, Graham Salisbury's **Calvin Coconut** series, including ***Calvin Coconut: Kung Fooey*** (P–I) follow an exuberant young boy in his adventures at home and at school in Hawaii. Although there are many moments of humor, there are also serious themes, such as when Calvin finds the courage to stand up for a friend. Nikki Grimes's ***Almost Zero: A Dyamonde Daniel Book*** (P–I), the third book in her series, also explores serious issues with humor and grace. Lenore Look's ***Ruby Lu, Star of the Show*** (P–I) similarly combines humor and serious issues as third-grader Ruby worries about the changes at home with her father losing his job and her mother going out to work. Look's **Alvin Ho** books about a fearful second-grade boy, including ***Alvin Ho: Allergic to Dead Bodies, Funerals, and Other Fatal Circumstances*** (P–I), liberally sprinkled with sketches by LeUyen Pham, are similar. Stephanie Greene's ***Happy Birthday, Sophie Hartley*** (P–I) also appeals to fans of easy-to-read, humorous stories of growing up.

Clementine (P), the first book in Sara Pennypacker's series, was a *New York Times* bestseller. The engaging protagonist is both hysterically funny and extremely lovable, and Marla Frazee's inspired illustrations reflect both extremes. ***The Talented Clementine, Clementine's Letter, Clementine: Friend of the Week***, and ***Clementine and the Family Meeting*** (all P) continue the adventures of a young girl finding her own voice in her loving family and the wider world of school. We now take a close look at *Clementine*.

* * *

A CLOSE LOOK AT
Clementine

As in many works of contemporary realistic fiction, character drives the everyday life stories in Sara Pennypacker's *Clementine* (P) and the books that follow. Eight-year-old Clementine lives with her little brother, artist mother, and father in the basement apartment of the building that her father manages. Her school and the building that she lives in are integral settings that serve to reveal character and advance the plot. Partially because her father is the building manager—although you might think that Clementine would do so anyway—she knows everyone in the building and has her own way of describing them all—not always flattering. This tells the reader a lot about Clementine's character, as does the fact that she and her mother look out of their ground-level kitchen window and Clementine knows who comes and goes by their feet. Similarly, in school, the interactions she has with her principal reveal a great deal about her personality.

Her best friend, Margaret, a bit more than a year older, lives in the building with her mother and older brother (who is *not* Clementine's boyfriend, as she is careful to remind us). Clementine's helpful nature is apparent when Margaret cuts a chunk of her own hair trying to get glue out of it. Clementine offers to help, with disastrous results. Then she helps again by coloring Margaret's rather bald scalp with lovely orange curls, just like her own. When the permanent marker curls don't make Margaret's mother happy, Clementine cuts off her own hair in sympathy and Margaret uses the green permanent marker to make curls for her. Clementine never blames Margaret, not even when she is engaged in a discussion with the principal. In fact, Clementine worries about the principal because the principal thinks that Clementine is not paying attention, which Clementine always does—just not to the things her teachers want her to focus on. In fact, Clementine pays such careful attention that she

Clementine is a character—both literally and figuratively— in **Clementine** *and the other chapter books in the series by Sara Pennypacker.*

solves a problem that her father is baffled by. It seems that Clementine possesses her own brilliance.

P R O F I L E

Sara Pennypacker

I start by making up a character. I make this character very real. I imagine what she likes for breakfast, what he thinks is unfair in this world, how she fits into her family, what he loves to do most. Then, when I feel I know and care about this character, I ask him or her, "What's wrong?" And I try to imagine what he or she might answer.

Sara Pennypacker loves to write, but she has a problem: She gets too many ideas. She says they are everywhere and tells young writers to keep a writer's notebook and take it with them everywhere; she does. She also does a lot of revising, wanting her books to be as perfect as possible. She says that each Clementine book takes close to a year to write.

There are now five Clementine volumes. Sara has also taken over the **Flat Stanley** series beginning with *Flat Stanley's Worldwide Adventure, Book Two: The Great Egyptian Grave Robbery*, released in 2009.

 To learn more about Sara Pennypacker, go to CengageBrain.com to access the Education CourseMate website where you will find links to relevant websites.

The language play is laugh-out-loud funny. When Clementine is trying to find a name for a pet, she goes into the bathroom to find a good word; her new cat's name, "Moisturizer," is much better than the name she gave to a former kitten, "Laxative." Chafing under her "fruit name," she refers to her little brother with a series of vegetable names: "Radish," "Pea Pod," "Celery." Her first-person narration reveals her character, with an almost breathless retelling of her adventures. Clementine, like Ramona, is a dynamo. Just one glimpse at the cover illustration, with Clementine standing on one hand, the other pressed to the wall, both feet pressed to opposite walls, tongue out, and red curls awry, tells young readers that they want to be her friend.

Series books are not only written for young readers developing their ability to handle extended texts with ease. They are also available to and remain popular with readers of all ages. In the sections that follow, we discuss other popular contemporary realistic fiction series books that are not transitional chapter books.

Novels in Verse

We consider novels in verse as poetry in Chapter 4, but many are contemporary realistic fiction as well. Sharon Creech's **Love that Dog** (I) is a beautifully told story of a young boy who at first resists his teacher's attempts to get him to write poetry. As the year progresses, he learns to express himself through poetry, and we watch as he comes to terms with the loss of a beloved companion. The sequel, **Hate that Cat** (I), continues his story as he opens himself up to loving a new pet. Lindsay Lee Johnson uses poetry to tell the story of Phoebe, abandoned by both mother and father, in **Soul Moon Soup** (I–A). This hauntingly beautiful novel follows Phoebe as she discovers her inner resources and the healing power of art and nature.

Steven Herrick's **Naked Bunyip Dancing** (I–A), with illustrations by Beth Norling, is a novel in verse from Australia that explores the often humorous trials and joys of self-discovery as the students in Class 6C begin to learn about things that are strange "school subjects" for them—Bob Dylan, poetry, belly dancing, yoga—and discover their hidden talents as they prepare for an end-of-the-year concert. In **Locomotion** (I–A), Jacqueline Woodson tells the story of eleven-year-old Lonnie Collins Motion, who lost both of his parents in a fire. He lost his little sister, too, even though she survived the fire, because they were placed in different foster homes. His pervasive grief and loneliness begin to lift when his teacher gives him a great gift—she asks him to "write it down before it leaves your brain,"

and Lonnie begins to write his life in free verse. This exquisite award-winning book and its sequel, **Peace, Locomotion** (I–A), a collection of primarily epistolary poems, reminds us of the power of words to shape our lives.

The difficulties of beginning middle school are captured by Nikki Grimes in **Planet Middle School** (I–A). An athlete, twelve-year-old Joy worries about being labeled a "tomboy," about her changing relationship with her best friend, about boys. Issues of gender-role expectations in life and in sports give this coming-of-age novel an interesting depth.

Graphic Novels

Novels with graphics that are a significant part of the storytelling are yet another format that young readers enjoy and, fortunately for them, more graphic novels are being produced. Graphic novels are not always realistic fiction, although that is what we focus on here; you will find graphic novels mentioned in several other chapters in this text.

Many of the transitional chapter books discussed previously rely on both text and illustration to tell a story, but occupy a place somewhere between illustrated book and graphic novel because the text seems to carry most of the narrative. For example, Cherise Mericle Harper's **Just Grace and the Double Surprise** (P–I), the seventh book in the series, includes Grace's "map of me," her charts and lists, and her cartoon drawings, all of which relate aspects of her feelings and her view of the world. Lincoln Peirce's **Big Nate: In a Class by Himself** (I–A) and James Roy's **Max Quigley: Technically Not a Bully** (I) appeal to readers with their combination of text and illustration. Jeff Kinney's **Diary of a Wimpy Kid** (I–A) is very popular, with its hand-printed format and cartoons punctuating every page. With **Diary of a Wimpy Kid: Rodrick Rules** (I–A), we follow Greg into middle school, with his adolescent angst exacerbated by older brother Rodrick and tattletale younger brother Manny. Underneath it all, Greg's obvious sense of humor keeps him, and the book, lighthearted.

In a more serious vein, Jacqueline Wilson's graphic novel, **Best Friends** (I), is an uncompromising look at how adults make decisions and children have to live with them. The story is told through a deft combination of art and speech, with the characters of Gemma and her friend Alice very realistic in their anguish about being parted and in their determination to remain "best friends forever," even as they learn to make other friends.

Raina Telegemeier based her graphic novel, **Smile** (I), on her own experiences with orthodontia. Much more than a chronicle of the agony of bad teeth, this story portrays growing up, discovering self, and finding true friendships, with all of the accompanying heartaches and joys. Moving from middle to high school is a traumatic time for some adolescents, and Neil has another complication. His best friend's mother is trying to force the library to ban the fantasy series that Neil and Danny love. Told as two stories, Neil's alongside excerpts from the fantasy series, M. K. Reed's **Americus** (A), with illustrations by Jonathan David Hill, depicts a young man who is learning what is worth fighting for.

Greg Neri's graphic novel, **Yummy: The Last Days of a Southside Shorty** (A), is based on the life of Robert "Yummy" Sandifer, an eleven-year-old Southside Chicago Black Disciples gang member. As the story unfolds, it is difficult to decide whether Yummy was a victim or a killer—or both. Illustrations by Randy DuBurke add emotional depth.

Award-winning picturebook artist Don Wood's venture into the graphic novel form, **Into the Volcano** (I–A), is an adventure/survival story, a mystery, and a bit of fantasy vividly brought to life through the detailed, colorful illustrations and snappy dialogue. There's even a bit of science thrown in as two unlikely heroes, brothers Duffy and Sumo, travel through a volcano on the island nation of Kocalaha.

Picturebooks and Novels

Although transitional chapter books, series books, novels in verse, and graphic novels are becoming increasingly prevalent in contemporary realistic fiction, most of this genre is in more traditional picturebook or prose novel formats. Unless otherwise noted, the books we discuss in the following sections are primarily prose novels, with some representative picturebooks. These stories range widely in style, theme, and structure, adding to the rich array of books to entice young readers into the world of contemporary realistic fiction. We turn to that array with a consideration of some of the most popular subgenres of fiction found in contemporary realism.

• • DISTINCTIVE TYPES • •

In addition to varied formats, contemporary realistic fiction contains different types, or subgenres, of stories as well. Some frequently asked for by young readers include adventure and survival stories, realistic animal stories, mysteries and thrillers, and sports stories.

Adventure and Survival Stories

Marked by especially exciting, fast-paced plots, adventure and survival stories captivate readers who are eager to discover what happens next. Often the central problem is a conflict between person and nature. The best adventure stories also contain multidimensional characters who control much of the action and who change as a result of the action. Many young readers who enjoy a compelling plot prefer adventure stories. **Into the Volcano** (I–A), discussed previously, is a good example of a graphic novel that is an adventure/survival story. Likewise, Graham Salisbery's series hero, Calvin Coconut, embarks on an adventure of his own in **Calvin Coconut: Hero of Hawai'i** (P–I), an adventure story that is a transitional chapter book.

Classic adventure stories include Jean Craighead George's **My Side of the Mountain** (A) and **Julie of the Wolves** (A), a wonderful story of the clash of cultures and coming of age that is as gripping today as it was when it won the Newbery Medal in 1973. Another novel that remains timeless, Gary Paulsen's **Hatchet** (I–A) is still one of the most popular adventure stories today. Readers also enjoy **Brian's Winter** and **Brian's Return** (I–A), in which Paulsen explores possible endings to this exciting adventure story set in the woods of northeastern Canada. These novels focus on Brian's conflict with nature, but also include some internal conflict as Brian struggles with himself in an attempt to cope with his parents' divorce. Will Hobbs's novels are always multilayered and gripping, and **Take Me to the River** (I) is no exception. In Tor Seidler's **Brothers Below Zero** (I), sibling rivalry results in two brothers struggling to stay alive in a terrible snowstorm, with the interpersonal conflict leading to the conflict with nature.

Sharon Creech's novel **The Wanderer** (I–A), a Newbery Honor book, revolves around several conflicts: internal struggles with the self, struggles between individuals, and a struggle with nature—in this case the sea. Sophie, thirteen, is sailing across the ocean with her uncles and two thirteen-year-old cousins, Cody and Brian, when a tremendous storm threatens their lives and calls forth courage they did not know they possessed. Told in a series of journal entries from Sophie and Cody, this is a complex, beautifully crafted story.

In **Red Midnight** (I), Ben Mikaelsen's young protagonist, twelve-year-old Santiago, and his younger sister demonstrate great courage and resourcefulness as they flee Guatemala after guerrilla soldiers attack their village. The overland adventure soon gives way to their struggle with the ocean as they try to reach the United States by sea kayak. Also struggling to survive the horrors of war, Chanda and her siblings, Iris and Soly, are caught up in a rebel invasion of their grandmother's village in a fictitious African countryside in Allan Stratton's **Chanda's Wars**, sequel to **Chanda's Secrets** (A). As Iris and Soly are forced into military slavery, the contrast between the inhumanity of their situation and the strength of their characters is apparent.

Animal Stories

Animal stories are about realistic relationships between human beings and animals, most commonly horses or dogs, or about realistic animal adventures. When they focus on an animal-human relationship, this relationship is usually a vehicle for maturation by the central human character. Good animal stories have engaging characters that grow and change as a result of their experience with an animal. Many of these books are very moving, often provoking a strong emotional response.

In **Snook Alone** (I), by Marilyn Nelson with illustrations by Timothy Basil Ering, it is the animal character who has to survive. When Snook and his owner, a monk, visit a remote, deserted island in the Indian Ocean, bad weather comes up and his owner is forced to leave without him. Nelson's lyrical text, full of repetition, cadence, and metaphor, depicts Snook's life on the island until "one day the good ending came." In picturebook form for younger readers, Margaret Wild's **Harry & Hopper** (P), illustrated by Freya Blackwood, presents a challenging topic—the death of a beloved pet. Harry grieves by remembering his special dog, and readers grieve along with him as those memories bring Hopper back, if only fleetingly.

The focal animal in Helen Frost's **Diamond Willow** (I) is also a dog. Set in interior Alaska, this story blends an animal story and a survival tale, with some magical realism as well. The protagonist of Kate DiCamillo's **Because of Winn-Dixie** (I), ten-year-old India Opal Buloni, loves her new dog from the first moment she sees him in the Winn-Dixie grocery store. His canine companionship eases her longing for her mother, helps her develop friendships in her new town, and opens up communication with her taciturn father. A loving relationship between girl and dog is also at the center of Deborah Wiles's **Each Little Bird that Sings** (I), in which the young protagonist is forced to make a very difficult choice when caught in a flood with her dog and younger cousin. The consequences of her choice, while heart wrenching, offer an opportunity for her to grow in compassion and understanding.

Phyllis Reynolds Naylor's **Shiloh** (I–A) is an outstanding example of a realistic animal story. Winner of the 1992 Newbery Medal, **Shiloh** presents a profound ethical dilemma as experienced by eleven-year-old Marty Preston, who rescues and then falls in love with a stray dog that has been abused. His family and community expect him to return the dog to his rightful owner, even though Judd has mistreated Shiloh. Marty, however, feels that a higher principle supports his keeping the dog. Intermediate-grade readers, in the midst of developing their own moral code as they begin to encounter ideas and experiences that cause them to think about values, can do so in the safety of the story world of **Shiloh**.

The protagonist of Patricia Reilly Giff's **Wild Girl** (I), Lidie moves from Brazil to New York to join her father, who runs a stable at a racetrack. She is already an accomplished rider, but her father and brother still think of her as the little girl they left behind. She struggles to show them how mature and accomplished she really is, by riding the new filly, Wild Girl. In Joseph Monninger's **Finding Somewhere** (I–A), two girls, sixteen and eighteen years of age, leave unhappy homes behind when they "steal" an old horse destined to be put down and embark on a road trip west, heading for Wyoming, a place where Speed can be a "free" horse before he dies. Along the way, they discover a lot about themselves and the unexpected consequences that always follow choices.

Mysteries and Thrillers

A thriller uses suspense, tension, and excitement as primary elements of the narrative, and usually the villain is known to both the hero of the tale and the reader. The focus of a thriller is, in a sense, the pursuit of evil by good, and thriller writers seek to evoke excitement and fear in their readers. A mystery is also marked by suspense, but the villain or cause of the problem is hidden from both protagonist and reader. The focus in a mystery story is a question—Who did it? Where is it? What happened?—and the action centers on finding the answer to that question. Although they are usually exciting, they rely less on excitement and fear than do thrillers. The best of these books revolve around an intriguing problem and contain well-developed characters who work to solve the problem. They feature fast-paced action. In the case of mysteries, a logical solution is usually foreshadowed through the careful presentation of clues. Writer Nancy Werlin distinguishes between mysteries and thrillers, which "tend to be about nasty people doing bad, illegal, and/ or unethical things" (2006, p. 529). Many children go through a phase in which mysteries are all they want to read; adolescents often devour thrillers. Fortunately, there are some excellent books for children of all ages, some of which are also series books.

Young readers who love mysteries are happy to find that mysteries are often also series chapter books. Elizabeth Levy, Donald Sobol, Seymour Simon, and Marjorie Sharmat are some of the writers who, for many years now, have provided younger readers with brief, exciting mysteries that satisfy their desire to figure things out. Sharon Draper's **Clubhouse Mysteries** series features four engaging elementary-school boys who just can't resist a mystery, even if it involves being trapped in a tunnel, as in *Lost in the Tunnel of Time* (P–I). Draper also incorporates real issues and information, in this case about the Underground Railroad in Cincinatti. In her *Shadows of Caesar's Creek* (P–I), the four friends end up, literally, in a canoe with no paddle and are rescued by the chief of the Shawnee Nation of Ohio. This opportunity helps them learn about local Native American history. This series has few illustrations but supports readers with brief chapters and uncomplicated language.

The **Sammy Keyes** books, by Wendelin Van Draanen, are a bit more challenging to read, but also very popular. In *Sammy Keyes and the Psycho Kitty Queen* (I), Sammy finds a dead cat on her thirteenth birthday and gets involved in solving yet another mystery. *Sammy Keyes and the Night of Skulls* (I) involves a Halloween adventure that leads Sammy and her friends into a much bigger mystery. Sammy is a super sleuth with a great sense of humor, who navigates with verve the life of a young adolescent.

Blue Balliett's first novel, *Chasing Vermeer* (I), is a puzzle, an adventure, and a mystery that needs solving. From the beginning of this intriguing novel, Balliett invites readers to participate in helping the three young protagonists solve the mystery of the missing Vermeer, and they are more than willing to give it a try. The second and third books in this series, *The Wright 3* and *The Calder Game* (I), are equally intriguing. In *The Calder Game* the action moves to England when Calder Pillay travels there with his father. When Calder goes missing, his friends Tommy and Petra, and elderly neighbor Mrs. Sharp, fly over to help find him. There are a few too many coincidences in all of these books, but the fast-paced action pulls young readers along and the theme of creative thinking appeals as well. These and other books, such as Trenton Lee Stewart's **The Mysterious Benedict Society** series (I) keep intermediate-grade children reading and guessing.

Anthony Horowitz ended his very popular **Alex Rider** series of thrillers with *Scorpia Rising* (I), in which his teenage hero finally defeats his enemies and embarks on what might be a relative normal life for a teen. Jon Scieszka capitalizes on young readers' interest in mysteries and thrillers with his *Guys Read: Thriller* (I–A), the second book in his **Guys Read** library, containing ten short stories by popular authors. Despite the title, girls who like thrillers like this book also.

An interesting mystery from Great Britain, Alex Shearer's *Canned* (I) is unpredictable and funny, as well as gruesome and exaggerated, introducing Fergal and Charlotte, eccentric children who form a tentative partnership when they discover unusual contents in the unlabeled cans they both collect. Andrea Beaty's *Cicada Summer* (I) is a thought-provoking, gripping multilayered story. In Siobhan Dowd's *The London Eye Mystery* (I–A), twelve-year-old Ted and his older sister join together to solve the mysterious disappearance of their cousin, Salim. Ted turns out to be a terrific detective, as the effects of his Asperger's syndrome, one of which is a very logical brain, work to his advantage. Chris Rylander's multilayered novel *The Fourth Stall* (I) is told from the point of view of the unlikely hero, a sixth-grade boy who runs a business involving solving problems of all kinds from the fourth stall of an unused boys bathroom in his school. Themes exploring bullying, honor, and friendship add depth, and the dry humor of the direct address engages readers.

Pete Hautman's *Blank Confession* (A) uses multiple points of view to explore the mystery that begins when Shayne Blank walks into the police station and confesses to a murder. Despite this confession, suspense lies in figuring out what really happened.

There are many mysteries that have delighted readers for many years. Joan Lowry Nixon's psychic mysteries and Lois Duncan's eerie novels satisfy older readers, and Mary Downing Hahn's novels are always intriguing. E. L. Konigsburg's *Silent to the Bone* (A), Carol Plum-Ucci's *The Body of Christopher Creed* (A), and Robert Cormier's chilling *The Rag and Bone Shop* (A) also provide adolescent mystery fans with intriguing books to read and think about.

Norma Fox Mazer's psychological thriller, *The Missing Girl* (A) gets into the minds of five sisters who are being stalked, with one eventually kidnapped and imprisoned by a very dangerous man; the man's point of view alternates with those of three of the sisters in this chilling tale. Nancy Werlin's *The Rules of Survival* (A) is a perfect example of how the tension of fear can catch and keep a reader turning the pages. Kevin Brooks's *Black Rabbit Summer* (A) is filled with social commentary as two teens disappear. One is wealthy and popular, the other poor and ignored, and the responses to the two disappearances reflect a stunning indifference to "ordinary" people. Harlan Coben's *Shelter* (A) is the first in the new **Mickey Bolitar** series by this best-selling author of adult mystery thrillers. The ending leaves readers eager for the next book. *The Boxer and the Spy* (A), by Robert Parker, combines mystery and a sports story as the protagonist, Terry, trains as a boxer and investigates a friend's apparent suicide.

Sports Stories

As demonstrated by ***The Boxer and the Spy***, good sports stories are almost always more than just stories about a sport. In sports stories, the action revolves around a sport and the thrills and tensions that accompany that particular sport, but it is the characters and how they use sports in their lives that carry the narrative. Dean Schneider (2011), a middle-school teacher, agrees, arguing that excellent sports stories are examples of the power of narrative when the subject is something that matters to young readers. Like mysteries, some sports stories are series books as well, such as the **Gym Shorts** series mentioned previously, and Lisa Yee's ***Bobby the Brave (Sometimes)*** (P–I). A small number of sports books with girls as central characters have broadened the scope of the genre and often explore the issues raised by sexism in sports. Some sports stories examine the issue of racism. In Michael Williams's ***Now Is the Time for Running*** (A), soccer is a vehicle for exploring racism, xenophobia, politics, and the plight of refugees in contemporary South Africa. The best of these books, such as Walter Dean Myers's ***Slam!*** (A), balance the descriptions of the sport with the development of the story, in which the central character grows in some way due to the challenges he or she faces because of participation in the sport. Often, sports serve as a metaphor for life

The third book in John Coy's **Four for Four** series, ***Love of the Game*** (I–A), four middle-school friends and sports lovers find that adjusting to middle school means they need to balance individual talents and interests with the desire to stick together, as they have always done. In Coy's ***Box Out*** and ***Crackback*** (A), the sport is a frame for the protagonists confronting difficult issues and decisions about life. In ***Whale Talk*** (A) Chris Crutcher deftly combines a story about swimming with an exploration of male friendships and high school social stratification in a gripping coming-of-age story.

Rather than describing how sports shape a child's life, Ron Koertge explores how being unable to continue a beloved sport affects a young boy's life in ***Shakespeare Bats Cleanup*** (I–A). Combining poetry and sports in a moving contemporary story, Koertge presents a young man driven to writing by boredom. He is home with mononucleosis, unable to play baseball, and he begins to read and write poetry, trying out different poetic forms. He uses his writing to come to terms with the recent death of his mother and with his changing role among his peers when his illness leaves him too weak to resume his role as baseball star. A novel in verse, a sports story, and a portrait of a young man growing up as he creates a new identity for himself, this novel in verse represents the richness and complexity of contemporary realistic fiction. In ***Shakespeare Makes the Playoffs*** (A), Kevin is fourteen, still passionate about baseball and good at writing poetry, and now involved with a girlfriend, who doesn't share those passions. He meets a new girl who is every bit as adept at words as he is and confronts the age-old dilemma: What should he do? Forming relationships with others and understanding yourself are two themes in this novel, and are found in much of the contemporary realistic fiction available today.

• • THEMES • •

Themes in contemporary realistic fiction are as many and varied as life itself. To make things even more confusing, most books explore more than one theme. How, for example, would you classify ***Pictures of Hollis Woods***? Is it a story about family, coming of age, friendship, or self-discovery? It is all of these and more, depending on the story an individual reader creates during reading. It is helpful to think of books according to themes, as young readers often want to read several books that relate to a single theme; many teachers, too, enjoy constructing thematic units (discussed in Chapters 11 and 12) with their students. The thematic Teaching Ideas in this book, such as Teaching Idea 7.2, are examples of how to make these connections. Themes that are important to authors sometimes arise from events in authors' own lives, although they are not necessarily autobiographical novels. Suggestions for discovering congruencies between authors' lives and their books are presented in Teaching Idea 7.3.

Growing Up

Not surprisingly, many of the most popular books for children and adolescents are about growing up. Indeed, it is difficult to find a piece of contemporary realistic fiction that is not about this universal quest. The path to adulthood is not always clear for our children; they must mark their own way. Books that portray a character struggling toward adulthood allow readers to see themselves reflected and provide an opportunity for thinking about how they might respond to varied real life situations. There are numerous picture storybooks for primary-grade readers that depict realistic characters trying to cope with growing up. Many of these books deal with children's increasing independence from adults as well as with the fear and delight that accompany that independence. Many of these books are discussed in Chapter 3 or appear in that booklist.

Study an Author's Work and Life

COMMON CORE STATE STANDARDS

This Teaching Idea does not address specific Common Core English Language Arts standards. It does, however, offer students the opportunity to understand that writing is influenced by personal history, a key idea to understanding the idea of ideology in text, and their own resources for writing.

Choose an author who writes realistic fiction, either novels or picture storybooks, and has also written an autobiography. With your students, read the autobiography and some of their realistic fiction books and discuss how events in the author's life influenced his or her books. For example, there is a clear link between Cynthia Rylant's early years and some of her early picturebooks and novels, and the same is true of Patricia Polacco. In her autobiography, Lois Lowry makes clear connections between her life and her writing, as do Chris Crutcher, Jack Gantos, and Walter Dean Myers.

The following are some questions you might want to pursue:

- What were the major influences in the author's life?
- How did events from the author's life influence her or his writing?
- What parallels can you find between her stories and her life?
- What does the author say about the relation between his life and his art?

Common themes in realistic fiction for children center on a variety of issues embedded in the larger process of growing up, developing peer relationships, and coping with often demanding family relationships. Themes in contemporary realistic fiction change as society changes, as art reflects life. Writers explore the issues that interest them in stories both tragic and humorous.

The characters in books for older readers continue to struggle for independence, often confronting conflicting feelings, difficult moral choices, and personal challenges along the way. They are engaged in a process of constructing their identity, trying to find out who they are, what they like and do not like, and what they will and will not do. Several of Kevin Henkes's books explore the thrill and the terror of moving from childhood to adolescence. In *Junonia* (I) we experience the emotions of Alice, who turns ten and learns, slowly and sadly, to accept that changes are a part of life no matter how much she wishes things would stay the same. In the Newbery Award–winning *The Higher Power of Lucky* (I), Susan Patron lovingly portrays a young girl who is living with her stepmother in a small desert town, in a trailer, and wondering just where she fits into the world. Over the course of the story, she discovers just what her "higher powers" are. By the end she seems ready to embark on the work of becoming an adult, secure in the knowledge that she is loved by her guardian, Brigitte. We watch her grow in the two sequels, *Lucky Breaks* (I) and *Lucky for Good* (I).

David Almond's *My Name Is Mina* (I) is a lyrical look into the heart and mind of one of the protagonists in his acclaimed novel, *Skellig* (I). Mina is different from her peers, more introspective, well-read, interested in quirky experiences and ideas. Her journal, written to herself, about her fears and feelings, allows readers to participate as she makes many discoveries about herself and her world. Lynne Rae Perkins won the Newbery Award for her beautiful coming-of-age novel *Criss Cross* (I–A), in which three fourteen-year-old neighbors—Debbie, from Perkins's *All Alone in the Universe* (I–A), Hector, and Lenny—are on the brink of moving from childhood into adolescence as their paths crisscross over the spring and summer. Thirty-eight vignettes, narrated primarily by either Debbie or Hector, come together in a quiet, beautifully told story. Set in a small town, perhaps in the recent past, this is a gentle, contemplative novel. In the thirteen short stories in *Hey, 13!* (A), Gary Soto captures thirteen perspectives on being thirteen, with its attendant joys, frustrations, and even danger.

Sometimes where and when a character lives creates extra challenges for that character. Monika

Schroder's **Saraswati's Way** (A) depicts the struggles of young Akash to follow his dream to continue his education even though he is poor, his father has died, and his grandmother sends him out to work to earn money for the family. Set in India, this story illuminates the universal urge to follow one's dream. Another book set in India, Deborah Ellis's **No Ordinary Day** (A) tells the story of a preadolescent girl, Valli, orphaned, desperately poor, living on the streets of Kolkata, and displaying signs of leprosy. In spite of this grim situation, this story is ultimately one of hope and determination.

Amjed Qamar creates a compelling character, fourteen-year-old Nazia, in **Beneath My Mother's Feet** (A), a haunting coming-of-age novel set in Karachi, Pakistan. When her father loses his job and her brother steals her dowry, Nazia and her mother have to go to work as housecleaners, a significant change in status. As Nazia struggles to adjust to her new life, she begins to realize that she has choices to make and that each choice carries a cost. Urdu words heighten the setting, and a glossary is thoughtfully included. Padma Venkatraman's travels in the Andaman Islands in the Bay of Bengal gave rise to her novel, **Island's End** (A). She tells the story of a young woman honored to have been chosen as her tribe's spiritual leader, who matures as she struggles to do what she knows is right while also attempting to gain their trust. She is determined to preserve their unique culture in the face of contact with the modern world.

Jeanette Winter explores the struggle to grow up and obtain an education under the Taliban in **Nasreen's Secret School: A True Story from Afghanistan** (P). This picturebook is based on a true story from modern Afghanistan. The turmoil in Afghanistan during the Taliban is also the setting for Deborah Ellis's **The Breadwinner** and **Parvanna's Journey** (I), highlighting both the horrible circumstances of that country and the courageous resilience of children. Trent Reedy's **Words in the Dust** (A) is set in Afghanistan and presents the life of a young Afghani girl, disfigured by a cleft lip and hindered by lack of schooling and a social structure that views women as property. Her life improves with some help from the American army, but it is mostly her own courage that opens the world to her.

The war on terror forms the background for Cory Doctorow's **Little Brother** (A), a chilling look at the encroachment of individual freedom that accompanied the government's response to the attacks of 9/11. Political repression in Nigeria is the setting for Beverley Naidoo's **The Other Side of Truth** (I–A), a Carnegie Award winner. This is a spellbinding story of two children who flee from Nigeria to London after their mother is killed. At first, their life in London is almost as dangerous as staying in Nigeria would have been, and they struggle to stay safe and be together. Modern Bethlehem is the setting for Randa Abdel-Fattah's **Where the Streets Had a Name** (I–A). Living in Israeli-occupied Bethlehem means that fear and the potential for bloodshed are a part of life. Enmity among Arabs, Christians, and Jews is also part of the fabric of daily existence, but the friendship a thirteen-year-old Hayaat, a Muslim, and Samy, a Christian defies this cultural barrier. This novel offer young readers the opportunity to begin to understand what it might be like to live under occupation. In J. L. Powers' **This Thing Called the Future** (A), living with the constant threat of AIDS is a reality in fourteen-year-old Khosi Zulu's life, just part of a lower-middle-class life in a South African township. Torn between modern and traditional beliefs, Khosi seeks help for her mother even as she negotiates the difficult role of a young woman caught between worlds.

Some books explicitly explore growing up within a racist and classist society. In **The Absolutely True Diary of a Part-Time Indian** (A), Sherman Alexie depicts the hopes and dreams of fourteen-year-old Junior, who leaves the "rez" to attend a white school in a well-to-do nearby town. Issues of race, class, and exceptionality make this novel both funny and painful, but ultimately triumphant. Jacqueline Woodson writes compellingly about race and poverty in novels such as **Miracle's Boys** (A), as well as in her novels in verse, discussed previously. Judith Ortiz Cofer in **Call Me Maria** (I–A); Joseph Bruchac in **The Heart of a Chief** (A); Cynthia Leitich Smith in **Indian Shoes** (I); Gary Soto in **Buried Onions** (A); and Laurence Yep in **Thief of Hearts** (A) explore race, poverty, and prejudice, and their influence on characters' lives. Walter Dean Myers's many books touch on race, and often poverty, in one way or another as he explores growing up as an African American. His novel, **Monster** (A), the story of a young black boy from a good family living in a neighborhood that made it easy to get caught up in a crime that he did not intend, won the first Printz Award. Written as part screen play and part journal entries, this novel considers what it is like to be young, black, and male in contemporary America.

In Angela Johnson's **The First Part Last** (A), sixteen-year-old Bobby becomes a father and realizes what that means. Told from Bobby's first-person point of view, this complex novel speaks to the rarely considered bond between a teenage father and his child.

Sometimes special challenges exist because the protagonist, like many of today's children, straddles two cultures—the one they were born into and the one they are living in. The issue of cultural dislocation and biculturalism is not a simple one, and there are no simple answers given in Andrea Cheng's *Honeysuckle House* (I), the story of two young Chinese American girls and their families. When fourth grader Sarah is assigned the role of special friend to Tina, a newly arrived immigrant from China, Sarah resents her. She is justly upset at her teacher's assumption that a shared first-culture heritage will make the girls friends. As Sarah and Tina get to know each other, they do become friends but not because they are both of Chinese origin. This story explores growing up and the immigrant experience, complete with incidents of subtle racism and the trauma of adjusting to new family circumstances.

Uma Krishnaswami looks at biculturalism from a different perspective in *Naming Maya* (I–A). In this story, a young Indian American girl travels from New Jersey to Chennai, in southern India, when her mother must return to sell her father's house. Not only does Maya have to contend with leaving her home and reconnecting with her friends in Chennai, but she is traveling with her mother, and they haven't really spoken much since her parents' bitter divorce. Once in India, Maya discovers a lot about herself and her family, and also learns that she can be herself in two very different parts of the world. A different look at this same issue, Jane Kurtz's *Jakarta Missing* (I–A) explores the realities of adjusting to life in the United States after living in Africa, and how this adjustment varies tremendously. Not everyone, it seems, can be happy in one place. The protagonist of Kashmira Sheth's *Blue Jasmine* (I) is also twelve, and she misses her home in India terribly when she and her family relocate to Iowa City, Iowa. Both of these books offer realistic yet hopeful depictions of the challenges that learning to live in a new culture can create.

An Na's Printz Award–winning *A Step from Heaven* (A) tells the story of Young Ju's wrenching departure from Korea and her beloved grandmother, her childhood and adolescence in the United States, and her eventual triumph over her abusive father and the grinding poverty that has plagued her family. Told in a series of short, present-tense, first-person narratives, this story has an immediacy that almost compels readers to feel the emotions with which Young Ju wrestles.

Many of the series books discussed earlier explore growing up—some, like the **Clementine** series, with humor. Other writers turn to humor as well. Louis Sachar underscores the funny yet poignant process of growing up in novels for intermediate-grade readers, such as *There's a Boy in the Girls' Bathroom* (I) and his Newbery Medal winner, *Holes* (I). This book breaks

many of the rules—it is both contemporary and historical; the characters are ludicrous; the circumstances are implausible; there are too many coincidences; and it's not truly realistic—which serves only to heighten the humor. By the end of the story, readers are cheering for Stanley Yelnats and laughing as they do. Humor is relatively scarce in contemporary realistic fiction for adolescent readers, however, with most books exploring serious issues from a serious perspective.

Peer Relationships

Part of growing up involves learning to interact with ever-widening worlds and with a wide variety of people. These relationships run the gamut from enmity to close friendship to romance. Books that explore peer relationships mirror many of the concerns that young readers have about their own lives. Today's books explore a wide range of relationships among peers: some characters are noble, some are loyal, but most are simply ordinary beings. Because young people value acceptance by their friends, they are highly susceptible to peer pressure. Books reflect their vulnerability and their strengths.

In *Ten Miles Past Normal* (I–A), Frances O'Roark Dowell tells the story of a perfectly normal girl who finds herself feeling anything but normal in her first month of high school. We take a close look at that story here.

* * *

A CLOSE LOOK AT
Ten Miles Past Normal

The setting in Frances O'Roark Dowell's *Ten Miles Past Normal* is a familiar one to many teens: a small town, bordered by rural areas, with a large consolidated high school drawing adolescents from across the county. No wonder that Janie is having a difficult time settling in to her new high school life. And of course, she doesn't have lunch with any of her friends from middle school. What makes things even worse is going to school with a clump of straw in her hair or, the opening scene in the novel, the day she got on the bus wearing shoes reeking of goat poop.

As Janie tells the story of the beginning of her high school experience, we discover that she used to be "normal," before she talked her parents into moving to the small farm where they raise goats. Her father is a college professor, her mother now embraces living close to nature and blogs about it, and her little sister is at that cute stage that makes her hard to live with. Beginning high school is not what Janie expected, and she does what many adolescents do when their lunch period isn't shared by any of their friends—she hides out in the library. She also goes along with her best friend and joins a music group that jams together one afternoon a week, hoping that they will become friends with a cute guy who smiles at them in the halls. What she finds at "jam band" is not what she expected. Instead of "cute guy," she is befriended by a very tall senior named "Monster," who teaches her to play bass guitar. At the same time, she is working with her best friend on a school project, and this time *she* is the one who came up with the idea to focus on Mrs. Brown, an older woman who was part of the local civil rights movement. None of the things that happen to Janie are remarkable. What is remarkable is her voice.

As Janie narrates her story, we come to know her well. She is philosophical and articulate. She also talks to the goats that she milks every morning, having funny, insightful conversations with her favorite. She loves her parents even though they embarrass her frequently and seem to have failed to see that she is no longer a child. She is lonely, but she works to change that. Slowly, she does, meeting a new friend during lunch in the library, getting to know the people in Jam Band, and spending time with Mrs. Brown, who teachers her about quiet courage.

Janie is aware she is just a small part of the world, but that she can "live large," can make a difference in the world. As she tells us, ". . . that's when I feel the big feeling again—the one I felt the first time I picked up Monster's bass—that strange sense that I'm becoming larger. Just by sitting here listening. Just by understanding how large a person's life can be" (Dowell, p. 139). This theme of growing up and becoming a part of the broader world is integral to this story. So, too, is becoming your own person and embracing your own uniqueness. Janie learns to assert herself with her best friend, pursuing her own interests while staying friends. She also comes to embrace her "Farm World" identity. When Verbana, Janie's library friend, tells her that she's "ten miles past normal," Janie thinks: "I've realized that when you move beyond normal, the road you're on doesn't necessarily take you to the land of the abnormal or the weird or the freakish. Instead you might find yourself in a place where people build Freedom Schools and have the courage to live large. It's a place where people don't worry too much when they get a little goat poop on their shoes" (Dowell, 208–209). Janie has a philosophical yet quietly humorous voice. Not normal, perhaps, but she is someone most young adolescents might want to get to know.

Many picture storybooks involve making new friends, going to school, and learning to share are some of the things that children learn to do as they widen their circle of friends. Other books about peer relationships are series chapter books that offer humor as well as reassurance that boys and girls are not alone in their feelings. These "school stories," form a solid foundation for the more complex stories and relationships that students will encounter as they mature.

P R O F I L E

Frances O'Roark Dowell

dvice to young writers: Read, read, read, write, write, write. You have to practice to get good at writing. So if you're serious about writing, make time to write every day. If you don't know what to write about, write about your life. Keep a journal. Do character sketches of people you go to school with.

Frances O'Roark Dowell readily admits to not being perfect. On her website, she confesses to young writers that her first drafts need a lot of work, and she does a lot of revision. She does her work on a computer, often writing at night after her children are asleep. She finds ideas everywhere, what she reads, her own life experiences, and odd things she thinks about as she's going about her daily life. She has a richly varied life to think about. Born in Germany to a father in the armed services, she has also lived in Virginia, Kansas, Texas, Massachusetts, Tennessee, and several towns in North Carolina. She, her husband, and their two sons now live in Durham, North Carolina.

Frances's books include ***Dovey Coe*** (I–A), which won the Edgar Award, the bestselling ***The Secret Language of Girls*** and its sequel ***The Kind of Friends We Used to Be*** (both I–A), and ***Shooting the Moon*** (I–A), which was awarded the Christopher Medal.

To learn more about Frances, go to CengageBrain.com to access the Education CourseMate website where you will find links to relevant websites.

Sometimes school stories are serious. The protagonist in A. S. King's **Everybody Sees the Ants** (A) endures daily bullying at school. His lack of self-confidence and family problems become too much for the ironically named Lucky to bear, and he escapes into dreams about his grandfather, who was missing in action in Vietnam, dreams from which he emerges as if he had really been with his grandfather, sometimes clutching an object, such as his grandfather's wedding band. Lost when his grandfather was lost, the ring opens up a new relationship with his father just as the story ends. Lisa Yee's **Warp Speed** (I–A) also involves bullying. Marley, a seventh-grade student, is the object of verbal and physical torment, the physical traces of which are easy to hide from his mother, who is blind. And Marley himself feels invisible. The challenges of middle school are realistically portrayed in this very readable novel. Yee's other books, such as **Millicent Min, Girl Genius** and **Stanford Wong Flunks Big-Time** also explore life at Rancho Rosetta Middle School with both seriousness and humor.

Esme Raji Codell's **Sahara Special** and **Sing a Song of Tuna Fish: Hard-to-Swallow Stories from Fifth Grade** (I) are wonderfully funny school stories. Steven Herrick's **Naked Bunyip Dancing** (I–A), discussed previously as a novel in verse, reveals the emotions of students in one class, often humorously, and Andrew Clements offers a funny story about twin boys who are beginning the sixth grade in **Lost and Found** (I).

Friendships in as well as out of school are the subject of many books for young readers. Kate DiCamillo and Alison McGhee's **Bink & Gollie** (P) is a funny but true-to-life look at a friendship between two very different girls. Their different personalities are amplified by Tony Fucile's illustrations, which also convey a significant part of the story line. With three chapters and eighty-two pages, this accessible book appeals to readers moving beyond picturebooks but not quite ready for full-length novels. Gary Paulsen's **Masters of Disaster** (I) is a hilarious tale of the ridiculous antics of three boys told in a brief chapter book. In his **Liar, Liar: The Theory, Practice, and Destructive Properties of Deception** (I), the protagonist gets himself into serious predicaments with his outrageous lies, but because he's a nice kid at heart, he redeems himself and even creates a new and much improved family dynamic. This, and the sequel, **Flat Broke** (I) are brief chapter books, with common and believable problems solved in a realistic, yet humorous manner.

In **The Cruisers: Checkmate** (I), the second book of his **The Cruisers** series, Walter Dean Myers depicts the relationships among four friends, all students at a Harlem, New York middle school for gifted and talented kids. Dana Reinhardt's **The Summer I Learned to Fly** (I–A) also relies on strong characterization. Drew is in that endless summer between seventh and eighth grades, a loner at loose ends until she meets Emmett in the alley behind her mother's cheese shop. As the first real friendship of her life blooms, Drew learns to take a chance and move beyond her rather restricted comfort zone to help a friend.

Grace Lin's **The Year of the Rat** (I) presents the distress that Pacy feels when her best friend moves and her new friends don't really act like friends. Pacy is Chinese, and she is acutely aware of the fact that she is now the only Asian American student in the school. Kevin Henkes's **Bird Lake Moon** (I) is a quiet book that follows two young boys as they tentatively begin a friendship during a summer vacation even as they are each struggling with serious family problems— divorce in one case and death in the other. Jacqueline Woodson's Newbery Honor book, **After Tupac and D Foster** (A) depicts a close friendship among three young adolescent girls and their close connection to the music of Tupac Shakur, whose lyrics inspire the girls to discover their own "big purpose" in life.

Romance is often part of growing up, and the beginnings of romantic feelings for another is a strand in many novels for intermediate-grade readers, the best of which have multilayered themes. Martha, the protagonist in Kevin Henkes's **Olive's Ocean** (I), a Newbery Honor winner, is twelve; she is about to spend the summer at her grandmother's house in Cape Cod when she is given a diary entry written by Olive, a recently deceased classmate, in which Olive had written that she had hoped to become Martha's friend. This affects how Martha thinks about herself, her life, her peers, and the world. As she wonders about what might have been, she is thrust into what will be as she awakens to her first crush and to the truth that her beloved grandmother is getting old. Martha's realization that she is not the center of the universe is compellingly perceptive.

Sometimes an interest in romance becomes dangerous. In **Speak** (A), Laurie Halse Andersen explores some of the emotional consequences of date-rape. Sharon Flake uses the medium of the short story in **Who Am I without Him? Short Stories about Girls and the Boys in Their Lives** (A) to explore identity and romance. This is a hard-hitting look at the dynamics of love relationships for black adolescents. In the ten first-person narratives that make up this collection, we see girls both weak and strong as they are engaged in figuring out how romantic relationships can work in today's world. Pete Hautman's **The Big Crunch** (A) is an unusual romance story in that it depicts a relationship that, on the surface, is not at all romantic. The action occurs across one year, beginning in the fall, and readers are privy to both Wes and June's thoughts. Told from a third-person limited point of view, the novel, like their relationship, unfolds calmly but compellingly.

Just as sexual identity has become part of the dialogue in the United States, it has also become part of literature for young readers. Although there are a few contemporary realistic fiction picturebooks for younger readers that attempt to help children develop tolerance for different lifestyles, none are without flaws. There are, however, a number of excellent contemporary realistic novels for adolescent readers that explore gender identity.

Jacqueline Woodson's *From the Notebooks of Melanin Sun* and *The House You Pass on the Way* (A) grapple with identity issues involving sexual preference and race in contemporary culture. David Levithan, in *Boy Meets Boy* (A), creates a setting in which homosexuality is no big deal, a setting in which he can then explore typical high school love relationship issues, only with gay characters. David LaRochelle's *Absolutely, Positively Not . . .* (A) is both humorous and heartwarming as sixteen-year-old Steven realizes that he is gay and that it is okay to be gay. The reactions of his friends and family are reassuringly supportive.

As children mature, their relationships become more complex. Often the unevenness of the onset of adolescence creates gulfs between good friends: one is interested in the opposite sex, one isn't; one is physically mature, one isn't. Adolescence also brings with it increasing pressures to experiment with the dangerous side of life—drugs and alcohol, sex, brushes with the law—and books for advanced readers often contain characters who struggle with a personal crisis as they seek to stand up for what they value and at the same time maintain their friendships.

Growing up is difficult for most, and special challenges can make it even more difficult to negotiate the world of school, friends, and family. A small but growing number of books for children demonstrate society's increasing awareness of the emotional and physical demands and accomplishments of those with exceptionalities. The trend in the field has shifted from nearly absolute neglect, to the appearance of occasional secondary characters, to the occasional book in which the main character has special needs. In today's literature, people's attitudes toward individuals with special needs are not always positive and do not always improve. At the same time, however, we also find many books in which characters with exceptionalities are loved and cherished by their families. We also find books in which the protagonists with special needs are not passive; instead, they are often heroes. The International

Board on Books for Youth (IBBY) has a list of excellent international books about characters with special needs, and the Schneider Family Award was established to recognize the best books about characters with special needs. To learn more about this award, go to CengageBrain.com to access the Education CourseMate website, where you will find links to relevant websites pertaining to these resources.

The protagonist in Sharon Draper's *Out of My Mind* (I–A) has a loving and supportive family, but no one at school knows that she has a photographic memory or how very intelligent she is because she has severe cerebral palsy. It is not until Melody gets a computer that can speak for her that her intelligence is recognized, and she becomes much more connected to the outside world. This outside world is not always kind, however, and prejudice against people with disabilities causes a teacher and classmates to do something that robs Melody of an honor she has earned. Even that does not stop her, and she confronts her teacher and her classmates.

Some books explore specific learning challenges. Jack Gantos writes from the point of view of a young boy with attention deficit hyperactivity disorder (ADHD) in the popular **Joey Pigza** books (I). Gantos's breathless run-on sentences leave readers almost as frantic as Joey. The first-person point of view allows peers and adults to glimpse what life might be like for children with this disorder. *Joey Pigza Loses Control* is a 2001 Newbery Honor book; *I Am Not Joey Pigza* (I) is a surprise fourth book in what was billed as a trilogy. The protagonist of Patricia Reilly Giff's *Eleven* (I) can't read words, is afraid of the number eleven, and finds an old newspaper clipping that triggers fragments of frightening memories. Because he is unable to read, he enlists a new girl at school, an avid reader, to help him uncover the secrets of his past.

In Pat Schmatz's *Bluefish* (A), Travis has completely tuned out of school. Who could blame him given that he's always been identified as "stupid" and has grown up feeling angry and alone. When he meets an unusual girl, who calls herself Velveeta, and a compassionate and generous teacher, he begins to feel that he just might not be so stupid after all, as he learns to read both books and his world.

Two picturebooks, Aliki's *Marianthe's Story: Painted Words, Spoken Memories* (P) and Helen Recorvitz's *My Name Is Yoon* (P), consider how young children adjust to life in an American school when they move with their families from another country. Although these books are suitable for primary-grade children, they can certainly be the beginning of a conversation about the topic with older children as well. In *Clara Lee and the Apple Pie*

Dream (P–I), written by Jenny Han with illustrations by Julia Kuo, a young Korean American third grader learns that hard work and good decisions trump blind luck as she competes for the honor of being "Miss Apple Pie," in spite worrying that her Korean heritage makes her not quite American enough. This is the first in what readers hope will become a series.

Family Relationships

Family relationships are also important to children and adolescents, and contemporary books present varied pictures of family life. These books portray not only two-parent families but also communal, one-parent, and extended families, families headed by divorced or separated parents, families headed by homosexual parents, and children living alone without adults. As traditional, culturally assigned roles have evolved and changed, so too have books for young readers.

Family stories have changed in other ways as well. Fathers receive increasing attention in books for children and adolescents; where they had once been ignored, they are now recognized as viable literary characters. Fictional mothers now run the full range of likeable to despicable characters, just as they do in real life. Contemporary realistic fiction also considers such subjects as sibling rivalry or learning to accept stepsisters or stepbrothers. In addition to happy, well-adjusted children from safe, loving homes, there are children who are victims of child abuse, abandonment, alcoholism, neglect, and a whole range of society's ills. These characters are often cynical, bitter, disillusioned, and despondent, but also can be courageous and strong.

The charming new series of chapter books by Atinuke about family life in modern Africa, offers young readers the wonderful opportunity to experience life as **Anna Hibiscus** does. Anna lives in a large extended family in "Amazing Africa." In the third book in the series, *Good Luck, Anna Hibiscus!* (P–I), she helps other children weather a drought; the fourth, *Have Fun, Anna Hibiscus!* (P–I), finds her flying to Canada to spend time with her white grandmother, a stranger to her. Illustrations by Lauren Tobia capture Anna's spirit perfectly. Atinuke and Tobia work with a picturebook format to present *Anna Hibiscus' Song* (N–P), in which she discovers how others in her family express their happiness and realizes that she does it by bursting into song. The series is based on the author's own childhood in Nigeria.

Jacqueline Woodson's picturebook, *Pecan Pie Baby* (P), illustrated by Sophie Blackall tells an old story in a new way. Young Gia is less than thrilled about her single-mother's pregnancy and isn't happy at the way mention of it seems to invade every aspect of her life. Her voice is authentic, and readers young and old will understand her reluctance to overcome the impending arrival of the "ding dang baby." The relationship between Gia and her mother is clearly loving and calm. Similarly, John Coy's *Two Old Potatoes and Me* (P) celebrates the relationship between fathers and children, even in divorce.

Julia Alvarez has four books in her **Tía Lola** series, *How Tía Lola Came to Visit Stay, How Tía Lola Learned to Teach, How Tía Lola Saved the Summer*, and *How Tía Lola Ended Up Starting Over* (all I). Tía Lola is a composite of all of the wonderful aunts that Alvarez grew up with, and these stories are full of warmth and humor.

The Penderwick family—four girls and their widowed father—first appeared in Jeanne Birdsall's *The Penderwicks: A Summer Tale of Four Sisters, Two Rabbits, and a Very Intersting Boy* (I), which won the National Book Award. In *The Penderwicks on Gardham Street* (I), the girls have grown up a bit and their father remarries. In *The Penderwicks at Point Mouette* (I), three of the sisters and their friend, Jeffrey, go on vacation in Maine with their beloved aunt, while the oldest sister goes with a friend to the shore and father and his wife and baby head to England. To Skye, the second oldest sister, this separation of the family is frightening, and she struggles to be the responsible sister-in-charge. *Lexie* (P–I), by Audrey Couloumbis, portrays the conflicting emotions of ten-year-old Lexie, whose family has changed dramatically. Her parents have divorced and, instead of spending time with her father in their beach house, she has to welcome his fiancé and her two sons.

Most families aren't perfect, even when they appear to be, as Gary Schmidt depicts in *Trouble* (I–A). The Smith family has a perfect life—a beautiful house in a beautiful setting, important ancestors, and three achievement-oriented children. The oldest, Franklin, is admired by all, most of whom fail to notice that he is arrogant and a bully, especially in the way he treats his younger brother, Henry. When Franklin is terribly injured in an automobile accident and his older sister withdraws to her room, Henry begins to understand that trouble can find anyone, anywhere.

Nikki Grimes explores the idea of home and family in *The Road to Paris* (I–A), winner of a Coretta Scott King Honor Award, in which young Paris is separated from her brother, Malcolm, when they are abandoned yet again by their mother. Sent to a foster family that lives outside of New York City, which had always been her home, biracial Paris initially has trouble fitting in and making friends; she certainly is not going to learn to love her new family. Of course, she eventually does, and she also learns to feel proud of her own accomplishments and make friends. When her mother reappears, repentant and seemingly responsible, Paris must make a difficult decision—does she join her mother and be reunited with her beloved brother, or does she stay with the foster family she has come to feel a part of?

The situation that Rits, a thirteen-year-old Dutch boy, finds himself in is dire. His mother is in a mental institution, his father is off with his girlfriend, and Rits is sent to a depressed and neglectful uncle's house for the summer. In spite of this, the humor in Mariken Jongman's *Rits* (A), realized through the protagonist's approach to the world, makes this a buoyant, moving story.

The protagonist of Claudia Mills's *The Totally Made-Up Civil War Diary of Amanda MacLeish* (I) is struggling with turmoil at home, desperately wishing that her parents would stay together, that things would be like they used to be. This struggle is mirrored in the school assignment she is working on, a diary of a fictional girl whose brothers fight on opposite sides of a war. In Audrey Couloumbis's *Jake* (I), the ten-year-old protagonist is living a happy, well-adjusted life with his mother when she ends up in the hospital and his life turns upside down. As he adjusts to his estranged grandfather's presence and is surrounded by help from friends and neighbors, he learns an important lesson about what family means.

A serious look at what it means to be a family is also found in Berlie Doherty's *The Girl Who Saw Lions* (A). Rosa's mother wants to adopt a child of Tanzanian heritage, and Rosa is worried about what that will mean for her. In Tanzania, Abela's mother dies of AIDS and she is smuggled into England by her uncle, who intends to sell her; when she wanders into a school, though, Abela is saved from that fate. Eventually, she and Rosa become sisters. Told through first-person narratives of Rosa and Abela, and Abela's third-person adult narrative, the story is unflinching in its depiction of the horrors that Abela suffered.

Family forms and reforms, and, sometimes, new relationships are forged. In Naomi Hirahara's *1001 Cranes* (A), twelve-year-old Angela Kato is sent to Los Angeles to live with her aunt and grandparents because her parents are on the brink of divorce. Of course, she does not want to go and so arrives with a great deal of resentment. She works in the family's flower shop, where they sell 1001 crane displays. As time passes Angela's resentment melts and her self-esteem grows, and she develops a relationship with her prickly grandmother. Jackie Brown's *Little Cricket* (I) recounts the story of a twelve-year-old Hmong girl who flees her home in Laos for a refugee camp in Thailand and three years later immigrates to St. Paul, Minnesota, with her older brother and grandfather. Their adjustment to life in America is not easy as their family structures and expectations are severely challenged in their new environment.

In the Printz Honor book *Stuck in Neutral* (A), an unusual and disturbing novel, Terry Trueman takes readers inside the mind of Shawn, a very bright boy with very bad cerebral palsy—he cannot control his muscles, which means he cannot speak. Those around him think he is profoundly developmentally disabled, but instead he has the gift of almost total recall of everything he hears. He's afraid that his father is planning to kill him, and he's telling us his story. Trueman informs readers in an afterword that he has a son who is very much like the protagonist in this novel. In a companion novel, *Cruise Control* (A), Trueman tells the other story, the story of the healthy and talented brother and his conflicted feelings about living with Shawn. A third novel, *Inside Out* (A), is a disturbing portrait of a young man with adolescent-onset schizophrenia.

Mark Haddon won the 2003 Whitbread Book of the Year Award for his portrayal of a young man with Asperger's, a syndrome on the autism spectrum, in *The Curious Incident of the Dog in the Night-Time* (A). Haddon wisely decides to tell Christopher's story through Christopher's own eyes, and readers are privy to both the obsession and the brilliance of his mind. As he pursues the solution to the mystery behind the killing of his neighbor's dog, he discovers things about his parents that destroy the world as he has always known it. At the same time, he discovers his own strength. Interestingly, this crossover book is marketed for both adult and adolescent audiences. In Siobhan Dowd's *The London Eye Mystery* (A), discussed previously, the protagonist has Asperger's syndrome, and his logical, literal brain helps him successfully solve the mystery. Ten-year-old Caitlin, protagonist of Kathryn Erskine's National Book Award–winning *Mockingbird* (I) also has Asperger's syndrome. Her older brother, who was her champion, the person who explained the world when she was confused, has died, and her single father is unable to cope. As Caitlin struggles with her relationships to the outside world, but especially to her father, she helps him learn how to heal.

The protagonist in Joan Bauer's *Close to Famous* (I) has managed to disguise her inability to read or write by memorizing everything she hears. In this way she has taught herself to be a wonderful baker, and it is this skill that not only helps her adjust to life in a new place, but also puts her in a situation in which she can get the help she needs.

Dyscalculia is the main problem for Kathryn Erskine's fourteen-year-old protagonist in **The Absolute Value of Mike** (I–A) in which the conflict between father, a mathematician, and son, who struggles with math, is resolved over an unusual summer. Living with his elderly great aunt and uncle isn't what Mike thought it would be like, but it turns out to be exactly what he needs to help him discover his own value.

In Jennifer Richard Jacobson's **Small as an Elephant** (I), the young protagonist has spent years trying to protect his mentally unstable mother. Jack awakes in a campground in Acadia National Park,

Maine, to find that she has left him alone. Afraid that authorities might take him away from her, he attempts to get himself home to Boston. When he finds his grandmother waiting for him in southern Maine, he discovers that his mother can be helped and that he has a home to wait in until she's ready to be with him again.

Just as in life, sometimes the families of fictional protagonists are torn apart by war. The war in Iraq is part of the setting for Nora Raleigh Baskin's **The Summer before Boys** (I) in which best friends who are also aunt and niece are in that in-between

TEACHING IDEA 7.4

Mirror Texts for English Learners

ELL

COMMON CORE STATE STANDARDS This Teaching Idea does not address specific Common Core English Language Arts standards but does represent best practices in teaching the English Language Arts as identified by the National Council of Teachers of English and the International Reading Association.

In multiethnic, multilingual classes, children's literature is a powerful tool. Chosen carefully, books used in the classroom can convey a message of inclusiveness and welcome to students who might otherwise feel like outsiders in the English speaking context of most US schools. Children's books can accurately represent a child's cultural background, include his or her home language, and/or explore ideas and issues such as immigration, language learning, or accepting cultural differences. Books such as these stimulate discussion among children and invite English language learners to share their own stories. As students who are so often marginalized, it is vital that they also have the opportunity to see that their languages and cultures are important enough to be included in books, and that they, themselves, have important expertise to share with their classmates.

Here are some titles to begin an inclusive classroom collection.

Ada, Alama Flor, **Gathering the Sun: An Alphabet in Spanish and English** (1997)

Aliki, **Marianthe's Story: Painted Words and Spoken Memories** (1998)

Applegate, Katherine, **Home of the Brave** (2008)

Bunting, Eve, **A Day's Work** (1997)

———, **One Green Apple** (2006)

Cheng, Andrea, **Grandfather Counts** (2003)

Choi, Yangsook, **The Name Jar** (2003)

Cummings, Mary, **Three Names of Me** (2006)

Deitz Shea, Pegi, **The Whispering Cloth** (1996)

Ho, Minfong, **Hush! A Thai Lullaby** (2000)

Kurtz, Jane, **Fire on the Mountain** (1998)

Kyuchukov, Hristo, **My Name Was Hussein** (2004)

Levine, Ellen, **I Hate English!** (1995)

Look, Lenore, **Uncle Peter's Amazing Chinese Wedding** (2006)

McDonnell, Christine, **Goyangi Means Cat** (2011)

Mobin-Uddin, Asma, **The Best Eid Ever** (2007)

Nobisso, Josephine, **In English, of Course** (2003)

Parry, Florence H. & Ted Lewin, **Day of Ahmed's Secret** (1995)

Perez, Amada Irma, **My Diary from Here to There/Mi diario de aqui hasta alla** (2009)

Recorvits, Helen, **My Name Is Yoon** (2003)

Shihab Nye, Naomi, **Sitti's Secrets** (1997)

Williams, Karen Lynn, **My Name Is Sangoel** (2009)

Wolf, Bernard, **Coming to America: A Muslim Family's Story** (2003)

time of thirteen. As if that weren't enough stress, Julia's mother is sent to Iraq and she goes to live with Eliza's family. Not only is her mother gone, but Julia is also putting childhood behind her and taking tentative steps into adulthood. In **Alice Bliss** (A), by Laura Harrington, the main character is also on the cusp of womanhood and very close to her father. When he is shipped to Iraq after joining the National Guard, her world is shaken as she must learn how to live without him.

The categories under which we loosely group contemporary realistic fiction are only a convenient way to discuss this genre. Every book belongs in multiple categories, be it format, subgenre, or theme. Taken as a whole, contemporary realistic fiction is as richly diverse as our society, reflecting the varied lives of young people today. It is also a wonderful resource for creating a message of inclusiveness and welcome for all students. Teaching Idea 7.4 suggests some picturebooks that teachers of all might find useful as a starting point for discussing inclusiveness. Other books and authors can be found in Chapter 1, as well as Chapters 3 through 10.

Contemporary Realistic Fiction in the Classroom

Young readers enjoy contemporary realistic fiction, and this genre is often a way to entice reluctant readers to taste the joys of a good book. These books are often passed around from reader to reader as children discover themselves in the pages. Such books can also open windows on other people and other worlds, offering children the opportunity to "try on" other lives for the period of time it takes them to read a book and to ponder it later. Reading contemporary realistic fiction stories that are set in different locales, contain characters that are culturally diverse, and explore the lives of a variety of people helps young readers learn about others. Knowing that not everyone is like ourselves expands our worlds. Understanding that there are many ways to think about the world allows us to grow as human beings. Knowing people from diverse cultures through books is a first step toward building a global perspective for an increasingly global world. Engaging with varied contemporary realistic fiction is an effective way to develop understanding and tolerance. It is also a first step toward recognizing our common humanity—the wishes, fears, and needs we all share, regardless of culture.

Any well-stocked classroom library contains many contemporary realistic fiction titles. These books should represent a wide range of reading levels, a diversity of authors, and a range of types and themes. Handing a reluctant reader just the right book is a powerful experience, and often that book is a piece of realistic fiction. Realistic fiction also generates interesting class and small group discussions. Comparing books of similar types or themes can help students learn about literature as they closely examine how different authors approach comparable tasks. Reading a wide range of books can also help students develop knowledge of their own preferences as readers. Experiences with contemporary realistic fiction can also give them the opportunity to develop their critical stance as they learn to view protagonists' choices in the light of the setting and events of the story. This, in turn helps readers understand that who they are and what they do determines, in part, what happens to them, and that they are in turn influenced by the things that happen, thus extending an understanding of the "unity of character and action" to their own lives.

Having many titles on hand means that teachers can readily incorporate realistic fiction in thematic units, building on students' interests or curricular demands by making available numerous appropriate and timely books.

Fine contemporary realistic fiction rings with truth. It offers readers multiple lenses through which to view the world and themselves, allowing them to become finer people—more compassionate, more knowledgeable, more heroic than they are in real life. Realistic fiction can be the mirror and the window in which we readers see our better selves.

SUMMARY

Books of contemporary realistic fiction are plausible stories set in today's world. The characters often seem like people we know, and the plots consist of events and actions that can and do occur in everyday life. Realistic fiction includes early chapter books, novels in verse, and graphic novels. Series books are extremely popular with young readers, each with a memorable character who ties the books together. Realistic fiction also includes subgenres such as adventure stories, animal stories, mysteries and thrillers, and sports stories. Contemporary realism explores a number of themes, including growing up, peer and family relationships, and other contemporary, sometimes sensitive, issues. Children enjoy realistic fiction, and teachers find these books an essential part of a classroom library.

Booklist

Although there are some picturebooks included in this list, many more can be found in the booklist for Chapter 3.

✳ Indicates some aspect of diversity

Adventure and Survival

Creech, Sharon, **The Wanderer** (2000) (I–A)

Dillon, Eilis, **The Lost Island** (1954/2006) (I)

Ellis, Deborah, **No Ordinary Day** (2011) (I–A)

✳ George, Jean Craighead, **Julie of the Wolves** (1972) (A)

_____, **My Side of the Mountain** (1959) (A)

McCaughrean, Geraldine, **White Darkness** (2007) (A)

✳ Mickelson, Ben, **Red Midnight** (2002) (I)

Paulsen, Gary, **Brian's Return** (1999) (I–A)

_____, **Brian's Winter** (1996) (I–A)

_____, **Dog Song** (1985) (I–A)

_____, **Hatchet** (1987) (I–A)

Philbrick, Rodman, **The Young Man and the Sea** (2004) (I–A)

Salisbury, Graham, **Lord of the Deep** (2001) (I–A)

Seidler, Tor, **Brothers Below Zero** (2002) (I)

Sloan, Holly Goldberg, **I'll Be There** (2011) (A)

Smith, Roland, **Peak** (2007) (I)

Wilson, N. D., **Leepike Ridge** (2007) (I)

✳ Woods, Brenda, **Saint Louis Armstrong Beach** (2011) (I–A)

Animal Stories

Castillo, Lauren, **Melvin and the Boy** (2011) (P)

Daly, Cathleen, **Prudence Wants a Pet** (2011) (P)

DiCamillo, Kate, **Because of Winn-Dixie** (2000) (I)

Farley, Walter, **The Black Stallion** (1947/2008) (I–A)

Haas, Jessie, **Runaway Radish** (2001) (I)

Hearne, Betsy, **The Canine Connection: Stories about Dogs and People** (2003) (A)

Hurwitz, Johanna, **One Small Dog** (2000) (I)

Naylor, Phyllis Reynolds, **Shiloh** (1991) (I–A)

Resau, Laura, **Star in the Forest** (2010) (I)

Rodowsky, Colby, **Not My Dog** (1999) (P–I)

Mystery Stories/Thrillers

Balliett, Blue, **Chasing Vermeer** (2004) (I)

Beaty, Andrea, **Cicada Summer** (2008) (I)

Bloor, Thomas, **The Memory Prisoner** (2000) (A)

Bowler, Tim, **Storm Catchers** (2003) (A)

Brooks, Kevin, **Black Rabbit Summer** (2008) (A)

Cormier, Robert, **The Rag and Bone Shop** (2001) (A)

✳ Dowd, Siobhan, **The London Eye Mystery** (2008) (I–A)

Feinstein, John, **Cover-Up: Mystery at the Super Bowl** (2007) (I)

Fienberg, Anna, **Number 8** (2007) (A)

Hahn, Mary Downing, **All the Lovely Bad Ones** (2008) (I–A)

Hiaasen, Carl, **Hoot** (2002) (I)

Konigsburg, E. L., **From the Mixed-Up Files of Mrs. Basil E. Frankweiler** (1967) (I)

_____, **Silent to the Bone** (2000) (A)

Parker, Robert, **The Boxer and the Spy** (2008) (A)

Plum-Ucci, Carol, **The Body of Christopher Creed** (2000) (A)

Stewart, Trenton Lee, **The Mysterious Benedict Society and the Perilous Journey** (2008) (I)

Van Draanen, Wendelin, **Sammy Keyes and the Hollywood Mummy** (2001) (I)

_____, **Sammy Keyes and the Psycho Kitty Queen** (2004) (I)

Werlin, Nancy, **Double Helix** (2004) (A)

_____, **The Rules of Survival** (2008) (A)

Sports Stories

Coy, John, **Box Out** (2008) (A)

_____, **Crackback** (2007) (A)

Cochrane, Mick, **The Girl Who Threw Butterflies** (2009) (I)

Crutcher, Chris, **Deadline** (2007) (A)

_____, **Whale Talk** (2001) (A)

Deuker, Carl, **Gym Candy** (2007) (A)

Koertge, Ron, **Shakespeare Bats Cleanup** (2003) (I–A)

_____, **Shakespeare Makes the Playoffs** (I–A)

Lipsyte, Robert, **The Contender** (1997) (A)

_____, **Yellow Flag** (2007) (A)

Lynch, Chris, **Iceman** (1994) (A)

_____, **Shadow Boxer** (1993) (A)

✳ Myers, Walter Dean, **Slam!** (1996) (A)

Powell, Randy, **Run If You Dare** (2001) (A)

_____, **Three Clams and an Oyster** (2002) (A)

Russo, Marisabina, **House of Sports** (2002) (I)

Williams, Michael, **Now Is the Time for Running** (2011) (A)

Coming of Age

✳ Atkins, Catherine, **Alt Ed** (2003) (A)

Bauer, Cat, **Harley, Like a Person** (2000) (A)

Bauer, Joan, *Hope Was Here* (2000) (A)

_____, *Stand Tall* (2002) (A)

Bauer, Marion Dane, *On My Honor* (1986) (A)

Blume, Judy, *Are You There God? It's Me, Margaret* (1970) (I)

Clements, Andrew, *The Janitor's Boy* (2000) (I)

_____, *Troublemaker* (2011) (I-A)

Creech, Sharon, *Granny Torrelli Makes Soup* (2003) (I)

_____, *Love that Dog* (2001) (I)

_____, *Walk Two Moons* (1994) (I-A)

Cummings, Priscilla, *Red Kayak* (2004) (I-A)

Dessen, Sarah, *The Truth about Forever* (2004) (A)

Fergus, Maureen, *Exploits of a Reluctant (But Extremely Goodlooking) Hero* (2007) (I)

✳ Flake, Sharon, *Who Am I without Him? Short Stories about Girls and the Boys in Their Lives* (2004) (A)

Gantos, Jack, *Jack on the Tracks: Four Seasons of Fifth Grade* (1999) (I)

Gauthier, Gail, *Saving the Planet and Stuff* (2003) (A)

Graves, Bonnie, *No Copycats Allowed* (1998) (P)

_____, *Taking Care of Trouble* (2002) (P)

✳ Hamilton, Virginia, *Plain City* (1993) (A)

Hannigan, Katherine, *Ida B: . . . And Her Plans to Maximize Fun, Avoid Disaster and (Possibly) Save the World* (2004) (I)

_____, *True (— Sort Of)* (2011) (I)

Henkes, Kevin, *Olive's Ocean* (2003) (I)

✳ Johnson, Angela, *The First Part Last* (2003) (A)

✳ _____, *Gone from Home: Short Takes* (1998) (A)

✳ Jones, Traci L., *Silhouetted by the Blue* (2011) (I-A)

✳ Kim, Derek Kirk, *Good as Lily* (2007) (A)

Koertge, Ron, *Margaux with an X* (2006) (A)

_____, *Stoner and Spaz* (2002) (A)

Konigsburg, E. L., *The Outcasts of 19 Schuyler Place* (2004) (A)

Mass, Wendy, *Leap Day* (2004) (I-A)

McKay, Hilary, *The Exiles* (1991) (I-A)

_____, *The Exiles at Home* (1993) (I-A)

_____, *The Exiles in Love* (1998) (I-A)

✳ Myers, Walter Dean, *Monster* (1999) (A)

✳ _____, *145th Street Stories* (2000) (A)

Naylor, Phyllis Reynolds, *Almost Alice* (2008) (A)

_____, *Dangerously Alice* (2007) (A)

_____, *Lovingly Alice* (2004) (I)

Nelson, Theresa, *Ruby Electric* (2003) (I-A)

✳ Nilsson, Per, *Heart's Delight* (2003) (A)

Patron, Susan, *The Higher Power of Lucky* (2008) (I)

_____, *Lucky Breaks* (2009) (I)

_____, *Lucky for Good* (2011) (I)

Reinhardt, Dana, *The Summer I Learned to Fly* (2011) (A)

✳ Rosenberry, Vera, *Vera Rides a Bike* (2004) (P)

Sternberg, Julie, *Like Pickle Juice on a Cookie* (2011) (P)

Tolan, Stephanie, *Surviving the Applewhites* (2002) (I-A)

Weeks, Sarah, *Guy Time* (2000) (I)

Wolff, Virginia Euwer, *True Believer* (2001) (A)

Yee, Lisa, *Warp Speed* (2011) (I)

✳ Yum, Hyewon, *The Twins Blanket* (2011) (N)

Zephaniah, Benjamin, *Gangsta Rap* (2004) (I-A)

Challenges: Immigration, Race, Class

✳ Alexie, Sherman, *The Absolutely True Diary of a Part-Time Indian* (2007) (A)

✳ Aliki, *Marianthe's Story: Painted Words and Spoken Memories.* (1996) (P)

✳ Brown, Jackie, *Little Cricket* (2004) (I)

✳ Bruchac, Joseph, *The Heart of a Chief* (2001) (A)

✳ Cheng, Andrea, *Honeysuckle House* (2004) (I)

✳ Cofer, Judith Ortiz, *Call Me Maria* (2006) (I-A)

✳ Krishnaswami, Uma, *Naming Maya* (2004) (I-A)

✳ Kurtz, Jane, *Jakarta Missing* (2001) (I-A)

✳ Myers, Walter Dean, *Monster* (1999) (A)

✳ Na, An, *A Step from Heaven* (2001) (A)

✳ Perkins, Mitale, *Monsoon Summer* (2004) (I-A)

✳ Recorvitz, Helen, *My Name Is Yoon* (2003) (P)

✳ Sheth, Kashmira, *Blue Jasmine* (2004) (I)

✳ Smith, Cynthia Leitich, *Indian Shoes* (2002) (I)

✳ Soto, Gary, *Buried Onions* (2006) (A)

✳ Woods, Brenda, *Emako Blue* (2004) (I-A)

✳ Woodson, Jacqueline, *Miracle's Boys* (2000) (A)

Challenges: War

Cooney, Caroline B., *Diamonds in the Shadow* (2007) (A)

✳ Dorros, Arthur, *Under the Sun* (2004) (A)

✳ Ellis, Deborah, *The Breadwinner* (2004) (I)

✳ _____, *Parvanna's Journey* (2004) (I)

Hof, Marjolijn, *Against the Odds* (2011) (I-A)

Holmes, Sara Lewis, *Operation Yes* (2011) (I)

✳ Marsden, John, *Tomorrow, When the War Began* (1993) (A)

✳ _____, *While I Live* (2007) (A)

McCormick, Patricia, *Purple Heart* (2009) (A)

Parry, Rosanne, *Heart of a Shepherd* (2010) (I)

✳ Rosoff, Meg, *How I Live Now* (2004) (A)

Peer Relationships

✳ Alexie, Sherman, *The Absolutely True Diary of a Part-Time Indian* (2007) (A)

Anderson, Laurie Halse, *Speak* (1999) (A)

_____, *Twisted* (2007) (A)

Banks, Kate, *Lenny's Space* (2007) (I)

Bauer, Marion Dane, *The Double-Digit Club* (2004) (I)

Bloor, Edward, *Tangerine* (1997) (A)

Bradby, Marie, *Some Friend* (2004) (I)

Brande, Robin, *Evolution, Me & Other Freaks of Nature* (2007) (A)

Brashares, Ann, *The Second Summer of the Sisterhood* (2003) (A)

_____, *The Sisterhood of the Traveling Pants* (2001) (A)

✳ Choldenko, Gennifer, *If a Tree Falls at Lunch Period* (2007) (I)

Codell, Esme Raji, *Sahara Special* (2003) (I)

———, *Sing a Song of Tuna Fish: Hard-to-Swallow Stories from Fifth Grade* (2004) (I)

Dowell, Frances O'Roark, *Phineas L. MacGuire . . . Gets Slimed!* (2007) (P–I)

———, *The Secret Language of Girls* (2004) (I)

✳ Draper, Sharon, *The Battle of Jericho* (2003) (A)

Easton, Kelly, *White Magic: Spells to Hold You* (2007) (I)

✳ Fine, Anne, *Jamie and Angus Together* (2007) (P–I)

✳ Flake, Sharon, *Broken Bike Boy and the Queen of 33rd Street* (2007) (I)

Fredericks, Mariah, *Love* (2007) (I)

Gauthier, Gail, *A Girl, a Boy, and a Monster Cat* (2007) (P–I)

✳ Gipi, *Garage Band* (2007) (A)

Going, K. L., *Fat Kid Rules the World* (2003) (A)

✳ Graff, Lisa, *The Thing about Georgie* (2007) (I)

✳ Hamilton, Virginia, *Bluish* (1999) (I)

Henkes, Kevin, *Bird Lake Moon* (2008) (I)

✳ Herrick, Steven, *Naked Bunyip Dancing* (2008) (I–A)

Hickey, Caroline, *Cassie Was Here* (2007) (I)

Juster, Norton, *Neville* (2011) (P)

Kerrin, Jessica Scott, *Martin Bridge: Sound the Alarm!* (2007) (P–I)

Kimmell, Elizabeth Cody, *Visiting Miss Caples* (2000) (I–A)

Korman, Gordon, *No More Dead Dogs* (2000) (I)

Koss, Amy Goldman, *The Girls* (2000) (I–A)

✳ Lin, Grace, *The Year of the Rat* (2008) (I)

McGhee, Alison, *Snap* (2004) (I)

✳ McKay, Hilary, *Indigo's Star* (2003) (A)

O'Connor, Barbara, *Fame and Glory in Freedom, Georgia* (2003) (I)

O'Dell, Kathleen, *Ophie out of Oz* (2004) (I)

Paterson, Katherine, *Bridge to Terabithia* (1977) (I)

✳ ———, *Flip-Flop Girl* (1994) (I)

Peirce, Lincoln, *Big Nate on a Roll* (2011) (I)

Perkins, Lynn Rae, *All Alone in the Universe* (1999) (I–A)

———, *Criss Cross* (2005) (I–A)

Pyle, Kevin C., *Blindspot* (2007) (I)

Sachar, Louis, *Marvin Redpost #7: Super Fast, Out of Control!* (2000) (P)

———, *There's a Boy in the Girls' Bathroom* (1987) (I)

Schmatz, Pat, *Bluefish* (2011) (A)

✳ Seuling, Barbara, *Robert and the Happy Endings* (2007) (P–I)

✳ Sneve, Virginia Driving Hawk, *Lana's Lakota Moons* (2007) (I)

✳ Soto, Gary, *Mercy on these Teenage Chimps* (2007) (I)

Spinelli, Jerry, *Eggs* (2007) (I)

Tarshis, Lauren, *Emma-Jean Lazarus Fell out of a Tree* (2007) (I)

✳ Walter, Mildred Pitts, *Suitcase* (1999) (I)

Weaver, Will, *Defect* (2007) (A)

Wiles, Deborah, *Aurora County All-Stars* (2007) (I)

Wilson, Jacqueline, *Best Friends* (2008) (I)

✳ Woodson, Jacqueline, *After Tupac and D Foster* (2008) (A)

✳ ———, *I Hadn't Meant to Tell You This* (1994) (A)

✳ ———, *Last Summer with Maizon* (1990) (A)

✳ Yee, Lisa, *Millicent Min, Girl Genius* (2003) (I)

✳ Yoo, David, *The Detention Club* (2011) (I)

✳ Zimmer, Tracie Vaughn, *Reaching for Sun* (2007) (I)

Family Relationships

Avi & Rachel Vail, *Never Mind! A Twin Novel* (2004) (I)

Birdsall, Jeanne, *The Penderwicks on Gardam Street* (2008) (I)

Brooks, Bruce, *Vanishing* (1999) (I)

Brooks, Martha, *Being with Henry* (2000) (A)

Cart, Michael, *Necessary Noise: Stories about Our Families as They Really Are* (2003) (A)

✳ Cheng, Andrea, *The Key Collection* (2003) (P–I)

Clements, Andrew, *The School Story* (2001) (I)

Conly, Jane Leslie, *Trout Summer* (1995) (I)

———, *While No One Was Watching* (1998) (I–A)

Couloumbis, Audrey, *Getting Near to Baby* (1999) (I)

———, *Lexie* (2011) (I)

Creech, Sharon, *Heartbeat* (2004) (I)

✳ ———, *Ruby Holler* (2002) (I)

Dessen, Sarah, *Dreamland* (2000) (A)

Doherty, Berlie, *The Girl Who Saw Lions* (2008) (A)

✳ Fine, Anne, *The Jamie and Angus Stories* (2002) (P)

Fleischman, Paul, *Seek* (2001) (A)

✳ Fletcher, Ralph, *Uncle Daddy* (2001) (I)

Flinn, Alex, *Nothing to Lose* (2004) (A)

Giff, Patricia Reilly, *Pictures of Hollis Woods* (2002) (I–A)

✳ Grimes, Nikki, *The Road to Paris* (2008) (I–A)

Henkes, Kevin, *The Birthday Room* (1999) (I)

✳ Hirahara, Naomi, *1001 Cranes* (2008) (A)

Hof, Marjolijn, *Mother Number Zero* (2011) (I)

Holt, Kimberly Willis, *Keeper of the Night* (2003) (A)

✳ Johnson, Lindsay Lee, *Soul Moon Soup* (2002) (I–A)

Kinney, Jeff, *Diary of a Wimpy Kid* (2008) (I–A)

———, *Rodrick Rules (Diary of a Wimpy Kid)* (2008) (I–A)

Koss, Amy Goldman, *Stranger in Dadland* (2001) (I)

Kurtz, Jane, *Jakarta Missing* (2001) (I–A)

Lisle, Janet Taylor, *How I Became a Writer and Oggie Learned to Drive* (2002) (I)

Martin, Ann M., *Ten Rules for Living with My Sister* (2011) (I)

✳ McDonnell, Christine, *Goyangi Means Cat* (2011) (P)

✳ McKay, Hilary, *Forever Rose* (2008) (A)

✳ ———, *Saffy's Angel* (2002) (A)

✳ Medina, Meg, *Tia Isa Wants a Car* (2011) (P)

Mills, Claudia, *The Totally Made-Up Civil War Diary of Amanda MacLeish* (2008) (I)

Newman, John, *Mimi* (2011) (I)

Paterson, Katherine, ***Jacob Have I Loved*** (1980) (A)

_____, ***The Same Stuff as Stars*** (2002) (I)

Plummer, Louise, ***A Dance for Three*** (2000) (A)

＊ Ryan, Pam Muñoz, ***Becoming Naomi Leon*** (2004) (I)

Schumacher, Julie, ***Black Box*** (2008) (A)

_____, ***Grass Angel*** (2004) (I)

Sones, Sonya, ***One of Those Hideous Books where the Mother Dies*** (2004) (I–A)

_____, ***What My Mother Doesn't Know*** (2001) (A)

＊ Woodson, Jacqueline, ***Miracle's Boys*** (2000) (A)

Additional resources to accompany this chapter can be found on the Education CourseMate website. Go to CengageBrain.com to access a variety of interactive study tools and useful resources including Video Conversations with children's book authors and illustrators, a searchable children's literature database, glossary flashcards, online activities, tutorial quizzes, links to relevant websites, and more.

Historical Fiction

Travis's firefly was, in fact, the only one spotted that night. Although I knew the fireflies would return in a year, it felt like the extinction of a species. How sad to be the last of your kind, flashing your signal in the dark, alone, to nothingness. But I was not alone, was I? I had learned that there were others of my kind out there.

—JACQUELINE KELLY
The Evolution of Calpurnia Tate, p. 258

There was silence when Jason closed the book at the end of chapter twenty-one. Calpurnia, better known as Callie Vee, had just had an enlightening conversation with her grandfather while her brothers were catching fireflies at the other end of their long front porch. After Callie Vee asked him if girls could be scientists, too, Grandfather had told her about women who had made important contributions to science. Previously, Jason's group of fifth graders had discussed Calpurnia's struggle to develop her interest in science by helping her naturalist grandfather collect and identify his specimens, and how her embroidery, piano, and cooking lessons—all of which prepared her to become a young lady—interfered with her time in the field and laboratory. What at first had seemed almost comical, for Calpurnia has a dry wit evident as she narrates her story, was now quite serious. Taking advantage of the silence, Jason asked his students to sit and think for a moment, and then to write in their response journals about what Calpurnia said. This theme—feeling alone because you are somehow "different," and then learning that there are others like you—would become an idea that these readers would return to again and again as they shared many other novels during the school year.

In historical fiction, the past is re-created as the stories of people who seem real to us. As history becomes a story about characters we know and even care about, it gives us the opportunity to vicariously experience life in the past. It also allows us to consider historical issues and events as having had real consequences for the real people who lived them, rather than as abstract concepts, understanding that those who lived in the past had some of the same hopes, fears, dreams, and struggles that we have today. Students such as those reading **The Evolution of Calpurnia Tate** (I–A) are lucky; through historical fiction they can connect with their history in a way no textbook can offer them.

Defining Historical Fiction

History is a story, the story of the world and its people and of cultures that rise and fall across time. Historical fiction tells the stories of history; as a distinct genre, it consists of imaginative narratives deliberately grounded in the facts of our past. It is not biography (discussed in Chapter 9), which focuses on the life of an actual person, or nonfiction (discussed in Chapter 10), which focuses on historical fact, but rather uses facts to re-create a time and place. Outstanding authors weave historical facts into the fabric of a fictional story about people both real and imagined. Historical fiction is realistic—the events could have occurred, and the people portrayed could have lived (and sometimes really did)—but it differs from contemporary realistic fiction in that the stories are set in the past rather than the present. As Christopher Ringrose describes it, "The alternative world one is invited to enter has an additional dimension: one of time as well as space" (2007).

Some books, such as Louisa May Alcott's **Little Women** (I–A), that we now think of as historical fiction, began as contemporary realism. These books are different from true historical fiction in that the author was not attempting to describe life or events in the past, but rather life and events in the author's present. These books have become historical solely because of the passage of time. It's easy to notice that some books created as contemporary realistic fiction many decades ago are no longer contemporary. It's more difficult, however, with books such as Katherine Paterson's **The Great Gilly Hopkins** (I–A). The story events and themes in that novel can certainly be considered contemporary, yet there are nuances in the setting and character development that make it clear that this is not a twenty-first century contemporary novel. Where the past begins is an intriguing question, but for the purposes of this chapter, historical fiction is writing set in a time that has already occurred, a time that the author has deliberately evoked as historical.

Some historical fiction stories are more grounded in specific facts or events than are others, such as when authors include real events and people in their imaginative stories. Irene Hunt's **Across Five Aprils** (A), a classic story of the Civil War, is filled with names, dates, newspaper accounts of real battles as well as realistic political and social detail woven into a moving story. Kenneth Oppel built on a fictional persona who "lived" in the past when he wrote **The Dark Endeavor: The Apprenticeship of Victor Frankenstein** (A), set in Geneva in the late 1700s, creating a carefully researched but wholly fictional prequel to another novel, Mary Shelley's **Frankenstein.** Andrew Lane did much the same with Arthur Conan Doyle's Sherlock Holmes character in his fictional creation of the great detective's childhood. **Death Cloud (Sherlock Holmes: The Legend Begins)** (I–A) presents fourteen-year-old Sherlock solving his first crime, with a lot of action and humor.

Some authors set their stories in times past but do not specifically explore any major historical events or especially important people. Still, these authors know a great deal about the time and place in which their stories are set, and the facts that they

On Your Education CourseMate

CONVERSATION WITH AVI

In a conversation with Lee Galda, Avi, author of Newbery Award–winning **Crispin: The Cross of Lead**, and two sequels, **Crispin: At the Edge of the World** and **Crispin: The End of Time** (all I–A), talks about how he prepared to write the first book. Go to CengageBrain.com to access the Education CourseMate website and watch the video conversation with Avi.

Questions to Consider

1. How did Avi prepare to write the dialogue? Why did he consider this so important? What is the result for you as a reader?

2. Why is it important to include factual information to make a fictional story "true" in terms of its setting?

weave into their narratives are what make their books historically rich. Avi, whose **Crispin: The Cross of Lead** (I–A) won the Newbery Award, not only carefully researched life in the Middle Ages in Britain, but also studied the language of the time in order to make the setting and style both vivid and accurate.

Authentic, vivid details make good stories also good history. Joseph Bruchac creates a vivid world with both physical details and carefully articulated beliefs in **The Winter People** (I–A), a story of an Abenaki boy caught in the midst of the French and Indian War. Karen English creates a vivid picture of life in the Deep South of the 1950s in **Francie** (I–A), a Coretta Scott King Honor book that explores issues of racism, human worth, and dignity that transcend time and place. Shenaaz Nanji's **Child of Dandelions** (A) is filled with strong sensory details of life in Uganda during the early 1970s. Clare Vanderpool re-created small-town Kansas during the Depression with such detail that she won a Newbery Medal for **Moon over Manifest** (I), a riveting story of love and redemption.

Some stories are based on memories from the authors' own lives or the lives of their ancestors. Mildred Taylor's Logan family saga, including the

Newbery Medal–winning **Roll of Thunder, Hear My Cry** (A), is based on the stories of her family, but the events of their lives have been sifted, artistically arranged, and presented as engaging stories. Louise Erdrich writes about her own family's history in **The Birchbark House, The Game of Silence**, and **The Porcupine Year** (I), recounting the moving story of the life of a young Ojibwe girl and her family living in the upper Midwest during the mid-nineteenth century. Based on research by the author's mother and sister, these novels are full of the homely details of life in one Ojibwe group in that time and place. We look closely at **The Porcupine Year** later in this chapter. In the Newbery Medal–winning **Bud, Not Buddy** (I), Christopher Paul Curtis creates memorable secondary characters who are based on his grandfathers, but he notes in his afterword that he learned most of what he knows about the Depression through research. Linda Sue Park, a Korean American writer, won the Newbery Medal for **A Single Shard** (A), a novel about a medieval Korean boy who becomes a master potter. Although her ancestors were Korean, she still had to do a great deal of research to be able to capture the place and time accurately. Family experience may have triggered these novels, but it took significant research and talented writers to turn that into good historical fiction.

Historical fiction sometimes surprises readers because it can also take the form of an adventure story, as in Iain Lawrence's **The Convicts, The Cannibals**, and **The Castaways** (I), Sally Gardner's **The Red Necklace** (A), or Julia Golding's **The Diamond of Drury Lane: A Cat Royal Adventure**, set in England. Geraldine McCaugrean's **The Glorious Adventures of the Sunshine Queen** (I–A), set during the heyday of Mississippi riverboats, and **Stop the Train!** (I–A), set in a railroad town on the western prairie during the Westward expansion, are both historical fiction and adventure stories. Historical fiction can also be a mystery, as in Tess Hilmo's **With a Name Like Love** (I–A), set in 1957 Arkansas, or Eleanor Updale's **Johnny Swanson** (I), set in post–World War I England. The issues that eleven-year-old Johnny wrestles with—bullying and being bullied; being scammed and being a con artist; lying and its consequences—are articulated within the historical time and place, yet speak directly to today's readers.

Sometimes historical fiction is also a romance novel. Sonia Gensler's **The Revenant** (A), set in 1896 at the Cherokee National Female Seminary in Tahlequah, Oklahoma, is both mystery and romance novel. Dianne Gray's **Together Apart** (A), while rich in historical details, is also an engaging romance.

Historical fiction also may be an animal story, as in Kate Thompson's two horse stories, **Highway Robbery** (I–A), set in highwayman Dick Turpin's England, and **Most Wanted** (I–A), set in ancient Rome.

Historical fiction may be a verse novel, as in Karen Hesse's story of the Great Depression, **Out of the Dust** (A), Jen Bryant's **Ringside, 1925: Views from the Scopes Trial** (A), or Pamela Porter's wrenching **I'll Be Watching** (A), set in small town Saskatchewan in 1941. Thanhha Lai's National Book Award–winning novel in verse, **Inside Out & Back Again** (A), reveals a young Vietnamese girl's fears, hopes, and dreams as she flees her war-torn country and settles in Alabama. Even though historical fiction is realistic, it may contain fantasy elements, like the time travel in Jane Yolen's **The Devil's Arithmetic** (A); the connection of stories occurring in two different times, as in Susan Cooper's **Victory** (I); or episodes of magic realism, as in Christopher Paul Curtis's **The Watsons Go to Birmingham, 1963**. Genre-blurring novels such as these could be called fantasy, but their carefully constructed historical setting makes them, at their core, historical fiction.

Matt Phelan's **Storm in the Barn** (I–A) contains magic realism, and we chose to discuss this book in our chapter on fantasy. Yet it won the Scott O'Dell Award for historical fiction, and it is also a graphic novel. His latest graphic novel, **Around the World** (I–A), begins in 1872 with Phileas Fogg proposing to travel around the world in eighty days (from the Jules Verne novel), then moves into three separate stories, all of which are based on true events of epic journeys. Julie Chibbaro uses the journal form in her story of a sixteen-year-old girl who helps research the cause of a major typhoid outbreak in 1906. **Deadly** (I–A) is illustrated by Jean-Marc Superville Sovak. Historical fiction also appears in many picturebooks and as series chapter books, as in Patricia McKissack's **Scraps of Time** series (P–I), in which each book recounts the story behind an African American family's keepsakes. What makes these books historical is their historical setting and the importance of that setting to the story.

No matter what form it takes, outstanding historical fiction shows that history is created by people, that people experience historical events in individual ways, that people living now are tied to those who lived in the past through a common humanity, and that human conditions of the past shape our perceptions of the present, our lives today. Historical fiction offers readers the opportunity to travel across time and place and thus to find themselves.

A Brief History of Historical Fiction

As the United States developed as a country, writers told the story of that development in historical fiction for young readers. Books such as Carol Ryrie Brink's *Caddie Woodlawn* (I), winner of the 1936 Newbery Medal, and Laura Ingalls Wilder's 1938 Newbery Honor–winning **On the Banks of Plum Creek** (I) were popular with children and librarians alike. Historical fiction became even more popular during the years of World War II (Marcus, 2008). Walter Edmonds's **The Matchlock Gun** (I), set in the pre-colonial era in upstate New York, won the 1942 Newbery Award, followed by Elizabeth Janet Gray's **Adam of the Road** (I) in 1943, and Esther Forbes's **Johnny Tremain** (I–A) in 1944. In the two decades that followed, many of the Newbery winners and Honor books were historical fiction, including Scott O'Dell's **Island of the Blue Dolphins** (I–A), a haunting story about a young native girl. O'Dell's was one of the first critically successful attempts to go beyond the generally white, European perspective present in most historical fiction for young readers, one which often resulted in the presence of racism or sexism that reflected not only the historical setting, but the attitudes of the author at the time of writing. Many of these early novels proved problematic because of this.

In the 1960s, with the civil rights movement in full swing, books for young readers began to change as new voices appeared. Writers such as Virginia Hamilton, Mildred Taylor, Yoshiko Uchida, and Joseph Bruchac brought new points of view to historical fiction. Gradually, the genre began to reflect the history of everyone in the United States—African American, Native American, Asian American, and Latino as well as European—with stories of the lives of ordinary girls and boys, rich and poor, urban and rural, captivating a new audience of readers. Still, much of the historical fiction published each year tells the stories of history from a white perspective, no matter how sensitive an author might be.

Some are not well documented and present misinformation to young readers, and it is important to consider authenticity when evaluating historical fiction. For example, Native American scholars and children's book critics have faulted Ann Rinaldi's **My Heart Is on the Ground: The Diary of Nannie Little Rose, a Sioux Girl, Carlisle Indian School, PA 1880** (I) for glossing over the horrors of the Indian schools in nineteenth-century America and including multiple inaccuracies of fact and perception. Knowing this, looking for more accurate fiction about the Indian school experience would be important.

In general, however, historical fiction series are good introductions to historical fiction for many of today's young readers. These series, such as the **Royal Diaries** (I), **Dear America** (I), **American Adventures** (I), and **American Girl** (I), were developed and marketed to attract even greater numbers of young readers to historical fiction. Many of these books, such as Siobhan Parkinson's **Kathleen: The Celtic Knot** (I) and Jane Kurtz's **Saba: Under the Hyena's Foot** (I) are very well done, written by outstanding authors and filled with a masterful blend of historical fact and period detail within an engaging fictional story. Kathryn Lasky's **Elizabeth I: Red Rose of the House of Tudor** (I), which presents Elizabeth's life in the years immediately preceding the death of her father, Henry VIII, is another series book that stands on its own merits as an excellent piece of historical fiction. The best of these books, with their engaging format, offer readers a glimpse of life as it was lived by a historical, albeit fictional, child, often a female, someone whose voice is rarely heard in other histories.

In 1982, Scott O'Dell, a noted writer of award-winning historical fiction, established the Scott O'Dell Award for Historical Fiction, to be given to a writer from the United States for a meritorious book published the preceding year. O'Dell hoped that this award would interest new writers in working within the historical fiction genre, and thus provide young readers more books that would help them understand the historical background that has helped shape their world. It seems that his desire has been realized, for historical fiction seems to be enjoying continued popularity; many new novels set in the past are published for young readers each year. Historical fiction has, if anything, gained in popularity, and currently many seasoned and fresh writers are producing wonderful narratives that continue to engage young readers.

In the remainder of this chapter we:

- Consider aspects of quality in historical fiction
- Explore historical fiction grouped by the time period in which it is set
- Discuss the place of historical fiction in the classroom

Considering Quality in Historical Fiction

The best historical stories come from good storytellers who are well acquainted with the facts; good historical fiction is grounded in facts but not restricted by them.

An author may use historical records to document events, but the facts serve only as a framework for the story. The trick is to make that material such a part of the background—in the setting, the events, the characterizations, the language, and the ideas—that readers may not consciously notice most of them, yet they are fundamental in shaping the story. Good historical fiction meets the criteria for *all* good narratives: it has well-developed characters and integral themes; it tells an engaging story with well-crafted language; and,

FIGURE 8.1

Considering Quality in Historical Fiction

Historical Accuracy

- Events and attitudes are consistent with historical evidence and appropriate to the time period.

- Social issues are portrayed honestly, without condoning bias for race, gender, or other differences.

Literary Quality

- The work meets the criteria for all good narratives.

- The setting is integral to the story and evokes a vivid historical time consistent with historical and geographical evidence.

- The language patterns are historically authentic and in keeping with the mood and characterization, yet still understandable to readers.

- Characters are well developed—with feelings, values, and behavior that reflect the historical period.

- The plot is based on authentic facts that are subordinate to the story itself.

- The theme echoes larger historical concerns and is important to today's readers.

- Illustrations, if present, enhance an understanding of plot, setting, characterization, and theme through the use of realistic details and artistic choices.

in the case of picturebooks, it contains beautiful and appropriate art. Beyond this, it meets criteria that are particular to the genre. Figure 8.1 is a summary of things to think about when considering quality in historical fiction.

• • HISTORICAL ACCURACY • •

Historical fiction should be consistent with historical evidence; narrative events and characters' attitudes and beliefs should be appropriate to the time portrayed. The story, though imaginative, must remain within the limits of the chosen historical background, avoiding distortion and anachronism. Historical accuracy, however, presents an interesting dilemma, one related to the discussion of ideology in Chapter 2. Although we can know "facts" about our past, we know these facts only in light of the present. Every generation of historians, to some degree, interprets the past by using the concerns of their own experiences and their present lives as a lens. For example, a book like Esther Forbes's classic Revolutionary War story, **Johnny Tremain** (A), written during a time of great patriotic fervor, is not at all critical of war. James Lincoln Collier and Christopher Collier's **My Brother Sam Is Dead** (A), written during the Vietnam conflict (1974), presents a very different picture of the same war (Taxel, 1984). Both stories deal with the same set of "facts," but their implications are radically different because they are written from different perspectives, perspectives influenced by the time and place that shaped the writing. Any presentation of history is an interpretation, but good historical fiction creates as true a picture of the past as an author can craft. Historical "accuracy," then, is always influenced by who the author is and when the author is writing, and by how the author understands the historical experience within his or her own life.

Historical accuracy can create problems with racism and sexism as well as other biases. When writing about periods of time in which racism and sexism were a significant part of the culture, authors must take care to portray these social issues honestly while at the same time not condoning them. In Ann Turner's **Nettie's Trip South** (I–A), the issue of slavery is in the foreground; it is slavery that marked the South before the Civil War, and it is slavery that sickens young Nettie. In **Walks Alone** (I), Brian Burks describes the often-vicious approach to the Apache taken by the U.S. Army. Jerry Spinelli's **Milkweed** (A) and Gary Schmidt's **Mara's Stories: Glimmers in the Darkness** (I–A) depict the racism and violence of Nazi-occupied Europe but do so in a way that helps readers understand how horrible it was as well as appreciate the personal courage of those caught up in the Holocaust. Historical fiction may have to portray racism and sexism for historical accuracy, but the stories themselves should not be racist or sexist.

Noteworthy historical novels do not overgeneralize; they do not lead the reader to believe, for example, that all Native Americans or all young women in the Middle Ages are similar to characters in any one story. Each character is unique, just as each of us is, and although the novelist focuses on one person in a group, it should be clear that the character is only one person, not representative of everyone. When Karen Cushman's Newbery Honor–winning **Catherine, Called Birdy** (A) was published, several critics took Cushman to task for creating a character who was a literate female living in the Middle Ages. Women, they said, were not literate and, what's more, didn't act independently. In fact, most women indeed were not literate and were completely under the control of men. Some noted historical figures were different, however, and it is these whom Catherine most resembles. She is not meant to represent "all" medieval women, but rather to stand as one specific, fictional woman. She is unique, but not anachronistic; she is possible, reflecting feelings, behavior, values, and language of the time, as well as her individuality. Indeed, several historical fiction novels published in the recent past, such as Kevin Crossley-Holland's **Crossing to Paradise** (A), feature spirited and courageous young women who challenge historical stereotypes without being anachronistic.

• • SETTING • •

Setting is a crucial element in evaluating historical fiction because setting distinguishes this genre most dramatically. The setting must be authentic and consistent with historical and geographical evidence. Clear and vivid details of setting enable readers to create mental images of the time and place in which the events occur. Historical milieu is integral to the plot of historical fiction; it determines characters' beliefs and actions. Just as setting in fantasy and science fiction helps make those stories believable, setting in historical fiction helps make those stories seem real. Often, the particular setting of a story mirrors the larger political and social setting in which the story occurs, as it does in Mildred Taylor's stories set in Mississippi during the Great Depression. The racism present in a small section of Mississippi is mirrored in the state, the region, and the country as a whole; the specific setting serves as symbol for a larger historical occurrence. Teaching Idea 8.1 describes a way to explore settings and help students learn about descriptive writing.

TEACHING IDEA 8.1

Writing Connection: Descriptive Techniques

 **COMMON CORE STATE STANDARDS**

This Teaching Idea addresses the English Language Arts Common Core, Writing standard 10, grades 3 through 12. The suggestions in this Teaching Idea may need to be adapted to suit your particular grade level and the needs of your students.

Select several historical fiction books to compare literary descriptions of historical settings, then:

- Read aloud several books that describe the same region or historical period.
- Ask students to compare selections and illustrations.
- Discuss with students which descriptions are more evocative and which use the most sensory details.
- Ask students to decide which books help them understand the place and time best.

- Have students use the techniques they have discussed to create original descriptions of a real place they know.

Any number of books with vivid settings, grouped by period or place, are appropriate. Often the historical fiction that you select can be complemented by nonfiction and other genres. This can also be done using picturebooks, with students turning the visual information into written text.

• • CHARACTERIZATION • •

Characters in historical fiction should believe and behave in a manner that is in keeping with the times in which they live. Authors who attribute contemporary values to historical figures run the risk of creating an *anachronism*, mistakenly placing something in the wrong historical period. Sometimes this is difficult to determine, as mentioned previously. Characters in historical fiction engage with events of the past in ways that demonstrate the human agency and consequences of history.

• • PLOT AND THEME • •

History is filled with a tremendous amount of raw material for exciting plots and themes. Events must be plausible, if not actual; they should help propel the narrative line. For example, Christopher Paul Curtis's **Elijah of Buxton** (I), a Newbery Honor book, is set in an actual place and based on true events. A master storyteller, Curtis took these historical facts and wove a heartbreaking yet also hilarious story of a young boy coming to understand what it meant to live freely in a settlement in Ontario, Canada, while his people were enslaved in the United States, just a few miles away. In Mildred Taylor's **Roll of Thunder, Hear My Cry** (I–A), a Newbery Award–winner, the rural Mississippi area where the Logan family lives, with its dominant culture of racism, reflects the larger picture of racial struggle in America at that time. As African Americans across the country struggled for a humane, just existence, so do the characters in the novel.

Themes that are developed through facts and narrative usually reflect both a macrocosm of the era (for example, a war for independence) and the microcosm of the story (for example, a struggle for personal independence). In the best historical fiction, the theme is evident in both the unique story and the larger historical context.

• • STYLE • •

Language should be in keeping with the period and the place, particularly in dialogue. Today's readers, however, have difficulty understanding archaic language. Accomplished authors synthesize language that has the right tone or sound for a period but is understandable to contemporary readers. Avi wrote **Crispin: The Cross of Lead** in a medieval verse form and then "translated" it into more understandable language in order to capture the rhythm of language at that time but not use language that would hinder readers.

Noted writer Rosemary Sutcliff explains how she works appropriate language into her writing:

I try to catch the rhythm of a tongue, the tune that it plays on the ear, Welsh or Gaelic as opposed to Anglo-Saxon, the sensible workmanlike language which one feels the Latin of the ordinary Roman citizen would have translated into. It is extraordinary what can be done by the changing or transposing of a single word, or by using a perfectly usual one in a slightly unusual way: "I beg your pardon" changed into "I ask your pardon." . . . This is not done by any set rule of thumb; I simply play it by ear as I go along. (1973, pp. 307–308)

The character's thoughts should also reflect the time and place. Any metaphors, similes, or images that describe what a character is thinking or feeling must be appropriate to the setting. In Michael Dorris's **Morning Girl** (I), set in 1492 on a Bahamian island that will soon be visited by Christopher Columbus, Morning Girl, a young Taino, thinks about her brother:

The world fits together so tightly, the pieces like pebbles and shells sunk into the sand after the tide has gone out, before anyone has walked on the beach and left footprints.

In our house, though, my brother was the footprints. (p. 14)

Morning Girl's world is bounded by the sand and the sea; it is fitting that she should think of life in those terms. Authentic language patterns and word choices that are in keeping with the mood and characterization help create excellent historical fiction.

• • ILLUSTRATIONS • •

In recent years, a number of excellent historical fiction picturebooks have been published. Many of them, such as **Henry's Freedom Box**, are discussed in Chapter 3. These books contain not only well-written, riveting stories but also beautiful illustrations that support and enhance the story. Illustrations in picturebooks of historical fiction must meet the criteria for quality of illustration in any picturebook. In addition, they must be historically accurate, providing realistic details of life in that historical period as well as reflecting, interpreting, and elaborating character and action. Excellent illustrations enhance the story and use realistic details to reflect an understanding of the setting, plot, and characterization.

Jacqueline Woodson's **Show Way** (P–I) received a Newbery Honor Award for her text, and Hudson Talbott's illustrations are also brilliant. This picturebook traces the history of Woodson's family over nine generations, from slavery to today, as each of

Set more than one hundred years ago, **The Evolution of Calpurnia Tate** *explores the struggles of growing up in a way that resonates with children today.*

them fashioned a "show way" quilt in different artistic ways. While the original quilts literally "showed the way" to escaping slaves, from Great-grandma Soonie onward, each woman fashioned her "quilt" in a unique manner—Jacqueline's is books. The metaphor of strength, determination, pride, and fierce love shines from the words and Talbott's detailed illustrations—all held together by a quilt motif.

We now turn to a close look at an outstanding piece of historical fiction, Jacqueline Kelley's **The Evolution of Calpurnia Tate** (I–A).

✳ ✳ ✳
A CLOSE LOOK AT
The Evolution of Calpurnia Tate

There is a hint as to the setting and theme in the title of this engaging novel. Calpurnia, herself, is indeed "evolving," as she is moving from childhood to adolescence, with all of the difficult changes that entails.

The society in which she lives is also evolving, as women's roles are beginning to change. Calpurnia is also learning about the theory of evolution, a very exciting new idea as the twentieth century approaches. The story begins in the summer of 1899, one of the hottest ever remembered in Texas, where eleven-year-old Calpurnia lives with her grandfather, her parents, and her six brothers—three older and three younger—on a ranch on the banks of the San Marcos River, where they grow pecans and cotton. The attitudes of that time and place are integral to the story, among them the debate about Darwin's work and its implications for the Book of Genesis; the restrictions placed on women, who didn't even have the right to vote; the lack of educational opportunities for women; and the expectations that young ladies would become accomplished in the feminine arts such as sewing, music, and cooking.

Many of the secondary characters in **Calpurnia** are well developed, especially Grandfather. During that hot summer, Calpurnia overcomes her fear of her forbidding Grandfather and asks him a question that had occurred to her as she was doing her daily "scientific observation." Grandfather suggests that she, herself, could answer it if she thought hard enough and, a little later, hands her a copy of Darwin's *The Origin of the Species*, and her work as a scientist and her relationship with her grandfather begins to flourish. Grandfather's many comments on the sorry state of education, his instruction in the scientific method, his enjoyment of whiskey (he even tries to make whiskey from pecans), and his memories of the Civil War all help develop him as a quirky, loving man, and all are important to the evolution of the character of Calpurnia.

It is apparent from the first chapter that Calpurnia is not a "typical" girl. She remarks that the worst thing about the heat "was the women who suffered the most in their corsets and petticoats." She tells us that it also "brought [her] freedom" because during the heat of the afternoon, when everyone else was napping, she went down to the river bank, floating in the water and observing nature. She envies the men being able to shave off their beards and, when her request to cut her long hair is not approved, began shortening it, inch by inch, with embroidery scissors, a telling irony. She writes to the local newspaper to suggest that they should publish the temperature in the shade, rather than in the sun because no one ever stood in the sun; they did. In just the first six pages, Jacqueline Kelly paints a vivid picture of a young girl who is smart, clever, kind, and interested in the world.

As the narrative progresses, we watch as Calpurnia's relationship with her grandfather becomes stronger and see her struggle with her embroidery, her piano recital, and cooking lessons.

Most of all, we feel her frustration at being forced away from what she wants to do: spend time in field and laboratory with her grandfather. It is also apparent that she is trying to hold on to her family relationships as they have existed since she can remember; her response to a potential romance between her oldest brother and a young woman is laugh-out-loud funny.

The combination of humor and seriousness works well in this novel and weaves throughout the plot as well as the character development. For example, when Calpurnia and her grandfather discover what may be a new species of vetch, they have photographs made and send them off to the Smithsonian Institution. The scene is which they talk the photographer into taking the pictures is very humorous, as is the piano recital, Grandfather's first sip of his homemade pecan liquor, and many other scenes in the story. Each event reveals a bit more about Calpurnia as well as about life in Texas in the last months of 1899. When she awakens on New Year's Day 1900, she awakens to a rare blanket of snow. Because she is Calpurnia, she leaves the house before anyone is up, walking out into the snow, noting what she sees. When she sees "skittery" bird tracks, she thinks "Of course they were confused; the last snow had been decades ago. If a finch lived for only two years, how could it pass along the idea of something it had never seen to the next generation? Did the word disappear from the finch

PROFILE

Jacqueline Kelly

I have wanted to write my whole life.

Jacqueline Kelly moved from New Zealand to Vancouver Island, British Columbia, Canada, growing up in the rain forests on the island before moving to a completely different landscape and climate: the desert of El Paso, Texas. After college Jacqueline practiced medicine before returning to school to get a law degree. After practicing law, she turned to writing fiction, and *The Evolution of Calpurnia Tate* was her first novel.

To learn more about Jacqueline Kelly, go to CengageBrain.com to access the Education CourseMate website, where you will find links to relevant websites.

language, from finch society? How could any species survive the snow if the word for it died out? The finch race, all the other races, would be unprepared. It would have to put out quantities of seed and suet, hay and ham, and in this way provide for all the links

TEACHING IDEA 8.2

Thematic Exploration: Self-Knowledge

COMMON CORE STATE STANDARDS

This Teaching Idea addresses the Common Core English Language Arts, Reading: Literature standard 3, grades 1 through 4. It is also useful as an introduction to other activities addressed in standard 3, grades 5 through 8. The suggestions in this Teaching Idea may need to be adapted to suit your particular grade level and the needs of your students.

Calpurnia Tate is engaged in discovering who she is, what she is passionate about, and how she can do what she wants to do in the world she lives in. She's thinking of these things in 1899; young readers still think about them in the twenty-first century. As she matures, Calpernia comes to know what is truly "her." Her curiousity, her ability to observe and take scientific notes, her ability to sketch the things she sees, as well as her desire to try to please her parents even when she resists becoming a young lady are all attributes that Calpurnia comes to know about herself.

Ask students to consider the knowledge they have of themselves. They might want to write a list poem or an acrostic, or name, poem, for Calpurnia or for themselves, in which they list character traits. An example of a possible beginning to Calpurnia's name poem might be: "Curioius/Always wondering/Looking at her world/Posing hypotheses/Useless at embroidery/Rebellious." Or they might simply write a journal entry discussing what Calpurnia discovered about herself or what they have discovered about themselves. This activity can also be linked to other books and other genres that explore this same theme.

along the food chain" (p. 337). Walking in the snow, she realizes that "anything is possible." And then she turns, exchanges a long look with her grandfather, who is watching her from the window, and "runs for the warmth" of her home. And in that moment it is clear that Calpurnia will continue to evolve into an extraordinary young woman, embracing science while also cherishing family.

History through Historical Fiction

Historical fiction can be organized and studied in several ways: as a genre, as an example of literary excellence, by theme, by chronological period, or according to the topics in a social studies curriculum. In any case, well-written stories will "establish human and social circumstances in which the interaction of historical forces may be known, felt, and observed" (Blos, 1992). We present historical fiction chronologically, and then consider how to explore particular historical settings as well as important themes across history; other ways of considering historical fiction are explored in the Teaching Ideas and in Chapter 12.

• • PREHISTORIC • • AND ANCIENT TIMES

Prehistoric times, the ancient period before written records were kept, are wrapped in the shrouds of antiquity. Scientists theorize about the daily life and culture of ancient peoples by observing archeological fragments of life and making inferences from shards of pottery, weapons, or bits of bone. Authors draw from the findings of archaeologists, anthropologists, and paleontologists to create vivid tales of life as it might have been. Because there are no written records to refer to, authors rely on the theories that these scientists create around the facts they do have.

Although novels of prehistoric times are not plentiful, those that do exist are often set in distant lands around the Mediterranean Sea or in ancient Britain. The best fiction about prehistoric people does more than re-create possible settings and events of the past. It engages itself with themes basic to all persons everywhere: the will to survive, the need for courage and honor, the growth of understanding, the development of compassion. Peter Dickinson's series **The Kin**, which includes **Suth's Story, Noli's Story, Po's Story,** and **Mana's Story** (I–A), takes readers back two hundred thousand years but grapples with issues important today. War and peace, the power of

language and the thought it enables, loving relationships, and community are some of the themes that connect these stories with our own times.

Stories of ancient times sometimes focus on life in early Mediterranean civilizations. Julius Lester's **Pharaoh's Daughter: A Novel of Ancient Egypt** (A) is a fictional account of the biblical story of Moses that contains well-developed characters and complex themes. Vicky Alvear Shecter's **Cleopatra's Moon** (A) is based on the historical evidence of one of the children of Cleopatra and Mark Anthony, Cleopatra Selene, artfully blending fact and fiction. Susan Fletcher writes imaginatively of life in a Persian harem during the time of Scheherazade in **Shadow Spinner** (A), a suspenseful story with a resourceful female protagonist and intriguing details of time.

Rosemary Sutcliff's novels of ancient Britain, such as the recently reissued **Frontier Wolf** (A), are masterful evocations of their time; they also provide sensitive insights into the human spirit. Sutcliff's heroes live and die for values and principles that we embrace today. Much like high fantasy, a very different genre, her stories reveal the eternal struggle between goodness—that which we value—and evil—the forces that work to destroy it.

• • THE MIDDLE AGES • •

The dissolution of the Roman Empire signaled the beginning of that part of the medieval period sometimes referred to as the Middle Ages, spanning roughly from 500 to the early 1500s A.D. There is some recorded history of these times, and writers breathe life into the shadowy figures of the history of this period. In **Bloodline Rising** (A), a companion to **Bloodline** (A), Katy Moran moves from the world of Constantinople during the Byzantine Empire to seventh-century Britain in a riveting adventure story that also re-creates these worlds with vivid detail. Although not technically a novel because it is actually a collection of brief plays, Laura Amy Schlitz's **Good Masters! Sweet Ladies! Voices from a Medieval Village** (I) won the Newbery Medal. This gathering of monologues and dialogues from fictional children from ages ten through fifteen is filled with details of life in medieval England, a variety of topics, wonderful period vocabulary, and a great deal of humor. Robert Byrd's illustrations add beautifully to the overall effect. In a gripping adventure for older readers, Michael Cadnum chose to re-create an actual historical event in Norman England, one shrouded in mystery to this day, in his **The King's Arrow** (A), a story filled with action, violence, and gritty details.

Others construct novels that blend fact and legend, as in Michael Morpurgo's retelling of **Sir Gawain** *and the Green Knight* (I–A). In the past ten years, there have been a number of outstanding narratives set in the Middle Ages, both fantasy and literary lore, as discussed in Chapter 6, and more realistic fictional narratives. Elizabeth Wein combines historical fiction and fantasy as she links ancient Britain and ancient Africa in her acclaimed Arthurian/Aksumite cycle. The books, *The Winter Prince, A Coalition of Lions, The Sunbird, The Lion Hunter,* and *The Empty Kingdom* (A) move from sixth-century Great Britain to sixth-century Africa as Goewin, princess of Britain, travels to African Aksum (today's Eritrea and Ethiopia) and helps forge an alliance between ancient Britain and the African kingdom.

Steeped in Arthurian legend but based on facts about the history of Britain and Ethiopia, these riveting narratives postulate a believable connection between the two ancient kingdoms, forged by unforgettable characters. Are they fantasy, or are they historical fiction? One could argue for both, as we do, by discussing them in Chapter 6 as well. The same blurring of genre lines can be seen in Kevin Crossley-Holland's *Arthur* trilogy, *The Seeing Stone, At the Crossing Places*, and *King of the Middle March* (I–A) because of the close connection with Arthurian legend. There is no fantasy in *Crossing to Paradise* (I–A), where Gatty's story is told as she journeys to the Holy Land and back home, where we first met her in *The Seeing Stone*, profoundly changed by her quest. K. M. Grant's *Blood Red Horse* (A), also set during the Crusades and containing some elements of fantasy, is an exciting adventure tale, a romance, and a terrific horse story, while also illuminating the effect of the Crusades on relations between the Arabs and the west, effects that permeate our lives today.

Avi's *Crispin: The Cross of Lead, Crispin: At the Edge of the World*, and *Crispin: The End of Time* (all I–A) are exciting adventure stories as Crispin follows his quest. In these books the sights, sounds, tastes, and smells, as well as the customs and beliefs of the period, are so vivid that readers are left with the feeling of having traveled through time. Karen Cushman's *The Midwife's Apprentice* (I–A), winner of the 1996 Newbery Medal, also weaves an array of details about daily life in Britain into a compelling narrative. The mundane, often distasteful details of the lives of the common folk in the Middle Ages form the rich background against which a young girl discovers her worth. Cushman's other books set in the Middle Ages, *Matilda Bone, Catherine, Called Birdy*, and *Alchemy and Meggy Swann* (all I–A), are also filled with details that sweep readers into the midst of life in England at that time. Readers who have enjoyed Avi's and Cushman's books might want

to go on to read Odo Hirsch's *Yoss* (A), a novel of the Middle Ages for slightly older readers that explores many of the themes that appear in *Crispin*.

Other fine stories explore the medieval period in other parts of the world. Constance Leeds's *The Silver Cup* (I) is set in Germany in 1095. Rich with details of time and place, this story portrays a friendship between two young women—one Christian and one Jewish—as they struggle against the intolerance of their cultures. Frances Temple's *The Beduins' Gazelle* (A) is set in the midst of a war between Beduin tribes in 1302. Jill Paton Walsh tells the story of the fall of Constantinople in 1453 in *The Emperor's Winding Sheet* (I–A). Tracy Barrett's *Anna of Byzantium* (A) is a graphic novel of the life of a brilliant woman in the eleventh-century Byzantine Empire, a difficult time in history for strong women. Janet Rupert's *The African Mask* (A) is set in eleventh-century Nigeria. Linda Sue Park's *A Single Shard* (A), set in medieval Korea, won a Newbery Medal for her exquisite description of time and place and development of a protagonist whom readers come to care about. Mette Newth's *The Transformation* (A), set in Greenland in the mid-1400s, explores the impact of Christian Europeans on the beliefs and culture—indeed, on the well-being—of the Inuit. This is a novel that presents a place and time that is unfamiliar to most readers, considers profound questions of theology and culture, and is also a riveting adventure as well as a tender love story.

● ● THE RENAISSANCE AND ● ● THE AGE OF EXPLORATION

Whether in real life or in books, mysterious or dangerous explorations of the unknown mesmerize us all. Accounts of navigation of the New World intrigue today's children as much as travels to the moon or Mars do. Explorers of the past and present need the same kind of courage and willingness to face the unknown. Stories of explorations range from tales of the early Vikings to those set in the age of European exploration—Columbus and after.

In 1992, the five-hundredth anniversary of Columbus's famous 1492 voyage brought forth many books to mark the anniversary. These books also reflected a growing trend in children's literature: some told the "other side" of the story, presenting Columbus from the point of view of the Native Americans who were present when he landed, or of Europeans who were skeptical of his motives. Books like Jane Yolen's *Encounter* (I–A) and Pam Conrad's *Pedro's Journal* (I) help present a more balanced picture of the impact of the age of exploration. The powerful writing and clever structure of Michael Dorris's **Morning Girl** (I) allow young readers to experience "firsthand" the shock of Columbus's invasion of the Taino Indian islands.

In a verse novel set in the sixteenth century in the Caribbean, Margarita Engle weaves together the tales of five narrators: two legendary lovers, two actual historical figures—a pirate and a conquistador—and a fictional slave in **Hurricane Dancers: The First Caribbean Pirate Shipwreck** (A). Their stories intersect and the action intensifies when a hurricane destroys the pirate ship and the pirate, his slave, and his prisoner, the conquistador, manage to reach Cuba, separately, where they, along with the star-crossed lovers, wrestle with their own struggles. Copious notes and a bibliography add historical details.

Michael Cadnum's **Ship of Fire** (I–A) is based on actual events during Sir Francis Drake's raid on the Spanish port of Cadiz in 1587. The protagonist, a young doctor, not only finds adventure and acts courageously but also is forced to question the English hero, Drake. Is he truly a hero or simply a pirate stealing for Queen Elizabeth? These questions elevate this exciting novel beyond just an adventure story.

The Renaissance is a fascinating time in history, but few books for children explore this era in Europe, and even fewer are set in other parts of the world. Pilar Molina Llorente's **The Apprentice** (I) is set in Renaissance Florence and depicts the lives of middle-class merchants and famous artists alike. Linda Sue Park sets **The Kite Fighters** (I) in Seoul, Korea.

• • COLONIAL THROUGH • • POST–REVOLUTIONARY WAR TIMES

Immigrants began sailing to America in the late sixteenth century, some seeking adventure and financial gain, some escaping religious persecution, some traveling as missionaries, and some seeking political freedom. Economic and social conditions made the New World attractive to people who were willing to sacrifice the known for the possibilities of a promising unknown. The settlements by the English at Roanoke, Jamestown, Plymouth, and Boston are vivid settings for stories based on early colonial life. Historical fiction set after Europeans came to North America is plentiful.

By the end of the seventeenth century, the early settlers were well established in their new communities and were stern guardians of their religious views, pious behavior, and moral standards. The hysteria that gripped the people of Salem, Massachusetts, in the days of the witch hunts grew out of the political, economic, and social forces of the community.

Kathryn Lasky's **Beyond the Burning Time** (A) explores some of the hidden passions that might have stoked the fires of Salem and brings to life the way people lived, believed, and sometimes died in that place and time. In her classic **The Witch of Blackbird Pond** (I–A), winner of the 1959 Newbery Medal, Elizabeth George Speare reveals how guilt by association occurs in Old Salem when a young girl and the old woman she has befriended are accused of witchcraft. Ann Turner's **Father of Lies** (A) presents a new scenario. The protagonist is a teenage girl who suffers, unbeknown to herself or those around her, from bipolar disorder. These books artfully blend fact and fiction to create a vivid picture of people and their lives during colonial times. As Turner states in the end matter when she is discussing the blend of truth and fiction in this novel, "It reminds us of how easy it is to be swayed by events; how easy it is to judge and condemn others; and how easy it is to be mortally wrong." Lessons from the past can, indeed, be applicable to the present.

The history of America is incomplete without stories of Native Americans. In the past their story was told, if at all, by European Americans who often characterized them in stereotyped ways. A growing number of writers now give more accurate portrayals of Native American cultures and a more objective picture of the five-hundred-year clash between the European and Native American cultures. Stories for younger children may present a simple view of the interaction between Europeans and Native Americans, but this view should not rely on stereotypes. Stories for older readers often consider the complexities inherent in the clash between two cultures, such as Elizabeth George Speare's novel about the faltering friendship of a white boy and an Indian boy in the 1700s, **The Sign of the Beaver** (I–A). Many people criticize Speare for her non-Native point of view. This is a book that students can critique and learn from.

Stories that reflect a Native American point of view concerning these times are still scarce, however, as are those that depict the lives and struggles of the many Africans brought as slaves before the turn of the century. Notable exceptions include Michael Dorris's **Guests** and **Sees behind Trees** (I) as well as Joseph Bruchac's **The Arrow over the Door** (I) and **Pocahontas** (I–A). In Joyce Rockwood's **To Spoil the Sun** (A), the story of the devastation of smallpox is vivid and moving. Rain Dove, a young Cherokee girl, finds her life destroyed when the disease arrives along with the white man.

The eighteenth century was an interesting and tumultuous time, with disease wreaking havoc in Europe and ships carrying people around the globe with greater and greater frequency. L. A. Meyer captures the dangers and excitement of mid-eighteenth-century life in **Bloody Jack: Being an Account of the Curious Adventures of Mary "Jacky" Faber, Ship's Boy** and its sequel, **Curse of the Blue Tattoo: Being an Account of the Misadventures of Jacky Faber, Midshipman and Fine Lady** (I–A). These tales of high adventure on the seas differ from most others in one remarkable way—the protagonist is female. Based on a true event, Mary Hooper's **Newes from the Dead** (A) recounts the experience of young Anne Green, hanged but not killed in seventeenth-century England. Told in the alternating voices of Anne and a medical student, this novel is well researched and documented with a bibliography and author's note.

There was also great upheaval in many countries around the world during this time, including Great Britain. Jane Yolen and Robert Harris again combine their talents in **Prince Across the Water** (I–A), set during the Scottish rebellion to replace King George with Bonnie Prince Charlie. The age-old desire of young men to go to war to prove their mettle plays itself out against a meticulously detailed setting and a thorough understanding of the role of clan and honor in the Highlander culture of the day. Another collaboration between Yolen and Harris, **The Queen's Own Fool: A Novel of Mary Queen of Scots** (I–A), brings another exciting piece of Scottish history to young readers.

Wars wrapped the globe in this period, and the American Revolutionary War was one of the most significant. Stories of this war were once quite one-sided: the Tories, or loyalists, were bad, the Patriots good. A more balanced picture began to appear in the 1970s with **My Brother Sam Is Dead** (A), and this trend has continued. Since then, the divided loyalties in colonial families or communities and the true horror of war have usually been in the foreground of fiction about this era. Janet Lunn, one of Canada's best-known writers for children, explores just these topics in **The Hollow Tree** (A), a gripping account of a young girl's harrowing journey north from New Hampshire to Canada to join other loyalist families even though her own family is divided in its allegiance.

Gary Paulsen's **Woods Runner** (I) is set in the early days of the American Revolutionary War in the wilderness of the colony of Pennsylvania. Thirteen-year-old Samuel lives in two worlds: the woods, where he tracks and hunts to help feed his family, and the cabin, where he lives with his parents in a small, isolated community of other settlers. He knew about the war, but is caught off guard when his community is attacked and his parents taken prisoner.

His determination to rescue them takes him to New York City, where they are being held in a British jail. Strong characterization and a vividly detailed setting make this gripping adventure story a very engaging read. Themes centering around independence, maturation, and the horrors of war are relevant for today's readers. Paulsen also includes factual explanations of certain aspects of the history that frames the book, such as how people communicated in 1776. Rather than disrupt the narrative flow, these snippets of information add to the experience.

Recently, several books that tell part of the story of the American Revolution through the eyes of a slave have highlighted the irony of a country fighting for freedom while enslaving others. M. T. Anderson's **The Astonishing Life of Octavian Nothing, Traitor to the Nation, Volume I: The Pox Party** (A), winner of the National Book Award and a Printz Honor book, and **Volume II: The Kingdom on the Waves** (A) are crossover books that straddle the young adult and adult market. Nevertheless, they represent a new direction in historical fiction of this period as sweeping epics that explore issues of race and class even as they explore issues of freedom. In **Chains** and the sequel, **Forge** (both A), novels for younger adolescents, Laurie Halse Anderson holds up the institution of slavery against the Patriots' desire for freedom from Britain. In **Chains**, the young protagonist, Isabel, a slave, hopes that the British, who had abolished slavery in England, would be better than the Patriots, but finds that not to be the case. The plot is packed with the historical events of this tumultuous time as well as events in Isabel's life, and the setting is carefully detailed, even down to the peculiar and unsavory smells. Each chapter opens with a quote culled from varied sources that highlights the thought of the time and serves to comment on the action in the chapter, often ironically. End material containing an interview with Anderson and acknowledgements clarify what is from the historical record and what is fiction.

Jefferson's Sons: A Founding Father's Secret Children (I–A) by Kimberly Brubaker Bradley offers yet another perspective on this peculiar combination of struggling for political freedom while practicing slavery. Set in the very early nineteenth century, the novel tells three stories, two of Jefferson's sons by slave Sally Hemings and one of a boy who was close to them. An endnote discusses the historical record and how Bradley's fiction does not contradict anything that is considered fact, though so little is known that there is ample room for speculation.

A picture storybook set in the mid-eighteenth century, Verla Kay's **Hornbooks and Inkwells** (P) explores life in a one-room schoolhouse somewhere on the frontier. The lively rhyming text, deft character development in very few words, and S. D. Schindler's detailed illustrations make this a very engaging, and unusual, school story. Set sometime in the late eighteenth or early nineteenth centuries, Diane Browning's *Signed, Abiah Rose* (P) gives young readers a taste of what it was like to be a girl at that time and of the early days of folk art in the United States. Abiah Rose is discouraged from being a serious artist, a profession for men, and, when she pursues her art, is instructed to not sign her paintings. She does not, in fact, sign them with her name but with a cleverly concealed rose in every one.

• • WESTWARD EXPANSION • • AND THE CIVIL WAR

After the American Revolution, the nineteenth century saw the citizens of the new United States continue to move westward. National identity was seriously challenged; the question of slavery became a national debate, and immigrants from Europe, Africa, and Asia (both voluntary and involuntary) brought their despair and sometimes their hopes and dreams to a new land. It was an interesting century, filled with amazing contradictions. As the United States grew, the native peoples' lands continued to shrink, and their cultures were almost obliterated. As the nation expanded, indentured Chinese, lured to America by the promise of work, were exploited as they built the transcontinental railroad. As the new nation prospered, Africans and others continued to be ripped from their homelands, forcibly transported, and doomed to endure a life of slavery. As the nation became industrialized, the quality of life improved for some and grew worse for many. Children's books explore these contradictions from many viewpoints, telling the story of the growth of a nation and the consequences of that growth.

The Westward Migration

Americans were on the move from the beginning. Those moving called it expansion; those who were displaced saw it as invasion. In either case, life required great physical strength and often, the ability to endure loneliness. People worked hard by necessity, providing their own food, clothing, shelter, and entertainment. Themes of loneliness, hardship, and acceptance of what life brings are threaded through many excellent novels about the pioneers and their struggle to tame a wild land.

These themes are evident in Joyce Carol Thomas's descriptions of the courage and dignity of a young black woman determined to own her own land. *I Have Heard of a Land* (P–I) presents the inspiring story of one woman who symbolizes all who homesteaded the American West, braving isolation, the wilderness, and nature's vagaries to forge a home for themselves. Loretta Ellsworth's *The Shrouding Woman* (I), set on the prairie, presents a quiet story of grief and recovery along with a description of a job that is all but extinct today—the shrouding of the dead by women trained to do so. In *Prairie Whispers* (I), Frances Arrington uses the setting to create a mood of foreboding and isolation. *Nothing Here but Stones: A Jewish Pioneer Story* (I–A) by Nancy Oswald tells the fictional story of a real group of Russian Jews who struggled to create a new home in the Colorado mountains.

Going west was an adventure story to many, and Will Hobbs's *Jason's Gold* (A) is a spine-tingling account of a young boy's adventures in the Klondike during the Alaskan gold rush. Michael Cadnum explores a similar story in the California gold fields in *Blood Gold* (I–A). This gripping adventure story takes readers from Panama to San Francisco by ship and then on to the gold fields, as the young narrator pursues an acquaintance who left his pregnant girlfriend in Philadelphia. The suspense is high, the plot twists and turns, and the settings are vivid.

During these times, the clash of cultural values between European settlers and Native Americans resulted in numerous conflicts, from grisly battles in which hundreds were killed to more personal conflicts in which individuals who had come to know one another as friends had to choose between friendship and loyalty to their own people.

The famous 1804–1805 voyage of Meriwether Lewis and William Clark is emblematic of the interest the U.S. government had in expanding westward. Until recently, stories of their expedition were told from the viewpoint of the two leaders or the soldiers who accompanied them. The minting of the Sacajawea "gold" dollar, however, came with not one but several stories about this brave Native American woman who helped lead Lewis and Clark through a large part of the upstream Missouri River and into the Rocky Mountains. Joseph Bruchac's *Sacajawea* (I–A) is a brilliant, thoughtful recounting of the voyage told in alternating points of view—Sacajawea's and William Clark's. Clark's chapters begin with excerpts from the diaries he kept on the journey; Sacajawea's begin with stories that her people told. Each brings a unique perspective to the grand adventure, and their mutual respect and growing friendship are evident. Those who enjoy graphic novels will want to read Nick Bertozzi's *Lewis & Clark* (A), which highlights the relationship between the two friends and the difficulties of their expedition.

The two hundredth anniversary of this epic journey occurred in 2004–2005, accompanied by the appearance of more books. Kate McMullan tells the story of the journey from the point of view of the youngest member of the group in *My Travels with Capts. Lewis and Clark by George Shannon* (I–A). McMullan used not only public records but also family documents—she is a direct descendant of George Shannon—to create a first-rate adventure story. The story is also filled with great detail about people and places and is a chronicle of the growth of a boy called Pup because he was so young. Stephen Ambrose also creates a fictional diary of George Shannon in *This Vast Land* (A). Allan Wolf tells the same story from the perspective of thirteen participants on the journey, one of which is the dog, Seaman, in *New Found Land: Lewis and Clark's Voyage of Discovery* (A).

Fortunately, some stories about the westward expansion reflect the views of someone other than the white settlers. Laurence Yep writes of the life of the Chinese laborers in *The Traitor: 1885* (I–A), part of his ten-volume **Gold Mountain Chronicles** series. In *Dragons of Silk* (I–A), he chronicles the linked stories of women who were silk workers, beginning in 1835 and crossing the generations through 2011, as one family moved from China to Chinatown to New York City. This wide sweep of time demonstrates how our present is rooted in our past.

Cornelia Cornelissen tells of the forcible removal of the Cherokee to Oklahoma in *Soft Rain: A Story of the Cherokee Trail of Tears* (I). In the first three books

of a planned cycle of novels, Louise Erdrich tells of the effects of encroachment by whites on the Ojibwe people in *The Birchbark House*, a National Book Award winner, *The Game of Silence*, a Scott O'Dell Award winner, and *The Porcupine Year* (ALL). Teaching Idea 8.3 offers a way to help students notice how varying perceptions of events influence the way we think of those events. We now take a close look at *The Porcupine Year* along with the other books in this ongoing series.

* * *

A CLOSE LOOK AT
The Porcupine Year

Beginning with *The Birchbark House* (I), Louise Erdrich chronicles the life and times of a young Ojibwe girl, Omakayas, and her extended family. In the first book of the series, we spend a year with seven-year-old Omakayas, a year that begins with small joys, such as her older sister and the beautiful place she lives, and small irritations, such as her younger brother, Pinch. As the year passes, her community is stricken by smallpox, an often-fatal disease introduced by white settlers who are also encroaching on the Ojibwe lands. In *The Game of Silence*, several canoes filled with people driven from their land join Omakayas's people, even as her people are being forced by the government to leave their beloved island. *The Porcupine Year* continues the story as Omakayas and her extended family set off across Minnesota rivers and lakes to their destination, Lake of the Woods, on the border between the United States and Canada.

TEACHING IDEA 8.3

Discussion: Compare Perceptions of a Historical Event

COMMON CORE STATE STANDARDS This Teaching Idea addresses the Common Core English Language Arts, Reading: Literature standard 9, grades 6 and 7. The suggestions in this Teaching Idea may need to be adapted to suit your particular grade level and the needs of your students.

Collect several books, both historical fiction and nonfiction, that describe a historical event such as the first Thanksgiving, the westward expansion on the Great Plains, or the Civil War. Read these with your students. Compare them, considering such questions as the following:

- Who is telling the story?
- What is the narrator's perception of the events?

- What factors influence that perception?
- How do perceptions differ across books?

An effective follow-up activity is to ask students to role-play from different perspectives.

The setting of the north woods, rivers, and lakes in all of the novels is lovingly described; it is evident that Erdrich cherishes the places she writes about. Set within this natural beauty, the social setting in which Omakayas lives her life seems almost idyllic, until the larger society—the encroaching white settlers—disrupts the community's life with disease and forces them to leave their island to seek an uncertain future. At the same time, Omakayas is growing from child to woman, learning her own gifts and responsibilities, and beginning to discover her own strength.

The Porcupine Year is a year in which Omakayas, her family, and a few others take everything they can carry that will help them settle into a new life and travel from the shores of Lake Superior to join their relatives on an island in Lake of the Woods. They are well prepared but meet with danger and disaster along the way. As they are dying from starvation when caught by winter after being robbed of their food, tools, and weapons, Omakayas saves them by following her heart. Her strength of character has been building throughout the three novels, with each new challenge representing an occasion for growth, and by the time she and her family reach their destination, she has transformed, heart and body, into a woman.

All three novels are full of the small details of life—how they dressed, ate, hunted, gardened, interacted with one another, worked together as a team—and Ojibwe words, with a glossary and pronunciation guide to aid nonfluent readers. Both heighten the experience of joining with Omakayas on her adventures as she journeys toward her new future and adulthood.

P | R | O | F | I | L | E

Louise Erdrich

Louise Erdrich is a versatile, gifted writer for adults and young readers. Her novel for adults, *Love Medicine*, is often studied in high school English classes. Her series for young readers, beginning with **The Birchbark House**, a National Book Award finalist, is inspired by research and stories from her Ojibwe (also known as Chippewa) family. The second book in the series, **The Game of Silence**, won the Scott O'Dell Award for Historical Fiction. **The Porcupine Year** is the third book in the planned, multibook series. Louise Erdrich owns a bookstore for children and adults, Birch Bark Books, in Minneapolis.

Slavery, the Civil War, and Its Aftermath

Slavery was a part of American life from early colonial days until long after the Emancipation Proclamation. Many chapters of American history are grim, and those involving slavery and the Civil War are among the worst. Slavery shamed a nation of people who professed to believe in freedom, and the war was a long, savage contest that tore the country apart and caused many deaths. Historical fiction of this period describes antebellum life as well as the turmoil and tragedy of the bloody war years. The years preceding the Civil War were a bleak period in American history, although individual acts of compassion and heroism did occur. A notable children's book that has captured the antebellum period is Ann Turner's picturebook **Nettie's Trip South** (I–A), which depicts the horror of slavery as seen through the eyes of a white girl from the North who is on a train trip to the South. In another picturebook, Elisa Carbone tells the fictional story of a real person, James Smith, in **Night Running: How James Escaped with the Help of His Faithful Dog** (P–I). Full-bleed double-page spreads by E. B. Lewis pull the reader into this story of courage and love between boy and dog. There are many other outstanding picturebooks that tell stories of escaping slaves and the Underground Railroad. Patricia Polacco's **January's Sparrow** (I) tells the story of a real family, the Crosswhites, who flee slavery in Kentucky, crossing the Ohio and heading to Michigan via the Underground Railroad. Once in Marshall, Michigan, they feel safer, but the realities of the Fugitive Slave Act catch up to them and they are found by the people they fled. When the town of Marshall stands for them against the slave catchers, they manage to escape to Canada, returning to Michigan after the Emancipation Proclamation. This heartwarming story offers much to think and talk about. Christopher Paul Curtis's **Elijah of Buxton** (I–A), set in Canada and Michigan, also describes the tenuous nature of freedom in the North for those who fled slavery.

Julius Lester uses the multiple voices of enslaved Africans and their owners to depict an actual event—the largest auction of slaves in American history on March 2 and 3, 1859, in Savannah, Georgia. **Day of Tears** (A), Lester's 2006 Coretta Scott King Award–winning novel in dialogue, is a stunning indictment of the institution of slavery and those who participated in it.

Avi's novel of the Civil War, **Iron Thunder: The Battle between the Monitor & the Merrimac** (I) is set in Brooklyn, New York, during the war. In an interesting portrayal of the class differences that existed at that time, Avi creates a memorable character, thirteen-year-old Tom, whose father is killed fighting for the Union. Tom takes a job in the ironworks where the "iron-clad" Monitor is being constructed and, in the process, sets himself on a perilous course. A confrontation with Confederate spies, the opportunity to join the Monitor's crew, and detailed, vivid battle scenes contribute to the fast-paced plot. In **The Storm before Atlanta** (I–A), Karen Schwabach re-creates the harsh realities of the Civil War as seen through the eyes of an eleven-year-old drummer boy. Joseph Bruchac presents a native American perspective on the Civil War in **March toward the Thunder** (I–A) through the eyes of a fifteen-year-old Abenaki Indian from Canada. Both of the protagonists in these novels discover that war is every bit as complex as life, only more difficult to endure.

Although **The River between Us** (A) begins and ends in 1916, Richard Peck re-creates life during the Civil War in a small Illinois town on the Mississippi River. When fifteen-year-old Howard, his father, and his two younger brothers arrive in Grand Tower, Illinois, to visit his grandparents and Great Aunt Delphine and Grand Uncle Noah, he and the reader are immediately swept up in Grandma Tilly's stories and transported into the world of the Civil War. Border states, such as Illinois, and especially the southern regions of those states, reflected the larger division in the country. Further, the Mississippi was the main thoroughfare for the center of the country, and North and South mingled, even after the beginnings of the war, through the trade between New Orleans and the North. This setting is integral to the story that Grandma Tilly unfolds of the mysterious Calinda and the beautiful Delphine, who came North from New Orleans on one of the last riverboats. With this story, Peck raises questions about how the United States considers race and what it meant to be a free person of color in that time and place.

Mildred Taylor reached back in time in her ongoing chronicle of the Logan family in **The Land** (A), the story of Paul-Edward, Cassie Logan's grandfather. The son of a white man and his former slave, Paul-Edward is privileged and educated, but also a young black man in the post–Civil War South. Blacks distrust his whiteness, whites discriminate against him because of his blackness, and he needs to find in himself the strength to craft the life that he wants because society is determined to thwart him. Taylor, arguably one of our most important contemporary authors, is unflinching in her examination of what life was like for African Americans in the postwar era.

● ● **IMMIGRATION AND THE** ● ●
INDUSTRIAL REVOLUTION

Beyond the far-reaching effects of the Civil War were other changes in the United States. Westward expansion continued, and millions of immigrants came from distant lands, dreaming of freedom and hoping to create a better life. Their stories are familiar stories, repeated over and over at family gatherings where young children cluster around their elders. Historical fiction contains a wealth of immigrant stories for all ages. Many books describe the conditions that led families to leave their country and migrate to America; others focus on the difficulties and hardships endured during and after immigration.

Patricia Reilly Giff sets **Nory Ryan's Song** (I–A) in 1845 in Ireland, just at the beginning of the potato famine. Although Nory is only twelve, her strength of character and gritty determination help her save her family and friends from starvation before she begins her own journey to America. That journey and its happy ending are described in the sequel, **Maggie's Door** (I–A). Nory is a mother as her story continues in **Water Street** (I–A), set in Brooklyn in the late nineteenth century as the famous bridge is being built. Karen Hesse's **Brooklyn Bridge** (I–A) is set in the same location in the early twentieth century. The famous bridge stands as a metaphor for bridges between old and new worlds, between generations, and between friends in this combination of romance, comedy, and ghost story.

In **A House of Tailors** (I–A), Patricia Reilly Giff relates the story of thirteen-year-old Dina, who flees Germany after being accused of spying against the Germans during the Franco-Prussian War. Dina hopes to leave her work as a seamstress, but when she arrives in Brooklyn in 1870, she finds that her uncle's house is as full of sewing as her father's was. As Dina adjusts to life in America, she also comes to value her talent as a seamstress and to realize that although she may love her American life, she will always long to return to Germany. This duality in the immigrant experience is beautifully captured by Allen Say in his Caldecott Medal–winning picturebook, **Grandfather's Journey** (P–I–A), set in the first half of the twentieth century. Avi sets **City of Orphans** (I–A) in 1893 New York City as he explores the underlying disparity in wealth and the arrogance of those who held power. The immigrant experience as portrayed in this novel is difficult and dangerous, but not without hope.

Margi Preus created an action-filled story of adventure on the high seas. Based on the true story of a fourteen-year-old Japanese boy who was rescued by an American whaling ship in 1841, **Heart of a Samurai: Based on the True Story of Nakahama Manjiro** (I–A), a Newbery Honor–winning novel, explores an important occurrence that resulted in the opening of Japan to the Western world. Turn-of-the-century Japan is the setting for Alan Gratz's **Samurai Shortstop** (A), a multilayered novel that explores honor, familial duty, and generational differences. The protagonist struggles with older boys in his boarding school, his father's aversion to all things Western, and his own love of baseball as he seeks to honor his family's samurai values in an increasingly modern Japan.

While the West was being settled and immigrants were pouring into the thriving cities of the East, rural and small-town America seemed quiet and peaceful. Several stories set around the turn of the century give a glimpse of life as it was lived in small towns in the East, away from the high drama of life on the frontier or in bustling urban centers. Gary Schmidt bases the Newbery Honor book, **Lizzie Bright and the Buckminster Boy** (I–A), on a true story. In 1911, Maine officials forced African American, Native American, and foreign-born residents to leave Malaga Island because they wanted to use the island as a tourist attraction. Schmidt takes this incident and weaves the story of Turner Buckminster III, son of the new congregational preacher, and Lizzie Bright Griffin, granddaughter of Malaga's African American preacher. The gripping drama contains multiple conflicts—not the least between Turner and his father—that reveal both the worst and the best sides of humanity as townspeople engage in a struggle for human dignity that is sparked by the desire for money and power. Jennifer Holm's **Our Only May Amelia** and **The Trouble with May Amelia** (both I) depict the joys and sorrows of turn-of-the-century life in Washington State while they also explore gender roles. Amelia, like Calpurnia Tate, strains against the restrictions of being a girl in that time.

Many major events are the catalysts for novels for young readers. The Johnstown Flood of 1889 was the result of the failure of a dam, but also the result of the very classist society of that time. Jame Richards's novel in verse, **Three Rivers Rising: A Novel of the Johnstown Flood** (A), is both social commentary and a very exciting adventure story. Deborah Hopkinson's **Into the Firestorm: A Novel of San Francisco, 1906** (I) is a carefully researched story of one boy's experience in the famous fire. Choosing between self-preservation and helping others becomes a defining moment in young Nick's life. Another famous fire is at the climax of Margaret Peterson Haddix's **Uprising** (A), which portrays the abysmal working conditions at the Triangle Shirtwaist Factory in New York City. Three main characters, a young Italian immigrant, a Russian immigrant who tries to organize the women in the factory, and a wealthy young woman who becomes involved in the struggle of these young women for safe and humane working conditions, allow Haddix to present a tapestry of the way people lived in that time and place. Katherine Paterson's **Bread and Roses, Too** (A) tells the moving story of the 1912 "Bread and Roses" mill strike in Lawrence, Massachusetts. Her compelling characterization, as always, puts a human face on history.

● ● WORLD WAR I ● ●
AND ITS AFTERMATH

There are not many books set during World War I, in either picturebook or novel form, but the books that do exist are outstanding. Recently, there have been several books that examine both the events and the nature of this war from the perspective of those left behind as well as those on the front lines. In Iain Lawrence's **Lord of the Nutcracker Men** (I–A), young Johnny's world has been profoundly affected. With his father in France and his mother working in a distant munitions plant, Johnny must leave London for the safety of his aunt's countryside home. He takes with him the nutcracker men and toy soldiers that his father made for him before leaving, and his army grows with each soldier his father carves and sends him from the front. As the war continues, both the soldiers and the letters from his father get more and more frightening, while Johnny learns to take responsibility for himself. Although Johnny's anguish is in the foreground, his father's letters also reveal the true horrors of the front.

Michael Morpurgo's **Private Peaceful** (A) moves from the front to the idyllic past of turn-of-the-century rural England as Private Thomas (Tommo) Peaceful spends a sleepless night trying to remember his past. His memories, told in a series of vignettes, recount his childhood and adolescence in the company of his older brother, Charlie, and their best friend, Molly. The brothers are so close that even though Tommo loves Molly, Charlie's marriage to her does not destroy their relationship. When Charlie goes to war, Tommo lies about his age to follow him. Morpurgo explores the brutality of not only the war but the people who engage in it. The ending is a profound condemnation of the killing of others, for any reason.

In the summer of 1925, it was hot—very hot—in New York City, the setting of Walter Dean Myers's **Harlem Summer** (A). Sixteen-year-old Mark needs a summer job, anything that will keep him from having to work for his uncle, an undertaker. He takes a job downtown at *The Crisis* publishing office, wondering how he fits in with the "new Negroes" working there—people such as Dr. W.E.B. DuBois and Langston

Hughes. And besides, it's just a job; his real passion is his saxophone and the music of Fats Waller. When Fats gets Mark involved in gangster activity and into the bad graces of the notorious Dutch Schultz, Mark must figure out how to solve his problem, quickly. Poignant and humorous, this is a terrific coming-of-age story and an entertaining glimpse of life in Harlem in 1925. Jen Bryant's ***Ringside, 1925: Views from the Scopes Trial*** (A) offers another view of the way thought was changing in the United States. A small town in Iowa in 1929 is the setting for Anne Ylvisaker's ***The Luck of the Buttons*** (I). This beautifully written novel is a mystery story, a coming-of-age story, and a portrait of one special family living in a calm and innocent time.

• • THE GREAT DEPRESSION • •

Stories of the Depression years portray America in times of trouble. The beginning of the period is generally considered to be the stock market crash of 1929. Then, stories of ruined businessmen jumping from skyscrapers filled the headlines of daily newspapers. Now, stories for children describe the grim effects of living in poverty. Mildred Taylor's books about Cassie Logan and her family, ***Song of the Trees*** (I), ***Roll of Thunder, Hear My Cry*** (A), ***Let the Circle Be Unbroken*** (A), ***The Friendship*** (A), and ***Mississippi Bridge*** (A), show rural poverty and prevailing racism. Young Cassie and her extended family, including Paul-Edward's widow (Cassie's grandmother) and David Logan (her father), live on their own farm. Owning their own land was unusual for African Americans in Mississippi at that time, and it is a source of pride for Cassie. She doesn't really understand why her father has to leave the family to find work to pay the taxes, however. Nor does she understand the prevalent racism that surrounds her because she has been protected by her loving family. In the Newbery Medal–winning ***Roll of Thunder, Hear My Cry***, Taylor vividly portrays the physical, social, and political setting through Cassie's eyes as Cassie begins to discover the truth about where she lives and the compelling reasons for holding on to their land. The Logan saga is the most complete chronicle of the Jim Crow era available for young readers. As such, it illuminates key threads of our history and identity as a nation.

TEACHING IDEA 8.4

Genre Study: Compare Treatment of a Theme across Genres

 **COMMON CORE STATE STANDARDS** This Teaching Idea addresses the Common Core English Language Arts, Reading: Literature standard 9, grades 3 through 8. The suggestions in this Teaching Idea may need to be adapted to suit your particular grade level and the needs of your students.

Select a theme that crosses the boundaries of time, such as the effects of homelessness on people's lives. Gather primary sources, such as current or historical newspapers and magazines and contemporary and historical fiction and nonfiction. Ask students to read and respond to their reading, then to compare these experiences to their reading of a textbook or encyclopedia on the same topic. Discuss the different ways of knowing—cognitive and emotional—that these readings generate.

The following are titles that deal with homelessness during the Great Depression and today:

Contemporary Fiction

Bunting, Eve, ***Fly Away Home*** (1991) (I)

Fox, Paula, ***Monkey Island*** (1991) (A)

Johnson, Lindsay Lee, ***Soul Moon Soup*** (2002) (I–A)

Tolan, Stephanie, ***Sophie and the Sidewalk Man*** (1992) (I)

Historical Fiction

Bartoletti, Susan Campbell, ***Christmas Promise*** (2001) (P)

Choldenko, Gennifer, ***Al Capone Does My Shirts*** (2004) (I–A)

Curtis, Christopher Paul, ***Bud, Not Buddy*** (1999) (I)

DeFelice, Cynthia, ***Nowhere to Call Home*** (1999) (I–A)

Peterson, Jeanne Whitehouse, ***Don't Forget Winona*** (2000) (I)

Nonfiction

Coombs, Karen Mueller, ***Children of the Dust Days*** (2000) (I)

Jen Bryant builds on a specific incident—the kidnapping and subsequent death of the Lindbergh baby in 1932—in *The Trial* (I–A). This novel in poems introduces us to twelve-year-old Katie and the world of small-town New Jersey during the Depression as seen through Katie's eyes. Katie finds herself inside the courtroom at the Hauptmann trial, helping her Uncle Jeff, a reporter who needs help taking notes because he has broken his arm. Because Katie, in all her innocence, is there, we can see the trial through fresh eyes, eyes that wonder about guilt and innocence.

Karen Hesse's Newbery Medal–winning *Out of the Dust* (A), also discussed in Chapter 4, is unrelenting in its depiction of life in the Oklahoma dust bowl; the story is softened only by the sensitivity of its heroine and its own poetic form. Told through the poems of young Billie Jo, the novel captures the combination of hope and despair that reflects the time and place; it also captures the pain of adolescence at any time in any place. Teaching Idea 8.4 offers suggestions for exploring the theme of homelessness, a common occurrence during the Depression, across different genres.

Other stories set during this time are less grim. In Gennifer Choldenko's *Al Capone Does My Shirts* (I–A), Moose worries about his father losing his job and their home, but he also copes with his sister's autism and their mother's emotional trauma; the daily life of his family, living on Alcatraz; and his increasing maturity. Although Christopher Paul Curtis's Newbery Medal–winning *Bud, Not Buddy* (I) does involve death, homelessness, and racism, its overall tone is one of hope mixed with poignant humor. Richard Peck's Newbery Medal–winning *A Year down Yonder* and Newbery Honor–winning *A Long Way from Chicago: A Novel in Stories* (I–A) are set in the Depression-era small-town Midwest. In both books, the characterization and humor, as well as the sense of place and time, are outstanding. Particia Reilly Giff's *R My name Is Rachel* (I–A) depicts the changes in lifestyle for a family who is forced to move from New York City to upstate New York. The children are left alone when the father leaves to find work, but they each rise to the occasion, doing what they can to hold the family together.

Andrea Davis Pinkney sets *Bird in a Box* (I) in a small upstate New York town in 1937 as Joe Louis prepares to take on James Braddock for the heavyweight championship of the world. Not only was this an athletic challenge, but it also challenged the color barrier in American sports and the pervasive racism in American life. Pinkney's three protagonists, a preacher's daughter, an abused child, and a lonely orphan, become friends as they struggle toward their individual dreams and root for the Brown Bomber, a symbol of African American hope and pride.

● ● WORLD WAR II ● ●
AND ITS AFTERMATH

The years 1933 to 1946 encompassed Adolf Hitler's rise and fall in Germany and Japanese military activity in the Pacific, as well as the maneuvering of the Soviet Union to annex other countries. World War II brought into vivid awareness humanity's potential inhumanity, particularly toward our fellow human beings. The horrors of the period were so unthinkable that it was several decades before the story was told in books for young people. The children who read these books today are reading about the world of their grandparents and great-grandparents; these stories connect with many family histories.

Stories Set in Europe and Asia

The familiar adage that those who do not know the past are condemned to repeat it is adequate cause for attending to the tragedy of the Holocaust. The books describing Hitler's reign of terror, with its effects ultimately on all people, are a good place to begin. Many emphasize—some in small ways, others in larger—that in the midst of inhumanity there can be small acts of human kindness.

Despite their grimness, some books are affirmative: young people work in underground movements, strive against terrible odds, plan escapes, and struggle for survival. Some books show heroic resistance, in which characters fight back or live with dignity and hope in the face of a monstrous future. Jane Yolen's *The Devil's Arithmetic* (A) is a graphic, moving account of being a Jew in Poland during the Nazi persecution. Using the fantasy device of a time slip, Yolen plunges her young protagonist into the life that her aunt and her aunt's best friend endured at the hands of the Nazis. A less graphic book appropriate for upper-elementary-school readers is Lois Lowry's Newbery Medal–winning *Number the Stars* (I). Lowry tells the story of how one Danish family saves the lives of their friends, the Rosens. The contrast between the implications of Nazi rule for the Jewish Ellen and the Christian Annemarie is striking.

Based on a true event during the war, Bebe Dumon Tak weaves an amazing story in *Soldier Bear* (I–A), translated from the Dutch by Laura Watkinson and illustrated by Philip Hopman. In this novel, which won the Batchelder Award, a small group of Polish soldiers flee the invading Russians and escape to Iran. There, they join the British army and adopt a bear cub, who becomes a member of their unlikely group of five men, one bear, and a monkey. Susan Lynn Meyer sets her story of resistance in the Vichy French countryside in *Black Radishes* (I). Eleven-year-old Gustave and his family flee Paris in 1940 for the relative safety of the countryside. Unfortunately, that safety is only relative, and the war continues to be a struggle for the family. Kathleen Benner Duble's **Phantom in the Snow** (I–A) begins in the United States but moves to the Italian Alps, as she fictionalizes the action of a real, elite group of military skiers. This novel is packed with detail and adventure.

Norway is the setting for Mary Casanova's **The Klipfish Code** (I)—the story of two children sent to the safety of an island to live with their grandfather and aunt, and how the war came with them. As the children struggle to adjust to a very different life, and to cope with the loneliness and fear of not knowing what is happening to their parents, young Marit decides to act to aid her country, doing what she can to hinder the Nazis during the occupation. Annika Thor's Batchelder Award–winning **A Faraway Island** (I–A) began the story of young Stephie as she flees Nazi-occupied Vienna for a rugged island off the coast of Sweden, which is continued in **The Lily Pond** (I–A), translated from the Swedish by Linda Schenck. In this second novel, Stephie is allowed to enroll in the school on the mainland, where she struggles to define herself and her role. She falls in love, which creates a difficult situation, discovers the growing Nazi ideology in Sweden, and continues to worry about the fate of her parents, trapped in Nazi Vienna. These are the first two in a quartet of books about Stephie and her sister.

William Durbin's **The Winter War** (I–A), set during the Soviet invasion of Finland in 1939, portrays the cunning and heroism of the Finns—some of them young boys—who used the snow and cold and their skill on skis to defeat the invading army. Ruta Sepetys's **Between Shades of Gray** (A) tells a story not frequently found in literature for young readers. In Lithuania of 1941, fifteen-year-old Lina, her mother, and her younger brother are sent to Siberia as their father is arrested and taken away. The life-threatening hardships that Lina and her family and those deported with her endure is balanced by the hope for the future that she continues to believe in. Based on the author's family history, this fictionalized recounting of the dark days of the Stalinist Soviet Union rings with truth.

Karen Hesse, intrigued by an article she read, began to research the Warsaw ghetto and Jewish resistance in Poland and wrote **The Cats in Krasinski Square** (I), a picturebook with a spare, poetic text and muted, lovely illustrations. The illustrations fill in details of time and place, and Hesse's words convey fear, determination, and the small joys of life in this story of resistance. Marisabina Russo's **I Will Come Back for You: A Family in Hiding during World War II** (P–I) is based on her own family story. In spare words and evocative illustrations, Russo recounts how one Jewish family lived in hiding during the Holocaust years. Although the ending is not totally happy, it is realistic and satisfying with what is left of the family immigrating to New York to begin a new life.

Stories about life in Europe after the war explore how people began to mend their shattered lives. Mirjam Pressler's **Halinka** (A) explores the emotional damage of war through the eyes of a young girl sent to a home for troubled girls in Germany in the postwar years. This story, translated from the German, is truly a universal tribute to the power of love.

Despite the fact that American armed forces fought for four years in the Pacific, few children's and adolescent novels are set in this locale. Roland Smith's **Elephant Run** (I), set in Burma, is a war story and a thrilling adventure as well as an animal story—in this case, elephants. Padma Venkatraman's **Climbing the Stairs** (A), a novel set in the India of 1941 during the British occupation, is a coming-of-age story within a country, and a world, in turmoil.

A novel set in Korea under the control of the Japanese, Linda Sue Park's **When My Name Was Keoko** (A) chronicles the life of the children of a Korean scholar, revealing the small, quiet triumphs and the abiding fear of an oppressed people. Set within the larger historical context of the war, the struggles of Sun-hee, forced to take the Japanese name of Keoko, and her brother Tae-yul, renamed Nobuo, are revealed in alternating first-person points of view. What is happening in Korea is mirrored in the family's life, and the hope at the end of the novel is only slightly dimmed by the communist threat in the North.

Stories Set in North America

Some stories that take place during World War II are set in North America. Some of these are about children who were evacuated from Europe. In Phoebe Stone's **The Romeo and Juliet Code** (I), an eleven-year-old girl and her parents evacuate London during the blitz and go to the coast of Maine to live. Her parents, however, soon leave, mysteriously. This coming-of-age spy story has just the right amount of suspense for intermediate readers.

Some stories explore the ugly side of life in the United States during the war, as do those that chronicle the shameful internment of Japanese Americans; still others explore the lives of children whose fathers, uncles, and big brothers were fighting in the war abroad. Winifred Conkling's **Sylvia & Aki** (I) is the fictionalized story of an unlikely friendship between two very real girls. Together they challenged the racism that affected the Japanese and Latino residents of California. These true events ended with a court decision that led to the desegregation of California schools and, eventually, the rest of the country.

Ken Mochizuki's ***Baseball Saved Us*** (ɪ) describes how one Japanese American family was uprooted and transported to an internment camp in the middle of the desert. Even when the war was over, ugly feelings against Japanese Americans ran high, especially on the West Coast. Virginia Euwer Wolff's ***Bat 6*** (ɪ–A), set in 1949 in a small Oregon town, explores how the wounds that were opened by the war continued to fester long after the war's end, culminating in a terrible incident during a girl's community baseball game.

There were strong feelings on the East Coast as well, with German Americans as the target. Janet Taylor Lisle's ***The Art of Keeping Cool*** (A), which takes place in a community located on the heavily fortified Rhode Island coast, explores the hatred in the community through the character of Abel Hoffman, a refugee artist. The story also depicts the havoc that hatred has wreaked in the life of one family.

Ellen Klages's Newbery Medal–winning ***The Green Glass Sea*** (ɪ) and the sequel, ***White Sands, Red Menace*** (ɪ–A), are set in the American Southwest and center around the creation of the atomic bomb and the implications of what occurred in Hiroshima and Nagasaki. The tensions between those in favor of and opposed to atomic research and weapons are mirrored in the tensions within families and friendships. Anne Ylvisaker's ***Little Klein*** (ɪ) is set in 1949 in a rural river town and perfectly captures the freedom enjoyed by boys who could roam the countryside. The Klein family and the dog who loves the youngest, Little Klein, are memorable characters who make this bygone America come to life.

Several picturebooks present aspects of life at this time as well. Jacqueline Woodson's ***Coming on Home Soon*** (P), with Caldecott Honor–winning illustrations by E. B. Lewis, is a poignant story of a young girl's yearning for her mother, who goes North to find work because "they are hiring Colored women in Chicago." This story reminds us that even when children are safe they, too, are profoundly affected by war. Lila Judge's ***One Thousand Tracings: Healing the Wounds of World War II*** (P) is based on a true story of one American family's effort to relieve the suffering of the postwar German people.

• • THE 1950S THROUGH • • THE 1980S: POLITICAL AND SOCIAL TURMOIL

The end of World War II brought with it change in the social organization of the world and the lifestyles of many people. Peace was not long-lasting; soon the world was disturbed by the Cold War and the Korean, Vietnam, and Cambodian conflicts, as well as by other less-publicized wars. In the United States, the civil rights movement forever altered the status quo, and the role of women in society also changed dramatically. Books set amid the issues and events of these decades are becoming more plentiful. Deirdre Baker (2007) speculates that this may be the result of the increasing tensions of our own time; stories of the Cold War remind us that sometimes tensions are resolved without wars. Linda Sue Park sets her novel ***Keeping Score*** (ɪ) in America at the time of a Cold War conflict, the Korean War, with a young girl's view of the damage that war can cause. Newbery Honor–winning ***Breaking Stalin's Nose*** (ɪ–A) by Eugene Yelchin is set in a dangerous and difficult time in the Soviet Union. At any moment, anyone can be arrested by the secret police and thrown in prison; most do not return. Ten-year-old Sasha worships Stalin, wants to join the Young Pioneers, and is steeped in communist beliefs until the night his own father, a member of the state security, is taken from their home in the middle of the night. Sasha begins to question the beliefs that he has held dear and to understand the costs to a society of fear and persecution. Narrated in Sasha's voice, this brief novel with dramatic black-and-white illustrations is a powerful introduction to a time and place that many young readers read about only in textbooks.

David Almond's ***The Fire-Eaters*** (ɪ–A) captures the tension of the Cold War at a specific time—when Kennedy and Khrushchev were arguing over Cuba and it seemed that nuclear war was inevitable. Set in rural England, this spellbinding novel brings this historical time to young readers who live with their own set of global tensions. Tim Wynne-Jones's ***Rex Zero and the End of the World; Rex Zero, King of Nothing;*** and ***Rex Zero, The Great Pretender*** (all ɪ–A) are set in Ottawa, Canada, during the 1960s. He captures perfectly the undercurrent of uneasiness, sometimes erupting into terror, that permeated the Western world at that time, all within a story of an often-funny and always endearing young boy just beginning to grow up and out into the wider world. In Deborah Wiles's ***Countdown*** (ɪ–A), "duck and cover" becomes all too real when the Cuban Missle Crisis heats up. Poor Fanny Chapman just wants everything peaceful—in the world, her family, and her own self as she negotiates her way from childhood to adolescence. Wiles intersperses her narrative with primary source material from 1962, creating a documentary novel that is a knockout. Some other excellent books set during the Cold War are Karen Cushman's ***The***

Loud Silence of Francine Green (I–A), Ursula Dubosarsky's *The Red Shoe* (A), and Iain Lawrence's *Gemini Summer* (I–A).

People such as Mildred Taylor's Cassie Logan and her brothers were at the front of the line during the civil rights movement, and many authors now tell their stories. Christopher Paul Curtis's *The Watsons Go to Birmingham—1963* (I–A), a Newbery Honor book, explores the experiences and feelings of ten-year-old Kenny and his family as they drive from Flint, Michigan, to Birmingham, Alabama, to visit Grandma. Alternately funny and deadly serious, the novel captures the tenor and the tragedy of the times. Sharon Draper dramatizes the integration of Central High School in Little Rock, Arkansas, in *Fire from the Rock* (A). Rita Williams-Garcia explores the black power movement of the late 1960s in *One Crazy Summer* (I–A). This very readable book won both a Coretta Scott King Author Award and a Newbery Honor. With minimal text and full-bleed, double-page spreads, Shane Evans presents a fictionalized version of the 1963 march on Washington, which ended with Martin Luther King's stirring *I Have a Dream* speech. *We March* (P–I–A) captures that day.

Cynthia Kadohata's *Kira-Kira* (I–A) is set in the early 1960s and follows Katie and her family as they move from a Japanese community in Iowa to the Deep South of Georgia, where they encounter racism and unabashed curiosity. When Katie's beloved older sister Lynn dies, Katie helps her family realize that there is, indeed, hope in the future. As Lynn has taught her, the world is *kira-kira*, shining. Kadohata won a Newbery Medal for this moving depiction of one family's experience. In *Outside Beauty* (A), set in the 1980s, she tells a story of sisterly bonds as a family of four sisters, and as many fathers, are separated when their mother is unable to care for them.

Historical fiction set during the conflict in Vietnam and the aftermath in Cambodia is becoming more plentiful. Like those about World War II, some of these books are set in the midst of the conflict and consider the lives of children in the war zones. Others are set in North America, Australia, or other countries and deal with such issues as children fleeing the war to find a new life; the experiences of children whose grandfathers, uncles, and fathers went to war; the impact of returning veterans on family life; and the deep divisions in America during the Vietnam conflict. Walter Dean Myers explores issues of race as well as issues surrounding the Vietnam conflict in his powerful *Fallen Angels* (A). In *Letters from Wolfie* (A), Patti Sherlock effectively portrays the deep divisions in the United States during the Vietnam conflict. When Mark's older brother leaves for Vietnam, Mark becomes convinced that he should send his beloved dog, Wolfie, to the army to be used as a scout dog. Mark's reasons for doing so are as jumbled as his feelings in this emotionally wrenching story.

Few stories are told from the point of view of the Vietnamese, Thai, Cambodian, or Hmong people who endured the war in their own homelands. National Book Award–winning *Inside Out & Back Again* (A) previously mentioned, is a beautifully crafted novel in verse by Thanhha Lai in which she tells the story of her family's escape from Saigon and their struggles as they adjust to life in Alabama. Living in poverty, racism, religious differences, the strength of family, and the importance of friendship are integral themes that speak to today's readers. This book was also a Newbery Honor winner.

Jack Gantos's *Dead End in Norvelt* (A) won a Newbery Award for his funny yet poignant portrayal of life in a small Pennsylvania town in 1962. A semi-autobiographical story, this book presents odd-ball characters with great affection and portrays an important summer in the life of an adolescent who learns that he can change his own behavior. Kimberly Willis Holt's *When Zachary Beaver Came to Town* (A), winner of the National Book Award, is set in a sleepy Texas town during the Vietnam conflict. The historical details are rich, and the characters' lives reflect the times in which they live even as the novel focuses on life issues rather than historical ones. Gary Schmidt's *The Wednesday Wars* (I–A), a Newbery Honor Award winner, is both side-splittingly funny and deeply poignant. A very compelling coming-of-age story set in 1967, the novel follows Holling Hoodhood across the course of a school year as he learns a great deal about himself and how the world works. As his teacher, Mrs. Baker, whose husband is serving in Vietnam, tells him, "A comedy isn't about being funny . . . [It's] about characters who dare to know that they may choose a happy ending after all" (p. 262). In the National Book Award finalist *Okay for Now* (I–A), a companion novel, Schmidt reveals the story of Holling's nemesis, Doug Swieteck. We now take a close look at this engaging story.

* * *

A CLOSE LOOK AT
Okay for Now

As Doug Swieteck and his family are about to leave Brooklyn to move to upstate New York, where his father has found a job after being fired, Holling Hoodhood stops by to give Doug the jacket that New York Yankee Joe Pepitone had given Holling when he, Doug, and another boy played catch with Pepitone and another player. Because his older brother had

In **Okay for Now**, the companion to **The Wednesday Wars**, *Gary Schmidt tells the story of a troubled boy who learns to let others care for him.*

taken the cap that Pepitone gave him, Doug was thrilled, even though puzzled, when Holling handed him the jacket. As the story progresses, it becomes a symbol of what is possible as Doug struggles with his dysfunctional family, small-town life, and adolescence.

Doug's narrative voice is set in the first few lines: "Joe Pepitone once gave me his New York Yankees baseball cap. I'm not lying. He gave it to me. To me, Doug Swieteck. To me." This is our first glimpse at Doug's capacity for awe, his need, based on past behavior, to assure readers and himself that he is being truthful, and his amazement that something wonderful has happened to him. This voice continues throughout the novel, as many things, both wonderful and difficult, happen in the first year he spends in the small town of Marysville.

Doug is a complex character. From what he tells us, we know that he is abused by his brothers, and that everyone, including his mother, is abused by his father, although the extent of that abuse is revealed only little

by little across much of the novel. We also gradually become aware that Doug cannot read. For example, he waits outside of the library for it to open even though the sign on the door clearly says that it is closed; in his new job as a delivery boy, he needs to ask for help finding streets even though he has a map. Fortunately for Doug, a few perceptive teachers also become aware of this and he does eventually learn. These teachers, one of the librarians who is also an artist, the customers on his delivery route, his own mother, and a girl who befriends him sense something in Doug that has been hidden: intelligence, kindness, possibility for love.

As we watch Doug struggle at home, at work, and at school, we also see him lie to himself as well as to everyone around him. He is unwilling to reveal his troubles, so unwilling that even when his gym teacher insists that he remove his shirt to play on the "skins" team, he refuses. We find out why when the teacher will not let the issue drop. Even as the poignant story unrolls, humor abounds. Doug's voice is tough, tender, and wry. Many of the predicaments he finds himself in are laugh-out-loud funny, whereas the next page evokes tears, much like the rollercoaster ride that is Doug's life.

The secondary characters in **Okay for Now** all have some dimension that is hidden from us because they are hidden from even Doug at the beginning of the story. His and our first impression of the girl he meets on his first day in Marysville is not positive; Doug is sure she is making fun of him. As we see him begin to trust her, and then begin to fall in love with her, we also see the results of Doug gradually shedding his defensive shell and beginning to trust the world. We, along with him, come to know that even those who seem really awful, such as the gym teacher, the school principal, his brothers and his father, have humanity. One of the more poignant revelations is when Doug's brother cries and, for the first time in the novel, Doug uses his name instead of "the jerk" or "my stupid brother." In the end, even Principal Peattie turns out to have a core of kindness.

This novel is woven with themes that run through each chapter. We see the power of art to alter a person's view of himself as Doug learns to draw using Audubon prints as his models. We understand how art applies to life, such as when the nobility that he sees in the eyes of the brown pelican allows him to see the nobility in the eyes of some of those around him. Trust in others, the courage to be vulnerable, and, above all, the power of love are themes that hold the novel together. Set during the Vietnam conflict, the echoes of that war are apparent in the adults Doug interacts with as well as in his own home. And, of course, the New York Yankees complete the picture. Against this backdrop, we see Doug learning that he is, indeed, okay for now.

P R O F I L E

Gary Schmidt

I write for the huge pleasure it brings, to create a work that a young reader would pick up. . . . It seems to me that we as a culture need to be bringing our best word to our children—our finest and most important resource. . . .

Gary Schmidt holds a PhD in medieval literature and teaches English at Calvin College in Grand Rapids, Michigan, living nearby in a 150-year-old farmhouse with his large family. In addition to his work teaching at Calvin College, he is on the faculty at Hamline University in St. Paul, Minnesota, where he teaches in the MFA program in writing for children. Author of several books for young readers, Gary has won two Newbery Honors, the first for *Lizzie Bright and the Buckminster Boy* and the second for *The Wednesday Wars*. He is also the author of numerous academic articles and books.

To learn more about Gary Schmidt, go to CengageBrain.com and visit the Education CourseMate website where you will find links to relevant websites.

Zimbabwe in the 1980s is the setting for Jason Wallace's *Out of Shadows* (A). Post–civil war Zimbabwe is a dangerous place; the larger setting of tense race relations and violence is mirrored in the smaller story of homophobia, bullying, and racism. There is no time period that young readers cannot explore through historical fiction. As time passes, our past enlarges. Fortunately, interest in places and people around the world has increased as well. Stories of the past from around the world offer us a wonderful resource for helping children, and ourselves, discover our own connections with humanity throughout history, to make sense of our present through our past, and to think about our future in new ways.

Historical Fiction in the Classroom

History is made by people—people with strengths and weaknesses who experience victories and defeats. It reflects what they do, what they say, and what they are. Authors of books set in the past want young readers to understand that history is full of human beings—real people like themselves. Today's youth don't know a world without computers, technology, rapid transportation, and modern communication. When they read good historical fiction, however, they can imagine themselves living in another time and place. They can speculate about how they would have reacted and how they would have felt. They can read about ordinary people acting heroically. By doing so, they begin to understand the impact one person can have on history.

Historical fiction can help children discover their own place in the history of their world; it can give them a sense of the historical importance of their own lives. Well-written historical fiction can make the past alive, real, and meaningful to children who are living today and who will shape the world of tomorrow.

Reading historical fiction can help children realize that they are players on the historical stage and that their lives, too, will one day become part of history. As they read historical fiction, they come to realize the human drama inherent in history as well as the common themes that reach across time and cultures. Historical fiction offers students opportunities that history textbooks do not. Students who read trade books in addition to textbooks learn more than students who do not.

There are many ways to explore historical fiction with young readers. The body of this chapter is organized around historical fiction grouped to explore particular times in history. Historical fiction can also be used to study the elements of fiction because excellent historical fiction anchors characters, plot, and theme in a particular time and place through language that also reflects that time and place. Following, we briefly describe two other ways of working with historical fiction in the classroom: presenting historical eras through multiple genres and exploring themes through historical fiction in combination with other genres. Indeed, the Common Core English Language Arts standards call for this kind of study.

Historical fiction can be linked to other genres: poetry, folklore, fantasy, biography, and nonfiction can be combined with historical fiction in the study of a particular time and place. For example, teachers who want their students to come to know about life in medieval England might want to combine folklore (such as the legends that surround King Arthur) with fantasy set in that period as well as with books that combine fantasy with historical fiction (such as the novels of Elizabeth Wein and Kevin Crossley-Holland) and the straightforward history of historical fiction (such as *Crispin; Yoss; Catherine, Called Birdy*; and *The Midwife's Apprentice*). The many fine works of nonfiction provide another way to explore the era. Together, these books provide a series of reading experiences that leave young readers so steeped in the time and place that they understand how people lived and thought as well as how that influenced subsequent generations.

The first time one fifth-grade teacher tried using historical fiction, poetry, biography, and nonfiction instead of the social studies text for the study of the American Revolution, she was unsure of the possible outcomes. She asked students to read one novel, some poetry, one biography, and one informational book on that historical period. In addition, they read an encyclopedia account of one of the events described in the novel. The students then critically examined the presentations in the various sources. The teacher modeled the process, and they worked in collaborative learning groups to discuss their findings. The class concluded that no single book could have given them the basis for understanding that they gained from their wide reading. The children begged their teacher to use the same approach for the next social studies unit.

Another teacher worked with her third-grade children to develop a study plan for a unit on early settlers in America. She filled the room with many sources of information, including books, records, poetry, films, and pictures. The students spent several days exploring the material and making suggestions about topics that interested them. Their list included the pilgrims, Plymouth Rock, the *Mayflower*, and the first Thanksgiving. The group organized the ideas into reasonably logical categories, and students chose topics they wanted to pursue, identified sources of information, and began the research for the study. Examining the past in this way helped students begin to understand human behavior, the ways that people and societies interact, the concept of humans as social beings, and the values that make people human.

When studying the same period of time with his eighth-grade students, another teacher successfully combined historical fiction set in colonial times with some of the excellent nonfiction available about those times, such as **Sir Walter Ralegh and the Quest for El Dorado** (A) by Marc Aronson. This allowed his students to understand how the political systems and religious thought in England influenced the structures and thought of colonial America.

Thematically organized instruction is yet another way to explore historical fiction. History is always repeating itself, and many stories set in the past explore issues that are important to people today. Understanding human nature and social patterns can result from thinking about themes found in historical

fiction and linking them to books in other genres and to our own lives. People have common needs; these universal needs can be identified as themes that permeate social interactions. For example, the quest for freedom and respect, the struggle between good and evil or between love and hate, and the determination to seek a better life are themes that are as old as time and as current as today. Historical fiction contains the stories of many people caught up in such struggles. Reading a number of books that explore the same theme across different periods of history allows students to understand the similarities of human needs across time; looking at books that explore the same theme in different cultures allows students to understand the similarities of human needs across peoples.

Prejudice is an issue that permeates many of the books discussed in this chapter, many of the books of contemporary realism discussed in Chapter 7, and many of the fantasy and science fiction novels discussed in Chapter 6. You will find issues of prejudice in the biographies of people who faced it in various forms and in the nonfiction accounts of segregation, women in the workforce, and life for immigrants, to name but a few subjects. Another prevalent theme is the cultural dislocation experienced by immigrants, both a timeless and a contemporary issue. Many fantasy novels, contemporary fiction novels, and biographies can be combined with historical fiction to explore this theme.

The possibilities for thematic combinations across genres as well as within the historical fiction genre are many, as are the times and places that young readers can explore. There are resources available to help teachers identify books to use. An annotated bibliography published yearly by the Children's Book Council and the National Council for the Social Studies, *Notable Children's Trade Books in the Field of Social Studies*, is one such resource. This is available from either organization and is also published in the April/May issue of the journal *Social Education*. Other resources present books by theme. These and other resources mentioned in Chapter 1 will help you construct powerful reading experiences for your students.

SUMMARY

When teachers put wonderful stories set in the past into the hands of children, the past comes alive for those students. By reading historical fiction, students see that history was lived by people who—despite their different dress, customs, and habits—were a lot like we are. Whether they are confronting the plague in

Europe during the Middle Ages, fleeing from soldiers in the American West, or watching a young father go to war, today's readers can vicariously experience the events of the past. When children are immersed in a compelling story, history comes to life. It is only then that it becomes real and important, that it becomes meaningful for young readers.

In the following Booklist, we present some titles of picturebooks of historical fiction. A few are discussed in the body of this chapter, but most are additional titles. A mix of old favorites and new titles, most of these books are appropriate for primary and intermediate readers. They can be used across all grades to introduce ideas, events, and historical periods to all students.

Booklist

The picturebooks in this list are appropriate for primary and intermediate readers unless otherwise specified.
✳ Indicates some aspect of diversity
✳ Browning, Diane, **Signed, Abiah Rose** (2010)
✳ Bruchac, Joseph, **Crazy Horse's Vision,** illustrated by S. D. Nelson (2007) (I–A)
✳ Carbone, Elisa, **Night Running,** illustrated by E. B. Lewis (2008)
✳ Dillon, Leo & Diane Dillon, **Jazz on a Saturday Night** (2001)
✳ Feelings, Tom, **The Middle Passage** (1995) (A)
✳ Garland, Sherry, **The Lotus Seed,** illustrated by Tatsuro Kiuchi (1993)
✳ Grifalconi, Ann, **Ain't Nobody a Stranger to Me,** illustrated by Jerry Pinkney (2007)
Hall, Donald, **Ox Cart Man,** illustrated by Barbara Cooney (1979)
Harvey, Brett, **My Prairie Christmas,** illustrated by Deborah Kogan Ray (1993)
✳ Hesse, Karen, **The Cats in Krasinski Square,** illustrated by Wendy Watson (2004)
✳ Hopkinson, Deborah, **Sweet Clara and the Freedom Quilt,** illustrated by James Ransome (2003)
Houston, Gloria, **The Year of the Perfect Christmas Tree,** illustrated by Barbara Cooney (1988)
✳ Howard, Elizabeth Fitzgerald, **Aunt Flossie's Hats (and Crab Cakes later),** illustrated by James Ransome (1990)
✳ Innocenti, Roberto, **Rose Blanche,** (1985) (A)
Kay, Verla, **Hornbooks and Inkwells,** illustrated by S. D. Schindler (2011)
✳ Lowry, Lois, **Crow Call,** illustrated by Bagram Ibatoulline (2009)
Martin, Jacqueline Briggs, **Grandmother Bryant's Pocket** (1996)
✳ Maruki, Toshi, **Hiroshima no Pika** (1980) (I–A)
✳ McKissack, Patricia, **Never Forgotten,** illustrated by Leo & Diane Dillon (2011) (I)
✳ Mitchell, Margaree King, **Uncle Jed's Barbershop,** illustrated by James Ransome (1993)
✳ Oppenheim, Shulamith Levey, **The Lily Cupboard:**

A Story of the Holocaust, illustrated by Ronald Himler (1992)
✳ Polacco, Patricia, **January's Sparrow** (2010) (I)
✳ _____, **Just in Time, Abraham Lincoln** (2011)
✳ _____, **Pink and Say** (1994) (I)
✳ Raven, Margot Theis, **Night Boat to Freedom,** illustrated by E. B. Lewis (2006)
✳ Russo, Marisabina Russo, **I Will Come Back for You** (2011)
✳ Say, Allen, **Grandfather's Journey** (1993)
Stevenson, James, **Don't You Know There's a War On?** (1992)
✳ Thomas, Joyce Carol, **I Have Heard of a Land,** illustrated by Floyd Cooper (1998)
✳ Turner, Ann, **Nettie's Trip South,** illustrated by Ronald Himler (1987) (I–A)
✳ Winter, Jeanette, **Follow the Drinking Gourd** (1988)
✳ Woodson, Jacqueline, **Coming on Home Soon,** illustrated by E. B. Lewis (2004)
✳ _____, **The Other Side,** illustrated by E. B. Lewis (2001)
✳ Yin, **Coolies,** illustrated by Chris Soentpiet (2001)
Yolen, Jane, **All Those Secrets of the World,** illustrated by Leslie Baker (1991)
✳ _____, **Encounter,** illustrated by David Shannon (1992) (I)
_____, **My Uncle Emily** (2010)

 Additional resources to accompany this chapter can be found on the Education CourseMate website. Go to CengageBrain .com to access a variety of interactive study tools and useful resources including Video Conversations with children's book authors and illustrators, a searchable children's literature database, glossary flashcards, online activities, tutorial quizzes, links to relevant websites, and more.

Biography and Memoir

- **Defining Biography and Memoir**

- **A Brief History of Biography and Memoir for Young Readers**

- **Considering Quality in Biography and Memoir**
  Accuracy
  Setting and Plot
  Portrayal of Subject
  Style
  Theme
  Illustrations
  A CLOSE LOOK AT   *Dave the Potter*

- **Variety in Biographical Subjects**
  Political and Military Leaders
  A CLOSE LOOK AT   *The Notorious Benedict Arnold*
  Philosophers and Religious Leaders
  Scientists and Inventors
  Adventurers and Explorers
  A CLOSE LOOK AT   *Almost Astronauts: 13 Women Who Dared to Dream*
  Practitioners of the Arts
  Sports Heroes
  Extraordinary Ordinary People

- **Biography and Memoir in the Classroom**
  Building a Biography Collection
  Using Biography with Other Genres to Study an Era
  Organizing Biography by Theme

- **Summary**

- **Booklist**

Jane often climbed her favorite tree,
which she named Beech.
She would lay her cheek against its trunk
and seem to feel the sap
flowing beneath the bark.
Jane could feel her own heart
beating,
beating,
beating.

—PATRICK MCDONNELL
Me…Jane*

Trinh sighed with pleasure as she read the final page of Caldecott Honor winner **Me…Jane** (P). "She really did it," she murmured to herself. Trinh leaned back in the beanbag chair tucked into the corner of her third-grade classroom and started to leaf through the pages of the book once again.

Trinh's third-grade teacher, Sam, had introduced his students to several biographical picturebooks over the last month. **Me…Jane** was one of many he had read aloud to the class, spending time discussing the back pages in particular of each book to help students understand that the people, and the stories, in the picturebooks were real. For example, after reading **Me…Jane** with Trinh and her classmates, Sam had led the students in closely examining the original photographs Patrick McDonnell used as inspiration for his illustrations. The class then visited two major Jane Goodall websites, read Jeanette Winter's biographical picturebook **The Watcher: Jane Goodall's Life with the Chimps** (P), and even explored a few pages of Goodall's *The Chimpanzees of Gombe: Patterns of Behavior*.

As they discussed the information presented in the picturebooks about Jane Goodall, about Eleanor Roosevelt in **Eleanor, Quiet No More** (P–I), about Amelia Earhart in **Night Flight: Amelia Earhart Crosses the Atlantic** (P), and more famous individuals, the students began to recognize that these individuals' attitudes and determination helped them to succeed in reaching their goals despite obstacles. It is not surprising that many of the students, like Trinh, seek out these biography picturebooks to pursue in independent reading time, finding the "happy endings" of the biographies sometimes more satisfying than those in fictional tales.

Defining Biography and Memoir

Biographies, autobiographies, and memoirs are narratives; they all tell the story of the life or a portion of the life of a real person. Autobiographies and memoirs are written by the subject him- or herself. Biographies and autobiographies range from mostly fictional to authentic—the genre straddles the boundary between fiction and nonfiction. Memoirs are interpretive accounts in which facts and events in the life of the author are selected, arranged, and constructed in order to bring out a particular theme or personality trait. Memoirs certainly contain facts, but they are based upon and interpreted through memory.

Biographies and memoirs may be episodic; that is, the author may highlight a particular part or parts of a life to illustrate the subject's character or to explore an especially important event in the life of the subject. In episodic biographies, writers can present a number of details within a manageable length, providing young readers the details they relish without sacrificing authenticity. Often episodic biographies are presented in picturebook format. Although this format forces authors to carefully select only the essentials of the story, the illustrations often offer a way for the essence of the subject and emotions of the episode to be captured without words.

Sometimes episodic biographies center around the early years of the subject, as in Catherine Brighton's ***Keep Your Eye on the Kid: The Early Years of Buster Keaton*** (P), in which she uses comic book frames to reflect the action. She also includes a brief bibliography, a list of Keaton's films, and an author's note, so that readers can discover more about the life of this man as an adult. Don Brown focuses on the early years of Thomas Edison in ***A Wizard from the Start: The Incredible Boyhood and Amazing Inventions of Thomas Edison*** (P–I).

Robert Burleigh's ***Langston's Train Ride*** (I) is an excellent example of an episodic biography that focuses on a pivotal event in the life of the subject. For Langston Hughes, this event was the train trip when he wrote his beautiful poem "The Negro Speaks of Rivers" and realized that he was a poet. Through the device of Langston's reflection about his life as he traveled, Burleigh is able to present other facts about

him as well. Burleigh's newest episodic biographical picturebook, ***Night Flight: Amelia Earhart Crosses the Atlantic*** (P), captures Earhart's first solo flight across the Atlantic in 1932 in lyrical prose and captivating illustrations by Wendell Minor.

Other biographies are more complete, spanning the entire life of a subject. Some, for primary- and intermediate-grade readers, are simplified, presenting what is in effect an outline of the subject's life. Over-simplification can result in an incomplete picture of both the individual and the times (Saul, 1986). David Adler's many biographies for primary-grade readers are examples of simplified biography. Even though they are factual, they contain few details and are most useful as an introduction to important people in history; some argue that their very simplification amounts to distortion. On the other hand, Barbara Kerley's Sibert Honor–winning ***What to Do about Alice? How Alice Roosevelt Broke the Rules, Charmed the World, and Drove Her Father Teddy Crazy*** (P–I) presents the life of this interesting woman from childhood through adulthood in a manner that intrigues young readers. Even biographies for younger readers can rely on fact and original source material, as Kerley's does. Biographies for older readers are even more inclusive of fact and source documents. Russell Freedman's wonderful ***Lincoln: A Photobiography*** (I–A) set a near standard for use of original sources in biographies for intermediate and young adult readers, even earning the Newbery Medal in 1988. It is filled with archival photographs, documented through multiple sources, and written with passion and verve.

Biographies also vary according to presentation. Some biographies focus on a single individual, whereas

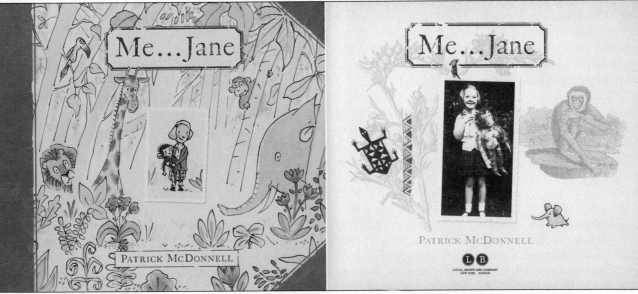

*Patrick McDonnell's illustrations in **Me...Jane** reflect actual photographs of Jane Goodall.*

others are collective biographies, or biographies about several individuals. These usually focus around a theme or other unifying principle. Tanya Lee Stone's Sibert Award–winning **Almost Astronauts: 13 Women Who Dared to Dream** (I–A), discussed later in this chapter, discusses the "Mercury 13" women as a group, but also explains a little bit of each individual's background and the battles they fought in their efforts to become the first women astronauts in the United States. Laurie Halse Anderson chose to look at other "unsung" female heroes in **Independent Dames: What You Never Knew about the Women and Girls of the American Revolution** (P–I). Anderson's humorous text is complimented by Matt Faulkner's illustrations, and young readers learn about some amazing girls and women. A timeline, additional facts, bibliography, web resources, and an index add to the information presented in the text itself.

A Brief History of Biography and Memoir for Young Readers

Biography was once regarded as an opportunity for young people to read about people they might emulate. For example, they might strive to be as honest as Abraham Lincoln or as brave as Lewis and Clark. Biographers in the nineteenth and early twentieth centuries wrote only about the good qualities of their subjects. During this period of intense nationalism, these writers deified America's heroes in a conscious effort to provide children with a set of role models, even if the depictions of these role models were false. Early biographies often did not include source material; documentation was rare. It was also difficult to separate fact from opinion because most biographers did not attempt to do so. Accuracy was less important than story, it seemed. Further, most of the early biographies were about white men of fame, and many were in multivolume series.

Fortunately, contemporary biographers are more likely to consider their subjects in a less adulatory and more realistic manner. We now view biography not as an opportunity for moral enlightenment, but as a chance for children to learn about themselves as they learn about the lives and times of people who made or are making a significant impact on the world (Herman, 1978). With this altered view of the role of biography have come books that focus on people who are not heroes. Today, there are biographies of ordinary, contemporary people living out their lives, such as Claire Nivola's **Planting the Trees of Kenya: The Story of Wangari Maathai** (P), a brilliantly told

and illustrated story of the Kenyan woman who rallies the women of her country to plant trees. Eventually, they are joined by men and children, and even soldiers. Wangari Maathai, a contemporary hero, won the Nobel Peace Prize in 2004.

There are even biographies of villains, such as James Cross Giblin's **The Life and Death of Adolf Hitler** (A) and Steve Sheinkin's **The Notorious Benedict Arnold** (I–A). The genre has also grown to encompass the diversity that exists in the world. Perhaps it has not grown quickly enough, but it is no longer as difficult to find excellent biographies of African American, Native American, Asian American, Latino, and international subjects. Biographies of all kinds of people allow young readers to understand both history and the contemporary world.

Still today, some very engaging biographies are biographical fiction, consisting almost entirely of imagined conversations and reconstructed events in the life of an individual. Barbara Kerley's **The Extraordinary Mark Twain (According to Susy)** (I) is a fictionalized story within a story; Susy, Mark Twain's daughter, writes her own biography of her famous father, which she claims will set the record straight on who he is. Joseph Bruchac's **Pocahontas** (I–A), told in alternating chapters by Pocahontas and John Smith, is another intriguing work of biographical fiction. Both books are classified as fiction, but they are based in part on factual evidence about a real person's life.

Memiors are an increasingly popular form of autobiographical writing in which an individual explores his or her own life; they are truthful, without necessarily being completely true. Francisco Jiménez's memoirs, **The Circuit: Stories from the Life of a Migrant Child** and **Breaking Through** (I–A), are stories about his life as a migrant child. They are classified as fiction. Roald Dahl's **More about Boy: Roald Dahl's Tales from Childhood** (I–A) is also often listed as fiction. In contrast, Ed Young's **The House Baba Built: An Artist's Childhood in China** (I), also a memoir, is more frequently classified as biography than fiction, yet both books are stories about their lives as recalled by the authors. The line is a fine one and is made even more complicated by such books as Milton Meltzer's **Lincoln: In His Own Words** and **Frederick Douglass: In His Own Words** (A), in which the author uses selections from the speeches and writings of his subjects, connected by his own commentary, to create a form very much like a memoir.

Today, most biographies for young readers are authentic biographies, well-documented stories about individuals in which even the dialogue is based on some record of what was actually said or written by particular people at particular times. Today's biographers also often rely on illustrations to convey information, whether in picturebooks or full-length formats. Picturebook biographies are increasingly popular and present a subject through both text and art. In Rosemary Bray's **Martin Luther King** (P–I), Malcah Zeldis's folk art paintings brilliantly depict the important moments of King's life and evoke the spirit of the times and of the man himself. Illustrated biographies often make use of archival photographs and other documents, such as newspaper clippings, to present visual information that complements and extends the text. Melissa Sweet's mixed-media illustrations for Jen Bryant's Caldecott Honor–winning **A River of Words: The Story of William Carlos Williams** (I) earned a spot on the *New York Times* top ten illustrated books for 2008. This terrific book is filled with Williams's own words, with lines from his poems often incorporated into the accompanying illustrations.

Any good biography illuminates the interaction between an individual and historical events, demonstrating how a person's time and culture influence his or her life even as that person influences his or her time and culture. Today, we are fortunate to have vivid and accurate portrayals of the *people* of history, stories that make history come alive for young readers.

In this chapter we will:

- Consider how to determine the quality of a biography or memoir
- Explore the wide variety of biographical subjects
- Discuss examples of outstanding biographies
- And suggest the power of using biography in the classroom

Considering Quality in Biography and Memoir

Biographies and memoirs are stories of people's lives and, like all narratives, are evaluated in terms of the characterization, the presentation of plot and setting, the style of the writing, the unifying theme, and, in the case of picturebooks or illustrated books, the quality and contribution of the illustrations. As biographies, they are also subject to special considerations because they are portraits of real people, complete with both strengths and weaknesses. Further, biographies and memoirs must present accurate depictions of the time and place in which the subject lived. Even biographical fiction and memoirs should be grounded in fact and should present authentic information about a person's life and times

FIGURE 9.1

Considering Quality in Biography and Memoir

Accuracy and Social Details

- The story is grounded in fact. Source material is noted for biography.
- The facts and story line are seamlessly integrated.
- The details are vivid, accurate, and linked to the individual's accomplishments.

Portrayal of the Subject

- The subject's character is well developed and multidimensional.
- The author avoids stereotypes.

Style

- The writing style is comprehensible and engaging.
- Complex topics are explained adequately.

Theme

- There is a unifying theme that highlights the special qualities of the subject.

Illustrations

- The illustrations help the reader visualize the time and place.
- The illustrations illuminate the character of the subject.

in an engaging style. Figure 9.1 presents a brief list of criteria for evaluating biography and memoir.

• • ACCURACY • •

Increasingly, biographers for young readers rely heavily on primary sources; good biographies are always grounded in fact. Biographies need to present both a vivid and an accurate picture of the life and the times of the subject. As is true of historical fiction, accuracy is a complex criterion. Careful biographers do not go beyond the facts as we know them today, but they do interpret these facts through the eyes of the present. Consider, for example, how early biographies of Rosa Parks present her as a woman who sat down in the front of the bus because she was tired. Later portraits, such as **Rosa Parks: My Story** (I), reflect society's acknowledgment of the careful organization of the civil rights movement and present her action as the planned, deliberate attempt to confront unjust practices and laws that it was.

Authentic biographies are anchored by primary sources: letters, diaries, collected papers, and photographs. They usually contain lists of sources the author consulted and address the author's process. Biographical fiction goes well beyond what is known about a subject; it would be a mistake to think of it as a factual resource. Like historical fiction, it offers enough intriguing facts to encourage the reader to learn more about the real person and real events. Memoirs, too, are not meant to be a source of facts, but rather an evocation of a subject's life in the subject's own words. Both biographical fiction and memoir, however, should be truthful.

Russell Freedman's Newbery Award–winning **Lincoln: A Photobiography** (I–A) exemplifies what an authentic biography should be. Freedman is always careful to distinguish fact from opinion and truth from legend. He presents a significant amount of interesting historical detail. His text includes many direct quotations from Lincoln, all set off with quotation marks. These quotations, the historical facts, and social details are all taken from sources listed at the end of the book. Freedman follows the text with a sampling of Lincoln's famous quotations, with sources indicated, along with the sources for the quotations that begin each chapter. After these are a list and description of historic sites having to do with Lincoln's life, a description of source books about Lincoln, acknowledgments, and a useful five-page index. This end material and the photographs of historical documents that appear throughout the text all attest to the integrity and thoroughness of this biography.

In an interesting departure from the norm, Candace Fleming uses archival material not only to support but actually to format her book **Ben Franklin's Almanac: Being a True Account of the Good Gentleman's Life** (I–A). Fleming patterns her book on Franklin's own *Poor Richard's Almanack*, organizing her information around the major interests in Franklin's life—science, public service, family, time in France—and including reproductions of etchings, paintings, and cartoons of the time along with Franklin's own words. The originality in the design of the book is matched by the authenticity of its content.

Judging the accuracy of a biographer's presentation is not easy unless one happens to be an expert on the subject. Asking yourself the following questions can help you judge the accuracy of a biography: What sources did the author use? Are these sources documented? Does the account of the subject's life seem truthful according to what you already know? Are unnecessary generalizations about the people of the time or stereotypes of gender, ethnic, or racial groups evident? With memoirs, it is slightly different, as the "sources" for most memoirs are, in fact, memories, or perhaps diaries, with supporting detail from family and friends.

• • SETTING AND PLOT • •

A subject's personality and accomplishments are more understandable when they are presented against a rich and vivid depiction of the social details of life. Readers enjoy these social details, relishing the minutiae of another person's life. Further, settings need to depict the cultural forces that influenced the development of the subject's character and accomplishments. Careful biographers find a balance between telling everything and telling just enough to portray a person's life accurately, in an interesting manner. Many subjects of biographies for children had lives that were touched with pain, suffering, and great hardship; many great achievements were won at great cost. These issues must be carefully but honestly presented in biographies for young readers.

Good examples of this can be found in many biographies of Dr. Martin Luther King Jr. The times that shaped Dr. King were not easy times; he grew up in a country deeply divided by racism. In any biography of King written for young readers, the social climate needs to be honestly portrayed in a way that is understandable to children without being overwhelming. Balancing the needs of the audience and the accuracy of the story is especially difficult when writing for primary-grade readers. Rosemary Bray's **Martin Luther King** (P) is an outstanding example of the achievement of this balance, in part because of the strength of the illustrations. So, too, are Doreen Rappaport's **Martin's Big Words: The Life of Dr. Martin Luther King, Jr.** (P), with illustrations by Bryan Collier, and **My Brother Martin: A Sister Remembers Growing Up with the Rev. Dr. Martin Luther King Jr.** (P–I), written by King's sister, Christine King Farris. Tonya Bolden's **M.L.K.: Journey of a King** (I–A) combines a riveting text with more than eighty photographs to highlight King's philosophy of nonviolence and loving one's neighbor.

Similarly, photographs and archival documents—including police record fingerprints—help describe the time and political situation that fifteen-year-old Claudette Colvin faced as captured in Philip Hoose's **Claudette Colvin: Twice toward Justice** (I–A). The book details the teen's largely unknown story of refusing to give up her seat on a Montgomery bus some months before Rosa Park's well-known refusal that sparked the city's famous bus protest. The story helps the young reader better understand the climate of the time and why Claudette was not selected as the "face" of the protest.

Peter Sís's moving memoir, ***The Wall: Growing Up behind the Iron Curtain*** (I–A), a Caldecott Honor book, depicts his personal history through young adulthood as it was shaped by his harsh life in Soviet-occupied Czechoslovakia during the Cold War. Through text and brilliant illustrations, Sís presents a moving portrait of one boy's struggle for freedom as well as his artistic freedom of expression, which represents the struggle of the Czech nation itself.

Whether complete or episodic, authentic biography or memoir, the particular events that shaped a subject's life form the basis of a biographical plot. Although some present the subject's entire lifetime, good biographers do not plod through tedious detail about everything that happened in that life. Biographers have an array of facts available to them; how they select from those facts and craft an engaging story is up to them. Certainly, all events presented as facts should be accurate.

Good authors document their facts and also differentiate between fact and opinion, or fact and legend, similar to the work in solid nonfiction. Diane Stanley and Peter Vennema do an excellent job of this in their biography ***Bard of Avon: The Story of William Shakespeare*** (I). In a foreword, they alert their readers to the problems of fact they encountered; not much is known about the details of Shakespeare's early life. In their text, they make careful use of qualifying words and phrases, such as *if so*

and *perhaps*, to alert readers to theory, opinion, and educated guesses.

By selecting key events in a subject's life and presenting them vividly, biographers illuminate their subject and keep a reader's interest with plots that blend factual background with a good story.

• • PORTRAYAL OF SUBJECT • •

Good biographers consider their subjects as individuals rather than as paragons, and individuals are multidimensional. The strengths *and* weaknesses of individuals are presented in excellent biographies, such as ***This Land Was Made for You and Me: The Life and Songs of Woody Guthrie*** (A) by Elizabeth Partridge. Guthrie's failings as well as his strengths and the harsh times in which he created his songs are vividly portrayed. Good biographies also avoid implying that the greatness of the subject was implicit from birth. They avoid weaving background knowledge or prescient knowledge of latent talents into unlikely conversations (Herman, 1978). Exaggerating the good qualities of a subject results in *hagiography*—the telling of the life of a saint—or the creation of a legend. Biographies are about real people, not legendary figures. The same is true of memoirs: fine authors seek to depict themselves and the events that shaped them as honestly as possible.

The biographer's point of view and interest in the subject should be apparent, as should the biographer's purpose. The same subject may be treated differently by different biographers. Teaching Idea 9.1 explores this idea.

TEACHING IDEA 9.1

Compare Biographies about One Person

COMMON CORE STATE STANDARDS

This Teaching Idea addresses Common Core English Language Arts, Reading: Informational Text standard 9, grades K through 3 and 6 through 8.

Ask your students to compare and evaluate different biographies about the same person by having them do the following:

1. Choose two biographies about the same person and read them.

2. Decide which biography gives the best idea of what the person was really like. How does it accomplish this?

3. Decide which tells the most about the person's accomplishments.

4. Decide which is more informative and which is more interesting.

Students can also compare biographies written from different perspectives:

1. Compare a biography written before 1980 with one written within the past five years.

2. Describe the differences in the way the subject is viewed or the way similar events are reported.

3. Decide which is more informative and which is more interesting.

• • STYLE • •

Authors make choices about what they say and how they say it. Even when a story is well grounded in verifiable fact, as in authentic biography, it still represents an author's choice of facts, structure, and language. Good biographies incorporate the language and customs of the times. The dialogue should reflect how the subject is likely to have talked with enough authenticity that readers get a true picture but are not overwhelmed by archaic or idiosyncratic speech patterns. For example, Joseph Bruchac's biography of Sitting Bull, *A Boy Called Slow: The True Story of Sitting Bull* (I), is told in the cadence of the storyteller and includes some Lakota words. Deborah Heiligman uses Charles and Emma Darwin's journals, diaries, and letters in *Charles and Emma: The Darwins' Leap of Faith* (A). Look for language that rings true to the characters but is not overwhelmingly archaic or full of dialect.

• • THEME • •

The theme of a biography is the unifying element behind the story. Facts are merely facts until they are subordinated to a theme and a structure that allows them to make a statement with universal application and appeal. Fighting against injustice, struggling for independence, or working for human rights happens around the world and in many different ways. Each individual story builds its own theme; combined, the stories highlight the resilience and courage of human beings. Look for books that contain a theme with universal application and appeal.

• • ILLUSTRATIONS • •

If the biography is a picturebook, the illustrations must present the setting and the subject in an accurate manner. Illustrations often provide the interesting details that the brief text of a picturebook biography lacks. For example, in *Balloons over Broadway: The True Story of the Puppeteer of Macy's Parade* (P–I), Melissa Sweet's mixed-media collages capture the balloon-creater Tony Sarg's joyful enthusiasm for his work. The stunning portrayal of a relatively unknown, but gifted, artist was highly deserving of its 2012 Sibert Award.

As we discuss in Chapter 3, illustrators, through choice of media, technique, and style, work with the text to present a particular vision, in this case, their particular vision of a biographical subject, the time, and the place. Picturebook biographies are as varied in their illustrations as they are varied in their subjects, and these illustrations serve to not only provide details

but to interpret character and enhance theme and mood. Whether realistic oil paintings, cartoon panel art, watercolor spot art, collage, photographs, or any of the many other ways illustrators are able to create their visions, excellent illustrations add visual power to the story of an individual's life.

Biographers also make use of archival photographs, when they are available, to highlight their subjects' personalities and lives. Orbis Pictus Award–winning *Through My Eyes* (I–A) by Ruby Bridges contains reproductions of photographs taken during the tense times when schools in the South were forcibly integrated. They allow readers to compare the innocence and courage of a young girl with the hatred and ugliness of the adults who opposed integration. Look for illustrations that include interesting details and illuminate the character of the subject.

We now take a close look at *Dave the Potter: Artist, Poet, Slave* (P–I) by Laban Carrick Hill and illustrated by Bryan Collier, a picturebook biography for younger readers that exemplifies these qualities of excellence. For more information about Bryan Collier, read his profile in Chapter 3.

❊ ❊ ❊
A CLOSE LOOK AT
Dave the Potter: Artist, Poet, Slave

In 2011, the American Library Association awarded the Coretta Scott King Illustrator Award to Bryan Collier for his artistic interpretation of Laban Carrick Hill's lyrical biography of Dave the Potter. The same year, *Dave the Potter: Artist, Poet, Slave* also received a Caldecott Honor Award.

As Hill describes in the detailed back pages of the book, Dave the Potter is an important figure in the history of American art, yet very little is known about him. Born into slavery at the beginning of the 1800s, Dave became a potter in the Edgefield, South Carolina, area. The numerous pots he created are extraordinary for their size, and their beauty helps define the functional Edgefield pottery tradition. Dave's pots are particularly unusual, though, because of the poetic verses he inscribed on many. More than one hundred pots were signed and dated by Dave, and many of those also bear short verses. This was during a historical period when slaves were not allowed to learn to read or write, so Dave's verses, publically declaring his literacy, are even more special.

In the back pages of the book, Hill and Collier explain the source material they used in great detail. An attractive three-page spread titled "Dave:

Laban Carrick Hill's lyrical verse and Bryan Collier's beautiful illustrations help capture the essence of poet and artist in **Dave the Potter***.*

A Life" is nearly a mini-biography in itself. Hill presents in prose the details of Dave's life in language easily understood by young readers. For example, to explain why Dave never wrote a last name, he states: "[Dave] would sometimes just sign his name. He only had a first name because slaves were not allowed to have family names, like 'Hill' or 'Collier.'" The information on the spread is broken beautifully by samples of Dave's verses that did not appear in the main parts of the book, allowing the young reader to see that actual source material.

This spread serves as an elaboration on the facts already captured in the lyrical verse of the main text. In addition to this spread, Hill and Collier further include personal notes explaining the research they did for the book and their own passion for the research and the topic, as well as a short bibliography and a list of the available websites about Dave. These details help to establish the accuracy of the biography and are particularly important given the nature of the lyrical verse used. Details in the three-page spread also help to better explain the social world of Dave's time.

The verses used throughout the main section of the text are very well crafted. The lines concisely capture not just the facts about Dave and his life, but also the essence of his situation. Without the text stating it outright, students can easily comprehend that Dave's life was challenging and the work he did immensely difficult.

The illustrations help convey the same message, highlighting Dave's immense concentration on his work and the strength he must have had to maneuver the pots. The illustrations also hint at the personal strength Dave must have had as well. Dave is portrayed as very serious and somber, and colors used in the pictures are dark and golden. Smaller images captured in the collage backdrops show slaves bent over working in the cotton fields, sheds, and simple wood dwellings that were likely slave quarters as well as a large, white, columned building representing the owner's house.

One page spread in the middle of the book is more hopeful, although perhaps bittersweet. The verse describes a large jar that Dave could nearly climb into and suggests he would be embraced by it

P R O F I L E

Laban Carrick Hill

Poetry is a tool that I often reach for, especially when I'm challenged.

Laban Carrick Hill has published more than 25 books including poetry, nonfiction, and fiction for children and young adults. He is perhaps best known for his nonfiction books, including *Harlem Stomp*, a 2004 National Book Award Finalist book. Hill is particularly interested in American identity, and thus in researching and writing about the African American experience in the United States and the various people in its history. He has taught courses on African American Literature and is a core faculty member in

a creative writing master of fine arts program. He serves as the codirector of the Writers Project of Ghana, promoting literary culture and literacy in Ghana through writing and reading groups, a small press, and other activities.

Hill's interest in Dave the Potter was piqued in 2003 after viewing one of Dave's pots during a lecture; this led to Hill doing further research on Dave and eventually starting the book on his life. While writing about Dave, Hill continued with his research and took an increasingly active role in trying to better understand Dave, reading and rereading Dave's poems and even trying to throw a few pots himself.

Hill used poetic nonfiction to capture the life of Dave the Potter in a children's picturebook biography. Speaking about his choice to use lyrical verse for the book, he has explained it took him more than a year to begin writing about Dave the Potter. When he finally began to try it in verse, it simply felt like the right way to honor Dave, who was himself a poet (Menon, 2010). From then on, the writing was much easier.

To learn more about Hill, go to CengageBrain.com to access the Education CourseMate website, where you will find links to relevant websites.

---

if he did. The illustration depicts Dave, eyes closed and a slight smile, face full of both longing and joy, with a tree behind him that is blanketed in faces suggestive of Dave's family and friends. Juxtaposed with the only full verse of Dave's in the main text ("I wonder where is all my relation/ friendship to all- and, every nation"), this particular spread helps capture the essence of Dave and what we understand and can discern about his life and his work.

Dave the Potter: Artist, Poet, Slave is an outstanding example of quality in a biographical picturebook and of excellence for all children's and young adult biography. From the lyrical text that directly speaks to the reader, to a gatefold spread that entices the reader to place his or her hands over Dave's to create a pot, to the well-presented research and source materials, this book truly stands out as a stellar example.

Variety in Biographical Subjects

Looking at biography in terms of historical period is perhaps the most common way of using biography in the classroom. Like historical fiction, biography can

help students envision what life was like in the past, and we discuss this later in the chapter. Here, however, we categorize biography according to the people whom the biographies portray. Because the subject, or person whom the biography is about, is the reason for biography, we look to the subject as a way to classify biographical narratives.

Doing so also makes it easier to talk about biography in terms of broad human themes. Political and military leaders seek either to control or to lead their people toward specific goals; issues of power, vision, and honor permeate the biographies of these leaders. Philosophers and religious leaders seek to articulate principles on which we might live; their lives are spent considering the role of human beings and higher entities. Many of these leaders exemplify or demonstrate their principles simply by living a holy life, however that might be defined, thus convincing others of the truth of their ideas. Artists of all kinds—musicians, dancers, writers, painters, craftsmen, filmmakers, and entertainers—all try to present their inner visions to the world; they often struggle to realize their talent and to find acceptance for their innovations. Scientists and inventors, too, seek to discover, understand, and create new ideas and opportunities for their fellow human beings; they often face a long struggle for recognition, during which they must persevere to reach their goals. Adventurers and explorers, propelled by their innate curiosity, spend their lives exploring new places and new challenges. Sports heroes work hard to attain a level of excellence that allows them to succeed. And the extraordinary ordinary people who live lives with dignity and strength change the world, one person at a time. An exploration of all these types of biographical subjects can inspire readers to think about their own place in the world today.

• • POLITICAL AND • • MILITARY LEADERS

For good or for ill, political and military leaders help shape the course of history. Biographies for young readers have long focused on the presidents, most frequently examining the unique histories and bigger-than-life stories of George Washington, Abraham Lincoln, the Roosevelts, and John F. Kennedy. Books such as Anne Rockwell's *Big George: How a Shy Boy Became President Washington* (P–I) and Doreen Rappaport's *Jack's Path of Courage: The Life of John F. Kennedy* (P–I) follow this trend and focus on particular traits and experiences of these men as teenagers and how this affected their taking of office. Rockwell examines some negative personality traits of the revered Washington, including his temper and diffidence around strangers. Rappaport discusses some of the things JFK faced down in his teenage years, such as the ongoing competition among his brothers and the family pressure to go into politics.

Esteemed children's biographer Russell Freedman takes a close look at Frenchman Marquis de Lafayette in *Lafayette and the American Revolution* (I–A). With his normal straight-forward, well-researched style, Freedman details young Lafayette's secret trip to the United States, against the wishes of his king and his family, leading to his role during the American Revolution and the role of the French overall in the battles. Freedman's engaging style, and the excellent attention to factual details, well backed up by a thorough bibliography, makes this an outstanding biography of a more unknown political figure. Archival paintings add interest.

The husband-wife team of Andrea Davis Pinkney and illustrator Brian Pinkney present a beautifully constructed picturebook on the famous Sojourner Truth in *Sojourner Truth's Step-Stomp Stride* (P–I). A conversational style and vivid, energetic illustrations help make this an excellent read-aloud to introduce primary-grade readers to the strong-willed Sojourner Truth and even broach the subject of slavery.

Other political biographies highlight lesser-known figures such as Sarah Edmonds, a young woman who pretended to be a man in order to serve in the Civil War. Carrie Jones's *Sarah Emma Edmonds Was a Great Pretender: The True Story of a Civil War Spy* (P–I) and Marissa Moss's *Nurse, Solider, Spy: The Story of Sarah Edmonds, A Civil War Hero* (P–I) both take a look at the unique Sarah Edmonds, who spent a good deal of her childhood pretending to be a boy. Keeping up the premise to become part of the Civil War Union Army, Sarah actually took on a number of roles to spy on the Confederate Army. Moss's book focuses on more vignettes and is slightly sparser than Jones's version, but both highlight the unique qualities of Sarah Edmonds and are well-supported by their bibliographies.

We now take a close look at a biography of another interesting American political leader, Benedict Arnold, who both supported and betrayed his country.

* * *
A CLOSE LOOK AT
The Notorious Benedict Arnold: A True Story of Adventure, Heroism, & Treachery

Biographies of villains, although still fairly unusual, are on the rise. The best of these examine the subject's background, tracing the experiences that over time may have had ramifications on later behavior. This is not to excuse the villains' acts in any way, but to offer some context. For example, James Cross Giblin is crystal clear in his Sibert Award–winning *The Life and Death of Hitler* that he considers Hitler a very evil man and that Hitler's thoughts and ideas, which he carefully and accurately records, were repugnant.

Like Giblin, Steve Sheinkin does not shy away from describing the violent temper or the traitorous acts of Benedict Arnold. But Arnold is a unique character in American history, at one time seen as a hero and great solider even by George Washington. Sheinkin delights in the story of this contradictory man and his rise and fall from greatness. He takes this fascinating story and makes his biography just that—a fascinating, action-adventure book.

The Notorious Benedict Arnold reads like an exciting novel. Scenes build upon one another and the real subjects feel like well-developed characters of a historical book. It is easy for the reader to be engrossed in the story and difficult to put down the book. Despite, or perhaps because, of this style, Sheinkin includes a very rich source notes section explaining in careful detail the accuracy of each sentence and statement. A letter from Sheinkin describing his interest in the subject, and his research also

P R O F I L E

Steve Sheinkin

Yes, it's true, I used to write history textbooks. . . .But I don't do that kind of thing anymore. Now I try to write history books that people will actually read voluntarily.

Steve Sheinkin wanted to write a book about Benedict Arnold for many years. In his acceptance speech for the Boston Globe–Horn Book Nonfiction Award, Sheinkin details his process to finally write the book, after obsessively researching Benedict Arnold since the late 1990s. Sheinkin sees Benedict Arnold as a wonderful American symbol, a historical figure who "leaves no doubt that a person, like a country, can do both great and terrible things" (Sheinkin, 2012).

Sheinkin's background as a history textbook writer, and his own interest in history, helps make him a passionate writer of children's biography. His conversational, humorous style helps to convey important details of his subjects' lives as he attempts to get young readers excited about historical figures and the major events they experienced.

Sheinkin is also the author of a graphic novel series, **Rabbi Harvey**.

To learn more about Sheinkin, go to CengageBrain.com to access the Education CourseMate website, where you will find links to relevant websites.

reminds readers of the book's theme, already readily apparent throughout the story—the idea that American history, and American historical figures, are all a bit good and bad.

Benedict is very well developed as a "character" throughout the book, depicted as a complicated man with a difficult past. Sheinkin naturally avoids stereotypes in his description of Benedict, but also keeps all of the major figures in the biography as well developed as is reasonable. The book is an example of the best of children's and young adult biography, and understandably won the 2012 YALSA Award for Excellence in Nonfiction for Young Adults and the 2011 Boston Globe–Horn Book Nonfiction Award. It soars because of its passionate, enthusiastic attention to Benedict Arnold as a person with a complicated past, an uncertain future, and the determination and cleverness to either succeed or fail miserably.

Biographies such as this allow students to consider subjects' unique strengths, as described in Teaching Idea 9.2.

• • PHILOSOPHERS AND • • RELIGIOUS LEADERS

As we live in an increasingly interconnected world, it is increasingly important to understand the thoughts and beliefs of other people. Books about philosophers and religious leaders help introduce young readers to timeless ideas and new ones alike. Many great philosophers and religious leaders have left their mark on the world. Born more than 2,500 years ago, Confucius was one of them. Russell Freedman celebrates his influence in **Confucius: The Golden Rule** (I). Although Confucius was born poor and had a homely appearance, his charm and intelligence helped him become a revered teacher and philosopher. His progressive ideals, such as equality and treating others as oneself, have been studied and argued for more than twenty-five centuries. Freedman teaches us not only who Confucius was but how he thought and how his precepts have echoed across time, as, for example, Jesuit missionaries read his teachings during the sixteenth century and realized the similarities between Confucius's thinking and their own Christian precepts. The liberal use of quotations from the *Analects* of Confucius help present the man while also stimulating the minds of readers: "Do you want to know what knowledge is? When you know something, recognize that you know it, and when you don't know something, recognize that you don't know it. That's knowledge."

• • SCIENTISTS AND INVENTORS • •

Just as philosophers seek to articulate their particular beliefs and share them with the world, scientists and inventors seek to discover, understand, and create new knowledge and possibilities. Often their search begins with careful observation of the world around them. Charles Darwin's observations aboard the HMS Beagle contributed to the development of his evolutionary theories. Kathleen Krull's **Charles Darwin** (I–A) is a clearly written, well-paced biography for middle-school readers in a more traditional format, while Alice McGinty does the same for intermediate readers

TEACHING IDEA 9.2

Thematic Connection: Self-Knowledge

COMMON CORE STATE STANDARDS   This Teaching Idea addresses Common Core English Language Arts, Reading: Informational Text standard 3, grades K through 5 and 6 through 8.

There are many biographies in which one of the pivotal events is the subject's recognition of his or her own talent or strength. This is evident in Francisco Jiménez's **Breaking Through** (I–A), Robert Burleigh's **Langston's Train Ride** (I), and William Miller's **Zora Hurston and the Chinaberry Tree** (P–I) as well as many other books. As you read books such as these with your students, ask them to consider how the subject's realization altered his or her life. Then ask them to think about themselves. Do they have a dream? A special talent? A special strength?

---

in **Darwin** (I) with a bit more emphasis on his personality. Deborah Heiligman takes a different approach for the older reader in her young adult **Charles and Emma: The Darwins' Leap of Faith** (A). Heiligman takes a look at the relationship between Charles and his wife, Emma, and how it affected both the development of Darwin's evolutionary theories and his beliefs about religion, as well as the interplay of the two.

Jane Goodall's name is known all over the world as the woman who studied chimpanzees in Tanzania's Gombe Reserve, and, today, as the woman who roams the globe speaking about the importance of conservation. Sudipta Bardhan-Quallen's contribution to the outstanding Up Close series, **Up Close: Jane Goodall** (A), is a detailed look at the life's work of this remarkable woman, one who sparked controversy when she became attached to the very animals she studied. The harsh reality of her struggle to fund her work, the criticism her work engendered, and her difficulty juggling her professional and personal lives are balanced by a portrait of a woman and a scientist who continues to work tirelessly to help the world understand the importance of taking care of our wild places. An index, bibliography, source notes, and photographs bolster Bardhan-Quallen's text. Two picturebook biographies aimed at much younger readers try to highlight Jane's dedication to pursue her childhood dreams of working with chimpanzees, Patrick McDonnell's **Me...Jane** (P–I) and Jeannette Winter's **The Watcher: Jane Goodall's Life with the Chimps** (P–I), mentioned earlier.

Geniuses in mathematics, physics, and the more abstract sciences are more rarely portrayed in biographies for young readers. But the larger than life, Nobel-winning quantum physicist Richard Feynman is captured brilliantly in Jim Ottaviani's **Feynman** (A), a graphic novel for adolescents. The brilliant colors and graphic novel format fit the subject perfectly and manage to convey the exuberant essence of Feynman. A different format also works well to capture Ben Franklin and his many skills; Alan Schroeder and John O'Brien's **Ben Franklin: His Wit and Wisdom from A–Z** (P–I) offers a cunningly detailed alphabet book that serves as a nice introduction to later, longer biographies of the well-known figure.

• • ADVENTURERS • • AND EXPLORERS

It is not unusual for scientists to also be explorers as they pursue their scientific questions by traveling in search of answers. Such is the case with John Wesley Powell, who led the first recorded expedition down the Green and Colorado Rivers as he mapped and studied the flora and fauna of a large portion of the Grand Canyon in 1869. In Deborah Kogan Ray's **Down the Colorado: John Wesley Powell, the One-Armed Explorer** (I), single pages of text with facing illustrations chronicle Powell's early life through his service in the Civil War. As he explores the Grand Canyon, double-page illustrations and quotes from Powell's journals and letters allow the reader to also experience the majesty of the canyon. A map, timeline, author's note, chronology, and bibliography add important information about the man and his journey.

Those who leave home to confront physical challenges or explore unknown places often become heroes. Grand exploits, such as climbing Mt. Everest or crossing the South Pole by dogsled, capture the imagination of the world. The solo flight of Amelia Earhart across the Atlantic is captured in picturebook fashion in Robert Burleigh's **Night Flight: Amelia Earhart Crosses the Atlantic** (P–I). The illustrations by Wendell Minor capture the excitement; Earhart was only the second person to attempt this feat, and the first woman. For older readers, Candace Fleming's **Amelia Lost: The Life and Disappearance of Amelia Earhart** (I–A) uses alternating chapters to describe Amelia's early life and her later career, and the mystery of her disappearance and search to find her and her missing plane.

Now, we take a close look at a collective biography for older readers that describes the actions of a group of women adventurers, Tanya Lee Stone's **Almost Astronauts: 13 Women Who Dared to Dream** (I–A).

* * *

A CLOSE LOOK AT
Almost Astronauts: 13 Women Who Dared to Dream

Stone begins her volume with an engaging look at a reunion of the Mercury 13; many of the original group of women are gathered to watch the 1999 launch of the space shuttle on its STS-93 mission, the first mission commanded by a woman. The opening is littered with black-and-white archival photographs and detailed with actual quotes from the countdown. The writing style is straightforward and smooth, easily describing any complicated subjects at the same time as compelling the reader to turn the page and see what happens next. Hints are made about the immense determination and sacrifice of a few women and a government secret to be revealed within the book. The very first chapter of **Almost Astronauts** is setting the scene not just for a terrific true story, but also an outstanding example of children's biography.

Stone lives up to expectations set in that very first chapter. **Almost Astronauts** chronologically describes the efforts of several women to become part of the NASA space program. The use of archived newspapers, articles, photographs, and even hidden documents from government files help to explain the prejudice and trials these women faced. The focus is placed on the small group of women, the Mercury 13, who were encouraged to be tested for suitability for spaceflight by Randolph Lovelace, chairman of NASA's Life Sciences Committee in the early 1960s.

Stone begins with the story of Jerrie Cobb, the central figure in the flight of the Mercury 13. The testing she underwent is detailed, and as each individual woman is added to the group, readers learn a bit about their impressive backgrounds and their experiences with testing. Soon the story turns to the political fight of the women to be part of the astronaut program. Stone keeps the interest high with quick paragraphs labeled with the date (month and year) and the progress of the movement. Layers of history are added on with segments devoted to other related political happenings of the time, more details about the individual women of the group, and a gradual development to the state of women astronauts today.

PROFILE

Tanya Lee Stone

Anytime I can do primary source research I do, especially when I'm writing about people who are alive.

Prolific writer Tanya Lee Stone was formerly a children's books editor, and then began doing her own writing. She has written teen novels and picturebooks, but the majority of her writing is nonfiction.

Tanya explains that she starts her writing by focusing on a topic that grabs her interest. She does not worry about format to begin. **Almost Astronauts**, for example, started as a picturebook filled with poetry, but because of the scope of the story became a longer nonfiction book. She believes all children writers should be careful to choose topics that they are truly curious and passionate about.

Tanya has won several awards for her writing, including the 2010 Sibert Medal for **Almost Astronauts**.

To learn more about Stone, go to CengageBrain.com to access the Education CourseMate website, where you will find links to relevant websites.

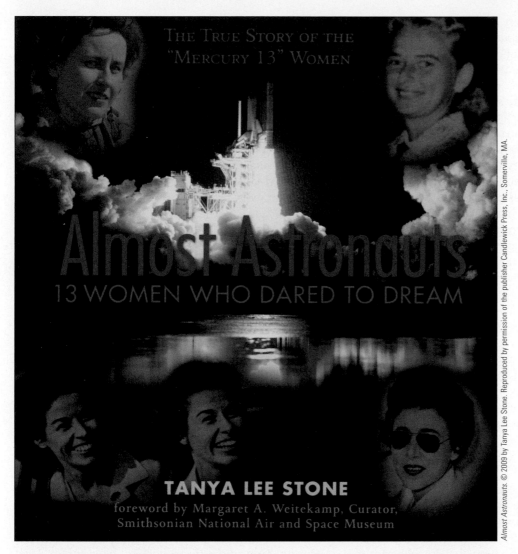

Almost Astronauts *details the fight of the "Mercury 13 women" to prove women could be astronauts.*

The continuous use of archival photographs (most frequently as full-page spreads and appearing nearly every two to three pages) grasps the reader's eye and helps to illuminate concepts described in the text.

The endpages of ***Almost Astronauts*** are filled with rich details about source material. Stone offers a letter explaining her attraction to the topic and her process of developing the book, even including a link to the poetry she originally wrote about each of the women portrayed. An appendix charts all the women who were invited to take the tests and the general results, a bibliography includes web and print resources, and a stunning list of source notes demonstrate the immense research that went into this book. Although ***Almost Astronauts*** excels with its attractive design and engaging, thorough style, it is possible that the research behind it could be considered its strongest point.

• • PRACTITIONERS • •
OF THE ARTS

There are many wonderful biographies of painters, sculptors, musicians, filmmakers, dancers, artisans, and writers who have successfully presented their visions to the world. The success is often hard won, however, and stories about these individuals often portray their struggles as thoroughly as they celebrate their successes.

Increasingly, those who write for children and young adults are creating autobiographies and memoirs that allow young readers to see the struggles of authors they admire. Both Ed Young's ***The House Baba Built: An Artist's Childhood in China*** (P–I) and Allen Say's ***Drawing from Memory*** (I–A) are new memoirs that feature their experiences as young artists. Both books are beautifully presented and offer insight to the detailed work of the well-known author-illustrators; Say's book was even awarded a Sibert Honor. Biographies about writers are important resources for exploring what it means to be a writer and for extending children's knowledge of the authors whose works they enjoy reading.

The artist Alexander Calder is the subject of Tanya Lee Stone's **Sandy's Circus: A Story about Alexander Calder** (P–I), illustrated by Boris Kulikov. In this biography for younger readers, Stone focuses on Calder's early years, when he made things out of the many bits and pieces that his parents provided for him. Studying both engineering and art, he continued his childhood passion and eventually created his famous circus, in which small figures made of wire, wood, cloth, and other scrap materials came alive as the springs, strings, and levers he built made them "leap, run, and dance." The illustrations do full justice to Calder's creativity, and an author's note, sources, and a photograph of Calder performing his circus offer additional information to curious readers.

The exciting, early life of pantomime artist Marcel Marceau is captured in picturebook form in Gloria Spielman's **Marcel Marceau: Master of Mime** (P). The use of his talent for impressions remarkably helped many Jewish children escape from German-occupied France to the safety of Switzerland, and is a little-known fact about the famous mime.

• • SPORTS HEROES • •

Sports heroes, like famous artists, often have the opportunity to work for a better world because of the esteem in which others hold them. Jackie Robinson epitomizes both the talent that it takes to be a heroic sports figure and the dedication that is necessary to use that position to benefit others. Sharon Robinson's moving tribute to her father, **Promises to Keep: How Jackie Robinson Changed America** (I–A), combines narrative reconstruction of the major events in his life with family photographs and letters. She presents the life of the man who broke the color barrier in major league baseball and who then went on to become an activist in politics and the struggle for civil rights. Although not all sports heroes have the opportunity to affect the world in the manner Jackie Robinson did, good sports biographies are more than just sources of information about heroic exploits in the sports arena.

The intriguing story of several famous baseball players is described in an episodic biography about the unique summer of 1941, **The Unforgettable Season: The Story of Joe DiMaggio, Ted Williams and the Record-Setting Summer of '41** (P–I). Author Phil Bildner tells the tale with terrific pacing and reassures readers that he believes another exciting summer like that will come again to the sport.

Muhammad Ali is the subject of two recent biographies that contextualize his outstanding physical abilities with his moral courage as he confronted the racism that surrounded him, especially after he refused to serve in the Vietnam War. Jonah Winter's **Muhammad Ali: Champion of the World** (P), illustrated by François Roca, borrows from Genesis as he "introduces" Jack Johnson and Joe Louis, predecessors—great in their own right—to Ali, the champion of the world. The variations in font make the text visually as well as verbally powerful and highlight the "fight" that Ali had with the world, while Roca's realistic oil paintings offer visual depictions of Ali's accomplishments. Charles R. Smith Jr.'s biography for older readers, **Twelve Rounds to Glory: The Story of Muhammad Ali** (A), illustrated by Bryan Collier, tells much the same story in more detail. The rhyming text—much like Ali's signature rhymes—clearly indicates Smith's admiration for the man, both as boxer and as human being, as he highlights not only the fights, but Ali's outspokenness against racism, against the Vietnam War and his final fight with Parkinson's disease.

• • EXTRAORDINARY • •
ORDINARY PEOPLE

Not everyone has a recognizable, outstanding talent. Most people are actually quite ordinary. Sometimes, however, the dignity and grace with which ordinary people live their lives make them extraordinary. Memoirs such as Nawuth Keat and Martha Kendall's **Alive in the Killing Fields: Surviving the Khmer Rouge Genocide** (A), authentic biographies such as George Sullivan's **Tom Thumb: The Remarkable True Story of Man in Miniature**, (I–A) and biographical fiction such as Joseph Bruchac's **Sacajawea** (I–A) depict the acts of ordinary people. The heroes of these stories are not sports or movie stars, politicians or generals, artists or philosophers, but persons whose strength of character makes them extraordinary in some way. For example, Sacajawea's knowledge, bravery, and intelligence made her an integral part of Lewis and Clark's expedition instead of just the wife of one of their interpreters.

Sometimes it surprises us that people who are now considered famous or heroic, such as Ruby Bridges, Rosa Parks, or Malcolm X, were in fact people with no particular reputation, talent, or position that would indicate eventual fame. The four young people who refused to move from the Woolworth's lunch counter, featured in Andrea and Brian Pinkney's poetic biographical picturebook **Sit-In: How Four Friends Stood Up by Sitting**

Down (P–I) were not famous before the event. The wonderfully researched book (even working into the verse the exact foods the teens ordered) highlights their determination to make things better. There were many women like Elizabeth Cady Stanton, women who wanted the right to vote, but Stanton stood up and fought for her rights, as Tanya Lee Stone depicts in **Elizabeth Leads the Way: Elizabeth Cady Stanton and the Right to Vote** (P–I), with illustrations by Rebecca Gibbon. Today, Stanton's name is forever linked with the cause she worked for.

Others whose lives are worth reading and thinking about still aren't famous—but they are exemplary. Quietly told stories of people who did not create headlines can also have a strong and lasting impact on young readers. The memoir **Leon's Story** (I–A), written by Leon Walter Tillage and illustrated with collage art by Susan L. Roth, won a Boston Globe–Horn Book Award for nonfiction. In this small book, Tillage tells the story of his life as the son of an African American sharecropper, growing up in North Carolina during the 1940s. As a young boy, he learns to endure the racism and bigotry of his surroundings while keeping intact his own dignity and sense of worth. His experiences lead him directly to being involved in the civil rights movement.

And, sometimes, ordinary people are simply the first to try an extraordinary feat. Chris Van Allsburg exciting's first nonfiction title, **Queen of the Falls** (P–I), captures the danger and thrill of Annie Taylor's attempt to go over Niagara Falls in a barrel, and then sadly details how her attempts to use this feat to make money did not pan out.

Biography and Memoir in the Classroom

Biography can help young readers develop their concepts of historical time; they can discover ideas and empathize with historical characters. Those who read biographies learn that all people have the same basic needs and desires. They begin to see their lives in relation to those of the past, learn a vast amount of social detail about the past, and consider the human problems and relationships of the present in the light of those in the past.

Biography can enliven a social studies curriculum; in conjunction with historical fiction and nonfiction, it can illuminate a time and place by telling the story of an individual. It can also support studies in music and art; many fine biographies of artists and musicians explore both their lives and their creative endeavors. An exploration of themes is enriched by including biographies. Picturebook biographies about artists can even be used to teach visual literacy.

Memoirs can serve as models for young readers as they develop their own or those of an older friend or family member. Other biographies serve as excellent examples of how to use source material to craft an engaging and accurate story. Some memoirs provide access to primary source material for students to use in their own research. A biography collection is an important part of any classroom or school library.

BUILDING A BIOGRAPHY COLLECTION

A collection of biographies needs to be wide in scope and representative of diverse people. If there are biographies of women and people of color that speak to your subject, be sure to include them in your collection. If there are not, you may want to consider with your students why there are no biographies of, for example, ancient female explorers, and why biographies of modern female explorers are now available. Taking into account the biographies and memoirs of ordinary people that are available today, consider with your students why someone might become the subject of a biography, a concept explored in Teaching Idea 9.3. Using this approach, children can begin to see how the world has changed and how historical and current social conditions influence individuals' potential.

USING BIOGRAPHY WITH OTHER GENRES TO STUDY AN ERA

As we discuss in other chapters, it is often quite effective to read across genres. When you do this, students not only learn about the focus of study but also further develop their understanding of genre constraints and possibilities. If, for example, you link literature with social studies, you can combine historical fiction, biography, and nonfiction to study a particular time or place. Experiences in each genre offer readers different opportunities that, taken together, can help them learn not only the "facts" about particular people and particular places but also the human story that has become history.

If you want students to really understand the reasons for and the impact of the civil rights movement, for example, you might want to read biographies of Gandhi, Martin Luther King Jr., and Malcolm X. Trace the development of Gandhi's ideas in the work of King, and compare King with Malcolm X. Then

Who Becomes a Biographical Subject?

This Teaching Idea addresses Common Core English Language Arts, Writing standard 8, grades K through 5.

Ask your students to consider what types of people are most likely to become the subjects of biographies. Which people are most likely to have several biographies written about them? Ask students to consider whether the subjects of biography have changed in the past thirty years. Have them follow this procedure:

1. Go to the library or search on the Internet to find out how many biographies have been written about a particular individual. List authors, titles, and dates of publication.

2. Check the school library holdings to ascertain what kinds of people are subjects of biographies written within the past thirty years. List subjects, authors, titles, and dates of publication.

3. Summarize the data from items 1 and 2 and make generalizations based on the data.

4. Discuss the findings, considering these questions: Who is in favor? Who is not? What kinds of people are the subjects of biographies or memoirs in any given year? Are there any observable trends?

---

bring in the stories of such people as Rosa Parks, Leon Tillage, and Ruby Bridges, some poetry from Langston Hughes (and his biographies), and historical fiction such as **Roll of Thunder, Hear My Cry** (A) or **The Watsons Go to Birmingham—1963** (I–A). Nonfiction, such as Chris Crowe's **Getting Away with Murder: The True Story of the Emmett Till Case** (A), supplements biography to provide added facts, while the stories told in biographies enhance the fiction.

• • ORGANIZING BIOGRAPHY • •
BY THEME

Biography, like fiction, includes stories of people who explore their world, fight for freedom, revolt against oppression, immigrate, establish new nations, and struggle for survival and human rights. Biographies can complement historical and realistic fiction that develop similar themes, or themes can be explored primarily through biographies. There are several biographical series—for example, the **Extraordinary People** series, published by Children's Book Press; the **Black Americans of Achievement** series, published by Chelsea; and Enslow's **African-American Biography, Hispanic Biography, World Writers**, and **Historical Americans** series—which present biographies about various people engaged in similar struggles. There are also collective biographies,

mentioned earlier in this chapter, which present brief biographies of a number of people who are linked in some way.

You can collect books that illustrate a particular theme, such as the struggle for human rights. By studying the lives of diverse people from around the world and across history, students can come to understand the universal struggles of humankind. Why do people around the world struggle for human rights? How are these struggles similar across nations and time? How do they vary according to age and culture? Exploring these kinds of questions can lead to a better understanding of humanity and one's place in it.

For example, you might want to consider the human desire to explore new places. Many biographies focus on explorers, both ancient and modern. Sir Walter Raleigh explored the New World; Sally Ride explored space. The theme of exploration can be widened to include those who explore the boundaries of science. Those people who have made scientific and technological breakthroughs are curious, dedicated individuals, just as many geographic explorers are. Biographies of famous scientists and inventors can enrich students' concepts of what it means to be an explorer. Artists and musicians who break new ground can also be considered explorers. Thus, a general theme like exploration or human rights can be woven from many varying biographies and even complemented by fiction and nonfiction.

Biographies of artists and musicians also can support the study of art and music. They can be compared in terms of the driving force that shaped the lives of their subjects: What caused them to pursue their talents with such passion and success? Biographies of female artists and musicians can be explored as examples of triumph over discrimination and then related to the general theme of human rights.

A great number of writers and illustrators of books for children have written biographies and memoirs, including a series of autobiographies for primary-grade readers published by Richard Owens. These biographies can be read for any number of purposes—to discover information about the writers, to learn about the effect on the writer's work of the time and place in which the writer lived, to develop an understanding of what it means to be a writer, and to extend knowledge of the authors whose works children enjoy reading.

Biography has become one of the most diverse, interesting, and popular genres in literature for young readers. Wise adults build on children's fascination with real stories and the details about the lives of others by using biography to explore both contemporary and historical people, events, and ideas.

SUMMARY

Biographies and memoirs tell the stories of the people who shaped and are shaping our history. Reading these books helps children and adolescents understand that people make history and that these people have strengths and weaknesses, as we all do. Understanding the humanity behind the greatness allows readers to dream of their own accomplishments and to know they are possible.

Booklist

* Indicates some aspect of diversity

Political and Military Leaders

Andronik, Catherine, **Hatshepsut, His Majesty, Herself** (2001) (I)

Aylesworth, Jim, **Our Abe Lincoln: An Old Tune with New Lyrics** (2009) (P–I)

* Bolden, Tanya, **M.L.K.: Journey of a King** (2008) (I–A)

* _____, **Up Close: W.E.B. Du Bois: A Twentieth-Century Life** (2008) (A)

Brown, Don, **Teedie: The Story of Young Teddy Roosevelt** (2009) (P–I)

* Bruchac, Joseph, **A Boy Called Slow: The True Story of Sitting Bull** (1994) (P–I)

* _____ **Crazy Horse's Vision** (2000) (P)

* Burchard, Peter, **Frederick Douglass: For the Great Family of Man** (2003) (A)

Cooper, Ilene, **Jack: The Early Years of John F. Kennedy** (2003) (I–A)

Cooper, Michael L., **Up Close: Theodore Roosevelt** (2010) (A)

* Demi, **Genghis Khan** (2009) (P–I)

Donnelly, Matt, **Theodore Roosevelt: Larger than Life** (2003) (A)

Fleming, Candace, **Ben Franklin's Almanac: Being a True Account of the Good Gentleman's Life** (2003) (I–A)

_____, **The Lincolns: A Scrapbook Look at Abraham and Mary** (2008) (I)

_____, **Our Eleanor: A Scrapbook Look at Eleanor Roosevelt's Remarkable Life** (2005) (I)

Freeman, Russell, **Lafayette and the American Revolution** (2010) (I)

_____, **Lincoln: A Photobiography** (1987) (I–A)

Fritz, Jean, **The Great Little Madison** (1989) (A)

Giblin, James Cross, **The Amazing Life of Benjamin Franklin** (2000) (I)

_____, **The Life and Death of Adolf Hitler** (2002) (A)

_____, **The Rise and Fall of Senator Joe McCarthy** (2009) (I)

* Gormley, Beatrice, **Barack Obama: Our 44th President** (2008) (P–I)

* Grimes, Nikki, **Barack Obama: Son of Promise, Child of Hope** (2008) (P–I)

Gulotta, Charles, **Extraordinary Women in Politics** (1998) (I)

Hendricks, John, **John Brown: His Fight for Freedom** (2009) (I)

Holzer, Harold, **Father Abraham: Lincoln and His Sons** (2011) (A)

Jones, Carrie, **Sarah Emma Edmonds was a Great Pretender: The True Story of a Civil War Spy** (2011) (P–I)

Kerley, Barbara, **What to Do about Alice: How Alice Roosevelt Broke the Rules, Charmed the World, and Drove Her Father Crazy** (2008) (P–I)

* King Farris, Christine, **My Brother Martin: A Sister Remembers Growing Up with the Rev. Dr. Martin Luther King Jr.** (2003) (P–I)

Kraft, Betsy Harvey, **Theodore Roosevelt: Champion of the American Spirit** (2003) (A)

Krull, Kathleen, **Harvesting Hope: The Story of Cesar Chavez** (2003) (P–I)

_____, **Hillary Rodham Clinton: Dreams Taking Flight** (2008) (P)

_____, **Kubla Khan: The Emperor of Everything** (2010) (I)

_____, **Lives of Extraordinary Women: Rulers, Rebels (and What the Neighbors Thought)** (2000) (I)

_____, **Lives of the Presidents: Fame, Shame (and What the Neighbors Thought)** (1998) (I)

Krull, Kathleen, & Paul Brewer, **Lincoln Tells a Joke: How Laughter Saved the President (and the Country)** (2010) (P–I)

Marrin, Albert, **The Great Adventure: Theodore Roosevelt and the Rise of Modern America** (2007) (A)

_____, **Old Hickory: Andrew Jackson and the American People** (2004) (A)

Mills, Judie, **Robert Kennedy** (1998) (A)

Moss, Marissa, **Nurse, Soldier, Spy: The Story of Sarah Edmonds, a Civil War Hero** (2011) (P–I)

Murphy, Jim, **The Crossing: How George Washington Saved the American Revolution** (2010) (I–A)

_____, **The Real Benedict Arnold** (2007) (A)

* Myers, Walter Dean, **Malcolm X: A Fire Burning Brightly** (2000) (I–A)

Pinkney, Andrea Davis, **Sojourner Truth's Step-Stomp Stride** (2010) (P–I)

Provensen, Alice, **The Buck Stops Here: The Presidents of the United States** (2011) (P–I)

Rappaport, Doreen, **Abe's Honest Words: The Life of Abraham Lincoln** (2008) (I)

_____, **Eleanor, Quiet No More** (2009) (P–I)

_____, **Jack's Path of Courage: The Life of John F. Kennedy** (2010) (P–I)

Rockwell, Anne, **Big George: How a Shy Boy Became President Washington** (2009) (P–I)

* Rumford, James, **Sequoyah: The Cherokee Man Who Gave His People Writing** (2004) (I)

Sheinkin, Steve, **The Notorious Benedict Arnold: A True Story of Adventure, Heroism, & Treachery** (2010) (A)

* Stanley, Diane, **Saladin: Noble Prince of Islam** (2002) (I)

St. George, Judith, **Stand Tall, Abe Lincoln** (2008) (P–I)

Thimmesh, Catherine, **Madame President: The Extraordinary, True (and Evolving) Story of Women in Politics** (2004) (I)

Philosophers and Religious Leaders

* Demi, **Buddha** (1996) (I)

* _____, **The Dalai Lama: A Biography of the Tibetan Spiritual and Political Leader** (1998) (I)

* _____, **Gandhi** (2001) (I)

* _____, **Muhammad** (2003) (I)

* Freedman, Russell, **Confucius: The Golden Rule** (2002) (I)

* Nelson, S. D., **Black Elk's Vision: A Lakota Story** (2010) (I)

Scientists and Inventors

Armstrong, Jennifer, **Audubon: Painter of Birds in the Wild Frontier** (2003) (P–I)

Bardhan-Quallen, Sudipta, **Up Close: Jane Goodall** (2008) (A)

Brown, Don, **Odd Boy Out: Young Albert Einstein** (2004) (P)

_____, **A Wizard from the Start: The Incredible Boyhood and Amazing Inventions of Thomas Edison** (2010) (P–I)

Collins, Mary, **Airborne: A Photobiography of Wilbur and Orville Wright** (2003) (I)

D'Agnese, Joseph, **Blockhead: The Life of Fibonacci** (2010) (I)

Davies, Jacqueline, **The Boy Who Drew Birds: A Story of John James Audubon** (2004) (P–I)

Engle, Margarita, **Summer Bird: The Butterflies of Maria Merian** (2010) (P–I)

Fisher, Leonard Everett, **Alexander Graham Bell** (1999) (I)

Gerstein, Mordicai, **Sparrow Jack** (2003) (I)

Heiligman, Deborah, **Charles and Emma: The Darwins' Leap of Faith** (2009) (A)

* Krensky, Stephen, **A Man for All Seasons: The Life of George Washington Carver** (2008) (P–I)

Krull, Kathleen, **Albert Einstein** (2009) (I)

_____, **The Boy Who Invented TV: The Story of Philo Farnsworth** (2009) (P–I)

_____, **Charles Darwin** (2010) (A)

_____, **They Saw the Future: Oracles, Psychics, Scientists, Great Thinkers, and Pretty Good Guessers** (1999) (I)

Lasky, Katherine, **The Man Who Made Time Travel** (2003) (I)

Matthews, Tom, **Always Inventing: A Photobiography of Alexander Graham Bell** (1999) (I)

McDonnell, Patrick. **Me . . . Jane** (2011) (P)

McGinty, Alice B., **Darwin** (2009) (I)

Mitchell, Don, **Driven: A Photobiography of Henry Ford** (2010) (I)

Old, Wendie, **To Fly: The Story of the Wright Brothers** (2002) (I–A)

Ottaviani, Jim, **Feynman** (2011) (A)

Ray, Deborah Kogan, **Down the Colorado: John Wesley Powell, the One-Armed Explorer** (2007) (I)

_____, **The Flower Hunter: William Bartram, America's First Naturalist** (2004) (P–I)

Reef, Catherine, **Sigmund Freud: Pioneer of the Mind** (2001) (A)

Schroeder, Alan, **Ben Franklin: His Wit and Wisdom from A–Z** (2011) (P–I)

Severance, John, **Einstein: Visionary Scientist** (1999) (I)

Sís, Peter, **The Tree of Life: A Book Depicting the Life of Charles Darwin: Naturalist, Geologist & Thinker** (2003) (I–A)

Winter, Jeanette, **The Watcher: Jane Goodall's Life with the Chimps** (2011) (P)

Adventurers and Explorers

Aronson, Marc, **Sir Walter Ralegh and the Quest for El Dorado** (2000) (A)

✳ Blumberg, Rhoda, **York's Adventures with Lewis and Clark: An African-American's Part in the Great Expedition** (2004) (I)

Burleigh, Robert, **Night Flight: Ameila Earhart Crosses the Atlantic** (2011) (P)

✳ Grimes, Nikki, **Talkin' about Bessie: The Story of Aviator Elizabeth Coleman** (2002) (I)

Fleming, Candace, **Amelia Lost: The Life and Disappearance of Amelia Earhart** (2011) (I–A)

Ray, Deborah Kogan, **Down the Colorado: John Wesley Powell, the One-Armed Explorer** (2007) (I)

Weatherford, Carole Boston, **I, Matthew Henson: Polar Explorer** (2008) (P–I)

Yaccarino, Dan, **The Fantastic Undersea Life of Jacques Cousteau** (2009) (P–I)

Zaunders, Bo, **Feathers, Flaps, and Flops: Fabulous Early Fliers** (2001) (I)

Artists, Artisans, and Filmmakers

Bernier-Grand, Carmen, **Frida: ¡Viva la vida! Long Live Life!** (2008) (I–A)

Brighton, Catherine, **Keep Your Eyes on the Kid: The Early Years of Buster Keaton** (2008) (P)

Brown, Don, **Mack Made Movies** (2003) (P–I)

Christensen, Bonnie, **Fabulous!: A Portrait of Andy Warhol** (2011) (P)

Debon, Nicolas, **Four Pictures by Emily Carr** (2003) (I–A)

Greenberg, Jan, **Romare Bearden: Collage of Memories** (2003) (P–I)

Greenberg, Jan, & Sandra Jordan, **Action Jackson** (2002) (P–I)

_____, **Andy Warhol: Prince of Pop** (2004) (A)

_____, **Christo and Jeanne-Claude: Through the Gates and Beyond** (2008) (I)

Harvey, Jeanne Walker, **My Hands Sing the Blues: Romare Bearden's Childhood Journey** (2010) (P–I)

Hill, Laban Carrick, **Dave the Potter: Artist, Poet, Slave** (2010) (P)

Krull, Kathleen, **Jim Henson: The Guy Who Played with Puppets** (2011) (P)

Ross, Michael Elsohn, **Salvador Dalí and the Surrealists: Their Lives and Ideas** (2003) (A)

Rubin, Susan Goldman, **Wideness and Wonder: The Life and Art of Georgia O'Keefe** (2011) (I)

Selznick, Brian, **The Houdini Box** (2001) (I–A)

Slaymaker, Melissa Eskridge, **Bottle Houses: The Creative World of Grandma Prisbrey** (2004) (P)

Spielman, Gloria, **Marcel Marceau: Master of Mime** (2011) (P)

Stanley, Diane, **Michelangelo** (2000) (I)

Stone, Tanya Lee, **Sandy's Circus: A Story about Alexander Calder** (2008) (P)

Sweet, Melissa, **Balloons over Broadway: The True Story of the Puppeteer of Macy's Parade** (2011) (P–I)

Wallner, Alexandra, **Grandma Moses** (2004) (P)

Warhola, James, **Uncle Andy's: A Fabulous Visit with Andy Warhol** (2003) (P)

_____, **Uncle Andy's Cats** (2009) (P)

Musicians and Dancers

Anderson, M. T., **Strange Mr. Satie** (2003) (P)

Christensen, Bonnie, **Woody Guthrie: Poet of the People** (2001) (P–I)

Cline-Ransome, Lesa, **Before There Was Mozart: The Story of Joseph Boulogne, Chevalier de Saint-George** (2011) (P–I)

Freedman, Russell, **Martha Graham: A Dancer's Life** (1998) (A)

✳ _____, **The Voice that Challenged a Nation: Marian Anderson and the Struggle for Equal Rights** (2004) (I–A)

Gerstein, Mordicai, **What Charlie Heard** (2002) (P–I)

✳ Lang, Lang, & Michael French, **Playing with Flying Keys** (2008) (A)

✳ Parker, Robert Andrew, **Piano Starts Here: The Young Art Tatum** (2008) (P–I)

Partridge, Elizabeth, **This Land Was Made for You and Me: The Life and Songs of Woody Guthrie** (2002) (A)

✳ Pinkney, Andrea Davis, **Ella Fitzgerald: The Tale of a Vocal Virtuosa** (2002) (P–I)

Rappaport, Doreen, **John's Secret Dreams: The Life of John Lennon** (2004) (P–I)

Reich, Susanna, **Clara Schumann: Piano Virtuoso** (1999) (I)

Rubin, Susan Goldman, **Music Was It: Young Leonard Bernstein** (2011) (I–A)

Rusch, Elizabeth, **For the Love of Music: The Remarkable Story of Maria Anna Mozart** (2011) (P–I)

✳ Ryan, Pam Muñoz, **When Marian Sang: The True Recital of Marian Anderson: The Voice of a Century** (2002) (P–I)

Sís, Peter, **Play, Mozart, Play!** (2006) (P)

✳ Tallchief, Maria, & Rosemary Wells, **Tallchief: America's Prima Ballerina** (1999) (I)

❋ Weatherford, Carole Boston, *Before John Was a Jazz Giant: A Song of John Coltrane* (2008) (P)

Winter, Jeanette, *Sebastian: A Book about Bach* (1999) (P)

Writers

Bolden, Tonya, *Up Close: W. E. B. Du Bois* (2009) (A)

Brown, Monica, *Pablo Neruda: Poet of the People* (2011) (P–I)

Bryant, Jen, *A River of Words: The Story of William Carlos Williams* (2008) (I)

❋ Burleigh, Robert, *Langston's Train Ride* (2004) (I)

❋ Cooper, Floyd, *Coming Home: From the Life of Langston Hughes* (1994) (I)

Crutcher, Chris, *King of the Mild Frontier: An Ill-Advised Autobiography* (2003) (A)

Dahl, Roald, *More about Boy: Roald Dahl's Tales from Childhood* (1984/2010) (A)

Fleischman, Sid, *The Trouble Begins at 8: A Life of Mark Twain in the Wild, Wild West* (2008) (A)

Gantos, Jack, *Hole in My Life* (2002) (A)

Glaser, Linda, *Emma's Poem: The Voice of the Statue of Liberty* (2010) (P–I)

❋ Herrera, Juan Felipe, *The Upside Down Boy/El niño de cabeza* (2000) (P)

Kerley, Barbara, *The Extraordinary Mark Twain (According to Susy)* (2010) (I)

_____, *Walt Whitman: Words for America* (2004) (I)

Krull, Kathleen, *The Boy on Fairfield Street: How Ted Geisel Grew Up to Become Dr. Seuss* (2004) (P–I)

_____, *The Road to Oz: Twists, Turns, Bumps, and Triumphs in the Life of L. Frank Baum* (2008) (P–I)

Lasky, Kathryn, *A Brilliant Streak: The Making of Mark Twain* (1998) (I)

Lowry, Lois, *Looking Back: A Book of Memories* (1998) (I)

Madden, Kerry, *Up Close: Harper Lee* (2009) (A)

McDonough, Yona Zeldis, *Louisa: The Life of Louisa May Alcott* (2009) (I)

Metselaar, Menno, & Ruud van der Rol, *Anne Frank: Her Life in Words and Pictures* (2010) (I)

❋ Murphy, Jim, *Pick and Shovel Poet: The Journeys of Pascal D'Angelo* (2000) (I–A)

❋ Myers, Walter Dean, *Bad Boy: a Memoir* (2001) (A)

Nobleman, Marc Tyler, *Boys of Steel: The Creators of Superman* (2008) (I–A)

Paulsen, Gary, *Guts: The True Stories behind Hatchet and the Brian Books* (2001) (I–A)

Reef, Catherine, *Ernest Hemingway: A Writer's Life* (2009) (A)

_____, *Jane Austen: A Life Revealed* (2011) (I–A)

Say, Allen. *Drawing from Memory* (2011) (I–A)

Scieszka, Jon, *Knucklehead: Tall Tales & Mostly True Stories about Growing Up Scieszka* (2008) (I–A)

Spinelli, Jerry, *Knots in My Yo-Yo String: The Autobiography of a Kid* (1998) (I)

Stanley, Diane, & Peter Vennema, *Bard of Avon: The Story of William Shakespeare* (1992) (I)

Warren, Andrea, *Charles Dickens and the Street Children of London* (2011) (I–A)

Winter, Jeanette, *Beatrix: Various Episodes from the Life of Beatrix Potter* (2003) (P)

Young, Ed, & Libby Koponen, *The House Baba Built: An Artist's Childhood in China* (2011) (P–I)

Younger, Barbara, *Purple Mountain Majesties: The Story of Katharine Lee Bates and "America the Beautiful"* (1998) (P)

Sports Heroes

❋ Bolden, Tonya, *The Champ: the Story of Muhammad Ali* (2004) (I)

❋ Bruchac, Joseph, *Jim Thorpe's Bright Path* (2004) (I)

❋ Cooper, Floyd, *Jump! From the Life of Michael Jordan* (2004) (P–I)

❋ De La Peña, Matt, *A Nation's Hope: The Story of Boxing Legend Joe Louis* (2011) (P)

❋ Debon, Nicolas, *The Strongest Man in the World: Louis Cyr* (2007) (I)

Hopkinson, Deborah, *Girl Wonder: A Baseball Story in Nine Innings* (2003) (P)

❋ Krull, Kathleen, *Wilma Unlimited: How Wilma Rudolph Became the World's Fastest Woman* (1996) (P–I)

❋ Myers, Walter Dean, *The Greatest: Muhammad Ali* (2001) (I–A)

❋ Robinson, Sharon, *Promises to Keep: How Jackie Robinson Changed America* (2004) (I–A)

❋ Smith, Charles R., Jr., *Black Jack: The Ballad of Jack Johnson* (2010) (I)

❋ _____, *Twelve Rounds to Glory: The Story of Muhammad Ali* (2007) (A)

Tavares, Matt, *Henry Aaron's Dream* (2010) (P–I)

❋ Winter, Jonah, *Muhammad Ali: Champion of the World* (2008) (P)

❋ Wise, Bill, *Louis Sockalexis: Native American Baseball Pioneer* (2007) (I)

Extraordinary Ordinary People

❋ al-Windawi, Thura, *Thura's Diary: My Life in Wartime Iraq* (2004) (I–A)

Anderson, Laurie Halse, *Independent Dames: What You Never Knew about the Women and Girls of the American Revolution* (2008) (P–I)

Bang, Molly, *Nobody Particular: One Woman's Fight to Save the Bays* (2000) (I–A)

❋ Barakat, Ibtisam, *Tasting the Sky: A Palestinian Childhood* (2007) (I–A)

Blumenthal, Karen, *Mr. Sam: How Sam Walton Built Wal-Mart and Became America's Richest Man* (2011) (I)

Bogacki, Tomek, *The Champion of Children: The Story of Janusz Korczak* (2010) (I)

❋ Bridges, Ruby, *Through My Eyes* (1999) (I–A)

Brown, Don, *Kid Blink Beats the World* (2004) (P–I)

❋ Bruchac, Joseph, *Pocahontas* (2003) (I–A)

✳ _____, *Sacajawea* (2000) (I–A)

✳ Coleman, Evelyn, *The Riches of Osceola McCarty* (1998) (I)

✳ D'Adamo, Francesco, *Iqbal* (2003) (I–A)

✳ Dash, Joan, *The World at Her Fingertips: The Story of Helen Keller* (2001) (A)

✳ Engle, Margarita, *The Surrender Tree: Poems of Cuba's Struggle for Freedom* (2008) (A)

✳ Erdich, Liselotte, *Sacagawea* (2003) (P–I)

Fleming, Candace, *The Great and Only Barnum: The Tremendous, Stupendous Life of Showman P. T. Barnum* (2009) (I)

✳ Fradin, Dennis Brindell, & Judith Bloom Fradin, *Fight On!: Mary Church Terrell's Battle for Integration* (2003) (I)

✳ _____, *Ida B. Wells: Mother of the Civil Rights Movement* (2000) (I–A)

✳ Gold, Alison Leslie, *A Special Fate: Chiune Sugihara: Hero of the Holocaust* (2000) (A)

✳ Greenfield, Eloise, *How They Got Over: African Americans and the Call of the Sea* (2003) (P)

✳ Grovenar, Alan, *Osceola: Memories of a Sharecropper's Daughter* (2001) (I)

✳ Halfman, Janet, *Seven Miles to Freedom: The Robert Smalls Story* (2008) (P–I)

✳ Hamilton, Virginia, *Many Thousand Gone: African Americans from Slavery to Freedom* (1993) (I–A)

Hurst, Carol Otis, *Rocks in His Head* (2001) (P–I)

✳ Jiménez, Francisco, *Breaking Through* (2001) (I–A)

✳ _____, *The Circuit: Stories from the Life of a Migrant Child* (1997) (I–A)

✳ Keat, Nawuth, *Alive in the Killing Fields: Surviving the Khmer Rouge Genocide* (2010) (A)

Lang, Glenna, & Marjory Wunsch, *Genius of Common Sense: Jane Jacobs and the Story of the Death and Life of Great American Cities* (2009) (A)

✳ Lobel, Anita, *No Pretty Pictures: A Child of War* (1998) (A)

✳ Marx, Trish, *One Boy from Kosovo* (2000) (I)

McCully, Emily Arnold, *Manjiro: The Boy Who Risked His Life for Two Countries* (2008) (P)

✳ _____, *My Heart Glow: Alice Cogswell, Thomas Gallaudet, and the Birth of American Sign Language* (2008) (P)

_____, *Wonder Horse: The True Story of the World's Smartest Horse* (2010) (P)

✳ Monceaux, Morgan, & Ruth Katcher, *My Heroes, My People: African Americans and Native Americans in the West* (1999) (I)

Moss, Marissa, *The Bravest Woman in America* (2011) (P)

Nelson, Vaunda Micheaux, *Bad News for Outlaws: The Remarkable Life of Bass Reeves, Deputy U.S. Marshall* (2009) (I)

✳ Nivola, Claire, *Planting the Trees of Kenya: The Story of Wangari Maathai* (2008) (P)

✳ Pinkney, Andrea Davis, *Let It Shine: Stories of Black Women Freedom Fighters* (2000) (I–A)

✳ Pressler, Mirjam, *Anne Frank: A Hidden Life* (2000) (A)

Say, Allen, *Music for Alice* (2004) (P–I)

✳ Siegal, Aranka, *Memories of Babi* (2008) (I–A)

Stauffacher, Sue, *Tille the Terrible Swede: How One Woman, a Sewing Needle, and a Bicycle Changed History* (2011) (P)

Steig, William, *When Everybody Wore a Hat* (2003) (P)

Stone, Tanya Lee, *Almost Astronauts: 13 Women Who Dared to Dream* (2009) (A)

_____, *Elizabeth Leads the Way: Elizabeth Cady Stanton and the Right to Vote* (2008) (P)

Sullivan, George, *Tom Thumb: The Remarkable True Story of a Man in Miniature* (2011) (I–A)

✳ Tillage, Leon Walter, *Leon's Story* (1997) (I–A)

Van Allsburg, Chris, *Queen of the Falls* (2011) (P–I)

Wadsworth, Ginger, *First Girl Scout: The Life of Juliette Gordon Low* (2011) (I–A)

✳ Warren, Andrea, *Escape from Saigon: How a Vietnam War Orphan Became an American Boy* (2004) (I–A)

✳ Wolf, Bernard, *Coming to America: A Muslim Family's Story* (2003) (P)

Additional resources to accompany this chapter can be found on the Education CourseMate website. Go to CengageBrain .com to access a variety of interactive study tools and useful resources including Video Conversations with children's book authors and illustrators, a searchable children's literature database, glossary flashcards, online activities, tutorial quizzes, links to relevant websites, and more.

Nonfiction

At 1:10 all the weighing and measuring is over. "Done!" proclaims Daryl. And then to the chick he says gently, "You rest for a while." He'll be up to feed it in four hours. Good thing Daryl practiced this sort of thing when his own baby son was born three years ago.

The rest of us are tired but elated.

"A worthy replacement for Bill," Jeff pronounces.

"Cool!" says Daryl. "We're up to eighty-seven again!"

—SY MONTOGOMERY
Kakapo Rescue: Saving the World's Strangest Parrot, p. 67

As Leslie shows her class the photograph of the tiny kakapo chick curled up next to an eggshell, the third graders cheer. They have been deeply engrossed in the story of Sy Montgomery and Nic Bishop's ten-day experience working with the New Zealand National Kakapo Recovery Team on Codfish Island. Respecting the strong narrative flow and subtle humor in the book, Leslie has been sharing a short chapter each day after lunch, much like she shared **The Tale of Despereaux** earlier in the year. But the gorgeous photographs help remind the students that this is not a work of fiction. They have begun to eagerly check the related kakapo recovery website; some chart the number of living kakapos, and others find the YouTube videos of their favorite birds. Even her most fervent fiction readers are caught up in the topic of animal extinction and browse through Martin Jenkins's **Can We Save the Tiger?** during free time. Using rich nonfiction children's literature, Leslie has ignited her students' enthusiastic foray into scientific inquiry.

Defining Nonfiction

Children and adolescents have a desire to *know*, and when they discover that books are a place to find answers, they embark on a journey of lifelong learning. They turn to nonfiction literature to feed their hunger for facts, ideas, and concepts. The term *nonfiction* describes books of information and fact about any topic. Nonfiction books are distinguished from fiction by their emphasis. Although both may tell a story, and both may include fact, in nonfiction, the facts and concepts are uppermost, with storytelling perhaps used as an expressive technique. In fiction, the story is uppermost, with facts sometimes used to support it. The key lies in the emphasis of the writer, which in nonfiction should be on the facts and concepts being presented. It is these that must be truthful, verifiable, and understandable.

The nonfiction now being published has great appeal to young readers. Writers select topics that interest children, and many of the topics they select fit nicely into an existing school curriculum. A recent push for including more nonfiction reading across the curriculum has led to increasing work with nonfiction in English and language arts as well as the content areas. It also has drawn attention to the various types of nonfiction, from argumentative prose to literary nonfiction, and the importance of exposing children to all types.

Regardless of particular type, nonfiction books today invite readers with spacious, well-designed the reader right there in the action, making even mundane moments exciting. Because she is not a scientist, she explains things in layman's terms and presents answers to the questions young readers are likely to have, perhaps because she personally is wondering the same things. This style allows for clear delineation between her observations and reactions as well as the facts that are known about the kakapos, including the details of what exactly the Recovery Team has learned. Montgomery explains this emphasis on the facts of the ten-day visit explicitly in the back matter of the book as well, stating that "as with all the books we write in this series, most of our research is done on site" (p. 73).

In the last few pages of the book, Montgomery shares a chance encounter she and Bishop had with a kakapo while hiking. Her earnest, emotional retelling captures the passion she has come to feel about saving these birds, the role humans have played in their loss, as well as the role humans will need to play if the kakapos will be ultimately saved

from extinction. The afterword directs readers to the Kakapo Recovery website so that they can continue to follow the lives of the individual birds they have come to love from the book and learn more about the work of the Recovery Team.

Fewer nonfiction books support a study of mathematics than support either science or social studies, although several are published each year. Mathematics programs today reflect a philosophy in which fiction and nonfiction literature fit naturally. Today, we present mathematical problems in context, draw on children's background knowledge to solve them, and model strategies for alternate ways to solve problems.

Many mathematics lessons begin with a story—a story with a problem that can be solved through a mathematical process. Teachers invite children to propose as many different strategies as possible to try to solve the problem. Together, they apply each strategy and evaluate its accuracy and efficiency. They learn that there are alternative ways to come up with

P | R | O | F | I | L | E | S

Sy Montgomery

To research books, Sy Montgomery has been chased by an angry silverback gorilla in Zaire, bitten by a vampire bat in Costa Rica, and handled a wild tarantula in French Guiana. She has been deftly undressed by an orangutan in Borneo, hunted by a tiger in India, and swum with piranhas, electric eels, and dolphins in the Amazon.*

Sy Montgomery is the author of both adult and children's nonfiction animal books, particularly known for her children's titles on unusual, often endangered, animals. Although not a scientist herself, she is a passionate conservationist. She wants her books to reach as many people as she can, explaining: "We are on the cusp of either destroying this sweet, green Earth—or revolutionizing the way we understand the rest of

animate creation. It's an important time to be writing about the connections we share with our fellow creatures."

Montgomery is currently working with Nic Bishop on another new title for the **Scientists in the Field** series, this time on the tapirs of Brazil.

Nic Bishop

Switching from adult to children's books was quite easy, for me, . . . as a photographer, very little change is needed. Even the youngest of children can interpret sophisticated images of nature. So I invest all the same skills and effort in photographing for children that I do for adults. The work is every bit as rewarding, and I'm happy to say, a lot more fun.**

The son of a biologist, Nic Bishop grew up in Bangladesh,

the Sudan, and New Guinea. As an adult, he spent seventeen years living in New Zealand, where he also worked on a PhD in biology. His love for adventuring and the outdoors combined with his love for photography, and he published his first photojournalism book, *Untouched Horizons*, in 1989 on the South Island wilderness landscapes. That book led to several others for adults on New Zealand's natural history and eventually to his well-known nonfiction children's books.

Nic spends enormous amounts of time capturing each of the amazing photographs found in his books.

 To learn more about Sy Montgomery or Nic Bishop and his photo process, go to CengageBrain .com to access the Education CourseMate website, where you will find links to relevant websites.

the right answer. Stories that are structured around numbers and counting, such as Pat Hutchins's classic, *The Doorbell Rang* (P), or Felicia Bond's *Tumble Bumble* (P) are especially useful for primary teachers who want to link mathematics and reading.

There are also many beautiful counting books and books that allow children to practice numeral recognition, such as Stephen Johnson's *City by Numbers* (P). These books encourage children to develop their visual skills as they look for numerals or count items on the artistically beautiful pages. Other books explain mathematical concepts, such as David Adler's *Mystery Math: A First Book of Algebra* (I) and Richard Evan Schwartz's engaging *You Can Count on Monsters* (I–A). Schwartz has created a special monster creature for each prime number; each page of the book represents a number 1 through 100 and the prime monsters work together to show the numbers. The concept of prime numbers and factor trees is a little more understandable when it involves little monsters!

Measurement and size are explored in Steve Jenkins's *Actual Size* (P–I) and *Prehistoric Actual Size* (P–I). Jenkins's amazing cut-paper collages appear again in these oversize books containing life-size illustrations of creatures, or parts thereof. The white backdrop emphasizes the relative sizes of the creatures in the books as compared to one another and invites young readers to compare themselves to the creatures depicted. Just how big is a gorilla's hand, anyway? Ben Hillman's *How Big Is It?: A Big Book All about Bigness* (P) combines a conversational text and manipulated photographs that allow young readers to see the actual size of twenty-two animals, objects, and places. Ken Robbins's *For Good Measure: The Ways We Say How Much, How Far, How Heavy, How Big, How Old* (P–I) uses gorgeous photographs to introduce children to the vocabulary of measurement.

Jon Scieszka's *Math Curse* (I), illustrated by Lane Smith, is a wonderfully funny book that underscores how we use mathematics in our daily lives and presents interesting mathematical puzzles for children to figure out. The outrageous humor in the book is so infectious that children enthusiastically engage in the mental arithmetic the book calls for.

The journal *Teaching Children Mathematics* reviews books that relate to mathematics instruction, as do *Language Arts, The Reading Teacher*, and *The Horn Book Magazine*.

• • SOCIAL STUDIES • •

Just as in science, the content of social studies evolves as changes in the world result in new configurations of countries and people. New communications technology makes the world seem much smaller than it used to be and increases our interest in other people and places. Children have more books than ever to select from as they pursue their interests in the past and present.

Many nonfiction books cover such topics as geography and maps, life in the past, and the social structures and customs of various cultures, past and present. Children are quite naturally interested in others, where they come from, and in the world around them; this natural curiosity and openness to people makes them receptive to books that explore the global community, past and present.

Sound historical detective work marks Scott Reynolds Nelson's *Ain't Nothing but a Man: My Quest to Find the Real John Henry* (I), written in collaboration with Marc Aronson. The reader, along with Nelson, follows the clues as Nelson finds them—photographs, census data, prison records, and other sources—and learns that John Henry might have been a convict, and most likely died of silicosis and was buried along with hundreds of other African American convicts forced to work on the railroad. A simple discovery—that there are no American statues that honor Klu Klux Klan victims—led to the deep research behind Susan Campbell Bartoletti's *They Called Themselves the K.K.K.: The Birth of an American Terrorist Group* (A). Bartoletti uses congressional documents, archival photographs, excerpts from slave narratives, and historical quotes to present the rise of the group and its political force. Her presentation highlights the extensive inquiry work she did, and a comprehensive annotated bibliography and source notes help provide further context for this significant book.

Faraway places and people are brought close in good nonfiction. Ted and Betsy Lewin visited Mongolia to see the Naadam, a sporting event held throughout Mongolia. In *Horse Song: The Naadam of Mongolia* (P–I), they focus on a race in which young boys gallop for fourteen miles across the Gobi Desert on their stallions. The watercolor illustrations are gorgeous as well as informative, the text succinct and vivid, and the end material provides interesting additional information about a nomadic culture so remote that most of us will never experience it. Although not strictly nonfiction, the beautiful watercolor and gouache paintings in Claire Nivola's *Orani: My Father's Village* (P–I) introduce readers to 1950s Sardinia as Nivola recounts her annual summer visits to the small town from which her father immigrated. The perspective here of an American child on a visit adds an additional detail when Nivola captures her feelings on returning to New York City each fall.

Current issues, and the most recent current events, in social studies find their way into children's books. In *Trapped: How the World Rescued 33 Miners from 2,000 Feet below the Chilean Desert* (I–A), Marc Aronson puts the reader right into the mine with the thirty-three men, but also allows the reader to view top-side events in detail as well. The extensive back matter and a discussion of geological and economic conditions near the mine offers better understanding of why the collapse occurred. Karen Blumenthal's *Bootleg: Murder, Moonshine, and the Lawless Years of Prohibition* (A) focuses on the Prohibition, but covers the drinking habits of Americans into present day, discussing Red Ribbon Week and substance abuse. Don Brown's *America Is under Attack: September 11, 2001: The Day the Towers Fell* (P–I) marks the tenth anniversary of the event in a picturebook.

History is also an important subject in nonfiction. American history is presented from fresh perspectives in such books as Tom Feelings's *Middle Passage: White Ships/Black Cargo* (A) and

Patricia and Fredrick McKissack's *Christmas in the Big House, Christmas in the Quarters* (I). Russell Freedman's *Who Was First?: Discovering the Americas* (I–A) invites readers to consider how the Americas have been "discovered" by many people at many times in history. He presents historical theories with accompanying evidence that both supports and refutes them. Kadir Nelson's stunning illustrations and the use of an unknown narrator speaking about her ancestors help to present an overview of African American history in a very intimate fashion in *Heart and Soul: The Story of America and African Americans* (I).

World War II is the setting for Susan Campbell Bartoletti's *Hitler Youth: Growing Up in Hitler's Shadow* (A), a deeply disturbing but also moving account of some of the young people caught up in the Hitler Youth movement. Voices of those who were enthusiastic Hitler Youth members, those who were part of the resistance, and those persecuted by the Third Reich help Bartoletti create a book that sparks discussion of values and the consequences of one's actions. *Candy Bomber* (I) by Michael O. Tunnell also captures part of World War II, specifically 1945 Berlin and the work of pilot Gail Halvorsen, who brought candy to the local children via airlift. Award-winning nonfiction author Russell Freedman offers perspectives into the causes of War World II by examining World War I in his newest stunning photo-filled book, *The War to End All Wars: World War I* (A).

New facts about history are presented in Chris Crowe's *Getting Away with Murder: The True Story of the Emmett Till Case* (A), in which the 1955 murder of a young black boy and the speedy acquittal of his white murderers is portrayed. Crowe also discusses how this incident galvanized people across the nation and helped provoke the civil rights movement of the 1960s. *Birmingham Sunday* (I–A) by Larry Dane Brimner takes a look at this time period, too, presenting the 1963 racial bombing in Birmingham's Sixteenth Street Baptist Church, but tracing the events preceding it by starting with discussion of the 1954 *Brown vs. the Board of Education* landmark case.

Places, how they evolved, and how people lived there are another important topic in social studies. An American icon is the focus of a collection of portraits from 108 contemporary writers and artists, *Our White House: Looking in, Looking out* (I–A). A patchwork of general history of the White House; interesting, unique stories about it; and major events that occurred are followed by support material that includes the *Our White House* website. *If You Lived Here: Houses of the World* (P–I) by

Giles Laroche showcases sixteen homes through beautiful cut-paper collages that demonstrate a wide variety of dwellings worldwide. Laroche uses empathy and wonder to help students begin to compare the homes to others, starting each page with "If you lived here..." Richard Michelson's ***Tuttle's Red Barn: The Story of America's Oldest Family Farm*** (P) chronicles social and economic changes over four centuries. Mary Azarian's woodcuts are worth poring over for details of dress, buildings, tools, and other artifacts.

Books such as these are easy to find. The Children's Book Council's "Notable Trade Books in Social Studies" list is available from the council and published in the April/May issue of the journal *Social Education*; they are reviewed in journals such as *The Horn Book Magazine, Language Arts*, and *The Reading Teacher*. Teaching Idea 10.4 offers suggestions for how to help students explore further the ideas presented in these books by examining their own family histories.

● ● LANGUAGE, LITERATURE, ● ● AND THE ARTS

Children's books that explore language are wonderful resources for an integrated language arts curriculum. Alphabet books, books about traditional parts of speech, histories of language, and books about writing are becoming more plentiful. Don Robb's ***Ox, House, Stick: The History of Our Alphabet*** (I), illustrated by Anne Smith, traces the transformations of each letter, weaving in history and interesting bits of information. Punctuation takes on a new dimension in Robin Pulver's ***Punctuation Takes a Vacation*** (P), a primary-grade version of the popular adult book *Eats, Shoots and Leaves*.

Books like Brian Cleary's ***But and For, Yet and Nor: What Is a Conjunction?*** (P) explore the parts of speech. Ruth Heller is known for her brightly illustrated, eye-catching books about the parts of speech, including ***Mine, All Mine: A Book about Pronouns*** (P–I). The rhyming text is surrounded by double-page illustrations visually depicting the pronouns. Heller's books give concrete and intriguing examples of what many students feel is boringly remote. Robin Pulver explores grammar in ***Silent Letters Loud and Clear*** (P–I), Gene Baretta talks homophones in ***Dear Deer*** (P-I), and Loreen Leedy has fun with similes in ***Crazy Like a Fox: A Simile Story*** (P–I). Older readers meet a comprehensive and witty editor in ***Grammar Girl Presents the Ultimate Writing Guide for Students*** (A) by "Grammar Girl" Mignon Fogarty, host of the *Grammar Girl* podcast and website.

A series of books by Marvin Terban explores wordplay in titles such as ***Guppies in Tuxedos: Funny Eponyms*** (I). Jon Agee's books, such as ***Elvis Lives! and Other Anagrams*** (I), are also interesting to students exploring what we can do with the English language. Loreen Leedy and Pat Street present interesting sayings in ***There's a Frog in My Throat! 440 Animal Sayings a Little Bird Told Me*** (P) with illustrations to increase the fun.

TEACHING IDEA 10.4

Thematic Connection: Learning about Family History

COMMON CORE STATE STANDARDS

This Teaching Idea addresses the Common Core English Language Arts, Writing: standard 8, grades K through 5, and standard 7, grades 3 through 5 and 6 through 8.

Students are always interested in finding out about themselves and their families and friends. Ask students to interview their older family members about family history. Then, after students have described that history—either orally or in writing—have them use their research skills, with the help of the school librarian, to find nonfiction books that offer information about some aspect of that history. For example, if a student's great-grandparents emigrated from eastern Europe in the 1940s, look for books that present that history. If a student's grandfather fought in the Vietnam conflict, look for books about that war. Students' family histories can then be put in the context of what the students discovered through their research. For upper elementary grade and middle-school students, this can take the form of a paper—one that is grounded in personal history.

Studies of books and authors often accompany composition instruction. These studies work best if they transcend the usual biographical information to get at the essence of what writers and illustrators do—create books. Leonard Marcus does just that in many books, including *The Wand in the Word: Conversations with Writers of Fantasy* (I–A) and his newest book of conversations, *Show Me a Story! Why Picture Books Matter: Conversations with 21 of the Worlds' Most Celebrated Illustrators* (I–A). Marcus explores how authors and illustrators work together to create picturebooks in *Side by Side: Five Favorite Picture-Book Teams Go to Work* (I–A). These books help students not only understand the complexities of the writing process but also recognize the artistry of the books they read and enjoy. Used in combination with the memoirs and biographies described in Chapter 9, they offer young readers an opportunity to get to know some of their favorite writers and illustrators. Outstanding books like these for teaching the English language arts are selected each year by a committee of the National Council of Teachers of English and published in *Language Arts*.

In addition to the many fine biographies of musicians and artists also explored in Chapter 9, a variety of nonfiction books explore aspects of music and art. Just as other subject areas are enhanced when well-written and beautifully designed books become a part of the curriculum, the study of art and music is made more vivid when accompanied by beautiful books.

Several series books that explore elements of art, including Philip Yenawine's *Lines* (P–I), and books that help readers learn to look at paintings, such as Gladys Blizzard's *Come Look with Me: Animals in Art* (I), are excellent resources for those interested in learning more about fine art. Susan Fillion highlights art collection in *Miss Etta and Dr. Claribel: Bringing Matisse to America* (I–A). Jean Tucker introduces children to photography in *Come Look with Me: Discovering Photographs with Children* (I), another book in the **Come Look with Me** series. The **Looking at Paintings** series, by Peggy Roalf, is organized around what a viewer sees in a painting. Two books in this series are *Children* and *Flowers* (I). Each volume contains nineteen full-color reproductions of paintings accompanied by a text that presents a history of the artist and information about technique and style.

The Painter's Eye: Learning to Look at Contemporary American Art (A) is a fascinating book that explains complicated concepts in an understandable fashion. Jan Greenberg and Sandra Jordan define and give examples of the elements of art and principles of design that artists use to create paintings. They also present the postwar American artists themselves through conversations, photographs, and brief anecdotes about their childhoods and their work. The text begins with a useful table of contents and includes brief biographies of the artists, a list and description of the paintings discussed, a glossary, a bibliography, an index, and suggestions for further reading. Greenberg and Jordan's *The Sculptor's Eye: Looking at Contemporary American Art* (A) is an excellent introduction to the concepts of contemporary sculpture.

A number of books explain different artistic processes and the creation of different products, inviting children to create collages, make paper, or design structures. Others explore bridges, buildings, and other objects as architectural art. Salvatore Rubbino's *A Walk in London* (P) uses mixed-media illustrations to capture the major landmarks in London; it pairs nicely with his earlier *A Walk in New York* (P) to highlight major architectural differences in the two cities.

Books about music and dance also are available. Ashley Bryan visually interprets music through his brilliantly colored, cut-paper illustrations in *Let It Shine: Three Favorite Spirituals* (I). Walter Dean Myers explores music in *blues journey* (I) and *Jazz* (I), both brilliantly illustrated by Christopher Myers. Historical events, great musicians, forms, and instruments are all touched on. These books are so compelling that they seem to be music themselves. Siena Cherson Siegel explores another art form in her memoir, *To Dance: A Ballerina's Graphic Novel* (I), illustrated by Mark Siegel. In *Dance* (P), Bill T. Jones and Susan Kuklin add few words to visually stunning photographs of Jones dancing.

Now, we take a close look at another book that centers on dance, but also presents an important American historical event, Sibert Award–winning *Ballet for Martha: Making Appalachian Spring* (P–I).

* * *

A CLOSE LOOK AT
Ballet for Martha: Making Appalachian Spring

Smiling, joyful dancers clad in white bonnets and blue gowns leap off the cover of Jan Greenberg and Sandra Jordan's beautiful picturebook *Ballet for Martha: Making Appalachian Spring*. The book details the collaboration between choreographer

The team of authors Jan Greenberg and Sandra Jordan and illustrator Brian Floca capture the tale of the creative team behind the American ballet in **Ballet for Martha: Making Appalachian Spring**.

Martha Graham, composer Aaron Copland, and set designer Isamu Noguchi to create the American ballet *Appalachian Spring*. Emphasis placed throughout is on how the work of all three combined to create an American dance masterpiece and stresses repeatedly that the ballet would not have existed without the hard work of all three artists.

Greenberg and Jordan use elegant, poetic language to detail the creative process behind *Appalachian Spring*. The text is sparse, but each phrase seems carefully calculated to perfectly capture an image. The images add up, in a straightforward chronological order, to tell the story of how the artists combined efforts to create the ballet. Quotes from Graham, Copland, and Noguchi are sprinkled throughout and allow the artists to literally tell the story in their own words. Greenberg and Jordan's additions help translate what might otherwise have been confusing for young readers.

The use of lyrical language, something becoming increasingly common in nonfiction for children (think of the texts earlier mentioned in this chapter, for example Sidman's **Swirl by Swirl**), distinguishes this book and adds a unique and engaging quality to the beautifully spare text. It is perhaps in the area of design, however, where **Ballet for Martha** most clearly excels. White space is used tremendously well throughout the book. The watercolor illustrations of wide skies, and vast, spare backdrops, are occasionally broken with a sudden close-up of vigorously moving dancers. The text as well employs the use of white space to set apart sentences into stanzas or to break a line and lend emphasis to a particular phrase or image.

The design matches well to the three main figures of the book. Martha Graham was well known for her modern approaches to dance and the use of spare, angular forms. Aaron Copland was inspired by the wide, open spaces of America. Isamu Noguchi had designed many sets for Martha Graham's ballets and was used to customizing sets to her unique ideas of dance. Greenberg, Jordan, and Floca's decision to match the design of their book to the style of Graham, Copland, and Noguchi's work adds additional understanding of the ballet *Appalachian Spring* for young readers in an inspiring, and certainly nondidactic, fashion.

The rich back matter of the book includes short biographies of each artist with an archival photograph, an extensive bibliography, and references for the original quotes used throughout the book. Even these back pages are beautifully designed with small sketches of dancers from the ballet appearing in the margins.

The attention to accuracy, the gorgeous illustrations, and the engaging text that takes on a complicated topic and makes it comprehensible make **Ballet for Martha** an outstanding example of a nonfiction picturebook.

Whether the subject is science, mathematics, social studies, language, or the arts, many beautiful nonfiction

P R O F I L E S

Jan Greenberg and Sandra Jordan

Our tenth book, Ballet for Martha: Making Appalachian Spring, began with a trip to the awesome Isamu Noguchi Garden Museum in Long Island City to see an exhibit of Noguchi's stage sets... Since we are collaborators, we were curious about how Martha worked with her troupe, as well as with Aaron, the composer, and with Isamu, the sculptor.*

Jan Greenberg and Sandra Jordan have collaborated on several award-winning nonfiction books; in fact, every one of their books has been an ALA Notable Book or an ALA Best Book for Young Adults, in addition to receiving a number of Sibert Award Honors and other honors. They met when Jan submitted her first novel to Farrar, Straus and Giroux, where Sandra was then editor in chief of children's

books. Ten years later, they collaborated on their first book, *The Painter's Eye*, and have created more than a dozen books together since then.

Jan and Sandra's work focuses on art and artists, particularly American artists. They have made it a point to talk to living artists to decide upon subjects they think would interest young readers as well as to interview living artists for their insights on the topics they ultimately select.

Brian Floca

There's a real narrative arc to the piece, a fine sense of process, and a rewarding payoff at book's end when the dance is premiered. It's a great text, and I hope that with the illustrations I've added a piece to the puzzle.**

Brian Floca is an illustrator and author of several books, both nonfiction and fiction. An

undergraduate class taken at Rhode Island School of Design with author and illustrator David Macaulay led to an introduction to the author Avi, and Brian ultimately began illustrating some of Avi's work. Brian now illustrates for several authors, but also has written and illustrated his own books, including two Sibert Honor–winning titles, *Lightship* and *Moonshot: The Flight of Apollo 11*. He has also taught classes on children's book writing and illustrating.

Brian has an extensive website including a blog, videos of him at work in the studio, portfolio pieces, and links to another website he contributes to with other children's authors and illustrators.

To learn more about Jan Greenberg, Sandra Jordan, or Brian Floca's website, go to CengageBrain .com to access the Education CourseMate website, where you will find links to the relevant websites.

---

children's books present more depth of information than can be contained within the pages of a textbook. The well-written texts of these books do not just inform; they provide models of effective nonfiction prose. The illustrations illuminate concepts and present information visually, bringing life and vitality to the topic under scrutiny. Children learn about the world from the many fine nonfiction books that are available, as they learn how to be critical consumers of information.

Nonfiction in the Classroom

Adults selecting books for young readers often give short shrift to nonfiction, assuming that stories and poetry are more appealing or are in some way superior to nonfiction. They aren't. Many young readers prefer nonfiction to fiction; their insatiable curiosity about the world is fueled by nonfiction books. As

they mature, many continue to prefer nonfiction, wanting to read to learn. Excellent nonfiction books allow children to learn about a particular topic, and when that matches children's interests, reading nonfiction is fun, just as reading fiction is fun.

We learn best by fitting new information into a coherent frame or schema. When children seek out information for themselves, identify what is relevant, and use it for meaningful goals, they become more efficient at storing and retrieving facts. Furthermore, nonfiction is readily available on virtually any topic and for almost any level of understanding. This rich and vast array of materials generates an interest and excitement that encourages children to find out about their world.

Reading for information relates to other language uses; it is part of the scheme of the total language system. Children do read to learn in assigned textbooks, but they read to learn with enthusiasm and excitement in specialized, excellent nonfiction. Compared to a textbook, a trade book can reveal the point of view of the

*Reprinted with permission from www.jangreenbergsandrajordan.com.
**Reprinted with the permission of the author from http://brianflocablog.blogspot.com.

author more directly, focus on an individual or a topic with a sharper light, and present specialized information that often gives readers a broader understanding. Trade books provide reading and learning opportunities for readers of all ages and skill levels. Textbooks, written with a generic grade-level student in mind, cannot. Trade books also provide the opportunity for greater depth of study, as they offer more information about individual topics than any one textbook could hold.

• •   TYPES OF NONFICTION   • •

The style of nonfiction trade books varies widely, but all excellent nonfiction uses interesting writing, rich language, and appropriate terminology. This writing can be classified into several types, and it is becoming increasingly important for teachers to be aware of these classifications. Changes to the 2009 Reading Framework of the National Assessment of Progress (NAEP) and widespread adoption of the Common Core standards point to an increased focus on nonfiction reading. In these documents, in recent research, and in education circles, however, the terms *nonfiction, informational text*, and *expository text* are often used in quite different, even contradictory, ways.

In the beginning of this chapter we defined *nonfiction* quite globally, stating that nonfiction is text in which the emphasis is on the facts and concepts being presented. We acknowledged that some nonfiction may use narrative styles to present these facts. This global definition is purposefully inclusive, but as teachers we do want to be certain our students learn to read and understand all types of nonfiction writing. Different types of nonfiction require different skills and strategies for comprehension. If we do not have a good understanding of the different types of nonfiction texts, we may think we have taught students to read "nonfiction text" when we actually have not.

Cognitive psychologists have long used the term *expository text* to distinguish text that has the primary purpose "to communicate information so that the reader might learn something" (Weaver & Kintsch, 1991, p. 230) and add the important note that this expository text must follow a nonnarrative (or "expository") text structure. Expository texts vary from narrative texts under this definition not only because of their purpose, but also because of their differences in text structure. This issue of text structure is where the definition of *nonfiction text* can get rather muddy.

Nonfiction, or text that focuses on truthful, verifiable facts, can be in several formats. NAEP's 2009 list perhaps most clearly defines what types American students are asked to be able to read and understand: argumentative and persuasive texts,

procedural texts and documents, and expository texts, which they define as those that do not follow a story structure and "present information, provide explanations and definitions, and compare and contrast" (National Assessment Governing Board [NAGB], 2008, p. 60). NAEP also mentions that students should read and comprehend "literary nonfiction," which they explain "employ[s] distinctly literary elements and devices [often a narrative or story structure] to communicate [its] message and to make [its] content more accessible to readers" (NAGB, 2008, p. 8). As is noted in this chapter, many of the exemplary nonfiction trade books published today use a narrative structure in at least part of their contents.

The caution for educators is simply to be aware of this. When the importance of teaching expository text is mentioned in standards, or when teachers are told they must teach more informational texts, we must recognize that this means teaching students to read *all* types of nonfiction text. Teachers should strive to share nonfiction trade books that represent a variety of text structures beyond the popular narrative/story structure. Books that use procedural structures or include procedural documents in sidebars, that include argumentative/persuasive essays, or those that employ traditional expository structure (compare and contrast, main idea and detail, etc.) are as important as "literary nonfiction" trade books. Students can be taught to recognize and comprehend the difference structures. The criteria of excellence presented in this chapter can be used to seek out the best books representing all of these types of nonfiction. Excellent nonfiction of all types provides many rich opportunities for learning.

• •   CRITICAL READING   • •
AND THINKING

Learning is more than the laying on of discrete areas of information; it requires an active response from students, an interpretation or reconstruction of new information in relation to what they already know. Rather than simply teaching a body of facts for students to memorize, effective teachers help students learn to think critically. Teaching Idea 10.5 offers some suggestions for helping students recognize what they are learning from nonfiction texts, put it in their own words, and determine what they still need to know as they become experts about a particular topic in preparation for writing about it.

Critical reading and thinking are basic to a lifetime of learning. The schemata we develop as we read to learn influences all subsequent knowledge. Thinking readers, called critical readers, evaluate

TEACHING IDEA 10.5

Read First, Write Later

This Teaching Idea addresses the Common Core English Language Arts, Writing standard 10, grades 3 through 5 and 6 through 8, and standard 7, grades 5 through 8.

Teachers often discover that students' science and social studies reports sound all too much like the entries in their encyclopedias. The ideas offered here will help students learn to write in their own voice, use a variety of resources, and synthesize information instead of copying it from an encyclopedia.

Collect many resources on science and social studies topics for the classroom library. Keep in mind the following suggestions for enriching students' learning experience:

- Have your students keep journals as they read, in which they write down what they are learning *and* what they think about what they are learning. They can do this by using the left-hand side of each double-page spread for notes and the right-hand side for comments.

- At regular intervals, have students answer these questions in writing: "What do I know already?" "What do I want to learn?"

- Have students explain to a classmate what they have learned and what they are still trying to find out.

- Be sure that students use a variety of books to search for answers to their questions. As they read for this purpose, have them take notes about their discoveries.

- When they have read widely, talked about their discoveries, and written about what they are learning and how they feel about it, then it is time for them to draft a report. Talk with them about the importance of writing it in their own voice. Give them guidelines for what you want them to produce.

new information in light of what they already know, compare many sources instead of accepting only one point of view, and make judgments about what they read. If one goal of education is to develop informed, thinking, participating citizens, then helping children learn to read critically is essential.

The person who believes that anything found in print is the truth—the whole truth—is at a disadvantage relative to one who has learned to check sources, compare reports, and evaluate. Young readers do not question what they read when they are given one textbook that is held up as embodying the final and complete truth on its subject. They do learn to question and evaluate as they read if we encourage them to make comparisons among different sources, including nonfiction trade books. We can encourage critical thinking by asking students to see what different books have to say about the same topic or to use their own knowledge and experiences to judge the quality of an idea or piece of information.

Readers of all ages can verify information found in books by checking it against observations made in real life. They can also assess an author's qualifications, look at the documentation provided, and critically

evaluate the books they read, much as we suggest in Figure 10.1, the evaluation checklist at the beginning of this chapter. Many of the nonfiction books we've discussed in this chapter encourage readers to adopt a critical stance based on research and observation, collect and analyze data, draw conclusions, make inferences, and test hypotheses. Books that draw the reader into research help develop an observant critical stance that spills over from books into daily life.

SUMMARY

There are many outstanding books of nonfiction on virtually any topic for a wide range of readers. Awards such as the Orbis Pictus and the Sibert establish criteria that recognize quality in nonfiction. When children are given excellent nonfiction books to explore topics of interest, they learn a great deal about those topics. They learn more than they would from textbooks or encyclopedias alone because the intriguing formats of nonfiction books make them intrinsically more interesting to read and because trade books contain more detailed information. When reading nonfiction, children also have the opportunity to experience well-written, organized expository prose that can then serve as a model for their own informational writing. Further, reading several nonfiction books provides a perfect opportunity to think critically—evaluating and verifying information by making comparisons with experience and with other books.

Booklist

Because the subjects, and the examples, of excellent nonfiction for young readers are almost inexhaustible, here we present the titles that have won the Sibert and Orbis Pictus Awards. These titles include both biography and other types of nonfiction; all are excellent.

The Robert Sibert Award Books

2001

Sir Walter Ralegh and the Quest for El Dorado, by Marc Aronson (Clarion)
HONOR BOOKS: *The Longitude Prize*, by Joan Dash, illustrated by Susan Petricic (Farrar, Straus and Giroux); *Blizzard*, by Jim Murphy (Scholastic); *My Season with Penguins: An Antarctic Journal*, by Sophie Webb (Houghton Mifflin); *Pedro and Me: Friendship, Loss, and What I Learned*, by Judd Winick (Henry Holt)

2002

Black Potatoes: The Story of the Great Irish Famine, 1845–1850, by Susan Campbell Bartoletti (Houghton Mifflin)
HONOR BOOKS: *Surviving Hitler: A Boy in the Nazi Death Camps*, by Andrea Warren (HarperCollins); *Vincent van Gogh*, by Jan Greenberg and Sandra Jordan (Delacorte); *Brooklyn Bridge*, by Lynn Curlee (Atheneum)

2003

The Life and Death of Adolf Hitler, by James Cross Giblin (Clarion)
HONOR BOOKS: *Six Days in October: The Stock Market Crash of 1929*, by Karen Blumenthal (Atheneum); *Hole in My Life*, by Jack Gantos (Farrar, Straus and Giroux); *Action Jackson*, by Jan Greenberg and Sandra Jordan, illustrated by Robert Andrew Parker (Roaring Brook); *When Marian Sang*, by Pam Muñoz Ryan, illustrated by Brian Selznick (Scholastic)

2004

An American Plague: The True and Terrifying Story of the Yellow Fever Epidemic of 1793, by Jim Murphy (Clarion)
HONOR BOOK: *I Face the Wind*, by Vicki Cobb, illustrated by Julia Gorton (HarperCollins)

2005

The Voice that Challenged a Nation: Marian Anderson and the Struggle for Equal Rights, by Russell Freedman (Clarion)
HONOR BOOKS: *Sequoyah: The Cherokee Man Who Gave His People Writing*, by James Rumford (Houghton Mifflin); *The Tarantula Scientist*, by Sy Montgomery, illustrated by Nic Bishop (Houghton Mifflin); *Walt Whitman: Words for America*, by Barbara Kerley, illustrated by Brian Selznick (Scholastic); *People Writing*, by James Rumford (Houghton Mifflin)

2006

Secrets of a Civil War Submarine: Solving the Mysteries of the H. L. Hunley, by Sally M. Walker (Carolrhoda)
HONOR BOOK: *Hitler Youth: Growing Up in Hitler's Shadow*, by Susan Campbell Bartoletti (Scholastic)

2007

Team Moon: How 400,000 People Landed Apollo 11 on the Moon, by Catherine Thimmesh (Houghton Mifflin)
HONOR BOOKS: *Freedom Riders: John Lewis and Jim Zwerg on the Front Lines of the Civil Rights Movement*, by Ann Bausum (National Geographic); *To Dance: A Ballerina's Graphic Novel*, by Siena Cherson Siegel (Simon & Schuster); *Quest for the Tree Kangaroo: An Expedition to the Cloud Forest of New Guinea*, by Sy Montgomery (Houghton Mifflin)

2008

The Wall: Growing Up behind the Iron Curtain, by Peter Sís (Farrar, Straus and Giroux)

HONOR BOOKS: *Lightship*, by Brian Floca (Simon & Schuster); *Nic Bishop Spiders*, by Nic Bishop (Scholastic)

2009

We Are the Ship: The Story of Negro League Baseball, by Kadir Nelson (Hyperion)
HONOR BOOKS: *Bodies from the Ice: Melting Glaciers and Rediscovery of the Past*, by James M. Deem (Houghton Mifflin); *What to Do about Alice? How Alice Roosevelt Broke the Rules, Charmed the World, and Drove Her Father Teddy Crazy!*, by Barbara Kerley, illustrated by Edwin Fotheringham (Scholastic)

2010

Almost Astronauts: 13 Women Who Dared to Dream, by Tanya Lee Stone (Candlewick)
HONOR BOOKS: *The Day-Glo Brothers: The True Story of Bob and Joe Switzer's Bright Ideas and Brand-New Colors*, by Chris Barton, illustrated by Tony Persiani (Charlesbridge); *Moonshot: The Flight of Apollo 11*, by Brian Floca (Atheneum); *Claudette Colvin: Twice Toward Justice*, by Phillip Hoose (Farrar, Straus and Giroux)

2011

Kakapo Rescue: Saving the World's Strangest Parrot, by Sy Montgomery, illustrated by Nic Bishop (Houghton Mifflin)
HONOR BOOKS: *Ballet for Martha: Making Appalachian Spring*, by Jan Greenberg and Sandra Jordan, illustrated by Brian Floca (Roaring Brook); *Lafayette and the American Revolution*, by Russell Freedman (Holiday House)

The Orbis Pictus Award Books

1990

The Great Little Madison, by Jean Fritz (Putnam)
HONOR BOOKS: *The Great American Gold Rush*, by Rhoda Blumberg (Bradbury); *The News about Dinosaurs*, by Patricia Lauber (Bradbury)

1991

Franklin Delano Roosevelt, by Russell Freedman (Clarion)
HONOR BOOKS: *Arctic Memories*, by Normee Ekoomiak (Henry Holt); *Seeing Earth from Space*, by Patricia Lauber (Orchard)

1992

Flight: The Journey of Charles Lindbergh, by Robert Burleigh and Mike Wimmer (Philomel)
HONOR BOOKS: *Now Is Your Time! The African-American Struggle for Freedom*, by Walter Dean Myers (HarperCollins); *Prairie Vision: The Life and Times of Solomon Butcher*, by Pam Conrad (HarperCollins)

1993

Children of the Dust Bowl: The True Story of the School at Weedpatch Camp, by Jerry Stanley (Crown)
HONOR BOOKS: *Talking with Artists*, by Pat Cummins (Bradbury); *Come Back, Salmon*, by Molly Cone (Sierra Club)

1994

Across America on an Emigrant Train, by Jim Murphy (Clarion)
HONOR BOOKS: *To the Top of the World: Adventures with Arctic Wolves*, by Jim Brandenburg (Walker); *Making Sense: Animal Perception and Communication*, by Bruce Brooks (Farrar, Straus and Giroux)

1995

Safari beneath the Sea: The Wonder of the North Pacific Coast, by Diane Swanson (Sierra Club)
HONOR BOOKS: *Wildlife Rescue: The Work of Dr. Kathleen Ramsay*, by Jennifer Owings Dewey (Boyds Mills); *Kids at Work: Lewis Hine and the Crusade against Child Labor*, by Russell Freedman (Clarion); *Christmas in the Big House, Christmas in the Quarters*, by Patricia and Fredrick McKissack (Scholastic)

1996

The Great Fire, by Jim Murphy (Scholastic)
HONOR BOOKS: *Dolphin Man: Exploring the World of Dolphins*, by Laurence Pringle, photographs by Randall S. Wells (Atheneum); *Rosie the Riveter: Women Working on the Home Front in World War II*, by Penny Colman (Crown)

1997

Leonardo da Vinci, by Diane Stanley (Morrow)
HONOR BOOKS: *Full Steam Ahead: The Race to Build a Transcontinental Railroad*, by Rhoda Blumberg (National Geographic); *The Life and Death of Crazy Horse*, by Russell Freedman (Holiday House); *One World, Many Religions: The Way We Worship*, by Mary Pope Osborne (Knopf)

1998

An Extraordinary Life: The Story of a Monarch Butterfly, by Laurence Pringle, illustrated by Bob Marstall (Orchard)
HONOR BOOKS: *A Drop of Water: A Book of Science and Wonder*, by Walter Wick (Scholastic); *A Tree Is Growing*, by Arthur Dorros, illustrated by S. D. Schindler (Scholastic); *Charles A. Lindbergh: A Human Hero*, by James Cross Giblin (Clarion); *Kennedy Assassinated! The World Mourns: A Reporter's Story*, by Wilborn Hampton (Candlewick); *Digger: The Tragic Fate of the California Indians from the Missions to the Gold Rush*, by Jerry Stanley (Crown)

1999

Shipwreck at the Bottom of the World: The Extraordinary True Story of Shackleton and the Endurance, by Jennifer Armstrong (Crown)
HONOR BOOKS: **Black Whiteness: Admiral Byrd Alone in the Antarctic**, by Robert Burleigh, illustrated by Walter Lyon Krudop (Atheneum); **Fossil Feud: The Rivalry of the First American Dinosaur Hunters**, by Thom Holmes (Messner); **Hottest, Coldest, Highest, Deepest**, by Steve Jenkins (Houghton Mifflin); **No Pretty Pictures: A Child of War**, by Anita Lobel (Greenwillow)

2000

Through My Eyes, by Ruby Bridges and Margo Lundell (Scholastic)
HONOR BOOKS: **At Her Majesty's Request: An African Princess in Victorian England**, by Walter Dean Myers (Scholastic); **Clara Schumann: Piano Virtuoso**, by Susanna Reich (Clarion); **Mapping the World**, by Sylvia Johnson (Atheneum); **The Snake Scientist**, by Sy Montgomery, illustrated by Nic Bishop (Houghton Mifflin); **The Top of the World: Climbing Mount Everest**, by Steve Jenkins (Houghton Mifflin)

2001

Hurry Freedom: African Americans in Gold Rush California, by Jerry Stanley (Crown)
HONOR BOOKS: **The Amazing Life of Benjamin Franklin**, by James Cross Giblin, illustrated by Michael Dooling (Scholastic); **America's Champion Swimmer: Gertrude Ederle**, by David Adler, illustrated by Terry Widener (Harcourt); **Michelangelo**, by Diane Stanley (HarperCollins); **Osceola: Memories of a Sharecropper's Daughter**, by Alan Govenar, illustrated by Shane W. Evans (Hyperion); **Wild and Swampy**, by Jim Arnosky (HarperCollins)

2002

Black Potatoes: The Story of the Great Irish Famine, 1845–1850, by Susan Campbell Bartoletti (Houghton Mifflin)
HONOR BOOKS: **The Cod's Tale**, by Mark Kurlansky, illustrated by S. D. Schindler (Putnam); **The Dinosaurs of Waterhouse Hawkins: An Illuminating History of Mr. Waterhouse Hawkins, Artist and Lecturer**, by Barbara Kerley, illustrated by Brian Selznick (Scholastic); **Martin's Big Words: The Life of Dr. Martin Luther King, Jr.**, by Doreen Rappaport, illustrated by Bryan Collier (Hyperion)

2003

When Marian Sang: The True Recital of Marian Anderson: The Voice of a Century, by Pam Muñoz Ryan, illustrated by Brian Selznick (Scholastic)
HONOR BOOKS: **Confucius: The Golden Rule**, by Russell Freedman, illustrated by Frédéric Clément (Levine); **The Emperor's Silent Army: Terracotta Warriors of Ancient China**, by Jane O'Connor (Viking); **Phineas**

Gage: A Gruesome but True Story about Brain Science, by John Fleischman (Houghton Mifflin); **Tenement: Immigrant Life on the Lower East Side**, by Raymond Bial (Houghton Mifflin); **To Fly: The Story of the Wright Brothers**, by Wendie Old, illustrated by Robert Andrew Parker (Clarion)

2004

An American Plague: The True and Terrifying Story of the Yellow Fever Epidemic of 1793, by Jim Murphy (Clarion)
HONOR BOOKS: **Empire State Building: When New York Reached for the Skies**, by Elizabeth Mann, illustrated by Alan Witschonke (Mikaya); **In Defense of Liberty: The Story of America's Bill of Rights**, by Russell Freedman (Holiday House); **Leonardo: Beautiful Dreamer**, by Robert Byrd (Dutton); **The Man Who Made Time Travel**, by Kathryn Lasky, illustrated by Kevin Hawkes (Farrar, Straus and Giroux); **Shutting Out the Sky: Life in the Tenements of New York, 1880–1924**, by Deborah Hopkinson (Orchard)

2005

York's Adventures with Lewis and Clark: An African-American's Part in the Great Expedition, by Rhoda Blumberg (HarperCollins)
HONOR BOOKS: **Actual Size**, by Steve Jenkins (Houghton Mifflin); **The Race to Save the Lord God Bird**, by Phillip Hoose (Farrar, Straus and Giroux); **Secrets of the Sphinx**, by James Cross Giblin (Scholastic); **Seurat and La Grande Jatte: Connecting the Dots**, by Robert Burleigh (Abrams); **The Voice That Challenged a Nation: Marian Anderson and the Struggle for Equal Rights**, by Russell Freedman (Clarion)

2006

Children of the Great Depression, by Russell Freedman (Clarion)
HONOR BOOKS: **ER Vets: Life in an Animal Emergency Room**, by Donna Jackson (Houghton Mifflin); **Forbidden Schoolhouse: The True and Dramatic Story of Prudence Crandall and Her Students**, by Suzanne Jurmain (Houghton Mifflin); **Genius: A Photobiography of Albert Einstein**, by Marfe Ferguson Delano (National Geographic); **Hitler Youth: Growing Up in Hitler's Shadow**, by Susan Campbell Bartoletti (Scholastic); **Mosquito Bite**, by Alexandra Siy and Dennis Kunkel (Charlesbridge)

2007

Quest for the Tree Kangaroo: An Expedition to the Cloud Forest of New Guinea, by Sy Montgomery, photographs by Nic Bishop (Houghton Mifflin)
HONOR BOOKS: **Gregor Mendel: The Friar Who Grew Peas**, by Cheryl Bardoe (Abrams); **Freedom Walkers: The Story of the Montgomery Bus Boycott**, by Russell Freedman (Holiday House); **John Muir: America's First Environmentalist**, by Kathryn Lasky (Candlewick); **Something out of Nothing: Marie Curie**

and Radium, by Carla Killough McClafferty (Farrar, Straus and Giroux); **Team Moon: How 400,000 People Landed Apollo 11 on the Moon**, by Catherine Thimmesh (Houghton Mifflin)

2008

M.L.K.: Journey of a King, by Tonya Bolden (Abrams) HONOR BOOKS: **Black and White Airmen: Their True History**, by John Fleischman (Houghton Mifflin); **Spiders**, by Nic Bishop (Scholastic); **Helen Keller: Her Life in Pictures**, by George Sullivan (Scholastic); **Muckrakers**, by Ann Bausum (National Geographic); **Venom**, by Marilyn Singer (Darby Creek)

2009

Amelia Earhart: The Legend of the Lost Aviator, by Shelley Tanaka, illustrated by David Craig (Abrams) HONOR BOOKS: **George Washington Carver**, by Tonya Bolden (Abrams); **The Lincolns: A Scrapbook Look at Abraham and Mary**, by Candace Fleming (Schwartz & Wade); **Washington at Valley Forge**, by Russell Freedman (Holiday House); **We Are the Ship: The Story of Negro League Baseball**, by Kadir Nelson (Hyperion); **When the Wolves Returned: Restoring Nature's Balance in Yellowstone**, by Dorothy Hinshaw Patent, illustrated by Dan and Cassie Hartman (Walker)

2010

The Secret World of Walter Anderson, by Hester Bass, illustrated by E.B. Lewis (Candlewick) HONOR BOOKS: **Almost Astronauts: 13 Women Who Dared to Dream**, by Tanya Lee Stone (Candlewick); **Darwin: With Glimpses into his Private Journal and Letters**, by Alice McGinty (Houghton Mifflin); **The Frog Scientist**, by Pamela Turner (Houghton Mifflin); **How Many Baby Pandas?**, by Sandra Markle (Walker); **Noah Webster: Weaver of Words**, by Pegi Deitz Shea (Calkins Creek).

2011

Ballet for Martha: Making Appalachian Spring, by Jan Greenberg and Sandra Jordan, illustrated by Brian Floca (Roaring Brook) HONOR BOOKS: **Birmingham Sunday**, by Larry Dane Brumner (Calkins Creek); **Candy Bomber: The Story of the Berlin Airlift's "Chocolate Pilot,"** by Michael O. Tunnell (Charlesbridge); **If Stones Could Speak: Secrets of Stonehenge**, by Marc Aronson (National Geographic); **Journey into the Deep: Discovering New Ocean Creatures**, by Rebecca L. Johnson (Millbrook); **Mammoths and Mastodons: Titans of the Ice Age**, by Cheryl Bardoe (Abrams)

Additional resources to accompany this chapter can be found on the Education CourseMate website. Go to CengageBrain .com to access a variety of interactive study tools and useful resources including Video Conversations with children's book authors and illustrators, a searchable children's literature database, glossary flashcards, online activities, tutorial quizzes, links to relevant websites, and more.

11

Literature-Based Instruction: Kindergarten through Third Grade

- **Children's Literature and Emergent Literacy**

- **Literature-Based Instruction**

- **Reading Aloud**

- **Supporting Children's Growing Literary Understanding**

- **Oral Language and Literature**
  Discussion
  Storytelling by Children
  Choral Speaking
  Drama

- **Variations of Literature-Based Instruction**
  Using Literature with Emergent and Beginning Readers
  Using Literature to Integrate the Curriculum
  Literature Study with Primary-Grade Readers

- **Assessment**

- **Summary**

Annette Bronsky's first-grade class is embarking on an exciting intellectual and creative journey: they are hearing and discussing David Wiesner's postmodern version of **The Three Pigs** for the first time. What happens when you think you know a story, and your background of experience turns out to be more of a hindrance than a help? What we see the children doing, with help from Annette, is to try to fit the story into their already well-developed schema for the Three Pigs tale, and then to discard their preconceived interpretations because they do not make sense in terms of Wiesner's new version.

Even the front cover of the storybook provides some "cognitive dissonance" for the children, as they note that the story is not called **The Three Little Pigs,** but rather **The Three Pigs:**

> STEVEN: The Three *Grownup* Pigs.
> NATHAN: Yeah, they're real pigs.
> NORMAN: They're—they look like three real pigs. And in the other stories, the other pigs didn't really look a lot like real pigs.
> TEACHER: What a good observation. Anything else? Morgan?
> MORGAN: They're pigs like animal pigs, and the other ones are like people pigs.
> TEACHER: These are animal or people pigs—oh—what do you mean by people pigs?
> STEVEN: Like they walk on their two feet. They talk.
> TEACHER: So the other ones [the pigs in the other versions the children had already heard] reminded you of people because they walked and they talked, but do they look like real pigs?
> MANDY: And they wear clothes.
> NATHAN: These are going to die.

This discussion is interesting because the children are already seeing a difference between versions of the tale they already know quite well and suggest that this story will be different: they draw a distinction between "animal pigs," which look real (and therefore, as Nathan observes, might "die" like real pigs), and "people pigs," which are fantasy characters.

As the story proceeds, the children are in familiar territory: the pigs build their houses of straw, sticks, and bricks, and the wolf comes to threaten them. At this point, when the wolf blows down the house of straw, the children experience their first real cognitive jolt. The wolf's huffing and puffing literally blows the first pig out of his own story! It's important to note that the text conforms to the traditional versions of the story and states that the wolf ate the first pig. However, the speech balloon for the pig reads, "Hey! He blew me right out of the story!" The children struggled mightily to make sense of this in terms of what they already knew:

> STEVEN: It looks like he's falling out of the story.
> MELANIE: It says, "I'll blow your house in like the other one."
> ANTHONY: I don't think he's in the story.
> TEACHER: That's a good observation. The pig just said, "He blew me right out of the story!"

STEVEN: 'Cause it looks like he's falling.

MANUEL: It looks like he's falling . . . out. It doesn't make sense.

TEACHER: Look at what it says up here: ". . . and ate the pig up."

KEITH: That's how the real story was.

TEACHER: Right. So here it said, "He huffed and he puffed and he blew the house in . . . and ate the pig up." But the pig's saying. "Hey! He blew me right out of the story!"

DOMINIQUE: Huh?

MANUEL: How does he eat him up?

STEVEN: Maybe he jumped out of the story with him and ate him.

DOMINIQUE: Pretend he was, maybe he was just joking that he ate him up.

TEACHER: These are all good things. Yes, Alex.

ALEX: Maybe he thought when he blew the house down he might have ate a lot of straw and thought he ate the pig.

TEACHER: Let's turn the page and see what happens.

MELANIE He *thinks* he eats the pig.

TINA: He mighta eat a lot of sticks.

MELANIE: He might've ate all the sticks.

STEVEN: Yeah, he's going . . . there's a circle with no sticks around him.

MELANIE: He's going, "This doesn't taste very good."

In this long excerpt, we see the children struggling greatly to make sense of the obvious contradiction between what the words say—"and ate the pig up"—(along with their previous background knowledge) and the illustration, which shows the pigs being blown out of the frame of the story. When all three pigs are outside the space of their own story, they decide to fold up the pages of their own story to make a paper airplane and escape. At this point, Keith suggested, "Maybe the plane will go out of control and go back to another script and the story will continue." Melanie suggested, cleverly, that "then they might meet themselves," a sophisticated metaphysical idea! What happens is that the pigs enter two more stories, however, and leave them rather quickly. In the first case, they fly into a version of *Hey Diddle Diddle* and take the cat with the fiddle along with them. In the second case, they fly into a vaguely medieval story about a dragon guarding a golden rose and take the dragon along with them. At this point they are in a place with many storyboards and many possible stories:

MANUEL: This is weird because this story's [points to the picture] going into this story. And this is another one. The fish are like floating in nowhere.

TINA: This is—this is like a picture story!

ANTHONY: And there's no talking in it.

DOMINIQUE: It's like a bunch of pictures.

MANUEL: This story is going into *every* story. The fish are going crazy and going *everywhere*. In that picture and in that picture!

DOMINIQUE: It's like a bunch of picture frames all over the place and you could go into any story!

At this point, the children understand the freedom that the pigs have: they are in a veritable library of stories and could enter any one of them. But they decide to go back to their own story, taking the dragon and the cat with them.

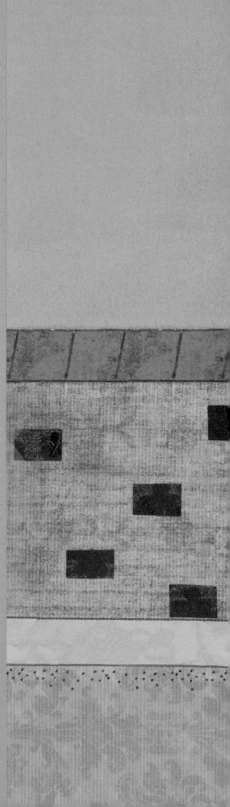

When they return, the wolf comes to the door, but the dragon scares it away, and the pigs and their other story friends live happily ever after. After the story ends, they discuss the dragon:

MORGAN: The dragon saved—the dragon saved them.
TEACHER: You're right.
MEL: Good thing they got him out of the story because if they just went back into this they would have gotten eaten.
TEACHER: You're right. Keith?
KEITH: I know. This all makes sense. They probably had it all planned out because they told the dragon to come and they would scare the wolf.

In this small series of excerpts from a much longer discussion, the children shift from being slightly puzzled that the pigs on the front cover are "real" pigs rather than "people" pigs, and then settling into the story they expect and already know quite well. When the first pig gets blown out of the story, they tenaciously cling to their previous knowledge of how a Three Pigs story proceeds, until it becomes impossible to apply this previous knowledge to the creative alternative that Wiesner offers. In the end, the children understand and appreciate this new version, with Keith's theory that "they probably had it all planned out" to go to different stories to find animals (like the dragon) that would help them defeat the wolf.

Children's Literature and Emergent Literacy

For many decades now, we have known that children who have experiences with books in their homes and preschools are more ready to embark on literacy learning when they begin formal education in kindergarten. Many researchers have explored the experiences that a literacy-rich home environment provides, with six general conclusions. First, literacy learning begins early in life and continues throughout development. Second, oral language and literacy are developed concurrently. Third, literacy learning is both a social and a cognitive process. Fourth, learning to read and write is a developmental process that occurs over time and evidences general patterns shaped by individual differences across children. Fifth, this learning is deeply rooted in cultural and family communication patterns. Finally, reading children's literature, especially within the family, has a special, important role in literacy learning (Strickland, Galda, & Cullinan, 2004). It is through repeated exposure to books that children begin to understand that those squiggles on the page are words, that white space separates those words, and that those words refer to objects, characters, and ideas that children can think about and are often captured in the illustrations that accompany the words. When these repeated encounters with books are pleasant, as they always should be, children begin to develop a positive attitude toward books and reading. Books become a source of pleasure, entertainment, refuge, and emotional satisfaction. These positive early experiences are the beginning of the development of life-long readers.

Literature-Based Instruction

More than thirty years ago, Holdaway (1979) explored the structures of these rich literacy experiences at home and how they might inform school practices. He argued that important components of these home experiences can be re-created in a classroom in which children's literature is a central component of daily life. Both children who come from literature-rich homes and children who have had infrequent experiences at home benefit from spending time with good books in the classroom. Good literature provides a strong foundation for building a literacy curriculum in the preschool and primary grades. Students need good literature to feed their minds and to practice their developing reading skills. Good books support children who are learning to read and think about themselves and their world; they help us hand down the magic—a love of reading—while also helping children develop as fluent readers, writers, and oral language users, as well as thoughtful people. A rich and positive experience with children's literature in school helps children develop a positive attitude toward books and their self-efficacy, or belief that they can make sense of those books. This develops their motivation to embark on the hard work of learning how to read.

Literature from all genres provides a rich array of resources for preschool and primary-grade teachers. Picturebooks from all genres, of course, provide endless opportunities for reading aloud and discussion. The easy-to-read books for emergent readers such as Lobel's **Frog and Toad** series support children's initial attempts at making sense of text. Transitional chapter books that provide support for those readers who are ready to move beyond picturebook-length texts allow newly independent readers to hone their newly developed skills in the most effective way possible—reading interesting books. These special kinds of books also support children as they learn to write; children quite naturally borrow patterns and structures from what they read as they create their own stories, poems, and nonfiction material. These same books also provide opportunities for oral language experiences, such as drama, choral reading, storytelling, and discussion—opportunities for students to speak as well as listen. Children's books provide a perfect opportunity for integrating the English language arts: reading, writing, listening, and speaking. Children's books also provide opportunities for children to develop their visual literacy skills as they learn to "read the pictures" in picture storybooks and the illustrations in nonfiction. Teaching Idea 11.1 suggests ways of helping children explore literature in primary-grade classrooms, practices that promote learning with literature. Books support all curriculum areas; many teachers try to integrate not just the English language arts, but also science, mathematics, and social studies, as well as art and music, through the use of children's books. Teachers who use this approach link curriculum areas by teaching reading and writing in conjunction with a topic in a particular area. They select children's books about that area and use them as the texts through which students practice reading skills and strategies. For example, many primary grades focus on the community in their social studies curriculum. Using that focus to develop a thematic unit around the idea of belonging to a number of different communities can allow teachers to integrate their curriculum in a way that makes it meaningful to their students' lives. The books are resources for reading, information gathering, and stimulating discussions, and they act as models as students craft their own writing.

Although you can certainly find curriculum guides and book study guides that provide step-by-step ideas for building a curriculum around literature, we encourage you to think for yourself. Think about your students—what they are interested in, what they know how to do, what they need to learn, and how they like to learn. Then think about your curriculum—what you need to teach, how much time you have to teach it, and what materials you have available. Consider how literature can help you create meaningful and effective learning experiences for your students. One essential tool in this enterprise is a classroom library. Teaching Idea 11.2 presents guidelines for building a classroom library that will support a literature-based curriculum for the primary grades.

Cengage Learning/Wadsworth

Even toddlers benefit from spending time with books, looking at them on their own, and hearing them read by others.

TEACHING IDEA 11.1

Ways to Explore Literature in Preschool and Primary-Grade Classrooms

 **COMMON CORE STATE STANDARDS** The suggestions in this Teaching Idea are foundational for all of the Common Core English Language Arts, Reading: Literature standards. Depending on how they are implemented, individual suggestions may address standards 1 through 6 in grades 2 and 3, as well as 7 and 9 in grade 3.

Exploring literature with students increases students' desire to read on their own. When the teacher reads aloud, tells stories, and gets students to talk about books, students respond by increasing the number of books they read, which leads to enhanced reading skill and motivation to read more, a lovely cycle that results in increased ability and knowledge.

- Read aloud. You are modeling what good reading is and exposing students to the high-quality literature you choose while creating opportunities for students to learn basic concepts such as directionality, story/poem/nonfiction structures, page turns, concept of word, literary language.

- Retell stories and poems. Retelling makes stories and poems a natural part of talk. Students will soon retell stories and poems to younger children and to their peers.

- Create a picture story. Tell a story in pictures as a sequence of drawings, a comic strip, collage, stylized frieze, or a story map inset with small pictures. This helps students recognize literary elements and structures, such as setting, plot, dialogue, and conclusion.

- Talk about books. Make talk about books a natural part of every day. Enthusiasm is contagious; share your enthusiasm for books.

- Recast old tales. List the basic elements of an old tale and ask your students to write their own stories using the same elements in a modern setting. Create a comparison chart with elements from the students' stories; they will realize that basic stories can be retold endlessly.

- Dramatize stories or scenes. Role-play characters confronting one another, working their way out of dilemmas. Improvisation makes literature memorable and helps students "own" it.

- Keep reading logs as places to record books students have read. Share these with parents.

- Identify themes, or big ideas. Encourage students to think about books that have similar themes. This helps students make connections among books and see patterns in literature.

- Organize a classroom library with books that reflect many cultural groups. Try to include books written in your students' home language(s) if possible. Bilingual books are an important part of any library collection. Ask students to consider alternate ways to organize books; discuss pros and cons of each way, and as a group decide which method works best.

- Draw story structures. Stories proceed in circular ways, along a straight line with rising action, or in interrelated sequences of events. Discuss how the plot "looks" and draw or graph memorable events in a shape that makes the structure understandable.

- In groups, plan choral readings of poems or a readers' theatre reading of stories. Discuss how the words of the author should sound, and why. Doing this helps students make the link between sound and meaning.

There are many ways to enact a literature-based literacy curriculum. Such a curriculum varies along many dimensions, including curricular goals, learning activities, and selection of books. In a study of how literature-based programs look in varied classrooms, Hiebert and Colt (1989) describe how the programs vary along two main dimensions: the instructional format and the selection of literature. The variations are linked to the amount of teacher control in each dimension, ranging from teacher-led instruction to independent application in terms of instructional format, and from teacher-selected to student-selected material in terms of literature. Most current literature-based programs fall somewhere along this continuum.

Some programs are marked by a high degree of teacher control; teachers select the materials and

Create a Classroom Library

COMMON CORE STATE STANDARDS This Teaching Idea does not address specific Common Core English Language Arts, Reading: Literature standards but is foundational for all of the grades 2 and 3 standards.

Research shows that when there is a classroom library, students read 50 percent more books than when there is not. Classroom libraries provide easy access to books, magazines, and other materials. To make sure your classroom library is attractive and inviting, follow these guidelines.

Collect books that are:

- Good examples of literature
- About diverse people and cultures
- Written in English, in students' home language(s), and bilingual
- Suitable for recreational reading
- Of varied reading levels
- "Touchstone" books, enduring favorites
- Use collection to rotate books as they relate to curriculum topic or literary focus

Organize books:

- In consultation with students
- In a simple manner

- In a way that accommodates routine changes in focus
- So that book covers, not spines, are visible when possible

Include such support materials as:

- Story props, including flannel boards and felt board stories and figures
- Reocrded files, DVDs, and other useful technology available that will enhance students' experiences with books
- Puppets
- Posters, bulletin boards, dust jackets

Provide a comfortable, quiet space:

- Where students can read privately or sit and relax
- That is away from vigorous activity
- That features an appealing display of books

---

lead the instruction. Other programs are marked by student selection of materials and student direction of their own learning with less teacher intervention. All sorts of variations and combinations of student independence and teacher direction are possible. In some cases, you will want to select materials that will help students learn something they need to know in order to progress in the curriculum. In other cases, you and your students will negotiate what is to be explored, how it will be explored, and which materials will be used. Often, students will independently select books and decide what to do with them, either within parameters that you have set or entirely on their own. Of course, all students need the time and space to read books of their own choosing just for fun.

For more than thirty years, research also has explored the ways in which teachers enact a literature-based curriculum. Some of the many books, classic and current, about this topic are listed in Figure 11.1. Journals such as *Language Arts, Journal of Children's Literature*, and *The Reading Teacher* contain articles written by classroom teachers and by university researchers that inform us about the difficulties and benefits of literature-based instruction. Many language arts and reading textbooks also explain in great detail ways of structuring such a curriculum. Later in this chapter, we present the ways some particular primary-grade teachers structured their curriculum using literature; we do the same for intermediate- and middle-school teachers in Chapter 12. As you read these two chapters, think about the children and the books you know and how you might adapt these ideas for your own classroom.

FIGURE 11.1

Resources for a Literature-Based Curriculum for Elementary Grades

See also Figure 1.5, Resources for Considering Culturally Diverse Literature, and Figure 4.3, Resources for the Poetry Teacher.

Bamford, Rosemary, and Janice Kristo, editors, *Making Facts Come Alive: Choosing Quality Nonfiction Literature K–8*

Blatt, Gloria, editor, *Once upon a Folktale: Capturing the Folklore Process with Children*

Bosma, Betty, *Fairy Tales, Fables, Legends, and Myths*

Cullinan, Bernice E., editor, *Invitation to Read: More Children's Literature in the Reading Program*

Daniels, Harvey, and Nancy Steineke, *Mini-Lessons for Literature Circles*

Daniels, Harvey, and Steven Zemelman, *Subjects Matter: Every Teacher's Guide to Content-Area Reading*

Galda, Lee, Shane Rayburn, and Lisa Stanzi, *Looking through the Faraway End: Creating a Literature-Based Curriculum with Second Graders*

Hancock, Marjorie, *A Celebration of Literature and Response: Children, Books, and Teachers in K–8 Classrooms*

Hefner, Christine, and Kathryn Lewis, *Literature-Based Science: Children's Books and Activities to Enrich the K–5 Curriculum*

Hickman, Janet, and Bernice E. Cullinan, *Children's Literature in the Classroom: Weaving Charlotte's Web*

Hickman, Janet, Bernice E. Cullinan, and Susan Hepler, *Children's Literature in the Classroom: Extending Charlotte's Web*

Hill, Bonnie, Nancy Johnson, and Katherine Schlick Noe, editors, *Literature Circles and Response*

Holland, Kathleen, Rachel Hungerford, and Shirley Ernst, editors, *Journeying: Children Responding to Literature*

Lattimer, Heather, *Thinking through Genre: Units of Study in Reading and Writing Workshops 4–12*

Laughlin, Mildred, and Terri Street, *Literature-Based Art and Music: Children's Books and Activities to Enrich the K–5 Curriculum*

Martinez, Miriam, and Nancy Roser, *What a Character! Character Study as a Guide to Literary Meaning Making in Grades K–8*

McMahon, Susan, and Taffy Raphael, editors, *The Book Club Connection: Literacy Learning and Classroom Talk*

Moss, Jay, *Teaching Literature in the Elementary School: A Thematic Approach*

Peterson, Ralph, and Maryann Eeds, *Grand Conversations: Literature Groups in Action*

Roser, Nancy, and Miriam Martinez, editors, *Book Talk and Beyond: Children and Teachers Respond to Literature*

Samway, Katharine, and Gail Whang, *Literature Study Circles in a Multicultural Classroom*

Schlick Noe, Katherine, and Nancy Johnson, *Getting Started with Literature Circles*

Short, Kathy, *Literature as a Way of Knowing*

Short, Kathy, and Kathleen Pierce, editors, *Talking about Books: Literature Discussion Groups in a K–8 Classroom*

Sorensen, Marilou, and Barbara Lehman, editors, *Teaching with Children's Books: Paths to Literature-Based Instruction*

Wooten, Deborah, and Bernice Cullinan, *Children's Literature in the Reading Program: An Invitation to Read*

Young, Terrell, *Happily Ever After: Sharing Folk Literature with Elementary and Middle School Students*

Zarnowski, Myra, *Making Sense of History: Using High-Quality Literature and Hands-On Experiences to Build Content Knowledge*

Reading Aloud

One primary way that teachers help children grow as engaged, responsive readers is to read aloud. Reading aloud is one of the most common and easiest means of sharing books. It is a pleasurable experience for all when done well, and it has a positive impact on students' reading development. Reading aloud not only helps young children become readers, but also helps older children become better readers. Reading aloud extends students' horizons, introduces them to literature they might not read on their own, offers alternate worlds and lifestyles for them to think about, increases the experiential base from which to view the world, and models good reading (Galda & Cullinan, 2003). Reading aloud to young children also demonstrates print- and book-handling concepts such as left-to-right and top-to-bottom directionality, page turning, and the role of print and pictures in telling a story or presenting a concept. The many reasons for reading aloud are summarized here. Reading aloud:

- Introduces new vocabulary
- Displays interesting sentence patterns
- Presents a variety of forms of language
- Shows various styles of written language
- Develops a sense of story, poetry, or exposition
- Motivates children to read more
- Provides ideas for students' writing
- Enriches students' general knowledge
- Models the sound of fluent reading
- Adds pleasure to the day

Reading aloud to children creates a "space" in the school day that allows teachers to encourage a number of types of cognitive and affective growth. In a school climate where many teachers may feel under pressure to spend little time in storybook read-alouds, this intellectual and emotional richness provides an argument to justify what we know is a potentially meaningful literacy experience for children. Some of the "spaces" created by reading aloud to children are the following:

- *A supportive, intimate, and emotionally rich space*—to share personal experience that relates to stories, to laugh and cry together, to consider foundational questions about what it means to be human. In this space, both teachers and children feel comfortable to express themselves honestly and openly. Through the medium of story, children may talk about sensitive or complicated issues in an uninhibited and deep way.

- *A space for play, pleasure, and spontaneity*—unleashing children's creativity and sense of fun. Children become immersed in the world of the story or use the story as the platform for an expression of their own imagination. Children and teachers alike can participate in these playful and exuberant "performances." There is concern, these days, about the absence of time to play in young children's lives—preschool and kindergarten have become much more prescriptive and skill-oriented, for example, and a lot of play seems rather individual—for example in video games and so forth. The read-aloud situation creates a space for "school-sanctioned" play, especially if the read-alouds are interactive and follow the children's interpretive trajectories rather than the teacher's. The "spaces" and time for play are extremely limited in many preschool, kindergarten, and primary classrooms; however, viewing the read-aloud as such a playful space provides a way of subverting the tightly scripted programs that so often characterize current literacy curricula.

- *A space for imagining, speculating, critiquing, and reflecting*. Read-alouds provide occasions for children to share alternative interpretations, put themselves in the place of story characters for vicarious experiences, and assume different stances and perspectives, "stretching" their cognitive abilities. One of the chief joys of stories is to see the world from a different lens, and thereby to increase children's capacities for imagining the world from an entirely different perspective. In turn, this capacity allows children to critique their own worlds and to imagine a more just and equitable society.

- *A space for creating an interpretive community*. During read-alouds, children have the opportunity to socially construct meaning. Together, children and the teacher work cooperatively to build and shape literary interpretation. This cooperative meaning-building makes children who are part of a dynamic literary community where everyone's voice is heard and respected.

- All in all, read-alouds provide *a space for responding to "art"* in the broadest sense of that term. Children pursue the impulse to interpret and know; the impulse to personalize and connect stories to their own lives; and the impulse to imaginatively liberate themselves from the contingencies of life. This is what all art does: it allows us to know in new ways, perceive ourselves and others in new ways, and it frees our imaginative capacities.

There are some guidelines to consider when selecting books to read aloud, the most important of which is to select books that are well written. Books of quality abound, as we discuss in Chapters 3 through 10, and it is a waste of precious time to read second-rate materials. Good books pique children's interest and invite them to read them—or others like them—independently. Sometimes teachers will read an inferior book "because the children love it," but students will love good books even more. Select books that will influence and expand children's literary tastes.

Find out which books are already familiar by asking children to list their favorites and then build from there, selecting old favorites as well as books that children will probably not discover on their own. Use read-aloud time to share the special books that you want your students to know. Introduce children to all of an author's books by reading aloud from one of them and telling them where to find the rest.

Reading from outstanding examples of all types of literature can help expand children's literary tastes. Reading some books slightly above students' reading abilities extends their language; they usually comprehend more than they can read. Most books can be understood on several levels, but do consider your students' capabilities as you choose. Select books that you want to make part of the whole-class experience, books that you want to become part of the shared knowledge in your classroom.

When reading aloud to children, know your material before you begin. Preparation is important, especially when reading poetry, where the phrasing and cadence carry so much of the meaning. Preparation also helps you decide on the mood and tone that you want to set and allows you to learn special names or refrains. It is important to be thoroughly familiar with the content of the material you read aloud.

When reading, use a natural voice, with inflections and modulations befitting the book. Avoid greatly exaggerated voice changes and overly dramatic gestures, unless the book calls for that. Read slowly, enunciate clearly, project your voice directly, and maintain eye contact with your listeners as much as possible. Teachers who read aloud with their noses in the book soon lose their audience. Some brief guidelines for reading aloud are:

- Read the book ahead of time; be familiar with it.
- Give a brief description of the book, why you chose it, or how it relates to something you are doing as a class to establish a context for the listeners.
- Begin reading aloud slowly; quicken the pace as listeners are drawn into the book.

- Look up from the book frequently to maintain eye contact.
- Interpret dialogue meaningfully.
- Read entire books, if possible, or read a chapter or more per day to sustain meaning.
- If reading a picturebook, hold the book so that the children can "read" the illustrations while listening to the text.
- Make reading aloud a highlight in the day, and ask for your students' complete attention.

Media adaptations of books are also an important part of primary-grade classrooms. Teaching Idea 11.3 suggests how to make sure the adaptations you use are of excellent quality.

Supporting Children's Growing Literary Understanding

Sensitive teachers help children make connections between their own lives and the books they read. Cochran-Smith (1984) documented how one preschool teacher did this with her class as she demonstrated how to make connections between text and life and between life and text. Wolf and Heath (1992) describe the way two children incorporate the literature that is read to them into their own lives. Asking questions and making connections to books helps children become avid readers. When teachers demonstrate how to do this, students learn that the stuff of their own lives is sometimes mirrored in the books they read.

Connections between life and text are at the core of children's experiences with literature, but connections among books and popular culture texts are important as well. As children read and listen to stories, they begin to build their personal storehouse of literary understanding. They begin to recognize thematic connections across stories, similarities in plot structures and characterization, and distinctive styles in text and illustration. Teachers can encourage this kind of understanding by drawing on their knowledge of how literature works and by planning a literature curriculum that contains books selected specifically to help students make connections among texts—connections that result in a deeper understanding of what literature is and how it works.

Teachers enhance their students' growing literary understandings when they structure opportunities for students to make links across books, or *intertextual* connections. Learning about the world of literature is

TEACHING IDEA 11.3

Select Media for Your Classroom

COMMON CORE STATE STANDARDS — This Teaching Idea addresses Common Core English Language Arts, Reading: Literature standard 7, grades 2 and 3 and are foundational for meeting standard 7 in grades 4 through 8.

- Set your goals. Think about why you want to use media. If you want to extend your students' time with print, then you will want material that is connected to books you have in your classroom library or that includes text. If you want to use media to help students practice visual literacy skills or to encourage them to compare across media, then you will want to find materials that suit these goals.

- Consider the literary value of the original work; a good film, tape, or video cannot improve a bad book.

- Consider if the medium is appropriate to the literary work. Does it enrich and expand the work?

- Consider the audience. Are the book and media materials appropriate for your students? Adaptations that dilute a work of art to make it accessible to a younger audience are inauthentic and misleading.

- Consider the quality of the materials. Media materials should be technically excellent; clear sound and visual reproduction are vital.

- Check the American Library Association for their Notable Children's Recordings, Notable Children's Videos, and Great Interactive Software for Kids lists.

 To learn more about these lists, go to CengageBrain.com to access the Education CourseMate website, where you will find links to relevant websites.

---

an ongoing process as students come to recognize similarities and differences in plot structures, characters, and themes. As with connecting books to life, connecting books to other books adds dimension to future reading and responding. Wide reading (many varied books) and deep reading (many books in a particular genre, by a particular author, with a particular structure, and so on) acquaint children with the world of literature and help them learn a lot about specific aspects of that world.

Oral Language and Literature

Oral language is central to many book extension activities in the primary grades. These range from the spontaneous recommendation of a book by its reader to discussions during or following a read-aloud, to dramatic reenactment, storytelling, or choral speaking. Good for all students, oral activities offer English language learners and students not ready to read support for developing oral language as they interact with literature. Effective oral language activities may be extensive or brief, but they always help children share and explore their responses to the books they read.

• • DISCUSSION • •

Book discussions are wonderful ways to help children learn about literature and how it works. These discussions, often spontaneous, present moments that allow teachers to explore books with students. We invite you to reread the opening vignette of this chapter, where we reproduce part of a discussion of David Wiesner's **The Three Pigs**, in which the pigs have the opportunity of visiting several stories after being blown out of their own familiar tale. Specifically, we invite you to analyze what the teacher does (and does not do) to orchestrate the discussion.

First, the teacher seems to follow the children's lead, encouraging them to listen to one another's ideas and praising them rather than asking questions or making statements that position her as the prime knower; in fact, she stays out of the way of the children's meaning-making and encourages the children to talk to one another a great deal. These exchanges among children are called "cross-talk" by linguists because they are not directed to the teacher, but among the children themselves as they construct an interpretation. There is some struggle, as Wiesner's story does not follow the traditional versions with which the children are familiar, but the teacher is quite comfortable with this struggle. In essence, she hands the power of meaning-making

TEACHING IDEA 11.4

Response to Literature for English Language Learners

ELL

COMMON CORE STATE STANDARDS

This Teaching Idea addresses Common Core English Language Arts, Reading: Literature standards 1 through 6, grades 2 and 3.

English language learners are often able to show what they know through alternative methods of response. Students benefit from response options such as using graphic representation or illustration. One of the best ways for English language learners to respond is verbally. These students may be able to share their ideas and opinions in a one-on-one conference with a teacher or with a response partner. They can also share in small and large group discussions with support from the teacher. Storytelling, choral speaking, and drama are other activities that English language learners can participate in to the best of their ability. Not only do these activities help these learners grow as readers of literature, they provide opportunities for them to use and develop their oral English language skills.

over to the children. We suggest that, when children are given this power, they tend to rise to the occasion and come up with an interpretation that makes sense without a great deal of scaffolding from the teacher. This is not to say that the teacher is absolved of all responsibility, however: notice how the one time she intervenes directly is to point out, very clearly, the tension and dissonance between what the words of the story say ("and ate the pig up") and what the illustration and speech balloon show (that the pig is not harmed but has been indeed blown out of the story). It is at this critical juncture that the teacher chooses to intervene.

We suggest that, as you read stories aloud to children, you choose your interventions just as carefully and wisely. Asking questions to which you already know the answer is not the way to encourage children's critical and inferential thinking; in fact, these sorts of questions (which we might call "What's on my mind?" questions because you are testing the children's knowledge rather than helping them construct an interpretation) should be used very sparingly, if at all. If "What's on my mind?" questions predominate, children become docile, telling you what they think you want to hear rather than becoming actively engaged in their own meaning-making.

When young children engage in regular discussions of books, they grow tremendously as readers/listeners. The responses of other students inform everyone. The guidance of a teacher who listens closely and helps children articulate what they are trying to say transforms talk into educationally productive discussions. These discussions allow all students an opportunity to share what they know;

they are effective with both English speakers and English language learners (Boyd & Galda, 2011). Teaching Idea 11.4 offers specific suggestions for those students who are learning English.

STORYTELLING BY CHILDREN

Young children's writing skills seldom match their oral language skills before the end of their elementary-school years. Storytelling activities contribute to their sense of story and provide opportunities for developing and expanding language. A strong read-aloud program is vital; children will use the literary language they hear in creating their own stories.

Wordless books are an excellent stimulus to storytelling. Because the story line depends entirely on the illustrations, children become much more aware of the details in the pictures. These books provide a structure—plot, characters, theme—and so provide a framework on which to build stories. Another excellent resource for storytelling is the folklore collection in the child's classroom. These stories, once told orally, are perfect for classroom storytelling. Beginning with familiar tales helps children feel confident of their ability to tell a story orally, and they soon experiment with new tales.

CHORAL SPEAKING

Choral speaking—people speaking together—can be adapted for any age level. For the youngest, it may mean joining in as a refrain is read aloud. Young children unconsciously chime in when you read aloud passages that strike a sympathetic chord. Rhythm and repetition in language, both of which are conducive to choral speaking, are found in abundance, especially in folklore, poetry, and patterned picture storybooks.

When introducing choral speaking, read aloud two or three times the text you are using so that the rhythm of the language can be absorbed by your listeners. Encourage them to follow along with hand clapping until the beat is established. Favorite texts, which become unconsciously committed to memory after repeated group speaking, stay in the mind as treasures to be savored for years.

Students feel comfortable taking part in choral speaking; they are members of a group. This is an effective practice with fluent readers, struggling readers, and English language learners. Choral speaking supports unsure readers; they do not risk the embarrassment that comes from being singled out. Most important, the students become a community of learners. Joining together in group routines solidifies the sense of community.

• • DRAMA • •

Children engage in imaginative play almost instinctively. They re-create what they see on television, in everyday life, and in their books as they express their thoughts and feelings in the guise of characters and roles. Informal dramatic play capitalizes on children's natural desire to pretend and can be the forerunner of numerous drama experiences. These experiences can promote dialogue among students and between students and teachers that allows children to explore their responses to literature. Dramatic activities provide opportunities to discuss and reflect on a book, as well as to perform it.

Many forms of drama can be explored in the classroom. Variations include pantomime, using body movements and expression but no words; interpreting, enacting, or re-creating a story or a scene; and improvising, extending, and extrapolating beyond a story or a poem.

Pantomime is silent. In pantomime, a story or meaning is conveyed solely through facial expressions, shrugs, frowns, gestures, and other forms of body language. The situations, stories, or characters that are pantomimed should be ones that children are familiar with, recognize easily, or want to explore further.

Re-enacting a story can immediately follow a read-aloud session. Children can identify necessary roles, discuss what is important to say exactly like it was said in the story, and even round up some rudimentary props.

Interpretation involves a dramatic oral reading of a story that children are interested in. This activity builds enthusiasm for reading and develops oral reading skills. It also encourages children to discuss characters, their personalities, and how they might talk, given their personalities and the situation facing them in the story.

Older children enjoy *improvisation* and *role-playing*. Improvisation involves going beyond acting out the basic story line. It begins with a supposition, often about plot or characterization, which goes beyond the story itself. Wondering about what happens next, or what would happen *if*, spurs improvisation. Role-playing allows students to assume a role and interact with others in roles. It is usually done with brief, specific incidents from stories. This activity allows students to explore and discuss meaningful episodes in stories, various characters' points of view, and characters' motivations.

Readers' theatre involves children working closely with a book to make their own scripts. Students read orally from student-generated scripts that are based on selections from literature. There is little to no movement, facial expression, or gestures; the words stand alone. Often, this activity is a vehicle for students discovering the role of the narrator in the stories they read. It is difficult to portray action without movement, and the role of the narrator takes care of that problem. Teaching Idea 11.5 offers more detailed instructions for doing readers' theatre.

Variations of Literature-Based Instruction

There are many ways to be an effective teacher who uses literature as the foundation of the curriculum. Here are descriptions of how three exemplary teachers work in very different ways with their primary-grade students. In her own manner, each is teaching to many Common Core standards and is a model of the professional standards developed by the International Reading Association.

• • USING LITERATURE • •
WITH EMERGENT AND
BEGINNING READERS

Betty Shockley Bisplinghoff's class provided a good opportunity for watching many things that can happen with literature as first-grade students learn to read (Galda, Shockley, & Pellegrini, 1995). The school picture of Betty's class shows seventeen children—African American, Asian American, and European

TEACHING IDEA 11.5

How to Prepare for Readers' Theatre Performances

 COMMON CORE STATE STANDARDS

This Teaching Idea addresses the Common Core English Language Arts, Reading: Literature standards 1, 2, 3, 5, 7, grade 1, and standards 1, 2, 3, grade 2.

1. Select a story with lots of dialogue and a strong plot. The best stories have a taut plot with an "and then" quality to pique your students' interest and make them want to know what will happen next.

2. Discuss with students the number of characters needed, including one or more narrators who read the parts between the dialogue.

3. Have students adapt the story to a play script format, deleting unnecessary phrases like "he said."

4. Assign roles and allow students to practice. Students work best with a partner or a director who can advise them on whether the character is coming through in the reading.

5. For the finished production, have performers sit or stand side by side, with the narrators off to one side and slightly closer to the audience. Readers stand statue-still, holding their scripts. When not in a scene, readers may turn around or lower their heads (Sloyer, 1982).

American—although across the school year the number of students ranged from sixteen to twenty-two. These students varied widely in their reading ability when they entered Betty's classroom: some were reading fairly fluently, some were at a beginning first-grade level, but most were below grade level.

There are two adults in the picture, Betty and her aide. The school itself is a medium-size K through 5 school in which 74 percent of the students are eligible for free or reduced-fee lunch. Both school and classroom look like many others, but what happened in Betty's classroom was special, and the sound of children reading, writing, singing, and talking together was almost constant.

Generally, Betty organized her day around oral sharing time, writing workshop, independent reading, and whole-class reading instruction in the mornings, with afternoons devoted to math, science or social studies, and center time. Children's books were part of each segment of the day. Betty used picturebooks, some of which were highly patterned and thus predictable, and some of which had an oversize format; she also used transitional readers and early chapter books to support her students' developing abilities.

Picturebooks

Literally hundreds of picturebooks spilled from the shelves in Betty's classroom. There was a sumptuously stocked reading corner in the far right-hand part of the room, under some windows that looked out onto trees and grass. These books were always available for students to browse through during free time; children could also select them for their independent reading. Boxes of picturebooks sat on the stage as well. The stage was where Betty went for whole-class instruction, where students gathered to share their writing, and where students shared books by reading them, talking about them, telling stories, singing, and presenting dramas.

Betty read picturebooks aloud several times a day for a variety of purposes. Sometimes, she read a book aloud simply because it was a good book and she wanted to share it with her students. Most often, any book read aloud connected in some way to something the children were studying, whether that was frogs or patterns in writing, a particular author or illustrator, or a certain phonics pattern. Especially at the beginning of the year, the picturebooks that Betty selected were often patterned, predictable texts that supported the reading development of the many emergent and beginning readers in her classroom.

Patterned, Predictable Texts

We know that children become literate in different ways and at different rates of development. We also know that children who have experience with

Spending time with good books is the best way to become an avid reader.

literature before they come to school begin school with an advantage. They are already emergent readers, readers who have some concepts about how print works. One of the best ways that preschool and early elementary teachers can help children develop these concepts is to read to them. When the books that are read are highly patterned and thus predictable, it is easier for children to figure out how print works (Holdaway, 1979).

Children search for patterns as they learn. They like to find things that match, words that rhyme, and phrases that are repeated. Many books are predictable because of their repetitive sequences, cumulative sequences, rhyme and rhythm, or familiar cultural sequences such as numbering, days of the week, or months of the year. Betty often read from books like these. When she could, she used enlarged versions of these stories so that students could see the words. Then she was able to help them make connections between sounds and print, and learn about concepts of print, such as top to bottom, left to right, and the functions of capitals, periods, and white spaces.

Patterned stories also formed the basis of rich oral language activities as students learned structures and patterns that they called upon to do storytelling and drama. These performances were quite interactive; if a student forgot an important word or phrase, his peers were happy to supply it for him. These patterned stories also made their way into the students' own stories, both oral and written. Sharing time, which once had focused on brief accounts of events from the children's lives, eventually featured elaborate accounts of these events, with students

incorporating book language and patterns into their own stories. In their writing, students often borrowed stock characters, basic plot structures, or literary phrases. These "borrowings" helped build the students' resources and abilities for both oral and written language production.

Easy Readers and Transitional Chapter Books

As is the case in many classrooms, Betty's students were not all at the same reading level, so her collection included picturebooks that were more difficult than the patterned texts we have discussed. It also included some easy reading for newly independent readers, such as Arnold Lobel's **Frog and Toad** series, and transitional chapter books of many genres.

As the most advanced readers in the class grew ready for more extended text, Betty introduced the class to the **Frog and Toad** series. After she read aloud from one of the books, she told students that several other books were written about the same characters; she made sure students knew where they were on the shelves. As the more advanced readers began to read them, they often had an attentive audience, with two or three of their peers gathered around them. As the students in the class came to know the stories well through repeated readings, the struggling readers were able to "read" them as well, calling on their memory and the illustrations to supplement their reading skills. By the end of the year, everyone had read all of this and other series.

The more advanced readers moved on to transitional chapter books, which gave them the opportunity to read extended text over time. Because the texts of these books are arranged in chapters, these students felt a sense of accomplishment—they could now read chapter books. It also gave them practice in reading stories that were a bit more complex than many of the picturebooks they were familiar with. No student abandoned picturebooks altogether. Betty's collection was so extensive that even the most fluent reader could find a picturebook with a challenging text. As readers became increasingly fluent, they moved on to longer versions of transitional chapter books and eventually into longer novels with an episodic structure.

Betty's literature-based literacy instruction offered her students the opportunity to read, write, speak, and listen for meaningful purposes. Quite often these purposes were related to the positive value these students had learned to place on being engaged with a good book.

• • USING LITERATURE • •
TO INTEGRATE THE CURRICULUM

Karen Bliss's first-grade class was experiencing literature-based instruction of a different kind. Using the science curriculum as a basis, Karen created and maintained a single theme across the year as she and her students explored the idea of interdependence. This theme involved a study of oceans for the first seven months of the school year. Her students were so interested in what they were doing that their reading, writing, listening, and speaking activities, as well as most of their social studies and science, were linked to their exploration of the oceans of the world. They learned geography, wrote extensively about the oceans and seas and the various continents they border, read extensively from fiction, nonfiction, and poetry, and painted many beautiful pictures of the oceans and their inhabitants. Their language activities were motivated and purposeful as they read books to research and wrote to explain. One of their big projects was a group-authored book on penguins, an animal they had become intrigued with during their studies. Working together and independently, they read children's books about penguins, wrote about penguins based on the models they found in the trade books they were reading, revised their writing, and published a class book about penguins. A parent made copies of the book for each student and for the classroom and school libraries. As they were learning about science and geography—and penguins—they were also learning to read, write, speak, and listen with fluency and effectiveness.

By structuring the content of the learning tasks within a thematic framework and exploring them through quality children's literature, Karen built in integration and meaningfulness. Excellent children's books are easy to find for almost any theme you might want to explore. Whether you link thematic study to the science or social studies curriculum, or both, as Karen did, or to the language arts curriculum, a thematic organization offers children the opportunity to learn about language while they are learning through the language of literature.

• • LITERATURE STUDY • •
WITH PRIMARY-GRADE READERS

The children in Lisa Stanzi's second-grade reading group were learning about reading and writing, as well as listening and speaking, as they engaged in the study of literature. Lisa's elementary school had an unusual way of organizing reading instruction. For seventy minutes each morning, students in a particular grade level were grouped according to ability, with each group receiving instruction from one teacher. Each of the two second-grade teachers worked with a group, and specialists worked with the other groups. Lisa's group consisted of five students from her own class and six to seven from the other second-grade class; all were reading at or above grade level. In spite of this, the group was quite heterogeneous in many ways. Some were struggling at a second-grade reading level; others were fluent at a fourth-grade level. The students were from many parts of the world—China, India, and Africa, as well as the United States. Several were English language learners. Further, they all had varying levels of experience with books.

Lisa was in the process of moving from a basal-based reading curriculum to a more literature-based curriculum, hoping to transform her "reading" group into something that looked more like a book discussion group or literature study group. To accomplish this, she gathered hundreds of trade books that supported the six themes that appeared in the system-mandated basal reader and planned her lessons around the literature in the basal text, the books she offered the children for independent reading, and those she read aloud. The books ranged from very easy to more difficult picturebooks, fiction, poetry, and nonfiction, and included easy readers and transitional chapter books with a range of difficulty. When she introduced the first whole-class chapter book in November, Lisa read it aloud; by the end of the year, the students were reading chapters at home in the evening in preparation for the next day's discussion. Every day for seventy minutes, her "literature group," as they called themselves, read, wrote, and talked about literature (Galda, Rayburn, & Stanzi, 2000).

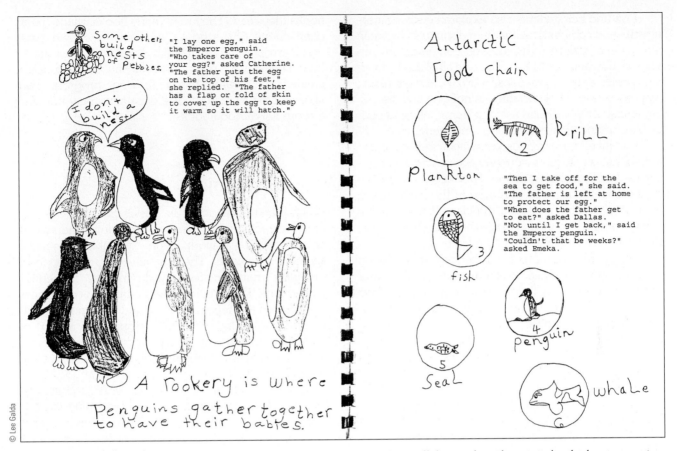

After reading and studying a series of informational books, Karen's class collaborated on their own book about penguins.

Lisa taught reading and the language arts through literature, using both the stories, poems, and nonfiction found in the basal text and the hundreds of trade books that the children read. Oral discussion of literature was at the heart of her reading program, and she spent a significant amount of time helping her students learn to talk about books. Although Lisa worked on decoding skills and strategies with those students who needed this work, as well as on vocabulary development, her focus was on comprehension strategies, which are directly linked to children's being able to read and respond to a book. In this way she was much like Betty, incorporating reading instruction when her students were engaged in reading children's books and responding to students' strengths and weaknesses. She also taught her students about literature by teaching them about literary elements, about how to make connections between what they read and their own lives, and about how to make connections among texts.

Lisa's students learned about what authors do by talking about the books they were reading. They studied authors and their work across the year. Students become interested in authors' and illustrators' lives

when they discover connections between writers' and artists' life experiences and their work. Teachers like Lisa often set up author or illustrator studies by doing the following:

- Choose an author or illustrator whose work students like, and read as many of the person's books as possible.

- Help students make some generalizations about the person's work.

- Make a comparison chart or display that demonstrates similarities and differences across several books.

- Locate biographical information about the person. Many children's book authors and illustrators have wonderful websites.

- Read and discuss the information students gather.

- Make some generalizations about how the person's life influenced his or her work.

- Help students prepare a display that depicts the connections they found between the person's life and work.

Lisa and her students also explored genre characteristics and conventions, trying to distinguish between fantasy and realism, historical and contemporary settings, fiction and nonfiction. They did all of this by reading widely, writing in response journals, and discussing what they read. They delighted in noticing and discussing an author's particular use of a literary element such as plot, setting, characterization, and theme.

Lisa planned her language arts and reading curriculum so that her students would engage in meaningful discussions that considered theme. They began the year by talking about families as portrayed in the picturebooks they were reading, exploring the idea "What makes a family?" As they continued to read and talk about books, they frequently linked them by theme because that was something that Lisa did as she talked with them. When teachers comment that a book reminds them of another book because they are both "about the same idea," and then discuss theme, students emulate that behavior. Lisa continued to notice theme as students read various stories in picturebooks and novels across the year. She asked explicit questions about thematic ideas and encouraged her students to think deeply about themes and to link books with each other.

On one spring morning, the group talked about the relationships that the characters in Sid Fleischman's **The Whipping Boy** (I) have with each other; they hypothesized about characters' motives for some of their actions. Sarah commented that she thought the prince didn't want to go back to his castle. Chris thought that the prince really liked another character, and Brett agreed that they might become friends. Cameron moved the discussion to another level with his perceptive comment: "On the inside he likes him, but on the outside he's just mean." They went on to discuss the characters and their own experiences as they wrestled with the idea that a person can be different on the inside from the way he or she is on the outside. Discussions like this prompted Chris to make a comment that revealed the heart of what Lisa did with books when he said, "In here we read differently. Here we think about what we read." These eight-year-olds had, by the end of the year, a very sophisticated understanding of theme and relished a discussion that centered on themes they found in the books they read.

Lisa also helped her students develop their visual literacy skills as she taught them how to "read" the illustrations in their basal reader and in the books in the classroom. In many group discussions, the children pored over illustrations as they sought to determine a mood, defend a theme, or describe a setting or character.

Lisa's young readers spent the year honing their reading skills while engaging in often passionate discussions of the stories, poems, novels, and nonfiction books they read. They read many books, made many connections across books and with their own lives, and learned a lot about themselves and about literature. They were able to do this because their teacher created a literature-based reading program that allowed time to read, choice of reading material, and a room full of good books.

Assessment

When literature abounds in classrooms, there is less time for traditional assessment procedures than when children are busy working on "gradable" products, such as worksheets. There is, however, more opportunity for what some teachers describe as "authentic" assessment. This type of assessment involves observing children as they are reading and responding to literature, examining the work they produce as part of their reading and responding, and talking with them about what they are doing. It also involves assessing yourself as a teacher—looking critically at your planning, at the daily life of your classroom, and at your students' literacy development to determine what is and is not effective practice. The focus is on what children can do and are doing, as teachers gather artifacts, observe student behaviors, listen to students talk, and record what goes on.

You will want to keep records that represent what your students are doing in the classroom and how they are performing. These records may include artifacts that children produce, such as reading logs or response journals. Children's response activities often involve products, such as pictures they paint or writing they produce. Save these so that you can inform yourself about students' understanding of and response to the books they are reading. Reading tests, such as informal reading inventories or standardized tests, become part of the record as well.

Notes from observation of students as they select books and as they read and respond to books provide a picture of what they are actually doing in the classroom. Watch to see if your students select books they can read and are likely to enjoy. If they are not yet reading fluently, see if they can retell the story through the illustrations. Find out how your students select books and whom they ask for suggestions. Discover whom they read with and where they like to read. Keep track of how your students respond to the books they read and examine the kinds of things they do. Notice the writing they do in response, and note how often they choose art or dramatic activities as response options. Watch students as they engage in these activities, looking for demonstrations of their engagement with and understanding of the books they read. As you observe, jot down brief notes about what you are seeing. If you use mailing labels to write on, you can affix them to a sheet of paper in each child's record. As you keep adding notes, you build a picture of each child's reading behaviors.

Notes from listening to their conversations about literature provide information about students' comprehension and response, just as an analysis of their oral reading provides information about their decoding strategies. Listening to children discuss books is a good way to assess their development as readers. Note the kinds of things they talk about, whether they attend to others' ideas, and whether others' ideas enrich their own reading and responding. This helps you know what you need to focus on in your instruction. Ask individual children to read aloud to you on a regular basis and note the skills and strategies they call on as they decode unfamiliar text. This helps tell you what you need to teach.

As you engage in these assessment activities, you will find that you learn things about your students that inform the instructional decisions you make. You will find yourself teaching more effectively as you focus on students rather than on a standard curriculum. This focus is crucial to a literature-based literacy curriculum.

SUMMARY

There are many ways to structure literature-based instruction for young children. Reading aloud and oral language activities such as discussion, time to read, a rich choice of reading material, and a purposeful classroom are basic to a successful program. Some teachers use literature to teach reading, writing, listening, and speaking. They seek out patterned, predictable texts, easy readers, and transitional chapter books to provide their students with rich literary experiences. Other teachers use children's books to support a thematic organization that links several areas of the curriculum. The books become a resource for practicing the English language arts, and they provide learning content about a particular theme. Still other teachers teach students about literature through literature-based instruction, even as they teach them how to read, write, and respond—and to discuss the books they read. There are as many ways to structure literature-based instruction as there are teachers and classrooms full of children. In all cases, however, teachers pay careful attention to what their students are doing, assessing their progress in order to plan instruction.

Additional resources to accompany this chapter can be found on the Education CourseMate website. Go to CengageBrain .com to access a variety of interactive study tools and useful resources including Video Conversations with children's book authors and illustrators, a searchable children's literature database, glossary flashcards, online activities, tutorial quizzes, links to relevant websites, and more.

Response-Centered, Literature-Based Instruction in Intermediate Grades and Middle School

- **Response-Centered Literature Instruction**

- **Teaching Literature across the Year**
  - Book Club
  - Reading Workshop

- **Teaching Individual Books**
  - Scaffolded Reading Experiences (SRE)

- **Connecting Literature Study and Writing**

- **Using Literature to Transform the Larger Curriculum**

- **Assessment**

- **Summary**

Dr. Death faced me across the kitchen table. He touched my hand with his long curved fingers. I caught the scent of tobacco that surrounded him. I saw the black spots on his skin. Dad was telling him the story: my disappearance in the night, my sleepwalking. I heard in his voice how scared he still was, how he thought he'd lost me. I wanted to tell him again that I was all right, everything was all right.

—DAVID ALMOND
Skellig, p. 122

The students in George's sixth-grade class are scattered around the room in small groups, heatedly discussing David Almond's **Skellig** (I–A), a Michael L. Printz Honor book. They have just finished the part where Michael and Mina visit Skellig in the night, and Michael's father awakes to find him gone. They are trying to decide just what or who Skellig is. Is he an angel? A vagrant? A figment of Mina and Michael's overactive imaginations? An apparition sent to comfort Michael during his newborn sister's medical crisis?

Because there is so much to think and talk about, so many things to figure out, George is reading this brief novel aloud so that everyone is, quite literally, on the same page. The surreal story has gripped everyone, and students ask George to go back a few chapters to reread some of the earlier descriptions of Skellig. Many students have asked their parents to buy them their own copy of the book; others are hoping that it will be offered through the book club that their class participates in. Later, George will ask his students to talk about the genre that **Skellig** belongs in, another query that will provoke lively discussion.

Reading and talking together about books that provoke strong responses are making these sixth-grade students more avid readers. These activities are also helping them become better readers because their desire to understand and be able to participate in class discussions is strong. These students are lucky to have the opportunity to engage with good books on a regular basis, to have time to talk about them with their peers, and to have opportunities to respond in journals, projects, and more formal papers. Both fluent and still struggling readers are caught up in the ideas that Almond is exploring and are actively creating meaning as they read. And they're enjoying it!

Response-Centered Literature Instruction

There are many ways to make literature a central part of intermediate-grade and middle-school instruction. Chapter 2 discussed a transactional view of reading literature and the goals of a response-centered curriculum. In this chapter, we explore different instructional frameworks that focus on developing intermediate-grade and middle-school students' responses and literary understanding as they engage with books.

As discussed in Chapter 2, the primary goal of a response-centered curriculum is to engage readers in the act of reading responsively. The focus is not on the works of literature, nor on the topics or skills, but on "the mind of the reader as it meets the book—the response" (Purves, Rogers, & Soter, 1990). A response-centered curriculum recognizes and encourages diversity among readers, recognizes and encourages connections among readers, and "recognizes that response is joyous" (Purves, Rogers, & Soter, 1990, p. 56). In this curriculum, the teacher provides a variety of books, time to read and explore them, time to talk and write about them, and time to draw and dramatize from them. In addition, teachers provide opportunities for students to enjoy the collaborative company of peers with whom to explore similarities and differences in responses. The teacher also helps students find the language with which to articulate their responses and challenges them to understand why they respond as they do (Purves, Rogers, & Soter, 1990).

A second goal is to build on the engagement that a response-centered curriculum fosters in order to develop children's awareness of the world of literature and of how words work (Benton, 1984) in literature. This goal is focused on helping children learn language and learn about it and its use in literature through reading. Although this is especially important in the primary grades, it also remains a central focus in a response-centered curriculum for the intermediate-grade and middle-school grades in a more advanced manner.

A third goal is to give children the opportunity to learn about themselves and their world through books, to learn *through* language. The virtual experiences possible through story, the emotional expansion that is possible with poetry, and the exposure to information about the world that comes from nonfiction all increase children's knowledge of themselves and their worlds. And this increased knowledge widens children's horizons and makes even more learning possible.

The three essential ingredients of a response-based curriculum—time and choice, reading aloud, and activities that support children's developing understanding of literature—are all elements in the frameworks discussed next. First, we will look at two ways to organize a response-based literature curriculum for the entire year, and then explore some methods for teaching individual books with a focus on students' responses. In each case, the suggested instruction allows for students' need for time to read, choices about how they read and respond, and scaffolding as they grow in their understanding of how literature works.

Teaching Literature across the Year

We know that children need both time to read and choices about what to read, how to read, and whom to read with.

> Allowing children time to be with books in the classroom, rather than assigning them to a certain number of books to be read on their own time, teaches them to value books. When time is set aside for reading and responding to literature, students know that this is viewed as important by their teacher. So, too, does reading to and with a class help to convince students of the value and the pleasures of reading. (Galda, 1988, p. 100)

The difficulty is finding a way to create this time and space for choice in the school day on a regular basis, especially in the upper elementary and middle-school grades when an increasing amount of complex content must be covered. The amount of independent reading children do in school, particularly when the texts are appropriately challenging, is significantly related to gains in reading achievement (Kuhn et al. 2006; Samuels & Wu, 2003). Researchers estimate that the typical primary-school child reads silently only seven or eight minutes per day. By the middle grades, silent reading time averages only fifteen minutes per school day. No one can become skilled at anything practiced only seven to fifteen minutes a day (Taylor, Frye, & Maruyama, 1990; West, Stanovich, & Mitchell, 1993).

We might think that we can solve the problem of tight schedules and too little time for reading in the classroom by assigning reading as homework. Research has found that students are more likely to read outside of school if the teacher reads aloud in school and if they have a period of independent silent reading during school (Fielding, Wilson, & Anderson, 1986). If we want students to read, we must tempt them with good stories, poems, and nonfiction, and show them that we value reading by devoting a significant amount of time to it in the classroom. It is also important, however, that students have time to respond to what they have read with peers, with their teachers, and on their own. Further, students need opportunities to make choices about what they read. As we discussed earlier, responses and preferences are highly individualistic. Although you as a teacher need to be able to help students select books they will like and that are appropriately challenging, and although you can and should make suggestions and assign books and response activities at times, children also need to be able to make their own choices about the books they read. They also should be able to make choices at times about what they want to do when they are finished with a book. Some children might like to write, others to talk, and others to sit quietly and think.

Teachers help students become knowledgeable about themselves as readers by providing both guidance and the freedom to choose books. Some teachers choose to use literature frameworks such as Reading Workshop, which allows children a fairly full range of choice; they can frequently choose nearly any book they would like to read. Other teachers use frameworks such as Book Club, which encourages teachers to provide revolving curriculum-based classroom collections for children to choose from. Whatever the approach, the idea that they can choose what they want to read has changed the way many children feel about reading.

As children become confident readers, they learn with teacher scaffolding to recognize what books they can read and what books they might like to read. They begin to know which authors and illustrators they like.

And they learn where to go for recommendations about books—to the teacher, the librarian, family and friends, other students in their class. Good readers know how to find books for themselves.

Year-long programs or frameworks for a response-based literature curriculum are often built around this important notion of time and choice. The two described here, Book Club and Reading Workshop, are widely used in the intermediate and middle grades.

• • BOOK CLUB • •

Book Club (McMahon, Raphael, Goatley, et al. 1997) was developed by classroom teachers in conjunction with university researchers. It is structured to include multiple opportunities for language use and easily accommodates thematic studies in a language arts curriculum or links between language arts and other curricular areas. The developers of Book Club also created a corollary program, Book Club for Middle School (Raphael, Kehus, & Damphousse, 2001), for middle-school students. The elements and background in the Book Club for Middle School program are the same as those in the original Book Club, but the sample units, themes, and lessons are geared specifically toward middle-school classrooms.

Book Club is grounded in a sociocultural perspective on language and learning and in response theory, discussed in Chapter 2. A sociocultural perspective reflects an understanding that language first develops through social interaction and eventually becomes internalized as thought. During this

Reading with friends means that students can discuss what they read, and that increases both pleasure and understanding.

© Cengage Learning/Wadsworth

interaction, learning occurs when individuals work on tasks in the company of others more knowledgeable who guide them. Through this interaction, individuals develop their own sense of self and of others, and they learn to use language in particular forms within particular contexts (McMahon, Raphael, & Goatley, 1997). Because readers are reading and responding to literature in Book Club, this perspective includes the idea that readers read within a social context and construct their responses over time as they read and share their thinking with others. These theoretical concepts shape the structure of Book Club. This includes reading, writing, small-group discussions, whole-class interactions, and multiple opportunities for instruction.

Reading

If we want our students to read more, then we have to provide time for them to read during the school day. Book Club does just this. The reading in Book Club differs from the traditional independent silent reading because the books are selected by the teacher or by both the teacher and the students, in an effort to explore a theme or curricular area. Criteria for selection include literary quality, substance, age-appropriateness, thematic connection, and difficulty; the book must be sufficiently engaging and stimulating that students will want to think, write, and talk about it.

The whole class may be reading the same book, or the class may divide into smaller groups, or book clubs, with each book club reading a different book, all relating to the unifying theme. Reading may be done individually, in pairs (often called buddy reading), through teacher read-alouds, or with the support of CDs or recordings. The point is that everyone has time to read an age-appropriate book so that he or she will be able to respond to it through writing and discussion. For struggling readers, this offers the opportunity to see what reading is all about—engaging with interesting ideas and compelling language—because many struggling readers never have the opportunity to work with age-appropriate texts.

Writing

After reading, students have the opportunity to write about what they are reading. This writing may be unstructured journal writing, but more often it will be structured by the teacher through the use of "think sheets" or questions and tasks that both support students' developing responses and offer alternative ways for students to think and talk about books. Writing helps students articulate their developing understandings about text and prepares them for an oral discussion of these texts. The writing component can also include more sustained writing activities.

Talking about Texts with Peers: The Book Club

After reading and writing, students meet in small, heterogeneous, peer-led discussion groups, or book clubs, to talk about their responses, to ask questions, and to compare ideas. These discussions offer students the opportunity to build on their personal responses within the social context of the group, to use oral language to talk about books in meaningful ways, to learn how to conduct themselves as a member of a group, and to serve as a resource for others.

Community Share: Whole-Class Interactions

Both preceding and following the book club discussions, the class as a whole talks together about the book they are reading. This is called "community share." Before reading, the teacher might focus students on strategies and skills they will need as they read, write, and talk about their book. Specific literary elements might be presented to guide students in their understanding of an author's craft. Following book club meetings, the teacher might bring up interesting ideas that have come up in book clubs, or she might raise questions that she would like the class to consider. At any time she could choose to read aloud from another book that explores the focal theme and ask students to consider their developing ideas in light of this additional experience. These brief whole-class activities serve as means to maintain a community of readers that stretches across individual book clubs. They also add to the richness and diversity of the social interaction around the target book.

Opportunities for Instruction

Teachers who use Book Club have various opportunities for instruction, including the writing and thinking tasks they set for their students and the focus they provide during community share. In some classrooms, this is enough. In others, there is a need for more extensive direct instruction in reading and language arts.

A group of teachers and university researchers developed what they call Book Club Plus (Raphael, Florio-Ruane, George, et al. 2004) in response to their need to ensure enough instructional time around reading. Book Club Plus provides a structured opportunity for reading and language arts instruction in guided reading groups. The texts read in these groups are thematically related to the Book Club book, but are at students' instructional level rather than at their age level. Thus, students get practice thinking and talking about books that engage their emotions and also get intensive instructional support from their teacher (Raphael, Florio-Ruane, & George, 2001).

Book Club, Book Club for Middle School, and Book Club Plus provide a framework that is based on sound theory and research yet is flexible enough that teachers can use the framework to support the needs of their students and the demands of their curriculum. The invariant structure of time to read, time to think and write, time to talk with peers, and time to interact as a whole class, coupled with multiple opportunities for instruction, supports the literacy learning of diverse students in diverse contexts. It allows teachers to present thematically focused units of study that provide students with opportunities to learn about themselves and others and to grapple with powerful ideas, while at the same time developing their reading, writing, listening, and speaking skills and learning about how literature works.

Another activity that promotes talk among peers is described in Teaching Idea 12.1.

TEACHING IDEA 12.1

Response-Centered Project Ideas for Individual Books

 **COMMON CORE STATE STANDARDS**   Various ideas in this Teaching Idea address Common Core English Language Arts, Reading: Literature standards 2, 3, 9, grades 4, 5, 6 and standards 2, 3, grades 7 and 8.

Following are project ideas ready to be given to students as they explore an individual book or make comparisons across books.

Present for a Character

If you were going to give the main character a present, what would it be? Create the present in 3-D. Then write a short essay explaining why you selected this present.

Recipes

If you were to publish a cookbook related to this book, what recipes would you include? Make up three recipes and explain in a short essay why each would make a good companion piece to this book. You might even experiment in the kitchen!

Theme Song

Create a theme song for this book. You should have at least three stanzas and a refrain. Create your own tune or select a well-known tune as the music. Write a short essay explaining why you selected this tune (for example, Does it convey the theme of the book?) and why you chose the particular incidents from the book to include in your stanzas.

Family Tree

Create a family tree for the main character. For each relative of the main character, draw a picture of the relative and write a paragraph explaining what he or she is like and how he or she is important to the main character. You may want to include the character's friends as well as family.

Character Scrapbook

Create a character scrapbook (about eight pages) for the main characters. What types of things would he or she include in a personal scrapbook? What dates would the scrapbook include?

Newspaper

Create a newspaper about a day during the book. What might be the front page news? Include editorials, advertisements, and more that relate to the main characters in the story and their actions.

Comparison Paper

Compare your book with a similar book you have read. Your comparison book might be similar in genre, style, or content. Write an essay explaining which book you like better and why. Think about style, point of view, story, content, structure, and characters in your response.

Once/Now Essay

Write a "once/now" essay (Once this character was x, but now this character is y because . . .). The essay should be about one of the main characters in your book. Support your ideas with examples from the text.

New Ending or New Chapter

Rewrite the ending of your book or write a new chapter. Make sure that your writing style fits with the author's style and that the events in your new ending or chapter make sense in the context of the events that occur in the book.

• • READING WORKSHOP • •

In the upper grades, and especially in middle schools, teachers often use the workshop as an organizing structure for reading and writing instruction. In her books *In the Middle: New Understandings about Writing, Reading, and Learning* (1998) and *The Reading Zone: How to Help Kids Become Skilled, Passionate, Habitual, Critical Readers* (2007), Nancie Atwell describes how the workshop runs in her classroom. She often begins each class with a brief "mini-lesson" about literature, focusing on what she has noticed her students need to learn or what in the curriculum they are ready to learn, such as supporting their growing literary understanding, working toward more independent book selection, or even scaffolding their independent use of reading skills or strategies. Her students then read independently. Following the reading, they write a letter or an entry in a dialogue journal to a peer or to her. Because the recipient of the letter writes back, these letters serve the social function that is so important to reading. The partners engage in a written conversation about books. As an alternative to the letters, students sometimes discuss their books orally in pairs or small groups.

Variations on Atwell's reading workshop abound. In some, rather than students selecting their own books all year, teachers might offer students the opportunity to select from a collection that relates to the curriculum. Some teachers add occasional response-centered projects in which students choose from a variety of creative ways to respond to a book they have read and share the book and their experience with their classmates.

In other classrooms, the reading workshop is integrated with a writing workshop, and students learn to pace themselves in their reading and writing; to expect brief, explicit instruction from their teacher; and to interact with their peers in a structured manner. Recently, some teachers have begun to add technological aspects to their reading workshops, from encouraging the use of online discussions to a full-blown Electronic Reading Workshop with online reading, blogs, e-journals, online discussions, and technology-based projects (Larsen, 2007). Whether the reading workshop follows the more traditional mode, takes on aspects of technology, or combines with a writing workshop, the structure offers choice about what to read, allows time to read and respond, and provides someone to "talk" with about reading. Teaching Idea 12.2 offers a way to promote the exchange of critical opinions among students.

TEACHING IDEA 12.2

Create a Classroom Reader's Choice Award

COMMON CORE STATE STANDARDS   This Teaching Idea does not address specific Common Core English Language Arts standards but does allow students to demonstrate their growing critical abilities in evaluation of books. It can be extended to other media as well. The suggestions in this Teaching Idea may need to be adapted to suit your particular grade level and the needs of your students.

To help your students learn to rely on one another's opinions as they select books, create a "Classroom Choices Award" file. Ask students to do the following:

1. Conduct a survey to determine their favorite books.

2. Write the titles of books they especially like on index cards.

3. Give book talks to promote the reading of their favorite books.

4. Create a file from the index cards for students to browse through when selecting books.

5. Rate each book read by marking the index card from 0 to 5 and adding a one-sentence comment.

6. At the end of the year, add up the ratings to determine the "best" books.

7. Share this list with students who will be in the classroom next year. It makes a great summer reading list!

Teaching Individual Books

Although supporting students' literary understanding is certainly part of Book Club and Reading Workshop, as well as other year-round response-centered, literature-based programs, the occasional teaching of individual books can allow for more specific opportunities to scaffold students' literary growth. Focusing as a group on a particular book allows a teacher to promote the deep understanding of that book, its literary elements, and the particular way it is crafted, and it helps lead to student understanding of what literature is and how it works. Students begin to create intertextual connections, or links across books, that scaffold their literary understanding in general.

For example, deep discussion about the characters in a specific book gradually enables students to make comparisons among characters from various stories. These comparisons can lead to generalizations about character types that children will meet as they read widely. Similarly, discussing plot results in the identification of various kinds of plots, which leads to understanding about archetypal plots that underlie literature. In a quest story, for example, a character begins at home, leaves in search of something important (an object, a person, self-knowledge), and returns home changed in some way. When students read and discuss such books, they can pinpoint characters' strengths and weaknesses, identify problems they must solve, and discover similarities and differences in the characters' quests, thus building an understanding of quest tales. Teaching Idea 12.3 offers some suggestions for helping English language learners acquire the vocabulary of literary discussion, although the ideas would work with many different students.

Finding similarities and differences in the underlying conflicts of stories also helps readers make connections among books. The connections build an understanding of literature. Some books revolve around several conflicts; others have only one or two central conflicts. Discussing these conflicts, or problems, helps readers notice their presence in stories and gives them another dimension along which to connect various stories. In the same way, consideration of themes often brings about an important recognition of the various ways that different authors treat the same general theme. Readers read similar stories about particular themes in many different books.

Children who explore how literature works also learn to look at books as works of art crafted by a writer. They notice the language that the writer uses and learn to appreciate the nuances that distinguish one writer from another. Students use their knowledge about literature in their own writing, incorporating patterns, structures, themes, character types,

TEACHING IDEA 12.3

Teaching the Language of Literature to English Language Learners

 This Teaching Idea does not address specific Common Core English Language Arts standards but does provide foundational knowledge that will enable all students to fully participate in activities that directly address the standards.

More proficient English language learners who have acquired basic, interpersonal vocabulary can learn the academic language structures and vocabulary associated with discussing and writing about literature. Many teachers use Venn diagrams to help students compare and contrast two similar books. If they also explicitly teach the language and structures embedded in comparisons, they offer support to those who are not already fluent in that register. By frequently using and defining literary terms such as *character development, point of view,* or *parallel plots* (including using these terms when listening and responding to students during a discussion), teachers offer English language learners the words they need to fully articulate their responses. By offering frames that promote comparison, such as "The setting in these two stories is similar because . . . yet also different because . . ." or "The protagonist in this story is . . . while the protagonist in that story is . . . ," teachers model how to use language to compare.

and language they have encountered. Books build on books, stories lean on stories, and children become knowledgeable readers and writers. Through carefully planned encounters with particular books, teachers can help their students delight in the artistry and interconnections in literature.

As students begin to link a particular book they deeply understand to another work in some way, they begin to better understand and appreciate all literature. This concept is also basic to learning; some cognitive psychologists have come to define *learning* as the search for patterns that connect. The following framework, Scaffolding Reading Experience (SRE), emphasizes deep understanding of a particular book or text. Over time, in-depth experiences with specific books and stories can help lead to students' development of more general literary understandings.

● ● SCAFFOLDED READING ● ● ● EXPERIENCES (SRE)

Taking the time to focus on students' experiencing one particular book in depth involves much planning on behalf of the teacher. How will you engage students with the book at its beginning? How will you scaffold students' understanding as they work through challenging sections? What discussions and activities will help students to internalize what they

have learned from the book? The Scaffolded Reading Experience (SRE) is a flexible framework that can be used by teachers to assist students in understanding, learning from, and enjoying reading a particular text selection (Graves & Graves, 2003). The SRE involves two phases. The first is a planning phase, in which the teacher considers (1) the purpose for teaching the particular book or text, (2) the text itself, including its themes, vocabulary, and more, and (3) the group of students who will be working with the text—their needs, strengths, and interests. Thinking through the interaction of these three variables in the planning phase leads teachers to the second phase: implementation. In this phase the teacher plans prereading, during-reading, and postreading activities that will help the particular group of students reach the goals set out in the purpose for working with this specific text.

The SRE can be designed for use with a variety of student populations, including English language learners (Fitzgerald & Graves, 2004) and special education students (Graves, Graves, & Braaten, 1996); many types of texts, from multicultural short stories to historical primary documents (Cooke, 2002); and with an array of purposes, including those with a response-centered focus (Liang, 2004).

The Scaffolded Reading Experience is well grounded in theory and provides an excellent, flexible

© Cengage Learning/Wadsworth

Time spent reading is the best predictor of success as a reader.

framework for teaching individual works of literature in the classroom. The planning phase reminds teachers to take the time to carefully consider why they are choosing this particular text to teach from the multitude of others available. Using the framework helps teachers present thorough, well-planned experiences with a specific book—introducing characters, plots, themes, literary elements, and even skills in responding that a class can use as points of reference when connecting with other literature in the future. Teaching Idea 12.4 offers suggestions for creating a response-centered scaffolded reading experience.

Enjoying and Responding— A Seventh-Grade SRE Experience

Cari, a seventh-grade teacher who uses a response-centered, literature-based curriculum in her language arts classroom, chose to use the SRE framework to teach the short story "The Truth about Sharks" by Joan Bauer from Jerry and Helen Weiss's (1997) collection **From One Experience to Another** (A). Cari first thought carefully about her purpose for teaching the story, the story itself, and her students. She determined that her purpose for teaching the story was two-fold: she wanted to help her students better understand

TEACHING IDEA 12.4

Create a Response-Centered SRE

 **COMMON CORE STATE STANDARDS**

This Teaching Idea does not pertain to specific Common Core English Language Arts standards but is a basic framework for implementing activities that could address any one of the standards for grades 4 through 8.

Try your hand at planning a response-centered SRE for a particular group of students and a special book you want to teach. Follow these steps.

Planning Phase

1. *Students.* Think about the group of students you will be teaching. What are their interests? Reading and responding strengths? Reading and responding weaknesses?

2. *Text.* Think about the particular book you have chosen. What is its theme? What genre is it? Is the vocabulary difficult? Are there points that will need to be clarified for your students? Have your students read any similar books?

3. *Response-centered purpose.* Why did you choose this particular book for this group of students; in other words, why are you taking the time to share this book in particular? What do you hope students will learn when you read this book as a class? What are your goals for teaching this book? Remember that this is a response-based SRE so your purpose should focus on encouraging students' responses to the book in some way.

Consider these three questions carefully. Then, once you are certain you have thought about the students, text, and purpose thoroughly, and how they all interplay with one another, you can move on to the next step.

Implementation Phase

1. *Prereading activities.* Plan what you will do to prepare and motivate students to read the book. Remember that you do not want to stifle students' responses to the book so your prereading activities will be fairly brief.

2. *During-reading activities.* How will students be reading the book? Will they read silently? Read with a partner? Listen to you read aloud? Or do all of these things? Plan carefully to decide what mode of reading will work best for each part of the book.

3. *Postreading activities.* What activities will students do after they have read sections of the book? After reading the entire book? What sorts of opportunities will you give students to respond to the text, share their responses, explore their responses and their peers' responses in more depth, and connect their experiences and understanding of the book to others they have read?

different ways they might respond to literature, and she also wanted them to enjoy and engage with a well-written modern short story. Based on the interaction of these three elements, her purpose, the text, and her students, Cari then moved to the implementation phase and planned pre-, during-, and postreading activities.

During the prereading phase, Cari began by modeling a response. She shared a response she had while recently watching a movie and explained that responding to a movie, television show, or book is more than just liking or disliking it. Through her sharing, she introduced her class to a few possible ways someone might respond to a text: making connections to other books, movies, or events; thinking about parts particularly liked or disliked; or perhaps thinking about the way the literature was written (the "craft" of the book).

After discussing these possible ways to respond, and several others the students generated, Cari asked the students to record at least four of their responses to the short story as they were reading it. She suggested they record their responses on a grid with two headings: "Why I want to remember this part or what I was thinking while reading this part" and "The page number and paragraph of this part." Knowing the importance of modeling, Cari then started reading aloud the story, stopping and modeling how to record responses she was having to the story. After a few pages, the students continued reading silently or in pairs, stopping at least four times on their own to respond on their grids.

Once the during-reading activities were complete, Cari moved the class to postreading activities. The exciting plot of the story—particularly the false accusation of shoplifting—had captivated the students and they were eager to discuss it. Cari built on this by starting the postreading activities, with students sharing their general reactions and impressions of the story in small groups. As Cari moved around the room joining in discussions, she asked questions to help students think more deeply about the story, such as: "Do you think you would have been able to speak up as quickly as Beth [the main character] did?" "Have you ever been accused of doing something you didn't do? How did you react?" "Why do you think the author titled this story 'The Truth about Sharks'?" When the discussions were beginning to wind down, Cari asked the students to share the responses they had written. As a class, the students and Cari noted how differently people responded to the same story and even the same parts of it. Cari then reminded the class about some

of the possible ways to respond to a text they had brainstormed earlier, and students offered examples of some of their responses that fit into the various generated categories. In this class discussion, Cari emphasized the idea of using multiple ways to respond to help better understand a text and your individual reaction to it.

The next day, Cari gave the students some time to continue responding to the story individually or in small groups. Students could choose to talk in small groups, write longer responses to the story on their own, or even draw their reactions to the story as a whole. After this short period of continued responding, the students gathered for a postreading dramatic activity, in which they imagined the main characters from the story were appearing on the "Cari Show." Students took on the roles of both the main characters and audience members of the show and asked and answered questions about their actions in the story. Some students even took on the roles of other "guests" on the show and pretended to be main characters from other books and stories commonly read by the class, now appearing on the "Cari Show" to quiz and question the characters from "The Truth about Sharks."

Through Cari's Scaffolded Reading Experience with "The Truth about Sharks," her students learned a bit more about ways of responding. They also discovered some engaging characters and plot events that they will be able to easily use as references when discussing new stories with one another.

Connecting Literature Study and Writing

Many teachers use literature as a foundation for their language arts curriculum. They might ask students to read short stories, poems, fiction, and nonfiction that complement the basal series they use, or they might use literature to help students develop their literary knowledge. Many teachers also use literature as an important component of their writing program, teaching their students to appreciate the wordsmithery demonstrated by the writers, to explore structures and styles as they relate to mood and tone, or to use the books they read as models for their own writing. Students who write read differently from those who do not write. When students are learning the craft of writing, they are sensitive to what other writers do and adopt some of the strategies as their own.

Students who read are better writers than those who do not read. The only source of knowledge sufficiently rich and reliable for learning about written language is the writing already done by others. We learn to write by reading what others have written; we enrich our repertoire of language possibilities by reading what others have said. Hearing and reading good stories, poems, and nonfiction develops vocabulary, sharpens sensitivity to language, and fine-tunes a sense of writing styles. These benefits may be especially important in regard to nonfiction. Students who read nothing but textbooks have no way of knowing just how graceful nonfiction writing can be, and they have no understanding of how different expository structures and techniques can support concept development or build arguments. No wonder their research papers read like encyclopedia entries!

Teachers who use literature to integrate reading and writing talk about how aspects of published writers' styles crop up in student writing, about how familiar structures are borrowed and used in new ways. Students of all ages do this—borrow from the books they read—to their great advantage. Teachers can capitalize on this by structuring lessons that focus students on exploring how language works in the books they are reading and how they can use their newfound knowledge to produce their own texts.

Students can observe how changing the point of view alters a story or the presentation of information. They can study how setting influences character and events, and how the same story can be told in a variety of ways. They can consider the words and the arrangements of those words in favorite stories, poems, and nonfiction texts. Structure can be explored in this way as well, as young readers experiment with the forms they find in the books they read. Students can notice and discuss the wide variety of topics that successful authors explore in poetry, fiction, and nonfiction, and consider the topics they know about and are interested in exploring further through their own writing. No matter what point you might want to make about writing, there is a book to help you make it clear.

Books about writing for students in intermediate grades and middle school are listed in Figure 12.1.

Being surrounded by good models of writing helps students learn to write well in a variety of genres. Students usually receive a great deal of exposure to stories but are often asked to write reports or poems without much experience in reading these genres. Textbooks in content areas are not always well written, and the amount of poetry that students encounter in basal reading series is simply inadequate. Susan, who teaches seventh graders, knows that she has to give students consistent and sustained opportunities to read and explore poetry before she can expect them to study it or write it. Consequently, from the beginning of the school year, she makes poetry available for students to read and share. She regularly reads or

FIGURE 12.1

Good Books about the Writing Process

Bauer, Marion Dane, *Our Stories: A Fiction Workshop for Young Authors*

_____, *What's Your Story? A Young Person's Guide to Writing Fiction*

_____, *A Writer's Story: From Life to Fiction*

Esbensen, Barbara Juster, *A Celebration of Bees: Helping Children Write Poetry*

Fletcher, Ralph, *How Writers Work: Finding a Process that Works for You*

_____, *Live Writing: Breathing Life into Your Words*

_____, *Poetry Matters: Writing a Poem from the Inside Out*

_____, *Writer's Notebook: Unlocking the Writer within You*

Graves, Donald, *Experiment with Fiction*

_____, *Investigate Nonfiction*

_____, *Explore Poetry*

Janeczko, Paul, *How to Write Poetry*

Livingston, Myra Cohn, *I Am Writing a Poem about . . . : A Game of Poetry*

, *Poem-Making: Ways to Begin Writing Poetry*

Stanek, Lou Willett, *Thinking Like a Writer*

Yolen, Jane, *Take Joy: A Book for Writers*

_____, *Take Joy: A Writer's Guide to Loving the Craft*

recites poetry to her students, and she takes pains to find poetry that relates to other books they are reading.

This time spent with poetry is necessary because many of Susan's students begin the year afraid of poetry; it is that funny kind of writing that they find difficult to understand and have learned to dislike because of excessive analysis or handwriting practice. Seven years of answering literal questions about poetry take their toll. Because Susan gives her students time to enjoy poetry, however, they are ready to join her enthusiastically when she is ready to focus on poetry in her writing curriculum. Armed with many books of and about poetry, Susan devises a series of lessons that combine reading and discussing poetry, talking about form and poetic devices, and experimenting with writing various types of poetry using different poetic devices.

For six weeks, her three seventh-grade classes spend their fifty minutes a day immersed in reading and writing poetry. The boundaries between reading and writing workshops blur, and they are truly reading like writers—and writing like the readers they are. One student, an avid horse-lover, produced the following poem:

SHOW

We dance into the ring,
a flash of chestnut.
Together,
we can work miracles.
And she dances,
her hooves barely touching the ground.
At "X" we salute the judge.
She nods, and we move on.
At "C" we canter,
a rollicking gait,
and I dare not give her her head.
She, too, is strong.
When we are done
once more we salute the judge
and when we leave, there is also
a flash of blue.
Later, after the show,
I am alone with her in a yellow-green meadow.
We canter.
This time her head is free.
The wind spreads the grass afore us
like a race track.
And she is the horse
And she is winning.

Can you tell that this young woman has enjoyed reading the many books of free verse that Susan has placed in her classroom library?

Using literature to connect many areas of the curriculum helps students learn; it makes sense to them to link the various things they are learning across the day. Using literature to connect the English language arts is critical. Students learn language—reading, writing, listening, and speaking—best when they make connections among these language domains. Another way to use literature is to select books that can help alter your teaching so that it becomes a challenge to students to think about themselves, our society, and the way the world works.

Using Literature to Transform the Larger Curriculum

Asking students to read widely about the ideas you are exploring in your classroom encourages them to discover what they are interested in and to delve deeply into that interest. This, in turn, means they are more likely to discover differing perspectives and new ways to think about things. Reading widely also provides an important opportunity for critical reading and thinking. Through wise selection, teachers can transform their curriculum, as Banks & Banks (1993) suggest, so their students come to consider knowledge as being shaped by culture and learn to consider ideas, issues, and events within a framework that embraces diversity.

For example, Jon wanted his sixth graders to think about current issues and events, and he began with homelessness, sure that this would generate some heated discussion. He began by asking his students to answer questions in writing. He wanted them to write because doing so meant that they had to take a stance. They answered the following:

1. What are the characteristics of homeless people?
2. What are the causes of homelessness?
3. Can't homeless people just get jobs?
4. What should the government do about homelessness?

After students had the opportunity to think about and answer these questions, he asked them to discuss them in small groups, with one person in the group being responsible for recording all of their answers on an *anonymous*, brief chart that they could share via the document projector. Had his white board not been broken, he could have used that technology to share their ideas.

The whole class then discussed the answers that students gave, categorizing them and discussing the assumptions inherent in each category. For example, some students assumed that homeless people are alcoholics, or lazy, or only male. Jon then shared some recent articles from the local paper and discussed the assumptions the reporters held. Later in the week, he read a book that explored homelessness. He chose a picturebook, Eve Bunting's *Fly away Home* (I) because it challenges many of the assumptions that his students demonstrated. A homeless father, who has a job, and his son live in an airport because the mother has died and the father's salary is insufficient to continue to pay their rent. He then suggested other books, at various reading levels, in which homelessness was present.

Teaching to transform a curriculum relies on a good collection of culturally diverse books—books from mainstream and parallel cultures, including American children's literature and international literature that present a wide variety of perspectives on the human experience. Chapters 3 through 10 describe the books and how to build a culturally diverse collection. Here we offer yet another way to think about the books you teach with—considering them in light of the perspectives they present, the picture of the world the author presents. The most effective books invite readers to explore alternative ways of thinking and living; they invite reader transformation and promote cross-cultural affective understanding. If you select books that do this, you will be able to teach your students to consider various perspectives and read critically.

Writing about multicultural education, Banks and Banks (1993) distinguish among the contributions approach, the additive approach, the transformation approach, and the social action approach. The *contributions approach* is certainly the easiest way to incorporate culturally diverse literature into your curriculum. Using this approach, you select books that, for example, celebrate heroes and holidays from various cultures. Spending time reading about Dr. Martin Luther King Jr. in January is a common practice that falls into this category. This approach does not integrate culturally diverse books and issues into the curriculum and is not likely to promote critical reading and thinking.

The *additive approach*, in which "content, concepts, themes, and perspectives are added to the curriculum without changing its basic structure" (Banks & Banks, 1993, p. 201), involves incorporating literature by and about people from diverse cultures into the mainstream curriculum without changing the curriculum. For example, Thanksgiving might still be part of a unit on holidays, but having students read Michael Dorris's *Guests* (I), a slim novel about the first Thanksgiving, told from the perspective of Moss, a young Native American boy whose family has invited the pilgrims to feast with them, would be "adding" cultural diversity to the traditional view of Thanksgiving. This approach, like the contributions approach, does not fundamentally transform thinking. The *transformation approach* "changes the basic assumptions of the curriculum and enables students to view concepts, issues, themes, and problems from several ethnic perspectives and points of view" (Banks & Banks, 1993, p. 203). In this approach, the Thanksgiving unit would become a unit exploring cultural conflict. Students might read *Guests*, discuss the irony in the term *Thanksgiving*, study historical documents, and read Marcia Sewall's *People of the Breaking Day* (I). They would consider the colonization of America from the perspectives of those who were colonized as well as from the perspectives of those who came looking for a better life. This kind of experience can lead to the habit of considering ideas, issues, and events from a variety of perspectives—critical thinking. This kind of teaching is not occasional or superficial; it involves a consideration of diversity as a basic premise.

The *social action approach* adds striving for social change to the transformation approach. In this approach, students are taught to understand, question, and do something about important social issues. After reading a number of books, both fiction and nonfiction, about recent immigrants to North America, students might write letters to senators, representatives in Congress, and newspaper editors to express their opinions about some of the new immigration policies in the United States.

If you examine your own teaching, it is easy to determine where you stand in your current practice. Wherever you are now in your development as a responsive teacher, you can alter your curriculum and classroom practices to include a variety of perspectives. Judy, a fifth-grade teacher, sought to transform her curriculum by finding books that reflect the themes and issues she explores in social studies, in which the focus is on American history.

Judy has always combined language arts and social studies instruction through children's literature, but this year she decides to do more than select books that illuminate the historical periods she is covering. First, she organizes her social studies and language arts curriculum around the theme of progress and cultural conflict, hoping to create a climate in her classroom whereby her diverse students will question what we mean by "progress" and will begin to see the history of the United States from multiple perspectives. Because the notion of progress often includes environmental issues, she decides to connect her theme to that portion of the science curriculum that covers ecology and environmental issues as well.

Judy begins the year by starting at the beginning, at least from the mainstream perspective. A study of Columbus and his "discovery" of the Americas provides an interesting introduction to the importance of perspective in interpreting historical events. Such books as Betsy Maestro's *The Discovery of the Americas* (I), Jane Yolen's *Encounter* (P–I), and Pam Conrad's *Pedro's Journal* (I) add contrast to the account of the age of exploration in the social studies text. Classic biographies of Columbus, in which he is praised as a great man, such as the d'Aulaires' *Columbus* (P–I), are compared to more recent texts, such as Vicki Liestman's *Columbus Day* (I) and Milton Meltzer's *Columbus and the World around Him* (A). These readings provide a perfect context for learning to critically assess nonfiction texts.

At the same time, the whole class is reading Michael Dorris's *Morning Girl* (I), sometimes aloud, sometimes silently, and students are writing about the book and discussing it after each chapter. The fifth graders have really come to know Morning Girl and Star Boy as people, and they have begun to talk about what a peaceful life the Taino had. Then the book ends with an excerpt from Columbus's journal in which he disparages the Taino as having no language and being fit only for slavery. What a shock! This experience helps these young readers see the power of perspective and the conflict that "progress," in this case the exploration of new lands, can bring.

With this strong beginning, it is easy for students to continue to explore the idea of progress and cultural conflict through the social studies topics they study and the literature they read. Both the Civil War and westward expansion are illuminated as historical periods when they are viewed as instances of cultural conflict, and they are made memorable through the reading and discussion of evocative books. Reading such picturebooks as Ann Turner's *Nettie's Trip South* (I–A) and Patricia Polacco's *Pink and Say* (I) and *January's Sparrow* (I–A), such biographical works as Mary E. Lyons's *Letters from a Slave Girl: The Story of Harriet Jacobs* (I–A) and Russell Freedman's *Lincoln: A Photobiography* (I–A), and many novels such as those mentioned in Chapter 8, becomes an important experience for these students as they discuss, from a variety of perspectives, the ideas of states'

rights and secession, slavery, and emancipation. The Civil War becomes not just an event in the history of their country but another example of cultural conflict and resolution.

The study of westward expansion is given breadth and impact through the reading of such nonfiction books as Russell Freedman's *An Indian Winter* (A), Leonard Everett Fisher's *The Oregon Trail* (A), and Dee Brown's *Wounded Knee: An Indian History of the American West* (A), adapted by Amy Ehrlich for young readers from Brown's original *Bury My Heart at Wounded Knee: An Indian History of the American West*. These books, along with novels such as those mentioned in Chapter 8, help students understand not only the exhilaration of moving to a new land, taming it, and making it your own but also the agony of living through the destruction of your people, values, and way of life.

The story of immigration in America is also a story of cultural conflict and change, and Judy's class explores Shaun Tan's *The Arrival*, and then goes on to read and discuss both fiction and nonfiction that chronicle the difficulties of adjusting to a new culture, many titles of which are discussed in Chapters 8 and 10. This becomes a subtheme that continues through the year and expands into family history projects.

By integrating social studies and literature within a meaningful thematic framework, Judy is able to transform her social studies curriculum from a study of history to a study of progress and cultural conflict in history. She also is able to incorporate the idea of cultural perspective in her science curriculum when the class studies ecology and the environment. Adding a Native American perspective to the discussion of the use of natural resources helps her students see that there are at least two sides to every issue. For example, although farming the prairie meant food for an expanding American population, it also meant severe loss of topsoil and destruction of the natural habitat for several species, which were also destroyed as a result. This in turn led to the starvation of Native Americans, who relied on hunting the prairie to feed their people. Faced with facts like these, students find it easier to understand and admire alternative perspectives, such as the Native American attitude toward natural resources. Rather than being held up as an example of an "undeveloped" or naïve cultural attitude or a quaint and amusing belief, the Native American reverence for nature becomes a prophetic lesson for all.

Judy chooses books that she hopes will provoke discussions of cultural conflict and perspective—books to engage students who read at different levels, books from a variety of genres. She provides time to read and gives students the opportunity to think, write, and talk about what they are reading. By bringing students together around meaningful books, Judy enables them to explore issues in history and science that are still important today. This in turn leads to discussions of contemporary issues, discussions that allow students to question previously held beliefs and form lasting values.

Judy has transformed her curriculum into one that not only allows her students to learn the "facts" of history and to practice their reading and comprehension skills but also offers them multiple opportunities to think critically. As they read, wrote about, and discussed the books she assigned, they learned a great deal. They learned to read with greater comprehension through her instruction in comprehension strategies and their application of those strategies to their reading assignments. They learned about the history of the United States. They learned to recognize various perspectives on the events of history. And, Judy hopes, they learned how to be more critical in their reading and thinking.

Assessment

No matter how you structure your response-centered, literature-based curriculum, assessment will be an important part of what you do. It is impossible to be a responsive teacher unless you are carefully observing your students. A literature-based classroom provides many opportunities for assessment, even though it uses far fewer worksheets. Teachers understand that standardized tests are part of the school year, but they also develop assessment practices that can inform them of their students' progress on a regular basis as the Common Core Standards require. Figure 12.2 lists some ideas that teachers can use as part of an ongoing assessment.

One such idea is a formal observation of students as they are doing what has been assigned. For example, a teacher can sit next to and formally observe a book club discussion group, evaluating the group's effectiveness based on predetermined criteria that have been shared with the students beforehand. Most teachers develop an observation form that allows them to check off or briefly describe whatever it is they are observing. Students know when and how they will be observed, and these observations take place periodically during the school year. This allows teachers to assess current progress and document individual students' growth over the course of the year.

The curriculum usually also includes gradable "products" that students generate. These, too, become an important component of any teacher's assessment. Students can evaluate their own success and progress by compiling a portfolio that reflects their best efforts. Asking students to look at their work and select materials that demonstrate what they have learned is a powerful step toward the practice of self-evaluation, a necessary skill for independent learners. See Strickland, Galda, & Cullinan (2004) and Galda & Graves (2007) for more extended discussion of assessment and teaching with literature.

FIGURE 12.2

Things to Observe about Reading Literature

This figure suggests assessment practices endorsed in the professional standards developed jointly by the International Reading Association and the National Council of Teachers of English.

- What books are your students reading, and how long are they taking to read them? Use reading logs; observe library behavior.

- How do your students decide which books to select? Observe library behavior; ask students to describe in writing how they make their choices.

- How do your students feel about reading? Use a reading attitude survey.

- Are your students good conversationalists about books? Observe a group discussion; ask students to self-evaluate their group behavior.

- Do your students comprehend the books they are reading? Are they engaged with the books? Observe students' comments during discussion; use artifacts that students produce such as journal or literature log entries.

SUMMARY

There are many ways to structure response-centered, literature-based instruction in the intermediate grades and middle school. Some teachers choose to use year-long frameworks such as Book Club or Reading Workshop. Both frameworks allow for social inter-action around literary events, time spent reading, and opportunities for students to respond in writing and by talking with peers. Other teachers might choose to work on response-centered instruction more in depth with individual books throughout the year. These teachers might use the SRE (Scaffolded Reading Experience) framework to foster students' understanding and enjoyment of the book and promote deep understanding. Over time, these experiences with individual books help students begin to make intertextual connections that build their general literary understanding.

Teachers also might infuse literature into their curriculum in other ways. Many teachers combine literature study and writing, using the books students read as resources for and examples of good writing. Others work toward transforming the curriculum they teach by using literature that provides students with alternative perspectives. All of these ways of incorporating literature into the curriculum are supported by assessment practices that keep teachers informed about how their students are performing.

Teaching with a response-centered, literature-based approach helps readers think about themselves and their world and expand their ideas about people, places, history, current events, and important issues. It helps students learn to read and think critically, considering multiple points of view. Books and the right kind of teaching can transform much more than the curriculum. They can transform lives.

Additional resources to accompany this chapter can be found on the Education CourseMate website. Go to CengageBrain.com to access a variety of interactive study tools and useful resources including Video Conversations with children's book authors and illustrators, a searchable children's literature database, glossary flashcards, online activities, tutorial quizzes, links to relevant websites, and more.

Appendix A
Selected Children's and Adolescent Book Awards

American Library Association Awards

• • • JOHN NEWBERY MEDAL • • •
AND HONOR BOOKS

The John Newbery Medal, established in 1922 and named for an eighteenth-century British publisher and bookseller, the first to publish books for children, is given annually for the most distinguished contribution to literature for children published in the United States in the preceding year. This award is administered by the Association for Library Service to Children, a division of the American Library Association.

1922

The Story of Mankind
by Hendrik Willem van Loon (Liveright)

HONOR BOOKS: *The Great Quest*, by Charles Hawes (Little, Brown); *Cedric the Forester*, by Bernard Marshall (Appleton); *The Old Tobacco Shop*, by William Bowen (Macmillan); *The Golden Fleece and the Heroes Who Lived before Achilles*, by Padraic Colum (Macmillan); *Windy Hill*, by Cornelia Meigs (Macmillan)

1923

The Voyages of Doctor Doolittle
by Hugh Lofting (HarperCollins)

HONOR BOOKS: No record

1924

The Dark Frigate
by Charles Hawes (Little, Brown)

HONOR BOOKS: No record

1925

Tales from Silver Lands
by Charles Finger (Doubleday)

HONOR BOOKS: *Nicholas*, by Anne Carroll Moore (Putnam); *Dream Coach*, by Anne Parrish (Macmillan)

1926

Shen of the Sea
by Arthur Bowie Chrisman (Dutton)

HONOR BOOK: *Voyagers,* by Padraic Colum (Macmillan)

1927

Smoky, the Cowhorse
by Will James (Scribner's)

HONOR BOOKS: No record

1928

Gay-Neck: The Story of a Pigeon
by Dhan Gopal Mukerji (Dutton)

HONOR BOOKS: *The Wonder Smith and His Son*, by Ella Young (Longman); *Downright Dencey*, by Caroline Snedeker (Doubleday)

1929

The Trumpeter of Krakow
by Eric P. Kelly (Macmillan)

HONOR BOOKS: **Pigtail of Ah Lee Ben Loo**,
by John Benett (Longman); **Millions of Cats**,
by Wanda Gág (Coward-McCann); **The Boy
Who Was**, by Grace Hallock (Dutton); **Clearing
Weather**, by Cornelia Meigs (Little, Brown);
Runaway Papoose, by Grace Moon (Doubleday);
Tod of the Fens, by Elinor Whitney (Macmillan)

1930

Hitty, Her First Hundred Years
by Rachel Field (Macmillan)

HONOR BOOKS: **A Daughter of the Seine**, by
Jeanette Eaton (HarperCollins); **Pran of Albania**,
by Elizabeth Miller (Doubleday); **Jumping-Off
Place**, by Marian Hurd McNeely (Longman);
Tangle-Coated Horse and Other Tales, by Ella
Young (Random House); **Vaino**, by Julia Davis
Adams (Dutton); **Little Blacknose**, by Hildegarde
Swift (Harcourt)

1931

The Cat Who Went to Heaven
by Elizabeth Coatsworth (Macmillan)

HONOR BOOKS: **Floating Island**, by Anne Parrish
(HarperCollins); **The Dark Star of Itza**, by Alida
Malkus (Harcourt); **Queer Person**, by Ralph
Hubbard (Doubleday); **Mountains Are Free**,
by Julia Davis Adams (Dutton); **Spice and the
Devil's Cave**, by Agnes Hewes (Knopf); **Meggy
Macintosh**, by Elizabeth Janet Gray (Doubleday);
Garram the Hunter, by Herbert Best (Doubleday);
Ood-Le-Uk the Wanderer, by Alice Lide and
Margaret Johansen (Little, Brown)

1932

Waterless Mountain
by Laura Adams Armer (Random House)

HONOR BOOKS: **The Fairy Circus**, by Dorothy P.
Lathrop (Macmillan); **Calico Bush**, by Rachel Field
(Macmillan); **Boy of the South Seas**, by Eunice
Tietjens (Coward-McCann); **Out of the Flame**,
by Eloise Lownsbery (Longman); **Jane's Island**,
by Marjorie Allee (Houghton Mifflin); **Truce of the
Wolf and Other Tales of Old Italy**, by Mary
Gould Davis (Harcourt)

1933

Young Fu of the Upper Yangtze
by Elizabeth Foreman Lewis (Winston)

HONOR BOOKS: **Swift Rivers**, by Cornelia Meigs
(Little, Brown); **The Railroad to Freedom**, by
Hildegarde Swift (Harcourt); **Children of the Soil**,
by Nora Burglon (Doubleday)

1934

Invincible Louisa
by Cornelia Meigs (Little, Brown)

HONOR BOOKS: **The Forgotten Daughter**, by
Caroline Snedeker (Doubleday); **Swords of Steel**,
by Elsie Singmaster (Houghton Mifflin); **ABC
Bunny**, by Wanda Gág (Coward-McCann); **Winged
Girl of Knossos**, by Erik Berry (Appleton); **New
Land**, by Sarah Schmidt (McBride); **Big Tree of
Bunlahy**, by Padraic Colum (Macmillan); **Glory of
the Seas**, by Agnes Hewes (Knopf); **Apprentice of
Florence**, by Ann Kyle (Houghton Mifflin)

1935

Dobry
by Monica Shannon (Viking)

HONOR BOOKS: **Pageant of Chinese History**, by
Elizabeth Seeger (Random House); **Davy Crockett**,
by Constance Rourke (Harcourt); **A Day on
Skates**, by Hilda Van Stockum (HarperCollins)

1936

Caddie Woodlawn
by Carol Ryrie Brink (Macmillan)

HONOR BOOKS: **Honk the Moose**, by Phil Stong
(Trellis); **The Good Master**, by Kate Seredy
(Viking); **Young Walter Scott**, by Elizabeth Janet
Gray (Viking); **All Sail Set**, by Armstrong Sperry
(Winston)

1937

Roller Skates
by Ruth Sawyer (Viking)

HONOR BOOKS: **Phoebe Fairchild: Her Book**,
by Lois Lenski (Stokes); **Whistler's Van**, by
Idwal Jones (Viking); **Golden Basket**, by Ludwig
Bemelmans (Viking); **Winterbound**, by Margery
Bianco (Viking); **Audubon**, by Constance Rourke
(Harcourt); **The Codfish Musket**, by Agnes Hewes
(Doubleday)

1938

The White Stag
by Kate Seredy (Viking)

HONOR BOOKS: ***Pecos Bill***, by James Cloyd Bowman (Little, Brown); ***Bright Island***, by Mabel Robinson (Random House); ***On the Banks of Plum Creek***, by Laura Ingalls Wilder (HarperCollins)

1939

Thimble Summer
by Elizabeth Enright (Holt)

HONOR BOOKS: ***Nino***, by Valenti Angelo (Viking); ***Mr. Popper's Penguins***, by Richard and Florence Atwater (Little, Brown); ***"Hello the Boat!"***, by Phyllis Crawford (Holt); ***Leader by Destiny: George Washington, Man and Patriot***, by Jeanette Eaton (Harcourt); ***Penn***, by Elizabeth Janet Gray (Viking)

1940

Daniel Boone
by James Daugherty (Viking)

HONOR BOOKS: ***The Singing Tree***, by Kate Seredy (Viking); ***Runner of the Mountain Tops***, by Mabel Robinson (Random House); ***By the Shores of Silver Lake***, by Laura Ingalls Wilder (HarperCollins); ***Boy with a Pack***, by Stephen W. Meader (Harcourt)

1941

Call It Courage
by Armstrong Sperry (Macmillan)

HONOR BOOKS: ***Blue Willow***, by Doris Gates (Viking); ***Young Mac of Fort Vancouver***, by Mary Jane Carr (HarperCollins); ***The Long Winter***, by Laura Ingalls Wilder (HarperCollins); ***Nansen***, by Anna Gertrude Hall (Viking)

1942

The Matchlock Gun
by Walter D. Edmonds (Putnam)

HONOR BOOKS: ***Little Town on the Prairie***, by Laura Ingalls Wilder (HarperCollins); ***George Washington's World***, by Genevieve Foster (Scribner's); ***Indian Captive: The Story of Mary Jemison***, by Lois Lenski (HarperCollins); ***Down Ryton Water***, by Eva Roe Gaggin (Viking)

1943

Adam of the Road
by Elizabeth Janet Gray (Viking)

HONOR BOOKS: ***The Middle Moffat***, by Eleanor Estes (Harcourt); ***Have You Seen Tom Thumb?***, by Mabel Leigh Hunt (HarperCollins)

1944

Johnny Tremain
by Esther Forbes (Houghton Mifflin)

HONOR BOOKS: ***These Happy Golden Years***, by Laura Ingalls Wilder (HarperCollins); ***Fog Magic***, by Julia Sauer (Viking); ***Rufus M.***, by Eleanor Estes (Harcourt); ***Mountain Born***, by Elizabeth Yates (Coward-McCann)

1945

Rabbit Hill
by Robert Lawson (Viking)

HONOR BOOKS: ***The Hundred Dresses***, by Eleanor Estes (Harcourt); ***The Silver Pencil***, by Alice Dalgliesh (Scribner's); ***Abraham Lincoln's World***, by Genevieve Foster (Scribner's); ***Lone Journey: The Life of Roger Williams***, by Jeannette Eaton (Harcourt)

1946

Strawberry Girl
by Lois Lenski (HarperCollins)

HONOR BOOKS: ***Justin Morgan Had a Horse***, by Marguerite Henry (Rand McNally); ***The Moved-Outers***, by Florence Crannel Means (Houghton Mifflin); ***Bhimsa, the Dancing Bear***, by Christine Weston (Scribner's); ***New Found World***, by Katherine Shippen (Viking)

1947

Miss Hickory
by Carolyn Sherwin Bailey (Viking)

HONOR BOOKS: ***Wonderful Year***, by Nancy Barnes (Messner); ***Big Tree***, by Mary and Conrad Buff (Viking); ***The Heavenly Tenants***, by William Maxwell (HarperCollins); ***The Avion My Uncle Flew***, by Cyrus Fisher (Appleton); ***The Hidden Treasure of Glaston***, by Eleanore Jewett (Viking)

1948

The Twenty-One Balloons
by William Pène du Bois (Viking)

HONOR BOOKS: *Pancakes-Paris*, by Claire Huchet Bishop (Viking); *Li Lun, Lad of Courage*, by Carolyn Treffinger (Abingdon); *The Quaint and Curious Quest of Johnny Longfoot*, by Catherine Besterman (Bobbs); *The Cow-Tail Switch and Other West African Stories*, by Harold Courlander (Holt); *Misty of Chincoteague*, by Marguerite Henry (Rand McNally)

1949

King of the Wind
by Marguerite Henry (Rand McNally)

HONOR BOOKS: *Seabird*, by Holling C. Holling (Houghton Mifflin); *Daughter of the Mountains*, by Louise Rankin (Viking); *My Father's Dragon*, by Ruth Stiles Gannett (Random House); *Story of the Negro*, by Arna Bontemps (Knopf)

1950

The Door in the Wall
by Marguerite de Angeli (Doubleday)

HONOR BOOKS: *Tree of Freedom*, by Rebecca Caudill (Viking); *The Blue Cat of Castle Town*, by Catherine Coblentz (Random House); *Kildee House*, by Rutherford Montgomery (Doubleday); *George Washington*, by Genevieve Foster (Scribner's); *Song of the Pines*, by Walter and Marion Havighurst (Winston)

1951

Amos Fortune, Free Man
by Elizabeth Yates (Aladdin)

HONOR BOOKS: *Better Known as Johnny Appleseed*, by Mabel Leigh Hunt (HarperCollins); *Gandhi: Fighter without a Sword*, by Jeanette Eaton (Morrow); *Abraham Lincoln, Friend of the People*, by Clara Ingram Judson (Follett); *The Story of Appleby Capple*, by Anne Parrish (HarperCollins)

1952

Ginger Pye
by Eleanor Estes (Harcourt)

HONOR BOOKS: *Americans before Columbus*, by Elizabeth Baity (Viking); *Minn of the Mississippi*, by Holling C. Holling (Houghton Mifflin); *The Defender*, by Nicholas Kalashnikoff (Scribner's);

The Light at Tern Rock, by Julia Sauer (Viking); *The Apple and the Arrow*, by Mary and Conrad Buff (Houghton Mifflin)

1953

Secret of the Andes
by Ann Nolan Clark (Viking)

HONOR BOOKS: *Charlotte's Web*, by E. B. White (HarperCollins); *Moccasin Trail*, by Eloise McGraw (Coward-McCann); *Red Sails to Capri*, by Ann Weil (Viking); *The Bears on Hemlock Mountain*, by Alice Dalgliesh (Scribner's); *Birthdays of Freedom, Vol. 1*, by Genevieve Foster (Scribner's)

1954

. . . and now Miguel
by Joseph Krumgold (HarperCollins)

HONOR BOOKS: *All Alone*, by Claire Huchet Bishop (Viking); *Shadrach*, by Meindert DeJong (HarperCollins); *Hurry Home, Candy*, by Meindert DeJong (HarperCollins); *Theodore Roosevelt, Fighting Patriot*, by Clara Ingram Judson (Follett); *Magic Maize*, by Mary and Conrad Buff (Houghton Mifflin)

1955

The Wheel on the School
by Meindert DeJong (HarperCollins)

HONOR BOOKS: *The Courage of Sarah Noble*, by Alice Dalgliesh (Scribner's); *Banner in the Sky*, by James Ullman (HarperCollins)

1956

Carry on, Mr. Bowditch
by Jean Lee Latham (Houghton Mifflin)

HONOR BOOKS: *The Secret River*, by Marjorie Kinnan Rawlings (Scribner's); *The Golden Name Day*, by Jennie Lindquist (HarperCollins); *Men, Microscopes, and Living Things*, by Katherine Shippen (Viking)

1957

Miracles on Maple Hill
by Virginia Sorensen (Harcourt)

HONOR BOOKS: *Old Yeller*, by Fred Gipson (HarperCollins); *The House of Sixty Fathers*, by Meindert DeJong (HarperCollins); *Mr. Justice Holmes*, by Clara Ingram Judson (Follett); *The Corn Grows Ripe*, by Dorothy Rhoads (Viking); *Black Fox of Lorne*, by Marguerite de Angeli (Doubleday)

1958

Rifles for Watie
by Harold Keith (Crowell)

HONOR BOOKS: ***The Horsecatcher***, by Mari Sandoz (Westminster); ***Gone-Away Lake***, by Elizabeth Enright (Harcourt); ***The Great Wheel***, by Robert Lawson (Viking); ***Tom Paine***, ***Freedom's Apostle***, by Leo Gurko (HarperCollins)

1959

The Witch of Blackbird Pond
by Elizabeth George Speare (Houghton Mifflin)

HONOR BOOKS: ***The Family under the Bridge***, by Natalie Savage Carlson (HarperCollins); ***Along Came a Dog***, by Meindert DeJong (HarperCollins); ***Chucaro: Wild Pony of the Pampa***, by Francis Kalnay (Harcourt); ***The Perilous Road***, by William O. Steele (Harcourt)

1960

Onion John
by Joseph Krumgold (HarperCollins)

HONOR BOOKS: ***My Side of the Mountain***, by Jean Craighead George (Dutton); ***America Is Born***, by Gerald W. Johnson (Morrow); ***The Gammage Cup***, by Carol Kendall (Harcourt)

1961

Island of the Blue Dolphins
by Scott O'Dell (Houghton Mifflin)

HONOR BOOKS: ***America Moves Forward***, by Gerald W. Johnson (Morrow); ***Old Ramon***, by Jack Schaefer (Houghton Mifflin); ***The Cricket in Times Square***, by George Selden (Farrar, Straus and Giroux)

1962

The Bronze Bow
by Elizabeth George Speare (Houghton Mifflin)

HONOR BOOKS: ***Frontier Living***, by Edwin Tunis (World); ***The Golden Goblet***, by Eloise McGraw (Coward-McCann); ***Belling the Tiger***, by Mary Stolz (HarperCollins)

1963

A Wrinkle in Time
by Madeleine L'Engle (Farrar, Straus and Giroux)

HONOR BOOKS: ***Thistle and Thyme***, by Sorche Nic Leodhas (Holt); ***Men of Athens***, by Olivia Coolidge (Houghton Mifflin)

1964

It's Like This, Cat
by Emily Cheney Neville (HarperCollins)

HONOR BOOKS: ***Rascal***, by Sterling North (Dutton); ***The Loner***, by Ester Wier (McKay)

1965

Shadow of a Bull
by Maia Wojciechowska (Simon & Schuster)

HONOR BOOK: ***Across Five Aprils,*** by Irene Hunt (Follett)

1966

I, Juan de Pareja
by Elizabeth Borton de Treviño (Farrar, Straus and Giroux)

HONOR BOOKS: ***The Black Cauldron***, by Lloyd Alexander (Holt); ***The Animal Family***, by Randall Jarrell (Pantheon); ***The Noonday Friends***, by Mary Stolz (HarperCollins)

1967

Up a Road Slowly
by Irene Hunt (Follett)

HONOR BOOKS: ***The King's Fifth***, by Scott O'Dell (Houghton Mifflin); ***Zlateh the Goat and Other Stories***, by Isaac Bashevis Singer (HarperCollins); ***The Jazz Man***, by Mary H. Weik (Simon & Schuster)

1968

From the Mixed-Up Files of Mrs. Basil E. Frankweiler
by E. L. Konigsburg (Simon & Schuster)

HONOR BOOKS: ***Jennifer, Hecate, Macbeth, William McKinley, and Me, Elizabeth***, by E. L. Konigsburg (Simon & Schuster); ***The Black Pearl***, by Scott O'Dell (Houghton Mifflin); ***The Fearsome Inn***, by Isaac Bashevis Singer (Scribner's); ***The Egypt Game***, by Zilpha Keatley Snyder (Simon & Schuster)

1969

The High King
by Lloyd Alexander (Holt)

HONOR BOOKS: ***To Be a Slave***, by Julius Lester (Dial); ***When Shlemiel Went to Warsaw and Other Stories***, by Isaac Bashevis Singer (Farrar, Straus and Giroux)

1970

Sounder
by William H. Armstrong (HarperCollins)

HONOR BOOKS: **Our Eddie**, by Sulamith Ish-Kishor (Pantheon); **The Many Ways of Seeing: An Introduction to the Pleasures of Art**, by Janet Gaylord Moore (World); **Journey Outside**, by Mary Q. Steele (Viking)

1971

Summer of the Swans
by Betsy Byars (Viking)

HONOR BOOKS: **Kneeknock Rise**, by Natalie Babbitt (Farrar, Straus and Giroux); **Enchantress from the Stars**, by Sylvia Louise Engdahl (Simon & Schuster); **Sing Down the Moon**, by Scott O'Dell (Houghton Mifflin)

1972

Mrs. Frisby and the Rats of NIMH
by Robert C. O'Brien (Simon & Schuster)

HONOR BOOKS: **Incident at Hawk's Hill**, by Allan W. Eckert (Little, Brown); **The Planet of Junior Brown**, by Virginia Hamilton (Macmillan); **The Tombs of Atuan**, by Ursula Le Guin (Simon & Schuster); **Annie and the Old One**, by Miska Miles (Little, Brown); **The Headless Cupid**, by Zilpha Keatley Snyder (Simon & Schuster)

1973

Julie of the Wolves
by Jean Craighead George (HarperCollins)

HONOR BOOKS: **Frog and Toad Together**, by Arnold Lobel (HarperCollins); **The Upstairs Room**, by Johanna Reiss (HarperCollins); **The Witches of Worm**, by Zilpha Keatley Snyder (Simon & Schuster)

1974

The Slave Dancer
by Paula Fox (Bradbury)

HONOR BOOKS: **The Dark Is Rising**, by Susan Cooper (McElderry)

1975

M. C. Higgins, the Great
by Virginia Hamilton (Macmillan)

HONOR BOOKS: **Figgs and Phantoms**, by Ellen Raskin (Dutton); **My Brother Sam Is Dead**, by James Lincoln and Christopher Collier (Four Winds); **The Perilous Guard**, by Elizabeth Marie Pope (Houghton Mifflin); **Philip Hall Likes Me. I Reckon Maybe**, by Bette Greene (Dial)

1976

The Grey King
by Susan Cooper (McElderry)

HONOR BOOKS: **The Hundred Penny Box**, by Sharon Bell Mathis (Viking); **Dragonwings**, by Laurence Yep (HarperCollins)

1977

Roll of Thunder, Hear My Cry
by Mildred Taylor (Dial)

HONOR BOOKS: **Abel's Island**, by William Steig (Farrar, Straus and Giroux); **A String in the Harp**, by Nancy Bond (McElderry)

1978

Bridge to Terabithia
by Katherine Paterson (HarperCollins)

HONOR BOOKS: **Ramona and Her Father**, by Beverly Cleary (Morrow); **Anpao: An American Indian Odyssey**, by Jamake Highwater (HarperCollins)

1979

The Westing Game
by Ellen Raskin (Dutton)

HONOR BOOKS: **The Great Gilly Hopkins**, by Katherine Paterson (HarperCollins)

1980

A Gathering of Days: A New England Girl's Journal, 1830–32
by Joan Blos (Scribner's)

HONOR BOOK: **The Road from Home: The Story of an Armenian Girl** by David Kherdian (Greenwillow)

1981

Jacob Have I Loved
by Katherine Paterson (HarperCollins)

HONOR BOOKS: **The Fledgling**, by Jane Langton (HarperCollins); **A Ring of Endless Light**, by Madeleine L'Engle (Farrar, Straus and Giroux)

1982

A Visit to William Blake's Inn: Poems for Innocent and Experienced Travelers
by Nancy Willard (Harcourt)

HONOR BOOKS: ***Ramona Quimby, Age 8***, by Beverly Cleary (Morrow); ***Upon the Head of the Goat: A Childhood in Hungary, 1939–1944***, by Aranka Siegel (Farrar, Straus and Giroux)

1983

Dicey's Song
by Cynthia Voigt (Simon & Schuster)

HONOR BOOKS: ***The Blue Sword***, by Robin McKinley (Greenwillow); ***Doctor De Soto***, by William Steig (Farrar, Straus and Giroux); ***Graven Images***, by Paul Fleischman (HarperCollins); ***Homesick: My Own Story***, by Jean Fritz (Putnam); ***Sweet Whispers, Brother Rush***, by Virginia Hamilton (Philomel)

1984

Dear Mr. Henshaw
by Beverly Cleary (Morrow)

HONOR BOOKS: ***The Wish Giver: Three Tales of Coven Tree***, by Bill Brittain (HarperCollins); ***A Solitary Blue***, by Cynthia Voigt (Simon & Schuster); ***The Sign of the Beaver***, by Elizabeth George Speare (Houghton Mifflin); ***Sugaring Time***, by Kathryn Lasky (Macmillan)

1985

The Hero and the Crown
by Robin McKinley (Greenwillow)

HONOR BOOKS: ***The Moves Make the Man***, by Bruce Brooks (HarperCollins); ***One-Eyed Cat***, by Paula Fox (Bradbury); ***Like Jake and Me***, by Mavis Jukes (Knopf)

1986

Sarah, Plain and Tall
by Patricia MacLachlan (HarperCollins)

HONOR BOOKS: ***Commodore Perry in the Land of Shogun***, by Rhoda Blumberg (Lothrop, Lee & Shepard); ***Dogsong***, by Gary Paulsen (Bradbury)

1987

The Whipping Boy
by Sid Fleischman (Greenwillow)

HONOR BOOKS: ***On My Honor***, by Marion Dane Bauer (Clarion); ***A Fine White Dust***, by Cynthia Rylant (Bradbury); ***Volcano***, by Patricia Lauber (Bradbury)

1988

Lincoln: A Photobiography
by Russell Freedman (Clarion)

HONOR BOOKS: ***Hatchet***, by Gary Paulsen (Bradbury); ***After the Rain***, by Norma Fox Mazer (Morrow)

1989

Joyful Noise: Poems for Two Voices
by Paul Fleischman (HarperCollins)

HONOR BOOKS: ***In the Beginning: Creation Stories from around the World***, by Virginia Hamilton (Harcourt); ***Scorpions***, by Walter Dean Myers (HarperCollins)

1990

Number the Stars
by Lois Lowry (Houghton Mifflin)

HONOR BOOKS: ***Afternoon of the Elves***, by Janet Taylor Lisle (Orchard); ***Shabanu: Daughter of the Wind***, by Suzanne Fisher Staples (Knopf); ***The Winter Room***, by Gary Paulsen (Orchard)

1991

Maniac Magee
by Jerry Spinelli (Little, Brown)

HONOR BOOK: ***The True Confessions of Charlotte Doyle,*** by Avi (Orchard)

1992

Shiloh
by Phyllis Reynolds Naylor (Simon & Schuster)

HONOR BOOKS: ***Nothing but the Truth***, by Avi (Orchard); ***The Wright Brothers: How They Invented the Airplane***, by Russell Freedman (Holiday House)

1993

Missing May
by Cynthia Rylant (Orchard)

HONOR BOOKS: ***What Hearts***, by Bruce Brooks (HarperCollins); ***The Dark Thirty: Southern Tales of the Supernatural***, by Patricia McKissack (Knopf); ***Somewhere in the Darkness***, by Walter Dean Myers (Scholastic)

1994

The Giver
by Lois Lowry (Houghton Mifflin)

HONOR BOOKS: **Crazy Lady!**, by Jane Leslie Conly (HarperCollins); **Dragon's Gate**, by Laurence Yep (HarperCollins); **Eleanor Roosevelt: A Life of Discovery**, by Russell Freedman (Clarion)

1995

Walk Two Moons
by Sharon Creech (HarperCollins)

HONOR BOOKS: **Catherine, Called Birdy**, by Karen Cushman (Clarion); **The Ear, the Eye and the Arm**, by Nancy Farmer (Orchard)

1996

The Midwife's Apprentice
by Karen Cushman (Clarion)

HONOR BOOKS: **The Great Fire**, by Jim Murphy (Scholastic); **The Watsons Go to Birmingham—1963**, by Christopher Paul Curtis (Delacorte); **What Jamie Saw**, by Carolyn Coman (Front Street); **Yolanda's Genius**, by Carol Fenner (McElderry)

1997

The View from Saturday
by E. L. Konigsburg (Simon & Schuster)

HONOR BOOKS: **A Girl Named Disaster**, by Nancy Farmer (Orchard); **The Moorchild**, by Eloise McGraw (McElderry); **The Thief**, by Megan Whalen Turner (Greenwillow); **Belle Prater's Boy**, by Ruth White (Farrar, Straus and Giroux)

1998

Out of the Dust
by Karen Hesse (Scholastic)

HONOR BOOKS: **Lilly's Crossing**, by Patricia Reilly Giff (Delacorte); **Ella Enchanted**, by Gail Carson Levine (HarperCollins); **Wringer**, by Jerry Spinelli (HarperCollins)

1999

Holes
by Louis Sachar (Farrar, Straus and Giroux)

HONOR BOOK: **A Long Way from Chicago**, by Richard Peck (Dial)

2000

Bud, Not Buddy
by Christopher Paul Curtis (Delacorte)

HONOR BOOKS: **Getting Near to Baby**, by Audrey Coloumbis (Delacorte); **26 Fairmount Avenue**, by Tomie dePaola (Putnam); **Our Only May Amelia**, by Jennifer L. Holm (HarperCollins)

2001

A Year Down Yonder
by Richard Peck (Dial)

HONOR BOOKS: **Hope Was Here**, by Joan Bauer (Putnam); **The Wanderer**, by Sharon Creech (HarperCollins); **Because of Winn-Dixie**, by Kate DiCamillo (Candlewick); **Joey Pigza Loses Control**, by Jack Gantos (Farrar, Straus and Giroux)

2002

A Single Shard
by Linda Sue Park (Clarion)

HONOR BOOKS: **Everything on a Waffle**, by Polly Horvath (Farrar Straus & Giroux); **Carver: A Life in Poems**, by Marilyn Nelson (Front Street)

2003

Crispin: The Cross of Lead
by Avi (Hyperion)

HONOR BOOKS: **The House of the Scorpion**, by Nancy Farmer (Simon & Schuster); **Pictures of Hollis Woods**, by Patricia Reilly Giff (Random House); **Hoot**, by Carl Hiaasen (Knopf); **A Corner of the Universe**, by Ann Martin (Scholastic); **Surviving the Applewhites**, by Stephanie Tolan (HarperCollins)

2004

The Tale of Despereaux: Being the Story of a Mouse, a Princess, Some Soup, and a Spool of Thread
by Kate DiCamillo (Candlewick)

HONOR BOOKS: **Olive's Ocean**, by Kevin Henkes (Greenwillow); **An American Plague: The True and Terrifying Story of the Yellow Fever Epidemic of 1793**, by Jim Murphy (Clarion)

2005

Kira-Kira
by Cynthia Kadohata (Simon & Schuster)

HONOR BOOKS: **Lizzie Bright and the Buckminster Boy**, by Gary Schmidt (Clarion);

Al Capone Does My Shirts, by Gennifer Choldenko (Putnam); *The Voice that Challenged a Nation: Marian Anderson and the Struggle for Equal Rights*, by Russell Freedman (Clarion)

2006

Criss Cross
by Lynne Rae Perkins (HarperCollins)

HONOR BOOKS: *Whittington*, by Alan Armstrong, illustrated by S. D. Schindler (Random House); *Hitler Youth: Growing Up in Hitler's Shadow*, by Susan Campbell Bartoletti (Scholastic); *Princess Academy*, by Shannon Hale (Bloomsbury); *Show Way* by Jacqueline Woodson, illustrated by Hudson Talbott (Putnam)

2007

The Higher Power of Lucky
by Susan Patron, illustrated by Matt Phelan (Simon & Schuster)

HONOR BOOKS: *Penny from Heaven*, by Jennifer L. Holm, (Random House); *Hattie Big Sky*, by Kirby Larson (Delacorte); *Rules*, by Cynthia Lord (Scholastic)

2008

Good Masters! Sweet Ladies! Voices from a Medieval Village
by Laura Amy Schlitz (Candlewick)

HONOR BOOKS: *Elijah of Buxton*, by Christopher Paul Curtis (Scholastic); *The Wednesday Wars*, by Gary D. Schmidt (Clarion); *Feathers*, by Jacqueline Woodson (Putnam)

2009

The Graveyard Book
by Neil Gaiman (HarperCollins)

HONOR BOOKS: *The Underneath*, by Kathi Appelt (Simon & Schuster); *The Surrender Tree: Poems of Cuba's Struggle for Freedom*, by Margarita Engle (Holt); *Savvy*, by Ingrid Law (Dial); *After Tupac and D Foster*, by Jacqueline Woodson (Putnam)

2010

When You Reach Me
by Rebecca Stead (Random House)

HONOR BOOKS: *Claudette Colvin: Twice Toward Justice*, by Phillip Hoose (Farrar, Straus and Giroux); *The Evolution of Calpurnia Tate*, by Jacqueline Kelly (Holt); *The Mostly True Adventures of Homer P. Figg*, by Rodman Philbrick (Scholastic); *Where the Mountain Meets the Moon*, by Grace Lin (Little, Brown)

2011

Moon over Manifest
by Clare Vanderpool (Delacorte)

HONOR BOOKS: *Dark Emperor and Other Poems of the Night*, by Joyce Sidman, illustrated by Rick Allen (Houghton Mifflin); *Heart of a Samurai*, by Margi Preus (Abrams); *One Crazy Summer*, by Rita Williams Garcia (HarperCollins); *Turtle in Paradise*, by Jennifer Holm (Random House)

2012

Dead End in Norvelt
by Jack Gantos (Farrar, Straus and Giroux)

HONOR BOOKS: *Breaking Stalin's Nose*, by Eugene Yelchin (Holt); *Inside Out & Back Again*, by Thanhha Lai (HarperCollins)

• • • • RANDOLPH CALDECOTT • • • •
MEDAL AND HONOR BOOKS

The Randolph Caldecott Medal, established in 1938 and named for a nineteenth-century British Illustrator of books for children, is given annually to the Illustrator of the most distinguished picturebook for children published in the United States in the preceding year. This award is administered by the Association for Library Service to Children, a division of the American Library Association.

1938

Animals of the Bible
by Helen Dean Fish, illustrated by Dorothy P. Lathrop (Lippincott)

HONOR BOOKS: *Seven Simeons*, by Boris Artzybasheff (Viking); *Four and Twenty Blackbirds*, by Helen Dean Fish, illustrated by Robert Lawson (Stokes)

1939

Mei Li
by Thomas Handforth (Doubleday)

HONOR BOOKS: *The Forest Pool*, by Laura Adams Armer (Longman); *Wee Gillis*, by Munro Leaf, illustrated by Robert Lawson (Viking); *Snow White and the Seven Dwarfs*, by Wanda Gág

(Coward-McCann); *Barkis*, by Clare Newberry (HarperCollins); *Andy and the Lion*, by James Daugherty (Viking)

1940

Abraham Lincoln
by Ingri and Edgar Parin D'Aulaire (Doubleday)

HONOR BOOKS: *Cock-a-Doodle Doo . . .* , by Berta and Elmer Hader (Macmillan); *Madeline*, by Ludwig Bemelmans (Viking); *The Ageless Story*, by Lauren Ford (Dodd, Mead)

1941

They Were Strong and Good
by Robert Lawson (Viking)

HONOR BOOK: *April's Kittens* by Clare Newberry (HarperCollins)

1942

Make Way for Ducklings
by Robert McCloskey (Viking)

HONOR BOOKS: *An American ABC*, by Maud and Miska Petersham (Macmillan); *In My Mother's House*, by Ann Nolan Clark, illustrated by Velino Gerrera (Viking); *Paddle-to-the-Sea*, by Holling C. Holling (Houghton Mifflin); *Nothing at All*, by Wanda Gág (Coward-McCann)

1943

The Little House
by Virginia Lee Burton (Houghton Mifflin)

HONOR BOOKS: *Dash and Dart*, by Mary and Conrad Buff (Viking); *Marshmallow*, by Clare Newberry (HarperCollins)

1944

Many Moons
by James Thurber, illustrated by Louis Slobodkin (Harcourt)

HONOR BOOKS: *Small Rain: Verses from the Bible*, selected by Jessie Orton Jones, illustrated by Elizabeth Orton Jones (Viking); *Pierre Pigeon*, by Lee Kingman, illustrated by Arnold E. Bare (Houghton Mifflin); *The Mighty Hunter*, by Berta and Elmer Hader (Macmillan); *A Child's Good Night Book*, by Margaret Wise Brown, illustrated by Jean Charlot (Scott); *Good Luck Horse*, by Chih-Yi Chan, illustrated by Plao Chan (Whittlesey)

1945

Prayer for a Child
by Rachel Field, illustrated by Elizabeth Orton Jones (Macmillan)

HONOR BOOKS: *Mother Goose*, illustrated by Tasha Tudor (Walck); *In the Forest*, by Marie Hall Ets (Viking); *Yonie Wondernose*, by Marguerite de Angeli (Doubleday); *The Christmas Anna Angel*, by Ruth Sawyer, illustrated by Kate Seredy (Viking)

1946

The Rooster Crows
illustrated by Maud and Miska Petersham (Macmillan)

HONOR BOOKS: *Little Lost Lamb*, by Golden MacDonald, illustrated by Leonard Weisgard (Doubleday); *Sing Mother Goose*, by Opal Wheeler, illustrated by Marjorie Torrey (Dutton); *My Mother Is the Most Beautiful Woman in the World*, by Becky Reyher, illustrated by Ruth Gannett (Lothrop, Lee & Shepard); *You Can Write Chinese*, by Kurt Weise (Viking)

1947

The Little Island
by Golden MacDonald, illustrated by Leonard Weisgard (Doubleday)

HONOR BOOKS: *Rain Drop Splash*, by Alvin Tresselt, illustrated by Leonard Weisgard (Lothrop, Lee & Shepard); *Boats on the River*, by Marjorie Flack, illustrated by Jay Hyde Barnum (Viking); *Timothy Turtle*, by Al Graham, illustrated by Tony Palazzo (Viking); *Pedro, the Angel of Olvera Street*, by Leo Politi (Scribner's); *Sing in Praise: A Collection of the Best Loved Hymns*, by Opal Wheeler, illustrated by Marjorie Torrey (Dutton)

1948

White Snow, Bright Snow
by Alvin Tresselt, illustrated by Roger Duvoisin (Lothrop, Lee & Shepard)

HONOR BOOKS: *Stone Soup*, by Marcia Brown (Scribner's); *McElligot's Pool*, by Dr. Seuss (Random House); *Bambino the Clown*, by George Schreiber (Viking); *Roger and the Fox*, by Lavinia Davis, illustrated by Hildegard Woodward (Doubleday); *Song of Robin Hood*, edited by Anne Malcolmson, illustrated by Virginia Lee Burton (Houghton Mifflin)

1949

The Big Snow
by Berta and Elmer Hader (Macmillan)

HONOR BOOKS: **Blueberries for Sal**, by Robert McCloskey (Viking); **All around the Town**, by Phyllis McGinley, illustrated by Helen Stone (Lippincott); **Juanita**, by Leo Politi (Scribner's); **Fish in the Air**, by Kurt Wiese (Viking)

1950

Song of the Swallows
by Leo Politi (Scribner's)

HONOR BOOKS: **America's Ethan Allen**, by Stewart Holbrook, illustrated by Lynd Ward (Houghton Mifflin); **The Wild Birthday Cake**, by Lavinia Davis, illustrated by Hildegard Woodward (Doubleday); **The Happy Day**, by Ruth Krauss, illustrated by Marc Simont (HarperCollins); **Bartholomew and the Oobleck**, by Dr. Seuss (Random House); **Henry Fisherman**, by Marcia Brown (Scribner's)

1951

The Egg Tree
by Katherine Milhous (Scribner's)

HONOR BOOKS: **Dick Whittington and His Cat**, by Marcia Brown (Scribner's); **The Two Reds**, by William Lipkind, illustrated by Nicholas Mordvinoff (Harcourt); **If I Ran the Zoo**, by Dr. Seuss (Random House); **The Most Wonderful Doll in the World**, by Phyllis McGinley, illustrated by Helen Stone (Lippincott); **T-Bone, the Baby Sitter**, by Clare Newberry (HarperCollins)

1952

Finders Keepers
by William Lipkind, illustrated by Nicholas Mordvinoff (Harcourt)

HONOR BOOKS: **Mr. T. W. Anthony Woo**, by Marie Hall Ets (Viking); **Skipper John's Cook**, by Marcia Brown (Scribner's); **All Falling Down**, by Gene Zion, illustrated by Margaret Bloy Graham (HarperCollins); **Bear Party**, by William Pène du Bois (Viking); **Feather Mountain**, by Elizabeth Olds (Houghton Mifflin)

1953

The Biggest Bear
by Lynd Ward (Houghton Mifflin)

HONOR BOOKS: **Puss in Boots**, by Charles Perrault, illustrated and translated by Marcia Brown (Scribner's); **One Morning in Maine**, by Robert McCloskey (Viking); **Ape in a Cape**, by Fritz Eichenberg (Harcourt); **The Storm Book**, by Charlotte Zolotow, illustrated by Margaret Bloy Graham (HarperCollins); **Five Little Monkeys**, by Juliet Kepes (Houghton Mifflin)

1954

Madeline's Rescue
by Ludwig Bemelmans (Viking)

HONOR BOOKS: **Journey Cake, Ho!**, by Ruth Sawyer, illustrated by Robert McCloskey (Viking); **When Will the World Be Mine?**, by Miriam Schlein, illustrated by Jean Charlot (Scott); **The Steadfast Tin Soldier**, by Hans Christian Andersen, illustrated by Marcia Brown (Scribner's); **A Very Special House**, by Ruth Krauss, illustrated by Maurice Sendak (HarperCollins); **Green Eyes**, by A. Birnbaum (Capitol)

1955

Cinderella, or the Little Glass Slipper
by Charles Perrault, translated and illustrated by Marcia Brown (Scribner's)

HONOR BOOKS: **Books of Nursery and Mother Goose Rhymes**, illustrated by Marguerite de Angeli (Doubleday); **Wheel on the Chimney**, by Margaret Wise Brown, illustrated by Tibor Gergely (Lippincott); **The Thanksgiving Story**, by Alice Dalgliesh, illustrated by Helen Sewell (Scribner's)

1956

Frog Went A-Courtin', edited by John Langstaff, illustrated by Feodor Rojankovsky (Harcourt)

HONOR BOOKS: **Play with Me**, by Marie Hall Ets (Viking); **Crow Boy**, by Taro Tashima (Viking)

1957

A Tree Is Nice
by Janice May Udry, illustrated by Marc Simont (HarperCollins)

HONOR BOOKS: **Mr. Penny's Race Horse**, by Marie Hall Ets (Viking); **1 Is One**, by Tasha Tudor (Walck); **Anatole**, by Eve Titus, illustrated by Paul Galdone (McGraw-Hill); **Gillespie and the Guards**, by Benjamin Elkin, illustrated by James Daugherty (Viking); **Lion**, by William Pène du Bois (Viking)

1958

Time of Wonder
by Robert McCloskey (Viking)

HONOR BOOKS: *Fly High, Fly Low*, by Don Freeman (Viking); *Anatole and the Cat*, by Eve Titus, illustrated by Paul Galdone (McGraw-Hill)

1959

Chanticleer and the Fox
adapted from Chaucer, illustrated by Barbara Cooney (Crowell)

HONOR BOOKS: *The House that Jack Built*, by Antonio Frasconi (Harcourt); *What Do You Say, Dear?*, by Sesyle Joslin, illustrated by Maurice Sendak (Scott); *Umbrella*, by Taro Yashima (Viking)

1960

Nine Days to Christmas
by Marie Hall Ets and Aurora Labastida, illustrated by Marie Hall Ets (Viking)

HONOR BOOKS: *Houses from the Sea*, by Alice E. Goudey, illustrated by Adrienne Adams (Scribner's); *The Moon Jumpers*, by Janice May Udry, illustrated by Maurice Sendak (HarperCollins)

1961

Baboushka and the Three Kings
by Ruth Robbins, illustrated by Nicolas Sidjakov (Parnassus)

HONOR BOOK: *Inch by Inch* by Leo Lionni (Obolensky)

1962

Once a Mouse . . .
by Marcia Brown (Scribner's)

HONOR BOOKS: *The Fox Went Out on a Chilly Night*, by Peter Spier (Doubleday); *Little Bear's Visit*, by Else Holmelund Minarik, illustrated by Maurice Sendak (HarperCollins); *The Day We Saw the Sun Come Up*, by Alice E. Goudey, illustrated by Adrienne Adams (Scribner's)

1963

The Snowy Day
by Ezra Jack Keats (Viking)

HONOR BOOKS: *The Sun Is a Golden Earring*, by Natalie M. Belting, illustrated by Bernarda Bryson (Holt); *Mr. Rabbit and the Lovely Present*, by Charlotte Zolotow, illustrated by Maurice Sendak (HarperCollins)

1964

Where the Wild Things Are
by Maurice Sendak (HarperCollins)

HONOR BOOKS: *Swimmy*, by Leo Lionni (Pantheon); *All in the Morning Early*, by Sorche Nic Leodhas, illustrated by Evaline Ness (Holt); *Mother Goose and Nursery Rhymes*, illustrated by Philip Reed (Atheneum)

1965

May I Bring a Friend?
by Beatrice Schenk de Regniers, illustrated by Beni Montresor (Atheneum)

HONOR BOOKS: *Rain Makes Applesauce*, by Julian Scheer, illustrated by Marvin Bileck (Holiday); *The Wave*, by Margaret Hodges, illustrated by Blair Lent (Houghton); *A Pocketful of Cricket*, by Rebecca Caudill, illustrated by Evaline Ness (Holt)

1966

Always Room for One More
by Sorche Nic Leodhas, illustrated by Nonny Hogrogian (Holt)

HONOR BOOKS: *Hide and Seek Fog*, by Alvin Tresselt, illustrated by Roger Duvoisin (Lothrop); *Just Me*, by Marie Hall Ets (Viking); *Tom Tit Tot*, by Evaline Ness (Scribner's)

1967

Sam, Bangs and Moonshine
by Evaline Ness (Holt)

HONOR BOOK: *One Wide River to Cross*, by Barbara Emberley, illustrated by Ed Emberley (Prentice)

1968

Drummer Hoff
by Barbara Emberley, illustrated by Ed Emberley (Prentice)

HONOR BOOKS: *Frederick*, by Leo Lionni (Pantheon); *Seashore Story*, by Taro Yashima (Viking); *The Emperor and the Kite*, by Jane Yolen, illustrated by Ed Young (World)

1969

The Fool of the World and the Flying Ship
by Arthur Ransome, illustrated by Uri Shulevitz (Farrar, Straus and Giroux)

HONOR BOOK: *Why the Sun and the Moon Live in the Sky*, by Elphinstone Dayrell, illustrated by Blair Lent (Houghton)

1970

Sylvester and the Magic Pebble
by William Steig (Windmill)

HONOR BOOKS: ***Goggles!***, by Ezra Jack Keats (Macmillan); ***Alexander and the Wind-Up Mouse***, by Leo Lionni (Pantheon); ***Pop Corn and Ma Goodness***, by Edna Mitchell Preston, illustrated by Robert Andrew Parker (Viking); ***Thy Friend, Obadiah***, by Brinton Turkle (Viking); ***The Judge***, by Harve Zemach, illustrated by Margot Zemach (Farrar, Straus and Giroux)

1971

A Story, a Story
by Gail E. Haley (Atheneum)

HONOR BOOKS: ***The Angry Moon***, by William Sleator, illustrated by Blair Lent (Atlantic/Little); ***Frog and Toad Are Friends***, by Arnold Lobel (HarperCollins); ***In the Night Kitchen***, by Maurice Sendak (HarperCollins)

1972

One Fine Day
by Nonny Hogrogian (Macmillan)

HONOR BOOKS: ***If All the Seas Were One Sea***, by Janina Domanska (Macmillan); ***Moja Means One: Swahili Counting Book***, by Muriel Feelings, illustrated by Tom Feelings (Dial); ***Hildilid's Night***, by Cheli Durán Ryan, illustrated by Arnold Lobel (Macmillan)

1973

The Funny Little Woman
retold by Arlene Mosel, illustrated by Blair Lent (Dutton)

HONOR BOOKS: ***Anansi the Spider***, adapted and illustrated by Gerald McDermott (Holt); ***Hosie's Alphabet***, by Hosea, Tobias, and Lisa Baskin, illustrated by Leonard Baskin (Viking); ***Snow-White and the Seven Dwarfs***, translated by Randall Jarrell, illustrated by Nancy Ekholm Burkert (Farrar, Straus and Giroux); ***When Clay Sings***, by Byrd Baylor, illustrated by Tom Bahti (Scribner's)

1974

Duffy and the Devil
by Harve Zemach, illustrated by Margot Zemach (Farrar, Straus and Giroux)

HONOR BOOKS: ***Three Jovial Huntsmen***, by Susan Jeffers (Bradbury); ***Cathedral: The Story of Its Construction***, by David Macaulay (Houghton)

1975

Arrow to the Sun
adapted and illustrated by Gerald McDermott (Viking)

HONOR BOOK: ***Jambo Means Hello*** by Muriel Feelings, illustrated by Tom Feelings (Dial)

1976

Why Mosquitoes Buzz in People's Ears
retold by Verna Aardema, illustrated by Leo and Diane Dillon (Dial)

HONOR BOOKS: ***The Desert Is Theirs***, by Byrd Baylor, illustrated by Peter Parnall (Scribner's); ***Strega Nona***, retold and illustrated by Tomie dePaola (Prentice Hall)

1977

Ashanti to Zulu: African Traditions
by Margaret Musgrove, illustrated by Leo and Diane Dillon (Dial)

HONOR BOOKS: ***The Amazing Bone***, by William Steig (Farrar, Straus and Giroux); ***The Contest***, retold and illustrated by Nonny Hogrogian (Greenwillow); ***Fish for Supper***, by M. B. Goffstein (Dial); ***The Golem***, by Beverly Brodsky McDermott (Lippincott); ***Hawk, I'm Your Brother***, by Byrd Baylor, illustrated by Peter Parnall (Scribner's)

1978

Noah's Ark
illustrated by Peter Spier (Doubleday)

HONOR BOOKS: ***Castle***, by David Macaulay (Houghton Mifflin); ***It Could Always Be Worse***, retold and illustrated by Margot Zemach (Farrar, Straus and Giroux)

1979

The Girl Who Loved Wild Horses
by Paul Goble (Bradbury)

HONOR BOOKS: ***Freight Train***, by Donald Crews (Greenwillow); ***The Way to Start a Day***, by Byrd Baylor, illustrated by Peter Parnall (Scribner's)

1980

Ox-Cart Man
by Donald Hall, illustrated by Barbara Cooney (Viking)

HONOR BOOKS: ***Ben's Trumpet***, by Rachel Isadora (Greenwillow); ***The Garden of Abdul Gasazi***, by Chris Van Allsburg (Houghton Mifflin)

1981

Fables
by Arnold Lobel (HarperCollins)

HONOR BOOKS: **The Bremen-Town Musicians**, by Ilse Plume (Doubleday); **The Grey Lady and the Strawberry Snatcher**, by Molly Bang (Four Winds); **Mice Twice**, by Joseph Low (McElderry); **Truck**, by Donald Crews (Greenwillow)

1982

Jumanji
by Chris Van Allsburg (Houghton Mifflin)

HONOR BOOKS: **Where the Buffaloes Begin**, by Olaf Baker, illustrated by Stephen Gammell (Warne); **On Market Street**, by Arnold Lobel, illustrated by Anita Lobel (Greenwillow); **Outside over There**, by Maurice Sendak (HarperCollins); **A Visit to William Blake's Inn**, by Nancy Willard, illustrated by Alice and Martin Provensen (Harcourt)

1983

Shadow
by Blaise Cendrars, translated and illustrated by Marcia Brown (Scribner's)

HONOR BOOKS: **When I Was Young in the Mountains**, by Cynthia Rylant, illustrated by Diane Goode (Dutton); **A Chair for My Mother**, by Vera B. Williams (Greenwillow)

1984

The Glorious Flight: Across the Channel with Louis Blériot
by Alice and Martin Provensen (Viking)

HONOR BOOKS: **Ten, Nine, Eight**, by Molly Bang (Greenwillow); **Little Red Riding Hood**, retold and illustrated by Trina Schart Hyman (Holiday House)

1985

St. George and the Dragon
retold by Margaret Hodges, illustrated by Trina Schart Hyman (Little, Brown)

HONOR BOOKS: **Hansel and Gretel**, retold by Rika Lesser, illustrated by Paul O. Zelinsky (Dodd, Mead); **Have You Seen My Duckling?**, by Nancy Tafuri (Greenwillow); **The Story of Jumping Mouse**, by John Steptoe (Lothrop, Lee & Shepard)

1986

The Polar Express
by Chris Van Allsburg (Houghton Mifflin)

HONOR BOOKS: **The Relatives Came**, by Cynthia Rylant, illustrated by Stephen Gammell (Bradbury); **King Bidgood's in the Bathtub**, by Audrey Wood, illustrated by Don Wood (Harcourt)

1987

Hey, Al
by Arthur Yorinks, illustrated by Richard Egielski (Farrar, Straus and Giroux)

HONOR BOOKS: **The Village of Round and Square Houses**, by Ann Grifalconi (Little, Brown); **Alphabetics**, by Suse MacDonald (Bradbury); **Rumpelstiltskin**, adapted and illustrated by Paul O. Zelinsky (Dutton)

1988

Owl Moon
by Jane Yolen, illustrated by John Schoenherr (Philomel)

HONOR BOOK: **Mufaro's Beautiful Daughters: An African Tale**, adapted and illustrated by John Steptoe (Lothrop, Lee & Shepard)

1989

Song and Dance Man
by Karen Ackerman, illustrated by Stephen Gammell (Knopf)

HONOR BOOKS: **The Boy of the Three Year Nap**, by Allen Say (Houghton Mifflin); **Free Fall**, by David Wiesner (Lothrop, Lee & Shepard); **Goldilocks and the Three Bears**, adapted and illustrated by James Marshall (Dial); **Mirandy and Brother Wind**, by Patricia McKissack, illustrated by Jerry Pinkney (Knopf)

1990

Lon Po Po: A Red Riding-Hood Story from China
adapted and illustrated by Ed Young (Philomel)

HONOR BOOKS: **Bill Peet: An Autobiography**, by Bill Peet (Houghton Mifflin); **Color Zoo**, by Lois Ehlert (Lippincott); **Hershel and the Hanukkah Goblins**, by Eric Kimmel, illustrated by Trina Schart Hyman (Holiday House); **The Talking Eggs**, by Robert D. San Souci, illustrated by Jerry Pinkney (Dial)

1991

Black and White
by David Macaulay (Houghton Mifflin)

HONOR BOOKS: **"More More More," Said the Baby: 3 Love Stories**, by Vera B. Williams (Greenwillow); **Puss in Boots**, by Charles Perrault, translated by Malcolm Arthur, illustrated by Fred Marcellino (Farrar, Straus and Giroux)

1992

Tuesday
by David Wiesner (Clarion)

HONOR BOOK: **Tar Beach**
by Faith Ringgold (Crown)

1993

Mirette on the High Wire
by Emily Arnold McCully (Putnam)

HONOR BOOKS: **The Stinky Cheese Man and Other Fairly Stupid Tales** by Jon Scieszka and Lane Smith, illustrated by Lane Smith; (Viking); **Working Cotton**, by Sherley Anne Williams, illustrated by Carole Byard (Harcourt); **Seven Blind Mice**, by Ed Young (Philomel)

1994

Grandfather's Journey
by Allen Say (Houghton Mifflin)

HONOR BOOKS: **In the Small, Small Pond**, by Denise Fleming (Holt); **Owen**, by Kevin Henkes (Greenwillow); **Peppe the Lamplighter**, by Elisa Bartone, illustrated by Ted Lewin (Lothrop, Lee & Shepard); **Raven: A Trickster Tale from the Pacific Northwest**, by Gerald McDermott (Harcourt); **Yo! Yes?**, by Chris Raschka (Orchard)

1995

Smoky Night
by Eve Bunting, illustrated by David Diaz (Harcourt)

HONOR BOOKS: **John Henry**, by Julius Lester, illustrated by Jerry Pinkney (Dial); **Swamp Angel**, by Anne Isaacs, illustrated by Paul O. Zelinsky (Dutton); **Time Flies**, by Eric Rohmann (Crown)

1996

Officer Buckle and Gloria
by Peggy Rathmann (Putnam)

HONOR BOOKS: **Alphabet City**, by Stephen Johnson (Viking); **The Faithful Friend**, by Robert D. San Souci, illustrated by Brian Pinkney (Simon & Schuster); **Tops and Bottoms**, by Janet Stevens (Harcourt); **Zin! Zin! Zin! A Violin**, by Lloyd Moss, illustrated by Marjorie Priceman (Simon & Schuster)

1997

Golem
by David Wisniewski (Clarion)

HONOR BOOKS: **Hush! A Thai Lullaby**, by Minfong Ho, illustrated by Holly Meade (Orchard); **The Graphic Alphabet**, by David Pelletier (Orchard); **The Paperboy**, by Dav Pilkey (Orchard); **Starry Messenger**, by Peter Sís (Farrar, Straus and Giroux)

1998

Rapunzel
by Paul O. Zelinsky (Dutton)

HONOR BOOKS: **Harlem**, by Walter Dean Myers, illustrated by Christopher Myers (Scholastic); **The Gardener**, by Sarah Stewart, illustrated by David Small (Farrar, Straus and Giroux); **There Was an Old Lady Who Swallowed a Fly**, by Simms Taback (Viking)

1999

Snowflake Bentley
by Jacqueline Briggs Martin, illustrated by Mary Azarian (Houghton Mifflin)

HONOR BOOKS: **Duke Ellington**, by Andrea Davis Pinkney, illustrated by Brian Pinkney (Hyperion); **No, David!**, by David Shannon (Blue Sky); **Snow**, by Uri Shulevitz (Farrar, Straus and Giroux); **Tibet: Through the Red Box**, by Peter Sís (Farrar, Straus and Giroux)

2000

Joseph Had a Little Overcoat
by Simms Taback (Viking)

HONOR BOOKS: **The Ugly Duckling**, by Hans Christian Andersen, illustrated by Jerry Pinkney (Morrow); **A Child's Calendar**, by John Updike, illustrated by Trina Schart Hyman (Holiday House); **Sector 7**, by David Wiesner (Clarion); **When Sophie Gets Angry—Really, Really Angry…**, by Molly Bang (Blue Sky)

2001

So You Want to Be President?
by Judith St. George, illustrated by David Small (Philomel)

HONOR BOOKS: **Casey at the Bat: A Ballad of the Republic Sung in the Year 1888**, by Ernest

Lawrence Thayer, illustrated by Christopher Bing (Handprint); *Click, Clack, Moo: Cows that Type*, by Doreen Cronin, illustrated by Betsy Lewin (Simon & Schuster); *Olivia*, by Ian Falconer (Simon & Schuster)

2002

The Three Pigs
by David Wiesner (Clarion)

HONOR BOOKS: *The Dinosaurs of Waterhouse Hawkins*, by Barbara Kerley, illustrated by Brian Selznick (Scholastic); *Martin's Big Words: The Life of Dr. Martin Luther King, Jr.*, by Doreen Rappaport, illustrated by Bryan Collier (Hyperion); *The Stray Dog*, by Marc Simont (HarperCollins)

2003

My Friend Rabbit
by Eric Rohmann (Roaring Brook)

HONOR BOOKS: *The Spider and the Fly*, by Mary Howitt, illustrated by Tony DiTerlizzi (Simon & Schuster); *Hondo & Fabian*, by Peter McCarty (Holt); *Noah's Ark*, by Jerry Pinkney (SeaStar)

2004

The Man Who Walked between the Towers
by Mordicai Gerstein (Roaring Brook)

HONOR BOOKS: *Ella Sarah Gets Dressed*, by Margaret Chodos-Irvine (Harcourt); *What Do You Do with a Tail Like This?*, by Steve Jenkins and Robin Page (Houghton Mifflin); *Don't Let the Pigeon Drive the Bus!*, by Mo Willems (Hyperion)

2005

Kitten's First Full Moon
by Kevin Henkes (Greenwillow)

HONOR BOOKS: *The Red Book*, by Barbara Lehman (Houghton Mifflin); *Coming on Home Soon*, by Jacqueline Woodson, illustrated by E. B. Lewis (Putnam); *Knuffle Bunny: A Cautionary Tale*, by Mo Willems (Hyperion)

2006

The Hello, Goodbye Window
by Norton Juster, illustrated by Chris Raschka (Hyperion)

HONOR BOOKS: *Rosa*, by Nikki Giovanni, illustrated by Bryan Collier (Holt); *Zen Shorts*, by Jon J. Muth (Scholastic); *Hot Air: The (Mostly) True Story of the First Hot-Air Balloon Ride*, by Marjorie

Priceman (Simon & Schuster); *Song of the Water Boatman and Other Pond Poems*, by Joyce Sidman, illustrated by Beckie Prange (Houghton Mifflin)

2007

Flotsam
by David Wiesner (Clarion)

HONOR BOOKS: *Gone Wild: An Endangered Animal Alphabet*, by David McLimans (Walker); *Moses: When Harriet Tubman Led Her People to Freedom*, by Carole Boston Weatherford, illustrated by Kadir Nelson (Hyperion)

2008

The Invention of Hugo Cabret
by Brian Selznick (Scholastic)

HONOR BOOKS: *Henry's Freedom Box: A True Story from the Underground Railroad*, by Ellen Levine, illustrated by Kadir Nelson (Scholastic); *First the Egg*, by Laura Vaccaro Seeger (Roaring Brook); *The Wall: Growing Up behind the Iron Curtain*, by Peter Sís (Farrar, Straus and Giroux); *Knuffle Bunny Too: A Case of Mistaken Identity*, by Mo Willems (Hyperion)

2009

The House in the Night
by Susan Marie Swanson, illustrated by Beth Krommes (Houghton Mifflin)

HONOR BOOKS: *A Couple of Boys Have the Best Week Ever*, by Marla Frazee (Harcourt); *How I Learned Geography*, by Uri Shulevitz (Farrar, Straus and Giroux); *A River of Words: The Story of William Carlos Williams*, by Jen Bryant, illustrated by Melissa Sweet (Eerdmans)

2010

The Lion & the Mouse
by Jerry Pinkney (Little, Brown)

HONOR BOOKS: *All the World*, by Liz Garton Scanlon, illustrated by Marla Frazee (Beach Lane); *Red Sings from Treetops: A Year in Colors*, by Joyce Sidman, illustrated by Pamela Zagarenski (Houghton Mifflin)

2011

A Sick Day for Amos McGee
by Philip C. Stead, illustrated by Erin E. Stead (Roaring Brook)

HONOR BOOKS: *Dave the Potter: Artist, Poet, Slave*, by Laban Carrick Hill, illustrated by Bryan Collier (Little, Brown); *Interrupting Chicken*, by David Ezra Stein (Candlewick)

2012

A Ball for Daisy
by Chris Raschka (Schwartz & Wade)

HONOR BOOKS: *Blackout*, by John Rocco (Hyperion); *Grandpa Green*, by Lane Smith (Roaring Brook); *Me . . . Jane*, by Patrick McDonnell (Little, Brown)

• • • CORETTA SCOTT KING • • • AWARD AND HONOR BOOKS

These awards, administered by the Social Responsibilities Round Table and the American Library Association, recognize an outstanding African American Author and Illustrator whose work commemorates and fosters the life, work, and dreams of Dr. Martin Luther King Jr., as well as honoring the courage and determination of Coretta Scott King to continue to work for peace and world brotherhood. Prior to 1974, the Coretta Scott King Award was given to AUTHORS only.

1970

AUTHOR AWARD: *Martin Luther King, Jr.: Man of Peace*
by Lillie Patterson (Garrand)

1971

AUTHOR AWARD: *Black Troubador: Langston Hughes*
by Charlemae Rollins (Rand McNally)

1972

AUTHOR AWARD: *17 Black Artists*
by Elton C. Fax (Dodd, Mead)

1973

AUTHOR AWARD: *I Never Had It Made*
by Jackie Robinson as told to Alfred Duckett (Putnam)

1974

AUTHOR AND ILLUSTRATOR AWARDS: *Ray Charles*
by Sharon Bell Mathis, illustrated by George Ford (Crowell)

1975

AUTHOR AWARD: *The Legend of Africania*
by Dorothy Robinson (Johnson)

ILLUSTRATOR AWARD: No award given

1976

AUTHOR AWARD: *Duey's Tale*
by Pearl Bailey (Harcourt)

ILLUSTRATOR AWARD: No award given

1977

AUTHOR AWARD: *The Story of Stevie Wonder*
by James Haskins (Lothrop, Lee & Shepard)

ILLUSTRATOR AWARD: No award given

1978

AUTHOR AWARD: *Africa Dream*
by Eloise Greenfield (Crowell)

AUTHOR HONOR BOOKS: *The Days When the Animals Talked: Black Folk Tales and How They Came to Be*, by William J. Faulkner (Follett); *Marvin and Tige*, by Frankcina Glass (St. Martin's Press); *Mary McCleod Bethune*, by Eloise Greenfield (Crowell); *Barbara Jordan*, by James Haskins (Dial); *Coretta Scott King*, by Lillie Patterson (Garrard); *Portia: The Life of Portia Washington Pittman, the Daughter of Booker T. Washington*, by Ruth Ann Steward (Doubleday)

ILLUSTRATOR AWARD: *Africa Dream*, illustrated by Carole Byard, text by Eloise Greenfield (Crowell)

1979

AUTHOR AWARD: *Escape to Freedom*
by Ossie Davis (Viking)

AUTHOR HONOR BOOKS: *Benjamin Banneker*, by Lillie Patterson (Abingdon); *I Have a Sister—My Sister Is Deaf*, by Jeanne Whitehouse Peterson (HarperCollins); *Justice and Her Brothers*, by Virginia Hamilton (Greenwillow); *Skates of Uncle Richard*, by Carol Fenner (Random House)

ILLUSTRATOR AWARD: *Something on My Mind*, illustrated by Tom Feelings, text by Nikki Grimes (Dial)

1980

AUTHOR AWARD: *The Young Landlords*
by Walter Dean Myers (Viking)

AUTHOR HONOR BOOKS: *Movin' Up*, by Berry Gordy (HarperCollins); *Childtimes: A Three-Generation Memoir*, by Eloise Greenfield and Lessie Jones

Little (HarperCollins); ***Andrew Young: Young Man with a Mission***, by James Haskins (Lothrop, Lee & Shepard); ***James Van Der Zee: The Picture Takin' Man***, by James Haskins (Africa World Press); ***Let the Lion Eat Straw***, by Ellease Southerland (Scribner's)

ILLUSTRATOR AWARD: ***Cornrows***, illustrated by Carole Byard, text by Camille Yarbrough (Coward-McCann)

1981

AUTHOR AWARD: ***This Life***
by Sidney Poitier (Knopf)

AUTHOR HONOR BOOK: ***Don't Explain: A Song of Billie Holiday***
by Alexis De Veaux (HarperCollins)

ILLUSTRATOR AWARD: ***Beat the Story Drum Pum-Pum***
by Ashley Bryan (Simon & Schuster)

ILLUSTRATOR HONOR BOOKS: ***Grandmama's Joy***, illustrated by Carole Byard, text by Eloise Greenfield (Collins); ***Count on Your Fingers African Style***, illustrated by Jerry Pinkney, text by Claudia Zaslavsky (Crowell)

1982

AUTHOR AWARD: ***Let the Circle Be Unbroken***
by Mildred Taylor (Dial)

AUTHOR HONOR BOOKS: ***Rainbow Jordan***, by Alice Childress (Coward-McCann); ***Lou in the Limelight***, by Kristin Hunter (Scribner's); ***Mary: An Autobiography***, by Mary E. Mebane (Viking)

ILLUSTRATOR AWARD: ***Mother Crocodile***
by John Steptoe (Delacorte)

ILLUSTRATOR HONOR BOOK: ***Daydreamers***, illustrated by Tom Feelings, text by Eloise Greenfield (Dial)

1983

AUTHOR AWARD: ***Sweet Whispers, Brother Rush***
by Virginia Hamilton (Philomel)

AUTHOR HONOR BOOK: ***This Strange New Feeling***
by Julius Lester (Dial)

ILLUSTRATOR AWARD: ***Black Child***
by Peter Magubane (Knopf)

ILLUSTRATOR HONOR BOOKS: ***All the Colors of the Race***, illustrated by John Steptoe, text by Arnold Adoff (Lothrop, Lee & Shepard); ***I'm Going to Sing: Black American Spirituals***, illustrated by Ashley Bryan (Simon & Schuster); ***Just Us Women***, illustrated by Pat Cummings, text by Jeanette Caines (HarperCollins)

1984

AUTHOR AWARD: ***Everett Anderson's Goodbye***
by Lucille Clifton (Holt)

SPECIAL CITATION: ***The Words of Martin Luther King, Jr.***, compiled by Coretta Scott King (Newmarket)

AUTHOR HONOR BOOKS: ***The Magical Adventures of Pretty Pearl***, by Virginia Hamilton (HarperCollins); ***Lena Horne***, by James Haskins (Coward-McCann); ***Bright Shadow***, by Joyce Carol Thomas (Avon); ***Because We Are***, by Mildred Pitts Walter (Lothrop, Lee & Shepard)

ILLUSTRATOR AWARD: ***My Mama Needs Me***, illustrated by Pat Cummings, text by Mildred Pitts Walter (Lothrop, Lee & Shepard)

1985

AUTHOR AWARD: ***Motown and Didi***
by Walter Dean Myers (Viking)

HONOR BOOKS: ***Circle of Gold***, by Candy Dawson Boyd (Apple); ***A Little Love***, by Virginia Hamilton (Philomel)

ILLUSTRATOR AWARD: No award given

1986

AUTHOR AWARD: ***The People Could Fly: American Black Folktales***
by Virginia Hamilton (Knopf)

AUTHOR HONOR BOOKS: ***Junius over Far***, by Virginia Hamilton (HarperCollins); ***Trouble's Child***, by Mildred Pitts Walter (Lothrop, Lee & Shepard)

ILLUSTRATOR AWARD: ***The Patchwork Quilt***, illustrated by Jerry Pinkney, text by Valerie Flournoy (Dial)

ILLUSTRATOR HONOR BOOK: ***The People Could Fly: American Black Folktales***, illustrated by Leo and Diane Dillon, text by Virginia Hamilton (Knopf)

1987

AUTHOR AWARD: ***Justin and the Best Biscuits in the World***
by Mildred Pitts Walter (Lothrop, Lee & Shepard)

AUTHOR HONOR BOOKS: ***Lion and the Ostrich Chicks and Other African Folk Tales***, by Ashley Bryan (Simon & Schuster); ***Which Way Freedom***, by Joyce Hansen (Walker)

ILLUSTRATOR AWARD: ***Half a Moon and One Whole Star***, illustrated by Jerry Pinkney, text by Crescent Dragonwagon (Macmillan)

ILLUSTRATOR HONOR BOOKS: *Lion and the Ostrich Chicks and Other African Folk Tales*, by Ashley Bryan (Simon & Schuster); *C.L.O.U.D.S.*, by Pat Cummings (Lothrop, Lee & Shepard)

1988

AUTHOR AWARD: *The Friendship*
by Mildred Taylor (Dial)

AUTHOR HONOR BOOKS: *An Enchanted Hair Tale*, by Alexis De Veaux (HarperCollins); *The Tales of Uncle Remus: The Adventures of Brer Rabbit*, by Julius Lester (Dial)

ILLUSTRATOR AWARD: *Mufaro's Beautiful Daughters: An African Tale*
by John Steptoe (Lothrop, Lee & Shepard)

ILLUSTRATOR HONOR BOOKS: *What a Morning! The Christmas Story in Black Spirituals*, illustrated by Ashley Bryan, selected by John Langstaff (Macmillan); *The Invisible Hunters: A Legend from the Miskito Indians of Nicaragua*, illustrated by Joe Sam, compiled by Harriet Rohmer, Octavio Chow, and Morris Vedaure (Children's Book Press)

1989

AUTHOR AWARD: *Fallen Angels*
by Walter Dean Myers (Scholastic)

AUTHOR HONOR BOOKS: *A Thief in the Village and Other Stories*, by James Berry (Orchard); *Anthony Burns: The Defeat and Triumph of a Fugitive Slave*, by Virginia Hamilton (Knopf)

ILLUSTRATOR AWARD: *Mirandy and Brother Wind*, illustrated by Jerry Pinkney, text by Patricia McKissack (Knopf)

ILLUSTRATOR HONOR BOOKS: *Under the Sunday Tree*, illustrated by Amos Ferguson, text by Eloise Greenfield (HarperCollins); *Storm in the Night*, illustrated by Pat Cummings, text by Mary Stolz (HarperCollins)

1990

AUTHOR AWARD: *A Long Hard Journey: The Story of the Pullman Porter*
by Patricia and Frederick McKissack (Walker)

AUTHOR HONOR BOOKS: *Nathaniel Talking*, by Eloise Greenfield, illustrated by Jan Spivey Gilchrist (Black Butterfly); *The Bells of Christmas*, by Virginia Hamilton (Harcourt); *Martin Luther King, Jr., and the Freedom Movement*, by Lillie Patterson (Facts on File)

ILLUSTRATOR AWARD: *Nathaniel Talking*, illustrated by Jan Gilchrist, text by Eloise Greenfield (Black Butterfly)

ILLUSTRATOR HONOR BOOKS: *The Talking Eggs*, illustrated by Jerry Pinkney, text by Robert D. San Souci (Dial)

1991

AUTHOR AWARD: *The Road to Memphis*
by Mildred Taylor (Dial)

AUTHOR HONOR BOOKS: *Black Dance in America*, by James Haskins (Crowell); *When I Am Old with You*, by Angela Johnson (Orchard)

ILLUSTRATOR AWARD: *Aida*, illustrated by Leo and Diane Dillon, told by Leontyne Price (Harcourt)

1992

AUTHOR AWARD: *Now Is Your Time! The African American Struggle for Freedom*
by Walter Dean Myers (HarperCollins)

AUTHOR HONOR BOOKS: *Night on Neighborhood Street*, by Eloise Greenfield, illustrated by Jan Spivey Gilchrist (Dial)

ILLUSTRATOR AWARD: *Tar Beach*
by Faith Ringgold (Crown)

ILLUSTRATOR HONOR BOOKS: *All Night, All Day: A Child's First Book of African American Spirituals*, by Ashley Bryan (Simon & Schuster); *Night on Neighborhood Street*, illustrated by Jan Spivey Gilchrist, text by Eloise Greenfield (Dial)

1993

AUTHOR AWARD: *The Dark Thirty: Southern Tales of the Supernatural*
by Patricia McKissack (Knopf)

AUTHOR HONOR BOOKS: *Mississippi Challenge*, by Mildred Pitts Walter (Bradbury); *Sojourner Truth: Ain't I a Woman?*, by Patricia and Frederick McKissack (Scholastic); *Somewhere in the Darkness*, by Walter Dean Myers (Scholastic)

ILLUSTRATOR AWARD: *The Origin of Life on Earth: An African Creation Myth*, illustrated by Kathleen Atkins Wilson, retold by David Anderson (Sights Productions)

ILLUSTRATOR HONOR BOOKS: *Little Eight John*, illustrated by Wil Clay, text by Jan Wahl (Lodestar); *Sukey and the Mermaid*, illustrated by Brian Pinkney, text by Robert D. San Souci (Four Winds); *Working Cotton*, illustrated by Carole Byard, text by Sherley Anne Williams (Harcourt)

1994

AUTHOR AWARD: **Toning the Sweep**
by Angela Johnson (Orchard)

AUTHOR HONOR BOOKS: **Brown Honey in Broomwheat Tea**, by Joyce Carol Thomas, illustrated by Floyd Cooper (HarperCollins); **Malcolm X: By Any Means Necessary**, by Walter Dean Myers (Scholastic); **Soul Looks Back in Wonder**, edited by Phyllis Fogelman, illustrated by Tom Feelings (Dial)

ILLUSTRATOR AWARD: **Soul Looks Back in Wonder**, illustrated by Tom Feelings, edited by Phyllis Fogelman (Dial)

ILLUSTRATOR HONOR BOOKS: **Brown Honey in Broomwheat Tea**, illustrated by Floyd Cooper, by Joyce Carol Thomas (HarperCollins); **Uncle Jed's Barbershop**, illustrated by James Ransome, text by Margaree King Mitchell (Simon & Schuster)

1995

AUTHOR AWARD: **Christmas in the Big House, Christmas in the Quarters**
by Patricia and Frederick McKissack (Scholastic)

AUTHOR HONOR BOOKS: **The Captive**, by Joyce Hansen (Scholastic); **I Hadn't Meant to Tell You This**, by Jacqueline Woodson (Delacorte); **Black Diamond: Story of the Negro Baseball League**, by Patricia and Frederick McKissack (Scholastic)

ILLUSTRATOR AWARD: **The Creation**, illustrated by James Ransome, text by James Weldon Johnson (Holiday House)

ILLUSTRATOR HONOR BOOKS: **The Singing Man**, illustrated by Terea D. Shaffer, text by Angela Shelf Medearis (Holiday House); **Meet Danitra Brown**, illustrated by Floyd Cooper, text by Nikki Grimes (Lothrop, Lee & Shepard)

1996

AUTHOR AWARD: **Her Stories: African American Folktales, Fairy Tales, and True Tales**
by Virginia Hamilton, illustrated by Leo and Diane Dillon (Blue Sky)

AUTHOR HONOR BOOKS: **The Watsons Go to Birmingham—1963**, by Christopher Paul Curtis (Delacorte); **Like Sisters on the Homefront**, by Rita Williams-Garcia (Delacorte); **From the Notebooks of Melanin Sun**, by Jacqueline Woodson (Scholastic)

ILLUSTRATOR AWARD: **The Middle Passage: White Ships/Black Cargo**
by Tom Feelings (Dial)

ILLUSTRATOR HONOR BOOKS: **Her Stories**, illustrated by Leo and Diane Dillon, text by Virginia Hamilton (Blue Sky); **The Faithful Friend**, illustrated by Brian Pinkney, text by Robert D. San Souci (Simon & Schuster)

1997

AUTHOR AWARD: **Slam**
by Walter Dean Myers (Scholastic)

AUTHOR HONOR BOOKS: **Rebels against Slavery: American Slave Revolts**, by Patricia and Frederick McKissack (Scholastic)

ILLUSTRATOR AWARD: **Minty: A Story of Harriet Tubman**, illustrated by Jerry Pinkney, text by Alan Schroeder (Dial)

ILLUSTRATOR HONOR BOOKS: **The Palm of My Heart: Poetry by African American Children**, illustrated by Gregorie Christie, edited by Davida Adedjouma (Lee & Low); **Running the Road to ABC**, illustrated by Reynold Ruffins, text by Denize Lauture (Simon & Schuster); **Neeny Coming, Neeny Going**, illustrated by Synthia Saint James, text by Karen English (Bridgewater Books)

1998

AUTHOR AWARD: **Forged by Fire**
by Sharon M. Draper (Simon & Schuster)

AUTHOR HONOR BOOKS: **Bayard Rustin: Behind the Scenes of the Civil Rights Movement**, by James Haskins (Hyperion); **I Thought My Soul Would Rise and Fly: The Diary of Patsy, a Freed Girl**, by Joyce Hansen (Scholastic)

ILLUSTRATOR AWARD: **In Daddy's Arms I Am Tall: African Americans Celebrating Fathers**, illustrated by Javaka Steptoe, text by Alan Schroeder (Lee & Low)

ILLUSTRATOR HONOR BOOKS: **Ashley Bryan's ABC of African American Poetry**, by Ashley Bryan (Simon & Schuster); **Harlem**, illustrated by Christopher Myers, text by Walter Dean Myers (Scholastic); **The Hunterman and the Crocodile**, by Baba Wagué Diakité (Scholastic)

1999

AUTHOR AWARD: **Heaven**
by Angela Johnson (Simon & Schuster)

AUTHOR HONOR BOOKS: **Jazmin's Notebook**, by Nikki Grimes (Dial); **Breaking Ground, Breaking Silence: The Story of New York's African Burial Ground**, by Joyce Hansen and Gary McGowan (Holt); **The Other Side: Shorter Poems**, by Angela Johnson (Orchard)

ILLUSTRATOR AWARD: *I See the Rhythm*, illustrated by Michele Wood, text by Toyomi Igus (Children's Book Press)

ILLUSTRATOR HONOR BOOKS: *I Have Heard of a Land*, illustrated by Floyd Cooper, text by Joyce Carol Thomas (HarperCollins); *The Bat Boy and His Violin*, illustrated by E. B. Lewis, text by Gavin Curtis (Simon & Schuster); *Duke Ellington: The Piano Prince and His Orchestra*, illustrated by Brian Pinkney, text by Andrea Davis Pinkney (Hyperion)

2000

AUTHOR AWARD: *Bud, Not Buddy* by Christopher Paul Curtis (Delacorte)

AUTHOR HONOR BOOKS: *Francie*, by Karen English (Farrar, Straus and Giroux); *Black Hands, White Sails: The Story of African-American Whalers*, by Patricia and Frederick McKissack (Scholastic); *Monster*, by Walter Dean Myers (HarperCollins)

ILLUSTRATOR AWARD: *In the Time of the Drums*, illustrated by Brian Pinkney, text by Kim L. Siegelson (Hyperion)

ILLUSTRATOR HONOR BOOKS: *My Rows and Piles of Coins*, illustrated by E. B. Lewis, text by Tololwa M. Mollel (Clarion); *Black Cat*, by Christopher Myers (Scholastic)

2001

AUTHOR AWARD: *Miracle's Boys* by Jacqueline Woodson (Putnam)

AUTHOR HONOR BOOKS: *Let It Shine! Stories of Black Women Freedom Fighters*, by Andrea Davis Pinkney, illustrated by Stephen Alcorn (Harcourt)

ILLUSTRATOR AWARD: *Uptown* by Bryan Collier (Holt)

ILLUSTRATOR HONOR BOOKS: *Freedom River*, by Bryan Collier (Hyperion); *Only Passing Through: The Story of Sojourner Truth*, illustrated by R. Gregory Christie, written by Anne Rockwell (Random House); *Virgie Goes to School with Us Boys*, illustrated by E. B. Lewis, written by Elizabeth Fitzgerald Howard (Simon & Schuster)

2002

AUTHOR AWARD: *The Land* by Mildred Taylor (Fogelman)

AUTHOR HONOR BOOKS: *Money-Hungry*, by Sharon G. Flake (Hyperion); *Carver: A Life in Poems*, by Marilyn Nelson (Front Street)

ILLUSTRATOR AWARD: *Goin' Someplace Special*, illustrated by Jerry Pinkney, written by Patricia McKissack (Simon & Schuster)

ILLUSTRATOR HONOR BOOKS: *Martin's Big Words*, illustrated by Bryan Collier, written by Doreen Rappoport (Hyperion)

2003

AUTHOR AWARD: *Bronx Masquerade* by Nikki Grimes (Dial)

AUTHOR HONOR BOOKS: *The Red Rose Box*, by Brenda Woods (Putnam); *Talkin' about Bessie: The Story of Aviator Elizabeth Coleman*, by Nikki Grimes (Orchard)

ILLUSTRATOR AWARD: *Talkin' about Bessie: The Story of Aviator Elizabeth Coleman*, illustrated by E. B. Lewis, written by Nikki Grimes (Orchard)

ILLUSTRATOR HONOR BOOKS: *Rap a Tap Tap: Here's Bojangles—Think of That*, illustrated by Leo and Diane Dillon (Blue Sky); *Visiting Langston*, illustrated by Bryan Collier (Holt)

2004

AUTHOR AWARD: *The First Part Last* by Angela Johnson (Simon & Schuster)

AUTHOR HONOR BOOKS: *Days of Jubilee: The End of Slavery in the United States*, by Patricia and Frederick McKissack (Scholastic); *Locomotion*, by Jacqueline Woodson (Putnam); *The Battle of Jericho*, by Sharon M. Draper (Simon & Schuster)

ILLUSTRATOR AWARD: *Beautiful Blackbird* by Ashley Bryan (Simon & Schuster)

ILLUSTRATOR HONOR BOOKS: *Almost to Freedom*, illustrated by Colin Bootman, written by Vaunda Micheaux Nelson (Carolrhoda); *Thunder Rose*, illustrated by Kadir Nelson, written by Jerdine Nolen (Silver Whistle)

2005

AUTHOR AWARD: *Remember: The Journey to Integration* by Toni Morrison (Houghton Mifflin)

AUTHOR HONOR BOOKS: *The Legend of Buddy Bush*, by Sheila Moses (McElderry); *Who Am I without Him? Short Stories about Girls and the Boys in Their Lives*, by Sharon Flake (Hyperion); *Fortune's Bones: The Manumission Requiem*, by Marilyn Nelson (Front Street)

ILLUSTRATOR AWARD: *Ellington Was Not a Street*, illustrated by Kadir Nelson, written by Ntozake Shange (Simon & Schuster)

ILLUSTRATOR HONOR BOOKS: *God Bless the Child*, illustrated by Jerry Pinkney, written by Billie Holiday and Arthur Herzog Jr. (Amistad); *The People Could Fly: The Picturebook*, illustrated by Leo and Diane Dillon, written by Virginia Hamilton (Knopf)

2006

AUTHOR AWARD: *Day of Tears: A Novel in Dialogue*
by Julius Lester (Hyperion/Hyperion)

AUTHOR HONOR BOOKS: *Maritcha: A Nineteenth-Century American Girl*, by Tonya Bolden (Abrams); *Dark Sons*, by Nikki Grimes (Hyperion); *A Wreath for Emmett Till*, by Marilyn Nelson, illustrated by Philippe Lardy (Houghton Mifflin)

ILLUSTRATOR AWARD: *Rosa*, illustrated by Bryan Collier, written by Nikki Giovanni (Holt)

ILLUSTRATOR HONOR BOOKS: *Brothers in Hope: The Story of the Lost Boys of Sudan*, by R. Gregory Christie (Lee & Low)

2007

AUTHOR AWARD: *Copper Sun*
by Sharon Draper (Simon & Schuster)

AUTHOR HONOR BOOKS: *The Road to Paris*, by Nikki Grimes, (Putnam/Penguin)

ILLUSTRATOR AWARD: *Moses: When Harriet Tubman Led Her People to Freedom*, illustrated by Kadir Nelson, written by Carole Boston Weatherford (Hyperion)

ILLUSTRATOR HONOR BOOKS: *Jazz*, illustrated by Christopher Myers, written by Walter Dean Myers (Holiday House); *Poetry for Young People: Langston Hughes*, illustrated by Benny Andrews, edited by David Roessel and Arnold Rampersad (Sterling)

2008

AUTHOR AWARD: *Elijah of Buxton*
by Christopher Paul Curtis (Scholastic)

AUTHOR HONOR BOOKS: *November Blues*, by Sharon M. Draper (Simon & Schuster); *Twelve Rounds to Glory: The Story of Muhammad Ali*, by Charles R. Smith Jr., illustrated by Bryan Collier (Candlewick)

ILLUSTRATOR AWARD: *Let it Shine*
by Ashley Bryan (Simon & Schuster)

ILLUSTRATOR HONOR BOOKS: *The Secret Olivia Told Me*, by Nancy Devard, written by N. Joy (Just Us Books); *Jazz on A Saturday Night*, by Leo and Diane Dillon (Scholastic)

2009

AUTHOR AWARD: *We Are the Ship: The Story of Negro League Baseball*
by Kadir Nelson (Hyperion)

AUTHOR HONOR BOOKS: *Keeping the Night Watch*, by Hope Anita Smith (Holt); *The Blacker the Berry*, by Joyce Carol Thomas (HarperCollins); *Becoming Billie Holiday*, by Carole Boston Weatherford (Boyds Mills)

ILLUSTRATOR AWARD: *The Blacker the Berry*, illustrated by Floyd Cooper, written by Joyce Carol Thomas (HarperCollins)

ILLUSTRATOR HONOR BOOKS: *We Are the Ship: The Story of Negro League Baseball*, by Kadir Nelson (Hyperion); *The Moon over Star*, by Jerry Pinkney, text by Dianna Hutts Aston (Dial); *Before John Was a Jazz Giant*, by Sean Qualls, text by Carole Boston Weatherford (Holt)

2010

AUTHOR AWARD: *Bad News for Outlaws: The Remarkable Life of Bass Reeves, Deputy U. S. Marshall*
by Vaunda Micheaux Nelson, illustrated by H. Gregory Christie (Carolrhoda)

AUTHOR HONOR BOOK: *Mare's War*, by Tanita S. Davis (Knopf)

ILLUSTRATOR AWARD: *My People*
by Charles R. Smith, text by Langston Hughes (Atheneum)

ILLUSTRATOR HONOR BOOK: *The Negro Speaks of Rivers*, by E.B. Lewis, text by Langston Hughes (Disney)

2011

AUTHOR AWARD: *One Crazy Summer*
by Rita Williams-Garcia (HarperCollins)

AUTHOR HONOR BOOKS: *Lockdown*, by Walter Dean Myers (HarperCollins); *Ninth Ward*, by Jewell Parker Rhodes (Little, Brown); *Yummy: The Last Days of a Southside Shorty,* by G. Neri, illustrated by Randy DuBurke (Lee & Low)

ILLUSTRATOR AWARD: *Dave the Potter: Artist, Poet, Slave*, by Bryan Collier, text by Laban Carrick Hill (Little, Brown)

ILLUSTRATOR HONOR BOOK: *Jimi Sounds Like a Rainbow: A Story of the Young Jimi Hendrix*, by Javaka Steptoe, text by Gary Golio (Clarion)

2012

AUTHOR AWARD: **Heart and Soul: The Story of America and African Americans** by Kadir Nelson (HarperCollins)

AUTHOR HONOR BOOKS: **The Great Migration: Journey to the North**, by Eloise Greenfield, illustrated by Jan Spivey Gilchrist (HarperCollins); **Never Forgotten**, by Patricia C. McKissack, illustrated by Leo and Diane Dillon (Random House)

ILLUSTRATOR AWARD: **Underground: Finding the Light to Freedom,** by Shane W. Evans (Roaring Brook)

ILLUSTRATOR HONOR BOOK: **Heart and Soul: The Story of America and African Americans**, by Kadir Nelson (HarperCollins)

• • • **PURA BELPRÉ AWARD** • • •

The Pura Belpré Award, established in 1996, presented biennially until 2009 when it became an annual award, honors a Latino/Latina writer and illustrator whose work best portrays, affirms, and celebrates the Latino cultural experience in an outstanding work of literature for children and youth. It is cosponsored by the Association for Library Service to Children, a division of the American Library Association, and the National Association to Promote Library Services to the Spanish Speaking, an ALA affiliate. The award is named in honor of Pura Belpré, the first Latina librarian in the New York Public Library. As children's librarian, storyteller, and AUTHOR, she enriched the lives of Puerto Rican children in the United States through her pioneering work of preserving and disseminating Puerto Rican folklore.

1996

NARRATIVE AWARD: **An Island Like You: Stories of the Barrio** by Judith Ortiz Cofer (Orchard)

NARRATIVE HONOR BOOKS: **The Bossy Gallito/ El Gallo de Bodas: A Traditional Cuban Folktale**, by Lucía González, illustrated by Lulu Delacre (Scholastic); **Baseball in April and Other Stories**, by Gary Soto (Harcourt)

ILLUSTRATION AWARD: **Chato's Kitchen**, illustrated by Susan Guevara, text by Gary Soto (Putnam)

ILLUSTRATION HONOR BOOKS: **Pablo Remembers: The Fiesta of the Day of the Dead**, by George Ancona (Lothrop, Lee & Shepard) (also available in a Spanish-language edition; **Pablo recuerda: la fiesta de día de los muertos**); **The Bossy Gallito/El gallo de bodas: A Traditional Cuban Folktale**, illustrated by Lulu Delacre, text by Lucía González (Scholastic); **Family Pictures/ Cuadros de Familia**, by Carmen Lomas Garza, Spanish text by Rosalma Zubizarreta (Children's Book Press)

1998

NARRATIVE AWARD: **Parrot in the Oven: Mi vida** by Victor Martinez (HarperCollins)

NARRATIVE HONOR BOOKS: **Laughing Tomatoes and Other Spring Poems/Jitomates risuenos y otros poemas de primavera**, by Francisco X. Alarcón, illustrated by Maya Christina Gonzalez (Children's Book Press); **Spirits of the High Mesa**, by Floyd Martinez (Arte Público Press)

ILLUSTRATION AWARD: **Snapshots from the Wedding**, illustrated by Stephanie Garcia, text by Gary Soto (Putnam)

ILLUSTRATION HONOR BOOKS: **In My Family/En mi familia**, by Carmen Lomas Garza (Children's Book Press); **The Golden Flower: A Taino Myth from Puerto Rico**, illustrated by Enrique O. Sánchez, text by Nina Jaffe (Simon & Schuster); **Gathering the Sun: An Alphabet in Spanish and English**, illustrated by Simon Silva, text by Alma Flor Ada, Spanish text by Rosa Zubizarreta (Lothrop, Lee & Shepard)

2000

NARRATIVE AWARD: **Under the Royal Palms: A Childhood in Cuba** by Alma Flor Ada (Simon & Schuster)

NARRATIVE HONOR BOOKS: **From the Bellybutton of the Moon and Other Summer Poems/ Del ombligo de la luna y otro poemas de verano**, by Francisco X. Alarcón, illustrated by Maya Christina Gonzalez (Children's Book Press); **Laughing Out Loud, I Fly: Poems in English and Spanish**, by Juan Felipe Herrera, illustrated by Karen Barbour (HarperCollins)

ILLUSTRATION AWARD: **Magic Windows**, by Carmen Lomas Garza (Children's Book Press)

ILLUSTRATION HONOR BOOKS: **Barrio: Jose's Neighborhood**, by George Ancona (Harcourt); **The Secret Stars**, illustrated by Felipe Dávalos, text by Joseph Slate (Cavendish); **Mama and Papa Have a Store**, by Amelia Lau Carling (Dial)

2002

NARRATIVE AWARD: ***Esperanza Rising*** by Pam Muñoz Ryan (Scholastic)

NARRATIVE HONOR BOOKS: ***Breaking Through***, by Francisco Jiménez (Houghton Mifflin); ***Iguanas in the Snow***, by Francisco X. Alarcón, illustrated by Maya Christina Gonzalez (Children's Book Press)

ILLUSTRATION AWARD: ***Chato and the Party Animals***, illustrated by Susan Guevara, text by Gary Soto (Putnam)

ILLUSTRATION HONOR BOOKS: ***Juan Bobo Goes to Work***, illustrated by Joe Cepeda, retold by Marisa Montes (HarperCollins)

2004

NARRATIVE AWARD: ***Before We Were Free*** by Julia Alvarez (Random House)

NARRATIVE HONOR BOOKS: ***Cuba 15***, by Nancy Osa (Delacorte); ***My Diary from Here to There/Mi diario de aquí hasta allá***, by Amada Irma Pérez (Children's Book Press)

ILLUSTRATION AWARD: ***Just a Minute: A Trickster Tale and Counting Book***, by Yuyi Morales (Chronicle)

ILLUSTRATION HONOR BOOKS: ***First Day in Grapes***, illustrated by Robert Casilla, text by L. King Pérez (Lee & Low); ***The Pot that Juan Built***, illustrated by David Diaz, text by Nancy Andrews-Goebel (Lee & Low); ***Harvesting Hope: The Story of Cesar Chavez***, illustrated by Yuyi Morales, text by Kathleen Krull (Harcourt)

2006

NARRATIVE AWARD: ***The Tequila Worm*** by Viola Canales (Random House)

NARRATIVE HONOR BOOKS: ***César: ¡Sí, se puede! Yes, We Can!***, by Carmen T. Bernier-Grand, illustrated by David Diaz (Marshall Cavendish); ***Doña Flor: A Tall Tale about a Giant Woman with a Great Big Heart***, by Pat Mora, illustrated by Raul Colón (Random House); ***Becoming Naomi León***, by Pam Muñoz Ryan (Scholastic)

ILLUSTRATION AWARD: ***Doña Flor: A Tall Tale about a Giant Woman with a Great Big Heart***, illustrated by Raul Colon, text by Pat Mora (Random House)

ILLUSTRATION HONOR BOOKS: ***Arrorró, mi niño: Latino Lullabies and Gentle Games***, illustrated by Lulu Delacre (Lee & Low); ***César: ¡Sí, se puede! Yes, We Can!***, illustrated by David Diaz, text by Carmen T. Bernier-Grand (Marshall Cavendish); ***My Name Is Celia/Me llamo Celia:***

The Life of Celia Cruz/ La vida de Celia Cruz, illustrated by Rafael Lopez, text by Monica Brown (Rising Moon)

2008

NARRATIVE AWARD: ***The Poet Slave of Cuba: A Biography of Juan Francisco Manzano*** by Margarita Engle, illustrated by Sean Qualls (Holt)

NARRATIVE HONOR BOOKS: ***Frida: ¡Viva la vida! Long Live Life!***, by Carmen T. Bernier-Grand, (Marshall Cavendish); ***Martina the Beautiful Cockroach: A Cuban Folktale***, by Carmen Agra Deedy, illustrated by Michael Austin (Peachtree); ***Los Gatos Black on Halloween***, by Marisa Montes, illustrated by Yuyi Morales (Holt)

ILLUSTRATION AWARD: ***Los Gatos Black on Halloween***, illustrated by Yuyi Morales, text by Marisa Montes (Holt)

ILLUSTRATION HONOR BOOKS: ***My Name Is Gabito: The Life of Gabriel García Márquez/Me llamo Gabito: la vida de Gabriel García Márquez***, illustrated by Raul Colon, text by Monica Brown. (Rising Moon); ***My Colors, My World/Mis colores, mi mundo***, illustrated and text by Maya Christina Gonzalez (Children's Book Press)

2009

AUTHOR AWARD: ***The Surrender Tree: Poems of Cuba's Struggle for Freedom*** by Margarita Engle (Holt)

AUTHOR HONOR BOOKS: ***Just in Case***, by Yuri Morales (Roaring Brook); ***Reaching Out***, by Francisco Jimenez (Houghton Mifflin); ***The Storyteller's Candle/La velita de los cuentos***, by Lucia Gonzalez, illustrated by Lulu Delacre (Children's Book Press)

ILLUSTRATOR AWARD: ***Just in Case***, by Yuri Morales (Roaring Brook)

ILLUSTRATOR HONOR BOOKS: ***Papa and Me***, illustrated by Rudy Gutierrez, written by Arthur Dorros (HarperCollins); ***The Storyteller's Candle/La velita de los cuentos***, by Lulu Delacre, written by Lucia Gonzalez (Children's Book Press); ***What Can You Do with a Rebozo***, illustrated by Amy Cordova, written by Carmen Tafolla (Ten Speed)

2010

AUTHOR AWARD: ***Return to Sender*** by Julia Alvarez (Knopf)

AUTHOR HONOR BOOKS: ***Diego: Bigger than Life***, by Carmen T. Bernier-Grand, illustrated by David Diaz

(Marshall Cavendish); *Federico Garcia Lorca*, by Georgina Lázaro, illustrated by Enrique S. Moreiro (Scholastic)

ILLUSTRATOR AWARD: *Book Fiesta!: Celebrate Children's Day/Book Day; Celebremos el dia de los ninos/El dia de los libros*, illustrated by Rafael López, written by Pat Mora (HarperCollins)

ILLUSTRATOR HONOR BOOKS: *Diego: Bigger than Life*, illustrated by David Diaz, written by Carmen T. Bernier Grand (Marshall Cavendish); *Gracias Thanks*, illustrated by John Parra, written by Pat Mora (Lee & Low); *My Abuelita*, illustrated by Yuyi Morales, written by Tony Johnston (Harcourt)

2011

AUTHOR AWARD: *The Dreamer* by Pam Muñoz Ryan, illustrated by Peter Sís (Scholastic)

AUTHOR HONOR BOOKS: *90 Miles to Havana*, by Enrique Flores-Galbis (Roaring Brook); *The Firefly letters: A Suffragette's Journey to Cuba*, by Margarita Engle (Holt); *¡Ole! Flamenco*, by George Ancona (Lee & Low)

ILLUSTRATOR AWARD: *Grandma's Gift*, illustrated and written by Eric Velasquez (Walker)

ILLUSTRATOR HONOR BOOKS: *Dear Primo: A Letter to My Cousin*, illustrated and written by Duncan Tonatiuh (Abrams); *Fiesta Babies*, illustrated by Amy Córdova , written by Carmen Tafolla (Crown); *Me, Frida*, illustrated by David Diaz, written by Amy Novesky (Abrams)

2012

AUTHOR AWARD: *Under the Mesquite* by Guadalupe Garcia McCall (Lee & Low)

AUTHOR HONOR BOOKS: *Hurricane Dancers: The First Caribbean Pirate Shipwreck*, by Margarita Engle (Holt); *Maximillian and the Mystery of the Guardian Angel: A Bilingual Lucha Libre Thriller*, written by Xavier Garza (Cinco Puntos)

ILLUSTRATOR AWARD: *Diego Rivera: His World and Ours*, illustrated and written by Duncan Tonatiuh (Abrams)

ILLUSTRATOR HONOR BOOKS: *The Cazuela that the Farm Maiden Stirred*, illustrated by Rafael López, written by Samantha R. Vamos (Charlesbridge); *Marisol McDonald Doesn't match/Marisol McDonald no combina*, illustrated by Sara Palacios, written by Monica Brown (Lee & Low)

● ● ● ● ROBERT F. SIBERT ● ● ● ● AWARD

The Robert F. Sibert Award, established in 2001, is sponsored by Bound to Stay Bound Books, Inc., in honor of its longtime president, Robert F. Sibert. It is administered by the Association of Library Service to Children, a division of the American Library Association, and seeks outstanding informational books written and illustrated to present, organize, and interpret verifiable, factual material for children. The complete list of award winners can be found at the end of Chapter 10.

● ● ● LAURA INGALLS WILDER ● ● ● MEDAL

The Laura Ingalls Wilder Medal, established in 1954 and named for its first winner, the Author of the Little House books, is given to an Author or Illustrator whose books, published in the United States, have made a substantial and lasting contribution to literature for children. Between 1960 and 1980, the Wilder Award was given every five years. From 1980 to 2001, it was awarded every three years. Beginning in 2001, it has been awarded every two years. This award is administered by the Association for Library Service to Children, a division of the American Library Association.

1954	Laura Ingalls Wilder
1960	Clara Ingram Judson
1965	Ruth Sawyer
1970	E. B. White
1975	Beverly Cleary
1980	Theodor S. Geisel (Dr. Seuss)
1983	Maurice Sendak
1986	Jean Fritz
1989	Elizabeth George Speare
1992	Marcia Brown
1995	Virginia Hamilton
1998	Russell Freedman
2001	Milton Meltzer
2003	Eric Carle
2005	Laurence Yep
2007	James Marshall
2009	Ashley Bryan
2011	Tomie dePaola

• • • MARGARET A. • • •
EDWARDS AWARD

The Margaret A. Edwards Award, established in 1988, honors an author's lifetime achievement for writing books that have been popular over a period of time. The annual award is administered by the Young Adult Library Services Association, a division of the American Library Association, and sponsored by *School Library Journal*. It recognizes an Author's work in helping adolescents become aware of themselves and addressing questions about their role and importance in relationships, society, and in the world.

1988	S. E. Hinton
1990	Richard Peck
1991	Robert Cormier
1992	Lois Duncan
1993	M. E. Kerr
1994	Walter Dean Myers
1995	Cynthia Voigt
1996	Judy Blume
1997	Gary Paulsen
1998	Madeleine L'Engle
1999	Anne McCaffrey
2000	Chris Crutcher
2001	Robert Lipsyte
2002	Paul Zindel
2003	Nancy Garden
2004	Ursula Le Guin
2005	Francesca Lia Block
2006	Jacqueline Woodson
2007	Lois Lowry
2008	Orson Scott Card
2009	Laurie Halse Anderson
2010	Jim Murphy
2011	Sir Terry Pratchett
2012	Susan Cooper

• • • MICHAEL L. PRINTZ • • •
AWARD

The Michael L. Printz Award, established in 2000, is administered by the Young Adult Library Services Association, a division of the American Library Association. The award honors the Author of an outstanding young adult book.

2000

Monster
by Walter Dean Myers (HarperCollins)

HONOR BOOKS: *Skellig*, by David Almond (Delacorte); *Speak*, by Laurie Halse Anderson (Farrar, Straus & Giroux); *Hard Love*, by Ellen Wittlinger (Simon & Schuster)

2001

Kit's Wilderness
by David Almond (Delacorte)

HONOR BOOKS: *Many Stones*, by Carolyn Coman (Front Street); *The Body of Christopher Creed*, by Carol Plum-Ucci (Harcourt); *Angus, Thongs, and Full-Frontal Snogging*, by Louise Rennison (HarperCollins); *Stuck in Neutral*, by Terry Trueman (HarperCollins)

2002

Step from Heaven
by An Na (Front Street)

HONOR BOOKS: *The Ropemaker*, by Peter Dickinson (Delacorte); *Heart to Heart: New Poems Inspired by Twentieth-Century American Art*, by Jan Greenberg (Abrams); *Freewill*, by Chris Lynch (HarperCollins); *True Believer*, by Virginia Euwer Wolff (Simon & Schuster)

2003

Postcards from No Man's Land
by Aidan Chambers (Dutton)

HONOR BOOKS: *The House of the Scorpion*, by Nancy Farmer (Simon & Schuster); *My Heartbeat*, by Garret Freymann-Weyr (Houghton Mifflin); *Hole in My Life*, by Jack Gantos (Farrar, Straus and Giroux)

2004

The First Part Last
by Angela Johnson (Simon & Schuster)

HONOR BOOKS: *A Northern Light*, by Jennifer Donnelly (Harcourt); *Keesha's House*, by Helen Frost (Farrar, Straus and Giroux); *Fat Kid Rules the World*, by K. L. Going (Putnam); *The Earth, My Butt and Other Big Round Things*, by Carolyn Mackler (Candlewick)

2005

How I Live Now
by Meg Rosoff (Random House)

HONOR BOOKS: *Airborn*, by Kenneth Oppel (EOS); *Chanda's Secrets*, by Allan Stratton (Annick); *Lizzie Bright and the Buckminster Boy*, by Gary Schmidt (Clarion)

2006

Looking for Alaska
by John Green (Dutton)

HONOR BOOKS: *Black Juice*, by Margo Lanagan (Allen & Unwin); *I Am the Messenger*, by Markus Zusak (Random House); *John Lennon: All I Want Is the Truth, a Photographic Biography*, by Elizabeth Partridge (Viking); *A Wreath for Emmett Till*, by Marilyn Nelson (Houghton Mifflin)

2007

American Born Chinese
by Gene Luen Yang (Macmillan)

HONOR BOOKS: *The Astonishing Life of Octavian Nothing, Traitor to the Nation: Volume I: The Pox Party*, by M. T. Anderson (Thorndike); *An Abundance of Katherines*, by John Green (Penguin); *Surrender*, by Sonya Hartnett (Candlewick); *The Book Thief*, by Markus Zusak (Knopf)

2008

The White Darkness
by Geraldine McCaughrean (HarperTempest)

HONOR BOOKS: *Dreamquake: Book Two of the Dreamhunter Duet*, by Elizabeth Knox (Frances Foster Books); *One Whole and Perfect Day*, by Judith Clarke (Front Street); *Repossessed*, by A. M. Jenkins (HarperTeen); *Your Own, Sylvia: A Verse Portrait of Sylvia Plath*, by Stephanie Hemphill (Knopf)

2009

Jellicoe Road
by Melina Marchetta (HarperCollins)

HONOR BOOKS: *The Astonishing Life of Octavian Nothing, Traitor to the Nation, Volume II: The Kingdom on the Waves*, by M. T. Anderson (Candlewick); *The Disreputable History of Frankie Landau-Banks*, by E. Lockhart (Hyperion); *Nation*, by Terry Pratchett (HarperCollins); *Tender Morsels*, by Margo Lanagan (Knopf)

2010

Going Bovine
by Libba Bray (Delacorte)

HONOR BOOKS: *Charles and Emma: The Darwins' Leap of Faith*, by Deborah Heligman (Holt); *The Monstromulogist*, by Richard "Rick" Yancey (Simon &Schuster); *Punkzilla*, by Adam Rapp (Candlewick); *Tales from the Madman Underground: An Historical Romance, 1973*, by John Barnes (Viking)

2011

Ship Breaker
by Paolo Bacigalupi (Little, Brown)

HONOR BOOKS: *Nothing*, by Janne Teller (Athenuem); *Please Ignore Vera Dietz*, by A.S. King (Knopf); *Revolver*, by Marcus Sedgwick (Roaring Brook Press); *Stolen*, by Lucy Christopher (Chicken House/Scholastic)

2012

Where Things Come Back
by John Corey Whaley (Atheneum)

HONOR BOOKS: *Jasper Jones*, by Craig Silvey (Knopf); *The Returning*, by Christine Hinwood (Dial); *The Scorpio Races*, by Maggie Stiefvater (Scholastic); *Why We Broke Up*, by Daniel Handler, art by Maria Kalman (Little, Brown)

• • • **THEODORE SEUSS GEISEL AWARD** • • •

The (Theodore Seuss) Geisel Award, established in 2006, is given annually to the Author and Illustrator of the most distinguished American book for beginning readers published in English in the United States during the preceding year.

2006

Henry and Mudge and the Great Grandpas
by Cynthia Rylant, illustrated by Sucie Stevenson (Simon & Schuster)

HONOR BOOKS: *Hi! Fly Guy*, by Tedd Arnold (Scholastic); *A Splendid Friend, Indeed*, by Suzanne Bloom (Boyds Mills); *Cowgirl Kate and Cocoa*, by Erica Silverman, illustrated by Betsy Lewin (Harcourt); *Amanda Pig and the Really Hot Day*, by Jean Van Leeuwen, illustrated by Ann Schweninger (Dial)

2007

Zelda and Ivy: The Runaways
by Laura McGee Kvasnosky (Candlewick)

HONOR BOOKS: *Mercy Watson Goes for a Ride*, by Kate DiCamillo, illustrated by Chris Van Dusen (Candlewick); *Move Over, Rover!*, by Karen Beaumont, illustrated by Jane Dyer (Harcourt); *Not a Box*, by Antoinette Portis (HarperCollins)

2008

There Is a Bird on Your Head
by Mo Willems (Hyperion)

HONOR BOOKS: **First the Egg**, by Laura Vaccaro Seeger (Roaring Brook); **Hello, Bumblebee Bat**, by Darrin Lunde, illustrated by Patricia J. Wynne (Charlesbridge); **Jazz Baby**, by Lisa Wheeler, illustrated by R. Gregory Christie (Harcourt); **Vulture View**, by April Pulley Sayre, illustrated by Steve Jenkins (Holt)

2009

Are You Ready to Play Outside?
by Mo Willems (Hyperion)

HONOR BOOKS: **Chicken Said, "Cluck!"**, by Judyann Ackerman Grant, illustrated by Sue Truesdell (HarperCollins); **One Boy**, by Laura Vaccaro Seeger (Roaring Brook); **Stinky**, by Eleanor Davis (Little Lit Library); **Wolfsnail: A Backyard Predator**, by Sarah C. Campbell, illustrated by Sarah C. Campbell and Richard P. Campbell (Boyds Mills)

2010

Benny and Penny in the Big No-No!
written and illustrated by Geoffrey Hayes (Toon Books)

HONOR BOOKS: **I Spy Fly Guy!**, written and illustrated by Tedd Arnold (Scholastic); **Little Mouse Gets Ready**, written and illustrated by Jeff Smith (Toon Books); **Mouse and Mole: Fine Feathered Friends**, written and illustrated by Won Herbert Yee (Houghton Mifflin); **Pearl and Wagner: One Funny Day**, by Kate McMullan, illustrated by R.W. Alley (Dial)

2011

Bink and Gollie
by Kate DiCamillo and Alison McGhee, illustrated by Tony Fucile (Candlewick)

HONOR BOOKS: **Ling & Ting: Not Exactly the Same!**, written and illustrated by Grace Lin (Little, Brown); **We Are in a Book!**, written and illustrated by Mo Willems (Hyperion)

2012

Tales for Very Picky Eaters
written and illustrated by Josh Schneider (Clarion)

HONOR BOOKS: **I Broke My Trunk**, written and illustrated by Mo Willems (Hyperion); **I Want My Hat Back**, written and illustrated by Jon Klassen (Candlewick); **See Me Run**, written and illustrated by Paul Meisel (Holiday)

• • •   **SCHNEIDER FAMILY BOOK AWARD**   • • •

The Schneider Family Book Awards honor an Author or Illustrator for a book that embodies an artistic expression of the disability experience for child and adolescent audiences.

2004

YOUNG CHILDREN BOOK: **Looking Out for Sarah** by Glenna Long (Charlesbridge)

MIDDLE SCHOOL BOOK: **A Mango Shaped Space**, by Wendy Mass (Little, Brown)

TEEN BOOK: **Things Not Seen**, by Andrew Clements (Philomel)

2005

YOUNG CHILDREN BOOK: **My Pal Victor/Mi amigo, Victor** by Diane Gonzales Bertrand, illustrated by Robert Sweetland (Raven Tree)

MIDDLE SCHOOL BOOK: **Becoming Naomi Leon**, by Pam Muñoz Ryan (Scholastic)

TEEN BOOK: **My Thirteenth Winter: A Memoir**, by Samantha Abeel (Orchard)

2006

YOUNG CHILDREN BOOK: **Dad, Jackie, and Me** by Myron Uhlberg, illustrated by Colin Bootman (Peachtree)

MIDDLE SCHOOL BOOK: **Tending to Grace**, by Kimberly Newton Fusco (Knopf)

TEEN BOOK: **Under the Wolf, Under the Dog**, by Adam Rapp (Candlewick)

2007

YOUNG CHILDREN BOOK: **The Deaf Musicians** by Pete Seeger and Paul DoBois Jacobs, illustrated by Gregory Christie (Putnam)

MIDDLE SCHOOL BOOK: **Rules**, by Cynthia Lord (Scholastic)

TEEN BOOK: **Small Steps**, by Louis Sachar (Delacorte)

2008

YOUNG CHILDREN BOOK: **Kami and the Yaks** by Andrea Stenn Stryer, illustrated by Bert Dodson (Bay Otter Press)

MIDDLE SCHOOL BOOK: **Reaching for Sun**, by Tracie Vaughn Zimmer (Bloomsbury)

TEEN BOOK: **Hurt Go Happy**, by Ginny Rorby (Starscape)

2009

YOUNG CHILDREN BOOK: **Piano Starts Here: The Young Art Tatum** by Robert Andrew Parker (Random House)

MIDDLE SCHOOL BOOK: **Waiting for Normal**, by Leslie Connor (HarperCollins)

TEEN BOOK: **Jerk, California**, by Jonathan Friesen (Penguin)

2010

YOUNG CHILDREN BOOK: **Django** by Bonnie Christensen (Roaring Brook)

MIDDLE SCHOOL BOOK: **Anything but Typical**, by Nora Raleigh Baskin (Simon & Schuster)

TEEN BOOK: **Marcelo in the Real World**, by Francisco X. Stork (Scholastic)

2011

YOUNG CHILDREN BOOK: **The Pirate of Kindergarten** by George Ella Lyon, illustrated by Lynne Avril (Atheneum)

MIDDLE SCHOOL BOOK: **After Ever After**, by Jordan Sonnenblick (Scholastic)

TEEN BOOK: **Five Flavors of Dumb**, by Antony John (Dial)

2012

YOUNG CHILDREN BOOK: no award given

MIDDLE SCHOOL BOOK: **Close to Famous**, by Joan Bauer (Viking); **Wonderstruck: A Novel in Words and Pictures**, by Brian Selznick (Scholastic)

TEEN BOOK: **The Running Dream**, by Wendelin Van Draanen (Knopf)

National Council of Teachers of English Awards

● ● ● THE AWARD FOR ● ● ● EXCELLENCE IN POETRY FOR CHILDREN

The NCTE Award for Excellence in Poetry for Children, established in memory of Jonathan Cullinan (1969–1975), is given to a living American poet in recognition of an outstanding body of poetry for children. The award is administered by the National Council of Teachers of English and was given annually from 1977 to 1982; currently, the award is presented every three years. The poet receives a citation. A medallion designed by Karla Kuskin is available for use on dust jackets of all the poet's books. An archival collection of the poets' books is housed at the Children's Literature Research Center, Andersen Library, at the University of Minnesota. Another collection is housed at Boston Public Library in the David McCord Room.

1977   David McCord
1978   Aileen Fisher
1979   Karla Kuskin
1980   Myra Cohn Livingston
1981   Eve Merriam
1982   John Ciardi
1985   Lilian Moore
1988   Arnold Adoff
1991   Valerie Worth
1994   Barbara Esbensen
1997   Eloise Greenfield
2000   X. J. Kennedy
2003   Mary Ann Hoberman
2006   Nikki Grimes
2009   Lee Bennett Hopkins
2011   J. Patrick Lewis

● ● ● ORBIS PICTUS AWARD ● ● ● AND HONOR BOOKS

The Orbis Pictus Award, established in 1990, is administered by the National Council of Teachers of English and honors the Author of an outstanding nonfiction book. The complete list of award winners can be found at the end of Chapter 10.

International Reading Association Awards

• • • IRA CHILDREN'S • • • BOOK AWARD

The IRA Children's Book Award, established in 1975, sponsored by the Institute for Reading Research and administrated by the International Reading Association, is presented for a children's book published in the preceding year by an Author who shows unusual promise. Since 1987, the award has been presented for both picturebooks and novels. Currently, the award is given for both fiction and nonfiction in each of three categories: primary, intermediate, and young adult. Books originating in any country are eligible. For books written in a language other than English, the IRA committee first determines if the book warrants an English translation and, if so, extends to it an additional year of eligibility.

1975

Transport 7-41-R
by T. Degens (Viking)

1976

Dragonwings
by Laurence Yep (HarperCollins)

1977

A String in the Harp
by Nancy Bond (McElderry)

1978

A Summer to Die
by Lois Lowry (Houghton Mifflin)

1979

Reserved for Mark Anthony Crowder
by Alison Smith (Dutton)

1980

Words by Heart
by Ouida Sebestyen (Little, Brown)

1981

My Own Private Sky
by Delores Beckman (Dutton)

1982

Good Night, Mr. Tom
by Michelle Magorian (Penguin, Great Britain; HarperCollins, USA)

1983

The Darkangel
by Meredith Ann Pierce (Little, Brown)

1984

Ratha's Creature
by Clare Bell (Simon & Schuster)

1985

Badger on the Barge
by Janni Howker (Greenwillow)

1986

Prairie Songs
by Pam Conrad (HarperCollins)

1987

PICTUREBOOK: **The Line Up Book** by Marisabina Russo (Greenwillow)

NOVEL: **After the Dancing Days**, by Margaret Rostkowski (HarperCollins)

1988

PICTUREBOOK: **Third Story Cat** by Leslie Baker (Little, Brown)

NOVEL: **The Ruby in the Smoke**, by Philip Pullman (Knopf)

1989

PICTUREBOOK: **Rechenka's Eggs** by Patricia Polacco (Philomel)

NOVEL: **Probably Still Nick Swansen**, by Virginia Euwer Wolff (Holt)

1990

PICTUREBOOK: **No Star Nights** by Anna Egan Smucker (Knopf)

NOVEL: **Children of the River**, by Linda Crew (Delacorte)

1991

PICTUREBOOK: ***Is This a House for Hermit Crab?*** by Megan McDonald (Orchard)

NOVEL: ***Under the Hawthorn Tree***, by Marita Conlon-McKenna (O'Brien Press)

1992

PICTUREBOOK: ***Ten Little Rabbits*** by Virginia Grossman (Chronicle)

NOVEL: ***Rescue Josh McGuire***, by Ben Mikaelsen (Hyperion)

1993

PICTUREBOOK: ***Old Turtle*** by Douglas Wood (Pfeiffer-Hamilton)

NOVEL: ***Letters from Rifka***, by Karen Hesse (Holt)

1994

PICTUREBOOK: ***Sweet Clara and the Freedom Quilt*** by Deborah Hopkinson, illustrated by James Ransome (Knopf)

NOVEL: ***Behind the Secret Window: A Memoir of a Hidden Childhood***, by Nelly Toll (Dutton)

1995

PICTUREBOOK: ***The Ledgerbook of Thomas Blue Eagle*** by Gay Matthaei and Jewel Grutman, illustrated by Adam Cvijanovic (Thomasson-Grant)

NOVEL: ***Spite Fences***, by Trudy Krisher (Bantam)

NONFICTION: ***Stranded at Plimoth Plantation 1626***, by Gary Bowen (HarperCollins)

1996

PICTUREBOOK: ***More than Anything Else*** by Marie Bradby and Chris Soentpiet (Orchard)

NOVEL: ***The King's Shadow,*** by Elizabeth Adler (Farrar, Straus and Giroux)

NONFICTION: ***The Case of the Mummified Pigs and Other Mysteries in Nature,*** by Susan Quinlan (Boyds Mills)

1997

PICTUREBOOK: ***The Fabulous Flying Fandinis*** by Ingrid Slyder (Cobblehill)

NOVEL: ***Don't You Dare Read This***, Mrs. ***Dunphrey***, by Margaret Peterson Haddix (Simon & Schuster)

NONFICTION: ***The Brooklyn Bridge***, by Elizabeth Mann (Mikaya)

1998

YOUNGER READER: ***Nim and the War Effort*** by Milly Lee and Yangsook Choi (Farrar, Straus and Giroux)

OLDER READER: ***Moving Mama to Town***, by Ronder Thomas Young (Orchard)

NONFICTION: ***Just What the Doctor Ordered: The History of American Medicine***, by Brandon Marie Miller (Lerner)

1999

YOUNGER READER: ***My Freedom Trip: A Child's Escape from North Korea*** by Frances and Ginger Park (Boyds Mills)

OLDER READER: ***Choosing Up Sides***, by John Ritter (Philomel)

NONFICTION: ***First in the Field: Baseball Hero Jackie Robinson***, by Derek Dingle (Hyperion)

2000

YOUNGER READER: ***The Snake Scientist*** by Sy Montgomery (Houghton Mifflin)

OLDER READER: ***Bud, Not Buddy***, by Christopher Paul Curtis (Delacorte); ***Eleanor's Story: An American Girl in Hitler's Germany***, by Eleanor Ramrath Garner (Peachtree)

NONFICTION: ***Molly Bannaky***, by Alice McGill (Houghton Mifflin)

2001

YOUNGER READER: ***Stranger in the Woods*** by Carl R. Sams II and Jean Stoick (Carl R. Sams II Photography)

OLDER READER: ***Jake's Orphan***, by Peggy Brooke (DK Publishing); ***Girls Think of Everything***, by Catherine Thimmesh (Houghton Mifflin)

NONFICTION: ***My Season with Penguins***, by Sophie Webb (Houghton Mifflin)

2002

PRIMARY FICTION: ***Silver Seeds*** by Paul Paolilli and Dan Brewer (Viking)

PRIMARY NONFICTION: ***Aero and Officer Mike***, by Joan Plummer Russell (Boyds Mills)

INTERMEDIATE FICTION: ***Coolies***, by Yin (Philomel)

INTERMEDIATE NONFICTION: ***Pearl Harbor Warriors***,

by Dorinda Makanaonalani Nicholson and Larry Nicholson (Woodson House)

YOUNG ADULT FICTION: **A Step from Heaven**, by An Na (Front Street)

YOUNG ADULT NONFICTION: **A Race against Nuclear Disaster at Three Mile Island**, by Wilborn Hampton (Candlewick)

2003

PRIMARY FICTION: **One Leaf Rides the Wind** by Celeste Davidson Mannis (Viking)

PRIMARY NONFICTION: **The Pot that Juan Built**, by Nancy Andrews-Goebel (Lee & Low)

INTERMEDIATE FICTION: **Who Will Tell My Brother?**, by Marlene Carvell (Hyperion)

INTERMEDIATE NONFICTION: **If the World Were a Village: A Book about the World's People**, by David Smith (Kids Can Press)

YOUNG ADULT FICTION: **Mississippi Trial, 1955**, by Chris Crowe (Fogelman Books)

YOUNG ADULT NONFICTION: **Headin' for Better Times: The Arts of the Great Depression**, by Duane Damon (Lerner)

2004

PRIMARY FICTION: **Mary Smith** by Andrea U'ren (Farrar, Straus and Giroux)

PRIMARY FICTION: **Uncle Andy's: A Faabbbulous Visit with Andy Warhol**, by James Warhola (Penguin Books)

INTERMEDIATE FICTION: **Sahara Special**, by Esmé Raji Codell (Hyperion)

INTERMEDIATE NONFICTION: **Carl Sandburg: Adventures of a Poet**, by Penelope Niven (Harcourt)

YOUNG ADULT FICTION: **Buddha Boy**, by Kathe Koja (Farrar, Straus and Giroux)

YOUNG ADULT NONFICTION: **At the End of Words: A Daughter's Memoir**, by Miriam Stone (Candlewick)

2005

PRIMARY FICTION: **Miss Bridie Chose a Shovel** by Leslie Conner, illustrated by Mary Azarian (Houghton Mifflin)

PRIMARY NONFICTION: **Eliza and the Dragonfly**, by Susie Calwell Rinehart, illustrated by Anisa Claire Hovemann (Dawn)

INTERMEDIATE FICTION: **The Golden Hour**, by Maiya Williams (Amulet)

INTERMEDIATE NONFICTION: **Buildings in Disguise**, by Joan Marie Arbogast (Wordsong)

YOUNG ADULT FICTION: **Emako Blue**, by Brenda Woods (Putnam)

YOUNG ADULT NONFICTION: **The Burn Journals**, by Brent Runyon (Knopf)

2006

PRIMARY FICTION: **Russell the Sheep** by Rob Scotton (HarperCollins)

PRIMARY NONFICTION: **Night Wonders**, by Jane Ann Peddicord (Charlesbridge)

INTERMEDIATE FICTION: **The Bicycle Man**, by David L. Dudley (Clarion)

INTERMEDIATE NONFICTION: **Americans Who Tell the Truth**, by Robert Shetterly (Dutton)

YOUNG ADULT FICTION: **Black and White**, by Paul Volponi (Viking)

YOUNG ADULT NONFICTION: **JAZZ ABZ: An A to Z Collection of Jazz Portraits**, by Wynton Marsalis and Paul Rogers (Candlewick)

2007

PRIMARY FICTION: **Tickets to Ride: An Alphabetical Amusement** by Mark Rogalski (Running Press)

PRIMARY NONFICTION: **Theodore**, by Frank Keating (Simon & Schuster)

INTERMEDIATE FICTION: **Blue**, by Joyce Moyer Hostetter (Boyds Mills)

INTERMEDIATE NONFICTION: **Something Out of Nothing: Marie Curie and Radium**, by Carla Killough McClafferty (Farrar, Straus and Giroux)

YOUNG ADULT FICTION: **Leonardo's Shadow: Or, My Astonishing Life as Leonardo da Vinci's Servant**, by Christopher Grey (Simon & Schuster)

YOUNG ADULT NONFICTION: **The Poet Slave of Cuba: A Biography of Juan Francisco**, by Margarita Engle Manzano (Holt)

2008

PRIMARY FICTION: **One Thousand Tracings: Healing the Wounds of World War II** by Lita Judge (Hyperion)

PRIMARY NONFICTION: **Louis Sockalexis: Native American Baseball Pioneer**, by Bill Wise, illustrated by Bill Farnsworth (Lee & Low)

INTERMEDIATE FICTION: **The Silver Cup**, by Constance Leeds (Viking)

INTERMEDIATE NONFICTION: **Tracking Trash: Flotsam, Jetsam, and the Science of Ocean Motion**, by Loree Griffin Burns (Houghton Mifflin)

YOUNG ADULT FICTION: **Red Glass**, by Laura Resau (Random House)

YOUNG ADULT NONFICTION: **Tasting the Sky: A Palestinian Childhood**, by Ibtisam Barakat (Farrar, Straus and Giroux)

2010

PRIMARY FICTION: **All the World** by Liz Garton Scanlon, illustrated by Marla Frazee (Beach Lane)

PRIMARY NONFICTION: **Building on Nature: The Life of Antoni Gaudi** (Holt)

INTERMEDIATE FICTION: **The Beef Princess of Practical County**, by Michelle Houts (Delacorte); **The Evolution of Calpurnia Tate**, by Jacqueline Kelly (Holt)

INTERMEDIATE NONFICTION: no award given

YOUNG ADULT FICTION: **When You Reach Me**, by Rebecca Stead (Wendy Lamb)

YOUNG ADULT NONFICTION: no award given

2011

PRIMARY FICTION: **Wanted: The Perfect Pet** by Fiona Roberton (Penguin)

PRIMARY NONFICTION: **My Heart Is Like a Zoo**, by Michael Hall (HarperCollins)

INTERMEDIATE FICTION: **Mockingbird**, by Kathryn Erskine (Penguin)

INTERMEDIATE NONFICTION: no award given

YOUNG ADULT FICTION: **Split**, by Swati Avasthi (Knopf)

YOUNG ADULT NONFICTION: **How They Croaked: The Awful Ends of the Awfully Famous**, by Georgia Bragg, illustrated by Kevin O'Malley (Walker)

International Awards

• • • LIBRARY ASSOCIATION • • • CARNEGIE MEDAL

Instituted in 1936 to mark the centenary of the birth of Andrew Carnegie, philanthropist and benefactor of libraries, the Library Association Carnegie Medal is awarded annually for an outstanding book for children written in English receiving its first publication in the United Kingdom during the preceding year.

1936 Arthur Ransome, **Pigeon Post**

1937 Eve Garnet, **The Family from One End Street**

1938 Noel Streatfeild, **The Circus Is Coming**

1939 Eleanor Doorly, **The Radium Woman** (biography of Marie Curie)

1940 Kitty Barne, **Visitors from London**

1941 Mary Treadgold, **We Couldn't Leave Dinah**

1942 "B.B." (D. J. Watkins-Pitchford), **The Little Grey Men**

1943 No award

1944 Eric Linklater, **The Wind on the Moon**

1945 No award

1946 Elizabeth Goudge, **The Little White Horse**

1947 Walter de la Mare, **Collected Stories for Children**

1948 Richard Armstrong, **Sea Change**

1949 Agnes Allen, **The Story of Your Home** (NONFICTION)

1950 Elfrida Vipont, **The Lark on the Wing**

1951 Cynthia Harnett, **The Wool-Pack**

1952 Mary Norton, **The Borrowers**

1953 Edward Osmond, **A Valley Grows Up** (NONFICTION)

1954 Ronald Welch, **Knight Crusaders**

1955 Eleanor Farjeon, **The Little Bookroom**

1956 C. S. Lewis, **The Last Battle**

1957 William Mayne, **A Grass Rope**

1958 Philippa Pearce, **Tom's Midnight Garden**

1959 Rosemary Sutcliff, **The Lantern Bearers**

1960 Ian W. Cornwall and Howard M. Maitland, **The Making of Man** (NONFICTION)

1961 Lucy M. Boston, **A Stranger at Green Knowe**

1962 Pauline Clark, **The Twelve and the Genii**

1963 Hester Burton, **Time of Trial**

1964 Sheena Porter, **Nordy Bank**

1965 Philip Turner, **The Grange at High Force**

1966 No award

1967 Alan Garner, **The Owl Service**

1968   Rosemary Harris, **The Moon in the Cloud**

1969   K. M. Peyton, **The Edge of the Cloud**

1970   Edward Blishen and Leon Garfield, **The God beneath the Sea**

1971   Ivan Southall, **Josh**

1972   Richard Adams, **Watership Down**

1973   Penelope Lively, **The Ghost of Thomas Kempe**

1974   Mollie Hunter, **The Stronghold**

1975   Robert Westall, **The Machine Gunners**

1976   Jan Mark, **Thunder and Lightnings**

1977   Gene Kemp, **The Turbulent Term of Tyke Tyler**

1978   David Rees, **The Exeter Blitz**

1979   Peter Dickinson, **Tulku**

1980   Peter Dickinson, **City of Gold**

1981   Robert Westall, **The Scarecrows**

1982   Margaret Mahy, **The Haunting**

1983   Jan Mark, **Handles**

1984   Margaret Mahy, **The Changeover**

1985   Kevin Crossley-Holland, **Storm**

1986   Berlie Doherty, **Granny Was a Buffer Girl**

1987   Susan Price, **The Ghost Drum**

1988   Geraldine McCaughrean, **A Pack of Lies**

1989   Anne Fine, **Goggle-Eyes**

1990   Gillian Cross, **Wolf**

1991   Berlie Doherty, **Dear Nobody**

1992   Anne Fine, **Flour Babies**

1993   Robert Swindells, **Stone Cold**

1994   Theresa Breslin, **Whispers in the Graveyard**

1995   Philip Pullman, **Northern Lights**

1996   Melvin Burgess, **Junk**

1997   Tim Bowler, **River Boy**

1998   David Almond, **Skellig**

1999   Aiden Chambers, **Postcards from No Man's Land**

2000   Beverly Naidoo, **The Other Side of Truth**

2001   Terry Pratchett, **The Amazing Maurice and His Educated Rodents**

2002   Sharon Creech, **Ruby Holler**

2003   Jennifer Donnelly, **A Gathering Light**

2004   Frank Cottrell Boyce, **Millions**

2005   Mal Peet, **Tamar**

2007   Meg Rosoff, **Just in Case**

2008   Philip Reeve, **Here Lies Arthur**

2009   Siobhan Dowd, **Bog Child**

2010   Neil Gaiman, **The Graveyard Book**

2011   Patrick Ness, **Monsters of Men**

● ● ●   **HANS CHRISTIAN**   ● ● ●
ANDERSEN AWARD

The Hans Christian Andersen Award, established in 1956, is given biennially and administered by the International Board on Books for Young People. It is given to one Author and, since 1966, to one Illustrator in recognition of his or her entire body of work. A medal is presented to the recipient.

1956

Eleanor Farjeon, Great Britain

1958

Astrid Lindgren, Sweden

1960

Erich Kästner, Germany

1962

Meindert DeJong, USA

1964

René Guillot, France

1966

AUTHOR: Tove Jansson, Finland

ILLUSTRATOR: Alois Carigiet, Switzerland

1968

AUTHORS: James Krüss, Germany, and José Maria Sanchez-Silva, Spain

ILLUSTRATOR: Jiri Trnka, Czechoslovakia

1970

AUTHOR: Gianni Rodari, Italy

ILLUSTRATOR: Maurice Sendak, USA

1972

AUTHOR: Scott O'Dell, USA

ILLUSTRATOR: Ib Spang Olsen, Denmark

1974

AUTHOR: Maria Gripe, Sweden

ILLUSTRATOR: Farshid Mesghali, Iran

1976

AUTHOR: Cecil Bodker, Denmark
ILLUSTRATOR: Tatjana Mawrina, USSR

1978

AUTHOR: Paula Fox, USA
ILLUSTRATOR: Otto S. Svend, Denmark

1980

AUTHOR: Bohumil R'ha, Czechoslovakia
ILLUSTRATOR: Suekichi Akaba, Japan

1982

AUTHOR: Lygia Bojunga Nunes, Brazil
ILLUSTRATOR: Zbigniew Rychlicki, Poland

1984

AUTHOR: Christine Nöstlinger, Austria
ILLUSTRATOR: Mitsumasa Anno, Japan

1986

AUTHOR: Patricia Wrightson, Australia
ILLUSTRATOR: Robert Ingpen, Australia

1988

AUTHOR: Annie M. G. Schmidt, Holland
ILLUSTRATOR: Dusan Kallay, Czechoslovakia

1990

AUTHOR: Tormod Haugen, Norway
ILLUSTRATOR: Lisbeth Zwerger, Austria

1992

AUTHOR: Virginia Hamilton, USA
ILLUSTRATOR: Kveta Pacovská, Czechoslovakia

1994

AUTHOR: Michio Mado, Japan
ILLUSTRATOR: Jörg Müller, Switzerland

1996

AUTHOR: Uri Orlev, Israel
ILLUSTRATOR: Klaus Ensikat, Germany

1998

AUTHOR: Katherine Paterson, USA
ILLUSTRATOR: Tomi Ungerer, France

2000

AUTHOR: Ana Maria Machado, Brazil
ILLUSTRATOR: Anthony Browne, United Kingdom

2002

AUTHOR: Aidan Chambers, United Kingdom
ILLUSTRATOR: Quentin Blake, United Kingdom

2004

AUTHOR: Martin Waddell, Ireland
ILLUSTRATOR: Max Velthuijs, The Netherlands

2006

AUTHOR: Margaret Mahy, New Zealand
ILLUSTRATOR: Wolf Erlbruch, Germany

2008

AUTHOR: Jurg Schubiger, Switzerland
ILLUSTRATOR: Roberto Innocenti, Italy

2010

AUTHOR: David Almond, United Kingdom
ILLUSTRATOR: Jutta Bauer, Germany

• • •   **MILDRED L. BATCHELDER AWARD**   • • •

The Mildred L. Batchelder Award, established in 1966, is given by the Association of Library Service to Children of the American Library Association to the publisher of the most outstanding book of the year that is a translation, published in the United States, of a book that was first published in another country. In 1990, honor books were added to this award. Due to space considerations, only the winners are included in this list. The original country of publication is given here.

1968

The Little Man
by Erich Kastner, translated by James Kirkup, illustrated by Rick Schreiter (Knopf), Germany

1969

Don't Take Teddy
by Babbis Friis-Baastad, translated by Lise Somme McKinnon (Scribner's), Norway

1970

Wildcat under Glass
by Alki Zei, translated by Edward Fenton (Holt), Greece

1971

In the Land of Ur
by Hans Baumann, translated by Stella Humphries (Pantheon), Germany

1972

Friedrich
by Hans Peter Richter, translated by Edite Kroll (Holt), Germany

1973

Pulga
by S. R. Van Iterson, translated by Alison and Alexander Gode (Morrow), Netherlands

1974

Petros' War
by Alki Zei, translated by Edward Fenton (Dutton), Greece

1975

An Old Tale Carved out of Stone
by A. Linevsky, translated by Maria Polushkin (Crown), Russia

1976

The Cat and Mouse Who Shared a House
by Ruth Hurlimann, translated by Anthea Bell, illustrated by the AUTHOR (Walck), Germany

1977

The Leopard
by Cecil Bødker, translated by Gunnar Poulsen (Simon & Schuster), Denmark

1978

Konrad
by Christine Nostlinger, illustrated by Carol Nicklaus (Watts), Germany

1979

Rabbit Island
by Jörg Steiner, translated by Ann Conrad Lammers, illustrated by Jörg Müller (Harcourt), Germany

1980

The Sound of the Dragon's Feet
by Alki Zei, translated by Edward Fenton (Dutton), Greece

1981

The Winter when Time Was Frozen
by Els Pelgrom, translated by Maryka and Rafael Rudnik (Morrow), Netherlands

1982

The Battle Horse
by Harry Kullman, translated by George Blecher and Lone Thygesen-Blecher (Bradbury), Sweden

1983

Hiroshima No Pika
by Toshi Maruki (Lothrop, Lee & Shepard), Japan

1984

Ronia, the Robber's Daughter
by Astrid Lindgren, translated by Patricia Crampton (Viking), Sweden

1985

The Island on Bird Street
by Uri Orlev, translated by Hillel Halkin (Houghton Mifflin), Israel

1986

Rose Blanche
by Christophe Gallaz and Roberto Innocenti, translated by Martha Coventry and Richard Graglia (Creative Education), Italy

1987

No Hero for the Kaiser
by Rudolf Frank, translated by Patricia Crampton (Lothrop, Lee & Shepard), Germany

1988

If You Didn't Have Me
by Ulf Nilsson, translated by Lone Tygesen-Blecher
and George Blecher, illustrated by Eva Eriksson
(McElderry), Sweden

1989

Crutches
by Peter Hatling, translated by Elizabeth D.
Crawford (Lothrop, Lee & Shepard), Germany

1990

Buster's World
by Bjarne Reuter, translated by Anthea Bell (Dutton),
Denmark

1991

Two Long and One Short
by Nina Ring Aamundsen (Houghton Mifflin),
Norway

1992

The Man from the Other Side
by Uri Orlev, translated by Hillel Halkin (Houghton
Mifflin), Israel

1993

No award

1994

The Apprentice
by Molina Llorente, translated by Robin Longshaw
(Farrar, Straus and Giroux), Spain

1995

The Boys from St. Petri
by Bjarne Reuter, translated by Anthea Bell (Dutton),
Denmark

1996

The Lady with the Hat
by Uri Orlev, translated by Hillel Halkin (Houghton
Mifflin), Israel

1997

The Friends
by Kazumi Yumoto, translated by Cathy Hirano
(Farrar, Straus and Giroux), Japan

1998

The Robber and Me
by Josef Holub, edited by Mark Aronson, translated
by Elizabeth Crawford (Holt), Germany

1999

Thanks to My Mother
by Schoschana Rabinovici, translated by James
Skofield (Dial), Germany

2000

The Baboon King
by Anton Quintana, translated by John
Nieuwenhuizen (Walker), Holland

2001

Samir and Yonatan
translated by Arthur A. Levine (Scholastic), Israel

2002

How I Became an American
by Karin Gündisch (Cricket), Germany

2003

The Thief Lord
by Cornelia Funke (Scholastic), Germany

2004

Run, Boy, Run
by Uri Orlev (Houghton Mifflin) Israel

2005

The Shadows of Ghadames
by Joëlle Stolz (Delacorte), France

2006

An Innocent Soldier
by Josef Holub (Levine), Germany

2007

The Pull of the Ocean
by Jean-Claude Mourlevat (Delacorte), France

2008

Brave Story
by Miyuki Miyabe (VIZ Media), Japan

2009

Moribito: Guardian of the Spirit
by Nahoko Uehashi (Scholastic), Japan

2010

A Faraway Island
by Annika Thor, translated by Linda Schenck
(Scholastic), Sweden

2011

A Time of Miracles
by Anne-Laure Bondoux, translated by Y. Maudet
(Delacorte), France

2012

Soldier Bear
by Bibi Dumon Tak, translated by Laura Watkinson
(Eerdmans), Netherlands

Other Awards

● ● ● EZRA JACK KEATS ● ● ● AWARD

This award, first presented in 1985, is administered by the Ezra Jack Keats Foundation and the New York Public Library. The award was originally given biennially to a promising new writer. Beginning in the year 2001, the award has been given annually to an ILLUSTRATOR as well as to a writer. The award honors work done in the tradition of Ezra Jack Keats, using the criteria of appeal to young children, storytelling quality, relation between text and illustration, positive reflection of families, and the multicultural nature of the world. The award is presented at the Early Childhood Resource and Information Center of the New York Public Library. Funded by the Ezra Jack Keats Foundation, the recipient receives a monetary award and a medallion.

1985

The Patchwork Quilt
by Valerie Flournoy, illustrated by Jerry Pinkney
(Dial)

1987

Jamaica's Find
by Juanita Havill, illustrated by Anne Sibley O'Brien
(Houghton Mifflin)

1989

Anna's Special Present
by Yoriko Tsutsui, illustrated by Akiko Hayashi (Viking)

1991

Tell Me a Story, Mama
by Angela Johnson, illustrated by David Soman
(Orchard)

1993

Tar Beach
by Faith Ringgold (Crown)

1995

Taxi! Taxi!
by Cari Best, illustrated by Dale Gottlieb (Little, Brown)

1997

Calling the Doves
by Juan Felipe Herrera, illustrated by Elly Simmons
(Children's Book Press)

2001

WRITER: **Henry Hikes to Fitchburg**
by D. B. Johnson (Houghton Mifflin)

ILLUSTRATOR: **Uptown**, by Bryan Collier (Holt)

2002

WRITER AND ILLUSTRATOR: **Freedom Summer**
by Deborah Wiles; illustrated by Jerome Lagarrigue
(Simon & Schuster)

2003

WRITER AND ILLUSTRATOR: **Ruby's Wish**
by Shirin Yim Bridges, illustrated by Sophie Blackall
(Chronicle)

2004

WRITER: **Yesterday I Had the Blues**
by Jeron Ashford Frame (Ten Speed Press)

ILLUSTRATOR: **My Name Is Yoon**, illustrated by Gabi
Swiatkowska (Farrar, Straus and Giroux)

2005

WRITER: **Going North**
by Janice Harrington (Farrar, Straus and Giroux)

ILLUSTRATOR: **The Night Eater**, illustrated by Jerome Lagarrigue (Scholastic)

2006

WRITER: **My Best Friend**
by Mary Ann Rodman (Viking)

ILLUSTRATOR: **Silly Chicken**, illustrated by Yunmee Kyong (Viking)

2007

WRITER: **For You Are a Kenyan Child**
by Kelly Cunnane (Simon & Schuster)

ILLUSTRATOR: **Mystery Bottle**, illustrated by Kristen Balouch (Hyperion)

2008

WRITER: **Leaves**
by David Ezra Stein (G. P. Putnam's Sons)

ILLUSTRATOR: **The Apple Pie that Papa Baked**, illustrated by Jonathan Bean (Simon & Schuster)

2009

WRITER: **Garmann's Summer**
by Stian Hole (Eerdmans)

ILLUSTRATOR: **Bird**, by Shadra Strickland (Lee & Low)

2010

WRITER: **Most Loved in All the World**
by Tonya Hegamin (Houghton Mifflin)

ILLUSTRATOR: **Only a Witch Can Fly**, by Taeeun Yoo (Macmillan)

• • • BOSTON GLOBE–HORN • • • BOOK AWARDS

The Boston Globe–Horn Book Awards have been presented annually since 1967 by the *Boston Globe* newspaper and *The Horn Book Magazine*. Through 1975, two awards were given, one for outstanding fiction and one for outstanding picturebook. In 1976, the award categories were changed to fiction or poetry, nonfiction, and picturebook. A monetary gift is awarded to the winner in each category.

1967

FICTION: **The Little Fishes**
by Erik Christian Haugaard (Houghton Mifflin)

PICTUREBOOK: **London Bridge Is Falling Down!**, illustrated by Peter Spier (Doubleday)

1968

FICTION: **The Spring Rider**
by John Lawson (Crowell)

FICTION HONOR BOOKS: **Young Mark**, by E. M. Almedingen (Farrar); **Dark Venture**, by Audrey White Beyer (Knopf); **Smith**, by Leon Garfield (Pantheon); **The Endless Steppe**, by Esther Hautzig (Crowell)

PICTUREBOOK: **Tikki Tikki Tembo,** by Arlene Mosel, illustrated by Blair Lent (Holt)

PICTUREBOOK HONOR BOOKS: **Gilgamesh: Man's First Story**, retold and illustrated by Bernarda Bryson (Holt); **Rosie's Walk**, by Pat Hutchins (Macmillan); **Jorinda and Joringel**, text by Jacob and Wilhelm Grimm, illustrated by Adrienne Adams (Scribner's); **All in Free but Janey**, text by Elizabeth Johnson, illustrated by Trina Schart Hyman (Little, Brown)

1969

FICTION: **A Wizard of Earthsea**
by Ursula Le Guin (Houghton Mifflin)

FICTION HONOR BOOKS: **Flambards**, by K. M. Peyton (World); **Turi's Poppa**, by Elizabeth Borton de Treviño (Farrar, Straus and Giroux); **The Pigman**, by Paul Zindel (HarperCollins)

PICTUREBOOK: **The Adventures of Paddy Pork**
by John S. Goodall (Harcourt)

PICTUREBOOK HONOR BOOKS: **New Moon Cove**, by Ann Atwood (Scribner's); **Monkey in the Jungle**, text by Edna Mitchell Preston, illustrated by Clement Hurd (Viking); **Thy Friend**, **Obadiah**, by Brinton Turkle (Viking)

1970

FICTION: **The Intruder**
by John Rowe Townsend (Lippincott)

FICTION HONOR BOOK: **Where the Lilies Bloom**, by Vera and Bill Cleaver (Lippincott)

PICTUREBOOK: **Hi, Cat!**, by Ezra Jack Keats (Macmillan)

PICTUREBOOK HONOR BOOK: **A Story, a Story**, by Gail Haley (Simon & Schuster)

1971

FICTION: **A Room Made of Windows** by Eleanor Cameron (Little, Brown)

FICTION HONOR BOOKS: **Beyond the Weir Bridge**, by Hester Burton (Crowell); **Come by Here**, by Olivia Coolidge (Houghton Mifflin); **Mrs. Frisby and the Rats of NIMH**, by Robert C. O'Brien (Simon & Schuster)

PICTUREBOOK: **If I Built a Village** by Kazue Mizumura (HarperCollins)

PICTUREBOOK HONOR BOOKS: **If All the Seas Were One Sea**, by Janina Domanska (Macmillan); **The Angry Moon**, retold by William Sleator, illustrated by Blair Lent (Little, Brown); **A Firefly Named Torchy**, by Bernard Waber (Houghton Mifflin)

1972

FICTION: **Tristan and Iseult** by Rosemary Sutcliff (Dutton)

PICTUREBOOK: **Mr. Gumpy's Outing**, by John Burningham (Holt)

1973

FICTION: **The Dark Is Rising** by Susan Cooper (McElderry)

FICTION HONOR BOOKS: **The Cat Who Wished to Be a Man**, by Lloyd Alexander (Dutton); **An Island in a Green Sea**, by Mabel Esther Allan (Simon & Schuster); **No Way of Telling**, by Emma Smith (McElderry)

PICTUREBOOK: **King Stork**, by Trina Schart Hyman (Little, Brown)

PICTUREBOOK HONOR BOOKS: **The Magic Tree**, by Gerald McDermott (Holt); **Who, Said Sue, Said Whoo?**, by Ellen Raskin (Simon & Schuster); **The Silver Pony**, by Lynd Ward (Houghton Mifflin)

1974

FICTION: **M. C. Higgins, the Great** by Virginia Hamilton (Macmillan)

FICTION HONOR BOOKS: **And Then What Happened, Paul Revere?**, by Jean Fritz (Coward-McCann); **The Summer after the Funeral**, by Jane Gardam (Macmillan); **Tough Chauncey**, by Doris Buchanan Smith (Morrow)

PICTUREBOOK: **Jambo Means Hello**, by Muriel Feelings, illustrated by Tom Feelings (Dial)

PICTUREBOOK HONOR BOOKS: **All Butterflies**, by Marcia Brown (Scribner's); **Herman the Helper**, by Robert Kraus, illustrated by Jose Aruego and Ariane Dewey (Windmill); **A Prairie Boy's Winter**, by William Kurelek (Houghton Mifflin)

1975

FICTION: **Transport 7-41-R** by T. Degens (Viking)

FICTION HONOR BOOK: **The Hundred Penny Box**, text by Sharon Bell Mathis, illustrated by Leo and Diane Dillon (Viking)

PICTUREBOOK: **Anno's Alphabet**, by Mitsumasa Anno (HarperCollins)

PICTUREBOOK HONOR BOOKS: **She Come Bringing Me that Little Baby Girl**, text by Eloise Greenfield, illustrated by John Steptoe (Lippincott); **Scram, Kid!**, text by Ann McGovern, illustrated by Nola Langner (Viking); **The Bear's Bicycle**, text by Emilie Warren McLeod, illustrated by David McPhail (Little, Brown)

1976

FICTION: **Unleaving** by Jill Paton Walsh (Farrar, Straus and Giroux)

FICTION HONOR BOOKS: **A String in the Harp**, by Nancy Bond (McElderry); **A Stranger Came Ashore**, by Mollie Hunter (HarperCollins); **Dragonwings**, by Laurence Yep (HarperCollins)

NONFICTION: **Voyaging to Cathay: Americans in the China Trade**, by Alfred Tamarin and Shirley Glubok (Viking)

NONFICTION HONOR BOOKS: **Will You Sign Here, John Hancock?**, text by Jean Fritz, illustrated by Trina Schart Hyman (Coward-McCann); **Never to Forget: The Jews of the Holocaust**, by Milton Meltzer (HarperCollins); **Pyramid**, by David Macaulay (Houghton Mifflin)

PICTUREBOOK: **Thirteen**, by Remy Charlip and Jerry Joyner (Four Winds)

PICTUREBOOK HONOR BOOKS: **The Desert Is Theirs**, text by Byrd Baylor, illustrated by Peter Parnall (Scribner's); **Six Little Ducks**, by Chris Conover (Crowell); **Song of the Boat**, text by Lorenz Graham, illustrated by Leo and Diane Dillon (Crowell)

1977

FICTION: **Child of the Owl** by Laurence Yep (HarperCollins)

FICTION HONOR BOOKS: **Blood Feud**, by Rosemary Sutcliff (Dutton); **Roll of Thunder, Hear My Cry**, by Mildred Taylor (Dial); *The Machine Gunners*, by Robert Westall (Greenwillow)

NONFICTION: *Chance, Luck and Destiny*, by Peter Dickinson (Little, Brown)

NONFICTION HONOR BOOKS: *Watching the Wild Apes*, by Betty Ann Kevles (Dutton); *The Colonial Cookbook*, by Lucille Recht Penner (Hastings); *From Slave to Abolitionist*, by Lucille Schulberg Warner (Dial)

PICTUREBOOK: *Grandfa' Grig Had a Pig and Other Rhymes without Reason from Mother Goose*, by Wallace Tripp (Little, Brown)

PICTUREBOOK HONOR BOOKS: *Anno's Counting Book*, by Mitsumasa Anno (Crowell); *Ashanti to Zulu: African Traditions*, text by Margaret Musgrove, illustrated by Leo and Diane Dillon (Dial); *The Amazing Bone*, by William Steig (Farrar, Straus and Giroux)

SPECIAL CITATION: *The Changing City and the Changing Countryside*, by Jörg Müller (McElderry)

1978

FICTION: *The Westing Game* by Ellen Raskin (Dutton)

FICTION HONOR BOOKS: *Ramona and Her Father*, by Beverly Cleary (Morrow); *Anpao: An American Indian Odyssey*, by Jamake Highwater (Lippincott); *Alan and Naomi*, by Myron Levoy (HarperCollins)

NONFICTION HONOR BOOKS: *Settlers and Strangers: Native Americans of the Desert Southwest and History as They Saw It*, by Betty Baker (Macmillan); *Castle*, by David Macaulay (Houghton Mifflin)

NONFICTION: *Mischling, Second Degree: My Childhood in Nazi Germany*, by Ilse Koehn (Greenwillow)

PICTUREBOOK: *Anno's Journey*, by Mitsumasa Anno (Philomel)

PICTUREBOOK HONOR BOOKS: *The Story of Edward*, by Philippe Dumas (Parents); *On to Widecombe Fair*, text by Patricia Lee Gauch, illustrated by Trina Schart Hyman (Putnam); *What Do You Feed Your Donkey On? Rhymes from a Belfast Childhood*, collected by Collette O'Hare, illustrated by Jenny Rodwell (Collins)

1979

FICTION: *Humbug Mountain* by Sid Fleischman (Little, Brown)

FICTION HONOR BOOKS: *All Together Now*, by Sue Ellen Bridgers (Knopf); *Silas and Ben-Godik*, by Cecil Bodker (Delacorte)

NONFICTION: *The Road from Home: The Story of an Armenian Girl*, by David Kherdian (Greenwillow)

NONFICTION HONOR BOOKS: *The Iron Road: A Portrait of American Railroading*, text by Richard Snow, photos by David Plowden (Four Winds); *Self-Portrait: Margot Zemach*, by Margot Zemach (Addison-Wesley); *The Story of American Photography: An Illustrated History for Young People*, by Martin Sandler (Little, Brown)

PICTUREBOOK: *The Snowman*, by Raymond Briggs (Random House)

PICTUREBOOK HONOR BOOKS: *Cross-Country Cat*, text by Mary Calhoun, illustrated by Erik Ingraham (Morrow); *Ben's Trumpet*, by Rachel Isadora (Greenwillow)

1980

FICTION: *Conrad's War* by Andrew Davies (Crown)

FICTION HONOR BOOKS: *The Night Swimmers*, by Betsy Byars (Delacorte); *Me and My Million*, by Clive King (Crowell); *The Alfred Summer*, by Jan Slepian (Macmillan)

NONFICTION: *Building the Fight against Gravity*, text by Mario Salvadori, illustrated by Saralinda Hooker and Christopher Ragus (McElderry)

NONFICTION HONOR BOOKS: *Childtimes: A Three-Generation Memoir*, text by Eloise Greenfield, illustrated by Jerry Pinkney, and with photos (Crowell); *Stonewall*, text by Jean Fritz, illustrated by Stephen Gammell (Putnam); *How the Forest Grew*, text by William Jaspersohn, illustrated by Chuck Eckart (Greenwillow)

PICTUREBOOK: *The Garden of Abdul Gasazi*, by Chris Van Allsburg (Houghton Mifflin)

PICTUREBOOK HONOR BOOKS: *The Gray Lady and the Strawberry Snatcher*, by Molly Bang (Greenwillow); *Why the Tides Ebb and Flow*, text by John Chase Bowden, illustrated by Marc Brown (Houghton Mifflin)

SPECIAL CITATION: *Graham Oakley's Magical Changes*, by Graham Oakley (Simon & Schuster)

1981

FICTION: ***The Leaving***
by Lynn Hall (Scribner's)

FICTION HONOR BOOKS: ***Ida Early Comes over the Mountain***, by Robert Burch (Viking); ***Flight of the Sparrow***, by Julia Cunningham (Pantheon); ***Footsteps***, by Leon Garfield (Delacorte)

NONFICTION: ***The Weaver's Gift***, text by Kathryn Lasky, photos by Christopher Knight (Warne)

NONFICTION HONOR BOOKS: ***You Can't Be Timid with a Trumpet: Notes from the Orchestra***, by Betty English (Lothrop, Lee & Shepard); ***The Hospital Book***, text by James Howe, photos by Mal Warshaw (Random House); ***Junk Food, Fast Food, Health Food: What America Eats and Why***, by Lila Perl (Clarion)

PICTUREBOOK: ***Outside over There***, by Maurice Sendak (HarperCollins)

PICTUREBOOK HONOR BOOKS: ***Where the Buffaloes Begin***, text by Olaf Baker, illustrated by Stephen Gammell (Warne); ***On Market Street***, text by Arnold Lobel, illustrated by Anita Lobel (Greenwillow); ***Jumanji***, by Chris Van Allsburg (Houghton Mifflin)

1982

FICTION: ***Playing Beatie Bow***
by Ruth Park (Simon & Schuster)

FICTION HONOR BOOKS: ***The Voyage Begun***, by Nancy Bond (Simon & Schuster); ***Ask Me No Questions***, by Ann Schlee (Holt); ***The Scarecrows***, by Robert Westall (Greenwillow)

NONFICTION: ***Upon the Head of the Goat: A Childhood in Hungary, 1939–1944***, by Aranka Siegal (Farrar, Straus and Giroux)

NONFICTION HONOR BOOKS: ***Lobo of the Tasaday***, by John Nance (Pantheon); ***Dinosaurs of North America***, text by Helen Roney Sattler, illustrated by Anthony Rao (Lothrop, Lee & Shepard)

PICTUREBOOK: ***A Visit to William Blake's Inn: Poems for Innocent and Experienced Travelers***, by Nancy Willard, illustrated by Alice and Martin Provensen (Harcourt)

PICTUREBOOK HONOR BOOK: ***The Friendly Beasts: An Old English Christmas Carol***, by Tomie dePaola (Putnam)

1983

FICTION: ***Sweet Whisper, Brother Rush***
by Virginia Hamilton (Philomel)

FICTION HONOR BOOKS: ***Homesick: My Own Story***, by Jean Fritz (Putnam); ***The Road to Camlann***, by Rosemary Sutcliff (Dutton); ***Dicey's Song***, by Cynthia Voigt (Simon & Schuster)

NONFICTION: ***Behind Barbed Wire: The Imprisonment of Japanese Americans during World War II***, by Daniel Davis (Dutton)

NONFICTION HONOR BOOKS: ***Hiroshima No Pika***, by Toshi Maruki (Lothrop, Lee & Shepard); ***The Jewish Americans: A History in Their Own Words: 1650–1950***, by Milton Meltzer (Crowell)

PICTUREBOOK: ***A Chair for My Mother***, by Vera B. Williams (Greenwillow)

PICTUREBOOK HONOR BOOKS: ***Friends***, by Helme Heine (McElderry); ***Yeh-Shen: A Cinderella Story from China***, text by Ai-Ling Louie, illustrated by Ed Young (Philomel); ***Doctor De Soto***, by William Steig (Farrar, Straus and Giroux)

1984

FICTION: ***A Little Fear***
by Patricia Wrighton (McElderry)

FICTION HONOR BOOKS: ***Archer's Goon***, by Diana Wynne Jones (Greenwillow); ***Unclaimed Treasures***, by Patricia MacLachlan (HarperCollins); ***A Solitary Blue***, by Cynthia Voigt (Simon & Schuster)

NONFICTION: ***The Double Life of Pocahontas***, by Jean Fritz (Putnam)

NONFICTION HONOR BOOKS: ***Queen Eleanor: Independent Spirit of the Medieval World: A Biography of Eleanor of Aquitaine***, by Polly Schoyer Brooks (Lippincott); ***Children of the Wild West***, by Russell Freedman (Clarion); ***The Tipi: A Center of Native American Life***, by David and Charlotte Yue (Knopf)

PICTUREBOOK: ***Jonah and the Great Fish***, by Warwick Hutton (McElderry)

PICTUREBOOK HONOR BOOKS: ***Dawn***, by Molly Bang (Morrow); ***The Guinea Pig ABC***, by Kate Duke (Dutton); ***The Rose in My Garden***, text by Arnold Lobel, illustrated by Anita Lobel (Greenwillow)

1985

FICTION: ***The Moves Make the Man***
by Bruce Brooks (HarperCollins)

FICTION HONOR BOOKS: ***Babe: The Gallant Pig***, by Dick King-Smith (Crown); ***The Changeover: A Supernatural Romance***, by Margaret Mahy (McElderry)

NONFICTION: **Commodore Perry in the Land of the Shogun**, by Rhoda Blumberg (Lothrop, Lee & Shepard)

NONFICTION HONOR BOOKS: **Boy**, by Roald Dahl (Farrar, Straus and Giroux); **1812: The War Nobody Won**, by Albert Marrin (Simon & Schuster)

PICTUREBOOK: **Mama Don't Allow**, by Thacher Hurd (HarperCollins)

PICTUREBOOK HONOR BOOKS: **Like Jake and Me**, text by Mavis Jukes, illustrated by Lloyd Bloom (Knopf); **How Much Is a Million?**, text by David M. Schwartz, illustrated by Stephen Kellogg (Lothrop, Lee & Shepard); **The Mysteries of Harris Burdick**, by Chris Van Allsburg (Houghton Mifflin)

SPECIAL CITATION: **1, 2, 3**, by Tana Hoban (Greenwillow)

1986

FICTION: **In Summer Light**
by Zibby Oneal (Viking)

FICTION HONOR BOOKS: **Prairie Songs**, by Pam Conrad (HarperCollins); **Howl's Moving Castle**, by Diana Wynne Jones (Greenwillow)

NONFICTION: **Auks, Rocks, and the Odd Dinosaur: Inside Stories from the Smithsonian's Museum of Natural History**, by Peggy Thomson (Crowell)

NONFICTION HONOR BOOKS: **Dark Harvest: Migrant Farmworkers in America**, text by Brent Ashabranner, photos by Paul Conklin (Dodd, Mead); **The Truth about Santa Claus**, by James Cross Giblin (Crowell)

PICTUREBOOK: **The Paper Crane**, by Molly Bang (Greenwillow)

PICTUREBOOK HONOR BOOKS: **Gorilla**, by Anthony Browne (Knopf); **The Trek**, by Ann Jonas (Greenwillow); **The Polar Express**, by Chris Van Allsburg (Houghton Mifflin)

1987

FICTION: **Rabble Starkey**
by Lois Lowry (Houghton Mifflin)

FICTION HONOR BOOKS: **Georgia Music**, by Helen V. Griffith (Greenwillow); **Isaac Campion**, by Janni Howker (Greenwillow)

NONFICTION: **The Pilgrims of Plimoth**, by Marcia Sewall (Simon & Schuster)

NONFICTION HONOR BOOKS: **Being Born**, text by Sheila Kitzinger, photos by Lennart Nilsson

(Grosset & Dunlap); **The Magic Schoolbus at the Waterworks**, text by Joanna Cole, illustrated by Bruce Degen (Scholastic); **Steamboat in a Cornfield**, by John Hartford (Crown)

PICTUREBOOK: **Mufaro's Beautiful Daughters**, by John Steptoe (Lothrop, Lee & Shepard)

PICTUREBOOK HONOR BOOKS: **In Coal Country**, text by Judith Hendershot, illustrated by Thomas B. Allen (Knopf); **Cherries and Cherry Pits**, by Vera B. Williams (Greenwillow); **Old Henry**, text by Joan Blos, illustrated by Stephen Gammell (Morrow)

1988

FICTION: **The Friendship**
by Mildred Taylor (Dial)

FICTION HONOR BOOKS: **Granny Was a Buffer Girl**, by Berlie Doherty (Orchard); **Joyful Noise: Poems for Two Voices**, by Paul Fleischman (HarperCollins); **Memory**, by Margaret Mahy (McElderry)

NONFICTION: **Anthony Burns: The Defeat and Triumph of a Fugitive Slave**, by Virginia Hamilton (Knopf)

NONFICTION HONOR BOOKS: **African Journey**, by John Chiasson (Bradbury); **Little by Little: A Writer's Education**, by Jean Little (Viking)

PICTUREBOOK: **The Boy of the Three-Year Nap**, text by Diane Snyder, illustrated by Allen Say (Houghton Mifflin)

PICTUREBOOK HONOR BOOKS: **Where the Forest Meets the Sea**, by Jeannie Baker (Greenwillow); **Stringbean's Trip to the Shining Sea**, text by Vera B. Williams, illustrated by Jennifer and Vera B. Williams (Greenwillow)

1989

FICTION: **The Village by the Sea**
by Paula Fox (Orchard)

FICTION HONOR BOOKS: **Eva**, by Peter Dickinson (Delacorte); **Gideon Ahoy!**, by William Mayne (Delacorte)

NONFICTION: **The Way Things Work**, by David Macaulay (Houghton Mifflin)

NONFICTION HONOR BOOKS: **The Rainbow People**, by Laurence Yep (HarperCollins); **Round Buildings, Square Buildings, and Buildings that Wiggle Like a Fish**, by Philip M. Isaacson (Knopf)

PICTUREBOOK: **Shy Charles**, by Rosemary Wells (Dial)

PICTUREBOOK HONOR BOOKS: *Island Boy*, by Barbara Cooney (Viking); *The Nativity*, illustrated by Julie Vivas (Harcourt)

1990

FICTION: *Maniac Magee*
by Jerry Spinelli (Little, Brown)

FICTION HONOR BOOKS: *Saturnalia*, by Paul Fleischman (HarperCollins); *Stonewords*, by Pam Conrad (HarperCollins)

NONFICTION: *The Great Little Madison*, by Jean Fritz (Putnam)

NONFICTION HONOR BOOK: *Insect Metamorphosis: From Egg to Adult*, text by Ron and Nancy Goor, photos by Ron Goor (Simon & Schuster)

PICTUREBOOK: *Lon Po Po: A Red Riding-Hood Story from China*, by Ed Young (Philomel)

PICTUREBOOK HONOR BOOK: *Chicka Chicka Boom Boom*, text by Bill Martin Jr. and John Archambault, illustrated by Lois Ehlert (Simon & Schuster)

SPECIAL CITATION: *Valentine and Orson*, by Nancy Ekholm Burkert (Farrar, Straus and Giroux)

1991

FICTION: *The True Confessions of Charlotte Doyle*
by Avi (Orchard)

FICTION HONOR BOOKS: *Paradise Cafe and Other Stories*, by Martha Brooks (Joy Street); *Judy Scuppernong*, by Brenda Seabrooke (Cobblehill)

NONFICTION: *Appalachia: The Voices of Sleeping Birds*, text by Cynthia Rylant, illustrated by Barry Moser (Harcourt)

NONFICTION HONOR BOOKS: *The Wright Brothers: How They Invented the Airplane*, by Russell Freedman (Holiday House); *Good Queen Bess: The Story of Elizabeth I of England*, text by Diane Stanley and Peter Vennema, illustrated by Diane Stanley (Four Winds)

PICTUREBOOK: *The Tale of the Mandarin Ducks*, by Katherine Paterson, illustrated by Leo and Diane Dillon (Dutton)

PICTUREBOOK HONOR BOOKS: *Aardvarks, Disembark!*, by Ann Jonas (Greenwillow); *Sophie and Lou*, by Petra Mathers (HarperCollins)

1992

FICTION: *Missing May*
by Cynthia Rylant (Orchard)

FICTION HONOR BOOKS: *Nothing but the Truth*, by Avi (Orchard); *Somewhere in the Darkness*, by Walter Dean Myers (Scholastic)

NONFICTION: *Talking with Artists*, by Pat Cummings (Bradbury)

NONFICTION HONOR BOOKS: *Red Leaf, Yellow Leaf*, by Lois Ehlert (Harcourt); *The Handmade Alphabet*, by Laura Rankin (Dial)

PICTUREBOOK: *Seven Blind Mice*, by Ed Young (Philomel)

PICTUREBOOK HONOR BOOK: *In the Tall, Tall Grass*, by Denise Fleming (Holt)

1993

FICTION: *Ajeemah and His Son*
by James Berry (HarperCollins)

FICTION HONOR BOOK: *The Giver*, by Lois Lowry (Houghton Mifflin)

NONFICTION: *Sojourner Truth: Ain't I a Woman?*, by Patricia and Fredrick McKissack (Scholastic)

NONFICTION HONOR BOOK: *Lives of the Musicians: Good Times, Bad Times (and What the Neighbors Thought)*, text by Kathleen Krull, illustrated by Kathryn Hewitt (Harcourt)

PICTUREBOOK: *The Fortune Tellers*, by Lloyd Alexander, illustrated by Trina Schart Hyman (Dutton)

PICTUREBOOK HONOR BOOKS: *Komodo!*, by Peter Sís (Greenwillow); *Raven: A Trickster Tale from the Pacific Northwest*, by Gerald McDermott (Harcourt)

1994

FICTION: *Scooter*
by Vera B. Williams (Greenwillow)

FICTION HONOR BOOKS: *Flour Babies*, by Anne Fine (Little, Brown); *Western Wind*, by Paula Fox (Orchard)

NONFICTION: *Eleanor Roosevelt: A Life of Discovery*, by Russell Freedman (Clarion)

NONFICTION HONOR BOOKS: *Unconditional Surrender: U. S. Grant and the Civil War*, by Albert Marrin (Simon & Schuster); *A Tree Place and Other Poems*, text by Constance Levy, illustrated by Robert Sabuda (McElderry)

PICTUREBOOK: *Grandfather's Journey*, by Allen Say (Houghton Mifflin)

PICTUREBOOK HONOR BOOKS: *Owen*, by Kevin Henkes (Greenwillow); *A Small Tall Tale from the Far Far North*, by Peter Sís (Knopf)

1995

FICTION: *Some of the Kinder Planets* by Tim Wynne-Jones (Orchard)

FICTION HONOR BOOKS: *Jericho*, by Janet Hickman (Greenwillow); *Earthshine*, by Theresa Nelson (Orchard)

NONFICTION: *Abigail Adams, Witness to a Revolution*, by Natalie Bober (Simon & Schuster)

NONFICTION HONOR BOOKS: *It's Perfectly Normal: Changing Bodies, Growing Up, Sex, and Sexual Health*, text by Robie H. Harris, illustrated by Michael Emberley (Candlewick); *The Great Fire*, by Jim Murphy (Scholastic)

PICTUREBOOK: *John Henry*, by Julius Lester, illustrated by Jerry Pinkney (Dial)

PICTUREBOOK HONOR BOOK: *Swamp Angel*, text by Anne Isaacs, illustrated by Paul O. Zelinsky (Dutton)

1996

FICTION: *Poppy* by Avi, illustrated by Brian Floca (Orchard)

FICTION HONOR BOOKS: *The Moorchild*, by Eloise McGraw (McElderry); *Belle Prater's Boy*, by Ruth White (Farrar, Straus and Giroux)

NONFICTION: *Orphan Train Rider: One Boy's True Story*, by Andrea Warren (Houghton Mifflin)

NONFICTION HONOR BOOKS: *The Boy Who Lived with the Bears: And Other Iroquois Stories*, text by Joseph Bruchac, illustrated by Murv Jacob (HarperCollins); *Haystack*, text by Bonnie and Arthur Geisert, illustrated by Arthur Geisert (Houghton Mifflin)

PICTUREBOOK: *In the Rain with Baby Duck*, text by Amy Hest, illustrated by Jill Barton (Candlewick)

PICTUREBOOK HONOR BOOKS: *Fanny's Dream*, text by Caralyn Buehner, illustrated by Mark Buehner (Dial); *Home Lovely*, by Lynne Rae Perkins (Greenwillow)

1997

FICTION AND POETRY: *The Friends* by Kazumi Yumoto, translated by Cathy Hirano (Farrar, Straus and Giroux)

FICTION AND POETRY HONOR BOOKS: *Lily's Crossing*, by Patricia Reilly Giff (Delacorte); *Harlem*, by Walter Dean Myers, illustrated by Christopher Myers (Scholastic)

NONFICTION: *A Drop of Water: A Book of Science and Wonder*, by Walter Wick (Scholastic)

NONFICTION HONOR BOOKS: *Lou Gehrig: The Luckiest Man*, by David Adler, illustrated by Terry Widener (Harcourt); *Leonardo da Vinci*, by Diane Stanley (Morrow)

PICTUREBOOK: *The Adventures of Sparrowboy*, by Brian Pinkney (Simon & Schuster)

PICTUREBOOK HONOR BOOKS: *Home on the Bayou: A Cowboy's Story*, by G. Brian Karas (Simon & Schuster); *Potato: A Tale from the Great Depression*, by Kate Lied, illustrated by Lisa Campbell Ernst (National Geographic Society)

1998

FICTION AND POETRY: *The Circuit: Stories from the Life of a Migrant Child* by Francisco Jiménez (University of New Mexico Press)

FICTION AND POETRY HONOR BOOKS: *While No One Was Watching*, by Jane Leslie Conly (Holt); *My Louisiana Sky*, by Kimberly Willis Holt (Holt)

NONFICTION: *Leon's Story*, by Leon Walter Tillage, illustrated by Susan L. Roth (Farrar, Straus and Giroux)

NONFICTION HONOR BOOKS: *Martha Graham: A Dancer's Life*, by Russell Freedman (Clarion); *Chuck Close up Close*, by Jan Greenberg and Sandra Jordan (DK Publishing)

PICTUREBOOK: *And If the Moon Could Talk*, by Kate Banks, illustrated by Georg Hallensleben (Farrar, Straus and Giroux)

PICTUREBOOK HONOR BOOKS: *Seven Brave Women*, by Betsy Hearne, illustrated by Bethanne Andersen (Greenwillow); *Popcorn: Poems*, by James Stevenson (Greenwillow)

1999

FICTION: *Holes* by Louis Sachar (Farrar, Straus and Giroux)

FICTION HONOR BOOKS: *The Trolls*, by Polly Horvath (Farrar, Straus and Giroux); *Monster*, by Walter Dean Myers, illustrated by Christopher Myers (HarperCollins)

NONFICTION: *The Top of the World: Climbing Mount Everest*, by Steve Jenkins (Houghton Mifflin)

NONFICTION HONOR BOOKS: *Shipwreck at the Bottom of the World: The Extraordinary True Story of Shackleton and the* Endurance, by Jennifer Armstrong (Crown); *William Shakespeare and the Globe*, by Aliki (HarperCollins)

PICTUREBOOK: **Red-Eyed Tree Frog**, by Joy Cowley, illustrated by Nic Bishop (Scholastic)

PICTUREBOOK HONOR BOOKS: **Dance**, by Bill T. Jones and Susan Kuklin, illustrated by Susan Kuklin (Hyperion); **The Owl and the Pussycat**, by Edward Lear, illustrated by James Marshall (HarperCollins)

SPECIAL CITATION: **Tibet: Through the Red Box**, by Peter Sís (Farrar, Straus and Giroux)

2000

FICTION: **The Folk Keeper**
by Franny Billingsley (Simon & Schuster)

FICTION HONOR BOOKS: **King of Shadows**, by Susan Cooper (McElderry); **145th Street: Short Stories**, by Walter Dean Myers (Delacorte)

NONFICTION: **Sir Walter Ralegh and the Quest for El Dorado**, by Marc Aronson (Clarion)

NONFICTION HONOR BOOKS: **Osceola: Memories of a Sharecropper's Daughter**, collected and edited by Alan Govenar, illustrated by Shane W. Evans (Hyperion); **Sitting Bull and His World**, by Albert Marrin (Dutton)

PICTUREBOOK: **Henry Hikes to Fitchburg**, by D. B. Johnson (Houghton Mifflin)

PICTUREBOOK HONOR BOOKS: **Buttons**, by Brock Cole (Farrar, Straus and Giroux); **A Day, a Dog**, by Gabrielle Vincent (Front Street)

2001

FICTION AND POETRY: **Carver: A Life in Poems**
by Marilyn Nelson (Front Street)

FICTION AND POETRY HONOR BOOKS: **Everything on a Waffle**, by Polly Horvath (Farrar, Straus and Giroux); **Troy**, by Adèle Geras (Harcourt)

NONFICTION: **The Longitude Prize**, by Joan Dash, illustrated by Dusan Petricic (Farrar, Straus and Giroux)

NONFICTION HONOR BOOKS: **Rocks in His Head**, by Carol Otis Hurst, illustrated by James Stevenson (Greenwillow); **Uncommon Traveler: Mary Kingsley in Africa**, by Don Brown (Houghton Mifflin)

PICTUREBOOK: **Cold Feet**, by Cynthia DeFelice, illustrated by Robert Andrew Parker (DK Publishing)

PICTUREBOOK HONOR BOOKS: **Five Creatures**, by Emily Jenkins, illustrated by Tomek Bogacki (Farrar, Straus and Giroux); **The Stray Dog**, retold and illustrated by Marc Simont (HarperCollins)

2002

FICTION AND POETRY: **Lord of the Deep**
by Graham Salisbury (Delacorte)

FICTION AND POETRY HONOR BOOKS: **Amber Was Brave, Essie Was Smart**, by Vera B. Williams (Greenwillow); **Saffy's Angel**, by Hilary McKay (McElderry)

NONFICTION: **This Land Was Made for You and Me: The Life and Songs of Woody Guthrie**, by Elizabeth Partridge (Viking)

NONFICTION HONOR BOOKS: **Handel, Who Knew What He Liked**, by M. T. Anderson, illustrated by Kevin Hawkes (Candlewick); **Woody Guthrie: Poet of the People**, by Bonnie Christensen (Knopf)

PICTUREBOOK: **"Let's Get a Pup!" Said Kate**, by Bob Graham (Candlewick)

PICTUREBOOK HONOR BOOKS: **I Stink!**, by Kate McMullan, illustrated by Jim McMullan (HarperCollins); **Little Rat Sets Sail**, by Monika Bang-Campbell, illustrated by Molly Bang (Harcourt)

2003

FICTION AND POETRY: **The Jamie and Angus Stories**
by Anne Fine, illustrated by Penny Dale (Candlewick)

FICTION AND POETRY HONOR BOOKS: **Feed**, by M. T. Anderson (Candlewick); **Locomotion**, by Jacqueline Woodson (Putnam)

NONFICTION: **Fireboat: The Heroic Adventures of the** John J. Harvey, by Maira Kalman (Putnam)

NONFICTION HONOR BOOKS: **To Fly: The Story of the Wright Brothers**, by Wendie C. Old, illustrated by Robert Andrew Parker (Clarion); **Revenge of the Whale: The True Story of the Whaleship** Essex, by Nathaniel Philbrick (Putnam)

PICTUREBOOK: **Big Momma Makes the World**, by Phyllis Root, illustrated by Helen Oxenbury (Candlewick)

PICTUREBOOK HONOR BOOKS: **Dahlia**, by Barbara McClintock (Farrar, Straus and Giroux); **Blues Journey**, by Walter Dean Myers, illustrated by Christopher Myers (Holiday House)

2004

FICTION AND POETRY: **The Fire Eaters**
by David Almond (Delacorte)

FICTION AND POETRY HONOR BOOKS: **God Went to Beauty School**, by Cynthia Rylant (HarperTempest); **The Amulet of Samarkand:**

The Bartimaeus Trilogy, **Book One**, by Jonathan Stroud (Hyperion)

NONFICTION: ***An American Plague: The True and Terrifying Story of the Yellow Fever Epidemic of 1793***, by Jim Murphy (Clarion)

NONFICTION HONOR BOOKS: ***Surprising Sharks***, by Nicola Davies, illustrated by James Croft (Candlewick); ***The Man Who Went to the Far Side of the Moon: The Story of Apollo 11 Astronaut Michael Collins***, by Bea Uusma Schyffert (Chronicle)

PICTUREBOOK: ***The Man Who Walked Between the Towers***, by Mordicai Gerstein (Roaring Brook Press)

PICTUREBOOK HONOR BOOKS: ***The Shape Game***, by Anthony Browne (Farrar, Straus and Giroux); ***Snow Music***, by Lynne Rae Perkins (Greenwillow)

2005

FICTION AND POETRY: ***The Schwa Was Here*** by Neal Schusterman (Dutton)

FICTION AND POETRY HONOR BOOKS: ***Kalpana's Dream***, by Judith Clarke (Front Street); ***A Wreath for Emmett Till***, by Marilyn Nelson (Houghton)

NONFICTION: ***The Race to Save the Lord God Bird***, by Phillip Hoose (Kroupa/Farrar)

NONFICTION HONOR BOOKS: ***Good Brother, Bad Brother***, by James Cross Giblin (Clarion); ***Michael Rosen's Sad Book***, by Michael Rosen, illustrated by Quentin Blake (Candlewick)

PICTUREBOOK: ***Traction Man Is Here!***, by Mini Grey (Knopf)

PICTUREBOOK HONOR BOOKS: ***That New Animal***, by Emily Jenkins, illustrated by Pierre Pratt (Foster/Farrar); ***The Hello, Goodbye Window***, by Norton Juster, illustrated by Chris Raschka (di Capua/Hyperion)

2006

FICTION AND POETRY: ***The Miraculous Journey of Edward Tulane*** by Kate DiCamillo, illustrated by Bagram Ibatoulline (Candlewick)

FICTION AND POETRY HONOR BOOKS: ***Yellow Elephant: A Bright Bestiary*** (Harcourt) by Julie Larios, illustrated by Julie Paschkis; Yellow Star, by Jennifer Roy (Marshall Cavendish)

NONFICTION: ***If You Decide to Go to the Moon***, by Faith McNulty, illustrated by Steven Kellogg (Scholastic)

NONFICTION HONOR BOOK: ***A Mother's Journey***, by Sandra Markle, illustrated by Alan Marks (Charlesbridge); ***Wildfire***, by Taylor Morrison (Lorraine/Houghton)

PICTUREBOOK: ***Leaf Man***, by Lois Ehlert (Harcourt)

PICTUREBOOK HONOR BOOKS: ***A True Story in Which a Baby Hippo Loses His Mama during a Tsunami, but Finds a New Home, and a New Mama***, by Jeanette Winter (Harcourt); ***Sky Boys: How They Built the Empire State Building***, by Deborah Hopkinson, illustrated by James E. Ransome (Random House)

2007

FICTION AND POETRY: ***The Astonishing Life of Octavian Nothing, Traitor to the Nation, Volume I: The Pox Party*** by M. T. Anderson (Candlewick)

FICTION AND POETRY HONOR BOOKS: ***Clementine***, by Sara Pennypacker, illustrated by Marla Frazee (Hyperion); ***Rex Zero and the End of the World***, by Tim Wynne-Jones (Kroupa/Farrar)

NONFICTION: ***The Strongest Man in the World: Louis Cyr***, by Nicolas Debon (Groundwood)

NONFICTION HONOR BOOKS: ***Tracking Trash: Flotsam, Jetsam, and the Science of Ocean Motion***, by Loree Griffin Burns (Houghton); ***Escape!***, by Sid Fleischman (Greenwillow)

PICTUREBOOK: ***Dog and Bear: Two Friends, Three Stories***, by Laura Vaccaro Seeger (Roaring Brook)

PICTUREBOOK HONOR BOOKS: ***365 Penguins*** by Jean-Luc Fromental, illustrated by Joelle Jolivet (Abrams); ***Wolves***, by Emily Gravett (Simon & Schuster)

2008

PICTUREBOOK: ***At Night*** by Jonathan Bean (Farrar, Straus and Giroux)

PICTUREBOOK HONOR BOOKS: ***Fred Stays with Me!***, by Nancy Coffelt, illustrated by Tricia Tusa (Little); ***A Couple of Boys Have the Best Week Ever***, by Marla Frazee (Harcourt)

FICTION AND POETRY: ***The Absolutely True Diary of a Part-Time Indian***, by Sherman Alexie, illustrated by Ellen Forney (Little, Brown)

FICTION AND POETRY HONOR BOOKS: ***Shooting the Moon*** by Frances O'Roark Dowell (Simon & Schuster); ***Savvy***, by Ingrid Law (Dial)

NONFICTION: ***The Wall***, by Peter Sís (Farrar, Straus and Giroux)

NONFICTION HONOR BOOK: **Frogs**, by Nic Bishop (Scholastic); **What to Do about Alice?**, by Barbara Kerley, illustrated by Edwin Fotheringham (Scholastic)

2009

PICTUREBOOK: **Bubble Trouble**
by Margaret Mahy, illustrated by Polly Dunbar (Clarion)

PICTUREBOOK HONOR BOOKS: **Old Bear**, by Kevin Henkes (Greenwillow); **Higher! Higher!**, by Leslie Patricelli (Candlewick)

FICTION: **Nation**, by Terry Pratchett (HarperCollins)

FICTION HONOR BOOKS: **The Astonishing Life of Octavian Nothing: Traitor to the Nation, Volume II: The Kingdom on the Waves**, by M. T. Anderson (Candlewick); **The Graveyard Book**, by Neil Gaiman (HarperCollins)

NONFICTION: **The Lincolns: A Scrapbook Look at Abraham and Mary**, by Candace Fleming (Random House)

NONFICTION HONOR BOOKS: **The Way We Work**, by David Macauley with Richard Walker (Houghton); **Almost Astronauts: 13 Women Who Dared to Dream**, by Tanya Lee Stone (Candlewick)

2010

PICTUREBOOK: **I Know Here**
by Laurel Croza, illustrated by Matt James (Groundwood)

PICTUREBOOK HONOR BOOKS: **The Lion and the Mouse**, by Jerry Pinkney (Little, Brown); **It's a Secret!**, by John Burningham (Candlewick)

FICTION: **When You Reach Me**, by Rebecca Stead (Random House)

FICTION HONOR BOOKS: **The Dreamer**, by Pam Muñoz Ryan, illustrated by Peter Sís (Scholastic); **A Conspiracy of Kings**, by Megan Whalen Turner (Greenwillow)

NONFICTION: **Marching for Freedom: Walk Together, Children, and You Don't Grow Weary**, by Elizabeth Partridge (Viking)

NONFICTION HONOR BOOKS: **Anne Frank: Her Life in Words and Pictures**, by Merino Metselaar and

Ruud van der Roi (Roaring Brook); **Smile**, by Raina Telegmeier (Scholastic)

2011

PICTUREBOOK: **Pocketful of Posies: A Treasury of Nursery Rhymes**
by Sally Mavor (Houghton)

PICTUREBOOK HONOR BOOKS: **Dark Emperor and Other Poems of the Night**, by Joyce Sidman, illustrated by Rick Allen (Houghton); **Pecan Pie Baby**, by Jacqueline Woodson, illustrated by Sophie Blackall (Putnam)

FICTION: **Blink & Caution**, by Tim Wynne-Jones (Candlewick)

FICTION HONOR BOOKS: **Chime**, by Franny Billingsley (Dial); **Anna Hisiscus**, by Atinuke (Kane Miller)

NONFICTION: **The Notorious Benedict Arnold: A True Story of Adventure, Heroism, & Treachery**, by Steve Sheinkin (Roaring Brook)

NONFICTION HONOR BOOKS: **Into the Unknown: How Great Explorers Found Their Way by Land, Sea, and Air**, by Stewart Ross, illustrated by Stephen Biesty (Candlewick); **Can We Save the Tiger?**, by Martin Jenkins, illustrated by Vicky White (Candlewick)

● ● ●   HOW TO UPDATE   ● ● ●
CURRENT LISTINGS
AND FIND OTHER AWARDS

There are almost two hundred different awards given for children's and adolescent books; each has its own unique selection process and criteria. Some awards are chosen by adults, some by children, and some by young adults; some are international, some state or regional; some are for a lifetime of work, some for one book. We used the comprehensive listing of various award winners in *Children's Books: Awards and Prizes*, published by the Children's Book Council. This publication is updated periodically. We also used websites of professional organizations for the most up-to-date information. A search of the Internet will allow you to access most award lists.

Appendix B

Resources

● ● ● **BOOK SELECTION AIDS** ● ● ●

Adventuring with Books: Grades Pre-K–6 (13th edition), edited by Amy A. McClure and Janice V. Kristo (National Council of Teachers of English, 2002). A comprehensive list of books selected for their merit and potential use in the classroom. Approximately two thousand new books are annotated with several hundred from previous editions listed by genre. New editions are prepared periodically.

Best Science and Technology Reference Books for Young People, edited by H. Robert Malinowsky (Greenwood, 1991). Reviews science and technology resources and recommends grade levels for sci-tech reference books.

Books to Help Children Cope with Separation and Loss (4th edition), compiled by Masha Kabakow Rudman, Kathleen Dunne Gagne, and Joanne E. Bernstein (Bowker, 1993). 514 pages. Discussion of bibliotherapy with annotated lists of books grouped by category, such as adoption, divorce, and disabilities.

Children's Books: Awards and Prizes, compiled and edited by the Children's Book Council (1996). 497 pages. A comprehensive list of honors awarded to children's books. Awards chosen by adults and children are grouped by state, national, and international designations.

Children's Books from Other Countries, edited by Carl M. Tomlinson (Scarecrow Press, 1998). An annotated bibliography of more than seven hundred titles for children, containing both translated books and books from English-speaking countries other than the United States, published between 1950 and 1996.

Children's Books in Print (Bowker, annual). A comprehensive index of all children's books in print at time of publication. Author, title, and illustrator indexes give pertinent publishing information. A directory of publishers and addresses is included.

Children's Catalog (Wilson, annual). A comprehensive catalogue classified by Dewey decimal system, with nonfiction, fiction, short stories, and easy books. Five-year cumulations and annual supplements are available.

Children's Literature Review (Gale Research). Articles about authors and topics of interest with excerpts from reviews of the works of each author. Since 1976, new volumes have been added periodically.

Continuum Encyclopedia of Children's Literature, edited by Bernice E. Cullinan and Diane G. Person (Continuum International, 2005). A comprehensive collection of author and illustrator biographies, and topic and genre entries about children's literature in the major English-speaking countries.

Elementary School Library Collection (25th edition), edited by Linda Homa (Bro-Dart, 2000). A comprehensive bibliography of print and nonprint materials for school media collections. Dewey decimal subject classification, age level, and brief annotations.

For Reading Out Loud!, by Elizabeth Segel and Margaret Mary Kimmel (Bantam Dell, 1991). A guide to selecting books for sharing with young people and techniques for sharing them. Subject, title, and author index.

Hey! Listen to This: Stories to Read Aloud, edited by Jim Trelease (Penguin, 1992). Selections from literature to read to primary-grade children. Trelease adds intriguing background information about each excerpt.

Jewish Children's Books: How to Choose Them, How to Use Them, by Marcia Posner (Hadassah, 1986). 48 pages. Summaries, themes, discussion guides, questions and activities, and further resources are given for more than thirty books.

Kaleidoscope: A Multicultural Booklist for Grades K–8 (4th edition), edited by Nancy Hansen-Krening, Elaine M. Aoki, and Donald T. Mizokawa (National Council of Teachers of English, 2003). Hundreds of fiction and nonfiction texts for elementary and middle-school students, featuring culturally diverse populations.

Library Services for Hispanic Children: A Guide for Public and School Librarians, edited by Adela Artola Allen (Oryx Press, 1987). 201 pages. Articles on professional issues related to library service for Hispanic children. Annotated bibliographies of children's books in English about Hispanics, recent noteworthy children's books in Spanish, computer software, and resources about Hispanic culture for librarians.

Newbery and Caldecott Medal Books: 1986–2000: A Comprehensive Guide to the Winners (Horn Book/Association for Library Service to Children, 2001). A continuing collaboration features book summaries, selected excerpts, reviews, acceptance speeches, and biographical essays about the winners.

The New Read-Aloud Handbook (5th edition), by Jim Trelease (Penguin, 2001). An enthusiastic argument for why we should read to children, techniques for reading aloud, and a treasury of more than a thousand books that work well as read-alouds.

Pass the Poetry, Please (3rd edition), by Lee Bennett Hopkins (HarperCollins, 1998). A well-informed author describes engaging interviews with outstanding poets. Hopkins includes comments from interviews and insights into the poets' work and suggests ways to use poetry with children.

Read to Me: Raising Kids Who Love to Read (2nd edition), by Bernice E. Cullinan (Scholastic, 2006). A book that encourages parents to make reading a central part of children's lives and shows them how to do it.

Selected Jewish Children's Books, compiled by Marcia Posner (Jewish Book Council, 1991). Annotated list of books containing Jewish content and values, categorized by topic and age levels.

Subject Guide to Children's Books in Print (Bowker, annual). Approximately 140,000 titles are grouped under seven thousand subject categories. This indispensable reference helps you find books on specific topics.

Subject Index to Poetry for Children and Young People, compiled by Violet Sell (Core Collection Books, 1982). 1,035 pages. An index of poetry organized by subject with a code for title and author.

With Women's Eyes: Visitors to the New World, 1775–1918, edited by Marion Tinling (University of Oklahoma Press, 1993). 204 pages. Twenty-seven European women who visited America between 1775 and 1918 tell about their experiences.

The World through Children's Books, edited by Susan Stan (Scarecrow, 2002). An annotated bibliography of more than seven hundred titles for children containing both translated books and books from English-speaking countries other than the United States, and including books written by authors residing in the United States but set in other countries, published between 1996 and 2000.

● ● ● GENERAL REFERENCE ● ● ● BOOKS ABOUT AUTHORS AND ILLUSTRATORS

Author Talk: Conversations with Judy Blume, Bruce Brooks, Karen Cushman, Russell Freedman, Lee Bennett Hopkins, James Howe, Johanna Hurwitz, E. L. Konigsburg, Lois Lowry, Ann M. Martin, Nicholasa Mohr, Gary Paulsen, Jon Scieszka, Seymour Simon, and Laurence Yep, by Leonard S. Marcus (Simon & Schuster, 2000). Interviews with well-known children's writers.

Caldecott Medal Books: 1938–1957, by Bertha Mahony Miller and Elinor Whitney Field (Horn Book, 1958). Artists' acceptance speeches and biographical articles of the Caldecott Medal winners. See also more recent editions.

Celebrating Children's Books, edited by Betsy Hearne and Marilyn Kaye (Lothrop, Lee & Shepard, 1981). Articles about their craft by the foremost authors writing for children today. The essays in this collection appear in honor of Zena Sutherland.

Children's Book Illustration and Design (Vol. 1, 1992; Vol. 2, 1998), edited by Julie Cummins (PBC International). Each book is a showcase for the work of about eighty illustrators of children's books selected by a knowledgeable critic.

From Writers to Students: The Pleasures and Pains of Writing, edited by Jerry Weiss (International Reading Association, 1979). 113 pages. Interviews with nineteen noted authors who reveal the inside story on their writing, including Judy Blume, Mollie Hunter, Milton Meltzer, Mary Rodgers, and Laurence Yep.

Illustrators of Children's Books: 1744–1945, edited by Bertha E. Mahony, Louise Payson Latimer, and Beulah Folmsbee (Horn Book, 1947). 527 pages. *Illustrators of Children's Books: 1946–1956*, edited by Bertha Mahony Miller, Ruth Hill Viguers, and Marcia Dalphin (Horn Book, 1958). 229 pages. *Illustrators of Children's Books: 1957–1966*, edited by Lee Kingman, Joanna Foster, and Ruth Giles Lontoft (Horn Book, 1968). 295 pages. *Illustrators of Children's Books: 1967–1976*, edited by Lee Kingman, Grace Allen Hogarth, and Harriet Quimby (Horn Book, 1978). 290 pages. *Illustrators of Children's Books: 1977–1986*, edited by Lee Kingman (Horn Book, 1987). Biographical sketches and discussion of artists' techniques.

Meet the Authors and Illustrators, by Deborah Kovacs and James Preller (Scholastic, 1991). Sixty creators of favorite children's books talk about their work.

Newbery and Caldecott Medal Books: 1956–1965, edited by Lee Kingman (Horn Book, 1965). 300 pages. *Newbery and Caldecott Medal Books:*

1966–1975, edited by Lee Kingman (Horn Book, 1975). *Newbery and Caldecott Medal Books: 1976–1985*, edited by Lee Kingman (Horn Book, 1987). *Newbery Medal Books: 1922–1955*, edited by Bertha Mahony Miller and Elinor Whitney Field (Horn Book, 1955). Acceptance speeches and biographical sketches about the winners.

Oxford Companion to Children's Literature, compiled by Humphrey Carpenter and Mari Prichard (Oxford University Press, 1984). Includes nearly two thousand entries, more than nine hundred of which are biographical sketches of authors, illustrators, printers, and publishers. Other entries cover topic and genre issues and plot summaries of major works.

Pauses: Autobiographical Reflections of 101 Creators of Children's Books, by Lee Bennett Hopkins (HarperCollins, 1995). Biographical information and excerpts from interviews with authors and illustrators.

Secret Gardens, by Humphrey Carpenter (Houghton Mifflin, 1985). A book about the authors who wrote during the years called the golden age of children's literature in the late nineteenth and early twentieth centuries.

Something about the Author (Gale Research). In more than 120 volumes, extensive biographical information, photographs, publication records, awards received, and quotations about thousands of authors and illustrators of children's books.

Speaking for Ourselves: Autobiographical Sketches by Notable Authors of Books for Young Adults, edited by Donald R. Gallo (National Council of Teachers of English, 1990). Includes brief first-person statements from writers about writing and a bibliography for each writer.

Speaking for Ourselves, Too, edited by Donald R. Gallo (National Council of Teachers of English, 1993). More autobiographical sketches by notable authors of books for adolescents. Also includes brief first-person statements from writers about writing and a bibliography for each writer.

Speaking of Poets: Interviews with Poets Who Write for Children and Young Adults, edited by Jeffrey S. Copeland (National Council of Teachers of English, 1993). *Speaking of Poets: Interviews with Poets Who Write for Children and Young Adults 2*, edited by Jeffrey S. and Vicki L. Copeland (National Council of Teachers of English, 1994). Brief biographies and substantial interviews, followed by individual bibliographies.

Talking with Artists (Vol. 1, 1992; Vol. 2, 1995; Vol. 3, 1999), edited by Pat Cummings (Bradbury). Children's book illustrators talk about their work.

• • • PERIODICALS ABOUT • • • CHILDREN'S LITERATURE

Book Links: Connecting Books, Libraries, and Classrooms, American Library Association, published six times a year. Features booklists, interviews, teaching guides, and theme-related bibliographies to help teachers and librarians bring literature to children in ways that make connections across the curriculum.

Bookbird: A Journal of International Children's Literature, edited by Siobhán Parkinson and Valerie Coghlan; past editor-in- chief Meena G. Khorana. A refereed journal published quarterly by the International Board on Books for Young People, Nonnenweg 12 Postfach, CH-4004 Basel, Switzerland. The journal provides a forum to exchange experience and information among readers and writers in fifty nations of the world. Includes analyses of children's literature in particular regions—for example, children's literature of Latin America.

Booklist, American Library Association, published biweekly September through August, once each in July and August. Reviews children's, adolescent, and adult books and nonprint materials. Periodic bibliographies on a specific subject, reference tools, and commentary on issues are invaluable.

Bulletin of the Center for Children's Books, Graduate School of Library and Information Science of the University of Illinois at Urbana-Champaign, distributed by the University of Illinois Press, published monthly, except August. One of the few journals to include critical starred reviews of books rated as * (books of special distinction), R (recommended), Ad (additional), M (marginal), NR (not recommended), SpC (special collection), SpR (special reader). Curriculum use and developmental values are assigned when appropriate.

CBC Features. Children's Book Council, published semiannually. A newsletter about current issues and events, free and inexpensive materials, materials for Children's Book Week, topical bibliographies, and essays by publishers and authors or illustrators.

Children and Libraries: The Journal of the Association for Library Service to Children. Articles of interest to teachers and librarians on current issues, specialized bibliographies, acceptance speeches by the Newbery and Caldecott Award winners, conference proceedings, and organizational news.

Children's Literature Association Quarterly. Children's Literature Association. Book reviews and articles on British and American children's literature, research, teaching children's literature, theater, and conference proceedings. Special sections on current topics of interest, poetry, censorship, awards, and announcements.

The Horn Book Magazine, published bimonthly. A review journal with intelligent commentary by the editor and invited writers, and articles by creators of children's books, publishers, critics, teachers, and librarians. Ratings include starred reviews for outstanding books and comprehensive reviews of recommended books. Also includes Newbery and Caldecott acceptance speeches, biographical sketches of winners, and Boston Globe–Horn Book Award winners. Announces children's literature conferences and events. Cumulative indexes with ratings for all books published appear in *The Horn Book Guide* twice a year.

Language Arts. A journal published monthly from September through May by the National Council of Teachers of English. A book review column reviews current recommended books for children. Profiles on authors and illustrators; articles on using books in the classroom, response to literature, and writing as an outgrowth of reading literature.

The New York Times Book Review. Includes occasional columns of reviews written by authors, illustrators, or reviewers. Special section in spring and fall features children's books; annual list of the ten best illustrated books of the year.

Publishers Weekly. Published by Reed Elsevier with a spring and fall special edition on children's books. Diane Roback is senior children's book editor, Jennifer M. Brown is forecasts editor, and Joy Bean is associate editor. Both positive and negative reviews of books and news articles of interest to publishers, teachers, librarians, and authors. Interviews with authors, illustrators, and publishers are regular features.

The Reading Teacher. International Reading Association, published nine times a year. A column of reviews of current children's books is a regular feature. Articles appear on the use of books in the classroom, special bibliographies, cross-cultural studies, and research using children's books in reading programs.

Scholastic Instructor, edited by Terry Cooper, Scholastic, published eight times a year. Teachers and librarians write feature articles about trends, new books, and authors and illustrators of note. Bernice E. Cullinan is editor of the primary-grade poetry column; Paul Janeczko is editor of the intermediate-grade poetry column. Conducts an annual poetry writing contest for children.

School Library Journal. Published eleven times a year. Includes articles on current issues and reviews of children's books written by practicing librarians. Information is given about conferences and library services. Also includes an annual "Best Books of the Year" column and a cumulative index of starred reviews.

School Library Media Research: Refereed Research Journal of the American Association of School Librarians. Published online at www.ala.org. Includes research articles on censorship, using books in the classroom, research, library services, and current issues.

Science and Children. Published eight times a year by the National Science Teachers Association. Monthly column of reviews of informational books on science topics, plus an annual list of recommended books chosen by NSTA/Children's Book Council Liaison Committee.

Young Adult Library Services: The Journal of the Young Adult Library Services Association. Articles of interest to teachers and librarians on current issues, specialized bibliographies, acceptance speeches by the Printz Award winner, conference proceedings, and organizational news.

Note: Each professional organization and journal publisher has an online website. Check the Internet for listings of current events and features.

Professional References

Aldana, P. (Ed.). (2004). *Under the spell of the Moon: Art for children from the world's great illustrators.* Toronto, Ontario: Groundwood.

Alexander, L. (1970). Identifications and identities. *Wilson Library Bulletin 45*(2), 144–148.

Apol, L. (1998). "But what does this have to do with kids?": Literary theory and children's literature in the teacher education classroom. *Journal of Children's Literature, 24*(2), 32–46.

Appelt, K. (2002). *Poems from homeroom: A writer's place to start.* New York: Holt.

Arizpe, E., & Styles, M. (2003). *Children reading pictures: Interpreting visual texts.* New York: Routledge Falmer.

Aronson, M. (March/April 2011). New Knowledge. *The Horn Book Magazine, 87*(2), 57–62.

Atwell, N. (1998). *In the middle: New understandings about reading, writing, and learning.* Portsmouth, NH: Heinemann.

_____. (2007). *The reading zone: How to help kids become skilled, passionate, habitual, critical readers.* New York: Scholastic.

Bader, B. (1976). *American picturebooks from Noah's art to the beast within.* Old Tappan, NJ: Macmillan.

_____. (2002, November/December). How the little house gave ground; The beginnings of multiculturalism in a new, black children's literature. *The Horn Book Magazine, 78,* 657–673.

_____. (2003a). Multiculturalism takes root. *The Horn Book Magazine, 79,* 143–162.

_____. (2003b). Multiculturalism in the mainstream. *The Horn Book Magazine, 79,* 265–291.

_____. (2006). Krik, krik, krik: How Aardema & Co. attuned us to African folklore. *The Horn Book Magazine, 82,* 651–658.

_____. (2007, March/April). For the McKissacks, Black is boundless. *The Horn Book Magazine, 83,* 149–156.

_____. (2010). Folklore: It's a different story. *The Horn Book Magazine, 86,* 19–27.

_____. (2011). Nonfiction: What's really new and different and what isn't. *The Horn Book Magazine, 87*(6), 41–46.

Baker, D. F. (2006). Special effects: What makes a good fantasy? *The Horn Book Magazine, 82,* 621–625.

_____. (2007). Why is the Cold War hot? *The Horn Book Magazine, 83,* 655–660.

Bamford, R., & Kristo, J. (Eds.). (1997). *Making facts come alive: Choosing quality nonfiction literature K–8.* Norwood, MA: Christopher-Gordon.

Bang, M. (2002). *Picture this: How pictures work.* San Francisco, CA: Chronicle.

Banks, J. A., & Banks, C. A. M. (1993). *Multicultural education: Issues and perspectives* (Third edition). Boston: Allyn & Bacon.

Bauer, M. D. (1992). *What's your story? A young person's guide to writing fiction.* New York: Clarion.

_____. (1995). *A writer's story: From life to fiction.* Boston: Houghton Mifflin Harcourt.

_____. (1996). *Our stories: A fiction workshop for young authors.* Boston: Houghton Mifflin Harcourt.

Beach, R., Thein, A. H., & Parks, D. (2007). Perspective-taking as transformative practice in teaching multicultural literature to white students. *English Journal, 97*(2), 54–60.

_____. (2008). *High school students' competing social worlds: Negotiating identities and allegiances in response to multicultural literature.* New York: Erlbaum.

Benton, M. (1984). The methodology vacuum in teaching literature. *Language Arts, 61,* 265–275.

_____. (1992). *Secondary worlds: Literature teaching and the visual arts.* Buckingham, UK: Open University Press.

Benton, M., & Benton, P. (2008). Forty years on: Touchstones now. *Children's literature in Education, 39,* 135–140.

Bishop, R. S. (1997). Multicultural literature for children: Making informed choices. In V. J. Harris (Ed.), *Teaching multicultural literature in grades K–8* (pp. 37–54). Norwood, MA: Christopher-Gordon.

_____. (2007). *Free within ourselves: The development of African American children's literature.* Portsmouth, NH: Heinemann.

_____. (Ed.). (1994). *Kaleidoscope: A multicultural booklist for grades K–8.* Urbana, IL: National Council of Teachers of English.

Blake, Q. (2006). *Magic pencil: Children's book illustration today.* London: The British Council and the British Library.

Blatt, G. (Ed.). (1993). *Once upon a folktale: Capturing the folklore process with children.* New York: Teachers College Press.

Blos, J. (1992). Perspectives on historical fiction. In R. Ammon & M. Tunnell (Eds.), *The story of ourselves: Teaching history through children's literature* (pp. 11–17). Portsmouth, NH: Heinemann.

Bogdan, D. (1990). In and out of love with literature: Response and the aesthetics of total form. In D. Bogdan & S. Straw (Eds.), *Beyond communication: Reading comprehension and criticism* (pp. 109–137). Portsmouth, NH: Heinemann.

Booth, D., & Moore, B. (1988). *Poems please! Sharing poetry with children.* Markham, Ontario: Pembroke.

Bosma, B. (1992). *Fairy tales, fables, legends, and myths: Using folk literature in your classroom.* New York: Teachers College Press.

Botkin, B. A. (1944). *A treasury of American folklore.* New York: Crown.

Boyd, M. P., & Galda, L. (2011). *Real talk in elementary classrooms: Effective oral language practice.* New York: Guilford.

Britton, J. (1970). *Language and learning.* London: Penguin.

Brooks, W., & McNair, J. (2008). *Embracing, evaluating, and examining African American children's and young adult literature.* Lanham: Scarecrow.

Brown, B., & Glass, M. (1991). *Important words: A book for poets and writers.* Portsmouth, NH: Boynton/Cook.

Bruchac, J. (1997). *Tell me a tale: A book about storytelling.* San Diego: Harcourt Brace.

Burrows, A. T. (1979). Profile: Karla Kuskin. *Language Arts, 56,* 934–939.

Cameron, E. (1969). *The green and burning tree.* New York: Little, Brown.

Campbell, P. (2004). Vetting the verse novel. *The Horn Book Magazine, 80,* 611–616.

Card, O. S. (1990). *How to write science fiction and fantasy.* Cincinnati, OH: Writer's Digest.

Carle, E. (2002). *The art of Eric Carle.* New York: Philomel.

Carrington, V., & Luke, A. (2003). Reading homes and families: From postmodern to modern? In A. van Kleeck, S. A. Stahl, & E. B. Bauer (Eds.), *On reading books to children: Parents and teachers* (pp. 231–252). Mahwah, NJ: Lawrence Erlbaum.

Carter, B. (2005). Privacy please. *The Horn Book Magazine, 81,* 525–534.

_____. (2010). Not the Newbery: books that make readers. *The Horn Book Magazine, 86*(4), 52–56.

Carter, J. B. (Ed.). (2007). *Building literacy connections with graphic novels: Page by page, panel by panel.* Urbana, IL: National Council of Teachers of English.

Charles, Z., & Robinson, L. (2008). *Over rainbows and down rabbit holes: The art of children's books.* Amherst, MA: Eric Carle Museum of Picture Book Art.

Chatton, B. (1993). *Using poetry across the curriculum: A whole language approach.* Phoenix, AZ: Oryx.

Cherland, M. (1992). Gendered readings: Cultural restraints upon response to literature. *The New Advocate, 5,* 187–198.

Cianciolo, P. J. (1976). *Illustrations in children's books.* Dubuque, IA: Brown.

_____. (1997). *Picture books for children* (Fourth edition). Chicago: American Library Association.

Cochran-Smith, M. (1984). *The making of a reader.* Norwood, NJ: Ablex.

Coles, R. (1989). *The call of stories: Teaching and the moral imagination.* Boston: Houghton Mifflin.

Colomer, T., Kummerling-Melibauer, B., & Silva-Diaz, C. (2010). *New Directions in Picturebook Research.* New York: Routledge.

Cooke, C. (2002). *The effects of scaffolding multicultural short stories on students' comprehension and attitudes.* Paper presented at the 31st Annual Meeting of the National Reading Conference, Miami, FL.

Cooper, S. (1981/1996). *Dreams and wishes: Essays on writing for children.* New York: Simon & Schuster.

Corso, G. (1983). Comment. In P. B. Janeczko (Ed.), *Poetspeak* (p.11). New York: Bradbury.

Cox, M. E., & Lang, A. (1893). *Cinderella: Three hundred and forty-five variants.* London: D. Nutt.

Cullinan, B. E. (Ed.). (1992). *Invitation to read: More children's literature in the reading program.* Newark, DE: International Reading Association.

Cullinan, B., Scala, M., Schroder, V., & Lovett, A. (1995). *Three voices: An invitation to poetry across the curriculum.* York, ME: Stenhouse.

Cummings, P. (Ed.). (1992). *Talking with artists* (Vol. 1). New York: Bradbury.

Cummins, J. (2004). Accessing the International Children's Digital Library. *The Horn Book Magazine, 80,* 145–151.

Cunningham A. E., & Stanovich, K. E. (1998). What reading does for the mind. *American Educator, Spring/Summer,* 8–15.

Daniels, H., & Steineke, N. (2004). *Mini-lessons for literature circles.* Portsmouth, NH: Heinemann.

Daniels, H., & Zemelman, S. (2004). *Subjects matter: Every teacher's guide to content-area reading.* Portsmouth, NH: Heinemann.

Darigan, D. L. (2001). NCTE poetry award recipient X. J. Kennedy. *Language Arts, 78,* 295–299.

Denman, G. A. (1988). *When you've made it your own: Teaching poetry to young people.* Portsmouth, NH: Heinemann.

Dillon, D. A. (1978). Perspectives: David McCord. *Language Arts, 55,* 379–385.

Doonan, J. (1993). *Looking at pictures in picture books.* Stroud, Glouchestershire: Thimble.

Dyson, A. H. (2003). *The brothers and sisters learn to write: Popular literacies in childhood and school culture.* New York: Teachers College Press.

Egoff, S. (1981). *Thursday's child: Trends and patterns in contemporary children's literature.* Chicago: American Library Association.

Eisner, W. (2008). *Comics and sequential art.* New York: Norton.

Enciso, P. (1994). Cultural identity and response to literature: Running lessons from Maniac McGee. *Language Arts, 71,* 524–533.

Erdrich, L. (1993). *Love medicine.* New York: Holt.

Ernst, S., & McClure, A. (2004). Profile: A poem is a house for words; NCTE Profiles: Mary Ann Hoberman. *Language Arts 81b*(3) 212–213.

Esbensen, B. J. (1975). *A celebration of bees: Helping children write poetry.* Minneapolis, MN: Winston.

———. (1995). *A celebration of bees: Helping children write poetry.* New York: Holt.

Evans, D. (2008). *Show & tell: Exploring the fine art of children's book illustration.* San Francisco: Chronicle.

Evans, J. (2009). *Talking beyond the page: Reading and responding to picturebooks.* New York: Routledge.

Farmer, P. (1979). *Beginnings: Creation myths of the world.* New York: Atheneum.

Feitelson, D., Kita, B., & Goldstein, Z. (1986). Effects of listening to series stories on first graders' comprehension and use of language. *Research in the Teaching of English, 20,* 339–356.

Fielding, L., Wilson, P. T., & Anderson, R. (1986). A new focus on free reading: The role of trade books in reading instruction. In T. E. Raphael & R. E. Reynolds (Eds.), *The contexts of school-based literacy* (pp. 149–160). New York: Random House.

Fish, S. (1980). *Is there a text in this class? The authority of interpretive communities.* Cambridge, MA: Harvard University Press.

Fisher, C. J., & Natarella, M. A. (1982). Young children's preferences in poetry: A national survey of first-, second-, and third-graders. *Research in the Teaching of English, 16*(4), 339–354.

Fitzgerald, J., & Graves, M. F. (2004). *Scaffolding reading experiences for English language learners.* Norwood, MA: Christopher-Gordon.

Fletcher, R. (1996). *Writer's notebook: Unlocking the writer within you.* New York: HarperCollins.

———. (1999). *Live writing: Breathing life into your words.* New York: HarperCollins.

Fletcher, R. (2000). *How writers work: Finding a process that works for you.* New York: HarperCollins.

———. (2002). *Poetry matters: Writing a poem from the inside out.* New York: HarperTrophy.

Fogarty, Mignon. (2011). Grammar Girl Presents the Ultimate Writing Guide for Students. Illustrated by Erwin Haya. New York: St. Martin's Griffin.

Fox, D., & Short, K. (Eds.). (2003). *Stories matter: The complexity of cultural authenticity in children's literature.* Urbana, IL: National Council of Teachers of English.

Fox, M. (1993). *Radical reflections: Passionate opinions on teaching, learning and living.* San Diego: Harcourt Brace.

Frohardt, D. C. (1999). *Teaching art with books kids love.* Golden, CO: Fulcrum Resources.

Frost, R. (1939). The figure a poem makes. *Collected poems of Robert Frost.* New York: Holt Rinehart Winston.

Frye, N. (1970). *The educated imagination.* Bloomington: Indiana University Press.

Galda, L. (1982). Assuming the spectator stance: An examination of the responses of three young readers. *Research in the Teaching of English, 16,* 1–20.

———. (1988). Readers, Texts and contexts: A response-based view of literature in the classroom. *The New Advocate, 2*(2), 92–102.

———. (1990). A longitudinal study of the spectator stance as a function of age and genre. *Research in the Teaching of English, 24,* 261–278.

———. (1998). Mirrors and windows: Reading as transformation. In T. E. Raphael & K. H. Au (Eds.), *Literature-based instruction: Reshaping the Curriculum* (pp. 1–12). Norwood, MA: Christopher-Gordon.

———. (2007/May). *Talent, turmoil, and tension: Adolescent literature today.* Annual Couper Lecture, Binghamton University, the State University of New York.

Galda, L., & Cullinan, B. E. (2003). Literature for literacy: What research says about the benefits of using trade books in the classroom. In J. Flood, D. Lapp, J. R. Squire, & J. M. Jensen (Eds.), *Handbook of research on teaching the English language arts* (Second edition, pp. 640–648). Old Tappan, NJ: Macmillan.

Galda, L., & Graves, M. F. (2007). *Reading and responding in the middle grades: Approaches for all classrooms.* Boston: Allyn & Bacon.

Galda, L., Ash, G. E., & Cullinan, B. E. (2000). Children's literature. In M. L. Kamil, P. B. Mosenthal, P. D. Pearson, & R. Barr (Eds.), *Handbook of reading research* (Vol. III, pp. 361–379). Mahwah, NJ: Erlbaum.

Galda, L., Rayburn, S., & Stanzi, L. C. (2000). *Looking through the faraway end: Creating a literature-based curriculum with second graders.* Newark, DE: International Reading Association.

Galda, L., Shockley, B. S., & Pellegrini, A. D. (1995). Sharing lives: reading, writing, talking, and living in a first-grade classroom. *Language Arts, 72,* 334–339.

Glazer, J. I. (1985). Profile: Lilian Moore. *Language Arts, 62,* 647–651.

Goodman, K. S. (1985). Transactional psycholinguistics model: Unity in reading. In H. Singer & R. B. Ruddell (Eds.), *Theoretical models and processes of reading* (Third edition, pp. 813–840). Newark, DE: International Reading Association.

Graves, D. (1989). *Experiment with fiction.* Portsmouth, NH: Heinemann.

_____. (1989). *Investigate nonfiction.* Portsmouth, NH: Heinemann.

_____. (1992). *Exploring poetry: The reading/writing teacher's companion.* Portsmouth, NH: Heinemann; Toronto: Irwin.

Graves, M. F., & Graves, B. B. (2003). *Scaffolding reading experiences to promote success* (Second edition). Norwood, MA: Christopher-Gordon.

Graves, M. F., Graves, B. B., & Braaten, S. (1996). Scaffolded reading experiences for inclusive classrooms. *Educational Leadership, 53*(5), 14–16.

Greenberg, J., & Jordan, S. (1991). *The painter's eye: Learning to look at contemporary American art.* New York: Delacorte.

_____. (1993). *The sculptor's eyes: Looking at contemporary American art.* New York: Delacorte.

Greenlaw, M. J. (1994). Profile: Barbara Juster Esbensen. *Language Arts, 71,* 544–548.

Grimal, P. (1965). *Larousse world mythology.* Seacaucus, NJ: Chartwell.

Grossman, F. (1991). *Listening to the bells: Learning to read poetry by writing poetry.* Portsmouth, NH: Boynton/Cook.

Guthrie, J., & Wigfield, A. (2000). Motivation and engagement in reading. In M. L. Kamil, P. B. Mosenthal, P. D. Pearson, & R. Barr (Eds.), *Handbook of reading research* (Vol. III, pp. 403–422). Mahwah, NJ: Erlbaum.

Hall, S. (1990). *Using picture storybooks to teach literary devices.* Westport, CT: Oryx.

Hamilton, V. (1993). Everything of value: Moral realism in the literature for children. *Journal of Youth Services in Libraries, 6,* 364–377.

Hancock, M. (2007).*Celebration of literature and response: Children, books, and teachers in K–8 classrooms* (Third edition). Englewood Cliffs, NJ: Prentice-Hall.

Hansen, S. (2004). *Fourth and fifth graders' poetry preferences before and after classroom poetry experiences: A case study.* (Plan B project submitted to the faculty of Graduate School of the University of Minnesota in partial fulfillment for the requirements for the degree of Master of Arts.)

Hansen-Krening, N., Aoki, E. M., & Mizokawa, D. T. (Eds.) (2003). *Kaleidoscope: A multicultural booklist for grades K–8* (Fourth edition). Urbana, IL: National Council of Teachers of English.

Harris, V. (1992). *Teaching multicultural literature in grades K–8.* Norwood, MA: Christopher-Gordon.

_____. (1997). *Using multiethnic literature in the K–8 classroom.* Norwood, MA: Christopher-Gordon.

Harrison, D. L., & Cullinan, B. (1999). *Easy poetry lessons that dazzle and delight.* New York: Scholastic.

Harste, J. C., Woodward, V. A., & Burke, C. L. (1984). Examining our assumptions: A transactional view of literacy and learning. *Research in the Teaching of English, 18*(1), 84–108.

Heard, G. (1989). *For the good of the earth and sun: Teaching poetry.* Portsmouth, NH: Heinemann.

_____. (1995). *Writing toward home: Tales and lessons to find your way.* Portsmouth, NH: Heinemann.

_____. (1999). *Awakening the heart: Exploring poetry in elementary and middle school.* Portsmouth, NH: Heinemann.

Hefner, C., & Lewis, K. (1995). *Literature-based science: Children's books and activities to enrich the K–5 curriculum.* Phoenix, AZ: Oryx.

Hemphill, L. (1999). Narrative style, social class, and response to poetry. *Research in the Teaching of English, 33,* 275–302.

Herman, G. B. (1978). "Footprints in the Sands of Time": Biography for Children. *Children's Literature in Education 9*(2), 85–94.

Hewitt, G. (1988). *Today you are my favorite poet: Writing poems with teenagers.* Portsmouth, NH: Heinemann.

Hickman, J. (1981). A new perspective on response to literature: Research in an elementary school setting. *Research in the Teaching of English, 115,* 343–354.

Hickman, J., & Cullinan, B. E. (1989). *Children's literature in the classroom: Weaving Charlotte's web.* Norwood, MA: Christopher-Gordon.

Hickman, J., Cullinan, B. E., & Hepler, S. (1995). *Children's literature in the classroom: Extending Charlotte's web.* Norwood, MA: Christopher-Gordon.

Hiebert, E. H., & Colt, J. (1989). Patterns of literature-based reading instruction. *The Reading Teacher, 43,* 14–20.

Hill, B., Johnson, N., & Noe, K. S. (Eds). (1995). *Literature circles and response.* Norwood, MA: Christopher-Gordon.

Holland, K., Hungerford, R. & Ernst, S. (Eds.). (1993). *Journeying: Children responding to literature.* Portsmouth, NH: Heinemann.

Hopkins, L. B. (1978). Profile: Aileen Fisher. *Language Arts, 55,* 868–870.

_____. (1987). *Pass the poetry, please.* New York: Harper & Row.

_____. (1991). Profile: Valerie Worth. *Language Arts, 68,* 499–501.

———. (1995). *Pauses: Autobiographical reflections of 101 creators of children's books.* New York: HarperCollins.

Hunt, J. (2007). Epic fantasy meets sequel prejudice. *The Horn Book Magazine, 83*, 645–653.

Iser, W. (1978). *The act of reading: A theory of aesthetic response.* Baltimore: The Johns Hopkins University Press.

Jackson, J. (1992). Paper presented at the Holmes-Hunter Lecture, University of Georgia, Athens.

Jalongo, M. R. (2004). *Young children and picture books* (Second edition). Washington, DC: National Association for the Education of Young Children.

Janeczko, P. (1983). *Poetspeak: In their work, about their work: A selection.* Scarsdale, NY: Bradbury.

———. (1990). *The place my words are looking for: What poets say about and through their work.* New York: Bradbury.

———. (1994). *Poetry from A to Z: A guide for young writers.* New York: Simon & Schuster.

———. (2001). *How to write poetry.* New York: Scholastic.

———. (2002). *Seeing the blue between: Advice and inspiration for young poets.* Cambridge, MA: Candlewick.

Kennedy, X. J., & Kennedy, D. M. (1982). *Knock at a star: A child's introduction to poetry.* Boston: Little, Brown.

Kiefer, B. Z. (1986). The child and the picture book: Creating live circuits. *Children's Literature Association Quarterly, 11*, 63–68.

———. (1995). *The potential of picturebooks.* Englewood Cliffs, NJ: Prentice-Hall.

Koertge, R. (2006). What makes a good poem? Tell the truth, but tell it slant. *The Horn Book Magazine, 82*, 535–539.

Kress, G., & van Leeuwen, T. (2006). *Reading images: The grammar of visual design* (Second edition). London: Routledge.

Kuhn, M., et al. (2006). Teaching children to become fluent and automatic readers. *Journal of Literacy Research, 38*, 357–388.

Kumar, L. (2007). Nikki Grimes. *Something about the author.* Farmington Hills MI: Gale.

Kuskin, K. (1980). *Dogs and dragons, trees and dreams.* New York: Harper & Row.

Langer, J. (1995). *Envisioning literature: Literary understanding and literature instruction.* New York: Teachers College Press.

Larrick, N. (1991). *Let's do a poem: Introducing poetry to children through listening, singing, chanting, impromptu choral reading, body movement, dance, and dramatization; including 98 favorite songs and poems.* New York: Delacorte.

Larson, L. C. (2007). *A case study exploring the "new literacies" during a fifth-grade electronic reading workshop.* Doctoral dissertation, Kansas State University.

Laster, L. (2011). *Reading fantastic literature: Science fiction and fantasy for young readers.* Unpublished manuscript. University of Minnesota.

Lattimer, H. (2003). *Thinking through genre: Units of study in reading and writing workshops 4–12.* Portland, ME: Stenhouse.

Laughlin, M., & Street, T. (1991). *Literature-based art and music: Children's books and activities to enrich the K–5 curriculum.* Phoenix, AZ: Oryx.

Lehman, B. A., Freeman, E. B., & Scharer, P. L. (2010). *Reading globally, K–8: connecting students to the world through literature.* Thousand Oaks, CA: Corwin.

Lehr, S. (Ed.). (2001). *Beauty, brains and brawn: The construction of gender in children's literature.* Portsmouth, NH: Heinemann.

Lehr, S. S. (1991). *The child's developing sense of theme: Responses to literature.* New York: Teacher's College Press.

Lester, J. (2004). *On writing for children and other people.* New York: Dial.

Lewis, C. (1997). The social drama of literature discussion in a fifth/sixth grade classroom. *Research in the Teaching of English, 31*, 163–204.

———. (2000). Limits of identification: The personal, pleasurable, and critical in reader response. *Journal of Literacy Research, 32*, 253–266.

———. (2001). *Literacy practices as social acts: Power, status, and cultural norms in the classroom.* Mahwah, NJ: Erlbaum.

Lewis, D. (2001). *Reading contemporary picturebooks: Picturing text.* New York: Routledge Falmer.

Lewis, J. P. (2009). Interview with Carolyn Brodie. www.jpatricklewis.com/teachers_interview1.shtml. Retrieved April 2009.

Liang, L. A. (2004). *Scaffolding middle school students' comprehension of and response to narrative text.* Paper presented at the meeting of the National Reading Conference, San Antonio, TX.

Livingston, M. C. (1990). *Climb into the bell tower.* New York: Harper & Row.

———. (1991). *Poem-making: Ways to begin writing poetry.* New York: HarperCollins.

———. (1997). *I am writing a poem about . . . : A game of poetry.* New York: McElderry.

Lunge-Larsen, L. (2004). *Folklore for today's children.* Speech given for Book Week at the University of Minnesota.

MacDonald, M. R., & Sturm, B. W. (2001). *The storyteller's sourcebook: A subject, title, and motif index to folklore collections for children, 1983–1999.* Detroit: Gale.

MacLean, M., Bryant, P. E., & Bradley, L. (1987). Rhymes, nursery rhymes and reading in early childhood. *Merrill-Palmer Quarterly, 33*, 225–281.

Maloch, B. (2002). Scaffolding student talk: One teacher's role in literature discussion groups. *Reading Research Quarterly, 37*, 94–112.

Many, J. E., & Wiseman, D. L. (1992). The effects of teaching approach on third-grade students' response to literature. *Journal of Reading Behavior, 24*, 265–287.

Marcus, L. S. (2008). *Minders of make-believe: Idealists, entrepreneurs, and the shaping of American children's literature.* New York: Houghton Mifflin.

_____. (2008). *Pass it down: Five picture-book families make their mark.* New York: Walker & Company.

Marcus, L. S., Curley, J. B., & Ward, C. (2007). *Children should be seen: The image of the child in American picture book art.* Amherst, MA: Eric Carle Museum of Picture Book Art.

Martin, M. (2004). *Brown gold: Milestones of African-American children's picture books, 1845–2002.* New York: Routledge.

Martinez, M., & Roser, N. (2005). *What a character!: Character study as a guide to literary meaning making in grades K–8.* Newark, DE: International Reading Association.

Martinez-Roldan, M. (2003). Building worlds and identities: A case study of the role of narratives in bilingual literature discussions. *Research in the Teaching of English, 37*, 491–526.

Matulka, D. (2008). *A picture book primer: Understanding and using picture books.* Westport CT: Libraries Unlimited.

McClure, A. (1985). *Children's response to poetry in a supportive literary context.* Unpublished doctoral dissertation. Ohio State University.

McClure, A., Harrison, P., & Reed, S. (1990). *Sunrise and songs: Reading and writing poetry in an elementary classroom.* Portsmouth, NH: Heinemann.

McGee, L. M. (1992). An exploration of meaning construction in first graders' grand conversations. In C. K. Kinzer & D. J. Leu (Eds.), *Literacy research, theory, and practice: Views from many perspectives* (pp. 177–186). Forty-first yearbook of the National Reading Conference. Chicago: National Reading Conference.

McGinley, W., & Kamberelis, G. (1996). "Maniac Magee and Ragtime Tumpie": Children negotiating self and world through reading and writing. *Research in the Teaching of English, 30*, 75–113.

McIntyre, E., Kyle, D. W., & Moore, G. H. (2006).A primary-grade teacher's guidance toward small-group dialogue. *Reading Research Quarterly, 41*, 36–66.

McMahon, S., & Raphael, T. (Eds.). (1997). *The book club connection: Literacy learning and classroom talk.* New York: Teachers College Press.

Meltzer, M. (1976). Where do all the prizes go? The case for nonfiction. *The Horn Book Magazine, 52*, 21–22.

Menon, S. (2010). Laban Carrick Hill: Bowling us over by Shanti Menon. *School Library Journal.* www.schoollibraryjournal.com/slj/newsletters/ newsletterbucketextrahelping/886525-443/laban _carrick_hill_bowling_us.html.csp.

Michaels, J. (2004). Pulp fiction. *The Horn Book Magazine, 80*, 299–306.

Miller-Lachman, L. (1992). *Our family, our friends, our world: An annotated guide to significant multicultural books for children and teenagers.* New Providence, NJ: Bowker.

Moebius, W. (1986). Introduction to picturebook codes. *Word and Image, 2*, 141–158.

Moll, L. (1994). Literacy research in community and classrooms: A sociocultural approach. In R. B. Ruddell, M. R. Ruddell, & H. Singer (Eds.), *Theoretical models and processes of reading* (Fourth edition, pp. 179–207). Newark, DE: International Reading Association.

Moller, K., & Allen, J. B. (2000). Connecting, resisting, and searching for safer places: Students respond to Mildred Taylor's *The Friendship. Journal of Literacy Research, 32*, 145–186.

Moss, J. (1996). *Teaching literature in the elementary school: A thematic approach.* Christopher-Gordon.

National Council of Teachers of English. (1983). Statement on censorship and professional guidelines. *The Bulletin, 9*(1–2), 17–18.

Nieto, S. (2002). *Language, culture, and teaching: Critical perspectives for a new century.* Mahwah: NJ: Erlbaum.

Nikolajeva, M. (2010). *Power, Voice and Subjectivity in Literature for Young Readers.* New York: Routledge.

Nikolavja, M., & Scott, C. (2001). *How picturebooks work.* New York: Garland.

No author noted. (2005). *The art of reading: Forty illustrators celebrate reading is fundamental's 40th anniversary.* New York: Dutton.

No author noted. (2006). *Why did the chicken cross the road?* New York: Dial.

No author noted. (2007). *Artist to Artist: 23 Major Illustrators Talk to Children about Their Art.* Amherst, MA: Eric Carle Museum of Picture Book Art.

No author noted. (2007). *Knock, knock!* New York: Dial.

No author noted. (2012). *The best children's books of the year: 2012 edition. Books published in 2011.* Distributed by Teachers College Press.

Nodelman, P. (1988). *Words about pictures: The narrative art of children's picture books.* Athens: University of Georgia Press.

_____. (1996). *The pleasures of children's literature* (Second edition). White Plains, NY: Longman.

_____. (1997). Fear of children's literature: What's left (or right) after theory? In S. L. Beckett (Ed.), *Reflections* of change: Children's literature since 1945. Westport, CT: Greenwood.

Nodelman, P., & Reimer, M. (2003). *The pleasure of children's literature* (Third edition). Boston: Allyn & Bacon.

Nye, N. S., & Bryan, A. (2000). *Salting the ocean: 100 poems by young poets.* New York: Greenwillow.

Odland, N. (1982). Profile: John Ciardi. *Language Arts, 59,* 872–874.

Opie, L., & Opie, P. (1951). *The Oxford dictionary of nursery rhymes.* London: Oxford University Press.

_____. (1974). *Classic fairy tales.* London: Oxford University Press.

Pantaleo, S. (2008). *Exploring student response to contemporary picturebooks.* Toronto: University of Toronto Press.

Patterson, E., Schaller, M., & Clemens, J. (2008). A closer look at interactive writing. *The Reading Teacher, 61*(6), 496–497.

Pavonetti, L. (2011). *Bridges to understanding: Envisioning the world through children's eyes.* Lanham, MD: Scarecrow.

Payton Walsh, J. (2007). A ghostly quartet. *The Horn Book Magazine, 80,* 245–252.

Pellowski, A. (1984). *The story-vine: A source book of unusual and easy-to-tell stories from around the world.* Old Tappan, NJ: Macmillan.

Peterson, R., & Eeds, M. (2007). *Grand conversations: Literature groups in action.* New York: Scholastic.

Pillar, A. M. (1983). Aspects of moral judgment in response to fables. *Journal of Research and Development in Education, 16*(3), 37–40.

Porter, E. J. (1980). Profile: Myra Cohn Livingston. *Language Arts, 57,* 901–903.

Pratt, L., & Beaty, J. (1999). *Transcultural children's literature.* New York: Merrill.

Pressley, M., Dolezal, S. E., Raphael, L. M., Mohan, L., Roehrig, A. D., & Bogner. L. (2003). *Motivating primary grade students.* New York: Guilford.

Propp, V. (1958). *Morphology of the folktale.* Minneapolis, MN: University of Minnesota Press.

Purves, A. C., Rogers, T., & Soter, A. D. (1990). *How porcupines make love II: Teaching a response-centered literature curriculum.* New York: Longmans.

Quintero, E., & Rummel, M. K. (1997). *American voices: Webs of diversity.* New York: Prentice-Hall.

Rabkin, E. S. (1976). *The fantastic in literature.* Princeton: Princeton University Press.

Raphael, T. E., Florio-Ruane, S., & George, M. (2001). Book club plus: A conceptual framework to organize literacy instruction. *Language Arts, 79,* 159–168.

Raphael, T. E., Florio-Ruane, S., George, M., et al. (2004). *Book club plus: A literacy framework for the primary grades.* Lawrence, MA: Small Planet Communications.

Raphael, T. E., Kehus, M., & Damphousse, K. (2001). *Book club for middle school.* Lawrence, MA: Small Planet Communications.

Ringrose, C. (2007). A journey backwards: History through style in children's fiction. *Children's Literature in Education, 38,* 207–218.

Robinson, L. (2008). Travels through time and genre. In L. Robinson & Z. Charles (Eds.), *Over rainbows and down rabbit holes: The art of children's books* (pp. 16–34). Santa Barbara, CA, & Amherst, MA: Santa Barbara Museum of Art & The Eric Carle Museum of Picture Book Art.

Rosenberg, L. (2005). Reviewing poetry. *The Horn Book Magazine, 81,* 375–378.

Rosenblatt, L. M. (1938/1976). *Literature as exploration.* New York: Noble & Noble.

_____. (1978). *The reader, the text, the poem: The transactional theory of literary work.* Carbondale: Southern Illinois University Press.

Roser, N. L., Martinez, M., Furhken, C., et al. (2007). Characters as guides to meaning. *The Reading Teacher, 60,* 548–559.

Roser, N., & Martinez, M. (Eds.). (1995). *Book talk and beyond: Children and teachers respond to literature.* Newark, DE: International Reading Association.

Salisbury, M. (2004). *Illustrating children's books: Creating pictures for publication.* London: Quarto.

_____. (2007). *Play pen: New children's book illustration.* London: Laurence King.

Samuels, S. J., & Wu, Y. C. (2003). *How the amount of time spent on independent reading affects reading achievement: A response to the National Reading Panel.* www.tc.umn.edu/~samue001. Retrieved November 13, 2008.

Samway, K. D., & Whang, G. (1995). *Literature study circles in a multicultural classroom.* York, ME: Stenhouse.

Saul, W. (1986.) Living proof: Children's biographers of Marie Curie. *School Library Journal, 33,* 103–108.

Sawyer, R. (1962). *The way of the storyteller.* New York: Viking.

Schlick Noe, K., & Johnson, N. (1999). *Getting started with literature circles.* Norwood, MA: Christopher-Gordon.

Schneider, D. (2011). What makes a good . . . sports novel? *The Horn Book Magazine, 87,* 68–72.

Schwarcz, J. (1982). *Ways of the illustrator.* Chicago: American Library Association.

Seale, D. & Slapin, B. (Eds.). *A broken flute: The native experience in books for children.* Berkeley: University of California American Studies Center.

Sebesata, S. E., & Monson, D. L. (2003). Reading preferences. In J. Flood, D. Lapp, J. R. Squire, & J. M. Jensen, (Eds.), *Handbook of research on* teaching the English language arts (Second edition, pp. 835–847). Old Tappan, NJ: Macmillan.

Seeger, P., & Jacobs, P. D. (2000). *Pete Seeger's storytelling book.* San Diego: Harcourt.

Selznick, B. (2008). Caldecott medal acceptance. *The Horn Book Magazine 84*(4), 393–406.

Shapiro, K., & Beum, R. (1975). *A prosody handbook.* New York: Harper & Row.

Sheinkin, S. (2012). The notorious Benedict Arnold. *The Horn Book Magazine, 88*(1), 19–23.

Short, K. (1997). *Literature as a way of knowing.* York: ME: Stenhouse.

Short, K. G., & Pierce, K. M. (Eds.). (1990). *Talking about books: Creating literate communities.* Portsmouth, NH: Heinemann.

Short, K. G., & Pierce, K. M. (Eds.). (1998). *Talking about books: Literature discussion groups in a K–8 classroom.* Portsmouth, NH: Heinemann.

Shulevitz, U. (1985). *Writing with pictures: How to write and illustrate children's books.* Lakewood, NJ: Watson-Guptill.

Sipe, L. R. (1998). Individual literary response styles of first and second graders. In T. Shanahan and F. V. Rodriguez-Brown (Eds.), *Forty-seventh yearbook of the National Reading Conference* (pp. 76–89). Chicago: National Reading Conference.

———. (1999). Children's response to literature: Author, text, reader, context. *Theory into Practice, 38*, 120–129.

———. (2000). "Those two gingerbread boys could be brothers": How children use intertextual connections during storybook readalouds. *Children's Literature in Education, 31*, 73–90.

———. (2001). Picturebooks as aesthetic objects. *Literacy Teaching and Learning: An International Journal of Early Reading and Writing, 6*, 23–42.

———. (2002). Contemporary urban children respond to Peter Rabbit: Making a text culturally relevant. In M. Mackey (Ed.), *Beatrix Potter's Peter Rabbit: A children's classic at 100* (pp. 3–18). Lanham, MD: The Children's Literature Association and Scarecrow.

———. (2008). *Storytime: Young children's literary understanding in the classroom.* New York: Teachers College Press.

Sipe, L. R., & Brightman, A. (2009). A young child's interpretation of page breaks in contemporary picturebooks. *Journal of Literacy Research, 41*, 68–103.

Sipe, L. R., & McGuire, C. E. (2006). Young children's resistance to stories. *The Reading Teacher, 60*, 6–13.

———. (2008). "The stinky cheese man" and other fairly postmodern picturebooks for children. In S. Lehr, (Ed.), *Shattering the looking glass: challenge, risk, and controversy in children's literature* (pp. 273–288). Norwood, MA: Christopher-Gordon.

Sipe, L. R., & Pantaleo, S. (2008). *Postmodern picturebooks: Play, parody, and self-referentiality.* New York: Routledge Falmer.

Sloan, G. D. (1981). Profile: Eve Merriam. *Language Arts, 58*, 957–962.

———. (2009). Northrop Frye in the elementary classroom. *Children's Literature in Education, 40*(2), 120–135.

Sloyer, S. (1982). *Readers theatre: Story dramatization in the classroom.* Urbana, IL: National Council of Teachers of English.

Smith, F. (1978). *Understanding reading* (Second edition). New York: Holt.

Smith, H. (Ed.). (2004). *The Coretta Scott King awards, 1970–2004.* Chicago: American Library Association.

Sorensen, M., & Lehman, B. (Eds.). (1995). *Teaching with children's books: Paths to literature-based instruction.* Urbana, IL: National Council of Teachers of English.

Spooner, A. (2010). A profile of Jerry Pinkney. *The Horn Book Magazine, 86*, 25–30.

Stan, S. (Ed.). (2002). *The world through children's books.* Lapham, MD: Scarecrow.

Stanek, L. W. (1994). *Thinking like a writer.* New York: Random House.

Staples, S. F. (2008). Speech given at the International Reading Association Annual Meeting, Book, and Author Luncheon. Atlanta, GA.

Stephens, J. (1992). *Language and ideology and children's fiction.* London: Longman.

Stevenson, D. (2006). Finding literary goodness in a pluralistic world. *The Horn Book Magazine, 82*, 511–517.

Stewart, S. L. (2008). Beyond borders: Reading "other" places in children's literature. *Children's Literature in Education, 39*, 95–105.

Stott, J. C. (1987). Spiraled sequence story curriculum: A structuralist approach to teaching fiction in the elementary grades. *Children's Literature in Education, 18*, 148–163.

Strickland, D. S., Galda, L., & Cullinan, B. E. (2004). *Language arts: learning and teaching.* Belmont, CA: Wadsworth.

Sumara, D. J. (1996). *Private readings in public: Schooling and the literary imagination.* New York: Peter Lang.

Sutcliff, R. (1973). History is people: In V. Haviland (Ed.). *Children and literature: Views and reviews* (pp. 307–308). Glenview, IL: Scott Foresman.

Sutherland, R. (1985). Hidden persuaders: Political ideologies in literature for children. *Children's Literature in Education, 16*, 143–157.

Taxel, J. (1984). The American Revolution in children's fiction: An analysis of historical meaning and narrative structure. *Curriculum Inquiry, 14*(1), 7–55.

Taylor, B. M., Frye, B., & Maruyama, G. (1990). Time spent reading and reading growth. *American Educational Research Journal, 27*, 351–362.

Terry, A. (1974). *Children's poetry preferences: A national survey of upper elementary grades.* Urbana, IL: National Council of Teachers of English.

Thomas J. T., Jr. (2007). *Poetry's playground: The culture of contemporary American children's poetry.* Detroit: Wayne State University Press.

Thompson, S. (1955–1958). *Motif-index of folk-literature* (Vol. 1–5). Bloomington, IN: Indiana University Press.

Thompson, T. (2008). *Adventures in graphica: Using comics and graphic novels to teach comprehension, 2–6.* Portland, ME: Stenhouse.

Tolkien, J.R.R. (1938/1964). *Tree and leaf.* London: Unwin.

Tomlinson, C. (2002). An overview of international children's literature. In S. Stan (Ed.), *The world through children's books* (pp. 3–26). Lapham, MD: Scarecrow.

———. (Ed.). (1998). *Children's books from other countries.* Lapham, MD: Scarecrow.

Tucker, B. (2009). Gotthold Ephraim Lessing's Laocoon and the lessons of comics. In S. Tabachnick (Ed.). *Teaching the graphic novel* (pp. 28–35). New York: The Modern Language Association.

Varley, P. (2002). As good as reading? Kids and the audiobook revolution. *The Horn Book Magazine, 78*, 251–262.

Weaver, C. A., & Kintsch, W. (1991). Expository text. In R, Barr, M. L. Kamil, P. Mosenthal, & P. D. Pearson (Eds.), *Handbook of reading research* (Vol. 2, pp. 230–245). Mahwah, NJ: Lawrence Erlbaum.

Weiss. M. J., & Weiss, H. S. (1997). *From one experience to another: Award winning authors sharing real-life experiences through fiction.* New York: Doherty.

Werlin, N. (2006). Working with fear: What makes a good . . . thriller? *The Horn Book Magazine, 82*, 529–532.

West, R., Stanovich, K., & Mitchell, H. (1993). Reading in the real world and its correlates. *Reading Research Quarterly, 28*, 34–50.

White, M. L. (1988). Profile: Arnold Adoff. *Language Arts, 65*, 584–588.

Wolf, S. A., & Heath, S. B. (1992). *The braid of literature: Children's worlds of reading.* Cambridge, MA: Harvard University Press.

Wolfe, G. K. (1986). *Critical terms for science fiction and fantasy.* New York: Greenwood.

Wong, J. (2002). *You have to write.* New York: Margaret K. McElderry.

Wood, K. D., Roser, N. L., & Martinez, M. (2001). Collaborative literacy: Lessons learned from literature. *The Reading Teacher, 55*, 102–111.

Wooten, D. A., & Cullinan, B. E. (2009). *Children's literature in the reading program: An invitation to read* (Third edition). Newark, DE: International Reading Association.

Yolen, J. (2000). *Touch magic: Fantasy, faerie and folklore in the literature of childhood.* Little Rock, AR: August House.

———. (2003). *Take joy: A book for writers.* Waukesha, WI: Writer Books.

———. (2006). *Take joy: A writer's guide to loving the craft.* Cincinnati: OH: Writer's Digest.

Young, T. (2003). *Happily ever after: Sharing folk literature with elementary and middle school students.* Newark, DE: International Reading Association.

Zarnowski, M. & Giblin, J. C. (2006). *Making sense of history: Using high-quality literature and hands-on experiences to build content knowledge.* New York: Scholastic.

Zipes, J. (1979). *Breaking the magic spell: Radical theories of folk and fairy tales.* Lexington, KY: University Press of Kentucky.

Children's Literature References

Aardema, Verna. (1975). **Why Mosquitoes Buzz in People's Ears: A West African Tale**. Illustrated by Leo Dillon and Diane Dillon. New York: Dial.

Abdel-Fattah, Randa. (2010). **Where the Streets Had a Name**. New York: Scholastic.

Ada, Alma Flor, & F. Isabel Campoy. (2009). **¡Muu, Moo! Rimas de animales/Animal Nursery Rhymes**. Illustrated by Viví Escrivá. New York: HarperCollins.

Ada, Alma Flor, F. Isabel Campoy, & Alice Schertle. (2003). **¡Pío Peep! Traditional Spanish Nursery Rhymes**. Illustrated by Viví Escrivá. New York: HarperCollins.

Adams, Richard. (1972). **Watership Down**. New York: Macmillan.

Addams, Charles. (1967). **The Charles Addams Mother Goose**. New York: Windmill.

Adlington, L. J. (2008). **Cherry Heaven**. New York: Greenwillow.

Adoff, Arnold. (1973). **Black Is Brown Is Tan**. Illustrated by Emily Arnold McCully. New York: HarperCollins.

———. (1975). **Make a Circle, Keep Us In: Poems for a Good Day**. Illustrated by Arnold Himler. New York: Dell.

———. (1982). **All the Colors of the Race: Poems**. Illustrated by John Steptoe. New York: HarperCollins.

———. (1995). **My Black Me: A Beginning Book of Black Poetry**. New York: Penguin.

———. (1997). **I Am the Darker Brother: An Anthology of Modern Poems by African Americans**. New York: Simon & Schuster.

———. (2011). **Roots and Blues: A Celebration**. Illustrated by R. Gregory Christie. New York: Clarion.

Aesop. (2011). **Aesop's Fables: A Pop-Up Book of Classic Tales.** Illustrated by Chris Beatrice & Bruce Whatley. New York: Simon.

Agee, Jon. (2003). **Z Goes Home**. New York: Hyperion.

———. (2009). **Orangutan Tongs: Poems to Tangle Your Tongue**. New York: Hyperion.

———. (2011). **My Rhinoceros**. New York: Scholastic.

Ahlberg, Allan. (2011). **Previously**. Illustrated by Bruce Ingman. Somerville MA: Candlewick.

Ahlberg, Janet, & Allan Ahlberg. (1986). **The Jolly Postman or Other People's Letters**. Boston: Little, Brown.

Ajmera, Maya. (2004). **Be My Neighbor**. Illustrated by John D. Ivanko. Watertown, MA: Charlesbridge.

Alarcón, Francisco X. (2008). **Animal Poems of the Iguazú/Animalario del Iguazú**. Illustrated by Maya Cristina Gonzalez. San Francisco: Children's Book Press.

Alcott, Louisa May. (1868/1968). **Little Women**. New York: Little, Brown.

Alexander, Elizabeth, & Marilyn Nelson. (2007). **Miss Crandall's School for Young Ladies & Little Misses of Color: Poems**. Illustrated by Floyd Cooper. Hornsdale, PA: Wordsong.

Alexander, Lloyd. (1964/1999). **The Book of Three**. New York: Holt, Rinehart & Winston/Holt.

Alexie, Sherman. (2007). **The Absolutely True Diary of a Part-Time Indian**. Illustrated by Ellen Forney. New York: Little, Brown.

Aliki. (1998). **Marianthe's Story: Painted Words and Spoken Memories**. New York: HarperCollins.

Alley, Zoe B. (2008). **There's a Wolf at the Door**. Illustrated by R. W. Alley. New York: Roaring Brook.

———. (2010). **There's a Princess in the Palace**. Illustrated by R. W. Alley. New York: Roaring Brook.

Almond, David. (1999). **Skellig**. New York: Delacorte.

———. (2004). **The Fire-Eaters**. New York: Knopf.

———. (2008). **Savage**. Illustrated by Dave McKean. Cambridge, MA: Candlewick.

———. (2009). **Raven Summer**. New York: Delacorte.

———. (2011). **My Name Is Mina**. New York: Delacorte.

Alvarez, Julia. (2001). **How Tía Lola Came to Visit Stay**. New York: Knopf.

———. (2002). **Before We Were Free**. New York: Knopf.

———. (2009). **Return to Sender**. New York: Knopf.

———. (2010). **How Tía Lola Learned to Teach**. New York: Knopf.

———. (2011). **How Tía Lola Ended Up Starting Over**. New York: Knopf.

———. (2011). **How Tía Lola Saved the Summer**. New York: Knopf.

Ambrose, Stephen. (2003). **This Vast Land**. New York: Random House.

Ammon, Richard. (2007). **An Amish Year**. Illustrated by Pamela Patrick. Honesdale, PA: Windsong.

Anderson, Ho Che. (2003). **King: A Comics Biography of Martin Luther King, Jr.** Washington: Fantagraphics.

Anderson, Laurie Halse. (1999). *Speak*. New York: Farrar, Straus and Giroux.

———. (2008). *Chains*. New York: Simon & Schuster.

———. (2008). *Independent Dames: What You Never Knew about the Women and Girls of the American Revolution*. Illustrated by Matt Faulkner. New York: Simon & Schuster.

———. (2010). *Forge*. New York: Atheneum.

Anderson, M. T. (2006). *The Astonishing Life of Octavian Nothing, Traitor to the Nation, Volume 1: The Pox Party*. Cambridge, MA: Candlewick.

———. (2008). *The Astonishing Life of Octavian Nothing, Traitor to the Nation, Volume II: The Kingdom on the Waves*. Cambridge, MA: Candlewick.

Anderson, Sara. (2007). *Fruit*. Brooklyn, NY: Handprint.

Andrews, Jan. (2011). *When Apples Grew Noses and White Horses Flew: Tales of Ti-Jean*. Illustrated by Dušan Petričić. Toronto, Ontario: Groundwood.

Angelou, Maya. (2008). *Amazing Peace: A Christmas Poem*. Illustrated by Steve Johnson & Lou Fancher. New York: Schwartz & Wade.

Anno, Mitsumasa. (1986). *Anno's Counting Book*. New York: HarperCollins.

Anonymous. (1971). *Go Ask Alice*. New York: Simon & Schuster.

Appelbaum, Susannah. (2009). *The Hollow Bettle*. New York: Knopf.

———. (2010). *The Tasters Guild*. New York: Knopf.

———. (2011). *The Shepard of Weeks*. New York: Knopf.

Appelt, Kathi. (2008). *The Underneath*. Illustrated by David Small. New York: Atheneum.

———. (2010). *Keeper*. New York: Atheneum.

Ardizzone, Edward. (1955). *Little Tim and the Brave Sea Captain*. New York: Walck.

Armstrong, Jennifer. (1998). *Shipwreck at the Bottom of the World: The Extraordinary True Story of Shackleton and the Endurance*. New York: Crown.

———. (2006). *Once upon a Banana*. Illustrated by David Small. New York: Simon & Schuster.

Arnold, Caroline. (2006). *The Terrible Hodag and the Animal Catchers*. Illustrated by John Sanford. Honesdale, PA: Windsong.

———. (2007). *Giant Sea Reptiles of the Dinosaur Age*. Illustrated by Laurie Caple. New York: Clarion.

Arnold, Marsha Diane. (2006). *Roar of a Snore*. Illustrated by Pierre Pratt. New York: Dial.

Arnosky, Jim. (2002). *Field Trips: Bug Hunting, Animal Tracking, Bird Watching, and Shore Walking with Jim Arnosky*. New York: HarperCollins.

———. (2008). *The Brook Book: Exploring the Smallest Streams*. New York: Dutton.

———. (2010). *Slow Down for Manatees*. New York: Putnam.

Aronson, Marc. (2000). *Sir Walter Ralegh and the Quest for El Dorado*. New York: Clarion.

———. (2010). *If Stones Could Speak: Unlocking the Secrets of Stonehenge*. Washington, DC: National Geographic.

———. (2011). *Trapped: How the World Rescued 33 Miners from 2,000 Feet below the Chilean Desert*. New York: Atheneum.

Arrington, Frances. (2003). *Prairie Whispers*. New York: Philomel.

Asimov, Issac. (1969). *Words from the Myths*. Tiptree, Colchester Essex: Signet.

Atinuke. (2010). *Anna Hibiscus*. Illustrated by Lauren Tobia. Tulsa, OK: Kane Miller.

———. (2011). *Anna Hibiscus' Song*. Illustrated by Lauren Tobia. Tulsa, OK: Kane Miller.

———. (2011). *Good Luck, Anna Hibiscus*. Illustrated by Lauren Tobia. New York: Kane Miller.

———. (2011). *Have Fun, Anna Hibiscus*. Illustrated by Lauren Tobia. New York: Kane Miller.

———. (2011). *The No.1 Car Spotter*. Illustrated by Warwick Johnson Cadwell. New York: Kane Miller.

Auch, Mary Jane, & Herm Auch. (2007). *Beauty and the Beaks: A Turkey's Cautionary Tale*. New York: Holiday House.

Aulnoy, Madame (Marie-Catherine). (1892). *The Fairy Tales of Madame d'Aulnoy, Newly Done into English*. Illustrated by Clinton Peters. London: Lawrence and Bullen.

Avi. (1995). *Poppy*. Illustrated by Brian Floca. New York: Orchard.

———. (1998). *Poppy and Rye*. Illustrated by Brian Floca. New York: Avon.

———. (1999). *Ragweed*. Illustrated by Brian Floca. New York: Avon.

———. (2000). *Ereth's Birthday*. Illustrated by Brian Floca. New York: HarperCollins.

———. (2002). *Crispin: The Cross of Lead*. New York: Hyperion.

———. (2003). *Silent Movie*. Illustrated by C. B. Mordan. New York: Simon & Schuster.

———. (2007). *Iron Thunder: The Battle between the Monitor & the Merrimac: A Civil War Novel*. New York: Hyperion.

———. (2008). *Crispin: At the Edge of the World*. New York: Hyperion.

———. (2010). *Crispin: The End of Time*. New York: Balzer + Bray.

———. (2011). *City of Orphans*. New York: Atheneum.

Azarian, Mary. (2005). *A Gardener's Alphabet*. Boston: Houghton Mifflin Harcourt.

Babbitt, Natalie. (1975). ***Tuck Everlasting***. New York: Farrar, Straus and Giroux.

Bacigalupi, Paolo. (2010). ***Ship Breaker***. New York: Little, Brown.

Backmeister, Rhoda W. (1940/1968). ***Stories to Begin On***. New York: Dutton.

Baek, Matthew. (2008). ***Be Gentle with the Dog, Dear!***. New York: Penguin.

Baker, Jeannie. (1988). ***Where the Forest Meets the Sea***. New York: HarperCollins.

———. (2004). ***Home***. New York: Greenwillow.

———. (2010). ***Mirror***. Somerville, MA: Candlewick.

Baker, Keith. (2010). ***LMNO Peas***. New York: Simon & Schuster.

———. (2011). ***No Two Alike***. New York: Simon & Schuster.

Balliett, Blue. (2004). ***Chasing Vermeer***. Illustrated by Brett Heliquist. New York: Scholastic.

———. (2006). ***The Wright 3***. Illustrated by Brett Heliquist. New York: Scholastic.

———. (2008). ***The Calder Game***. Illustrated by Brett Heliquist. New York: Scholastic.

Balnes, Becky. (2008). ***Your Skin Holds You In***. Washington, DC: National Geographic.

Bang, Molly. (1987). ***The Paper Crane***. New York: Greenwillow.

———. (1996). ***Ten, Nine, Eight***. New York: HarperCollins.

———. (2002). ***Dawn***. New York: SeaStar.

Bania, Michael. (2004). ***Kumak's Fish: A Tall Tale from the Far North***. Portland, OR: Alaska Northwest.

Banks, Kate. (2007). ***Fox***. Illustrated by Georg Hallensleben. New York: Farrar, Straus and Giroux.

Banyai, Istvan. (2005). ***The Other Side***. San Francisco, Chronicle.

Barakat, Ibtisam. (2007). ***Tasting the Sky: A Palestinian Childhood***. New York: Farrar, Straus and Giroux.

Bardhan-Quallen, Sudipta. (2008). ***Up Close: Jane Goodall***. New York: Viking.

Bardoe, Cheryl. (2010). ***Mammoths and Mastodons: Titans of the Ice Age***. New York: Abrams.

Baretta, Gene. (2010). ***Dear Deer***. New York: Square Fish.

Barner, Bob. (2007). ***Penguins, Penguins, Everywhere!***. San Francisco: Chronicle.

Barrett, Tracy. (1999). ***Anna of Byzantium***. New York: Delacorte.

Barrie, James M. (1911/1950). ***Peter Pan***. New York: Scribner.

———. (2004). ***Child of the Dark Prophecy***. New York: Philomel.

———. (2005). ***Shadows on the Stars***. New York: Philomel.

———. (2006). ***The Eternal Flame***. New York: Philomel.

———. (2008). ***Merlin's Dragon***. New York: Philomel.

———. (2009). ***Doomraga's Revenge***. New York: Philomel.

———. (2010). ***Ultimate Magic***. New York: Philomel.

Barron, T. A. (2007). ***The Day the Stones Walked***. Illustrated by William Low. New York: Philomel.

Barrows, Annie. (2008). ***Ivy + Bean Take Care of the Babysitter***. Illustrated by Sophie Blackall. San Francisco: Chronicle.

———. (2009). ***Ivy + Bean Doomed to Dance***. Illustrated by Sophie Blackall. San Francisco: Chronicle.

———. (2011). ***Ivy + Bean: No News Is Good News***. Illustrated by Sophie Blackall. New York: Scribner.

Bartoletti, Susan Campbell. (2001). ***Christmas Promise***. New York: Blue Sky.

———. (2005). ***Hitler Youth: Growing Up in Hitler's Shadow***. New York: Scholastic.

———. (2010). ***They Called Themselves the K.K.K.: The Birth of an American Terrorist Group***. Boston: Houghton Mifflin.

———. (2011). ***Naamah and the Ark at Night***. Illustrated by Holly Meade. New York: Candlewick.

Bates, Katharine Lee. (2004). ***America the Beautiful***. Illustrated by Chris Gall. London: Little, Brown.

Bauer, Joan. (2011). ***Close to Famous***. New York: Viking.

Bauer, Marion Dane. (2009). ***The Longest Night***. Illustrated by Ted Lewin. New York: Holiday House.

———. (2010). ***The Very Little Princess: Zoey's Story***. Illustrated by Elizabeth Sayles. New York: Random House.

———. (2011). ***The Very Little Princess: Rose's Story***. Illustrated by Elizabeth Sayles. New York: Random House.

Baum, L. Frank. (1900).***The Wizard of Oz***. Illustrated by Evelyn Copelman, adapted from the illustrations by W. W. Denslow. New York: Grosset & Dunlap.

Bean, Jonathan. (2007). ***At Night***. New York: Farrar, Straus and Giroux.

Beaty, Andrea. (2008). ***Cicada Summer***. New York: Amulet.

Bemelmans, Ludwig. (1939/1962). ***Madeline***. New York: Viking.

Berner, Rotraut Susanne. (2009). ***Definitely Not for Little Ones: Some Very Grimm Fairy-Tale Comics***. Translated by Shelley Tanaka. Toronto, Ontario: Groundwood.

Bernhard, Derga. (2011). ***While You Are Sleeping: A Lift-the-Flap Book of Time around the World***. New York: Charlesbridge.

Bertozzi, Nick. (2011). ***Lewis & Clark***. New York: First Second.

Bierhorst, John. (1993). *The Hungry Woman: Myths and Legends of the Aztecs*. New York: Quill.

Biggs, Brian. (2011). *Everything Goes: on Land*. New York: Balzer + Bray.

Bildner, Phil. (2011). *The Unforgettable Season: The Story of Joe DiMaggio, Ted Williams and the Record-Seeing Summer of '41*. Illustrated by S. D. Schindler. New York: Putnam.

Billingsley, Franny. (2011). *Chime*. New York: Dial.

Birdsall, Jeanne. (2005). *The Penderwicks: A Summer Tale of Four Sisters, Two Rabbits, and a Very Interesting Boy*. New York: Knopf.

_____. (2008). *The Penderwicks on Gardam Street*. New York: Knopf.

_____. (2011). *The Penderwicks at Point Mouette*. New York: Knopf.

Bishop, Nic. (2008). *Frogs*. New York: Scholastic.

_____. (2010). *Lizards*. New York: Scholastic.

Blake, William. (1789). *Songs of Innocence and Experience*. Princeton, NJ: Princeton University Press.

Blizzard, Gladys. (1992). *Come Look with Me: Animals in Art*. Charlottesville, VA: Thomasson-Grant.

Blume, Judy. (1970). *Are You There God? It's Me, Margaret*. Englewood Cliffs, NJ: Bradbury.

_____. (1975). *Forever*. Scarsdale, NY: Bradbury.

Blumenthal, Karen. (2011). *Bootleg: Murder, Moonshine, and the Lawless Years of Prohibition*. New York: Roaring Brook.

Bodeen, S. A. (2008). *The Compound*. New York: Feiwel and Friends.

Bolden, Tonya. (2004). *The Champ: The Story of Muhammad Ali*. Illustrated by Gregory Christie. New York: Random House.

_____. (2007). *M.L.K.: The Journey of a King*. Illustrated by Bob Adelman. New York: Abrams.

Bond, Felicia. (2000). *Tumble Bumble*. New York: HarperCollins.

Bondoux, Anne-Laure. (2010). *A Time of Miracles*. Translated by Y. Maudet. New York: Delacorte.

Bonner, Hannah. (2007). *When Fish Got Feet, Sharks Got Teeth, and Bugs Began to Swarm: A Cartoon Prehistory of Life Long before Dinosaurs*. Washington, DC: National Geographic.

Booraem, Ellen. (2011). *Small Persons with Wings*. New York: Dial.

Borden, Louise. (2006). *Across the Blue Pacific: A World War II Story*. Illustrated by Robert Andrew Parker. Boston: Houghton Mifflin.

Bortz, Fred. (2011). *Seven Wonders of Space Technology*. Minneapolis, MN: Twenty-First Century.

Boston, Lucy M. (1954/2002). *The Children of Green Knowe*. San Diego, CA: Harcourt.

Bottner, Barbara. (2010). *Miss Brooks Loves Books! (and I don't)*. Illustrated by Michael Emberley. New York: Knopf.

Bradley, Kimberly Brubaker. (2011). *Jefferson's Sons: A Founding Father's Secret Children*. New York: Dial.

Bray, Rosemary. (1995). *Martin Luther King*. Illustrated by Malcah Zeldis. New York: Greenwillow.

Breen, Steve. (2007). *Stick*. New York: Dial.

Brett, Jan. (2011). *Beauty and the Beast*. New York: Putnam Juvenile.

Bridges, Ruby. (1999). *Through My Eyes*. New York: Scholastic.

Briggs, Raymond. (1970). *Jim and the Beanstalk*. New York: Coward-McCann.

_____. (2006). *The Puddleman*. London: Red Fox.

Brighton, Catherine. (2008). *Keep Your Eyes on the Kid:The Early Years of Buster Keaton*. Brookfield, CT: Roaring. Brook.

Brimner, Larry Dane. (2010). *Birmingham Sunday*. Honesdale, PA: Boyds Mills.

Brink, Carol Ryrie. (1935/1973). *Caddie Woodlawn*. Illustrated by Trina Schart Hyman. New York: Simon & Schuster.

Broach, Elise. (2008). *Masterpiece*. Illustrated by Kelly Murphy. New York: Holt.

Brooks, Gwendolyn. (1963). *Selected Poems*. New York: Harper & Row.

Brooks, Kevin. (2008). *Black Rabbit Summer*. New York: Scholastic.

Brooks, William. (1990). *A Telling of the Tales*. Illustrated by Richard Egielski. New York: Harper & Row.

Brown, Charlotte Lewis. (2006). *The Day the Dinosaurs Died*. Illustrated by Phil Wilson. New York: HarperCollins.

Brown, Dee. (1993). *Wounded Knee: An Indian History of the American West*. Adapted by Amy Erlich. New York: Holt.

Brown, Don. (2010). *A Wizard from the Start: The Incredible Boyhood and Amazing Inventions of Thomas Edison*. New York: Houghton Mifflin.

_____. (2011). *America Is under Attack: September 11, 2001: The Day the Towers Fell*. New York: Roaring Brook.

Brown, Jackie. (2004). *Little Cricket*. New York: Hyperion.

Brown, Marc Tolon. (2011). *Arthur Turns Green*. New York: Little, Brown.

Brown, Margaret Wise. (1947). *Goodnight Moon*. Illustrated by Clement Hurd. New York: Harper.

Brown, Monica. (2010). *Waiting for the Biblioburro*. Illustrated by John Parra. Berkeley, CA: Tricycle.

Browne, Anthony. (1983/2002). *Gorilla*. Cambridge, MA: Candlewick.

_____. (1987). *Piggybook*. New York: Knopf.

_____. (1990). *Changes*. New York: Knopf.

_____. (1998). *Voices in the Park*. New York: DK.

_____. (1999). *Willy's Pictures*. Cambridge, MA: Candlewick.

_____. (2004). *Into the Forest*. Cambridge, MA: Candlewick.

_____. (2007). *My Brother*. New York: Farrar, Straus and Giroux.

_____. (2010). *Me and You*. New York: Farrar, Straus and Giroux.

Browning, Diane. (2010). *Signed, Abiah Rose*. Berkeley, CA: Tricycle.

Bruchac, Joseph, & James Bruchac. (2003). *How Chipmunk Got His Stripes: A Tale of Bragging and Teasing*. Illustrated by Jose Aruego & Ariane Dewey. New York: Puffin.

Bruchac, Joseph. (1994). *A Boy Called Slow: The True Story of Sitting Bull*. Illustrated by Rocco Baviera. New York: Philomel.

_____. (1996). *Between Earth and Sky: Legends of Native American Sacred Places*. Illustrated by Thomas Locker. San Diego, CA: Harcourt.

_____. (1997). *Eagle Song*. Illustrated by Dan Andreasen. New York: Dial.

_____. (1998). *The Arrow over the Door*. New York: Dial.

_____. (1998). *The First Strawberries*. Illustrated by Anna Vojtech. New York: Puffin.

_____. (2000). *Sacajawea*. San Diego, CA: Silver Whistle.

_____. (2001). *The Heart of a Chief*. New York: Penguin.

_____. (2002). *The Winter People*. New York: Dial.

_____. (2003). *Pocahontas*. Orlando, FL: Silver Whistle.

_____. (2008). *March toward the Thunder*. New York: Dial.

_____. (2008). *Ringside, 1925: Views from the Scopes Trial*. New York: Knopf.

_____. (2011). *Dragon Castle*. New York: Dial

Bryan, Ashley. (2002). *Beautiful Blackbird*. New York: Simon & Schuster.

_____. (2007). *Let It Shine: Three Favorite Spirituals*. New York: Simon & Schuster.

Bryant, Jen. (2004). *The Trial*. New York: Knopf.

_____. (2008). *A River of Words: The Story of William Carlos Williams*. Illustrated by Melissa Sweet. Grand Rapids, MI: Eerdmans.

Bunce, Elizabeth C. (2008). *A Curse Dark as Gold*. New York: Levine.

Bunting, Eve. (1991). *Fly away Home*. Illustrated by Ronald Himler. New York: Clarion.

_____. (1994). *Smoky Night*. Illustrated by David Diaz. San Diego, CA: Harcourt.

_____. (2006). *One Green Apple*. Illustrated by Ted Lewin. New York: Clarion.

Burkert, Nancy Elkholm. (1972). *Snow White*. New York: Farrar, Straus and Giroux.

Burkert, Rand. (2011). *Mouse and Lion*. Illustrated by Nancy Ekholm Burkert. New York: Scholastic.

Burks, Brian. (1998). *Walks Alone*. San Diego, CA: Harcourt.

Burleigh, Robert. (2004). *Langston's Train Ride*. Illustrated by Leonard Jenkins. New York: Orchard.

_____. (2011). *Night Flight: Amelia Earhart Crosses the Atlantic*. Illustrated by Wendell Minor. New York: Simon & Schuster.

Burton, Virginia Lee. (1939). *Mike Mulligan and His Steam Shovel*. Boston: Houghton Mifflin.

Cadnum, Michael. (2003). *Ship of Fire*. New York: Viking.

_____. (2004). *Blood Gold*. New York: Viking.

_____. (2008). *The King's Arrow*. New York: Viking.

Caldecott, Randolph. (1878). *The House that Jack Built*. London: Routledge.

Carbone, Elisa Lynn. (2008). *Night Running: How James Escaped with the Help of His Faithful Dog*. Illustrated by E. B. Lewis. New York: Random House.

Carle, Eric. (1981). *The Very Hungry Caterpillar*. New York: Philomel.

_____. (1989). *The Very Busy Spider*. New York: Philomel.

Carmi, Daniella. (2000). *Samir and Yonatan*. New York: Levine.

Carnesi, Monica. (2012). *Little Dog Lost: The True Story of a Brave Dog Named Baltic*. New York: Nancy Paulsen Books.

Carroll, Lewis. (1865/1992). *Alice's Adventures in Wonderland*. Illustrated by John Tenniel. New York: Morrow.

_____. (1871/1977). *Through the Looking Glass*. Illustrated by John Tenniel. New York: St. Martin's.

_____. (2007). *Jabberwocky*. Illustrated by Christopher Myers. New York: Hyperion.

_____. (2008). *Alice in Wonderland*. Illustrated by Lisbeth Zwerger. London: Penguin.

Casanova, Mary. (2007). *The Klipfish Code*. Boston: Houghton Mifflin.

_____. (2007). *To Catch a Burglar*. Illustrated by Omar Rayyan. New York: Aladdin.

Catalanotto, Peter, & Pamela Schembri. (2008). *The Veteran's Day Visitor*. New York: Holt.

Catalanotto, Peter. (2007). *Ivan the Terrier*. New York: Atheneum.

Cauley, Lorinda Bryan. (1983). *Jack and the Beanstalk*. New York: Putnam.

Cazet, Denys. (2003). *Minnie and Moo: Will You Be My Valentine?*. New York: HarperCollins.

Chalk, Gary. (1993). *Yankee Doodle*. New York: Dorling Kindersley.

Chase, Richard. (2003). *The Jack Tales*. Boston: Sandpiper.

Cheng, Andrea. (2004). *Honeysuckle House*. Asheville, NC: Front Street.

———. (2008). *Where the Steps Were*. Honesdale, PA: Wordsong.

Cherry, Lynn, & Gary Braasch. (2008). *How We Know What We Know about Our Changing Climate: Scientists and Kids Explore Global Warming*. Nevada City, CA: Dawn.

Chibbaro, Julie. (2011). *Deadly*. Illustrated by Jean-Marc Superville Sovak. New York: Atheneum.

Child, Lauren. (2000). *Beware of the Storybook Wolves*. New York: Scholastic.

———. (2002).*Who's Afraid of the Big Bad Book?*. New York: Hyperion.

Chin, Jason. (2009). *Redwoods*. New York: Roaring Brook.

———. (2011). *Coral Reefs*. New York: Roaring Brook.

Choldenko, Gennifer. (2004). *Al Capone Does My Shirts*. New York: Putnam.

Church, Caroline Jayne. (2007). *Digby Takes Charge*. New York: McElderry.

Ciardi, John. (1959). *The Reason for the Pelican*. Philadelphia: Lippincott.

———. (1961). *I Met a Man*. Boston: Houghton Mifflin.

———. (1961). *The Man Who Sang the Sillies*. Philadelphia: Lippincott.

———. (1962). *You Read to Me, I'll Read to You*. Philadelphia: Lippincott.

———. (1964). *You Know Who*. Philadelphia: Lippincott.

———. (1966). *The Monster Den: Or Look What Happened at My House—and to It*. Philadelphia: Clarion.

Cisneros, Sandra. (1991). *The House on Mango Street*. New York: Vintage.

Cleary, Brian. (2010). *But and For, Yet and Nor: What Is a Conjunction?*. Minneapolis, MN: Millbrook.

Clements, Andrew. (2007). *Dogku*. Illustrated by Tim Bowers. New York: Atheneum.

———. (2008). *Lost and Found*. Illustrated by Mark Elliott. New York: Atheneum.

Climo, Shirley. (1989). *The Egyptian Cinderella*. Illustrated by Ruth Heller. New York: Crowell.

———. (1993). *The Korean Cinderella*. Illustrated by Ruth Heller. New York: HarperCollins.

———. (1995). *Atalanta's Race: A Greek Myth*. Illustrated by Alexander Koshkin. New York: Clarion.

———. (1996). *The Irish Cinderlad*. Illustrated by Loretta Krupinski. New York: HarperCollins.

———. (2002). *Tuko and the Birds: A Tale from the Philippines*. Illustrated by Francisco X. Mora. New York: Holt.

———. (2005). *Monkey Business: Stories from around the World*. Illustrated by Erik Brooks. New York: Holt.

Cline-Ransome, Lesa. (2007). *Young Pelé: Soccer's First Star*. Illustrated by James Ransome. New York: Schwartz & Wade.

Coben, Harlan. (2011). *Shelter: A Mickey Bolitar Novel*. New York: Putnam.

Codell, Esme Raji. (2003). *Sahara Special*. New York: Hyperion.

———. (2004). *Sing a Song of Tuna Fish: Hard-to-Swallow Stories from Fifth Grade*. New York: Hyperion.

Cofer, Judith Ortiz. (1995). *An Island Like You: Stories of the Barrio*. New York: Orchard.

Cofer, Judith. (2004). *Call Me Maria*. New York: Orchard.

Coffelt, Nancy. (2007). *Fred Stays with Me!*. Illustrated by Tricia Tusa. Boston: Little, Brown.

Colfer, Eoin. (2008). *Airman*. New York: Hyperion.

Collier, Bryan. (2003). *Uptown*. New York: Holt.

Collier, James Lincoln, & Christopher Collier. (1974). *My Brother Sam Is Dead*. Old Tappan, NJ: Macmillan.

Collins, Suzanne. (2008). *The Hunger Games*. New York: Scholastic.

———. (2009). *Catching Fire*. New York: Scholastic.

———. (2010). *Mockingjay*. New York: Scholastic.

Collodi, Carlo. (1883/1983). *Pinocchio*. Illustrated by Lorenzo Mattotti. New York: Lothrop, Lee & Shephard.

Colum, Padraic. (2010). *The Children of Odin: The Book of Northern Myths*. Illustrated by Willy Pogani. Charleston, SC: CreateSpace.

Compestine, Ying Chang. (2011). *Crouching Tiger*. Illustrated by Yan Nascimbene. Somerville, MA: Candlewick.

Compton, Kenn, & Joanne Compton. (1993). *Jack the Giant Chaser: An Appalachian Tale*. New York: Holiday House.

Conkling, Winifred. (2011). *Sylvia & Aki*. Berkeley, CA: Tricycle.

Conrad, Pam. (1991). *Pedro's Journal*. Honesdale, PA: Caroline House.

Coombs, Karen Mueller. (2000). *Children of the Dust Days*. Minneapolis, MN: Carolrhoda.

Cooper, Elisha. (2010). *Beaver Is Lost*. New York: Schwartz & Wade.

———. (2010). *Farm*. London: Orchard.

Cooper, Susan. (1966). *Over Sea, Under Stone*. San Diego, CA: Harcourt.

———. (1973). *Greenwitch*. New York: McElderry.

———. (1973). *The Dark Is Rising*. Illustrated by Alan E. Cober. New York: Atheneum.

———. (1974). *The Grey King*. New York: McElderry.

_____. (1977). *Silver on the Tree*. New York: McElderry.

_____. (1991). *The Selkie Girl*. New York: Aladdin.

_____. (2006). *Victory*. New York: Simon & Schuster.

Cormier, Robert. (1974). *The Chocolate War*. New York: Knopf.

_____. (2001). *The Rag and Bone Shop*. New York: Delacorte.

Cornelissen, Cornelia. (1999). *Soft Rain: A Story of the Cherokee Trail of Tears*. New York: Delacorte.

Cottin, Menena. (2008). *The Black Book of Colors*. Illustrated by Rosana Faria. Translated by Elisa Amado. Toronto, Ontario: Groundwood.

Coudray, Philippe. (2011). *Benjamin Bear in Fuzzy Thinking: A Toon Book*. Translated by Leigh Stein. New York: Toon.

Couloumbis, Audrey. (2010). *Jake*. New York: Random House.

_____. (2011). *Lexie*. New York: Random House.

Cowley, Joy. (2006). *The Wishing of Biddy Malone*. Illustrated by Christopher Denise. New York: Puffin.

Coy, John. (2003). *Two Old Potatoes and Me*. Illustrated by Carolyn Fisher. New York: Knopf.

_____. (2007). *Crackback*. New York: Scholastic.

_____. (2008). *Box Out*. New York: Scholastic.

_____. (2011). *Love of the Game*. New York: Feiwel and Friends.

Crausaz, Anne. (2010). *Seasons*. San Diego, CA: Kane Miller.

Creech, Sharon. (2000). *The Wanderer*. New York: HarperCollins.

_____. (2001). *Love that Dog*. New York: HarperCollins.

_____. (2004). *Heartbeat*. New York: HarperCollins.

_____. (2008). *Hate that Cat*. New York: Joanna Cotler Books.

Crews, Donald. (2002). *Inside Freight Train*. New York: Scholastic.

Crews, Nina. (2004). *The Neighborhood Mother Goose*. New York: Greenwillow.

_____. (2006). *Below*. New York: Holt.

_____. (2011). *Jack and the Beanstalk*. New York: Holt.

_____. (2011). *The Neighborhood Sing-Along*. New York: Greenwillow.

Crossley-Holland, Kevin. (1998). *The World of King Arthur and His Court: People, Places, Legend and Lore*. Illustrated by Peter Malone. New York: Dutton.

_____. (2001). *The Seeing Stone*. New York: Scholastic.

_____. (2002). *At the Crossing Places*. New York: Scholastic.

_____. (2004). *King of the Middle March*. New York: Scholastic.

_____. (2008). *Crossing to Paradise*. New York: Levine.

Crowe, Chris. (2003). *Getting Away with Murder: The True Story of the Emmett Till Case*. New York: Penguin.

Croza, Laurel. (2010). *I Know Here*. Illustrated by Matt James. Toronto, Ontario: Groundwood.

Crutcher, Chris. (2001). *Whale Talk*. New York: Greenwillow.

Cunnane, Kelly. (2011). *Chirchir Is Singing*. Illustrated by Jude Daly. New York: Schwartz & Wade.

Curlee, Lynn. (2008). *Mythological Creatures: A Classical Bestiary: Tales of Strange Beings, Fabulous Creatures, Fearsome Beasts, & Hideous Monsters from Ancient Greek Mythology*. New York: Atheneum.

Curtis, Christopher Paul. (1995). *The Watsons Go to Birmingham—1963*. New York: Delacorte.

_____. (2004). *Bud, Not Buddy*. New York: Delacorte.

_____. (2007). *Elijah of Buxton*. New York: Scholastic.

_____. (2012). *The Mighty Miss Malone*. New York: Wendy Lamb Books.

Cushman, Karen. (1994). *Catherine, Called Birdy*. New York: Clarion.

_____. (1995). *The Midwife's Apprentice*. New York: Clarion.

_____. (2000). *Matilda Bone*. New York: Clarion.

_____. (2006). *The Loud Silence of Francine Green*. New York: Clarion.

_____. (2010). *Alchemy and Meggy Swann*. Boston: Houghton Mifflin Harcourt.

d'Aulaire, Ingri, & Edgar Parin d'Aulaire. (1955). *Columbus*. Garden City, NY: Doubleday.

_____. (1967). *Norse Gods and Giants*. New York: Doubleday.

Dahl, Roald. (2010). *More about Boy: Roald Dahl's Tales from Childhood*. Illustrated by Quentin Blake. New York: Farrar Straus and Giroux.

Daly, Jude. (2010). *Sivu's Six Wishes: A Taoist Tale*. Grand Rapids MI: Eerdmans.

Daly, Niki. (2006). *Happy Birthday, Jamela!*. New York: Farrar, Straus and Giroux.

Dashner, James. (2009). *The Maze Runner*. New York: Delacorte.

_____. (2010). *The Scorch Trials*. New York: Delacorte.

_____. (2011). *The Death Cure*. New York: Delacorte.

David, Laurie, & Cambria Gordon. (2007). *The Down-to-Earth Guide to Global Warming*. New York: Scholastic.

Davidson Mannis, Celeste. (2003).*The Queen's Progress: An Elizabethan Alphabet*. Illustrated by Bagram Ibatoulline. New York: Penguin.

Davies, Nicola. (2005). *Surprising Sharks*. Illustrated by James Croft. Cambridge, MA: Candlewick.

_____. (2011). *Talk, Talk, Squawk! A Human's Guide to Animal Communication*. Illustrated by Neal Layton. Somerville, MA: Candlewick.

Davol, Marguerite W. (1997). *The Paper Dragon*. Illustrated by Robert Sabuda. New York: Simon & Schuster.

de la Mare, Walter. (1968). *Songs of Childhood*. Nineola, NY: Dover.

de la Pena, Matt. (2011). *A Nation's Hope: The Story of Boxing Legend Joe Louis*. Illustrated by Kadir Nelson. New York: Dial.

Debon, Nicolas. (2003). *Four Pictures by Emily Carr*. Toronto, Ontario: Groundwood.

deBrunhoff, Jean. (1933). *The Story of Babar*. New York: Random House.

deBrunhoff, Laurent. (2003). *Babar's Museum of Art*. New York: Abrams.

Deedy, Carmen Agra. (2007). *Martina the Beautiful Cockroach: A Cuban Folktale*. Illustrated by Michael Austin. Atlanta, GA: Peachtree.

DeFelice, Cynthia. (1999). *Nowhere to Call Home*. New York: Farrar, Straus and Giroux.

deFombelle, Timothee. (2009). *Toby Alone*. Illustrated by Francois Place. Translated by Sarah Ardizzone. Somerville, MA: Candlewick.

_____. (2010). *Toby and the Secrets of the Tree*. Illustrated by Francois Place. Translated by Sarah Ardizzone. Somerville, MA: Candlewick.

deGroat, Diane. (2007). *Last One in Is a Rotten Egg!*. New York: HarperCollins.

Delacre, Lulu. (1989). *Arroz con Leche: Popular Songs and Rhymes from Latin America*. New York: Scholastic.

Della Chiesa, Carol. (2011). *Adventures of Pinocchio*. New York: Aeterna.

Dematons, Charlotte. (2004). *The Yellow Balloon*. Honesdale, PA: Boyds Mills.

Demi. (2004). *The Hungry Coat: A Tale from Turkey*. New York: McElderry.

_____. (2007). *The Legend of Lao Tzu and the Tao TeChing*. New York: Simon & Schuster.

deVarennes, Monique. (2007). *The Jewel Box Ballerinas*. Illustrated by Ana Juan. New York: Schwartz & Wade.

Diakité, Baba Wagué. (2007). *Mee-Ann and the Magic Serpent*. Toronto, Ontario: Groundwood.

DiCamillo, Kate, & Alison McGhee. (2010). *Bink & Gollie*. Illustrated by Tony Fucile. Somerville, MA: Candlewick.

DiCamillo, Kate. (2000). *Because of Winn-Dixie*. Cambridge, MA: Candlewick.

_____. (2003). *The Tale of Despereaux: Being the Story of a Mouse, a Princess, Some Soup, and a Spool of Thread*. Illustrated by Timothy Basil Ering. Cambridge, MA: Candlewick.

Dickinson, Peter. (1988). *Eva*. New York: Delacorte.

_____. (1998). *Noli's Story*. New York: Grosset & Dunlap.

_____. (1998). *Po's Story*. New York: Grosset & Dunlap.

_____. (1998). *Suth's Story*. New York: Grosset & Dunlap.

_____. (1999). *Mana's Story*. New York: Grosset & Dunlap.

Dillon, Leo, & Diane Dillon. (1998). *To Everything There Is a Season*. New York: Scholastic.

_____. (2007). *Mother Goose: Numbers on the Loose*. San Diego, CA: Harcourt.

Doctorow, Cory. (2008). *Little Brother*. New York: HarperCollins.

Dodds, Dayle Ann. (2003). *Where's Pup?*. Illustrated by Pierre Pratt. New York: Penguin.

Dodge, Mary Mapes. (1865/1915). *Hans Brinker; or The Silver Skates*. New York: Scribner.

Doherty, Berlie. (2008). *The Girl Who Saw Lions*. Amsterdam: Facet.

Donnio, Sylviane. (2007). *I'd Really Like to Eat a Child*. Illustrated by Dorothée de Monfreid. New York: Random House.

Dorris, Michael. (1992). *Morning Girl*. New York: Hyperion.

_____. (1994). *Guests*. New York: Hyperion.

_____. (1996). *Sees behind Trees*. New York: Hyperion.

Dowd, Siobhan. (2007). *The London Eye Mystery*. New York: David Fickling.

Dowell, Frances O'Roark. (2001). *Dovey Coe: A Novel*. New York: Simon & Schuster.

_____. (2004). *The Secret Language of Girls*. New York: Atheneum.

_____. (2008). *Shooting the Moon*. New York: Atheneum.

_____. (2010). *The Kind of Friends We Used to Be*. New York: Atheneum.

_____. (2011). *Ten Miles Past Normal*. New York: Atheneum.

Dowson, Nick. (2011). *North: The Amazing Story of Arctic Migration*. Illustrated by Patrick Benson. Somerville, MA: Candlewick.

Draper, Sharon M. (2007). *Fire from the Rock*. New York: Dutton.

_____. (2010). *Out of My Mind*. New York: Atheneum.

_____. (2006). *Lost in the Tunnel of Time*. New York: Aladdin.

_____. (2011). *Shadows of Caesar's Creek*. Illustrated by Jesse Joshua Watson. New York: Aladdin.

Duble, Kathleen Benner. (2011). *Phantoms in the Snow*. New York: Scholastic.

Dubosarsky, Ursula. (2007). *The Red Shoe*. New Milford, CT: Roaring Brook.

Duffy, Chris. (2011). *Nursery Rhyme Comics: 50 Timeless Rhymes by 50 Celebrated Cartoonists*. New York: First Second.

Duke, Kate. (2007). *The Tale of Pip and Squeak*. New York: Dutton.

Dumon Tak, Bibi. (2011). *Solider Bear*. Illustrated by Philip Hopman. Translated from the Dutch by Laura Watkinson. Grand Rapids, MI: Eerdmans.

Dunbar, Polly. (2007). *Penguin*. Cambridge, MA: Candlewick.

Dunrea, Olivier. (2008). *Boo-Boo*. Boston: Houghton Mifflin.

_____. (2008). *Peedie*. Boston: Houghton Mifflin.

Durbin, William. (2008). *The Winter War*. New York: Random House.

Edgeworth, Maria. (1864). *The Purple Jar*. Routledge.

Edmonds, Walter D. (1941). *The Matchlock Gun*. New York: Putnam.

Egielski, Richard. (2000). *The Gingerbread Boy*. New York: HarperCollins.

Ehlert, Lois. (1989). *Color Zoo*. New York: HarperCollins.

_____. (1991). *Red Leaf, Yellow Leaf*. San Diego, CA: Harcourt.

_____. (2008). *Oodles of Animals*. San Diego, CA: Harcourt.

_____. (2011). *RRRalph*. New York: Beach Lane.

Eliot, T. S. (1939/1982). *Old Possum's Book of Practical Cats*. London: Faber and Faber.

Elliott, David. (2008). *On the Farm*. Illustrated by Holly Meade. Cambridge, MA: Candlewick.

Ellis, Deborah. (2000). *The Breadwinner*. Toronto, Ontario: Douglas & McIntyre.

_____. (2004). *Parvanna's Journey*. Oxford: Oxford University Press.

_____. (2011). *No Ordinary Day*. Toronto, Ontario: Groundwood.

Ellsworth, Loretta. (2002). *The Shrouding Woman*. New York: Holt.

Emberley, Rebecca. (2009). *Chicken Little*. Illustrated by Ed Emberley. New York: Roaring Brook.

England, Kathryn. (2007). *Grandfather's Wrinkles*. Illustrated by Richard McFarland. Brooklyn, NY: Flashlight.

Engle, Margarita. (2006). *The Poet Slave of Cuba: A Biography of Juan Francisco Manzano*. Illustrated by Sean Qualls. New York: Holt.

_____. (2008). *The Surrender Tree: Poems of Cuba's Struggle for Freedom*. New York: Holt.

_____. (2011). *Hurricane Dancers: The First Caribbean Pirate Shipwreck*. New York: Holt.

English, Karen. (2004). *Hot Day on Abbott Avenue*. Illustrated by Javaka Steptoe. New York: Clarion.

_____. (2007). *Francie*. New York: Square Fish.

Erdrich, Louise. (1999). *The Birchbark House*. New York: Hyperion.

_____. (2005). *The Game of Silence*. New York: HarperCollins.

_____. (2008). *The Porcupine Year*. New York: HarperCollins.

Ericsson, Jennifer. (2007). *A Piece of Chalk*. Illustrated by Michelle Shapiro. New Milford, Conn.: Roaring Brook.

Ernst, Lisa Campbell. (2004). *The Turn-Around, Upside-Down Alphabet Book*. New York: Simon & Schuster.

Erskine, Kathryn. (2010). *Mockingbird*. New York: Philomel.

_____. (2011). *The Absolute Value of Mike*. New York: Penguin.

Esbensen, Barbara Juster. (1984). *Cold Stars and Fireflies*. New York: HarperCollins.

_____. (1986). *Words with Wrinkled Knees: Animal Poems*. New York: Crowell.

_____. (1992). *Who Shrank My Grandmother's House? Poems of Discovery*. Illustrated by Eric Beddows. Toronto, Ontario: University of Toronto Press.

_____. (2000). *The Night Rainbow*. Illustrated by Helen Davie. New York: Scholastic.

Evans, Shane W. (2011). *Underground: Finding the Light to Freedom*. New York: Roaring Brook.

_____. (2012). *We March*. Illustrated by London Ladd. New York: Roaring Brook.

Farjeon, Eleanor. (1951). *Poems for Children*. Philadelphia: Lippincott.

_____. (1960). *The Children's Bells: A Selection of Poems*. New York: H. Z. Walck.

Farmer, Nancy. (1994). *The Ear, the Eye, and the Arm: A Novel*. New York: Orchard.

_____. (2002). *The House of the Scorpion*. New York: Atheneum.

_____. (2004). *The Sea of Trolls*. New York: Atheneum.

_____. (2007). *The Land of the Silver Apples*. New York: Atheneum.

_____. (2009). *The Islands of the Blessed*. New York: Atheneum.

Feelings, Tom. (1995). *Middle Passage: White Ships/ Black Cargo*. New York: Dial.

Feiffer, Jules. (1997). *Meanwhile*. New York: HarperCollins.

Felix, Monique. (1988). *The Story of a Little Mouse Trapped in a Book*. La Jolla, CA: Green Tiger.

Field, Eugene. (2008). *Wynken, Blynken and Nod*. Illustrated by Giselle Potter. New York: Random House.

Fillion, Susan. (2011). *Miss Etta and Dr. Claribel: Bringing Matisse to America*. Boston: Godine.

Fine, Anne. (2007). *Jamie and Angus Together*. Illustrated by Penny Dale. Cambridge, MA: Candlewick.

Fisher, Aileen. (1962). *Like Nothing at All: Out in the Dark and Daylight*. Illustrated by Leonard Weisgard. New York: HarperCollins.

———. (1980). *Anybody Home?* Illustrated by Susan Bonners. New York: Crowell.

———. (1983). *Rabbits, Rabbits*. Illustrated by Gail Niemann. New York: Harper & Row.

———. (1988). *The House of a Mouse*. Illustrated by Joan Sandin. New York: HarperCollins.

———. (1991). *Always Wondering*. Illustrated by Joan Sandin. New York: HarperCollins.

———. (2001). *Sing of the Earth and Sky: Poems about Our Planet and the Wonders Beyond*. Illustrated by Karmen Thompson. Honesdale, PA: Wordsong.

Fisher, Catherine. (2003). *The Oracle Betrayed*. New York: HarperCollins.

———. (2004). *The Sphere of Secrets*. New York: HarperCollilns.

———. (2005). *Day of the Scarab*. New York: HarperCollins.

———. (2010). *Incarceron*. New York: Dial.

———. (2010). *Sapphique*. New York: Dial.

Fisher, Leonard Everett. (1984). *Olympians: Great Gods and Goddesses of Ancient Greece*. New York: Holiday House.

———. (1990). *The Oregon Trail*. New York: Holiday House.

Fitzhugh, Louise. (1964). *Harriet the Spy*. New York: Harper & Row.

Flake, Sharon. (2004). *Who Am I without Him? Short Stories about Girls and the Boys in Their Lives*. New York: Hyperion.

Fleischman, Paul. (1988). *Joyful Noise: Poems for Two Voices*. New York: HarperCollins.

———. (1989). *I Am Phoenix*. Illustrated by Ken Nutt. New York: HarperCollins.

———. (2000). *Big Talk: Poems for Four Voices*. Illustrated by Beppe Giacoppe. Cambridge, MA: Candlewick.

———. (2007). *Glass Slipper, Gold Sandal: A Worldwide Cinderella*. Illustrated by Julie Paschkis. New York: Holt.

Fleischman, Sid. (1978). *McBroom and the Beanstalk*. Boston: Little, Brown.

———. (1986). *The Whipping Boy*. New York: Greenwillow.

———. (2009). *The Dream Stealer*. Illustrated by Peter Sís. New York: Greenwillow.

Fleming, Ann Marie. (2007). *The Magical Life of Long Tack Sam: An Illustrated Memoir*. New York: Riverhead.

Fleming, Candace. (2003). *Ben Franklin's Almanac: Being a True Account of the Good Gentleman's Life*. New York: Atheneum.

———. (2011). *Amelia Lost:The Life and Disappearance of Amelia Earhart*. New York: Schwartz & Wade.

Fleming, Denise. (1996). *Lunch*. New York: Holt.

———. (1998). *In the Small, Small Pond*. New York: Holt.

———. (2000).*The Everything Book*. New York: Holt.

———. (2001). *Barnyard Banter*. New York: Holt.

———. (2010). *Sleepy, Oh So Sleepy*. New York: Holt.

———. (2011). *Shout! Shout It Out!*. New York: Holt.

Fletcher, Susan. (1989). *Dragon's Milk*. New York: Atheneum.

———. (1993). *Flight of the Dragon Kyn*. New York: Atheneum.

———. (1996). *Sign of the Dove*. New York: Atheneum.

———. (1998). *Shadow Spinner*. New York: Atheneum.

———. (2010). *Ancient, Strange, and Lovely*. New York: Atheneum.

Floca, Brian. (2003). *The Racecar Alphabet*. New York: Simon & Schuster.

———. (2007). *Lightship*. New York: Simon & Schuster.

———. (2009). *Moonshot: The Flight of Apollo 11*. New York: Simon & Schuster.

Florian, Douglas. (1997). *In the Swim: Poems and Paintings*. San Diego, CA: Harcourt Brace.

———. (1999). *Winter Eyes*. New York: Greenwillow.

———. (2002). *Summersaults: Poems and Paintings*. New York: Greenwillow.

———. (2003). *Autumnblings*. New York: Greenwillow.

———. (2006). *Handsprings*. New York: Greenwillow.

———. (2011). *A Dazzling Display of Dogs*. Illustrated by Michael Wertz. Berkeley, CA: Tricycle.

Fogarty, Mignon. (2011). *Grammar Girl Presents the Ultimate Writing Guide for Students*. Illustrated by Erwin Haya. New York: St. Martin's Griffin.

Fogliano, Julie. (2012). *And Then It's Spring*. Illustrated by Erin E. Stead. New York: Holt.

Forbes, Esther. (1943). *Johnny Tremain*. Boston: Houghton Mifflin.

Forester, Victoria. (2008). *The Girl Who Could Fly*. New York: Feiwel and Friends.

Fox, Mem. (1983). *Possum Magic*. Illustrated by Julie Vivas. San Diego: Harcourt.

———. (1997). *Whoever You Are*. San Diego, CA: Harcourt.

———. (2004). *Where Is the Green Sheep?*. Illustrated by Judy Horacek. San Diego, CA: Harcourt.

Fox, Paula. (1991). *Monkey Island*. New York: Orchard.

Franco, Betsy. (2009). *Zero Is the Leaves on the Tree*. Illustrated by Shino Arihara. Berkeley, CA: Tricycle.

Franklin, Kristine. (2003). *The Grape Thief*. Somerville, MA: Candlewick.

Frasier, Debra. (1995). *On the Day You Were Born*. San Diego, CA: Harcourt.

Frazee, Marla. (2006). *Roller Coaster*. New York: Voyager.

_____. (2008). *A Couple of Boys Have the Best Week Ever*. Orlando: Harcourt.

Freedman, Deborah. (2007). *Scribble*. New York: Random House.

Freedman, Russell. (1987). *Lincoln: A Photobiography*. New York: Clarion.

_____. (1987). *Lincoln: A Photobiography*. New York: Clarion.

_____. (1992). *An Indian Winter*. New York: Holiday House.

_____. (2002).*Confucius:The Golden Rule*. Illustrated by Frederic Clement. New York: Levine.

_____. (2004). *The Voice that Challenged a Nation: Marian Anderson and the Struggle for Equal Rights*. New York: Clarion.

_____. (2007). *Who Was First? Discovering the Americas*. New York: Clarion.

_____. (2010). *Lafayette and the American Revolution*. New York: Holiday House.

_____. (2010). *The War to End All Wars: World War I*. New York: Clarion.

French, Fiona. (1999). *Anancy and Mr. Dry-Bone*. London: Frances Lincoln.

Freymann, Saxton. (2006). *Baby Food*. Illustrated by Joost Elfers. New York: Scholastic.

_____. (2006). *Dog Food*. Illustrated by Joost Elfers. New York: Scholastic.

_____. (2006). *Fast Food*. Illustrated by Joost Elfers. New York: Scholastic.

Frost, Helen. (2006). *The Braid*. Detroit: Thorndike.

_____. (2008). *Diamond Willow*. New York: Farrar, Straus and Giroux.

_____. (2008). *Monarch and Milkweed*. Illustrated by Leonid Gore. New York: Atheneum.

Funke, Cornelia. (2002). *The Thief Lord*. New York: Scholastic.

_____. (2003). *Inkheart*. New York: Scholastic.

_____. (2004). *Dragon Rider*. New York: Scholastic.

_____. (2005). *Inkspell*. New York: Scholastic.

_____. (2007). *Igraine the Brave*. New York: Scholastic.

_____. (2008). *Inkdeath*. New York: Scholastic.

Gág, Wanda. (1928). *Millions of Cats*. New York: Coward-McCann.

_____. (2006). *More Tales from Grimm*. Minneapolis, MN: University of Minnesota Press.

_____. (2006). *Tales from Grimm*. Minneapolis, MN: University of Minnesota Press.

Gaiman, Neil. (2008). *The Graveyard Book*. Illustrated by David. McKean. New York: HarperCollins.

Galdone, Paul. (1979). *Jack and the Beanstalk*. New York: Clarion.

Gall, Chris. (2006). *Dear Fish*. New York: Little, Brown.

_____. (2008). *There's Nothing to Do on Mars*. New York: Little, Brown.

Gantos, Jack. (2000). *Joey Pigza Loses Control*. New York: Farrar, Straus and Giroux.

_____. (2007). *I Am Not Joey Pigza*. New York: Farrar, Straus and Giroux.

_____. (2011). *Dead End in Norvelt*. New York: Farrar, Straus and Giroux.

Garden, Nancy. (1982). *Annie on my Mind*. New York: Farrar, Straus and Giroux.

Gardner, Sally. (2008). *The Red Necklace: A Story of the French Revolution*. New York: Dial.

Gauthier, Gail. (2007). *A Girl, a Boy, and a Monster Cat*. Illustrated by Joe Cepeda. New York: Putnam.

_____. (2008). *A Girl, a Boy, and Three Robbers*. Illustrated by Joe Cepeda. New York: Putnam.

Gee, Maurice. (2009). *Salt*. Custer, WA: Orca.

Geisel, Theodore. (1957).*The Cat in the Hat*. New York. Random House.

_____. (1989). *And to Think I Saw It on Mulberry Street*. New York: Random House.

Geisert, Arthur. (2008). *Hogwash*. Boston: Houghton Mifflin Harcourt.

_____. (2010). *Country Road ABC: An Illustrated Journey through America's Farmland*. Boston: Houghton Mifflin Harcourt.

Gensler, Sonia. (2011). *The Revenant*. New York: Knopf.

George, Jean Craighead. (1959). *My Side of the Mountain*. New York: Dutton.

_____. (1972). *Julie of the Wolves*. New York: Harper & Row.

George, Kristine O'Connell. (2001). *Toasting Marshmallows: Camping Poems*. Illustrated by Kate Kiesler. New York: Clarion.

_____. (2002). *The blue between*. In P. Janeczko, *Seeing the blue between: Advice and inspiration for young poets* (pp. 82–84). Cambridge, MA: Candlewick.

_____. (2005). *Fold Me a Poem*. Illustrated by Lauren Stringer. San Diego, CA: Harcourt.

_____. (2011). *Emma Dilemma: Big Sister Poems*. Illustrated by Nancy Carpenter. New York: Clarion.

Geras, Adele. (2001). *Troy*. San Diego: Harcourt.

Gershator, Phyllis. (2005). *Sky Sweeper*. Illustrated by Holly Meade. New York: Farrar, Straus and Giroux.

Gerson, Mary-Joan. (1994). *Why the Sky Is Far Away: A Nigerian Folktale*. Illustrated by Carla Golembe. Boston: Little, Brown.

Gibbons, Gail. (2007). *The Vegetables We Eat*. New York: Holiday House.

Giblin, James Cross. (2002).*The Life and Death of Adolf Hitler*. New York: Clarion.

Gidwitz, Adam. (2010). *A Tale Dark & Grimm*. New York: Dutton.

Giff, Patricia Reilly. (1997). *Lily's Crossing*. New York: Delacorte.

_____. (2000). *Nory Ryan's Song*. New York: Delacorte.

_____. (2002). *Pictures of Hollis Woods*. New York: Random House.

_____. (2003). *Maggie's Door*. New York: Random House.

_____. (2004). *A House of Tailors*. New York: Random House.

_____. (2008). *Eleven*. New York: Random House.

_____. (2008). *Water Street*. New York: Yearling.

_____. (2009). *Wild Girl*. New York: Wendy Lamb Books.

_____. (2011). *R My Name Is Rachel*. New York: Wendy Lamb Books.

Gifford, Peggy. (2008). *Moxy Maxwell Does Not Love Stuart Little*. Photographs by Valorie Fisher. New York: Schwartz & Wade.

_____. (2008). *Moxy Maxwell Does Not Love Writing Thank-You Notes*. Photographs by Valorie Fisher. New York: Schwartz & Wade.

Giovanni, Nikki. (2006). *Rosa*. Illustrated by Bryan Collier. New York: Holt.

Global Fund for Children. (2007). *Global Babies*. Watertown, MA: Charlesbridge.

Goble, Paul. (1984). *The Gift of the Sacred Dog*. New York: Aladdin.

Golding, Julia. (2008). *The Diamond of Drury Lane*. New York: Roaring Brook.

Goldstein, Bobbye S. (1992). *Inner Chimes: Poems on Poetry*. Honesdale, PA: Wordsong.

Gonyea, Mark. (2005). *A Book about Design: Complicated Doesn't Make It Good*. New York: Holt.

_____. (2007). *Another Book about Design: Complicated Doesn't Make It Bad*. New York: Holt.

Goodman, Susan. (2003). *Skyscraper: From the Ground Up*. Illustrated by Michael Doolittle. Boston: Hornbook.

Gorbachev, Valeri. (2007). *Red Red Red*. New York: Philomel.

Gore, Al. (2007). *An Inconvenient Truth:The Crisis of Global Warming*. New York: Penguin.

Gore, Leonid. (2007). *Danny's First Snow*. New York: Simon & Schuster.

Grady, Cynthia. (2012). *I Lay My Stitches Down: Poems of American Slavery*. Illustrated by Michele Wood. Grand Rapids, MI: Eerdmans.

Graham, Joan Bransfield. (1994). *Splish Splash*. Boston: Houghton Mifflin.

_____. (1999). *Flicker Flash*. Boston: Houghton Mifflin.

Grahame, Kenneth. (1908/1961). *The Wind in the Willows*. New York: Scribner.

Grant, K. M. (2005). *Blood Red Horse*. New York: Walker.

Gratz, Alan. (2008). *Samurai Shortstop*. New York: Penguin.

Graves, Bonnie. (1998). *No Copycats Allowed*. Illustrated by Abby Carter. New York: Hyperion.

_____. (2002). *Taking Care of Trouble*. Illustrated by Robin Preiss Glasser. New York: Penguin.

Gravett, Emily. (2006). *Wolves*. New York: Simon & Schuster.

_____. (2007). *Meerkat Mail*. New York: Simon & Schuster.

_____. (2007). *Orange Pear Apple Bear*. New York: Simon & Schuster.

_____. (2008). *Monkey and Me*. New York: Simon & Schuster.

_____. (2010). *The Rabbit Problem*. New York: Simon & Schuster.

_____. (2011). *Blue Chameleon*. New York: Simon & Schuster.

Gray, Dianne. (2002). *Together Apart*. Boston: Houghton Mifflin.

Gray, Elizabeth Janet. (1942). *Adam of the Road*. New York: Viking.

Greaves, Margaret. (1990). *Tattercoats*. Illustrated by Margaret Chamberlain. New York: Clarkson N. Potter.

Greenberg, Jan, & Sandra Jordan. (1991). *The Painter's Eye: Learning to Look at Contemporary American Art*. New York: Delacorte.

_____. (1993). *The Sculptor's Eye: Looking at Contemporary American Art*. New York: Delacorte.

_____. (2010). *Ballet for Martha: Making Appalachian Spring*. Illustrated by Brian Floca. New York: Roaring Brook.

Greene, Stephanie. (2010). *Happy Birthday, Sophie Hartley*. Boston: Clarion.

_____. (2010). *Princess Posey and the First Grade Parade*. Illustrated by Stephanie Roth Sisson. New York: Putnam.

_____. (2011). *Princess Posey and the Perfect Present*. Illustrated by Stephanie Roth Sisson. New York: Penguin.

Greenfield, Eloise. (1978). *Honey, I Love and Other Love Poems*. New York: Crowell.

_____. (1991). *Night on a Neighborhood Street*. Illustrated by Jan Spivey Gilchrist. New York: Dial.

_____. (1993). *Nathaniel Talking*. Illustrated by Jan Spivey Gilchrist. Danbury, CT: Writers & Readers.

_____. (2006). *The Friendly Four*. Illustrated by Jan Spivey Gilchrist. New York: HarperCollins.

_____. (2011). *The Great Migration: Journey to the North*. Illustrated by Jan Spivey Gilchrist. New York: Amistad.

Gregory, Valiska. (1992). *Through the Mickle Woods*. New York: Little, Brown.

Grey, Mini. (2005). *Traction Man Is Here*. New York: Knopf.

_____. (2006). *The Adventures of the Dish and the Spoon*. New York: Knopf.

_____. (2008). *Traction Man Meets Turbo Dog*. New York: Knopf.

Grimes, Nikki. (1994). *Meet Danitra Brown*. Illustrated by Floyd Cooper. New York: HarperCollins.

_____. (1996). *Come Sunday*. Grand Rapids, MI: Eerdmans.

_____. (2001). *A Pocketful of Poems*. Illustrated by Javaka Steptoe. New York: Clarion.

_____. (2001). *Danitra Brown Leaves Town*. Illustrated by Floyd Cooper. New York: HarperCollins.

_____. (2002). *Bronx Masquerade*. New York: Dial.

_____. (2002). *My Man Blue*. Illustrated by Jerome Lagarrigue. New York: Penguin.

_____. (2004). *What Is Goodbye?*. Illustrated by Raul Colón. New York: Hyperion.

_____. (2005). *Danitra Brown, Class Clown*. Illustrated by E. B. Lewis. New York: HarperCollins.

_____. (2005). *It's Raining Laughter*. Illustrated by Miles C. Pinkney. Honesdale, PA: Boyds Mills.

_____. (2008). *Oh, Brother!*. Illustrated by Mike Benny. New York: HarperCollins.

_____. (2008). *The Road to Paris*. New York: Penguin.

_____. (2010). *Almost Zero: A Dyamonde Daniel Book*. Illustrated by Christie R. Gregory. New York: Putnam.

_____. (2011). *Planet Middle School*. New York: Bloomsbury.

Grimm, Jacob, & Wilhelm Grimm. (2003). *The Juniper Tree and Other Tales from Grimm*. Illustrated by Maurice Sendak. Translated by Lore Segal. New York: Farrar, Straus and Giroux.

_____. (2004). *The Annotated Brothers Grimm*. Translated and edited by Maria Tatar. New York: W. W. Norton.

_____. (2007). *The Bremen Town Musicians*. Illustrated by Lisbeth Zwerger. Translated by Anthea Bell. New York: Minedition.

_____. (2011). *German Popular Stories*. Illustrated by George Cruikshank. Nabu.

_____. (2011). *Kinder- und Hausmärchen*. Ulan.

Guthrie, Woody. (2004). *New Baby Train*. Illustrated by Marla Frazee. London: Little, Brown.

Gutierrez, Elisa. (2005). *Picturescape*. Vancouver, Canada: Simply Read.

Guy, Ginger Foglesong. (2007). *Perros! Perros! Dogs! Dogs! A Story in English and Spanish*. Illustrated by Sharon Glick. New York: Greenwillow.

Haddix, Margaret Peterson. (2007). *Uprising*. New York: Simon & Schuster.

Haddon, Mark. (2003). *The Curious Incident of the Dog in the Night-Time*. New York: Doubleday.

Hale, Shannon, & Dean Hale. (2008). *Rapunzel's Revenge*. Illustrated by Nathan Hale. New York: Bloomsbury.

_____. (2010). *Calamity Jack*. New York: Bloomsbury.

Haley, Gail E. (1986). *Jack and the Bean Tree*. New York: Knopf.

_____. (1988). *Jack and the Fire Dragon*. New York: Random House.

_____. (1992). *Mountain Jack Tales*. New York: Penguin.

Hall, Michael. (2011). *Perfect Square*. New York: Greenwillow.

Hamilton, Virginia. (1967). *Zeely*. New York: Macmillan.

_____. (1971/2002). *The Planet of Junior Brown*. New York: Simon & Schuster.

_____. (1974). *M.C. Higgins, the Great*. New York: Simon & Schuster.

_____. (1985). *The People Could Fly: American Black Folktales*. Illustrated by Leo & Diane Dillon. New York: Knopf.

_____. (1988). *In the Beginning: Creation Stories from around the World*. Illustrated by Barry Moser. San Diego, CA: Harcourt Brace Jovanovich.

_____. (1995). *Her Stories: African American Folktales, Fairy Tales, and True Tales*. Illustrated by Leo Dillon & Diane Dillon. New York: Blue Sky.

_____. (1996). *When Birds Could Talk and Bats Could Sing: The Adventures of Bruh Sparrows, Sis Wren, and Their Friends*. Illustrated by Barry Moser. New York: Blue Sky.

_____. (1997). *A Ring of Tricksters: Animal Tales from America, the West Indies, and Africa*. Illustrated by Barry Moser. New York: Blue Sky.

_____. (2000). *The Girl Who Spun Gold*. New York: Blue Sky.

_____. (2003). *Bruh Rabbit and the Tar Baby Girl*. Illustrated by James Ransome. New York: Blue Sky.

_____. (2004). *The People Could Fly: The Picture Book*. Illustrated by Leo & Diane Dillon. New York: Knopf.

_____. (2004). *Wee Winnie Witch's Skinny: An Original African American Scare Tale*. Illustrated by Barry Moser. New York: Scholastic.

_____. (2006). *M. C. Higgins, the Great*. New York: Aladdin.

Han, Jenny. (2011). *Clara Lee and the Apple Pie Dream*. Illustrated by Julia Kuo. New York: Little, Brown.

Hardy, Janice. (2009). *The Shifter*. New York: Balzer + Bray.

———. (2010). *Blue Fire*. New York: Balzer + Bray.

———. (2011). *Darkfall*. New York: Balzer + Bray.

Harley, Avis. (2000). *Fly with Poetry: An ABC of Poetry*. Honesdale, PA: Wordsong.

———. (2001). *Leap into Poetry: More ABC's of Poetry*. Honesdale, PA: Wordsong.

Harper, Charise Mericle. (2011). *Just Grace and the Double Surprise*. Boston: Houghton Mifflin Harcourt.

Harper, Charley. (2008). *Charley Harper 123s*. Pasadena, CA: AMMO.

Harper, Jessica. (2010). *I Barfed on Mrs. Kenly*. Illustrated by Jon Berkeley. New York: Putnam.

Harrington, Janice N. (2004). *Going North*. Illustrated by Jerome Lagarrigue. New York: Farrar, Straus and Giroux.

———. (2007). *The Chicken-Chasing Queen of Lamar County*. Illustrated by Shelley Jackson. New York: Farrar, Straus and Giroux.

Harrington, Laura. (2011). *Alice Bliss*. New York: Viking.

Harris, Robie. H. (2011). *Who Has What? All about Girls' Bodies and Boys' Bodies*. Illustrated by Nadine Bernard Westcott. Somerville, MA: Candlewick.

Harrison, David L. (2007). *Piggy Wiglet and the Great Adventure*. Illustrated by Karen Stormer Brooks. Honesdale, PA: Wordsong.

Harrison, David. (1999). The future me. In Harrison, D., & B. Cullinan. (1999). *Easy Poetry Lessons that Dazzle and Delight* (p. 47). New York: Scholastic.

Hart, Jane. (1989). *Singing Bee! A Collection of Favorite Children's Songs*. Illustrated by Anita Lobel. New York: Lothrop Lee & Shepard.

Hautman, Pete. (2010). *Blank Confession*. New York: Simon & Schuster.

———. (2011). *The Big Crunch*. New York: Scholastic.

Hawkes, Kevin. (2007). *The Wicked Big Toddlah*. New York: Random House.

Hawkins, Colin, & Jacqui Hawkins. (2004). *Fairytale News*. Cambridge, MA: Candlewick.

Hawthorne, Nathaniel. (1851/1893). *A Wonder Book for Boys and Girls*. Boston: Houghton Mifflin.

Hayes, Joe. (2000). *Little Gold Star/Estrellita de oro: A Cinderella cuento*. Illustrated by Gloria Osuna Perez and Lucia A. Perez. El Paso, TX: Cinco Puntos.

———. (2004). *La llorona/The Weeping Woman: An Hispanic Legend Told in Spanish and English*. Illustrated by Vicki Trego Hill & Mona Pennypacker. El Paso, TX: Cinco Puntos.

Hegamin, Tonya, C., & Marilyn Nelson. (2008). *Pemba's Song: A Ghost Story*. New York: Scholastic.

Heiligman, Deborah. (2009). *Charles and Emma: The Darwins' Leap of Faith*. New York: Holt.

Heller, Ruth. (1997). *Mine, All Mine: A Book about Pronouns*. New York: Grosset & Dunlap.

Hemphill, Stephanie. (2007). *Your Own, Sylvia: A Verse Portrait of Sylvia Plath*. New York: Knopf.

Henderson, Kathy. (2006). *Lugalbanda: The Boy Who Got Caught Up in a War*. Illustrated by Jane Ray. Cambridge, MA: Candlewick.

Henkes, Kevin. (2003). *Olive's Ocean*. New York: Greenwillow.

———. (2003). *Wemberly's Ice-Cream Star*. New York: HarperCollins.

———. (2004). *Kitten's First Full Moon*. New York: Greenwillow.

———. (2007). *A Good Day*. New York: Greenwillow.

———. (2008). *Bird Lake Moon*. New York: Greenwillow.

———. (2011). *Junonia*. New York: Greenwillow.

———. (2011). *Little White Rabbit*. New York: Greenwillow.

———. (2011). *Old Bear*. New York: Greenwillow.

Hennessy, B. G. (2006). *The Boy Who Cried Wolf*. Illustrated by Boris Kulikov. New York: Simon & Schuster.

Hermsen, Ronald. (2007). *The Story of Giraffe*. Illustrated by Guido Pigni. Honesdale, PA: Front Street.

Herrick, Steven. (2008). *Naked Bunyip Dancing*. Illustrated by Beth Norling. Asheville, NC: Front Street.

Hesse, Karen. (1997). *Out of the Dust*. New York: Scholastic.

———. (2004). *The Cats in Krasinski Square*. Illustrated by Wendy Watson. New York: Scholastic.

———. (2008). *Brooklyn Bridge*. New York: Feiwel and Friends.

Hicks, Betty. (2008). *Basketball Bats*. Illustrated by Adam McCauley. New York: Roaring Brook.

———. (2008). *Goof-Off Goalie*. Illustrated by Adam McCauley. New York: Roaring Brook.

Hill, Laban Carrick. (2003). *Harlem Stomp! A Cultural History of the Harlem Renaissance*. New York: Little, Brown.

———. (2010). *Dave the Potter: Artist, Poet, Slave*. Illustrated by Bryan Collier. New York: Little, Brown.

Hillenbrand, Jane. (2006). *What a Treasure!*. Illustrated by Will Hillenbrand. New York: Holiday House.

Hillman, Ben. (2007). *How Big Is It? A Big Book All about Bigness*. New York: Scholastic.

Hills, Tad. (2010). *How Rocket Learned to Read*. New York: Schwartz & Wade.

Hilmo, Tess. (2011). *With a Name Like Love*. New York: Farrar, Straus and Giroux.

Hinds, Gareth. (2010). *The Odyssey*. Cambridge, MA: Candlewick.

Hinton, S. E. (1967). *The Outsiders*. New York: Viking.

Hirahara, Naomi. (2008). *1001 Cranes*. New York: Delacorte.

Hirsch, Odo. (2004). *Yoss*. New York: Random House.

Ho, Minfong, & Saphan Ros. (1996). *Brother Rabbit: A Cambodian Tale*. Illustrated by Jennifer Hewitson. New York: Lothrop, Lee & Shepard.

Hoban, Tana. (2000). *Cubes, Cones, Cylinders, and Spheres*. New York: HarperCollins.

Hobbs, Will. (2000). *Jason's Gold*. New York: HarperCollins.

_____. (2011). *Take Me to the River*. New York: Harper.

Hoberman, Mary Ann. (1957). *All My Shoes Come in Twos*. New York: Little, Brown.

_____. (1998). *The Llama Who Had No Pajama: 100 Favorite Poems*. Illustrated by Betty Fraser. San Diego, CA: Harcourt.

_____. (2001). *Fathers, Mothers, Sisters, Brothers: A Collection of Family Poems*. Boston: Little, Brown.

_____. (2007). *A House Is a House for Me*. Illustrated by Betty Fraser. New York: Penguin.

_____. (2007). *I'm Going to Grandma's*. Illustrated by Tiphanie Beeke. San Diego, CA: Harcourt.

Hodges, Margaret. (1984). *St. George and the Dragon: A Golden Legend*. Illustrated by Trina Schart Hyman. Boston: Little, Brown.

_____. (2004). *Merlin and the Making of the King*. Illustrated by Trina Schart Hyman. New York: Holiday House.

_____. (2006). *Dick Whittington and His Cat*. Illustrated by Melisande Potter. New York: Holiday House.

Hogrogian, Nonny. (1981). *Cinderella*. New York: Greenwillow.

Holm, Jennifer L. (1999). *Our Only May Amelia*. New York: HarperCollins.

_____. (2011). *The Trouble with May Amelia*. New York: Atheneum.

Holt, Kimberly Willis. (1999). *When Zachary Beaver Came to Town*. New York: Holt.

_____. (2007). *Piper Reed, Navy Brat*. Illustrated by Christine Davenier. New York: Holt.

_____. (2008). *Piper Reed, the Great Gypsy*. Illustrated by Christine Davenier. New York: Holt.

Holtz, Thomas R. (2007). *Dinosaurs: The Most Complete, Up-to-Date Encyclopedia for Dinosaur Lovers of All Ages*. Illustrated by Luis V. Rey. New York: Random House.

Hooks, William. (1987). *Moss Gown*. Illustrated by Donald Carrick. New York: Clarion.

Hooper, Mary. (2008). *Newes from the Dead*. New York: Holt.

Hoose, Phillip. (2004). *The Race to Save the Lord God Bird*. New York: Farrar, Straus and Giroux.

_____. (2009). *Claudette Colvin: Twice toward Justice*. New York: Square Fish.

Hopkins, Lee Bennett. (1999). *Been to Yesterdays: Poems of a Life*. Illustrated by Charlene Rendeiro. Honesdale, PA: Boyds Mills.

_____. (2007). *Today and Today*. Illustrated by G. Brian Karas. New York: Scholastic.

_____. (2008). *Americans at War: Poems Selected by Lee Bennett Hopkins*. Illustrated by Stephen Alcorn. New York: Simon & Schuster.

_____. (2009). *Sky Magic*. Illustrated by Mariusz Stawarski. New York: Dutton.

_____. (2011). *Dizzy Dinosaurs: Silly Dino Poems*. Illustrated by Barry Gott. New York: HarperCollins.

_____. (2011). *I Am the Book*. Illustrated by Yayo. New York: Holiday House.

Hopkinson, Deborah. (2005). *Under the Quilt of Night*. Illustrated by James Ransome. New York: Simon & Schuster.

_____. (2006). *Into the Firestorm: A Novel of San Francisco, 1906*. New York: Knopf.

_____. (2008). *Abe Lincoln Crosses a Creek*. Illustrated by John Hendrix. New York: Random House.

_____. (2012). *A Boy Called Dickens*. Illustrated by John Hendrix. New York: Schwartz & Wade.

Horacek, Petr. (2007). *Butterfly, Butterfly*. Cambridge, MA: Candlewick.

Horowitz, Anthony. (2011). *Scorpia Rising*. New York: Penguin.

Hort, Lenny. (2003). *The Seals on the Bus*. Illustrated by G. Brian Caras. New York: Holt.

Howitt, Mary Botham. (1839). *Hymns and Fire-Side Verses*. London: Darton.

Huck, Charlotte. (1989). *Princess Furball*. Illustrated by Anita Lobel. New York: Greenwillow.

Hughes, Langston. (2008). *The Dream Keeper and Other Poems*. Illustrated by Brian Pinkney. New York: Knopf.

Hunt, Irene. (1964). *Across Five Aprils*. Chicago: Follett.

Hunter-Gault, Charlayne. (2012). *To the Mountaintop: My Journey through the Civil Rights Movement*. New York: Flash Point.

Hutchens, Pat. (1971). *Rosie's Walk*. New York: Aladdin.

Hutchins, Hazel. (2004). *A Second Is a Hiccup: A Child's Book of Time*. Illustrated by Kady MacDonald Denton. New York: Levine.

Hutchins, Pat. (1986). *The Doorbell Rang*. New York: Greenwillow.

Inns, Christopher. (2007). *Peekaboo Puppy and Other Pets*. London: Kingfisher.

Intriago, Patricia. (2011). *Dot*. New York: Farrar, Straus and Giroux.

Isaac, Anne. (2000). *Swamp Angel*. Illustrated by Paul O. Zelinsky. New York: Puffin.

Isadora, Rachel. (2000). *1 2 3 Pop!*. New York: Viking.

———. (2001). *ABC Pop!*. New York: Penguin.

———. (2007). *The Princess and the Pea*. New York: Putnam.

———. (2007). *The Twelve Dancing Princesses*. New York: Putnam.

———. (2007). *Yo, Jo!*. San Diego, CA: Harcourt.

———. (2008). *The Fisherman and His Wife*. New York: Putnam.

———. (2008). *Uh-Oh!*. San Diego, CA: Harcourt.

———. (2009). *Hansel and Gretel*. New York: Putnam.

Issa, Kobayashi. (1973). *Don't Tell the Scarecrow, and Other Japanese Poems*. New York: Scholastic.

Jablonski, Carla. (2010). *Resistance: Book 1*. Illustrated by Leland Purvis. New York: First Second.

Jackson, S., & E. Colon. (2010). *Anne Frank: The Anne Frank House Authorized Graphic Autobiography*. New York: Hill and Wang.

Jacobs, Joseph. (1965). *Tom Tit Tot*. Illustrated by Evaline Ness. New York: Scribner.

———. (1968). *English Fairy Tales*. New York: Bodley Head.

Jacobson, Jennifer Richard. (2011). *Small as an Elephant*. Somerville, MA: Candlewick.

Jacques, Brian. (1986). *Redwall*. Illustrated by Brian Chalk. New York: Philomel.

Jagendorf, Moritz. (1988). *Noodlehead Stories from around the World*. New York: Random House.

Janeczko, Paul B., & J. Patrick Lewis. (2006). *Wing Nuts: Screwy Haiku*. Illustrated by Tricia Tusa. New York: Little, Brown.

Janeczko, Paul. (1993). *A Poke in the I: A Collection of Concrete Poems*. Illustrated by Christopher Rashka. Cambridge, MA: Candlewick.

———. (1993). *Looking for Your Name: A Collection of Contemporary Poems*. New York: Orchard.

———. (2000). *Stone Bench in an Empty Park*. Illustrated by Henri Silberman. New York: Orchard.

———. (2001). *Dirty Laundry Pile: Poems in Different Voices*. Illustrated by Melissa Sweet. New York: HarperCollins.

———. (2005). *A Kick in the Head: An Everyday Guide to Poetic Forms*. Illustrated by Chris Raschka. Cambridge, MA: Candlewick.

———. (2007). *Hey, You! Poems to Skyscrapers, Mosquitoes, and Other Fun Things*. Illustrated by Robert Rayevsky. New York: HarperCollins.

Jansson, Tove. (1995). *Tales from Moominvalley*. New York: Farrar, Straus and Giroux.

Jarrie, Martin. (2005). *ABC USA*. New York: Sterling.

Jay, Allison. (2005). *ABC: A Child's First Alphabet Book*. New York: Penguin.

Jeffers, Oliver. (2006). *Lost and Found*. New York: Philomel.

Jenkins, Emily. (2006). *Love You when You Whine*. Illustrated by Sergio Ruzzier. New York: Farrar, Straus and Giroux.

———. (2006). *Toys Go Out: Being the Adventures of a Knowledgeable Stingray, a Toughy Little Buffalo, and Someone Called Plastic*. Illustrated by Paul O. Zelinsky. New York: Schwartz & Wade.

———. (2008). *Toy Dance Party: Being the Further Adventures of a Bossyboots Stingray, a Courageous Buffalo, and a Hopeful Round Someone Called Plastic*. Illustrated by Paul O. Zelinsky. New York: Schwartz & Wade.

———. (2011). *Toys Come Home: Being the Early Experiences of an Intelligent Stingray, a Brave Buffalo, and a Brand-New Someone Called Plastic*. Illustrated by Paul O. Zelinsky. New York: Schwartz &Wade.

Jenkins, Martin. (2011). *Can We Save the Tiger?*. Illustrated by Vicky White. Cambridge, MA: Candlewick.

Jenkins, Steve, & Robin Page. (2003). *What Do You Do with a Tail Like This?*. Illustrated by Steve Jenkins. Boston: Houghton Mifflin.

———. (2008). *Sisters & Brothers: Sibling Relationships in the Animal World*. Boston: Houghton Mifflin.

Jenkins, Steve. (1995). *Biggest, Strongest, Fastest*. Boston: Houghton Mifflin.

———. (2004). *Actual Size*. Boston: Houghton Mifflin.

———. (2005). *Animals in Flight*. Boston: Houghton Mifflin.

———. (2005). *Prehistoric Actual Size*. Boston: Houghton Mifflin.

———. (2007). *Living Color*. Boston: Houghton Mifflin.

———. (2011). *Just a Second*. Boston: Houghton Mifflin Harcourt.

Jiménez, Francisco. (1997). *The Circuit: Stories from the Life of a Migrant Child*. Albuquerque, NM: University of New Mexico Press.

———. (2001). *Breaking Through*. Boston: Houghton Mifflin.

Jinks, Catherine. (2010). *Living Hell*. Boston: Harcourt.

Jocelyn, Marthe. (2011). *Ones and Twos*. Illustrated by Nell Jocelyn. Toronto, ON: Tundra.

Johnson, Angela. (2003). *I Dream of Trains*. Illustrated by Loren Long. New York: Simon & Schuster.

———. (2003). *The First Part Last*. New York: Simon & Schuster.

———. (2010). *The Day Ray Got Away*. Illustrated by Luke La Marca. New York: Simon & Schuster.

Johnson, Crockett. (1955). *Harold and the Purple Crayon*. New York: Harper & Brothers.

Johnson, D. B. (2000). *Henry Hikes to Fitchburg*. Boston: Houghton Mifflin.

_____. (2002). *Henry Builds a Cabin*. Boston: Houghton Mifflin.

_____. (2003). *Henry Climbs a Mountain*. Boston: Houghton Mifflin.

_____. (2004). *Henry Works*. Boston: Houghton Mifflin.

_____. (2007). *Four Legs Bad, Two Legs Good!*. Boston: Houghton Mifflin.

Johnson, David A. (2006). *Snow Sounds: An Onomatopoeic Story*. Boston: Houghton Mifflin Company.

Johnson, Lindsay Lee. (2002). *Soul Moon Soup*. Asheville, NC: Front Street.

Johnson, Rebecca L. (2010). *Journey into the Deep: Discovering New Ocean Creatures*. Minneapolis, MN: Millbrook.

Johnson, Stephen. (2003). *City by Numbers*. New York: Viking.

Johnson-Davies, Denys. (2005). *Goha, the Wise Fool*. Illustrated by Hag Hamdy Mohamed Fattouh. New York: Philomel.

Jones, Bill T., & Susan Kuklin. (1998). *Dance*. New York: Hyperion.

Jones, Carrie. (2011). *Sarah Emma Edmonds Was a Great Pretender: The True Story of a Civil War Spy*. Illustrated by Mark Oldroyd. Minneapolis, MN: Carolrhoda.

Jongman, Mariken. (2008). *Rits*. Asheville, NC: Front Street.

Jonnell, Lynne. (2007). *Emmy and the Incredible Shrinking Rat*. Illustrated by Jonathan Bean. New York: Holt.

Jonnell, Lynne. (2008). *Emmy and the Home for Troubled Girls*. Illustrated by Jonathan Bean. New York: Holt.

Joosse, Barbara. (1991). *Mama, Do You Love Me?*. Illustrated by Barbara Lavallee. San Francisco: Chronicle.

_____. (1998). *¿Me quieres, mama?*. Illustrated by Barbara Lavallee. San Francisco: Chronicle.

Joyce, William. (2011). *The Man in the Moon*. New York: Atheneum.

Judge, Lila. (2007). *One Thousand Tracings: Healing the Wounds of World War II*. New York: Hyperion.

_____. (2011). *Red Sled*. New York: Atheneum.

Juster, Norton. (2006). *The Hello, Goodbye Window*. Illustrated by Chris Raschka. New York: Hyperion.

_____. (2008). *Sourpuss and Sweetie Pie*. New York: Scholastic.

Kadohata, Cynthia. (2006). *Kira-Kira*. New York: Alladin.

_____. (2008). *Outside Beauty*. New York: Atheneum.

Kamm, Katja. (2006). *Invisible*. New York: North-South.

Kannenberg, G. (2008). *500 Essential Graphic Novels: The Ultimate Guide*. New York: Collins Design.

Karas, G. Brian. (2010). *Young Zeus*. New York: Scholastic.

_____. (2010). *The Village Garage*. New York: Holt.

Kathleen Krull. (2010). *Charles Darwin*. Illustrated by Boris Hulikov. New York: Viking.

Kato, Yukiko. (2011). *In the Meadow*. Illustrated by Komako Sakai. Translated by Yuki Kaneko. New York: Enchanted Lion.

Kay, Verla. (2011). *Hornbooks and Inkwells*. Illustrated by S. D. Schindler. New York: Putnam.

Keat, Nawuth, & Martha Kendall. (2010). *Alive in the Killing Fields: Surviving the Khmer Rouge Genocide*. Washington, D.C.: National Geographic.

Keats, Ezra Jack. (1962). *The Snowy Day*. New York: Viking.

Keenan, Sheila. (2000). *Gods, Goddesses and Monsters: A Book of World Mythology*. New York: Scholastic.

Keller, Laurie. (2007). *Do unto Otters: A Book about Manners*. New York: Holt.

Kellogg, Steven. (1988). *Johnny Appleseed*. New York: HarperCollins.

_____. (1991). *Jack and the Beanstalk*. New York: Morrow.

Kelly, Jacqueline. (2009). *The Evolution of Calpurnia Tate*. New York: Holt.

Kendall, Carol. (1959). *The Gammage Cup*. San Diego, CA: Harcourt.

_____. (1965). *The Whisper of Glocken*. San Diego, CA: Harcourt, Brace & World.

Kennedy, X. J. (1975). *One Winter Night in August, and Other Nonsense Jingles*. Illustrated by David M. McPhail. New York: Simon & Schuster.

Kennedy, X. J., & Dorothy Kennedy. (2002). *Talking Like the Rain*. Illustrated by Jane Dyer. New York: Little, Brown.

Kerley, Barbara. (2008). *What to Do about Alice: How Alice Roosevelt Broke the Rules, Charmed the World, and Drove Her Father Teddy Crazy*. Illustrated by Edwin Fotheringham, NY: Scholastic.

_____. (2010). *The Extraordinary Mark Twain (According to Susy)*. Illustrated by Edward Fotheringham. New York: Scholastic.

Kessler, Liz. (2008). *Philippa Fisher's Fairy Godsister*. Illustrated by Katie May. Cambridge, MA: Candlewick.

Kilaka, John. (2006). *True Friends: A Tale from Tanzania*. Groundwood.

Kimmel, Eric A. (1988). *Anansi and the Moss-Covered Rock*. Illustrated by Janet Stevens. New York: Holiday House.

_____. (2011). *Cactus Soup*. Illustrated by Phil Huling. New York: Cavendish.

_____. *Anasi Goes Fishing*. Narrated by Jerry Terheyden. Pine Plains, NY: Live Oak Media.

Kinerk, Robert. (2007). *Clorinda Takes Flight*. Illustrated by Steven Kellogg. New York: Simon & Schuster.

King Farris, Christine. (2003). *My Brother Martin: A Sister Remembers Growing Up with the Rev. Dr. Martin Luther King, Jr.* New York: Simon & Schuster.

King, A. S. (2011). *Everybody Sees the Ants*. New York: Little, Brown.

Kinney, Jeff. (2007). *Diary of a Wimpy Kid*. New York: Amulet.

———. (2008). *Diary of a Wimpy Kid: Rodrick Rules*. New York: Amulet.

Kipling, Rudyard. (1912). *Just So Stories*. Garden City, NC: Doubleday.

Klages, Ellen. (2006). *The Green Glass Sea*. New York: Viking.

———. (2008). *White Sands, Red Menace*. New York: Viking.

Klass, David. (2010). *Stuck on Earth*. New York: Farrar, Straus and Giroux.

Klassen, Jon. (2011). *I Want My Hat Back*. Somerville, MA: Candlewick.

Klise, Kate. (2007). *Imagine Harry*. Illustrated by M. Sarah Klise. San Diego, CA: Harcourt.

Knight, Eric. (1940). *Lassie Come-Home*. New York: Holt, Rinehart & Winston.

Koertge, Ron. (2003). *Shakespeare Bats Cleanup*. Cambridge, MA: Candlewick.

———. (2012). *Shakespeare Makes the Playoffs*. Cambridge, MA: Candlewick.

Konigsburg, E. L. (2000). *Silent to the Bone*. New York: Atheneum.

Kostecki-Shaw, Jenny Sue. (2011). *Same, Same But Different*. New York: Holt.

Kratter, Paul. (2004). *The Living Rain Forest*. Boston: Charlesbridge.

Kraus, Joanna H. (2007). *A Night of Tamales & Roses*. Illustrated by Elena Caravela. Summit, NJ: Shenanigan.

Krilanovich, Nadia. (2011). *Chicken, Chicken, Duck!*. Berkeley, CA: Tricycle.

Krishnaswami, Uma. (2004). *Naming Maya*. New York: Farrar, Straus and Giroux.

Kromhout, Rindert. (2007). *Little Donkey and the Birthday Present*. Illustrated by Annemarie van Haeringen. Translated by Marianne Martens. New York: North-South.

Kundhardt, Dorothy. (2001). *Pat the Bunny*. New York: Golden.

Kurtz, Jane. (2000). *Faraway Home*. Illustrated by E. B. Lewis. San Diego CA: Harcourt.

———. (2001). *Jakarta Missing*. New York: Greenwillow.

———. (2003). *Saba: Under the Hyena's Foot*. Middleton, WI: Pleasant.

Kuskin, Karla. (1975). *Near the Window Tree: Poems and Notes*. New York: Harper & Row.

———. (1980). *Dogs and Dragons, Trees and Dreams: A Collection of Poems*. New York: Harper & Row.

———. (1997). *The Upstairs Cat*. New York: Clarion.

———. (1998). *The Sky Is Always in the Sky*. Illustrated by Isabelle Derveaux. New York: Laura Geringer Books.

———. (2000). *I Am Me*. New York: Simon & Schuster.

———. (2003). *Moon, Have You Met My Mother? The Collected Poems of Karla Kuskin*. Illustrated by Sergio Ruzzier. New York: Laura Geringer Books.

Kwon, Yoon-duck. (2007). *My Cat Copies Me*. La Jolla, CA: Kane Miller.

L'Engle, Madeleine. (1962). *A Wrinkle in Time*. New York: Ariel.

———. (1973). *A Wind in the Door*. New York: Farrar, Straus and Giroux.

———. (1978). *A Swiftly Tilting Planet*. New York: Farrar, Straus, and Giroux.

La Fontaine, Jean. (2007). *The Complete Fables of Jean de La Fontaine.* Translated by Narmon R. Shapiro. Champaign, IL: University of Illinois Press.

Lagerlöf, Selma. (1906–1907/1991). *The Wonderful Adventures of Nils*. Minneapolis, MN: Skandisk.

Lai, Thanhha. (2011). *Inside Out & Back Again*. New York: Harper.

Lakin, Patricia. (2007). *Rainy Day*. Illustrated by Scott Nash. New York: Dial.

Lane, Andrew. (2011). *Death Cloud (Sherlock Holmes: The Legend Begins)*. New York: Farrar, Straus and Giroux.

Lang, Andrew. (2007). *The Blue Fairy Book*. Fairfield: IA: 1st World Library—Literary Society.

Laroche, Giles. (2011). *If You Lived Here: Houses of the World*. Boston: Houghton.

LaRochelle, David. (2005). *Absolutely, Positively Not. . . .* New York: Levine.

———. (2007). *The End*. Illustrated by Richard Egielski. New York: Levine.

Lasky, Kathryn. (1996). *Beyond the Burning Time*. New York: Scholastic.

———. (1999). *Elizabeth I: Red Rose of the House of Tudor*. New York: Scholastic.

———. (2011). *Silk & Venom: Searching for a Dangerous Spider*. Illustrated by Christopher G. Knight. Cambridge, MA: Candlewick.

Lawrence, Iain. (2001). *Lord of the Nutcracker Men*. New York: Delacorte.

———. (2005). *The Cannibals: The Curse of the Jolly Stone Trilogy, #2*. New York: Random House.

_____. (2005). *The Convicts: The Curse of the Jolly Stone Trilogy, #1*. New York: Random House.

_____. (2006). *Gemini Summer*. New York: Delacorte.

_____. (2007). *The Castaways: The Curse of the Jolly Stone Trilogy, #3*. New York: Random House.

Lawrence, Louise. (2002). *Children of the Dust*. London: Random House.

Le Guin, Ursula. (1968). *A Wizard of Earthsea*. Illustrated by Ruth Robbins. Boston: Houghton Mifflin.

Leaf, Munro. (1936). *The Story of Ferdinand*. Illustrated by Robert Lawson. New York: Penguin.

Lear, Edward. (1846/1980). *A Book of Nonsense*. New York: Metropolitan Museum of Art and Viking.

Lee, Suzy. (2008). *Wave*. San Francisco: Chronicle.

Leeds, Constance. (2007). *The Silver Cup*. New York: Viking.

Leedy, Loreen, & Pat Street. (2003). *There's a Frog in My Throat! 440 Animal Sayings a Little Bird Told Me*. New York: Holiday House.

Leedy, Loreen. (2008). *Crazy Like a Fox: A Simile Story*. New York: Holiday House.

Lehman, Barbara. (2004). *The Red Book*. Boston: Houghton Mifflin.

_____. (2006). *Museum Trip*. Boston: Houghton Mifflin.

_____. (2007). *Rainstorm*. Boston: Houghton Mifflin.

_____. (2008). *Trainstop*. Boston: Houghton Mifflin.

_____. (2011). *The Secret Box*. Boston: Houghton Mifflin.

Leprince de Beaumont, Jeanne-Marie (1979). *Beauty and the Beast*. New York: Random.

Lester, Julius. (1987). *The Tales of Uncle Remus: The Adventures of Brer Rabbit*. Illustrated by Jerry Pinkney. New York: Dial.

_____. (1988). *More Tales of Uncle Remus: Further Adventures of Brer Rabbit, His Friends, Enemies, and Others*. Illustrated by Jerry Pinkney. New York: Dial.

_____. (1990). *Further Tales of Uncle Remus: The Misadventures of Brer Rabbit, Brer Fox, Brer Wolf, the Doodang, and Other Creatures*. Illustrated by Jerry Pinkney. New York: Dial.

_____. (1994). *John Henry*. Illustrated by Jerry Pinkney. New York: Penguin.

_____. (2000). *Sam and the Tigers*. Illustrated by Jerry Pinkney. New York: Penguin.

_____. (2002). *Pharaoh's Daughter: A Novel of Ancient Egypt*. New York: HarperCollins.

_____. (2005). *Day of Tears*. New York: Hyperion.

_____. (2005). *The Old African*. New York: Penguin.

Levine, Anna. (1999). *Running on Eggs*. New York: Cricket.

Levine, Ellen. (2007). *Henry's Freedom Box*. Illustrated by Kadir Nelson. New York: Scholastic.

_____. (2007). *Henry's Freedom Box*. Illustrated by Kadir Nelson. New York: Scholastic.

Levine, Gail Carson. (1997). *Ella Enchanted*. New York: HarperCollins.

_____. (2011). *A Tale of Two Castles*. New York: HarperCollins.

Levithan, David. (2003). *Boy Meets Boy*. New York: Knopf.

Lewin, Ted, & Betsy Lewin. (2008). *Horse Song: The Naadam of Mongolia*. Illustrated by Ted Lewin. New York: Lee & Low.

Lewin, Ted. (1997). *Fair!*. New York: HarperCollins.

Lewis, C. S. (1950). *The Lion, the Witch, and the Wardrobe*. Illustrated by Pauline Baynes. London: Geoffrey Bles.

Lewis, J. Patrick, & Paul B. Janeczko. (2008). *Birds on a Wire: A Renga 'round Town*. Illustrated by Gary Lippincott. Honesdale, PA: Wordsong.

Lewis, J. Patrick. (1998). *Doodle Dandies: Poems that Take Shape*. Illustrated by Lisa Desimini. New York: Atheneum.

_____. (2004). *Scien-Trickery: Riddles in Science*. Illustrated by Franz Remkiewicx. Orlando, FL: Silver Whistle.

_____. (2006). *Once upon a Tomb: Gravely Humorous Verses*. Illustrated by Simon Bartram. Cambridge, MA: Candlewick.

Lewis, Richard. (1994). *All of You Was Singing*. Illustrated by Ed Young. New York: Aladdin.

Liestman, Vicki. (1991). *Columbus Day*. Minneapolis, Carolrhoda.

Light, John. (2007). *The Flower*. Illustrated by Lisa Evan. Swindon, UK: Child's Play International.

Lillegard, Dee. (2007). *Who Will Sing a Lullaby?*. Illustrated by Dan Yaccarino. New York: Knopf.

Lin, Grace. (2008). *The Year of the Rat*. New York: Little, Brown.

_____. (2009). *Where the Mountain Meets the Moon*. New York: Little, Brown.

_____. (2010). *Ling & Ting: Not Exactly the Same*. New York: Little, Brown.

Lindberg, Reeve. (1993). *Johnny Appleseed: A Poem*. Illustrated by Kathy Jakobsen. Boston: Little, Brown.

Lipsyte, Robert. (1967/1997). *The Contender*. New York: HarperCollins.

Lisle, Janet Taylor. (2002). *The Art of Keeping Cool*. New York: Aladdin.

Livingston, M. C. (1979). *O Silver of Liver and Other Poems*. New York: Atheneum.

_____. (1991). *Lots of Limericks*. Illustrated by Rebecca Perry. New York: McElderry.

_____. (1991). *Poem-Making: Ways to Begin Writing Poetry*. New York: HarperCollins.

_____. (1993). *Abraham Lincoln: A Man for All the People*. Illustrated by Samuel Perry. New York: Holiday House.

_____. (1994). *Keep on Singing: A Ballad of Marion Anderson*. Illustrated by Samuel Byrd. New York: Holiday House.

_____. (1994). *Riddle-Me Rhymes*. Illustrated by Rebecca Perry. New York: Simon & Schuster.

_____. (1995). *Call Down the Moon*. New York: Simon & Schuster.

Llorente, Pilar Molina. (1994). *The Apprentice*. New York: Farrar, Straus and Giroux.

Lloyd, Saci. (2010). *The Carbon Diaries 2017*. New York: Holiday House.

Lobel, Anita. (2002). *One Lighthouse, One Moon*. New York: HarperCollins.

Lobel, Arnold. (1970). *Frog and Toad Are Friends*. New York: Harper & Row.

_____. (1983). *The Book of Pigericks: Pig Limericks*. New York: Harper & Row.

_____. (1986). *The Random House Book of Mother Goose*. New York: Random House.

Look, Lenore. (1999). *Love as Strong as Ginger*. Illustrated by Stephen Johnson. New York: Simon & Schuster.

_____. (2011). *Alvin Ho: Allergic to Dead Bodies, Funerals, and Other Fatal Circumstances*. Illustrated by LeUyen Pham. New York: Schwartz & Wade.

_____. (2011). *Ruby Lu, Star of the Show*. Illustrated by Stef Choi. New York: Atheneum.

Louie, Ai-Ling. (1982). *Yeh Shen: A Cinderella Story from China*. Illustrated by Ed Young. New York: Philomel.

Lovelace, Maud Hart. (1940). *Betsy-Tacy*. New York: Crowell.

Lowry, Lois. (1989). *Number the Stars*. Boston: Houghton Mifflin.

_____. (1993). *The Giver*. Boston: Houghton Mifflin.

_____. (2000). *Gathering Blue*. Boston: Houghton Mifflin.

_____. (2004). *Messenger*. Boston: Houghton Mifflin.

_____. (2009). *Gooney Bird Is So Absurd*. Illustrated by Middy Thomas. Boston: Houghton Mifflin.

_____. (2011). *Bless This Mouse*. Illustrated by Eric Rohmann. New York: Houghton Mifflin.

_____. (2011). *Gooney Bird on the Map*. Illustrated by Middy Thomas. Boston: Houghton Mifflin.

Luján, Jorge Elias. (2004). *Rooster/Gallo*. Illustrated by Manuel Monroy. Ontario, Canada: Groundwood.

Lunge-Larsen, Lise. (2003). *The Troll with No Heart in His Body*. Illustrated by Betsy Bowen. Boston: Sandpiper.

_____. (2004). *The Hidden Folk: Stories of Fairies, Dwarves, Selkies, and Other Secret Beings*. Illustrated by Beth Krommes. Boston: Houghton Mifflin.

_____. (2011). *Gifts from the Gods: Ancient Words & Wisdom from Greek & Roman Mythology*. Illustrated by Gareth Hinds. Boston: Houghton Mifflin Harcourt.

Lunn, Janet. (2000). *The Hollow Tree*. New York: Viking.

Lynch, Chris. (2008). *Cyberia*. New York: Scholastic.

_____. (2009). *Monkey See, Monkey Don't*. New York: Scholastic.

_____. (2010). *Prime Evil*. New York: Scholastic.

Lyon, George Ella. (2011). *All the Water in the World: The Water Cycle in Poetry*. Illustrated by Katherine Tillotson. New York: Atheneum.

_____. (2011). *Which Side Are You On? The Story of a Song*. Illustrated by Christopher Cardinale. El Paso, TX: Cinco Puntos.

Lyons, Mary E. (1992). *Letters from a Slave Girl: The Story of Harriet Jacobs*. New York: Scribner.

_____. (1995). *The Butter Tree: Tales of Bruh Rabbit*. Illustrated by Mireille Vautier. New York: Holt.

Macaulay, David, & Richard Walker. (1998). *The Way We Work: Getting to Know the Amazing Human Body*. Boston: Houghton Mifflin.

Macaulay, David. (1981). *Cathedral: The Story of Its Construction*. New York: Sandpiper.

_____. (1982). *Castle*. Boston: Graphia.

_____. (1990). *Black and White*. Boston: Houghton Mifflin.

_____. (1995). *Shortcut*. Boston: Houghton Mifflin.

_____. (2003). *Mosque*. Boston: Houghton Mifflin.

_____. (2010). *Built to Last*. Boston: Houghton Mifflin.

MacDonald, Margaret Read. (2011). *The Boy from the Dragon Palace: A Folktale from Japan*. Illustrated by Sachiko Yoshikawa. Park Ridge, IL: Whitman.

MacDonald, Ross. (2003). *Achoo! Bang! Crash! The Noisy Alphabet*. Brookfield, CT: Roaring Brook.

MacLachlan, Patricia. (1980). *Arthur, for the Very First Time*. New York: Harper & Row.

MacLeod, Elizabeth. (2007). *I Heard a Little Baa*. Illustrated by Louise Phillips. Toronto, Ontario: Kids Can.

Maestro, Betsy. (1990). *The Discovery of the Americas*. New York: Lathrop, Lee & Low.

Mahy, Margaret. (2009). *The Magician of Hoad*. New York: McElderry.

Makhijani, Pooja. (2007). *Mama's Saris*. Illustrated by Elena Gomez. Boston: Little, Brown.

Mammano, Julie. (2007). *Rhinos Who Rescue*. San Francisco: Chronicle.

Mandel, Peter. (2011). *Jackhammer Sam*. Illustrated by David Catrow. New York: Roaring Brook.

Manna, Anthony, & Soula Mitakidou. (2011). *The Orphan: A Cinderella Story from Greece*. Illustrated by Giselle Potter. New York: Schwartz & Wade.

Manning, Maurie. (2003). *The Aunts Go Marching*. Illustrated by Sandra D'Antonio. Honesdale, PA: Boyds Mills.

Marcantonio, Patricia Santos. (2005). *Red Ridin' in the Hood: and Other Cuentos*. Illustrated by Renato Alarcão. New York: Farrar, Straus and Giroux.

Marcus, Leonard S. (2001). *Side by Side: Five Favorite Picture-Book Teams Go to Work*. New York: Walker.

_____. (2006). *The Wand in the Word: Conversations with Writers of Fantasy*. Cambridge, MA: Candlewick.

_____. (2012). *Show Me a Story! Why Picture Books Matter: Conversations with 21 of the World's Most Celebrated Illustrators*. Somerville, MA: Candlewick.

Markle, Sandra. (2007). *Outside and Inside Woolly Mammoths*. New York: Walker.

Marrin, Albert. (2012). *Black Gold: The Story of Oil in Our Lives*. New York: Knopf.

Marshall, James. (1993). *A Pocketful of Nonsense*. New York: Artists and Writers Guild.

_____. (1998). *Goldilocks and the Three Bears*. New York: Puffin.

Martin, Bill, Jr. (1967). *Brown Bear, Brown Bear, What Do You See?*. Illustrated by Eric Carle. New York: Holt.

Martin, Jacqueline Briggs. (1998). *Snowflake Bentley*. Illustrated by Mary Azarian. Boston: Houghton Mifflin.

_____. (2010). *The Chiru of High Tibet*. Illustrated by Linda Wingerter. Boston: Houghton Mifflin.

Martin, Rafe. (1985). *Foolish Rabbit's Big Mistake*. Illustrated by Ed Young. New York: Putnam.

_____. (1992). *The Rough-Face Girl*. Illustrated by David Shanon. New York: Putnam.

_____. (1993). *The Boy Who Lived with Seals*. Illustrated by David Shannon. New York: Putnam.

_____. (1996). *Mysterious Tales of Japan*. Illustrated by Tatsuro Kiuchi. New York: Putnam.

_____. (1997). *Dear as Salt*. Illustrated by Vladyana Krykorka. Toronto, Ontario: Scholastic Canada.

_____. (1998). *The Brave Little Parrot*. Illustrated by Susan Gaber. New York: Putnam.

_____. (2000). *The Language of Birds*. Illustrated by Susan Gaber. New York: Putnam.

_____. (2007). *The Shark God*. Illustratedby David Shannon. New York: Scholastic.

Martinez, Victor. (1996). *Parrot in the Oven: My Vida*. New York: HarperCollins.

Matthews, Tina. (2007). *Out of the Egg*. Boston: Houghton Mifflin.

Mavor, Sally. (2010). *Pocketful of Posies: A Treasury of Nursery Rhymes*. Boston: Houghton Mifflin.

Mazer, Norma Fox. (2007). *Has Anyone Seen My Emily Greene?*. Illustrated by Christine Davenier. Cambridge, MA: Candlewick.

_____. (2008). *The Missing Girl*. New York: HarperCollins.

Mbitu, Ngangur, & Ranchor Prime. (1997). *Essential African Mythology: Stories that Change the World*. London: Thorsons.

McBratney, Sam. (2005). *One Voice, Please: Favorite Read-aloud Stories*. Illustrated by Russell Ayto. Cambridge, MA: Candlewick.

McCarthy, Anne. (2007). *A Closer Look*. New York: Greenwillow.

McCaughrean, Geraldine. (2002). *Gilgamesh the Hero*. Oxford: Oxford University Press.

_____. (2002).*My Grandmother's Clock*. Illustrated by Stephen Lambert. Boston: Houghton Mifflin.

_____. (2003). *Stop the Train!*. New York: HarperCollins.

_____. (2011). *The Glorious Adventures of the Sunshine Queen*. New York: Harper.

McClintock, Barbara. (2005). *Cinderella*. New York: Scholastic.

McCloskey, Robert. (1941). *Make Way for Ducklings*. New York: Viking.

McCord, David. (1970). *For Me to Say*. Illustrated by Henry B. Kane. New York: Little, Brown.

_____. (1977). *One at a Time*. Illustrated by Henry Bugbee Kane. Boston: Little, Brown.

_____. (1999). *Every Time I Climb a Tree*. Illustrated by Marc Simont. New York: Little, Brown.

McCormick, Patricia. (2006). *Sold*. New York: Hyperion.

McCully, Emily Arnold. (1997). *Mirette on the High Wire*. New York: Penguin.

_____. (2004). *Squirrel and John Muir*. New York: Farrar, Straus and Giraux.

McDermott, Gerald. (1978). *The Stonecutter*. New York: Penguin.

_____. (1992). *Zomo the Rabbit: A Trickster Tale from West Africa*. San Diego, CA: Harcourt.

_____. (1993). *Raven: A Trickster Tale from the Pacific Northwest*. San Diego, CA: Harcourt.

_____. (1994). *Coyote: A Trickster Tale from the American Southwest*. San Diego, CA: Harcourt.

_____. (2003). *Creation*. New York: Dutton.

_____. (2005). *Jabuti and Tortoise*. Boston: Sandpiper.

_____. (2009). *Pig-Boy: A Trickster Tale from Hawai'i*. Boston: Houghton Mifflin.

_____. (2011). *Monkey: A Trickster Tale from India*. San Diego, CA: Harcourt.

McDonnell, Christine. (2011). *Goyangi Means Cat*. Illustrated by Steve Johnson & Lou Fancher. New York: Viking.

McDonnell, Patrick. (2011). *Me . . . Jane*. New York: Little, Brown.

McEntire, Myra. (2011). *Hourglass*. New York: Egmont.

McGill, Alice. (2008). *Way up and over Everything*. Illustrated by Jude Daly. Boston: Houghton Mifflin Harcourt.

McGinty, Alice. (2009). *Darwin*. Ilustrated by Mary Azarian. New York: Houghton Mifflin.

McKinley, Robin. (1988). *The Outlaws of Sherwood*. New York: Greenwillow.

_____. (1997). *Rose Daughter*. New York: Greenwillow.

_____. (1999). *Beauty*. New York: HarperCollins.

_____. (2000). *Spindle's End*. New York: Putnam.

McKissack, Fredrick. (1994). *Christmas in the Big House, Christmas in the Quarters*. New York: Scholastic.

McKissack, Patricia C. (2011). *Never Forgotten*. Illustrated by Leo & Diane Dillon. New York: Schwartz & Wade.

McKissack, Patricia C., & Onawumi Jean Moss. (2005). *Precious and the Boo Hag*. Illustrated by Kyrsten Brooker. New York: Atheneum.

McLeod, Bob. (2006). *SuperHero ABC*. New York: HarperCollins.

McLimans, David. (2006). *Gone Wild*. New York: Walker.

McMillan, Bruce. (2007). *How the Ladies Stopped the Wind*. Illustrated by Gunnella. Boston: Houghton Mifflin.

McMullan, Kate. (2004). *My Travels with Capts. Lewis and Clark by George Shannon*. New York: Cutler.

McPhail, David. (2011). *Boy, Bird, and Dog*. New York: Holiday House.

Medina, Meg. (2011). *Tía Isa Wants a Car*. Illustrated by Claudio Muñoz. Somerville, MA: Candlewick.

Melmed, Laura Krauss. (2004). *Rainbabies*. Illustrated by Jim LaMarche. New York: HarperCollins.

Meltzer, Milton. (1990). *Columbus and the World around Him*. New York: Watts.

_____. (1993). *Lincoln: In His Own Words*. San Diego, CA: Harcourt.

Meltzer, Milton. (1995). *Fredrick Douglass: In His Own Words*. San Diego, CA: Harcourt.

Merriam, Eve. (1962). *There Is No Rhyme for Silver*. New York: Atheneum.

_____. (1964). *It Doesn't Always Have to Rhyme*. New York: Atheneum.

_____. (1992). *The Singing Green: New Selected Poems for All Seasons*. Illustrated by Kathleen Collins Howell. New York: Morrow.

_____. (1994). *Higgle Wiggle: Happy Rhymes*. New York: Morrow.

Messner, Kate. (2011). *Over and Under the Snow*. Illustrated by Christopher Silas Neal. San Francisco: Chronicle.

Metzger, Steve. (2011). *Detective Blue*. Illustrated by Tedd Arnold. London: Orchard.

Meyer, Louis A. (2002). *Bloody Jack: Being an Account of the Curious Adventures of Mary "Jacky" Faber, Ship's Boy*. San Diego, CA: Harcourt.

_____. (2004). *Curse of the Blue Tattoo: Being an Account of the Misadventures of Jacky Faber, Midshipman and Fine Lady*. San Diego, CA: Harcourt.

Meyer, Susan Lynn. (2010). *Black Radishes*. New York: Delacorte.

Michelson, Richard. (2006). *Across the Alley*. Illustrated by E. B. Lewis. New York: Penguin.

_____. (2007). *Tuttle's Red Barn: The Story of America's Oldest Farm*. Illustrated by Mary Azarian. New York: Putnam.

_____. (2008). *As Good As Anybody*. Illustrated by Raul Colón. New York: Random House.

Mikaelsen, Ben. (2002). *Red Midnight*. New York: HarperCollins.

Milgrim, David. (2006). *Time to Get Up, Time to Go*. New York: Clarion.

Miller, Ron. (2011). *Seven Wonders beyond the Solar System*. Minneapolis, MN: Twenty-First Century.

Miller, William. (1994). *Zoa Hurston and the Chinaberry Tree*. Illustrated by Cornelius Van Wright & Ying-Hwa Hu. New York: Lee & Low.

Mills, Claudia. (2008). *The Totally Made-Up Civil War Diary of Amanda MacLeish*. New York: Farrar, Straus and Giroux.

Milne, Alan Alexander. (1924). *When We Were Very Young*. New York: Dutton.

_____. (1927). *Now We Are Six*. New York: Dutton.

Milnes, Gerald. (1999). *Granny, Will Your Dog Bite and Other Mountain Rhymes*. Illustrated by Kimberly Bulcken Root. Little Rock, AR: August House Littlefolk.

Miranda, Anne. (1997). *To Market, to Market*. Illustrated by Janet Stevens. San Diego, CA: Harcourt.

Mitchell, Margaree King. (2012). *When Grandmama Sings*. Illustrated by James Ransome. New York: Amistad.

Mitchell, Stephen. (2008). *Genies, Meanies, and Magic Rings: Three Tales from the Arabian Nights*. Illustrated by Tom Pohrt. New York: Walker.

Mochizuki, Ken. (1993). *Baseball Saved Us*. Illustrated by Dom Lee. New York: Lee & Low.

Mohr, Nicholasa. (1973). *Nilda: A Novel*. New York: Harper & Row.

_____. (1988). *In Nueva York*. Houston, TX: Arte Publico.

Monninger, Joseph. (2011). *Finding Somewhere*. New York: Delacorte.

Montgomery, L. M. (1908). *Anne of Green Gables*. New York: Page.

Montgomery, Sy. (1999). *The Snake Scientist*. Illustrated by Nic Bishop. Boston: Houghton Mifflin.

_____. (2004). *The Tarantula Scientist*. Boston: Houghton Mifflin.

_____. (2010). *Kakapo Rescue: Saving the World's Strangest Parrot*. Illustrated by Nic Bishop. Boston: Houghton Mifflin Harcourt.

Moore, Clement Clarke. (1823/1992). *A Visit from St. Nicholas*. Illustrated by Elmer and Berta Hader. New York: Rosen.

Moore, Lilian. (1982). *Something New Begins: New and Selected Poems*. New York: Simon & Schuster.

_____. (1984). *I Feel the Same Way*. New York: Simon & Schuster.

_____. (1992). *Adam Mouse's Book of Poems*. Illustrated by Kathleen Gary McCord. New York: Simon & Schuster.

_____. (1997). *Poems Have Roots*. New York: Simon & Schuster.

_____. (2004). *Here in Harlem: Poetry in Many Voices*. New York: Holiday House.

_____. (2006). *Jazz*. Illustrated by Christopher Myers. New York: Holiday House.

Mora, Pat. (2005). *Doña Flor*. Illustrated by Raul Colón. New York: Knopf.

_____. (2009). *Gracias/Thanks*. Illustrated by John Perra. New York: Lee & Low.

Morales, Yuyi. (2007). *Little Night*. Brookfield, CT: Roaring Brook.

Moran, Katy. (2009). *Bloodline*. Somerville, MA: Candlewick.

_____. (2011). *Bloodline Rising*. Somerville, MA: Candlewick.

Mordecai, Martin. (2009). *Blue Mountain Trouble*. New York: Levine.

Morley, Jacqueline. (1999). *Egyptian Myths*. Illustrated by Giovani Caselli. Lincolnwood, IL: Peter Bedrick Books.

Morpurgo, Michael. (2004). *Private Peaceful*. New York: Scholastic.

_____. (2004). *Sir Gawain and the Green Knight*. Cambridge, MA: Candlewick.

Morris, Carla. (2007). *The Boy Who Was Raised by Librarians*. Illustrated by Brad Sneed. Atlanta, GA: Peachtree.

Morris, Gerald. (2003). *The Ballad of Sir Dinadan*. Boston: Houghton Mifflin.

_____. (2011). *The Adventures of Sir Gawain the True*. Boston: Houghton Mifflin Harcourt.

Moss, Marissa. (2011). *Nurse, Solider, Spy: The Story of Sarah Edmonds, a Civil War Hero*. Illustrated by James Hendrix. New York: Abrams.

Munro, Roxie. (2011). *Hatch!*. New York: Marshall Cavendish.

Muntean, Michaela. (2006). *Do Not Open This Book!*. New York: Scholastic.

Murphy, Jim. (2003). *An American Plague: The True and Terrifying Story of the Yellow Fever Epidemic of 1793*. New York: Clarion.

Murphy, Sally. (2011). *Pearl Verses the World*. Illustrated by Heather Potter. Somerville, MA: Candlewick.

Myers, Christopher. (2000). *Wings*. New York: Scholastic.

_____. (2005). *Lies and Other Tall Tales*. Collected by Zora Neale Hurston. New York: HarperCollins.

Myers, Walter Dean. (1988). *Fallen Angels*. New York: Scholastic.

_____. (1996). *Slam!*. New York: Scholastic.

_____. (1997). *Harlem*. Illustrated by Christopher Myers. New York: Scholastic.

_____. (1999). *Monster*. Illustrated by Christopher Myers. New York: HarperCollins.

_____. (2003). *blues journey*. Illustrated by Christopher Myers. New York: Holiday House.

_____. (2006). *Jazz*. Illustrated by Christopher Myers. New York: Holiday House.

_____. (2007). *Harlem Summer*. New York: Scholastic.

_____. (2011). *Looking Like Me*. Illustrated by Christopher Myers. Pine Plains, NY: Live Oak Media.

_____. (2011). *The Cruisers: Checkmate*. New York: Scholastic.

Na, An. (2001). *A Step from Heaven*. Asheville, NC: Front Street.

Naidoo, Beverley. (2011). *Aesop's Fables*. Illustrated by Piet Grobler. New York: Frances Lincoln.

_____. (1999). *The Other Side of Truth*. New York: HarperCollins.

Nanji, Shenaaz. (2008). *Child of Dandelions*. Honesdale, PA: Wordsong.

Napoli, Donna Jo. (1993). *The Magic Circle*. New York: Dutton.

_____. (1996). *Zel*. New York: Dutton.

_____. (1999). *Crazy Jack*. New York: Delacorte.

_____. (1999). *Spinners*. New York: Dutton.

_____. (2000). *Beast*. New York: Dutton.

_____. (2011). *Treasury of Greek Mythology: Classic Stories of Gods, Goddesses, Heroes & Monsters*. Illustrated by Christina Balit. Washington, DC: National Geographic.

Naylor, Phyllis Reynolds. (1991). *Shiloh*. New York: Atheneum.

NCBLA, & David McCullough. (2008). *Our White House: Looking In, Looking Out*. Cambridge, MA: Candlewick.

Neil, Philip. (1994). *King Midas*. Illustrated by Isabelle Brent. Boston: Little, Brown.

Nelson, Kadir. (2008). *We Are the Ship: The Story of Negro League Baseball*. New York: Hyperion.

_____. (2011). *Heart and Soul: The Story of America and African Amercians*. New York: Balzer + Bray.

_____. (2011). *Heart and Soul: The Story of America and African Americans*. New York: HarperCollins.

Nelson, Marilyn. (2001). *Carver: A Life in Poems*. Asheville, NC: Front Street.

_____. (2005). *A Wreath for Emmett Till*. Illustrated by Philippe Lardy. Boston: Houghton Mifflin.

_____. (2010). *Mirror Mirror: A Book of Reversible Verse*. New York: Dutton.

_____. (2012). *Snook Alone*. Illustrated by Timothy Basil Ering. Cambridge, MA: Candlewick.

Nelson, Scott Reynolds, & Marc Aronson. (2008). *Ain't Nothing but a Man: My Quest to Find the Real John Henry*. Washington, DC: National Geographic.

Neri, G. (2010). *Yummy: The Last Days of a Southside Shorty*. Illustrated by Randy DuBurke. New York: Lee & Low.

Nesbet, Anne. (2012). *The Cabinet of Earths*. New York: HarperCollins.

Nesbit, E. (1999). *Five Children and It*. Illustrated by Paul O. Zelinsky. New York: Morrow.

Ness, Patrick. (2008). *The Knife of Never Letting Go*. Cambridge, MA: Candlewick.

_____. (2009). *The Ask and the Answer*. Somerville, MA: Candlewick.

_____. (2010). *Monsters of Men*. Somerville, MA: Candlewick.

_____. (2011). *A Monster Calls: A Novel*. Illustrated by James Kay. Somerville, MA: Candlewick.

Newman, Marc. (2011). *Polar Bears*. New York: Holt.

Newth, Mette. (2000). *The Transformation*. New York: Farrar, Straus and Giroux.

Nicholls, Sally. (2011). *Season of Secrets*. New York: Levine.

Niland, Deborah. (2006). *Annie's Chair*. New York: Walker.

Nivola, Claire. (2008). *Planting the Trees of Kenya: The Story of Wangari Maathai*. Illustrated by Rebecca Gibbon. New York: Holt.

_____. (2011). *Orani: My Father's Village*. New York: Farrar, Straus and Giroux.

Noble, Trinka Hakes. (2007). *The Legend of the Cape May Diamond*. Illustrated by E. B. Lewis. Farmington Hills, MI: Sleeping Bear.

Nolan, Dennis. (2011). *Sea of Dreams*. New York: Roaring Brook.

Nolen, Jerdine. (2003). *Big Jabe*. Illustrated by Kadir Nelson. New York: HarperCollins.

_____. (2007). *Pitching in for Eubie*. Illustrated by E. B. Lewis. New York: HarperCollins.

Norton, Mary. (1953). *The Borrowers*. Illustrated by Beth and Joe Krush. San Diego, CA: Harcourt.

Noyes, Deborah. (2007). *Red Butterfly: How a Princess Smuggled the Secret of Silk out of China*. Illustrated by Sophie Blackall. Cambridge, MA: Candlewick.

_____. (2007). *When I Met the Wolf Girls*. Illustrated by August Hall. Boston: Houghton Mifflin.

Nye, Naomi Shihab. (1994). *Sitti's Secrets*. Illustrated by Nancy Carpenter. New York: Four Winds.

_____. (1997). *Habibi*. New York: Simon & Schuster.

_____. (2001). *19 Varieties of Gazelle: Poems of the Middle East*. New York: Greenwillow.

_____. (2008). *Honeybee: Poems & Short Prose*. New York: Greenwillow.

_____. (2011). *There Is No Long Distance Now: Very Short Stories*. New York: Greenwillow.

Nyeu, Tao. (2010). *Bunny Days*. New York: Dial.

O'Brien, Robert C. (1971). *Mrs. Frisby and the Rats of NIMH*. Illustrated by Zena Bernstein. New York: Atheneum.

O'Connell, Caitlin, & Donna M. Jackson. (2011). *The Elephant Scientist*. Photographs by Caitlin O'Connell & Timothy Rodwell. Boston: Houghton.

O'Conner, George. (2004). *Kapow!*. New York: Simon & Schuster.

_____. (2010). *Zeus: King of the Gods*. New York: First Second.

O'Connor, Jane. (2007). *Ready, Set, Skip!*. Illustrated by Ann James. New York: Viking.

O'Dell, Scott. (1960). *Island of the Blue Dolphins*. Boston: Houghton Mifflin.

Oberman, Sheldon. (1994). *The Always Prayer Shaw*. Illustrated by Ted Lewin. Honesdale, PA: Boyds Mills.

Okorafor, Nnedi. (2011). *Akata Witch*. New York: Viking.

Olaleye, Isaac. (2000). *In the Rainfield: Who Is the Greatest?*. Illustrated by Ann Grifalconi. New York: Scholastic.

Onishi, Satoru. (2007). *Who's Hiding?*. La Jolla, CA: Kane Miller.

Opie, Iona. (1988). *Tail Feathers from Mother Goose: The Opie Rhyme Book*. Boston: Little, Brown.

_____. (1996). *My Very First Mother Goose*. Illustrated by Rosemary Wells. Cambridge, MA: Candlewick.

_____. (1999). *Here Comes Mother Goose*. Illustrated by Rosemary Wells. Cambridge, MA: Candlewick.

_____. (2007). *Mother Goose's Little Treasures*. Illustrated by Rosemary Wells. Cambridge, MA: Candlewick.

Oppel, Kenneth. (1997). *Silverwing*. New York: Simon & Schuster.

_____. (2000). *Sunwing*. New York: Simon & Schuster.

_____. (2003). *Firewing*. New York: Simon & Schuster.

_____. (2007). *Darkwing*. Illustrated by Keith Thompson. New York: Eos.

_____. (2011). *This Dark Endeavor: The Apprenticeship of Victor Frankenstein*. New York: Simon & Schuster.

Ord, Colon. (2007). *Magic Moving Images: Animated Optical Illusions*. St. Albans, Hertfordshire: Tarquin.

Ormerod, Jan, & David Lloyd. (1990). *The Frog Prince*. New York: Lothrop, Lee & Shepard.

Orozco, Jose-Luis. (1999). *De Colores and Other Latin American Folksongs for Children*. Illustrated by Elisa Kleven. New York: Puffin.

Orr, Wendy. (2010). *The Princess and Her Panther*. Illustrated by Lauren Stringer. New York: Beach Lane.

Osborne, Mary Pope. (1996). *Favorite Norse Myths*. Illustrated by Troy Howell. New York: Scholastic.

_____. (2000). *Kate and the Beanstalk*. Illustrated by Giselle Potter. New York: Atheneum.

_____. (2002). *The Land of the Dead*. New York: Hyperion.

_____. (2002). *The One-Eyed Giant*. New York: Hyperion.

Osborne, Mary Pope. (2003). *Sirens and Sea Monsters*. New York: Hyperion.

_____. (2003). *The Gray-Eyed Goddess*. New York: Hyperion.

_____. (2004). *Return to Ithaca*. New York: Hyperion.

Oswald, Nancy. (2004). *Nothing Here but Stones: A Jewish Pioneer Story*. New York: Holt.

Ottaviani, Jim. (2011). *Feynman*. Illustrated by Leland Myrick. New York: First Second.

Owens, Mary Beth. (2007). *Panda Whispers*. New York: Dutton.

Page, Robin. (2008). *Sisters and Brothers: Sibling Relationships in the Animal World*. Illustrated by Steve Jenkins. Boston: Houghton Mifflin.

Paolini, Christopher. (2003). *Eragon*. New York: Knopf.

_____. (2005). *Eldest*. New York: Knopf.

_____. (2008). *Brisinger*. New York: Knopf.

_____. (2011). *Inheritance: Or the Vault of Souls*. New York: Knopf.

Park, Linda Sue. (2000). *The Kite Fighters*. Boston: Houghton Mifflin.

_____. (2001). *A Single Shard*. New York: Clarion.

_____. (2002). *When My Name Was Keoko*. New York: Clarion.

_____. (2007). *Tap Dancing on the Roof: Sijo (Poems)*. Illustrated by Istvan Banyai. New York: Clarion.

_____. (2008). *Keeping Score*. New York: Clarion.

_____. (2010). *A Long Walk to Water: Based on a True Story*. Boston: Clarion.

Parker, Robert B. (2008). *The Boxer and the Spy*. New York: Philomel.

Parkinson, Siobhan. (2003). *Kathleen: The Celtic Knot*. Middleton, WI: Pleasant.

_____. (2008). *Blue Like Friday*. New York: Roaring Brook.

Parks, Rosa. (1992). *Rosa Parks: My Story*. New York: Dial.

Parks, Van Dyke, & Malcolm Jones. (1986). *Jump! The Adventures of Brer Rabbit*. Illustrated by Barry Moser. San Diego, CA: Harcourt.

_____. (1989). *Jump On Over! The Adventures of Brer Rabbit and His Family*. Illustrated by Barry Moser. San Diego, CA: Harcourt.

_____. (1987). *Jump Again! More Adventures of Brer Rabbit*. Illustrated by Barry Moser. San Diego, CA: Harcourt.

Partridge, Elizabeth. (2002). *This Land Was Made for You and Me: The Life and Songs of Woody Guthrie*. New York: Viking.

Paterson, Katherine. (1977). *Bridge to Terabithia*. Illustrated by Donna Diamond. New York: HarperCollins.

_____. (1978). *The Great Gilly Hopkins*. New York: HarperCollins.

_____. (1992). *The King's Equal*. New York: HarperCollins.

_____. (2008). *Bread and Roses, Too*. New York: Sandpiper.

Patron, Susan. (2008). *The Higher Power of Lucky*. New York: Alladin.

_____. (2009). *Lucky Breaks*. New York: Atheneum.

_____. (2011). *Lucky for Good*. New York: Atheneum.

Paulsen, Gary. (1987). *Hatchet*. New York: Atheneum.

_____. (1996). *Brian's Winter*. New York: Delacorte.

_____. (1999). *Brian's Return*. New York: Delacorte.

_____. (2010). *Masters of Disaster*. New York: Wendy Lamb Books.

_____. (2010). *Woods Runner*. New York: Wendy Lamb Books.

_____. (2011). *Liar, Liar: The Theory, Practice, and Destructive Properties of Deception*. New York: Wendy Lamb Books.

_____. (2012). *Flat Broke*. New York: Wendy Lamb Books.

Pearce, Philippa. (1958). *Tom's Midnight Garden*. Philadelphia, PA: Lippincott.

Pearson, Mary. (2008). *The Adoration of Jenna Fox*. New York: Holt.

Peck, Richard. (2002). *A Year Down Yonder*. New York: Penguin.

_____. (2003). *The River Between Us*. New York: Dial.

_____. (2004). *A Long Way from Chicago: A Novel in Stories*. New York: Penguin.

_____. (2011). *Secrets at Sea: A Novel*. Illustrated by Kelly Murphy. New York: Dial.

Peirce, Lincoln. (2010). *Big Nate: In a Class by Himself*. New York: HarperCollins.

Pendziwol, Jean E. (2005). *The Red Sash*. Illustrated by Nicolas Debon. Berkeley, CA: Groundwood.

Pennypacker, Sara. (2007). *The Talented Clementine*. Illustrated by Marla Frazee. New York: Hyperion.

_____. (2008). *Clementine*. Illustrated by Marla Frazee. New York: Hyperion.

_____. (2008). *Clementine's Letter*. Illustrated by Marla Frazee. New York: Hyperion.

_____. (2009). *Flat Stanley's Worldwide Adventures, Book Two: The Great Egyptian Grave Robbery*. Illustrated by Macky Pamintuan. New York: Harper.

_____. (2010). *Clementine, Friend of the Week*. Illustrated by Marla Frazee. New York: Hyperion.

_____. (2011). *Clementine and the Family Meeting*. Illustrated by Marla Frazee. New York: Hyperion.

Pérez, Amada Irma. (2007). *Nana's Big Surprise/Nana, qué sorpresa!*. Illustrated by Maya Christina Gonzalez. San Francisco: Children's Book Press.

Perkins, Lynne Rae. (1999). *All Alone in the Universe*. New York: Greenwillow.

_____. (2003). *Snow Music*. New York: Greenwillow.

_____. (2005). *Criss Cross*. New York: Greenwillow.

_____. (2007). *Pictures from Our Vacation*. New York: Greenwillow.

Perrault, Charles. (1982). *Histoire ou Contes du Temps Passé, avec des Moralités*. Italy: Tallone.

_____. (1999). *Contes de ma Mère l'Oye*. New York: French and European Publications.

Peters, Lisa Westberg. (2003). *Our Family Tree: An Evolution Story*. Illustrated by Lauren Stringer. San Diego, CA: Harcourt.

Peterson, Jeanne Whitehouse. (2000). *Don't Forget Winona*. New York: Joanna Cotler Books.

Phelan, Matt. (2009). *The Storm in the Barn*. Somerville, MA: Candlewick.

_____. (2011). *Around the World*. Somerville, MA: Candlewick.

Philip, Neil. (1994). *King Midas*. Illustrated by Isabelle Brent. Boston: Little, Brown.

Pierce, Tamora. (2011). *Mastiff*. New York: Random House.

_____. (2011). *Tortall and Other Lands: A Collection of Tales*. New York: Random House.

Pinkney, Andrea Davis. (1998). *Duke Ellington: The Piano Prince and His Orchestra*. Illustrated by Brian Pinkney. New York: Hyperion.

_____. (2006). *Peggony-Po: A Whale of a Tale*. New York: Hyperion.

_____. (2010). *Sit In: How Four Friends Stood Up by Sitting Down*. Illustrated by Brian Pinkney. New York: Little, Brown.

_____. (2010). *Sojourner Truth's Step-Stomp Stride*. Illustrated by Brian Pinkney. New York: Hyperion.

_____. (2011). *Bird in a Box*. New York: Little, Brown.

Pinkney, Brian. (2000). *The Adventures of Sparrowboy*. New York: Simon & Schuster.

Pinkney, Jerry. (2000). *Aesop's Fables*. New York: SeaStar.

_____. (2006). *The Little Red Hen*. New York: Penguin.

_____. (2007). *Little Red Riding Hood*. New York: Little, Brown.

_____. (2009). *The Lion & the Mouse*. New York: Little, Brown.

Piper, Watty. (1930). *The Little Engine that Could*. New York: Platt & Munk.

Plum-Ucci, Carol. (2000). *The Body of Christopher Creed*. San Diego, CA: Harcourt.

Polacco, Patricia. (1994). *Pink and Say*. New York: Philomel.

_____. (1995). *Babushka's Mother Goose*. New York: Philomel.

_____. (2000). *The Butterfly*. New York: Philomel.

_____. (2009). *January's Sparrow*. New York: Philomel.

Pollock, Penny. (1995). *The Turkey Girl: A Zuni Cinderella Story*. Illustrated by Ed Young. Boston: Little, Brown.

Porter, Pamela. (2011). *I'll Be Watching*. Toronto, Ontario: Groundwood.

Potter, Beatrix. (1902/2000). *The Tale of Peter Rabbit*. New York: Warne.

Pratchett, Terry. (2010). *I Shall Wear Midnight*. New York: Harper.

Pratt, Kristin Joy. (1992). *A Walk in the Rain Forest*. Nevada City, CA: Dawn.

_____. (1994). *A Swim through the Sea*. Nevada City, CA: Dawn.

Prelutsky, Jack. (1984). *The New Kid on the Block*. Illustrated by James Stevenson. New York: Greenwillow.

_____. (1989). *Circus*. New York: Aladdin.

Pressler, Mirjam. (1998). *Halinka.* **Translated by Elizabeth D. Crawford**. New York: Holt.

_____. (2007). *Let Sleeping Dogs Lie*. Translated by Erik J. Macki. Asheville, NC: Front Street.

Preus, Margi. (2010). *Heart of a Samurai: Based on the True Story of Nakahama Manjiro*. New York: Amulet.

_____. (2011). *Celebritrees: Historic & Famous Trees of the World*. Illustrated by Rebecca Gibbon. New York: Holt.

Prince, April Jones. (2006). *What Do Wheels Do All Day?*. Illustrated by Giles Laroche. Boston: Houghton Mifflin.

Pringle, Laurence. (1997). *Everybody Has a Belly Button*. Honesdale, PA: Boyds Mills.

_____. (2011). *Billions of Years, Amazing Changes: The Story of Evolution*. Illustrated by Steve Jenkins. Honesdale, PA: Boyds Mills.

Proddow, Penelope. (1982). *Art Tells a Story: Greek and Roman Myths*. Minneapolis, MN: Book Sales.

Provensen, Alice. (1982). *The Mother Goose Book*. Illustrated by Martin Provensen. London: Hamlyn.

Pullman, Philip. (1995). *The Golden Compass*. New York: Knopf.

_____. (1997). *The Subtle Knife*. New York: Knopf.

_____. (2000). *The Amber Spyglass*. New York: Knopf.

Pulver, Robin. (2003). *Punctuation Takes a Vacation*. Illustrated by Lynn Rowe Reed. New York: Holiday House.

_____. (2008). *Silent Letters Loud and Clear*. Illustrated by Lynn Rowe Reed. New York: Holiday House.

Qamar, Amjed. (2008). *Beneath My Mother's Feet*. New York: Atheneum.

Quattlebaum, Mary. (2006). *Sparks Fly High: The Legend of Dancing Point*. New York: Farrar, Straus and Giroux.

Quigley, Mary. (2007). *Granddad's Fishing Buddy*. Illustrated by Stéphanie Jorisch. New York: Dial.

Raczka, Bob. (2010). *Guyku: A Year of Haiku for Boys*. Illustrated by Peter Reynolds. Boston: Houghton Mifflin.

_____. (2011). *Lemonade: And Other Poems Squeezed from a Single Word*. Illustrated by Nancy Doniger. NY: Roaring Brook.

Ramirez, Antonio. (2006). *Napi Goes to the Mountain*. Illustrated by Domi. Toronto, Ontario: Groundwood.

Ransome, James E. (2011). *New Red Bike!*. New York: Holiday House.

Rappaport, Doreen. (2001). *Martin's Big Words: The Life of Dr. Martin Luther King, Jr.* Illustrated by Bryan Collier. New York: Hyperion.

_____. (2001). *Martin's Big Words: The Life of Dr. Martin Luther King, Jr.* Illustrated by Bryan Collier. New York: Hyperion.

_____. (2009). *Eleanor, Quiet No More*. Illustrated by Gary Kelley. New York: Hyperion.

_____. (2010). *Jack's Path of Courage: The Life of John F. Kennedy*. Illustrated by Matt Tavares. New York: Hyperion.

Raschka, Chris. (1993). *Yo! Yes?*. New York: Orchard.

_____. (2011). *A Ball for Daisy*. New York: Schwartz & Wade.

Rascol, Sabina. (2004). *The Impudent Rooster*. Illustrated by Holly Berry. New York: Dutton.

Rash, Andy. (2004). *Agent A to Agent Z*. New York: Levine.

Rasmussen, H., Marilyn Nelson, & Pamela Espeland. (2011). *A Little Bitty Man and Other Poems for the Very Young*. Illustrated by Kevin Hawkes. Somerville, MA: Candlewick.

Rathman, Peggy. (1995). *Officer Buckle and Gloria*. New York: Penguin.

Raven, Margot Theis. (2006). *Night Boat to Freedom*. Illustrated by E. B. Lewis. New York: Farrar, Straus and Giroux.

Rawlings, Marjorie Kinnan. (1939). *The Yearling*. New York: Scribner.

Ray, Deborah Kogan. (2007). *Down the Colorado: John Wesley Powell, the One-Armed Explorer*. New York: Farrar, Straus and Giroux.

Ray, Mary Lyn. (2001). *Mud*. Illustrated by Lauren Stringer. San Diego: Harcourt.

_____. (2011). *Stars*. Illustrated by Marla Frazee. New York: Beach Lane.

Recorvits, Helen. (2003). *My Name Is Yoon*. Illustrated by Gabi Swiatkowska. New York: Farrar, Straus and Giroux.

Reed, M. K. (2011). *Americus*. Illustrated by Jonathan David Hill. New York: First Second.

Reedy, Trent. (2011). *Words in the Dust*. New York: Levine.

Reeve, Philip. (2001). *Mortal Engines*. New York: Scholastic.

_____. (2003). *Predator's Gold*. New York: Scholastic.

_____. (2005). *Infernal Devices*. New York: Scholastic.

_____. (2006). *The Darkling Plain*. New York: Scholastic.

_____. (2008). *Here Lies Arthur*. New York: Scholastic.

_____. (2010). *Fever Crumb*. New York: Scholastic.

_____. (2011). *A Web of Air*. New York: Scholastic.

_____. (2011). *Scrivener's Moon*. New York: Scholastic.

Reibstein, Mark. (2008). *WabiSabi*. Illustrated by Ed Young. New York: Little, Brown.

Reid, Barbara. (2005). *The Subway Mouse*. New York: Scholastic.

Reinhardt, Dana. (2011). *The Summer I Learned to Fly*. New York: Wendy Lamb Books.

Reinhart, Matthew, & Robert Sabuda. (2011). *Encyclopedia Mythologica: Dragons and Monsters Pop-Up*. Cambridge, MA: Candlewick.

Reiser, Lynn. (2003). *Ten Puppies*. New York: HarperCollins.

_____. (2006). *Hardworking Puppies*. San Diego, CA: Harcourt.

_____. (2007). *My Way/A mi manera: A Margaret and Margarita Story*. New York: Greenwillow.

Rey, H. A. (1941). *Curious George*. Boston: Houghton Mifflin.

Richards, Jame. (2010). *Three Rivers Rising: A Novel of the Johnstown Flood*. New York: Knopf.

Ries, Lori. (2007). *Fix It, Sam*. Illustrated by Sue Ramá. Watertown, MA: Charlesbridge.

Rinaldi, Ann. (1999). *My Heart Is on the Ground: The Diary of Nannie Little Rose, a Sioux Girl, Carlisle Indian School, PA 1880*. New York: Scholastic.

Riordan, Rick. (2005). *The Lightning Thief*. New York: Hyperion.

———. (2011). *The Son of Neptune*. New York: Hyperion.

Ritz, Karen. (2010). *Windows with Birds*. Honesdale, PA: Boyds Mills.

Roalf, Peggy. (1993). *Children*. New York: Hyperion.

———. (1993). *Flowers*. New York: Hyperion.

Robb, Don. (2007). *Ox, House, Stick: The History of Our Alphabet*. Illustrated by Anne Smith. Watertown, MA: Charlesbridge.

Robberecht, Thierry. (2007). *Sam Tells Stories*. Illustrated by Philippe Goossens. New York: Clarion.

Robbins, Ken. (2010). *For Good Measure: The Ways We Say How Much, How Far, How Heavy, How Big, How Old*. New York: Roaring Brook Press.

Robinson, Sharon. (2004). *Promises to Keep: How Jackie Robinson Changed America*. New York: Scholastic.

Rockwell, Anne. (2009). *Big George: How a Shy Boy Became President Washington*. Illustrated by Matt Phelan. New York: Harcourt.

Rockwood, Joyce. (2003). *To Spoil the Sun*. New York: Holt.

Rogers, Gregory. (2007). *Midsummer Knight*. New Milford, Conn.: Roaring Brook.

Rohmann, Eric. (2002). *My Friend Rabbit*. Brookfield, CT: Roaring Brook.

———. (2011). *Bone Dog*. New York: Roaring Brook.

Root, Phyllis. (2002). *Big Momma Makes the World*. Illustrated by Helen Oxenbury. Cambridge, MA: Candlewick.

———. (2004). *If You Want to See a Caribou*. Illustrated by Jim Meyer. Boston: Houghton Mifflin.

Rose, Caroline Starr. (2012). *May B.: A Novel*. New York: Schwartz & Wade.

Rose, Deborah Lee. (2000). *Into the A, B, Sea: An Ocean Alphabet*. Illustrated by Steve Jenkins. New York: Scholastic.

Rosen, Michael J. (2011). *The Hound Dog's Haiku: And Other Poems for Dog Lovers*. Illustrated by Mary Azarian. Somerville, MA: Candlewick.

Rotner, Shelley. (2006). *Senses at the Seashore*. Minneapolis, MN: Millbrook.

Rowling, J. K. (1998). *Harry Potter and the Sorcerer's Stone*. Illustrated by Mary Grandpre. New York: Scholastic.

Roy, James. (2009). *Max Quigley: Technically Not a Bully*. Boston: Houghton Mifflin Harcourt.

Rubbino, Salvatore. (2009). *A Walk in New York*. Cambridge, MA: Candlewick.

———. (2011). *A Walk in London*. Cambridge, MA: Candlewick.

Rumford, James. (2001). *Traveling Man: The Journey of Ibn Battuta 1325–1354*. Boston: Houghton Mifflin.

———. (2003). *Seeker of Knowledge: The Man Who Deciphered Egyptian Hieroglyphs*. Boston: Sandpiper.

Rumford, James. (2004). *Sequoyah: The Cherokee Man Who Gave His People Writing*. Boston: Houghton Mifflin.

———. (2007). *Beowulf: A Hero's Tale Retold*. Boston: Houghton Mifflin.

———. (2010). *Tiger and Turtle*. New York: Roaring Brook.

Rupert, Janet. (1994/2005). *The African Mask*. New York: Backinprint.com.

Russo, Marisabina. (2011). *I Will Come Back for You: A Family in Hiding during World War II*. New York: Schwartz & Wade.

Ryan, Pam Muñoz. (2010). *The Dreamer*. Illustrated by Peter Sís. New York: Scholastic.

Rylander, Chris. (2011). *The Fourth Stall*. New York: Walden Pond.

Rylant, Cynthia. (1996). *Henry and Mudge*. Illustrated by Sucie Stevenson. New York: Simon & Schuster.

———. (2010). *Brownie & Pearl See the Sights*. Illustrated by Brian Biggs. New York: Beach Lane.

———. (2011). *Annie and Snowball and the Book Bugs Club*. Illustrated by Sucie Stevenson. New York: Simon Spotlight.

Sabuda, Robert, & Matthew Reinhart. (2007). *Encyclopedia Prehistorica: Mega Beasts*. Cambridge, MA: Candlewick.

Sabuda, Robert. (1992). *Saint Valentine*. New York: Simon & Schuster.

———. (1995). *Arthur and the Sword*. New York: Atheneum.

———. (1995). *Arthur and the Sword*. New York: Atheneum.

———. (1997). *King Tutankhamen's Gift*. New York: Simon & Schuster.

Sachar, Louis. (1987). *There's a Boy in the Girl's Bathroom*. New York: Knopf.

———. (1998). *Holes*. New York: Farrar, Straus and Giroux.

Saint-Exupery, Antoine de. (1943). *The Little Prince*. San Diego, CA: Harcourt.

Salisbury, Graham. (2011). *Calvin Coconut: Hero of Hawai'i*. Illustrated by Jacqueline Rogers. New York: Wendy Lamb Books.

———. (2011). *Calvin Coconut: King Fooey*. Illustrated by Jacqueline Rogers. Wendy Lamb Books.

Salley, Coleen. (2002). *Epossumondas*. Illustrated by Janet Stevens. Orlando, FL: Harcourt.

———. (2006). *Epossumondas Saves the Day*. Illustrated by Janet Stevens. Orlando, FL: Harcourt.

San Souci, Robert D. (1989). *The Talking Eggs: A Folktale from the American South*. Illustrated by Jerry Pinkney. New York: Dial.

———. (1994). *Sootface: An Ojibwa Cinderella Story*. Illustrated by Daniel San Souci. New York: Delacorte.

———. (1995). *The Faithful Friend*. Illustrated by Brian Pinkney. New York: Simon & Schuster.

———. (1998). *Cendrillon: A Caribbean Cinderella*. Illustrated by Brian Pinkney. New York: Simon & Schuster.

San Souci, Robert D., & Jane Yolen. (1993). *Cut from the Same Cloth: American Women of Myth, Legend, and Tall Tale*. Illustrated by J. Brian Pinkney. New York: Philomel.

Satrapi, Marjane. (2004). *Persepolis: The Story of a Childhood*. New York: Pantheon.

———. (2005). *Persepolis 2: The Story of a Return*. New York: Pantheon.

Savadier, Elivia. (2006). *Time to Get Dressed!*. New Milford, CN: Roaring Brook.

Savage, Stephen. (2011). *Where's Walrus?*. New York: Scholastic.

Say, Allen. (1993). *Grandfather's Journey*. Boston: Houghton Mifflin.

———. (2002). *Home of the Brave*. Boston: Walter Lorraine Books.

———. (2011). *Drawing from Memory*. New York: Scholastic.

Sayre, April Pulley. (2008). *Trout Are Made of Trees*. Illustrated by Kate Endle. Watertown, MA: Charlesbridge.

Scanlon, Liz Garton. (2009). *All the World*. Illustrated by Marla Frazee. New York: Beach Lane.

Schertle, Alice. (2007). *Very Hairy Bear*. Illustrated by Matt Phelan. San Diego, CA: Harcourt.

Schlitz, Laura Amy. (2007). *Good Masters! Sweet Ladies! Voices from a Medieval Village*. Illustrated by Robert Byrd. Cambridge, MA: Candlewick.

———. (2007). *The Bearskinner: A Tale of the Brothers Grimm*. Illustrated by Max Grafe. Cambridge, MA: Candlewick.

Schmatz, Pat. (2011). *Bluefish*. Somerville, MA: Candlewick.

Schmidt, Gary D. (2001). *Mara's Stories: Glimmers in the Darkness*. New York: Holt.

———. (2004). *Lizzie Bright and the Buckminster Boy*. New York: Clarion.

———. (2007). *The Wednesday Wars*. New York: Clarion.

———. (2008). *Trouble*. New York: Clarion.

———. (2011). *Okay for Now*. New York: Clarion.

Schneider, Christine. (2004). *I'm Bored!*. Illustrated by Hervé Pinel. New York: Clarion.

Schon, Isabel. (1983). *Doña Blanca and other Hispanic Nursery Rhymes and Games*. Minneapolis, MN: Denison.

Schories, Pat. (2004). *Breakfast for Jack*. Asheville, NC: Front Street.

Schroder, Monika. (2010). *Saraswati's Way*. New York: Farrar, Straus and Giroux.

Schroeder, Alan. (2011). *Ben Franklin: His Wit and Wisdom from A–Z*. Illustrated by John O'Brien. New York: Holiday House.

Schulman, Janet. (2008). *Pale Male: Citizen Hawk of New York City*. Illustrated by Meilo So. New York: Random House.

———. (2008). *Pale Male: Citizen Hawk of New York*. Illustrated by Meilo So. New York: Random House.

Schwabach, Karen. (2010). *The Storm before Atlanta*. New York: Random House.

Schwartz, Alvin. (1990). *Whoppers: Tall Tales and Other Lies*. Illustrated by Glen Rounds. New York: HarperTrophy.

Schwartz, David M. (1998). *G is for Googol: A Math Alphabet Book*. Illustrated by Marissa Moss. New York: Ten Speed.

———. (2001).*Q is for Quark: A Science Alphabet Book*. Illustrated by Kim Doner. New York: Ten Speed.

Schwartz, Richard Evan. (2010). *You Can Count on Monsters*. London: Peters.

Scieszka, Jon. (1989). *The True Story of the Three Little Pigs*. Illustrated by Lane Smith. New York: Viking.

———. (1992). *The Stinky Cheese Man and Other Fairly Stupid Tales*. Illustrated by Lane Smith. New York: Viking.

———. (1994). *The Book that Jack Wrote*. New York: Viking.

———. (1995). *Math Curse*. Illustrated by Lane Smith. New York: Viking.

———. (2004). *Science Verse*. Illustrated by Lane Smith. New York: Viking.

———. (2005). *Seen Art?*. Illustrated by Lane Smith. New York: Viking.

Scieszka, Jon. (Ed.). (2011). *Guys Read: Thriller*. New York: Walden Pond.

Scott, Elaine. (2011). *Space, Stars, and the Beginning of Time: What the Hubble Telescope Saw*. New York: Clarion.

Seder, Rufus Butler. (2007). *Gallop!*. New York: Workman.

———. (2008). *Swing! A Scanimation Picture Book*. New York: Workman.

Seeger, Laura Vaccaro. (2007). *Dog and Bear: Two Friends, Three Stories*. New Milford, CN: Roaring Brook.

———. (2010). *What If?*. New York: Roaring Brook.

Seidler, Tor. (2002). *Brothers Below Zero*. New York: Laura Geringer Books.

Sellier, Marie. (2007). *Legend of the Chinese Dragon*. Illustrated by Catherine Louis and Wang Fei. New York: North-South.

Selznick, Brian. (2007). *The Invention of Hugo Cabret*. New York: Scholastic.

———. (2011). *Wonderstruck*. New York: Scholastic.

———. (2007). *The Invention of Hugo Cabret*. New York: Scholastic.

———. (2011). *Wonderstruck: A Novel in Words and Pictures*. New York: Scholastic.

Sendak, Maurice. (1963). *Where the Wild Things Are*. New York: HarperCollins.

Sepetys, Ruta. (2011). *Between Shades of Gray*. New York: Philomel.

Serafini, Frank. (2008). *Looking Closely across the Desert*. Toronto, Ontario: Kids Can Press.

———. (2008). *Looking Closely along the Shore*. Toronto, Ontario: Kids Can Press.

———. (2008). *Looking Closely inside the Garden*. Toronto, Ontario: Kids Can Press.

———. (2008). *Looking Closely through the Forest*. Toronto, Ontario: Kids Can Press.

Seuss, Dr. (1957). *The Cat in the Hat*. New York: Random House.

Sewall, Marcia. (1990). *People of the Breaking Day*. New York: Atheneum.

Sfar, Joann. (2003). *Little Vampire Goes to School*. New York: Simon & Schuster.

Shange, Ntozake. (2004). *Ellington Was Not a Street*. New York: Simon & Schuster.

———. (2012). *Freedom's a-Callin Me*. Illustrated by Rod Brown. New York: Amistad/Collins.

Shannon, David. (1998). *No, David!*. New York: Scholastic.

———. (1999). *David Goes to School*. New York: Scholastic.

———. (2002). *David Gets in Trouble*. New York: Scholastic.

———. (2005). *David Smells!*. New York: Blue Sky.

Shannon, George. (2007). *Rabbit's Gift*. Illustrated by Laura Dronzek. San Diego, CA: Harcourt.

Shea, Pegi Deitz. (1996). *The Whispering Cloth*. Illustrated by Anita Riggio & You Yang. Honesdale, PA: Boyds Mills.

Shearer, Alex. (2008). *Canned*. New York: Scholastic.

Shecter, Vicky Alvear. (2011). *Cleopatra's Moon*. New York: Scholastic.

Sheen, Dong Il, and Jae-Soo Lin. (2002). *Yellow Umbrella*. La Jolla, CA: Kane Miller.

Sheinkin, Steve. (2010). *The Notorious Benedict Arnold: A True Story of Adventure, Heroism, & Treachery*. New York: Roaring Brook.

Shelley, Mary. (1991). *Frankenstein* (reissue). New York: Bantam.

Shepard, Aaron. (2006). *One-Eye! Two-Eyes! Three-Eyes! A Very Grimm Fairy Tale*. Illustrated by Gary Clement. New York: Atheneum.

Sherlock, Patti. (2004). *Letters from Wolfie*. New York: Viking.

Shertle, Alice. (2009). *Button Up! Wrinkled Rhymes*. Illustrated by Petra Mathers. San Diego, CA: Harcourt.

Sheth, Kashmera. (2004). *Blue Jasmine*. New York: Hyperion.

Shulman, Polly. (2010). *The Grimm Legacy*. New York: Putnam.

Sidman, Joyce. (2003). *The World According to Dog: Poems and Teen Voices*. Boston: Houghton Mifflin.

———. (2006). *Butterfly Eyes and Other Secrets of the Meadow: Poems*. Illustrated by Beth Krommes. Boston: Houghton Mifflin.

———. (2006). *Meow Ruff*. Illustrated by Michelle Berg. Boston: Houghton Mifflin.

———. (2006). *Song of the Water Boatman and Other Pond Poems*. Illustrated by Becky Prange. Boston: Houghton Mifflin.

———. (2009). *Red Sings from Treetops: A Year in Colors*. Illustrated by Pamela Zagarenski. Boston: Houghton Mifflin.

———. (2010). *Dark Emperor & Other Poems of the Night*. Illustrated by Rick Allen. Boston: Houghton Mifflin.

———. (2010). *Ubiquitous: Celebrating Nature's Survivors*. Illustrated by Beckie Prange. Boston: Houghton Mifflin.

———. (2011). *Swirl by Swirl: Spirals in Nature*. Illustrated by Beth Krommes. Boston: Houghton Mifflin.

Sidney, Margaret. (1963). *The Five Little Peppers and How They Grew*. New York: Grosset & Dunlap.

Siegel, Siena Cherson. (2006). *To Dance: A Ballerina's Graphic Novel*. Illustrated by Mark Siegel. New York: Simon & Schuster.

Sierra, Judy. (1996). *Nursery Tales around the World*. Illustrated by Stefano Vitale. New York: Clarion.

———. (1996). *Wiley and the Hairy Man*. Illustrated by J. Brian Pinkney. New York: Lodestar.

Silverman, Erica. (1999). *Raisel's Riddle*. Illustrated by Susan Gaber. New York: Farrar, Straus and Giroux.

Silverstein, Shel. (1964). *The Giving Tree*. New York: Harper & Row.

———. (1981). *A Light in the Attic*. New York: HarperCollins.

Siméon, Jean-Pierre. (2007). *This Is a Poem that Heals Fish*. Illustrated by Olivier Tallec. Brooklyn: Enchanted Lion.

Simon, Seymour. (1992/2007). *Our Solar System*. New York: HarperCollins.

_____. (1993). *Wolves*. New York: HarperCollins.

_____. (2006). *The Brain: Our Nervous System*. New York: HarperCollins.

_____. (2006). *The Heart: Our Circulatory System*. New York: HarperCollins.

_____. (2008). *The Human Body*. New York: HarperCollins.

_____. (2011). *Butterflies*. New York: HarperCollins.

Singer, Issac Bashevis. (1968). *When Shlemiel Went to Warsaw and Other Stories*. Illustrated by Margot Zemach. New York: Farrar, Straus and Giroux.

_____. (1976). *Naftali the Storyteller and His Horse, Sus*. Illustrated by Margot Zemach. New York: Farrar, Straus and Giroux.

Singer, Marilyn. (2007). *City Lullaby*. Illustrated by Carll Cneut. New York: Clarion.

_____. (2010). *Mirror Mirror: A Book of Reversible Verse*. Illustrated by Jósee Masse. New York: Dutton.

Sís, Peter. (2007). *The Wall: Growing Up behind the Iron Curtain*. New York: Farrar, Straus and Giroux.

Skurzynski, Gloria. (2010). *This Is Rocket Science: True Stories of the Risk-Taking Scientists Who Figure Out Ways to Explore Beyond Earth*. Washington, DC: National Geographic.

Smith, Charles R., Jr. (2007). *Twelve Rounds to Glory: The Story of Muhammad Ali*. Illustrated by Bryan Collier. Cambridge, MA: Candlewick.

Smith, Cynthia Leitich. (2001). *Rain Is Not My Indian Name*. New York: HarperCollins.

_____. (2002). *Indian Shoes*. Illustrated by Jim Madsen. New York: HarperCollins.

Smith, Lane. (2011). *Grandpa Green*. New York: Roaring Brook.

Smith, Roland. (2007). *Elephant Run*. New York: Hyperion.

Snyder, Laurel. (2011). *Bigger than a Bread Box*. New York: Random House.

So, Meilo. (2004). *Gobble, Gobble, Slip, Slop: A Tale of a Very Greedy Cat*. New York: Knopf.

Soto, Gary. (1997). *Buried Onions*. San Diego, CA: Harcourt Brace.

_____. (2011). *Hey 13!*. New York: Holiday House.

Souhami, Jessica. (1999). *No Dinner! The Story of the Old Woman and the Pumpkin*. Tarrytown, NY: Cavendish.

_____. (2006). *Sausages*. London: Frances Lincoln.

Speare, Elizabeth George. (1958). *The Witch of Blackbird Pond*. Boston: Houghton Mifflin.

_____. (1983). *The Sign of the Beaver*. Boston: Houghton Mifflin.

Spielman, Gloria. (2011). *Marcel Marceau: Master of Mime*. Illustrated by Manon Gauthier. Minneapolis, MN: Kar-Ben.

Spinelli, Eileen. (2007). *Callie Cat, Ice Skater*. Illustrated by Anne Kennedy. Morton Grove, IL: Whitman.

Spinelli, Jerry. (2003). *Milkweed*. New York: Knopf.

Spyri, Johanna. (1879–1880). *Heidi*. New York: Platt & Peck.

St. George, Judith. (2000). *So You Want to Be President?*. Illustrated by David Small. New York: Philomel.

Stampler, Ann Redisch. (2010). *The Rooster Prince of Breslov*. Illustrated by Eugene Yelchin. New York: Clarion.

Stanley, Diane, & Peter Vennema. (1992). *Bard of Avon: The Story of William Shakespeare*. New York: Morrow.

Stanley, Diane. (1990). *Fortune*. New York: Morrow.

_____. (1997). *Rumplestiltskin's Daughter*. New York: Scholastic.

_____. (2002). *Joan of Arc*. New York: HarperCollins.

_____. (2011). *The Silver Bowl*. New York: Harper.

Staples, Suzanne Fisher. (1989). *Shabanu*. New York: Knopf.

_____. (1993). *Haveli*. New York: Knopf.

Stead, Philip C. (2010). *A Sick Day for Amos McGee*. Illustrated by Erin E. Stead. New York: Roaring Brook.

Stead, Rebecca. (2009). *When You Reach Me*. New York: Wendy Lamb Books.

Steig, William. (1969). *Sylvester and the Magic Pebble*. New York: Windmill.

_____. (1990/2010). *Shrek!*. New York: Farrar, Straus and Giroux.

Stephens, John. (2011). *The Emerald Atlas*. New York: Knopf.

Steptoe, John. (1969). *Stevie*. New York: Harper & Row.

_____. (1987). *Mufaro's Beautiful Daughters*. New York: Lothrop, Lee & Shepard.

_____. (1989). *The Story of Jumping Mouse*. New York: HarperCollins.

Stevens, Janet, & Susan Stevens Crummel. (2011). *The Little Red Pen*. Illustrated by Janet Stevens. Boston: Harcourt.

Stevenson, Robert Louis. (1885). *A Child's Garden of Verses*. New York: Philomel.

_____. (2006). *The Moon*. Illustrated by Tracy Campbell Pearson. New York: Farrar, Straus and Giroux.

Stewart, Sarah. (2004). *The Friend*. Illustrated by David Small. New York: Farrar, Straus & Giroux.

Still, James. (1996). *Jack and the Wonder Beans*. Lexington, KY: The University Press of Kentucky.

Stone, Phoebe. (2011). *The Romeo and Juliet Code*. New York: Levine.

Stone, Tanya Lee. (2008). *Elizabeth Leads the Way: Elizabeth Cady Stanton and the Right to Vote*. Illustrated by Rebecca Gibbon. New York: Holt.

_____. (2008). *Sandy's Circus: A Story about Alexander Calder*. Illustrated by Boris Kulikov. New York: Viking.

_____. (2009). *Almost Astronauts: 13 Women Who Dared to Dream*. Somerville, MA: Candlewick.

Straparola, Giovanni Francesco. (1899). *Le piacevolinotti di M. Giovanfrancesco Straparola*. Ann Arbor, MI: University of Michigan Library.

Stratton, Allan. (2004). *Chanda's Secrets*. Toronto, Ontario: Annick.

_____. (2008). *Chanda's Wars*. New York: HarperCollins.

Strete, Craig Kee. (1979). *When Grandfather Journeys into Winter*. New York: Greenwillow.

_____. (1995). *The World in Grandfather's Hands*. New York: Clarion.

Stryer, Andrea Stenn. (2007). *Kami and the Yaks*. Illustrated by Bert Dodson. Palo Alto, CA: Bay Otter.

Sullivan, George. (2011). *Tom Thumb: The Remarkable True Story of a Man in Miniature*. New York: Clarion.

Sutcliff, Rosemary. (1954). *The Eagle of the Ninth*. New York: Walck.

_____. (2007). *Frontier Wolf*. Honesdale, PA: Front Street.

Swanson, Susan. (2008). *The House in the Night*. Illustrated by Beth Krommes. Boston: Houghton Mifflin.

Sweet, Melissa. (2011). *Balloons over Broadway: The True Story of the Puppeteer of Macy's Parade*. New York: Houghton Mifflin.

Swinburne, Stephen. (2002). *The Woods Scientist*. Boston: Houghton Mifflin.

Taback, Simms. (1999). *Joseph Had a Little Overcoat*. New York: Viking.

Tafuri, Nancy. (2007). *The Busy Little Squirrel*. New York: Simon & Schuster.

Tak, Bibi Dumon. (2011). *Soldier Bear*. Illustrated by Philip Hopman. Translated by Laura Watkinson. Grand Rapids, MI: Eerdmans.

Tan, Shaun. (2007). *The Arrival*. New York: Levine.

_____. (2009). *Tales from Outer Suburbia*. New York: Scholastic.

_____. (2011). *Lost and Found: Three by Shaun Tan*. New York: Levine.

Taylor, Ann, & Jane Taylor. (1804). *Original Poems for Infant Minds by Several Young Persons*. New York: Garland.

Taylor, Mildred. (1976). *Roll of Thunder, Hear My Cry*. New York: Dial.

_____. (1981). *Let the Circle Be Unbroken*. New York: Dial.

_____. (1985). *Song of the Trees*. New York: Dial.

_____. (1987). *The Friendship*. New York: Dial.

_____. (1990). *Mississippi Bridge*. New York: Dial.

_____. (2001). *The Land*. New York: Fogelman.

Taylor, Sarah Stewart. (2010). *Amelia Earhart: This Broad Ocean*. Illustrated by Ben Towle. New York: First Second.

Tchana, Katrin H. (2006). *Changing Woman and Her Sisters: Stories of Goddesses from around the World*. Illustrated by Trina Schart Hyman. New York: Holiday House.

Telgemeier, Raina. (2003). *Inside Out*. New York: HarperCollins.

_____. (2004). *Cruise Control*. New York: HarperCollins.

_____. (2010). *Smile*. New York: Graphix.

Temple, Frances. (1994). *The Beduins' Gazelle*. New York: HarperCollins.

Terban, Marvin. (1998). *Guppies in Tuxedos: Funny Eponyms*. Illustrated by Giulio Maestro. Boston: Houghton Mifflin.

Thimmesh, Catherine. (2006). *Team Moon: How 400,000 People Landed Apollo 11 on the Moon*. Illustrated by Douglas B. Jones. Boston: Houghton Mifflin.

Thomas, Jan. (2007). *What Will Fat Cat Sit On?*. San Diego, CA: Harcourt.

Thomas, Joyce Carol. (1993). *Brown Honey in Broomwheat Tea*. Illustrated by Floyd Cooper. New York: HarperCollins.

_____. (1995). *Gingerbread Days*. New York: HarperCollins.

_____. (1998). *I Have Heard of a Land*. Illustrated by Floyd Cooper. New York: HarperCollins.

_____. (2000). *Hush Songs: African American Lullabies*. Illustrated by Brenda Joysmith. New York: Hyperion.

_____. (2008). *The Blacker the Berry*. Illustrated by Floyd Cooper. New York: HarperCollins.

Thomas, Patricia. (2008). *Red Sled*. Illustrated by Chris Demarest. Honesdale, PA: Boyds Mills.

Thompson, Kate. (2009). *Highway Robbery*. New York: Greenwillow.

_____. (2010). *Most Wanted*. New York: Greenwillow.

_____. (2010). *The White Horse Trick*. New York: Greenwillow.

Thong, Roseanne. (2007). *Tummy Girl*. Illustrated by Sam Williams. New York: Holt.

Thor, Annika. (2009). *A Faraway Island*. New York: Delacorte.

_____. (2011). *The Lily Pond*. Translated by Linda Schenck. New York: Delacorte.

Tillage, Leon Walter. (1997). **Leon's Story**. Illustrated by Susan L. Roth. New York: Farrar, Straus and Giroux.

Tjong Khing, Thé. (2007). **Where Is the Cake?**. New York: Abrams.

Tolan, Stephanie S. (1992).**Sophie and the Sidewalk Man**. New York: Four Winds.

Tolkien, J.R.R. (1937). **The Hobbit**. New York: Random House.

_____. (1954). **Fellowship of the Ring**. London: Allen & Unwin.

Travers, P. L. (1934). **Mary Poppins**. London: Harper Collins.

Trueman, Terry. (2000). **Stuck in Neutral**. New York: HarperCollins.

Tucker, Jean. (1994). **Come Look with Me: Discovering Photographs with Children**. Charlottesville, VA: Thomasson-Grant.

Tullet, Herve. (2011). **Press Here**. San Francisco: Chronicle.

Tunnell, Michael O. (2010). **Candy Bomber**.Watertown, MA: Charlesbridge.

Turner, Ann. (1987). **Nettie's Trip South**. Illustrated by Roland Himler. Old Tappan, NJ: Macmillan.

_____. (2011). **Father of Lies**. New York: HarperTeen.

Turner, Pamela S. (2009). **The Frog Scientist**. Illustrated by Andy Comins. Boston: Houghton Mifflin. (Paperback reissue in 2011.)

_____. (2010). **Project Seashore**. Photographed by Scott Tuason. Boston: Houghton Mifflin.

Ungar, Richard. (2007). **Even Higher**. Toronto, Ontario: Tundra.

Ungerer, Tomi. (2009). **The Moon Man**. London: Phaidon.

Updale, Eleanor. (2011). **Johnny Swanson**. New York: David Fickling.

Ursu, Anne. (2011). **Breadcrumbs**. New York: Walden Pond.

Vail, Rachel. (1998). **Over the Moon**. Illustrated by Scott Nash. New York: Orchard.

Valente, Catherynne M. (2011). **The Girl Who Circumnavigated Fairyland in a Ship of Her Own Making**. Illustrated by Ana Juan. New York: Feiwel and Friends.

Van Allsburg, Chris. (1981). **Jumanji**. Boston: Houghton Mifflin.

_____. (1983). **The Wreck of the Zephyr**. Boston: Houghton Mifflin.

_____. (1985). **The Polar Express**. Boston: Houghton Mifflin.

_____. (1986). **The Stranger**. Boston: Houghton Mifflin.

_____. (1995). **Bad Day at Riverbend**. Boston: Houghton Mifflin.

_____. (2002). **Zathura**. Boston: Houghton Mifflin.

_____. (2011). **Queen of the Falls**. New York: Houghton Mifflin.

Van Draanen, Wendelin. (2004). **Sammy Keyes and the Psycho Kitty Queen**. Illustrated by Dan Yaccarino. New York: Knopf.

_____. (2011). **Sammy Keyes and the Night of Skulls**. New York: Knopf.

Van Fleet, Matthew. (2007). **Dog**. Illustrated by Brian Stanton. New York: Simon & Schuster.

Van Laan, Nancy. (1995). **Sleep, Sleep, Sleep: A Lullaby for Little Ones around the World**. Illustrated by Holly Meade. Boston: Little, Brown.

Vanderpool, Clare. (2010). **Moon over Manifest**. New York: Delacorte.

van Eekhout, Greg. (2011). **The Boy at the End of the World**. New York: Bloomsbury.

Varon, Sara. (2006). **Chicken and Cat**. New York: Scholastic.

_____. (2007). **Robot Dreams**. New York: First Second.

Venkatraman, Padma. (2008). **Climbing the Stairs**. New York: Putnam.

_____. (2011). **Island's End**. New York: Putnam.

Vennema, Peter. (1988). **Shaka, King of the Zulus**. Illustrated by Diane Stanley. New York: HarperCollins.

Voigt, Cynthia. (2011). **Young Fredle**. Illustrated by Louise Yates. New York: Knopf.

Waddell, Martin. (2008). **Tiny's Big Adventure**. Illustrated by John Lawrence. Somerville, MA: Candlewick.

Waldman, Neil. (1999). **The Starry Night**. Honesdale, PA: Wordsong.

Walker, Alice. (2007). **Why War Is Never a Good Idea**. Illustrated by Stefano Vitale. New York: HarperCollins.

Wallace, Jason. (2011). **Out of Shadows**. New York: Holiday House.

Wallenfels, Stephen. (2009). **POD**. Honesdale, PA: Namelos.

Walsh, Ellen Stoll. (2007). **Mouse Shapes**. San Diego, CA: Harcourt.

_____. (2010). **Balancing Act**. New York: Beach Lane.

Walsh, Jill Paton. (1986). **The Green Book**. Illustrated by Lloyd Bloom. New York: Farrar, Straus and Giroux.

_____. (2004). **The Emperor's Winding Sheet**. Ashville, NC: Front Street.

Ward, Helen. (2004). **Unwitting Wisdom: An Anthology of Aesop's Fables**. San Francisco: Chronicle.

_____. (2008). **Varmints**. Illustrated by Marc Craste. Cambridge, MA: Candlewick.

Wardlaw, Lee. (2011). **Won Ton: A Cat Tale Told in Haiku**. Illustrated by Eugene Yelchin. New York: Holt.

Watt, Mélanie. (2007). **Chester**. Toronto, Ontario: Kids Can Press.

_____. (2008). **Chester's Back!**. Toronto, Ontario: Kids Can Press.

Wattenberg, Jane. (2000). *Henny Penny*. New York: Scholastic.

Weaver, Tess. (2007). *Cat Jumped In!*. Illustrated by Emily Arnold McCully. New York: Clarion.

Webb, Sophie. (2000). *My Season with Penguins: An Antarctic Journal*. Boston: Houghton Mifflin.

———. (2004). *Looking for Seabirds: Journal from an Alaskan Voyage*. Boston: Houghton Mifflin.

———. (2011). *Far from Shore: Chronicles of an Open Ocean Voyage*. Boston: Houghton Mifflin.

Weeks, Sarah. (2006). *Ruff! Ruff! Where's Scruff?*. Illustrated by David A. Carter. San Diego, CA: Harcourt.

———. (2006). *Counting Ovejas*. Illustrated by David Diaz. New York: Atheneum.

Weill, Cynthia, & K. B. Basseches. (2007). *ABeCedarios: Mexican Folk Art ABCs in English and Spanish*. Photographed by Moisés Jiménez and Armando Jiménez. El Paso. TX: Cinco Puntos.

Wein, Elizabeth. (1993). *The Winter Prince*. New York: Atheneum.

———. (2003). *A Coalition of Lions*. New York: Viking.

———. (2004). *The Sunbird*. New York: Viking.

———. (2007). *The Lion Hunter*. New York: Viking.

———. (2008). *The Empty Kingdom*. New York: Viking.

Wells, Robison. (2011). *Variant*. New York: HarperTeen.

Wells, Rosemary. (1979). *Max's First Word*. New York: Dial.

———. (2006). *Max's ABC*. New York: Viking.

———. (2008). *Max's Bunny Business*. New York: Penguin.

Werlin, Nancy. (2008). *The Rules of Survival*. New York: Penguin.

Westerfeld, Scott. (2011). *Goliath*. Illustrated by Keith Thompson. New York: Simon Pulse.

Whatley, Bruce. (2001). *Wait! No Paint!*. New York: HarperCollins.

Wheeler, Lisa. (2007). *Jazz Baby*. Illustrated by R. Gregory Christie. San Diego, CA: Harcourt.

White, E. B. (1952). *Charlotte's Web*. Illustrated by Garth Williams. New York: HarperCollins.

Wiesner, David. (1991). *Tuesday*. New York: Clarion.

———. (2001). *The Three Pigs*. New York: Clarion.

———. (2006). *Flotsam*. New York: Clarion.

———. (2010). *Art & Max*. New York: Clarion.

Wild, Margaret. (1998). *Our Granny*. Illustrated by Julie Vivas. New York: Sandpiper.

———. (1999). *Jenny Angel*. New York: Viking.

———. (2000). *Tom Goes to Kindergarten*. Illustrated by David Legge. Park Ridge, IL: Whitman.

———. (2003). *Kiss! Kiss!*. Illustrated by Bridget Strevens-Marzo. New York: Simon & Schuster.

———. (2007). *Piglet and Papa*. Illustrated by Stephen Michael King. New York: Abrams.

———. (2007). *Woolvs in the Sitee*. Illustrated by Anne Spudvilas. Honesdale, PA: Boyds Mills.

———. (2008). *Lucy Goosey*. Illustrated by Ann James. Surry Hills, New South Wales: Little Hare.

———. (2010). *Fox*. St. Leonards, NSW: Allen & Unwin.

———. (2011). *Harry & Hopper*. Illustrated by Freya Blackwood. New York: Feiwel and Friends.

Wilder, Laura Ingalls. (1937). *On the Banks of Plum Creek*. New York: Harper & Brothers.

Wildsmith, Brian. (2007). *Hare and the Tortoise*. Oxford: Oxford Childrens.

Wiles, Deborah. (2005). *Each Little Bird that Sings*. Orlando, FL: Harcourt.

———. (2010). *Countdown*. New York: Scholastic.

Willard, Nancy. (1981). *A Visit to William Blake's Inn: Poems for Innocent and Experienced Travelers*. New York: Harcourt Brace Jovanovich.

———. (1989). *East of the Sun and West of the Moon*. Illustrated by Barry Moser. San Diego, CA: Harcourt.

Willems, Mo. (2003). *Don't Let the Pigeon Drive the Bus!*. New York: Hyperion.

———. (2004). *Knuffle Bunny: A Cautionary Tale*. New York: Hyperion.

———. (2004). *The Pigeon Finds a Hot Dog*. New York: Hyperion.

———. (2005). *The Pigeon Has Feelings, Too!*. New York: Hyperion.

———. (2005). *The Pigeon Loves Things that Go!*. New York: Scholastic.

———. (2006). *Don't Let the Pigeon Stay Up Late!*. New York: Hyperion.

———. (2007). *Knuffle Bunny Too: A Case of Mistaken Identity*. New York: Hyperion.

———. (2008). *The Pigeon Wants a Puppy*. New York: Hyperion.

———. (2011). *Hooray for Amanda & Her Alligator! 6 1/2 Surprising Stories about 2 Surprising Friends*. New York: Balzer + Bray.

Willey, Margaret. (2001). *Clever Beatrice: An Upper Peninsula Conte*. Illustrated by Heather Solomon. New York: Atheneum.

———. (2004). *Clever Beatrice and the Best Little Pony*. Illustrated by Heather Solomon. New York: Atheneum.

Williams, Marcia. (2000). *Bravo, Mr. William Shakespeare*. Cambridge, MA: Candlewick.

———. (2004). *Tales from Shakespeare*. Cambridge, MA: Candlewick.

Williams, Margery. (1922). *The Velveteen Rabbit*. New York: George H. Doran.

Williams, Michael. (2011). *Now Is the Time for Running*. New York: Little, Brown.

Williams-Garcia, Rita. (2010). *One Crazy Summer*. New York: Amistad.

Wilson, April. (1999). *Magpie Magic*. New York: Dial.

Wilson, Jacqueline. (2008). *Best Friends*. Illustrated by Nick Sharratt. New York: Roaring Brook.

Winter, Jeanette. (2003). *The House that Jack Built*. New York: Puffin.

_____. (2007). *The Tale of Pale Male: A True Story*. San Diego, CA: Harcourt.

_____. (2009). *Nasreen's Secret School: A True Story from Afghanistan*. New York: Beach Lane.

_____. (2010). *Biblioburro: A True Story from Colombia*. New York: Beach Lane.

_____. (2011). *The Watcher: Jane Goodall's Life with the Chimps*. New York: Schwartz & Wade.

Winter, Jonah. (2008). *Muhammad Ali: Champion of the World*. Illustrated by François Roca. New York: Random House.

_____. (2008). *Roberto Clemente: Pride of the Pittsburg Pirates*. Illustrated by Raul Colón. New York: Simon & Schuster.

_____. (2008). *Steel Town*. Illustrated by Terry Widener. New York: Simon & Schuster.

_____. (2011). *Born and Bred in the Great Depression*. Illustrated by Kimberly Bulcken Root. New York: Schwartz & Wade.

Wisniewski, David. (1998). *The Warrior and the Wise Man*. New York: HarperCollins.

Wittenstein, Vicki Oransky. (2010). *Planet Hunter: Geoff Marcy and the Search for Other Earths*. Honesdale, PA: Boyd Mills.

Wolf, Allan. (2004). *New Found Land: Lewis and Clark's Voyage of Discovery*. Cambridge, MA: Candlewick.

Wolff, Virginia Euwer. (1993). *Make Lemonade*. New York: Holt.

_____. (1998). *Bat 6*. New York: Scholastic.

_____. (2001). *True Believer*. New York: Atheneum.

Wong, Janet S. (2003). *Minn and Jack*. Illustrated by Genevieve Cote. New York: Farrar, Straus and Giroux.

_____. *The Dumpster Diver*. Illustrated by David Roberts. Cambridge, MA: Candlewick.

Wood, Don. (2008). *Into the Volcano: A Graphic Novel*. New York: Blue Sky.

Woodson, Jacqueline. (1994). *From the Notebooks of Melanin Sun*. New York: Blue Sky.

_____. (1997). *The House You Pass on the Way*. New York: Delacorte.

_____. (2000). *Miracle's Boys*. New York: Putnam.

_____. (2003). *Locomotion*. New York: Putnam.

_____. (2004). *Coming on Home Soon*. Illustrated by E. B. Lewis. New York: Putnam.

_____. (2005). *Show Way*. Illustrated by Hudson Talbott. New York: Putnam.

_____. (2008). *After Tupac and D Foster*. New York: Putman.

_____. (2008). *Rex Zero, the King of Nothing*. New York: Farrar, Straus and Giroux.

_____. (2009). *Peace, Locomotion*. New York: Penguin.

_____. (2010). *Pecan Pie Baby*. Illustrated by Sophie Blackall. New York: Penguin.

_____. (2010). *Rex Zero, the Great Pretender*. New York: Farrar, Straus and Giroux.

Worth, Valerie. (1994). *All the Small Poems and Fourteen More*. Illustrated by Natalie Babbitt. New York: Farrar, Straus and Giroux.

Wright, Barbara. (2012). *Crow*. New York: Random House.

Wright, Blanche Fisher. (2010). *The Real Mother Goose*. New York: General Books.

Wyeth, Sharon Dennis. (1998). *Something Beautiful*. New York: Doubleday.

Wyndham, Robert. (1998). *Chinese Mother Goose Rhymes*. Illustrated by Ed Young. New York: Puffin.

Wynne-Jones, Tim. (2007). *Rex Zero and the End of the World*. New York: Farrar, Straus and Giroux.

Yaccarino, Dan. (2011). *All the Way to America: The Story of a Big Italian Family and a Little Shovel*. New York: Knopf.

Yagawa, Sumiko. (1987). *The Crane Wife*. New York: Morrow.

Yang, Gene Luen. (2006). *American Born Chinese*. New York: Roaring Brook.

Yee, Lisa. (2003). *Millicent Min: Girl Genius*. New York: Scholastic.

_____. (2005). *Stanford Wong Flunks Big-Time*. New York: Scholastic.

_____. (2011). *Warp Speed*. New York: Scholastic.

_____. (2012). *Bobby the Brave (Sometimes)*. New York: Scholastic.

Yee, Paul, & J. P. Wang. (2004). *A Song for Ba*. Toronto, Ontario: Groundwood.

Yee, Wong Herbert. (2007). *Abracadabra! Magic with Mouse and Mole*. Boston: Houghton Mifflin.

_____. (2007). *Who Likes Rain?*. New York: Holt.

Yelchin, Eugene. (2011). *Breaking Stalin's Nose*. New York: Holt.

Yenawine, Phillip. (1991). *Lines*. New York: Museum of Modern Art.

Yep, Laurence. (1997). *Thief of Hearts*. New York: HarperCollins.

_____. (2003). *The Traitor: 1885*. New York: HarperCollins.

_____. (2011). *Dragons of Silk*. New York: Harper.

Yezerski, Thomas F. (2011). *Meadowlands: A Wetlands Survival Story*. New York: Farrar.

Ylvisaker, Anne. (2007). *Little Klein*. Cambridge, MA: Candlewick.

———. (2011). *The Luck of the Buttons*. Somerville, MA: Candlewick.

Yolen, Jane, & Andrew Fusek Peters. (2010). *Switching on the Night: A Very First Book of Bedtime Poems*. Illustrated by G. Brian Karas. Somerville, MA: Candlewick.

Yolen, Jane, & Robert Harris. (2001). *The Queen's Own Fool: A Novel of Mary, Queen of Scots*. Illustrated by Cynthia Von Buhler. New York: Philomel.

———. (2004). *Prince across the Water*. New York: Philomel.

Yolen, Jane. (1988). *The Devil's Arithmetic*. San Diego, CA: Harcourt.

———. (1990). *Tam Lin: An Old Ballad*. Illustrated by Charles Mikolaycak. San Diego: Harcourt.

———. (1992). *Encounter*. Illustrated by David Shannon. San Diego, CA: Harcourt.

———. (1994). *Sleep Rhymes around the World*. Honesdale, PA: Wordsong.

———. (1996). *Sky Scrape/City Scape: Poems of City Life*. Honesdale, PA: Wordsong.

———. (1997). *Wings*. Illustrated by Dennis Nolan. San Diego, CA: Harcourt.

———. (2000). *How Do Dinosaurs Say Goodnight?*. Illustrated by Mark Teague. New York: Blue Sky.

———. (2000). *Not One Damsel in Distress: World Folktales for Strong Girls*. Illustrated by Susan Guevara. San Diego, CA: Silver Whistle.

———. (2003). *Sword of the Rightful King: A Novel of King Arthur*. San Diego, CA: Harcourt.

———. (2004). *Fine Feathered Friends: Poems for Young People*. Hornsdale, PA: Wordsong.

———. (2010). *Foiled*. Illustrated by Mike Cavallaro. New York: First Second.

———. (2011). *Birds of a Feather*. Illustrated by Jason Stemple. Honesdale, PA: Wordsong.

———. (2011). *Snow in Summer: Fairest of Them All*. New York: Philomel.

Yorinks, Arthur. (1999). *The Alphabet Atlas*. Illustrated by Adrienne Yorinks. Delray Beach, FL: Winslow.

Young, Ed, & Libby Koponen. (2011). *The House Baba Built: An Artist's Childhood in China*. New York: Little, Brown.

Young, Ed. (1989). *Lon Po Po: A Red-Riding Hood Story from China*. New York: Philomel.

———. (1992). *Seven Blind Mice*. New York: Philomel.

———. (2004). *The Sons of the Dragon King: A Chinese Legend*. New York: Atheneum.

———. (2006). *My Mei Mei*. New York: Philomel.

Zelinsky, Paul O. (1986). *Rumpelstiltskin.* New York: Penguin.

———. (1997). *Rapunzel*. New York: Penguin.

Zemach, Harve. (1973). *Duffy and the Devil: A Cornish Tale*. Illustrated by Margot Zemach. New York: Farrar, Straus and Giroux.

Zindel, Paul. (1968). *The Pigman*. New York: HarperCollins.

Zolotow, Charlotte. (1972). *William's Doll*. Illustrated by William Pene DuBois. New York: HarperCollins.

———. (1995). *The Old Dog*. Illustrated by James Ransome. New York: HarperCollins.

Zusak, Markus. (2006). *The Book Thief*. New York: Knopf.

Author and Title Index

Notes:
- Titles in bold indicate series books.
- *Titles in bold italics indicate individual children's books.*
- *Titles in italics indicate books or periodicals about children's literature.*
- Page numbers in *italics* indicate author profiles.
- Page numbers followed by *(2)* or *(3)* indicate two or three separate discussions.

SUBJECT INDEX

Notes:
- **_Titles in bold italics indicate children's books._**
- _Titles in italics indicate books or periodicals about children's literature._
- Page numbers in _italics_ indicate text features including figures, profiles, and teaching ideas.
- Page numbers followed by (2) or (3) indicate two or three separate discussions.

Touchstones in the History of Children's Literature

1950s

1959 Philippa Pearce
Tom's Midnight Garden

1957 Dr. Seuss
The Cat in the Hat

1956 Gwendolyn Brooks
Bronzeville Boys and Girls

1952 Anne Frank
Anne Frank: The Diary of a Young Girl

1952 Mary Norton
The Borrowers

1952 E. B. White
Charlotte's Web
ILLUSTRATED BY GARTH WILLIAMS

1950 Beverly Cleary
Henry Huggins

1950 C. S. Lewis
The Lion, the Witch, and the Wardrobe

1940s

1947 Margaret Wise Brown
Goodnight Moon

1947 Alvin Tresselt
White Snow, Bright Snow
ILLUSTRATED BY ROGER DUVOISIN

1945 Lois Lenski
Strawberry Girl

1944 Robert Lawson
Rabbit Hill

1943 James Thurber
Many Moons
ILLUSTRATED BY MARC SIMONT

1942 Virginia Lee Burton
The Little House

1941 Robert McCloskey
Make Way for Ducklings

1941 H. A. Rey
Curious George

1930s

1939 Ludwig Bemelmans
Madeline

1938 Virginia Lee Burton
Mike Mulligan and His Steam Shovel

1937 J.R.R. Tolkien
The Hobbit

1934 Pamela Travers
Mary Poppins

1932 Laura Ingalls Wilder
Little House in the Big Woods
ILLUSTRATED BY GARTH WILLIAMS

1920s

1926 A. A. Milne
Winnie-the-Pooh
ILLUSTRATED BY E. H. SHEPARD

1922 Margery Williams
The Velveteen Rabbit
ILLUSTRATED BY WILLIAM NICHOLSON

1900s

1911 Frances Hodgson Burnett
The Secret Garden

1908 Lucy M. Montgomery
Anne of Green Gables

1908 Kenneth Grahame
Wind in the Willows

1903 Kate Douglas Wiggin
Rebecca of Sunnybrook Farm

1902 Beatrix Potter
The Tale of Peter Rabbit

1900 L. Frank Baum
The Wizard of Oz
ILLUSTRATED BY W. W. DENSLOW

1800s

1891 Carlo Colodi
Pinocchio

1891 James Whitcomb Riley
Rhymes of Childhood

1888 Ernest Thayer
Casey at the Bat

1886 Frances Hodgson Burnett
Little Lord Fauntleroy

1885 Randolph Caldecott
Hey Diddle Diddle and Baby Bunting

1885 Robert Louis Stevenson
A Child's Garden of Verses